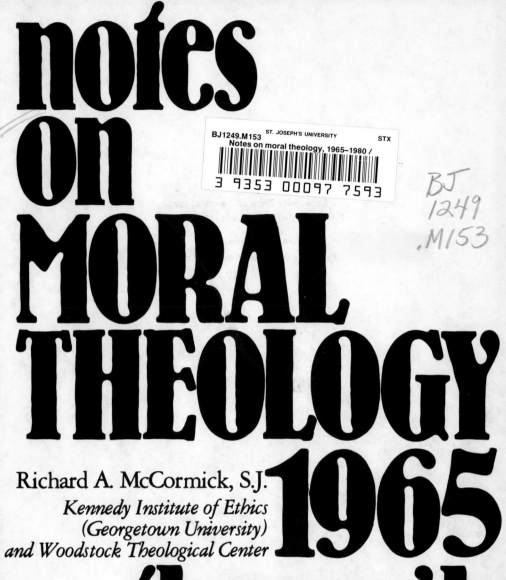

notes on MORAL THEOLOGY 1965

Richard A. McCormick, S.J.
Kennedy Institute of Ethics
(Georgetown University)
and Woodstock Theological Center

through 1980

University Press of America™

Copyright © 1981 by

University Press of America, Inc.
P.O. Box 19101, Washington, D.C. 20036

ISBN: 0-8191-1439-1 (Case)
0-8191-1440-5 (Perfect)

Library of Congress Catalog Card Number: 80-5682

FOR

Robert Drinan, S.J.,
Jesuit Priest and Congressman
And
Timothy S. Healy, S.J.,
Jesuit Priest and Educator

Both of whom, in different spheres,
translate moral concern into lived reality

PREFACE

In 1964, the late and highly esteemed John Courtney Murray, S.J., then the editor of *Theological Studies*, asked me to "have a try at" "Notes on Moral Theology" for that journal. I welcomed the opportunity but not without an appropriate dose of fear and trembling. After all, these critical surveys had been previously composed by such well-known scholars as John C. Ford, S.J., Gerald Kelly, S.J., John Connery, S.J., John Lynch, S.J., and Joseph Farraher, S.J.

During the first several years, the so-called "Notes" were a semi-annual publication, authored for one period of the year by Robert Springer, S.J., and the other by me. As time went on, the present prestigious editor of *Theological Studies*, Walter J. Burghardt, S.J., thought the overall purpose of the "Notes" could be achieved by a single annual roundup of the literature in moral theology. That task fell to me.

The Second Vatican Council, after noting that other theological disciplines should be renewed by livelier contact with the mystery of Christ and the history of salvation, stated bluntly: "Special attention needs to be given to the development of moral theology." Since that time (the Council closed Dec. 8, 1965) this "special attention" has been visited upon moral theology in unremitting fashion. *Notes on Moral Theology 1965-1980* reports and critiques this post-conciliar literature.

After some gentle *vires a tergo* from colleagues and friends, I yielded to the suggestion to bring out these "Notes" in a single volume with an index. The hope is that such a publication would make more readily available and more easily usable the vast literature of the past fifteen years in ethics and moral theology.

The composition of the "Notes," besides keeping its author off the streets and out of the air for two months of the year, has been an intellectual delight. It has, for one thing, forced me to read a great deal of material that was very enlightening and challenging. In the process of reporting and critiquing this literature, I have been led by my colleagues into several changes of mind on important and sometimes highly controversial subjects. In other words, I have been liberated from the isolation of my own perspectives, for better or for worse—and I am sure that there are more than a few who believe it has been for the worse.

v

Be that as it may the republication of these surveys provides me with the pleasurable opportunity of thanking those who make the "Notes" possible. First on such a list are my colleagues in ethics and moral theology whose disciplined and painstaking writing merits reporting and analysis. But also on that list must be included the names of Walter J. Burghardt, S.J. and Henry J. Bertels, S.J. As editor of *Theological Studies*, Father Burghardt has not only enthusiastically supported the idea of the "Notes;" he has, by his insightful reading and suggestions, contributed to them by reducing their inevitable shortcomings. Father Bertels, head librarian of the Woodstock Theological Center Library, is the most competent and cheerfully helpful librarian I have ever known. He has, with his able and friendly assistant, William J. Sheehan, C.S.B., made the task of assembling the literature to be reviewed, far less formidable than it would be. Future compositors of the "Moral Notes" will be fortunate if they enjoy such support. If they do, they will be as grateful as I am.

Finally, the reduced price of this volume (originally set at $22.50 for paper, $30 for cloth) was made possible by a generous grant from the Detroit Province of the Society of Jesus. For this I wish to thank the Very Reverend Michael Lavelle, S.J., Provincial of the Detroit Province.

Richard A. McCormick, S.J.

TABLE OF CONTENTS

CURRENT THEOLOGY: 1965
NOTES ON MORAL THEOLOGY

FUNDAMENTAL MORAL

For quite a few years now, theologians have, without disowning casuistry, disowned an excessively casuistic approach to the moral life. The effects of such an approach—a unilateral and cramping juridicism of outlook—are all too clear. S. Pinckaers, O.P., believes that behind the casuistic thought-patterns of some theology and much spoken doctrine is a certain concept of liberty, the notion of "liberty of indifference."[1] Being defined as the power to choose between this and that, the reasonable and unreasonable, for or against the law, this concept of liberty tends to manifest itself by staking out claims against all that is not itself. Autonomy is to be guarded, and this defensive attitude expresses itself in separation, negation, revolt. Now casuistic moral theology does not defend this concept of liberty, Pinckaers asserts, but too often its reflections seem to imply and even buttress it. With such a notion of freedom, the law appears as the expression of a foreign will making threatening claims. The dominant response of the person is fear, the dominant virtue obedience. The moralist and conscience itself become primarily concerned with acts in violation of obligation, with sins; hence they become almost arbitrators between man and the will of God.

Rather than this liberty, Pinckaers proposes what he calls the "liberty of perfection," one which takes root in a primitive and spontaneous sense of perfection and aspiration for the good. Instead of tension between liberty and law, where God is seen as the supreme legislator, the liberty of perfection views God as the sovereign good, all amiable, supremely worthy of friendship. Thus liberty should really be conceived as the ability to respond creatively, if progressively, to this great good. Moral theology must be primarily concerned with promotion of this response. This does not mean that obligation ceases to exist; rather it pertains, Pinckaers believes, to a certain "infancy level" of response where one has need of exterior aids and constraints—just as the budding artist must submit to a certain discipline and painful restraints to bring himself to a level of more profound and spontaneous response. The mature pass beyond the need of such guidelines simply because they do the things commanded spontaneously and with internal grasp of the value involved. Casuistic moral theology pertains to the level of constraint—the early level of pedagogy, so to speak—and it

EDITOR'S NOTE.—The present survey covers the period from January to June, 1965.

[1] S. Pinckaers, O.P., "La liberté en morale," *Revue ecclésiastique de Liège* 51 (1965) 86–102.

concerns itself with sin and imperfection precisely to lead to the fuller moral life of spontaneous creativity. Thus far Pinckaers.

Rather than say that the casuistry of sin is based on an inadequate concept of liberty, the liberty of indifference, I would prefer to say: the casuistry of sin is only one aspect of the search for God's will, and the liberty of indifference only one aspect of liberty. If we cannot do without the discernment of spirits, neither can we totally dispense with the casuistry of sin. Men, even the most mature, will never cease to live in a concrete and complex world where the accumulated wisdom of the past will have something (not everything) to say to them. Similarly, just as we need that aspect of liberty comprised by the phrase "liberty of indifference" (and not only for sinful but also for virtuous acts), so we need also that aspect of liberty which regards it as a gift, a power of spontaneous and creative response. Eventually, however, without liberty of indifference such a response would be meaningless. The real villain is neither liberty of indifference nor casuistry, but the mentality which decontextualizes them.

Whenever one writes "an essay in emphasis," he is exposed to the dangers of caricature and tends to build up false opposites. Pinckaers has not entirely escaped this danger—though his emphasis is certainly healthy. The more we can educate people to the idea that their liberty, rather than a sovereign autonomy to be jealously guarded from the claims of law, is a power of personal and creative response to the God behind all law, the more will we educate them to moral adulthood.

P. Anciaux has an excellent article on conscience and moral education.[2] Basically, he treats two points: the concept of conscience in the light of psychological data and contemporary philosophical thought, and the proper education of moral conscience in light of this concept.

Too often we encounter fragmentary notions of conscience which express only one side of it—for example, conscience as a judgment about that which is prohibited and allowed, or conscience as the reaction after an act, or conscience as the "voice of God." This latter is a notion which is generally deformed by a negative codalism or juridicism. Contrarily, Anciaux contends that before seeing conscience as a judgment or voice of any kind, one must view it as a capacity to be developed. It is the capacity to grasp the fundamental law, that is, that life is a task to be performed, a vocation to be realized in liberty. In other words, in the measure that a man progresses in "the age of reason," he grasps himself as responsible for his life, that his life must be assumed as response to a vocation or call. He seizes the fundamental

---

[2] P. Anciaux, "La conscience et l'éducation morales," *Collectanea Mechliniensia* 50 (1965) 3–31.

law of his existence. Therefore it is false and dangerous to reduce moral conscience to a cognitive or notional faculty in the abstract. Rather it is the faculty of knowing values as moral, scil., in so far as they are related to man's becoming what he ought to be, a person. This is a growing thing and therefore is tied up intimately with the personality structure which conditions man's life—above all, his social life.

Adopting a dynamic structure for the development of personality, Anciaux proceeds to point out what this means for moral education. Here he is especially good. Moral education must, above all, educate man to live according to his vocation. The climate of tenderness and love is most important in the early years—as contrasted with an exclusive concern with order and good external behavior. Immediately before the arrival at use of reason, the child is governed by a type of "mirror conscience," that is, by reflections from his parents. Hence the quality of the mirror is important. Parents will be eager to indicate not just what is to be done, but above all why. Identification and imitation in the early years do not stop at exterior conduct; they include also profound personal attitudes. Therefore the child must experience that the parents themselves are guided by the norms which they impose. Only so will he perceive objective values gradually.

Moral education will then emphasize the call to responsibility. Practically, parents will avoid unmotivated orders; furthermore, orders will be inspired by love and not only by expressions of impatience or the desire of peace and quiet. The youngster constantly harassed by unmotivated orders or contradictory ones becomes either the "wise little compliant" or the rebel—in either of which cases he is dependent on and bound to his parents in a way which impedes gradual maturity. Moral education depends almost totally on the persons of the educators. Their job: aid the youngster to become a person, to assume responsibility for himself. Only if he surpasses the stage of mirror conscience and dependence can he achieve the level of intersubjectivity. Only genuine love can get him that far.

J. Ghoos wrote a companion article to that of Anciaux, and it is difficult to believe that he was not peering over Anciaux's shoulder as he wrote.[3] The emphases are very close indeed. Ghoos's main concern is the development of conscience as a responsible personal undertaking, the shaping of a life project. He approaches his subject somewhat more theologically than Anciaux. Specifically, he seeks the proper place of authority, of commandments, of norms, of virtues in this developmental process and is at pains (successfully, I believe) to show that the personalism he advocates is not situationism. There is nothing new in the article, but there is a succession of

[3] J. Ghoos, "De morele ontwikkeling door het leven heen," *ibid.*, pp. 32–56.

balanced and worth-while assertions. For example, when treating the
authority of the Church in the enlightenment of conscience, his touch is deft.
Because we are spellbound by the immediate, we need in the moral life, just
as in every other aspect of life, the aid of authority. The norms proposed by
the magisterium are not heteronomous and foreign to man; they are rather
the demands of the love which is our life project. On the other hand, we must
guard against the idea that the Christian message can be harmonized for all
time by the language and thought patterns of a single era. In this type of
counterstatement Ghoos is not advocating the suppression of concrete norms,
but a truly virtuous and intelligent assessment of their place. As long as the
moral life continues to be conceived as a series of exterior acts in fulfilment
of precepts (instead of as a growth process in a basic orientation), we shall
need articles like this. Their continuing appearance is a painful reminder of
their necessity.

John Courtney Murray, S.J., once observed that "the American mind has
never been clear about the relation between morals and law."[4] The chief
manifestation (and mischief) of this confusion is the reformer's cry that
"there ought to be a law," that is, whatever is moral ought to be legislated.
Apparently this confusion is not restricted to America. Norman St. John-
Stevas notes its presence in England.[5] He asks the question: What is the
principle which guides us in deciding what moral rules are to be imposed by
law? The distinction used by the Wolfenden Committee between crime and
sin he feels is unsatisfactory, and for two reasons. First, most crimes are
moral offenses and therefore the distinction is unrealistic. Secondly, the
distinction is inappropriate because the state knows nothing of sin qua sin,
"though it may well be concerned with conduct contrary to the moral
standards accepted by the community which may incidentally also be
considered by the Church as sinful." The Wolfenden principle is, then, too
exclusive. On the other hand, there are those who would place no theoretical
limit to state power to legislate against immorality, on the grounds that the
state has a right to pass judgment on moral matters and to enforce this
judgment by law. St. John-Stevas rejects both of these positions as extremes
and accepts the principle that only those moral offenses which affect the
common good are fit subjects for legislation. What constitutes this "common
good"? Beyond the obvious factors (public order, civil peace, security of the
young, etc.), there is also the public consensus on morality. This is a varying
thing, more likely to be affected by public than private acts, but "one can-

[4] J. C. Murray, S.J., *We Hold These Truths* (New York: Sheed & Ward, 1960) p. 156.
[5] Norman St. John-Stevas, "Public Morality," *Wiseman Review*, Winter, 1964–65,
pp. 343–50. Cf. also THEOLOGICAL STUDIES 21 (1960) 233–34; 22 (1961) 234–38.

not say that no private act can ever affect it." Euthanasia, for example, is a private act but constitutes such a threat to the sanctity of life that it should be punishable by law.[6]

It is easy to agree with St. John-Stevas that the crime-sin distinction does not provide a sufficient theoretical basis for the relationship between morals and law; for it too easily leaves the impression that legality and morality are absolutely distinct. That this is not the case is brought out admirably by a series of editorials in *America*.[7] The editorials quickly state the obvious fact that law has an inherently moral purpose and go on to discuss the problems this raises in a pluralistic society. Because of law's undeniably moral purpose, it is too easy to think that only moral principle is relevant to decisions of public policy involving morals. Hence, too, the temptation to urge the enactment of one's moral convictions (which are largely derived from one's religious faith) into law. On the other hand, there is the extreme which would exclude the moral conscience from the public forum, as if what is good for men (the common good) has nothing to do with moral climate and moral convictions. *America* rather points to a sound middle ground. Laws which enact a society's moral code must express the convictions of the community. Such laws, representing a consensus of the community conscience, are elaborated through a process of rational reflection which must take into account the whole social reality with which the law must deal. The Catholic (and even more broadly, the religious man) may, indeed must, (1) attempt according to his capacity to exercise a creative influence on the formation of a public consensus by presenting his convictions, but (2) not "as doctrines revealed by God. . . but as convictions about the moral and human values that society exists to protect and to foster."[8]

As long as many Catholics are scandalized by the difference between a Catholic moral position on, for example, divorce and a Catholic position on the public policy concerning divorce, they show that they need a heavy dose of the message of these editorials. Otherwise not only will the cause of good law suffer, but also eventually the cause of good personal morality.

Contributing formatively to the public ethos is one thing; judging individual policies is quite another. In an interesting and on the whole excellent article Paul Ramsey, Harrington Spear Professor of Religion at Princeton

[6] Whether homosexual acts should fall into this category is becoming very difficult to judge. Homosexual literature increasingly argues for a change of law not because homosexuality involves private acts, but because a minority is being deprived of rights. Legal toleration could easily mean a type of social acceptance with enormous consequences for the public good.

[7] *America* 112 (1965) 280, 351, 450, 520–21, 747.

[8] *Ibid.*, p. 747.

University, discusses the relationship between the church and the magistrate (and to that extent between morality and political policy) in terms of the above distinction.[9] Ramsey insists that the churches in our time have done what they ought not to and thereby left undone what they ought to have done. Specifically, they have attempted to pronounce upon and influence *particular* policy decisions. In doing this, not only have they identified the moral precept with the political decision, thereby improperly narrowing the range of political decisions; they have also neglected what is their proper task as churches, the informing of "the ethos and conscience of the nation," and *therewith* the forming of the conscience of its statesmen. Ramsey means that "it is not the Church's business to recommend but only to clarify the grounds upon which the statesman must put forth his own particular decree ... to see to it that the word over which and through which statesmanship or government wins its victory is not an inadequate word." There has been, he asserts, a tendency for Americans to mark down "moral" and "immoral" beside specific policy decisions without first weighing carefully the nature of politics. In saying this, Ramsey does not mean to imply that morality should be left to professional ethicians; he means only that when moralists undertake to influence the opinion of a nation, they are responsible for the type of disciplined reflection which is in command of political realities. It is hard to think that Ramsey did not have in mind (though he nowhere says so) incidents similar to the one-page newspaper advertisments signed by hundreds of clergymen urging the President to stop the carnage in Vietnam.

Ramsey's remarks on policy decisions should not be confused with a completely different thing: the duty of bishops to inform their flocks of the spiritual and religious values involved in issues put to the electorate. Francis G. McManamin, S.J., provides a good overview of the activity of American Catholic bishops in this delicate area and the consequent obligation on the voter.[10]

A particular instance where morality and public policy interact is that of abortion. The sanctity of life is not only a moral concern; it is also a public and legal one. As such, policies which protect it must be elaborated out of a public consensus, as was pointed out earlier. Some recent writings provide examples of how influence may be brought to bear in the formation of public consensus.

Norman St. John-Stevas devotes two chapters of his recent book *The Right*

[9] Paul Ramsey, "The Church and the Magistrate," *Christianity and Crisis* 25 (1965) 136-40.

[10] Francis G. McManamin, S.J., "Episcopal Authority in the Political Order," *Continuum* 2 (1965) 632-38.

to Life to the thalidomide incidents.[11] The first chapter deals with the famous Liège case, in which Madame Suzanna van de Put—together with her mother, sister, husband, and a Dr. Jacques Casters as copartners—was tried for the murder-by-poison of her deformed baby. At the end of the six-day trial Madame van de Put and the other defendants were acquitted in a tumultuously popular verdict. St. John-Stevas sees the verdict as striking at one of the fundamental principles on which Western society is based.

The van de Put case, in effect, confers on the individual citizen a license to kill—a license with no clear limiting terms. To one person, life without sight will appear unbearable; to another, the absence of arms; to another, the lack of legs. Once the principle of the sanctity of life is abandoned, there can be no criterion of the right to life, save that of personal taste. For all its apparent benevolence, then, the Liège decision is a step back to the jungle from which society has, with infinite difficulty, emerged.

In a relentlessly logical manner St. John-Stevas exposes one argument after another as even poor pragmatism. For instance, Madame van de Put had pleaded that she took her child's life for what she regarded as the child's good. "I just thought you could not let a baby like that live. I thought it could never be happy in its whole life." Here St. John-Stevas quietly points to the totalitarian implications of depriving another of life on the grounds that *"in someone else's opinion*, the amount of unhappiness he is likely to endure in living will probably be greater than the amount of happiness."

P. Pas treats specifically the problem of handicapped children, whether the handicap be physical or psychic.[12] He places the whole discussion in the context of charity, insisting that it is charity which brings happiness under any circumstances—the charity others show us, but above all the charity we bring to our relations with others. Certainly this virtue is a parental duty and privilege, but it is also a community project. The entire community must preoccupy itself with the handicapped, as it actually has done. Modern prosthetic techniques show what can be done and what direction our charitable concern must take in the future. As for the psychically handicapped, Pas admits that their suffering has no meaning in itself; rather one must give it meaning. The suffering of these infants receives a meaning when they are loved. He concludes simply that killing is "to capitulate before the difficulties of life."

[11] Norman St. John-Stevas, *The Right to Life* (New York: Holt, Rinehart and Winston, 1964).

[12] P. Pas, "Vijfde gebod en gehandicapte kindern," *Collectanea Mechliniensia* 50 (1965) 167–91.

In a second chapter St. John-Stevas treats of abortion. Many who defend the practice on moral grounds appeal to the theory of retarded animation. St. John-Stevas does not deny the theoretical possibility of delayed animation but points out that "today, and indeed for a very considerable period, it has been accepted by biologists that there is no qualitative difference between the embryo at the moment of conception and at the moment of quickening. Life is fully present from the moment of conception."[13]

I am not as sure of biological opinion as St. John-Stevas is. But even were biologists to conclude that there is a qualitative difference between the embryo and the fetus at quickening (first movement), another article concludes that this would provide only indirect evidence at best about the presence of a soul.[14] Where the soul is concerned as the term of a creative act of God, we are dealing with things impervious to the *direct* measuring capacities of human instruments.

Catholic thinkers (and many others also) are, of course, aware of these truths. Their mention here is justified for two reasons. First, it serves as a reminder that their relatively peaceful possession in Catholic theological circles is in marked contrast to a growing public consensus. Secondly, the articles cited indicate how the religious conscience should operate to form (and transform) this consensus; for while the authors may hold their positions because of enlightenment from religious belief, they need not and do not urge them in these terms; rather they offer them as basically a human position.

John Lynch, S.J., once wrote that "while the principle of double effect endures, a moralist's life need never be dull."[15] As if to prove this, P. Knauer, S.J., has written a lengthy study of the double effect.[16] After complaining that standard interpretations of this principle put too much emphasis on the physical structure of the act (its causality) and thus fragment the total moral act into unreal parts, Knauer writes: "in the total objective structure of an action, that only constitutes the *finis operis* which is willed by the subject, not only materially but formally, to the exclusion of the physical elements on which the intention does not bear." Theologians would certainly admit this.

How does one know what is "formally" willed by the subject? The motive or reason for acting must be considered here. "The reason which one pro-

[13] *Op. cit.*, p. 32.

[14] Richard A. McCormick, S.J., "A Human Stand on Abortion," *America* 112 (1965) 877–81.

[15] Theological Studies 17 (1956) 169–70.

[16] P. Knauer, S.J., "La détermination du bien et du mal moral par le principe du double effet," *Nouvelle revue théologique* 87 (1965) 356–76.

poses does not remain exterior to the act, but it co-operates in the constitution of the '*finis operis*' itself of the act."

Therefore, in defining or describing that which is willed by the subject, one must include the motive; for this tells us eventually under what formality the act is willed. But the formality under which the act is willed is determined by the proportionate reason for acting. That is, since the motive must be included in the *finis operis*, and since this motive is actually the proportionate reason for acting, it is the proportionate reason which tells us under what aspect the act is willed. By doing this, it determines whether the evil effects enter formally into the intention or not. "To admit an evil without proportionate reason constitutes sin; the evil is no longer 'accidental' but enters into the object of our act. Contrarily, if there is a proportionate reason, the evil effect becomes by this very fact indirect. *An evil effect will be indirect or direct according to the presence or absence of a proportionate reason.*"[17] Knauer's basic thesis, then, is that what is directly willed or only indirectly willed is determined by the presence or absence of a proportionate reason, precisely because this determines the object willed.

To clarify the direction of Knauer's reasoning, I will present one of his own applications of it. Suppose a doctor uses a medicine with harmful effects after discovery of a more recent and better medicine. Now one who uses the older medicine after discovery of the better one can only do so because he had a different motive from that originally proposed (cure of the disease). This reason might be the avoidance of higher costs or even avoidance of extra work. This reason for acting enters into the very object of choice. Thus the object of choice would no longer be "to cure disease" but "to save money." But it is only a *proportionate* reason (one which aspires to the maximum realization of the value in question) which renders the evil effects indirect. Since the reason is not proportionate to the original goal in the case given, and since it enters into the very object of the act, the evil effects would enter into the choice directly and formally.

Knauer sees this same thinking verified in several other areas of moral theology: for instance, the treatise on co-operation. "Suppose an act of material co-operation with sin without proportionate reason; from the material co-operation that it was, the co-operation becomes formal." Acceptance of work in a drugstore where abortifacients are sold constitutes formal co-operation if there is no proportionate reason; with a reason, the co-operation is material. It is, then, simply the proportionate reason which decides the difference between the two types of co-operation. Knauer feels that the proportionate-reason principle as determinative of what is directly

[17] *Ibid.*, p. 365.

or indirectly willed should be used in explaining many tracts of moral theology: e.g., the casuistry of the lie, self-defense, theft in extreme need, probabilism, and the principle of totality. With regard to this last, he states that the principle of totality is nothing more than the double effect and is not a separate principle at all. "A medical operation to produce a cure consists formally in the removal of an obstacle to the cure. It can happen 'accidentally' that this obstacle is a member of the organism. In this case the removal of the organ as such is not willed directly, because it is justified by a proportionate reason."[18]

Summarily, then: proportionate reason determines under what aspect I will the act and therefore whether evil effects enter the will-act formally and directly. If the motive or reason is proportionate, the evil effects are only indirectly willed. Therefore the proportionate reason determines what is directly or indirectly willed.

I suspect that behind Knauer's treatment was the kind of vague dissatisfaction we all feel in certain complex instances of double effect where we manipulate the description of the act rather abstractly—almost to come up with a certain conclusion. For example (and Knauer uses this example), a man jumps out a fifty-story-high room to escape excruciating death by fire. As not infrequently presented, the action here is defined as "jumping out of a window." Every sane person squirms under this description of what is going on—and that is why some moralists have never allowed this type of thing. In order to be realistic here, one has to appeal to the motive to get an *objectum actus* in an acceptable sense. It is in generalizing off this example that Knauer, if I understand him correctly, appears to me to be imprecise. Let us change some words in the quotation just given on the principle of totality. "A medical operation in view of health consists formally in the removal of an obstacle to health. It can happen 'accidentally' that this obstacle is a living, nonviable fetus. In this case the removal of the fetus as such is not willed directly, because it is justified by a proportionate reason." One senses immediately that something is wrong here. If not, the quotation could be changed to the following: "A bombing mission in view of a nation's survival (by deterrence) consists formally in the removal of obstacles to this survival. It can happen 'accidentally' that this obstacle is the population of another nation. In this case removal (destruction) of the population as such is not willed directly, because it is justified by a proportionate reason."

If applied right down the line, this reasoning would destroy the concept of that which is intrinsically evil *ex objecto*. Knauer might disown this conclusion. But it is not clear to me that he could do so logically. Of course, his

[18] *Ibid.*, p. 373.

formulation is not necessarily wanting because it leads to such conclusions (for we cannot exclude the possibility that the conclusions are correct); it is vulnerable only if in doing so it proves inconsistent. I believe this is the case. I should like to comment on two points: first, the inconsistency; secondly, what appears to me to be the source of the problem.

First, the inconsistency. After identifying the traditional notion of *objectum actus* with physical structure or causality and rightly rejecting this as a sufficient determinant of the meaning of an action, Knauer makes proportionate reason so unqualifiedly the constitutive factor of the object of the act that causality or the external act is no longer functional at all. Hence he makes it theoretically possible to assume into an act as indirect and licit any means, providing it is necessary to a value or end envisaged. Knauer sees this impasse clearly and rejects it as a conclusion to his reasoning as follows: "If a nonjustified evil precedes the achievement of the end, it enters itself into the specification of the act: to kill to get money is to commit murder." This is certainly true, but it is not clear that Knauer can conclude it. Mere temporal precedence does not qualify an act or effect as evil, as Knauer himself admits. Therefore the above statement must mean that killing to get money is wrong because it is not justified. One wonders why not on Knauer's principles, if the proportionate reason is decisive; for then the object of the act can be defined by this motive. Knauer's only logical answer can be that the motive or reason is not proportionate. But this may be questioned. For example, to save the life of the mother is certainly a motive proportionate to the value with which the doctor is dealing when he treats a pregnant woman. Why it would not justify destroying the child if necessary is not clear. And if this is true, then it is equally licit to destroy one million enemy civilians (noncombatants) by people-bombing if this will act as an effective deterrent against loss of five million Americans. These deaths would be, in Knauer's terms, indirect because of the existence of a proportionate reason.

Secondly, the source of the problem. How did Knauer get to the point where his formulation seems open to this objection? It seems to me that he has failed to distinguish "proportionate reason" carefully. "Proportionate reason" can mean two things. Some proportionate reasons are identical with the good effect *as produced immediately by the cause* (or with the cause as producing this effect as one equally immediate with several others). Other proportionate reasons are motives "introduced from outside," so to speak, and superimposed on an external act whose basic meaning is already determined (because of its unique immediate effect). If I fail to make this distinction, nothing will prevent me from introducing the motive into an act which already has a basic meaning in human terms to alter it substantially. There is nothing wrong with doing this on the drawing boards; the chief objection to it is that it contravenes experience. When I destroy a child to save its mother, I may, if I care to, call this "mother-saving." But no amount of verbal shuffling can obscure what is clear to common sense, scil., that I will this (destruction of the child) directly, because it is the single immediate effect of what I am doing.

Why did Knauer fail to make this distinction clearly? I believe Knauer was led to gloss over the ambiguity in the term "proportionate reason" because he relies heavily on St. Thomas' use of self-defense against unjust aggression as an example of the double effect. St. Thomas regarded the death of an unjust aggressor resulting from an act of self-defense as indirectly voluntary. Because he supposes this as a case of double effect, Knauer must explain how the death of the aggressor was not an object of will. Therefore something else had to be this object of will, namely, self-defense—which, of course, is the motive or proportionate reason. Once he has accepted this as a case of indirect voluntary, clearly the external act cannot be that which tells me the *objectum actus* and what is directly and indirectly willed. Furthermore, he is in a position where any external act (regardless of its causality) can and must be defined (*objectum*) in terms of its motive. The problem here: most modern theologians find it extremely difficult to accept the death of the aggressor as an example of the double effect.

Once Knauer has begun in this way, one can understand his repugnance to using the external act in any way as constitutive of the object. He notes, for instance, that the physical character does not differ in murder and self-defense—which is certainly true. Therefore, if the physical structure is to be equated with the moral object, there is no differentiation at the level of object, and one must seek it elsewhere, that is, in the motive. Thus the motive enters the very notion of the object.

Where Knauer has abandoned the physical structure of the act altogether, I would prefer to say that it oftentimes helps to determine the moral object, though it is not always sufficient by any means. Moralists have always insisted that the object (*objectum actus*) may not be understood in a mere physical sense. To get the moral object, it is sometimes necessary to turn to the circumstances or the intention. For example, sometimes an act produces two immediate (causally) effects, so that only the intention will determine or specify the true moral object. At other times the circumstances enter into the object. Thus the moral object of a murderous act is not simply "killing a man" but "killing an innocent man." The object of the act of self-defense is not simply "killing a man" but "killing an unjust aggressor." The difference is not precisely in the motive but in an objective circumstance, and this circumstance distinguishes the two acts in a valid and humanly reasonable way. At still other times a physical evil (e.g., the death of a human being) is so uniquely the immediate effect of my action that it is unrealistic to talk about it as anything but a *direct* killing—whether this be done in service of a higher value or not.

Summarily, then, what Knauer is doing is this: he is trying to make the specification of the human act (*objectum*) move from the intention to the external act, rather than vice versa. Once this is done, anything not specified by one's good purpose is excludable from what is directly willed. Many anguishing problems could be solved if this could be done. However, "direct willing" is not just a phrase; it represents a psychological reality. It seems to me that experience itself supports our belief that our act gets basic moral specification from the object—that is, *from the external act reasonably understood, reasonably interpreted*.[19]

This understanding of *objectum actus* seems basic to any use of the double effect. For example, where co-operation is involved, Knauer says that it is precisely the proportionate reason which constitutes co-operation material. I believe it would be more accurate to say that co-operation is material because, being an act distinct from the sinner's, *it can be chosen and willed* without intending his sin. In order to establish this distinctness, one must return to the standard concept of *objectum actus*. Whether one actually does withhold his intention will, of course, depend largely on the proportionate reason. But even to postulate the possibility, the two acts must be distinguishable. The proportionate reason will not always give me this distinction. Furthermore, the distinction is often difficult in practice, and no doubt we have been guilty of making a few hairline distinctions and planting a few definitions to come up with certain attractive conclusions. But these weaknesses do not reflect any inadequacy in the moral principles; they rather reflect the complexity of material reality, which is continuous and inherently not totally intelligible. Nor do they mean that we can do without the concept of *objectum* as traditionally understood. If we jettison this notion altogether, we arrive at the point of suspension of ethical thought—basically, I would suggest, because we have abandoned our own experience as the stuff to be judged.

THEOLOGY OF THE NATURAL LAW

There has been a great deal of interesting writing on the natural law in the very recent past. The noted Scripture scholar John L. McKenzie, S.J.,

[19] Many of these same reflections are applicable to W. Van der Marck's *Love and Fertility* (New York: Sheed & Ward, 1965).

examines the biblical basis for the natural-law tradition.[20] His exegesis of the *loci classici* (Rom 1:19–21; 2:14–15) leads him to the conclusion that "Paul's thought is correctly summarized if we say that he regarded a morality of reason and nature as a morality that fails." Surely this conclusion is incontestable. When one approaches what we call the natural law in terms of its efficaciousness as a saving or salutary mediation (and this is Fr. McKenzie's approach[21]), there can be little doubt that the New Testament abrogates all law.[22] Surely also Fr. McKenzie is right when he rejects in the Pauline corpus any kind of "natural morality." On the other hand, I am unaware of any theologians who would seek the biblical basis for natural-law thinking in the existence of such a law as of itself efficacious, as a saving mediation. There is only one way of salvation: redemption by the blood of Christ. I am also unaware of any theologians who would hold that the existence and validity of natural law should be equated with "natural morality."[23]

Finally, Fr. McKenzie turns his attention to a totally different question, that of the possibility of a system of moral obligations in particular based on a rational consideration of nature. He rejects the possibility and contends that "Christian love offers a solution to all these problems, but we find the solution impractical." The problems referred to are the ethics of war, use of wealth, ownership of slaves, internal and external politics, sex, etc. McKenzie is unquestionably right in asserting that Christian love can find the solution to these problems. But it is not from mere perversity that I suggest that he is being frivolous when he states that this search excludes moral imperatives derived rationally from man's being. If he intends this seriously, then two points must be clearly stated.

First of all, the intelligibility of the ethical values of revelation (*lex Christi*) is dependent upon a rational (intuitive) knowledge by man of the ethical values discernible in his own being and experience (*lex naturae*). More practically, man would not understand the meaning of love, humility, trust in revelation unless his own ethical experience (founded on his being) was

---

[20] John L. McKenzie, S.J., "Natural Law in the New Testament," *Biblical Research* 9 (1964) 1–11.

[21] Cf. his phrases "no greater efficacy," "a saving power which belongs to Christ alone," "a morality that fails," "any salutary value to the observance," etc.

[22] Cf. S. Lyonnet, S.J., "Liberté chrétienne et loi de l'esprit," *Christus* 1–4 (1954) 6–27.

[23] For other reflections on natural law in the Bible, cf. Rudolph Schnackenburg, *The Moral Teaching of the New Testament* (New York: Herder and Herder, 1965) pp. 290–93; Jos. Fuchs, S.J., *Lex naturae: Zur Theologie des Naturrechts* (Düsseldorf, 1955) pp. 21–38. John Courtney Murray, S.J., is of the opinion that "it would not, of course, be difficult to show that the doctrine is, in germinal fashion, scriptural" (*We Hold These Truths* [New York: Sheed & Ward, 1960] pp. 296–97).

ground for a language which would make these notions naturally clear to him. Bruno Schüller, S.J., has made this point extremely well in an article in *Lebendiges Zeugnis*.[24] He points out that faith, in so far as it is knowledge, is knowledge mediated and negotiated by signs. The encounter, therefore, between the believing man and the revealing God is only possible because God makes use of language already familiar to man. Now man's ethical vocabulary is just as broad as his own natural ethical experience, his own ethical consciousness. Schüller says: "If, therefore, it is the natural ethical consciousness of man which grounds the expressive possibilities of human language, then it seems to follow that God through His revelation can only communicate to man that aspect of moral insight which man already knows by means of his natural ethical experience, or at least that which he can know."[25] Schüller concludes: "man is, therefore, only capable of hearing and giving intelligent belief to the ethical message of the New Testament because prior (logically) to the revelation of God's word he already grasps and expresses himself as an ethical being."[26] So, far from denying rational knowledge of a *lex naturae*, the *lex Christi* supposes it and is impossible without it.

Secondly, there is every indication that Fr. McKenzie is opposing two things between which there is and can be no real opposition: Christian love and the concrete demands of that love founded on man's being (the natural law). Far from denying the validity of what theologians call natural-law obligations, it is precisely because Christ charged us with love of the neighbor that He must be thought to have asserted them. One who would claim to love his neighbor while at the same time refusing to acknowledge the claims that the human person makes on this love would not accept and communicate with the total reality of that person. In failing to do so he would, incidentally, be underestimating the affirmation of the dignity and worth of men implied in Christ's very Incarnation (His God-*manhood*). How these claims are to be formulated is, of course, another thing. But they are there, and some of them are inseparable from the being of man. Hence they are inseparable from the privilege of loving him. And because man is reasonable, he can discover, if only with difficulty, the larger outlines of these demands. This is all that the authentic natural-law tradition asserts. In making such an assertion, it is not endorsing a "natural morality"; it is but insisting that a person's lovability may not be defined short of his full humanity. Being a work of God, man *as man* is a word of God.

[24] Bruno Schüller, S.J., "Wieweit kann die Moraltheologie das Naturrecht entbehren?" *Lebendiges Zeugnis*, March, 1965, pp. 41–65.
[25] *Ibid.*, pp. 47–48.
[26] *Ibid.*, p. 48.

Gregory Baum does not oppose the fact of natural law; rather he is uncomfortable with the term "natural law."[27] As for the word "natural," Fr. Baum claims that we have "no way of knowing whether a moral conviction which matures in the consciences of men is simply natural, or whether it is not partially the work of redemptive grace in them, grace of which Jesus is the sole mediator." If a moral conviction is alive in the consciences of men, he says, it is impossible to say whether this is due to human reflection or brought about under the influence of divine grace. Fr. Baum feels that the word "law" is unfortunate, because it suggests some kind of formulated law or set of laws.

Unfortunately, what the word "law" suggests to some or even many people is after a certain point beyond control. That is the way it is with words. That the word has led to a caricature of the thing in some quarters is probably true. That it must do so is a conclusion which strikes at the very possibility of any precise scientific terminology. That it is more inclined to lead to caricature than other words is a matter of opinion. I do not share Fr. Baum's discomfort with the word "natural," because I know of no theologian who understands the word as in the phrase "*natural* law" precisely as he does. He understands the word to mean those moral convictions arrived at without the aid of grace.

There are two problems with this understanding. First, the word "natural" as in the phrase "natural law" need not exclusively or even primarily refer to the cognitive aspects of this law, a point Fr. Baum's explanation supposes. It refers rather to the fact that the law is founded on the being of man, regardless of how he has factually come to know it. That is, it is derived from his nature as a human person. If Fr. Baum wants a truly misleading term, I suggest "the law of reason." This is misleading because it suggests that only those demands concluded to by rational reflection, without magisterial help or revelation, and with persuasiveness to most men here and now, may be said to pertain to the natural law. However, while admitting the physical capacity of the intellect (or perhaps better, of the person) to arrive at certain conclusions, theological literature is at one with papal statements in asserting that "divine revelation must be considered morally necessary so that those religious and moral truths which are not of their nature beyond the reach of reason in the present condition of the human race may be known with a firm certainty and with freedom from all error."[28]

My second problem with Fr. Baum's understanding of "natural" centers

[27] Gregory Baum, O.S.A., "The Christian Adventure—Risk and Renewal," *Critic* 23 (1965) 41–53.

[28] Pius XII, *Humani generis*, *AAS* 42 (1950) 561–62.

around the notion of grace. Even with regard to the cognitive aspects of natural law, theologians assert the physical capability of the intellect to grasp the law. This does not mean that grace is absent. Quite the contrary. Modern theologians insist on the fact that grace is busily operative here. However, grace is not a faculty; it is an aid for our faculties in their own proper operations. Therefore, when theologians use the word "natural" in this context, they do not mean to suggest the absence of grace, nor need the word itself suggest this.

A thoroughly competent and well-documented article by John J. Reed, S.J., discusses the natural law and its relation to the Church.[29] Fr. Reed insists that one element of the natural law is that it is "God-made," another that it is "man-discovered." Without thereby detracting from the importance of this latter aspect, he states that the more theologically significant element of the natural law is that it is God-made, that is, founded on the being of man. "It has the character of law precisely and only because it is an order established and willed by God, not because it is an order perceived by man." Because this law is founded on man's being and because man is reasonable, the law will be knowable "more or less," to use Fr. Reed's phrase. However, whether man arrives at a moral conclusion by rational reflection, or through the teaching of the Church, or even through revelation, this methodology is not constitutive of the law as natural. Thus the fact that something is also revealed does not mean that it is not of natural law. Therefore Reed feels it is very important to distinguish the source of the law from the source of our knowledge of the law. One can derive (and probably does so more often than we think) his certitude about a particular aspect of natural law from, for example, the magisterium without prejudice to the law's distinctive attribute as natural law. "Such a position does not cut off dialogue with the non-Catholic theologian or moral philosopher. On the contrary, it is a position more acceptable to him than the implication that he fails to see the cogency of the Catholic argument. He is, quite rightly, not prepared to admit that the Catholic has a reason or a degree of sincerity which he has not."

There are two points in this very helpful essay on which I should like to comment. First, there is the matter of arguments. Fr. Reed refers to the fact that in matters of natural law the arguments and analyses we make "demonstrate at least the reasonableness of a particular controverted position." This strikes me as being an extremely important point in ethical discussion. Any theologian who holds a natural law would assert that the good of human life,

[29] John J. Reed, S.J., "Natural Law, Theology, and the Church," THEOLOGICAL STUDIES 26 (1965) 40–64.

for example, is at the heart of this law. This must be intuitively clear to rational human beings.[30] It is also and almost equally clear that certain material norms with an absolute validity are inseparable from this intuition.[31] However, our ability to establish persuasively these material norms within a system may not rise above the level of reasonable consistency. This might explain the apparently paradoxical fact that one can be deeply convinced of a conclusion without being able to demonstrate his conviction persuasively to all or many. It also could explain why another can feel the urgent need to demonstrate and why he could deny the same conclusion for lack of demonstration. To admit this is not to stump for a complacent obscurantism. It is to admit that our perception of the implications of the primary principles of moral conduct is fragile and difficult. Certain truths about man's nature penetrate his consciousness gradually by historical processes and for the same reason are maintained only with difficulty. It is this very fact which suggests the inherent reasonableness of an authoritative magisterium.

The theological issue in many matters of natural law is one of expectation, expectation from ourselves and from the Church. What do we expect of ourselves in the area of "proof" where applications of the natural law are involved? Does it follow that because something pertains to the natural law, a convincing proof must be clear to all men, or most, or even many, and *now*? As for the Church, what have we a right to demand of the Church in vindication of her teaching on natural law? Is it not, up to a point, precisely because arguments are not clear, or at least not universally persuasive, that a magisterium makes sense in this area? At what point does our healthy impatience to understand muffle the voice most likely to speed the process? These remarks are not offered as special pleading of one sort or another. They simply raise a genuine and difficult issue. It is the issue of expectation. To expect too little of ourselves would be the abject abdication of reason. To expect too much would be a new rationalism and at root a subtle attack on our human condition and the divinely commissioned teaching authority which protects it. The line between abdication and exaltation of reason is not easy to draw.

Secondly, there is the matter of Church competence to teach the natural law infallibly. Fr. Reed maintains clearly and explicitly this competence. He

---

[30] Cf. B. Schüller, S.J., *art. cit.*, p. 47; also G. Grisez, *Contraception and the Natural Law* (Milwaukee: Bruce, 1965) p. 65.

[31] An interesting article contends that "in matters of supreme importance, in the basic issues, we have, characteristically and historically, tended to act in a uniform way." The article lists and illustrates these "centralmost drives or desires of personal existence." Douglas Straton, "The Meaning of Moral Law," *Andover Newton Quarterly* 57 (1965) 31–39.

explains the position as being clear from two facts. First, the Church has been charged with the whole of revelation. Secondly, a particular demand of natural law cannot be excluded from this totality, because it may be contained only implicitly and obscurely in the depositum, and the Church is the one competent to decide what is contained in revelation.

The Church's ability to teach the natural law infallibly is the subject of a good deal of recent discussion. In this country Gregory Baum has been especially emphatic on the point that the Church cannot teach the natural law with infallibility.[32] His reason: the Church's infallible competence is limited to revelation. The wording of conciliar documents (*doctrina de fide vel moribus*) refers simply to revelation, the "ethics revealed in the gospel."[33] Obviously Frs. Baum and Reed are at an impasse here, and I suspect that their disagreement is representative of a growing body of opinion on both sides of this question. The discussion will continue, and in the interests of ultimate clarity I should like to state certain difficulties with Fr. Baum's position which other theologians may share with me.

First of all, we may ask: Is what theologians call the natural law actually present, even though obscurely, in revelation? There are good reasons for thinking so. I do not refer merely to the *loci classici*. There is also the simple fact that the mediator of our salvation and the exemplar of Christian existence is the God-*man*. Furthermore, Christ and Paul, who are interested in nothing if not *Christian* morality, insist on the observance of natural-law prescriptions. Finally, Paul propagates the commands of natural-law morality as belonging to the *evangelium*.[34] Fr. Baum himself hints the germinal presence of natural-law morality in the revealed word of God when he writes: "Since the dignity of man is so powerfully revealed in the Scriptures and lies at the heart of the Christian message, we may even ask the question whether modern society, even while largely abandoning the Christian creed, has not retained, assimilated and developed an inherited Gospel theme."[35] I agree with this and wonder how the revealed dignity of man can fail to include

[32] *Commonweal* 81 (1965) 516–17; *Critic, art. cit.*, pp. 43–44, 50–51. Of the opposite opinion he says simply: "This is wrong." To these allegations George K. Malone attaches this note: "It is unusual that one side of this matter would be stated so apodictically by a council *peritus*, Gregory Baum, O.S.A., who writes about the Church: 'Her teachings regarding natural wisdom and the meaning and content of the natural law, however true they may be, and however authoritative her voice in pronouncing them, are not and can never be infallible'" (*American Ecclesiastical Review* 152 [1965] 102). The quotation from Baum is from *Commonweal*, Nov. 20, 1964, p. 286.

[33] *Critic, art. cit.*, p. 44.   [34] 1 Th 4:2; Phil 4:9; 1 Cor 7:10.

[35] *Critic, art. cit.*, p. 49.

precisely the dignity of *man*. Perhaps it is because Fr. Baum thinks of natural law as a code of rules that he finds it hard to discover it in the gospel.

Secondly, to speak of the natural law and the gospel morality as two different entities involves a false notion of the place of natural law in the *Heils-ordnung*. Is there any such thing as a natural law actually separable from the law of Christ? Hardly. There is rather only Christian morality. To admit a natural law and yet to conceive it independently from the law of Christ is to conceive it as a mere abstraction. The language itself of papal literature is abundantly suggestive of the integral position of the natural law in the law of Christ. This literature does not refer to two different moral laws, one natural, the other Christian. It often refers simply to "moral conduct,"[36] "truths of the moral order,"[37] "moral truths,"[38] "the field of morals."[39]

Thirdly, even if (*per impossibile*, I should think) the natural law was not integral to the gospel, the Church's prerogative to propose infallibly the gospel morality would be no more than nugatory without the power to teach the natural law infallibly. One could hardly propose what concerns *Christian men* without proposing what concerns *men*. The Church could hardly propose *Christian love* in any meaningful way without being able to propose the very suppositions of *any love*. In other words, and from this point of view alone, to propose the natural law is essential to the protection and proposal of Christian morality itself, much as certain philosophical truths are capable of definition because without them revealed truths are endangered. Furthermore, charity has no external act of its own. It can express itself only through acts of other virtues. But natural-law demands constitute the most basic demands of these virtues, simply because we can never escape the fact that it is *man* who is loving and to be loved. Would not, therefore, the ability to teach infallibly the dignity of man (certainly a revealed truth) without being able to exclude infallibly forms of conduct incompatible with this dignity be the ability infallibly to propose a cliché?

COMMUNICATIO IN SACRIS

The practical conclusions listed under title of *communicatio in sacris* will undergo considerable revision, perhaps even some drastic changes, in the months and years ahead. This should not be surprising; for adaptation has long been a part of Church discipline in this area. In a historical article covering the major shifts in Church practice over the centuries, Wilhelm de Vries,

---

[36] *AAS* 22 (1930) 579.   [37] *Ibid.*   [38] *AAS* 42 (1950) 561–62.
[39] *AAS* 46 (1954) 671–73.

S.J., calls attention to a gradual move away from earlier flexibility toward increasing rigidity.[40] Recent centuries have been stamped by a highly negative tone, the one found, for example, in canon 1258. De Vries insists on two points. First of all, even in her most severe directives the Church never contended that liturgical services in common with non-Catholics are "necessarily and intrinsically morally reprehensible." Secondly, to understand the negative tone of the Holy See's position, one must understand the theoretical basis. De Vries states that this "is to be looked for in the firm conviction of the Catholic Church that it is the one and only true Church of Christ, and that it alone has the right to offer legitimate public worship to God." Through the many oscillations of history this conviction is one of those "fixed points that remain always the same."

I wonder whether it is precisely this conviction of her uniqueness which completely explains the negative tone of ecclesiastical directives over the years. If there is a logical and necessary connection between awareness of uniqueness and negative attitudes on *communicatio*, I am afraid we are committed to negativism. Even the *Decretum de oecumenismo*,[41] assuredly one of the most irenic of conciliar documents, testifies repeatedly to the Church's awareness of her unique position. It seems, therefore, that her past negative attitudes would rather be traceable to the manner in which she expressed this conviction at various historical moments. At certain times—by force of circumstance and human frailty—the line of demarcation between full and imperfect membership in the Church was drawn in a polemical and divisive spirit because these were polemical and divisive times. At such times the Church tended to view separated groups as sources of danger and contamination. A kind of "war ethos" prevailed in which the term *sentire cum ecclesia* had, as R. Egenter notes,[42] a military ring. Practically, this spirit meant that the Church set herself apart and proclaimed her position by a process of dissociation, above all liturgically, because liturgy is the deepest expression of her faith and doctrines. Where, however, circumstances are greatly altered, the conviction of her uniqueness will manifest itself in different ways. In our time I believe the Church is attempting to signalize herself by a truly unique desire for unity with those still outside her visible precincts. Her desire for unity, while it never blurs the lines which separate or waters down her own belief that she is the one true Church, leads her to acknowledge a community

[40] Wilhelm de Vries, S.J., "Communicatio in sacris," in *The Church and Ecumenism* (= *Concilium* 4; New York: Paulist Press, 1965) pp. 18–40.

[41] *AAS* 57 (1965) 90–107; Latin text also available in *Nouvelle revue théologique* 87 (1965) 40–65.

[42] Richard Egenter, "Die Bedeutung des Sentire cum ecclesia im christlichen Ethos," *Trierer theologische Zeitschrift* 74 (1965) 1–14, at p. 3.

of heritage in spite of important differences. It leads her to dialogue, to mutual exchange, to co-operative social action, and to sharing—even liturgically, to some extent—if this will promote the unity so profoundly a part of her salvific mission. Obviously we have here an impulse which can yield different practical directives where *communicatio in sacris* is concerned.

Just what direction these practical directives might take is treated very thoroughly and competently by John Prah in an exploratory article presented in advance of the ratification of the *Decretum de oecumenismo*.[43] To determine what can be done, one must determine exactly what principles control *communicatio*. It is probably safe to say that most priests left the seminary with the conviction that the conclusions on common worship spelled out in canon law were unchangeable. They were explained in terms of external approbation of heresy or schism, danger of scandal, danger of perversion of faith. Thus the prohibition was traced to divine law itself, and when divine law is invoked in moral matters, it is all too easy to get locked into immutable positions. Certainly it is easy to agree with Fr. Prah that this analysis too readily obscured the contingent character of the conclusions.

Assuredly, if active participation in non-Catholic rites involves approbation of a false cult precisely as false, then clearly such participation will involve implicit denial of one's faith. Furthermore, if it is attended by scandal or danger of perversion, it will be prohibited to the extent that these dangers are imprudently incurred. Whether these hypotheses are realized concretely is a matter of variable fact. This point has been missed, can still be missed, and therefore must be made even more implicit.

For instance, whether active participation involves external approbation of false cult and denial of one's faith depends largely on the manner in which these rites are viewed by the Church. In an apologetic and defensive age, because the Church will tend to emphasize her uniqueness protectively by withdrawal from others, she will see these rites as from across a chasm, as separate *and therefore* as false rites. She will therefore view participation in these rites as a repudiation of allegiance to herself. Where her concern is less polemical, her approach to such rites will undergo a decided shift in emphasis. She will view them not so much as false rites but rather insist that "the brethren divided from us also use many liturgical actions of the Christian religion. These most certainly can truly engender a life of grace in ways that vary according to the condition of each church and community. These liturgical actions must be regarded as capable of giving access to the community of salvation."[44] Here she is viewing these rites not so much as false but rather

[43] John Prah, "Communicatio in sacris: Present Trends," *Proceedings of the Catholic Theological Society of America* 19 (1964) 41–60.
[44] *AAS* 57 (1965) 93.

as sources of grace for those still not in full communion with herself. Once this has been said, it is clear that participation in such rites need not imply repudiation of one's own faith.

As for scandal, this would above all take the form of approval of a separated sect, and therefore to some extent of separateness. This engenders the deceptive impression that unity has in fact been achieved. Such an impression is theologically scandalous, because it tends to weaken the faith of Catholics and makes it harder for all concerned to seek genuine union. In an apologetic age common worship is more likely to sharpen these sources of scandal. But in an era characterized by intelligent ecumenical aspirations, limited common worship can more readily suggest common heritage, the incompleteness but reality of existing ties, and the desire for full union.

The danger of perversion of faith mentioned in moral literature takes the form of indifferentism—not perhaps full-blown theological indifferentism, but at least the "indifferentist mentality." This mentality is more subtle and insidious than theological indifferentism. It is definable in terms of those whose constant association with sincere non-Catholics has led them to underesteem the sacraments, the authoritative aids of Church teaching, etc., so that eventually they come to regard full membership in the Catholic Church as an inherited misfortune. This attitude is all too virulent and one dare not underestimate it. However, this again is a factual and variable matter. It seems that limited common worship need not foster this mentality at all where sound instruction has prepared the way. In an ecumenical age well-informed Catholics could approach non-Catholic religious rites as the worship of fellow Christians whose membership in the Church is as yet incomplete. Far from minimizing obstacles, this spirit meets them head on, but with calm and patient charity rather than with the animosity of strategy or blind sentimentality. Because a strong and intelligent desire for union insists on facing obstacles honestly, the danger of perversion is enormously reduced. Indeed, such contact could quite easily be a source of edification and growth in one's faith.

It is doubtless this type of consideration which Fr. Prah had in mind when he wrote that "distinctions between the rites themselves and the modifying circumstances were not sufficiently marked off."

It is clear that the *Decretum de oecumenismo* has enlarged the approach to this subject. After indicating the desirability of prayer in common as "an effective means of obtaining the grace of unity and ... a true expression of the ties which still bind Catholics to their separated brethren," the Decree turns to worship properly so called.

Yet worship in common (*communicatio in sacris*) is not to be considered as a means to be used indiscriminately for the restoration of Christian unity. There are two main principles governing the practice of such common worship: first, the bearing witness to the unity of the Church, and second, the sharing in the means of grace. Witness to the unity of the Church very generally forbids common worship to Christians, but the grace to be had from it sometimes commends this practice. The course to be adopted, with due regard to all the circumstances of time, place, and persons, is to be decided by local episcopal authority, unless otherwise provided for by the Bishops' Conference according to its statutes, or by the Holy See.[45]

The interesting word here, as Enda McDonagh points out,[46] is *indiscretim*. "In the mind of canon law," he writes, "active participation in worship together (which seems certainly in question) would have been unthinkable as a means towards unity." The Decree does not take this point of view. In using the word *indiscretim* it actually implies that there are times when active common worship is in place. At the same time and secondly it implies recognition of the enormous practical difficulties which make of active common worship such a delicate thing. One of these difficulties mentioned by Gustave Thils[47] is the diversity of doctrine about the sacraments and particularly about the Eucharist. For this and similar reasons the Decree is content to present two general theological principles on *communicatio* and leave their application to local authority.

The first principle in control of common worship is the fact that liturgy bears witness to the unity of the Church. The second principle views liturgy from a different point of view; it sees it as a means of grace. Gregory Baum has indicated that these two principles move in opposite directions.[48] One forbids while the other favors. One must balance these carefully against each other to determine whether the prohibitive or permissive principle should predominate in individual instances.

The Council fathers were not content to state these two controlling principles; they also applied them in a general way. Thus, when one considers liturgy as a sign of unity, "significatio unitatis *plerumque* vetat communicationem." They immediately add: "gratia procuranda *quandoque* illam commendat." As a general rule, worship as a sign of unity will give rise to the dangers and problems because of which common worship has been and must continue to be prohibited.

I think it would be accurate to summarize the shift in emphasis introduced by the Decree in the following way. Formerly we had asked: When is common worship permissible because free of improper approbation, scandal, and

[45] *AAS* 57 (1965) 98.

[46] Enda McDonagh, "The Practice of Ecumenism," *Irish Theological Quarterly* 32 (1965) 141–50, at p. 145.

[47] G. Thils, "Le décret conciliaire sur l'oecuménisme," *Nouvelle revue théologique* 87 (1965) 231.

[48] Gregory Baum, O.S.A., "Communicatio in sacris," *Ecumenist* 2 (1965) 62.

danger of perversion? The factual answer to this question had been emphatically negative because of conditions flowing from a pre-ecumenical era. Actually, however, even the question asked was unilateral. The dangers adduced tell us what can be wrong with *communicatio*; they do not tell us positively what can commend it. More precisely, these three sources of the prohibition of common worship arise from an approach to liturgy as a sign of unity. Liturgy is certainly a sign of unity. But the Decree points out that it is also a means of grace. It is in giving more explicit and emphatic recognition to this fact that the Decree has effected a shift in approach. Previously, of course, we had instances of this aspect of *communicatio* where priests were permitted to administer the sacraments to dying non-Catholics. In these instances the role of liturgy to signify unity became subordinate to the over-all salvific mission of the Church. There could be other situations where *communicatio* is necessary as a means of grace, but in a larger and less obvious sense, and where it could lead to a similar subordination. That is, in specific cases common worship could be a very apt means of manifesting the unity of grace and baptism already existing between Christians, and thereby of promoting Christian unity and charity. Christian unity, being an essential aspect of the salvific mission of the Church, could dictate the momentary neglect of the liturgy as a sign of unity ". . . as long as the momentary neglect of the liturgy as sign of unity would not confuse the Christian conscience, or in particular, create the danger of indifferentism."[49] Equivalently, then, the Decree has said *per se non licet, per accidens licet,* and it has given us a fuller notion of the necessity which may lead to a judgment of licitness.

It is explicitly stated by the Decree that the practical course to be adopted is to be decided by local episcopal authority "unless otherwise provided for by the Bishops' Conference according to its statutes, or by the Holy See." Examples of such determination already exist in this country.

On June 11, 1965, the Archdiocese of St. Louis published its *Archdiocesan Directory on Ecumenism.* It is an admirable blend of prudence and initiative. After discussing the meaning of ecumenism and the *Decretum de oecumenismo,* it presents detailed directives with regard to *communicatio,* but states for its faithful that the norms "are given with full realization that future developments may cause them to be modified." Of particular interest is the statement on the Eucharist. The Directory states that the Eucharist is the sign and cause of unity and as such it is the goal towards which the ecumenical movement is directed. It continues:

Although there is theological discussion of the advisability of admitting members of other Christian Churches to Communion on specific occasions, the arguments

[49] Baum, *ibid.*

against open Communion in the present stage of the ecumenical era seem the more cogent. Generally speaking, Catholics look to the Eucharist as the sacrament of unity to be shared in by those who are already fully united. Inter-Communion is viewed as a goal to be attained rather than a means of achieving unity.

The Directory mentions "open" Communion, and that "in the present stage." It does not discuss the matter of individual (for lack of a better word) administration of Communion (or absolution) to a well-disposed non-Catholic Christian.

What is to be thought of such "individual" reception of these sacraments? Any policy on this point must return to the principles asserted in the *Decretum de oecumenismo*. There it is implied that the liturgy as a sign of unity is of great importance. But this sign of unity is not ultimate.[50] The over-all salvific mission of the Church must be the ultimate arbiter of policy. When this mission demands or strongly suggests it, common worship will be in place. Specifically, the Decree is suggesting that Christian unity is so essential a part of her salvific mission that when common worship will aid or promote it, this unity is to be considered as *gratia procuranda*. By way of general answer to the question of "individual" reception of absolution and Communion by well-disposed non-Catholic Christians, I would suggest the following formulation: If local ordinaries judge that individual reception will actually foster eventual unity among Christians without unduly occasioning the dangers associated with common worship, they will have judged that this vital aspect of the Church's mission has in fact taken precedence over the *signum unitatis*. This is an extremely delicate matter and one that local ordinaries will certainly want to weigh carefully. Practically, I do not believe that such individual reception of the sacraments should be invited or encouraged at the present time.

In mid-June (1965) the Catholic press published the text of *Interim Guidelines for Prayer in Common and Communicatio in sacris*. This document was issued by the Commission for Ecumenical Affairs of the U.S. Bishops. The Commission states that ultimately the Secretariate for Promotion of Christian Unity will present a directory applicable to the universal Church. In the meantime it offers certain recommendations.

The *Guidelines* text quotes liberally from the *Decretum de oecumenismo* but makes it more specific in places. For instance, with regard to the participation of Catholics in the official worship of other Churches, it states that the

[50] This is obvious in the attitude taken by the *Decretum* toward the separated Eastern Churches. There it is stated that "quaedam communicatio in sacris . . . non solum possibilis est sed etiam suadetur" (*AAS* 57 [1965] 102). Cf. also Augustin Cardinal Bea, "Il decreto conciliare sull'ecumenismo: L'Azione da svolgere," *Civiltà cattolica* 116 (1965) 9–22, at pp. 19–20.

Decretum does envisage such *communicatio*. Specifically, "Catholics may attend official services of other Churches which have special civic or social significance, especially weddings and funerals." While this is not new in every respect, still there is no mention of mere passive presence. With regard to the Eucharist, the document is very close to the St. Louis Directory. "At the present time, however, except in particular cases of members of the Eastern Orthodox Church, intercommunion with Christians in other denominations should not be permitted." This is a tentative conclusion and one can surmise that the document is concerned with open reception of the Eucharist on the part of non-Catholic Christians.

Recent literature and the *Decretum de oecumenismo* have, then, brought a more positive emphasis to the matter of common worship by making explicit the contingent character of the facts behind prohibition and by highlighting the all-too-often-neglected principle of *gratia procuranda*. Moral theologians will have to reconsider many of their practical conclusions in light of these principles.

DIGNITY OF THE HUMAN PERSON

Premarital intercourse has always been something of a practical problem for the young. This is to be expected. That it should be a theological problem of sorts might come as a surprise. Yet some recent literature, especially non-Catholic, has been concerned with the problem theologically. A sampling may help to show what is being said.[51] D. E. H. Whiteley had stated in the *Expository Times* that fornication is always a sin, and he had listed the reasons for his conclusion.[52] Most of the reasons listed were appeals either to its harmful effects, or to the psychic results of violation of conscience, or to the possibility of growing abuse if "anticipated marriage" between the engaged were allowed. In answer, R. E. Taylor points out the nonuniversal character of many of these arguments.[53] He concedes, of course, that to inflict psychological harm or to cause misery violates the command to love our neighbor,

[51] See also John A. T. Robinson, *Honest to God* (Philadelphia: Westminster Press, 1963) pp. 105–21; *The Honest to God Debate*, ed. David L. Edwards (Philadelphia: Westminste, Press, 1963); Arnold Lunn and Garth Lean, *The New Morality* (London: Blandford Press 1964) esp. pp. 56–72; Lunn and Lean, *The Cult of Softness* (London: Blandford Press, 1965); Francis Canavan, S.J., "Reflections on the Revolution in Sex," *America* 112 (1965) 312–15.

[52] D. E. H. Whiteley, "Important Moral Issues: I—Sex and Fornication," *Expository Times* 75 (1963) 36–39.

[53] R. E. Taylor, "Another Look at 'Anticipated' Marriage," *Expository Times* 76 (1965) 252–54.

and that the morality of premarital relations cannot be assessed apart from this great command.

Basically, however, an understanding of sin must come, he insists, more directly from an understanding of God's word itself. With regard to "anticipated marriage," the first question must be: Do Scripture and tradition tell us that it is *always* a sin? Taylor finds no evidence in Scripture condemnatory of sexual intercourse so long as marriage was definitely intended. *Porneia*, for example, is a general term for illicit intercourse, and it evidently includes promiscuous sexual relationships, but not clearly intercourse between those betrothed. The early Christians felt that present marriage consent (Taylor says inaccurately and continuously "mutual commitment") was a sufficient basis for life as man and wife. Ceremonies were highly desirable; their lack was not invalidating. He concludes that what morally legitimated sexual relations in both Jewish and Christian tradition was neither the blessing of the Church nor the permission of the state, but the freedom of the couple to marry and their commitment to do so. Therefore "churchmen may continue to teach that sexual relations *unaccompanied by a lifetime commitment are sin.*"

Paul Ramsey approaches the problem of sexual relations from a slightly different point of view.[54] First he presents an analysis of sexual intercourse. Ramsey sees intercourse as an act which is *of itself* both an act of love and procreative. He puts this very clearly and it would help to cite him exactly:

Whether or not an existing relation between the man and the woman is actually nourished and strengthened by their sexual intercourse, the act itself is an act of love. Whether or not a child in engendered, the act is in itself procreative. This means that sexual intercourse tends, of its own nature, toward the expression and strengthening of love and toward the engendering of children.

One could scarcely put the double *finis operis* of sexual intercourse more clearly. Neither love nor procreativity is present only when the parties decide to put their minds to it; these are the inner senses of intercourse. Secondly, Ramsey insists over and over again that "God has joined these two things together" in a single act. Thirdly, Ramsey suggests that the crucial question about premarital relations is this: "whether sexual intercourse as an act of love should ever be separated from sexual intercourse as an act of procreation." His answer: man may not separate these two inner senses and premarital intercourse does so.

[54] Paul Ramsey, "A Christian Approach to the Question of Sexual Relations outside of Marriage," *Journal of Religion* 45 (1965) 100–118.

Ramsey argues that as a general rule premarital intercourse is irresponsible activity. For when men attempt to put asunder entirely an act of sexual love from its procreative meaning, they must be sensitive to the responsibilities involved. In premarital intercourse they are not. First of all, where a contraceptive is not technically and humanly perfect, the irresponsibility is clear. Fornicators who ignore a two per cent defectibility rate in a contraceptive are just as irresponsible as two people who play Russian roulette where chances of death are only two in a hundred. Secondly, even where a perfect contraceptive removed from all human error is available and where man *can* separate acts of sexual love from procreation, *should* he? No, says Ramsey, for in doing so "no respect is paid, no honor given, to the fact that God joined sexual love and procreation together in our beings." ·Even a perfect contraceptive means a refusal of the image of God's creation (where love and creation combined) in our activity.

More precision is needed where relations between those engaged to be married are involved. Here Ramsey distinguishes marriage consent from the ceremonies of marriage. Therefore we must distinguish premarital relations from expressions of an existing marriage which is simply unannounced. Preceremonial relations are not necessarily premarital relations. "If they [the couple] mean to express the fact that their lives are united and that they now are willing to accept all that is entailed in sexual intercourse as their unity in one flesh ... then it is simply impossible for them to engage in *pre*marital sexual relations as this is understood in Christian teachings." If, on the other hand, the couple engages in something they know is *pre*marital in the authentic sense, they recognize their irresponsibility.

Anyone familiar with the writings of Paul Ramsey will appreciate the precise and provocative character of his thought. Particularly remarkable in this article, for one who does not take his departure from Catholic teachings, is Ramsey's insistence that intercourse is "at the same time and by virtue of its own tendencies, an act of love and an act of procreation." There are a few points in his interesting presentation which deserve comment.

First of all, Ramsey's proof for the immorality of premarital intercourse when a technically perfect contraceptive is used seems unpersuasive. He had argued that this completely separates the act of love from the sex act as procreative and thus amounts to a refusal to allow the image of God (in whom love and creativity always combine) in our activity. However, if the oneness of the unitive and procreative aspects of sex is honored in marriage even when perfect contraceptives are used, as Ramsey claims it can be, then it is clear that this honor can be manifested in ways other than in individual acts. The young man who sincerely intends to marry later and raise a family is showing honor to this union in Ramsey's terms, I should think, even though he indulges in premarital relations now.[55]

Secondly—and this point is common to Taylor and Ramsey—what is the relationship between individual marriage consents and competent authority? Taylor had remarked that "the Church did not have the power to validate or invalidate a marriage,"[56] for marriage is fundamentally a consensual thing. Ramsey, in clarifying his position as reported in *Time* magazine, wrote that "Christians in past ages believed that persons consenting together (whether before church or state, or not) have a performatory power that is so extraordinary that it creates an indissoluble bond that did not exist before between them."[57] Both Taylor and Ramsey would hold, I take it, that relations which express an already given consent (private, that is, and preceremonial) are not premarital in a moral sense and, to that extent, not immoral. It is here that I believe something more has to be said.

What Christians believed in the past in terms of what the Church actually did then is one thing; what the Church *can do* is quite another. The Church vindicates to herself competence over the marriage of the baptized in such a way that she can establish even diriment impediments to marriage.[58] She has the competence, in other words, to make demands which when not observed render the persons *inhabiles* to contract—even though they are *habiles* to consent. Furthermore, since not any contract was elevated by Christ to sacramentality but only a valid one, this *inhabilitas* would indirectly obtain for the sacrament also. Now if a person is for some reason or other *inhabilis* to contract, what in his case would "marriage consent" mean or achieve? This consent achieves its full effect in an ecclesial and social context. As long, then, as the Church has the right to make invalidating demands and actually does so (as she still does in our time where canonical form is concerned—whether she should is another question), lack of compliance with them means that consent is not effective in establishing a true marriage.

The terms "premarital" and "conjugal" must be understood in relation to the total reality of marriage. Marriage as totally understood is an ecclesial and social reality. Hence intercourse performed with what the parties call "marriage consent" is *premarital*, I should think, in the fullest moral sense. After all, is not one's ability to effect something by consent condi-

[55] For a helpful analysis of the morality of premarital relations, cf. Joseph Fuchs, S.J., *De castitate et ordine sexuali* (3rd ed.; Rome: Gregorian Univ. Press, 1963) pp. 45 ff., 99 ff.

[56] *Art. cit.*, p. 254.

[57] *Time* 85 (March 19, 1965) 15.

[58] A. DeSmet, *De sponsalibus et matrimonio* (Bruges, 1926) nos. 419–25, esp. n. 1, p. 362; M. Zalba, S.J., *Theologiae moralis summa* 3 (Madrid, 1958) nos. 1197 and 1334.

tioned by his ecclesial reality? Therefore I do not understand the abstract (and absolute) character of the performatory power which Ramsey and Taylor assert. This is not to underestimate such performatory power (for nothing can supply for consent[59]); it is rather to put it in its proper ecclesial context. As for the nonbaptized, it seems that the proper civil authority could make similar demands (whether it does beyond mere civil effects I do not know). Marriage consent is qualified by the ability to marry, and we dare not think of such ability apart from man's ecclesial and social context; for this would jeopardize the very goods marriage is intended to achieve.

Thirdly, Ramsey has spoken of the union of the procreative and unitive purposes of intercourse in the selfsame act and asked: Is it proper for man to put these asunder completely? It would be interesting if a man of Ramsey's shrewdness were to ask: *Can* man, even if he wants to, ever separate the two? That is, what assurance does man have, after he has altered the act in such a way that procreation is impossible, that he is still dealing with a true act of sexual love? How is such an act to be defined concretely and by what criteria?

Two articles in the *Homiletic and Pastoral Review*[60] attempt to face the premarital problem at a pastoral level. Their main point is that adolescent sexual problems must be situated within the context of the adolescent growth process. Once such problems are viewed as above all developmental problems, what can the priest do to aid the process of growth to maturity? The articles suggest that the priest—in any of his three roles of confessor, counselor, teacher—makes his best contribution by helping the adolescent to see and understand himself as a person and by aiding him in the understanding of the positive values of human sexuality. With regard to this latter, the priest will find very helpful Evelyn Millis Duvall's new book *Why Wait till Marriage?*[61] This is not a moral or religious treatise, but it contains a wealth of common sense couched persuasively for those for whom it was written.

Denis F. O'Callaghan discusses the case of the spy who desires to take his own life to protect his comrades, perhaps even his country, from the harm he could cause through revelation of classified information.[62] The case is interesting not merely or especially because in an era of cold war and arms

[59] W. Bertrams, S.J., "Efficacitas consensus matrimonialis naturaliter validi," *Periodica* 51 (1962) 288–300; H. Heimerl, "Ehewille–Eheschliessungsform–Ehegültigkeit," *Theologisch-praktische Quartalschrift* 113 (1965) 144–63.

[60] R. A. McCormick, S.J., "The Priest and Teen-Age Sexuality," *Homiletic and Pastoral Review* 65 (Feb., 1965) 379–87; 65 (March, 1965) 473–80.

[61] Evelyn Millis Duvall, *Why Wait till Marriage?* (New York: Association Press, 1965).

[62] Denis F. O'Callaghan, "May a Spy Take His Life?" *Irish Ecclesiastical Record* 103 (1965) 259–64.

races espionage is more frequent; it is above all pertinent as a test of our existing practical formulations concerning the sanctity and inviolability of human life. One of the most common of these formulations, as manifested in the distinction between direct and indirect killing, is the principle of double effect. O'Callaghan discusses thoroughly and accurately existing formulations, admitting that eventually every one runs into human complexities where the load seems too great for the formulation, especially if we have endowed it with a computer-like rigidity. One such instance, it is said, would be the inability of the terms direct–indirect self-killing adequately to grasp the real difference between suicide and self-sacrifice. Some direct self-killings conform humanly to the notion of sacrifice rather than to that of suicide—e.g., when done in a very noble cause. O'Callaghan, while admitting the moral relevance of this distinction, prefers to associate it with motive and ultimately finds direct killing of self for one's country "unacceptable both from the point of view of principle and the point of view of consequence."

It is interesting that those who prefer the categories suicide–sacrifice to direct–indirect self-killing (Leclercq, Huftier[63]) give as examples of sacrifice of self classic cases of indirect killing (e.g., the soldier who kills himself in the process of blowing up a fortress). I am inclined to agree with Fr. O'Callaghan that the spy may not take his own life, and for two reasons. First, the spy cannot be regarded as an unjust aggressor against his country, even though his human frailty may be the cause of harm to it; for unjust (materially unjust—which is all that is required) aggression supposes that an individual has left the sphere of his own rights and entered the sphere of another's. One simply performing vital activities, for example, even though they are harmful to others, cannot be said to have abandoned the sphere of his own rights. While we have a right to demand that those with deadly communicable diseases segregate themselves, we do not have a right to demand that they cease vital functions if this is our only protection. Somewhat similarly, reacting in accordance with human limitations under severe torture does not mean that I have left the sphere of my own rights and invaded that of my government's; for no government has the *right* to demand that I be superhuman. Hence, though the revelation under torture of secret information could be harmful to others, I doubt that such a probability would put the spy in the category of unjust aggressor. In making use of human agents with built-in limits, the government must be thought to understand and accept this calculated risk.

Secondly, even though the indirect voluntary leaves us scratching our

[63] J. Leclercq, *Leçons de droit naturel* 4: *Les droits et devoirs individuels* (Namur: Maison d'Editions, 1955) pp. 57–58; M. Huftier, in *L'Ami du clergé* 72 (1962) 297–303.

heads at times, it does represent a most human and common-sense distinction capable of handling the vast majority of sacrificial vs. suicidal situations. For this reason I would prefer to adhere to it even in the face of an unpopular solution, if such a solution constitutes my only solid reason for abandoning it.

Patrick Granfield, O.S.B., presents an admirably clear and thorough summary of moral thought on the right to silence.[64] Textbook literature has been generally content to rest its case for this right on a practical positive-law basis. That is, the defendant is bound to respond *secundum ordinem juris*, and civil codes do not demand confession of one's crime. This treatment easily leaves the impression that the right may not be natural. More current literature contends that the axiom *nemo tenetur tradere seipsum* expresses something rooted in man's very being, something which founds a natural, though not unlimited, right against self-incrimination. What is this something? Fr. Granfield summarizes the five most common arguments which point to the natural-law origin of the right to silence: (1) right to secrecy; (2) right to reputation; (3) exceptional character of the duty to perform heroic acts; (4) legitimate love of self; (5) dignity of the human personality. I must confess that whenever I encounter such abundance, I suspect that no one argument quite carries it off. Apparently Fr. Granfield shares this uneasiness when he concludes with a combination of 1 and 5: "the best argument for the right to silence is the fundamental dignity of man as God's superb creation, destined to perfect himself in a society. Man, endowed with liberty, has a certain dominion over his inner world. He has a right to his private and personal life." But this right has limits. Precisely because this dignity can be developed and maintained only within society is the right limited by the common good (Granfield prefers "maximal public order"); but precisely because the common good purposes the good of individuals is the limitation itself severely limited.

Another problem touching secrecy and through it the dignity of the individual is wire tapping. Traditional moral theology has said very little about this specific type of invasion of privacy. It has given two general principles: to search out another's secret demands a right to the knowledge and the use of licit means.[65] A recent article can help concretize the term "licitness of means."[66] While the two lawyers who discuss wire tapping do

[64] Patrick Granfield, O.S.B., "The Right to Silence," THEOLOGICAL STUDIES 26 (1965) 280–98.

[65] Robert E. Regan, O.S.A., *Professional Secrecy in the Light of Moral Principles* (Washington, D.C.: Catholic Univ. of America, 1943) p. 34.

[66] F. E. Inbau and Herman Schwartz, "Wiretapping: Yes or No?" *Christian Century* 82 (1965) 75–79.

not approach it from a moral point of view, much of what they say is very pertinent to the moral question.

Fred E. Imbau, of Northwestern University, argues in favor of wire tapping on the grounds that it is the only practical way of getting at the big racketeers. Furthermore, the fear of the ordinary citizen that police will have access to his private affairs (indiscretions, etc.) is unjustified, for wire tapping is neither cheap nor easy. It simply is not worth while unless it is done to get at the very serious criminal offender. Nor should we fear blackmail, for there are easier ways to go about this too. Finally, those who opt for wire tapping as a necessary police function want it permitted only after the police have obtained a court order.

Herman Schwartz, of the State University of New York (Buffalo), argues against the need of wire tapping on two basic grounds: danger to privacy is too great and the value of the wire tap is relatively minimal. As for privacy, he contends that the wire tap is inherently unlimitable. To tap the line of one person means to invade the privacy of many. Nor is the wire tap the only practical way of getting to the major criminal elements in society, a point admitted by not a few attorneys general. It is useful, of course, but a case for indispensability has not been made, "and in a free society one does not give the police drastic powers unless a need is conclusively shown." Finally, the wire tap is but one investigative technique made possible by the electronic revolution. Legitimation of this one technique will lead and has led to use of other devices (detectaphones, parabolic microphones, etc.).

We all share a strong revulsion against the criminally parasitic and we share an instinctive reaction that these people should be prevented at any cost. But these reactions, however wholesome, must be carefully controlled if we are to survive our own enthusiasms. The cost just may be too high. We may have indeed provided protection against criminal elements in society, but in the process we may have produced a society where it is hardly worth while being protected. I would suggest the following conclusions about the licitness of this means: wire tapping is *per se* illicit, *per accidens* licit— that is, illicit unless it is carefully restricted (1) by court order and surveillance (2) to instances of very serious crime or its threat (3) where no other means are practicable. Whether these conditions can ever be realized practically, *videant sapientiores*. But on paper Schwartz has the better of the argument. A society which enjoys privacy can unfortunately begin to take it for granted and badly underestimate its true worth. The road back is long and hard.

L. Beirnaert's interesting discussion of the modern problem of secrecy is more concerned with the subjective (personal) factors involved.[67] Even

---

[67] L. Beinaert, "Problèmes autour du secret," *Etudes*, March, 1965, pp. 334–40.

when all the standard protective conditions are fulfilled, the very idea of unburdening oneself to another retains a fearsome aspect and often blocks the genuine exchange so basic to modern organized charitable endeavors. Why? The secret is symbolic of our own personal dignity. Since we all possess a kind of instinctive urge to penetrate the secrets of others (a guarded secret contains a bit of defiance), we tend to storm the secrecy of others and thereby provoke the attitude of resistance; for the person is under attack. Therefore, in modern situations calling for self-unburdening, any exercise of power must be renounced in favor of a charity which seeks uniquely the good of the person. Otherwise the relationship may produce information for the dossier, but it will scarcely produce the real self-revelation necessary for the progress of the subject.

Rudolph Weiler presents a brief moral analysis of the use of narcotic stimulants in athletic events.[68] The first problem one faces here is one of definition. Weiler understands *das Doping* as meaning the "administration or use by healthy persons of substances foreign to the body in any form and of physiological substances in abnormal doses or in an abnormal way, with the single purpose of artificially and unfairly heightening competitive achievement." After listing what all would regard as medical examples (morphine, cocaine, etc.), he opines that ten times the daily dose of vitamins would probably fit his definition. Also to be included by affinity, so to speak, are psychic means of stimulation such as hypnosis. Rather surprisingly (to Americans), he includes use of oxygen by football players.

The essay concludes that use of stimulants as defined is to be morally interdicted on three grounds. First, it is harmful, or easily can be, to bodily health. Athletics purpose among other things enduring bodily health and conditioning. Any drugs which have an over-all negative effect on the whole person later on are irreconcilable with the human meaning of athletics. Secondly, drug stimulants offend the fairness and honesty inseparable from competitive sport, because they alter its basic suppositions and conditions. Furthermore, they deceive the public. Finally, these practices are (in many places) in violation of international agreements. Weiler's statements are general and he is careful not to venture beyond this general character. Serious sin can be present but is not often likely to be present.

Without gainsaying the validity of this analysis, I would prefer a slightly different approach. Victory is inseparable from the notion of competitive athletics. Because this struggle for victory sharpens personal skills and co-

[68] R. Weiler, "Das Doping und seine sittliche Beurteilung," *Theologisch-praktische Quartalschrift* 113 (1965) 164–67. For further remarks cf. THEOLOGICAL STUDIES 21 (1960) 589–90.

ordination, develops foresight through strategic thinking, intensifies co-op-eration and unselfishness through teamwork, enlarges toleration for adver-sity—in short, calls forth and promotes human qualities which reflect man's dignity and worth—it has always been honored as a *human* achievement. It is precisely because men bear the burden of this struggle that it is human-izing. To the extent that this burden is shifted to a drug, competition is de-humanized and therefore becomes dehumanizing. Little more need be said. In an age which already short-cuts many of its challenges through chemis-try, it is unfortunate that this form of dehumanization is actual and common enough to require moral analysis.

Underlying any legal (whether civil or canonical) stipulations about ob-scenity is a theological notion of the obscene. Theologians would readily admit to a feeling of vague dissatisfaction with the results of their attempts to make this notion precise and viable. Maurice Amen, C.S.C., summarizes for attorneys Church law on the obscene and especially the theological at-tempts to elaborate that notion.[69]

An excellent article by Peter R. Connolly offers some challenging reflec-tions.[70] While admitting that obscenity is comprised of both subjective and objective factors (scil., the objective *allectatio* is measured by the reactions of the individual), he feels that theological formulations of the obscene have tended to neglect the objective factors. This neglect manifests itself in our use of quantity of sexual detail as a criterion, whereas it is not quantity but quality (the spirit which animates the sexual detail) which distinguishes pornography from other literary genres. Unless we make this quality clear, *allectatio* will remain an ambiguous term containing indiscriminately the allure of the pornographic and the allure of things not pornographic, above all that of erotic realism.[71]

Erotic realism, Connolly insists, in spite of its treatment of sexual detail, is not pornographic. Genuine pornography is a subliterary type involving direct solicitation to lustful acts, whether in the mind or outside of it. It isolates physical sexuality from all context of spiritual or emotional feeling and imprisons the reader in the world of genital stimulation. Erotic realism, on the other hand, appeals to and builds up erotic feeling but contains it. It attempts to control and interpret the sexual experience of contemporary man. There is a continual reference to a larger and more total pattern. Thus,

[69] Maurice Amen, C.S.C., "The Church versus Obscene Literature," *Catholic Lawyer* 11 (1965) 21–32.

[70] Peter R. Connolly, "The Moralists and the Obscene," *Irish Theological Quarterly* 32 (1965) 116–28.

[71] Connolly includes in the literary type of "obscene writing" the scatological, the bawdy, and erotic realism. Clearly he is distinguishing obscenity from pornography.

whereas pornography is the verbal counterpart of lust, erotic realism "in the West has become a literary correlative for the state of romantic love as it evolved in that tradition." This article presents a convincing case that the two genres are antithetical despite superficial resemblances and that this difference is detectable even at the level of verbal texture.

Once the distinction between true pornography and other literary types (including the bawdy, the scatological, and erotic realism) has been made, two questions occur: (1) Has the Church been forbidding only pornography? (2) Should she have forbidden only pornography? As for the first question, I suspect we would have to say "no," and Connolly would suggest that it is precisely because of neglect of objective factors (which literary criticism is best suited to provide) that we have to answer in this way. I believe it is a reasonable reading of his meaning to say that he would answer the second question affirmatively. It is not hard to agree with Connolly here. If erotic realism, etc., are genuine literary types—and I am convinced they are—control were better left to sound education and to the principles covering individual moral risk. At any rate, Connolly's own sensitivity should make it clear to the theologian that an acceptable notion of pornography cannot be elaborated independently of literary criticism.

Nudity in films is not necessarily obscenity. But it does raise practical problems. There are at least two points of view from which one might approach nudity in films: that of artistic canons and that of practical policy. Because the two are distinct, they should be kept distinct. A press release of a statement by the Episcopal Committee for Motion Pictures, Radio, and Television wrote of films: "In itself nudity is not immoral and has long been recognized as a legitimate subject in painting and sculpture. However, in the very different medium of the motion picture it is never an artistic necessity." The Committee's statement went on to adopt a policy with regard to nudity: "The temptation for film-makers to exploit the prurient appeal of nudity in this mass medium is so great that any concession to its use, even for otherwise valid reasons of art, would lead to wide abuse." An editorial in *America* stated that the Episcopal Committee was stating a "*policy*, not a principle of moral philosophy or a canon of artistic criticism."[72] As a policy, the attitude voiced by the Episcopal Committee makes good common sense. Nor are the American bishops the only ones concerned about the temptation to exploitation. James Wall, editor of the *Christian Advocate* (Methodist), wrote: "The sight of bared breasts is of course not likely to do great harm to the American psyche. But the watering-down of the code that has occurred can mean only that a vast commercial enterprise is endeavoring to widen its economic base. . . . The proper use of nudity in

[72] *America* 112 (1965) 895.

Pawnbroker is doomed to be followed by productions so catering to mass prurience that though they reap quick profits they will eventually harm the entire community."[73] Since the Episcopal Committee was specifically interested in a policy approach, two questions remain open to discussion: (1) whether they should have said "it [nudity] is never an artistic necessity"; (2) whether *Pawnbroker* was the best vehicle for implementation of this policy. Such questions will probably be discussed for months, or even years.

CONTRACEPTION

Contraception continues to be (at the time of the composition of these Notes) the major moral issue troubling the Church. In an address to the College of Cardinals delivered June 24, 1965, Pope Paul VI stated that his special commission had not yet completed its work, but that he hoped to be able to make a statement soon.[74] By the time these Notes appear, that statement may have appeared. It was to be expected (given the general unrest on this matter, the now famous "holding" statement on June 23, 1964, the appointment and meeting of Pope Paul's special study commission, and the imminence of the fourth session of Vatican II) that the literature on contraception in the past six months would be voluminous. That expectation has not been disappointed. Only a few of the contributions can be reviewed here.[75]

What is the theological note for the Church's teaching on contraception? Frs. Ford and Kelly had earlier expressed the opinion that it is "very likely already taught infallibly *ex jugi magisterio*."[76] L. L. McReavy came to the same conclusion, that is, that it is "contained in, and guaranteed by, the ordinary and universal teaching of the Church, which cannot mislead."[77] Disagreeing with Fr. McReavy, Canon F. H. Drinkwater insists that we are not dealing with irreformable doctrine.[78] Since *Casti connubii* was not

---

[73] James M. Wall, "Toward Christian Film Criteria," *Christian Century* 82 (1965) 777.

[74] *Documentation catholique* 62 (1965) 1154–59. For a summary of the commission's task and the papal address to its members, cf. E. Tesson, S.J., in *Etudes*, May, 1965, pp. 724–30.

[75] For summaries of earlier contributions, cf. *Moral Problems and Christian Personalism* (= *Concilium* 5; New York: Paulist Press, 1965) pp. 97–154.

[76] John Ford, S.J., and Gerald Kelly, S.J., *Contemporary Moral Theology* 2 (Westminster, Md.: Newman, 1963) 277.

[77] L. L. McReavy, in *Clergy Review* 49 (1964) 707.

[78] F. H. Drinkwater, "Ordinary and Universal," *Clergy Review* 50 (1965) 2–22. This essay is also included in his book *Birth Control and Natural Law* (Baltimore: Helicon, 1965) pp. 39–66. Karl Rahner's statement in *America* 112 (June 12, 1965) 860 is ambiguous. He states that neither *Casti connubii* nor Pius XII's teaching is "absolutely formal or irreformable." He did not address himself to the question of the ordinary and universal magisterium, unless it was by implication.

an ex-cathedra pronouncement and since the same must be said of subsequent papal directives, Drinkwater's main concern is with McReavy's contention that the teaching on contraception is infallible from the ordinary and universal magisterium. His rather lengthy discussion of "ordinary and universal" contains the implicit conclusion that the immorality of contraception has not been taught in this way.

Without asserting that the immorality of contraception is infallible *ex jugi magisterio*, I am puzzled by Drinkwater's reasons for thinking it is not. Unless I am mistaken, his assertion is twofold.

First, he contends that during the past thirty-five years we have had "a whole generation of frozen silence, the silence of intellectual death, or at least of paralysis. . . . The point is that in such an atmosphere the true living voice of the ordinary and universal teaching of the Church is not to be easily heard. There is heard only, so to speak, a single gramophone record playing on and on."[79] There seem to be two implications here: first, that the "ordinary and universal" character of this teaching spans a period of only thirty-five years; secondly, that unless each bishop has made a profound personal study of the matter, the consent is speciously universal. As for the first implication, a book such as John T. Noonan's *Contraception: A History of Its Treatment by the Catholic Theologians and Canonists*[80] should be sufficient to bid it adieu. Secondly, while sympathizing with the Canon's fears of curialism and the all too human temptation to confuse infallibility with administrative centralization, I find it difficult to accept a concept of "ordinary and universal" which demands that each bishop have wrestled personally with the problem himself.[81] The essential of the concept concerns *that which is taught*, not why it is taught or how one arrived at the conclusion. The Church, being also a cultural phenomenon, will always carry along deadwood, both formulated and personal. But Canon Drinkwater's own description of infallibility as a kind of preventative *assistentia* might have suggested to him that such deadwood does not shackle the preventative assistance of the Holy Spirit.

His second assertion is that the immorality of contraception has not been the core teaching. Rather, the real truth being constantly preserved (and repeated in, for example, *Casti connubii*) is "the whole doctrine of Christian marriage, monogamous, fruitful, image of Christ and Church." Therefore,

---

[79] *Art. cit.*, pp. 18–19.

[80] Cambridge: Harvard Univ. Press, 1965.

[81] This idea of ordinary and universal is also presented in Baum's "Can the Church Change Her Position?" in *Contraception and Holiness* (New York: Herder and Herder, 1964).

far from denying an ordinary and universal (and therefore infallible) magisterium on marital morality, Canon Drinkwater is asserting it but interpreting its assertion. The Church has indeed been infallible *ex jugi magisterio* but the assertions of this magisterium have concerned "the whole doctrine of Christian marriage. . . ." As for contraception, "the contraception paragraph was an incidental detail, occasioned by a Lambeth Conference of those days."[82] This may be right, but there is little evidence in Canon Drinkwater's presentation to secure the point. On the face of it, the evidence is heavily weighed against this restrictive reading of the constant and universal teaching.

Unless I am mistaken, we have here one of the most basic theological issues in this entire discussion: Who can assert the *certain* criteria for a doctrine infallible from the universal and ordinary magisterium? Drinkwater is correct, it would seem, when he states that no one of the indications (he lists seven) is decisive. Yet, using his own criteria for what pertains to the universal and ordinary magisterium, I would have to say that where the immorality of contraception is concerned, he has opted for noninfallibility rather than justified this conclusion.

Gregory Baum holds that the Church's infallibility is not involved in the traditional teaching on contraception, but he holds this on different grounds, scil., the Church *cannot* teach infallibly the natural law.[83] Drinkwater obviously, though perhaps unwittingly, disagrees with Fr. Baum, since he holds that the Church has actually been teaching infallibly but only up to a certain point. Also in total disagreement with Fr. Baum is E. Schillebeeckx, who asserts not only the possibility but the fact of irreformable teaching on basic natural-law morality. He says: "We are in fact faced with the universal teaching of the bishops of the world, so that we cannot go back on it. Moreover, it is unthinkable that in such a vitally important question the Church would in fact err in teaching something that has not been declared infallibly."[84] Schillebeeckx, however, interprets the meaning of this teaching in a manner similar to that of Drinkwater.

As the discussion of contraception has continued, it has become obvious that methodological considerations are extremely important. Two articles deal with methodology.

Germain Grisez points out a series of equivocations and assumed premises

---

[82] Drinkwater, *art. cit.*, p. 18.

[83] Gregory Baum, "The Christian Adventure—Risk and Renewal," *Critic* 23 (1965) 41–53.

[84] E. Schillebeeckx, O.P., as reported in *Moral Problems and Christian Personalism*, p. 124.

which lead him to the conclusion that the controversy has been conducted with "almost incredible sloppiness."[85] He cites several examples of this philosophical untidiness. One is the word "intention." It can refer to the tendency of the will toward the good or the end, the tendency which leads to deliberation and eventually to choice. It can also refer to the act of the will which is the choice, the efficacious willing with a view to the end. Grisez's constant message (and one with which I agree) has been: personal problems, population problems, etc., do not tell us whether contraception is morally right or wrong. They rather point up more acutely the need of knowing whether it is right or wrong, and especially why.

Michael Dummett calls attention to the fact that very few of those convinced of the immorality of contraception are satisfied with available statements of the grounds of this immorality.[86] He insists, therefore, that this situation makes it "not less, but *more* incumbent on them [those who favor contraception] to scrutinize that view, and the possible grounds there may be for it, with the greatest care." He does not believe that the real case against contraception has been stated, and hence "those who have convinced themselves that they may safely reject the case against contraception are judging rashly, since it is impossible that they should have considered that case presented in the strongest version of which it should be capable." In the course of his presentation, Dummett gives what he considers to be the two possible sources of the evil of contraception and points out the problems with both of them.

I believe that everyone would concede the importance of methodology in moral discussion. And most would, in dispassionate moments, probably agree with Grisez that there has been an enormous amount of position taking. It is so hard to retain an open and balanced point of view, simply because so much seems to be at stake. On the one hand, there appears the health and happiness of married life itself; on the other, the integrity of morals and the indefectibility (in carefully defined contexts) of the Church's magisterium. However, as soon as one approaches the problem as "something at stake," he tends either to promote or to defend. Neither the promotional nor the defensive posture is a properly theological one. The theologian's task is understanding through open enquiry.

The notion of "open" enquiry may well be at the heart of many methodological problems. I should like to submit the following understanding for theological discussion. The effect of repeated authoritative Church pro-

[85] Germain Grisez, "Reflections on the Contraception Controversy," *American Ecclesiastical Review* 152 (1965) 324–32.

[86] Michael Dummett, "The Question of Contraception," *Clergy Review* 50 (1965) 412–27.

nouncements on a matter of this importance is a presumptive certitude of their correctness. (This supposes for the moment that the precise conclusion in question has not been irreformably taught.) Because there is presumptive *certitude*, prudence demands the acceptance of the conclusion in defect of prevailing contrary evidence. But because this certitude is *only* presumptive, circumstances can arise which will create a duty for the theologian to test it in the light of changing fact, increasing understanding of ethical theory, etc. This testing may appear to be an attempt to get at the same conclusions by other means; hence it may appear to be a defensive or apologetic tactic. The line between testing a teaching and defending it is indeed fine—so fine that not a few theologians have been trapped into a defensive mentality. But testing is not closed-minded apologetics; it is enquiry—but enquiry conducted with the conviction that a Catholic cannot begin as if the Church had never spoken or, if she did, as if this is momentarily irrelevant.

It is here that methodology becomes crucial. If, as some contend, the atmosphere within the Church for the past thirty-five years has prevented truly free discussion of this matter, then by the same token the doctrine has simply been insufficiently tested. It is here that I agree with Dummett that the teaching on contraception has not been presented in the strongest version of which it is capable.

But if the Church's magisterium enjoys certain presumptions, this does not exempt those who draw enlightenment from this teaching from contributing to its formation. The promised guidance of the Holy Spirit, far from rendering discussion and human co-operation unnecessary, rather demands it. In the past semester there have been several attempts to deepen our understanding of marital sexuality. I shall mention but three—and these in impoverishing summary.

Robert O. Johann, S.J., presented to the Catholic Theological Society of America (June, 1965) a paper entitled "Responsible Parenthood: A Philosophical View."[87] After determining the meaning of responsibility as above all stressing the fact that our actions are precisely responses of persons, and after rejecting two extreme forms of the ethics of responsibility, Fr. Johann develops the broad outlines of an ethics of responsibility which will avoid these extremes. Man's very personhood is a call to responsiveness to Being. "What this affirmation of Being requires, i.e., what actually constitutes an adequate response to Being in any particular situation, is a matter for discerning intelligence." This does not exclude universally binding norms.

[87] Fr. Johann very kindly allowed me the use of his manuscript. Quotations are taken directly from the talk as given. It will appear in the *Proceedings of the Catholic Theological Society of America*, Twentieth Annual Meeting, 1965.

"For we are not related to the Absolute and Infinite except through the mediation of the finite and relative." Reason discerns certain types of conduct as incompatible with man's fundamental call to responsiveness to Being. Thus, for example, reason discerns the radical distinction between the order of persons and the order of impersonal nature. Because persons are open to the Absolute, the order of persons participates in the value of the Absolute. Thus this order is necessarily included in one's orientation to God. In other words, one cannot love God without loving the neighbor. Therefore, any exploitative conduct offensive to the dignity of the person is intrinsically evil (e.g., racial discrimination, economic exploitation, rape, etc.). Fr. Johann insists that his general approach, since it is thoroughly ontological in character (founded on man's nature as person), is one of natural law which insists on the objectivity of the moral realm. But he equally insists that though man is concerned with the world's workings, "the importance of natural processes does not lie in their brute facticity." God did not intend that man simply observe the way things operate and leave them that way. Openness to Being is creative and inventive. Against this general background Johann approaches marital ethics.

Sex at the human level absorbs the brute facticity of biological function, and sexual union becomes the embodiment of mutual self-giving. The whole generative process becomes the co-operation of two lovers in the creation of new intelligence, a new freedom, a new person. Summarily, the human meaning of sex is the family. "And it is to this integral sense that man in his freedom and rationality is called to respond." Fr. Johann concludes that any use of sex which makes it a plaything is a failure in responsiveness—but not because "a biological process is interrupted." It is not the perversion of sex as a physical activity that is monstrous, but the perversion of reason in relation to the full human sense of sex. Hence, man's "intervention in natural processes is always justified when its issue is an enlargement of human meanings and possibilities." Fr. Johann concludes that when biological fertility begins to threaten the common work of raising and being a family and when abstention is itself also a threat, then modification of the physical processes so as to further the central reality (the family) is not to thwart the full meaning of sex but to promote it.

Gustave Martelet, S.J., of Lyons, takes a different point of view.[88] If the structure of sexuality is mere "brute facticity," then surely Johann's objections would be decisive. But Martelet insists that this is not so. After stating honestly and forcibly the arguments of present proponents of contra-

[88] Gustave Martelet, S.J., "Morale conjugale et vie chrétienne," *Nouvelle revue théologique* 87 (1965) 245–66.

ception, he reduces them to a single difficulty: the accusation of naturalism. That is, the traditional negative law proscribing contraception ties man to the yoke of the biological and physiological, thus subordinating his intelligence and freedom to the brute facticity of physical structures. In answer to this, Martelet points out that man is *conditioned* transcendence, that is, his intelligence and liberty meet certain thresholds of objectivity which he must adequately understand before asserting his power arbitrarily to intervene. Only when one understands the structure of sexuality adequately will he perceive a genuine spiritual sense in it—a sense which will remove it from the category of "brute facticity." Once this fuller dimension is clear, it is obvious that man actually attests his intelligence and liberty in respecting it and in assuming it as a sign of his creaturehood.

In order to grasp the full sense of sexuality, it is necessary to understand clearly two things: the meaning of the term "natural" and the relation of this to man's creaturely condition.

As for the term "natural," this is not to be understood as the metaphysically necessary. Nor is it to be taken as if "brute facticity" were normative in the narrow context of faculties and finalities. "Natural" rather refers to functionally integral structure. Even though there are variations in the structures of concreteness, beneath them and presupposed in their contingency is the permanence of structure itself. Heads may be all shapes and sizes, but beneath these contingencies is the integrality of the fact of having a head. So also with sexuality. "It is a fact that the sexuality which gives to love its most original language, does so within the generic context of fecundity which one may call natural to love."[89] Natural in what sense? In the sense that this fecundity constitutes an integral part of its structure and condition. One cannot say, then, that sexuality is human when it unites and simply biological when it procreates. In human sexuality the biological conditions the expression of love. That is, "it is to the same reality of life that human subjects, in their conjugal union, owe the sexual language of their love and, in this love, the fecundity (for the most part unforeseen) of their life."[90] If man attributes union to the person and procreation to nature, he is guilty of falsely spiritualizing sexuality. The systematic dissociation of life and love is a basic denial in the area of sexuality of man's conditioned transcendence. So much for the term "natural."

What is the relation of this functional structure to man's creaturely condition? It is here especially that Martelet attempts to show why this natural (scil., functional) structure cannot be regarded as "brute facticity." Procreation represents an astonishing *synergie* on the part of God and the

[89] *Ibid.*, p. 257.   [90] *Ibid.*, p. 249.

couple. By their loving union-in-one-flesh the couple places the indispensable condition for the divine co-operation. It is for this reason basically that human sexuality and the sexual act itself are not subordinate to man's arbitrary powers of intervention. If procreation were merely the production of a *thing* (not a person), it would be otherwise. Martelet puts it as follows:

Unless we are to say that in sexuality God finds Himself at the mercy of man, and that He thus passes to the level of a simple *component* of procreation, we must admit that He does not bind Himself to man without man himself being bound to God, and in the same ways. Now the bond of God with the human couple by and in the language of sexuality is sexuality itself. The nature—that is, the structure— is here the intermediary always endowed with the synergic relations of the couple and their God in view of the unlimited appearance of man. The bond which unites procreation by man and woman with creation (strictly so called) by God is, therefore, essentially objective, and here again functional. It is in respecting this structure in which is concealed—and therefore accomplished—the creative operation of God that the spouses, freely engaged in the intersubjective behavior of love, are bound to God in the same way in which God is bound to them. Being forbidden in their works to break the structural correlation which *disposes* the couple and their *work* to the irreplaceable work of God, man and woman united in a love which binds God Himself are, in their turn, bound by God. Therefore, every objective opposition to the structures which relate their love to the possibility of life would be an opposition to God Himself, who established this relationship in which His transcendent activity is hidden and operative.[91]

Because, then, God is bound to the couple through the structure of sexuality, they are bound to Him in the same structure. If this is true, Martelet asserts, one cannot refer to the structures of sexuality as "brute facticity." Rather, they reflect man as conditioned transcendence.

Germain Grisez's book *Contraception and the Natural Law*[92] appeared on the scene in early 1965. Since its appearance he has in several places repeated the reasoning that led him to conclude to the intrinsic immorality of contraception.[93] Grisez approaches the problem from the point of view of basic ethical theory. Too much earlier moral thought had failed in this respect, he feels, and had ended up jumping from what simply *is* in the natural order to what *ought to be*. Grisez criticizes these analyses very tellingly. His own theory begins with the fact that the first principles of practical reason have a basis in experience. These basic principles reflect the goods toward which human activity can be directed. While these goods are

---

[91] *Ibid.*, pp. 259–60.   [92] Milwaukee: Bruce, 1965.
[93] G. Grisez, *Contraception: Is It Always Wrong?* (Huntington: Our Sunday Visitor, 1965); cf. also *National Catholic Reporter*, April 21, 1965, p. 6.

equally basic, they are not equally good. However, no one can be rejected to maximize another. Intrinsic immorality is action which involves a rejection of one of these basic goods—a will turned against such a good. Now the beginning of human life (the procreative good) is one of these basic goods. Grisez's ultimate assertion is that those who practice contraception cannot help but reject the beginning of human life. Instead of being open to the procreative good, they are unwilling to permit it to be. Thus the malice of contraception is not in the external act alone nor in the will alone. It is rather in a form of external conduct which involves the will in a rejection of the procreative good. The practice of rhythm, on the contrary, need not involve the couple in an act of will directly opposed to the procreative good.

These are presented as but three examples of the type of reflection going on in the Catholic community. They all make excellent points. Johann establishes a personalistic context for the reading of natural law. Martelet makes very explicit the implications in the area of sexuality of man's conditioned transcendence.[94] Grisez highlights the basic goods which are at the heart of moral obligation. However, in my opinion, all three presentations raise grave problems. For example, Johann's reflections have provided an excellent basis for what theologians call the *individual* morality of marital conduct. This term refers to the constellation of circumstances (intentions, attitudes, desires, atmospheres, effects, etc.) which are the heart and soul of the conscious human experience. Man's personhood and with it his openness to Being make any exploitative conduct morally unacceptable at the *individual* level. But these considerations do not touch *specific* morality. Specific morality refers here to those minimal external requirements which distinguish coitus from other acts not coitus. Clearly these minimal requirements are not something that married people consciously reflect upon in their experience of marital relations. Nor do they adequately define the total experience. But at the level of minimal characteristics (note the modesty of purpose here), certain physiological elements of the sexual act will be included in its definition, for we are dealing with human sexuality, not angelic communication. If one fails to state these basic requirements within a coherent theory, it is hard to see how one can logically and consistently make a moral distinction between coitus and other presumably unacceptable

[94] Here he is very close to Pope John XXIII's statement in *Mater et magistra*: "Being fulfilled by a deliberate and conscious act, the transmission of life is subject as such to sacred, immutable, and inviolable laws of God, laws which all are obliged to accept and observe; hence no one is allowed to have recourse to means and methods that are licit with respect to the propagation of plant and animal life" (*AAS* 53 [1961] 447).

forms of sexual expression. This is by no means to state, as some have alleged, that contraceptive practices are equivalent to or will lead to sexual variants. It is to seek a principle of consistency. Either certain minimal physiological elements enter into a definition of coitus or they do not. If they do, the admission of this is not anchoring the person to "brute facticity." It is but admitting that man is, after all, man. Thus, when Fr. Johann says that man's "intervention in natural processes is always justified when its issue is an enlargement of human meanings and possibilities," I find no intelligible limitation here to exclude variants which, on the basis of all evidence (historical, anthropological, physiological, psychological, moral), must be repudiated. This is also the methodological point so sharply made by the renowned English philosopher G. E. M. Anscombe.[95]

On the other hand, Martelet's contention that the sexual structure is inviolable because it is the meeting ground, so to speak, for divine and human operations (just as the couple bind God in their activity and sexuality, so God binds them in their sexuality) is not totally convincing. Martelet had begun with the obvious procreative character of human sexuality, scil., from the fact of procreation. The binding-to-God or inviolability he asserts is therefore rooted in the fertile period of the sexual structure. Since, however, woman is known to be biphasic, would this suggest that the limit of this inviolability is not the structure itself, but the structure in so far as its meaning is derivable from its *biphasic* character? If this is so, not every intervention would be prohibited, but only a type of intervention which removes the good of *prolis* altogether or in unwarranted fashion from the marital scene.

Grisez's challenging analysis leaves me wondering whether he has attended sufficiently to the external act. He admits that the evil of contraception is not found exclusively in the will but is originated in external conduct which involves the will in a rejection of the procreative good. Unless I have misunderstood him, he has not sufficiently specified what this external conduct is. When he does so, the basis of his analysis may appear more traditional than it actually does.

I have always thought that the most basic methodological question where contraception (*not all of marital morality*) is concerned is the following: How does one determine the minimal elements required for coitus? Or even, how does one arrive at a criterion? Or even further, what is the proper ethical theory which will point toward clarity here?[96] I do not believe we have

[95] G. E. M. Anscombe, "Contraception and Natural Law," *New Blackfriars* 46 (1965) 517–21.

[96] Anscombe, *ibid.*, insists that the two questions (What is normal copulation? Why is contranormal copulation wrong?) must be kept separate. Agreed. But there is a point where the first is only answerable by a clear answer to the second.

found a totally satisfactory answer to these questions. The recent brush fire ignited by the pill has shown this clearly. The reason may be that we have been asking inadequate, unilateral questions. For example, traditional formulations, besides being affected by a heavy procreative emphasis, were to some extent also influenced by the effort to exclude the certainly impotent from marriage and simultaneously to allow for the validity of certainly sterile marriages. Equivalently, that means that theologians have been asking: What minimal definition of coitus is required to steer this middle course? This was and is an important jurisprudential question. But when theologians got an answer, perhaps it was easy, too easy, to conclude that they had fully defined the minimal requirements of coitus. Actually they had defined them to the extent of their question. I am not suggesting that theologians would have concluded to the permissibility of contraception, at least in some forms. Quite the contrary. I am suggesting that a larger context to the question might have provided the means for a more adequate understanding of traditional conclusions.

Recent revisionist efforts in the area of the pill have failed to persuade because they (e.g., Janssens, Reuss, Cardegna[97]) have operated within traditional formulations and begun from there. If the traditional questions were inadequate, theories constructed on their answers are necessarily going to share this inadequacy. Thus, in most recent writings we encounter the phrase "the substantially intact (or integral) marital act." The writers mean that when pill or diaphragm is used, the conjugal act remains "substantially intact." More concretely, they mean that there is vaginal semination and that this is all that is required for "substantial intactness." We have been saying something like this for years, but, as was noted above, this "intactness" is concluded largely from jurisprudential considerations and does not represent an adequate question. Revisionist writers who accept the phrase and build upon it make an enormous supposition, scil., that the marital act is truly intact in more than a jurisprudentially useful way. In other words, have they attended to the full reason why such a definition of coitus may be referred to as "substantially intact"?

Finally, to suggest further the inadequacy of our questions, one might point to their profound masculinity. The "substantially intact marital act" (as meaning vaginal semination) says nothing or very little about female participation in coitus. Yet we know that whereas masculine physiology represents relative uniformity, the female is biphasic or cyclic. She is fertile-

[97] L. Janssens, "Morale conjugale et progestogènes," *Ephemerides theologicae Lovanienses* 39 (1963) 787–826; J. M. Reuss, "Eheliche Hingabe und Zeugung," *Tübinger theologische Quartalschrift* 143 (1963) 454–76; F. Cardegna, S.J., "Contraception, the Pill, and Responsible Parenthood," THEOLOGICAL STUDIES 25 (1964) 611–36.

infertile and this biphasic character reaches into her psychology and spirituality. With this in mind, what does total sexual encounter between man and wife mean in personalistic terms? Or again, if all intercourse, even sterile intercourse, is symbolic, where do we derive the content of the symbol and what does this mean for the morality of marital intimacy? What is totally unitive coitus?[98] These questions are methodological in character, my only point being that we have not often asked this type of question.

One point of methodology is easy to overlook—indeed, it is bound to be overlooked. That is the atmosphere itself in which our gropings occur. Rarely has theological thought risen completely above the cultural climate which nourished the theological thinker. The Catholic community must face squarely the unencouraging fact that its present reflections are taking place in an atmosphere described by four hundred German physicians as "public sexualization."[99] These men are not strident and disoriented reformers, but keen and responsible observers of their age. They protest the fact that "the view that the meaning of human life is to be found in 'prosperity and pleasure-seeking' has become the guiding idea for the great majority of people." This powerful document must lead us to wonder how far we can trust ourselves and our own witness. If the characteristic danger of a mechanical and automated age is the submergence of the person, then our reflections on human sexuality are certainly going to share the effects of this submergence.[100] This conclusion has been brilliantly argued by Malcolm Muggeridge.[101] The point reaches paradoxical proportions when we remember that this is occurring at the very time we are extolling the person in our philosophical thought. This leads one to the conclusion that the "problem of contraception" is actually only symptomatic. To think that a pill or a coil will alleviate more than symptoms is to foster the very moral infantilism which nurtures the real problem so unsparingly—a point well made by Michel Roy, S.J.[102]

A committee preparatory to the Lambeth Conference of 1958 asked:

[98] W. Bertrams, S.J., concludes to the immorality of contraception precisely from a consideration of the character of conjugal love and the conjugal act: "De structura metaphysica amoris conjugalis," *Periodica* 54 (1965) 290–300. For a popular expression of the same idea, see Frank M. Wessling, in *National Catholic Reporter*, Jan. 6, 1965.

[99] "Four Hundred German Physicians Attack Propaganda for Contraception," *Herder Correspondence* 2 (1965) 122–24.

[100] For some interesting psychiatric-pastoral insights on this point, cf. André Lussier, "Psychoanalysis and Moral Issues in Marital Problems," *Cross Currents* 15 (1965) 57–67. Interesting sociological implications may be found in Lester A. Kirkendall's "Captives to the Double Standard," *Pastoral Psychology* 16 (1965) 23–32.

[101] Malcolm Muggeridge, "Down with Sex!" *Esquire* 63 (Feb., 1965) 72–74.

[102] Michel Roy, S.J., "Perspectives doctrinales sur l'aide aux couples en difficulté," *Supplément aux fiches documentaires du C.L.E.R.*, Jan.–Feb.–March, 1965, pp. 1–8.

"Is it possible that, by claiming the right to manipulate his physical processes in this matter, we may, without knowing or intending it, be stepping
over the boundary between the world of Christian marriage and what one
might call the world of Aphrodite—the world of sterile eroticism against
which the Church reacted so strongly (perhaps too strongly) in its early
days?"[103] If the question is legitimate, and it is, its urgency must bring us
to our knees; for is any attack upon Christianity more basic than the confusion of love and eroticism?

As the discussion continues, what is the position and responsibility of
the priest who must aid the faithful in the formation of their conscience?
Stanislaus de Lestapis, S.J., in discussing the papal statement of June 23,
1964, points out that the Pope demanded "that we change nothing with
respect to what the Church has taught us and still requires us to observe in
our lives."[104] The declarations of Pius XII continue to be the norm of our
conduct, for a "methodical examination is not a doubt." D. F. O'Callaghan,
while welcoming the current discussion, also concludes that a "doctrine
taught in an authoritative fashion must be accepted as binding at the
pastoral level."[105] This was also the position taken by John J. Lynch, S.J.,
in this journal.[106] What these well-respected theologians would say at the
present moment I do not know.

My own very fallible opinion would organize itself as follows. First, it
must be pointed out that the discussion first centered around the pill exclusively; only more recently has it broadened to the whole field of contraception. While many theologians are convinced that the same principles
which allow (or disallow) contraceptive use of the pill will allow (or disallow)
other forms of contraception which are not abortifacient in effect, this continuity of principle has not been as intensely the object of discussion as has
been the pill itself. Therefore, although there seems to be little room for a
theoretical position distinguishing the pill from other forms of contraception,
there might more easily be room for a practical attitude (for the present)
which makes this distinction.

I have been of the opinion that Pope Paul's intervention meant both to

---

[103] *The Family in Contemporary Society* (London: SPCK, 1959) p. 135.

[104] S. de Lestapis, S.J., "Techniques of Contraception or the Practice of Self-Restraint."
This is the translation of an article which originally appeared in *Prêtre et apôtre*, June–
July, 1965.

[105] D. F. O'Callaghan, in *Irish Ecclesiastical Record* 103 (1965) 180.

[106] J. J. Lynch, S.J., "Notes on Moral Theology," THEOLOGICAL STUDIES 26 (1965)
267–72. J. M. Reuss's "Suggestions pour une pastorale des problèmes du marriage et de la
fécundité," *Vie spirituelle, Supplément*, no. 72 (1965) 5–12, appeared earlier in *Theologie
der Gegenwart* 7 (1964) 134–39 and was written before the June 23, 1964, statement of
Pope Paul VI.

encourage theological thought and yet to repeat *authoritatively* the norms of Pius XII, especially with regard to the pill. I have never been able to read this intervention as merely disciplinary. Hence, I have felt that the official position of the Church as a guide of consciences has been the norms of Pius XII. Practically, this would mean that those who claim the privilege of enlightenment from the magisterium would reflect this magisterium in their advice and actions.

However, since the intervention of Paul VI, there has been a great amount of theological writing asserting the morality of intervention into the physical or biological processes of sexuality. There has also been a great deal of practical advice (in conference and confessional) along these lines. It is clear that the Pope (1) has reserved competence over this extremely important matter to himself, (2) knows the practical urgency of the decision, (3) is well informed on the literature, and (4) has promised to speak soon and authoritatively on the subject. If he fails to do so, one can only conclude that a state of practical doubt exists in the Church on this matter. In such a case it would be hard to deny the application of the principles of probabilism. This would mean that a confessor or priest would indicate to an enquirer that the matter is still under discussion and that he must be ready to receive with open and grateful heart the ultimate authoritative teaching of the magisterium. In the meantime it is not clear that he is acting immorally if his contraceptive use of the progestins is, from all other aspects, responsible.

It is important to note two aspects of this conclusion. First, it is strictly temporary in character. It is not and cannot be regarded as an acceptable resolution of this discussion. No conscientious married couple can rest satisfied with an analysis of their marital intimacy which states that it is at best only *probably* in accord with divine law, is only *probably* not a violation of God's law.

Secondly, the conclusion should not be identified with the claim of those who assert *as a principle* that Christian couples should "be allowed to decide the matter for themselves." This can only mean either of two unacceptable things. First, it might mean that the morality of contraception can only be decided with reference to individual circumstances. This, of course, prejudges the whole question. Secondly, it might mean that the couple is more capable than the magisterium of deciding whether contraception is intrinsically immoral. No Catholic who accepts the divine commission of the Church to enlighten consciences can accept this. It is important, therefore, to realize that the Church will continue to distinguish between determination of family size and determination of the means to implement this decision.

The point has been made recently by Ph. Delhaye, who asserts that "among the discourses delivered at the Council one will look in vain for declarations with a different orientation."[107]

VARIA ON THE SACRAMENTS

An excellent article by Donald P. Gray discusses the relation between liturgy and morality.[108] Gray shows in very convincing fashion that the moral life is the fulfilment or complement of the commitment made in liturgy. This essay is sparing and simple, but it makes a point which should dominate classroom treatment of the moral life.

In an era of general renewal and communal soul-searching, the question of parvity of matter in the Eucharistic fast may appear to be a museum piece. And indeed I think it is. The chief and perhaps only reason for discussing it is that such discussion may liberate us from the need of doing so in the future; that is, it may help us to lead the faithful to focus their attention where it should be, scil., on the meeting with Christ sacramentally rather than on the materialities which, while they are intended to prepare for this encounter, more often are distractions from it.

Several years ago Babbini had argued persuasively that parvity of matter is had in this law just as in all ecclesiastical law.[109] Basically, his point was that the arguments adduced to make an exception of the Eucharistic fast (both from intrinsic reasoning and from authority) were unconvincing. His line of reasoning was taken up by G. Rinaldi, who concluded that the arguments admitting parvity of matter in violation of the Eucharistic fast were "grave, plausible, strong, valid, weighty, cogent, and unexceptionable."[110] To those who might have missed the thrust of these dactylics, Rinaldi dismissed the opposing arguments as "deboli, poco cogenti et molto fragili." Clearly no one wants to die for such a cause.

Recently Rinaldi completed his series of articles with an attempt to determine precisely and concretely what this parvity of matter should be.[111] Appealing to the law of attendance at Sunday Mass and the estimate that a third part of the Mass is a "notable" omission, he concludes that "if one communicates with fifteen or twenty minutes lacking to the prescribed hour

[107] Ph. Delhaye, in *L'Ami du clergé* 75 (1965) 170.

[108] Donald P. Gray, "Liturgy and Morality," *Worship* 39 (1965) 28–35.

[109] Leone Babbini, O.F.M., "La legge del dijiuno eucaristico non ammette parvità di materia?" *Palestra del clero* 42 (1963) 923–28.

[110] G. Rinaldi, "La parvità di materia nella legislazione attuale del dijiuno eucaristico," *Perfice munus* 39 (1964) 141–48, 217–22.

[111] G. Rinaldi, "Determinazione della parvità di materia nel dijiuno eucaristico," *ibid.* 40 (1965) 92–99.

of fast, he commits a venial infraction." As for quantity, he finds an analogy in the laws of Lenten fast. Using 120–30 grams (roughly about four ounces) as that quantity which, when eaten between meals, constitutes a "notable" and grave violation of the fast, he suggests that less than this quantity of solid food (and liquids which are not liquors) should be regarded as a slight violation of the Eucharistic fast. As for liquors, 40–50 grams is the break-off point.

Unfortunately, I believe it is precisely this type of discussion which is calculated to bring Church law into deserved disrepute. The impossibility of making practical estimates of this kind without being arbitrary and offensive to common sense and Christian morals leads one to wonder why Rinaldi did not turn his attention originally to the very existence of grave matter in a law which has undergone substantial changes and been reduced almost to nothing. No one wants to assert lightly that a law which has always been regarded and accepted as grave (cf., for example, the imposing excusing causes under canon 858, §1) is no longer such. However, the gravity of an ecclesiastical law is to be measured intrinsically (by the gravity of the matter) and extrinsically (by the will of the legislator). As for the gravity of the matter, this will be measured by the relationship of the prescribed matter to a definite end and by the importance of that goal. One must suppose that the legislator will accommodate his intent to this relationship.

Now the end or goal of the Eucharistic fast may be said to be threefold: avoidance of the abuses mentioned by St. Paul (1 Cor 11:21); devout preparation for reception of the Eucharist; finally and especially, the honor and reverence owed to this august sacrament. Clearly there was a time when the stipulations of the fast were regarded as very conducive to these ends. While the general goals mentioned above have not changed, the constant and substantial reduction of the fast indicates that in the mind of recent popes it no longer conduces to these ends in the same way it did at other times. Indeed, one would have to conclude that facility of access to the Eucharist and reverent, active liturgical participation are regarded now as more likely to secure these goals. Therefore, the materialities of the fast no longer "multum conferunt ad bonum commune,"[112] the touchstone of serious matter where law is concerned. I am convinced, therefore, that this law no longer contains serious matter.

Be this as it may, three remarks may conclude this summary. First, it is obviously important that we avoid the insinuation that ecclesiastical laws are "only venial sins" at times and hence unimportant, or that the legislator is incapable of binding seriously. Secondly, the best manner of avoiding this

[112] M. Zalba, S.J., *Theologiae moralis summa* 1 (Madrid, 1957) 310.

impression is to get the whole emphasis of presentation of the Eucharistic fast out of the area of sin. Thirdly and practically, I believe it would be sound to present the fast in the following manner. "Do the best you reasonably can to observe the fast. If in spite of your best efforts you cannot or do not, you need not deprive yourself of Communion on this account—and there is no need for further worry."

Two points in marriage legislation which have always been sore points with non-Catholics are the requirement of canonical form for the validity of marriages involving a Catholic and the promise that all the children hereafter born of the union be baptized and educated in the Catholic faith (cf. canon 1061). It was inevitable and even desirable that these points be discussed.

With regard to canonical form, Franz Böckle, of the University of Bonn, points out that any ecumenical solution must be theologically sound.[113] Hence, for one thing, it must reckon with the dogmatic position of the Church on the identity between the contract and the sacrament; that is, wherever a marriage between baptized Christians is valid, it is also necessarily sacramental. The sacrament of matrimony gives the husband and wife an active share in the union between Christ and the Church; it is part of the life of the Church. Therefore, "the *de facto* identity of sacrament and contract demands that in some way or other the Church be present at the ceremony." Böckle rightly sees no overwhelming problem here, because the partners are the ministers of the sacrament. As baptized, they represent the Church in a real sense. Hence he proposes that the requirement of a priest should bind only for licitness, not validity.

The same conclusion is proposed by the noted canonist James I. O'Connor, S.J., in an article which reviews the advantages of this change from a practical point of view.[114] Pointing out that the supreme test of ecclesiastical legislation is the good of souls, he asks whether the present law conduces to this good. His answer: an unqualified "no." Present legislation is based on the evils (especially clandestinity) which gave rise to the decree *Tametsi,* and these evils are no longer a serious threat. The existing law is used by many Catholics as a device for a trial marriage. Those Catholics who obey the marriage laws are in a more disadvantageous position. Fr. O'Connor points out that "it is hardly conducive to the good of souls when those obedient to the law have to suffer through life while the disobedient can

[113] Franz Böckle, "Mixed Marriages: A Catholic View," *The Church and Ecumenism* (= *Concilium* 4; New York: Paulist Press, 1965) pp. 115–22.

[114] James I. O'Connor, S.J., "Should the Present Canonical Form Be Retained for the Validity of Marriage?" *Jurist* 25 (1965) 66–81.

derive notable benefit from their disobedience." To the objection that change in the legislation would result in the perpetual misery of many teenagers who marry in a burst of youthful blindness and fascination, he suggests that the validity of such marriages before a Protestant minister or civil authority would really be an enormous deterrent to the actual and more basic problem, youthful marriages.

Fr. O'Connor adduces many other arguments. For instance, the Church has the duty to promote the stability and sanctity of marriage. With a law where divorce with remarriage is easily obtainable (because of invalidity due to defect of canonical form), one can wonder whether the Church actually promotes this stability. Also, Catholics who marry outside the Church know that, practically speaking, they are precisely outside the Church. With this mentality there is easy loss of faith. "A change of law would leave them conscious that they are still members of the Church and thus tend to save both their faith and that of their offspring." Besides having ecumenical value, the position presented by Fr. O'Connor is very persuasive. At a time when dogmatic theology is redescribing the relations between Catholics and non-Catholic Christians, canon law should do the same.[115]

The problem of the *cautiones*, especially the promise to baptize and educate the children in the Catholic Church, is much thornier. There have been several suggestions for revision of Church law on mixed marriages over the past few years. First, it has been suggested that the law should forgo legal insistence on promises to baptize and raise the children Catholics. Presently this legal insistence takes the form of invalidity of the dispensation for a mixed marriage (and therefore of the marriage where disparity of cult, a diriment impediment, is concerned). It also involves refusal of the priest to officiate (hence often ends in invalidity through defect of form). Secondly, it has been suggested that even short of these legal measures the law should cease demanding the formal promise to raise the children as Catholics. Thirdly, the Church should allow marriage as a general policy even when the Catholic baptism and upbringing is not morally certain.

To approach the problem as if a change in canon law would ease the tensions involved labors under at least two weaknesses. First, it supposes that the source of tension and irritation is the means chosen by the Church to insist premaritally on the Catholic baptism and education of the children. Actually the problem seems to be more than that. It seems to be the basic

[115] The same conclusion is urged from another and perhaps more theological point of view by H. Heimerl, "Ehewille–Eheschliessungsform–Ehegültigkeit," *Theologisch-praktische Quartalschrift* 113 (1965) 144–63.

teaching that there is a divine-law duty on the Catholic party to raise his children Catholic. Secondly, such an approach neglects the connection between this basic duty (if it exists) and Church insistence on its fulfilment. Before the architects of new mixed-marriage laws can proceed with security, two basic moral issues must be faced.

First, is the duty to baptize and raise the children as Catholics a duty of divine-law origin incumbent on the Catholic party? Secondly, to what extent must and should the Church insist on this duty if it is truly of divine-law origin? The manner of the Church's insistence (the more properly legal sphere), if insistence is in place, will depend to some extent on how one answers these questions.

Is the duty to baptize and educate the children as Catholics a duty of divine law? Charles Curran contends that "it seems difficult to sustain a divine law obligation to raise all the children of mixed marriages in the Catholic faith."[116] The Catholic spouse has an obligation to see to the Catholic education of the children, but only if such an education would not be against the conscience and religious convictions of the non-Catholic partner. He argues from two principles. First, there is the principle of religious liberty. Granting that there is a conflict of rights, he denies that the conflict can be solved by appeal to the objective truth of one position, since religious liberty is based rather on the dignity of the human person sincerely striving to conform himself to God's will. Therefore he concludes that "the right to educate and raise his child in his own faith is a necessary consequence of his right to worship God according to the dictates of his own conscience."

Secondly, Fr. Curran argues from the ecumenical principle; that is, raising the child in another Christian faith cannot be viewed as a perversion. It is true that children not educated as Catholics would not receive the fulness of truth. "But it is not the difference between night and day and all or nothing. *Per se* it would only be a question of degree." The ecumenical spirit has taught us to take a different point of view toward non-Catholic Christians. As for the former Church documents insisting on the divine-law duty to raise the children Catholic, he believes that "the Church condemned any possibility of raising the children as non-Catholics based on false indifferentism. But today in the light of religious liberty and ecumenism there is a new and true basis for our proposed teaching."

Because, therefore, he denies the divine-law origin of the duty in question,

[116] Charles Curran, "The Mixed Marriage Promises—Arguments for Suppressing the *Cautiones*," *Jurist* 25 (1965) 83–91, at p. 91.

Curran's answer to the second question will be clear. The Church need not and in our time should not insist on this duty. Hence, also, her present legal insistence should go.

Robert G. Wesselmann disagrees with this analysis.[117] As for the argument from religious liberty, he contends that there are limits to religious liberty, limits defined by the rights of God, other men, and society. Where the Catholic education of the children is concerned, the non-Catholic is faced with the rights and duties of another. "Hence we are in an area where there is a just limit to the exercise of the right of religious freedom, especially when you consider that the non-Catholic can call off the marriage if he feels that he cannot sign the promises." If we say that, because of religious liberty there can be no duty of divine law incumbent on the Catholic to educate the children Catholic, would not the Church logically also have to allow divorced non-Catholics to marry Catholics if she must respect their conscience convictions to that extent?

As for the ecumenical principle adduced by Curran, Wesselmann regards it as false irenicism. To suppress or de-emphasize Catholic principles simply because they displease Christians of other faiths will never do. "I submit that the obligation of baptizing children in infancy, raising them as Catholics from infancy, and the policy of doing something about non-Catholic opposition to these ideas before mixed marriages are celebrated, are Catholic principles which cannot be suppressed . . . simply to secure good will from Christians of other faiths."

Because he is convinced that the duty is one of divine law, Wesselmann's answer to the second question follows suit. "It behooves the Church as a mother to insist that her children fulfil this obligation. . . . The Church is certainly obliged to do all that she can to induce her children to observe the law of God when they contract marriage." The limits on the manner or form of this insistence are the limits of prudence defined within the Church's divine commission. For a host of practical reasons Wesselmann is convinced that as a general policy the Church should refuse to allow mixed marriages where there is doubt about the faith of the children. And some form of *cautiones* remains in place to this end.

Ladislaus Örsy, S.J., had treated this problem earlier[118] and concluded that we must accept the following propositions: (1) the Catholic party to a mixed marriage has a right and a duty of immutable divine law to educate

---

[117] Robert Wesselmann, "The Mixed Marriage Promises—Arguments for Retaining the *Cautiones*," *ibid.*, pp. 92–105.

[118] Ladislaus Örsy, S.J., "The Religious Education of Children Born from Mixed Marriages," *Gregorianum* 54 (1964) 739–60.

all his children in the Catholic religion; (2) the Church has a right and duty to aid every Catholic contracting a mixed marriage to carry out his obligation. The form this help should take (whether legal or more generally pastoral) is another and a prudential question. Moreover, the duty to educate the children as Catholics is an affirmative one, and there could be extraordinary cases (indeed, have been) where omission of acts fulfilling this duty was tolerated by the Church. These are, above all, cases where the natural right to marry is otherwise jeopardized. Could the Church at the present time cease insisting *in general* on the fulfilment of this duty, in order to promote better relations with our non-Catholic brothers? Örsy does not think so. The only opening seems to be in the form of the insistence. But again, according to Wesselmann and others, the form of insistence is not the basic problem; it is the fundamental doctrine itself which offends.

My own tentative opinion corresponds to that of Franz Böckle when he answers the two basic questions as follows: "For the Catholic who is convinced of the divine mission of his Church the education of his children in the faith and the sacraments of this Church is an important divine command."[119] Secondly, "no ecclesiastical authority can dispense him from this; on the contrary he must be reminded of it and his readiness to comply must be required." I do not see how the Church would remain faithful to her convictions about herself if she denied the divine origin of this duty; and I do not see how she would fulfil her charge toward her children if she failed to remind them of this duty, especially, one might say, during an era of great ecumenical desire. I agree with Böckle that this situation is "an almost unbridgeable gap." Hans Dombois, a member of the Evangelical Church of Germany and professor at the University of Heidelberg, agrees that "if one party has convictions that are permanently unacceptable to the other for reasons of conscience, they should be advised not to marry because there is no solution for such a situation."[120]

I have seen no persuasive arguments against the divine-law origin of the duty to do all possible to baptize and educate the children as Catholics, though Fr. Curran has made about as strong a case as can be made. The explicit recognition of full religious liberty for all men does not argue against the divine-law origin of the duty in question; it simply exacerbates the practical problem and makes it more insoluble than ever. The fact that mixed marriages will continue to occur in which the Catholic abandons any determination to raise the children as Catholics is, of course, terribly regret-

[119] Böckle, *art. cit.*, p. 121.
[120] Hans Dombois, "Mixed Marriages: A Protestant View," in *The Church and Ecumenism*, p. 112.

table. Continued insistence on the Catholic's duty will not prevent or meet this situation. Granted. On the other hand, a regrettable situation does not argue to the nonexistence of a duty. As for the principle of ecumenism adduced by Fr. Curran, I see in the practical concessions made by the Catholic the germ of the very indifferentism he claims was behind earlier documents of the Church.[121] Finally, the duty asserted by Fr. Curran (to raise the children Catholic if this does not violate the conscience convictions of the non-Catholic) seems arbitrary in defect of a divine-law obligation.

Everyone admits that the painful dilemmas occasioned by mixed marriages are symptomatic of the deeper division within Christianity. I am afraid that individual couples will continue to feel the pains involved as long as the separation exists. Given this situation, perhaps some of the practical suggestions made by Leo J. Hayes can help to mitigate the tensions.[122] Fr. Hayes agrees that the only situation which offers any hope is the mixed marriage in which the non-Catholic is sincerely indifferentist, believing that one religion is as good as another. At least here there is a common crossing-ground where the dogmatic tenets of the Catholic Church can survive. In such a case the non-Catholic is not asked to abandon his right but "to predetermine the direction that his right is going to take." The most appropriate procedure, Fr. Hayes suggests, is that the non-Catholic party make his promises directly to the Catholic party and that the Catholic attest to the reception of such promises. He feels that there are two practical advantages to this. First, this puts the promises in the context of personal commitment between husband and wife. It is, after all, "within this personal family relationship that the actual decisions of free exercise of faith are to be made." Secondly, if the situation is actually one of the insoluble type, it is better that the Catholic partner come to this realization himself. These considerations merit attention, especially if it is true that the present form of the *cautiones* is not achieving its intended effect. But they scarcely solve the more basic problem.

THE SACRAMENT OF PENANCE

What is the proper age for the confession of youngsters? Renewed interest in this question as a pastoral-moral issue probably springs from the dis-

---

[121] B. Häring feels that advance agreement by the Catholic to have the child educated as a non-Catholic amounts to formal co-operation; this would seem to indicate that he regards the duty as of divine origin (*Lexikon für Theologie und Kirche* 7 [2nd ed.; Freiburg, 1962] 444).

[122] Leo J. Hayes, "Ideas of the 'Mixed Marriage' Promises," *Homiletic and Pastoral Review* 65 (1965) 574–80.

satisfaction of many, including parents, educators, and priests, with the results too often obvious in present practice. Many regret the routine and mechanical way youngsters are taught to rattle off a litany of horrors they did not commit and rarely understand. The effects of this can be disastrous. Here, it is claimed, we have the breeding ground of scruples, because youngsters steepen themselves in a narrowly moral attitude rather than in a genuinely religious one. The almost superstitious mentality with which the young often approach the sacrament prevents the building of a true personal and dialogical attitude toward this and other sacraments. Finally, many feel that early and indiscriminate introduction of youngsters to confession does not square well with contemporary evidence of human development.

Ludwig Bertsch, S.J.,[123] contends that in approaching this problem the key question is not the ability of the youngster to distinguish good from evil; rather it is his ability to make a genuine moral decision, to reach a sufficient development of freedom so that a basic option or commitment to ethical good (therefore, to the will of God) is possible. Thomas' "incipiens habere usum rationis"[124] is misleading here; for conscience involves more than just knowledge. It also involves "the vital conviction in one's inner self that the attitude assumed toward the good is bound up with one's own salvation or damnation."[125] This conviction, in turn, is dependent on the development of the whole man. Adopting a dynamic structure for this development, Bertsch sees a corresponding development in conscience— roughly, from early social and authoritarian conscience to personal conscience. It is only in the immediately prepubertal years that one can speak of a personal conscience, because only at this time does conscience disengage itself from those parental or peer influences and characteristics which suggest the term "authoritarian." Before this time, conscience decisions are, to a greater or lesser degree, mediated by others. Therefore it follows that the fundamental option which alone gives fully moral character to individual decisions is had only around the prepubertal years. Before this time, only the exceptional individual is capable of serious sin.

However, this does not mean that there are no moral choices (hence no sin) before this; for the development of a personal conscience is a gradual thing. Even in its earlier stages there can be a turning to God corresponding to the conditions of that age. The moral decisions possible at this age, when compared to fully personal moral decisions, suggest the relation between

[123] Ludwig Bertsch, S.J., "Der rechte Zeitpunkt der Erstbeicht," *Stimmen der Zeit* 175 (1965) 255–62.

[124] *Sum. theol.* 1–2, q. 89, a. 6.

[125] B. Häring, *The Law of Christ* 1 (Westminster, Md.: Newman, 1961) 139.

mortal and venial sin; that is, they are analogously moral decisions. Hence real but analogous moral conduct is possible.

Bertsch is convinced that the confession of youngsters must be adapted to the developmental character of the growth of conscience. He suggests, therefore, that seven-to-eight-year-olds should first be introduced to group expressions of sorrow and penitence. Eight-to-nine-year-olds could profitably then experience group sacramental confession. Shortly thereafter they will find themselves much better prepared for individual confession.

This suggestion is not new. Bishop Moors of Roermond (Holland) had directed that the first Communion be at age seven-to-eight, and first confession at age ten-to-eleven.[126] Before the first confession there· would be careful preparation. First, there would be repentance celebrations to inculcate the basic attitudes of renewal and conversion. After this phase there would be "personal" confessions during a parish celebration with absolution given to the group. Here the idea would be to teach that confession is more than a mere imitation of what youngsters have been taught to say. Finally, truly private confession would take place.

Pierre Ranwez, S.J., approaches the matter from a slightly different point of view.[127] The child must experience a double initiation: first into a sense of God, then into the meaning of sacramental symbols. The first initiation is "assured by the child's social life with its parents. They are the image of God, Father, Son, and Holy Spirit." Through parental love and tenderness the child is led to discover God's love. The second initiation can be achieved through "familiarity with reality-signs, by living in a well ordered home, where gestures, attitudes and realities stand out." What are these? Blessings, different bodily attitudes, meals together, material objects (door, table, book, etc.). Once this second initiation has been made, the child should be introduced to the totality of salvation brought to us in the economy of the sacraments; that is, he should receive confirmation, Holy Communion, and penance (this latter being a renewal of baptism).

Since the delay of sacramental confession is not infrequently based on the conviction that children cannot sin at the time they now learn to confess, Ranwez attacks the delay-solution here. The number of young children truly capable of sinning is probably rather low, he admits. But this is due to the type of education usually given. "It is not age . . . it is education which leads to liberty." Therefore, not delay but revision of approach is called for. This will include three elements: preparation, celebration, and

[126] J. Dreissen, in *Katechetische Blätter* 89 (1964) 494, as cited in Bertsch, p. 256.
[127] Pierre Ranwez, S.J., "The Sacraments of Initiation and the Age for First Confession," *Lumen vitae* 20 (1965) 9–24.

adequate subsequent education. Preparation refers, above all, to a home experience of affection, firm ruling, and forgiveness, where a child reaches a knowledge of God who calls, demands, and forgives. Conscience formation at this time should be general and positive, not the carefully docketed inventory of sins so common. As for celebration, Ranwez suggests a program very close to Bertsch's but without the delay. Subsequent education will include regularly arranged celebrations, emphasis on the social dimension of the child's fault, and the sacrament of penance.

I do not know what kind of reception these suggestions will receive in this country. They certainly merit serious study. But two remarks appear to be in place.

First, I believe that our confession discipline for the very young (supposing the possibility of some sin) should be based on the practical success or failure of the discipline in terms of over-all attitudes and fruits produced, rather than immediately on a theory of dynamic structure of conscience development which allows for a basic option only around the age of eleven or twelve. I would conclude this because even those who are convinced that a basic option is possible only in the immediately prepubertal years admit the existence of venial sin in youngsters before this time. In other words, there seems to be no necessary connection between the time of personal confession and the age of basic option.[128]

By this comment I do not mean to deny the value or validity of recent writings which take the position (which draws heavily from our increasing knowledge of the depth sciences and child psychology) that a basic option is possible only around the prepubertal years. Quite the contrary. This position corresponds very well with a widespread conviction that mortal sin is *practically* out of the question in the early years. I mean merely to point out that we are dealing with two distinct problems: (1) the time of the basic moral option and the criteria to determine this; (2) the confessional discipline for children. The problems are practically distinct, because all those involved in the discussion on the basic option admit the existence of true (if only analogous) moral acts, and therefore the possibility of venial sins, after attainment of the use of reason.[129]

[128] Whether psychologist Eve Lewis is excluding the possibility of sin in recommending delay of confession until at least the tenth year is not clear to me; cf. "Children and the Sacrament of Penance," *Month* 210 (1965) 28–36.

[129] Those who contend that a basic option is not possible until the prepubertal years face the problem of how venial sin is possible before this time—a fact which they admit. Those who contend that this basic option, being a profound, obscure, and preconscious thing made under the influence of grace, can exist without being accessible to direct human experience and the criteria of dynamic psychology face other problems. For example, why

Secondly, there seems to be real merit in the advisability of the generic confession for the very young (e.g., "I have not always done what our Lord wanted of me"), and even perhaps in the suggested preparatory steps leading to private confession. At least it would be worth while seeing further serious studies of generic confession based on the reactions of all concerned. The emphasis is away from the syntax and mathematics of individual sins and is placed more easily on the sacramental contact with the forgiving Christ. This provides a healthy background for a later and more searching examination of conscience. The lack of precision in such a confession should occasion no concern about sufficient matter. Perhaps we have made a good deal more than necessary of the problem of *expression* of sufficient matter.[130] I would prefer instructional emphasis on genuine contrition in the earliest years. Here Ranwez makes eminent good sense:

No confessor can be absolutely positive that he hears sufficient "matter" for absolution. All the more when a child recites a list of faults enumerated in a set examination of conscience can it be feared that this mechanical avowal hardly contains sufficient "matter." The child who makes a global accusation of his sins is certainly not doing worse. If his teachers have noticed that his moral conscience is sufficiently developed, there is reason to conclude that his behaviour has sometimes been that of a sinful Christian.

This consideration is sufficient for us to conclude that attempts to make the early confessional experience a sacramental one for the very young are reasonable and *propter homines* in the best sense of the sacramental axiom.

To suggest the possibility of generic confessions, especially group generic confessions for the very young, is one thing. It is hypothesized upon, among other things, the not unreasonable conclusion that mortal sin has not been committed. Generic confession for adults is, therefore, quite another thing. The suggestion of generic confession for adults as part of parish liturgical life has popped into the popular presses occasionally[131] and has been treated recently in at least two places.[132]

---

could this option not take place at age two or three? For further literature on the type of knowledge involved in this option, cf. Jos. J. Sikora, S.J., "Faith and the First Moral Choice," *Sciences ecclésiastiques* 17 (1965) 327–37; M. Flick, S.J., and Z. Alszeghy, S.J., "L'Opzione fondamentale della vita morale et la grazia," *Gregorianum* 41 (1960) 593–619, especially pp. 599–600. Anciaux has called attention to the fact that "a moral conscience, very naive as yet, becomes possible around the sixth or seventh year. . . . With most it becomes a fully *reflexive* conscience during youth." Cf. "La conscience et l'éducation morales," *Collectanea Mechliniensia* 50 (1965) 21 (emphasis added).

[130] For some practical remarks, cf. G. Kelly, S.J., in THEOLOGICAL STUDIES 24 (1963) 644–49.

[131] Brother Philip, F.S.C., in *National Catholic Reporter*, Jan. 27, 1965.

[132] Francis V. Manning, "Private Confession—Pros and Cons," *Pastoral Life* 13 (1965) 227–30; Daniel Lowery, C.SS.R., in *Liguorian* 53 (1965) 47–49.

The advantages of general confession reflect, it is contended, the disadvantages of private confession. Private confession places too much emphasis on externals, is too often routine, is an obstacle to frequent Communion (through fear of confession), is a source of scruples and bad spiritual direction, is time-consuming for the priest and prevents in this way more profound and lasting guidance, encourages the fear-psychology in avoidance of sin, etc. General confession, on the other hand, would place the emphasis on interior conversion and at the same time would make the sacrament more easily available to greater numbers, thereby encouraging more frequent Communion.

Any realistic discussion of this matter must, as both Frs. Manning and Lowery point out, face the issue of integrity. Succinctly stated, this refers to the duty of the penitent to confess his certain mortal sins according to their lowest moral species and number. In the light of this duty, the alternatives are not general vs. private confession, but general vs. specific confession. Privacy of confession follows to a large extent—and rather understandably, I should think—upon the demand of specific and numerical integrity. It is this demand which is the heart of the discussion; for it seems clearly to be of divine law.[133]

Those who argue for general confession treat the matter of integrity a bit too lightly, it would seem. In fact, I am afraid they often manifest the very attitude responsible for some of the harm occasioned by private confession, harm which they correctly regret. This attitude is one which looks upon integrity as "merely a requirement," "a legal fulfilment," "not at the heart of, often in the way of, true repentance." If this is one's attitude toward integrity, clearly trouble is ahead.

Actually, however, the demand of integrity must be understood from a consideration of the place of the Church in the lives and sacramental penance of Christians. The Church, holding the place of Christ, must judge authoritatively about concession of reconciliation to a penitent and direct his penance within the Church, because, as Rahner shows,[134] the sinner has sinned also against the Church. Only in such a framework does her binding (banning) and loosing yield real meaning. The demand of integrity rests directly on the ecclesial character of the sacrament of penance. Hence one who treats it lightly is really insensitive to the ecclesial character of the sacrament(s)—which is quite an insensitivity.

On the other hand, the fact that reconciliation with God must occur in an ecclesial and judicial context which demands integrity and highlights

---

[133] DB 899, 699, 574a.
[134] Karl Rahner, S.J., *Theological Investigations* 2 (Baltimore: Helicon, 1963) 135–74, esp. pp. 136 ff.

the *communal* aspect of grace, sin, and repentance, should not blind us to the fact that specific accusation of sin is also for our own good. Being men, the sincerity and depth of the contrition and purpose of amendment that we bring to the sacramental event can be intensified greatly through its externalization in accusation. To take any other point of view could easily underestimate our human condition.

If it is argued that general confession should be restricted to devotional confession, with the mortal sinners confessing privately and specifically, we are faced with the uncomfortable situation where those who seek private confession would ultimately be regarded as needing it. It is difficult to think of a more effective way to bring odium upon the sacrament in our time. Fr. Manning concludes that although integrity is not an open question (and therefore to that extent neither is general confession), much can be done to rethink and revise present discipline surrounding private confession. Specifically, he suggests that we could rethink frequency of confession, the age of the first confession, the law limiting the Eucharist by confession (scil., after commission of mortal sin), the possibility of face-to-face confession more frequently, education of penitents, and so on.

It is clear that public sacramental absolution was being practiced in Holland in some places. The Dutch bishops issued two documents on the point, one a general letter to the faithful (read in all Dutch churches March 28, 1965), the other a set of instructions to the clergy.[135] These documents are extremely interesting. Several points stand out. First, public penitential celebrations have a definite place in the life of the Church and are to be encouraged; for, besides emphasizing the ecclesial aspects of responsibility, sin, and forgiveness, these celebrations can and should act as a school for the faithful toward a more profound personal (and private) confession of sin. But by no means should private confession fall into desuetude as a result. Secondly, the documents warn against mechanical haste in private confession, thus underlining, it would seem, what seems to be the major source of the "problem of private confession." Thirdly, the bishops reaffirm the obligation of confessing expressly and privately mortal sins.[136] Fourthly, the use of the formula of absolution which the Church reserves for private confession is not justified in these public celebrations. Finally, as for the

[135] "Deux lettres collectives de l'épiscopat hollandais," *Documentation catholique* 62 (1965) 1170-79.

[136] To the faithful they refer to "l'obligation d'avouer *expressement* tout péché grave en confession" (1174). To the clergy they say: "Nous devons maintenir fermement l'obligation de confesser *en privé* les péchés graves ..." (1175). These are practical statements; that is, while integrity does not *de se* demand private confession, the duty of integrity does indeed practically issue in private confession.

sacramentality of these public celebrations, the bishops urge the clergy to refrain from any pronouncements on the matter, since this is a theological problem still under discussion. These documents strike me as being very balanced and useful, especially in their insistence on the ecclesial dimension of sin and private confession.[137]

With the introduction of the vernacular in the form of absolution, a number of dioceses are urging penitents to recite the act of contrition before entering the confessional, so that, after confession of sin, they can listen attentively to the form of absolution. Eugene J. Weitzel, C.S.V., treats the problems which might arise in the mind of the confessor from this practice.[138] One such problem is sufficient external expression of contrition. He rightly concludes that once there is internal contrition, the mere fact of making one's confession is sufficient external expression to constitute a valid sacramental sign. A slightly different question is the following: What expression of sorrow is necessary that the confessor may make the pastoral judgment as to sufficient sorrow? In organizing his answer to this question, Fr. Weitzel first cites the (privately obtained) opinion of John C. Ford, S.J., on the matter. While admitting that the "ordinary signs" enumerated in moral literature (spontaneous confession, sincere and humble accusation, a confession made in spite of difficulties, resolve to follow the confessor's advice, etc.) are sufficient assurance for the confessor, and insisting that a routinely recited act of contrition would not necessarily give the confessor the assurance he needs, Fr. Ford expressed the general opinion that it "is nevertheless advisable that penitents express their sorrow explicitly in confession,

---

[137] Th. van Eupen, C.SS.R., reviews three books which deal generally with the "crisis of the sacrament of penance in Holland" in an article "Biecht en Boeteviering," *Theologie en Zielzorg* 61 (1965) 113–18. The reviewer regards the first book, by J. Bommer (*De biecht in leer en praktijk—Een nieuwe benadering*), as not of great importance. The second (*De biecht—Verkondiging over de biecht*, by L. Bosse, O.F.M., and H. Borgert, C.SS.R.) reports the discussions of a commission appointed by Bishop Bekkers of 's Hertogenbosch to study the sacrament of penance. The book deals largely with the manner of presentation of the sacrament to the people and suggests emphasis on several points: e.g., what is sin, what not; the ecclesiastical dimension of the sacrament of penance. But the principles of practical celebration of the sacrament do not emerge clearly. Van Eupen devotes most of his article to the third book, by F. Heggen (*Boete-viering en private biecht*). Heggen proposes public confession, points to the fact that there were various forms of confession in the past, insists that penance must be an act of the community. Van Eupen criticizes the book on several scores: the confusion of the ecclesial with the community aspect of penance; the minimalizing of Trent's decree on penance; overdependence on Bonhoeffer and Robinson for its concept of sin. Finally, he contends that Heggen has adduced no real argument for the sacramentality of a penitential celebration without confession.

[138] Eugene J. Weitzel, C.S.V., "Judging Contrition in the Vernacular Confession," *Homiletic and Pastoral Review* 65 (1965) 307–13.

even by means of a formula, for this gives the priest a good presumption of sorrow."[139] Fr. Weitzel would prefer to say that in the confession of a well-instructed penitent there is no need to insist on explicit expression of sorrow. Only in cases where the penitent is either poorly instructed or doubtfully contrite would Weitzel recommend an express act of contrition.

Msgr. James Madden discusses the same question[140] and concludes that the formal recitation of an act of sorrow during the confession itself is useful for the more fruitful reception of the sacrament. But this does not mean that the recitation should occur during the imparting of absolution. Msgr. Madden would prefer to retain the custom of explicit contrition but before the imparting of absolution.

My own opinion is very close to that of Msgr. Madden. I would prefer to base a policy-conclusion to retain explicitly expressed contrition not precisely on the fact that expressed sorrow "gives the priest a good presumption of sorrow"[141] (which I would accept as sufficiently and generally present from other indications), but rather on the fact that not a few penitents seem to derive from the act of confession itself and from the subsequent exchange with the confessor a type of understanding and motivation which can aid them in eliciting a more profoundly sincere and satisfying act of sorrow. Furthermore, listening to the absolution meaningfully imparted will give the penitent a clearer idea of what the sacramental event should be, hence will provide a basis for deepening his contrition for future confessions. One might care to think twice, therefore, before adopting a general policy which would prevent penitents either from hearing the form of absolution or from eliciting an act of contrition after they have confessed.

[139] *Ibid.*, p. 308.

[140] James Madden, "The Act of Contrition at Confession," *Australasian Catholic Record* 42 (1965) 123–27.

[141] Francis J. Connell, C.SS.R., in *American Ecclesiastical Review* 152 (1965) 200–201, strongly urges "some explicit expression of contrition, so that he [the confessor] may be morally certain that the sacrament is being administered validly." I would place less emphasis on explicit expression for the reason given by Fr. Connell, because I doubt that it is that functional with regard to validity.

CURRENT THEOLOGY: 1966

NOTES ON MORAL THEOLOGY

RENEWAL IN MORAL THEOLOGY

In its Decree on Priestly Training (*Optatam totius*) the Second Vatican Council stipulated: "Other theological disciplines should also be renewed by livelier contact with the mystery of Christ and the history of salvation. *Special attention needs to be given to the development of moral theology.* Its scientific exposition should be more thoroughly nourished by scriptural teaching. It should show the nobility of the Christian vocation of the faithful, and their obligation to bring forth fruit in charity for the life of the world."[1]

It would be hard to read the italicized words as a compliment to what we might call "traditional moral theology." On the other hand, it must be noted that there has been in the past twenty years a genuine flowering in biblical, liturgical, and dogmatic studies. A renewal of moral theology could hardly precede these, given the inherent dependence of moral science on these disciplines. But the task is now urgent.

That task will be made appreciably easier by the availability of what must be one of the most compact and carefully written yet ranging articles to appear in some time. Joseph Fuchs, S.J., has made the brief conciliar paragraph cited above the subject of a lengthy study.[2] Fuchs points out that the primary object of moral theology must be the elaboration of the excellence of the Christian vocation. This makes it immediately clear that the character of the moral life will be seen as one of Christian response. The main fruit of this response will be charity, a charity which, being concerned with the life of the world, is the soul of the social virtues. The dominant context of moral thought will be the mystery of Christ and the history of salvation. In the wrong hands the more thorough biblical nourishment which alone provides this context could become either an abstract supernaturalism or a type of poetry and preachment. Fuchs's own writings should be enough to allay the fear of such prescientific evangelism.[3] It would be

EDITOR'S NOTE.—The present survey covers the period from January to June, 1966.

[1] Cf. *The Documents of Vatican II*, ed. Walter M. Abbott, S.J. (New York: Association Press, 1966) p. 452.

[2] Joseph Fuchs, S.J., "Theologia moralis perficienda: Votum Concilii Vaticani II," *Periodica* 55 (1966) 499–548.

[3] Cf. Diaz-Nava, S.J., "Enfoque cristiano de la teología moral," *Sal terrae* 54 (1966) 242–56, for an article which relies heavily on Fuchs's work in general moral.

well if this essay were translated and put into the hands of everyone plying anything remotely resembling moral theology.

The same might be said for the well-documented essay of Edward Hamel, S.J., which examines more in detail the Council's phrase *scientifica expositio, doctrina S. Scripturae magis nutrita*.[4] After showing the failure of earlier moral theologians to become more than precursors *in voto* of a biblical renewal in moral thought, Hamel turns his attention to the use of Scripture in current moral theology. He argues that a "return to the Bible" must carefully distinguish between the gospel, preaching, biblical theology, and scientific moral theology if the Bible is to be a doctrinal treasure rather than a mere arsenal for *dicta probantia*. There will always be something of a tonal hiatus between the morality of the New Testament and its scientific elaboration.[5] But this only says that moral theology is a science and that the Bible is not. It does not say that this science can hope to reach Christian maturity if its beginnings and inspiration are not profoundly biblical. Like Hamel's previous work, this article is both balanced and forward looking.

Franco Festorazzi also insists that moral theology cannot be simply equated with biblical morality.[6] It is rather the investigation of biblical thought conducted through reason illumined by faith. After treating of some of the methodological problems, Festorazzi points out that it is the appearance of the young discipline of biblical theology which provides the meeting ground for the moralist and the exegete.[7]

The Council insisted that renewal in moral theology must not be equated with abandonment of its scientific character. One of the most fruitful areas of recent scientific analysis emerges from the literature surrounding what we might call the fundamental option. Several conciliar statements seem to suggest, even suppose, this analysis of moral activity. The term "fundamental option" is used by theologians to refer to the free determination of oneself with regard to the totality of existence, the fundamental choice between love of self and love of the saving Lord. Because man's eternal salvation, his basic position for or against the God of salvation, is at stake in such choices, they must involve a man's total disposition of himself, out of the radical center of his being. Since this is the case, these

---

[4] Edward Hamel, S.J., "L'Usage de l'Ecriture sainte en théologie morale," *Gregorianum* 47 (1966) 53–85.

[5] This point does not come through as clearly as one would like in John L. McKenzie's "Law in the New Testament," *Jurist* 26 (1966) 167–80, at p. 171.

[6] Franco Festorazzi, "La Sacra Scrittura anima del rinnovamento della teologia morale," *Scuola cattolica* 94 (1966) 91–115.

[7] For a report of the conclusions of Spanish moral theologians on the renewal (especially biblical) of moral theology, cf. *Sal terrae* 54 (1966) 25–27.

choices will involve a depth of the person's being beyond formulating (or reflex) consciousness, and hence will escape adequate conceptual formulation.

This understanding of the root of moral activity has helped us immeasurably in understanding the meaning of mortal sin, and hence also the difference between mortal and venial sin.[8] It has also helped us to explain the so-called grades within the category of serious sin. It has deepened our knowledge of the meaning of conversion. Theological literature increasingly uses existential language in describing mortal sin and sees it as involving an act of fundamental liberty in the depths of the soul, where a man is totally present to himself and as such is called by God. Venial sin is, by contrast, a peripheral act committed at a less central depth of the soul and, as such, is compatible with the love of God still alive in the depths of the person. It is this existential concept of choice, not primarily the matter, which distinguishes mortal from venial sin. This doctrine is not new, of course; but one could say that it is being newly recovered and restored and its ramifications are being spelled out. However, its extension beyond the analysis of sinful conduct and its relationship to other dogmatic facts have not been carefully studied.

Bruno Schüller, S.J., discusses the fundamental option and attempts to show (with singular success, I believe) that it not only aids us in grasping more thoroughly the analogous character of mortal and venial sin, but also is the foundation for the analogy we must recognize in the area of good acts, of liberty, of law itself.[9] Thus, for example, we can and should speak of *honestum grave, honestum leve*. So, too, the notions of freedom and law are only analogous notions differing qualitatively when found in the area of grave or slight morality.

Take, for example, freedom, and specifically the freedom involved in venial sin. Suppose a man in the state of grace deliberately lies. He knows

[8] A recent example of an article which examines the pastoral, catechetical, and canonical implications of our deepened understanding of mortal sin is that of Robert P. O'Neil and Michael A. Donovan, "Psychic Development and Mortal Sin," *Pastoral Life* 14 (1966) 261–68. A choice involving a basic orientation of life demands an autonomy of judgment not achieved by children until the ages of 12–14. The authors' major conclusion is that confession should be delayed until this time. The authors seem to equate the sacrament of penance with *specific* and *private* confession. Until other possibilities (such as public penitential celebrations, eventually sacramental) are investigated, their conclusion does not recommend itself as necessarily the most helpful for the sacramental life of the child. Cf. THEOLOGICAL STUDIES 26 (1965) 654–58, and more recently J. Bulckens, "Première confession dans le cadre de l'école," *Collectanea Mechliniensia* 51 (1966) 192–226.

[9] Bruno Schüller, S.J., "Zur Analogie sittlicher Grundbegriffe," *Theologie und Philosophie* [bis 1965, *Scholastik*] 41 (1966) 3–20.

this is forbidden but he says to himself that his salvation is not involved. This means that he lies with his free will yet remains *conversus ad Deum* with the same free will which he used to disobey God. Moralists have frequently referred to such an act as *peccatum leve plene deliberatum*. Schüller believes that this gives away the fact that they are viewing freedom univocally. He insists that the freedom involved in mortal sin is qualitatively different from that involved in venial sin.

If one defines freedom as it is often defined (*positis omnibus ad agendum requisitis, potest* etc. . . . .), it actually appears to be operative in an identical manner in mortal and venial sin, in grave or slight good acts, hence to be a univocal notion. But this is to define freedom incompletely, in a purely formal way as active indifference in the face of a limited good. If we remember that in acting man takes hold of himself in a responsible way, engages himself and becomes his act, we can recognize a new dimension to freedom and see this dimension as the inner constitutive of decision. We can no longer miss the qualitative difference between the freedom involved in mortal and venial sin. We can, therefore, no longer speak of a *peccatum leve plene deliberatum*, or at least we must understand it differently.

Schüller enlightens nearly everything he touches, and this is true here of such things as *fides informis*, resistance to temptation, the good acts of one in the state of serious sin, and the concept of the oughtness of law itself.

CONTEXTUALISM VS. PRINCIPLES

The Council at least implies that Catholic moral theology will profit from contact with other moralities.[10] If the literature is a valid indication, the most lively issue in "other moralities" has been the discussion which we may entitle, certainly for lack of a better phrase, "contextualism vs. principles."[11] Assuredly this polarization can be very misleading, because, as James Gustafson (Yale) remarks,[12] the umbrellas of contextualism and principles have become so sprawling that they include thinkers whose views are as significantly different from each other as they are from persons gathered under the other umbrella. However, James A. Burtness, of the Lutheran Theological Seminary in St. Paul, does not believe that the wide variety of

[10] Cf. *The Documents of Vatican II*, p. 453.

[11] Max L. Stackhouse (Harvard) observes a disenchantment among the younger writers with both of these methods. They are producing papers "the methodological presuppositions of which are perhaps still obscure." Cf. "Technical Data and Ethical Norms: Some Theoretical Considerations," *Journal for the Scientific Study of Religion* 5 (1966) 191–203, at p. 194.

[12] James M. Gustafson, "Context versus Principles: A Misplaced Debate in Christian Ethics," *Harvard Theological Review* 58 (1965) 171–202, at p. 173.

positions in each category, and the overlapping of context and principle in most positions, necessarily invalidates the use of categories as a helpful device to describe a general trend.[13] Be this as it may, apparently it was once thought that a serious confrontation with the issues raised by "the new morality" or "situation ethics" would contaminate the streams of Catholic thought.[14] It is not to underestimate this danger to assert that quite the opposite effect is a legitimate hope.

The literature on this subject is enormous, and nothing more than a synoptic treatment can be attempted here. A good introduction to the discussion, especially to its more profound theological and dogmatic roots, would be Gustafson's article "Christian Ethics."[15] It contains a full bibliography. Paul Ramsey's recent *Deeds and Rules in Christian Ethics* is also helpful.[16] It is a critical introduction to the thought of men like Robinson, Frankena, and Lehmann. Similarly, Gustafson's survey in the *Harvard Theological Review* is the kind of article it is a pleasure to read.[17] Gustafson shows himself a careful, precise thinker with sensitivity for and appreciation of a point of view he does not necessarily share.

Gustafson contends that there are four basic points from which discourse on Christian ethics can and does begin: moral principles; accurate social or situational analysis; theological affirmations; the nature of the Christian life in Christ and the proper expression of this in moral conduct. It is impossible not to move toward the other three bases no matter what base one accepts as primary. The debate on contextualism vs. principles has tended to assume that the matter of how moral decisions are made could be separated from other considerations. Gustafson insists that if one argues against contextualism, one has to direct his argument to the theological and ethical reasons given for stress on the context. Similarly, if one argues against principles, one has to be particular about many questions often sloppily disposed of with rhetoric: from what sources are the principles derived (natural law, biblical revelation, ethos of the Christian community), how are principles used (for direction to goals, or for determination of right conduct), how are they interpreted (as prescriptive or illuminative)?

What is behind the stress on context which has led to situational moral

---

[13] James H. Burtness, "The New Morality," *Dialogue* 5 (1966) 10–17, at p. 16. Nearly the entire issue is devoted to the New Morality.

[14] *AAS* 48 (1956) 144–45.

[15] James M. Gustafson, "Christian Ethics," in *Religion*, ed. Paul Ramsey (Englewood Cliffs: Prentice-Hall, 1965) pp. 287–354.

[16] Paul Ramsey, *Deeds and Rules in Christian Ethics* (Scottish Journal of Theology Occasional Papers 11; Edinburgh, 1965).

[17] Cf. supra n. 12.

thinking? The proximate reasons are theological and/or epistemological. But James H. Burtness believes it is important to see the so-called "new morality" as part of a much larger historical movement.[18] He sees this movement as a massive shift from what he calls a spatial dualism of nature and supernature to a temporal dualism of old and new. Before Copernicus, man's understanding of reality was spatial ("ups" and "downs"); after Copernicus, time began to shape his understanding of things. Thus, the biologist used to be almost completely concerned with classification of permanent forms of life; now he works rather with the development of one form of life to another. Formerly we attributed an absoluteness to the law of supply and demand; now the relativities of Keynesian economics shape government policies. And so on.

Spatial dualism, according to Burtness, also affected man's approach to God.

For vast numbers of people in the Church, God has been defined specifically as the changeless who dwells above change, the timeless untouched by time, the absolute over against the relative. And that has often meant that theoretical statements, because they are about a changeless God, are themselves changeless. Theology, in this case, has to do with the timeless: God defined in terms of his attributes; the Trinity defined in terms of ontological inner-relationships; the Lord's Supper defined in terms of the spatial problem of the intertwining of bread and wine, body and blood; sin defined in terms of breaking God's absolute laws.[19]

Now, however, theologians lean toward the functional rather than the ontological: the Bible is the book of the acts of God; Christ is the man for others; sacrament is the occasion upon which God approaches the recipient; sin is a description of man's situation. This theological shift from space to time is accompanied by an ethical shift from absolutes to situations. When man lives in history rather than in the "spatial supernatural," Burtness asserts that there are no such things as ethical absolutes; there is only responsible decision. Even Marshal Dillon is beginning to find himself in more ambiguous situations. The remainder of Burtness' essay is a survey of modern situational theologians (e.g., Bonhoeffer, Sittler, Lehmann).

In an age of mass communications it was inevitable that this discussion would shift from tome to table talk. In the process of its popularization it has lost some of its theological rootage and precision, but none of its liveliness. The three best-known popular exponents of a "situation ethics" are

[18] Cf. supra n. 13.
[19] *Art. cit.*, p. 11.

Canon Douglas A. Rhymes,[20] Prof. Joseph Fletcher,[21] and Bishop John A. T. Robinson.[22] Since Rhymes and Fletcher have written during the past semester, my summary will consist of excerpts from their writings.

The first difficulty one encounters in making a précis and comments on Fletcher–Rhymes is the problem of rhetoric. It is here that Fletcher is at his best as a situationist. What he says of acts ("goodness is what happens to an act, it is not in the act itself") could be applied to his use of words: "meaning is what happens to a word, it is not in the word itself." Fletcher is dangerously close to the absolutism he abhors in adhering to this. Thus, Gustafson in his rather devastating review has noted that

"love" like "situation" is a word that runs through Fletcher's book like a greased pig. . . . Nowhere does Fletcher indicate in a systematic way his various uses of it. It refers to everything he wants it to refer to. It is the *only* thing that is intrinsically good; it *equals* justice; it is a formal *principle*; it is a *disposition*, it is a predicate and not a property, it is a ruling norm etc.[23]

Others have noted this same thing in Canon Rhymes. Robert E. Fitch, dean of the Pacific School of Religion, has gathered some of these phrases together under the rubric of fetish phrases: mature, adult, responsible, relational, provisional, contextual, etc. He refers to it all as "the flourishing of shibboleths. . . . We look up for the water of life, but are drowned under a cascade of clichés."[24] Similarly, Union Theological's Tom Driver, after calling attention to the neon words in this rhetoric ("maturity," "responsibility," "love"), asks simply: "Who can disagree with such statements?"[25] Bernard E. Meland, formerly of the University of Chicago, sees "maturity" and "responsibility" in Rhymes as weasel words. He asks: "Mature in what sense? Responsible to whom or what?"[26]

The matter of rhetoric is important beyond the fun poked at it by its critics. It constitutes a kind of methodology by incantation which makes it

[20] Douglas A. Rhymes, "The 'New' Morality," *Religion in Life* 35 (1966) 170–81. This article is a brief statement of the views expressed in Rhymes's book *No New Morality* (Indianapolis: Bobbs Merrill, 1965). Nearly the entire issue of *Religion in Life* is devoted to the New Morality and makes extremely interesting reading.

[21] Joseph Fletcher, *Situation Ethics* (Philadelphia: Westminster, 1966), as well as "Love is the Only Measure," *Commonweal* 83 (1966) 427–32.

[22] John A. T. Robinson, *Christian Morals Today* (Philadelphia: Westminister, 1964), as well as *Honest to God* (Philadelphia: Westminister, 1963) pp. 103–21.

[23] James M. Gustafson, "How Does Love Reign?" *Christian Century* 83 (1966) 654.

[24] Robert E. Fitch, in *Religion in Life* 35 (1966) 186.

[25] Tom Driver, *ibid.*, p. 200.

[26] Bernard E. Meland, *ibid.*, p. 194.

terribly hard to know what Fletcher is actually saying. Certainly he is against legalism; but we all are or should be. Certainly he is for maturity, responsibility, and love. But are we not all? The intent, then, is beyond dispute. When he spells out this intent, he waves before us a series of supposedly clear opposites which are neither clear nor clearly opposed: "brushing aside moral responsibility in favor of sticking to the rules"; "an ethic of responsible decision rather than obedience to law"; "love not law"; "principles are maxims not rules"; "love people, not principles." Rhymes uses many of the same couplets and asserts that Jesus does "not primarily call men to a code to be applied but to the demanding rule of love as the only absolute, to the working out of what love means in the existing situation."[27]

Obviously such rhetorical gestures cry out for several distinctions and it would be tedious to marshal them here. But their general effect is to jockey one into the position of not loving and caring in the situation if he insists on the validity of an absolute. This is the methodological point Paul Ramsey is constantly making when he talks about getting the terms of the debate straight. It is unsound to begin by defining what he calls "general-rule agapism" or "in-principled love" as readiness to obey a rule even though the action it calls for is seen not to be what love would directly require.[28] It is because in-principled love sees nothing of the kind that it adheres to its principles. It is precisely the love that is in it and which would be violated by departure from it which gives the principle its validity. Or as Ramsey himself puts it: "The fact that nothing other than *agape* makes a thing right or wrong does not mean that nothing is right or wrong."[29] To think otherwise would be to compromise love and actually to risk doing the unloving thing. Fletcher's rhetorical beginnings are, then, only justified if one has established their suppositions.

The only way to get at Fletcher's suppositions is through his conclusions. These conclusions, as I read them, could be stated in two propositions. (1) There is only one absolute: love. In whatever situation man finds himself, it is his call to work out the maximum response of love. (2) No negative principles have absolute validity in describing the character of this loving response.[30] Thus, practically, adultery may generally be immoral, but there can be the outside instance where it is the loving thing to do. No serious Christian moralist will quarrel with the first assertion. It is the second, or rather its suppositions, which constitute the heart of the matter.

---

[27] Rhymes, *art. cit.*, p. 178.

[28] Paul Ramsey, "Two Concepts of General Rules in Christian Ethics," *Ethics* 76 (1966) 192–207, at pp. 196–97.

[29] *Ibid.*, p. 195.

[30] I put it this way because, except for a few absolute negative prohibitions, I believe that Catholic moral theology is quite as situationist as Fletcher at his best.

Before one can defend this position other than arbitrarily, he must have answered the question: how does one go about making a moral judgment? As far as one can gather, Fletcher's answer to this would run as follows: evaluate the total situation, then do the loving thing. So far, no problem. But how does one determine what is the loving thing? Here Fletcher is very ambiguous. At one time the loving thing is the sum of the consequences of an act, so that if, by and large, more harm will result, the proposed activity would be unloving. At other times, as Herbert McCabe, editor of *New Blackfriars*, notes,[31] this caring is distinct from the act and its effects and seems to be only an inner psychological state. In other words, judgments of morality are assessments of the caring or loving thing to do in the situation; but it is not clear how one determines this. Obviously Fletcher has not made up his mind on how moral judgments are made. As long as this remains unclear, he can squeeze out of any epistemological corner, because he has none he calls his own. And as long as he has none he calls his own, one can only say that he has adopted a method (and its content-conclusions) without first solving the problems of methodology.

It would be ungracious to imply that no one else is guilty of this. We have all had our turn at it, and undoubtedly far more often than we realize. However, this cannot be allowed to blur the fact that rather than work his way back carefully to his premises, Prof. Fletcher has chosen to plug the holes where these premises begin to appear. Even when he unveils a premise, it remains a slippery word (e.g., nominalism) which he would prefer to bandy about rather than analyze. This is not to say that Fletcher is wrong; it is only to say that he has not shown satisfactorily on what grounds he could be right.

In his tightly reasoned *Commonweal* article, Fr. McCabe sets out to show why Fletcher is wrong in his suppositions. He begins by stating the issue: "Are there some things that you must never under any circumstances do?" If the answer is "yes," then Fletcher is wrong. The Fletcher-situationist says "no." McCabe's answer to this is a kind of *reductio ad dualismum*.

McCabe's basic point seems to be this. The New Moralist must contend in principle that *every* piece of behavior can pass as "loving." Therefore he must deny that any action is loving or unloving as such, specifically that any action is always unloving. McCabe sees this as an attack on the significance of human (bodily) behavior. He asserts: "I think that it is possible for them to hold this only because they believe that the adjective 'loving' is descriptive not of bodily behavior as such but of something else that accompanies it." If this is true, McCabe sees it rightly as inseparable from a

---

[31] Herbert McCabe, "The Validity of Absolutes," *Commonweal* 83 (1966) 432–37 and 439–40, at p. 439.

dualistic view of man, a view according to which values attach to events in an interior and invisible life which runs alongside of man's physical life. Love is not behavior; it accompanies behavior.

The accusation of dualism is, I believe, well aimed. If any activity can count as loving, we begin to sense that the word has lost its content, because human actions have lost their significance. To take but a single example— and that is all that is really needed[32]—is there a more disastrous sentence in recent theological literature than Fletcher's "sexual intercourse may or may not be an act of love"?[33] One can only make such a statement if he denies significance to this particular bit of human behavior. What Fletcher should have said (but could not on his suppositions) is: "this *act of love* may or may not be personally accompanied by appropriate sentiments of loving concern and othercenteredness, may or may not occur in circumstances which honor its meaning." Fletcher must deny that sexual intercourse as such is in any sense a loving act. For him it is neutral. It merits description as "loving" only when the parties put their minds to it. That means that ultimately it merits description as "loving" only *because* they put their minds to it. There have always been those who thought that sexual love were better off when confined to the mind. But have we not been battling such attacks on the significance of human behavior for centuries?

McCabe is right on target, therefore, when he points out that for Fletcher there is no such thing as sexual love; there is only sex accompanied by love. "Sex," Fletcher notes, "which does not have love as *partner* is wrong." The implications of this type of talk must be a terrible setback to all who feel that we have made genuine progress in extricating ourselves from the one-sidedness of the past in analyzing human love. For it is quite as effective an attack on the significance of human behavior as a narrow physicalism. On the other hand, perhaps we should not be surprised that our contemporary culture finds it more congenial to ask not *why* coitus is an act of love (an act which therefore makes demands of its participants), but *whether* it is.

But to McCabe's thoughtful essay one might apply the old axiom: *omnia dicta sunt vera, sed non omnia vera sunt dicta.* I mean that though McCabe has felled his demon, he has not shown, and did not really attempt to show, how one determines precisely what activities are always unloving and therefore generate absolute prohibitions. This is a far larger problem.

---

[32] If it can be shown that in one instance the situational suppositions involve an attack on the significance of human behavior, the method has been shown to fail. As Ramsey says: "A single exception to act-agapism and to summary-rule agapism would be sufficient to destroy these positions utterly and to establish general-rule agapism in at least some types of action" (*Ethics* 76 [1966] 196).

[33] *Commonweal* 83 (1966) 429.

It would be a serious mistake to treat Fletcher–Rhymes as mere ethical gadflies. I believe that they are saying something very important. First of all, over and beyond their healthy revulsion from mere conformism as the meaning of morality, they are articulating very persuasively what one can easily believe is the implicit moral position of the vast majority of Christian nonspecialists, especially when they face desperate situations. These writings, therefore, can speak a message to the theologian who sees his task as more than ivory-towerism. Secondly, they are raising a question for technical moral thought which has not been satisfactorily confronted by Catholic theologians—the problem of Christian moral knowing. Finally, one can suspect that the fact that this question has not received the attention in Catholic circles that it deserves stems at least partially from, and therefore passes judgment on, the working separation of moral theology from other theological disciplines.

John G. Milhaven, S.J., has turned his attention to this extremely interesting and important epistemological question and asked: how does one know inviolable values in this world?[34] One must know the answer to this question before the absoluteness of a moral position is clear. Failure even to ask the question has locked much modern Catholic moral thought in mere propositions without an adequately developed epistemology to support them. Fr. Milhaven suggests a two-pronged approach.

First, there are certain values which we recognize immediately and intuitively as absolute without need of further evidence of any kind. "If one discerns what can be the authentic love between a man and a woman, one recognizes its absolute worth. One sees that no man may seek to frustrate it or destroy it. . . . Once human love is understood, once the insight is had, man sees immediately its absolute worth." Milhaven feels that very few values fit this category. He mentions "love and honor and pity and pride and compassion and sacrifice." At another point he mentions the husband-wife friendship and *condigna prolis educatio* as absolute values.

Secondly, one recognizes acts as immoral when the empirical observation of a number of cases indicates that the act (e.g., divorce) will result in some absolute evil. By empirical evidence Milhaven means "the evidence of the probable or certain consequences of what is going to result from the act in question." It is only empirical evidence in this sense that shows that divorce will oppose the absolute values embedded in marriage. Moralists have been insufficiently aware of the decisive character of consequence-empiricism in most moral judgments, hence have remained wrapped in a rationalistic garb which is an unfashionable oddity to the contemporary thinker.

[34] John G. Milhaven, S.J., "Towards an Epistemology of Ethics," THEOLOGICAL STUDIES 27 (1966) 228–41.

I believe that Milhaven is right in asserting that too often we moral theologians have been content with derivative statements (e.g., "innocent human life is inviolable from direct attack") without examining the underlying epistemology. Such propositions do not establish a moral position, but simply formulate more or less accurately a moral position already taken. It is also beyond doubt that we have not always appreciated how many moral decisions are really dependent on the type of empirical evidence he describes.

But could it be that in making these quite valid points Milhaven has also raised a question to which his suggested epistemology does not adequately attend? I refer to the problem of Christian moral knowing. Perhaps one can outline the problem as follows. If the Church can and does go beyond the natural evidence of consequence-empiricism in her moral perceptions and teaching, this seems to mean a great deal for both theological methodology and epistemology.

As for theological methodology, it means that our analyses may not restrict themselves to consequence-empiricism, at least in those areas where this has happened. It also suggests that the function of empirical evidence is not merely probative, but also and perhaps even especially indicative. That is, such evidence also aids us—even where it is not "probative"—in arriving at insights. Finally, it suggests that the only type of evidence available for certain conclusions might be what Milhaven refers to as "rationalistic." Milhaven has asked for the "further evidence" behind some theological propositions. I am suggesting (and that only) that there may not be any of the type he seeks, simply because the theologian is only attempting to analyze and formulate a position which goes beyond available empirical evidence. Practically this means that we may be in situations where we must try to analyze as far as we can to the point of persuasion (using all evidence, even and especially empirical evidence) but not abandon a position for failure to arrive at a probative analysis based on empirical data.

Secondly, the epistemological question. If the moral perceptions of the Church go beyond the evidence of consequence-empiricism, one would expect this fact to affect our knowing processes. I mean that we would expect that, as a general rule, Church teachings would sharpen and sensitize our very perception of natural value. Human beings are dynamic beings who grow and mature in all aspects of their personalities, even their sensitivity to value. Furthermore, they are one, and it must be expected that their faith will affect their growth, including their knowing processes. Specifically, just as one would think that contact with the God-man in faith would enlarge and refine our sensitivity to human values, should we not also expect that the aid provided by Church teaching over the centuries should favorably affect our perception of value?[35]

I should like to present a single example of what I mean.[36] Milhaven asserts that the decisive evidence for the morality of sexual acts must be empirical—and recall that he means by this only a calculation of consequences. The supposition underlying such a statement must be that other sources (above all, the accumulated wisdom of revelation and Church teaching) cannot lead us or have not led us, if only gradually, to a perception of the meaning of coitus which relates it to the love of man and woman. However, I wonder if there is not a meaning to human coitus which we perceive beyond what scientific empiricism might prove.

Concretely, why is it wrong to assert: anyone who knows what the true love of man and woman is will know that adulterous coitus is immoral? Or in Milhaven's words, "it [adultery] betokens *by definition* the absence of a quality (love and/or fidelity) whose absolute value is seen intuitively on understanding what it is." I am suggesting that human sexual intercourse has a sense and meaning prior to the individual purposes of those who engage in it, a significance which is a part of their situation whether or not the partners turn their minds to it. It is an act of love, and therefore has a definition which relates it immediately to the love of man and woman—with all the demands of this love. Furthermore I am also suggesting that we can

[35] Paul Ramsey puts the question as follows: "I should not myself deny that man's natural sense of justice and injustice is able to penetrate to the person and into the meaning of the good for him deeply enough to discern some quite general principles that discriminate between the humane and the inhumane. But even if this were false, surely Christian theologians ought not to dismiss out of hand—rather it is their specific business to explore—the possibility that Christian faith and love affords mankind more than probable knowledge *into ethics*" ("Two Concepts of General Rules in Christian Ethics," p. 194).

[36] Is direct abortion another example? Many (including the Council fathers; cf. *Documents of Vatican II*, n. 27, p. 226) think so. Perhaps human life is not an "absolute value," as Fr. Milhaven understands "absolute" and "value." However, there is a good deal of evidence that human life must constitute a basic value in any realistic epistemology. First of all, human life is the most basic good and, as many believe, the object of the most basic right of man. If any good is capable of generating absolute prohibitions, one would think it would be this good. Secondly, the very difficulty we have had in developing a totally acceptable theological rationale for our positions on capital punishment, warfare, and repulsion of aggression is a kind of negative indication of the existence of a primitive grasp on the good that is human life, similar to the grasp on the good that is honor, compassion, etc. Milhaven's suggested distinction between the inviolability of the human *person* and the inviolability of human *physical life* needs much more discussion than it has yet had in theological literature.

come to know this meaning even if the scientific empiricism of our time has not proved it and cannot prove it. Finally I am suggesting that it is probably the full Christian experience which produces this refinement of sensitivity to *natural* values.[37]

All of this is not to underestimate consequence-empiricism; it is rather to suggest that the Church has gone beyond it and that her teaching can and does affect our value-perception. Growth in this type of knowledge is not appreciated in the twentieth century, but does that negate its reality and its validity as a source of moral truth?

PASTORAL PROBLEMS

What is the proper theological and pastoral attitude of the priest in dealing with the unfortunate situation of a person whose former sacramental and consummated marriage has collapsed and who is now "married" to another person and has several children by this second marriage? Perhaps the case is one wherein the innocent party has been deserted and has already attempted unsuccessfully to persevere in a life of celibacy. There are any number of possible variants. We are all familiar with these second marriages and we know that many of them are characterized by genuine love, permanence, and spiritual aspiration. Indeed it is precisely these qualities which make the problem so intractable.

Since validation of the existing second marriage is presumably out of the question, we also know that the alternatives which face the couple are excruciating. Separation seems to neglect the rights of the child, his need for both parents and a familial climate in his growth process. On the other hand, continued cohabitation will leave the couple proximately exposed to adulterous conduct. Furthermore the relationship will continue to be regarded as adulterous by the Catholic community—if the community is true to its convictions—and hence will close the door to a sacramental life. The problem is anguishing, to say the least.

Four recent articles have dealt with this situation, all from slightly different points of view. Dennis Doherty, O.S.B., uses the problem as a stimulus to ask a whole series of theological questions.[38] What, for instance, is the meaning of consummation? Doherty is suggesting that if consummation might be viewed more broadly than as mere physical completion of intercourse, it is possible to ask: what degree or level of consummation would or

[37] The word "natural" is highlighted to indicate that these perceptions do not constitute *religious belief.*

[38] Dennis Doherty, O.S.B., "The Problem of Divorce and Remarriage," *Marriage* 48 (1966) 12–18.

should involve indissolubility? Or again, is it necessary to enlarge our concept of valid consent by taking into account the acknowledged immaturity of many who marry as teen-agers? The gist of these questions in not precisely that we change what we hold (rejection of divorce with remarriage) but that we attempt to understand it better. These are legitimate questions and no one wants to see them tabled. Each age must face them anew in light of its advancing knowledge of the person and his acts, if theology is to avoid stagnation. However, one only hopes that this continuing theological task can be acquitted quietly and unsensationally without offering the cruel comfort born of false hopes.

M. Huftier's approach to the problem is pastoral.[39] Adverting to the possibility of total or partial separation (this latter meaning abstention from acts of conjugal intimacy), he then rather wryly remarks that "il reste. . . la majorité des cas." For these he makes two general pastoral suggestions.

First, it is important that the couple be clear on why they cannot receive the sacraments, especially the Eucharist. Huftier accepts this as a foregone conclusion. In elaborating this conclusion he stresses greatly the sign-dimension of both the sacraments and social conduct.[40] In both cases we are in the world of signs and are governed by the norms proper to this external order. Thus, the reception of penance and the Eucharist are visible signs of reconciliation and community with Christ in the Church, a kind of profession of faith. Similarly but contrarily, an adulterous situation is a visible pattern of life at odds with this community and its beliefs about marriage, a kind of external denial of this ecclesial faith. To admit to the public profession of faith (inseparable from reception of the Eucharist) one whose exterior situation constitutes a contradictory sign would be to deny the social or ecclesial significance of the sacrament and render it mendacious. "The Church, therefore, cannot give the sacraments to those whose social comportment is a contradictory sign to this faith."

Secondly, Huftier insists that the pastor of souls approach the problem not in terms of what the couple must do to return to the sacraments but rather with the explicit aim of deepening their Christian faith. He will support their fulfilment of their duties toward each other and the children. Even if they cannot receive the Eucharist, the priest will point out that the Church does not reject them and he will encourage their assistance at Mass and their continuing manifestation of conscience to a priest.

[39] M. Huftier, "Sur la séparation de divorcés remaries," *Ami du clergé* 76 (1966) 201–207.

[40] A similar analysis of the sign-value of the sacraments is given by E. Marcus, "Qui doit-on laisser accéder aux sacrements?" *Collectanea Mechliniensia* 51 (1966) 54–78, at p. 74.

G. Rossino's brief statement focuses exclusively on the moral demands.[41] If the adulterous situation is known in the place where the couple live, Rossino sees no alternative to separation whenever this is possible. If it is impossible (because of children, etc.), cohabitation may be continued if there is a serious resolve to avoid demonstrations of conjugal affection. If the couple arrive at this resolve, they may even receive the sacraments, but only if the situation is occult and likely to remain so.

Three moralists, two of them from the Netherlands, have approached what they term the problem of *concubinarii* largely in terms of the permissibility of participation in the Church's sacramental life.[42] They conclude that not all *concubinarii* are excluded in principle from receiving the sacraments. Those who cohabit in a "marital state of mind" because cohabitation is their only practical option may be allowed to receive the sacraments. By a "marital state of mind" the authors mean that the couple "possess the mental and emotional dispositions which are proper to marriage itself." They "consider themselves as married to each other" and want to fulfil their duties to their children.

They arrive at this conclusion by attempting to show that the three reasons adduced for exclusion of such individuals from the sacraments (individual disposition, ecclesiastical unworthiness, scandal) are not of absolute validity. For example, with regard to what they call "ecclesiastical unworthiness," they accept Huftier's general analysis but "wonder whether this opinion does not overstress the visible expression of holiness of the Church. After all, is the unity and holiness within which the sacraments can be true signs an absolute and indivisible holiness? Might it perhaps be possible to accept a holiness which is 'more or less' rather than simple 'is or is not'? Would it not be possible to draw into this the essential imperfection of man and of all that is human?"

This last article is disturbing, not because it raises a delicate question and takes a nontraditional stand, but because in doing so it is rather wooly in its attitude toward this second "marriage." Two examples of this ambiguity will have to suffice here.

First, the article treats all cases of second marriages (which cannot be regularized) in the same way under title of "people invalidly married who are unable to convalidate their marriage." The authors refer to such instances as situations with no "juridical solution." This is certainly true. But

---

[41] G. Rossino, "La questione spinosa delle convivenze illegittime," *Perfice munus* 61 (1966) 130–33.

[42] B. Peters, T. Beemer, and C. van der Poel, "Cohabitation in a 'Marital State of Mind,' " *Homiletic and Pastoral Review* 66 (1966) 566–77.

it obscures the fact that this lack of a juridical solution is sometimes simply an extension of a basic doctrinal position on divorce and remarriage, at others rather a matter of jurisprudential policy surrounding this doctrine. For example, there is no juridical solution when *ratum non consummatum* proceedings break down for lack of proof, even though the petitioner knows in his conscience that coitus did not occur. In this juridical instance the moral position on divorce and remarriage is not at stake in the same way it is in other cases. By leaving "juridical" thus loose and ambiguous, the authors manage to attribute more weight to "the marital state of mind" than it deserves. This tends to solve the underlying problem by reducing its real proportions. Indeed there are times when one wonders just how the authors do regard the first sacramental and consummated marriage.

A second example is their discussion of the "good dispositions" of the *concubinarii*. Their norm for such a disposition is: "How much real living Christianity is present despite this situation? Is there, in view of the situation, a sufficient visibly-lived Christianity?" They then face the question as to whether abstention from all conjugal intimacy "belongs to the signs of a living Christian mentality." This is certainly the case, they state, "when the partners cannot consider themselves as a married couple." But when they actually are in a "marital state of mind," the authors assert that it would be biologism to make this demand of them. Since they may be obliged in conscience to stay together, "it is hard to see how the positive meaning of sexual relations in regard to the love-relationship is different in this 'cohabitation in marital state of mind' from the same in a real marriage."

From this one might conclude that the authors would find objective justification for sexual intercourse at times. But they state immediately that "complete sexual relations remain *per se* beyond the realm of their state of life." At one point they assert that the mentality to live as brother-sister cannot be demanded as an absolutely necessary sign of their Christian mentality. At another point they refer to the serious effort of the couple to arrive at sexual mastery, even though failures might occur. This type of verbal sleight of hand unfortunately pervades the piece.

It is easy to agree with Peters–Beemer–van der Poel that the "marital state of mind," the willingness to educate the children, and the desire for sacramental participation are assuredly important aspects of the situation. They must not be forgotten. But they are not the only aspects. There is always the danger that a one-sided emphasis of these aspects could lead both priest and couple to view the present impasse as a juridical mistake of the past only. However, the past sacramental and consummated but broken marriage is not simply a matter of the past; it is, if our doctrine on divorce and remarriage means anything, as unavoidably a part of the *present* situation as the mature affection and the "marital state of mind." Here and now at least one of these *concubinarii* is irrevocably given to another. To allow the "marital state of mind" to obscure this fact or mitigate its demands is to analyze the present situation in terms of only one of its existential aspects. The present situation is not only a state of mind; it is a state of persons.

However, it is one thing to insist on this reality; it is quite another to say that its corollaries must receive immediate and emphatic attention. Where separation (total, or at least partial) is judged possible, this moral demand will be pointed out. On the other hand, many priests are convinced that some of these couples are not psychologically, morally, and spiritually equipped at the moment to do anything but live as man and wife. Any other alternative seems so often to represent a genuine moral impossibility for the present. To be sure, the moral demands do not thereby cease to exist; they are real, present, and crucial. But no less real is the present incapacity to meet them, sometimes even to understand them. Acknowledgment of this incapacity does not solve the dilemma, but perhaps it does suggest that a balanced pastoral approach might sometimes take the form of gradualism, which would view the moral demands as the term of a growth process. The wisdom of experience teaches us that the conclusions of moral principles often function more as goals toward which we must struggle than norms to which we can immediately conform—a point we moralists can easily forget.

If the gradual attitude just described is a sound Christian response to the situation, would not the general effort be to lead the couple to gather their strength through deepening of faith, that is, to lead them to the point where they can do justice both to the real claims of their present relationship and to the undeniably real meaning of their former ones? This process could easily take a good deal of time, and there is nothing in Catholic theology justifying anything but Christlike kindness and charity during this period of struggle and growth. But it must be conceived as a growth toward an ultimate resolution. Anything else is playing the ostrich.

The possibility that these trapped and suffering individuals could approach the sacraments is a question which can be legitimately asked. It is perhaps all the more legitimate when one considers the painful conclusion to which their growth must be expected to bring them. However, it is not clear to me how anything but a negative answer to this question is possible. Be this as it may, before one can answer the question about the sacraments, he must be clear on the moral status of these relationships, that is, that such couples are not truly husband and wife. Otherwise compassion and confusion will have become pastoral companions.[43]

[43] Two recent articles discuss historical aspects of indissolubility: F. Von Gunten, O.P.,

The number of articles appearing in recent years on the practical aspects of the sacrament of penance underlines what nearly everyone seems to be thinking: the discipline of this sacrament could stand reforming.[44] Before any reform can hope to be appropriate, the theology of the sacrament must be better understood. Brian Kelly, C.S.Sp., states the theological problem involved in the confession of devotion as follows: how can there be further forgiveness in the confession of devotion—and sacramental forgiveness at that—of what has already been forgiven?[45] The traditional explanation of the three reasons given in favor of devotional confession (occasion for direction of conscience, forgiveness of sin, increase of grace) do not answer this problem with satisfaction. Even Rahner's rather dazzling insights on the sacrament do not light up this more circumscribed issue.

To understand the confession of devotion, Kelly suggests, one must understand the notion of forgiveness. Forgiveness is not simply a legal statement of nonimputation; rather it is an interior refashioning whereby the sinner is both ontologically and psychologically set apart from sin. It is a many-sided process of liberation capable of indefinite increase and perfection. One's psychological opposition to sin, his spiritual distaste for it, his deepening inner revulsion is a part of the totality of this process. If forgiveness is viewed in this way, we must eventually define it as the production in the soul of the state of withdrawal from sin. In this sense the confession of devotion produces genuine forgiveness. Frequent confessions of devotion should, therefore, have the effect of increasing our spiritual antipathy to sin.

R. E. Modras contends that a faulty understanding of the efficacy of the sacraments plus an indiscriminating reading of authoritative encouragement given to devotional confession have led to formalism in confessional practice.[46] For many of the faithful, confession of devotion is a ritual regulated by the calendar rather than by a change of heart. "Unless his act of sorrow, his reaffirmation of conversion, is more intense than the previous conversion which characterized his supernatural condition, there is no actual increase of grace." Upon this Thomistic premise, Fr. Modras does not discourage frequent devotional confession, but he asks: "How many people are capable

---

"La doctrine de Cajétan sur l'indissolubilité du mariage," *Angelicum* 43 (1966) 62–72; H. Crouzel, S.J., "Séparation ou remariage selon les Pères anciens," *Gregorianum* 47 (1966) 472–94.

[44] If anyone has doubts, cf. Sister Lawrence, S.N.D., "The Sacrament of Penance—An Investigation," *Clergy Review* 51 (1966) 112–22.

[45] B. Kelly, C.S.Sp., "The Confession of Devotion," *Irish Theological Quarterly* 33 (1966) 84–90.

[46] Ronald E. Modras, "Frequent Devotional Confession," *Homiletic and Pastoral Review* 66 (1966) 650–58.

of having a change of heart or intensifying such a change once a week? Or once a month?"

This interesting article suggests two cautions. First, without gainsaying the theory which demands a more intense act of charity for an increase in sanctifying grace, one must be cautious about the meaning of the word "intense." When Modras questions the ability of people to "intensify their change of heart" weekly or monthly, he seems to locate the notion of intensity at the level of reflex awareness, perhaps even at the level of sensible feelings. Yet we know that our profound personal orientation toward God involves a depth of our person beyond the grasp of our reflex consciousness. Hence the acts which intensify this orientation will also reach to this depth. Therefore we dare not measure their intensity by our reflexly conscious experience of such intensity, as if intensity consisted of a kind of psychological muscle-flexing. Similarly it would be a mistake to identify our capacity for more intense conversion with a capacity we experience at the level of reflex awareness. And does not one do precisely this when he questions our ability to intensify our conversion more than once or twice a month?

Secondly, even though it may be true to say that an increase of grace takes place only "when a person strives for that increase by a more intense act of penance or love," this should not necessarily lead us to conclude to less frequent confession. For might not such an ultimate striving actually depend on a series of frequent confessions which do not in themselves achieve such intensity? Human growth is not discontinuous. It is easy to believe that we need a series of dispositive actions to prepare us for the type of act which would only occur as the culmination of such a series. In other words, routine acts performed with "equal intensity" can also deepen the stability of love or virtue, and this deepened stability may often be the springboard to greater intensity. This seems to be the way of growth—routinely, unobservably, day by day. This is the way the grass grows and it is the way marriages grow. Is it wrong to think that it is also the way love of God grows?

One could agree with Modras, therefore, that frequency of devotional confession is a highly individual thing and that some, perhaps many, devotional confessions are made in a magico-mechanical way. However, I would not regard the notion of intensity either as the heart of the problem or as the basis for a reduction in frequency. Other more tangible factors seem to govern frequency.[47]

The Apostolic Constitution *Paenitemini*, which completely reorganized the external penitential discipline of the Church, was promulgated Feb. 18,

[47] For some helpful remarks on making confession more meaningful, cf. A. Weigert, "One Art of the Confessor," *Review for Religious* 25 (1966) 484–88.

1966 in *L'Osservatore romano*.[48] The document is a beautiful summary of the Church's convictions about the nature and necessity of penance in general in the Christian life. One of the dominant concerns of the document is that penance, to merit the name, must spring from an interior disposition. In order to emphasize this, *Paenitemini* puts great stress on the personal responsibility and initiative of the faithful. Indeed, it was concern for precisely this personal responsibility which, according to Wilhelm Bertrams, S.J., led to the use of the phrase "substantial fulfilment" to describe the gravity of the law.[49]

Bertrams wrote in *L'Osservatore romano*, two days after the promulgation of the Constitution, what appears to have been a commissioned commentary.[50] He says:

What does "substantial violation" mean? We believe that the expression was deliberately chosen, above all to give greater prominence to the personal responsibility of each of the faithful before God, so that he may fulfil his mortification in a spirit of true sincerity and earnestness without insisting too much on the traditional limits of the distinction between a grave and a nongrave quantity for the violation of a precept. Consequently, a single nonobservance in the matter cannot be regarded as grave, while a repeated, habitual violation of the precept will certainly be regarded as grave.

Hence it must be said that the more sincere and serious one's will to observe the penitence on the days and in the manner established by the Church, the less serious should one consider a partial transgression. The graver the motive which excuses from observance, the less grave is nonobservance. If this reason is truly proportionately grave, all guilt undoubtedly ceases.

Bertrams is saying that the Constitution manifests the conviction that a casuistry of grave and slight *quantity* too easily defrauds penance of its interior spirit. But to regard a single day's violation as serious involves one immediately in this type of calculation. To avoid this, the phrase "substantial fulfilment" has been used to shift the undoubted gravity from the single day to the generality of the precept. The result: only a "repeated and habitual violation" is substantial nonfulfilment. Bertrams does not further specify what that might mean.

This reading of "substantial fulfilment" is presented by M. Zalba, S.J., Msgr. James Madden, G. Rossino, and "A. de B." of *Nouvelle revue théologique*.[51] As to what a substantial violation would concretely be, the ex-

[48] *L'Osservatore romano*, Feb. 17, 1966. The Latin text is also available in *AAS* 58 (1966) 177–98. An English translation is given in *Jurist* 26 (1966) 246–58.

[49] "Eorum substantialis observantia graviter tenet," *AAS* 58 (1966) 183.

[50] *L'Osservatore romano*, Feb. 20, 1966.

[51] M. Zalba, S.J., "La ley de ayuno y abstinencia," *Razón y fe* 173 (1966) 397–402;

pressions are deliberately left vague. A transgression on "one or other day" is not serious for Zalba. Madden says that he has "no desire to discuss how many Fridays in the course of the year would amount to a substantial number," though one could say that he had kept the Fridays if his omissions were occasional. Rossino leaves it at "habitual violation" and says of further numerical precision that "non mi sembra opportuno."

E. Regatillo, S.J., is altogether against this understanding of "substantial fulfilment."[52] Acknowledging that the phrase was chosen deliberately, he insists, however, that its meaning is not that the entire penitential discipline obliges gravely only *en globo*. The gravity applies to each day. His reasons are three. First, the word "substantial" does not mean what Bertrams says it means. Regatillo claims that the preparatory commission *De disciplina cleri et populi christiani*, of which he was a member, discussed whether fast and abstinence should be *sub levi* on each day and settled nothing. It was, he suggests, to avoid any residual doubt on the point that the expression used was chosen. Secondly, Bertrams' "habitual violation" would lead to so many varying interpretations that it would make the law ineffective, especially "if assessment had to be left to the conscience of the faithful." Finally, it is more reasonable that each day be grave because the fasts and abstinences have been reduced in number.

G. Huguera, S.J., after presenting this difference of interpretation, states his awareness of the growing tendency to interpret ecclesiastical laws according to Bertrams' understanding and concedes that "the legislator could make and impose such a law in this way"—perhaps to reduce the number of grave sins for violations of merely human laws.[53] Has he actually done so? Huguera concedes that Bertrams may well have spoken a rather official message; but because of the great practical impact this interpretation would have on other ecclesiastical and civil laws, he would prefer to await an authoritative declaration or at least a unanimous gathering of authoritative opinions.[54]

James Madden, "Changes in the Church's Penitential Discipline," *Australasian Catholic Record* 43 (1966) 137–52; G. Rossino, "Breve commento alla costituzione 'Paenitemini,'" *Perfice munus* 61 (1966) 258–62; *Nouvelle revue théologique* 88 (1966) 305–9.

[52] E. Regatillo, S.J., "Nueva ley de la abstinencia y del ayuno," *Sal terrae* 54 (1966) 194–209.

[53] G. Huguera, S.J., "La nueva ley sobre la abstinencia y el ayuno," *Sal terrae* 54 (1966) 323–42.

[54] Off in a corner by himself is Capuchin Bonaventure da Gangi. Not only is a single day substantial, but he specifies that grave matter on such a day would be seventy grams, because this was the milder doctrine taught until now by the authors. As if aware that he is alone on stage and that there are protesting voices in the wings, da Gangi adds: "Some-

Is it not rather disquieting that several commentators have seen in the word "substantial" a mitigation granted by the lawgiver? The same uneasiness is generated by the comments of Huguera and Regatillo. It seems all too easy to see in their remarks a rather voluntaristic concept of positive law—as if the lawgiver decides by fiat whether the thing prescribed is to bind gravely or not.[55] On the contrary, the lawgiver prescribes the thing, and its gravity is determined by its importance to the Christian way of life. It is the task of the responsible Christian (above all, the specialist) accurately to assess this importance.

No one has doubted the importance of external and communal penance, and the Church states her awareness of this in *Paenitemini*. Furthermore it is easy to see how fast and abstinence can retain importance as particular forms of penance.[56] The question is: what is important? I believe that increasingly experts will answer in this case: it is important that one's habitual conduct reflect appreciation and acceptance of this form of penance. By using the word "substantial," then, is *Paenitemini* doing anything more than acknowledging what the informed and sensitive Christian conscience should conclude? Rather than stating a mitigation of law, is not the Constitution only gently reminding specialists to take a long second look at their norms for interpreting obligation in ecclesiastical law—with a renewed appreciation of the responsibility of the individual if law is truly to achieve its aims in the Christian community?

If this reading of the document and especially of "substantial" is correct, then it is clear that this matter is important far beyond the issue which occasioned it. For the spirit behind *Paenitemini* will have repercussions on the reading of all ecclesiastical law and, of course, on the eventual revision of the code. In the meantime the least we can do is avoid the type of casuistry which obscures the interiority of genuine penance.

BUSINESS PROBLEMS

Any discussion of the practical problems relating to justice should begin with and constantly return to the positive and open attitudes so charac-

---

one could cast ridicule on this number of grams. But until he presents a better way for determining grave matter without destroying or denying its very existence, or evading the question he derides, I do not think one can contest my opinion." Cf. *Palestra del clero* 45 (1966) 372–75.

[55] The point made here is discussed in Joseph Fuchs's "Auctoritas Dei in auctoritate civili," *Periodica* 52 (1963), 3–18, at p. 10.

[56] The Italian bishops have dispensed their people from abstinence except during Lent. In Taiwan full abstinence was restored. These dispositions show how the importance of particular forms of penance varies according to circumstances.

teristic of the pastoral Constitution *On the Church in the Modern World*. The document contains a rather fully elaborated social theory and doctrine of man. One of the positive attitudes referred to is the genuinely creative and Christian concept of justice embedded in the document. Edward Hamel, S.J., has presented a valuable synthetic study of this notion as it is elaborated throughout the Constitution.[57] According to Vatican II, rights and justice are rooted in man's vocation as a personal and social being and therefore are based on the eminent dignity of the human person.

Hamel's brief discussion of the relationship of justice and charity is excellent. Charity brings a perspective to justice totally beyond a sterile juridicism. In the Christian economy "acts of justice are mediations, expressions, and participations of charity itself"—of the charity poured into our hearts by the Holy Spirit. The most basic task of charity toward others is recognition of and respect for their rights. "For there can be no true union of charity except between persons who acknowledge each other as *distinct*." The article has many other helpful analyses, and it would make fine corollary reading to what assuredly must be a basic document in the training of the contemporary priest, the pastoral Constitution *Gaudium et spes*.

For the past few years businessmen and moral theologians have been attempting to project, discuss, and clarify the moral questions inseparably a part of modern business. A nucleus of well-trained and interested specialists has been promoting these discussions. Prominent on the list are Raymond C. Baumhart, S.J., William J. Byron, S.J., Richard Athey, O.P., Thomas F. McMahon, C.S.V., Brother Leo Ryan, C.S.V., Thomas Garrett, S.J., John W. Cousins, C.P., and Henry Wirtenberger, S.J., to mention but a few. The form this has taken is the conference-dialogue involving both moral and business experts.

A single example of this type of exchange is the 1966 Conference on Business Morality, which dealt with the labyrinth of pricing. The morality of pricing cannot begin to be securely assessed without in-depth knowledge of the mechanics of current pricing theory and practice. Administered prices, price leadership, differing industry price structures, government regulations and guidelines—all of these and a host of other complicating factors make the determination of the just price simply harrowing. The results of the Conference, which gave heavy emphasis to the drug and automotive industries, are now published under title of *Justice and Pricing*.[58] The issue raised by all the papers in one form or other is: can the traditional theory

[57] Edward Hamel, S.J., "Justitia in constitutione pastorali 'Gaudium et spes' Concilii Vaticani II," *Periodica* 55 (1966) 315–53.

[58] *Justice and Pricing*, ed. Thomas F. McMahon, C.S.V. (Chicago, 1966).

of just price be applied to the pricing problems of the modern American economy? The answer would be a rather resounding "no."

These conferences were originally conceived as an opportunity for the moral theologian to inform himself of the theories and facts pertinent to a moral judgment. Richard L. Porter, S.J., takes a slightly different point of view.[59] He proposes seminars and workshops for businessmen where outside consultants are brought in. But "the effectiveness of such meetings will depend on the extent to which the businessmen get involved, find and work out moral principles for themselves and preach the value of these principles to each other." Specialists such as economists and moral theologians are available to the businessmen as resource persons, but the ultimate and major responsibility rests with the businessman himself.

If it is the businessman himself who must elaborate, with the aid of resource persons, a morality to fit his dizzily changing world, it is necessary that an awareness of the reality and complexity of his problems become a part of seminary training. For this we need a very special kind of specialist, one well enough versed in both morality and business that he can speak in simple but exact language to the nonspecialist seminarian. There is a growing body of literature useful for this purpose. One example would be Garrett's *Business Ethics*.[60] Further helpful entries can be found in *Economic Ethics Bibliography*, published by the Economics Department of South Dakota State University.

Many of the more difficult problems in business deal with decision-making and therefore are management problems. In a recent volume of *The Annals* totally devoted to moral issues, Arthur Selwyn Miller of George Washington University has discussed the moral problems of top management.[61] He contends that answers to questions about the ethical posture of American business demand reference to and analysis of the corporate nature of business. The giant corporations set the tone of American business. Hence business morality will be corporate morality. But executives and managers of corporations have multiple publics to whom they are responsible: shareholders, employees, consumers, suppliers to the corporation, the public at large, and so on. They must always seek to balance the interests of their several publics. Only a few standards for behavior are provided by officially

[59] Richard L. Porter, S.J., "The Economics of Business Ethics," *Advertiser's Digest* 31 (1966) 1–5.

[60] Thomas M. Garrett, S.J., *Business Ethics* (New York: Appleton-Century-Crofts, 1966).

[61] Arthur S. Miller, "Business Morality: Some Unanswered (and Perhaps Unanswerable) Questions," *The Annals* 363 (1966) 95–101. The volume also has interesting articles on the ethical aspects of insurance, advertising, and union policy.

imposed government rules (e.g., antitrust laws) and by the power position of the unions. Furthermore self-disciplining codes of behavior do not work, because "they would have no effective technique for enforcement and are written in such nebulous language as to leave large areas for interpretation." Miller concludes that until the modern corporation has been absorbed into political and economic theory by systematic analysis, one cannot hope to answer the basic moral questions of upper management.

The problems of middle management are perhaps even more anguishing. Middle managers are those executives who translate general policy and broader planning into workable procedures. In a very helpful study[62] Thomas F. McMahon, C.S.V., has pinpointed these moral problems as problems of pressure: from superiors for compliance, from family for time and affection, from peers in competition for advancement. For example, with regard to the first type of pressure, Fr. McMahon notes that top management can easily exert pressure through the common situations which require that the subordinate (1) produce "or else," (2) act unethically, (3) act ethically but without adequate provision to do so.

When middle managers are faced with a compliance contrary to their own moral convictions, they have three choices: (1) leave the company or resign their positions; (2) conform to their superior's wishes; (3) refuse to cooperate and thereby expose themselves to dismissal, demotion, or horizontal change where pressures are not so keen. McMahon states that most lower-echelon managers solve this type of problem by invoking "company policy." As for resignation, he suggests that "if resignation opens the position to unscrupulous individuals, I wonder if such an action is truly an example of Christian fortitude." McMahon wonders whether such a situation is not often analogous to that of the nurse assisting at immoral operations.

These are but two examples—and good ones—of articles which bring home to the theologian the forbidding complexity of the moral aspects of modern business. What is expected of the theologian in this area? At one point McMahon states that "it is my hope that moral theologians will suggest solutions to the problems of middle managers mentioned above." Perhaps it is only the wording one might regret here. It seems to suggest that the moral theologian should come up with practical moral solutions to these problems. Much more realistic are McMahon's subsequent remarks:

The work of theologians is to enlighten these consciences of businessmen about the moral aspects of their decision-making. Pertinent questions, elaboration of moral principles and the demands of the Christian vocation, and suggestions for alterna-

---

[62] Thomas F. McMahon, C.S.V., "Moral Problems of Middle Management," *Proceedings of the Catholic Theological Society of America* 20 (1966) 23–49.

tive courses of moral activity seem to fill the needs of businessmen more than do categorical pronouncements on issues of dubious relevancy.[63]

CIVIL DISOBEDIENCE

Civil disobedience is increasingly becoming a matter of moral concern. This is a healthy development if for no other reason than that it indicates a salutary respect for law and legal processes. However, the term "civil disobedience" is much more frequently used than clarified. It is applied, for instance, to practices which under analysis are neither precisely disobedient nor always civil. Such ambiguity in the use of the term means that the moral discussion of civil disobedience is often at sixes and sevens. Because one form of protest seems justified and has been called civil disobedience, it is sometimes alleged that all things loosely called civil disobedience are morally acceptable. For this reason one is often dissatisfied with the discussion without being able to pinpoint the source of his dissatisfaction.[64]

Mark R. MacGuigan, Associate Professor of Law at the University of Toronto, had earlier pointed out that there has always been a tradition within Catholic theology allowing for certain forms of disobedience.[65] St. Thomas held that, although per se there is a duty to obey civil law because political authority is derived from God, there are "some cases in which authority is defective in title or exercise and therefore not derived from God, and in such cases there is no obligation of obedience."[66] MacGuigan had indicated that this summary represents only a general attitude toward disobedience and its justification within a particular moral philosophy. It does not consider the forms disobedience might take. This is not to say that Thomas and later Scholastic thinkers did not allow active resistance; clearly they did, as their teaching on tyrannicide attests. But active resistance seems to have been reserved for the usurper of power. Only passive resistance (noncompliance with an unjust command) could be used against the

---

[63] In the pastoral Constitution *Gaudium et spes* we read: "Let the layman not imagine that his pastors are always such experts that to every problem which arises, however complicated, they can readily give him a concrete solution, or even that such is their mission. Rather, enlightened by Christian wisdom and giving close attention to the teaching authority of the Church, let the layman take on his own distinctive role" (*The Documents of Vatican II*, p. 244). Cf. also *America* 115 (1966) 182–184; *Time* 87 (1966) 82.

[64] An example of the type of statement which is in many respects healthy but ultimately dissatisfying is that of Waldo Beach, "Civil Disobedience and the Churches," *Christianity and Crisis* 26 (1966) 126–27.

[65] Mark R. MacGuigan, "Civil Disobedience and Natural Law," *Catholic Lawyer* 11 (1965) 118–29.

[66] For a recent popularization, cf. Timothy McDermott, O.P., "Must We Always Obey the Laws?" *New Blackfriars* 56 (1965) 418–22.

legitimate ruler who ruled unjustly in a given instance. The Scholastic tradition was developed outside the democratic context and hence did not deal specifically with resistance as a method of suasion.

It is only when nonviolent resistance to law is used as a form of suasion or advocacy that we have what modern writers call "civil disobedience." In the very interesting brochure, *Civil Disobedience*, attorney Richard Wasserstrom points out that the truly interesting thing about civil disobedience is "that its primary function is always an educative one."[67] Or as Harrop A. Freeman puts it, civil disobedience is "intentional action for ulterior reasons or goals,"[68] a democratic technique. For this reason the defense of civil disobedience has often been identified with the urgency of the goal.

The technique of disobedience-as-suasion can be used in a wide variety of circumstances. The general problem then becomes: in what circumstances is it morally acceptable to use violation of law as a form of advocacy? At this point it is only fair to say that this formulation of the question is in itself something of a point of view. It implies that mere advocacy of a just cause is not in itself enough to justify disobedience. Be that as it may, one can only hope to answer the question as stated (or frame it more accurately) if he has first determined the moral status of the individual violation of law in question. There are four points which continually recur in the recent literature. They may help us to isolate the issues and to assess the moral status of individual acts vis-à-vis the law.

1) *The claim of conscience.* All authors admit the duty to follow one's conscience when it forbids an act prescribed by law. In his helpful article on moral pre-emption, Joseph J. Farraher, S.J., discusses the attitude of the state toward conscience claims.[69] Since society is pluralistic and since the state is incompetent to judge the tenets founding conscience claims, the state "should respect any reasonable claim of conscience."[70] Farraher sug-

[67] Richard Wasserstrom, in *Civil Disobedience* (Center for the Study of Democratic Institutions, 1966) p. 18.

[68] Harrop A. Freeman, *ibid.*, p. 7.

[69] Joseph J. Farraher, S.J., "Moral Preemption: The Natural Law and Conscience-Based Claims in Relation to Legitimate State Expectations," *Hastings Law Journal* 17 (1966) 439–51.

[70] *Ibid.*, p. 443. With regard to conscientious objection to war, cf. *The Documents of Vatican II*, p. 292. The Council's statement is practical and does not enter the more problematic aspects of the matter. Some recent literature on conscientious objection: Andrea Piola, "Obiezione al servizio militare e diritto italiano dopo il Concilio," *Justitia* 19 (1966) 12–43; A. Messineo, "L'obiezione di coscienza al servizio militare," *Civiltà cattolica* 1 (1966) 263–67; L. Babbini, "Il Concilio Vaticano II e l'obiezione di coscienza," *Palestra del clero* 45 (1966) 649–50; Alan Geyer, "The Just War and the Selective Objector," *Christian Century* 83 (1966) 199–201; E. N. Beiser, "God and the Draft," *Commonweal* 83 (1966) 631–33.

gests that there should be evidence beyond mere assertion if the claim is to be honored as reasonable. One example of this evidence would be membership in a well-organized religion which publicly teaches the doctrine at variance with existing laws. If there is no sufficient evidence, the state need not honor the conscience claim and the individual is faced with the prospect of violation of law. If the conscience claim is genuine, there is no question of the subjective moral integrity of such violation.

Several authors have insisted that when this situation arises, there is not exactly a legal *right* to civil disobedience. As Bayard Rustin, long-time worker in civil-rights movements, puts it: "When a democratic society has willed through democratic processes to establish law, it is the duty of that society to insist that its members adhere to the law."[71] It is precisely the civil disobedient's willingness to accept suffering cheerfully that constitutes the force of his advocacy and gets other people to think about the wrongs of society.

2) *Procedural violation of law.* This refers to an open violation of law committed to provoke a juridical interpretation. The lunchcounter sit-ins in the South might be a good example of this. Mr. Freeman's long defenses of civil disobedience really seem to defend this type of thing. He shows, for example, that civil disobedience is a recognized procedure for challenging law or policy and for obtaining a court determination of the validity thereof. Furthermore, even when the highest court holds a law constitutional, the right of "disobedience" does not cease, for this would freeze as permanent law the Dred Scott, Plessy, and other decisions which have been reversed.

Several authors reject this as a proper concept of "disobedience." Though such practices are violations of an existing law, they are not, strictly speaking, disobedience. Thus, William T. Sweigert writes:

If the disobedience is under claim that the violated law—for example, a national or state statute or a local ordinance—contravenes the "supreme law" of the land and is, therefore, an "unconstitutional" impingement on some civil right, then, of course, the violation is more apparent than real and the issue must be resolved through the judicial channels provided by the state.[72]

Similarly Darnell Rucker contends that "civil disobedience is not a matter of challenging the legality of a law or of ascertaining the meaning of the law. It is a matter of a man rejecting a moral demand of his society at the same

[71] Bayard Rustin, in *Civil Disobedience*, p. 10. See also William T. Sweigert, "Moral Preemption: Claims of 'Right' under the Positive Law," *Hastings Law Journal* 17 (1966) 453–71, at pp. 461–62.

[72] Sweigert, *art. cit.*, p. 463.

time that he admits the legal right of his society over him."[73] Paul Ramsey and Wasserstrom have made the same point.[74] Therefore, in terms of legality only (and of morality in so far as it is affected by legality), true disobedience must be distinguished from a violation made under a genuine legal claim.

3) *The nature of coercion.* Everyone would admit that real violence must be excluded except in the most extreme circumstances where a society's structure is anarchical anyway. Indeed *civil* disobedience, besides referring to a violation of civil law, connotes nonviolent disobedience. However, some nonviolent acts not only violate a law but in doing so are or can be coercive. Such coercion must be taken into account if one is to judge the moral status of the violation adequately. But not all are agreed on the nature of coercion.

Joseph J. Farraher judged the lunchcounter sit-ins in the South morally justified "provided that the sitters were ready to accept service and pay for it if rendered, *and that they were otherwise orderly and clean according to accepted custom . . . .*"[75] Fr. Farraher attends explicitly only to lack of on-the-spot violence. While few would disagree with his ultimate judgment, it is not clear whether he regards the sit-in as otherwise coercive and to what extent this coercion must be weighed in a moral judgment.

Paul Ramsey believes that it is impossible to distinguish in one's conduct between discrimination and those who discriminate.[76] Therefore, when one lets loose the coercive force of sit-ins and boycotts, however legally justifiable they may be, he also necessarily opposes with nonviolent force the evildoers themselves. Therefore Ramsey insists that for the Christian such forms of protest also and especially involve the ethics of the use of force. After showing that resistance in the form of violent warfare was an application of the basic principle of "neighbor-regarding love," Ramsey suggests that in so far as sit-ins, boycotts, etc. are coercive, they must also be subjected to "the ancient principles and limitations justifying a Christian in taking up any use of force." For Ramsey, therefore, the moral status of these actions is not judged only in terms of legality and absence of on-the-spot violence.

Prof. Harry Prosch of Skidmore College has taken a completely different view of the force involved in violation of discriminatory laws or trespass laws which can be used to buttress discrimination.[77] He sees the very viola-

---

[73] Darnell Rucker, "The Moral Grounds of Civil Disobedience," *Ethics* 76 (1966) 142–45, at p. 143.

[74] Paul Ramsey, *Christian Ethics and the Sit-In* (New York: Association Press, 1961) p. 41; Wasserstrom, *op. cit.*, p. 18.

[75] Farraher, *art. cit.*, p. 449.   [76] Ramsey, *op. cit.*, p. 104.

[77] Harry Prosch, "Limits to the Moral Claim in Civil Disobedience," *Ethics* 75 (1965) 103–11. A point of view ("body rhetoric") not dissimilar from Prosch's is found in John

tion as a use of force, and he sees force as a weapon leading to absurdity. He explains himself as follows. These actions are claims expressed in action, and the action is one which forces a response. "You are not coercing them by violence. You are merely putting to them a question .... They must either act or not act in the face of your challenge ...." Prosch sees this as a use of force, albeit nonviolent. "Even though your action is non-violent, its first consequence must be to place you and your opponents in a state of war. For your opponents have only the same sort of choice that an army has: that of allowing you to continue occupying the heights you have moved onto, or of applying force—dynamic, active, violent force—to throw you back off them." Because the resister has forced his opponent out of the possibility of contending in the nonviolent arenas of moral persuasion and political maneuvering, his tactic is military rather than political. The only force the resister has used, it is true, is the inertia of his own body, but it creates a situation of force, because the opponent must either allow him to protest by disobedience or forcefully carry him away.

Darnell Rucker, in a carefully reasoned response, contends that Prosch has confused *civil* disobedience with defiance of authority.[78] The man who attempts to escape both command and punishment is the anarchist. The civil disobedient peaceably accepts the punishment for his act—a point Prosch has overlooked. And by this oversight he has eliminated what has long stood as the last bastion of the individual against his society short of rebellion.

These considerations on the nature of coercion show how complex is the judgment of this aspect of a transgression of law.

4) *Violation of a just law or ordinance to further a cause.* In discussing civil disobedience, most authors simply suppose that the violation in question is of an unjust law. But because the term "civil disobedience" does not of itself make this clear, some proponents of civil disobedience defend violation of a perfectly just law to promote a just cause or to protest an unjust situation. This is very close to the Ghandian Satyagraha.[79] The publicized suffering of the resister (in our time, jail sentence) is the heart of this form of protest. A good example would be street lie-ins bringing arrest for traffic obstruction.

This form of disobedience has not often been the object of careful study. Two statements are currently available. Sweigert sees this as a form of

---

H. Stassen's "The Rhetoric of Student Revolt," *Intercollegiate Review* 2 (1965) 200–207.

[78] Rucker, *art. cit.*, pp. 142–45.

[79] For an extremely interesting account of this, cf. Raghavan N. Lyer, in *Civil Disobedience*, pp. 19–25.

violence directed at the state and others in the state. "To say that unlawful interference with the person or property of others, or with the public property, need, or convenience, is a civil 'right' so long as others affected ...are not physically injured or their property physically damaged, nor any great commotion created, is, to say the least, an attenuation of the word violence."[80] Such actions, therefore, must be tested by the same principles as are applicable to rebellion. Only a careful distinction between the liberally interpreted civil rights of advocacy and demonstration on the one hand, and civil disobedience on the other, will ultimately protect these civil rights.

Farraher comes to much the same conclusion.[81] He sees this type of activity as a form of pressure put on the general public to correct an abuse in another area and says that it is never justified. The means of pressuring the public to correct certain evils must not include "interference with their rights nor cause them a loss of business or even cause them mental and emotional suffering."

This impoverishing summary of mine reveals at least how misleading it can be to discuss civil disobedience in general without isolating the issues involved in concrete violations of law. This failure to be particular will mean that the moral question will be reduced to the broader issues of contempt for law and defiance of authority on the one hand, or to the overriding natural justice of, e.g., the Negro cause on the other.[82] Certainly these broader concerns will be operative in any adequate moral analysis, but of themselves it is not clear that they decide every issue. There is still a distinction between a worthy cause and the means used to promote it. The means attractive to our instinctive sense of justice must submit to rational reflection if they are to continue to be in the service of noble goals. To defend *any* act of civil disobedience as long as it is done under *some* claim of advocacy is, in my judgment, to defend anarchy. At any rate, discussion of civil disobedience should be viewed as an attempt to insure the success of justice by restricting its promotion to responsible means.

OF LIFE AND DEATH

In his introduction to Paul Ramsey's occasional paper entitled *Again, The Justice of Deterrence*, James Finn, director of publications for The Council on Religion and International Affairs, wrote: "No moral philosopher on this side of the Atlantic has given as consistent, long term, and disciplined attention to the ethical shaping of nuclear policy as Paul Ramsey."[83] Anyone

---

[80] Sweigert, *art. cit.*, p. 464.   [81] Farraher, *art. cit.*, pp. 445–49.

[82] Cf., for example, *Homiletic and Pastoral Review* 65 (1965) 655–61.

[83] Paul Ramsey, *Again, The Justice of Deterrence* (Occasional paper for the Council on Religion and International Affairs; New York, 1965).

familiar with the literature on nuclear policy would admit this. For this reason this section will carry the name of this genial gentleman more frequently than his modesty would permit.

For the Catholic theologian, certainly the most notable recent utterance on war has been that of Vatican II in the pastoral Constitution *Gaudium et spes*. Ramsey's sympathetic and thoughtful essay on the Council's statement finds in the document three successive climactic declarations around which the whole can be organized.[84]

The first of these is the condemnation of any acts of war "aimed indiscriminately at the destruction of entire cities or of extensive areas along with their population." Ramsey does not hide his delight that the principle of discrimination so decisively controls the Council's statement. And no wonder. He has been urging this point of view for years.[85]

The second key idea is the treatment given to the fact and morality of deterrence. Deterrence, it is true, maintains only a "peace of a sort" (*pax quaedam*), and this "peace of a sort" is a good which must be bent toward the better yet to come. Nevertheless deterrence does not fall below the floor of the morally permissible. Ramsey tweaks some of his colleagues "who are liberally on their way to forgetting" Reinhold Niebuhr's statement: "to serve peace, we must threaten war without blinking the fact that the threat may be a factor in precipitating war."[86]

The third great pillar of the conciliar statement on war is the duty of all in the work of political reconstruction needed to change the conditions making war possible. Ramsey sees as the central question behind which the Council wished to put the full weight of its spiritual authority the following: "Can anyone, citizen or political leader, who believes not and labors not for the radical political reconstruction of the nation-state system, can he also be saved?" This is strong language, but anyone familiar with modern weaponry and the Council's statement would have to agree that it is not too strong. One can only think Christianly about war in our time if one's thoughts are an extension of one's passion and search for peace, a point made also by Henri de Riedmatten in his study of the conciliar statement.[87] Or as Lawrence Cardinal Shehan put it in his brief but excellent pastoral latter: "Even

[84] Paul Ramsey, "The Vatican Council on Modern War," Theological Studies 27 (1966) 179–203.

[85] For theological opinion as it touches this principle, cf. Richard S. Hartigan, "Noncombatant Immunity: Its Scope and Development," *Continuum* 3 (1965) 300–314.

[86] Reinhold Niebuhr, "From Progress to Perplexity," in *The Search for America*, ed. Huston Smith (Englewood Cliffs, 1959) p. 144.

[87] H. de Riedmatten, "L'Enseignement du concile sur la guerre et la paix," *Études*, Feb., 1966, pp. 247–56, at p. 247, where he insists that the document's section on peace has "une valeur normative stricte."

though our hands are embattled, then, our hearts must remain steadfastly peace-loving. Otherwise, at the peril of an escalation which could end in annihilation, we may fail to be responsive to the possibilities of reasonable and honorable negotiations."[88]

Joseph L. Allen examines the relevance of the just-war doctrine for modern war.[89] At the heart of the doctrine as applied to modern war Allen sees the teaching on noncombatant immunity. He then imagines a case where only direct city-bombing or its threat would deter. His conclusion: because keeping the rule (prohibiting indiscriminate acts of war) "would produce disastrous results . . . it is at least morally ambiguous to view non-combatant immunity as an absolute rule." He opts for a more "flexible" consequentialist ethics. In his summary Allen states that "some people will choose to be irrelevant rather than to imagine they might ever threaten or attack cities." Many of us would prefer to word this differently as follows: "Some people will see in their refusal to threaten or attack cities a depth of relevance all the more crucial because so often unperceived by the contemporary strategist." Relevance, after all, extends beyond the rather algebraic scenarios of the tactician. If I cannot defend myself except by immoral acts, the only conclusion is that I cannot defend myself.

The Bennett–Ramsey exchange in *America*[90] is interesting because two articulate and highly regarded theologians present positions which, it is safe to say, gather up two of the major currents[91] of Christian reaction to war and especially to war in Vietnam. Union Theological's John C. Bennett contends that our military actions in Vietnam are morally intolerable and politically self-defeating. The moral intolerability he locates in the acts of inhumanity we perpetrate (bombing of villages in South Vietnam, poisoning of crops, and—through our South Vietnamese allies—the torturing of prisoners). This type of thing he describes as "intolerably evil in itself." As if this were not enough, what we are doing is leading us into a political blind alley. Bennett urges that we turn our attention to the presuppositions underlying our policies in Vietnam. These are two: first, an anti-Communist obsession; secondly, our insistence that the struggle there is a test case of wars

[88] Lawrence Cardinal Shehan, "The Christian's Duties toward Peace," in *Catholic Messenger*, July 14, 1966, p. 5.

[89] Joseph L. Allen, "The Relevance of Christian Just War Doctrine for Modern War," in *Aspects of International Order* (New York: Hudson Institute, 1965) pp. 119–40.

[90] John C. Bennett and Paul Ramsey, in *America* 114 (1966) 616–22.

[91] For another current cf. Gordon Zahn, "Catholic Conscientious Objectors: A Portrait," *Continuum* 3 (1965) 329–37; Gulbert G. Rutenber, "Pacifism Revisted," *Andover Newton Quarterly* 6 (1966) 38–52.

of liberation. If we withdraw here, we can expect only proliferation on other fronts. Both of these suppositions he rejects.[92]

Ramsey's rebuttal of the alleged "moral intolerability" centers around the principle of discrimination in acts of war. He believes Bennett is in error both in principle and in fact. He errs in principle because "one should not first define some political or military action as 'intolerably evil in itself' or as 'morally intolerable' and then make ready to perform it under some circumstances." If something is intolerably evil in itself, nothing can justify it. He is factually in error because he has not shown that the central war (as distinguished from peripheral acts) is "evil in itself." Ramsey attributes this to a failure to grasp the nature of guerilla warfare. The insurgent strikes the civil population to subvert it. He strikes as few military targets as possible. This, of course, is totally immoral on any reading. But by fighting between, behind, and over the civilian population, it is *he* who has enlarged the extent of foreknowable but collateral damage done by the counterguerilla. "The onus of the wickedness of placing multitudes of peasants within range cannot be shifted to counterinsurgency," any more than we can blame the Russians for the enormous collateral damage which would result from *our* locating missile pads in the heart of downtown Chicago. Ramsey concludes that "the main design of the counterinsurgency mounted in Vietnam need not be and likely is *not* an inherently evil or morally intolerable use of armed force." As for the self-defeating character of our policy, he offers some rejoinders and qualifications.[93]

The pastoral Constitution *On the Church in the Modern World (Gaudium et spes)* is remarkable for what it chose not to say on the morality of deterrence. It simply noted that the accumulation of arms does serve as a deterrent and then added: "Many regard this state of affairs as the most effective way by which peace of a sort can be maintained between nations at the present time."[94] The morality of nuclear deterrence is still hotly debated.

In *Peace, the Churches and the Bomb* Dr. Walter Stein of the University of Leeds (England) had attacked Ramsey's defense of a deterrent based on fear of collateral damage.[95] Stein referred to this defense as a "radical abuse of

[92] Bennett has also presented these points and others in detail elsewhere: cf. *Christianity and Crisis* 26 (1966) 13–14, 33–34, 69–70, 165–66; also *Christian Century* 83 (1966) 104–13.

[93] For Ramsey's views on policy, cf. *Christian Century* 83 (1966) 909–13.

[94] This need not refer to the type of retaliation envisaged in Herman Kahn's "tit-for-tat" countercity deterrence. Cf. James C. Fleck, S.J., in *Christian Century* 83 (1966) 680–83.

[95] *Peace, the Churches and the Bomb*, ed. James Finn (New York: Council on Religion and International Affairs, 1965).

double-effect categories." Stein seems to mean that the collateral damage, once it is envisaged as a deterrent, would be directly willed and that this amounts to direct intent of evil that good may come of it. In the extremely interesting occasional paper referred to at the beginning of this section, Ramsey turns to the morality of deterrence in general,[96] and particularly to this objection. He agrees that "collateral deterrence" (deterrence through fear of collateral damage) does involve one in directly willing the deterrent effect, but that this is not necessarily to want or intend the damage itself.

To clarify his point Ramsey uses two analogies. The first is Dr. John Rock's experiments during the course of hysterectomies.[97] Over the years Rock had performed 211 hysterectomies. The operations were scheduled at a time when it was thought that the women would be ovulating. As a result Rock secured 34 ova, ranging from a two-day, two-cell egg to a 17-day ovum. Obviously a certain number of fertilized ova were going to be destroyed in this process. Since these deaths were the indirect effects of a properly targeted surgical action and unavoidable (a factual matter on which Ramsey passes no judgment), he asserts that the doctors could quite licitly "want all the goods in pure knowledge and for medical practice that were the immediate fruits of controlled attention to the indirect killing often involved in hysterectomies." One can bring the indirect, unavoidable deaths scientifically into prospect without directly willing them.

If, of course, Rock and associates had deliberately encouraged those patients requiring hysterectomies to get themselves pregnant shortly before the operation, or if the women had wanted to co-operate by securing in themselves an impregnated ovum, then there would have been complicity in bringing human life under the knife. In this instance death itself would have been radically wanted. It is Ramsey's contention that Stein conceives collateral deterrence in this second way, but he argues that it need not be so conceived.

Ramsey's second analogy, and the one he regards as the closest, is the case of a woman with a scarred uterus which will not carry another pregnancy to term. However, it is supposed that this medical determination is not made at the time of her last cesarean section, but afterward. The required hysterectomy is scheduled, but the woman subsequently discovers that she is pregnant. If the operation is performed, the death of the nonviable fetus would be indirect. However, because of the threat to her child, the woman resolves to attempt to bring it to viability. She is "deterred" by

[96] He also discusses deterrence by the ambiguity of the weapons themselves and by ambiguity about our intentions in their use.

[97] John Rock, M.D., *The Time Has Come* (New York: Knopf, 1963) pp. 184–85.

the "menace" to her child. And she can be deterred without wanting the death of the child. It is precisely the latter that she wants to avoid. She does not want the child menaced, but since the child is irremediably subjected to indirect menace, "she can without any malice at all *want the menace* to help her sustain the courage she will need in the months ahead." Just so with the menace to populations involved in the prospect of unavoidable collateral deaths.

I believe that Ramsey is unquestionably right in his basic contention that unavoidable collateral deaths need not be directly willed when I accept and desire the deterrent effect their prospect creates. But several points in this intriguing study merit comment.

First, Ramsey has at times worded the matter badly. He is a subtle and exact thinker. But as he hones his thought to precision, he builds hyphenated words, multiple parentheses, neologisms, and qualifications into a mounting tension where release, but not always clarity, is achieved with the period. What I think Ramsey means to say is this: it is morally legitimate to want the enemy to be moved (deterred) by the thought of the damage that may unavoidably and indirectly be visited on him as I perform a perfectly just act of war. To say this, Ramsey chooses the word "menace" and says, for example, that we may "want the menace that is there for its assured pressure." The word "menace" is ambiguous,[98] and hence the phrase "wanting the menace" will share this ambiguity and confuse rather than clarify the distinction Ramsey is trying to make. It too easily suggests directly intended damage as a threat. This is important, for I think that it is probably here that he has misled Stein and could easily mislead others.

Secondly, analogies are doomed to remain analogies. The difficulty with Ramsey's second analogy (the woman deterring herself during pregnancy from a hysterectomy) is what it suggests about the meaning and workings of deterrence. Indirect but unavoidable civilian damage associated with my legitimate acts of war can deter the enemy, or deter me from unloosing such a strike. The question is: when we speak of collateral deterrence, are we speaking of deterring ourselves or deterring the enemy? The latter, I should think. We deter him and, if he is capable of such a strike, he deters us. We do not exactly deter ourselves by the damage we might cause him. This

[98] Taken *actively* it can mean that I threaten you with damage and death. The active sense here (I will do something to you) carries the connotation of direct intent. Or it can mean that I want you to be moved by what I may have unavoidably and indirectly to do in the course of a perfectly just act of war. Taken *passively* it can refer to the damage and deaths themselves, either direct or indirect. Or it can refer to the fear and caution that will be present as a result of indirect, unavoidable death.

would be very noble (and is even an essential moral factor in weighing the decision to strike), but is it the way deterrence actually works? If it is not, then Ramsey's analogy has not illumined the problem of collateral damage.

Thirdly, in developing the first analogy (the Rock series of hysterectomies) Ramsey viewed the death of fertilized ova as indirect, hence as morally legitimate if unavoidable. Granted. But *unavoidable* is the issue. Ramsey wrote: "There is no universal affirmative obligation that women requiring hysterectomies should cease from the performance of the marriage act lest they become pregnant." Is there not a clear duty to do all that is reasonably possible to prevent the death of the fertilized ovum? This would indeed mean abstention from marital relations when morally possible if the probable effect of such intercourse would be the conception of human life. The point is important; for otherwise Ramsey is equivalently saying that there is no duty to try to avoid collateral civilian damage by warning the civilian population to evacuate areas around legitimate target sites. I believe there is such a duty whenever this is compatible with achievement of the military objective. This reflection points to the fact that use of collateral damage as a deterrent, while it is perfectly justifiable on paper, is or can be a very dangerous way of thinking in practice.

This is but a sampling of the enormous literature on war and peace. It will have to suffice for the present.

From killing the enemy to killing babies may appear to be an illegitimate jump. Indeed there are many who apparently see no connection between the two. This raises the suspicion that our indignation at the killings-in-combat may be far less *moral* indignation than we believe. Too often the very ones who protest most strongly against all killing in war are the very ones who not only silently tolerate abortions, but plead a liberalization of laws which, on all available evidence, would increase their number. This inconsistency is a curious restriction of humane and liberal thinking.

Francis Canavan, S.J., sees in the rush toward more liberalized abortion laws the workings of a kind of historical inevitability.[99] Infanticide is the next step to be taken. This inevitability is not the outgrowth of the logic of legal processes, for law does not work logically. Rather "it is because all the forces pushing us to this step are already in existence and there seems to be no force that can effectively resist them." The forces listed by Fr. Canavan are: secularism, liberalism, skepticism, distrust of absolute principles, abhorrence of suffering, the mass media, slogans and arguments; and most importantly, the motives for infanticide are already operative in the minds and

[99] Francis Canavan, S.J., "History Repeats Itself," *America* 114 (1966) 738–42.

hearts of many people. He sees all of this as symptomatic of a major shift in the value structure of our society.

Only one cloistered from the literature of the past several years will disagree with Fr. Canavan that it is a veritable campaign-for-abortion that is being waged. Of the countless articles that have come to my attention in the past months, that which appeared in the *Chicago Tribune*[100] followed exactly the structure outlined by Fr. Canavan.

In his straightforward article Herbert Ratner, M.D., sees this campaign at work even in the literature of Planned Parenthood.[101] In its pre-1964 editions of a pamphlet on birth control (*Plan Your Children*) the editors had asked: "Is it [birth control] an abortion? Definitely not. An abortion requires an operation. It kills the life of a baby after it has begun. It is dangerous to your life and health. It may make you sterile so that when you want a child you cannot have it. Birth control merely postpones the beginning of life."[102] These statements are omitted in the 1964 revision, and Ratner sees in the omission a "drastic shift in position."

There has been no lack of suggestions as to what should be done in face of this campaign.[103] Certainly one would hope that an increasing number of serious thinkers would become properly informed on all aspects of abortion. Toward this end it would be helpful to read Russell Shaw's fine booklet *Abortion and Public Policy* and Paul V. Harrington's series of articles.[104] Shaw makes a point (easily overlooked in this discussion) that the state has the duty to protect innocent human life. Existing laws at least represent an attempt in the direction of due process. In this connection one can wonder why those who oppose liberalization of abortion laws are accused of attempting to impose their "religious beliefs" on others. The fact, for example, that Vatican II has made a strong statement on abortion does not constitute one's position a religious belief.[105]

[100] Shirley Motter Linde, "Abortion: The Facts, the Controversy, the National Dilemma," *Chicago Tribune*, Feb. 13, 1966, pp. 16–20 and ff.

[101] Herbert Ratner, M.D., "A Doctor Talks about Abortion," *Report* 3 (1966) 20–22; *Catholic Mind* 64 (1966) 45–50.

[102] As cited in Ratner, *art. cit.*

[103] For example, *Commonweal* 83 (1966) 685; *National Review* 18 (1966) 308.

[104] Russell B. Shaw, *Abortion and Public Policy* (Washington: Family Life Bureau, 1966); Paul V. Harrington, "Abortion," *Linacre Quarterly* 32 (1965) 339–45; 33 (1966) 81–92, 153–169. With regard to psychiatry and abortion, cf. *Medico-Moral Newsletter* 2 (1966); *New Blackfriars* 47 (1966) 374–79; *Homiletic and Pastoral Review* 66 (1966) 643–49.

[105] "Furthermore, whatever is opposed to life itself, such as any type of murder, genocide, abortion, euthanasia or willful selfdestruction . . . all these things and others of their like are infamies indeed" (*The Documents of Vatican II*, p. 226).

Whether IUD contraception is certainly abortifacient is apparently still not known with certainty. The matter was unclear at the 1962 Conference on Intra-Uterine Contraceptive Devices—a conference which gathered many of the doctors (e.g., Margulies, Lippes, etc.) actively involved in studies on the devices.[106] Rudolph H. Ehrensing, M.D., has a long two-part article on the IUD, especially its method of operation.[107] He states that there are three possible modes of action: (1) local disruption of the already implanted ovum, (2) prevention of implantation, and (3) decrease of opportunities for the meeting of ovum and sperm, probably by stimulating the peristaltic action of the Fallopian tubes. His conclusion is that "the best evidence to date indicates the IUD acts as a safe and effective contraceptive, with a mode of action that could be recognized by the Church as moral."

However, even if the IUD operates by preventing implantation of the young embryo, Ehrensing contends that it is not killing human beings. His basis for this assertion: in human procreation and development, the individual mimics or re-enacts the development of the species. Thus "the developing embryo reaches the border of the spiritual in perhaps a few weeks or months, accomplishing what originally took millions of years."

Julian Pleasants, of Notre Dame's College of Science, takes strong exception to this analysis.[108] The idea presented by Ehrensing was popularized by Haeckel but it has been discredited by evolutionary biology, comparative embryology, and modern genetics. "The newly fertilized ovum has as much genetic information as the adult it will eventually be." All it needs from that time on is adequate nutrition and beneficent climate for it to reach its potential. Pleasants is saying that, as far as science is concerned, there is simply no reason for denying the humanity of the newly fertilized ovum.

While Pleasants agrees that the fertilized ovum is a human being, he argues that aborting such a fetus directly is not necessarily direct killing. "The act of abortion leads to the death of the fetus only when modern medicine does not know how to maintain such a fetus outside the womb." Because medicine may *in the future* be able to support the lives of fetuses outside the womb, Pleasants concludes that abortion is not *now* direct killing. It is passing strange that a student of the life sciences would understand the

---

[106] *Intra-Uterine Contraceptive Devices*, ed. Christopher Tietze and Sarah Lewit (New York: Excerpta Medica Foundation, 1962). This remains the situation, according to Robert E. Hall, M.D. In "Intrauterine Contraceptives: Questions and Answers," *Current Medical Digest* 33 (1966) 495–97, he says: "How does the IUCD work? This is still unknown."

[107] Rudolph H. Ehrensing, M.D., *National Catholic Reporter*, April 20, 1966, p. 6, and April 27, 1966, p. 6.

[108] Julian R. Pleasants, *ibid.*, May 11, 1966, p. 4.

term "direct killing" in such an unrealistic and basically static way. We may eventually be able to repair the heart pierced by a bullet, but until such happy days I am afraid that we shall have to continue to talk of direct killing when bullets pierce hearts and are intended to do so.

CONTRACEPTION

What is the status of the traditional teaching on contraception? This is, because of its enormous practical consequences and its unavoidably controversial character, an extremely delicate question. Furthermore one approaches the question with the foreknowledge that his remarks may be obsolete by the time they appear. At this moment in history the compositor of these Notes might well plead that since a papal statement seems imminent, it were better to allow the literature to go unreported. In the post-Sullivan era[109] he might also plead his celibacy. However, since understanding of the issues has been, still is, and will remain at the heart of the problem, neither of the above pleas will find support in sound theological methodology. It appears to me that an accurate answer to the question raised at the beginning of this paragraph must take into account three factors: (1) recent professional literature on contraception, (2) the conciliar statement, and (3) Pope Paul's statement of 1964.

The literature on contraception shows no tendency to abate. Quite the contrary. During the past semester it has been huge.

What are the issues involved in the contraceptive discussion? It has become increasingly obvious that they reach far beyond the moral liceity of contraceptive acts. They touch, for example, the nature of the Church and the teaching magisterium, the knowledge of natural law in general, the theological import of *consensus fidelium,* and the meaning of doctrinal development. Elsewhere I have tried—certainly not without revealing the limitations of a point of view—to develop these larger issues.[110]

In a remarkably short space Denis O'Callaghan has managed to summarize very accurately the theological differences of opinion in the Church.[111] He sees these differences as centering around principle, tradition, and authority. Indeed a reading of current literature would simply provide footnotes to his valuable summary. A brief sample will illustrate this.

Bishop Josef Maria Reuss continues to argue against Demmers, Kraus,

[109] Dan Sullivan, "Beast in the Belly vs. Union with the Beloved," *National Catholic Reporter,* June 29, 1966, p. 6.

[110] Richard A. McCormick, S.J., "Practical and Theoretical Considerations," in *The Problem of Population* (Notre Dame: University of Notre Dame Press, 1965) pp. 50–73.

[111] Denis O'Callaghan, "Dilemma in Birth Control," *Irish Ecclesiastical Record* 105 (1966) 232–45.

and Günthör that it has not been shown that every act of sexual union must be somehow ordained to procreation.[112] Hence he insists that the procreative orientation of coitus does not play a decisive role in the solution of the problem of contraception. L. Beirnaert also challenges the ordination of each individual coital act to procreation.[113] When one considers both the natural infecundity of the vast majority of sexual acts and the specifically human character of procreation ("the child is the fruit of dialogue"), Beirnaert contends that it becomes clear that the procreative aspect of coitus is not tied to individual acts.

Contrarily E. Garrigou sees marital intercourse as of itself apt for procreation and apt to express the mutual gift and love of the couple.[114] These two inbuilt purposes are inseparably united, so that "all contraception constitutes a desacralization of love. Voluntarily to separate the natural expression of love from its openness to life is to reduce the mutual self-gift to a simple possession."

Bernard Häring, C.SS.R., continues to focus his attention on the more general issue of responsible parenthood.[115] He very correctly distinguishes responsible parenthood from the cold reckoning of mere economic planning. John C. Ford, S.J., repeats his conviction that "the Church will not and cannot accept a radical revision—that is, a substantial change—in her basic traditional teaching."[116]

John T. Noonan contends that in so far as authority is concerned (scriptural, patristic, conciliar, papal), the condemnation of usury is more impressive than that of contraception.[117] He does not deny the authoritative character of the teaching on contraception, but wonders—in the light of our past experience with usury—how it might best be approached. He suggests that

---

[112] Josef Maria Reuss, "Zeugungsziel und eheliche Vereinigung," *Der Seelsorger* 36 (1966) 249–59. Reference to Demmers, Kraus, and Günthör can be found in Reuss's article.

[113] Louis Beirnaert, "Régulation des naissances et sexualité humaine," *Etudes*, Jan., 1966, pp. 21–31.

[114] E. Garrigou, "Immoralité de la contraception," *Ami du clergé* 76 (1966) 207–8. The same point is put in the form of a question by Vienna's Karl Hörmann; cf. "Moraltheologische Sonderbehandlung der Sterilisation?" *Theologisch-praktische Quartalschrift* 114 (1966) 31–35. Cf. also William F. Drummond, S.J., "Contraception Frustrates Nature," *Catholic World* 203 (1966) 202–6.

[115] Bernard Häring, C.SS.R., "Responsible Parenthood," in *The Vatican Council and the World Today* (Providence: Brown University, 1966), pages not numbered.

[116] John C. Ford, S.J., *ibid.*

[117] John T. Noonan, Jr., "Authority, Usury and Contraception," *Cross Currents* 16 (1966) 55–79. See also "Contraception," *Catholic World* 203 (1966) 153–56, where Noonan repeats in popular form some of the same ideas.

we must treat the absolute prohibition of contraception as a working rule but not as unchanging moral law. Specific moral rules enacted by the Church should be taken as sure guides for the periods for which they are enacted, but "they are not beyond reexamination and revision to preserve their purpose and to protect the permanent goods they safeguard."

Perhaps these examples will suffice to show that much recent literature merely repeats points previously made or pursues nuances previously suggested. The same is not true of the interesting article by R. S. Pendergast.[118] Fr. Pendergast begins by insisting that the structures of the world are indeed normative for man, and in this sense the traditional analysis was fundamentally sound. But what do the structures of the world tell us about how man's sexual activity can best further the work of building the world which God has given us? The answer given by the traditional analysis did not adequately answer this question. It attributed a finality to the *sexual mechanism* as such. This is erroneous, because mechanisms do not have finality; they simply do what they must do and are not normative for anything. Pendergast does not reject finality. Rather it is his thesis that only if we attend to the evolutionary concept of man do we enlarge the context sufficiently to determine this finality adequately. Once we have done this it will be clear, he contends, why a mechanistically conceived finality must be rejected and also why an analysis of contraception based on such finality is inadequate.

To enlarge the context of thought, Pendergast points out that evolutionary variations occur in the interests of survival. That is, some variations have greater survival value than others, and therefore are selected and propagated. In man it is the entire pattern of sexuality and conjugal life which has survival value, and it is this entire pattern which man must use his intelligence to further, not just one part of it (scil., procreation). Furthermore survival is survival in an environment and in harmony with that environment. Hence the purpose of man's sexual powers must be a pattern of action compatible with, harmonious with, the environment in which he lives.

Against this general background, Pendergast states that the over-all "substantial" purpose for man's sexual powers is the procreation and rearing of an ecologically optimum number of high-quality offspring. But this general purpose is specified in different environments. A birth rate which would have been optimal one hundred years ago no longer is, but it rather tends to bring man into conflict with his environment. Therefore the finality of

[118] R. S. Pendergast, S.J., "Some Neglected Factors of the Birth Control Problem," *Sciences ecclésiastiques* 18 (1966) 205–27.

sexual powers can be put as follows:

The organs and tissues which under one aspect constitute a sexual mechanism have genuine finality only insofar as they express and realize the general purpose for which the universe produced them, namely, the total pattern of conjugal life, and the particular specification of that general purpose which the intelligence recognizes as reasonable in relation to the here-and-now state of the world around them.

This being said, Pendergast concludes that the ultimate test of the worth of a sexual act is indeed its finality, but in this larger sense, scil., "whether it serves the purpose for which the universe produced man's sexual structure."

Pendergast next turns to the liceity of contraception. The sexual gift of one person to another must have real value. The act will have value, he says, if it contributes in a positive way to the pattern of sexual life between the spouses. All the coital acts should contribute to uniting the spouses in a procreative relationship, that is, a love relationship which is given a special character by the fact that it is intended to result in procreation and full education of an optimum number of high-quality human beings.

What acts actually contribute to uniting the spouses in this procreative relationship and build up their conjugal attitudes?

A morally good sex act must confirm the man and woman in their reproductive roles by either commemorating or foreshadowing occasions on which those roles are realized more fully in intercourse that is actually fruitful (insofar as the intention of the parties involved is concerned). An act in which the parties play roles that are essentially the same as they would play in a homosexual relationship is intrinsically evil because it goes contrary to the finality of sex.

The question which logically occurs here is the following: what acts allow the couple to play roles which are truly conjugal (and not homosexual)? Pendergast answers: those which do not disturb the symbolism of the act. If they disturb this symbolism and to the extent that they do, justifying causes are required for their use.

Pendergast's article is carefully wrought and deserves serious attention. It does not simply reject a traditional analysis by captious and ultimately confusing debating techniques, but brings to the discussion a dimension (evolution and its implications) not present in previous literature. I should like to put a single question to Fr. Pendergast in the hope that he will treat it more in detail at a future date: what constitutes the symbolism of the act? His own analysis thins out when he deals with this question; unless I am mistaken, it is a crucial point.

What did the Council say about contraception? This has been the object of a lively debate. Certainly the Council reaffirmed the teaching on contraception. But what does "reaffirm" mean? Several theologians understand this reaffirmation as a simple condemnation. This seems certainly to be the position of M. Zalba, S.J.[119] Unless I misread him, this is also the position of John C. Ford, S.J.[120]

However, others have seen this "reaffirmation" in a different light. They have seen the conciliar statement as a reminder that the tradition is with us, and that we cannot discuss the matter without taking cognizance of this tradition. The famous footnote 14, these authors would contend, simply calls attention to this tradition as the starting point for any realistic contemporary discussion. In their own way John L. Thomas, S.J.,[121] Gregory Baum, O.S.A.,[122] Donald Campion, S.J.,[123] and others have presented this approach to the Council's statement. It seems that John J. Lynch, S.J., is not far from this understanding of the document when he writes: "It would be reading entirely too much into the conciliar Constitution to maintain that the doctrinal status was affected in any substantial way by Vatican II."[124] It was this second sense of "reaffirmation" that I had in mind when I wrote in *America*: "The document, as everyone knows, did not decide the 'contraceptive question' simply because it did not intend to . . . . Thus no reading of the conciliar statement that attempts to squeeze from it either a resounding affirmation or a practical change on contraception will be very realistic."[125] The very intricacy of Ford's expert presentation of an opposing view

[119] M. Zalba, S.J., "De dignitate matrimonii et familiae fovenda," *Periodica* 55 (1966) 381–429. He refers to the conciliar statement as a "ratificationem documentorum istorum" (pp. 423–24) and adds (in footnote 32) "improbavit denuo improbatas vias quas memoravit." Throughout the article he rejects completely the idea of the existence of a practical doubt where contraception is concerned.

[120] John C. Ford, S.J., in *America* 114 (1966) 103–7 and 553–57.

[121] John L. Thomas, S.J., "What Did the Council Conclude on Contraception?" *America* 114 (1966) 294–96.

[122] Gregory Baum, O.S.A., "Birth Control—What Happened?" *Commonweal* 83 (1965) 369–71.

[123] Donald Campion, S.J., in *The Documents of Vatican II*, p. 256, n. 172.

[124] John J. Lynch, S.J., "The Contraceptive Issue: Moral and Pastoral Reflections," THEOLOGICAL STUDIES 27 (1966) 242–65, at p. 249.

[125] Richard A. McCormick, S. J., "The Council on Contraception," *America* 114 (1966) 47–48. It was this idea which was clumsily worded as follows: "The constitution On the Church in the Modern World says nothing explicitly about contraception." It should have read: ". . . says nothing explicitly of any great significance about contraception."

corroborates this reading. If the Council intended to condemn contraception in any significant way, one can only conclude that it failed to execute its intent.

As to the June, 1964 statement of Pope Paul VI, several remarks are in place. First, I believe that Ford and Lynch are unquestionably correct in their contention that this document referred especially to the pill. This was the issue at the time, and Paul VI addressed himself above all to that issue.

In the second place, it seems difficult to maintain that the statement was merely disciplinary. Why? For two reasons. First, one can doubt the competence of the Church to establish disciplinary decrees to regulate the intimate sexual lives of the faithful. Secondly, a disciplinary decree would have, in the circumstances, made little or no sense. As everyone knows, disciplinary decrees, like Church laws, are subject to excusation through proportionate reason. As disciplinary, the decree would have bound only in so far as there was no legitimate excusing cause. As soon as a couple would experience hardship from its observance (and what couple would not?), it would cease to bind them. Practically this would mean that Pope Paul had issued a disciplinary decree which would not bind in at least very many cases—hence which would be practically meaningless. One is hesitant to accuse the Supreme Pontiff of perpetrating an all but meaningless decree.

The statement was, therefore, a doctrinal one at least in its basic assertion. Its basic assertion was the present validity of norms established by Pius XII. "We say frankly that We do not so far see any adequate reason for considering the relevant norms of Pius XII superseded and therefore no longer obligatory." This was an authentic but noninfallible assertion by the Pontiff that there were no sufficient reasons in 1964 for modifying the norms of Pius XII. But he immediately added: "They should, therefore, be regarded as valid, at least as long as We do not consider Ourselves obliged in conscience to modify them." What is the present import of this statement?

Many interpret this as meaning that the norms of Pius XII must be said to be valid and binding in conscience unless and until the Pontiff says otherwise. On this understanding, these authors have found it impossible to grant the status of probability to opinions proposing a different point of view than the traditional. Or again, they have found it impossible to admit the existence of any practical doubt where contraception in general and contraception by pill in particular is concerned.

Without for the moment asserting the probability of any opinion or the existence of any practical doubt, I should like to offer an alternate approach to the statement of Pope Paul VI. The Pontiff must be understood to be asserting three things. (1) At the present time (1964) the arguments against the norms laid down by Pius XII are not persuasive or sufficient to bring traditional teaching into doubt. As noted above, this is a noninfallible but authentically magisterial declaration and will have practical effects for those who count it a privilege to share the enlightenment which Church teaching brings to human affairs. (2) As long as the arguments remain unpersuasive, these norms must be regarded as obligatory. (3) We (Pope Paul) are the *ultimate* judge as to whether the arguments and analyses against traditional norms are persuasive and conclusive.

But the statement cannot mean that only if and when the Pope speaks will it become clear that arguments are sound and persuasive. It cannot mean this simply because it could become clear that former arguments and positions are inadequate even without a papal statement. Furthermore, if the Pontiff were going to issue a modification of traditional teaching, such a modification would be plausible only on the supposition that it had already become clear *before his statement* that traditional teaching was inadequate. Certainly the Pope would not wish to reserve to himself the ability to recognize this clarity. And if it has become clear even before a papal statement, then can there be any objection to a couple's use of this clarity in their own conjugal life? Hardly.

The question, then, reduces itself to a matter of fact, to an assessment of the force of new (since 1964) analyses and arguments. Are these sufficiently cogent to have superseded the norms laid down by Pius XII—and also Pius XI—or at least to have rendered them doubtful?

There are many theologians who believe that recent analyses, together with the beginnings provided even before 1964, are sufficient to establish at least the probable moral liceity of contraception. It is not clear to me whether they mean by this (1) only that traditional arguments are inadequate or (2) that, even beyond this, it can be shown persuasively that contraceptive acts are positively permissible as justifiable by a sound and consistent analysis of conjugal intimacy. The point is important. If it is clear only that traditional arguments will not support the traditional conclusion, one might only be able to conclude (given the strong presumption in favor of the traditional position) that theologians had not done their homework sufficiently well. This is all the more understandable in light of the strong curial controls which, in the view of many, prevented adequate free discussion of this matter for a fairly prolonged period.

At any rate, it is easy to see how many priests might share the feelings of Msgr. Ralph J. Tapia when he says that "one might still be tempted to wonder, notwithstanding contrary opinions, whether the existing laws on contraception are the object of a purely theoretical doubt, which is admitted by all, or whether a practical doubt—ultimately freeing conscience—may legitimately be posited."[126]

[126] Ralph J. Tapia, "Burning Issues of Schema 13," *Homiletic and Pastoral Review* 66, (1966) 739–53, at p. 747. Msgr. Tapia has, I believe, worded his point unhappily when he says that "the main doubt revolves precisely around the divine or human origin of such laws." It would be more accurate to say that the substance of the law is certainly divine, although it may be questionable whether we have captured that substance in our formulations. Tapia's cautious insinuation that a practical doubt might surround traditional Catholic teaching on contraception should not be confused with the pastorally oriented remarks originally attributed to Julius Cardinal Doepfner (cf. *Documentation catholique* 63 [April 3, 1966] 669–70). In a letter to John Cardinal Heenan, Cardinal Doepfner points out that the remarks were not his own, but directives which appeared, not without his knowledge, for the use of marriage counselors. As for the content of the directives, "il s'agit uniquement d'un jugement subjectif porté sur l'attitude de personnes mariées qui s'efforcent honnêtement de vivre conformément à la loi de Dieu, mais qui éprouvent des difficultés de conscience en raison des circonstances concrètes de leur vie" (*Documentation catholique* 63 [May 15, 1966] 960).

CURRENT THEOLOGY: 1967

NOTES ON MORAL THEOLOGY: JANUARY–JUNE, 1967

OF PRINCIPLES AND DECISIONS

Vatican II suggested that "the ecumenical dialogue could start with discussions concerning the application of the gospel to moral questions."[1] Perhaps the Council was thinking of concrete moral questions such as the problem of racial justice, the problem of poverty, the problems of human sexuality, etc. However, such dialogue hardly begins when it happens upon the more fundamental problem of methodology. This is what the rather tired old discussion on situation ethics is all about. *Pace* Joseph Fletcher, it is far less concerned with Bertha's abortion than it is with the presuppositions of all of Bertha's decisions. It is both challenging and attempting to clarify the starting points for moral discourse. It is important to realize this; for if we reduce the discussion to a quibble over a few concrete norms, we miss its point and therefore its potential advantages.

Earlier, rather bellicose tactics ("legalist-relativist," "juridicism-antinomianism"[2]) are tending to disappear in favor of a calm attempt to understand what others are saying or trying to say. Such open and sincere attempts to understand can only lead to enrichment—whether this translates as honest disagreement, or reappraisal and eventual modification of one's theological categories.[3] Therefore, instead of casting up desperate alternatives and deepening the immobilism inseparable from extreme positions, recent literature appears to be engaged in the more creative task of balancing and unifying. This has manifested itself in at least two ways: the synthetic-conciliatory type of article, and the appearance of several attempts to formulate new principles.

First some examples of the former. Frederick S. Carney sees three basic positions in Christian ethics (principle at the center of Christian moral life; directional norms in Christian ethics; the relation of virtue to context) and contends that each of these basic positions has been arguing for something very important to the structure of moral decision.[4] In any adequate

[1] *The Documents of Vatican II*, ed. Walter M. Abbott, S.J. (New York: Association Press, 1966) p. 365.

[2] For an excellent treatment of the Pauline theology of law, cf. Joseph Fitzmyer, S.J., "St. Paul and the Law," *Jurist* 27 (1967) 18–36.

[3] A recent example is Norman H. G. Robinson's "Agape and Agapism," *Canadian Journal of Theology* 13 (1967) 79–85.

[4] Frederick S. Carney, "Deciding in the Situation: What Is Required?" *McCormick Quarterly* 20 (1967) 117–30.

theory each of these features must play its role. Nearly everyone will have reservations on Carney's suggestions as to how each of these elements can be understood to function within a single theory. However, the synthetic attempt is itself perhaps the most significant thing about the paper.

Louis Dupré examines two forms of situationism, one with a philosophical inspiration, one with a theological.[5] Each of these lines of thought he confronts with what he calls "objective" ethics. After presenting argument and counterargument, Dupré concludes that the "confrontation between objective morality and situation ethics calls for a theory that combines the subjective-creative with the objective-rational element of freedom. No moral system in the past has done full justice to both these elements." Dupré seems to be suggesting that situation ethics and objective morality represent only aspects of a totality and therefore that a dynamic concept of nature and a personal relation to God are not incompatible with absolute moral objectivity.

The adjustment Dupré calls for in both lines of thought strikes me as balanced and moderate. But it will probably appear to some as a sneaky bit of intrinsicalism. There is no question, for instance, where Dupré stands on one of the issues which, rightly or wrongly, is constantly catapulted into the heart of this discussion: the question of absolute concrete norms. He insists that the distinction between universal principles and less universal application of these principles "by no means implies that all concrete moral precepts allow of exceptions. Some acts are always and under any circumstances destructive of an essential human value." He gives adultery as an example.

John G. Milhaven, S.J., and David J. Casey, S.J., have presented a very useful summary of the theological background of contemporary contextualism.[6] They first summarize the works of its Continental precursors, then detail the position of individual contextualists such as Lehmann, Sittler, H. Richard Niebuhr, and Fletcher. The survey ends with brief sketches of the orientation of men like James Gustafson, John Bennett, and Paul Ramsey. The coauthors conclude that "a first view suggests that there is much here that could enrich the Catholic tradition and much that could be enriched by it." This is assuredly the case. Since Milhaven and Casey have crammed an enormous amount into a short space, it might be ungracious carping to suggest that they seem somewhat clearer on how contemporary contextualists could enrich Catholic tradition than vice versa.

[5] Louis Dupré, "Situation Ethics and Objective Morality," THEOLOGICAL STUDIES 28 (1967) 245–57.

[6] John G. Milhaven, S.J., and David J. Casey, S.J., "Introduction to the Theological Background of the New Morality," ibid., pp. 213–44.

Much of the ground covered by Milhaven–Casey is spelled out in terms of the basic motifs or emphases in contextualist literature by James B. Nelson (United Theological Seminary of the Twin Cities).[7] Nelson concludes his careful summary by suggesting that further dialogue is needed, not only between contextual ethics and the behavioral sciences, but between Protestant contextualism and Catholic thought.

In an interesting ecumenical effort, George G. Christian, O.P., and Ronald E. Whittall, speaking out of two different traditions and tendencies, assert that the controversy which has arisen between supporters of a natural-law morality and those espousing a situation ethic is pointless.[8] They suggest that quite possibly both sides are speaking of the same moral reality and trying to convey the same message, but that they begin with a different logical framework and language. After separate position papers which, given their brevity, are hardly totally adequate, they attempt to reconcile the differences in their approaches through a doctrine of Christian personalism. It is their conviction that conscience is the actual locus for the encounter of natural law and reasonable (prudential) judgment of the circumstances.

It would be hasty and eventually unfruitful, I believe, to conclude that the only difference or even the major difference in contemporary discussions of contextualism is one of language. It might be much nearer the truth to say that increasingly the difference appears to be one of emphasis. Whenever we emphasize one aspect of moral decision, we generally fail to take sufficient account of another.[9] Our failure becomes all the more pronounced and incorrigible when this single emphasis comes under attack and becomes an object of defense. Defensive attitudes have never been anything but notoriously poor guides to theological clarity and balance. Contextualists have emphasized one aspect of moral decision, natural-law proponents another. It may be a huge oversimplification to put it this way, but it seems that far more than we have sometimes realized we all are and must be contextualists; and we all are and must be adherents of natural law, even if we eschew the name.

Contextualist James Nelson has illustrated this, perhaps unwittingly, in a thought-provoking article.[10] After discussing the assumptions of the

[7] James B. Nelson, "The Moral Significance of the Church in Contemporary Protestant Contextual Ethics," *Journal of Ecumenical Studies* 4 (1967) 66–91.

[8] George G. Christian and Ronald E. Whittall, "Natural Law and Situation Ethics," *Insight* 5 (1967) 4–11.

[9] Some commentators have seen an example of this in John G. Milhaven's "Be Like Me! Be Free!" *America* 116 (1967) 584–86.

[10] James B. Nelson, "Contextualism and the Ethical Triad," *McCormick Quarterly* 20 (1967) 104–16.

contextualist method,[11] Nelson turns to the method itself and does some balancing. With Gustafson he notes that some (e.g., Sittler) have become contextualists because of an understanding of the God whose actions toward and claims upon men are always concrete and specific. The contextualism of others (e.g., H. Richard Niebuhr) is rooted in a social and responsive understanding of selfhood. Nelson believes that regardless of where one begins, the other two elements of the ethical triad (God, self, neighbor) are immediately involved. Hence he argues for a contextualism based upon a richer understanding of this triad.

For example, if moral decision depends upon the interpretation of and response to God's action, it also depends on my assessment of my neighbor's need. Here Nelson is especially perceptive. He insists that the neighbor's need may or may not be identical with his subjective feeling or desire. More generally, the neighbor's need is defined by his potentialities. But such potentialities are not self-evident. "Thus, the neighbor point of the triangle is driven back to the God point, for it is not only through scientific investigation but also through God's revelation as Creator that we know the potentialities of created being; it is not only through interpersonal communication but also through God's revelation in Jesus Christ that we know what constitutes true man and authentic human need." This is not only good contextualism, but it could stand as the manifesto of the contemporary Christian natural lawyer.

Similarly, Robert O. Johann, S.J., has provided what could serve as a corrective paradigm in current discussions.[12] Rejecting the crippling automatism involved in the notion that the moral life is simply a matter of bringing our choices into line with pre-established principles, he insists, however, that genuine personal choices always involve, at least implicitly, the adoption of a principle of conduct. "To be concerned, therefore, about rules of behavior is not to be morally hidebound. It is an effort, rather, to bring out the full implications of our choices and to see if, then, we still want to make them."[13]

[11] One such assumption is a relational value theory. This means, Nelson says, that value does not exist in and of itself apart from relationships. He cites Fletcher's statement as asserting the same thing: "Good and evil are extrinsic to the thing or action. . . ." It seems that these are totally different statements. One can admit that value does not exist apart from relationships without admitting that it is totally extrinsic to action. This is so because some actions, at the level of their external concreteness, have a stable relational significance and therefore constitute a part (not the whole) of the relationship in which value can exist. In this respect cf. Louis Janssens, *Mariage et fécondité* (Paris: Duculot, 1967) 111–12; THEOLOGICAL STUDIES 27 (1966) 616; Thomas Wassmer, S.J., *America* 117 (1967) 132.

[12] Robert O. Johann, S.J., "Rules and Decisions," *America* 117 (1967) 61.

[13] Johann refers in the course of his essay to the "dwindling defendants of natural law

These are but a few examples of the type of literature which will probably increase in the near future. Others have approached the practical problem of decision-making, especially in difficult circumstances, by attempting to formulate new practical principles. We shall mention three here: the principle of tension, the principle of overriding right, and the principle of compromise.

Peter Chirico, S.S., has attempted to discover a third way which will do justice both to Christian moral tradition and to contemporary insights.[14] He finds this third way in a "tension moiality." It is Chirico's contention that because of concupiscence man is incapable of affirming totally "his own being, his relationship to other men, and ultimately his relationship to God." He can only move toward such affirmation. Man's internal incapacity is externalized from time to time in concrete situations in which the various strands of the moral law are so interwoven that the performance of one imperative of the law renders the performance of another morally impossible. Thus the tension. In such circumstances the Christian's duty is to recognize and affirm (internally) all the values involved, and to attempt to implement them externally in so far as possible. The situation must be viewed as one of challenge to grow, to overcome gradually one's incapacity to the point where all values can be affirmed both internally and externally.

An example of the "tension" situation envisaged by Fr. Chirico is that wherein I am confronted with the obligation to speak the truth and the obligation to protect my neighbor's reputation by hiding the truth. Here are two values: my inner need to express myself truthfully, my concern for my neighbor's reputation. "Since I am morally incapable of manifesting these two values in the same response, I tell a simple untruth; for of the two values, the neighbor's reputation outweighs the moral imperative to be truthful."

However, Chirico does not regard such conduct as simply proper. Of the evasive tactic he says: "It is an untruth. It is a perversion of the expressive faculty." The only way one can avoid the harm involved (gradual loss of honest expressiveness) is to realize "that telling untruths, even in the circumstances involved, is an immoral aspect of a concrete act that must always be internally detested and externally avoided to the extent that this is possible." Why? Because one who lies, even for a good cause, helps make himself a liar. He harms himself. He can only counterbalance

---

theology." Would it not be more accurate to refer to the dwindling defendants of a *certain type* of natural-law theology?

[14] Peter Chirico, S.S., "Tension, Morality, and Birth Control," THEOLOGICAL STUDIES 28 (1967) 258–85.

this harmful aspect of untruthful speech by recognizing the elements of the problem, affirming all the values (internally) in the situation, recognizing the real significance of the tension situation as revealing his own weakness and the need to grow. Finally, when a Christian does what he can in these situations, "there is no sin, for there is no wilful turning away from God and creation."

Chirico applies this principle of tension to the contraceptive situation. A contraceptive act is, he believes, always wrong "because it is a conscious attempt to deny life-giving capacity to an act that is directed toward life-giving." It is wrong because "it does personal harm to the moral human beings who practice it." That is, it lowers their reverence for life. However, this evil effect of the contraceptive act can be minimized, but precisely because contraception is recognized as evil—"just as the evil effects of lying on one's personality are minimized precisely when one recognizes the evil of lying and does so [lies] only reluctantly." Now, in married life there are situations where it is morally impossible to affirm externally all the values of married life, values one is held to affirm (e.g., the personal relationship of husband and wife, the procreation of children, the upbringing of children). In such a dilemma "their concrete contraceptive acts of intercourse have positive value in that they truly manifest the concern of the spouses for one another and their mutual love for their children, but at the same time the specifically contraceptive aspect of these acts does them personal harm. The act considered in its totality is not simply good but ambivalent; it is permitted because of the moral incapacity of the parties. . . ."

In summary, Chirico sees his "tension principle" as representing a position midway between what he calls the absolutist and the situationist. With the absolutist he insists on the existence of absolute moral norms whose infringement is always wrong "because conscious infringement always involves moral harm to persons." With the situationist he agrees that there are times when a person may contravene these absolutes. A person may do this without sin not because these imperatives have lost their validity in the specific case (as the situationist would claim), but because the person is in a moral dilemma in which he is morally incapable of living up to all the imperatives of the moral law. The act *in concreto* is without blame, even though there are aspects to it that contravene moral absolutes.

There are certain aspects of this fascinating paper which are very attractive. For example, it relates concrete moral norms to human weakness in a way which is very consoling to those of us who identify easily with Trent's declaration (*DB* 792) about concupiscence: "fatetur et sentit." Furthermore, it does indeed bring more than an *ad hoc* casuistry to some urgent modern problems. However, it seems that Chirico's "principle of tension" is not without problems. I see them as two: the suppositions of the principle itself, and its application to contraception.

As for the principle, there are times, Chirico asserts, when one must perform an act *with immoral elements in it* if one is to realize obligatory values in one's external conduct. Precisely here a problem arises. Chirico seems to suppose that unless an external act achieves all possible values, it is morally evil, in the sense that it contains morally evil elements. Does this not mean ultimately that he has measured the objective moral quality of an act by its relation to an individual value? Should not this basic moral quality, the moral specification, be derived rather from the relation of the act to the whole hierarchy of values? It would seem so.

Perhaps it can be put as follows. Because we are finite, all our acts are metaphysically imperfect. They do not and cannot embody all values. This radical metaphysical limitation will obviously manifest itself at the level of concrete external activity. An act of worship is neither an act of chastity nor an act of social justice. Furthermore, some acts will include even material privations. This means that the moral question is not whether an act includes some material defects or privations, but whether in its concreteness it relates properly to the hierarchy of values. It is this relationship to the hierarchy of values which gives the act its objective moral significance. If the proper hierarchy of values is observed, the act is objectively moral, even though it fails to incarnate all values and to slough off all privations. It is this relationship to the totality of value which explains why moralists have always found it much more than verbalism to distinguish between "taking another's property" and "theft," between "material untruth" and "a lie." The materialities of these actions are often indistinguishable, but their objective moral significance is totally different, basically because in the concrete circumstances they relate differently to the hierarchy of values.

Take a single example. Chirico's analysis supposes that a material statement of untruth is morally wrong, is a "perversion of the expressive faculty." The moral wrong, he says, lies in the harm done the speaker (loss of honest expressiveness). It is this supposition that one might want to challenge. In other words, what is harmful to self and others is not precisely material untruth, but the misuse of human expressive powers. Now what concretely constitutes a misuse of these powers can only be determined in relation to their meaning and purpose. This meaning and purpose must be defined against the background of the hierarchy of values. This is, I believe, the basic insight of moral tradition over the years, though reflective reasoning has struggled mightily to reduce this to a viable formula.

"Material untruth" can only be said to be an invariable misuse of expressive powers if the adequately described purpose of speech is said to be "uttered truth." Such an analysis could easily appear to reflect a rather isolated and mechanistic notion of the finality of human expression, that is, one gathered without sufficient advertence to all possible specifying values. When one adverts to the hierarchy of values, one will conclude that the meaning and purpose of human expressive powers is not simply the communication of true information, but a communication between persons which respects and promotes their good precisely as persons in community.[15] Whether a particular utterance is a misuse of the power of expression will be determined, then, by weighing it against the demands of the total personal situation.

Therefore, when one utters an untruth—call it what we will: evasive tactics, mental reservation, or, less appropriately, a lie—to protect the professional secret, I see no misuse of speech. Therefore, I see no harm done the speaker or anyone else, and so I see nothing morally wrong. One who does this does not "make himself a liar" unless I have a prefabricated definition of a liar as one who utters untruths even when he should. He rather deepens his respect for himself, other persons, and also thereby for truth and truthful expression.

Summarily, where one's act observes the hierarchy of value, there seems to be no question of *moral* evil in the act. Chirico's "principle of tension" supposes there is moral evil in the act. A proper definition of our acts destroys this supposition.

A second difficulty with the "principle of tension" is its application to contraception. Use of the principle in this area supposes the solution of the very problem which has agitated us. Perhaps it can be put as follows. Either contraceptive intercourse embodies a denial of an absolute value or it does not. If it represents denial of an absolute value, then by definition this absoluteness will make it impossible to subordinate this value to any other, or to regard any other as prevalent. If the contraceptive act does not represent denial of an absolute value, then there is nothing immoral about it when it properly relates to the hierarchy of values. Our only problem is

---

[15] Dupré, *art. cit.*, p. 249. Dupré points out that the universal precept is not "to speak the truth under any circumstances" but rather "never to use language in a way which jeopardizes man's life in a community." There are times when material truth destroys the very values which veracity is meant to protect.

to learn to relate sexual expression more adequately to this hierarchy. Chirico, however, by making this subordination, has supposed that contraceptive intercourse does not embody a denial of an *absolute* value. This supposition may be right (and it is my opinion that it is). But then, why say there is anything immoral with contraception in the proper circumstances?[16] It is no more immoral than an "uttered untruth" to protect the professional secret. And if it is not immoral, then why is a "principle of tension" needed to justify it?

If the "principle of tension" seems to present certain difficulties, then perhaps Archbishop Denis E. Hurley's "principle of overriding·right" can be of help.[17] Adverting to situations such as the killing of an unjust aggressor and the taking of another's property when one is in extreme need, the Archbishop concludes that what is normally wrong becomes in these instances morally acceptable because of a circumstance. The circumstance is a clash between a right and a duty where the right prevails. For example, I have a duty to respect the life of another and I have a right to preserve my own life. Where I am attacked, there is a clash between this duty and this right—and the right prevails. Similarly, "I have a duty to respect the property of another, but I have a right to preserve my life. If my life is in danger, my right to life clashes with my duty to respect the other's property. My right predominates." The Archbishop sees this reasoning as applicable to many other areas such as sterilization, transplantation, and contraception. For example, writing of sterilization, he sees "the right to health and conjugal union clashing with the duty to preserve bodily integrity." The former prevails.

It seems that one's basic objection against Archbishop Hurley's "principle of overriding right" might be that it is not a principle at all. That is, it does not provide the means of solving a problem, but simply formulates a solution at which one has already arrived. Under analysis, the "principle" only asserts that if one duty is more important than another and I cannot do justice to both, then I must discharge that which is more important. Fair enough. But that does not tell me and cannot tell me which duty is more important or why it is so. This a genuine principle should do.

For example, in the case of extreme need, to say that my right to life predominates over my duty to respect my neighbor's property is simply a

<hr />

[16] Here the majority report of the Birth Control Commission is more accurate. It refers to the contraceptive act as involving "a material privation," "a negative element, a physical evil." Cf. *National Catholic Reporter*, April 19, 1967, and *Tablet*, May 6, 1967.

[17] Denis E. Hurley, O.M.I., "A New Moral Principle: When Right and Duty Clash," *Furrow* 17 (1966) 619–22. For subsequent discussion cf. *ibid.* 18 (1967) 167–70, 275–77.

way of saying that we have a basic grasp on the significance of human life and material goods and have decided, correctly of course, that material goods are for man. It is this judgment which is the basis for my decision—my principle, if you wish. Once we have understood the relationship between human life and material goods, we are able to assert the inherent limitations on the right to material goods. Therefore, it is only after I have taken a position on the hierarchy of values that I am positioned to see whether a certain form of conduct involving these values is promotive of human growth or not.

One could put the matter negatively as follows. Is it not precisely because we may have been one-sided or at least vague about the values of Christian marriage that we have been vague about the meaning of actions making procreation in marriage impossible? Would sterilization actually promote the long-run total good of the marriage in some instances or not? This is what the contraceptive controversy is all about. To say that "my right to conjugal union predominates over my duty to preserve bodily integrity" is not to offer a principle of solution to this question; it is rather to formulate a solution already arrived at on other grounds. And that is why Archbishop Hurley has not offered a principle at all.

What he does give us is a formulation. Is it a good formulation? I think not. It builds on the idea of a clash between right and duty. As the Archbishop says: "The discovery of the new . . . formula arose out of the realization that we have no general principle in our moral theology dealing with situations in which right and duty clash." This is true. But the reason is that a "precise statement of a moral duty takes account of such rights as may intervene in the matter concerned and, by delimiting both the right and the duty in conformity with the divine order from which they alike derive, it eliminates the very basis of a *contrary* right."[18] A genuine clash is only possible if there is no inherent limitation on rights and duties. But there are such limitations. Therefore, to adopt a formulation which speaks of a clash is both to suggest the illimitability of rights and duties and to entice others away from the hard work of delimiting such rights and duties. This is somewhat less than happy.

Charles E. Curran engages in a dialogue with Joseph Fletcher.[19] After faulting Fletcher on three ethical presuppositions (the notion of love, nominalism, and pragmatism), Curran wonders whether it is possible to

[18] L. L. McReavy, "When Right and Duty Clash—A New Moral Principle?" *Clergy Review* 52 (1967) 213–16, at p. 215.

[19] Charles E. Curran, "Dialogue with Joseph Fletcher," *Homiletic and Pastoral Review* 67 (1967) 821–29.

come to grips with difficult situations in a more realistic way than Catholic theology has hitherto managed to do. He proposes a theory of compromise based on the pervasive presence of sin in the structures of human existence.

In the face of the sinful situation man must do the best he can. The destructive and disruptive influence of sin frequently prevents man from doing what he would want to do in the given situation. The businessman might be forced to make kick-backs in order to stay in business. The laborer might have to kick in so much a day to be hired. The word "compromise" seems to fit such situations quite well.

Curran bases this "principle of compromise" on the sinfulness of the situation. When a woman is forced to have an abortion to save her life, there is, he says, something wrong in that situation. Similarly, when one must kill to protect innocent victims of mass hatred, there is something radically and sinfully ajar about that situation. The notion of compromise takes this into account and concludes: from one point of view the action is good, because it is the best that one can do. From another viewpoint the action is wrong; that is, it manifests the sinfulness of the situation. "Every such decision indicates that sin is forcing a person to do what he would not do under other conditions."

Curran is saying something very important: we have overrationalized moral decision to the neglect of its prudential aspects. Furthermore, there seems to be no problem with an analysis of the situation which sees the source of many anguishing problems in the radical sinfulness of the world. Indeed, many of our rather traditional categories (e.g., material and formal co-operation, double effect, counseling the lesser evil) are, so to speak, categories of compromise. They suppose a sinful world and go about determining the meaning of actions inextricably bound up with human hurt and/or moral evil.

If the "theory of compromise" is only a way of saying that we are not always responsible before God for our conduct, there is no difficulty with it. But I believe that Curran wants the theory to say more than this. The difficulty one might have with the "principle of compromise" is similar to the problem one has with Hurley's "principle of overriding right." In a sense it is not a theory or a principle at all, for it does not tell me which compromises it is reasonable to make.

To say that a compromise is good because it is "the best I can do" is to imply a judgment on an opposite course of action or on other alternatives. It is this judgment and its foundations which rectify or, better, justify a compromise. Those who obeyed the genocidal orders of their superiors under Nazism did, in a sense, "the best they could." It was the only way of saving their lives in a sinful situation. From this single example, however, one can see that "the best I can do" only means something acceptable in the moral order if I have decided that this "best" is better than its opposite or other alternatives. *This* decision I make on other grounds, not on a theory of compromise.

A compromising act, therefore, is only reasonable and possessed of minimal objective moral goodness if I know what values are being sacrificed, what preserved. Some compromises are worth making because only by compromise could my decision incarnate the greatest possible value. Others (see the example above) are not reasonably made. A theory of compromise does not tell me which. Therefore, to say that a certain act is "the best I can do" and then to say that this provides "the good aspect of the act" is to confuse the objective and subjective character of moral value—precisely because the buried judgment on alternative courses of action is left buried. In summary: in a sinful world, sometimes "the best I can do" is the very worst that could be done.

THE NATURAL LAW

Theological writing continues to reveal a vigorous interest in natural law. Undoubtedly there are those who still question why the *theologian* is concerned with natural law at all. Rather recently J. Ratzinger had argued that Christian social teaching, for example, should be developed not by natural-law considerations, but by mere submission of empirical social data to the "gospel as a value-measure."[20] Through such a procedure these facts would take on their ethically normative character. It was quite possibly Ratzinger, or at least the tendency exemplified in his suggestion, that stimulated Bruno Schüller, S.J., to return to his insistence on the existence and importance of the natural law for theological methodology.[21]

Schüller approaches the natural law from two points of view. First, he shows that the natural law (which he is careful to delimit and define in a way which allows a legitimate question to be put to Scripture) is a reality recognized in Scripture. Obviously, however, this does not mean that this reality is called by name in Scripture or that it can be identified with the teaching of the Stoa as found in St. Paul. If one would want more than

---

[20] J. Ratzinger, "Naturrecht, Evangelium und Ideologie in der katholischen Soziallehre," in von Bismarck and W. Dirks, *Christlicher Glaube und Ideologie* (Stuttgart, 1964) pp. 27 ff., as cited in Schüller.

[21] Bruno Schüller, S.J., "Zur theologischen Diskussion über die lex naturalis," *Theologie und Philosophie* 41 (1966) 481–503.

Schüller's own exegesis, then Schüller points to the fact that there are the likes of H. W. Schmidt, F. J. Leenhardt, J. Murray, C. K. Barrett, H. C. G. Moule, C. H. Dodd, and R. Bultmann to contend with.

Schüller's next question is: Is natural-law thinking and argumentation something Christian moral theology can dispense with? His answer is a resounding no. He repeats what he has written before, namely, that man is only capable of hearing and giving intelligent belief to the ethical message of the New Testament because prior (logically) to the revelation of God's word he already grasps and expresses himself as an ethical being. "From this experience all moral concepts and ideas receive their meaning for man." And it is precisely these moral concepts which form the only possible medium through which God can reveal the *lex Christi*. The fact that natural morality concerns him is for man his obediential potency that the law of Christ can concern him.[22] Hence theology itself can only progress in genuine understanding of the supernatural moral order when it critically reflects on that which is the necessary medium for the revelation of that order. Indeed, Schüller insists that the better theology understands the natural law, the more advantageously positioned it is to hear and understand the *lex Christi*.

Another major point made by Schüller is that natural-law reasoning is the only basis on which one can determine whether a revealed duty is transtemporal or time-conditioned. Suppose, for a moment, that the validity of a New Testament demand can only be known in faith. How could one know whether this is transtemporal in character or not? If the validity of the precept itself is guaranteed only through God's word, then also its continuing duration can only be guaranteed if this duration is an inner constitutive of the validity. But what New Testament demand carries with it a clear indication of transtemporality? However, if we understand a demand from its inner sense (natural-law reasoning), then we are positioned to discriminate between those things which oblige for all times and those which do not; for ultimately it is to one and the same reason that a demand owes its obliging force and the continuance of this obliging force.

Schüller's article is carefully wrought and deserves the serious attention of anyone trifling with the temptation to abandon the natural law as a luxury we can no longer afford.

Hans Rotter, a doctoral candidate in moral theology at Innsbruck, has

---

[22] Ratzinger's attempt to bypass natural morality and to use the "gospel as value-measure" is doomed according to Schüller; for man can only be in a position to understand the gospel as a value and a value-measure because logically prior to his belief he already has an interior grasp of what an ethical value is. But this grasp is precisely the content of natural law.

pursued Schüller's line of thought in an interesting article.[23] Since revealed morality is certainly intended to represent something more in our lives than an irrational gymnastic, the commands of Christ must be able to be grasped as values, specifically as possible realizations of love. Therefore, man must find in his own experience the ability to understand these demands. This much Schüller had said.

Now if this is so, how does revealed morality differ from natural morality? Schüller had pointed out that the imperatives of the two must be *verbally* the same. Rotter suggests that natural-law morality relates to the moral message of the New Testament in the same way that implicit faith relates to explicit faith. An act of faith contains more than is expressly formulatable. Similarly, the "yes" to the imperative of conscience contains theological and eschatological depths which can only be explicitated through revelation. Rotter believes, therefore, that the New Testament's moral message is a deepening and "radicalizing" of natural law. That is, it is precisely the radicality with which Christ addresses man, the unity of individual demands in love, that surpasses what we know naturally and in an explicit way. Ultimately, then, *as far as verbal content is concerned*, revelation in the area of morality brings an explicitation of the conscience-experience in a way and a depth not otherwise possible. It is in this sense that the moral message of Christianity brings no new (i.e., foreign to conscience) content—a point Schüller had also made.

Clearly, the relationship between revelation and natural law needs much more study. But it seems that the general lines of Rotter's thought might lead one to say that the magisterium has a teaching competence where natural law is concerned precisely because the Church is commissioned to teach revelation. Or again, the magisterium does not enjoy competence to teach natural law only because that law is extrinsically necessary for the protection of the basic gospel message. Rather, at one level there is and must be an identity between natural law and revealed morality. The command of love of God and neighbor is a specification—analogously, of course—of both natural morality and revealed morality. Similarly, even more concrete norms are—again, analogously—historical specifications of both natural and revealed morality. This is not to say that the magisterium of the Church may or should descend to detailed specifications of the demands of radical love.[24] An enlightened sensitivity to changing historical and cultural factors

[23] Hans Rotter, S.J., "Naturrecht und Offenbarung," *Stimmen der Zeit* 179 (1967) 283–92.

[24] On this point cf. the following for varying points of view: B. Schüller, S.J., "Die Autorität der Kirche und die Gewissensfreiheit der Gläubigen," *Der Männer-Seelsorger* 16 (1966) 130–43; F. Böckle, in *Concilium* 25, 3–6; Paul McKeever, "Theology and Natural Law," *Proceedings of the Catholic Theological Society of America* 21 (1966) 223–37.

suggests great caution here. It is only to say that here we have a point of view sharply distinguished from the separatism of those who divide morality into natural and revealed and invite the Church to concern herself all too exclusively with the latter.

But to affirm the existence of a natural moral order—that is, one grounded in the being of man as man—is to say very little about its content or the manner in which o __ determines this content. Most of the recent literature seems to represent an attempt to clarify these more specific points. And rightly so. One is understandably confused when one hears the "duty to respect one's neighbor" and "the prohibition of artificial insemination" both ascribed to the natural law, and without much distinction. The first is a formal, or at best a very general material, principle; the second is a rather detailed material norm. If a concept of the being of man and a moral order founded on it leads necessarily to such indiscriminate lumping of norms, then clearly it derives from a static concept of man which can never make its peace with contemporary sociology and anthropology.

Recent literature, then, represents a variety of attempts to formulate natural law in such a way that it is both founded on the being of man and yet appropriately aware of the historicity of this being. How this attempt is made differs with each author. Some emphasize especially the noetic aspects of natural law; others attempt to nuance the notion of nature. But a basic unity is discernible in the literature if one approaches it from the overriding concern mentioned above. We will mention only a few examples here.

At a three-day conference in 1965, German-speaking moral theologians discussed the meaning of natural law. Joseph Th. C. Arntz presented a carefully researched paper detailing the history of natural law within scholastic circles.[25] This interesting history reveals a snowballing process away from the balanced subjectivity of Thomas' presentation. Whereas St. Thomas understood by natural law in its strictest sense only the first practical principles (*principia naturaliter nota*),[26] subsequent theologians began to include in the notion also the conclusions derived from these principles. This is perfectly legitimate, of course; but increasingly these conclusions were thought to share the same timeless necessity as the principles and a certain immobilism set in.

In a brief essay Frederick S. Carney outlines, rather apologetically in-

---

[25] Jos. Th. C. Arntz, "Die Entwicklung des naturrechtlichen Denkens innerhalb des Thomismus," in F. Böckle, *Das Naturrecht im Disput* (Düsseldorf: Patmos, 1966) pp. 87–120. The book is summarized in *Stimmen der Zeit* 179 (1967) 383–85.

[26] For a recent study of natural law in Thomas, cf. Soeur Sainte-Marcelle-d'Auvergne, "De la matière du droit naturel," *Laval théologique et philosophique* 23 (1967) 116–45.

deed, a natural-law procedure for Christian ethics.[27] He believes that the only way the serious objections against natural law can be met is by a three-fold clarification: the area of law, the meaning of nature, and the relation of human nature to law.

Where law is concerned, Carney suggests that the term "natural law" has suffered from association with physical laws (which are universal) and civil laws (which are established by the will of men). To counterbalance this, he proposes that we must be concerned with the relational aspects of the material norms of natural law—that is, with those aspects of life which are cultural and epochal. This does not mean that natural law is subjective. Contrarily, there is a criterion by means of which norms and then actions can be assessed. That criterion is preservation and fulfilment of human life in the context where it is found. But rather than emphasize law as a body of norms, Carney prefers to see it as a process of reflection upon the normal functioning of human nature.

As for nature, he proposes that we conceive this in a rather general, empty-container fashion as "the full dimensions of man's being." In filling out what this means, Carney insists that our formulas must sufficiently cover the whole range of man's existence, and therefore must adequately account for the social dimension in human existence.

Finally, the article is at pains to show that natural-law thinking as proposed does not draw normative conclusions from nonnormative premises; for man's perception of his world is not merely fact-perception, but value-perception. Carney suggestively speaks of a "thouness" in the primordial perception of reality. He refers to the "built-in presence of felt obligation that may reside in its disarmingly factual exterior."

J. Etienne, with nearly every informed modern writer, rejects a concept of nature which mirrors God as a transcendental engineer who has preplotted man's course and embedded this plan in a multitude of concrete persons.[28] Such a caricature is a result of human imagination. Rather, man's essential dignity is in his rationality. This is his prerogative and his fundamental responsibility. In the depths of his being, man becomes conscious of his rationality as his basic endowment, and therefore his basic task. It is in his life, in the "given," that man is beckoned to answer the call of the spirit. Etienne feels that there are certain immutable traits which oblige the spirit of man to take the same paths in order to develop itself and reach greater

[27] Frederick S. Carney, "Outline of a Natural Law Procedure for Christian Ethics" *Journal of Religion* 47 (1967) 26–38.

[28] J. Etienne, "La nature est-elle un critère de moralité?" *Revue diocésaine de Namur* 20 (1966) 282–94.

potential. But since these constants are overlaid with personal and cultural histories, they are extremely hard to determine.

In recent months Franz Böckle has made several attempts to clarify the meaning of natural law.[29] It is Böckle's contention that the notion of nature, as grounding natural law, has confronted us in four different ways: as noetic capacity (*natura ut ratio*), as a metaphysical essence (*natura metaphysica*), as the metaphysical structure of the human act itself, and as concrete nature (especially with its biological and physiological structures). The last three of these contain obvious elements of truth, but it seems to be Böckle's contention that they provide insurmountable difficulties in grounding and explaining a natural law.

Take, for example, nature as meaning the metaphysical structure of the human act. According to this point of view, the foundation of natural law derives directly from the action itself. But the invariable structure of an action is extremely difficult to determine; for the point of departure in determining this metaphysical structure must be concrete human experience and reflexion. Such experience and reflexion, however, are time-conditioned. Actually, different acts get their proper significance only as part of a total development, of a whole life. To give a metaphysical structure to an act is to rip it from its context. Thus, marriage does not get its meaning from individual acts, but the individual act derives its significance from placement within the totality that is marriage. Böckle does not want to conclude that an intelligible structure must be denied to human acts, but only that we must be more aware of the cultural-historical setting in stating what that structure is.

Böckle then turns to what he regards as a proper understanding of natural law. Natural moral law has two senses: the strict and basic sense (primary), and the derived sense (secondary).

First, the primary sense. The unavoidable primary insights (Thomas' *naturaliter nota*, in contrast to what is discursively known) constitute the natural law in its most basic sense. However, the importance of these principles is not only or especially that they are the first normative assertions or principles of conduct. Nor must one view them as simply the unchanging source of derived conclusions. Rather, in these evident insights man experiences a transcendental "oughtness." This "oughtness" does not refer simply to the unavoidability of the principles. Before all else it speaks a transcendental claim to self-realization. In these principles man is bid to take up his existence, to commit himself freely to the project of his own formation and

[29] F. Böckle. "Rückblick und Ausblick," in *Das Naturrecht im Disput*, pp. 121–50; *Grundbegriffe der Moral* (Aschaffenburg: Pattloch, 1966) pp. 47–55; *Concilium, loc. cit.*

development. It is precisely in man's responsibility, grounded in his reason, that he shares in God's providence (eternal law), because, like God Himself, man is *sibi ipsi et aliis providens*.[30]

Therefore, the natural law is not first and foremost a formulated law at all; nor is it a handing down of general, sempiternally valid principles out of which concrete law (*Recht*) is constructed. The heart of natural law rests in this unconditioned "ought" which lies at the center of man's being.[31]

Second, the derived sense. It is here that natural law appears as formulated law. It is the sum of the universally valid formulated demands based on universal structures. What are the enduring structures pertaining to the essence of man? To discover this, Böckle appeals to a transcendental deduction, i.e., from the activity of man to those things which are necessary to its possibility. The results of this process show that the social nature of man, his spirituality, his freedom of decision, and perhaps a few more characteristics belong to the essence of man. In so far as we can draw moral demands immediately from these structures, we can speak of timelessly valid norms. "This is what Catholic theology means when it speaks of ultimately timeless and universally valid demands of natural law."[32]

It is clear that Böckle's writing derives from a strong emphasis on the noetic aspects of natural law.[33] It is out of this emphasis that he says that there are four ways of conceiving nature which come down to us in natural-law thinking. This seems inaccurate. The noetic origins of natural law are but one aspect of natural law. The metaphysical foundation is another. The structure of the concrete act is still another. No theory of natural law will be complete without all aspects, simply because all are dimensions of reality. Thus it is incorrect to set those who discuss a *natura metaphysica* (e.g., Fuchs) over against those who speak of *natura ut ratio*. Fuchs himself has written, for example: "The natural law must be considered, not as the sum of external universal laws, but as *internal* law comprising the totality of that moral norm which corresponds to the totality of man's being."[34]

Böckle's own splendid treatment of premarital coitus can serve as a good

---

[30] 1–2, q. 91, a. 2.

[31] Böckle has summarized his position elsewhere (*Concilium* 25, 4) as follows: "The best way of understanding natural law is to take it as the inner content of any concrete regulation of law and morality. This content is only visible and tangible *in a concrete and positive regulation of law and morality*." He refers to this content as a kind of legal essence underlying any law.

[32] *Grundbegriffe der Moral*, p. 50.

[33] In this respect cf. also D. C. Duivesteijn, "Reflexions on Natural Law," *Clergy Review* 52 (1967) 283–94.

[34] Joseph Fuchs, S.J., *Natural Law—A Theological Investigation* (New York: Sheed & Ward, 1965) p. 134.

example of what I mean.[35] After an enlightening discussion of Christian morality as a radical love morality, Böckle turns to the area of sexuality and attempts to establish its significance. In particular, he rightly asserts that we must know the sense and meaning of marital intercourse if we are to understand its meaning during the premarital period. He finds three meanings in sexual intercourse. (1) It is a symbol of unity. (2) It is an expression of mutual love. (3) It is an act of mutual knowledge. Briefly, it is a sign of a total personal relationship.

With these meanings established, Böckle states that one confronts immediately a decisive supposition for the fully meaningful act of coitus: the mutual will or intent of unity.[36] It is this very intent to make a total and lasting self-gift which constitutes marriage.[37] If coitus is a sign of a mutual and total gift of the person, then the persons must actually be in this relationship. Before such a moment (i.e., before marriage) man cannot give himself unreservedly in a consciously responsible manner; for without the exchange of a full responsibility for each other, the self-gift cannot achieve its deepest and most proper sense. But Christian love demands an inner preparedness for this full meaning. Therefore, Böckle concludes, Christian love excludes premarital coitus. "Seen in this light, every premarital and extramarital coitus is and remains ultimately false and cannot be reconciled with the criterion of radical love."

Now, what has happened here? Böckle has described the meaning of coitus and upon this meaning he has built a moral norm. In doing so he has used what some authors have called the "metaphysical structure of the act"— though certainly there must be a better word for the significance of an act than that. In other words, Böckle is dealing here with natural-law reasoning. He disguises this fact by saying that it is precisely *Christian* love which demands the preparedness for full responsibility for each other. Christian love certainly makes this demand. But one would think that any genuinely human love would also demand that coitus be a marital act. Indeed, this demand can only be understood as Christian if it is first a human demand.

[35] Franz Böckle and Josef Köhne, *Geschlechtliche Beziehungen vor der Ehe* (Mainz: Matthias-Grunewald-Verlag, 1967) pp. 7–37.

[36] Böckle uses the terms "Wille zur Bindung," "die Bereitschaft zur Hingabe der Person mit dem Willen zur Übernahme der vollen Verantwortung," and "Wille zur gegenseitigen dauerenden Hingabe und Bindung." These terms do not immediately translate into consent, but it is clear that Böckle means this.

[37] At this point Böckle has an excellent exposition of the social character of marital consent and its relation to legal form. See also Jack L. Stotts, "Sexual Practices and Ethical Thought," *McCormick Quarterly* 20 (1967) 131–45.

In the last analysis, therefore, Böckle is dealing with a legitimate specification of what it means to "take up one's existence," to "become what thou art." And he has proceeded by analysis of the structure of the act. Briefly, he has argued to a material norm in a way which, when he discusses natural law in general, he seems eager to find problematic. On Böckle's own terms, therefore, does not the natural law have to take account of all the elements he mentions if we are to get a truly complete statement of it?

George M. Regan, C.M., presents a fine summary of recent trends in natural-law thought.[38] He is particularly concerned with the meaning of human nature. Reviewing the work of Fuchs, Monden, Columba Ryan, and Charles Fay, Regan points to an increasing tendency to emphasize what he calls "concrete human nature" in elaborating natural-law theory. Abstract human nature refers to man's metaphysical being and is consequently realized in a univocal, universal, and essentially immutable way. "Concrete ... human nature," Regan says, "refers to man's physical being as realized existentially in different historical eras and in specific situations. In this latter usage, all man's being at a given moment becomes morally relevant." It is Regan's conviction that man in his concreteness deserves more stress in moral theory. "By continuing to emphasize this more concrete understanding of man, proponents of natural law may carry greater weight in the contemporary world."[39]

This is but a sampling. If one were to back away for a moment and attempt to generalize on the direction of natural-law discussion, he might conclude that it reveals three characteristics. (1) There is an increasing tendency to approach natural law more as a thought-structure than as a normative content. The basic assertion of this thought-structure would be: man's obligation is founded on man's being. (2) This thought-structure emphasizes, above all, rational creativity in human conduct. (3) It tends to recognize formal rather than material norms as universally valid principles of natural law. This last tendency undoubtedly stems from a renewed awareness of man's historicity, and reflects a desire to relate natural law more obviously to the totality of man's being.

It is easy to agree with these emphases, if for no other reason than that they are appropriately corrective. Traditional theology, at least in its popularizations, has too often left the impression that when one deals with the natural law he is simply unpacking basic principles which, when shined up

[38] George M. Regan, C.M., "Natural Law in the Church Today," *Catholic Lawyer* 13 (1967) 21–41; cf. also *Vie spirituelle, Supplément*, May, 1967, pp. 187–324.

[39] Cf. Ildefons Lobo, O.S.B., "Toward a Morality Based on the Meaning of History: The Condition and Renewal of Moral Theology," in *Concilium* 25, 25–45.

a bit, will reflect a rather comprehensive kaleidoscope of norms. There has to be a reaction to this type of thing. On the other hand, in retreating from such instant certainties and allowing full range to man's historical existence and creativity, must we not retain the courage to be concrete? Otherwise we can be left with a natural law so refined that it contemplates with equanimity the notion that "one man goes in for handball while another likes killing Jews and that is all there is to say about the matter."[40]

PENANCE

The directions of Vatican II on the sacrament of penance were sparing. The Council simply stated: "The rite and formulas for the sacrament of penance are to be revised so that they give more luminous expression to both the nature and effect of the sacrament."[41] What form should this revision take? The question is important far beyond the few lines given to the matter by the Council. Revision of the sacramental rites and formulas involves historico-dogmatic problems, questions touching existing pastoral structures, and, not least, matters of great import for moral theology; for sacramental practice in this area not only reflects moral instruction but shapes it to some extent, as our experience has shown. The maturity or infantilism of attitudes toward the Christian moral life, the formation of conscience, social responsibility, etc., relate intimately to the discipline of the sacrament of penance.

At the twenty-seventh North American Liturgical Week, John E. Corrigan had proposed two forms of communal penitential celebrations.[42] The first involves common preparation (including readings, prayer, examination of conscience), then private confession and absolution, finally common execution of penance. This has been proposed before and has been tried in quite a few places already. There seems to be no serious problem with it, except the very practical problem of getting people to come and stay long enough to bring it off.

The second possible development Fr. Corrigan investigates is general absolution given after public generic confession. He admits that the major obstacle to this is Trent's teaching on integrity where serious sin is concerned. He approaches this difficulty from two points of view. First, since mortal sin is a reversal of a fundamental decision regarding one's whole relationship

---

[40] John R. Carnes, "Whether There Is a Natural Law," *Ethics* 77 (1967) 122–29, at p. 128.

[41] *The Documents of Vatican II*, p. 161.

[42] John E. Corrigan, "Penance: A Service to the Community," in *Worship in the City of Man* (Washington: Liturgical Conference, 1966) pp. 108–17.

with God, it has to be admitted that this type of change does not happen as often as we think. Indeed, Corrigan suggests that mortal sin is really rather rare. If such is the case, integral confession of mortal sin will not be a frequent problem. The second approach to the problem is, he suggests, the meaning of "divine law" in Trent. Perhaps the Fathers used the phrase in a rather sprawling and general way which did not imply in every case a revealed teaching.

It is easy, and rather pleasant, to be able to agree with Corrigan that mortal sin is probably not as frequent as we are sometimes led to believe. However, I am not sure that this neutralizes the problem of integrity as much as he suggests. For two reasons. First, even though mortal sin is regarded as less frequent, it still exists as a reality. Diminished frequency does not rinse us clean of the problem of integrity, but only reduces the number to whom it applies. Secondly, even though the radical and self-disposing option which is mortal sin is not an everyday affair, our knowledge of its occurrence and of our basic position before God is not totally accessible to reflex or formulating consciousness. Hence Trent could not have taught the necessity of integrity only insofar as I am clear and certain about the existence of a bad option in my action. We simply do not have this type of clarity. Rather, as Monden notes,[43] what the priest must know and what the penitent must tell him "is not an adequate description of the sinner's situation, a perfectly true insight into the extent of his sinfulness. What the penitent tells him is only a sign of what he tells God. The confession of sins is a sincere *signifying*, to the extent of his insight and according to certain rules prescribed by the Church, of his being a sinner." It is to this sincere signifying that the law of integrity must be understood to apply.

Tübingen's Walter Kasper shows that at the heart of the sacrament is a hearing and following of God's word.[44] Ecclesiastical tradition contains many forms of this hearing and following. The official sacramental form through exclusion from and then reincorporation into the community was really an extraordinary form of bringing the sinner back to God. In the high Middle Ages, lay confession was regarded as the ordinary means of making peace after minor sins and as the extraordinary means after major sins. Though he does not elaborate the distinction between "minor" and "major" sins, Kasper suggests that there are many (e.g., familial) situations where this type of lay confession could be used with great profit.[45]

[43] Louis Monden, S.J., *Sin, Liberty and Law* (New York: Sheed & Ward, 1965) p. 47.

[44] Walter Kasper, "Confession outside the Confessional," in *The Sacraments: An Ecumenical Dilemma* (= *Concilium* 24; New York: Paulist Press, 1967) pp. 31–42.

[45] For an interesting variant, cf. "Anybody for Group Confession?" *National Catholic Reporter*, July 12, 1967, p. 4.

He next suggests common generic confession followed by common absolution. After describing the advantages of such a procedure, Kasper notes that it should not lead to the demise or devaluation of individual private confession. "For truly major sins this should remain as obligatory as it is now . . . ." It is clear that he regards "major" sins as relatively rare ("a most unusual situation for a practicing Christian to be in"). Here, it would seem, he confronts the same problems Corrigan faced.

Many years ago J. B. Hirscher had approached the question of public or common confession not from the liturgical but from the moral-pastoral point of view.[46] His question: What must the sacrament be to provide the best help for the penitent to develop the virtue of penance? In a fine article[47] Albert Höfer continues in this pastoral vein and asks: What should the sacramental sign be to give the best possible assistance to its personal performance?

Höfer begins his own suggestions by pointing out that the acts of the penitent are the matter of the sacrament, that is, cocauses. The penitent is a coplacer of the sacramental sign, an active celebrant of the sacrament. The sacrament will be only as effective as this personal co-operation is rendered possible within the sacrament. Since the sacraments effect what they signify, and since the penitent is a coplacer of this sign, Höfer insists that the penitent has a right of voice in determining the best form of these acts. The ritual cannot be determined in an aprioristic manner.

Höfer then takes each act of the penitent and attempts to discover what procedure will be most productive of genuine penance. Thus, even where recognition of sin is concerned, if a man views his conduct in the mirror of the Ten Commandments, he perceives only amorality, not sin. To see one's conduct as sin demands faith, confrontation with the living God. In other words, a confession liturgy without proclamation of the living God is unthinkable. Otherwise the penitent is left alone with his "confession mirror."

Similarly with sorrow. It is an interpersonal happening. Man confronts his conduct and distances himself from it, but always in relation to a Thou. Sorrow, therefore, supposes that one is confronted not only with his acts and norms for these acts, but with a living Thou. This supposes preaching in some form. Even confession itself is an interpersonal event. I confess to someone as much as I confess something. The best liturgical form of an interpersonal confession, according to Höfer, is prayer—a good example of this

[46] Cited and reviewed by A. Exeler in *Eine Frohbotschaft vom christlichen Leben* (Freiburg, 1959) pp. 50–52.

[47] Albert Höfer, "Öffentliche Beichten werden in Vorschlag gebracht," *Der Seelsorger* 37 (1967) 95–102.

being St. Augustine's *Confessions*. Augustine is confessing to the world, but above all to God; hence he falls frequently into prayer.

Höfer concludes from his study of modern man that he must not be left alone in placing his acts. A public penance-liturgy best avoids this isolation and is therefore a great pastoral aid. Ultimately, of course, he admits that a public penance-liturgy finds its best justification in newly gained insights into the relation between the sacraments and the Church as the "first sacrament." This relation, as a theological datum, must be experienceable by the Christian as a liturgical event.

When Höfer touches on the problem of integrity, he remarks that in the prayer-form of confession there should be no question of perfect integrity. A confession is integral when it is genuine before God and hides nothing. One can wonder whether Höfer is facing the problem in its fulness when he puts the matter this way. To overlook the fact that confession takes place before the community in its official representative (Höfer minimizes this) is to miss the very ecclesial dimension of the sacrament which all recent literature underscores.

A.-M. Roguet, O.P., also discusses community penitential celebrations.[48] It is clear that he refers only to celebrations involving public preparation and conclusion—with private confession and absolution. Roguet finds many advantages in these celebrations, but above all they would return the sacrament of penance to a position within the framework of a celebration of the Word of God. The sacrament of penance, like all liturgical celebrations, is a proclamation of the Word of God—a point contemporary practice obscures. In contemporary practice confession means only the revelation of faults. Ideally it should rather conform to the notion of *confiteri*, which is a much fuller reality. One would best translate it by "celebrate." Thus confession is a celebration consisting principally in proclaiming the sanctity of God, recalling the radical exigencies of His law, manifesting our own sinfulness, and finally, in last place, enumerating our sins. If such an enumeration is not founded on a confession of God's sanctity and our fundamental misery as sinners, it risks losing its religious character. Roguet does not confront the issue of integrity simply because his suggested communal celebrations do not raise it.

Paul Anciaux offers several pastoral remarks as guidelines toward a reordering of private confession in the totality of Christian life.[49] First, he insists that all liturgical symbols of conversion and reconciliation are rooted

---

[48] A.-M. Roguet, O.P., "Les célébrations communautaires de la pénitence," *Vie spirituelle* 116 (1967) 188–202.

[49] P. Anciaux, "Privatbeichte und gemeinschaftliche Bussfeier," *Theologie der Gegenwart*

in the mystery of the Church as a sacramental reality and consist in an extension of baptism. In this sense all sacraments are signs of conversion and ratification of reconciliation. If we grasp this close connection between baptism and the other sacraments, we will see more clearly the appropriate liturgical forms for the embodiment of the various moments of a sacrament.

Secondly, public celebrations can be fully effective only within the context of a corresponding pastoral care. If the community dimension does not assume its proper position in other areas of pastoral care, these communal celebrations will remain disengaged curiosities. Thirdly, confession (especially of devotion) must be set in the context of a changing pastoral attitude. Formerly our pastoral care was largely paternal and authoritative. Now it must become more community-oriented and co-operative. Confession must share in this development. Finally, Anciaux feels that we must discover for our time intermediate forms of confession which symbolize the gradual or "step-by-step" return of the converting sinner.

From this short survey it is clear that one of the major problems of a renewed liturgy for the sacrament of penance is the problem of integrity. Carl J. Peter met this problem head on in his careful study of integrity in the Council of Trent.[50] He first notes that consistency with and conformity to the message of Jesus as elaborated in Trent is a condition for fruitful development in penitential doctrine and discipline. He then asks: Was Trent's teaching on integral confession an elaboration of revealed truth or a disciplinary law pure and simple? Peter approaches this question by attending to two points: (1) the dogmatic binding character of Trent's teachings, particularly in its anathemas; (2) the meaning of *jus divinum* in Trent.

After reviewing the work of Umberg, Lennerz, Favre, Lang, Fransen, De Letter, and F. X. Lawlor, Peter concludes that not all the canons of Trent reject heresy in the strict sense of the term. But what of that canon concerned with the integrity of confession? The same is true here, since these canons obviously include also matter of purely ecclesiastical law. But his study leads him to reject the conclusion that the duty of integrity is purely disciplinary. "But as to the basic, hard fact of integral confession, that comes from God. At least for the Fathers of Trent, integrity was not one of those elements arising solely from the Church's determination of the sacrament; it was contained in or followed from Christ's institution."

10 (1967) 15–21. This article first appeared in its expanded form in *Collectanea Mechliniensia* 5 (1966) 606–17.

[50] Fr. Peter very kindly allowed me the use of his manuscript. It will appear in the *Proceedings of the Catholic Theological Society of America*, Twenty-second Annual Meeting, 1967.

Peter draws the same conclusion when he studies *jus divinum*. The phrase meant that integrity was not established by the Church. However, an object may be "established by God" (*jus divinum*) because at a particular point in history it is necessary for man if he is to enjoy the conditions required for salvation. Thus it represents God's will in these circumstances. Peter rejects this as the mind of Trent and states that integrity was willed by God as somehow established in His revelation through Christ. "To refuse to admit that this was the mind of Trent is hard to reconcile with the Acts."

Trent's message, Peter concludes, is that integral confession is a value revealed by God—neither absolute (there are other values and theology has always recognized them) nor merely of disciplinary ecclesiastical law. It must be approached in proper relation with other values. Could it be observed if there were generic confession and communal absolution with the obligation of confessing specifically within a definite period of time even though no strict necessity were involved? Peter refuses to judge the merits of such a proposal but does add: "I do not, however, think the Council of Trent can be invoked as an authority to exclude it."

Peter's excellent study makes it clear that Trent supposed some internal limits on the necessity of integrity. The precept is, in other words, an affirmative precept. Christ, and the Church authoritatively interpreting Christ's revelation, could not demand the impossible. Post-Tridentine moral teaching seized upon the concept of impossibility and built around it. Thus it has become traditional teaching that there is excuse from material integrity whenever an integral confession would be physically (e.g., the moribund) or morally impossible. It is morally impossible when it cannot be achieved without sacrificing some more important value, and hence without ultimately rendering the sacrament odious to men. In explaining this notion of moral impossibility, textbook theology has said that the notion is verified when there is simultaneously a need to confess and no confessor to whom one might confess without giving rise to the harm anticipated.

Therefore, when one approaches the question of public generic confession as it relates to integrity, he would probably ask two questions: (1) Does the contemporary situation correspond to a situation of moral impossibility? (2) If it does not, is moral impossibility the only justification for such generic confession?[51]

As for the first question, one might argue that the existence of only a single private penitential rite which fails to aid the penitent sufficiently in his acts (Höfer) and to emphasize the ecclesial character of sin and reconciliation

[51] For another and rather different approach, cf. F. J. Connell, C.SS.R., "Common Confession Rite," *American Ecclesiastical Review* 156 (1967) 409–12.

(Anciaux) constitutes a situation of moral impossibility. In other words, the values sacrificed by the absence of an occasional communal and generic confession are so great that such a confession is intermittently justified.

Is this a valid and reasonable point of view? I do not think so. First, the benefits of communal generic confession can be achieved, as Roguet notes, with communal penitential celebrations which include private confession and absolution.[52] Secondly, the concept of moral impossibility seems to suppose that there is a desire here and now to confess integrally, but a desire which is impeded. No such desire need be or would be present in the communal services envisaged. Therefore, I do not see that the proposed group confession fits the category of a morally impossible situation excusing from integrity. Hence, if such confession is to be reconciled with Trent's teaching on integrity, one would have to look elsewhere for justification.

That brings us to the second question: Is moral impossibility the only justification for a materially nonintegral confession of mortal sin? It seems to me that one might argue that Trent was speaking of integrity in confession as Trent knew confession. But confession was private at that time. Therefore, it was within the one-to-one relationship of private penance-rites that the notion of impossibility arose and was developed. Could one not suggest, then, that impossibility as the sole excuse from integrity is based on the supposition that only a private confessional rite is in question? Where private confession is not in question, is impossibility the only category allowing excuse from material integrity? Could not one argue that the integrity of a *public* or *communal* confession is sufficiently fulfilled if there is the intent at the time of confession to submit any mortal sins privately at the next opportunity? The point can at least be raised, and I suspect that there may be competent conciliar theologians ready to defend it.

However, is the question raised by common generic confessions merely one of conciliar interpretation? It seems also to be a basic dogmatic question and not an easy one to answer. It can be submitted that we know very little about integrity. We know that there are situations when material integrity is not required. And we know in a negative way why this is so. But we do not know positively how there can be excuse from material integrity, what happens when there is, and what resubmission of the omitted sin really means and effects. I mean that we do not adequately understand why a generic confession of serious sin constitutes a sufficient sacramental sign in some instances but not in others. We shall only begin to understand this when we understand why integrity is required at all. That is the root problem.

[52] This is also the point of view of G. Rossino in "Verso una confessione communitaria," *Perfice munus* 42 (1967) 336–42.

For example, is integrity a preliminary but psychologically indispensable step for genuine contrition, as Schmaus proposed? Or was P. Charles, S.J., nearer the truth when he centered attention on the character of judicial pardon and insisted that it is not a mechanical act but a personal one demanding full knowledge of what one grants?[53] Some years ago Dumont contended that the demand of integrity must be elaborated out of an adequate understanding of *reconciliation* with the Church.[54] Reconciliation, if it is not to be mere amnesty, demands an opening of the sinner to the Church, and an active opening of the Church to the sinner.

Only when we understand better the relation of an integral confession of serious sin to the process of sacramental forgiveness will we adequately understand the meaning of excusation from integrity and the limits of excusation. And until we understand these better, we will not be in a position to say with security whether a rite of communal generic confession with later private submission of serious sin is in accord with the substance of Trent's teaching.

There are also many unresolved practical problems to public confession, especially the problem raised by Anciaux (pastoral structures). These problems we solve, it is true, by experiment and experience. But since a basic dogmatic question underlies these practical concerns, would it not be premature and imprudent at the very least if our conduct failed to conform to directives similar to those issued by the French and Canadian episcopates?[55] Both decreed that in any communal celebrations of penance, confession and absolution were to be given privately and individually.

CELIBACY

Pope Paul's Encyclical on celibacy (*Sacerdotalis caelibatus*) represents the most recent episode of a very important conversation within the Catholic community. This discussion has been at near intensity pitch for some years now. Before turning to the Encyclical, it would be well to summarize some of the more recent literature.

Tübingen's Alfons Auer has written as fine an exposition of the meaning of celibacy as I have seen.[56] The priest, Auer argues, shows forth Christ the mediator. This basic function of the priesthood is given an impressive clari-

---

[53] Cf. also P. J. Hamell, "Penance and Judgment," *Furrow* 18 (1967) 322–29.

[54] C. Dumont, S.J., "La réconciliation avec l'église et la nécessité de l'aveu sacramentel," *Nouvelle revue théologique* 81 (1959) 577–97.

[55] For the statement of the French bishops, cf. *Documentation catholique* 64 (1967) 665–66; for that of the Canadian bishops, cf. *ibid.*, col. 286–87.

[56] A. Auer, "The Meaning of Celibacy," *Furrow* 18 (1966) 299–321. This is a translation of Auer's *Vom Sinn des Zölibates*.

fication by priestly celibacy. Indeed, "the celibate state of the priest can have its meaning and foundation nowhere else than in the signification and representation of Christ the mediator." The ministry of Christ the mediator is present in the triple ministry (priestly, teaching, and pastoral) of the Church. Auer discusses at length and with insight how this threefold ministry of Christ and the Church is signified and represented in a special way through the celibate state of the priest. He grants that this analysis leads only to the high suitability of a celibate priesthood. But he does state "that it seems to us that the reasons in favor of celibacy possess a clear if not absolutely overwhelming preponderance."

At the last session of the Council Bishop Alfred Ancel, auxiliary bishop of Lyons, presented a rather thorough review of the celibacy question to the bishops of Brazil and other countries.[57] However, since that time he has developed his ideas in *La croix*.[58] This latter presentation seems to represent his more mature and definitive thought.

Of the many excellent points made by Ancel, one stands out: the question of freedom and its implications. "Either the commitment to celibacy is free, or it is worthless." This freedom can mean either of two things. It can mean that a man wants the priesthood freely and with the greatest possible awareness, but only resigns himself to celibacy as a condition. Or it can mean that one wants with the same eagerness and liberty both celibacy and the priesthood. Ancel confesses that he believed that only a commitment of this second type existed; but experience has taught him differently. Therefore, he insists on stating the meaning of commitment to celibacy without equivocation.

If the hierachical authority, after having maturely reflected, thinks that it is more valuable for the fulfillment of the Church's mission that there be only celibate priests, it can decide thus, not in imposing celibacy on men who do not truly will it, but in choosing to be priests only men who, freely and in complete lucidity, directly will celibacy.

Now the law of celibacy does not mean that celibacy will be imposed on men who do not will it, who would only resign themselves to it. . .in order to be able to be priests. It means only those men will be accepted for the priesthood who desire, at the same time and in a completely free manner, to commit themselves to celibacy and keep it voluntarily.[59]

G. Griesl summarizes the minutes of a committee of experts of *Das Institut für Europäische Priesterhilfe*.[60] The group first outlined the reasons for the

[57] A. Ancel, "Le célibat sacerdotal," *Documentation catholique* 64 (1967) 727–50.
[58] Cf. *Pastoral Life* 15 (1967) 389–97.   [59] *Ibid.*, p. 391.
[60] G. Griesl, "Priesterberuf und personale Reife," *Theologie der Gegenwart* 10 (1967) 27–31.

appropriateness of the celibacy of the diocesan clergy, then the reasons for a change in law. Admitting that the Church has always regarded the relationship between ministry and celibacy as relative, Griesl details five reasons which might suggest change. Two of them stand out. First, the obligatory general connection between priestly office and celibacy actually can easily hide the charismatic character of celibacy. Secondly, a genuine personal decision or choice of celibacy might be better protected where celibacy is optional. Furthermore, such an option would actually increase the valuation of the celibate form of life, which loses some of its brilliance because it is imposed by law.

However, Griesl's group found great difficulties in any immediate change in law. Most problematic in their estimate would be the change in pastoral structures which is a presupposition for a change in law. A sudden change of law would make the already neglected care of priestly maturity even worse and give rise to problems among married priests far more tragic than those found among celibates. An appropriate transition would be experiment with a married diaconate. The heart of the problem, however, remains priestly maturity. This problem would not be lessened by a change in law.

Karl Rahner's most recent contribution adopts the literary form of a letter to a fellow priest.[61] The letter is impassioned, highly personal, and in places represents some of the strongest writing in the Rahnerian corpus. Rahner's remarks deal not so much with the possibility of a married priesthood as with the priest who is now a celibate. The priest's celibacy is not simply a barrier the Church has imposed. It is, under the grace of God, a free moral choice, a profound personal commitment. Celibacy represents a genuinely possible Christian existence only for those who will and choose it. Because we look too often to the future of Church law—hoping for a change—we reveal the fact that we have regarded celibacy, and perhaps lived it, more as an external conformism to an ecclesiastical injunction than as a personal choice. Thus the contemporary priest who discusses celibacy must distinguish celibacy in general from "my celibacy." The answer to the general abstract question is no answer to the individual's question. And the individual's question can be clarified only in conversation with God, by petitions for grace before the Crucified, and by a prayerful fight for preparedness to accept the folly of the cross.

Disowning the mantle of prophecy, Rahner makes four declarations of opinion. (1) He does not expect or wish that the Church will alter the discipline of celibacy for the Western rite. (2) The Church can and must im-

---

[61] K. Rahner, "Der Zölibat des Weltpriesters im heutigen Gespräch," *Geist und Leben* 40 (1967) 122–38.

prove the education of her seminarians to the meaning of celibacy. (3) She must be largehearted in her practice of dispensation. This is a matter of Church law only, and "Church law is not everything." (4) She can give the priesthood to married men. But ultimately Rahner is a strong voice for the appropriateness of a celibate ministry (we witness dramatically by our lives to what we proclaim). Of course, this witness can be given in other ways. But there can never be a true Christianity, he asserts, without a "no" to the obviousness of this world. Only the one who appreciates the radical nonconformity of Christianity will grasp the fact that this nonconformity must continually realize itself concretely.

Many of these same points are touched upon in other statements. Bernard Häring, for example, insists that priestly celibacy is a charism which has extraordinary value in our age of pansexualism.[62] Should those who definitively reject their celibacy be allowed to return to the active priesthood? Häring gives the same negative answer given by Ancel. After having made a solemn promise in which they affirmed their knowledge of celibacy and their free acceptance of it, how could they proclaim the morality of covenant, which is a morality of fidelity? A priest is not only a functionary; he is a witness of that which is at the heart of his message.

Cardinal Leger stresses the point made by Rahner: the discussion of a married clergy cannot be the occasion for irresoluteness about one's own priestly engagement and commitment to celibacy.[63] One looks back only to deepen his promise and to grasp its meaning more fully. Hence priestly fidelity to celibacy is a choice demanding constant rediscovery and renewal.

Felix Cardegna, S.J., discusses religious celibacy and finds in it a thunderous witness-value.[64] People are puzzled or intrigued by it, and may even ridicule it. "But very few, if any, can be neutral about it. It bothers them. *We* bother them. And that's exactly as it should be. It's in these moments that the whole thing is working as it should. Our celibacy is doing just what it should be doing. It's troubling others; raising a question in their minds . . . . " Cardegna has some highly salutary remarks about the meaning of loneliness and prayer in the celibate's life.

Charles Davis suggested earlier that the question raised by the celibate would be much more striking and effective if it were joined with a genuine poverty. "An eschatological sign is unconvincing when its bearer is securely ensconced in material comfort, whether personal or communal."[65] Such comfort simply shifts the accent of celibacy to the negation of sex.

[62] B. Häring, "Le célibat sacerdotal," *Documentation catholique* 64 (1967) 863.
[63] Paul-Emile Leger, "Le célibat ecclésiastique," *ibid.*, col. 155–62.
[64] Felix Cardegna, S.J., "Religious Celibacy," *Sacred Heart Messenger* 102 (1967) 16–19.
[65] Charles Davis, "Empty and Poor for Christ," *America* 115 (1966) 419–20.

By far the most intriguing study of a married priesthood is that of R. J. Bunnik.[66] Bunnik argues that the legal obligation of celibacy is only legitimate if ecclesiastical authority can give convincing proof that this particular law is necessary or at least very useful. If this proof is not at hand, then such a law must be viewed as an unlawful attack on human freedom and at best doubtfully valid.[67] After reviewing Scripture, history, theology, and the practical arguments *ex convenientia*, Bunnik concludes that "they do not lead to a conclusion that the unmarried state is necessary or evidently useful." He concludes that since the arguments are of limited value, "no obligation can be based on them. Consequently it must be doubted that the law of celibacy has any right to exist . . . ."[68]

Bunnik next turns his attention to the law invalidating the marriage of the priest (can. 1072). The right to marry is natural; the law of celibacy is disciplinary, and dispensation from this disciplinary law is dependent on a superior. But "it is extremely difficult to imagine that somebody's natural right to marry can be completely taken over by somebody else and can be made irrecoverable by a human law."[69] He concludes that the law, as unjustifiably impairing human freedom, represents an overstepping of competence on the Church's part, hence is an invalid law.

This very interesting article represents a rather radical challenge to existing discipline. But in my opinion it demands several important qualifications.

First, it is very misleading to state that the Church's present discipline, by demanding celibacy as a condition for ordination, represents a "disciplinary institution of charismata" or "creates or imposes charismata." Rather, the discipline insists that only those who have received this gift or charism should be allowed to take orders. This is not to "create" or "institute" charismata, and such journalese can only muddy the discussion. Indeed, it has muddied Bunnik's presentation at a critical point; for it leads him to distinguish the gift of virginity and the unmarried state in such a way that present Church law is read as imposing celibacy *even without the existence of the gift of celibacy.* Thus he concludes that "at present a candidate for the ecclesiastical ministry remains unmarried by virtue of legal prescript." Such a candidate "accepts a permanently unmarried condition only by virtue of

[66] R. J. Bunnik, "The Question of Married Priests," *Cross Currents* 15 (1965) 407–31; 16 (1966) 81-112. The article contains an excellent bibliography of the work done prior to 1965 and an appendix of selected citations from prominent churchmen on the matter of celibacy.

[67] This seems also to be the position of Hans Küng; cf. *National Catholic Reporter*, July 12, 1967, p. 5.

[68] *Art. cit.,* p. 97.   [69] *Ibid.,* p. 102.

legal obligation—unless he has personally received the gift of virginity beforehand."[70] Strictly speaking, of course, this latter is a true statement of what can happen; but it is not a true statement of the meaning of the law.

Existing discipline must be read as demanding that only those who receive the gift of virginity should accept ordination and be accepted for it. Clearly this supposes that the gift of virginity will be generously offered by the Spirit. It also supposes that this divine invitation will be accepted and embraced personally. A priestly celibacy which is not personally received and nurtured into a chosen state quickly sinks to a very tragic and dangerous externalism. Bunnik admits this when he notes that "only the person who can fully see this decision as a personal choice will be able to bring this great task to a happy conclusion."[71] Obviously, then, such a personal choice or commitment is the only state of affairs Church law could reasonably envisage. Hence Bunnik's statements that the "secular minister is unmarried, not on the strength of a charismatic vocation, but on the strength of the ecclesiastical institution" and "celibacy is not a free choice in itself, but the inevitable consequence of a free choice of something else" are caricatures of the sense of the law, as Ancel has noted.

It may factually be true that some priests, perhaps even more than some, have not really chosen their celibacy, but are only grittily grinning and bearing it as part of a package deal. One can only say that such tolerated celibacy remains a bad choice and is certainly not the situation envisaged in the Encyclical *Sacerdotalis caelibatus* and the discipline it reiterates.

Secondly, when Bunnik sets about to seek proofs for the usefulness of the existing law, he is therefore seeking proofs for a law which he reads as imposing celibacy on the majority of diocesan priests *even when the gift of virginity is not present*. This is tantamount to searching for the nutritious value of food I have already described as poison. Very few proofs are needed to disown such a law from the outset. Its interment would be tearless; for it is a law perpetuating a nonvalue, even a harmful existence. But Bunnik understands celibacy in this way, and since he does, one would expect his judgment of the values associated with a celibate ministry to be less than enthusiastic.

Be this as it may, it is the usefulness of the law properly understood which he should be attempting to assess. And this is assuredly a thoroughly legitimate question. When Bunnik seeks to weigh this usefulness, he naturally turns to the relationship between celibacy and ministry. No one contends that this relationship is necessary and Bunnik expressly concedes this. However, he seems to demand that celibacy be in a necessary relationship to

---

[70] *Ibid.*, p. 425.　　[71] *Ibid.*, p. 97.

ministry before it can be prescribed; for when he faces the possibility (which is the actual state of affairs) that the Church wants the prospective priest to choose both ministry and celibacy, he remarks that this is "beating around the bush, because it is still based on the supposition that *ministry and celibacy are necessarily connected.*"[72]

By no means. It is based only on the supposition that this connection is highly suitable and highly effective, and therefore is considered to incarnate a great value. It need not be a necessary good to be prescribed as obligatory—unless Bunnik would want to challenge the validity of all laws which do not impose a necessary good.[73] It need only represent a genuine value. In human affairs, of course, the choice and preservation of one value often mean the loss of others. The choice of general celibacy will certainly mean the sacrifice of other values (e.g., the witness of a married priesthood;[74] the presence of perhaps many highly qualified men in the ministry). Whether the present law is desirable depends on whether the over-all effectiveness of the general celibate witness properly compensates for these losses. This is the question we should be asking.

However, making this assessment is extremely difficult. One would suspect that in this area we are more than ever liable to the inducements of an unrecognized utilitarianism. Celibacy participates in the mystery of Christ and in the folly of the cross in a way which at least partially resists analysis by theological argument and counterargument. Furthermore, as a form of witness, its effects are in the spiritual order and impervious to the type of empiricism we cling to so ardently. Does this not mean that the full value of celibacy is terribly hard to come by? Does it not therefore mean that a

[72] *Ibid.*, p. 100.

[73] Perhaps he does wish to challenge such laws. At one point (p. 97) he states that "possibility, legitimacy, or usefulness have become necessity and obligation." Bunnik would seem to imply that necessity (by law) can only legitimately exist where necessity has existed before law. It is precisely this concept of law which one can challenge. The ordinary process of law is that a useful means (among several useful alternatives) has by reasonable determination of legitimate authority become law—hence necessary or obligatory. A useful (in itself) means does not become a necessary (in itself) means by legal prescription. A useful means first becomes law and then it becomes necessary—but in a totally different sense. It becomes morally necessary for those under the law. That is the way it is with law.

[74] I cannot agree with John A. O'Brien when he writes that "perhaps the major consideration which should prompt a re-examination of the celibacy requirement is the profound and far-reaching change which has occurred in recent years in the Church's thinking concerning marriage and specifically the conjugal act" ("Celibacy: Compulsory or Optional?" *Pastoral Life* 15 [1967] 398–410, at p. 408). The impression too easily left by this article is that we now give up marriage because it was thought in the past to be merely a concession to human lust and frailty. It is precisely when marriage appears in all its Christian splendor that celibacy makes its best sense.

judgment of the obsoleteness of a law requiring universal celibacy would be a very harrowing undertaking?

I would not conclude from this that a conclusion of obsoleteness can never be drawn, or that it will not become clear one day that a celibate priesthood is a luxury we cannot afford. This is a possibility and we must remain open to it. I mean rather that there are value-factors about celibacy and a generally celibate priesthood which run rather deep. It is deceptively easy to be triggerhappy when discussing the usefulness or uselessness of a law which, drawing on these value-factors, prescribes celibacy for all priests.

These are but a few examples of the writing which preceded Pope Paul's Encyclical *Sacerdotalis caelibatus*.[75] The timeliness of the Encyclical has been challenged,[76] and not without some reason. Without attempting a thorough analysis of the Encyclical, I should like to list six key affirmations around which it develops.

1) The gift of a priestly vocation and the gift of celibacy are distinct (n. 15). This point had been made by nearly all the literature prior to the Encyclical. Indeed, as Rahner notes, if the Church cannot recruit enough priests in general or in certain areas, she *must* renounce the demand of celibacy; for the duty to provide a sufficiency of pastoral care takes precedence over the legitimate desire that this care be witnessed to by the celibate commitment. However, even though a vocation to ministry and the gift of celibacy are distinct, a vocation is not definitive or operative, the Pope insists, without being tested and accepted by those who bear responsibility for the community.

2) Pope Paul constantly refers to celibacy as "suitable" (n. 18), "fitting" (n. 31), "appropriate" (n. 40), "helpful" (n. 44). In other words, the Encyclical is making no attempt to view celibacy as essentially or necessarily connected with the ministry. The eminent suitability of celibacy is based on its Christological, ecclesiological, and eschatological significance.

3) Celibacy is repeatedly referred to as a gift (nn. 34, 44, 60, 62, 63, 81), even a "very special gift" (n. 44) and one that we can only prepare for (n. 63). The Encyclical disowns any notion that the legislative arm of the Church can bring into being by fiat either the invitation to celibacy or the profound personal response of acceptance. But even though celibacy is a gift, Pope Paul asserts what the Council affirmed: his confidence that the Father will liberally grant this gift if the whole Church humbly and perseveringly begs for it.

[75] The citations used here are from the version issued by the United States Catholic Conference. The numbers refer to paragraph numbers.
[76] For example, cf. *National Catholic Reporter*, June 28, 1967.

4) Celibacy is a gift, but it must be personally chosen. For example, the Encyclical states that "in virtue of such a gift, corroborated by canon law, the individual is called to respond with free judgement and total dedication . . ." (n. 62). Again later Pope Paul refers to celibacy as a man's "total gift of himself" and adds: "The obligation of celibacy, which the Church adds as an objective condition to Holy Orders, becomes the candidate's own accepted personal obligation under the influence of divine grace" (n. 72). The Pope refers to existing discipline as "the law requiring a freely chosen and perpetual celibacy . . ." (n. 42). From these statements it is clear how unfortunate it is to refer to the celibacy of the diocesan clergy as based "not on the strength of a charismatic vocation, but on the strength of the ecclesiastical institution" (Bunnik). Celibacy by ecclesiastical discipline and celibacy by charismatic vocation are not mutually exclusive. The Church, it is true, cannot create charisms by law; she can, however, demand in her discipline (as long as it is fitting) that only those who feel charismatically called to celibacy present themselves for priestly ordination.

5) There is some indication in the Encyclical that the inchoate priestly or ministerial call and the call to consecrated virginity are not only distinct but quite definitely temporally separable. Thus candidates for the priesthood do not necessarily have the call to celibacy as yet. Indeed, the Encyclical is careful to insist that seminary education be such that it is favorable to the reception of this gift.[77]

6) Pope Paul acknowledged the fact that married ministers from other confessions have been and will continue to be admitted to the priesthood in special instances. This fact, however, must "not be interpreted as a prelude to its [celibacy] abolition" (n. 43).

The question of a married priesthood will almost certainly continue to be a touchy and controversial issue in the Catholic community. It concerns the intimate lives of individuals in a profound way, touches the public life of the Church, and has implications for some of the deepest ecumenical aspirations of the People of God. The issue is certainly not closed with the issuance of *Sacerdotalis caelibatus*, simply because discipline of its very nature invites

[77] For recent discussions of problems relating to priestly training, maturity, and celibacy, cf. C. W. Baars, M.D., "Love, Sexuality, and Celibacy," in *Sex, Love, and the Life of the Spirit* (Chicago: Priory Press, 1966) pp. 56–81; B. Gardey, O.P., "Conditions nouvelles d'un célibat permanent," *Vie spirituelle, Supplément*, Sept., 1966, 435–59; J. B. Rosenbaum, "A Psychoanalyst's Case for Celibacy," *Catholic World* 205 (1967) 107–10; F. D. MacPeck, S.J., "On the Significance of Celibacy," *Pastoral Life* 15 (1967) 209–16; E. Kennedy, "A Quiet Catholic Question," *America* 116 (1967) 147–48; F. J. Kobler, J. V. Rizzo, and E. Doyle, "Dating and the Formation of Religious," *Journal of Religion and Health* 6 (1967) 137–47; *Vie spirituelle, Supplément*, Feb., 1967, pp. 22–175.

constant re-examination. Such questions can be considered closed only at the terrible price of stagnation. Hence respectful and responsible discussion of these questions is a desideratum even after the Encyclical—but hardly without a thorough knowledge of the document.

To remain truly responsible,[78] it would seem that such discussion should not obscure, and hence undermine, the fact that ordained priests do *presumably* have a charism, and that *presumably* they have personalized this by deliberate choice, and that therefore they have a factual commitment in the moral order. This presumption can, of course, yield to the facts. If some priests have not assumed their celibacy by deliberate internal choice, or are incapable of doing so, their situation is indeed anomalous. It is that of one destined to wait out his days in a spiritually sterile and sclerotic bachelorhood. Such "reluctant" celibates, whether still active in the ministry or not, deserve the full compassion and charitable understanding of the Christian community. Something can and should be done for them in the juridical order. I am suggesting that they should be allowed to marry, or that their previous attempt to marry be recognized in the juridical order. This would not compromise a commitment. It would simply recognize juridically that there never was one. Juridical provisions, if they are in a balanced and healthy condition, attempt to conform to moral realities—to educate to them, to support them, and to recognize their limits. Or, as Cardinal Leger notes, "there are backward movements which are not infidelities, and the Church herself is today more understanding and more solicitous to correct these erroneous choices."[79]

OF WARS AND DRAFTS

In the literature touching war, two moral issues have received intensified attention. On one of them (selective conscientious objection) there is growing unanimity; on the other (the moral aspects of the war in Vietnam) there is deepening disagreement. A bit about each.

Recent Selective Service statutes establish three criteria to determine eligibility for the status of conscientious objector. (1) The objection must be based on religious training and belief. (2) It must be conscientious, i.e., sincerely held as binding in conscience. (3) The objection must be against all wars or war in any form. In *United States* v. *Seeger* (1965) the Supreme Court interpreted the first criterion as satisfied by "a given belief that is

[78] One is disappointed that a great weekly could not state its forthright disagreement with the decision of the Encyclical without betraying, in its choice of title, a sniggering arrogance; cf. "Bachelor Psychosis," *Commonweal* 86 (1967) 436.

[79] Cf. n. 63 above.

sincere and meaningful [and] occupies a place in the life of its possessor parallel to that filled by the orthodox belief in God of one who clearly qualifies for the exemption." In other words, the Court broadened the functional definition of religion to include Seeger's agnosticism and love of humanity. Subsequent decisions, therefore, granted conscientious-objection status to those opposed to all wars on religious or humanitarian grounds.[80]

In a helpful review article[81] Lawrence Minear studies the history of conscientious objection and concludes that since the last three centuries manifest a growing sensitivity to the complexities of conscience, our next logical step is, among other things, to provide protection to the conscience of the religious-humanitarian objector to a particular war—that is, to the selective conscientious objector.

It is precisely this position which has gained increasing support from theologians and religious leaders over the past few years. Paul Ramsey espoused it back in 1961.[82] In May, 1966, the 178th General Assembly of the United Presbyterian Church, U.S.A., urged Congress to examine proposals dealing with "those who cannot conscientiously serve in a particular war." The General Board of the National Council of Churches recommended on Feb. 23, 1967, the extension of present provisions "for those who are conscientiously opposed to a particular war, declared or undeclared." In April, 1967, the Methodist Board of Social Concerns also asked for statutory protection for the selective objector.

In several places Union Theological's Roger L. Shinn gathers these and similar statements and argues the case of selective conscientious objection.[83] The case rests basically on the fact that Christian tradition, in distinguishing just and unjust wars, has "put upon its people the moral burden of distinguishing between the justifiable and the unjustifiable war." It is true that many will conclude that the wars of their own country are righteous. But should all get locked into this majority judgment? "The rest of us must say that men of conscience have a right and responsibility to make moral decisions that may differ from those of the government." This is the heart of the issue, I should think.

Shinn agrees, of course, that it is impossible to go "all the way down" any road, whether it be the road of unlimited individual freedom or unlimited government. On some issues, he says, it is reasonable to let society have its

[80] For a scathing criticism of the theology involved in present provisions, cf. Michael Novak, "Draft Board Theology," *Commonweal* 86 (1967) 467–68.

[81] Lawrence Minear, "Conscience and the Draft," *Theology Today* 23 (1966) 60–72.

[82] Paul Ramsey, *War and the Christian Conscience* (Durham, N.C.: Duke Univ., 1961).

[83] Roger L. Shinn, "The Selective Conscientious Objector Again," *Christianity and Crisis* 27 (1967) 61–63; also *Testimony on Selective Conscientious Objection* (New York: Council for Christian Social Action, 1967).

way. Shinn does not explain where one draws the line, and it is precisely here that some opponents of selective conscientious objection have balked. Perhaps we can put the matter as follows. Can a line be drawn once selective conscientious objection is recognized by law? In other words, would not young men begin to take selective stances with respect to other laws (e.g., tax laws)? If conscience should be operative vis-à-vis all laws, would not the government have to respect conscientious objection in all cases?

Hardly. There is a rather sharp distinction between a tax law, for example, and draft laws which could involve one in killing. Contributing to a war by my taxes is one thing; killing in a war is another. The difference is that between more or less remote co-operation toward and direct participation in. Just as the common good strongly suggests that the government respect sincere selective conscientious objection to a particular war, so it is the same common good which will strongly suggest to the individual that rights in society (here legal protection of conscience claims) must be limited. A government can respect every conscience claim against any law only at the price of its own disappearance. The community consensus has affirmed in the past the reasonableness of a limitation on rights. I believe it will continue to do so. Hence it will admit the reasonableness of a distinction between more or less remote forms of co-operation in a cause one regards as unjust, and direct participation in this cause. And even if certain individuals fail to honor this distinction, serious thinkers and more sensitive citizens will, precisely because it is necessary for the preservation of that social stability which alone guarantees any freedom.

Recently John M. Swomley, Jr.,[84] and Harvey Cox[85] have supported the basic position of Shinn. Cox notes that protecting the selective conscientious objector "would conform to the fact that conscience seldom operates in the categorical way the law now requires but responds to different situations with different levels of moral approval or disapproval."

In November, 1966, the National Conference of Catholic Bishops emphasized the place of personal responsibility in decisions about war.[86] While the Catholic bishops took no explicit position on selective conscientious objection, they espoused the principle on which it rests. "No one is free to evade his personal responsibility by leaving it entirely to others to make moral judgments."

Vatican II's endorsement of laws which "make humane provisions for the

[84] John M. Swomley, Jr., "Conscience and the Draft," *Christian Century* 84 (1967) 833–35.

[85] Harvey Cox, "Reappraising the Draft," *Christianity and Crisis* 27 (1967) 73–74.

[86] "Statements of the National Conference of Catholic Bishops," *Catholic Mind* 65 (1967) 55–64, at p. 62.

case of those who for reasons of conscience refuse to bear arms" is probably too general to apply clearly to the selective conscientious objector. However, its teaching clearly supposes personal moral decision and responsibility. After condemning actions designed for the methodical extermination of an entire people, it stated that these actions, "as well as orders commanding such actions, are criminal. Blind obedience cannot excuse those who yield to them . . . . The courage of those who openly and fearlessly resist men who issue such commands merits supreme commendation."[87] To state that blind obedience is unacceptable and cannot excuse those who yield to immoral orders is clearly to imply the necessity of personal responsible decision in one's actions. The Council was saying unequivocally that no one may turn his conscience over to the state.

It was against such a background of mounting unanimity that the President's National Advisory Commission on Selective Service (Marshall Commission) made its report to the President in February, 1967.[88] During the deliberations of the Commission, two proposals were submitted to its membership for consideration. The first argued that the Selective Service Act be amended to eliminate the requirement that conscientious objection must be lodged against war in all forms. The second proposal suggested that the conscientious objector to a particular war should be excused from combatant service, but should be required to serve in a noncombatant military capacity under conditions of hardship, and even hazard, for a period perhaps even longer than the combatant.

It is not hard to believe that the first proposal was drafted under the guidance of the late John Courtney Murray, S.J. It reflects both his reasoning and his happy precision of formulation.[89] The proposal was structured on three assertions. First, the present statute incorporates the moral position of absolute pacifism. However, such a view does not represent the moral consensus of the American people. Hence, even though such a position should continue to be honored in a revised Selective Service Act, it should not be accorded its present position of privilege. Secondly, the classical doctrine on war holds that not all uses of military force are inherently immoral. A war may be just; it may also be unjust. Thirdly, though it is true that the decision to make war is the prerogative of duly established government and its decision founds for the citizen a presumption in favor of the legiti-

[87] *The Documents of Vatican II*, p. 292.
[88] *Who Serves When Not All Serve?* Report of the National Advisory Commission on Selective Service (Government Printing Office, 1967) pp. 48–51.
[89] J. C. Murray, S.J., *We Hold These Truths* (New York: Sheed & Ward, 1960) pp. 249–73.

macy of the war, "the citizen still is personally responsible for his own moral judgments on matters of public policy. He may not abdicate his own conscience into the hands of government. In making his moral judgment on the legitimacy of war he must assess the political and military factors in the case, but the judgment itself is to be a moral judgment."[90]

It is this principle which has led an increasing number of responsible spokesmen to speak in favor of selective conscientious objection. It is most unfortunate, therefore, that the Marshall Commission's majority report recommended against statutory recognition of selective pacifism. In doing so, it failed to deal realistically with the need and sanctity of personal responsibility. Its reasoning was even more unfortunate:

A determination of the justness or unjustness of any war could only be made within the context of that war itself. Forcing upon the individual the necessity of making that distinction—which would be the practical effect of taking away the Government's obligation of making it for him—could put a burden heretofore unknown on the man in uniform and even on the brink of combat, with results that could be disastrous to him, to his unit, and to the entire military tradition.[91]

Commonweal bitterly editorialized (and rightly, I believe) that "in a matter-of-fact tone and with virtually no dissimulation of language, the Marshall Commission simply says that individual moral responsibility is a threat to the nation."[92] It should not be too surprising, therefore, that the subsequent Military Selective Service Act of 1967 will satisfy no one. As *America* noted,[93] it not only perpetuates the injustices of former legislation, but eliminates the clause which allowed the Supreme Court in *U.S.* v. *Seeger* to broaden the definition of the religious conscientious objector to all wars.

The case for statutory protection of selective conscientious objection is, I believe, very strong. To a nation which has drawn so much of its vigor and creativity from freedom of conscience it should appear almost unassailable. Obviously, execution of such humane provisions would involve a mountain of practical difficulties. But these practical headaches, when weighed against the inescapable importance of personal moral responsibility, should operate merely as a challenge to American pragmatism and optimism. The Nuremberg trials indicate clearly that we expect individuals to exercise this responsibility. Vatican II indicates the very same thing. A nation that expects and honors personal responsibility in the face of commands which led to Nuremberg should recognize that it can do so consistently only if it expects

[90] *Op. cit.*, p. 49.   [91] *Ibid.*, pp. 50–51.
[92] "The Draft and Conscience," *Commonweal* 86 (1967) 139–41. Swomley criticizes the majority recommendation on other grounds; cf. *Christian Century* 84 (1967) 465–68.
[93] "The Selective Conscientious Objector," *America* 117 (1967) 73.

and honors personal responsibility in those choices which can lead to such ultimate instances. Or again, one who does not honor conscience claims about the morality of a particular war is a bit inconsistent in appealing to these claims when they touch the morality of acts within a particular war.

Since, therefore, personal responsibility is a requisite at all times, the government should do everything possible to give statutory recognition to conscience convictions. In doing so, it is not only supporting and educating to personal dignity, but serving its own best interest; for a government which penalizes sincere conscience objection to a particular war—as our government currently does—is one which is in principle penalizing the only court of appeal against commands such as those which led to Nuremberg. History shows how unenlightened and self-destructive this is. It is axiomatic that a parent who treats a child like a puppet is training a monster. It is altogether proper, therefore, that we continue to urge two points: (1) the individual's personal moral responsibility where participation in war is concerned;[94] (2) legal protection of conscience judgments representing the sincere exercise of this responsibility.[95]

When individuals exercise their personal responsibility by attempting moral judgments on the war in Vietnam, there is not nearly the unanimity that there is about the legal respect due to such judgments. The moral judgment of a particular war will bear on two aspects of that war: (1) the justice of the nation's cause; (2) the measure and manner of the force used. Both of these aspects elicit disagreement. Space permits only an example or two.

The justice of the cause. Philip Wogaman points out that the essence of traditional just-war doctrine, as a marginal morality in a sinful world, is that the presumption of the Christian must be against, not for, every particular war.[96] He centers his own attention on the condition that the war must be declared and waged by a duly constituted, or legitimate, authority. It is precisely here, he contends, that American intervention in Vietnam is wanting in moral legitimacy.

Wogaman presents several reasons for his conclusion. First, the origins of guerilla conflict trace back to popular revolution against the essentially irresponsible French rule in Indochina. The present government, with which we are aligned, is a lineal descendant of French rule, of an imposed rule.[97]

---

[94] For an extremely interesting and helpful list of questions aimed at a moral assessment of Vietnam, cf. *Ave Maria* 105 (1967) 6–15.

[95] For educational efforts to acquaint students with their right to conscientious objection, cf. " 'No' to the Draft," *Christian Century* 84 (1967) 715–16.

[96] Philip Wogaman, "Vietnam: A Moral Reassessment," *ibid.*, pp. 7–9.

[97] Gerhard A. Elston would also support this reasoning; cf. "Vietnam: Some Basic Considerations," *Catholic World* 205 (1967) 78–82.

Secondly, the settlement of 1954 provided for popular elections in July, 1956. The United States was not a signatory of this agreement and concurred with the Diem regime in disregarding this arbitrament by ballot. Thirdly, subsequent regimes in South Vietnam have derived authority from *de facto* possession of power, not from the concurrence of the people. Finally, U.S. intervention has no basis of authority beyond that of its own judgment and the invitation of irresponsible South Vietnam regimes. Summarily: the U.S. imposition of power serves neither the manifest wishes of the people nor the manifest judgment of the majority of peoples of the world.

Contrarily, Quentin L. Quade argues that the legitimacy of American policy in Vietnam must be judged with constant reference to one's estimate of the stakes involved.[98] It is Quade's contention that Vietnam generates far wider ripples than is readily appreciated.[99] If the force threatening Vietnam is merely indigenous with no further repercussions, then it would be hard to justify U.S. presence. But if the force is more than indigenous, then there are greater values at stake and a larger significance to the anguishing situation.

What is the larger significance, what are the greater values at stake in Vietnam? Without accepting any automatic "domino theory," Quade contends that China has raised the stakes beyond the confines of Vietnam because she (and Russia) have consistently viewed Vietnam as a test case for wars of national liberation. If the U.S. had not intervened in Vietnam, it would have been confronted with comparable, perhaps even more ominous, choices at a later date.

Quade sees a pattern in Communist activity. Its expansionist ambitions toward Western Europe, Greece, and Turkey were not simply given up; they were frustrated. Similarly, China's aspirations in Taiwan and Korea were not just abandoned; they were first contained. Quade believes, therefore, that we must approach the wars of liberation, elaborated by Krushchev and Lin Piao, in light of the expansionist aspirations of contemporary Communism. There will be no successful wars of liberation if they are contained. Our containment-war involves, therefore, the many values inseparable from the frustration of expansionist aims.

These summaries inevitably blunt the subtlety and range of both articles. And obviously they hardly make all the points that can and should be made. But they indicate serious attempts by concerned citizens to bring moral judgment to bear on American policy.[100] From a reading of this type of

[98] Quentin L. Quade, "Vietnam: Is the Price Too High?" *America* 116 (1967) 805–9.

[99] William V. O'Brien would agree with this; cf. "Comments on the Vietnam Debate," *Catholic World* 205 (1967) 169–70.

[100] For the assessment of the American bishops, cf. *Catholic Mind* 65 (1967) 62–63; see also *America* 116 (1967) 32.

article—and they are countless—it must be clear that the justice of a nation's cause can only be assessed when one commands a rather thorough knowledge of contemporary history and political realities.

The measure and manner of the force used. Alan Walker refers to attacks on noncombatants and concludes that "on this ground alone the Vietnam conflict is immoral and unjust because of the vast civilian suffering it is causing."[101] Furthermore, the measure of force employed in Vietnam is altogether disproportionate. In a just war the gains of victory must exceed the evils visited by war. It is Walker's belief that the destruction of life and devastation of land infinitely outweigh any ends that could be attained by victory. "Thus before the bar of Christian judgment the Vietnam war stands condemned."

The University of Akron's D. Gareth Porter claims that our prosecution of the war is limited only if one defines limited war in terms of the political aims which the government has proclaimed.[102] The restraining limits have not touched the means used. The United States has undertaken a bombing policy "which assumes as its primary effect an ever-increasing level of death and destruction in residential areas." Since our professed aim is to "force them to move toward negotiations" (in the words of Secretary McNamara), then the bombing can hardly be limited to surgical strikes against military targets which hardly touch Hanoi's willingness to pursue the war in the south. The bombing "must deeply affect civilian life itself."

Peter L. Berger distinguishes between the ambiguity of political decisions and the clarity of the moral horror in Vietnam.[103] Our prosecution of the war is simply criminal because its methods involve the killing of large numbers of helpless people. "There is no justification for methods of warfare that are in themselves criminal. And if a war cannot be fought except with these methods, then this war must be stopped—regardless of political costs."

Harvey Cox's position on the use of force in Vietnam seems clear.[104] He compares Vietnam to the 1937 (April 27) bombing of the Basque capital of Guernica. At that time "the indiscriminate bombing of women and children worked a wave of revulsion and rage around the world." However, we use incomparably more bombs on Vietnam in one night than the Germans used in the entire Spanish operation. "But we are incapable of an appropriate measure of abhorrence."

[101] Alan Walker, "Vietnam: Reappraisal from Down Under," *Christian Century* 84 (1967) 835–36.

[102] D. Gareth Porter, "Is This a Limited War?" *Commonweal* 86 (1967) 9–11.

[103] Peter L. Berger, "A Conservative Reflection about Vietnam," *Christianity and Crisis* 27 (1967) 33–35.

[104] Harvey Cox, "Our Own Guernica," *Commonweal* 86 (1967) 164–65.

Michael Novak speaks of the bombing of children and scorns as any defense for civilian damage the idea that "you can't put a bomb in a barrel."[105] Jay Neugeboren refers to the "murderous fact of U.S. actions," "the horror which goes on every day in Vietnam," and calls for massive civil disobedience.[106]

On the other hand, Ernest W. Lefever of the Brookings Institution contends that the term "indiscriminate bombing" has been indiscriminately used.[107] Of the bombing in the north he states that "it is in fact the most discriminating bombing in the history of aerial warfare." The problem in the south is, he admits, totally different. There the Vietcong have used civilians, including women and children, as protective cover for their terror activities.

For this reason the Americans go to extraordinary measures (i.e., beyond anything in previous warfare) to protect civilians, including warning, safe conduct, resettlement, emergency relief, economic assistance, and medical care. These measures, undertaken for political and humanitarian reasons, often interfere with military efficiency and result in greater United States casualites. *No national army in history has operated under stricter rules of political self-restraint than the Americans in Vietnam.* Even so, there are, regretfully, thousands of civilian casualties.[108]

The main lines of Paul Ramsey's thought are known to those familiar with the literature on the morality of war. He has put his thought clearly and concisely in a recent summary.[109] Ramsey is convinced that liberal religious and academic spokesmen have been hurling around the terms "murder," "inherently immoral," and "indiscriminate" in a way which hardly reflects their ordinary precision of thought and language. A just-war theorist, Ramsey accepts as the cardinal principle governing just conduct in war the principle of discrimination—the moral immunity of noncombatants from deliberate direct attack. Noncombatancy, however, is always a function of the current organization of nations and forces for war.

In insurgency warfare as we know it, the guerilla chooses to fight between, behind, and over the peasants, women, and children. He lives among the people like fish in water. It is *he*, therefore, who has enlarged the extent of foreknowable but collateral civilian damage. He has brought his own population into range and the onus for this should not be shifted to counterin-

---

[105] Michael Novak, "Humphrey at Stanford," *Commonweal* 86 (1967) 7–8.

[106] Jay Neugeboren, "Disobedience Now!" *ibid.*, pp. 367–69.

[107] Ernest W. Lefever, "Vietnam: Joining the Issues," *Catholic World* 205 (1967) 72–77.

[108] *Ibid.*, p. 73. On this cf. the comments of General Earle G. Wheeler, *U.S. News and World Report* 62 (Feb. 27, 1967) 42–43.

[109] Paul Ramsey, "Is Vietnam a Just War?" *Dialogue* 6 (1967) 19–29.

surgency. Therefore, the application of the principle of discrimination in insurgency warfare cannot be settled by a body count. Ramsey repeats his conviction that "the main design of the counterinsurgency mounted in Vietnam need not be and likely *is* not an inherently evil or morally intolerable use of armed force."

Elsewhere he asserts that our bombing, by its main design, has been directed at raising the cost of infiltration.[110] Thus it is against the infiltration, against the combatancy as such. However, on March 10, 1967, there was an air raid over North Vietnam no longer describable in these terms. It was the bombing of the Thainguygen iron-and-steel complex. War products constituted only a small percentage of the plant's output. "This," Ramsey insists, "was a blow against North Vietnamese society and against the will of that country's rulers by striking its people's stake in their future economic development." He sees it as a large step up the slope leading to total war; for we were no longer involved in raising the cost *of the infiltration* (and thus in meeting the combatancy), but we were involved in raising the costs *to North Vietnam*. Once this becomes our criterion, we have made ourselves conditionally willing to do inherently immoral things (Hiroshima, Nagasaki, etc.) if raising the costs upon Hanoi requires it.

I believe that Ramsey's analysis of the Thainguygen bombing (whether it is factually correct or not) points up a factor very important for moral analysis: the *temptation* to involve civilians as targets. The Vietnam war has two major characteristics. First, it is drawn out, frustrating, and dirty. It is not, by and large, a war made up of major set-piece battles. Rather, its ingredients are snipers, booby traps, napalm, underground fortresses, rice paddies, mortar lobs, snakes, disease, and civilian treachery. Secondly, it is a war of containment where our overriding aim is to tighten the noose around the enemy and bring him to the conference table. This combination of characteristics means that there is the inbuilt temptation to work on the enemy's morale—and therefore on his civilians. This is not to say that this has often happened or will necessarily happen. It is simply to say that the temptation is there. It is all the more urgent, therefore, that our own moral categories be capable of distinguishing collateral civilian death from direct strikes on civilians.

Two things have struck the compositor of these notes as he reviewed the recent literature on the moral aspects of the Vietnamese war. Both have to do with the principle of discrimination in the use of force.

First, it is clear that the notion of "inherent evil," "intrinsic evil," is with

---

[110] Paul Ramsey, "Over the Slope to Total War?" *Catholic World* 205 (1967) 166–68.

us to stay—at least for the duration of the war.[111] The very ones who reject the category when dealing with theological methodology are the ones who cling to it when discussing Vietnam, especially when condemning the war on the grounds of civilian loss.

Secondly, the use of these terms is terribly loose. They are used interchangeably with "slaughter" and "atrocity," and generally translate to mean dead or maimed bodies, dislocated civilians, etc. To remain human and promotive of the values we treasure, our outrage and indignation at the effects of the use of military force must be structured upon the cardinal principle of discrimination. Otherwise, as Ramsey notes, our vocabulary (and our indignation) is exhausted and spent when a genuinely immoral use of military force does occur.

The essential distinction is that between direct and collateral damage in the use of force. Our judgments may differ as to the actualities—whether certain military strikes are directly visited upon civilians or not. But to allow our outrage to build without benefit of this basic distinction is to plant the seed of total warfare in our own attitudes; for to identify civilian casualties with direct civilian slaughter is reductively to identify any killing with murder. It is, in Ramsey's phrase, to identify tragedy with wickedness. Such a confusion of categories forces one either to adopt absolute pacifism or—since this is unacceptable to the vast majority of us in our sinful world—to support countersociety strikes and obliteration bombing when they are necessary.

It is precisely here that some religious and academic spokesmen do their own cause most harm. We all shudder at the suffering and death brought by war. We all want a quick and lasting peace in Vietnam. But to agree with some spokesmen in their flabby and imprecise expression of this desire is to renounce in principle any use of force that ends up with maimed civilians. If there is anything which approaches indiscriminate bombing, it is *indiscriminate* horror at the evils of war; for here we have the mentality which breeds total-war thinking. In principle, such thinking forces us to abandon our basic freedoms to no defense or to an immoral one. Since Christian tradition has refused to accept this narrowing of options, it must resist the mentality behind it, a mentality revealed and made public by indiscriminate indignation. That is why Wogaman is so utterly right when he says that the breakdown and seeming irrelevance of the just-war doctrine in times of war

[111] For a recent study of intrinsic evil, cf. Thomas Wassmer, S.J., "Is Intrinsic Evil a Viable Term?" *Chicago Studies* 5 (1966) 307–14.

is not due to the doctrine itself, but to "the disinclination of Christians to perfect and apply it."[112]

CONTRACEPTION

In reaction to the rather inconclusive remarks of *Populorum progressio*[113] on birth regulation, the *Christian Century* editorialized that "Pope Paul has his hand on the doorknob. Will he open the door?"[114] Perhaps a better question, or at least a more theological question, would be this: Is the door locked or unlocked? Robert H. Springer, S.J., suggested in this journal that it is not only unlocked but already half open.[115] That could well be the case. Even so, the literature on marriage in general and on contraception in particular has continued to follow its rather fertile old ways.[116] Here I shall mention only two points which have come up for discussion in the past semester: the documents of the Papal Commission and the address of Pope Paul of Oct. 29, 1966.

The documents of the Papal Commission[117] represent a rather full summary of two points of view. They incorporate most of the important things which have been said on the subject of contraception over the past three or four years, plus a few very interesting and important nuances. The majority report, particularly the analysis in its "rebuttal," strikes this reader as much the more satisfactory statement. Many theologians are convinced that only an *act* analysis can do justice to the tenets of Christian tradition and the findings of contemporary empirical studies. It is precisely such an act analysis that the majority report attempts to develop and it is this analysis

[112] *Art. cit.*, p. 8.

[113] *AAS* 59 (1967) 257–99. Cf. also *Documentation catholique* 64 (1967) 1027–33; B. Sorge, S.J., "Come leggere l'enciclica 'Populorum progressio,' " *Civiltà cattolica* 118 (1967) 209–23, at pp. 212–13.

[114] *Christian Century* 84 (1967) 460.

[115] Robert H. Springer, S.J., in THEOLOGICAL STUDIES 28 (1967) 327–30.

[116] Cf. M. Huftier, "Morale chrétienne et régulation des naissances," *Ami du clergé* 77 (1967) 193–208, 209–12; G. M. Sirilla, S.J., "Family Planning and the Rights of the Poor," *Catholic Lawyer* 13 (1967) 42–51; J. Dominian, "Vatican II and Marriage," *Clergy Review* 52 (1967) 19–35; D. Quartier, "De verantwoorde methoden van geboortenregeling," *Collationes Brugenses et Gandavenses* 63 (1967) 126–35; J. Villain, "Un rapport sur la régulation des naissances," *Etudes*, March, 1967, pp. 338–43; D. Hickey, "The 1966 Theological Problem," *Furrow* 18 (1967) 91–99; *Palestra del clero* 66 (1967) 544–48, 612–13; M. Dayez, "L'Etat et le planning familial," *Revue diocésaine de Tournai* 22 (1967) 80–95, 130–43; *Sal terrae* 55 (1967) whole issue; J. Rötzer, "Empfängnisregelung—nur eine Frage der Technik?" *Theologisch-praktische Quartalschrift* 115 (1967) 164–76; L. Berg, "Von Ehe und Familie," *Trierer theologische Zeitschrift* 76 (1967) 54–58.

[117] Cf. n. 16 above.

which provides its most interesting feature. In sketchy and impoverishing outline I would say that the report seems to build in the following way.

1) The morality of sexual expression in marriage must be concluded from the meaning of the action.

2) The meaning of the action is gathered not from the implications of an intact biological structure, but from the essential meanings of human sexuality. These meanings can be stated as follows: responsible and generous fecundity, expression of mutual union and love. These are two of the basic values of conjugal life.

3) If these values are properly realized in the individual act, the act has good moral quality or objective rectitude. They are so realized if (a) the action is a dignified expression of mutual self-giving; (b) there is responsible fertility in the whole conjugal life.

4) Therefore, in so far as procreation as a value specifies the individual act, it is the fertility of the whole married life which does so. That is, infertile acts receive one dimension of their meaning or moral specification not from their individual procreative aptitude, but from the procreativity of the marriage as such. This means that, in one sense, infertile acts are incomplete and constitute with fertile acts one moral choice. Therefore, they receive their full moral quality from the relation to the fertile act—basically because the love they individually express culminates in fertility.

5) Therefore, if the fertile act is irresponsibly excluded, other infertile acts derive a bad specification from this single irresponsible decision until it is rectified. Hence the enormous responsibility on parents to make their decisions about family size truly responsible Christian choices.

One could, I believe, summarize the analysis operative in the majority report in the following syllogism. Each act of sexual union is, in its external concreteness, an expression of marital love. But this love culminates in fertility, and therefore finds a basic meaning in fertility. Therefore, each act gets a moral quality or specification from this fertility (i.e., the choices which pursue it or exclude it).

Obviously, this analysis provokes a great number of questions. There is much more work to be done in this area. But these beginnings look very promising. Side by side with the increasingly patent inadequacy of an analysis rooted in the notion of *actus naturae*,[118] these beginnings could lead one to believe that the position espoused by the majority report should be regarded as intrinsically the more probable and acceptable opinion.

That brings us to the matter of pastoral practice. Does the state of affairs

---

[118] Cf. Louis Janssens, *Mariage et fécondité* (Paris: Duculot, 1967).

as we now (August, 1967) find it justify the conclusion that the Church's traditional teaching on contraception is a matter of practical doubt? The current sticking point is said to be the address of Pope Paul VI to the Italian Society of Obstetricians and Gynecologists (52nd National Congress, Oct. 29, 1966).[119] In that statement, it will be recalled, Pope Paul reminded his hearers that "the norm until now taught by the Church, integrated by the wise instructions of the Council, demands faithful and generous observance. It cannot be considered not binding, as if the magisterium of the Church were in a state of doubt at the present time, whereas it is in a moment of study and reflection concerning matters which have been put before it as worthy of the most attentive consideration."

It was this statement, together with preceding teaching, which led Nicholas Halligan, O.P., to conclude that there is no practical doubt on the matter of contraception.[120] "When ... authoritative pronouncement or authentic judgment has been made in matters related to faith or morals, this [doubt] can no longer obtain." It is obvious that Halligan regards the October statement as either an "authoritative pronouncement or authentic judgment."

John Noonan has taken up the question of the October statement and sensitively disowned several scabrous attacks on the Holy Father's intelligence and good faith.[121] Because of Noonan's prestige, his analysis of the current situation will be studied carefully. His position can be stated in two propositions. (1) The rules governing the conduct of Catholics are not in doubt. (2) There is a doubt as to whether these norms constitute divine law.

Unless I am mistaken, this position presents grave problems to the theologian, if not to the lawyer. The problem can be outlined as follows. Noonan has argued, in his magisterial tome on contraception, that the Church's proscription of contraception might be read as a practical rule in support of abiding values. When the rule no longer functions as a support, it can and should change.

The term "practical rule" is ambivalent. It can mean at least two different things. First, it can refer to a simple legal directive. In this sense it would pertain to what we know as a disciplinary prescription. Second, it can refer to a time-conditioned understanding of a divine-law demand. That is, it can enuntiate what the Church understands the divine law to demand *in these*

---

[119] For English versions cf. *American Ecclesiastical Review* 166 (1967) 136–40; *Catholic Mind* 65 (1967) 59–62.

[120] Nicholas Halligan, O.P., "Doubt or No Doubt—The Papal Question," *American Ecclesiastical Review* 166 (1967) 257–67.

[121] John Noonan, "The Pope's Conscience," *Commonweal* 85 (1967) 559–60.

circumstances. Noonan accepts this second sense as the proper meaning of "practical rule" when he treats of the history of the teaching on contraception.

Yet, when he confronts the present situation, he contends that the traditional norms still bind certainly and will continue to bind until the Pope says otherwise, *even though there is a doubt as to whether they represent divine law.* Could it be that Noonan has begun to regard his "practical rule" as a mere disciplinary ruling? I believe so. And here is where the theologian balks.

Theologians would contend that the precise obliging force of papal statements on contraception is their doctrinal force. That is, authoritative Church interventions on questions of natural law are educative in the moral order. This educative aspect is the basic source of their obligatory power. In other words, the Catholic recognizes in the magisterium a divine commission to teach, to enlighten consciences. Because of this divine commission and the promise of aid in its execution, authentic noninfallible Church interpretations of natural law enjoy the presumption of correctness, and it is this presumption which founds the duty in prudence to accept in a human way these teachings; for we are all bound to prudence in the formation of our consciences. The obligation is not the result of a legal directive.

It seems that if Noonan is going to hold that the moral duty to avoid contraception is certain even though the divine-law duty is doubtful, he must regard the source of obligation to be a legal directive of some kind. This is what is theologically difficult to admit.

Once it is shown, therefore, that there are intrinsic reasons (good and probable) why the Church may change her teaching on contraception, it would seem that the foundation for a certain obligation has ceased to exist— precisely because the obligation never derived in the first place from a legal directive, but from a teaching or doctrinal statement. If the teaching statement becomes doubtful, does not the obligation also? And if the pertinence of past norms to divine law is doubtful, is not the teaching statement doubtful?

But, it has been claimed, the address of Pope Paul VI on Oct. 29, 1966, repudiated the existence of a doubt. Verbally, yes. But a careful reading of this address (wherein the Pope said explicitly that he was not making his decisive statement on contraception) will lead one to the conclusion that it could not have been a doctrinal or teaching statement. Noonan admits this when he asserts that the Pope was actually admitting a "doubt as to the divine immutable character of the law."[122] Only an authentic teaching state-

---

[122] *Ibid.*, p. 560.

ment is capable of dissipating a genuine doctrinal doubt.[123] And that is why I would agree with the many theologians who contend that the matter of contraception is as of now, at least for situations of genuine conflict, just where it was before the papal address—in a state of practical doubt.[124]

[123] One could, of course, challenge the existence of a doubt prior to Pope Paul's 1966 address; but that has become a difficult thing to do.

[124] For example, cf. B. Häring, "Aber wir Beichtväter . . .!" *Theologie der Gegenwart* 10 (1967) 40–43, at p. 41; *Sal terrae* 55 (1967) 128.

CURRENT THEOLOGY: 1968

NOTES ON MORAL THEOLOGY: JANUARY–JUNE, 1968

OF SIN AND DEATH

Sin has been the subject of several recent studies. Kevin F. O'Shea, C.SS.R., offers a criticism of the "saying no to God" catechesis of sin as insufficiently realistic, historical, and communitarian to convey the insights of biblical revelation on sin.[1] In biblical terms sin is the exclusion by an individual of the new covenant in his life. Similarly sin (better, Sin) is a powerful virus which entered the world as a personified force. It is a beaten but still violent power working itself out in history.

This reality, O'Shea argues, is not a matter of a single act. "It takes a whole lifetime, including death, to commit this kind of sin. Only then could there be, in an absolute sense, a final covenant rupture with the God of New Testament grace; only then could there be a definitive expression of the historical virus of evil in the personal life of a particular man."[2]

Upon this principle O'Shea builds an analysis of the sins committed during one's lifetime. During life there is the possibility of a genuine self-realization of the person against the God of covenant, "not in the total sense which can only take place in death, but in a true relative sense." If this occurs, several possibilities exist. First, sometimes the sin-act performed will involve ("dynamically and infallibly") a further course of personal life in a sin-state which leads to death-in-sin and the final sin. This sin-act is *mortal* sin. Secondly, during life there can be a true rupture of covenant with God without involving this sin-dynamism or sin-course unto death. This is *serious* sin. In this instance the spiritual or moral climate or atmosphere in which the person is immersed inhibits the inner character of the position taken from assuming its true proportions in that person. Serious sin represents a true basic option but "without the involvement of a life drive as a result." In a sin which is serious but not mortal, O'Shea sees the psychology as that of a person who wants to take a radical position before God and does so, "but at the same time he does not want to be that kind of person for good and all." A similar distinction is drawn between venial and slight sin. In venial sin there is a permissive attitude to the possibility of a serious crisis situation; in slight sin there is not.

[1] Kevin F. O'Shea, C.SS.R., "The Reality of Sin: A Theological and Pastoral Critique," THEOLOGICAL STUDIES 29 (1968) 241–59.

[2] *Ibid.*, p. 247.

The emphasis in O'Shea's article is on the distinction between serious and mortal sin. His descriptions of various sin-states contain a good deal that is psychologically plausible. But before accepting the distinction between serious and mortal sin, one should weigh the theological implications carefully. Basic to the distinction is the "final-option theory" developed in the writings of Glorieux, Boros, Schoonenberg, Schmaus, and others.[3] This theory distinguishes mortal sin from sin-unto-death. Only in death, it is contended, is a man capable of a perfectly free self-determination wherein he accepts or rejects salvation definitively. If he rejects it, we have sin-unto-death. Other prior serious acts have both a provisional and a preparatory character. O'Shea accepts the fact that the decisive and total rupture of covenant can happen only "in the projected course of a human lifetime climaxing in the personal position taken in death." It is in light of this tenet that he can distinguish between serious sin and mortal sin. Therefore it is in light of this, too, that one must assess the acceptability of the distinction.

Bruno Schüller, S.J., in a tightly written article, raises several serious difficulties against the final-option theory.[4] We shall mention only two here. But before doing so, it must be recalled that basic to the final-option theory is the assertion that God must call all individuals without exception in death, since only in death is man capable of definitive self-disposition.

First, Schüller argues that the theory denies the grace of forgiveness. Where traditional teaching says that every mortal sin is *of itself* definitive and that it is provisional only in virtue of the free grace of divine forgiveness, the final-option theory says that every sin before death is *of itself* only provisional because it originates out of lesser insight and freedom than is required for definitive decision. Therefore the possibility remaining to the mortal sinner to convert is not seen in this theory as grounded in the forgiving grace of God, but in the imperfection of every free self-disposition of earthly man. This means that the final-option theory must render the grace of forgiveness superfluous. Why? Because looking at himself and his acts, the "mortal sinner" is certain in advance that he will have the opportunity to convert back to God. He is certain of this because he knows that he was able to dissociate himself only provisionally from God and therefore did so only provisionally. God, therefore, could dissociate Himself only provisionally from the sinner. Because the sinner's decision was not definitive, God simply must offer Himself again as salvation, not from grace but from

---

[3] Michael Schmaus, "Death as Fulfillment," *Continuum* 5 (1967) 483–88.

[4] Bruno Schüller, S.J., "Todsünde—Sünde zum Tod?" *Theologie und Philosophie* 42 (1967) 321–40.

justice. Summarily, the sin-unto-death as absolutely irrevocable is unforgivable; mortal sin prior to this, as not definitive, needs no forgiveness purely from grace.

Schüller urges the argument from a slightly different aspect. In the New Testament the grace of forgiveness is seen as that given against one's deserts. Forgiveness by grace means that a man has brought his salvation history to an end. He is (*von sich aus*) a definitively damned person, but God makes a radically new start. Forgiveness by grace is the conversion of the end into a radically new start. Therefore it can only become a reality after a genuine end has occurred. Since, therefore, the final-option theory denies to man the possibility of putting a real end to his history with God during earthly life, it implicitly denies that God needs to place any new beginning in His history with man. And this is to render forgiveness as we know it in the New Testament superfluous.

According to Schüller, then, mortal sin and sin-unto-death are, in so far as they depend on the sinner alone, irreparable and decisive. The qualitative difference between the two depends not on the sinner's self-disposition, but on a radically gratuitous act of God. To say otherwise, as the final-option theory must, is to attack this forgiveness.

Schüller's second argument is that the only-provisional-mortal-sin is really slight sin. The defenders of the final-option theory believe that mortal sins remain mortal sins even when man turns only "provisionally" from God in this life. Schüller denies this. Each act, he argues, receives its special character from that to which it turns (*actus specificatur ab objecto*). From the fact that in mortal sin man turns from God his last end we can conclude what kind of freedom must be present in mortal sin. Precisely because the last end is that which is sought before and in all, mortal sin can only be a turning from God as last end if man, in so far as it depends on him, totally and definitively engages himself in a free decision. But totality and definitiveness are precisely the qualities absent in any sin but the sin-unto-death in the final-option theory. Therefore these sins simply cannot be mortal.

A careful study of Schüller's article will give one great pause about the final-option theory. Because the distinction between mortal and serious sin suggested by O'Shea seems to depend on this theory, it would appear to represent theological haste to embrace the distinction without further study.[5]

[5] G. Higuera, S.J., concludes that the distinction between mortal and serious sin is in its theological infancy and needs much more work before it can be of pastoral use: *Sal terrae* 56 (1968) 132–39.

In an excellent piece of theological reflection, John W. Glaser, S.J., faces the problem of the apparently frequent transition from grace to sin, life to death.[6] He suspects that something is wrong with our categories of thought when we are led to regard this change as really frequent. Synthesizing recent writings on the basic option, Glaser indicates that there are several levels of freedom from which our acts can be performed. There is a more peripheral or superficial level which does not represent a total engagement of the person. This is the level of slight morality. But there is a core freedom where man acts out of the center of his being. It represents the area of grave morality. Since this use of freedom is a total and definitive disposition of self, it must have a considerable degree of stability. This excludes the possibility of frequent fluctuations between affirmation and negation. Hence when such a fluctuation does occur in the external order, it would seem that its source in the person would not be the core freedom, but the more peripheral level of freedom which constitutes the dimension of *moralitas levis*.

However, Glaser notes that this explanation does not totally solve the problem of fluctuation in the external order. For this fluctuation often occurs in an area of serious matter. Now serious matter is by definition that which can call forth the core freedom of man when he has knowledge of this seriousness. At this point and to answer this problem, Glaser analyzes more closely the nature of what we call in moral theology "matter." He argues that the object of man's freedom (the created medium in which God's offer of Himself to the individual realizes itself) is the individual himself in all his concreteness as God-given task. But this individual is a developing being. Glaser takes sexuality as an example of this development. Man moves through various sexual stages (infancy, latency, adolescent object-relationships, etc.) to maturity. Therefore sexuality is not present in the life of an individual in a univocal way. Even though in its mature stage man's sexuality is capable of being the medium of an ultimate call from God to the very core of the person, it does not follow that it is so at all stages. Just as sexuality develops, so too does its ability to be the medium of an ultimate call from God. This would mean "that a given dimension of man as nature—e.g., his sexuality—could move from being an amoral reality through various stages of intensifying *moralitas levis* to the point where it becomes *moralitas gravis*."[7]

Glaser concludes by returning to the common phenomenon of those who seriously try to live a good life and find themselves in a "habit of serious sin"

[6] John W. Glaser, S.J., "Transition between Grace and Sin: Fresh Perspectives," THEOLOGICAL STUDIES 29 (1968) 260–74.

[7] *Ibid.*, p. 270.

and who therefore "experience the utter gloom of sin and the sudden sunshine after confession—and this perhaps on a weekly basis." These people, he concludes, are experiencing two realities: (1) a genuine transition from sin to repentance on the level of *moralitas levis*; (2) a release from the sense of guilt (of superego origin) which does not represent a transition from serious sin to grace.

Glaser's essay, besides synthesizing and applying the best recent thought (Rahner, Metz, Schüller) on the nature of the moral act,[8] has some fine pastoral insights. A few points in the article would seem to merit comment.

First of all, Glaser has faced creatively the problem of what we call habitual sin. It should be fairly clear that he is thinking of phenomena like habitual adolescent masturbation. His suggested solution: the external fluctuations experienced by an adolescent do not reflect real transitions between grace and sin (i.e., no mortal sin), because they pertain to the area of slight morality, *moralitas levis*.

It should be noted that *moralitas levis* is of itself an ambiguous term. It can mean two things. First, it can mean that even though the matter is serious, the individual does not respond with a serious moral act. By and large, traditional theology has approached the problem of habitual sin in this way.[9] It has looked for and found reasons for seeing reduced imputability in the face of what it called serious matter. Secondly, *moralitas levis* can mean that the matter itself is calculated to evoke only a peripheral act of freedom. In this more objective sense it is slight matter. It is in this sense that Glaser would view certain instances of adolescent sexual expression. And he does so precisely on the grounds that man is a developing being whose sexuality does not present itself to him univocally throughout life. At certain developmental

[8] For further discussion on the basic option and some of its pastoral implications, cf. R. A. McComick, S.J., "The Moral Theology of Vatican II," in *The Future of Ethics and Moral Theology* (Chicago: Argus, 1968) pp. 7–18.

[9] Thus recently Giordano Kunicic, O.P., insists that any re-evaluation must occur only in terms of subjective responsibility and pastoral practice. He rightly insists on the objectivity of the moral order, but then proceeds to identify this with one understanding of the meaning and malice of self-stimulation. Cf. "Verso un ridimensionamento della gravità del peccato solitario?" *Perfice munus* 43 (1968) 222–29. F. M. Marchesi, S.J., also treats of subjective imputability only ("Su la gravità del peccato solitario," *Palestra del clero* 47 [1968] 513–16). He argues that there is a presumption that normal Christian youths in the Mediterranean environment do commit serious sin when they are involved in masturbation. Both articles take dead aim at some statements of Bernard Häring, whose occasional ineffabilities do indeed make an inviting target. But both articles strike this reviewer as a bit unrealistic.

stages it is not generally capable of being the medium of an ultimate encounter with God.[10]

This is a very interesting and possibly fruitful way in on the problem. Obviously a good deal of work remains to be done and many precisions need to be made.[11] It is important to note that behind Glaser's analysis is a different manner of determining the seriousness or slightness of matter. Traditionally the object of freedom has been presented as "something out there" which I choose. This immediately endows the object of choice with a good deal of immutability. Thus in traditional categories infant masturbation would have the same objective meaning, hence the same objective deordination, as masturbation in adulthood. It is not hard to suspect that something is wrong here. Recent writings, however, have seen the object of choice as the individual himself in all his concreteness and relationships.[12] I mention this here because such a shift in emphasis, without destroying the objectivity of morality, will have important consequences in assessing the meaning of human actions, and consequently their gravity, and not least of all in the area of ecclesiastical law.[13]

A second observation could be in place by way of completion of Glaser's remarks. He had suggested that a youngster is not sinning seriously in individual acts of habitual masturbation. He had argued this on the basis of the developing character of human sexuality. Here something should be added. Precisely because human sexuality—better, the human person as sexed—is evolutionary, it can be stagnated. Masturbatory activity and its causes can represent an influential factor in this arrest. A person's very

---

[10] For some up-to-date and thoroughly realistic comments on the subject of masturbation, cf. "Tercer coloquio de profesores de teología moral," *Sal terrae* 56 (1968) 48–59. There are several interesting remarks in this summary. First, methodologically the Spanish moralists insist that masturbation must not be situated on the sexual-genital plane but rather on the personal. Secondly, they suggest that the traditional thesis on no parvity of matter must be submitted to serious and conscientious re-examination. Thirdly, they contend that if masturbation is truly symptomatic behavior, its occurrence in candidates for consecrated celibate life must be weighed in terms of the underlying causes. That is, one should attempt to determine whether the underlying causes are compatible with priestly and religious life. These remarks suggest what many of us have been thinking: in assessing the meaning of masturbatory activity in candidates to the priestly or religious life, much more attention must be given to over-all personal stability.

[11] For example, it can be doubted that Glaser would want to say simply that all sexual acts at a certain developmental stage are incapable of constituting serious matter.

[12] B. Schüller, S.J., *Gesetz und Freiheit* (Düsseldorf: Patmos, 1966) p. 43.

[13] For some recent suggestions, cf. Kevin T. Kelly, "Mortal Sin and Grave Matter," *Clergy Review* 52 (1967) 588–606; W. F. Allen, "Mortal Sin: Its Essence and Meaning," *Pastoral Life* 16 (1968) 445–49.

growth to the stage of *moralitas gravis* can be at stake in the attitude he takes toward the habit. Therefore, is there not the possibility of serious matter in this attitude and determination?

Concretely, if a youngster simply decides to neglect the existence of the habit altogether and to indulge it at whim, he is feeding and strengthening the underlying causes of such symptomatic behavior. Often enough these causes are the multiple anxieties inseparable from the growing process. If the youngster's outlook is irresponsible, then is he not compromising his growth toward maturity and *moralitas gravis*? Such knowing negligence would seem to be serious matter in the fullest sense. Hence I would not care to use the phrase *moralitas levis* as covering the whole range of choices facing a youngster caught in a sexual "habit of sin." His basic attitude toward his habit can and does confront him with a serious choice. But once this choice is properly made and endures, there is increasing conviction that the inconsistencies which occur thereafter are not serious sin—whether because of slightness of matter (Glaser) or reduced imputability (the more traditional view). Whatever point of view one adopts, I believe that lack of serious guilt in these cases is a safe pastoral presumption.

Should the adolescent be told this? Yes, as a general rule he should be, unless, of course, the presumption is not valid in his instance, or unless the information would do him more over-all harm than good. The much more important, indeed crucial, matter is how he is told. I would suggest that he be told two things. First, "each act is not something here and now for which you will be punished eternally in hell. It is precisely your challenge to get to the point where you are genuinely mature and free in sexual expression." Secondly, "the problem of masturbation in your life is a serious thing. It is a problem you want to grow through. Because this habit represents a serious challenge to your growth, it demands a serious response on your part, a resolute and adult attitude. As long as you maintain this, you are on the right path and are responding properly to your challenge."

Even though the habit of masturbation does represent a serious over-all challenge, nevertheless sin should not be the focus of pastoral treatment. Rather the emphasis should fall on the growing process toward full maturity through growth in over-all personal responsibility.

THE THEOLOGY OF REVOLUTION

Camilo Torres, the priest-turned-guerilla, once wrote: "Love of the neighbor must be efficacious. In the actual circumstances of Latin America, the minority which has power makes no decisions against its own interests. Therefore it is necessary to favor the seizure of power by the majority so that they can realize reforms for good. This is called 'revolution,' and if it is necessary for the realization of love of neighbor, then a Christian ought to be a revolutionary."[14] This conviction is increasingly being repeated, expanded, and refined throughout the Christian world to the point where it is almost a manifesto.

For instance, the March 27 issue of *Le monde* carried the conclusions of a conference on "Christianity and Revolution" held at Paris. It reads as follows:

> The situation of violence which reigns in the world because of the domination and misuse of the capitalistic system in all its forms, the impossibility of resolving the contradictions inherent in this system . . . by means of gradual reform, constitute the objectively necessary conditions of revolution. But the subjective conditions of revolution depend on the will of the men collectively committed to promote it. Revolution appears to us, therefore, as the only way possible and it supposes a radical change of political and economic structures. But there will not be a structural revolution without a cultural revolution. We are perfectly aware of the fact that this revolution implies a questioning of Christianity in its forms of thought, of expression, and of action. We are convinced that our commitment ought to identify itself with the struggle of the classes and of the oppressed masses to achieve their liberation, in France and elsewhere. The revolutionary struggle ties itself closely to the prospect of the construction of the kingdom of God without identifying itself with this kingdom. We acknowledge the right of every Christian as well as of every man to participate in this revolutionary process, including armed struggle. We express, as a community, our support for the believers who, because of their commitment, are put aside by their local church and feel themselves alone in the faith.[15]

This paragraph draws on and summarizes rather well much of what is being said about revolution in theological literature. This literature rather commonly presents an analysis of sociopolitical structures, a theological interpretation, and draws conclusions on these bases. Revolution is going to occur with or without the Church. It was perhaps this realization which led Harvey Cox to state that "we are trying to live in a period of revolution without a theology of revolution. The development of such a theology should be the first item on the theological agenda today."[16] However, Bishop Marcos McGrath (Santiago de Veraguas, Panama) has stated that "we already have a theology of revolution thanks to the encyclical *Populorum*

---

[14] Cited in Gaston Zananiri, "L'Eglise et la révolution en Amérique latin," *Ami du clergé* 78 (1968) 187–92, at 189.

[15] Cited in "La tentazione della violenza," *Civiltà cattolica* 119 (1968) 313–17, at 314.

[16] Harvey Cox, *The Secular City* (New York: Macmillan, 1965) p. 107.

Progressio, but what we need is a theology of violence which makes precise that which is legitimate and that which is not."[17] The difference in these two statements probably lies in the understanding of the word "theology." By theology I suspect that Cox would mean the broad underlying perspectives of a social ethic which support the more practical statements of *Populorum progressio*.

Be that as it may, the first thing to be said about revolution is that the meaning of the word is ambiguous. G. Zananiri[18] lists four general senses the term can have: violent insurrection unleashed before having exhausted the possibilities of dialogue; violent insurrection justified as a response to violence and out of desperation; pacific action undertaken to accelerate urgently-needed reforms; pacific action undertaken progressively over a period of time more or less determined (evolution). Thus the term can refer to everything from a simple military *Putsch* with or without bloodshed to radical socioeconomic changes within constitutionally established processes. This ambiguity is never totally overcome in some of the literature, but increasingly the term is understood in a sense close to that stated by the seventeen bishops of the Third World in their excellent statement: "a break with some system that no longer ensures the common good, and the establishment of a new order more likely to bring it about."[19]

What is the nature of this break? Gustavo Pérez-Ramírez, approaching revolution from the sociological point of view, concludes that there are several components which distinguish a true revolution from a simple *coup d'état* and other forms of aimless subversion.[20] For example, he insists that in a true revolution it is the relationships of man to man and classes to classes that are primarily affected. The relationship of men to things is secondary. Thus the true revolution has as its aim that "man should be the agent of, and take part as a subject in the achievement of his own advancement." The most important element of revolution, however, is ideology understood as a complex of norms and values. Therefore revolution, when described in structural terms, is "the transition from one given social system, morally authentic but with now obsolete values, to a new order in which the new system of social

---

[17] Cf. José de Broucker, "Has the Church Opted for Revolution?" *New Blackfriars* 49 (1968) 540–43, at 543.

[18] Zananiri, *art. cit.*, p. 187. Similar distinctions are repeated almost everywhere that revolution is discussed.

[19] Cf. "Gospel and Revolution," *New Blackfriars* 49 (1967) 140–48, at 141. The document is also available in *Catholic Mind* 66 (1968) 37–46.

[20] Gustavo Pérez-Ramírez, "The Church and the Social Revolution in Latin America," in *Faith and the World of Politics* (= *Concilium* 36; New York: Paulist Press, 1968) pp. 124–35.

control is authenticated by values and norms formerly considered a source of dissolution." This understanding of revolution as involving a "complex of norms and values" relates it immediately to theology.

The emphasis in recent theological literature has centered on two points: the relation of Christianity to revolution; the relation of Christianity to revolutionary violence. Here we can present only a sample of the articles touching on these two points.[21]

Relation of Christianity to Revolution

A good introduction to the study of the theology of revolution would be Paul J. Weber's excellent summary.[22] Weber highlights the premises and emphases of current theological writing in this area. For instance, the starting point of the Christian's approach to the total social fact of underdevelopment is a view of history. "Just-revolution" theologians reject a static view of history (creation is a finished work to be preserved) and build from the premise that history has a direction and that God is working in history. The biblical message shows us that this direction is toward greater justice, love, freedom. In working out this direction, God encounters human intransigence, especially as found in social structures which are oppressive and unjust and ultimately constitute a form of violence. It is this basic view of history which provides the substructure of the theology of revolution.

A specific example of this view of history would be a recent article by Johannes B. Metz.[23] Complaining of the privacy and individualism of transcendental, existential, and personalist theology, Metz calls for a "political theology."[24] Its primary task would be to reassess the relationship between eschatological faith and social life. "The eschatological promises of the biblical tradition—freedom, peace, justice, reconciliation—cannot be reduced to a private matter. They constantly force themselves into the sense of social responsibility." These promises are never simply identified with any given social situation, but we move toward them in social situations. Thus the eschatological promises render every social situation provisional and they necessarily render Christian attitudes toward social

---

[21] The literature used in this summary contains a rather full bibliography.

[22] Paul J. Weber, S.J., "A Theology of Revolution?" *Catholic World* 207 (1968) 220–23. For a different perspective, cf. Georges Morel, "Réflexions sur l'idée de révolution," *Etudes*, May, 1968, pp. 681–700.

[23] Johannes B. Metz, "The Church's Social Function in the Light of a 'Political Theology,'" *Concilium* 36 (n. 20 above) 2–18.

[24] This is also the emphasis of T. Westow, who states that "politics are the very heart of concern with the brother"; cf. "Violence and Brotherhood: A Case of 'trahison des clercs,'" *New Blackfriars* 49 (1968) 229–32.

situations critical. That is, because of its orientation toward the eschatological promises, faith develops a constantly fresh critical attitude toward its social environment. Metz sees the liberating function of the Church's criticism exercised in three ways: the defense of the individual, criticism of totalitarianism, and love as the principle of revolution. He argues that love must be interpreted in its social dimension and be made operative. "This means that it must be understood as the unconditional commitment to justice, freedom and peace *for others*." Understood in this way, love implies a criticism of mere force, but it may at times command revolutionary force.

Heinz-Dietrich Wendland (West Germany) argues that the gospel contains a revolutionary element.[25] He then seeks the connection between the revolutionary element in the Bible and revolution in history. This connection involves both an affinity and a distinction. As for the affinity, the Bible is at one with historical revolution in its eschatology. The coming of the kingdom confronts the Christian with the principle *societas semper reformanda*. This reformation is not precisely a Christian revolution, because the Christian's task is to humanize the secular orders. Or, in Richard Shaull's words, "as a political form of change, revolution represents the cutting edge of humanization."[26] The biblical revolution is distinct from historical revolution, because no historical revolution "opens the door to the reign of freedom, which at the same time offers the inexhaustible satisfaction of all human needs." Ultimately, therefore, Wendland understands the revolutionary element in the Bible as one with only indirect social repercussions. That is, the rule of God operates through the quiet and unarmed force of loving action and the service of Christian groups scattered throughout the world.

Princeton's Richard Shaull is one of the more prominent proponents of the theology of revolution in this country.[27] Shaull accepts the fact that God is at work in human history. And more specifically he states, with Dietrich von Oppen, that the revolutionary impact of Jesus is that all institutions lose their sacral character. They are merely functional and exist to serve men. If this attitude permeates a culture, then institutions will appear which are open, flexible, and subject to constant criticism. Creation of these institutions is the very context of human liberation; for they allow for the

[25] As in J. M. Lochman, "Ecumenical Theology of Revolution," *Scottish Journal of Theology* 21 (1968) 170–86. This article reports on the relevance of theology to revolution, discussions held at the World Conference on Church and Society (Geneva, 1966).

[26] *Ibid.*, p. 172.

[27] Richard Shaull, "A Theological Perspective on Human Liberation," *Ido-c*, no. 68, April 28, 1968. Cf. also "Theology and the Transformation of Society," *Theology Today* 25 (1968) 23–36.

discovery of selfhood and nourish a new will to shape the future. It is this discovery of selfhood and this new will to shape the future which are at the heart of the Negro revolution, the student uprisings, and the social unrest in the Third World. Because this is true, "then we should feel ourselves closely identified with this struggle and the achievement of this goal should be our central concern as Christians at this time." However, these movements have met with tremendous efforts on the part of those in power to preserve the *status quo*.

Shaull admits that one cannot prove the action of God in history. But to make the wager of faith is to bet that the symbols and stories which make up biblical tradition have the power to make transparent to us the deeper meaning of historical processes. Now the basic Christian symbols are death and resurrection. Personally, we move to maturity as we allow the old to collapse and the new to rise. This means that for the Christian birth is the fruit of death. We must understand not only personal but also social history in the light of these symbols. The collapsing of the old to allow the new to be born is a thought-structure connatural to the Christian. It is an outlook which suggests to him that he view social structures as functional and provisional, subordinate to the birth of the kingdom and human liberation. It is precisely *as Christians* that we are free of the self-imposed limitations of American liberalism (American liberals are for liberation of the depressed "as long as they do not upset too much the present system or run the risks of violence") and capable of shattering the systems of thought which give security but inhibit human liberation.

Some of these same emphases are present in the fine study of Rolland F. Smith, S.J.[28] Smith describes a historical Christianity as one which finds God revealing Himself in the events of history which are continually giving way to new events. The Christian distinguishes carefully the revelatory event from the Revealer, and is therefore continually ready to criticize and transcend particular revelatory events. Upon this notion of history Smith builds a distinction between revolution and rebellion. Revolution idealizes an event, whether past or future; it fixates forms and tends to absolutize them, whether these be political, economic, or religious. Rebellion, on the other hand, continually calls these forms into question. Following Camus, Smith sees the rebel as affirming a value in the present structures at the very time he is questioning and toppling them. The rebel, therefore, both criticizes the present and participates in it. Smith understands the new theology of hope with its stress on man's position between promise and

---

[28] Rolland F. Smith, S.J., "A Theology of Rebellion," *Theology Today* 25 (1968) 10–22.

fulfilment (Moltmann, Metz) as an attempt to set forth a historical Christianity and therefore a theology of rebellion.

These are but a few examples of the more speculative writings on the relationship of Christianity to revolution.[29] We may summarize by citing two sentences from the remarkable statement of the bishops of the Third World: "As soon as a system ceases to ensure the common good to the profit of some party involved, the Church must not merely condemn such injustice, but dissociate herself from the system of privilege, ready to collaborate with another that is better adapted to the needs of the time, and more just." Later the document asserts: "Christians and their pastors should know how to recognize the hand of the Almighty in those events that from time to time put down the mighty from their thrones and raise up the humble, send away the rich empty-handed, and fill the hungry with good things."[30] The first statement acknowledges the subordinate and provisional character of social structures. The second recognizes the action of God in the transformation of the structures. Such statements are straight out of the developing theology of revolution, and therefore tell us what it is at root all about: a search in the biblical message and symbols for a deeper understanding of man as a sociopolitical being. It is easy to agree with George Celestin[31] that these speculations are incomplete and sometimes simplistic. But even if there are loose ends, these beginnings are promising and exciting.

The Relation of Christianity to Revolutionary Violence

If Christian love involves an unconditioned commitment to justice, freedom, and peace for others, what concrete forms may this love take as it moves into the area of political and social structures? Vatican II stated: "Where public authority oversteps its competence and oppresses the people, these people should nevertheless obey to the extent that the objective common good demands. Still it is lawful for them to defend their own rights and those of their fellow citizens against any abuse of this authority, *provided that in so doing they observe the limits imposed by natural law and the gospel*."[32] What are these limits? Can violence be justified as a means toward urgently needed social change?

This is not an easy question to answer. First of all, the term "violence"

---

[29] For outlines of an ethic built on hope, cf. V. Eller, "The Ethic of Promise," *Christian Century* 85 (1968) 963–65.

[30] As in *Catholic Mind* 66 (1968) 40.

[31] George Celestin, "A Christian Looks at Revolution," *Listening* 3 (1968) 137–44.

[32] *The Documents of Vatican II*, ed. Walter M. Abbott, S.J. (New York: Association, 1966) pp. 284–85, emphasis added.

covers a broad spectrum of actions and human experiences, as Ivan Illich has pointed out.[33] For instance, violence against property and things is different from violence against persons. Generalizations ignore these marked differences at their own risk. Secondly, in the circumstances under discussion the problem of force confronts the Christian in a relatively new form. We are no longer dealing with the open aggression of one sovereign state against another (war), but rather with the concealed, legally protected, complex violence endemic in oppressive social structures. Violent response to such systemic injustice raises new questions, both tactical and moral. For instance, does violence inevitably beget violence and turn out to be self-defeating—hence disproportionate in a moral sense? To what extent is violent response to sclerotic social structures compatible with love of the oppressor? On the other hand, does nonviolence in the face of injustice actually end up supporting the unjust *status quo*? Is G. Thibon right when he concludes that systematic refusal of violence can lead straight to the reign of absolute violence?[34] Or does the use of violence absolutize the social structure one proposes to introduce and thus compromise the transcendence of eschatological faith? These are only some of the knotty questions this discussion raises.

Many of the responses to these questions have merely stated a rather general position on force without analyzing it at length or attempting to apply it. A few examples of this type of statement will suffice here. Dom Jorge (the Bishop of Santo Andres, Brazil) said on television that "armed revolution by the people is justified when oppression rules and famine wages obtain."[35] Similarly Mons. Fragoso (Bishop of Crateus, Brazil) asserted that "at times violence is the only possible way of liberating man from an established, permanent and grievous violence. We have to recognize that the mature conscience of the citizens has the right to opt for violence."[36] At the World Conference on Church and Society (Geneva, 1966) most of the delegates from South Africa and Latin America approved the use of force at times. Delegates from the more industrialized countries were more reserved.[37] Ultimately the Conference urged Christians not to resort to force, even in the most unfavorable circumstances. But it added that a question could arise "whether the violence which sheds blood in planned revolutions may

[33] Ivan Illich, "Violence: A Mirror for Americans," *America* 118 (1968) 568–70, at 570.

[34] G. Thibon, in *La Violence* (Paris: Desclée de Brouwer, 1967) p. 121.

[35] As cited in de Broucker, *art. cit.*, p. 542.

[36] Cf. Almeri Bezerra de Melo, "Revolution and Violence," *Ido-c*, no. 68, July 14, 1968, p. 11.

[37] Cf. Lochman, *art. cit.*, p. 177.

not be a lesser evil than the violence which, though bloodless, condemns whole populations to perennial despair."

Johannes Metz believes that Christian love "may in certain circumstances command something like revolutionary force. Where a social *status quo* is so full of injustice that it might equal that created by a revolutionary movement, then a revolution . . . cannot be ruled out in the name of love."[38] Richard Shaull is on record with the statement that "there may be some situations in which only the threat or use of violence can set the process of change in motion."[39] Paul Verghese is convinced that Christians certainly cannot completely oppose the counterviolence of protest if this means allowing systemic violence to continue and be disposed of at a pace chosen by the oppressor.[40] The Theological Commission of the Christian Peace Conference allowed in its report for the use of force as *ultima ratio*. Their reason: existing social relationships represent a structure of power which uses force in the most varied, even if concealed forms, to maintain the *status quo*.[41] These are all guarded statements, and frankly they do not help a great deal, but they do manifest a drift of thought.

Several essays I have recently[42] encountered contain a longer reflection on Christianity and revolutionary violence. Bishop McGrath first states the problem as it is often formulated:

> Where the few are established in power and this power is systematically used to augment their own interests and block efforts at improving the situation of the majority who are in need, then, these Christians say, violence is already present. To strike out against this violence requires no further ethical argument. It is merely self-defense.[43]

In commenting on this, Bishop McGrath makes several points. First, counterviolence can be against the system or against the persons enforcing the system. Generally it is against the persons. But it is precisely the system that needs to be changed. Furthermore, what will violence achieve? Certainly it will "throw the scoundrels out," but unless deliberately provoked revolution has clear goals and the means to reach them, it very easily represents another form of paternalism. It refuses to face the long uphill strug-

[38] Metz, *art. cit.* p. 14.
[39] As in Lochman, *art. cit.*, p. 176.
[40] Paul Verghese, "The Christian and the Revolutionary," *Theology Today* 25 (1968) 141–44.
[41] In "The Just Revolution," *Cross Currents* 18 (1968) 67–76, at 69.
[42] For an earlier study, cf. Karl Rahner, "The Theology of Power," *Theological Investigations* 4 (Baltimore: Helicon, 1966) 391–409.
[43] Marcos McGrath, "Development for Peace," *America* 118 (1968) 562–67.

gle the masses face before they can be brought to be the authors of their own improvement. McGrath also wonders whether Christians involved in violent revolution can maintain their values in whatever actions they initiate. Christians soon find themselves associated with those for whom terrorism and indiscriminate killing are a hobby. Add to this the fact that prolonged violence crushes the basic human and Christian values of life and respect for others. Adverting to the loss of mutual confidence in the people of Vietnam, Bishop McGrath asks: "How long will it take to rebuild the inner humanity of a people thus destroyed?" Finally McGrath rejects vehemently any generalization about the existence in Latin America of institutional violence of the kind justifying counterviolence.

Juan Luis Segundo, S.J., argues that to face realistically the question of violence in Latin America one has to demythologize certain notions and images.[44] First, it is true that the violence of the masses should be conceived of as a response to yet another existing violence under the guise of a legal regime. But things are not that easy. "Latin American social reality is not that of the jungle where violence is natural, nor is it that of developed countries where politics is concerned with the welfare of the people." Therefore the first problem with violence in South America is its very introduction. Life has to become so unbearable that the masses have nothing to lose. Then the right climate for revolution is created. But revolutionaries must take responsibility for creating this climate, since truly monstrous governments (e.g., Batista's in Cuba) are wisely avoided by those in power. There is a moral dilemma here.

Secondly, Segundo asserts that the real violence excercised by the unjust established order justifies in principle a violent response as self-defense. Yet how far can one carry this principle? That is, the general validity of the idea of self-defense does not tell us what means can be employed in self-defense. For example, certainly one threatened at gunpoint may draw in self-defense and fire on his aggressor. But could an individual, knowing his aggressor to be quicker on the draw, hide in the bushes and attack him from behind? Further, realizing his inability to take the aggressor by surprise in any way, could the innocent person kill one of his own friends and lay the responsibility on the enemy and get at him in this way? Segundo insists—and rightly—that Christ's message must guide not only causes but the means used.

Almeri Bezerra de Melo, a Brazilian priest, disagrees.[45] In an otherwise extremely interesting essay he grants that it is not difficult to demonstrate

[44] Juan Luis Segundo, S.J., "Christianity and Violence in Latin America," *Christianity and Crisis* 28 (1968) 31–34.
[45] Cf. de Melo, *art. cit.*

that the message of the Gospels is a message of peace and love, not of war and violence. But the Gospels also carry a message of liberation. "When we are considering the liberation of entire peoples, currently subjected to every kind of slavery, the end to be attained must take precedence over the means employed, and in the case under consideration these are revolutionary violence, armed insurrection." With the facile stroke of an *ipse dixit*, de Melo has adopted a principle which cuts him adrift from a long and cherished tradition. Not all traditions are wise, of course. But some of them are. And it is the peculiar danger of desperation to blur the distinction and render it ultimately irrelevant.

One of the great "revolutionary texts" constantly appealed to is that of Pope Paul VI in *Populorum progressio*. There the Pontiff had referred to situations where whole populations are the victims of injustice. In such situations "recourse to violence, as a means to right these wrongs to human dignity, is a grave temptation." He then added:

We know, however, that a revolutionary uprising—*save where there is manifest, long-standing tyranny which would do great damage to fundamental personal rights and dangerous harm to the common good of the country*—produces new injustices, throws more elements out of balance, and brings on new disasters. A real evil should not be fought against at the cost of even greater misery.[46]

The italicized phrase above is frequently cited as a good description of what is the case in several Latin American countries. Hence Paul VI was being cited as a champion of violent revolution. Recently the Pope has returned to the subject to straighten the records. In his general audience of March 27, 1968, in a speech commemorating the first anniversary of the publication of *Populorum progressio*, Pope Paul stated:

Thus, so it seemed to some . . . that when We denounced in the name of God the very grave needs in which so much of humanity suffers, We had opened the way to the so-called theology of revolution and of violence. Such an error is far from our thought and language. Revolution is altogether different from the positive, courageous, and energetic activity necessary in many instances to establish structures of social and economic progress.[47]

[46] *AAS* 59 (1967) 257–99, at 272, emphasis added.
[47] *AAS* 60 (1968) 258. Earlier Pope Paul, speaking of Latin America, had said in his message to the College of Cardinals at the end of 1967: "We invite the entire world to resist the temptation to violence in order to seek wisely and in a Christian way a dynamic and constructive peace, a source of development and civil progress" (*AAS* 60 [1968] 31). Similarly to the participants at the Conference of Teheran he once again rejected violence as a means to redress economic misery and ideological oppression (*AAS* 60 [1968] 285). In his August (1968) visit to Latin America the Pope reiterated his rejection of violent reform.

Civiltà cattolica jumped on the phrase "tentazione della violenza" as an opportunity to point out that what is characteristic about contemporary thought on violence is its theorization. Violence has always existed, but now we are theorizing it into a value.[48] Hence it is no longer contrasted with the evangelical spirit, but regarded as a consequence of it. In this sense the Christian is increasingly experiencing violence as a temptation, something presenting itself under the appearances of good. The editors of *Civiltà* rightly squirmed at this and warned against the temptation to extend the tolerability of violence beyond instances of evident and prolonged tyranny.

This inadequate roundup of opinion will indicate at least one thing: we are dealing here with one of the most exciting aspects of contemporary Christian thought. It is obvious that Christians are beginning to come alive to social responsibility. The tone is often militant, even at times somewhat unrestrained and uncritical. But beneath it all something wonderful is happening. To face this situation with a complete casuistry of licits and illicits would be tantamount to substituting a kind of Western moral imperialism for the existing financial imperialism. On the other hand, to rule out moral reflection as irrelevant is to play the deadly game of spiritual suicide. If a Christian dare not absolutize law and order at the expense of justice, neither can he allow efficacy of means to be the supreme criterion; for this would only prepare the rationale for tomorrow's totalitarianism. The Christian absolutizes only the eschatological promises; and it is in light of these that he must formulate his basic ethical questions about violence.

As a person cast between promise and fulfilment, the basic posture of the Christian would seem to be that of "involved transcendence," as Paul Verghese puts it. His witness is "to be basically in sympathy with the protest yet not be drawn into the maelstrom of hatred and destruction that counterviolence generates."[49] The Christian will not absolutely disown the cross of violence, but only the hatred so often its twin. A good practical summary of the moral judgments involved in preserving his "involved transcendence" is supplied by Bishop McGrath:

Each Christian must form his own conscience, but with an accurate knowledge of the situation he is in and a clear grasp of the principles and the dangers involved. He should look well, very well, before leaping. There must be real justification— as to the end, as to the means, as to a program and as to the likelihood of success, not only of the overthrow of a regime but of the program to follow. Let him re-

[48] *Civiltà cattolica* 119 (1968) 313–17.
[49] Verghese, *art. cit.*, p. 143.

member that our greatest commandment is to love our neighbor. Even if violence may be chosen, we may not hate.[50]

THE ETHICS OF HEART TRANSPLANTS

The December 3, 1967 transplant of the heart of Denise Ann Darvall to Louis Washkansky at Groote Schuur Hospital in Cape Town not only occasioned a flurry of similar attempts around the world[51] but also provoked a good deal of moral comment. The transplantation of organs had been rather thoroughly discussed in the literature over the past twenty-five years.[52] Hence the sudden resurgence of moral discussion of the subject at this time could look surprising. There are probably many reasons for this, but none seems more obvious than the symbolic character of the heart itself.[53] The

[50] McGrath, art. cit., p. 567.

[51] The publicity surrounding the first heart transplants has been widely regretted as irresponsible. Science reporter John Lear referred to the "optimistic ballyhoo" surrounding Washkansky's surgery as masking "some curious diversions from the normal behavior of the medical community" (Saturday Review, Feb. 3, 1968, p. 55). See also New England Journal of Medicine 278 (1968) 395.

[52] The most recent thorough discussion is that of Augustine Regan, C.SS.R., in Studia moralia 3 (New York: Desclee, 1965) 320–361, and Studia moralia 5 (1968) 179–200. Previous writing had stated that the principle of totality could not be used to justify organic transplantation. The only question was: did this principle exclude it? It is Regan's contention that transplantation inter vivos can and must be justified by the principle of totality. To do this, he must interpret the principle in a more personal way than has been customary. Rejecting that sense of community (so vigorously condemned by Pius XII) which sees it as a huge magnification of a physical organism in which the personal members are totally subordinate to the whole, Regan builds upon an understanding of person which sees "a natural order to other human persons that is in the very concept of human personality itself." By donating an organ, an individual can become (in carefully delimited circumstances) more fully a person; for by communicating to another of his very being, he has more fully integrated himself into the mysterious unity between person and person. The argument is carefully wrought, developed out of a wide acquaintance with previous literature, and—aside from a few quibbling points—very persuasive. In much the same sense G. Ziegler distinguishes between a physical understanding of the principle of totality and an altruistic understanding: "Moraltheologische Überlegungen zur Organstransplantation," Trier theologische Zeitschrift 77 (1968) 153–74. So also R. Egenter in Münchener theologische Zeitschrift 16 (1965) 167–78, and Theology Digest 16 (1968) 100–103; cf. also C. Bouchaud, "Réflexion morale," Cahiers Laënnec 26 (1966) 41–45.

[53] Wilfried Ruff, S.J., "Die Transplantation von Organen," Stimmen der Zeit 93 (1968) 155–64. However, one must not equate this symbolic character with erroneous notions about the presence of the soul. Surely Thomas O'Donnell, S.J., is correct when he says: "The human heart is a most important organ arising from a special adaptation of part of the circulatory system, but it has, theologically, no more intimate relation to the 'soul' than have the viscera or the eyes" (Linacre Quarterly 35 [1968] 36).

heart has been celebrated in song, story, and cult as the metonym for the person. And not without reason. Not only does it register human sensations and emotions in a dramatic way, but it is, as *Time* noted, "essential to life in a more immediate temporal sense than any other organ, even the brain. The human body can survive for years in a coma, with no conscious brain function—but only for minutes without a beating heart. So the presence of a heartbeat, along with breathing, has long been the basic criterion for distinguishing life from death."[54]

It is very likely the immediacy of this life-death motif which has occasioned so much moral concern and comment. The surgical virtuosity of the heart transplant represents a dramatic leap in man's power over life and death. A more extensive power over the life-death process means greater responsibility. And greater responsibility, if it is not to be muffed, demands a clear grasp of basic values. Thus the questioning and reappraisals. Or, as Sir Theodore Fox put it recently: "The more we know how to do things, the more we shall need to know just what we really want to do. . . . We shall have to learn to refrain from doing things merely because we know how to do them."[55]

Some of the moral comment has been flamboyant. For example, *Christianity Today* conjured up the ghoulish possibility of a black market in hearts and asked: "Might the mafia promise overnight delivery with anybody its prospective victim?"[56] The *Tablet* feared a horde of old men and women with other people's lungs, hearts, and kidneys, but their own ageing and senile brains.[57] Most intriguing was the vision of J. S. Hayes of a 130-year-old body consisting for the most part of prosthetic devices and lying partly in the hospital bed and partly on the surrounding shelves.[58] Most of the discussion, however, has been serious. It has settled around two general areas: the death of the "donor" and the prospects for the beneficiary.

The Death of the Donor

Because the donor must be dead and because the surgeon wants his heart as fresh as possible (before deterioration due to lack of oxygen), it is imperative to know when death occurs. Doctors have asked this question before, of

---

[54] "The Ultimate Operation," *Time* 90 (Dec. 16, 1967) 64–72, at 71.

[55] T. Fox, "Purposes of Medicine," in *Lancet* as cited in G. E. W. Wolstenholme's *Ethics in Medical Progress : With Specific Reference to Transplantation* (Boston: Little, Brown, 1966) p. 79. This book contains many enlightening remarks plus an appendix of highly useful documents.

[56] *Christianity Today* 12 (1968) 24–26.

[57] *Tablet* 222 (1968) 73–74.

[58] Cited in the *Medical-Moral Newsletter* 4 (1968) 32.

course; but until recently it was nearly always aimed at discovering when one ought to cease defense of life. Now it is asked to determine when one may profit from death. Eugene Tesson, S.J., catches this change in attitude in the face of approaching death with the phrase "cette impatience difficilement surmontable."[59] Simply put, cardiac transplants can involve divided loyalty on the part of the physician. Kenneth Vaux concretizes the point by suggesting that Clive Haupt (the second of the South African heart donors) was immediately treated as a potential heart donor rather than as a present stroke victim.[60]

Dr. Leonard R. Kass, a researcher in molecular biology, has highlighted the confidence problem involved in this tension. "Confidence of the patient in his doctor, and in his chances for recovery, are important for the patient's will to recover and sometimes for the recovery itself. Even when—or perhaps especially when—recovery is impossible, it would be reprehensible to add to the pain and grief the suspicion that the dying patient was being sacrificed for his value as spare parts."[61] This problem of a possible divided loyalty has led any number of commentators to insist on the necessity of two distinct teams, one for the care of the donor, the other for the transplant.[62]

When, then, is a person dead? The answer to this question might appear to the layman to be fairly simple. But the literature reveals that it is anything but simple.[63] As cardiac surgeon Donald Longmore notes, the statute books of the 1930's would have said that a man is dead when he has no spontaneous breathing or heartbeat.[64] With modern supportive and resuscitative devices, however, both of these conditions are reversible today, at least sometimes. Therefore from the clinical point of view it is increasingly clear that death is a complicated process consisting of a series of biological and cellular shutdowns. At a certain point along the way it is legitimate to say that "this

---

[59] Eugene Tesson, S.J., "Les greffes du coeur," *Etudes*, March, 1968, pp. 322–28, at 323.

[60] Kenneth Vaux, "The Heart Transplant: Ethical Dimensions," *Christian Century* 85 (1968) 353–56, at 353.

[61] Leon R. Kass, "A Caveat on Transplants," *Washington Post*, Jan. 14, 1968.

[62] For instance, cf. Tesson, *art. cit.*, p. 326; Wolstenholme, pp. 68–69; Ruth K. Franklin, "The Question of Transplants," *New Republic*, March 16, 1968, p. 7, where it is stated that in British hospitals no physician who is to be involved in transplanting an organ may also be in attendance on a would-be donor. Cf. also the *Journal of the American Medical Association* 204 (May 27, 1968) 805–6.

[63] An introduction to the scientific aspects of the discussion can be had in the *Medical-Moral Newsletter* 4 (1968) 17–20. See also *World Medical Journal* 14 (1967) 143–46; *JAMA* 204 (May 6, 1968) 423; *JAMA* 204 (June 24, 1968) 1197; *New England Journal of Medicine* 278 (June 27, 1968) 1425.

[64] Donald Longmore and M. Ross-Macdonald, "New Hearts for Old," *Month* 39 (1968) 172–77, at 174.

person is dead" or "there is here no longer a human person." What is that point? Since organs function but it is the person who lives and dies, the determination of this point involves not merely clinical knowledge but also a grasp of the meaning of person upon or against which a definition of the absence of personhood can be made. There is room, therefore, for many competences in the construction of a general definition of death. But obviously such a general definition should be carefully distinguished from verification of this definition in an individual case. Both judgments are necessary, of course, for the determination of death in a concrete instance, and hence for the practical conclusion about licit heart removal. The following remarks gather a few samples of how moral literature has dealt with the·problem of donor death where heart transplants are concerned.

It will be recalled that the criteria used by Dr. Barnard were: the heart is no longer working, the lungs are no longer working, and there are no longer any complexes on the ECG. Vittorio Marcozzi, S.J., has criticized these criteria.[65] First, he says, we must distinguish between true death and clinical death. True death for the believer refers to separation of soul and body. For the nonbeliever it designates that time when the processes of deterioration are irreversible. Clinical death, on the other hand, refers to lack of the basic vital functions (circulation, respiration, etc.). It is Marcozzi's contention, based on the authority of several eminent doctors, that Barnard's three criteria are not secure signs of real death, but only of clinical death. Citing German neurologist Walter Bushart and others, Marcozzi states that the brain can emit electric oscillations four days after the electroencephalogram is quiet. Barnard should, he says, have been aware of the bibliography on this point and aware of the fact that reputable doctors demand in addition to Barnard's criteria the test of time.

In a thoughtful article,[66] Eugene Tesson, S.J., applies the cessation of brain activity (the flat line on the encephalogram) as a criterion of death to two different situations: *coma dépassé* and *coma prolongé*.[67] In the former the cerebral system lacks all activity. Even if the other organs function (whether artificially or not), death is, he believes, beyond doubt. *Coma prolongé*, however, he describes as a slackening of cerebral activity, but not its total sup-

---

[65] V. Marcozzi, S.J., "Trapianto del cuore e problemi morali," *Civiltà cattolica* 119 (1968) 371–75.

[66] Tesson, *art. cit.*, and J. Daoust and R. Bourdon, "Les greffes du coeur," *Ami du clergé* 78 (1968) 217–18, which is a summary of Tesson.

[67] A similar distinction is made by Père Riquet as cited in *La foi et le temps* 1 (1968) 85–87.

pression. A return to consciousness is not excluded. Tesson sees a case of *coma prolongé* in that of the sick person whose survival will be brief, whose consciousness is lacking or at best intermittent. We are in this instance in the presence of a human being, and here medicine must fall back on its first principles.

Díaz-Nava, S.J., after adverting to the difference between clinical and real death, insists that surgeons must assure themselves of real death.[68] What, however, if the donor is not dead but is indeed totally past recovery? Díaz-Nava repeats the conviction of theologians that direct lethal intervention at this point must be viewed morally as homicide. He rejects the suggestion that there may be a parallel between hastening death here and heroic self-sacrifice for the neighbor. To this latter instance the practical rule of double effect can and must be applied. But hastening the death of the prospective heart donor resists such an analysis.

Stefano Tumbas, S.J., recalls the many possible definitions of death: clinical vs. biological, real vs. apparent, true vs. legal.[69] He acknowledges that modern medicine possesses the means to certify death but notes that there are shades of opinion as to what is considered essential to this determination. Arguing that organs function but man lives, Tumbas suggests that the fact that respiration and heartbeat can be continued artificially does not exclude the liceity of removing the heart—on condition that the cerebral functions are irreversibly destroyed.

In an article which is a model of lucidity and precision, John J. Lynch, S.J., has insisted with nearly all moralists that there must be "moral certainty of medical death."[70] Lynch states: "Real medical death may be defined as cessation of vital function beyond reasonable hope of resuscitation. But it is for doctors, not theologians, to determine the discernible signs by which real death can be verified in particular instances." It should be noted that Lynch has offered a general definition of death ("cessation of vital function beyond reasonable hope of resuscitation"). I believe that nearly everyone would accept this as a good working description[71] if vital function is understood in a very general way which allows it to be continually nuanced

[68] A. Faz. Díaz-Nava, "Ante el primer transplante de corazón humano," *Sal terrae* 56 (1968) 60–65.

[69] S. Tumbas, S.J., "Il trapianto del cuore," *Palestra del clero* 47 (1968) 298–302.

[70] John J. Lynch, S.J., "Ethics of the Heart Transplant," *America* 118 (1968) 194–95.

[71] Dr. M. F. A. Woodruff says: "I think it is important, however, to draw the attention of the non-medical people here to some of the difficulties. In the first place death cannot be defined as the loss of all vital functions because tissues removed from the body can be kept alive in cultures for possibly hundreds of years." Cf. Wolstenholme, p. 71.

by medical advances. Lynch's remarks show an enlightened sensitivity to the many competences involved where determination of death is concerned.[72]

Since many competences are involved in the construction of an acceptable definition of death, nearly everyone is calling for a high-level conference to establish practical guidelines. A move in the right direction was a committee established by Harvard University.[73] It included members from the faculties of medicine, public health, law, divinity, arts and sciences. The Harvard group concluded that a permanently nonfunctioning brain (irreversible coma) was criteriological of death. The flat encephalogram has "confirmatory value" in this determination. The following criteria of a nonfunctioning brain were offered: unreceptivity and unresponsivity (total unawareness of external stimuli and inner need, and complete unresponsiveness); no movements or breathing (one hour of observation is sufficient to satisfy this demand); no reflexes (eye pupils will not respond to direct bright light; no swallowing, yawning, or vocalization). It seems that the Harvard group has simply made concrete what Tesson refers to as *coma dépassé*.

Prospects for the Beneficiary

The problem of distinguishing a general moral statement from a concrete application of this statement arises under this title also. Moral literature states unanimously that cardiac transplants must involve reasonable hope of substantial benefit for the recipient. Otherwise this radical surgery would amount to simple experimentation on the recipient. Not only would this represent a dehumanizing manipulation of the person, but in this instance it could easily be tantamount to an act of direct killing. Therefore two questions have arisen around the word "experiment": (1) What amount of surgical experimentation is permissible in principle? (2) To what degree is the heart transplant at the present time experimental? The ultimate moral assessment of heart transplants depends on both judgments. But where the second question is concerned, the moral theologian can only report.

As for permissible experimentation in therapeutic procedures, Tesson is surely correct when he says that experimentation is the price of advance and that ultimate success involves some less certain attempts at the beginning.[74] Some experimentation, therefore, is unquestionably permissible. Ruff agrees

---

[72] I cannot completely agree with Frank J. Ayd, M.D., when he says: "The medical profession now is looking for moralists who will provide further guidelines for establishing a specific criterion for certifying that a person is dead" (*Medical-Moral Newsletter* 4 [1968] 20).

[73] "A Definition of Irreversible Coma," *Journal of the American Medical Association* 205 (1968) 337–40.

[74] Tesson, *art. cit.*, p. 327.

that medicine eventually has to apply new techniques to man, but stipulates that, if this is to remain responsible, all other proportionate pretests must have occurred with at least some success. Furthermore, the surgical team may not heighten the risks for the present patient in the interests of future patients.[75] Because of the temptation to do this, Vaux urges that the "ethical imperative of the hour is that concern for an individual and concern for humanity enrich each other."[76]

Lynch faces the problem of experimentation by defining the meaning of "reasonable hope" and "substantial benefit." Reasonable hope is by no means to be understood as a guarantee, but merely as a well-founded medical expectation. Substantial benefit should be interpreted principally in terms of prolongation of human life over a period of time long enough to compensate for the risks presently entailed in heart transplantation. He then rightly insists that "only competent medical authority can judge whether and when this condition is fulfilled."[77] Marcozzi goes beyond this general judgment. Relying on the statements of some medical experts, he finds it "difficult to give a tranquil yes" to the surgery at the present time.[78]

To what extent is the heart transplant actually experimental? As noted before, this is a medical judgment.[79] And presently this judgment revolves chiefly around one point: the problem of immunological rejection. What stands as a triumph for surgery remains a headache and even a defeat for biochemistry. Here I can only report how a few spokesmen have judged the matter at the time of this writing.

Dr. Norman E. Shumway describes heart transplants as a "clinical trial."[80] Dr. Christian Barnard regards them as "therapeutic."[81] These statements very likely represent a difference in emphasis rather than a genuine opposition in point of view. W. J. Dempster and associates reconcile this difference when they speak of cardiac transplantation as palliative "in that no proof exists that any given allotransplant will function normally indefinitely. Such palliation must always be weighed against other priorities, especially when account is taken of the very heavy burdens that transplantation imposes on all departments of a hospital."[82] It was their own opinion that the state of the rejection problem then (January, 1968) did not justify heart transplants.

---

[75] Ruff, *art. cit.*, p. 161.   [76] Vaux, *art. cit.*, p. 354.   [77] Lynch, *art. cit.*, p. 194.
[78] Marcozzi, *art. cit.*, p. 373. A very similar judgment is given by Ziegler, *art. cit.*, p. 172.
[79] A. S. Fox, "Heart Transplants: Treatment or Experiment?" *Science* 159 (1968) 374.
[80] *Time*, Jan. 19, 1968, p. 51.
[81] *Saturday Review*, Feb. 3, 1968, p. 56.
[82] W. J. Dempster et al., "Scientific, Technical, and Ethical Considerations in Cardiac Transplantation," *British Medical Journal*, Jan. 20, 1968, p. 178.

"Palliative" was also the term used by the conference of experts who met at the invitation of the Council for International Organizations of Medical Sciences in June, 1968. But the group did not exclude heart transplants.[83] It only concluded that they should be "resorted to only exceptionally at the present state of knowledge."

The Board of Medicine of the National Academy of Sciences referred to the procedure as "scientific investigation" not yet meriting the title "accepted therapy."[84] Hence, it continued, "the primary justification for this activity in respect to both the donor and recipient is that from the study will come new knowledge of benefit to others in our society." The Board regards cardiac transplants as falling under the "ethics of experimentation."

In summary, it can be said that there are some experts who regard cardiac transplants as medically unjustified in light of the present state of research on the immunological problem. Others are convinced that it is justified as palliative therapy in last-resort instances.

There are several other problems connected with heart transplants. One of them is the problem of supply if and when the surgery becomes an established form of therapy. Peter Riga contends that if a supply of hearts, kidneys, lungs, etc. cannot be guaranteed by voluntary donations, it would be quite possible (and moral) for the state to legislate that various organs be removed from all victims of violent death.[85] His reason: "Morally speaking such a legal procedure would only be an application of the state's prerogative and obligation to safeguard the *common good of the living*." There are many who would, I believe, shudder at this conclusion. The common good of the living is a very complicated matter. It involves not only material provisions but the manner of this provision. The already delicate balance between personal autonomy and social subordination would be, or at least could easily be, seriously threatened by such legislation. If this is the case, would it truly be for the common good? Riga's statement strikes me as a bit sweeping.

Another problem is that of hastening death. That jaunty polemicist Joseph Fletcher has declared that "speeding up a donor's death, when death is positively inevitable, may be justified if the transplant provides another human with valuable life."[86] This conclusion is consistent with Fletcher's sponsor-

[83] *New York Times*, June 15, 1968, p. 14.

[84] "Cardiac Transplantation in Man," *Journal of the American Medical Association* 204 (1968) 805–6.

[85] Peter J. Riga, "Heart Transplantation and Genetic Transmutations," *Catholic World* 207 (1968) 18–22.

[86] As in *Newsweek*, Dec. 18, 1967, p. 87. Much more cautious in this respect are the remarks of Charles Curran in "The Morality of Human Transplants," *Sign* 47 (1968) 22–29, at 28. Franz Böckle takes up the question whether it is permissible to remove organs

ship of euthanasia. But this latter thesis he has not really argued. He has simply promulgated it in a way describable as theological logomachy.[87] In this game a Mongoloid becomes an "embryonic anomaly." The decision not to use artificial means to sustain life becomes "bringing death about left-handedly." Euthanasia in certain instances is opposed to "just letting it all hang on chance" and is praised as "a responsible choice, a morally authentic decision." Those opposed to all of this are dubbed "vitalists" and "archaists." Fletcher clinches the argument with a few quick aphorisms: "Death is not always an enemy; it can sometimes be a friend and a servant." "Let the law favor living, not mere life."

These pyrotechnics can be tremendous fun. But ultimately it must be said that whatever case there is for hastening death, it cannot be made by appending the adjective "responsible" and "authentic" to what one wants to do. Not only is this slippery methodology; it is terrifying when the stakes get big. Consider the instance raised by Leon R. Kass.[88] A high-ranking governmental official suffers a massive heart attack and requires a new heart to survive. Might not even the best of physicians be tempted to ease up on the treatment of a critically-ill patient deemed less worthy? "Is it too far fetched," Kass asks, "to imagine that people might be asked to step forward and volunteer their organs under these circumstances? If no volunteers were available, would mercy-killing or murder be excusable in order to provide a new heart for the statesman? If we are willing to send men involuntarily to their death in battle for the welfare of their country, is it not conceivable that we may someday expand that notion of the general welfare to include the health of our leaders?"

I find in Joseph Fletcher's methodology and thought-patterns no strong resistance to this continuity of thought. Men have rejected such conclusions over the centuries not out of any blind vitalism, but out of a wholesome (if we may be allowed to play the game of adjectives this once) reverence for God's promises and presence to His human creatures—even His unconscious, preconscious, nascent, and dying creatures. In other words, they have in-

---

when death, properly defined, is immediately imminent and its occurrence is, by all medical experience, certain. He argues that in these instances death has very possibly already happened; for we get full certainty only considerably after the occurrence. Therefore Böckle does not absolutely exclude the permissibility of beginning to remove organs at this point, "bevor die letzte methodologische Sicherheit gewonnen ist" (as in Ziegler, p. 171). Ziegler rejects this on the grounds that a probable prognosis before death cannot replace a certain one after death.

[87] Joseph Fletcher, "The Right to Die," *Atlantic Monthly* 221 (April, 1968) 62–64.
[88] Kass, *art. cit.*

sisted that the very quality of life that we seek to heighten depends, among other things, on an unshakable respect for human existence itself. Recent history has taught us that departures from such "archaism" lead quickly to barbarism.

In this connection Père Riquet has remarked that "on peut, aujourd'hui, donner jusqu'a son coeur."[89] He asserts that in the heart transplant both human solidarity and Christian charity find a new and remarkable expression. The meaning here is clear. But are there not limits to the value of this type of talk? Our language not only expresses our thought but affects it. If the use of a cadaver's heart is seen as a "donation" and a great act of charity, there is the temptation to redefine the removal of a heart from a living person as "heart donation" and an act of charity. It can be hoped that theologians will prove at least as resolute in their rejection of this as the medical world has shown itself to be.

These are but some of the questions raised by heart transplants.[90] In the final analysis, it would represent Christian and theological myopia were we to approach this latest medical spectacular as simply another case in medical ethics. The heart transplant should remind us forcefully that we live amidst a knowledge explosion in all areas. The use of this knowledge for the promotion of genuine human values is our larger challenge. Peter Riga is certainly on target when he says that it is crucial that the Church exercise her vigilant and prophetic role over these new procedures, not judicially, but "to bring God's word of love and justice to bear on them so they are not used to destroy or manipulate men."

James M. Gustafson provides some excellent moral and social directives for the implementation of this larger task.[91] For example, he insists on the need for public discourse "for the sake of developing the awareness of man's own worthwhileness in the light of which knowledge can be put to the service of man." He calls for new institutions to make interdisciplinary interaction possible. He asks for a clearer formulation of the very values in question, so that these values can function as signposts of the direction the uses of contemporary science must take. And elsewhere[92] he asks theologians to stop muttering woolly generalizations about humanization and openness to the modern world and to get on with the task of becoming informed and precise.

[89] Riquet, art. cit., p. 87.

[90] For some more cf. G. Kunicic, "Trapianto del cuore: Considerazioni morali," *Perfice munus* 43 (1968) 322–30.

[91] James M. Gustafson, "Christian Humanism and the Human Mind," in *The Human Mind* (Amsterdam: North Holland Publ. Co., 1967) pp. 85–109, at 106–8.

[92] James M. Gustafson, "Toward Maturity in Decision-Making," *Christian Century* 85 (1968) 894–98.

Medical progress has in the past contributed to the process of humanization. If Gustafson's suggestions are taken seriously, there is every evidence that it will continue to do so, even in unforeseen ways.[93]

MORALITY AND THE MAGISTERIUM

Shortly before the issuance of *Humanae vitae*, John Cardinal Heenan wrote of the magisterium that "there is no more delicate subject in contemporary theology."[94] Where the ordinary papal magisterium is concerned, Cardinal Heenan suspects that "an article in the periodical *Concilium* is at least as likely to win their [theologians] respect as a papal encyclical. The decline of the magisterium is one of the most significant developments in the post-conciliar Church." It is not surprising, therefore, that there has been a good deal of writing in the past semester on the magisterium, especially as it touches morality.

What is responsible for this crisis? Gregory Baum, O.S.A., proposed earlier that a mythical understanding of the magisterium is being challenged by recent developments in the Church, and this challenge is accompanied by a loss of authority on the part of the magisterium.[95] By a mythical notion of the magisterium Baum means the view that the divine truths of salvation are in the possession of pope and bishops and that therefore these are positioned to pass along divine answers to religious questions.

Behind the contemporary challenge to this notion Baum discovers many factors. For example, the doctrinal development at Vatican II shocked and surprised many Christians. Positions proposed authoritatively in the past by the magisterium were modified or even reversed. Another factor is the extraordinary fate of many well-known theologians in the Catholic Church. Those suspect in the fifties and unable to write were the very ones who played a crucial role in Vatican II. Then, too, there is the cultural pluralism of the Catholic Church. Because the Church embraces those belonging to different cultural and intellectual environments, the faith will be formulated in different ways. The magisterium usually expresses itself in a way closer to one theological tradition than to another, and this is seen as partiality by the diverging tradition. Furthermore, doctrinal questions have arisen for which

[93] C. Edward Crowther, "A Change of Heart?" *Center Magazine* 1 (March, 1968) 85–86. Crowther points up the many ironies involved in a transplant from the colored Clive Haupt to the white Philip Blaiberg occurring in apartheid South Africa.

[94] John Cardinal Heenan, "The Authority of the Church," *London Tablet* 222 (1968) 488–90.

[95] Gregory Baum, O.S.A., "The Problem of the Magisterium Today," *Ido-c*, Doss. 67, 30/31/32/33.

answers are not available. The necessary research on historical documents is just beginning. This means that there are authoritative doctrinal statements whose full meaning we do not know. Baum also mentions the antirationalism of contemporary culture, its positivistic mentality, and the spirit of rebellion as contributing influences in the crisis.

In a long article Daniel Maguire has turned his attention to the magisterium and morality.[96] It is Maguire's contention that "the term 'infallible' does not in fact aptly describe the nature or function of the moral magisterium and that we should discontinue using that term in discussing the moral magisterium." Eight reasons are offered to support this conclusion. For example, it is argued that "the very nature of truth should make us cautious in speaking of infallibility." Reality, Maguire says, exceeds our conceptualizations and our knowledge of it. Human knowledge is for *homo viator* "never complete or entirely error free." Furthermore, he contends that "there is a conflict in the concept of an infallible statement made through the medium of fallible language." Meaning has a tendency to slip out from under verbal formulae. A third point made is that not all the bishops were happy with the word "infallible" at Vatican I. Finally, the author argues that the term "infallible" has connotations that are offensive and confusing.

Maguire is certainly correct in asserting that the term "infallible" does not aptly describe the nature or function of the moral magisterium as we have experienced it. But a large qualification might be made at this point. Some of his arguments (i.e., the ones given above) are not only targeted on infallibility in the moral magisterium, but they explode against the whole idea of infallibility in general. This not only represents scattershot aim, but it tends to dissipate the force of the very valid point Maguire is establishing. For example, the fact that "meaning has a tendency to slip out from under verbal formulae" hardly supports the conclusion of a "conflict in the concept of an infallible statement made through the medium of fallible language." Does it not mean only that we must find out what the language meant at the time to know what has been defined?

Maguire also reviews the relationship of natural law to the gospel, especially in terms of the competence of the magisterium. At several points he chides the author of these Notes, and not without some reason. The positions he questions certainly call for some qualification, and I am grateful for Maguire's reflections. David Leigh, S.J., presents a good overview of the entire discussion just mentioned.[97] He concludes that the limits and meaning

[96] Daniel Maguire, "Morality and the Magisterium," *Cross Currents* 18 (Winter, 1968) 41–65.

[97] David Leigh, S.J., "The Church as a Moral Guide," *American Ecclesiastical Review* 158 (1968) 385–98.

of the Church's infallible authority over morals represent insoluble problems unless there is clarification in several other areas. For example, greater clarity is needed on the interpretation of moral principles and the epistemology of moral knowledge. Similarly there is an urgent need for clarification of the extent of revelation and the relationship of the natural law to the formation of a Christian way of life in early Christianity.

Ultimately, however, Maguire is right, I believe, in saying that the infallible competence of the Church does not imply the power to proceed infallibly through the multiple judgments and informational processes required to apply these natural and gospel values to highly concrete instances. This restriction does not solve the question about competence to define the natural law. It merely suggests that, regardless of what position one prefers on this point, he should distinguish between the natural law in its basic imperatives, and derivations or applications of this law. It also suggests that a more realistic and fruitful avenue of enquiry is the authentic noninfallible moral magisterium.

The second part of Maguire's article deals with the authentic noninfallible magisterium. He believes that the moral magisterium in our time should present two characteristics. First, it should be prophetic. That is, it should be distinguished by its insight into the present and should pierce the blinding clouds that inevitably envelop human consciousness. The social encyclicals were genuinely prophetic documents. They braved the charge of left-wing radicalism to call for social reconstruction. Secondly, the magisterium must be dialogical. The truth is reached not in solitude but in the processes of communitarian existence. The Church must recognize herself as a participant in these processes and "not enter conversation trying to say the last word."

These emphases are healthy, and if they can avoid the traps of unilateralism they will prove very helpful. Not the least of the theologian's problems in relating Christianly and creatively to the magisterium is to avoid being selective about what could be prophetic. And that brings us to what is surely one of the most delicate theological problems surrounding discussion of the noninfallible moral magisterium: the relationship of theological research and writing to the teaching office of the Church.[98] The problem received a new poignancy with the publication of *Humanae vitae*.

Here we can review some statements on only one aspect of this relationship, i.e., dissent. Facing the problem of the scholar who disagrees on a particular

---

[98] For some official statements, cf. the collective pastoral of the Italian bishops, "Théologie et magistère," *Documentation catholique* 65 (1968) 507–18. This is summarized in *Herder Correspondence* 5 (1968) 111–14. See also the collective pastoral of the American hierarchy in *The Pope Speaks* 13 (1968) 48–97, at 89–93. Cf. especially the "Report on Doctrine" of the episcopal synodal commission in *Furrow* 19 (1968) 106–12.

point with the ordinary noninfallible magisterium, Austin B. Vaughan, president of the American Catholic Theological Society, states that the scholar may withdraw internal assent if he finds contrary reasons still compelling after he has accorded proper weight to the noninfallible teaching of the magisterium.[99] Vaughan believes that the theologian "still may not oppose it externally (directly) unless circumstances indicate that the magisterium now regards it as a matter open for discussion." Vaughan is aware of the difficulties of this position, the most obvious of which is that chief among the circumstances leading the magisterium to regard something as open for discussion is scholarly publication questioning a teaching.

In an article full of vintage certainties, Luigi Ciappi, O.P., touches on the duty of Catholics to adhere to the certain doctrine proposed by the magisterium of the Church.[100] The duty is grave, he says, because demanded by the duty of submitting oneself to the legitimate authority of the Church within the limits of its competence. "But, if in an exceptional case someone had clear arguments for doubting that the doctrine of the Church, not definitive and irreformable, is true, or that its decisions are just, he would not be held to internal assent, and yet the obligation of 'silent submission' would remain." Ciappi feels that the exceptional instance is realized not simply when a theologian is in the process of raising difficulties against magisterial teaching, but when new and convincing arguments are elaborated in favor of a contrary position. As for the publication of these findings, he believes that "one cannot admit good faith in one who discusses in public, especially if it is in books or reviews destined for the general public, the teaching or the decisions of the ordinary magisterium."

It is easy to agree with Daniel Maguire when he rejects this conclusion. He grants that the obligation not to contradict the doctrine of the magisterium in public speech and writing was a truism among Catholic moralists for years. But "it is hardly defensible today. . . . Presumably, if discussion is called for, theologians around the world can hardly communicate by word of mouth. They must write, and by now it would be obvious that there is no written word on theological subjects that might not be proclaimed from the housetops. Vital theological discussions can no longer be kept 'under wraps.' Pastoral difficulties result from this and must be met, but this new fact of life must be accepted."[101]

[99] Austin B. Vaughan, "The Role of the Ordinary Magisterium of the Universal Episcopate," *Proceedings of the Catholic Theological Society of America* 22 (1967) 1–19.

[100] Luigi Ciappi, O.P., "Crisis of the Magisterium, Crisis of Faith?" *Thomist* 32 (1968) 147–70.

[101] Maguire, *art. cit.*, p. 56. Bruno Schüller agrees that it is by no means self-evident that

In a remarkable article Bishop Carlo Colombo, president of the Theological Faculty of Milan, first describes the notion of freedom of research of the theological scholar.[102]

In this moment of research one is not obliged to start from the teaching of the authentic noninfallible magisterium as from a certain definitive datum: one can place it in discussion, using methodical doubt, as in any scientific discussion, and one is not obliged to arrive at conclusions always and under every aspect conformed to the teaching of tradition expressed in the ordinary magisterium. One could indicate in it some insufficiencies or perhaps even some errors of interpretation of divine truth. In such a case, which is not a daily occurrence, one would have the right and the duty not only of suspending his religious assent as a believer, but also of proposing the reasons which lead to doubting some truth of the common teaching, in order to aid the entire Church, and particularly its teachers. to attain a more exact knowledge of the truth.

Colombo next turns to the *right and duty* of the theologian to propose his reasons. Publication, he asserts, involves a delicate and important pastoral problem. It can re-enforce or diminish the faith of the community, depending on its manner and timing. Since the magisterium must guard not only the content but also the spirit and virtue of faith, it has a right of judgment and control over the pastoral aspect of theological publication.[103]

In a thoughtful essay George K. Malone reviews Colombo's remarks and argues convincingly that Colombo must be understood to be distinguishing between responsible and irresponsible publication of dissenting views.[104] Malone rightly contends that the Roman Catholic theologian enjoys full academic freedom with regard to the authentic noninfallible magisterium as long as commonly accepted academic standards are observed. This means that his publication is the result of scholarly research and that his conclusions (especially when they represent dissent) are offered with sobriety and circumspection. Of course, the mass media do pick up the results of such

one may not publicly dispute an authentic teaching when one has clear and convincing grounds for thinking the magisterium is in error. He rightly believes that there would seem to be an obligation to correct the error, unless a greater evil would ensue. And in assessing this greater evil, it must be remembered that a delay in retracting an erroneous decision could do great harm in the long run by undermining the faithful's confidence in the magisterium ("Bemerkungen zur authentischen Verkündigung des kirchlichen Lehramtes," *Theologie und Philosophie* 42 [1967] 534–51, at 544).

[102] Carlo Colombo, "Obbedienza al magistero ordinario," *Seminarium* 7 (1967) 527–42.

[103] For a balanced statement of this pastoral concern, cf. Stephen E. Donlon, S.J., in *New Catholic Encyclopedia* 6 (New York: McGraw-Hill, 1966) 122.

[104] George K. Malone, "Academic Freedom Revisited," *Chicago Studies* 7 (1968) 3–13.

research publication, and this can create difficult pastoral problems. Malone is convinced that the only alternatives to publication are unacceptable and ultimately provocative of more harm than good. Therefore he insists that in exercising its "right of judgment and control over the pastoral aspect of theological publication," the hierarchical magisterium must face the educative problem where it truly exists—at the pastoral level.[105] It may be seriously questioned whether "control . . . of theological publication" is in our day an apt means in any sense.

In an age when it is increasingly impossible to do theology exclusively in professional journals, theologians have a heavy responsibility in contributing to the solution of the pastoral problem just mentioned. They would go a long way toward discharging their responsibilities if in the diffusion of theological thought they scrupulously adhered to the pedagogical guidelines stated by the episcopal synodal commission on doctrine: "First of all, let what is certain and fundamental be proposed as the unshaken basis of the faith and of Christian life; then what is new should be presented in such a way that a fitting explanation will manifest the continuity in the faith of the Church; finally, hypotheses should be put forth with that degree of probability which they in fact enjoy and with attention to the ways in which it is foreseen it will be understood."[106]

John F. Dedek faces the problem of dissent by examining more closely the duties of a Catholic vis-à-vis authentic noninfallible teaching.[107] He sees two reasons why a Catholic is obliged to give religious assent to such teaching. First, prudence dictates this assent. The teaching of the authentic magisterium enjoys the presumption of truth. Secondly, assent is required by religious obedience; that is, the authentic teacher has authority from Christ "to bind the consciences of Christians in religious matters." Thus failure in this duty involves both temerity and disobedience.

Now neither of these reasons is absolute. The presumption can yield to

---

[105] Msgr. Philips has summarized the problem from the point of view of the theologian as follows: "No one forbids him to continue his investigations as long as he avoids throwing discredit, through spite or intellectual pride, on the declarations of the magisterium. In practice this man would have to observe great prudence in order to prevent a public debate in which sentence would be pronounced by a tribunal of incompetents. This attitude is demanded of him by the respect due not only to the magisterium, but also to his brethren in the faith whom it is not lawful to plunge rashly and without profit into inextricable conflicts of conscience" (*L'Eglise et son mystère au deuxième Concile du Vatican* 1 [Paris: Desclée, 1967] 323).

[106] Cf. *Furrow* 19 (1968) 111.

[107] John F. Dedek, "Freedom of the Catholic Conscience," *Chicago Studies* 7 (1968) 115–25.

contrary evidence. As for obedience, Dedek says that "the Church has the authority from God to command the faithful to accept with their minds certain doctrinal positions." But this obedience-motive brings us back to the juridical order, where the virtue of epikeia is operative. This means that it is the burden and freedom of conscience to judge the binding force and relevance of such precepts in one's own situation. Any other attitude would amount to mechanical obedience, which is no virtue at all and is fraught with dangers. Therefore, since the obedience-motive is one of the reasons calling for acceptance of noninfallible teaching, Dedek concludes that "the individual Christian conscience has the same kind of freedom before authentic noninfallible teaching as it does before Church law." That is, he must decide on other objective grounds the situational validity of authentic teaching. "He is first bound to judge and in the end to do only and always what he himself thinks is right." The precept to assent is "subject to the judgment of conscience."[108]

This is an intriguing analysis. It has unquestionable foundations in earlier dogmatic texts and in recent magisterial statements. Furthermore, a good case can be made for saying that some interventions of the magisterium reflect more the character of a decision, a practical *modus agendi*, than a teaching in the strict sense. Hence they would seem to invoke an obediential response rather than assent. However, where the *acceptance of teaching* is concerned, let us question for the moment the very existence of two distinct sources of duty (presumption of truth, obedience). In the face of teaching, the Catholic's duties, it would seem, are uniquely the consequence of the very existence of a teaching office in the Church.

The matter might be put as follows. Suppose that the command of obedience were actually a distinct reason for giving assent to noninfallible teaching. Obedience cannot be, as Dedek notes, mechanical. Therefore the individual "is first bound to judge and in the end to do only and always what he himself thinks right." In this case the object of the command would be to "accept with the mind," to use Dedek's phrase. Now the only reason for not "accepting with the mind" is contrary evidence. But does this not bring us back simply to the breakdown of the presumption favoring magisterial teach-

---

[108] A somewhat similar approach is presented by John G. Milhaven, S.J., in *National Catholic Reporter*, Aug. 7, 1968, p. 11. Milhaven writes: "If the authority can be wrong in the obedience he demands, then the subject can, in certain cases, be obliged to consider whether he is justified in obeying or whether, if he were to obey in this case, he would be abdicating his moral responsibility." I say "somewhat similar" because Milhaven seems to regard certain concrete actions as the object of the precept, where Dedek sees assent as its object.

ing? Similarly the binding force of this precept is, according to Dedek, "subject to the judgment of conscience." But what else can this mean except that such a command would be conditioned by contrary evidence? If it is not evidence that leads one to dispense himself from the command-to-assent, one's nonconformity with it would seem to be arbitrary. Therefore is it not difficult to see how the command postulated by Dedek adds anything not already present in the presumption based on the divinely constituted character of the magisterium?

On the other hand, perhaps the objection I have raised here overrationalizes the whole process of teaching and learning in the Church. Perhaps it cuts too fine and views the teaching process too uniquely from the point of view of the theologian rather than the ordinary faithful. Continued discussion of this point is certainly called for.

Nearly all of the literature touching on dissent from noninfallible teaching starts from the premise that such teaching generates per se a duty of "religious assent." This analysis has been with us for years and has a good deal to recommend it.[109] However, anyone familiar with theological literature will realize how difficult it has been for theologians to untangle the problems involved in this assent. Robert Springer, S.J., remarked in the June edition of these Notes that "the earlier epistemology demanding 'religious assent' to authentic teaching has been inadequate and in need of development."[110] Where Springer would locate the inadequacy is not clear, but most theologians would endorse his general statement, I believe, and would be in sympathy with attempts to rethink the question.

In reapproaching the relationship of the Catholic to noninfallible teaching, must we not begin by saying that our concept of the magisterium will be closely tied to our concept of the Church? The magisterium is, after all, the Church as she teaches. Now in the past a rather one-sidedly juridical model of the Church was common. Such a notion of the Church is bound to in-

---

[109] Vatican II spoke of "religiosum voluntatis et intellectus obsequium" but then added "ita nempe ut magisterium ejus supremum reverenter agnoscatur, et sententiis ab eo prolatis sincere adhereatur, juxta mentem et voluntatem manifestam ipsius" (*AAS* 57 [1965] 30). With regard to episcopal teaching, the faithful are told that they "religioso animi obsequio adhaerere debent" (*ibid.*, p. 29). Speaking to priests, Paul VI says in *Humanae vitae*: "Vos primi in ministerio vestro perfungendo exemplum sinceri obsequii edite, quod interius exteriusque ecclesiastico Magisterio tribuendum est" (*De propagatione humanae prolis recte ordinanda* [Rome: Typis Polyglottis Vaticanis, 1968] p. 35). Recently M. Flick, S.J., referred to "quel religioso ossequio di volontà e intelligenza" ("Teologia e magistero nel messagio dell'Episcopato italiano," *Civiltà cattolica* 119 [1968] 333–42, at 341).

[110] Robert H. Springer, S.J., "Notes on Moral Theology," THEOLOGICAL STUDIES 29 (1968) 279.

fluence the theology of the magisterium—specifically the nature of authentic teaching and the response due to it. If a heavily juridical notion of the Church prevails, is it not inevitable that a heavily juridical notion of the magisterium will accompany this? This means that the teaching office of the Church could be easily confused, to some extent or other, with the administrative (or disciplinary) office. When this happens, Church teaching can gradually take on characteristics which do not properly belong to teaching as such. Thus in the past we have spoken of "the binding force of papal teaching"; we have referred to it as "imposed" and "commanded." The response to teaching conceived in this manner is described with the terms "obedience," "submission," "acceptance," "assent." What I am tentatively suggesting is that assent, as the immediate proportionate response to authentic noninfallible teaching, could be a product of an overly juridical notion of the Church. Embedded in such a concept is a paternalistic attitude toward teaching where the teacher possesses the truth and the taught are dispensed from personal reflection and assimilation, and are asked simply to accept. The ultimate popular caricature of this juridical emphasis is: if you belong to the club, you keep the rules of the club.

The Second Vatican Council enlarged our notion of the Church by moving away somewhat from the juridical model. The dominant description of the Church became the People of God. If this notion of the Church is weighed carefully, would it not affect the notion of the Church as teacher? Just one of the effects would be a clearer separation of teaching and administration (discipline). In light of this separation, magisterial teachings would not be viewed as "imposed, commanded, demanding submission and obedience"; for these terms suggest disciplinary jurisdiction, not teaching authority. Rather, noninfallible Church teachings would be seen as offered to the faithful. Obviously, such teaching must still be viewed as authoritative, but the term "authoritative" would shed many of its juridical, and sometimes almost military, connotations. The proportionate response to authoritative teaching might not *immediately* be religious assent, even though such acceptance would generally follow.

Perhaps the matter could be put as follows. Because of its indisputable charism (we say nothing for the moment about the manner of its exercise), the hierarchical magisterium must be accepted as an authoritative teacher. That is, for a Catholic the teachings of the hierarchical magisterium enjoy an eminence not conceded to any other religious teacher. This means that its teachings will generate a presumption not enjoyed by other teaching authorities. In the past we have referred to this as a presumption that its teachings are correct, sound, and reliable.

It would seem that the *immediate* response to such a presumption in a concrete case is not assent, but rather more generally a religious docility and deference.[111] That is, the appropriate personal posture vis-à-vis an authoritative teacher and the presumptions generated by his authority is a kind of connatural eagerness to accept and adhere to his teaching. The actuation of this cast of mind and bent of will might be described in terms of a strong inclination which accompanies us as we go about the task of appropriating and assimilating a teaching. This strong inclination would concretize itself in several ways. First, it will mean respect and reverence for the person and his office, and continuing openness to his teaching. Secondly, it will mean a readiness to reassess one's own positions in light of this teaching, an attempt to see if this teaching can be supported on grounds other than those presented, and a humble realization of the limitations imposed by one's own background, etc. Thirdly, it will suggest a great reluctance to conclude that magisterial moral teaching is clearly erroneous even after one has concluded that the evidence, arguments, and analyses used to establish this teaching are inadequate. One would prefer, in all humility, to conclude for the present that the authentic teaching is positively doubtful rather than clearly erroneous. Finally, it will demand a style of external behavior which fosters respect and support for the magisterium. If a Catholic's conduct corresponds to these demands, he has brought to authoritative teaching a response he brings to no one else. He has, one would think, responded proportionately to the authority of the teacher. Such procedural respect and reverence will generally lead to assent, but assent is not the immediate proportionate response. And if dissent occurs, one would suspect that it could occur, as a general rule, only after the passage of a certain amount of time, since time is needed for the arduous reflection suggested here.

Ladislas M. Orsy, S.J., has argued for substantially the same idea as that presented here.[112] However, he retains the word "assent" and then defines it as follows:

It means to respect authority and to acknowledge it as coming from Christ. It means to be open to any teaching coming from authority and to acknowledge the charism of the Spirit in it; and at the same time it means to admit humbly that since the charism of infallibility is not in operation, the Spirit of God may well allow human fallibility to be present with divine wisdom.

---

[111] This would apply to those whose background and competence demands of them a personal reflection.

[112] Ladislas M. Orsy, S.J., "Questions about 'Human Life,'" *America* 119 (1968) 99. Cf. also the statement by twelve members of the Alma College faculty in *America* 119 (1968) 162–64.

If there is some merit to these skeletal suggestions (they certainly need much more rigorous analysis than space permits here), they would lead us away from the vocabulary of conformity which has dominated discussion about the noninfallible magisterium: "the binding force of an encyclical," "the obligation to assent," "obedience to the teaching." These are terms which all too easily reflect the magisterium of a Church conceived according to a dominantly juridical model. One can argue that obedience is not the proper word to describe one's reactions to a revered teacher, even a teacher revered out of the strong impulses of faith. Similarly, one could argue that authentic noninfallible teaching has no binding force strictly so called; it is simply teaching and enjoys the authority proper to the teacher in question.

If religious docility involving internal and external reverence, respect, openness, and careful reflection (generally issuing in assent) is the proper immediate response to authoritative noninfallible teaching, then several things would be clarified. First, the measure of one's loyalty to the magisterium is not precisely assent, but the docility and deference which generally (only this) issue in assent.[113] Secondly, since this is so, juridical sanctions against Catholics who conscientiously and responsibly dissent are out of place. Such sanctions only perpetuate a paternalistic notion of the Church and her teaching. Furthermore, by misidentifying the locus of loyalty, they might make genuine disloyalty harder to recognize and therefore ultimately easier to practice. Sanctions are in place for the reckless and irresponsible style of one's dissent. Thirdly, a doctrine which is offered in contrast to one which is imposed has the character of a gift. Our over-all concern should be to promote those conditions which facilitate a truly personal reception of this gift. For example, hierarchical concern and vigilance should be aimed above all at the education of the Catholic community: to the nature of noninfallible teaching and to the privilege that is ours in its possession; to the harsh responsibilities upon us of disciplined reflection if our personal reception of this gift leads ultimately to dissent; to an awareness of the many values and circumstances to be weighed where publicizing this dissent is in question.

This point of view suggests that achievement of the truth is a process in which all of us have a Christian responsibility. It is precisely and only by a truly personal appropriation of magisterial teaching that we will learn in the Church how our charity is to be expressed. If we simply hear and act, then the learning process of the Church will be short-circuited. The process of growth of knowledge in the Church demands that we hear, study, consult,

[113] This may appear to be a very subtle distinction from the traditional formulation. However, I believe it is significant. For to say that authentic moral teaching generates per se a duty of assent all too easily allows dissent to be confused with disloyalty.

and act. The result of this communal experience becomes the source of a new understanding and a fuller unfolding of basic human and Christian values. Dissent—honorable, respectful, responsible—is not so much a personal right (there are implied concessions of excessive juridicism in this type of talk); rather it is only the possible outcome of a respectful and docile personal reflection on noninfallible teaching. Such reflection is the very condition of progress in understanding in the Church. Dissent, therefore, as a possible outcome of this reflection, must be viewed as a part of that total approach whereby we learn. If it is seen as a challenge to papal authority or as disloyalty, we have by implication ruled personal reflection out of court and compromised our own growth in understanding.

THE MAGISTERIUM AND CONTRACEPTION BEFORE "HUMANAE VITAE"

In the last installment of these Notes a discussion on the papal address of Oct. 29, 1966, concluded as follows: "Only an authentic teaching statement is capable of dissipating a genuine doctrinal doubt. And that is why I would agree with the many theologians who contend that the matter of contraception is as of now, at least for situations of genuine conflict, just where it was before the papal address—in a state of practical doubt."[114] This conclusion was based on the opinion that the Oct. 29 statement of Pope Paul was not an authentic teaching statement.

John C. Ford, S.J., and John J. Lynch, S.J., have challenged the conclusion that the teaching on contraception was practically doubtful (and subject to probabilism), and especially they have challenged it on the grounds on which I argued it.[115] The particular point at issue between us was the condition of certainty or doubt in the Church as this situation was affected by Vatican II and the papal address of Oct. 29. An analysis of the situation in terms of these two documents is no longer adequate since the issuance of *Humanae vitae*. However, the state of the Church from 1966–68 is very helpful, perhaps even necessary, for an understanding of the over-all significance of *Humanae vitae*. That is, an understanding of *Humanae vitae* and the cognate problems it raises will depend to some extent on how one assesses the situation in the Church prior to the Encyclical. Furthermore, because of the established competence and humaneness of the authors, and

---

[114] THEOLOGICAL STUDIES 28 (1967) 799–800.

[115] John C. Ford, S.J., and John J. Lynch, S.J., "Contraception: A Matter of Practical Doubt?" *Homiletic and Pastoral Review* 68 (1968) 563–74. That the article is a counterstatement to the conclusions I drew is made explicit in the July issue of *HPR*, p. 810.

because the entire discussion touches sensitively on the matter of theological methodology, we stand to learn a great deal from a continuing exchange of views on this matter.

The Ford-Lynch argument was made in three steps: (1) the papal statement of June 23, 1964; (2) the doctrine of Vatican II; (3) the papal address of Oct. 29, 1966. The thrust of their paper was that these three documents prevented the existence of a contrary practical probability. A word on each of these documents is called for here.

With regard to the first point, I am in full agreement with Ford and Lynch. The Allocution of June 23, 1964 was an authentic noninfallible teaching statement. It was an authentic noninfallible assertion that the reasons adduced to that point were not sufficient to topple the norms of Pius XI and Pius XII. Those familiar with the articles published before that time would agree that they contained serious defects and inconsistencies, and that these shortcomings fully justified the judgment of Pope Paul.

As for Vatican II, Ford-Lynch state their conviction that the texts of the Council "deal with contraception and prohibit it." These Notes have discussed this matter at length before and it is unlikely that further prolonged discussion of the matter could do more than deepen trenches already dug and occupied.[116] However, since the discussion concerned not only the document itself but its relation to a practical doubt, several points bear repeating here.

First, it must be remembered that the Pope reserved the matter to himself. It is hardly likely, therefore, that the statement of Vatican II would be very definite or decisive. Indeed, those familiar with the *stylus curiae* recognize in the conciliar remarks a piece of masterful evasion. Hirschmann reminds us that the conciliar statement was very "cautious and open" and that the famous footnote 14 ends as follows: "With the doctrine of the magisterium in this state, this Holy Synod does not intend to propose immediately concrete solutions." [117] Such conciliar light-stepping is not to be wondered at when we read from a Council *peritus* and the editorial secretary of the subcommission which studied marriage questions: "The grave questions as to whether every act is subject to the end of procreation and whether an act of conjugal love in a generously lived marriage may not

---

[116] THEOLOGICAL STUDIES 27 (1966) 651.

[117] Johannes B. Hirschmann, "Eheliche Gewissenskonflikte und kirchliches Lehramt," *Geist und Leben* 41 (1968) 142–47, at 143.

find more independent expression are left quite open. *The Council deliberately refrained from giving a decision in this theological dispute.*"[118]

Secondly, Ford-Lynch introduced two letters from H. J. Cardinal Cicognani to Alfredo Cardinal Ottaviani. One of their purposes in introducing these letters, the authors stated, was "to throw light on the meaning which Pope Paul himself attached to the conciliar text when he signed it." It can be argued that if such letters are needed to illumine the meaning a signatory attaches to a text, then the text hardly speaks too clearly and convincingly for itself. Furthermore, it must be said that the letters adduced throw light on the desires and intentions of Pope Paul, not precisely on the meaning he "himself attached to the conciliar text when he signed it," as the authors asserted.

Finally, if Vatican II spoke so clearly and decisively on contraception, one is puzzled by Pope Paul's later remarks about the conciliar statement: "The new pronouncement awaited from the Church on the problem of the regulation of births is not thereby [by the Council] given, because We ourselves, having promised and having reserved the matter to ourselves, wanted to consider carefully the doctrinal and pastoral applications which have arisen regarding this problem in recent years...." [119]

The Council, then, was hardly the place to turn for the type of statement which would unequivocally and authoritatively settle a matter which it knew the Pope had reserved to himself. I cannot but agree with Donald Campion, S.J., when he asserts that it seems generally agreed now that the Council did not alter "the state of debate on the matter that had existed since Pope Paul's own announcement of June 23, 1964 of his creation of a commission to study questions in dispute about marriage and birth control." [120]

This brings us to the papal Allocution of Oct. 29, 1966. [121] It was the contention of these Notes that this Allocution did not represent a genuine teaching statement dealing with the doubts that had arisen since 1964.

---

[118] Victor L. Heylen, "Fostering the Nobility of Marriage and the Family," in *The Church Today*, ed. Group 2000 (Westminster: Newman, 1968) p. 117. This is also the conclusion of Michel Dayez: "En effet, le Concile n'a pas voulu condamner les nouvelles tentatives de solution selon lesquelles on peut, pour des motifs objectifs...recourir à la contraception. Il a même explicitement rejeté plusiers amendments qui visaient à introduire dans le texte conciliaire lui-même des formulations favorisant la présentation classique de la doctrine" (*Revue diocèsaine de Tournai* 22 [1967] 520).

[119] *AAS* 58 (1966) 1169.

[120] Donald R. Campion, S.J., and Gregory Baum, O.S.A., *Pastoral Constitution on the Church in the Modern World* (Westminster: Paulist Press, 1967) p. 43.

[121] *AAS* 58 (1966) 1166–70.

Ford-Lynch disagree with this conclusion. Their reasons are two. First, they are "mystified when any theologian imagines that a pope would attempt to deal with a problem like contraception by means of canonical legislation." I am too. But canonical legislation is not the only alternative to a teaching statement. It can be argued that the Pope was simply trying to calm the ruffled waters by suggesting an interim pastoral policy which would not make his genuine teaching more difficult than it should be. Still, a pastoral policy is not a teaching statement. [122]

Their second reason for regarding the Allocution as a doctrinal statement is that "Paul himself explicitly declares in the document that the norm he is insisting on is one which is 'constituted best and most sacred for everybody by the authority of the law of God, rather than by Our authority.'" Here we must recall two facts. First, Pope Paul did not at this time make his decisive statement. Alluding to the enormous complications and tremendous gravity of the subject, he said: "This is the reason why our response has been delayed and why it must be deferred for some time yet." Secondly, in an earlier Allocution to the Congress of the Italian Feminine Center, Pope Paul, referring to the ongoing work of his special birth-control commission, stated: "The magisterium of the Church cannot propose moral norms until it is certain of interpreting the will of God. And to reach this certainty the Church is not dispensed from research and from examining the many questions proposed for her consideration from every part of the world. This is at times a long and not an easy task." [123]

These two statements must be weighed in conjunction with each other. The following analysis is suggested. If the magisterium cannot propose (i.e., teach) moral norms "until it is certain of interpreting the will of God," then the traditional moral norms reiterated by Pope Paul at that time must have represented a *certain* teaching of the will of God. But if this was so, why would he have delayed his decisive statement and done so precisely on the grounds that time and research were needed to achieve certainty? The obvious conclusion would seem to be that the magisterium was not *certain* that these norms represented God's will. This conclusion is only re-enforced when one recalls the conclusions proposed by the majority of the papal study

---

[122] F. Bersini asks the following question: May someone in the meantime freely follow the opinion he holds better, as in the situation of doubt? His answer is interesting because it casts serious doubt on the teaching character of the statements of Vatican II and Pope Paul (Oct. 29, 1966): "La nostra risposta è negativa; perché, mentre la questione è posta allo studio dei competenti, il Concilio e il Summo Pontefice *vogliono che nella practica pastorale* si segua la dottrina tradizionale" (*Perfice munus* 43 [1968] 149–62, at 155–56, emphasis added).

[123] *AAS* 58 (1966) 218–24, at 219.

commission. If "to reach this certainty (*raggiungere questa certezza*) the Church is not dispensed from research," then surely the conclusions of this research group must have some bearing on the achievement or maintenance of certainty in this area. If it is argued that the papal delay was to be attributed to problems of pastoral presentation and not to uncertainty, we need only to return to Pope Paul's statement (Feb. 12, 1966) that the magisterium must be certain that it is proposing God's will when it proposes norms for conduct and that to reach this certainty "is at times a long and not an easy task." [124]

Summarily, then, if certainty is required to teach moral norms, and if research is required to achieve this certainty, and if the research sources produce anything but certainty, then the conclusion must be that the required certainty about these norms did not exist—hence that these norms could not be proposed (taught). And if this is so, how was the papal statement of Oct. 29, 1966 a true teaching statement? This would not mean that the traditional norms were seen to be incorrect. It simply means that it is not clear how they could then be taught as certainly interpreting God's will.

Let us put it this way. Given the certainty necessary to teaching binding moral norms (a certainty asserted by the Pope himself), what was one to think of the Pope's assertion that "the thought and norm of the Church are not changed"? This might have meant two things. (1) The traditional thought and norm are *certainly* the will of God. The evidence seems heavily weighted against such a reading if Pope Paul's statement about certainty and its indispensable sources is given due consideration. That is, if in February, 1966, the Pope needed the studies of the commission to achieve (*raggiungere*) the certainty necessary to propose moral norms, and if having received the majority report of the commission he achieved or maintained a certainty contrary to it, then perhaps we need a long, long discussion about the nature of the magisterium. We shall return to this point shortly. (2) The thought and norm just mentioned are not certainly the will of God, but they have not yet been formally reversed or formally admitted to be doubtful. The magisterium was not at that time prepared either to reverse these norms or to admit their doubtful character. In other words, the magisterium was certain only that it did not yet want formally and explicitly to modify or recall these norms. Such hesitation was, in my judgment, very understandable and very prudent. But certainty that the norms should not yet have been formally modified was not the same as certainty that they represented the will of God. The latter is a doctrinal certainty, the former is

[124] John Cardinal Heenan found the root of delay in the character of the devices which fall under the general term "contraception": *Tablet* 222 (May 18, 1968) 489.

not necessarily such. Expression of the latter certainty is a doctrinal or teaching statement, whereas expression of the former is not necessarily such.

What then of the papal insistence that "they [traditional norms] demand faithful observance"? In 1966 this conclusion only raised the question: why?[125] In other words, if the traditional norms were not clearly enough the will of God to allow a decisive statement to that effect, then the assertion that "the norms are still valid" simply had to rest on something other than the conviction that they were certainly the will of God. Consequently this assertion constituted something other than a doctrinal or genuine teaching statement. It was this line of reasoning that led me to the conclusion that the real doubts which had arisen since 1964 had not encountered a true teaching statement.[126] This in turn led to the assertion that contraception was in a state of practical doubt. [127] This still appears to me to have been a very defensible position.

We have dwelt at considerable length on this matter because of its importance to an understanding of the nature and function of the magisterium. In this perspective the discussion is far broader than the single issue which occasioned it. When weighty considerations are introduced against traditional norms of the natural law, and when a highly competent research group

[125] By simply referring to the 1964 statement, the Pope does not thereby issue a similar statement in 1966; for the 1964 statement was a teaching statement on the reasons adduced to that time. If the 1966 statement were to have had a similar force, it would have to have passed authoritatively on the theological thought since then, and specifically on the report of the commission. The Pope said of the commission's conclusions only that "they cannot be considered definitive."

[126] Cardinal Heenan's remarks do not appear to be those of a man faced with a genuine teaching statement; cf. *Tablet* 222 (1968) 489.

[127] Dayez (*art. cit.*, p. 520) held explicitly the conclusion of practical doubt: "Given the state of doctrinal research, given the evolution which is developing, given the positive and reasonable doubt touching the statement that 'every contraceptive method is *de se* evil,' it appears to me that a confessor cannot *demand*, under pain of refusal of absolution, that the penitent renounce a contraceptive method motivated by grave reasons of conjugal life." Hirschmann gingerly avoided saying explicitly that probabilism was operative where contraception is concerned. But his whole treatment implied this conclusion. For example, he insisted that probabilism does not amount to minimalism or laxism. Furthermore, he suggested that clinging to a teaching which did not by any means clearly raise the claim of last authority can lead one to place himself in the path of a fuller appearance of the truth and thereby inhibit the final dynamic of the Spirit in the Church (*art. cit.*, p. 145). These conclusions, it must be noted, do not resemble those which drew from the French episcopal commission on the family the following castigation: "Even though the work and research of moral specialists are legitimate and necessary, still it is astonishing that some Catholic authors allow themselves to solve the question authoritatively in advance of papal teaching" (*Documentation catholique* 65 [1968] 533).

is assembled to sort out these problems, and when this group fails to uphold traditional norms, and when a subsequent episcopal commission produces the same results, then the contention that the norms are still certain (certainly the will of God) because the magisterium has not yet modified them would seem to be a contention which asks the magisterium to bear a burden it can hardly carry. Iş it not asking it to be certain independently of the ordinary sources of clarity and certainty? At some point or other such a notion of the magisterium is all too easily a caricature of the teaching office of the Church.

Could we not put it this way? If a modification of traditional teaching is only plausible on the supposition that the inadequacy of traditional norms had already become clear *before the papal statement*, then it is not the official papal statement alone which gives this clarity. Norms are not certain up to the moment of modification, then suddenly uncertain or changed with the modifying statement. To say so is to adopt a theory of "magisterium by fiat." [128] Now if the state of uncertainty is not produced by a papal statement of modification, but is the condition of its possibility, this means that the state of uncertainty is gathered from the best available evidence prior to such a statement. This in turn suggests that the state of certainty is gathered from the best available evidence, not from a papal assertion about the state of certainty. [129] To imply anything else is once again to adopt a theory of magisterium by decree and to deny the validity of Pope Paul's assertion that research is required to achieve certainty.

In summary, what very probably underlay the exchange between Ford-Lynch and the compositor of these Notes was the relationship of the magisterium to theological investigation. This relationship constitutes what surely is one of the most important theological problems of the day. In broader

[128] Some of these same reflections can be urged against the guidelines produced in several American dioceses prior to the issuance of *Humanae vitae*. After calling attention to the direct and supreme jurisdiction of the Pope over all members of the Church, and referring to the Pope's insistence on the validity of existing (then) norms, the guidelines say: "In the light of that statement it is clear that neither priest in the confessional, nor Catholic teachers in public or private instruction, may say or imply that the teaching of the Catholic Church either permits or condones the use of means of contraception, be they mechanical, chemical or simply behavioral." The guidelines mentioned greater understanding and compassion; "we repeat, however, that he [the confessor] may not permit or condone the contraceptive practices mentioned above" (*National Catholic Reporter*, July 3, 1968, p. 6). A somewhat different emphasis is found in the letter of Bishop Bernhard Stein (Trier) to his priests (cf. *NCR*, May 22, 1968) and in the remarks of Bishop Sergio Mendez Arceo of Cuernavaca (cf. *Davenport Messenger*, May 16, 1968).

[129] The state of certainty, it would seem, is a fact, not precisely a doctrine about which the magisterium can teach.

perspective, it is simply one aspect of a changing notion of the magisterium. The style and structure of authority in the Church (not excluding teaching authority) are undergoing development. Not all aspects of this development are clear, but at the root of it there seems to be a growing decentralization. It is possible, of course, to carry this too far; it is also possible not to allow it to occur at all. Somewhere in the middle lies the truth. But at a time of painful and groping transition it is hard to find this middle. It is quite possible that it was these larger issues which were operative in our disagreement. And that brings us to *Humanae vitae*.

THE ENCYCLICAL "HUMANAE VITAE"

The problem prior to *Humanae vitae* was whether the positive doubts surrounding traditional teaching had encountered a true teaching statement. To view the problem in this way was, of course, to approach it from the restricted viewpoint of classical categories. Specifically, it was to imply that a true teaching statement would have destroyed, at least temporarily, any contrary practical probability. The focus of attention was on pastoral practice, once one had granted the existence of a genuine doctrinal doubt. It should not be forgotten that this discussion supposed the existence of a true doctrinal doubt. The problem after *Humanae vitae* is the extent to which this document, obviously a teaching statement, has truly solved the doubts.

Perhaps it were better to say that this is one of the problems occasioned by the Encyclical; for if anything is clear, it is that *Humanae vitae* is inseparable from questions far more basic than the issue which occasioned it. These larger issues have been stated very clearly by a group of theologians at Marquette University in the following way:

1) In the areas of human understanding which are proper to human reasoning, such as natural law, what is the function of the Church as the authoritative teacher of revelation?
2) What are the sources for the formulation of binding moral doctrine within the Christian community?
3) What is the precise role of the Pope as an authoritative teacher in these areas?
4) What is the role of the bishops, of the body of the faithful, and of the Church's theologians in formulating such moral teaching?
5) What qualifications may be attached to the individual Christian's assent to admittedly fallible statements of the merely authentic magisterium, especially when this involves practical judgments of grave consequence?[130]

These questions, touching as they do on the central nervous system of

[130] Cf. *Our Sunday Visitor*, Aug. 18, 1968.

Catholic belief and life, explain why *Humanae vitae* caused such a profound reaction in the Catholic community. [131] Obviously we cannot discuss these major theological themes here. [132] However, only their full discussion will position us to understand the phase of development we are presently experiencing. We can address ourselves only to the single assertion which is at the heart of the Encyclical: every contraceptive act is intrinsically evil. The following remarks may be gathered under three headings: (1) the analysis and argument of the Encyclical; (2) the relation of theological analysis to a doctrinal conclusion; (3) some pastoral notes and conclusions.

The Analysis and Argument of the Encyclical

After stating that each marriage act must remain open (*per se destinatus*) to the transmission of life, Pope Paul presents the following analysis.

That teaching, often set forth by the magisterium, is founded upon the inseparable connection, established by God and unable to be broken by man on his own initiative, between the unitive and procreative meanings, both of which are present in the conjugal act.

For by its intimate structure, the conjugal act, while most closely uniting husband and wife, also capacitates them (*eos idoneos etiam facit*) for the generation of new life, according to laws inscribed in the very being of man and woman. By safeguarding both of these essential aspects, the unitive and the procreative, the use of marriage preserves in its fulness the sense of true mutual love and its ordination to man's exalted calling to parenthood.[133]

The Encyclical argues, therefore, that coitus is a single act with two aspects or inner meanings, the unitive and procreative. It further argues that these two senses are by divine design inseparable, so that one who deliberately renders coitus sterile attacks its meaning as an expression of mutual self-giving. Thus we read later that contraceptive intercourse

[131] This reaction was not without its human inconsistencies. For example, one wonders whether the issue of collegiality would have been raised quite so sharply had the decision of Pope Paul been different. This issue should have been raised by theologians at a much earlier date. Similarly, in earlier days the celibacy of the theologian defending traditional teaching was underscored. This same celibacy seems a bit more tolerable where the theologian is presently a dissenter. Or again, the very ones who dissented most vigorously when *Mater et magistra* appeared are now the ones fervently urging that Rome has spoken.

[132] For example, the word *ecclesia* is used thirty-four times in the Encyclical, according to my hasty count. It would be interesting to study the theological implications of its various uses.

[133] *De propagatione humanae prolis recte ordinanda* (Rome: Typis Polyglottis Vaticanis, 1968) no. 12. This is a Latin version of *Humanae vitae*. Subsequent references will be to this text and by paragraph number.

removes, "licet solum ex parte, significationem et finem doni ipsius" (n. 13). It seems that the whole weight of the Encyclical's teaching that a contraceptive act is "intrinsece inhonestum" (n. 14) derives from this analysis. In fact, Pope Paul says just that. Because this is so, several remarks are in place.

First, the above analysis is not new. It will be recalled that *Casti connubii* approached the expression of marital love as a motive for sexual intercourse. In the years prior to the Second Vatican Council it became clear to theologians that this was an incomplete and imperfect analysis. They began to speak of the expression of marital love as one of the very inner senses (*finis operis*) of coitus. Several allocutions of Pius XII adopted this point of view. [134] In recent years Joseph Fuchs, S.J., was more than anyone else associated with systematizing this notion. Speaking of the relationship of the two meanings or aspects of coitus, Fuchs wrote in 1963:

The Creator so arranged the sexual act that it is simultaneously both per se generative and per se expressive of intimate oblative love. He has so arranged it that procreation would take place from an act intimately expressive of conjugal love and that this act expressive of conjugal love would tend toward procreation. Therefore an act which *of itself* does not appear to be apt for procreation is by this very fact shown to be one which does not conform to the intentions of the Creator. The same thing should be said about an act which *of itself* is not apt for the expression of oblative love. Indeed, an act which is not apt for procreation is by this very fact shown to be one which is *of itself* not apt for the expression of conjugal love; for the sexual act is one.[135]

Many of us accepted this approach for a number of years and argued that contraceptive interference could not be viewed as a merely biological intervention. [136] Rather, we argued, it was one which affected the very foundation of the act as procreative and hence as unitive of persons; for by excluding the child as the permanent sign of the love to be expressed in coitus, one

---

[134] For example, *AAS* 43 (1951) 850; *AAS* 48 (1956) 470.

[135] Joseph Fuchs, S.J., *De castitate et ordine sexuali* (3rd ed.; Rome: Gregorian Univ. Press, 1963) p. 45. Speaking in another place (p. 80) of the separability of the two aspects of coitus asserted by some non-Catholics, Fuchs wrote: "They do not sufficiently grasp that the Creator *united* this double aspect. The sexual faculty has but *one* natural actuation in which the generative and oblative aspects specify each other." These same analyses are present in the earlier edition (1959, p. 61) of Fuchs's work.

[136] Cf. R. A. McCormick, S.J., "Conjugal Love and Conjugal Morality," *America* 110 (1964) 38–42, and "Family Size, Rhythm, and the Pill," in *The Problem of Population* (Notre Dame: Univ. of Notre Dame Press, 1964) pp. 58–84.

introduced a reservation into coitus and therefore robbed it of that which makes it objectively unitive.

This analysis, even though it represents a genuine advance, rests ultimately on the supposition that every act of coitus has and therefore must retain a per se aptitude for procreation. [137] This supposition is accepted and clearly stated in *Humanae vitae*. The Encyclical's formulation and repetition of traditional teaching speaks of the necessity that each marital act "ad vitam humanam procreandam per se destinatus permaneat" (n. 11). [138] Furthermore, the Encyclical speaks of the restriction of man's dominion over the genital powers "because of their intrinsic ordination toward raising up life, of which God is the principle" (n. 13). Also, of coitus we read that "by its intimate structure coitus . . . capacitates them for the generation of new life . . ." (n. 12). Now the immediate and often-stated difficulty with such a contention is that, starting with an obsolete biology, it attributes a meaning to all coitus on the basis of what happens with relative rarity.

Unless I am mistaken, *Humanae vitae* reflects the strength of this difficulty in what appears to be almost a contradiction within the Encyclical. Speaking of coital acts during infertile periods, the Encyclical says that they are legitimate "cum non cesset eorum destinatio ad conjugum conjunctionem significandam roborandamque" (n. 11). The rather clear implication here is that any *destinatio ad procreationem* ceases. Otherwise why did the Encyclical not say "cum non cesset eorum per se destinatio ad procreationem"? Why did the document use the phrase "non cesset" of a single aspect of coitus, thereby implying that the other of the two ordinations or aspects did indeed cease? The unstated but obvious reason is that any *destinatio ad procreationem* is absent in infertile acts. And if it is absent, it is clearly separable from them. In these infertile acts the unitive and procreative aspects are separable. This means that at one point the Encyclical seems unwittingly to imply a factual separation of the unitive and procreative aspects of individual coital acts during the infertile period. At another (n. 12) the doctrine that each act must remain open to new life is said to rest on the inseparable connection between the procreative and unitive meanings "quae ambae in actu conjugali insunt."

A second point must be noted here. Theologians have found the per se aptitude for procreation of each act of coitus an extremely difficult analysis

---

[137] For a refutation of the validity of the argument, cf. G. Grisez, *Contraception and the Natural Law* (Milwaukee: Bruce, 1964) pp. 34–35.

[138] This wording seems to represent a great broadening of the notion of a forbidden contraceptive act. In *Casti connubii* those interventions were condemned in which the act was deprived of its natural power to procreate: *AAS* 22 (1930) 560.

to sustain, because it seems to imply and demand an unacceptable criterion for the assessment of the meaning of human actions. The criterion apparently inseparable from this analysis is an approach which measures the meaning of an act by examining its physiological structure. In any number of places in the Encyclical biological structure and the processes of nature are accepted as the determinants of meaning. [139] They are said to represent God's plan and therefore to be morally normative.

Contemporary theological thought insists that the basic criterion for the meaning of human actions is the person, not some isolated aspect of the person. Vatican II, while speaking of marriage and responsible parenthood, pointed out that the moral character of any procedure must be determined by objective standards "ex personae ejusdemque actuum natura desumptis." [140] It is interesting to note the shift in emphasis found in *Humanae vitae*. There the criterion is "ipsa matrimonii ejusque actuum natura" (n. 10).

It is important to understand what it means to say that the person is the criterion of the meaning of actions. Authors have always admitted that the total object (or significance) of an action cannot be identified merely with the physical object. Physical objects as such have no relation to the moral order. Thus "taking another's property" is only a physical act; it is not yet a moral object. Similarly "uttering an untruth" is only a physical act or object. The Majority Report points this out in the case of arms, whose use is good when in self-defense, but evil when turned to unjust killing. [141] The materiality of the act is not the same as its meaning.

If, however, "taking another's property" contains an attack on persons or a person, it contains the malice of theft (and is an unloving act). If "uttering an untruth" jeopardizes man's life in community, it contains the malice of a lie. After examination of the goals and conditions of the human person (his potentialities and relationships as known from all sources—above all, revelation), we have concluded to the meaning of material goods and man's relation to them. The basic common destiny of material goods allows us to conclude to the inherent limitations on property rights. Only those actions

---

[139] "Deus enim naturales leges ac tempora fecunditatis ita sapienter disposuit..." (no. 11); "humana ratio... biologicas deprehendit leges, quae ad humanam personam pertinent..." (no. 10); "actum amoris mutui, qui facultati vitam propagandi detrimento sit, quam Deus omnium Creator secundum peculiares leges in ea insculpsit..." (no. 13); "... leges conservans generationis..." (no. 13); "... conjuges legitime facultate utuntur, sibi a natura data; in altera vero, iidem impediunt, quominus generationis ordo suos habeat naturae processus..." (no. 16); "Qui limites non aliam ob causam statuuntur, quam ob reverentiam, quae toti humano corpori ejusque naturalibus muneribus debetur..." (no. 17).

[140] *AAS* 58 (1966) 1072.   [141] *Tablet* 221 (1967) 512.

which violate genuine property rights constitute an attack on persons and merit the name of theft. We say genuine property rights, i.e., rights as defined and delimited within the whole hierarchy of personal value. This relationship to the hierarchy of personal value we have encapsulated in the phrase "against his reasonable will." Therefore only those acts which take another's property against his reasonable will constitute the category of theft, and represent an attack on the person through those things which are necessary to personal growth and good. It is the total good of the person which has determined which physical acts are theft, which not. The same might be said of speech.

Clearly, then, significance does not refer to mere physical acts; rather it is an assessment of an action's relation to the order of persons, to the hierarchy of personal value. [142] This same methodology must also apply in the area of sexual ethics. The significance (the total moral object) must be determined as in other instances, by relating the physical act to the order of persons and by seeing it as an intersubjective reality.

Of course, sexuality is founded in biological realities, and just as obviously sexual intercourse, materially considered, has some orientation toward fecundation. We are not calling these "thresholds of objectivity" into question here. We are only suggesting that the meaning of sexual activity cannot be derived narrowly from biological materialities; for this does not take account of the full range and meaning of human sexuality. It is not the sexual organs which are the source of life, but the person. As the Majority Report noted, "the biological process in man is not some separated part (animality) but is integrated into the total personality of man." [143] Thus the material fecundity in this process gets its moral meaning from its finalization toward the goods which define marriage. This is what it means, one would think, to draw objective standards "ex personae ejusdem actuum natura." Just as we refuse to identify "taking another's property" with theft, so we must refuse to identify the physiological components with the full meaning of sexual actions.

The third point to be made about the argument of the Encyclical is its handling of the analysis made by the now famous Majority Report. This report had suggested that infecund acts (even those deliberately made such) are incomplete, and derive one aspect of their moral quality from their relationship to the fertile acts already placed or to be placed. This analysis is rejected by the Encyclical on the grounds that an act deprived of its

[142] W. Van der Marck, O.P., refers to this personal aspect of the act as "intersubjectivity" (*Toward a Christian Ethic* [Westminster: Newman, 1967] pp. 48–59).
[143] *Tablet, loc. cit.*

procreative power is intrinsically evil. But this is precisely the point to be shown. In my judgment the Encyclical does not succeed in doing this.

Relation of a Theological Analysis to a Doctrinal Conclusion

If the analysis and argument used in an authoritative moral teaching on natural law do not support the conclusions, what is one to think of these conclusions? Concretely, *Humanae vitae* taught the intrinsic immorality of every contraceptive act. At least very many theologians will agree that there are serious methodological problems, even deficiencies, in the analysis used to support this conclusion. What is one to say of the conclusion in these circumstances?

The Encyclical itself, after exhorting priests to be examples of loyal internal and external *obsequium*, [144] stated: "That *obsequium*, as you know well, obliges not only because of the reasons adduced, but rather (*potius*) because of the light of the Holy Spirit, which is given in a particular way to the pastors of the Church in order that they may illustrate the truth" (n. 28). This statement summarizes the accepted notion of the authoritative but noninfallible moral magisterium. It says in effect that the authoritative character of the teaching is not identified with the reasons adduced for it. On the other hand, it clearly implies that the certainty of the teaching cannot prescind from the adequacy of the analyses given. Establishing the proper balance is the problem we face.

It might be helpful to point out the extremes to be avoided where authoritative noninfallible teaching is concerned. One extreme is that the teaching is as good as the argument. This makes the pope just another theologian and destroys the genuinely authoritative character of the papal charism. It also implies a one-sidedly rationalistic epistemology of moral cognition. The other extreme is that the teaching is totally independent of the argument. This makes the pope an arbitrary issuer of decrees and edicts. It dispenses completely with the need of theological reflection and ends up ultimately as an attack on the *teaching* prerogatives of the Holy Father.

It is important to stress this point. If a teaching is considered valid independently of the reasons and arguments, then the possibility of objectively founded dissent is eliminated on principle. That is, if noninfallible teaching must be accepted independently of the reasons supporting it (understanding "reasons" in a broad, not excessively rationalistic, sense), on what grounds is dissent still possible? And if dissent is impossible, in what sense is the teaching noninfallible? At this point the truth of the teaching is

144 I have left the word *obsequium* untranslated because a satisfactory English equivalent is lacking. Several Latin scholars have suggested that "obedience" is too strong.

simply identified with the authority proposing it. And who has greater moral authority than the Sovereign Pontiff? Many of us will find it uncomfortable to live with a notion of noninfallible teaching which demands that it be treated as practically infallible. Somewhere between these two extremes lies the truth.

The middle ground between these extremes has traditionally been formulated in terms of a presumption to be granted to authentic noninfallible statements. This is a presumption that they are correct. [145] The strength of this presumption will vary in individual instances according to many circumstances too numerous to detail or discuss here. We have already suggested that the response generated by this presumption is religious docility of mind and will. Furthermore it was suggested that this docility would concretize itself in several ways. These ways include a readiness to reassess one's own position in light of the teaching and an attempt to discover whether the conclusion taught might be established on grounds other than those adopted by the magisterium. Finally it was stated that such steps will generally lead to full and grateful acceptance of the teaching. And this acceptance will manifest itself in one's decisions.

But precisely because we are dealing with noninfallible teaching, the steps which express one's radical docility and submission could end somewhat differently. This will not happen often; otherwise the magisterium would cease to be truly authoritative. [146] But if the very possibility is excluded on principle, then are we really dealing with noninfallible teaching? Now if the steps stimulated by docility are carefully and conscientiously taken, and one still finds it personally impossible to justify the doctrinal conclusion, it seems to me that the presumption supporting the doctrine prevails until a sufficient number of mature and well-informed members of the community share this same difficulty. Until this stage is reached, our difficulties will suggest to us our own limitations, if we are honest and realistic. But once it becomes clear that a large number of loyal, docile, and expert Catholics share this same difficulty, then it would seem that the presumption supporting the certain correctness of the teaching would be weakened, at least to the extent that the doctrine could be said to be doubtful. If the presumption would not be weakened in the instance just described, when would it ever be? At this point one would wonder whether such a doctrine could give rise to a certain obligation in conscience.

[145] Here some further precisions are probably in place. When the word "correct" is applied to moral teaching, it could mean "speculatively true," "a valid value judgment," "a justifiable jurisdictional act in protection of moral values," etc.

[146] G. Baum, O.S.A., "The Right to Dissent," *Commonweal* 88 (1968) 553–54.

How does all of this apply to the doctrine of *Humanae vitae* that a contraceptive act is "intrinsically evil" (n. 14) and "always illicit" (n. 16)? By way of preface it must be said that a theologian's answer to this question is only his own honest, conscientious, but very fallible opinion. He submits it to his colleagues for appraisal and correction, and then to the bishops for their prayerful consideration. It seems necessary to make this point because in recent years theological opinions, including some in these Notes, have occasionally been used as if they enjoyed doctrinal status. This being said, we may attempt an answer to the question raised by proceeding in stages.

First, in the past years a good number of theologians, after literally thousands of hours of diligent study and discussion, had concluded that the traditional norms as proposed by Pius XI and Pius XII were genuinely doubtful. That is, there were serious and positive reasons against them. I am convinced that for many of us the word "doubt" meant just that. [147] It did not mean certainty one way or the other, though increasingly many of us viewed the analysis presented in the Majority Report as by far the more probable and persuasive view. Hence, when *Humanae vitae* appeared, we read it eagerly looking for the new evidence or the more adequate analyses which led Paul VI to his reaffirmation of traditional norms.

Secondly, a rather well-educated guess would say that the vast majority of theologians will conclude that the analyses of *Humanae vitae* build upon an unacceptable identification of natural law with natural processes. That is, they will assert that the argument does not justify the conclusion.

Thirdly, at this point the theologian's docility will stimulate him to ask: Can the intrinsic immorality of contraception be established in some more acceptable way, and on other grounds? Possibly. But in the past six or seven years of intense discussion we have experienced little success, and not for lack of trying, to be sure. It is not that the arguments do not conclude with the force of mathematical demonstration. Few ethical arguments do, even the most suasive. It is rather that there seems to be no argument capable of sustaining the intrinsic malice of contraceptive acts, and a good deal of evidence which denies this thesis. Indeed, past attempts to establish the doctrine have imprisoned us, step by inexorable step, in totally unacceptable presuppositions.

This is not to say that a strong indictment of contraception is out of place. Quite the contrary. For very many people contraception could easily represent a way of life springing from and reflecting the materialism and

---

[147] We say "many" here because there are certainly some, perhaps quite a few, theologians who are convinced of the complete moral integrity of contraception, at least in certain circumstances.

secularism of Western man. We live in a contraceptive world where the pill (etc.) has assumed the character of a human panacea. Contraception cannot be viewed in isolation from basic attitudes toward life and sexuality. There is mounting evidence that in contemporary culture contraception is part and parcel of an attitudinal package that includes sterilization (even coerced), abortion, artificial insemination, and ultimately euthanasia. Furthermore, contraception might be associated with a certain amount of marital selfishness, marital infidelity, and premarital irresponsibility, though we must be careful here to document any generalizations we would make.

Perhaps it was a cultural criticism such as this which Paul Ricoeur had in mind when he wrote:

What gives force to the anti-contraceptive position are not, in my opinion, the arguments based on the meaning of "natural" and "unnatural," but an argument which is rarely made use of: the knowledge that contraception risks destroying the quality of the sexual act by making it facile and ultimately insignificant. I would develop the implicit argument of those who oppose contraception in these terms: Of course, birth control is necessary, but there is the danger that the meaning and value of sexuality will disappear. Today we are perhaps more worried about overcoming the fatality of reproduction. The price of this victory—a price costly from the point of view of psychology and spirituality—will inevitably become apparent. It may be that tomorrow's greatest problem will be to preserve the expressive and meaningful value of sexuality. But if this is tomorrow's problem, is it not already today's? Must we not, come what may, retain the distinction between natural and unnatural, not because this distinction is of value in itself, but because nature itself proposes an exterior limit to a man's demands on sex, and also maintains the sole objective bulwark capable of sustaining the quality of the sexual act?[148]

Ricoeur then added that

the partisans of birth control should be aware that contraception, considered as a simple technique in general, helps to precipitate sexuality into meaninglessness; it is probable that a rational use of contraception can only succeed where men are spiritually aroused to the need for maintaining the quality of the sexual language.[149]

Clearly Ricoeur himself believes that contraception can be put at the disposal of a responsible conjugal ethics and that it can be in the service of rational fertility rather than sterility. I am not arguing here that this approach to the question is persuasive or that it will lead to the conclusions of *Humanae vitae.* I am only suggesting that it seems to represent the only kind of approach left toward those conclusions. One might argue that we live in a

---

[148] *Cross Currents* 14 (1964) 246–47.   [149] *Ibid.,* p. 247.

culture where very many are not spiritually aroused to the need for maintaining the quality of sexual language. Sexual expression is more facile and
insignificant than ever. Its increasing mechanization poses a serious threat to
its viability as a human experience.

If we approach the question of contraception from this point of view,
could we arrive at the conclusion that it is intrinsically evil? I doubt it. We
would conclude only that it is dangerous and that the duty of the individual
couple is subject to their ability to detach the practice from these poisonous
concomitants. However, the dangers might be so considerable that ecclesiastical authority would wish to impose a norm of conduct in virtue of its
jurisdictional authority. There is some indication in the documents of the
magisterium that propositions about natural-law matters do at times conform more to jurisdictional precepts than to teaching. [150] If this were the case,
it would seem that the teaching would be, to use Daniel Maguire's phrase,
"open to the soothing influence of epikeia." [151] In any event, these reflections
do not lead to the conclusion of the intrinsic immorality or absolute illicitness of contraceptive acts.

If theologians have not been able to sustain the conclusion of intrinsic
malice, and if increasingly they have found sound theological reasons to
justify contraception at least in some instances (cf. the Majority Report),
on what grounds did the Pope reaffirm traditional teaching? It is not from
arrogance that one seeks to discover how Pope Paul VI arrived at the conviction that he must reaffirm traditional norms. Only when one knows
what factors were operative in this decision is he positioned to appropriate
the decision as fully as a docile and intelligent Catholic would desire. We are
dealing here, after all, with the natural law, as the Encyclical states. This
means that the exclusion of contraception is a demand based on man's being
as man. Now the demands of natural law are determined by evidence
gathered from many competences and evidence available to all of us. This
evidence either yields a reasonably convincing case or it does not.

If it does, should this not recommend itself to the reflections of at least
very many devoted and reflective Christians, and manifest itself in the
convictions of a majority of expert theologians and episcopal advisors, even

[150] For example, Pope John XXIII wrote in *Mater et magistra*: "It is clear, however, that
when the hierarchy has issued a *precept or decision* on a point at issue, Catholics are bound
to obey their directives. The reason is that the Church has the right and obligation, not
merely to guard the purity of ethical and religious principles, but also to intervene authoritatively when there is question of judging the application of these principles to concrete
cases" (*AAS* 53 [1961] 457).

[151] *Art. cit.*, p. 57.

though our formulations of this may be awkward?[152] It did not. How, then, are we to explain the reaffirmation? Pope Paul VI gives some hint of an explanation when he refers in *Humanae vitae* to the work of the Birth Control Commission. He states that its conclusions could not be considered definitive and gives as the special reason for this (*praesertim*) "because certain criteria of solutions had emerged which departed from the moral teaching on marriage proposed with constant firmness by the teaching authority of the Church" (n. 6). There are many other indications in the Encyclical that the Holy Father felt keenly the weight of tradition.[153] Ultimately, however, one must conclude that the constant proposal of a teaching by the Church guarantees not its absolute correctness (unless it is infallibly proposed) but only its longevity.

At this point perhaps the theologian ought to ask himself whether he has read the Encyclical properly. Certainly, before anyone concludes that the teaching of *Humanae vitae* is gravely doubtful or even in error, he must determine what that teaching is. To do that, he must have some hermeneutic for papal documents. We are familiar with the contention of theologians that earlier authoritative condemnations must be understood as condemnations of a teaching or tenet as it was then understood (e.g., religious liberty). Pius XII's elaboration of the principle of totality had to be read, theologians argued, in light of the totalitarian abuses of which he was so acutely aware and which he wished to counteract. And so on.

A concrete application of this method to *Humanae vitae* might suggest the following approach. Beneath the explicit and dated language of faculties and processes, of intrinsic evil and per se ordinations, there is a message which carries beyond these categories. Perhaps the document should be read as one which points a general direction and prophetically defends the great values of life and marital love. In other words, perhaps it can be read as delineating an ideal toward which we must work. Just as marriage is growth in unity, so the expression of marriage (marital intimacy) is an activity whose purity and

---

[152] Here it must be noted that many reactions to *Humanae vitae* were couched in terms of support or nonsupport for the Pope, of acceptance or rejection of his authority. Hence they cannot be reckoned a truly accurate guide of Catholic conviction on the issue at stake.

[153] For instance: ". . . ut saepenumero Decessores Nostri pronuntiaverunt . . ." (no. 4); ". . . Ecclesia congrua dedit documenta . . ." (no. 4); ". . . hinc constans Ecclesiae doctrina declarat . . ." (no. 10); ". . . quam constanti sua doctrina interpretatur . . ." (no. 11); "huiusmodi doctrina, quae ab Ecclesiae Magisterio saepe exposita est . . ." (no. 12); ". . . sicut Ecclesiae Magisterium pluries docuit . . ." (no. 14); "Ecclesia sibi suaeque doctrinae constat . . ." (no. 16); "Cum Ecclesia utramque hanc legem non condiderit, ejusdem non arbitra, sed tantummodo custos atque interpres . . ." (no. 18).

perfection we have not reached but for which we must constantly struggle. It is quite possible that we are collectively insensitive to this ideal.

However, if this is the basic message of the Encyclical, if it is outlining a horizon toward which we must move rather than a casuistry to which we must conform, then the integrity of marital relations would be determined by the couple's acceptance or rejection of this ideal in their present situation. If contraceptive acts were performed without a resolve or desire to grow toward this ideal, then they would be immoral. But as long as the couple resolve to do what they can to bring their marriage (and societal conditions) to the point where the fulness of the sexual act is possible, their practice of contraception would not represent moral failure.

I am not suggesting here that the Encyclical can or should be read in this manner. I doubt that it can. I am only attempting to illustrate how the theologian will exhaust every reasonable means to understand and defend authoritative teaching before he ultimately questions its validity. In this instance one feels particularly reluctant to develop a hermeneutic in the face of the practical statements of *Humanae vitae* precisely because such attempts will almost certainly provoke immediate howls that they are devious and ignominious attempts to water down the clear teaching of the Encyclical. And up to a point this reaction is justified. But those who insist on reading the Encyclical with theological literalism must live with the presuppositions of theological literalism. And in this instance that would be a hard life.

In the light of these reflections it is the opinion of the compositor of these Notes that the intrinsic immorality of every contraceptive act remains a teaching subject to solid and positive doubt. This is not to say that this teaching of *Humanae vitae* is certainly erroneous. [154] It is only to say that there are very strong objections that can be urged against it and very little evidence that will sustain it. One draws this conclusion reluctantly and with no small measure of personal anguish. With proper allowance made for one's own shortcomings, pride, and resistance, what more can a theologian say? He can say, of course, that the teaching is clear and certain simply because the papal magisterium has said so. But ultimately such an assertion must rest on the supposition that the clarity and certainty of a conclusion of natural-law morality are independent of objective evidence. In the discussion that has followed *Humanae vitae*, those who have supported the conclusions

---

[154] That is why I stated in the *National Catholic Reporter*: "I am not prepared to say that it is the only way traditional norms could be established and that therefore this teaching is *clearly inadequate*. More time and study are required to reach such a conclusion" (August 7, 1968, p. 9). "Gravely doubtful" is not the same as "clearly inadequate." This latter suggests reasonable certainty of error. There are other theologians whose position would be far stronger than this.

of the Encyclical have argued in just this way. I believe this is theologically unacceptable.

If other theologians, after meticulous research and sober reflection, share this opinion in sufficient numbers, if bishops and competent married couples would arrive at the same conclusion, it is difficult to see how the teaching would not lose the presumption of certainty ordinarily enjoyed by authoritative utterances. However, the ecclesial value of dissenting judgments in the present circumstances remains a problem in its own right.

Because of the proximity of the Encyclical and some unfortunate reactions associated with its issuance (unfortunate because agreement was allowed to be equated with loyalty, disagreement with disloyalty), one's honest expression of his theological opinion risks appearing as a kind of private magisterium that has entered into conflict with the authoritative papal magisterium. John Reed, S.J., was assuredly correct when he noted that "whatever the limits on one's obligation to accept the judgment of the latter [magisterium of the Church], one is certainly not entitled, either singly or in company with other theologians, to enter into conflict with it." [155] It is very difficult in the present circumstances to question the papal magisterium in one form or another without seeming to be in conflict with it. But the two notions (dissent from, in conflict with) are radically different. The theologian who conscientiously questions a particular teaching of the magisterium is deeply convinced that he is actually supporting and contributing to the magisterium. Indeed, the continuing health of the magisterium depends on his ability to do just this.

But he will be disinclined to discharge his duty of personal reflection if the results of his study are viewed as a private and defiant magisterium. The only ones capable of preventing this are the bishops. They are the magisterium in a way no theologian can claim to be. They must be in close contact with theologians (and the sources theologians draw upon), so that the best and most responsible Catholic thought will feed into the magisterium and shape its authoritative directives. If a much closer working relationship between the episcopal and theological community fails to mature, the theologian will be faced with only two alternatives, both of which are disastrous for himself and the Church: to abandon his honesty and integrity of thought, or to keep it and to become a private magisterium distinct from and sometimes in conflict with the genuine magisterium of the Church.

Some Pastoral Notes and Conclusions

We are too close to the neurological issue and too far from the solution to the great theological problems inseparable from the Encyclical to lay down

[155] THEOLOGICAL STUDIES 26 (1965) 59.

pastoral directives with any degree of confidence. Furthermore, such a task is properly that of the bishops. However, certain avenues of approach may be suggested here with the hope that they will stimulate others to make them more precise. We may touch on three points: bishops, bishops and priests, priests and the married.

Bishops. It is a mistake for an individual bishop or the conference of bishops to accept this, or any noninfallible teaching, without serious personal reflection and consultation. The teaching charism of bishops demands of them a truly personal reflection. The Dutch bishops gave us an example of this. They stated: "It is obvious, therefore, that your bishops will be able to give the guidance you so badly need only after consultation with theologians and other experts. This guidance will undoubtedly be given, but cannot be given until after some lapse of time." [156] It would seem that decisions to "support the Pope" without a true personal reflection are policy decisions. Such decisions can all too easily deprive the Pope and the faithful of the wisdom they have a right to expect from their bishops. They also fail to tell us whether the bishops are truly accepting and teaching a doctrine rather than just enforcing it. In this connection it must be said in all candor that the statements of several American bishops fail to distinguish "accepting the authority of the Pope" from "accepting what is authoritatively taught."

Bishops and priests. Given the fact that the teaching is noninfallible and error is possible (though one does not start with this emphasis in his own reflections), it is a mistake for bishops to insist on assent from their priests. We shall only grow in knowledge and understanding in the Catholic community if acceptance of this or any teaching is completely uncoerced, and if it represents, as far as possible, a truly personal assimilation, even though this assimilation may be somewhat delayed.

It would seem more appropriate that bishops, in dealing with their priests, should insist on a basic Christian and religious docility and the need for arduous reflection, study, and consultation. Bishops should do everything possible to encourage and facilitate a personal assimilation of authoritative teaching on the part of their priests. Secondly, they should insist on responsible conduct, whether one's study has issued in acceptance or dissent. Responsible conduct would include the following: respect for the Pope and his office; respect for the fact that he has a personal charism authoritatively to teach and lead the faithful. In other words, a priest's conduct will reflect a realization that the virtue of faith may not be weakened in the process of discussing one teaching which does not pertain to the faith.

Priest and faithful. It seems to me that the priest's first task is to distinguish for his faithful between his own personal opinion and authoritative

[156] *National Catholic Reporter*, Aug. 14, 1968, p. 5.

teaching. The Church needs the reflections and opinions of all of us. But our assimilation of any teaching is subject to our own imperfections and short-comings. Concretely, if a priest in his professional capacity (confessor, preacher, counselor) asserts that "it is legitimate to practice contraception in certain circumstances," this is his opinion. If he presents it as any more than this, is he not equivalently setting himself up as a teacher in conflict with a far more authoritative teacher? It is precisely the impossibility of doing this which constitutes the problem we are now facing.

The priest's second task is to aid the faithful toward a personal reflection and assimilation of the Encyclical. Just as growth in understanding in the Church depends on a careful reflection by the authentic teachers in the Church (the bishops), so their reflections remain incomplete if they are not informed by the uncoerced reflections of those most vitally concerned and most directly involved in the question—the married. Therefore anything a priest says must represent an aid to the faithful in forming their consciences. He should not attempt to form their conscience for them. This would represent a form of paternalism detrimental to personal and corporate growth.

Thirdly, we come inevitably to what in the past we have referred to as "confessional practice" or its equivalent. Perhaps the matter could be approached in the following way, pending further developments.

a) When asked, we must unambiguously state that the present but non-infallible teaching of the papal magisterium is that every contraceptive act is immoral. This conclusion should, of course, be stated within the context of a rounded assertion of the positive values contained in *Humanae vitae*.

b) The dissent of reflective and competent married people should be respected and the teaching on contraception should not be made a matter of denial of absolution.

c) The truly anguishing aspect of the problem has been put well by the National Association of Laymen Executive Board. They state: "We are, therefore, not concerned for ourselves but for the millions of silent Catholics on whom this decision will fall as an unnecessary and harsh burden. They will obey because this is the main thrust of their religious training—to obey. They have not been allowed to reach spiritual adulthood, so they have no way to make independent judgment. For them to disobey or ignore this edict would destroy the very root of their religious belief." [157] There is no genuinely satisfactory solution for these people in terms of a practical conclusion. Indeed, if there were such a solution, the problem would not exist in its present poignancy. But here we may propose two suggestions which may help priests structure their pastoral practice.

[157] *Ibid.*, Sept. 14, 1968, p. 2.

First, in the present circumstances (widespread public confusion, episcopal and theological dissent, difficulty of the doctrine, frequent good faith,
unclarity of related theological questions, etc.) this teaching should not be
allowed to become an issue of refusal of absolution. When the problem arises
in the confessional situation, the faithful should be encouraged, and they
should be urged to exercise Christian patience and confidence as the unanswered questions and difficulties connected with this problem work themselves
out.

Secondly, if a couple are trying to live responsibly their married life as
defined by the values stated in *Humanae vitae*, a strong case can be made for
saying that their individual acts of contraception should not be viewed by
them or judged by the confessor to be subjectively serious sin. [158] Furthermore, the statement just made suggests to theologians the need to determine
more precisely and satisfactorily what constitutes serious matter where the
practice of contraception is concerned. I realize that these pastoral notes do
not solve the basic underlying problems of the Encyclical and its application
to daily Catholic practice. But they do not intend to do this. They intend
only to formulate possible approaches—tentative and imperfect—during
difficult, transitional, and therefore challenging times.

[158] Three considerations suggest this conclusion. (1) *The difficulty of the faithful in understanding the doctrine.* Consider the following factors: confusion from priestly and theological
discussions; a sensate, pansexualized culture; hardness of the doctrine; discussion before
Humanae vitae and the expectations associated with it; subtlety of the argument; "asperas
vitae conditiones" of families and nations (no. 19); "sine dubio multis talis videbitur,
ut nonnisi difficulter, immo etiam nullo modo servari possit" (no. 20). (2) *The difficulty in
practicing the doctrine.* Note: "multosque labores postulat" (no. 20); "asceseos sit opus"
(no. 21); the grave difficulties of married life (no. 25); the fact that married people tend to
judge the importance of an act by its relation to the goals and values of married life, not by
a physiological openness, etc. (3) *The compassion and understanding urged by the Encyclical.*
"In their difficulties may married couples always find in the words and the heart of a
priest the echo of the voice and the love of the Redeemer" (no. 29). Similarly, "if sin should
still keep its hold over them, let them not be discouraged, but rather have recourse with
humble perseverance to the mercy of God" (no. 25). The Belgian hierarchy, after referring
to attempts of Catholics in difficult circumstances to adapt their behavior to the norms of
Humanae vitae, stated that "if they do not succeed immediately, they should not, however,
believe they are separated from God's love" (*Catholic Chronicle*, Sept. 6, 1968). In this
connection cf. the interesting remarks of John Dedek, "*Humanae vitae* and the Confessor,"
Chicago Studies 7 (1968) 221–24. Dedek believes that true evaluative cognition would be
lacking in very many instances in the present circumstances.

CURRENT THEOLOGY: 1969

NOTES ON MORAL THEOLOGY: JANUARY–JUNE, 1969

The Notes which follow focus on five principal issues: (1) reactions to the Encyclical *Humanae vitae*, (2) theology and authority, (3) morality and the competence of the magisterium, (4) the ethics of political protest, and (5) genetic engineering.

HUMANAE VITAE—A ROUNDUP OF REACTIONS

Over the years these Notes have devoted a good deal of space—even at times a disproportionate amount—to the intramural discussion of birth control. One would like to declare a temporary moratorium on the subject, but the quantity of literature disallows this. However, the compassionate reader will understand and share the compositor's determination to allow a brief roundup to suffice.

It is probably safe to say that comments on *Humanae vitae* in the past semester run the gamut between Ermenegildo Lio's assurance that the Encyclical contains "immutable and absolute proposals"[1] to Robert Springer's remark that "contraception is no longer the issue."[2] Lino Ciccone's commentary on *Humanae vitae* is not only very long (it takes him fifty-three pages to deliver his thoughts on nos. 1–6 of the Encyclical), but the article concludes with the ominous threat "(*continua*)."[3] Obviously we are getting a serialized version of what will be or could be a book—or three. But the suspense is not that great. It is very clear what Ciccone will be up to in forthcoming issues. The tone is set by his recall of what he styles "elementary reflections" on the magisterium, "since not a few theologians seem to be ignorant of them, at least in practice."

Edward MacKinnon, S.J., approaches *Humanae vitae* from the point of view of the principles of doctrinal development.[4] Behind every proposition affirmed as true are a conceptualization of reality and distinct presuppositions required for the meaningfulness of the truth-claim. Thus, for example, in a primitive culture which accepts devil possession as the cause of epilepsy, the witch doctor's report that someone is possessed by the devil will be accepted as true. *We* would distinguish

---

[1] *Osservatore Romano*, July 26, 1969.

[2] Robert Springer, S.J., "Notes on Moral Theology," THEOLOGICAL STUDIES 30 (1969) 264.

[3] L. Ciccone, "L'Enciclica 'Humanae vitae.' Analisi e commento," *Divus Thomas* 72 (1969) 3–58.

[4] Edward MacKinnon, S.J., "*Humanae vitae* and Doctrinal Development," *Continuum* 6 (1968) 269–75.

between accepting this as an observational report and accepting the background commitments used to frame this report. But such a distinction is not meaningful to the native.

Thus, where *Humanae vitae* is concerned, the meaning of the general principle asserted (each act must remain open to procreation) depends in part on the conceptual framework within which it is embedded. MacKinnon finds three general principles operative as a conceptual framework. First, the purposefulness of certain biological acts is seen in their natural ordination to a specific end. Second, human nature in itself and its essential relations is fundamentally unchangeable. Third, an interventionist view of divine providence prevails. By this MacKinnon understands the attitude that if we trust in God, He will provide for all of our needs. The acceptance of these principles is prerequisite to acceptance of the papal principle on rational rather than authoritative grounds. It is MacKinnon's contention that this frame of reference has undergone a revolutionary change in modern times. He concludes: "One cannot help but conclude that the doctrine defended in the encyclical is meaningful and philosophically defensible only within a conceptual framework which has already, or almost already, become obsolete through a process of conceptual revolution."[5]

One of the more provocative discussions is a panel presentation involving Ph. Delhaye, Jacques Etienne, Victor Heylen, Louis Janssens, and noted exegete Joseph Coppens.[6] Interestingly, Coppens, professor emeritus at Louvain, is the only one who seems to stand firmly behind the Encyclical. He believes that "the pope's main argument is not based in the first instance upon the guidance of the Spirit in his personal case, but upon the position that the teaching of the Encyclical is *constans ecclesiae doctrina*." Heylen rejects this completely on the grounds that we have identified as "tradition" what is little more than the persistence of a deterministic view of bodily functions tracing back to Galen. The teaching must be called constant within these limits. In an analysis close to that of MacKinnon, Heylen sees the basic issue as follows: "How can theological speculation break away from a scientific thought which limits it by closing off certain areas of reflection?"[7]

Among the many interesting points touched on by the panel, two stand out. First, several (Heylen, Delhaye, Janssens) emphasize the rather sharp differences between *Gaudium et spes* and *Humanae vitae* in their views of marriage and marital morality. Secondly, Delhaye and

[5] *Ibid.*, p. 275.

[6] "A Symposium on 'Humanae vitae' and the Natural Law," *Louvain Studies* 2 (1969) 211–53.

[7] *Ibid.*, p. 226.

Heylen severely criticize the pastoral of the French bishops in terms of its use of the principle of lesser evil. Delhaye remarks that to maintain that, whatever the situation, it is enough simply to choose the lesser evil "is to ignore the existence of intrinsic disorder." For this reason Delhaye says flatly that "the French statement goes too far." Heylen adds: "I agree wholeheartedly. Taken literally the French statement would bring about complete moral relativism."[8]

Not so, says Michel Dayez in his continuing commentary on *Humanae vitae*.[9] Indeed, such episcopal statements are really in agreement with the Encyclical but simply apply its message. It will be recalled that in no. 14 the Encyclical stated that "to justify conjugal acts made intentionally infecund, one cannot invoke as valid reasons the lesser evil . . . . " It then went on to explain that if it is sometimes licit to tolerate a lesser evil, it is never licit to do evil, "that is, to make into the object of a positive act of the will something which is intrinsically disorder . . . even when the intention is to safeguard or promote individual, family, or social well-being." Dayez believes it is incorrect to say that all recourse to the notion of lesser evil is excluded by this statement. Rather the document simply recalls that considerations advanced from the subjective order cannot justify on the objective plane. Thus, killing is objective disorder. But to kill in self-defense situates the *concrete moral quality* of the act, even though it cannot make it less of a disorder to kill anyone. Therefore Dayez sees no. 14 of the Encyclical saying that contraception is at times an inevitable evil, that a conflict of duties can exist which leads to the *tolerance* of a moral evil to promote a greater good or avoid a worse evil. To tolerate is not to take as a positive object of the will that which is intrinsic disorder. Rather it is to will positively a greater good, admitting that actually and concretely it is accessible only in *tolerating* an element of disorder.

It seems to me that Dayez has confused the issue and ultimately explained away the notion of intrinsic evil, whatever one might think of that term as a legitimate theological category.[10] That is, his argument would go somewhat as follows. Contraception is objective disorder. But to contracept for the good of the family yields the *concrete moral quality* of the act, even though it cannot make contraception less of a disorder. What Dayez seems to overlook is that what is said to be intrinsic

[8] *Ibid.*, p. 222.

[9] M. Dayez, "Pour comprendre 'Humanae vitae,'" *Confrontations* 1 (1968) 375–403, 577–603. The article containing Dayez's own problems with the Encyclical had not reached me at the time of this writing.

[10] For an interesting recent treatment, cf. E. Ranwez, "Intrinsèquement mauvais?" *La foi et le temps* 3 (1969) 289–95.

evil already has a basic *concrete moral quality* in traditional understanding. Specifically, contraception (traditionally and in the understanding of the Encyclical) is not a vague and general disorder like killing, which gathers objective moral quality by further circumstantial specification. It is precisely the meaning of the category "intrinsic evil" that it already has a basic moral quality.

Robert McAfee Brown finds what he calls the "fundamental principle" of the Encyclical (the inseparability of the unitive and procreative meanings of coitus) "false and grievously so."[11] So also Michigan's Carl Cohen, who says of this principle: "First, it is without good foundation. Second, it is false. Third, its denial is perfectly consistent with the larger doctrines of the Catholic Church regarding marriage. Fourth, it betrays an unwholesome, essentially instrumental view of sex. Fifth, it is a premise contradicted by the Church's own view of licit birth control."[12] In much more moderate tones Bernard Häring discusses the same principle and its consequences and finds it impossible to see, in terms of "openness to the transmission of life," how rhythm differs from contraceptive interferences.[13] He admits that there is need for a thorough study of the relationship between the unitive and procreative meaning of the marriage act, but finds the Encyclical's understanding mechanical. Charles Curran criticizes the teaching in terms of the theory of natural law operative beneath it—one which defines the moral action in terms of the physical structure of the act.[14]

Thomas Gilby, O.P., on the other hand, is convinced that "the Pope sees the subject at greater depth than his critics."[15] He believes that *Humanae vitae* faithfully represents and applies a constant tradition, scil., that sexuality is never to be taken as an exclusively interpersonal value. If this exhausts the message of the Encyclical, then surely Gilby is correct. But given its explicit language, is it not impossible to peel the document down to this message? P. E. Hodgson details the criticisms of the scientific world (*Nature, New Scientist, World Medicine, Lancet,* etc.).[16] He notes that the Encyclical shows

---

[11] Robert McAfee Brown, "*Humanae vitae:* A Protestant Reaction," in *Contraception: Authority and Dissent,* ed. Charles Curran (New York: Herder and Herder, 1969) pp. 193–215.

[12] C. Cohen, "Sex, Birth Control and Human Life," *Ethics* 79 (1969) 251–62.

[13] B. Häring, "The Inseparability of the Unitive-Procreative Functions of the Marital Act," in *Contraception: Authority and Dissent,* pp. 176–92.

[14] C. Curran, "Natural Law and Contemporary Moral Theology," *ibid.,* pp. 151–75.

[15] T. Gilby, O.P., "The Encyclical Abstraction," *New Blackfriars* 50 (1968) 94–102.

[16] P. Hodgson, "Scientific Reactions to 'Humanae vitae,'" *New Blackfriars* 50 (1969) 338–42. Cf. also H. Koester, "Ärztliche Überlegungen zu 'Humanae vitae,'" *Stimmen der Zeit* 94 (1969) 217–30.

little trace of scientific consultation and asserts that "the scientists and others who labored so long and fruitfully might be forgiven if they were to feel that their time had been wasted."

Philosopher Timothy Potts sees two arguments in *Humanae vitae*, the consequentialist (no. 17) and the central argument (no. 12).[17] The former he regards as valid only where large-scale and habitual contraception is concerned. The latter argument he finds logically inconsistent and he ultimately agrees with the Dutch Pastoral Assembly that "the encyclical's total rejection of contraceptive methods is not convincing on the basis of the arguments put forward."[18] The same could be said for Heythrop's John L. Russell.[19] He argues that in those instances where the preservation of physiological integrity clashes with the natural finality of the marriage as a whole, it is the latter which should prevail. Physiological processes are for the good of the person, not vice versa.

In his unhurried article, in which there is a good deal of casual wisdom, Gilby had suggested that the work leading to *Humanae vitae* was unsatisfactory. Specifically, he found the Minority Report wooden, the Majority Report woolly. Michael Dummett shares this judgment and claims that it was the impossibly bland tones of the Majority Report that may have led Pope Paul to his decision.[20] The minority presented, in Dummett's judgment, two serious problems which the majority treated with insufficient realism. These were (1) the argument from tradition and the effects of change on confidence in the magisterium, and (2) relationship and continuity with other areas of sexual behavior ("where do we draw the line?"). Since both of these problems have serious pastoral implications, he feels that the majority response to them had more influence in producing the Encyclical than the majority would care to think.

Philosopher James Good (University College, Cork) uses the Syllabus of Errors as an interpretative device in approaching *Humanae vitae*.[21] The Syllabus was greeted in 1864 with widespread opposition. Dupanloup created the distinction between *thèse* and *antithèse*. For Dupanloup, the Syllabus was speaking of a *thèse* situation, the state of society where everything was organized perfectly along Christian

---

[17] T. C. Potts, "The Arguments of *Humanae vitae*," *Month* 41 (1969) 144–55.

[18] *Tablet* (London) 223 (1969) 67–68.

[19] John L. Russell, "Contraception and the Natural Law," *Heythrop Journal* 10 (1969) 121–34.

[20] Michael Dummett, "The Documents of the Papal Commission on Birth Control," *New Blackfriars* 50 (1969) 241–50.

[21] James Good, "'Humanae vitae,' a Platonic Document," *Tablet* 223 (1969) 386–87.

lines. In such a state the principles of the Syllabus would find their full expression. However, we do not live in such a condition, but in one where the actual represents a recession from the ideal. We live in the *antithèse*. Just as the Syllabus was talking about an idyllic and Platonic world, so is *Humanae vitae*. It simply cannot be translated into real life as it stands. For example, ideally the "natural rhythms" might be an adequate child-spacing agent. Actually they are not. The Encyclical, therefore, is a *thèse* which makes sense only in terms of an *antithèse*. This translation from ideal to real Good puts as follows: "Contraceptive intercourse is generally evil but in married life it is lawful where there are serious reasons for it." Or more positively, "contraceptive intercourse in married life is good, but it may be abused, e.g., by selfishness."[22] Good admits that Dupanloup explained the Syllabus of Errors for a grateful Pius IX by explaining it away. His own reading does the same for *Humanae vitae*, but he is convinced that this is the only way one can live with its teaching.

In one of the more intriguing comments on *Humanae vitae*, Ieuan Ellis approaches the Encyclical according to a model suggested by the work of Reinhold Niebuhr.[23] Niebuhr had argued that Christian ethics is not concerned with a choice between an absolute belonging to a transcendental world or a relevant ethic attainable in this world. It is a compound of both and creates inescapable tension. Every moral decision places man "between an impossibility which constrains him and a possibility with which he must never be satisfied." The impossible ethical ideal is the law of love shown in the life of Jesus. Anything less would produce a relative moral effort, a second-best, calculative ethic.

Ellis suggests that this approach might be helpful in reading *Humanae vitae*. Pope Paul is also speaking about a dialectical situation. He has invoked what appears to be an impossible ethical ideal—the positioning of the transmission of human life in a transcendental context where these laws are seen as God's laws. But this ideal is to function dynamically by leading men to greater efforts, efforts which can be supported only by full participation in the life of the Church. Thus Ellis concludes that *Humanae vitae* represents a mode of ethical thinking which "is both a dynamic and more complex matter than some of the Pope's critics allow."[24]

Edward Hamel, S.J., offers a long and thorough commentary on the

---

[22] *Ibid.*, p. 387.

[23] Ieuan Ellis, "The Encyclical and Niebuhr's 'Impossible Possibility,'" *New Blackfriars* 51 (1969) 405-10.

[24] *Ibid.*, p. 410.

pastoral letters of the various episcopal conferences.[25] He concludes that there is nò contradiction between these pastoral letters and *Humanae vitae*, but rather a legitimate complementarity. There is, he admits, divergence in interpreting certain particular points of the Encyclical. There are tonal differences, and some rather remarkable differences in scientific precision. But his ultimate judgment on this variety is that "substantialia relinquit intacta." The Holy Father will be delighted to hear this—and perhaps a bit surprised.

John R. Quinn, Auxiliary Bishop of San Diego, has questioned some of the analyses presented in these Notes last year.[26] His Christian urbanity and the thoughtfulness of his essay make it a pleasure to exchange views with him. I shall not comment further on the biologized notion of natural law in the Encyclical nor on its discontinuities with *Gaudium et spes*. These criticisms have been made with almost tedious frequency by many reputable commentators. But two points do deserve notice.

After granting (*dato non concesso*) that the person is the exclusive factor in the determination of the meaning of human actions, Bishop Quinn wonders whose concept of person is to be normative. He writes:

The Pope assumes a definite perspective when he calls for an integral vision of man, man viewed not only in terms of earthly happiness and its demands, but rather in the light of man's calling to share in the Paschal Mystery, the communion of the Lord's death as well as His resurrection. If the person as the criterion for the meaning and morality of human acts is viewed apart from this dimension, purely in terms of earthly categories, then, of course, the Encyclical presents insurmountable problems, as indeed the Gospel itself does.[27]

Two remarks. First, those of us who have had great difficulty with the reasoning behind the central conclusion of the Encyclical should not, I would hope, be regarded too easily as viewing the person "purely in terms of earthly categories" or "only in terms of earthly happiness and its demands." Bishop Quinn seems to trace "insurmountable difficulties" precisely to this inadequate perspective. I feel sure that there are theologians who believe it is *Christian* wisdom which undergirds their dissent. Secondly, granted that we should all view the person

[25] Edward Hamel, S.J., "Conferentiae episcopales et Encyclica 'Humanae vitae,'" *Periodica* 58 (1969) 243-349.

[26] John R. Quinn, "'Humanae vitae': Forgotten Arguments on the Pope's Side," *Priest* 25 (1969) 260-63.

[27] *Ibid.*, p. 261.

from the papal perspective—"in light of man's calling to share in the Paschal Mystery," as Bishop Quinn puts it—how does this perspective prohibit intervention in the biological processes to achieve the values of marriage? One does not answer this question by appealing to a perspective; he does so by reasoning within a perspective. It is always possible, even dangerously easy, to dismiss the cross of Christ in theological reflection. On the other hand, if one appeals to the Paschal Mystery without further ado as the perspective which generates a concrete prohibition, he should spell out how and why this is so. Otherwise he has methodically lifted reflection on morals out of human range.

Secondly, Bishop Quinn alludes to the place of revelation in the knowledge of natural law and cites Pope Paul VI's teaching on contraception as a "teaching founded on the natural law, *illumined and enriched by divine revelation*." Bishop Quinn then says that "there arises for theology the task of showing how and where such a thing is contained in revelation." When faced with this problem of how and where this teaching is found in revelation, he suggests that we must give more attention to "pneumatic insight, the Church's ability to sense by the power of the Holy Spirit what is and what is not consonant with the Gospel teaching." Marriage is, after all, a sacrament for Christians and this leads Bishop Quinn to ask: "Could there be in the Magisterium an as yet unarticulated insight into some of these aspects of revelation?"

Several remarks are called for here. First, after saying that the papal position is founded on natural law *illumined and enriched by divine revelation*, Bishop Quinn says that "there remains for theology, then, the task of showing how and where such a thing is contained in revelation." Haven't we moved a bit fast here? The task of showing how and where such a thing is contained in revelation is a task which follows upon certainty that it is contained in revelation. A natural law *illumined and enriched by divine revelation* does not give this certainty. Moreover, once one realizes that theologians generally hold that revelation contains no new material moral content not present in natural law, the task will appear a bit formidable. Secondly, theologians would probably grant that there is such a thing as Harry McSorley's "pneumatic insight." But they might immediately add three postscripts. First, such insight is a heritage primarily of the *Church*—a point we shall return to later. Secondly, such "pneumatic insight" is chiefly concerned with the substance of the Christ-event, less obviously with detailed prescriptions of the natural law. Finally, past history shows us that there has also been in the pilgrim Church some amount of what we might call "stubborn reluctance" in the face of change and new evidence. The only way to distinguish "pneumatic insight" from "stubborn reluctance" is to bring to bear on a venerable moral tenet the fulness of Christian wisdom and reasoning. This is itself risky, of course, and not immune from error. But if it is not done, and the matter is settled too hastily by appeal to "pneumatic insight," the conversation has again drifted out of human range. I would agree, therefore, with Bishop Quinn that whatever evidence there is from revelation for an absolute prohibition of contraception is indeed in the category of "an as yet unarticulated insight."

This chronicle must end here, not for lack of further literature, but in deference to the demands of space.[28] But not before two impressions are recorded. First, as the discussion of the issues surrounding *Humanae vitae* continues, it cannot be emphasized too strongly that Christian thought is now, as it always has been, a child of its times. Far more than a Christian, be he layman or theologian, can reflexly grasp, his culture is the soil which nourishes and subtly influences his thought. This has to scare us. For contemporary Western culture appears to be pansexualized to almost incredible depths. It is not hard to argue persuasively that sexual expression in our times is flirting with the danger of losing its viability as a human experience. At the very time we abstractly extol interpersonal relations and the importance of sexuality within them, we find many of these actual relationships in ruins all about us. Therefore a generous purchase on a self-questioning

---

[28] Cf. James Madden, "Cases on Contraception," *Australasian Catholic Record* 46 (1969) 52–59; John R. Connery, S.J., "Pastoral Practice and *Humanae vitae*," *American Ecclesiastical Review* 160 (1969) 55–59; S. Lener, "Matrimonio e amore conjugale nella 'Gaudium et spes' e nella 'Humanae vitae,'" *Civiltà cattolica* 120 (1969) 22–33; G. Higuera, "El mensaje teológico-moral y evangélico de la 'Humanae vitae,'" *Sal terrae* 57 (1969) 163–78; G. Kunicic, "La contraccezione non colpevole?" *Perfice munus* 44 (1969) 342–48; Biagio Russo, S.J., "Un' umile risposta all'invito del Pontefice," *Palestra del clero* 48 (1969) 393–414; G. Saraggi, "Ancora sull'enciclica 'Humanae vitae,'" *Palestra del clero* 48 (1969) 58–65; B. da Gangi, "Responsabilità del professore di morale," *Palestra del clero* 48 (1969) 385–87; W. F. Allen, "*Humanae vitae:* Expressions. Reactions," *Pastoral Life* 17 (1969) 37–43; "*Humanae vitae* and Mixed Marriages," *One in Christ* 5 (1969) 208–12; Robert Y. O'Brien, "Comment on *Humanae vitae*," *Journal of Ecumenical Studies* 6 (1969) 87–89; D. Fitch, S.J., "*Humanae vitae* and Teaching Authority." *Homiletic and Pastoral Review* 69 (1969) 272–76; D. Fitch, S.J., "*Humanae vitae* and Reasonable Doubt," *Homiletic and Pastoral Review* 69 (1969) 516–23; James J. Mulligan, "Confessor, Penitent and *Humanae vitae*," *Homiletic and Pastoral Review* 69 (1969) 507–15; F.-J. Thonnard, "La morale conjugale selon saint Augustin," *Revue des études augustiniennes* 15 (1969) 113–31; John J. O'Callaghan, S.J., "Reflections on *Humanae vitae*," *Theology Digest* 16 (1968) 317–27; John Mahoney, S.J., "The Development of Moral Doctrine," *Clergy Review* 54 (1969) 260–70; W. Dunphy, C.SS.R., "Open to the Transmission of Life," *Australasian Catholic Record* 46 (1969) 129–36.

humility is in order for any realistic theologian as he weighs the importance of his own reflections in the area of human sexuality at this time in history.

Secondly, anyone who reads the current literature on *Humanae vitae* cannot help but notice that articles favoring the papal teaching manifest a heavy, almost exclusive concern with tradition and authority. Those which dissent are concerned largely with the analysis of evidence and reasoning. Obviously both aspects are important in Christian moral thought. But their relationship is still an uneasy and fragile thing in the Catholic community, especially at a time of escalating cultural antagonism to authority in general. And that is why much of the writing on the Encyclical is concerned with two headings which follow: (1) theology and authority; (2) the competence of the magisterium in the area of morals. Although there is some unavoidable overlapping in these headings, they may be treated distinctly.

THEOLOGY AND AUTHORITY

Biblical scholar John L. McKenzie, S.J., after distinguishing theology from proclamation, contends that the Church has no commission to theologize with authority.[29] She has a mandate to preach with authority. On the other hand, McKenzie admits that the Church has to theologize if she is to fulfil her mission of preaching. Otherwise she could not speak clearly to the world in which she lives. But the ultimate judge of the competence of the theologian is his peers. McKenzie believes, therefore, that theology will thrive best if it is carried on with that freedom which the private investigator has. Bishops should leave theology alone unless they are themselves theologians of demonstrated competence. Where they lack competence, bishops tend to use crozier-thumping as a theological argument.

Carlo Colombo takes a slightly different point of view.[30] On December 17, 1968, several European dailies published a "Declaration of 38 Theologians" in which the signatories insisted on the need for freedom of theological inquiry and suggested several practical steps whereby this could be assured.[31] The document affirmed with conviction the existence of the magisterium of the pope and of the bishops which, "under the Word of God, is at the service of the Church and of its preaching." But it insisted that the pastoral magisterium of proclamation could not supplant or hinder scientific theology and it rejected coercion as an appropriate method for dealing with potential theologi-

---

[29] John L. McKenzie, S.J., "Q.E.D.," *Critic* 27 (1969) 6–7, 99.

[30] Carlo Colombo, "Magistero e ricerca teologica," *Civiltà cattolica* 120 (1969) 70–76.

[31] *Documentation catholique* 66 (1969) 119–21.

cal error. It was this document which occasioned an article by Bishop Carlo Colombo on the magisterium and theological research.

After admitting the legitimacy of many of the statements in the Declaration, Colombo turns to what he regards as some "less clear points" in the document, the most notable of which is the relationship between the magisterium and theology. The Declaration had referred to the "pastoral" magisterium of the pope and bishops. Colombo argues that the nature and pastoral finality of the magisterium include also the authority to *judge* in matters of faith and the proclamation of the faith. The hierarchy, he insists, is not simply guardian of a deposit of faith; they are educators in the faith. They do not simply guard against error, but their more basic task is to form in the community a mentality of faith (*habitus fidei*). Therefore it is their right and duty to pass judgment on the pedagogy of the formation of faith in the community. Colombo thinks the theologian-authors of the Declaration have insisted unilaterally on their need of freedom and have ended up asking to be treated as a privileged class. They should have recalled more clearly the subordination of individual liberty to the demands of the formation of the faith in the community.

Here we have McKenzie objecting against crozier-thumping as a form of theological exchange and Colombo crying "privileged class" in the face of theological claims to freedom. Both points are well made, I believe. But they spring from an awareness of actual defects in the way theology and authority are relating. There have been ill-advised and coercive visits to the theological camp by ecclesiastical authorities, and there has been imprudent and untimely dissemination of theological speculation. But when these abuses are the focal point for further theoretical reflections on the relationship of theology to authority, we are likely to get a one-sided or at least incomplete statement.

For example, McKenzie is correct when he insists that theology is a scholarly affair, that its only authority is in its arguments and evidence, that one who will criticize it or its conclusions must avail himself somehow of scholarly tools, that therefore formal authority as such has no commission to theologize. But in his legitimate desire to reject incompetent meddling and bureaucratic brush-ups, has he unduly separated theology from proclamation? If theology is necessary for proclamation—a point McKenzie admits—and if the hierarchy are the authentic proclaimers of the gospel, then do they not have a legitimate interest in and concern for theology, even in some sense an authoritative concern? Therefore, rather than inviting the bishops to "stay out of theology," McKenzie should, I believe, urge them to translate their legitimate concern into a vigorous protection of its freedom. Perhaps this is what McKenzie actually had in mind.

But to remove theology in theory and totally from all authority not theological seems inevitably to remove it from any living relationship to proclamation. And this is to trivialize it. The Church is not simply a society for the advancement of learning, like a historical or mathematical society. She is a community which proclaims the faith and passes it along. Theology is in the service of and subordinate to the demands of this commission. Therefore, just as ecclesiastical authority is not authority to invade theology, so neither is theological freedom the same as isolation from the Christian community in the dissemination of theological thought.

On the other hand, Colombo's antipodal concern with the rights of authority leads him to an emphasis which theologians increasingly regard as incomplete. To the suggestion that the Congregation for the Doctrine of the Faith be expanded to include theologians from all schools of thought, Colombo notes:

The faith and authority of the Apostolic See is not, in fact, to be conceived as a *result* of the co-operating convergence (*l'apporto*) of the entire Christian community in its various riches and expressions. It is an original fact (*un fatto originario*), founded on a specific promise of Jesus Christ and a specific charism. For this, the make-up of the organs through which authority acts and expresses itself can facilitate and render more perfect its exercise and render our adherence easier. But it is not the foundation of authority itself nor of our adherence to it.[32]

Here it must be said that the fact that authority is "an original fact, founded on a specific promise of Jesus Christ and a specific charism" does not exempt this authority from the normal means of fulfilling its mandate. To underline authority as "an original fact" in the face of reasonable theological requests for more adequate curial representation all too easily suggests such exemption.

In summary, then, isolated insistence on his freedom can lead the theologian to undervalue the pastoral charism of the hierarchy and the benefits he derives from this as a Christian and a theologian. Isolated emphasis on the authority of the hierarchy risks devaluating the depth of theological work and the breadth of consultation required if the pastoral charism is to be exercised in a responsible and credible way. Something is always lost when friends pass unknowingly in the night. And that may have happened here. It is, therefore, the proper relationship of both indispensable charisms which insures the healthy

[32] *Ibid.*, p. 75.

functioning of each.[33] In other words, freedom is expanded by relating itself properly to authority. Authority is strengthened by guaranteeing the freedom of those who can aid it in constructing the forms which render it relevant and contemporaneous. Therefore both magisterial authority and theological freedom must be viewed within the total and continuing teaching-learning process of the Christian community.

Another article attempts to clarify this viewpoint by approaching the relationship of theology and the magisterium through the notion of teaching.[34] In the past many cultural factors[35] produced a notion of teaching in the Church which manifested three characteristics: (1) it unduly distinguished and separated the *docens* and *discens* function with a consequent almost unique emphasis on the right to teach, little being said about the duty incumbent on the teacher to learn; (2) it unduly identified the teaching function in the Church with a single group in the Church (the hierarchy); (3) it unduly isolated a single aspect of the teaching function (the judgmental). This notion of teaching laid heavy stress on the authority of the teacher and a correspondingly lesser stress on evidence and the processes whereby it is gathered. It also generated a theology of response which was heavily obediential in tone.

Radical changes affecting these same cultural factors have produced a renewed notion of teaching in the Church. This renewed approach shows these characteristics: (1) it sees the learning process as an essential part of the teaching process; (2) it regards teaching as a pluridimensional function, only a single aspect of which is the judgmental; (3) it therefore sees the teaching function as involving the charisms of many persons, not just that of the hierarchy. The repercussions of this notion of teaching are only now beginning to appear in the theology of the magisterium and the suggested style of its exercise. For example, without negating the authoritative character of papal or collegial-episcopal pronouncements, contemporary theology devotes more attention to evidence and sound analysis in assessing the ultimate meaning and value of such teachings. In other words, teaching must persuade,

[33] A very helpful statement on this relationship is had in Ladislas M. Orsy's "Academic Freedom and the Teaching Church," *Thought* 43 (1968) 485–98.

[34] Richard A. McCormick, S.J., "The Teaching Role of the Magisterium and of Theologians," *Proceedings of the Catholic Theological Society of America* 24 (1969); pagination unavailable at time of writing.

[35] For instance: the self-definition of the Church, the influence of the mass media on the learning processes, the manner of exercise of authority in the Church, the educational status of laity and clergy, the state of relations between ecclesial groups, educational theories and styles dominant in a particular culture.

not only command. Furthermore, there is a developing theology of response to authoritative noninfallible teaching which emphasizes a docile personal assimilation and appropriation of authentic teaching as the appropriate immediate response, rather than an unquestioning assent. Finally, the creative reflection of theologians and the prophetic charisms of all Christians are seen as utterly essential if the hierarchy is to express the faith in our times in a meaningful, contemporary, and persuasive way.

After listing the processes which pertain to the teaching function,[36] the article suggests that these processes together constitute the teaching function of the Church as she goes about her task of preserving and deepening the faith committed to her. When these functions are related to individuals within the Church, it might be possible to say that the teaching function is composed of three distinguishable components: the prophetic charism (very broadly understood so as to include all competences), the doctrinal-pastoral charism of the hierarchy, the scientific charism of the theologian. It is the interplay of these charisms which constitutes the full teaching function of the Church. And it is the proper and harmonious interplay of these functions which yields a healthy, vigorous, and effective magisterium.[37]

The article then argues that actually within the contemporary Church these functions are not relating harmoniously. That is, the style of teaching is seriously defective. And while there are many explanations for this, I have suggested that this lack of harmony can be attributed above all to the fact that the bishops have not concerned themselves sufficiently with the other (than judgmental) aspects of teaching. Specifically, too many have not taken with sufficient seriousness the other charisms involved in the total teaching function.[38] The article concludes that bishops must be much more involved in the learning processes of teaching than a preconciliar notion of the Church and of authority—hence of teaching—intimated. In our day

[36] (1) The search for new understanding by asking fresh questions, hypothesizing, testing old formulations, attempting new ones; (2) the discovery of the action of the Spirit in the Church by eliciting the insights of all competences, encouraging communication and dialogue among Christians, supporting individual charisms; (3) determination of the identifiable dimensions of Christian faith in our times by bringing the wisdom, reflection, experience of the entire Church to authoritative expression, either infallibly or in guidelines less than infallible; (4) the publication and circulation of this expression in an effective way through the various communications media.

[37] For an analysis very close to this, cf. Joseph E. Kerns, *How Does God Teach Us Morals?* (New York: Paulist, 1969) pp. 41–57.

[38] Cf. N. Schiffers, "Diskutiertes Lehramt: Kirchliche Autorität und Risiko der Gläubigen," *Theologisch-praktische Quartalschrift* 117 (1969) 22–38, at 31 ff.

the credible teacher is the most eager, humble, open-minded learner. But if this is to occur, there must be a radical change in the image and role of the bishop as we have come to experience it. The bishop can no longer be chosen above all for his ability to administer a sprawling, highly complex local institution. The effectiveness of teaching (and even more broadly, of episcopal leadership) in our day will depend on the effectiveness of the bishop in making his person and his position a rallying point for Christian thought and creative action. If this happens around the world, obviously the world will listen to (*obsequium*) the hierarchy, because it will be clear that the Church is speaking.

The question of the teaching roles of theology and the magisterium in the development of Catholic doctrine was raised concretely and dramatically by the dissent that followed *Humanae vitae*. Some observers felt that theologians who spoke a dissenting view were setting themselves up as a countervailing authority, a kind of competitive magisterium. Others accused them of sweeping, offensive, and unmeditated statements. The perspective of distance has allowed the dust to settle and created the atmosphere for a calm theological reflection on the forms and meaning of dissent. It is precisely this that Enda McDonagh provides in his thoroughly balanced and temperate evaluation of the situation experienced by theologians in the months immediately following issuance of the Encyclical.[39] He treats of the theologian's coresponsibility and notes that his work is for the community and must ultimately be tested by it. A "silence is safer" policy frequently means safer for the theologian, not the community. He therefore insists that open, competent discussion is a first responsibility of the theologian.

Undoubtedly, the dissent which provoked the most controversy was that originating in Washington and originally associated with "eighty-seven theologians."[40] It was rather unique because it was both public and organized. This style of dissent has been both defended and attacked. For instance, Ciccone believes that "affirmations as grave as this made after a simple reading of the Encyclical can be the fruit only of emotion, not of serious reflection."[41] James J. Mulligan criticizes the Washington statement as playing to the press in an appeal which

---

[39] Enda McDonagh, "Coresponsibility and the Theologian," *Furrow* 20 (1969) 172–84.

[40] There were others, but at a later date: e.g., the *Declaration of Twenty European Theologians* (including men of the stature of Auer, Fransen, Janssens, Schoonenberg, Böckle, Beemer, McDonagh). Cf. Ciccone, *art. cit.*, p. 14.

[41] Ciccone, *art. cit.*, p. 13.

became "more inflammatory than intelligible."[42] Vincent Zamoyta believes that one aspect of the statement "oversteps the bounds of prudence in this very important matter."[43] G. Kunicic argues that dissenting theologians forget that individuals are not the custodians and interpreters of the natural law.[44] One searches his vocabulary in vain for language strong enough to disown the judgment of Colin Burns.[45] Seeking the why of the public dissent of some priests and bishops, he finds "the unpalatable answer to this is that even dedicated priests are not above the lure of personal popularity." One can only hope that this lapse in Christian courtesy got into the pages of the venerable *Australasian Catholic Record* through a printers' conspiracy.

On the other hand, there are many defenders of the Washington statement. The very fact that a considerable number of prominent scholars of demonstrated loyalty felt compelled to take this step gives one great pause in one's judgment. Those with whom I have discussed the matter support their decision from a wide variety of viewpoints. All of them root eventually, of course, in the conviction that the central assertion of the Encyclical cannot be accepted as it stands. A single example will suffice. Bernard Häring, convinced of the erroneous nature of the doctrine, saw little hope for a revised statement in Pope Paul's lifetime, "unless the reaction of the whole Church immediately makes him realize that he has chosen the wrong advisors and that the arguments which these men have recommended as highly suitable for modern thought are simply unacceptable."[46]

Whatever one's individual judgment may be about public and organized dissent, it is clear that there are deep differences of opinion in the Catholic community on the incident. The matter is so complex and many-sided that it surely justifies the American bishops' request

[42] James J. Mulligan, *The Pope and the Theologians* (Emmitsburg: Mt. St. Mary's Seminary, 1968) p. 66.

[43] Vincent Zamoyta, "On *Humanae vitae:* A Search for Human Understanding," in *To Be a Man*, ed. George Devine (Englewood Cliffs: Prentice-Hall, 1969) pp. 82–92, at 88. The statement Zamoyta disapproves is: "Therefore, as Roman Catholic theologians. conscious of our duty and our limitations, we conclude that spouses may responsibly decide according to their conscience that artificial contraception in some circumstances is permissible and indeed necessary to preserve and foster the values and sacredness of marriage."

[44] G. Kunicic, *art. cit.*, p. 348.

[45] Colin Burns, "A Medical Commentary on Some Present Theological Opinions on the Encyclical," *Australasian Catholic Record* 46 (1969) 45–51, at 47–48. For an earlier example of genuine theological courtesy, cf. Maurice Bévenot, "A Problem at Trent and *Humanae vitae*," *Heythrop Journal* 10 (1969) 134–45.

[46] B. Häring, "The Encyclical Crisis," in *The Catholic Case for Contraception*, ed. D. Callahan (Toronto: Macmillan, 1969) pp. 77–91, at 78–79.

for dialogue between theologians and bishops on "the ways in which theological dissent may be effectively expressed, in a manner consistent with pastoral solicitude."[47] The following remarks are offered as a groping attempt to provide a framework for discussion of the style of dissent.

Dissent from authoritative noninfallible teaching is but a single aspect of the learning process of the Church. That is, it is the terminus of a sincere attempt to assimilate authentic teaching. Therefore the style of public dissent (private dissent does not raise the question of "style") must be determined by positioning it within this total learning process.

As part of the total learning process of the Church, public dissent should both reflect this learning process and contribute to it. It will *reflect* it by embodying the qualities of a truly Catholic response to authentic teaching. These qualities are: respect for the person and charism of the authentic teacher, proportionate docility, honesty combined with an awareness of one's own limitations. Public dissent which manifests these qualities will be: always respectful, generally reluctant, clearly open to correction and persuasion. It will *contribute* to the learning process by supporting all the component elements of the teaching-learning process. It was noted above that the teaching function of the Church includes at least three distinguishable components: the prophetic charism of the Christian, the pastoral charism of the hierarchy, the scientific charism of the theologian. Since it is the proper interplay of these charisms which yields a healthy and vigorous magisterium, dissent must contribute to this proper interplay.

It would seem that for a proper interplay of these functions certain "atmospheric conditions" must exist within the Church. This atmosphere is constituted by the preservation of certain values within the teaching-learning process: respect for the authority of the teacher, the confidence of the faithful in the openness of the teacher, a passionate devotion to truth and its sources, the freedom of scholarly research and publication, the existence of broad consultative procedures as the basis for the exercise of authoritative teaching, good relations between the persons exercising the various functions within the teaching process. If public dissent is to *contribute* to the learning process, its over-all effect must be to support and strengthen these values which constitute the atmosphere just mentioned.

Whether a particular style of dissent will support or undermine

---

[47] *Human Life in Our Day* (Washington, D.C.: United States Catholic Conference, 1968) p. 18.

these values depends on many circumstances peculiar to each situation: for example, the way authority is being exercised in the Church at a particular time, cultural attitudes toward authority, the extent of consultation prior to teaching, the temper and stability of the Christian faithful, the repute of the dissenter, the importance of the teaching, the weight of authority summoned in its proposal, the condition of the communications media, etc.

A careful comparison of these circumstantial factors with the values to be preserved might lead to the following general assertion as helpful in our time: *where dissent is both public and organized, it carries with it special risks, and hence demands special warrants.* Some of the *risks* in our day are: it appears to many to attack authority itself; it tends to polarize the persons exercising the various charisms within the teaching function; it tends to undermine the confidence of the faithful in the charism of the hierarchy; it tends to anticipate and prevent a truly personal reflection on the teaching by the faithful; it tends to associate theology with popular media rather than with serious, scholarly reflection.[48] The *warrants* are two: (1) other forms of less sensational dissent are ineffective (2) in circumstances where an unopposed error would cause great harm.

This harm would be traceable to two sources: first, the personal suffering of the faithful occasioned by the teaching if it touched their lives on a frequent basis; secondly, loss of credibility of the magisterium. Here it should be noted that in former times the credibility and effectiveness of the magisterium were associated with and measured by a high degree of uniformity of thought and expression, and unity of practice. In times which emphasize philosophical pluralism, rapid communications, historical consciousness and the tentative character of human formulations, the complexity of moral issues, the wide variety of competences needed in their solution, freedom of expression, etc., the credibility of the magisterium is less associated with uniformity than with openness, utter honesty, collegial procedures.

Therefore, given the availability of other styles of dissent and the fact that public organized dissent may easily disturb the proper interplay of the various charisms within the teaching function of the Church, the burden of proof would seem to be on those whose dissent

---

[48] Such considerations are summarized by the Belgian bishops when they say of the competent dissenter: "He must also beware of creating an unhealthy unrest or, a fortiori, of questioning the very principle of authority." The German bishops say: "In adopting this [dissenting] position he will have to give consideration to the laws of intra-Church dialogue and try to avoid giving any scandal."

is both public and organized. This is not to say that it is never justified. It is only to say that, in general, organized public dissent can easily threaten to derogate from certain values profoundly associated with the common good. If this is so, the dissenter must show that the good to be achieved is at least proportionate to the foreseeable harm. If he does this successfully—in so far as this is possible in the circumstances—he has shown that the style of his dissent is both reasonable and Christian.

MORALITY AND THE COMPETENCE OF THE MAGISTERIUM

One of the questions of very lively debate surrounding *Humanae vitae* was the Pope's relationship to consultative and collegial procedures. Diametrically opposed positions have appeared in the literature. Three articles cover the range of reactions rather well. H. Paul Le Maire, S.J., in a strong but respectful essay, contrasts the spirit of the Encyclical with that of Vatican II.[49] He finds that the Encyclical departs from Vatican II in four significant areas. First, there is the question of dialogue (with the world, with Christian churches, between pastors and laymen). *Humanae vitae* showed little evidence of this dialogue in the face of Vatican II's strong desires for it. Secondly, the role of a truly responsible laity was neglected. "If the Holy Spirit operates in and through all members of the Church, then all members of the Church should be taken seriously and their voice listened to." Thirdly, collegiality "died a premature death" with the Encyclical. Finally, the work of theologians was rejected without justifying reason. Le Maire concludes that if the Church continues along this path, "it will become the Church isolated from the world in which it lives; it will become a Church where authority speaks only to itself."

Francesco Marchesi, S.J., takes a completely opposite point of view.[50] He disagrees with Karl Rahner on the basis for dissent. Rahner had said that the fact that many of the papal commission disagree could be an element in one's dissent. Marchesi believes that this is a problem only for those who erroneously hold that the Church is a democracy where decisions are made by majority vote. Rather, "in virtue of this primacy, the pope can decide even by himself, according to his prudent and reflective judgment." Marchesi insists that "it would be a grave error to hold that the pope is, by divine will, con-

---

[49] H. Paul Le Maire, S.J., "*Humanae vitae* and the Spirit of Vatican II," *Philippine Studies* 17 (1969) 133–45.

[50] Francesco M. Marchesi, S.J., "Qualche rilievo su 'Riflessioni' di K. Rahner," *Palestra del clero* 48 (1969) 100–108.

ditioned in his doctrinal decisions by a dialogue with bishops, and the bishops by a dialogue with their faithful."[51]

Somewhere between these positions is that of Michael Walsh, S.J.[52] He grants that *Humanae vitae* was not a collegial act. But through the Encyclical and the enormous reactions to it, he senses that Catholics are becoming aware that all share in the responsibility of Christ's Church. This is the beginning of a lived collegiality. Walsh seems to be suggesting that perhaps it was a bit much to expect collegiality to burst fully mature on the scene. Rather we have to grope to it, and this may be the overriding meaning of the Encyclical-happening.

The question of the consultative and collegial relationships of the Holy Father has not stopped there. It has opened into a very interesting discussion of the competence of the magisterium in the area of morality. The discussion is immature as yet, but it is so vitally important that it deserves presentation at length, even if many loose ends remain.

Peter Huizing of Nijmegen endorses an analysis which those familiar with the literature will recognize as that of J. David, S.J.[53] Where the magisterium is concerned, it has a proper mission and competence in ethical questions in so far as these find an answer in the sources of revelation. In questions of natural law, the magisterium has only a negative competence. That is, it can teach that certain ethical assertions are in contradiction to revelation. But the more positive statements about specific natural-law demands do not pertain to the ecclesiastical magisterium (*Lehramt*) in the strictest sense. Rather they represent a use of the pastoral office (*Hirtenamt*), of a kind of directive power. This function of authority is purely subsidiary. When men reach sufficient maturity, the solution of natural ethical questions is to be left to their judgment and to the secular sciences. Huizing concedes that the community of the Church as a whole cannot in any historical moment neglect the technical-scientific aspects of moral questions, the concretizations of natural law. The Christian has a commission to form the world according to the specific content associated with a Christian vision. But this development of a natural innerworldly ethic is the task of the laity, not of the hierarchy.

Tübingen's Alfons Auer carries this line of thought even further.[54]

---

[51] *Ibid.*, p. 106.

[52] Michael J. Walsh, S.J., "Collegiality and the Encyclical," *Month* 41 (1969) 168–75.

[53] Peter Huizing, S.J., "'Göttliches Recht' und Kirchenverfassung," *Stimmen der Zeit* 94 (1969) 162–73. For J. David's position, cf. *Das Naturrecht in Krise und Läuterung* (Cologne, 1967).

[54] Alfons Auer, "Nach dem Erscheinen der Enzyklika 'Humanae vitae'—Zehn Thesen über die Findung sittlicher Weisungen," *Theologische Quartalschrift* 149 (1969) 75–85.

He writes from the conviction that with *Humanae vitae* the curtain has fallen on a certain form of magisterial moral teaching. Auer develops his thought in ten "theses" which might be summarized as follows. Because morality is at root the claim which reality makes on the human person, man's basic morality is an innerworldly one. Neither the Old nor the New Testament presented a new concrete innerworldly ethic. Rather they took over existing norms and popular ethical models, situated them within new perspectives, and dynamized them with fresh (e.g., salvational) motives. Later moral theology, in using Aristotelico-Stoic categories, did the same thing. Therefore, for Auer, concrete moral directives are, as immanent innerworldly realities, a product of the human spirit and can be clarified totally by man. Nor has the Church disputed this. Her teaching on natural law has said just that.

Yet the Church has always claimed a special competence in this area, a kind of special knowledge. In Auer's view, the process of secularization is seriously questioning this competence at the present time. He believes that the imposition of detailed innerworldly norms pertains to the Church's subsidiary function, not to her original function. That is, she took over this responsibility at a time when it was culturally and historically necessary. But when a society grows to intellectual maturity, these tasks must be abandoned. The Church should not retain subsidiary functions any longer than necessary, because in doing so she courts the danger of jeopardizing her essential mission for the sake of the only putatively essential.

Auer does not deny the right and duty of the Church to have a say in the delineation of concrete moral directives. Rather this competence must be conceived in a radically different way. It is above all a *criticizing* function. Because of sin, even spiritual man can flounder in his notions of morality. The statements of revelation about human life and history are—even after being appropriately demythologized—so helpful and clear that they must always operate as a critical measure. When a concrete moral directive endures this confrontation, the Church can point out the possibility and necessity of its Christian integration. But it will remain the product of the human spirit.

Thus the Church can and must propose moral norms, but rather than claiming any original competence, she will take over autonomously developed ethical directives and present them as helpful models for Christian living. This implies two things. First, if the Church proposes innerworldly norms which are established neither through revelation nor through a historically validated ethical consciousness, then the claim can be imposed only to the extent that the arguments ground it. Secondly, since autonomously developed ethical directives draw very heavily on experience, dialogue within the community must have a central position in the discovery of moral directives.

Louvain's Louis Janssens presents a point of view not too far from that of Auer, though it does differ in significant details.[55] After noting that the material content of Christian morality is identical with that of the natural law, he asserts that it is man's task to decipher and regulate the laws and values of created things. The Church certainly has a competence here, and for two reasons. First, the good of the community demands it. Authoritative proposal of moral norms is a pedagogical aid needed by sinful man. Secondly, the Church has a vocation, as the People of God, to be the living conscience of mankind. This vocation demands that the magisterium, in the name of the Church and as witness to the world, defend the poor, denounce injustice, and so on.

But in the discovery and proposal of concrete norms "dialogue is obviously demanded, *both* by the autonomy of man *and* the historicity of moral norms." By "autonomy" Janssens refers to the fact that the content of morality is within the domain of natural law. This being the case, if the magisterium proposes concrete moral norms, it places itself on the plane of human knowledge, "where the final word is given not to authority, but to the overriding validity of the reasons proposed." Even past errors of the magisterium indicate that in the domain of concrete moral norms it is not the argument of authority but the intrinsic value of the evidence which is decisive. By "historicity" Janssens refers to the fact that concrete moral norms develop in community through collaboration between those joined by fidelity to conscience. This fact also imposes dialogue as a means of discovering moral norms. "The magisterium, too, can intervene only after the fact, to compile norms which have developed in the life of the community, and to communicate them universally."[56] Janssens is close to Auer when he concludes by noting that if the pronouncements of the magisterium are the expression of the life of the People of God, they are heartily welcomed by both Church and world. If, contrarily, these pronouncements go against the lived experience of a great number of Christians and non-Christians, the reactions are negative.

Ph. Delhaye distinguishes two different domains where the magisterium operates, the doctrinal and the pastoral.[57] In this he echoes

[55] Louis Janssens, "Considerations of 'Humanae vitae,'" *Louvain Studies* 2 (1969) 231–53.

[56] *Ibid.*, p. 245.

[57] Ph. Delhaye, "Conscience et autorité ecclésiale," *La foi et le temps*, Jan.-Feb. 1969, pp. 5–35.

Huizing, but explains things a bit differently. In the doctrinal sphere the magisterium is making statements of truth or falsity. In the pastoral sphere her statements are rather prudential determinations, where more basic principles are in confrontation with social structures of the moment, and hence are variable. Thus we notice a considerable shift in emphasis and even some discontinuity in *Rerum novarum*, *Quadragesimo anno*, and *Mater et magistra*. That is to be expected. Times change.

Where morality is concerned, it is Delhaye's contention that the magisterium is generally involved in the pastoral domain, and it would be a mistake to interpret the documents of the magisterium as if they pertained to the level of theoretical moral. Thus he regards the controversy surrounding *Humanae vitae* as largely due to those myopic authors who have read the Encyclical as a theoretical moral statement rather than as a prudential pastoral counsel. Using this epistemological perspective, Delhaye sees *Humanae vitae* as a loud and well-targeted protest against modern eroticism and pansexualism. Its basic message is to caution those couples who use contraceptives (because they can do nothing else) against the danger of confusing responsible parenthood with a destructive hedonism. For Delhaye, the term "intrinsic evil" used in the Encyclical is really only a pastoral affirmation whose basic meaning is: avoid contraception as much as possible and use it only to preserve higher values. This message, he believes, should not be tightened into a doctrinal statement.

If Delhaye's interpretation of the Encyclical is correct, then the vast majority of theologians and episcopal conferences have been deceived about the problem it was facing and the answer it was giving.

Robert L. Cunningham approaches the relationship of authority to morality by distinguishing between one who is *in* authority and one who is *an* authority.[58] In-authority pertains, for example, to an officer in the army or the manager of a firm. Pronouncements of in-authority are, in a sense and up to a point, self-authenticating. That is, the authority makes things appropriate by saying so. For example, those in authority in baseball decide what is to count as a balk. These rules call for obedience and are defeasible not by showing that the command is inferior to another possible one, but by appeal to higher authority.

An-authority, on the contrary, is established by the ability to cite

---

[58] R. L. Cunningham, "Authority and Morals," in *Truth and the Historicity of Man* (the brochure program of 43rd annual meeting of the American Catholic Philosophical Association) pp. 20–29.

facts, make distinctions, give explanations, make predictions—summarily, by over-all expertise. Acceptance or "belief" is the proper response to an-authority, and the pronouncements of an-authority are defeasible by appeal to the facts. Thus the two types of authority are different. Possession of in-authority does not mean that an individual is an-authority. The precise difficulty in the Church is the fact that there are in the same persons (the pope, bishops) both types of authority. When this is the case, Cunningham suggests that in-authority is too easily confused with an-authority and, indeed, sometimes substitutes for it where moral issues are concerned. A symbol of this is the disagreement between in-authority (pope and bishops) and an-authority (theologians) on certain moral questions.

Walter Kerber, S.J., in a thoughtful article on moral-theological hermeneutics, contends that the distinction between the *Lehramt* and the *Hirtenamt* (with the Church's concrete moral declarations limited to this latter) is an unacceptable way to explain the concrete moral declarations of the magisterium, especially errors in magisterial teaching.[59] Among his several objections: Why should the pastoral office be less protected from error than the teaching office, when one sees its authority as genuinely theological rather then merely human? Secondly, for many years the Church has claimed a truly magisterial role in matters of moral law and bound the faithful to her statements. To have done this without competence would constitute a more fundamental mistake than any single declaration on a specific moral issue. Finally, the David-Huizing distinction does not sufficiently respect the profound inner relationship between revealed morality and natural law. Kerber concludes, therefore, that any past errors in Church teaching should not lead us to new limitations upon the teaching authority, but to a more adequate over-all theology of the teaching office.

We will not develop this more adequate theology unless we have a more exact notion of New Testament moral teaching. Kerber suggests that those who restrict the teaching competence of the Church in moral matters to revealed morality have an inadequate knowledge of the ethical message of the New Testament. They imply that New Testament morality is a rather full and enclosed moral system transtemporally valid. This is not the case. Contemporary hermeneutics makes it quite clear that very many concrete Scripture statements cannot be read as ethical directives for all time. They represent rather

[59] Walter Kerber, S.J., "Hermeneutik in der Moraltheologie," *Theologie und Philosophie* 44 (1969) 42–66.

concretizations of the *lex Christi* within a definite time and culture. Furthermore, these normative concretizations have been forged with the help of Hellenistic, Jewish, and Stoic philosophy—that is, from the consciousness of the time. It is clear, therefore, that many New Testament assertions cannot be simply identified with the *lex Christi*.

Hermeneutics makes it possible to disengage the transtemporal from the historically conditioned and in this sense to see the parts in the light of the whole. Now underlying all moral obligation is a general knowledge of what man should be, but a general knowledge which is visible and tangible only in concrete situations. In other words, what we call "natural law" is the basic inner assumption provided by man's understanding of himself, as Böckle has noted.[60] With the coming of Christ and acceptance of Him by the Christian as a model, this antecedent understanding, this horizon which underlies all obligations and persists through all concretizations, was profoundly affected. It is upon this basic inner understanding of man now deepened by Christ that New Testament morality builds, not upon everlastingly valid concrete propositions *ex clara scriptura*.

Franz Böckle has derived the teaching competence of the Church from precisely this notion of natural law. "Since Catholic theology lives in the conviction that, in Christ, something decisive has been revealed to man about himself, the Church is committed to the true image of man in this world. She must make an important contribution to man's true understanding of himself. But this understanding does not thereby get detached from his historical conditioning."[61]

Therefore both Kerber and Böckle are convinced that the Church has a doctrinal competence in the area of natural law. It would seem that they would argue the matter as follows. Because the natural moral law is at root man's self-understanding, and because this self-understanding has been decisively affected by Christ, it is clear that the Church has a doctrinal competence about what we call natural law. Or again, the self-understanding to be concretized at different times and in different cultures is not simply one of "natural man," but a self-understanding suffused with the influence of Christ. It is therefore one deeply influenced by revelation.

In this understanding natural law and revealed morality are very closely associated at the rather general level of man's self-understand-

---

[60] F. Böckle, ed., *Understanding the Signs of the Times* (*Concilium* 25; New York: Paulist, 1967) p. 4. Cf. also B. Schüller, S.J., "Wie weit kann die Moraltheologie das Naturrecht entbehren?" *Lebendiges Zeugnis*, March 1965, pp. 41–65.

[61] Böckle, *op. cit.*, p. 4.

ing. If such an explanation of natural law is one way of establishing the doctrinal competence of the Church in this area, it also suggests two notable limits upon this competence. First, when this self-awareness is concretized in norms and directives, not only are we dealing with the use of man's very fallible reasoning processes, but also with norms and directives embedded in the contingencies of history. Therefore the competence, while genuine, simply cannot be final or infallible in instances of such concretization. Secondly, since it is man's self-understanding that is the source of concrete moral norms, the exercise of Church competence demands a broad dialogical procedure.

Donald Wuerl, in a tightly written article, touches some of the emphases seen in Kerber.[62] He first shows that man's apprehension and delineation of a natural moral order (basic human responses and relational structures) is limited and conditioned. Not only are our perceptions filtered through our own situations and experiences, but we develop within a community and hence inherit the values which come to us from this community. Therefore, while we are capable of grasping a basic human value (his example: "thou shalt not kill the innocent"), specific questions remain. For example, who is innocent? The answer to such specific questions "will be mediated by the circumstances and the community in which man lives. And the specific direction given a man by his beliefs and experiences in a community will provide these conditions."[63]

Just as Israel's encounter with reality was conditioned by the experience at Sinai of God's presence, so Christ's intervention in human history and His gathering of peoples from all lands to be His Church means that "any consideration of man's basic orientation and his basic responses will now, to some extent, be conditioned by this fact." That is, Christ has given a direction to human existence. Therefore both the evaluation of basic human orientations and their translation into specific and practical guidelines will be made in light of the Christ-event.

Wuerl then notes that "given the impetus of Christ to the direction of man's life in history and given the conditioning of man's approach to reality that this necessarily entails, the disciple should expect the Church to teach officially in the area of natural moral order."[64] Therefore, when the Church teaches in the area of natural law,

---

[62] Donald Wuerl, "Natural Law, the Community and Authority," *Priest* 25 (1969) 272-82.

[63] For a similar analysis, cf. Daniel Callahan, "The Sanctity of Life," in *The Religious Situation 1969* (Boston: Beacon, 1969) pp. 297-336.

[64] *Ibid.*, p. 278.

Wuerl would contend that she is simply specifying basic human relational structures but within a value system. Sometimes these specifications are adequately known by reason and enthusiastically endorsed
by all men (e.g., premeditated destruction of human life). But there are
other areas where neither experienced reason nor revelation will yield
a clear relation to basic relational structures. As Wuerl sees it, "we
are in the wide areas of human responses that usually receive direction
from competent authority, the authority that is competent to speak for
the values that found and permeate the community."[65] In these areas
it is the function of competent authority to interpret and apply the
initial experience that gave rise to the community.

Ultimately, therefore, it would seem that Wuerl would understand
certain specifications of Church teaching as value judgments best
named "directives." Because this is their nature, he concludes that
"acceptance of directives of the magisterium in matters of faith and
morals no longer rests entirely upon the absolute internal intelligibility of those directives. Rejection of a given argument connected
with the explanation of a moral imperative does not necessarily permit
rejection of the teaching of the magisterium concerning that imperative."[66] In another paragraph Wuerl states that "he [the Catholic] is
not free to reject the official and authentic teaching of the Church
even if he concludes that the teaching in question depends heavily
upon an intellectual position he rejects."[67] This is so basically because these directives speak the Church's living re-evaluation and
application of the meaning given human life by Jesus.

Later I shall attempt to show why the affirmation that "acceptance
of directives... no longer rests entirely upon the absolute internal
intelligibility of those directives" is tenable not precisely because the
directives represent the judgments of competent authority, but because, *if authority has proceeded correctly*, it is in possession of a
wisdom which presumably surpasses the individual's.

Daniel Maguire views the competence of the magisterium in terms
of the notion of teacher.[68] Authority, he contends, can serve but not
substitute for any of the evaluative processes of moral inquiry. Thus
the good teacher is one who inspires, stimulates, sensitizes, encourages. "Authority" is a poor way of stating this because it suggests a
superior power of knowing which can bypass essential methods of ethi-

[65] *Ibid.*, p. 279.
[66] *Ibid.*, p. 281.
[67] *Ibid.*
[68] Daniel C. Maguire, "Teaching, Authority, and Authenticity," *Living Light* 6 (1969)
6–18.

cal reflection.[69] Maguire prefers "teaching influence" to "teaching authority" and says of the Christian teacher that his essential authority is his ability to perceive the truth and to transmit it. Therefore in the contemporary Church we have moved away from teachers who say the last word in an effort to close debate to teachers who seek to say important words calculated to enlarge and enrich the processes of debate.

It is clear that the articles summarized above start from different points of view, move in different directions, and sometimes even draw different conclusions. Yet when one stands back from them, I believe it possible to detect a single thread or theme running through nearly all of them: a much greater emphasis on human experience, reflection and analysis in the establishment of concrete moral norms, and a consequent insistence on broad consultative and collegial procedures. But in ecclesiastical documents the authoritative character of the declarations of the noninfallible moral magisterium is argued by appeal to the light of the Holy Spirit. Thus *Humanae vitae* (no. 28) stated that obedience is due to these teachings "not only because of the reasons adduced, but rather because of the light of the Holy Spirit which is given in a particular way to the pastors of the Church in order that they may illustrate the truth."

Any attempt to understand more adequately the role of authority in moral inquiry must attempt to relate these two elements. This should be done, it would seem, before drawing conclusions similar to those of Auer and Huizing about the noncompetence of the magisterium in the area of concrete moral directives. I believe this suggests above all the need to examine the concept of the assistance of the Holy Spirit; for it is this assistance to which appeal is made to establish the authority of the teaching.

Maguire asserts that the notion of the Spirit's assistance to the hierarchical leaders needs a good deal of work by theologians. It is his own conviction that this notion as it appears both in presentations of Pope Paul VI and in Vatican II has two major defects.[70] First, it is tendentially quietistic. That is, it too easily implies a power to achieve truth outside of human processes. Secondly, it suffers from in-

---

[69] Alois Müller also rejects "obedience" as the proper word to describe one's moral duties where teaching is concerned. Cf. "Authority and Obedience in the Church," in *War, Poverty and Freedom* (*Concilium* 45; New York: Paulist, 1966) pp. 71–88, at 73. For an excellent recent discussion of teaching and authority, cf. Jos. A. Komonchak, "Magisterium and Religious Assent," in *Contraception: Authority and Dissent*, pp. 101–26.

[70] Daniel C. Maguire, "Moral Inquiry and Religious Assent," in *Contraception: Authority and Dissent*, pp. 127–48.

nocence of history. A chastening trip through history will reveal any number of erroneous positions proposed by the magisterium. In terms very close to Cunningham's, Maguire therefore rejects a juridically conceived magisterium which wills moral insights into legitimacy. He states that "there is need for teaching officers in the Church to give voice to the truest insights of the community by stimulating the magisterial potential of the whole Church."[71]

I believe it is correct to say that the notion of the assistance of the Holy Spirit needs a good deal of theological attention. If it remains as opaque as it actually is in the documents of the magisterium, it is likely that the voice of the hierarchical magisterium will continue to be loudest and clearest when it says "authority and special assistance" and that of others loudest when it says "evidence and reasons." Both emphases are important, of course, but if they are left unrelated, are we not still vulnerable to the dangers of a simplistic notion of assistance?

What, then, is the meaning of "the assistance of the Spirit" where the authoritative noninfallible magisterium is concerned?[72] Anyone who undertakes to speak about the action of the Spirit, especially if he tries to explain how the Spirit works, realizes in advance that he is more than ever likely to end up with a theological foot in his mouth and make an utter fool of himself; for the operations of the Spirit are above all ineffable. Yet the possibility of gaining some understanding and the anticipation of charitable correction by others minimizes the arrogance of the attempt. With this in mind I should like to offer a possible approach.

In facing this question two extremes must be avoided. The first would explain the assistance of the Spirit to the magisterium in a way which dispenses with human processes. The second would simply reduce this assistance to human processes. The first is the notion of a special assistance by the Spirit which represents a new source of hierarchical knowledge, arcane and impervious to any criticism developed out of Christian experience, evidence, and reasoning. Such a notion of assistance results in a form of fideism which makes it difficult, if not impossible, to see how any authoritative utterance is not thereby practically infallible. Furthermore, this notion of assistance

[71] *Ibid.*, p. 148.

[72] I am supposing a radical difference between the infallible and noninfallible magisterium, though it is probably true to say that we have theologized (and catechized) about the two within a framework of continuity rather than analogy. Certainly many generations of Catholics have been taught to view the noninfallible magisterium as "just a little less than infallible."

is a summary edict of dissolution for the scholarly and theological fraternity.

The second extreme is such an emphasis on analysis and reasons that the action of the Spirit is simply identified with the shrewdest thinkers in the community and ultimately imprisoned in the best reasons they can unravel. This is an extreme for many reasons, not the least of which is that it is a form of neorationalism which overlooks the complexity and developmental character of moral cognition, especially by bypassing the real significance of the communitarian aspect of moral knowledge, and especially of the *sensus fidelium*. If the action of the Spirit is primarily directed to the Church as a whole, and secondarily and in subordination to the needs of the Church, to its pastors as pastors, then surely this fact must influence the emergence of moral knowledge, the operations of the magisterium, and the notion of the special assistance of the Holy Spirit to the magisterium.

It would seem that any explanation of the assistance of the Holy Spirit to the magisterium (noninfallible) must be adequate to four factors: (1) the judgmental competence of the hierarchy within the whole teaching process, (2) the activity of the Spirit in the formation of such judgment, (3) the possibility and fact of error in these judgments, and (4) the relevance of the experience and reflection of the whole Church in forming these judgments.

I should like to suggest that the middle course we seek is one which would associate the activity of the Spirit with human processes without identifying it with them. The nature of this association can perhaps be illumined by a reflection on error. When error occurs in human judgments, it would seem to occur in either of two ways: in the gathering of evidence or in the assessment of the evidence. Obviously there can be many reasons why either of these processes would function inadequately, but it is the breakdown of one of them to which judgmental error can be traced. If this is true, then is it not reasonable to think that at least the proper implementation of these processes is generally required to avoid error in complex decisions?

When this is applied to the magisterium, we might say that error could occur either through evidence-gathering or evidence-assessing.[73] Hence at least adequate evidence-gathering and evidence-assessing are required if error is to be avoided. Evidence-gathering is inadequate when consultation is not broad enough to allow the full wisdom stimu-

[73] Evidence is not to be understood here as data gathered by the physical sciences, where no prior assessment is part of the data itself. Rather evidence should be taken as including the reflections and judgments of those constituting the evidence.

lated by the Spirit's activity in the whole Church to emerge. Evidence-assessing breaks down when consideration of the evidence is insufficient to allow the Spirit to aid in the emergence of its meaning.[74] In the contemporary world these inadequacies would seem to be traceable to a failure in the fulness of the collegial process at all levels.

Now the magisterium of the Church has special advantages to overcome these handicaps in arriving at moral truth. First of all, bishops *as pastors* are in a unique position to be in contact with the convictions, problems, beliefs, joys, sufferings, and reflections of all groups in the local church. That is, they are positioned to consult the experience and convictions (the wisdom) of their flock. As *collegial pastors* they are in a position to pool this wisdom and weigh it through a process of dialogue and debate. In this sense the episcopal and papal magisterium have sources of information which exceed those available to anyone else. Summarily: negatively, the magisterium is in a wonderful position to reduce the barriers which bind the Spirit; positively, it is positioned to engage the total resources of the community and thus give the Spirit the fullest possible scope.[75]

Therefore, though we cannot capture in human categories the operations and assistance of the Holy Spirit, can we not identify the human processes within which the Spirit must be supposed to operate? And since the hierarchy is uniquely situated to implement these processes, is it not open to the assistance of the Spirit in a special way when it does so? That is, the ability of bishop-pastors (and through them the pope) to range beyond the isolation of their own reflections or those of restricted groups is the foundation for the confidence that in doing so they will be specially open to the Spirit and that their authentic pronouncements will show this.

Therefore who would doubt that when the magisterium actually draws upon the wisdom resident in the entire Church and actually submits itself to an adequate evaluative process, it is better positioned than any individual or group of individuals to relate this to Christian conduct? A prudent and sensitive Catholic would be willing to accept such conclusions precisely because (and providing that) he had the assurance that they proceeded from a store of wisdom far be-

[74] In an interesting article Gerard P. Kirk, S.J., maintains that *Humanae vitae* was a "crisis document" issued before true ripeness of the issues was achieved (*Continuum* 6 [1968] 288–94). This suggests the possibility that concrete moral directives are often in the category of more probable judgments. In the past we may have viewed them too often as virtually unconditioned judgments which settled matters definitively. This must be kept in mind in judging the meaning of error in moral teaching.

[75] Cf. Enda McDonagh, "Coresponsibility and the Theologian," *Furrow* 20 (1969) 184.

yond the solipsism of his own insights. And for this reason he would find it quite acceptable to say with *Humanae vitae* that acceptance of these judgments is owed "not only because of the reasons adduced, but rather because of the light of the Holy Spirit which is given in a particular way to the pastors of the Church in order that they may illustrate the truth." On the other hand, one may legitimately expect that this "light of the Holy Spirit" will manifest itself concretely in the "way the question itself is handled. That means in the solid presentation of proofs from human experience and with good arguments."[76]

When pastoral leaders do not implement these human processes where the matter in question demands it, one can wonder to what extent they may lay claim to the assistance of the Spirit.[77] Furthermore, even after these human means have been utilized, genuine error (not to be confused with prudential directives to be adapted later in the light of differing circumstances) might occur. Men are men, even in their collaboration with the Spirit. But in this case three things are to be noted. First, this error would probably be detectable only at a considerably later date as *certain* error—precisely because the wisdom of the entire Church had apparently gone into its formulation. Secondly, since error must be attributed to human frailty and not to the Holy Spirit, the error would be traceable, on closer examination, to factors which inhibited the fulness of these processes we have mentioned, even though at the time they seemed adequate. Thirdly, the error would reveal itself, to a greater or lesser extent, in the reasons and analyses used to elaborate the teaching. This is why, among other reasons, theologians must continue to subject the principles and arguments used in magisterial documents to the most careful scrutiny and

---

[76] Häring, in *The Catholic Case for Contraception*, p. 82.

[77] Karl Rahner has pointed out that the Roman pontiff and the bishops have a moral obligation to take "apt means" for discovering the truth where the infallible magisterium is to be exercised. He lists these means as follows: "constant recourse to Scripture, the theological work of exegetes, historians and dogmatic theologians, and the free untrammelled exchange of views, living contact with the instinct of faith which cannot err in the faithful as a whole, and ecumenical dialogue. The 'hierarchy of the truths of faith' must be respected, the spiritual and theological heritage of the Eastern Churches must be revived, there must be a frank and courageous dialogue with the spiritual and social realities of each age, the charismatic element in the Church must be taken seriously. A constant effort must be made to overcome the restricted outlook of the various schools, each of which is legitimate in itself, but which are too easily tempted to identify themselves with the mind and doctrine of the believing Church. And finally 'public opinion' in the Church must be adequately taken into account" (K. Rahner, in *Commentary on the Documents of Vatican II* 1 [New York: Herder and Herder, 1967] 214). This would be true a fortiori where the noninfallible magisterium is concerned.

criticism. It is the human way of distinguishing between truth and error in moral judgments.

But does not this explanation of the manner of operation of the authoritative magisterium derogate from papal prerogatives, from the supreme magisterium of the Holy Father? Marchesi was cited at the beginning of this section as follows: "In virtue of this primacy, the pope can decide even by himself, according to his prudent and reflective judgment."[78] To say anything else Marchesi regards as "grave error." It seems to me that the over-all thrust of recent writings as reviewed in this section is to deny outright Marchesi's statement, if "decide by himself" means independently of the processes whereby evidence is gathered and assessed, or in the face of very considerable contrary evidence. In other words, contemporary theological writings reject the identification of "primacy" with the ability to "decide by himself."

But this is not to deny primacy or to derogate from the supreme magisterium of the Holy Father. It is rather to raise this question: Within what processes and with what dependence on these processes is primacy to be exercised in our times if it is to function in a more than merely juridical way? To understand primacy as the ability to "decide by himself" could easily represent the reduction of primacy to a juridical abstraction and its contraction to a cultural form no longer adequate to the complex moral problems of a changing world. By this same token, to liberate it from this contraction and to search for more suitable ways for its exercise is not at all to derogate from the primacy. It could be to defend it against decay.

The point is important enough to suggest the value of a rewording. The juridical powers of the pope are not in question. In other words, the issue is not what the pope *can* do. That is a simple juridical statement. The issue is what he must do to acquire the information, knowledge, and evidence essential to doing what he can do. Those who say that "the pope need not consult" or "need not accept the advice of his consultative commissions" are making purely juridical statements. It is true in a juridical sense that the teaching authority of the pope is not limited by collegiality. But the Holy Father is limited by the evidence in support of the truth. He *can*, as possessor of a supreme magisterium, teach that something pertains to the natural law. But the exercise of this juridical power supposes that there is persuasive evidence supporting the teaching. Collegiality and consultation function in service of this evidence. Therefore, when the pope rejects

[78] For a similar statement, cf. Zamoyta, *op. cit.*, p. 91.

the suggestions of his consultants, the presumption is that he has persuasive contrary evidence. Otherwise why consult in the first place?

Archbishop Denis Hurley put the matter quite well: "To be acceptable in our time, it seems to me that primacy must operate in accordance with the practices of communication and consultation accepted in modern, responsible society, but remembering my own attitudes of only a few years ago I can fully understand the attitude of mind of Pope Paul and the Curia. It is a mistake, however, to identify the primacy and the monarchical expression of it."[79]

THE ETHICS OF POLITICAL PROTEST

On May 17, 1968, nine opponents of the war in Vietnam entered the local draft headquarters in Catonsville, Maryland, emptied four hundred 1-A files into wastebaskets, took them outside, and burned them with homemade napalm. On September 24, 1968, fourteen men, including five priests, removed nearly ten thousand 1-A draft files from Milwaukee's Selective Service boards and burned them with napalm in a square dedicated to America's war dead. On May 25, 1969, fifteen persons, including two priests and a seminarian, raided the draft files on Chicago's south side. Tar and red paint were poured over some files, others were taken outside and burned.

These incidents represent three of the more colorful acts of defiance in a growing series of obstructionist tactics which include everything from mill-ins and the blocking of traffic to the imprisonment of CIA or Dow Chemical recruiters. Reactions to these protests have been deeply divided. Some see them as an immoral invasion and destruction of private property and an infringement on the rights of others. Others see them as legitimate forms of "symbolic language" in the face of enormous injustices when other more democratic methods are of no avail. Whatever the effectiveness of the tactics of the Catonsville Nine (*et al.*) as an antiwar protest, there is little doubt that the action has made the ethics of protest a subject of keen interest.

Furthermore, raids on draft files have an importance beyond their own specificity. In a world where change is rapid, government huge and impersonal, the processes of persuasion (e.g., TV) out of the reach of most, legal processes tedious and cumbersome, sensitivity to suffering and deprivation sharper than ever, we may expect more situations where citizens will conclude that the only effective way to express their malaise is through an illegal form of dissent. For this reason it may be of some value to review the moral issues raised by the various forms of

[79] Denis Hurley, "Letter of Law and Lesson of Life," *Tablet* 223 (1969) 153.

protest. The recent literature touches on two points: the over-all morality of protest and the specific instance of raids on draft files.[80]

Peter Riga describes the broader biblical perspectives of Christian protest.[81] He finds the heart of truly Christian protest (as contrasted with mere political protest) in meekness. Therefore protest is not basically a tactic but an attitude, an attitude based on expectation and hope for the kingdom. The Christian witnesses to this hope and expectation by challenging the omnipotent demands and self-sufficiencies of human institutions. He is a protester by nature against egotism and hatred and their by-products: nationalism, racism, militarism, world poverty. And since the poor are always the victims of human institutional *hubris*, the whole Church must become the protesting spokesman for the poor in all their concrete needs.

The larger issues involved in protest are brought out in an almost classic confrontation between Abe Fortas and Boston University's Howard Zinn.[82] Fortas encourages dissent and protest, but the methods must be within the limits of the law. It is Fortas' contention that "the definition of objectives and the selection of those which will triumph are of fundamental importance to the quality of our society, of our own lives, and those of our descendants. But the survival of our society as a free, open, democratic community, will be determined not so much by the specific points achieved by the Negroes and the youth-generation as by the procedures—the rules of conduct, the methods, the practices—which survive the confrontations."[83] Some procedures Fortas sees as never permissible. For example, violence is understandable but intolerable. Damage to persons or property is never justified. As for violation of law, civil disobedience which challenges a law believed to be unjust or unconstitutional is permissible. But "civil disobedience... is never justified in our nation where the law being violated is not itself the focus or target of the protest."[84] Obviously Fortas is convinced that in our country viable alternatives to these measures do exist.

Zinn disagrees with Fortas at almost every turn. But his most basic disagreement is with regard to Fortas' attitude toward law. For Fortas, law and "the rule of law" constitute a kind of supreme value. In Zinn's

[80] For a general treatment of protest, cf. Jerome H. Skolnick, *The Politics of Protest* (New York: Ballantine, 1969).

[81] Peter Riga, "Toward a Theology of Protest," *Thomist* 33 (1969) 229–50.

[82] Abe Fortas, *Concerning Dissent and Civil Disobedience* (New York: Signet, 1968); Howard Zinn, *Disobedience and Democracy* (New York: Random House, 1968).

[83] Fortas, *op. cit.*, pp. 119–20.

[84] *Ibid.*, p. 124.

judgment, Fortas does not relate law to the values it must serve. Ultimately, therefore, his treatment of dissent shows us only the legal limits of protest, not the moral limits. Fortas is, in Zinn's opinion, a legalist pure and simple.

Take violence as an example. Fortas had excluded it absolutely as a form of protest. Zinn argues that Fortas has given neither moral nor practical grounds for this exclusion. Zinn is not a promoter of violence. He only argues that law is instrumentally in the service of human goods and values. Therefore he begins by describing civil disobedience as the "deliberate, discriminate violation of law for a vital social purpose."[85] Its aim is always to close the gap between law and justice. Civil disobedience is not only justifiable, but necessary when a fundamental human value is at stake. For government and its laws are not sacred; they are instruments serving certain ends: life, liberty, happiness. "The instruments are dispensable, the ends are not."[86] In this light he allows for violation of laws which are not in themselves obnoxious in order to protest a very important issue. "In each case, the importance of the law being violated would need to be measured against the importance of the issue."[87] As for tactics, Zinn's rejection of violent protest is largely a pragmatic determination and therefore is far from absolute. Those who engage in civil disobedience should choose tactics which are as nonviolent as possible, "consonant with the effectiveness of their protest and the importance of the issue. There must be a reasonable relationship between the degree of disorder [in the protest] and the significance of the issue at stake."[88] When civil disobedience moves from mild actions to disorder, to violence, these criteria should be kept in mind: the violence must be guarded, limited, aimed carefully at the source of injustice, and preferably directed against property rather than people.

The Fortas-Zinn debate almost symbolizes the attitudes of two sharply opposed groups in the American community. It might be tendentious but is not altogether inaccurate to suggest that these attitudes are captured in the slogans "law and order," "law and justice." The value of the Fortas-Zinn exchange is that it brings to the surface and dissects the suppositions underlying these attitudes. The pivotal differences seem to be the following three: (1) the meaning, function, and

---

[85] Zinn, op. cit., p. 119.

[86] Ibid., p. 120. This same emphasis is found in William Sloane Coffin, Jr. He urges that it is a Christian task to respect what is legal but to be more concerned with what is right. On these grounds he asserts that man never has the right to break the law, but upon occasion he may have the duty to do so. This is the case with the Vietnam war in Coffin's opinion (Christianity and Crisis 28 [1968] 8-11).

[87] Zinn, op. cit., p. 120.   [88] Ibid., p. 121.

uses of law; (2) the effectiveness of the ordinary democratic processes of persuasion and protest; (3) the urgency of the social issues being protested.

While both books score good points on these differences, Zinn's is the more challenging presentation in my opinion. But he leaves several key questions unanswered. For instance, he states that "if a specific act of civil disobedience is a morally justifiable act of protest, then the jailing of those engaged in that act is immoral and should be opposed, contested to the very end." This is a vast oversimplification. The "moral justifiability" of a protest is the precipitate of many complex judgments: the relative importance of the value at issue, an assessment of the state of its realization or deteriorization in a particular society, the state of democratic processes in this society, the level of violence existent in the society, the prospective support to be won by the protest, the sensitivity of the society to the value of law, etc. When such judgments are the necessary ingredients of a conclusion about "moral justifiability," it is clear that this conclusion is a prudential judgment, with a fairly high level of risk.

Therefore "morally justifiable" must mean that a person (or persons) has submitted to the processes of justification demanded of any socially responsible person. It does not mean, because of its complexity and prudential character, certainty that the protest is objectively justifiable. To insist that it is immoral to jail a "morally justifiable" protester is to forget this and grant a degree of clarity to the notion of "moral justifiability" which it rarely possesses. Such unreal and abstract thinking has the effect of absolutizing the right to dissent to the point where it negates another's right to an opposite opinion—another's right to dissent from the dissenter. It is clear that such thinking is, therefore, ultimately and in principle self-destructive. It is one of the functions of law to protect the right to dissent by refusing to absolutize it out of existence.

In a long and thorough study of political disobedience, Leslie J. Macfarlane of Ruskin College (Oxford, England) shows that those who engage in political disobedience must successfully pass through a four-stage process of justification: of the cause served by disobedience, of the rejection of political obligation, of the form of disobedience practiced, of the expected consequences.[89] Macfarlane does not set out to produce a well-defined set of principles. Rather his analysis aims at disclosing "a number of relevant points which are capable, after subjection to critical appraisal and refinement, of forming the basis for the

[89]Leslie Macfarlane, "Justifying Political Disobedience," *Ethics* 79 (1968) 24–55.

establishment of conditional principles of political disobedience."[90] He succeeds eminently.

Macfarlane makes many excellent points along the way, but it is his treatment of the means of protest which is most immediately pertinent to our discussion. Once ground for rejection of obligation has been shown, Macfarlane states that it is not difficult to justify that disobedience aimed at publicizing the cause and gaining public support. This objective itself will rule out many of the more questionable forms of violent action, because they would result in loss of adherents. Violent protest in the form of sabotage and wrecking runs the risk of injuring the innocent, but Macfarlane feels that against highly oppressive regimes (e.g., South Africa) it can be used. The same would be true where a state refuses to permit constitutional methods of protest and uses brute force to suppress them. But Macfarlane argues that failure to secure objectives through ordinary channels does not thereby justify political disobedience. It may only suggest the need to re-evaluate one's cause. The ability of other causes to realize their objectives in part or in whole suggests that effective constitutional machinery exists which could be utilized.

"Refusal to permit constitutional methods of protest" is a sprawling phrase. Brute force is not the only way this refusal can be achieved. A cramping institutionalism can be so effective in rendering dissent and protest ineffective that it might amount to "refusing to permit constitutional methods of protest." Robert B. Thigpen and Lyle A. Downing (Department of Government, Louisiana State University) suggest that precisely such an institutionalism is behind the rash of disruptive behavior we are experiencing on the American scene.[91] They claim that disruptive tactics must be seen not merely as dissent but above all as a desire to participate in making policy decisions. Thus Dean Rusk and other official spokesmen for the administration's policy in Vietnam were shouted down because they represented power, and a power which attempted to limit popular participation in decision-making. In this light the disruptions we witness must be regarded as demands for the power to participate, not as interferences with the rights of others to free expression. To the counterargument that truth comes from dialogue and discussion the authors respond that this confuses discussion with decision-making. Truth comes from the former, policy from the latter. In

[90] Ibid., p. 53.

[91] Robert B. Thigpen and Lyle A. Downing, "Power, Participation, and the Politics of Disruption," Christian Century 86 (1969) 973–75.

our time the power to participate in decision-making is a minimal prerequisite for popular acceptance of policy decisions.

The Thigpen-Downing article raises the obvious question: To what extent does institutional life in America (at all levels: governmental, collegiate, etc.) actually stifle participation in decision-making?

Lawyer-journalist John B. Sheerin, C.S.P., summarizes the main points of the Fortas–Zinn exchange.[92] He agrees with Fortas that a just law may not be violated to call attention to an unjust law, for "our big cities would be utterly chaotic if individuals were allowed to break laws that are just." But justice would be better served if grand juries and ordinary juries were given more discretion to consider the question of justice as well as the letter of the law in arriving at their decisions. As for violence, Sheerin does not reject it in theory or absolutely but contends that it is not permissible in our country here and now because "our democratic system is not beyond redemption."

Readers of these Notes familiar with the shrewd and insightful commentaries of John R. Connery, S.J., in the 1950's, will rejoice at his return to active writing on moral questions.[93] After stating that the right to protest is not absolute but must be exercised within the limits of justice and charity, Connery details what these limits are. His general statements about protest (justification of cause, calculus of effects, etc.) are very close to those of Macfarlane and represent good common sense. When he turns to the interesting question of methods of protest, Connery offers a general principle very similar to Zinn's: "From a moral standpoint the methods used should be proportioned to the values at stake."[94]

Connery then asks about the morality of violating just laws as a means of protesting injustice. His answer: if this were the only effective means of preventing serious injustice, it would be acceptable. In this perspective he is closer to Zinn than to Fortas. But he believes that there are so many legal avenues available that this situation would arise only very rarely. Furthermore, this procedure tends to alienate other citizens from the cause one espouses.

As for violent protest, Connery admits the difference between violence against persons and against property. But to leave the distinction there, as do some advocates of violent protest, is unsatisfactory because

[92] John B. Sheerin, C.S.P., "Civil Disobedience," *American Ecclesiastical Review* 160 (1969) 351–56.

[93] John R. Connery, S.J., "The Morality of Protest," *Jesuit Educational Quarterly* 32 (1969) 21–31.

[94] *Ibid.*, p. 26.

"it is precisely because of its relationship to a person that the violation of property takes on a moral aspect...."[95] This is an important point, I believe. One can get at a person very effectively through his possessions. It is precisely this close relationship of person and property which explains why Christians have always viewed beneficence as an act of charity toward the *person*, and theft as an assault on the *person*. Or, as Connery notes, a shopkeeper would often prefer a beating to the burning of his shop. Connery's conclusion is that violence against property to protest injustice is morally unacceptable.

I am not sure of Connery's reason for this conclusion. It seems to rest on a twofold basis: on the fact that traditional principles have never permitted violence against property except in defensive-warfare conditions, and on the judgment that we are not, whatever the injustices of our society, in a warfare situation. On the other hand, since he does allow for violation of a just law if this were the only effective means of preventing continued injustice, it is reasonable to believe that Connery would say the same of proportionate violence if it were the only effective means available. Perhaps he would call a situation which had degenerated to this extent a prewar situation.

One of the most interesting discussions of protest is that of Barbara Deeming.[96] Rejecting the violent tactics of people like Stokely Carmichael, Floyd McKissick, Andrew Kopland, and Carl Oglesby, she is at pains to show that the alternative is not meek petitioning. It is an open use of power which frustrates an antagonist's actions and policies. Yet it remains essentially nonviolent, because it refuses to injure the person of the antagonist. And this refusal to injure the person is precisely the genius of nonviolence. As Deeming puts it:

We can put *more* pressure on the antagonist for whom we show human concern. It is precisely solicitude for his person *in combination with* a stubborn interference with his actions that can give us a very special degree of control (precisely in our acting both with love, if you will—in the sense that we respect his human rights—and truthfulness, in the sense that we act out fully our objections to his violating *our* rights.[97]

Thus a double pressure is exerted on the antagonist: the pressure of defiance and the pressure of our respect for his life. This double pressure has the advantage of inhibiting the action of the adversary, but modulating his ability to strike back. Thus it contains the escalation of force.

[95] *Ibid.*, p. 29.
[96] Barbara Deeming, "On Revolution and Equilibrium," in *Delivered into Resistance* (New Haven: Advocate Press, 1969) pp. 18–49.
[97] *Ibid.*, p. 28.

Deeming has some intriguing insights into nonviolence and its tactical advantages. But there is one key point where her analysis seems less than adequate. It is the distinction between violent and nonviolent action. Deeming regards all actions which do not injure another's person as nonviolent. This solicitude for the person of the adversary is said to consist in a respect for his human rights. So far so good. But at this point the ethical legerdemain begins. Deeming defines what are basic freedoms, what are not. She says: "Some freedoms are basic freedoms and some are not. To impose upon another man's freedom to kill, or his freedom to help kill, to recruit to kill, is not to violate his person in a fundamental way."[98]

There are many who would reject the description of their participation in war as an exercise of their "freedom to kill." Obviously there is no such freedom. But just as obviously, if there is such a thing as a just war, then there is such a thing as freedom to participate in it. Or to reword Deeming: "To impose upon another man's freedom to go to war in a cause he judges just *is* to violate his person in a fundamental way." Summarily, Deeming's "refusal to injure the adversary" gives precious little assurance of genuine nonviolence if she retains competence to tell the adversary what his rights are and when he is really injured. This becomes all the clearer and more disconcerting when, in exercising this competence, Deeming skins property rights to the bone.

Now to the specific instance of draft-file raids. It is perhaps understandable that there have been very few outright defenses of these acts, probably because the odds against success are rather steep. But there have been reactions fitting midway between comment and support.

In several places Richard Shaull has called attention to the significance of draft-file raids.[99] He believes that the decisive factor is the realization by many of the participants of a basic colonialism in the structure of "the American way." In its relationships with other countries the United States dominates and uses these peoples for its own purposes. Similarly at home we have a situation he describes as "internal colonialism." We are a managed society with no opportunity to choose or shape our own future. This has been particularly true of the blacks. Therefore "what is required of us is not a shift of loyalty from one institution to another, but the re-structuring of social organizations and institutions from the ground up."[100] If we are to respond creatively to this situation, we must first realize our own part in this exploitation,

[98] *Ibid.*
[99] Richard Shaull, "Resistance and the Third World," in *Delivered into Resistance*, pp. 60–64; "Realism and Celebration," *Christianity and Crisis* 28 (1968) 272–73.
[100] "Resistance and the Third World," p. 62.

both as perpetrators and as victims. Once we do, we are in a position to break with the system in the very center of our beings, to reshape our values, to form communities which offer new collective self-identity, and to build new political power capable of confronting our present structures. Therefore Shaull sees the draft raids as symbolic actions announcing a break with an old order and an identification with the victimized.

One has the uneasy feeling that Shaull's interpretation of the draft-file raids dovetails a bit too neatly and conveniently with what he has been saying over the past three or four years about colonialism of structures. On the other hand, the documents produced by the various groups of file raiders do speak a language remarkably similar to Shaull's. The Catonsville group destroyed draft files not only because they represent misplaced power aloof from public dissent, but above all "to illustrate why our country is torn at home and is harassed abroad by enemies of its own creation."[101] It then issued a stinging condemnation of the quality of American life and reproached the "religious bureaucracy" for being an accomplice in war, hostile to the poor, and racist. The Milwaukee group protested against "the American way of death," a way which gives property greater value than life. It found the roots of the Vietnamese struggle converging in the soil of American values and priorities, and then undertook a scathing criticism of these values. The Chicago group referred to the "freedom [of the powerful] to increase their fortunes through exploitative foreign investments." In other words, while the groups were indeed protesting and resisting the war, they seemed to see it as only a single symptom of a whole exploitative system. It was this system and its values to which they were saying no, though it can be doubted whether all in the groups shared such sentiments.

Staughton Lynd reflects on these incidents with three questions.[102] (1) Is it right to destroy property? (2) What is the justification of disruptive resistance? Why not work for reform within the system? (3) Why did the perpetrators permit themselves to be arrested?

Lynd never really answers his first question. But he does get around to facing an obvious objection to property destruction. It is this: if a protester or resister who believes himself right and moral can do this, then he is inviting his adversary to do the same thing. This results in a "trial of brute strength" situation, an escalation to nowhere. Lynd believes that the draft-file raiders, by practicing disruption in a way which

[101] Cf. *Delivered into Resistance*. For the Chicago group, I rely on distributed mimeographed material.

[102] Staughton Lynd, "Letter from Jail: Telling Right from Wrong," in *Delivered into Resistance*, pp. 11–17.

kept the spirit of dialogue alive, avoided this. This they did precisely because it is their conviction that all people should act out their convictions more than we do in our society—as long as the distinction between damage to life and damage to property is accepted as a fundamental ground rule. Thus Lynd proposes that those who disagree with the Catonsville Nine should be able to burn the files of the American Civil Liberties Union.

As to the why of disruption, Lynd admits the extreme character of the act involved and admits that it might make change more difficult in the long run. To explain it, he distinguishes civil disobedience into two types: reformist and resistant. The reformist attempts to energize the conventional machinery into decision-making. Item: he breaks a law to create a constitutional test. Rejecting revolution (which attempts to destroy existing powers), the resistant explores the twilight zone between reform and revolution. His activity is suited to a prerevolutionary situation. He is involved in attacking evils which cannot be solved by administrative decision because they are too deep-seated. Not relying on the electoral process, the resistant undertakes "an experiment, a probing operation, which determines if revolution is required."

The resistant knows he will alienate some people. But Lynd finds it impossible to discover a yardstick which will measure the appropriateness of the tactic. Ultimately he concludes:

Perhaps the best that can be said is that if a person believes "deep in his heart" that he must take a certain action, if he has meditated over the act or if the act, suddenly presenting itself, still flowers from a deep root of reflection, above all if it is an action *he* will take, the consequences of which will fall first on his own shoulders—then any other person can only stand aside and let his friend go on.[103]

Perhaps this is the best that can be said after all. But there are those who will judge it a very weak best. Furthermore, there are times when Lynd's essay reads as a more structured apology for the draft-file raids. As such it rests on two basic points. First, it builds on the distinction between personal and property damage and the acceptance by a society of property damage as a reasonable way to act out one's convictions. This is terrifying if one generalizes it to the extent that Lynd does. Civilized societies reject this conclusion, doubtless because of a firm grasp of the intimate relationship between property and person. It is sadly ironical that the most outstanding examples of this relationship are the very victims of American economic imperialism in whose behalf these protests occur. These victims suffer *personally* because they have been systematically despoiled by exploitative practices.

[103] *Ibid.*, p. 14.

Secondly, Lynd's apologia rests on the assumption that we live in social conditions so desperate that they are describable as prerevolutionary. This is a judgment, of course, which some might care to contest.

The most interesting and enlightening statement I have seen is that of William Kunstler, chief counsel to the Catonsville Nine.[104] He makes a strong case for the power of jurors to follow their consciences in rendering their verdict—that is, to judge the law as well as the fact. There are times when a government so involves itself in a wretched policy that it has to be extricated by popular repudiation in a forum more immediately available than a ballot box. This forum is nullification by a jury. If the jury could judge both fact and law, then it could express the deep desires of the community it represents. Kunstler argues that the jury is, by its own inherent structure, the safety valve that must exist if our society is to accommodate itself to its own internal stresses and strains. Ultimately, therefore, Kunstler does not attempt to justify the act. Rather he suggests that whatever justification there is must be decided by the jury acting as the conscience of the community. In this sense the draft-file burners were throwing themselves on their fellow citizens.

Nearly everyone has a strong opinion on symbolic actions like these. They touch some of our most sensitive ideological nerves. Yet to elaborate a well-rounded moral judgment of them is extremely difficult. And this for two reasons.

First, they are full of contradictions. Their deep concern for some men seems like unconcern for others. They are accompanied by a profound and admirable passion, but also by an annoying rhetoric and even at times by a self-consciousness bordering on arrogance. There is some truth to nearly all the contentions of the resisters: that legal forms of protest are often ineffective in the ear of a government hard of hearing and sclerotic, that American economic policies frequently have oppressive effects, that the war in Vietnam may well represent a tragic misjudgment and a deep injustice, that Christian leadership has not always responded with proportionate vigor. Yet their statements reveal inescapable strains of political naïvete and too frequent doses of overkill. As tactics, such destructive actions alienate vast numbers of people, yet they find the young sympathetic. They strain one's concepts of rights, yet they do so in the pursuit of righteousness. They look like anarchy, yet they are acted out like peaceful liturgies. And so on. In short, these actions are at the periphery of free expression and they show all the inconsistencies of the borderline instance.

[104] William Kunstler, "Dissent and the Jury," in *Delivered into Resistance*, pp. 50–59.

Secondly, their claim to legitimacy rests on judgments about several very complex issues: the condition of democratic processes in our society, the justice of the war, the oppressiveness of our economic policies, the tolerance of a particular society for violence, the effect of this or that tactic, the apathy of the religious establishment, etc. These are extremely difficult questions.

It is not surprising, therefore, that it is both easy to defend these tactics and easy to condemn them. But it is easy only if one lifts out a single aspect of these actions and establishes this as crucial in his evaluation. This is precisely what has happened so often. For instance, the defender often talks exclusively in terms of the injustice of the war, but he ends up neglecting the real value played by law in the fabric of social security and stability. The condemner speaks only of property rights, and he generally fails to put these rights into the wider context of their social setting. Another defender talks of the systemic injustice of American economic policy, but he generally fails to acknowledge the enormous benefits, actual and potential, of American wealth. The condemner talks exclusively in terms of law and its violation, but he generally fails to relate law to its moral purposes.

Perhaps two points could be made by way of conclusion. First, one cannot judge such actions *in abstracto* as licit or illicit, even though there is a strong antecedent presumption against their licitness. Rather he must judge first the conditions or causes of protest and the effectiveness of other democratic processes in producing change. It is against this twofold consideration that these actions will be seen as proportionate or not. I believe it would be true to say that nearly everyone approves in retrospect the attempt made on Hitler's life. We could not do so if the taking of life had an absolute moral illicitness independent of circumstances. The same is true with the lesser destruction of property. If the protesters are right in their evaluation of the issues (especially the injustice of the war), and if effective means are no longer available to bring about a change within a reasonable time, then property damage, as a tactic and means of communication, would seem to be proportionate. But these are big ifs, and it probably takes a prophet to be sufficiently sure. The very definition of a prophet is one who sees clearly now what others only come to see later.

These men may be prophets in their assessments. They also may be deluded. Be this as it may, the prophet, genuine or deluded, has always suffered, and will continue to suffer in his time, simply because organized social life can only exist when it shapes itself around the national conscience.

And that brings us to a second remark. If these actions can be judged satisfactorily only in light of complex prior evaluations, what attitude should be taken after the fact? It is here that I believe Kunstler's point is well made. He had argued that the jury be allowed to judge such instances in terms of their consciences. On the presumption that the jury is a true reflection of the national conscience, what Kunstler is saying is that the morality of these borderline acts cannot be determined abstractly in every instance. Rather they must be judged in light of the evils they protest and the availability of other effective means of change. And for such an evaluation the national conscience may be the best guide; for even if the national conscience cannot compose and balance the many complex judgments to be made with certainty, still it can determine the practical limits of tolerable expression at a given point in history. The willingness of the resisters to submit to the jury judgment (if it is a true conscience judgment and fairly representative of the national conscience) is a test of their basic respect for organized social life.

But if the conscience of the nation is to be the basis of the judgment (as brought by a jury), it is important that the issue protested be sharply defined. Here one might fault some of the resisters. They have gone after the "system" of which the war is, in their judgment, a symbol. Their case becomes much less persuasive when it is dispersed in this way. Furthermore, it must be stated candidly that the resisters, by dressing their convictions in an enormous amount of rhetoric, have narrowed the basis of their appeal. Kunstler, in other words, is often much more persuasive than the groups he represents.

GENETIC ENGINEERING

Present medical techniques are enabling people with genetic deficiency to live and reproduce, and thus to add to the degeneration of the genetic pool. In this sense it has been said that the human race is bending under the burden of a genetic load. The situation is viewed with varying degrees of concern by the initiated—from bemused pooh-poohing to doomsday alarm. For example, according to Paul Ramsey's reading of the late Nobel Prize winner H. J. Muller, this degeneration amounts to a horrendous cul-de-sac. Muller sees the world after a few million years as one enormous hospital system wherein pitiful genetic relics spend their waning energy propping up their own feebleness. Mankind is doomed under its genetic load unless positive steps are taken to unburden it. Similarly Stanford's William Shockley sees the threat of genetic deterioration as one of the three chief threats dimming our bright future.[105] Others point out that man has been successful over a half-million years precisely through his variability and hybridization.[106]

Whatever the sane view may be, it is clear that with the cracking of the genetic code in our time by men like Crick, Watson, Nirenberg, and others, a whole new field of molecular medicine has been opened up.[107] There is a divergence of scientific opinion as to when some of the more exotic genetic interventions will be technically feasible.[108] But few doubt that within a relatively brief period genetic engineering will be a reality. The enormous importance of this can be stated in many ways. In the most general terms it can be said that man has uncovered secrets which give him control over human growth and evolution. Perhaps it was the profound and far-reaching implications of this that François Houtart had in mind when he stated, in a discussion on the moral concerns of the Church, that "the problem of tomorrow is the control of genetics."[109] If genetics is the problem of tomorrow, it is already the problem of today if we are to wrest from technology the dictation of policy in this vitally important sphere.

The possibilities laid open by research into the DNA molecule are many. But the most engaging and all-inclusive is human eugenics. Eugenics has been with us for some time, of course. But it has never really gotten off the ground—probably because, as Kingsley Davis notes, the social structures most relevant to genetics are those having to do with health, and with marriage and the family.[110] Briefly, with

[105] William Shockley, "Population Control or Eugenics," in *Genetics and the Future of Man*, ed. John D. Roslansky (New York: Appleton-Century-Crofts, 1966) pp. 65–105, at 70.

[106] Dimitri B. Shimkim, "Further Thoughts on the Biological Revolution," *Atlantic* 223 (1969) 46.

[107] For a good overview of the problem of genetic control and the options in facing it, cf. V. Elving Anderson, "Genetics, Society, and the Family," in *Birth Control and the Christian*, ed. W. O. Spitzer and C. L. Saylor (Wheaton, Ill.: Tyndale House, 1969) pp. 343–54.

[108] Cf., for example, Donald Fleming, "On Living in a Biological Revolution," *Atlantic* 223 (1969) 64–70; Edward L. Tatum, "The Possibility of Manipulating Genetic Change," in *Birth Control and the Christian*, pp. 51–61; P. Overhage, "Manipulationen an der Keimesentwicklung," *Stimmen der Zeit* 183 (1969) 32–44; K. H. Degenhardt, "Probleme der genetischen Manipulation," *ibid.*, pp. 375–82.

[109] F. Houtart, *The Eleventh Hour* (New York: Sheed and Ward, 1968) p. 46. Similarly Kingsley Davis says that "the deliberate alteration of the species for sociological purposes will be a more fateful step than any previously taken by mankind" (*Genetics and the Future of Man*, p. 204). Peter J. Riga spells out the anxieties being experienced over the new discoveries: "Modern Science and Ethical Dimension," *Catholic World* 209 (1969) 213–17.

[110] *Op. cit.*, p. 182.

mortality and reproduction. Profound human and religious convictions underpin these social structures and hence they resist easy modification.[111] But with a new awareness of genetic deterioration and new abilities to deal with it, these human and religious convictions will again be tested. Thus the appearance recently of moral writings on genetics.

In the literature we shall bring under review, eugenics is described as either positive or negative. Though this terminology is somewhat slippery and inconsistent at times, in general it can be said that negative eugenics refers to the correction or straining out of defective hereditary material. Obviously this could be done in the interests of individual or family health, or as part of an over-all eugenics program with the gene pool in mind. Examples of negative eugenics would be sterilization of a person with defective genes, or genetic counseling discouraging reproduction. Positive eugenics refers to the programing of desirable traits into the population as a whole, the achievement of human betterment by selective breeding of superior individuals to improve the gene pool. Now to a brief roundup of the moral literature admittedly still in its infancy.

Dr. Kurt Hirschhorn, after reviewing the various methods of genetic control and commenting on their feasibility, concludes that neither positive nor negative eugenics can improve the gene pool and simultaneously allow for adequate evolutionary improvement of the race.[112] Take donor insemination (AID) as a form of positive eugenics. Hirschhorn shows that fertilization of many women by a few men would tend to have adverse effects on the advantages present in genetic variability. The population would tend to be more alike in genetic characteristics and lose flexibility in adapting to environment. Such flexibility is one of the major factors in satisfactory evolutionary development. As for negative eugenics, attempts to reduce the fertility of sizable portions of the population would also prevent the passing along to future generations of favorable aspects of evolution. Improvement of the population through evolutionary selectivity demands a gene pool containing enormous variability. Hirschhorn, therefore, sees negative eugenics as helpful only on a restricted basis for individual cases.

His final ethical judgment is that "all maneuvers of genetic engineering must be judged for each individual and, in each case, must take

---

[111] For a ranging theological criticism of much eugenic utopianism and many eugenic values, cf. P. E. Hughes, "Theological Principles in the Control of Human Life," in *Birth Control and the Christian*, pp. 93–149.

[112] Kurt Hirschhorn, "On Re-doing Man: The Ethics of Genetic Engineering," *Commonweal* 88 (1968) 257–61.

primary consideration of the rights of the individual. This is impossible by definition in any attempt at positive eugenics."[113]

Interesting and balanced as Hirschhorn's essay is, it calls for several comments. First, there is an unreal separation between a judgment of practicality and a moral evaluation of some suggested programs. Perhaps this is to be expected from one who is professionally a scientist, not a theological ethician. The major portion of the paper is taken up with faulting positive and negative eugenics for the improvement of the gene pool. Hirschhorn sees the various proposals (e.g., Muller's sperm bank with AID) as inefficient for the very purposes envisaged, and this inefficiency is found in the lack of sufficient gene variability to allow evolutionary improvement. Hirschhorn regards this rejection as a judgment of mere inefficiency; for when he turns to an ethical judgment, he excludes positive eugenics on the grounds that it cannot consider the rights of individuals. However, it would seem that any eugenics program judged impractical because of adverse and deleterious effects on man's evolutionary development is thereby judged to be a massive attack on the human race in some sense, much as atomic fallout would be. This is not, I would think, a judgment of mere inefficiency. Does not such inefficiency amount to a radical violation of man's responsibility to his progeny, a kind of futuristic social injustice?

Secondly, the exclusion of such programs in terms of effects only (even after I admit that these effects are downright unjust) contains a hidden methodological suggestion, scil., that it is uniquely in terms of effects that the morality is to be assessed. There are still many moralists whose ethical judgments will not be strait-jacketed to a determination of effects, at least as this determination is often explained. Specifically, even if a massive program of AID were to prove beneficial for the genetic pool over the long haul, there are many theological ethicists who would reject it on other grounds.

Gabriel Fackre, after reviewing the kinds of control of life facing us (preventive manipulation—e.g., electrode implants in the brain; instant pacification—e.g., by sprays and gasses; prenatal programing—e.g., genetic surgery), seeks in the resources of Christian faith perspectives for decision-making.[114] He finds three crucial themes: responsibility, futurity, and realism. By responsibility Fackre means the motif asserting that man is to shape his own future. Futurity refers to the future-orientation of the Christian, the bent to and struggle for the *eschaton*

---

[113] *Ibid.*, p. 261.

[114] Gabriel Fackre, "Ethical Guidelines for the Control of Life," *Christianity and Crisis* 29 (1969) 68–72.

of peace, justice, and freedom. Realism is an acknowledgment of the lethal presence of sin in our cosmos, always ready to render man's best efforts ambiguous and discordant.

On the basis of these perspectives, he argues that it is not possible to accredit the prenatal programing of value choices that biological engineering may soon make possible. Mechanizing the choosing capacity is a violation of what is central to man's humanity. He means here the programing of value choices, but he leaves open the question of pre-designing social skills in certain cases. As for instant control by police forces, Fackre views this as immoral in light of Christian realism about the corruptibility of monolithic power. Finally, he allows for biotechnical manipulation within the boundaries of self-control, that is, those which will release from imprisonment and expand freedom of choice.

There are two aspects of Fackre's interesting paper which are noteworthy: first, the way he proceeds from basic Christian motifs or values to the concrete judgment; secondly, the fine sensitivity he shows to the many ways the *humanum* can be violated.

Union Theological's Roger Shinn offers a stimulating discussion of genetic manipulation in terms of the methodology underlying contemporary discussions of the matter.[115] He distinguishes two questions: What is possible in this area? What is desirable?

The most obviously ethical question touches desirability. Here Shinn calls our attention to the difficult questions underlying any assertions we might make. For example, he himself is favorably disposed to negative eugenics. But the question remains: How do we determine what is harmful and disposable? Heredity must be related to its environment before it can be called desirable or undesirable. As for positive eugenics, who shall determine and by what criteria what is a desirable endowment? Shinn feels that fallible men already impose enough erroneous judgments on their progeny without rushing in to add a more fateful hereditary load.

Shinn is a balanced thinker whose message is a wise one of caution about the unanswered questions and the assumptions underlying answers we might give. He comes closest to stating the values in light of which he might articulate these assumptions when he notes that genetic manipulation may enhance or threaten freedom. The problem, then, is to determine how much manipulation, what kind, etc., will enhance freedom. When properly fleshed out, freedom is an excellent criterion. But Shinn would admit, I am sure, that until we have described more in detail the nature of human freedom, we have not es-

[115] Roger Shinn, "Genetic Decisions: A Case Study in Ethical Method," *Soundings* 52 (1969) 299–310.

caped the perils inherent in genetic manipulation done in the interests of freedom; for until human freedom is related to the being of man, it almost certainly will be read by many as a loosening from the very goods and responsibilities that will assure human growth.

After a beautiful statement of the biblical understanding of man and his future, B. L. Smith proposes to see whether this view needs modification, particularly in view of the young disciplines of molecular biology, microbiology, and biochemistry.[116] What does the Christian say in face of the possibility of taking a strong hand in the biological formation of his own future?

Smith suggests three things. First, he recalls that man's function is to exercise dominion. If this includes control of our environment and other so-called euthenic changes (use of eyeglasses, surgical procedures), it can conceivably include genetic manipulation and the development of intellectually and physically superior types. Secondly, because we are sinful, we are always prone to abuse every advance in knowledge. And as our ability to affect our own personalities increases, so does the potential harm through abuse. Thirdly, the future of man has been shown in Christ. Christ is the one toward whom we press. Smith admits that these three are not issues on which biology can pronounce; but they are issues to which every biologist must give attention and to which he must make a full response.

It is not clear what Smith would say to various forms of bio-engineering or genetic control. He did not set himself this task. Yet there are those (e.g., Paul Ramsey, as we shall see) who would join issue with Smith over the implication that these three things are all that a Christian can say. Does not our past experience—including the gospel heritage, our failures and successes, our reflective history and growth—give us both the ability and the courage to be more concrete than Smith seems willing to be?

To this question Paul Ramsey responds with a resounding affirmative in the most thorough and satisfying study of the moral aspects of genetic control that I have yet seen.[117] Ramsey's thought, it is well known, is like spun glass—complicated but ultimately clear. He approaches

[116] B. L. Smith, "Biology and the Christian Faith," *Christianity Today* 13 (1969) 627–30, 683–86.

[117] Paul Ramsey, "Moral and Religious Implications of Genetic Control," in *Genetics and the Future of Man*, pp. 109–69. For further reflections by Ramsey, cf. *Hospital Progress* 49 (1968) 13; also his forthcoming "Shall We Clone a Man?" in *Ethics in the Medical and Technological Context*, ed. Kenneth Vaux (Fortress, 1969). We await eagerly the publication of Dr. John Fletcher's (Protestant Episcopal Theological Seminary, Alexandria, Va.) doctoral dissertation on the subject. It was worked out under the direction of Roger Shinn and is bound to be good.

the problem in two steps. First, he lifts up to view certain aspects of what it means "to intend the world as a Christian." Since being a Christian is a mode of being human and will affect one's values and ethical judgments, Ramsey first contrasts Christian eschatology with what he calls "genetic eschatology." Secondly, he then focuses on the question of means to be used in genetic control.

How does "intending the world as a Christian" affect one's ethical judgments where genetic control is concerned? To answer this, Ramsey first notes that the genetic crisis can be faced out of any number of basic interpretations of the meaning of man and his world. And out of this interpretation emerge the values which found one's ethical judgments. The Christian viewpoint will yield two results, one general and pervasive, the other more precise. First, the Christian will face the situation in faith. No matter how great the problem, no matter how gruesome the details of the genetic apocalypse, the Christian has known all along that an end must come, that one day there will be none like us to come after us. Therefore Christian hope in and for the future does not depend on denying the seriousness of lethal genetic mutations. The Christian hopes on in faith.[118]

Secondly, one who is, in Ramsey's words, oriented on the Christian *eschaton* and not exclusively on the genetic cul-de-sac knows that he is not bound to succeed in preventing genetic deterioration at all costs, any more than he is bound to prevent cooling of the sun at all costs. This means that he knows an ethic of means. Ramsey is quick to add that "this does not mean that he will do nothing. But it does mean that as he goes about the urgent business of doing his duty in regard to future generations he will not begin with the desired *end* and deduce his obligation exclusively from this. He will not define *right* merely in terms of conduciveness to the good end."[119]

Ramsey concedes that other interpretations of the world also put limits on the means of genetic control. But it is his point that underlying many of the eugenic proposals being made by geneticists is a view of man which is the fruit of "intending the world as a scientist or geneticist." In this view the basic human values are freedom and thought. The means of genetic control must always respect these values—for example, sterilization must always be voluntary. Ramsey, rightly I believe, sees these two values as an incomplete picture of the *humanum*. Man is more than the repository of thought and freedom. One who

[118] Cf. also P. E. Hughes, *op. cit.*, pp. 140–48.
[119] Ramsey, "Moral and Religious Implications of Genetic Control," p. 139.

views the world as a Christian will discover more elements in the nature of man deserving of respect and removed from human trespass.

Specifically—and here Ramsey moves to his second point, the evaluation of means of genetic control—it is the Christian teaching concerning the union of the two goods of sexuality which will largely preside over one's assessment of the means of control. By the "union of the two goods of sexuality" Ramsey means that the *spheres* of personal love and procreation should not be put asunder. He derives this inseparability of spheres from a Christian reflection on the Prologue of John and Ephesians 5. We procreate new beings like ourselves in the midst of our love for one another and "in this there is a trace of the original mystery by which God created the world because of His love." Therefore Ramsey concludes that "to procreate from beyond the sphere of love [AID, for example, or making human life in a test tube] or to posit acts of sexual love beyond the sphere of responsible procreation [by definition, marriage] means a refusal of the image of God's creation in our own."[120]

In the light of this principle Ramsey judges both negative and positive eugenics. As for the first, he accepts genetically motivated birth control. Secondly, where "genetic surgery" is concerned (direct action on the genotype to allow a couple to bear a child without some defective gene), Ramsey has no problem. If treatment to cure infertility is morally acceptable, then why not treatment to enable a couple to bear a child without defect? Thirdly, as for AID from genetically clean sperm frozen in banks (Muller's suggestion), Ramsey utterly rejects it as illicitly separating what God has joined together—the spheres of personal love and procreation. When he turns to positive eugenics, it is his judgment that there are too many problems and risks in this type of thing to make it acceptable. That is, we cannot prevent the goal-setting from drifting and oscillating out of control. To establish a process with this uncertainty would be irresponsible.

Perhaps the most radical moral evaluation of genetic programing is that of Michael Hamilton, canon at Washington Cathedral.[121] Hamilton's basic theological assumption is man's authorization to exercise dominion over the natural world, including his own body. Working off this assumption, Hamilton finds little difficulty with negative eugenics. Such decisions are, he contends, in principle similar to decisions about

[120] *Ibid.*, pp. 147–48.
[121] Michael Hamilton, "New Life for Old: Genetic Decisions," *Christian Century* 86 (1969) 741–44.

the use of new drugs and are controlled by the norms governing experimentation.[122]

Positive genetics are, of course, another thing. But Hamilton's enthusiasm scarcely abates here. Should we raise the I.Q. of our children by genetic intervention if this becomes feasible? He is convinced that we should, "because intelligence is clearly an asset in coping with our world and is in line with the evolutionary trends we are capable of discerning." In fact, he points out that this goal has been tacitly accepted by AID parents. He then provides his basic moral norm.

I believe that the guiding and limiting principles in positive eugenics should be the enhancement of health and intelligence and the preservation of the unique quality of man. That quality I take to be his capacity for free, conscious, and personal relationships with God and his neighbor. A man may lose his appendix, have a transplanted heart in his chest, improve his eyesight and hearing, choose the sex of his children, and for all these possibilities we should be grateful. But so to affect healthy men's minds that they were no longer capable of loving and hating or worshipping and repenting would be to destroy their nature as human beings, and therefore, in my judgment, would be wrong.[123]

Hamilton then turns to a more sinister venture, the growth in vitro of parahumans (cyborgs). He understands such beings as animal rather than robots and presents the word of an anonymous scientist that they would "look like humans, would be very good for domestic service, but are not really humans." Hamilton finds no a priori theological objection to production of these beings but regards their creation as impractical because cybernetic systems would probably have made them undesirable as a labor force by the time their production is feasible.

As to experiments in vitro with human material, he accepts them in the early stages of growth, "because they will cast light on normal pregnancies and will yield some information on how chromosomal mutations take place."[124] When confronted with the Christian conviction

---

[122] For some recent entries on experimentation, cf. Daedalus, Spring 1969, entire issue; R. Kautzky, "Scientific Progress and Ethical Problems in Modern Medicine," in Dilemmas of Tomorrow's World (Concilium 45; New York: Paulist, 1969) pp. 75–90. Unfortunately there is very little new in this latter article. It is, sad to say, becoming all too typical of the material appearing in Concilium, which increasingly leaves the impression of extraordinary haste rather than extraordinary diligence.

[123] Art. cit., p. 743.

[124] See also "Human Life in a Test-Tube," Tablet 223 (1969) 200–202. G. Higuera, S.J., discusses fertilization in vitro with the sperm of the husband and the ovum of the wife. In his judgment it is immoral in its circumstances, that is, unnatural by reason of place and method. Even though the sciences have much to say about "naturalness," the Church has the competence to describe this naturalness. For Higuera, fertilization in vitro presents the same moral objections as AIH ("Fecundación en laboratorio y moral," Sal terrae 57 [1969] 337–56, 403–16).

(stated so powerfully by Ramsey) that the spheres of responsible loving and procreation are inseparable, he responds: "I believe that the demand of love in relation to parenthood is fulfilled in ensuring that all children born into this world, by whatever means, be reared in a family."[125] This conclusion is based on the assertion that "parenthood in its deepest sense is not a biological but a *human* function—of a man and wife accepting responsibility for caring for and rearing a child."[126] It is to be expected, therefore, that Hamilton would raise no a priori theological objections against "cloning"—the vegetative, asexual production of a man from a single cell, the rough equivalent of the growth of a rose bush from the slip of another rose bush.

The interest of Hamilton's article lies not in the particular conclusions or judgments but in the implicit methodological assumptions and dominating values. Perhaps the best way to unpack these assumptions is to begin with a particular statement. He writes: "Parenthood in its deepest sense is not a biological but a *human* function—of a man and wife accepting responsibility for caring for and rearing a child." It was on this basis that Hamilton concluded that the demand of love in relation to parenthood is fulfilled in ensuring that all children born into this world, *by whatever means*, be reared in a family.

Here several things must be noted. In Christian conviction the same sexual love that generates becomes the parental love that nurtures. Parents do not love their children simply because the children are there and need love. They love them because they have loved each other and because the children are the visible fruit and extension of this love. That is why we have always said—sometimes clumsily to be sure—that conjugal love is by its very nature "ordained for the procreation *and education* of children, and finds in them its ultimate crown." Just as education is, in a sense, a continuation of procreation, so there is a basic identity and continuity in the love that procreates and the love that nurtures. Therefore to separate the acts which nurture from the act which generates and then to associate parental love only with the former is to undermine the very foundation of the love which nurtures. To limit the notion and love of parenthood to "caring for and rearing a child" is therefore a radical attack on several basic humano-Christian values (the meaning of human sexuality, the meaning of marriage and parenthood).

Secondly, Hamilton has provided some clue as to how he came to his remarkable conclusions. He has said that parenthood is not a biological but a human function. He then identified this human function with accepting responsibility for rearing a child. Summarily, caring for and

---

[125] *Art. cit.*, p. 743.   [126] *Ibid.*

rearing a child is human, procreating him is biological. But since parent-hood and parental love are obviously human, procreation as such does not pertain to them.

Here we are face to face once again with an all too familiar and pernicious dualism, where men love and care in many ways, but not in their sexual intercourse. Ultimately this assertion roots in a principle which depreciates the body and disallows its participation in the specifically human. In the area of human sexuality it has been a long up-hill struggle for Christianity to slough off the enticements of one or other form of dualism. Vatican II succeeded eminently when it referred to the child as the fruit of conjugal love. It was saying that man is not a parent or a loving parent only with his nurturing. He becomes a parent and a loving parent also in his sexual expression. It was insisting in principle that man does not relate, love, and hate with his mind exclusively or with his body exclusively. He relates, loves, and hates as man, as a mysterious psychosexual totality that is the "I." Some hint of Hamilton's dualistic instincts is seen in his assertion: "But so to affect healthy men's *minds* that they were no longer capable of loving or hating. . . ."

Thirdly, Hamilton's uneven bout with dualism brings him perilously close to a morality of goals. This means that if the goals are or appear to be desirable, then the means are evaluated as they move toward the goal. Hamilton does not quite go that far, but he is leaning. Thus experiments in vitro with human material are supported in the early stages because of the light they will cast on other pregnancies. "Cloning" is ultimately (but only temporarily, I must assume) rejected because present work with animals has resulted in a large percentage of monstrosities. Even should these be eliminated, "the advantages of such procedures would still be limited." This direction of thought is understandable; for if procreation does not pertain to parenthood or parental love but is something "merely biological," then we are only a quick illative away from seeing the product of conception as "something merely biological," at least up to a certain stage of development. And if this is the case, obviously experiments on this "something" will be assessed in terms only of the goals and ends.[127]

---

[127] Abortion is obviously a radical form of genetic control. While space does not permit a review of the recent literature on abortion, still it is difficult to leave unnoticed the wise remarks of Leroy Augenstein, chairman of the biophysics department at Michigan State University. Augenstein contends that abortion laws are a paradigm. That is, how we handle the question will determine how we handle or mishandle other life-issues such as genetic manipulation; for they are of a piece. And there is little question in his mind that we are badly mishandling the legal issue. It is his conviction that once we set up the apparatus for making a decision, we then almost insure what that decision will be, or at

Even a cursory reading of the literature on genetic control will make it clear that decisions in this area put in the balance some rather basic human values. For instance, V. E. Anderson ominously notes that "the more freedom of choice is allowed, the less effective any program toward a defined goal will be."[128] Donald Fleming remarks that according to the eugenic planners the control of biological inventory "is or ought to be a question of social policy rather than individual indulgence."[129] Up to now, many have viewed contraception as a right of the couple. It will increasingly be viewed by statesmen and biologists as a duty. Some genetic planners question the very nature of parenthood and the family. For example, Kingsley Davis finds the most fundamental obstacle to genetic control through reproductive selection in "a curious fact," the retention of the family.[130] A system where people are connected socially by birth and in which responsibility for the rearing of children is primarily given to those who procreate them is said to be "a very primitive mode of social organization."[131]

Furthermore, nearly everyone who writes on genetic controls is concerned about the kind of thoroughbred considered desirable, and especially about the persons and processes qualified to make this determination. These questions are all the more urgent when one recalls the total detachment from religion ascribed to many biological revolutionaries. Fleming, for example, cites Nobel Prize winner Francis Crick to the effect that "there is going to be no agreement between Christians and any humanists who lack their particular prejudice about the sanctity of the individual, and who simply want to try it scientifically."[132]

The stakes, then, are enormous. But here I should like to advert briefly to another issue in this discussion which can easily be over-

[128] *Op. cit.*, p. 352.   [129] *Art. cit.*, p. 68.   [130] *Op. cit.*, p. 183.
[131] *Ibid.*   [132] *Art. cit.*, p. 67.

least what values will be brought to bear in making it. The current proposals have almost totally ignored this fact. Hence they are setting patterns for our procedure in other areas (L. Augenstein, "It's Later Than We Think," *Ecumenist* 7 [1969] 41–43). Further recent literature on abortion includes: J. McLaughlin, S.J., "Abortion: Sweden and the U.S.," *Catholic Mind* 67 (1969) 24–32; "Illinois Bishops on Abortion," *ibid.*, pp. 59–64; *Documentation catholique* 66 (1969) 49 (Canadian bishops on abortion); J. O'Connor, "On Humanity and Abortion," *Natural Law Forum* 13 (1968) 127–33; John T. Noonan, "Deciding Who Is Human," *ibid.*, pp. 134–40; James E. Kraus, "Is Abortion Absolutely Prohibited?" *Continuum* 6 (1968) 436–40; James M. Gustafson, "The Transcendence of God and the Value of Human Life," *Proceedings of the Catholic Theological Society of America* 23 (1968) 96–108; R. F. Drinan, S.J., "Catholic Moral Teaching and Abortion Laws in America," *ibid.*, pp. 118–30; Richard A. McCormick, S.J., "Past Church Teaching on Abortion," *ibid.*, pp. 131–51; T. J. Harrington, "Legislation and Abortion," *Homiletic and Pastoral Review* 69 (1969) 685–90; James C. Fleck, S.J., "Canada Debates Abortion and Homosexuality," *Christian Century* 86 (1969) 354–58.

looked. It is the underlying one of theological methodology. Two previous entries (Ramsey, Hamilton) concretize the problem. Here we have two Christian thinkers in profound disagreement about the means of genetic control. When faced with the possibility of fecundation in vitro and AID, Hamilton states that he can find no a priori theological reasons for excluding such things. Ramsey, on the other hand, had insisted that a contemporary Christian reflection on Scripture leads us to conclude to the inseparability of the spheres of procreation and conjugal love. He then used this norm to exclude certain procedures of genetic control. In other words, he did find a priori theological reasons for excluding these things.

The issue of ethical theory suggested by this disagreement has been stated very well by James Gustafson: "Are there limits to man's tampering with human life which have a more direct relationship to religious beliefs?"[133] He rewords the point as follows: "It is clear that one does not have to have a Jewish or Christian theology in order to value human life. But does a Jewish or Christian theology which supports the moral principles which protect life in any way set limits, safeguards, or restrictions to what men are permitted to do with other human lives?" If one's answer here is yes—and I suspect that for most theologians it will be—he must then show how he derives these normative restrictions without becoming a biblical fundamentalist or a narrow natural-law legalist. This task is far from complete in the community of Christian moral theologians.

---

[133] James M. Gustafson, "Commentary on *The Sanctity of Life*," in *The Religious Situation 1969*, p. 347.

CURRENT THEOLOGY: 1970

NOTES ON MORAL THEOLOGY: APRIL–SEPTEMBER, 1970

In the past semester the literature touching moral questions has been so vast and variant that it suggests the contemporary ecological crisis and the advisability of rewards for the two-article professor in the years ahead. At any rate, these Notes are faced with a kind of "responsible authorhood" they have rarely faced before.

This makes this as good a time as any to call attention to the limitations of these Notes. Some limitations are obvious: one man with limited perspectives, reviewing a vast literature, in a small space, against a deadline. The upshot is that the compositor's opinions and reactions do not in every instance represent a fully elaborated position. Other limitations are not so obvious but are nonetheless real. I refer to the problem of objectivity in the selection of both areas to review and articles within the area. One tries to approach objectivity but realizes that his efforts must remain only partially successful.

The matter is mentioned here for two reasons. First, the brevity imposed on these reviews has occasionally left a wrong impression of the compositor's opinion, or has suggested underlying implications which subsequent exchange and discussion have shown to be nonexistent. Secondly and more importantly, brevity of comment, when it is critical, can border on unfairness to an author's thought. This is "mortally sinful" in the professional fraternity. But because the true professional can understand both the advantages and the handicaps of critical surveys, his forgiveness comes easy.

This being said, the present survey will focus on four issues: (1) tendencies in theological ethics, (2) situations of conflict, (3) the theology of ecology, (4) theology and divorce.

TENDENCIES IN THEOLOGICAL ETHICS

There has been a good deal of literature summarizing contemporary discussions and indicating future directions in Christian moral thought.[1]

[1] Cf., e.g., C. D. MacNiven, "Analytic and Existential Ethics," *Dialogue* 9 (1970) 1–19; F. J. Steinmetz, "Freiheit-Gesetz-Sünde: Über einige Schwerpunkte heutiger Moraltheologie," *Geist und Leben* 43 (1970) 64–71; Charles Reynolds, "A Proposal for Understanding the Place of Reason in Christian Ethics," *Journal of Religion* 50 (1970) 155–68; George L. Frear, "The Need for an Ongoing Dimension in Christian Ethics," *Journal of Religious Thought* 27 (1970) 18–27; Jack T. Sanders, "The Question of the Relevance of Jesus for Ethics Today," *Journal of the American Academy of Religion* 38 (1970) 131–46; Vernon J. Bourke, "Recent Trends in Ethics," *New Scholasticism* 44 (1970) 396–425; Hans Rotter, "Tendenzen in der heutigen Moraltheologie," *Stimmen der Zeit*, April, 1970, pp.

Some of this literature can be briefly reviewed under title of "tendencies in theological ethics." This review will necessarily be somewhat scattershot even though it can be organized under three distinct headings.

The New Morality

Nearly everybody has had a go at this subject by now, or at least one would have thought so. But the literature continues. Everyone involved in teaching Christian ethics should ponder the fascinating report of Leander E. Keck and James E. Sellers.[2] They argue that vital theology is always born out of the agony of faith and understanding precipitated by crisis. Unless we realize this, there will continue to be a hiatus between the places where men are living, dying, and being brutalized, and the places that have always been the repository of sources for thinking about these events.

Amid an exhortation to honesty in facing ethical situations, Rabbi Richard Israel (Director of B'nai B'rith Hillel Foundation at Yale) makes some interesting remarks about ethical concerns.[3] He distinguishes micro-ethics from macro-ethics. The former is that which is appropriate to relations between individuals. Macro-ethics deals with the larger problems of political power, war and peace, distribution of wealth, poverty, and race. In the past decade or so situationalism represented a micro-ethical attitude largely concerned with the relationships between individuals. When it did turn to the larger issues, it viewed them as though they were ethical problems between two people. Thus: "make love, not war." Now, however, macro-ethical attitudes are beginning to infect the micro-ethical framework. Politics has begun to infuse the interpersonal world. The language of collegians reflects this when it refers to the theft of a case of beer as "liberating a case of beer."

Rabbi Israel makes the extremely interesting point that in an interpersonal ethic, values tend to be relative. In macro-ethics, however, they tend to be absolute. For instance, only one thing is acceptable to

259–68; M. D. Chenu, "The Renewal of Moral Theology: The New Law," *Thomist* 34 (1970) 1–12; Hans Rotter, "Die Prinzipien der Moral," *Zeitschrift für katholische Theologie* 92 (1970) 167–82; M. J. Langford, "New Approaches to Natural Law," *Religious Studies* 4 (1968) 153–62; "Moral Theology in Italy," *Idoc*, June 13, 1970, pp. 20–24; John Cardinal Heenan, "La morale d'aujourd'hui," *Documentation catholique* 67 (1970) 284–88.

[2] Leander E. Keck and James E. Sellers, "Theological Ethics in an American Crisis," *Interpretation* 24 (1970) 456–81.

[3] Richard J. Israel, "The New Morality and the Rabbis," *Conservative Judaism* 24 (1969) 62–70.

the contemporary macro-ethical mind, not the ROTC or Dow thing. Israel's essay suggests several interesting questions. To what degree will macro-ethical absolutism begin to affect interpersonal morality? Also, to what degree are ethical postures really a product of an individual's situation? Would the enthusiastic American pacifist, for example, really be a pacifist if he lived in Israel?

Only recently an excellent article by James Gustafson came to my attention.[4] This essay is an example of Gustafson's remarkable ability to isolate drifts and trends with accuracy and fairness and to tell us where we are in a given problem area. Armed with a distinction made by Ernst Troeltsch in 1902 between an ethics of disposition, intention, conscience (*Gesinnungsethik*) and an ethics of laws, norms (*Objektivethik*), Gustafson shows how these general issues were present in St. Paul, St. Thomas, and Luther. And they are still alive today. Current discussion, both Catholic and Protestant, is determined by the prevalence of an antilegalist mood. Gustafson summarizes this mood with a list of contrasts (e.g., dynamic vs. static, open vs. closed, future-looking vs. orientation to past, creative responsibility vs. conformity to predefined order). Many of these distinctions reflect the more basic Troeltschian distinction. It comes as no surprise that Gustafson himself finds it "theologically, historically, sociologically and psychologically appropriate in our time to view moral existence as initiating and responding activity in a changing field of action ... to view oneself as the creative and responsible participant in the ongoing development of history...."[5] This has been Gustafson's dominant theological attitude and pastoral approach for some time. And he carries it with admirable balance; for he sees the need for more work not only on the problems of the formation of genuine Christian dispositions, but also on the formation of directions for these dispositions.[6]

If the genial Joseph Fletcher is alive and well—and he is[7]—it is not for lack of hatchet men.[8] Raising a lance and trying a round with Fletcher has become almost a hobby in moral theological circles. Four recent examples will suffice here. One of the longest and sharpest

[4] James M. Gustafson, "What is the Contemporary Problematic of Ethics in Christianity?" *Central Conference of American Rabbis Journal*, Jan., 1968, pp. 14–26.

[5] *Ibid.*, p. 25. Cf. also Gustafson's "What Ought I to Do?" *Proceedings of the American Catholic Philosophical Association*, 1969, pp. 56–70.

[6] See James M. Gustafson, "The Place of Scripture in Christian Ethics," *Interpretation* 24 (1970) 430–55.

[7] Joseph Fletcher and Thomas A. Wassmer, S.J., *Hello, Lovers* (Washington: Corpus Books, 1970).

[8] A recent example is Joseph Vadakumcherry, *Natural-Law-Morality versus Situationism in Morals* (Cochin: Mar Louis Memorial Press, 1969).

lances is that of Ignacio L. Götz, who concludes that "Fletcher has *in fact* placed his situationism outside the realm of Christian ethics."[9] Götz bases his conclusion on Fletcher's nominalism. Since "sinful" is something men never *are*, it is meaningless to speak of the Christian notion of atonement.

J. Charles King criticizes Fletcher's act-utilitarianism on several scores.[10] Its exposition in Fletcher's writings involves vicious circularity. That is, for Fletcher love (*agapē*) is the criterion of goodness. But if this is so, then seeking the neighbor's *good* cannot be a satisfactory account of the nature of love. King also faults Fletcher on the fact that he has overlooked the possibility of genuine moral principles which take full account of the peculiarities of individual situations. Without such principles a judgment of mere personal preference replaces a true moral judgment.

Auburn University's Robert Andelson contends that Fletcher cavalierly disregards the canons of logical argument.[11] Noting that Fletcher rightly claims that love universalizes its concern and that the neighbor is thus Everyman, Andelson insists that Everyman incorporates *all* whom a decision might conceivably affect, known and unknown, present and future. "Thus a loving decision must be one which is made not merely with reference to specific persons but also and more importantly in the light of principles applicable to personality as a general category." Similarly, if the neighbor is really Everyman, how does one adjudicate the competing claims of persons except in terms of abstract principles of good?

It would be inaccurate to say that Paul Ramsey has returned to the fray. He has never really left it during the past five or six years. Once again he argues that there are love-embodying and love-fulfilling rules governing crucial areas of human life.[12] The "new morality" would regard all principles as analogous to the tactical advice given a quarterback: punt on fourth down. Ramsey insists that in morality there are rules and principles which go beyond such tactical advice. I think he is right, but in this essay he has not carried the argument beyond what he has written at greater length elsewhere.

As the dust of the storm surrounding Fletcher's work has settled, two

[9] Ignacio L. Götz, "Is Fletcher's Situationism Christian?" *Scottish Journal of Theology* 23 (1970) 273–78.

[10] J. Charles King, "The Inadequacy of Situation Ethics," *Thomist* 34 (1970) 423–37.

[11] Robert V. Andelson, "Some Fundamental Inconsistencies in Fletcher's *Situation Ethics*," *Personalist* 51 (1970) 332–37.

[12] Paul Ramsey, "The Biblical Norm of Righteousness," *Interpretation* 24 (1970) 419–29.

impressions linger. First, we have been forcefully reminded that traditional moral approaches, at least in the hands of their latter-day prac-
titioners, have too easily underestimated the situational aspects, especially consequences, in decision-making. Secondly, this neglect has not
been and will hardly be adequately corrected within a presentation so
individualistic, systematically underdeveloped, and ultimately intellectually dissatisfying as that of Joseph Fletcher.

Charles Curran offers a ranging commentary on moral methodology.[13]
He centers his attention on faulty and one-sided methodological approaches. For instance, any moral theology which is to be truly Christian must take account of the full Christian mystery of "creation, sin,
incarnation, redemption and resurrection destiny." It is only such a full
view that allows us to avoid the extremes of uncritical acceptance of the
present or irresponsible devaluation of the present. Curran criticizes
both theological actualism (the attempt to perceive the will of God here
and now without giving enough importance to all the criteria, especially
rational criteria) and consequentialism (morality is determined only by
weighing the consequences of our acts). Curran is especially on target
in his criticism of Fletcherian consequentialism.[14] As he puts it, "there
always remains the problem of appraising the hierarchical importance
of the various consequences involved." For the Christian, frustration,
suffering, tragedy, and ultimately death must be viewed within the
perspectives of the paschal mystery. The problem of elaborating a
satisfying value system within the totality of Christian realities remains
one of the most important unfinished tasks in the field of Christian
morality.

Another very useful source on the new morality is John Macquarrie's
Three Issues in Ethics.[15] There is very little that is new in Macquarrie,
but his work summarizes expertly and in very simple language a good
deal that is going on in moral theology. His critique of the "new morality" is finely balanced. It concludes:

The traditional moral theology was too strongly tied to the notion of a fixed,
essential human nature, set in the midst of a static hierarchically ordered universe. Yet its basic method of approaching the problem of ethics was correct—
not through some special Christian concept of love or whatever it might be,
but through the study of man.[16]

[13] Charles Curran, "Methodological and Ecclesiological Questions in Moral Theology," *Chicago Studies* 9 (1970) 59–80.

[14] I say "Fletcherian" because I suspect that there is a rendering of consequentialism,
as yet not systematically developed, with which many of us could feel at home.

[15] John Macquarrie, *Three Issues in Ethics* (New York: Harper & Row, 1970).

[16] *Ibid.*, p. 42.

It is clear, therefore, that Macquarrie will hold hands with no one who would do away with natural law. "Indeed," he says, "I shall go further and claim that natural law is foundational to morality. It is the inner drive toward authentic personhood and is presupposed in all particular ethical traditions, including the Christian one." Of course, the interpretation of this law must keep pace with man's continually evolving self-understanding.

It is in his summary of man's contemporary self-understanding that Macquarrie is, I believe, especially perceptive. His exposition remains the best short treatment I have seen. He presents and explains thoroughly five characteristics of "the new man": (1) changing man— a being-on-the-way; (2) embodied man—a being-in-the-world; (3) social man—a being-with-others; (4) man as agent; (5) man come of age: responsibility. Clearly this new self-understanding is bound to bring new priorities and shifts of interest in the moral life.

Specificity of Christian Morality

A variety of contemporary currents—for example, secularization, ecumenism, the Church as teacher—have raised anew the question of the specificity of Christian morality. The question can be put in any number of ways, and one's answer to be sure will generally reflect the shape of his question. But in recent literature the formulation has been as follows: What is there about Christian morality that distinguishes it from one which is built on the authentically human, or one which Paul Ramsey referred to some years ago as "generally valid natural morality"?[17]

John Macquarrie's answer to this question is that the Christian ethic is not distinctive in its ultimate goals or its fundamental principles; these are shared with all serious-minded people of all traditions. Therefore the distinctiveness is not to be found in the concrete moral obligations derived from an authentic humanity but in the degree of explicitness surrounding the notion of authentic humanity. "The distinctive element is the special context within which the moral life is perceived. This special context includes the normative place assigned to Jesus Christ and his teaching—not, indeed, as a paradigm for external imitation, but rather as the criterion and inspiration for a style of life."[18]

J.-M. Aubert prepares the way for his own answer by studying the question in St. Thomas.[19] Thomas' point of view is gathered from his

[17] Paul Ramsey, *Basic Christian Ethics* (London: S.C.M. Press, 1953) p. 86.
[18] *Three Issues in Ethics*, p. 89.
[19] J.-M. Aubert, "La spécificité de la morale chrétienne selon saint Thomas," *Supplément* 92 (1970) 55–73. Cf. also R. Simon, "Spécificité de l'éthique chrétienne," *ibid.*,

treatment of the relation of human virtues to Christian virtues, and from his discussion of the relation between the law of Christ and human morality. With regard to the virtues, Aubert maintains that Thomas clarified a long patristic heritage by explaining the autonomy and value of human virtue. An earlier Augustinian concern to avoid Pelagianism tended to smother the human with the overwhelming gratuity and supremacy of the theological virtues. Thomas recovered this human aspect with no compromise on the supremacy of the theological order. For him charity was the form of the virtues, suffusing and dynamizing them, but leaving them intact as the genuinely human expressions or ways of charity.

With regard to law, Thomas taught that the law of Christ should animate and transfigure all of human life. This implies that human life already has a moral content to which charity will give a new sense. But Thomas insisted that the law of Christ adds of itself no new particular moral prescriptions. It introduces a new dynamism and power. The resultant new life is essentially a more total and divinized way of leading a human life, a human life having its own proper demands which man perceives by reason and conscience.

On the basis of his study Aubert concludes that it is faith which is the truly distinguishing (or formal) cause of the specificity of Christian morality. But this must be properly understood. Since there is only one destiny possible to all men, there is existentially only one morality common to Christians and non-Christians. That means that there is a *material* identity between Christian moral demands and those perceivable by reason. However, faith operates a distinctiveness in the manner and intentionality of living these common moral demands. That is, it renders explicit the presence of charity. The Christian builds a life style on this explicitness. Therefore

the specificity of Christian morality is found essentially in the very style of life, the manner of comporting oneself and of accomplishing the moral tasks which the Christian has in common with other men—a manner more dynamic, more assured, more joyous, more capable of following the example of Christ dying for other men. For it is ultimately the law of the cross which remains the essentially Christian model of the manner of practicing the moral law. . . .[20]

In several valuable studies Joseph Fuchs, S.J., pursues in depth the notion of "Christian intentionality" mentioned by Aubert.[21] It is Fuchs's

---

pp. 74-104. The entire issue is entitled "L'Ethique chrétienne à la recherche de son identité" and contains useful general essays.

[20] *Art. cit.*, p. 73.

[21] Joseph Fuchs, S.J., "Gibt es eine spezifisch christliche Moral?" *Stimmen der Zeit*

thesis that prescinding from this intentionality Christian morality is, in its materiality and concreteness, human morality. Therefore both Christians and non-Christians must seek the answers to moral questions by determining what is genuinely human. It is the intentionality brought to the authentically human which specifies Christian morality.

How are we to understand this intentionality? To explain it, Fuchs recalls that in the moral act there are two aspects: the specific act itself and through it one's self-realization with reference to an Absolute. This self-realization in relation to an Absolute is the decisive element in morality, even though we are not reflexly conscious of it. Thus there is "a certain intentionality which transcends and fulfils the individual moral act." Now the Christian does not relate himself to God only as the Absolute, but to God as Father, to God who gave us His love in the person of Christ, and who is in His Christ our salvation. It is this deep-seated stamp on our consciousness which is distinctive of Christian morality. Or, as Fuchs puts it: "This Christian intentionality is what makes the moral behavior of the Christian truly and specifically Christian, at every moment and in every aspect, even when it appears at first to be simply conduct conforming to human morality."[22] Everything the Christian does is an expression of this personal, conscious, and freely willed relation to the Father of Jesus Christ. This intentionality is present to us without explicit and systematic reflection on our part.

While Christian intentionality is the decisive element in Christian morality, there is another important aspect which Fuchs underlines. The Christian knows in faith and acknowledges certain realities which he alone can acknowledge: the person of Christ, the Holy Spirit at work in us, the message of salvation, the Church, the Christian community, the sacraments, teaching authority. Our relationship to these realities belongs to our being and must be realized in our conduct. It will do so at the level of a deeper and richer motivation.

Charles Curran has written an extremely interesting essay on the existence of a distinctively Christian social ethics.[23] His conclusion: "There is no distinctively Christian social ethics in the sense that Christians would possess a knowledge or a power that other non-Christians would not and could not possess." Ultimately he says this also of personal ethics. Furthermore, he concludes that not only is there no dis-

---

185 (1970) 99–112. See also his "Human, Humanist and Christian Morality," in *Human Values and Christian Morality* (Dublin: Gill and Macmillan, 1970) pp. 112–47. The Italian version is *Esiste una morale cristiana?* (Rome: Herder, 1970).

[22] Fuchs, *Human Values and Christian Morality*, p. 124.

[23] Charles Curran, "Is There a Distinctively Christian Social Ethic?" in *Metropolis: Christian Presence and Responsibility* (Notre Dame: Fides, 1970).

tinctively Christian social ethics in the above sense, "but likewise there can be no distinctively Christian attitudes, dispositions, or goals." This last statement is, I would assume, a denial of the thesis of James Gustafson; for Gustafson maintains that loyalty to the Christian gospel and faith evokes distinctively Christian attitudes, dispositions, intentions, goals and norms.[24]

Curran does not conclude that the churches should never speak out on concrete issues. Quite the contrary. They should, but in such a way that they enunciate the general Christian attitudes and principles relevant in the particular situation and "show how they arrive at their particular conclusion with the humble realization that they might be wrong and are not pretending to propose the only Christian solution to the problem."

A distinctively Christian ethic would involve, Curran argues, several false presuppositions. First, it presupposes that there is a great difference between Christians and non-Christians because Christians have been freed from sin and death and brought to new life by Christ. Contemporary theology, on the contrary, would maintain that God somehow offers His saving love to all men, even without explicit contact with the historical Jesus. Secondly, a distinctively Christian ethic builds off the view that the world is totally disfigured by sin (Lutheran) or the view that the natural is totally distinct from the realm of the supernatural (Catholic). These dichotomies are overturned by the contemporary theology of eschatology and of cosmic redemption. "The world is not just the area of the natural but the world embraces all the different aspects of the Christian mystery—creation, sin, incarnation, redemption and resurrection destiny." Thirdly, a distinctively Christian ethic supposes that creation and redemption (or the human and the Christian) are separated, if not opposed. Contrarily, redemption brings creation to completion.

Perhaps three remarks would not be out of place here. First, I would agree that these arguments are convincing reasons for saying that human morality (natural law) and Christian morality are *materially* identical. This is what nearly everyone (e.g., Fuchs, Aubert, Macquarrie, Rahner) is saying these days.[25] The light of the gospel does not bring something distinct from the human, but helps us to discover what is

---

[24] James M. Gustafson, *Christ and the Moral Life* (New York: Harper & Row, 1968) pp. 238–71.

[25] On the other hand, B. Häring writes: "Some people, including certain Catholic theologians, still have the incredible idea that the moral teaching of the New Testament adds no new content to the natural law, that it only offers new motives. This is actually worse than the moral doctrine of Pelagius . . ." (*Road to Relevance* [New York: Alba,

authentically human. Perhaps this is what Curran means. But I wonder if he has formulated it exactly. He denies a distinctively Christian ethic "in the sense that Christians would possess a knowledge or a power that other non-Christians would not and could not possess." It seems to me that if the light of the gospel can aid in the discovery of truly human solutions to our problems, then those who have the gospel have a source of knowledge which others not exposed to the gospel do not have. Whatever *material content* this light of the gospel leads to, it will always be utterly human, not beyond or at variance with the human and the reasonable.

Secondly, Curran states in the course of his study that "the natural law approach, from a theological perspective, embodies certain theological presuppositions which argue against its continued use in contemporary moral theology. Catholic theology and Catholic practice were never able to integrate the natural law approach into the total Christian perspective." Ultimately Curran opts for the phrase (used by Vatican II) "human experience," because "it avoids the theological problem created by the presupposition of the natural as an area unaffected both by the transforming and redeeming aspects of the resurrection as well as subject to the limitations and disfigurement of sin."

Undoubtedly there is a better term for natural law, but I do not believe that the basic notion necessarily involves the "presupposition of the natural as an area unaffected both by the transforming and redeeming aspects of the resurrection...." Sometimes the natural law has been spoken of in this way. Indeed, one could say that a handle for this separatist thinking was provided by Vatican I's notion of natural law. Edward Hamel, S.J., in a careful study, has shown that "Vatican I in some sense considers nature and grace as if they were two not only distinct but separate entities.... It speaks as if 'natural' knowledge of God occurred outside of all influence of grace, outside the economy of salvation."[26]

1970] p. 66). It is hard to know just what and whom Häring has in mind. For his phrase "no new content" seems hardly an accurate rendering of the thought of men like Fuchs and Rahner. I am not sure where Paul Ramsey stands here. He seems to argue for the permanence of marriage on exclusively Christian grounds. "It was the inseverability of Christ's covenant with us that, touching the covenants among men, made for the inseverability of the marriage bond" (*Interpretation* 24 [1970] 428). If Ramsey means this ("made for") literally, he would have to say that there is a specifically Christian material content in the moral life.

[26] Edward Hamel, S.J., "Lumen rationis et lux evangelii," *Periodica* 59 (1970) 215–49, at 247.

However, Hamel shows that Vatican II integrated the abstract, notional, objective, separatist treatment into a richer perspective and was able to bring out the unity of human morality within the Christian dispensation. This unity comes out in any number of places in the documents of the Council. For instance, *Gaudium et spes* states that "faith throws a new light on everything, manifests God's design for man's total vocation, and thus directs the mind to solutions which are *fully human*."[27] Also: "But only God, who created man to His own image and ransomed him from sin, provides a fully adequate answer to these questions. This He does through what He has revealed in Christ His Son, who became man. Whoever follows after Christ, the perfect man, *becomes himself more of a man*."[28] Therefore the notion of human morality (natural law), when properly integrated as in Vatican II, need not embody "certain theological presuppositions which argue against its continued use in contemporary moral theology."

My third question is closely related to the first two. Curran denies that there are distinctively Christian moral dispositions, intentions, attitudes. Perhaps I do not understand his intent here. But it seems that if Vatican II invites us to consider contemporary social problems "in the light of the gospel and human experience," and if it asserts that "faith ... directs the mind to solutions that are fully human," then it is precisely through Christian dispositions and attitudes that the authentically human may be deeply and accurately grasped. In an order where redemption completes creation, and where men remain human even though addressed by revelation and grasped by grace (in other words, where the human and Christian are integrated and the human thereby brought to its own highest perfection), is this not to be expected?

At this point it is helpful to ask how the light of the gospel relates to human morality. Hamel has done just that.[29] First, the grace of Christ, by neutralizing or removing impediments to the secure use of reason (pride, bad faith, passion, etc.), exercises a liberating effect. Under its influence man discovers more easily and readily what is authentically human. Secondly and more positively, the light of the gospel furnishes us with a knowledge of man's integral vocation. Only if the fulness of man's vocation is the backdrop for moral reflection will our solutions be truly and fully human; for only then will we consider all the elements and dimensions of the problem.

If it is the light of the gospel which gives us knowledge of the integral

[27] Cf. *The Documents of Vatican II*, ed. Walter M. Abbott, S.J. (New York: Guild Press, 1966) p. 209.

[28] *Ibid.*, p. 240 (n. 41).   [29] *Art. cit.*

vocation of man, is it. not possible and to be expected that this knowledge will issue in distinctive attitudes and intentions? I have in mind what Fuchs calls "transcendental" norms (e.g., the following of Christ, leading a sacramental life, the life of faith, etc.).[30] Gustafson's "attitudes, dispositions, intentions, goals and norms" are very close, I would think, to Fuchs's transcendental norms.

James Bresnahan, S.J., in an exceptionally fine summary of the ethical perspectives of Rahner's thought, has caught very well the direction of contemporary writing on the question of a distinctive Christian ethic.[31] First, he points out that since Christian ethics is the objectification in Jesus Christ of what every man experiences of himself in his subjectivity, "it does not and cannot add to human ethical self-understanding as such any material content that is, in principle, 'strange' or 'foreign' to man as he exists and experiences himself in this world."[32] Secondly, however, Bresnahan correctly insists that a man within the Christian community has access to a privileged articulation, in objective form, of this experience of subjectivity. Precisely because the resources of Scripture, dogma, and Christian life are the fullest available "objectification" of the common human experience, "the articulation of man's image of his moral good that is possible within historical Christian communities remains privileged in its access to enlarged perspectives on man." This statement is an excellent testimony to the radical unity of the human and the Christian.[33]

[30] Fuchs, "Gibt es eine spezifisch christliche Moral?" p. 101. Cf. also Raymond F. Collins, "Christian Personalism and the Sermon on the Mount," *Andover Newton Quarterly* 10 (1969) 19–30.

[31] James F. Bresnahan, S.J., "Rahner's Christian Ethics," *America* 123 (1970) 351–54.

[32] A different point of view and one not purged of separatism is that of R. Coste, "Loi naturelle et loi évangélique," *Nouvelle revue théologique* 92 (1970) 76–89. Coste uses the term *mutation radicale* to describe the relation of human morality and evangelical morality, and states that "it is no longer man who is the measure of ethical demand, as in the natural law; it is God Himself in the exemplarity of the Word Incarnate" (p. 84). Again, after describing evangelical love of neighbor in terms of pardon of offenses, love of enemies, nonviolence, etc., he concludes: "What an astronomical distance we have thus been carried from the natural law!" (p. 85). To the first statement we must insist that man indeed is the measure of ethical demand, but because of the God-man we now know more profoundly what is authentically human. To the second statement we must insist that Coste's description of evangelical love of neighbor is not "an astronomical distance from the natural law" but rather its finest explicitation. What underlies Coste's "separatism" is a dated notion of natural law.—It is ultimately the lack of any notion of human morality that underlies the unsuccessful struggles of Jack T. Sanders to find an ethical relevance for Jesus. For he criticizes the notion that an ethical principle coming from Jesus might be expected "to stand on its own." This rather clearly separates the human from the Christian. Cf. *Journal of the American Academy of Religion* 38 (1970) 131–46.

[33] So are some sentences by Enda McDonagh. For instance, "for the theological study

Regardless of how one formulates the specific character of Christian morality, should not the historical Christian communities reflect a distinctively Christian *concern* in the face of human problems? Our corporate embarrassment at this formulation of the question is itself some indication of the kind of answer the question deserves.

The Sense of Sin

John G. Milhaven treats of the new sense of sin.[34] In the past, Christians were taught that mortal sin was the deliberate choice of a single act of a specified sort. Unless the sinner repented, eternal punishment was the result. The "vindictive" mentality, basically juridical in character, undergirded this notion. Now, however, the contemporary Catholic views God as "a divine father, a divine husband, a divine lover." This dominant attitude, Milhaven believes, has led to a new sense of sin. He sees this as one founded in "positive obligation." That is, "to what extent is the action loving? To what extent does it bring about good consequences in human experience?" This positive attitude generates a corresponding negative norm for evaluating sin. "A sin will be grave to the extent that it is a failure to love, i.e., a responsibility for the presence of bad consequences, or the absence of good consequences, in human experience." In other words, a sin will be grave to the extent that it hurts or fails to help myself or another.

How does this norm of gravity operate? According to Milhaven, it has three characteristics. It is rarely identified with individual acts, it usually occurs only over a period of time ("because in everyday life it generally takes time to hurt a person seriously"), and it is generally a sin of omission—a failure to do something ("I did not concern myself with troubles of members of my family").[35] In summary, it is Milhaven's conviction that the contemporary Christian views sin not as an individual act but as a "continuing failure to act lovingly in innumerable situations over a period of time."

---

of morality accepting the human in all its fulness is one necessary starting point. It is this human which is then illuminated by the person, teaching, and achievement of Jesus Christ" ("Towards a Christian Theology of Morality," *Irish Theological Quarterly* 37 [1970] 187–98, at 197). Or: "The experience of Jesus Christ is regarded as normative because he is believed to have experienced what it is to be human in the fullest way and at the deepest level" (p. 196). This is also the sense of G. Bortolaso's statement that "the gospel certainly contains more than a pure order of reason, but this latter is contained in the gospel in a full and total manner" ("Il fondamento dei valori," *Civiltà cattolica* 121 [1970] 268–75, at 275).

[34] John G. Milhaven, "A New Sense of Sin," *Critic* 28 (1970) 14–21.

[35] Cf. also the editorial "Il peccato di omissione, oggi" *Civiltà cattolica* 121 (1970) 209–13.

Few will doubt that there is a good deal to be said in favor of the emphases Milhaven discusses. For instance, sins of omission need much more attention not only theologically but in popular catechesis. This is especially true in the area of social morality. However, some questions remain, as is bound to happen when one is depicting broad trends within the confines of a brief essay. Only a single point will be lifted out of Milhaven's treatment for discussion here: the relationship of sin to the individual act.

Increasingly one hears it said that "there can be no act such that its commission or omission alone is mortally sinful."[36] Statements such as this are rooted in a healthy reaction against an earlier excessive juridicism in our attitudes toward sin. Morality was viewed all too mechanically in terms of the external act. In correcting this view, there is a real danger of a reaction—a reaction which contains, in a different direction, the one-sidedness of the view against which it reacts. Concretely, a contemporary view of sin can all too easily divorce it almost totally from human activity and end up with an antihuman spiritualism. Actually, basic freedom, the freedom required for serious moral acts, can operate only in human acts. Our challenge, one with enormous pastoral implications, is to formulate the relationship of basic freedom to the individual act in a balanced and realistic way.[37]

Those who deny that any single act can be the occasion of a radical change (fundamental option) frequently assert that man cannot commit himself totally in a single personal act because the act occurs in a few moments, is brief, etc. If an act is understood in the way implied, then the statement is very likely correct. But this understanding can easily reflect a very unreal notion of a human act. Take adultery, for example. This can be described in two ways, abstractly or integrally. Abstractly, adultery can be said to occur in a very brief period of time. It is as brief as its mere physical occurrence. But more integrally viewed, adultery includes a larger experience: the meetings, thoughts, desires, plans, effects as foreseen, the vacillations, and so on. In other words, realistically viewed, adultery is a whole relationship brought to this culmination. Most often it is the culmination of a process including many components. Is it not this totality which a person must be said to choose, not simply and abstractly extramarital intercourse? If the entire experience is understood as the full meaning of the action, then is there not good reason for thinking that adultery could indeed

---

[36] Robert P. O'Neill and Michael A. Donovan, *Sexuality and Moral Responsibility* (Washington: Corpus, 1968) p. 57 and *passim*.

[37] For a treatment manifesting this balance, cf. Fuchs, *Human Values and Christian Morality*, pp. 98–111.

and presumably does elicit a serious moral response? This same analysis is true in other areas if the single act is understood in more human and integral terms. I believe that this is how "grave matter" must be explained to remain true to contemporary psychological data on freedom.

This discussion is far from complete. But as it continues, the following might prove helpful as guidelines. (1) Actions must be realistically defined before attempting to relate them to the use of our basic freedom. (2) Even when they have been realistically defined and are seen as capable of provoking a serious moral response, they may do so much less frequently than we have thought or think. Furthermore, even the most realistic definition remains general and abstract. It does not and cannot tell us what the individual is meaning, doing, suffering, experiencing as he performs the realistically defined action. (3) The moment of serious choice need not and perhaps often does not coincide with the performance of an individual action, but rather coincides with the full existential realization of its importance in one's life. This realization could break through at any number of points in the process which goes to make a realistically defined action.

SITUATIONS OF CONFLICT

Several years ago these pages reviewed three articles which dealt with situations of conflict, that is, situations in which an individual seemed trapped by circumstances into realizing one value in his choice only at the expense of another.[38] That these situations are real and frequent is clear. For instance, a couple with five children feel a deep responsibility toward these children and decide that they cannot enlarge their family further if the children are to be raised decently. On the other hand, they conclude that the support and growth of their marriage demands regular sexual expression. Within the confines of official magisterial teaching they feel that they cannot satisfy both of these duties. The aforementioned articles were attempts to develop a principled approach to situations of this kind. Beyond doubt they were saying something of substantial value, but their formulations were in my judgment far from precise and left them vulnerable to rather obvious objections.[39]

[38] THEOLOGICAL STUDIES 28 (1967) 753-60.

[39] The discussion continued in Denis E. Hurley, O.M.I., "In Defense of the Principle of Overriding Right," THEOLOGICAL STUDIES 29 (1968) 301-9; Norbert Rigali, S.J., "The Unity of the Moral Order," *Chicago Studies* 8 (1969) 125-43. The criticisms I raised against Curran's principle of compromise were largely concerned with the formulation, not with the substance, of the statements. Roderick Hindery criticizes the substance of the principle as applied to contraception; cf. *Cross Currents* 20 (1970) 331-36.

Over the past few months there have been at least four attempts to come to grips with problems like this. Nearly all of these have been rather obviously inspired by the problems raised by *Humanae vitae*.[40] But all of them have implications far beyond this single issue. Indeed, three of the essays use the Encyclical only as a springboard into the area of general moral theory. Because of their enormous importance for moral theology, they deserve a thorough presentation.

Using the analogy of physical laws, Peter Chirico, S.S., argues that specific moral laws, which are simply expressions of the general moral law enunciated in the two great commandments, have four qualities.[41] They are universal (applicable to the totality of occurrences), abstract (have reference to one specific relevant aspect of the relationship of persons), ideal (presuppose "other things being equal"), and copresent (converge with other laws relevant to the same situation). Thus, the prohibition of lying inculcates a single aspect of the concrete relationship of persons. But "since the truth conveying aspect of any concrete speaking is never the total meaning of that speaking, the command to tell the truth is but a specific law representing a single abstract ideal out of the total number of abstract ideals that are globally expressed in the first and second commandments."[42]

Now in concrete situations there are often present several values, each represented by a specific moral law. That is, specific moral laws are copresent. What is to be done when several laws are copresent in a situation? Chirico gives the following three directives. First, the agent must attempt to implement each value involved—for example, he must try to save both his own life and that of his assailant. Secondly, if he cannot, he should choose in the direction of the preponderance of values. Which value and law is to receive preference cannot be decided beforehand but must be judged according to the concrete facts of each situation. Thirdly, the agent may not simply choose the greater value

[40] For some recent comment on *Humanae vitae*, cf. James E. Allen, "How Catholics Are Making up Their Minds on Birth Control," *Christian Century* 87 (1970) 915–18; Norman R. C. Dockeray, "An Anglican's Reflections on *Humanae vitae*," *Downside Review* 88 (1970) 233–45; Johannes Messner, "Ehemoral und Entscheidungsethik," *Hochland* 62 (1970) 1–19; Richard J. Connell, "A Defense of *Humanae vitae*," *Laval théologique et philosophique* 26 (1970) 57–88; Charles N. R. McCoy, "*Humanae vitae:* Perspectives and Precisions," *New Scholasticism* 44 (1970) 265–72; F. Nagy, "Sur un ouvrage récent consacré à l'encyclique 'Humanae vitae,'" *Science et esprit* 22 (1970) 99–110; M. John Farrelly, O.S.B., "The Principle of the Family Good," THEOLOGICAL STUDIES 31 (1970) 262–74; Miran Vodopivec, "Humanbiologische und pastoralmedizinische Marginalien zu 'Humanae vitae,'" *Theologische Quartalschrift* 150 (1970) 256–61.

[41] Peter Chirico, S.S., "Morality in General and Birth Control in Particular," *Chicago Studies* 9 (1970) 19–33.

[42] *Ibid.*, p. 23.

and let it go at that. He must, for example, *regret* taking the life of his assailant even as he does so, and work to eliminate the conditions which generate such choices. Chirico concludes: "I have to proceed according to my capabilities, and this will involve many imperfect acts that constitute the best that I can do."

He then applies this to birth control. Sexual intercourse embodies three values: the relationship of husband to wife, the creative movement to offspring, the responsibility to already existing children and society. Each of these values is an aspect of the supreme law enunciated in the two great commandments and therefore each is rendered intelligible by an abstract, universal, ideal, specific law. Since all these laws pertain to the same act, we may speak of the copresence of three laws: the law of integral personal relationship, the law of integral intercourse, the law of total responsibility. All of these laws must be respected in the unique situation of the couple. They cannot be collapsed into a single law—for example, "every act must remain open to procreation" or "as long as the couple is generally responsible, it is permissible to use contraceptives." Chirico puts it this way: "Each couple in each act of intercourse starts from a unique situation in which the unlimited demands of the first and second commandments as expressed abstractly in the three laws mentioned above must be uniquely applied so as to yield the greatest possible growth for the couple and for society."[43]

Practically, Chirico concludes that contraception can be justified in individual instances, but that it "can only be tolerated to the extent that there are other and greater values that necessitate intercourse here and now and yet also dictate the avoidance of further children." He judges this view to be consonant with *Humanae vitae*. That is, it "does not deny the content of *Humanae vitae*. Nor does it repeat it. It is, rather, an attempt to fulfill it." This fulfilling consists in supplying the context within which papal statements should be read. And this context, Chirico argues, is the fact that in concrete situations specific moral imperatives are copresent and in a sense competitive with other no less valid imperatives.

This analysis, while containing many strains of Chirico's earlier thought, represents a genuine corrective and advance. In the past, Chirico had seen *moral* evil in an act which did not achieve all possible values. For example, his earlier analysis supposed that a material statement of untruth is a "perversion of the expressive faculty" even when this untruth was uttered to protect the most solemn secret. Thus he concluded that there are times when one must perform an act with

[43] *Ibid.*, p. 31.

immoral elements in it. This implied that the moral quality of an individual act was being measured by reference to only one value, even though the act was permissible because of the "tension" situation.

Now, however, Chirico sees the moral quality of the act emerging only after the concrete act has been related to all the values involved. This is what he means by saying that the choice or decision must take seriously all the copresent laws. After this evaluation has been made, we are in a position to assess the moral quality of the act. This is, I would think, a more accurate account of the specification of moral quality.

Without at all wishing to challenge the conclusions Chirico draws with regard to contraception and, by implication, with regard to other matters (indeed, I would agree with them), still I wonder whether his present formulation has completely ironed out all the wrinkles present in his earlier analysis. Perhaps there is some reason to doubt it. That reason may be discernible in his formulation of moral laws. He sees these as abstract and absolute statements rooted in a value. For example, since integral intercourse is one value in sexual expression, there is the "law of integral intercourse." This law is, of course, copresent with other laws, and the moral quality of an act takes shape "from the total value of the concrete act in the life of the person in question."

It is off this analysis that Chirico disowns the term "objective evil." In his opinion this is a misleading term, since it "can only refer to a deviation from some abstract ideal law and so it too is an abstraction." Furthermore, to call such deviation even objective sin "is to begin to insinuate a moral judgment that can only emerge from the total value of the concrete act in the life of the person in question."[44]

The problem one might raise here is the very notion of moral law Chirico presents. If moral laws and rules are to be formulated as Chirico explains them, then indeed the notion of "objective evil" is an abstraction. That is, if moral laws are abstract, ideal statements *which take no account of other values in their very formulation* (e.g., the moral "law of integral intercourse"), then to speak of a violation of them is meaningless. And if "objective evil" means violation of law understood in this way, then we can bid a tearless adieu to the notion. But is this a proper accounting of moral laws? A lingering sense of discomfort leads me to think it may not be.

Let us take the question of theft. According to Chirico's analysis, in extreme situations there would be two values involved: the value of private property and the value of self-preservation or individual life.

[44] *Ibid.*, p. 32.

Hence there are two laws copresent in some situations: the law to preserve one's own life and the law against taking another's property. In other words, there is a moral law for each value. These laws can be composed, balanced, or reconciled only "in the life of the person in question"; for "a moral judgment can only emerge from the total value of the concrete act in the life of the person in question."

Actually, are moral laws restricted to imposing a single isolated value? It can be doubted. Just as human values exist in a total, sometimes very complicated, and sinful context, so laws derived from them try to reflect this total context. Moral norms, therefore, represent attempts to sort out and order the relationship of several values in possible situations and then to formulate this ordering as accurately as possible. The formulation of the law or norm occurs only after we reflect on the two or more copresent values and relate them as best we can. In other words, it is not isolated values which generate norms, but human situations, situations in which many values are or can be interwoven.

Thus, traditional wisdom has refused to say simply that there is a moral law against taking another's property. Rather, after reflecting on experience and on all the values involved in it, Christian thinkers have said that there is a moral law prohibiting the taking of another's property *against his reasonable will.* It is this which is prohibited. This is properly the law, or at least a useful negative formulation of it. And this kind of norm is not the isolated thing Chirico's laws are. It is a generalization, admittedly imperfect, brought to term out of reflection on many situations and experiences. And therefore it refers to kinds of human action. Because it speaks of kinds of human action (and not isolated aspects of an act), it is possible to speak meaningfully, if only generally, of actions which violate this norm. And if this is so, is it not possible to speak of "objective evil"? This Chirico cannot do, because his laws do not refer to human actions, but only to isolated aspects of actions.

With this single reservation, Chirico's paper is extremely interesting and enlightening. And perhaps even this reservation can be reduced to mere quibbling. I suspect it can. Whatever the case may be, Chirico seems to admit *ambulando* the point made here. His treatment concludes with a whopping and undisguised category of action and moral norm: "Contraception, thus, can only be tolerated to the extent that there are other and greater values that necessitate intercourse here and now and yet also dictate the avoidance of further children."[45] This is a

---

[45] *Ibid.,* p. 31.

moral norm, I would think. And because it is not a norm built on a single value, it speaks not merely of an aspect of an action but of kinds of human actions. Therefore it can be violated by kinds of human action. And to that extent this kind of action can be said to be objectively evil, even if the norm does not and cannot tell us whether this or that individual is performing this kind of action.

Chirico had rightly urged theologians to provide the fuller context for the reading of papal teaching, and made an interesting attempt in this direction himself. Charles Robert makes a similar attempt.[46] The pastoral letter of the French bishops on *Humanae vitae* had referred to a "veritable conflict of duties" confronting some couples. Robert argues that this phrase opens the way for our return to a great moral tradition which should be the context for interpreting not only *Humanae vitae* but many other instances of conflicting values. He uses the French reference as a stimulus to discover how a "conflict of duties" should be faced in Christian ethics.

St. Thomas' treatment of self-defense serves as Robert's model. The basic structure of Thomas' approach is extremely simple. There is a complete lack of complicated jargon such as tolerance of evil, choosing the lesser evil, direct and indirect voluntary. Rather, Thomas sees the situation as one involving two goods (integrity of my life and that of the aggressor) which cannot be realized in the same moment. The assailant has put me in the position of choosing one good which, in the circumstances, can only be realized to the detriment of the other. The good preferred (my own life) is not necessarily a greater good; it is simply "nearer and more urgent." In such a desperate situation this good or effect alone is intended, while the other effect is unintended. However, this act done with good intent can be immoral if it is not proportionate. That is, the means must be chosen with moderation, so vengeance and other malicious sentiments do not vitiate the good intent. The entire moral question focuses on the moderation or the proportionate character of the means.

Nor is self-defense an isolated instance in Thomas. The theme of "objective obstacle" (*impedimentum*) leads Thomas to the same analysis in other areas. For instance, Robert finds a similar infrastructure in Thomistic analysis of theft in evident and urgent need. In this case all the themes of objective conflict arise: two fundamental but in the circumstances contradictory goods, imminence of peril, urgency. He believes Thomas is using the principle of double effect in this instance, as well as in his treatment of capital punishment, warfare, and so on.

[46] Charles Robert, "La situation de 'conflit': Un thème dangereux de la théologie morale d'aujourd'hui," *Revue des sciences religieuses* 44 (1970) 190–213.

Robert argues that this approach does not involve the use of a bad means to a good end; for once the means is seen as the only way of exiting from an impasse, of realizing one of two fundamental but mutually exclusive goods, it is this good which engages and specifies the intent. It is in this context that one must understand *Humanae vitae* when it says: "It is not licit, even for the (gravest reasons, to do evil so that good may follow therefrom, that is, to make into the object of a positive act of the will something which is intrinsically disorder" (n. 14). The second part of this statement ("that is, to make into the object of a positive act of the will...") explains how the first must be understood. One only *"does evil* so that good may follow" when the evil is "the object of a positive act of the will." The Latin of the original is "in id voluntatem conferre." Robert contends that Thomas' analysis reveals that in cases of objective conflict of goods, the will does not "in id conferre."

Robert's reliance on an earlier study by Peter Knauer, S.J., is obvious and acknowledged. In a recent essay Knauer himself applies his general theory of double effect to the question of contraception.[47] It hardly needs to be recalled that Pope Paul VI taught in *Humanae vitae* that each conjugal act must remain open to the transmission of life. Knauer wonders whether this conclusion follows from the general principle that married love must remain basically open to the transmission of life. To bring a child into the world without the capacity to raise him properly is a misuse of marriage. Such conduct is in contradiction to the deepest sense of the conjugal act, and therefore in a genuine sense lacks true openness to the procreation and education of human life. On the other hand, a couple could intervene into the fertility of their union precisely out of responsibility for a prospective child. Knauer concludes with this general criterion: if an intervention into the fertility of a conjugal act happens *against* the child (e.g., out of egoism), there is illicit birth control. But intervention into this fertility in the interests of the possible child has nothing to do with *direct* contraception.

This leads Knauer to a description of direct contraception. The statements of Pius XI and Paul VI are accurate if we understand "de industria" or "intentionally" correctly: in a moral-theological sense rather

---

[47] P. Knauer, S.J., "Überlegungen zur moraltheologischen Prinzipienlehre der Enzyklika 'Humanae vitae,'" *Theologie und Philosophie* 45 (1970) 60–74. The earlier study is "La détermination du bien et du mal moral par le principe du double effet," *Nouvelle revue théologique* 87 (1965) 356–76.

than just a psychological sense. Even the popes, however, did not achieve this understanding.

Knauer describes the distinction with an example from medicine. In a leg amputation the psychological attention of the surgeon is focused on a skilful removal of the leg. This removal is the concrete thing that is attended to and willed by him. But the morality of the act is not determined on this level of mere physical happening or psychological intention. It is only after we determine what value the act seeks to serve that we determine its morality. If in the circumstances the act is the best possible way to insure the life and health of the patient, then in a *moral* sense what is intended is not the taking of the leg, but the health of the patient. If, contrarily, the reason is not commensurate, the amputation would be a mutilation in the moral sense. In summary, the *psychological* intention (skilful removal of an organ) is not the same as the *moral* intent (healing through removal of an obstacle to health).

In the moral sense, therefore, that physical evil is direct or *de industria* when it is caused or permitted without a truly commensurate reason. Applied to birth control, this means that "an intervention into the fertility of a conjugal act grounded precisely in responsibility for the transmission of life is not contraception in the moral sense, but is distinguished from contraception in the same way a medically justified amputation is different from a radically illicit mutilation."[48] The physical evil would be indirect in the moral sense.

This analysis is simply an application of Knauer's over-all interpretation of the double effect, an interpretation he presented some five years ago, but which he substantially clarified several years later.[49] Since his thought has been widely quoted and appears to be rather widely accepted, it deserves continued attention. Here I will present the core ideas as they are presented in Knauer's revised version. Knauer's basic thesis is that moral evil consists in the permission or causing of a physical evil which is not justified by a commensurate reason. In explaining this, he leans heavily on St. Thomas. In Thomas' discussion of self-defense, "effect" is not used simply as a correlative of "cause" but in a more general sense. "Aspect" would be a better way to render it. Thus, self-defense, rather than a strict effect, is really an aspect of the action. Similarly, the *finis operis* of an act is not derived simply from its external effect, but is really that aspect of the act which is willed. For example, almsgiving is not just a physical act;

[48] *Ibid.*, p. 66.

[49] P. Knauer, S.J., "The Hermeneutic Function of the Principle of Double Effect," *Natural Law Forum* 12 (1967) 132–62.

it gets its sense and becomes a moral act through the intention of the donor.

Knauer argues that it is with this in mind that we must understand the terms "direct" and "indirect." In the past we have tied these terms too closely to physical causality. Actually, "the permission or causing of a physical evil is direct or indirect as there is or is not present a commensurate reason"; for when there is a commensurate reason, this reason "occupies the same area as what is directly willed and alone determines the entire moral content of the act. If the reason of an act is commensurate, it alone determines the *finis operis*, so that the act is morally good."[50] This commensurate reason engages the intent in a *moral* sense, and the associated physical evil is indirect.

How important this thesis is practically becomes clear when we see how Knauer applies it throughout the realm of concrete decisions. For example, a lie consists in telling what is false without commensurate reason and "therefore directly or formally causes the error of another." Theft is "the taking of the property of another without commensurate reason." Mutilation is surgery without a commensurate reason.[51] Contraception is intervention into the fertility of the conjugal act without commensurate reason. In all these instances, when there is a commensurate reason, the moral content of the act is not the physical evil but the commensurate reason. The physical evil is then indirect.

The practical consequences of this analysis are clear in a paragraph which is a good summary of Knauer's presentation:

In the case of an ectopic pregnancy it is almost certain that the woman together with an unborn child will die if the fetus is not removed as early as possible. The "insight" that this is immoral is scarcely demonstrable to any doctor. It is agreed that direct killing is forbidden. But in my opinion some scholastic moralists have assumed incorrectly that the saving of the mother, which in the normal case is probable if there is immediate removal of the ectopic fetus, is a direct killing. Negative laws (You shall not kill, You shall not speak an untruth, You shall not take the property of another) are understandable only as the prohibition of direct and therefore formal permission or causing of these physical evils (death, error, loss of property etc.) in cases where by definition there is no commensurate reason. Whether there is a violation of a commandment (that is, whether an act is murder, lying, theft) can be ascertained only if it is established that the reason for the act in its existential entirety is not commensurate. Without a commensurate reason an evil is always willed di-

---

[50] *Ibid.*, p. 141.

[51] Knauer believes, therefore, that the principle of totality is identical with the principle of double effect.

rectly, even if the attention is not expressly directed to the evil but it is desired that there be no such evil.[52]

If one raises the objection here that a good end does not justify a bad means, Knauer would respond: true, but such a principle supposes that the means is *morally* evil. But this is only so if the permission or production of a physical evil is not justified by a commensurate reason. In other words, one must not assume that the means is bad just because it involves physical evil. It becomes morally evil as means if the physical evil is not justified by a commensurate reason.

Obviously the notion of commensurate reason is so utterly central to his thesis that its meaning must be spelled out carefully. Knauer stresses the fact that a reason is not commensurate because it is sincere, meaningful, or even plain important. It is commensurate if the value realizable here and now by measures involving physical evil in a premoral sense is not in the long run undermined and contradicted by these measures but supported and maximized. The present action achieves the value as effectively as possible in the long run. For instance, "a refusal to bear children is only commensurately grounded if it is ultimately in the interests of the otherwise possible child."[53]   I shall return to this notion below.

Bruno Schüller, S.J., in an extremely interesting study, approaches conflict situations from a slightly different point of view, but ends up with a structure ultimately compatible with the thought of Knauer and Chirico.[54] There are two types of norms: those that apply in all thinkable circumstances and are exceptionless; those that apply in normal circumstances or as a rule. Those in the first category are valid independently of circumstances. They are norms such as "thou shalt love God with thy whole heart," "thou shalt not kill another unjustly," and so on. Those in the second category are valid only in determined conditions. In this sense they are contingent norms. For example, one must generally keep the entrusted secret. In the past we have put into the first category some synthetic norms such as "every intervention into the fertility of sexual intercourse is forbidden." It is Schüller's contention that most of these synthetic judgments are contingent and conditional norms and suffer exceptions, sometimes frequent exceptions. His

---

[52] *Ibid.*, pp. 149–50. For an analysis of abortion very similar to Knauer's, cf. Bernard Häring, "A Theological Evaluation," in *The Morality of Abortion*, ed. John T. Noonan, Jr. (Cambridge: Harvard Univ. Press, 1970) pp. 123–45, at 136–37.

[53] "Überlegungen," p. 73.

[54] B. Schüller, S.J., "Zur Problematik allgemein verbindlicher ethischer Grundsätze," *Theologie und Philosophie* 45 (1970) 1–23.

study focuses on killing and on remarriage after divorce as instances where rethinking might be called for.

Schüller argues his case by appeal to what he modestly calls a "hypothesis." His hypothesis: all moral norms touching our concrete conduct with our fellow men and the world are really conclusions or applications of more general "preference rules." Norms based on these "preference rules" are absolute and exceptionless only if they command a value which cannot concur with another more important value. These "preference rules" are reductively one rule with several formulations. Stated negatively, it reads: put in a position where he will unavoidably cause evil, man must discover which is the worst evil and avoid it. Stated positively, this is its formulation: put before two concurring but mutually exclusive values, man should discover which merits preference and act accordingly. These statements imply that a physical evil can be caused or permitted only if it is demanded by a proportionate good.

Schüller offers two reasons in support of his hypothesis. The first is less an argument than an induction from contemporary experience and conviction. Put simply, these norms in control of concrete conduct appear more and more to be conditioned principles. For example, many would put the prohibition against contraception as follows: the use of contraception is forbidden unless avoidance of pregnancy is justified and abstention would be harmful to the good of the couple. Underlying this formulation is the conviction that obviously something is of greater value than the physical evil done by contraceptive intervention.

Similarly with the lie. The principle that "every falsehood is a lie" is not absolute. Those who say it is cannot answer satisfactorily the conflict situation where secrets must be kept. The traditional answer here (broad mental reservation) is no answer, since in the context such mental reservation is really a falsehood. Schüller contends that falsehood is an attack on value and morally wrong from the fact that error and lack of trust are visited on the neighbor *without proportionate reason*. Therefore, when traditional theology used broad mental reservation to justify falsehood in certain cases, it was really saying: this is morally licit because it avoids an evil greater than my neighbor would suffer through his deception and error. Or positively, the choice of falsehood represents the preference of a greater value in circumstances where two concurring values are mutually exclusive.

Schüller's second reason to support his hypothesis is the relative character of our conduct where our neighbor is concerned. That is, the aim of our conduct in dealing with others is not absolute good, but relative good. Since this is the case, it is always in principle thinkable that this good could be copresent with another good and that we would have to determine to which to give preference. Therefore, in the moral assessment of actions that have only a relative value, this value must always be assessed in relation to another possibly concurrent relative value to discover whether it merits preference or not.

Traditional theology has been aware of this in distinguishing *benevolentia* from *beneficentia*. There is a limit to what our *beneficentia* can do. Therefore traditional theology tried to work out conflict situations through an *ordo caritatis*. But it did not follow up logically on this by seeing all concrete innerworldly areas in the light of the preference principles buried in the *ordo caritatis*.

All of this means, of course, that concrete norms can have exceptions. Traditional theology has always admitted this but in at least two instances (direct killing of the innocent and *ratum et consummatum* marriage) has maintained that only God, as Creator and Lord, has the power to allow such exceptions. Schüller questions this restriction and wonders why men with their power of judgment should not be able to apply the preference principle to even these areas.

As for killing the innocent (or oneself, for that matter), Schüller believes that the prohibition can only be grounded in the fact that the life of such a man deserves preference before other concurring values. It is precisely within this value structure that traditional theology has argued for the permissibility of capital punishment and self-defense. For Schüller, killing is just as illicit as the good (which is realized through it) is not proportionate to the evil of destruction of life. This formulation does not radically alter traditional conclusions, but it does make some conflict situations discussable. In these situations Schüller would put the question squarely: Is there actually no good thinkable which could come into conflict with my life or that of an innocent man and deserve preference? Bodily life is not, after all, the highest good, even though it is the most fundamental.

Schüller next turns to marriage. The Church's traditional teaching (absolute indissolubility of a *ratum et consummatum* marriage) lacks inner coherence and smacks strongly of legal positivism when viewed in light of the preference principle. Take, for example, the Pauline and Petrine privileges. Basically, these are concessions to human weakness, *in favorem fidei*; that is, to remain unmarried could prevent conversion to the faith or perseverance in it. Is this not to admit that there is a higher value than the bond of marriage? In this instance this higher value is the faith. Why does God not grant the same concession to the weakness of the Christian couple who cannot in all best will live together? To live unmarried is beyond their strength, and experience shows that insistence on this is a real danger to their faith too.

Therefore, when one studies both the words of Jesus on indissolubility and the Pauline privilege, it becomes clear that Paul operated with the conviction that this is the way to read the Lord's words in this situation. Concretely, upholding indissolubility in these instances is at the price of peace and danger to the faith. In such conflict situations, peace and faith merit preference. The Church took over this power of interpretation and came to realize over the years that all marriages are dissoluble except *ratum et consummatum* unions. But Schüller is convinced that this conviction is only a step in the process of interpretation of her powers by the Church and that this process has not come to an end. In the future he anticipates a widening of application of the basic preference principle even to *ratum et consummatum* marriages.

I have dwelt on these articles at considerable length because of their thoughtfulness and the great theoretical and practical importance of their subject matter. For instance, all conclude in one way or another that the physically direct doing of evil or harm is not really decisive. This assertion would challenge many textbook conclusions in the areas of abortion, sterilization, contraception, co-operation, killing, to mention but a few. Doubtless there are those who will judge this literature a sneaky and left-handed way of getting around the clear practical directives of *Humanae vitae*. Others will broaden the attack and see in such reflections the slippery slope to "situation ethics." It remains a regrettable fact that too often labels are libels. Even where they are not, they are rarely the product of an open and disciplined reflection. And that is what is essential here.

It seems to me that all four articles are dealing with a single basic problem, and a very good one: When and how does physical evil become moral evil? Deception, suffering, intervention into fertility, amputation, ignorance, loss of repute, death—these are of themselves physical evils. When does causing or permitting them become immoral? All the articles above come to the same conclusion (though in Chirico's case less explicitly): the causing of physical evil becomes immoral when it occurs without proportionate reason.

The textbook tradition on this matter has been unsatisfactory or at least incomplete. Robert and Knauer suggest that the reason is that the relation of evil to the will was seen too restrictedly in terms of mere physical causality. Thus, when fetal death was the sole immediate effect of a procedure, it was said to be direct abortion. This one-sided emphasis on physical causality abandons, they contend, the pure and simple lines of the Thomistic analysis and leads ultimately to a confusion of psychological and moral directness. Because of this confusion we regard many things as directly intended which are really only directly intended psychologically. Moral directness is determined not by this psychological intent but by the presence or absence of a commensurate reason. Once this reason is present, the evil caused remains indirect.

Schüller, without a similar emphasis on directness and indirectness, studies those exceptional instances where traditional formulations have allowed for some degree of physical harm, e.g., theft in extreme need. The formulations allowing for this he sees deriving from an underlying preference-principle by which values are weighed against each other prior to the emergence of a formulation of moral licitness or illicitness. This preference-principle implies that physical evil becomes moral evil when it is caused without proportionate reason.

I believe there is something very important in the direction of these analyses, for two reasons. First, there is evidence to suggest that our contemporary notion of direct intent of evil, with its very close reliance on direct physical causality, may have narrowed and distorted rather than advanced the original Thomistic analysis. For instance, not a few theologians are uncomfortable with the conclusion that removing a pregnant Fallopian tube is licit, whereas shelling out the fetus and leaving a healthy tube intact is not. Discomfort, of course, is hardly a Christian reason for abandoning a hard saying. But if this discomfort is intellectual, it is an excellent reason for questioning the saying. Certainly there is logic and consistency in the traditional analysis, but is it possible that this logic and consistency occur within the confines of a notion of directness that may itself be distorted? We cannot dismiss this possibility out of hand.

Secondly, I believe Schüller has convincingly argued that behind our formulated norms in control of concrete conduct is a more general preference-principle from which these norms derive. If this is true, we must reapproach some traditional conclusions to see if they square with this derivation. Several years ago I made a probe in this direction where abortion is concerned and wrote:

History reveals a constant sharpening and delimiting of the category of abortion. The development was controlled by the categories of thought and scientific information available at the time. Contemporary formulations are the precipitate of this development process. As such, they are only the best we have. They hinge on two concepts: *direct* and *innocent*. Now it would seem that *innocent* is concluded from the injustice involved in war, aggression, capital offenses. That is, certain recognized injustices defined the category of innocence.

The conclusion: it is morally tolerable to kill directly only where injustice is involved. Therefore, abortion is seen as an act whose basic moral quality is determined within the justice-injustice category.

If, however, one distills from the three examples of morally tolerable killing a more general *ratio* (sc., that behind justice-injustice is a more general category, sc., *higher personal value*), then abortion as a form of forbidden killing might be recognized as that not justified by the hierarchy of personal value.[55]

This approach is very close to Schüller's key idea. As this important discussion continues, I should like to raise three points where greater clarity would be a help.

The first point concerns the notions of direct and indirect. If Schüller's ultimate justification for causing or permitting physical harm is a preference-principle, it is not clear what role or importance the traditional notions of directness and indirectness play in his analysis. On the other hand, Knauer adheres to this terminology but redefines it in a way which leads to the complete distinction between moral and psychological directness. This does violence to one's sense of reality. The criticisms offered by Grisez on this point seem accurate.[56]

Secondly, how do we, or even *can* we, know that the reason for permitting or causing harm is commensurate? Clearly, this question stems from Knauer's formulation of commensurate reason. For Knauer, a reason is commensurate if the manner of the present achievement of a value will not undermine but support the value in the long run and in the whole picture. This is a sound description of proportionality. But who can confidently make such a judgment? An individual? Hardly. It seems to demand a clairvoyance not granted to many mortals and would paralyze decision in most cases. For example, what individual can say whether this present abortion will, in the long haul, undermine or promote the value of maternal and fetal life? This is especially true if the individual in question has a great stake in the abortion and presumably, therefore, is more focused on the immediate impasse than on the long-term stakes. Knauer does not resolve this problem adequately.[57] Nor does Schüller. He only adverts to the fact that a determination of the hierarchy of values is very difficult. But stated in this way, the problem suggests easily and naturally the desirability of resources and perspec-

---

[55] Richard A. McCormick, S.J., "Past Church Teaching on Abortion," *Proceedings of the Catholic Theological Society of America* 23 (1968) 131–51, at 150.

[56] Germain C. Grisez, *Abortion: The Myth, the Realities and the Arguments* (Washington: Corpus, 1970).

[57] He does insist on "rigorous objective criteria" (p. 154) but does not go into any detail on what they might be. His essentially evasive answer to Noonan's question (p. 162) about the hypothetical case of a woman who commits adultery to rescue her children from a concentration camp only points up this lack.

tives which can be supposed to be larger than the individual's, that is, the need of scientific moral theology and the desirability of a magisterium.

This brings us to the third point. If it is precisely the lack of proportionate reason which makes the causing of physical evil wrong (indeed, inherently evil), then moral prohibitions issued by the magisterium must be conceived as value judgments on the presence or absence of proportionate reason in certain concrete forms of conduct. If this is the case, the explicit formulations of the magisterium, especially absolute prohibitions, must be tested and interpreted in light of this understanding of moral teaching. Has the magisterium conceived its past prohibitions in this way? It can be doubted. If the magisterium had actually conceived its prohibitions in this way, would the practical conclusions be substantially different? In some instances I suspect they would, though the matter is extremely difficult and extremely delicate.

The teaching of the recent magisterium on AIH (artificial insemination by husband) provides a good example here. In 1949 Pius XII prohibited AIH. Before his statement, the licitness of AIH was espoused by a fair number of reputable theologians. As for the reasoning of Pius XII, in 1949 he referred to the "procreation of life according to the will and plan of the Creator . . . this is in harmony with the dignity of the marriage partners, with their bodily and spiritual nature, and with the normal and happy development of the child."[58]

In 1951 Pius XII elaborated the argument as follows:

To reduce the cohabitation of married persons and the conjugal act to a mere organic function for the transmission of the germ of life would be to convert the domestic hearth, sanctuary of the family, into nothing more than a biological laboratory. Hence in our address of Sept. 29, 1949, to the international congress of Catholic doctors, we formally excluded artificial insemination from marriage. The conjugal act in its natural structure is a personal action, a simultaneous mutual self-giving which, in the words of Holy Scripture, effects the union "in one flesh." This is much more than the mere union of two germs, which can be brought about also artificially, that is, without the natural action of the spouses. The conjugal act, as it is planned and willed by nature, implies a personal co-operation, the right to which the partners have mutually conferred on each other in contracting marriage.[59]

It seems that the point of Pius' argument is this: AIH is not human because the child so born is not the fruit of an act *in itself* the expression of personal love. Now the hidden assumption here is this: the child must always be conceived of an act in itself a personal expres-

---

[58] *AAS* 41 (1949) 559–61.   [59] *AAS* 43 (1951) 850.

sion of love; for to proceed otherwise would turn marriage into a biological laboratory.

It can be argued that this conclusion is a value judgment. And I think it is *generally* true. That is, if procreation were commonly to occur via AIH, we would have taken a long step toward biologizing and mechanizing marriage. Why? Because sexual intercourse would begin to lose its sense and this in itself is an attack on marriage because it is an attack on the typical expression of marriage. The child is the fruit of love (cf. Vatican II), the enduring incarnation of the husband-wife two-in-oneness. Hence, he should come into being through the act which is the typical expression of this love. Otherwise, he could gradually become a "thing" of the marriage.

But Pius XII said of AIH: "absolute eliminanda est." The reasoning supports the general prohibition: AIH is per se (generally) immoral. Or again, it is certainly wrong to substitute AIH for natural intercourse when this is not required. But if the couple is having sexual relations and cannot conceive, would the reasoning offered by Pius XII hold? Would AIH here tend to turn marriage into a biological laboratory? This is not clear, unless there are other circumstances in the culture which would support this conclusion.

The above reflections lead one to ask: What is the nature of Pius XII's prohibition? It seems that the Pope thought he was clarifying a demand of the natural law. And indeed, this may be true. But when we think of a "demand of the natural law," we too often think of something immutable and absolute, derived from the nature of things. Actually, the force of the papal argument seems to derive from effects, i.e., what would happen if AIH were permitted. Such arguments are conclusive only in so far as the foreseen dangers are unavoidable. If AIH even in exceptional instances would lead to the biologizing of marriage, then the conclusion "absolute eliminanda est" is justified.[60] But if the evil effects follow only when there is a general practice of AIH without necessity, then it would be possible to admit the licitness of the exceptional instance. The point I am making is that the form of argument used by Pius XII seems to be, at root, a value judgment. This of itself says nothing about the validity of the conclusion. It only underlines the relative and culturally conditioned character of the judgment; for value judgments are made in cultural circumstances and can vary

---

[60] There is increasing evidence that this may be the case in our culture. Margaret Mead points out that we will soon have babies without love-making. At the University of Michigan 18 women have already been successfully inseminated from sperm frozen up to 2½ years. Cf. George C. Anderson, "Playing God with Human Beings," *Christian Ministry* 1 (1970) 12–14.

with different cultural conditions. It also suggests that such judgments, especially when they represent absolute prohibitions, may be closer to laws than to teachings.

This section should not close without the salutary admission that if individuals need the magisterium to rise above the limits of their own perspectives in assessing proportionality over the long haul, they will be appropriately hesitant to rely exclusively on their own perspectives in questioning these magisterial value judgments.

TOWARD AN ETHICS OF ECOLOGY

The usual article on ecology starts with some now familiar facts.[61] Every year Americans junk 7 million cars, 48 billion cans, 20 million tons of paper. Our industries pour out 165 million tons of waste and belch 172 million tons of fumes and smoke into the sky. We provide 50% of the world's industrial pollution. An average of 3000 acres of oxygen-producing earth a day (1,000,000 a year) fall beneath concrete and blacktop. The average American puts 1500 pounds of pollutants into the atmosphere each year. Furthermore, there is no end in sight. It is estimated that there will be between 6 and 7 billion people in the world by the year 2000 (there are 3.5 billion now) and 25 billion within the next 100 years. Our ecosphere, it is said, can support only 6–8 billion. This figure will be reached in 30 years. Therefore, with an increase of people, depletion of resources, and unchecked pollution, we are on a collision course with our environment. Eco-catastrophe is predictable and it is made of three elements: people, resources, and pollution—too many of the first using too much of the second causing too much of the third. The result: a mass attack on a limited environment. As Paul Ehrlich put it: "The causal chain of the deterioration [of the environment] is easily followed to its source. Too many cars, too much pesticide, inadequate sewage treatment plants, too little water, too much CO_2, all can be traced easily to *too many people*."[62]

In the face of this apocalyptic peril, we are beginning to hear of a "theology of ecology," "ecological ethics," "land ethics." What is it all about? It is all about man's failure to live up to his responsibilities of stewardship of the earth (and through it, of himself) and the recovery of sanity in this area. The literature is so vast that it resists orderly

[61] *Time*, Feb. 2, 1970, pp. 56–63.

[62] Cited in Bruce Wrightsman, "Man, Manager or Manipulator of the Earth," *Dialog* 9 (1970) 214. Statements such as Ehrlich's have been challenged as oversimplifications; cf. Robert L. Schueler, "Ecology—The New Religion?" *America* 122 (1970) 292–95, at 294.

review. We can only show drifts and trends.[63] But in general most of the literature attempts to identify the problem and offer the direction of a solution. Since nearly all the authors find the basic problem in a priority of values sustained by an attitude toward man and his world, they find the ultimate solution in a change in this basic world view. It may be useful to organize this kaleidoscopic review in three stages: origin of the problem, proposed solutions, several more notable contributions.

Origin of the Problem

What is behind our ecological mess? Peter Riga believes it is a whole mentality and value system: the consumer mentality.[64] "More things represent human fulfillment." This basic value judgment is obvious in our insane adoration of the GNP. He calls for a whole change of mind and value. J. Barrie Shepherd says much the same thing.[65] Man's present attitude to the material world views it as a giant cookie jar. This consumer-to-a-commodity attitude toward the world reveals a theology which regards the world as a vale of tears to be endured to achieve heavenly bliss in a world to come. If we can reap some returns from the world in the meantime, so much the better. Therefore we profit, pleasure, and pollute.

Similarly, Douglas Daetz traces the problem to our attempt to have too much for too many.[66] Ian Carrick feels that scientific development has caught the Church and Christians unprepared. We have developed a theology of salvation in terms of personal relationship to God but not in terms of the natural order.[67]

[63] For an excellent bibliography, cf. Kenneth P. Alpers, "Starting Points for an Ecological Theology," *Dialog* 9 (1970) 226–35. Mention can also be made here of recent related work in the area of medical ethics. Cf. Donald Dial *et al.*, "Human Experimentation," *Duke Divinity School Review* 35 (1970) 47–63; Charles E. Curran, "Moral Theology and Genetics," *Cross Currents* 20 (1970) 64–82; Charles Curran, "Theology and Genetics: A Multi-faceted Dialogue," *Journal of Ecumenical Studies* 7 (1970) 61–89; Kenneth Vaux, "Cyborg, R.U. Human? Ethical Issues in Rebuilding Man," *Religion in Life* 39 (1970) 187–92; H. L. Smith, "Religious and Moral Aspects of Population Control," *ibid.*, 193–204; James M. Gustafson, "Basic Ethical Issues in the Biomedical Fields," *Soundings* 53 (1970) 151–80; J. G. Milhaven, "How Far Has God Shared His Dominion with Man?" *American Ecclesiastical Review* 162 (1970) 57–63; Sean Cahill, "Euthanasia: Problematic of Morality and Law," *Laurentianum* 11 (1970) 36–54, 154–88; Paul Ramsey, *Fabricated Man* (New Haven: Yale Univ. Press, 1970). The literature on abortion is simply too immense even to list here.

[64] Peter Riga, "Ecology and Theology" *Priest* 26 (1970) 16–21.

[65] J. Barrie Shepherd, "Theology for Ecology," *Catholic World* 211 (1970) 172–75.

[66] Douglas Daetz, "No More Business as Usual," *Dialog* 9 (1970) 171–75.

[67] Ian Carrick, "A Right Involvement with Nature," *Frontier* 13 (1970) 31–33.

The editors of *Triumph* state that the present disequilibrium is not physical but moral, and its human consequences are not primarily physical but moral.

We hear complaints of physical discomfort, but they are not convincing. Clevelanders who can no longer swim in Lake Erie have easy access to chlorinated pools. Smarting eyes, a cough, are occasionally annoying to Angelinos, but as between that physical pain and the pain of giving up automobiles, the choice is not even close. What really agitates contemporary America, what is really responsible for the ecology craze, is a psychic breakage, a brutal severance of those connections with reality, both natural and supernatural, which allow a man to be a man.[68]

The statement does not specify what these "connections" are.

Ian G. Barbour views the crisis as a result of attitudes toward nature and technology.[69] Where nature is concerned, man is portrayed as over against nature rather than as an integral part of it. Our technological mentality is thing-oriented rather than person-(or life-)oriented, a characteristic made visible, for example, in our Vietnam policy, where we use military power to solve social and political problems.

What lies behind these attitudes toward nature and man's relation to it? In a widely-quoted article published several years ago, Lynn White, Jr., had stated: "Both our present science and our present technology are so tinctured with orthodox Christian arrogance toward nature that no solution for our ecological crisis can be expected from them alone. Since the roots of our trouble are so largely religious, the remedy must also be essentially religious."[70] To what extent is "orthodox Christian arrogance" a justifiable term?[71]

James Megivern admits that popular renditions of Genesis have contributed to a gladiatorial concept of man's relation to the world.[72] But he then sets the record straight. "The God of the Bible makes abundantly clear by his own actions that to be lord does not mean to dominate, plunder, and destroy, but to foster, encourage, and bless." Megivern uses the Cain story as a parable for all time of man's sinful

---

[68] "Ecology: Whose Rebellion?" *Triumph* 5 (March, 1970) 41.

[69] Ian G. Barbour, "An Ecological Ethic," *Christian Century* 87 (1970) 1180–84.

[70] Lynn White, Jr., "The Historical Roots of Our Ecological Crisis," *Science* 155 (1967) 1203–7, at 1207.

[71] For some recent literature on the theology of progress, cf. Joseph Fuchs, S.J., "De progressu humano," *Periodica* 58 (1969) 613–39, translated in his *Human Values and Christian Morality*, pp. 178–203; Ivan Illich, "The Church, Change and Development," *Dialog* 9 (1970) 91–93; François Houtart, "The Church and Development," *Concurrence* 1 (1969) 176–83; Paul Surlis, "Transforming the World," *Furrow* 21 (1970) 227–41.

[72] James J. Megivern, "Ecology and the Bible," *Ecumenist* 8 (1970) 69–71.

mismanagement: when man destroys his brother, he pollutes the earth; when he pollutes the earth, he destroys his brother and himself.

Bruce Wrightsman's thoughtful article faults White on three scores: (1) he misinterprets Genesis; (2) the predominantly exploitative attitude ascribed to Western man is one-sided—there are at least three other major attitudes operative today; (3) a change in religious attitudes is a far too simple solution to the problem.[73] As for Genesis, Wrightsman points to the two strains in Genesis, one of which is stewardship. Dominion must be understood in terms of responsible stewardship. If the exploitative attitude is not supported by a correct exegesis of Genesis where did it originate? Wrightsman believes it may stem from "a distinction which is fundamentally incompatible with the Bible, but in whose terms the Bible has unfortunately been read for nearly 20 centuries." He refers to a kind of dualism between the celestial and terrestrial, the spiritual and material, which has deep roots in Plato and Aristotle.

Karlfried Froehlich rejects the charge that Christianity has any special complicity in the ecological crisis; for such a contention "does too much honor to the progressive spirit of Christianity in its ecclesiastical and philosophical manifestations."[74]

Frederick Elder's recent book *Crisis in Eden* sets up a dichotomy between "exclusionists" (who see man as separate from and elevated above the natural world) and "inclusionists" (who see man as an integral part of nature).[75] He claims that Christian tradition has been strongly exclusionist. Donald E. Gowan criticizes this dichotomy, especially as Elder attempts to bolster the desired inclusionist view with biblical evidence.[76] Genesis affirms both the lordship of man and his inescapable and intimate unity with nature. In this sense neither inclusionist nor exclusionist approaches are adequate. Gowan insists that the Bible is not at all damaging to our ecological concerns but could actually be the basis for a renovation of perspective.

Yes, the Bible says that man dominates nature, uses it for his own purposes *and has a right to do so*. But since man's well-being depends ultimately on the well-being of nature, he must use it responsibly and with respect for the natural order. But the biblical foundation for respect of the natural order is to be found in respect for man.

[73] Wrightsman, *art. cit.*, pp. 200–214.

[74] Karlfried Froehlich, "The Ecology of Creation," *Theology Today* 27 (1970) 263–76, at 269.

[75] Frederick Elder, *Crisis in Eden: A Religious Study of Man and Environment* (New York: Abingdon, 1970).

[76] Donald E. Gowan, "Genesis and Ecology: Does 'Subdue' Mean 'Plunder'?" *Christian Century* 87 (1970) 1188–91.

This intimate unity of man and nature is treated very well by Richard Leliaert, O.S.C.[77] Focusing on Rom 8:19–25, he points out that "the earth was made by God to share in man's present and future destiny. Man has a solidarity with his earth, yet in God's eyes he is also its steward." Ian Carrick stresses the same theme.[78] The relationship of man to his world is one of partnership. This delivers us from a theology which views nature as hostile, thereby undermining any coherent purpose for creation. Rather, man and world are to grow together, to be rescued together, to share a common destiny. "Resurrection is necessary for our understanding of the meaning and purpose of creation."

This quick overview gives some idea of how theological literature is identifying the problem. In general summary, it could be said that the current ecological problem reflects a distorted hierarchy of values ultimately rooted in a one-sided conquest conception of man's relationship to his world. An inaccurate popular accounting of Judeo-Christian sources may have involved Christendom in some measure of environmental guilt.

Proposed Solutions

The editors of the London *Tablet*, commenting on an ecological report of the Church of England's Board of Social Responsibility, stated: "The report is more precise in diagnosing the disease than in prescribing cures for it."[79] This is probably inevitable. If the problem is radically attitudinal, the solution is a change of attitudes. To comtemporary technological man, this kind of solution never appears very precise. Nevertheless, it is the substance of most conclusions in the current literature. For instance, John B. Cobb, Jr., of the Claremont School of Theology, is convinced that the ecological problem can only be met satisfactorily if we develop a perspective on nature which gives it a value in itself— "a concern for the subhuman world for its own sake."[80]

Kenneth P. Alpers believes that "the development of an adequate theological response to current environmental issues will not be found by beginning with deductions from Christian sources and dogmas, but by first looking at the complex nature of the environment itself. Unless we are listening we will not be heard."[81] Such listening will give us

---

[77] Richard Leliaert, O.S.C., "All Things Are Yours," *Homiletic and Pastoral Review* 70 (1970) 573–78.

[78] Carrick, *art. cit.*   [79] "Man and His World," *Tablet* 224 (1970) 122–23.

[80] John B. Cobb, Jr., "The Population Explosion and the Rights of the Subhuman World," *Idoc*, Sept. 12, 1970, pp. 41–62. The entire issue is devoted to ecology. Cf. also Cobb, "Ecological Disaster and the Church," *Christian Century* 87 (1970) 1185–87.

[81] Alpers, *art. cit.*

a context for reflection which Alpers calls "the ecological perspective." This perspective includes an awareness of the limits of the earth's resources, an understanding of the complex, dynamic, and interdependent character of the ecosystem.

Ian Barbour believes that recent religious thought provides trends which will build a theology in support of an ecological ethic.[82] These trends he sees as a new theology of nature built on process thought, a fresh awareness of man's unity with nature, and a sharper understanding that secular existence is the sphere of our religious responsibility.

J. Barrie Shepherd asks: Where do we get a new vision, how do we construct a new theology to meet the situation? Shepherd turns to Judeo-Christian sources in order to recapture the conviction that the world is not a dumb spectator but an active participant in the Fall and redemption.[83] Froehlich sees the root of the problem in human *hybris*, the limitless desire to dominate the world.[84] Therefore humility is needed, a humility which takes limits into its frame of reference. The Christian who knows the humble and sacrificial Lord should be the first to introduce humility and sacrifice into our relation to the world. Thus the contemporary asceticism must be ecological restraint. It will mean a radical reconsideration of all we formerly took for granted: the unchecked expansion of national economy, the right to have as many children as a couple desires, etc. This is the tone of much of the theological literature on ecology.

Naturally, a change in basic attitudes must eventually translate into concrete action. Froehlich referred to a "radical reconsideration of all we formerly took for granted." Concretely, not only must we husband and distribute our resources more carefully without compounding the pollution problem, but we must slow down or limit population growth. It is precisely here that the problem gets especially sticky, for at this point the word "coercion" begins to appear. Paul Ehrlich proposes to set up a powerful governmental agency, the Department of Population and Environment (DPE), whose task it would be to "take whatever steps are necessary to establish a reasonable population size in the United States and to put an end to the steady deterioration of our environment."[85] The University of California's Garrett Hardin reported to presidential counsel John Erlichman: "In the long run, voluntarism is insanity. The result will be continued uncontrolled population growth."[86] Gowan speaks of the "acceptance of unimagined controls on activities and groups."[87]

[82] Barbour, *art. cit.*   [83] Shepherd, *art. cit.*   [84] Froehlich, *art. cit.*

[85] Paul R. Ehrlich, *The Population Bomb* (New York: Ballantine, 1968) p. 138.

[86] Cited in Roger Shinn, "Population and the Dignity of Man," *Christian Century* 87 (1970) 442–48.

[87] Gowan, *art. cit.*

The basic human and moral issue here is relating national goals and priorities to individual freedom. Traditionally, the determination of family size has been regarded and guarded as a sacred personal right, a value of the highest priority. On the other hand, it has been argued that personal preferences in both developed and underdeveloped countries yield reproductive figures which to some ecological eyes spell disaster.[88] This alleged failure in individual ecological rationality constitutes a strong temptation for government to move in on the determination of family size.

The delicate relation of national planning to individual freedom needs a great deal more study. But one could hardly make a better start on the matter than with the reflections of Roger Shinn.[89] Shinn points out that the contemporary situation calls for revision of inherited values and ethical criteria. "The question is how the concern for life that created the ethic may today require its revision." Shinn is no bandwagoner; he is a careful and balanced ethicist. He sees that in revising the sense of his own relationship to nature and his fellow men, man is faced with the "most difficult ethical problem connected with population: the problem of human freedom." When Shinn relates this value to the urgency of population pressures, he walks his tightrope well— steady and down the middle between destructive coercion and destructive freedom. Between these two stark alternatives he finds room for economic pressures, prestige systems, taxation, skilfully contrived propaganda. Yet even these Shinn ultimately views as regrettable compromises. His finest paragraph could stand as an ethical charter in this entire matter. "In any crisis society qualifies personal rights, but part of ethical wisdom is to avoid crises that permit only destructive choices, and another part of wisdom is to maintain a maximum of human integrity even in crisis. Certainly any humane population policy will seek a maximum of free decision, a minimum of coercion."[90]

Shinn's essay is a loud and clear shout that the quality of life is a profoundly complex notion that defies reduction to a simple quantitative calculus. I believe that we Americans are peculiarly liable to miss this. *America*'s reminder that we are a pragmatic people is well taken.[91] We take the step forward and *then* think of the premium to be paid for progress. Isolated tactical decisions replace over-all human strategy. This is what the ecological crisis is all about. Our pragmatism leads us to short cuts. And, as *America* noted, "there is no call for pragmatic short-cuts when the value in balance is personal freedom. We can clean up our pollution. We may not be able to recover our liberty."

---

[88] Cf. Schueler, *art. cit.*, p. 294.   [89] Shinn, *art. cit.*   [90] *Ibid.*, p. 448.
[91] "Safeguarding the Quality of Life," *America* 122 (1970) 548.

Several Notable Contributions

This last consideration brings us to two articles on ecology which in my judgment are a considerable cut above the average. The first is by H. Paul Santmire of Wellesley College.[92] Santmire claims that America has ecological schizophrenia: we venerate nature (thus camping, sailing, surfing), yet we venerate the Gross National Product as the criterion of national health and virtue. How can we so intensely adore yet so violently abuse our land? Santmire seeks the answer in history.

In the nineteenth century the American mind was captivated by two apparently contradictory quasi-religious approaches to nature. The first Santmire refers to as "nature vs. civilization." In this approach the individual seeks deity, virtue, and vitality in communion with nature. But this seeking is accompanied by a negative element: a withdrawal from the organized city of man. Since God is found by the individual in communing alone with nature, it is permissible, even obligatory, to let the city stew in its sin. Thus Santmire can refer to this mentality as involving an "irresponsible political ethic of withdrawal." This cultural phenomenon was historically paralleled by several utopian religious groups who manifested dissatisfaction with the sociopolitical *status quo* by withdrawal. "In a word, the American passion for nature in the nineteenth century and beyond . . . was predicated on a flight from oppressive social realities to God in nature. Thereby that American passion functioned as an unconscious (if not conscious) force which undergirded an increasingly unjust status quo in the burgeoning industrial city of man."[93]

At the same time, however, another quasi-religious approach emerged. Santmire calls it "civilization vs. nature." The steam locomotive was a symbol of the economic forces and enthusiasm let loose at this time. We sang about it and its ability to leap rivers, grind rocks into powder, trample down hills. Ultimately, this view depicted nature as a "reality defined . . . by its openness to manipulation and exploitation."

It is Santmire's contention that these two quasi-religious approaches survive today. The religion of nature is present in our cult of the simple rustic life symbolized in the media by the enduring popularity of a thing like *Bonanza*. The religion of civilization survives in our cult of impulsive manipulation. By this latter Santmire refers to the idolization of technical reason: competence, know-how, expertise, efficiency,

---

[92] H. Paul Santmire, "Ecology and Schizophrenia: Historical Dimension of the American Crisis," *Dialog* 9 (1970) 175–92.

[93] *Ibid.*, p. 178.

"get the job done" are national virtues. We manipulate the environment without question. Here the symbol is *Mission Impossible*.

Summarily, Santimire contends that nature has been a dilemma for American society. We worship it, yet we exploit it. We work in the city while dreaming of the country; we work on the SST and live in ranch houses to escape the noise of the city. At a deeper level Santmire argues that, for some, nature functions as an escape from anxiety before an uncertain future; for others, it is a refuge from a decaying society. Both attitudes have the same rootage: a rejection by Americans of authentic life in history. This rejection is at the heart of our ecological problems.[94]

Santmire's study is a brilliant piece of social criticism and provides a context for understanding a host of things from beards and blue jeans to drugs, sun bathing, sexuality, hippie communes, and political styles.

The second article I wish to point up is that of Joseph Sittler of the University of Chicago Divinity School.[95] In effect, Sittler is attempting to analyze in theological terms what Santmire had uncovered by historical analysis. His theme is both simple and profound. All reality is itself ecological, that is, relational. Thus, the fundamental concepts of Scripture are relational terms: God, man, love, sin, hate, grace, covenant, restoration, redemption, salvation, faith, hope. Since all reality is relational, it must be viewed or beheld as such. Where nature is concerned, it must be viewed with ecological glasses, and therefore within the full splendor of its constitutive relationships. For the Christian, this means an "ecological understanding of man whose father is God *but whose sibling is the whole creation*." It is precisely a nonrelational or isolated view of nature which is behind our ecological problems. Therefore Sittler states that "this way of regarding things is an issue that the religious community has got to attend to before it gets to the more obvious moral, much less the procedural and pedagogical problems." He sees this way of regarding things as "the fundamental task of religious and theological responsibility in the ecological issue."[96]

Now the key area where post-Enlightenment man has failed to think

[94] Thomas S. Derr faults an underlying romanticized deism in much contemporary ecological literature, an attitude which "wants man to live in harmony with nature, on nature's given immutable terms." Cf. "Man against Nature," *Cross Currents* 20 (1970) 263–75.

[95] Joseph Sittler, "Ecological Commitment as Theological Responsibility," *Idoc*, Sept. 12, 1970, pp. 75–85.

[96] *Ibid.*, p. 79.

relationally is the area of creation and redemption. We have separated the two, or, as Sittler puts it, "we suppose that redemption is a historical drama which leaves untouched and has no meaning for and cannot be celebrated in terms of the care of creation." But this is not the case. Precisely because redemption cannot be thought of apart from creation, pollution of the earth (creation) is *Christianly* blasphemous. But our separation of creation and redemption—our nonecological theology, so to speak—allows us to act in this blasphemous way. What is called for is a recovery of the relationship of creation and redemption.

Sittler is saying equivalently that Santmire's "cult of the simple rustic life" and "cult of impulsive manipulation" can coexist in contemporary Western culture because we have wrenched redemption from creation. Once this separation is achieved, it is Christianly irrelevant whether we reverence or ravish the earth. In this sense, Sittler's paper is a plea for a genuinely Christian metaphysics. If we cling to our old categories and simply squeeze a few moral and procedural mandates from them, we will only be sweeping our contemporary filth under the rug. Furthermore, his paper suggests that unless we do get a genuinely Christian outlook anything we do is going to be an extension of the very separatism which has occasioned our problems and will simply exacerbate them. The efficient American mind will, of course, scarcely see this; it will roll up its technological sleeves, flex its muscles, and jump into the task—and simply add to the mess.[97]

Sittler has, I think, gotten to the heart of the matter: several centuries of nonrelational, nonecological thinking about creation-redemption. But whether optimism or pessimism is the proper reaction to his analysis is a good question. There are at least two reasons for pessimism. First, is there any realistic hope of unlocking the confusion of our corporate minds so that the creation-redemption continuity gets straightened out? The separatism that exists (and allows us to stride through the world with Olympian arrogance) is a product of many influences, was long in developing, has hardened into profound personal and social attitudes and values, and is reinforced by complex economic policies and structures. Denis Hayes has put the point in this way:

How do you eliminate the automobile from a society which posits the pretentious coat-of-arms of the Cadillac as its highest form of grandeur? How do you combat the vested billions of dollars in Detroit? How do you challenge the vested billions of dollars of the petroleum complex (especially after the

[97] For an interesting essay on how to go about making social decisions in a technological society, cf. Donald W. Shriver, Jr., "Technological Change and Multi-valued Choice," *Soundings* 53 (1970) 4–19.

opening of the Alaskan North Slope)? How do you fight something in which nearly every American family has a couple thousand dollars in vested interests, and whose advertising is a mainstay of American communications?[98]

How *do* you? A good question.

Secondly, the current ecological crisis is so utterly urgent that something drastic has to be done now. Does this not almost guarantee that what we will do will not be the product of Sittler's holistic attitude toward creation-redemption, but will proceed from the very attitudes which led to the crisis? If this is true, our present practical responses will represent a stopgap tidying-up of industrial procedures, good for a generation or two at most.

I think it would be a fair even if mini-statement of the theological dimensions of the ecological problem to say that man has a responsibility for his earth and through it for himself and his fellow men. The very first step in fulfilling this responsibility is establishing a correct attitude toward the relationship of man to the world. The unity of creation-redemption is central here. The second step is one of communication of this attitude. Both steps are moral concerns of the first magnitude. And the second step may even be the more difficult. Neither the scientific nor the theological community can undertake the process alone. Perhaps even together and in dialogue they will remain isolated and ineffective. But try they must. And that is why John E. T. Hough is right when he says that "scientists and theologians must learn together the humbling and noble art of listening and learning as members one of another and joint heirs of the advancing Kingdom of God."[99]

THEOLOGY AND DIVORCE

Melchite Archbishop Elias Zoghbi proposed to the fourth session of the Second Vatican Council that it consider a pastoral practice more closely resembling the *oikonomia* of the Eastern Churches where divorce and remarriage are concerned. "There is here," he stated, "an exegetical, canonical, and pastoral problem which cannot be ignored. It is a matter for the Church to decide on the opportuneness of admitting a new cause for dispensation analogous to those which she has introduced in virtue of the Petrine Privilege."[100] Since that time, there

---

[98] Denis Hayes, "Environmental Action," *Theology Today* 27 (1970) 256-62, at 260.

[99] John E. T. Hough, "Geneva Conference on Technology and the Future," *Christian Century* 87 (1970) 948-49. That such conversation is essential in the medical field also is clear from Walter G. Muelder's remarks in "The Identity and Dignity of Man," *Nexus* 13 (1970) 1-8, 26-29.

[100] *Civiltà cattolica* 4. 116 (1965) 603.

has been a good deal of writing on divorce and Zoghbi's intervention is often considered to be the stimulus for it.[101]

There are three distinct levels to the discussion, as Zoghbi indicates: the theology of marriage (especially its biblical sources), canonical practice, and pastoral attitudes toward the divorced and remarried. There is, of course, an inner unity and dependence of these three levels. What we say about marriage and its indissolubility will influence the shape of canonical practice and pastoral attitudes. Similarly, canonical and pastoral practice can influence the growth and integrity of doctrine. It is understandable, therefore, that much of the literature slides almost imperceptibly back and forth among the three dimensions of the problem and becomes in the process a bit difficult to review coherently. Central to all the literature, however, is an underlying notion of marriage. If that is kept in mind, perhaps some semblance of unity can be preserved here.

First, some literature with a more pronounced doctrinal emphasis. Several general review articles provide a "feel" for the direction of contemporary writing. W. J. O'Shea offers what appears to be a very competent summary presentation of the recent literature on the exceptive clauses of Matthew and the general biblical teaching on divorce.[102] O'Shea believes that the biblical evidence on divorce is ambiguous. "This ambiguity is confirmed: by the lack of unanimity on the question among the Fathers . . . ; by the wide variation found in the practice of the Christian Churches; and by the maze of interpretations proposed by biblical scholars. . . ."[103] As for a change in the teaching of the Church, he concludes that "the New Testament teaching is not so clear that it precludes the possibility of such a change."

Another fine critical review of recent literature is that of George Vass, S.J.[104] The article summarizes the recent work of Steininger, C. Duquoc, J. C. Margot, Moingt, Huizing, and Russo. Vass finds laudable points but deficiencies in nearly all these presentations. Indeed, he sees the stage of discussion we are presently in as a "fight between a not fully mature theology against an entrenched canonical

---

[101] A very thorough bibliography of the most important material can be found in William W. Bassett, "Divorce and Remarriage: The Catholic Search for a Pastoral Reconciliation," *American Ecclesiastical Review* 162 (1970) 100–105. The *Revue de droit canonique* 21 (March–Dec., 1971) arrived just as these Notes were going to press. It is totally devoted to the questions discussed in these pages.

[102] W. J. O'Shea, "Marriage and Divorce: The Biblical Evidence," *Australasian Catholic Record* 167 (1970) 89–109.

[103] *Art. cit.*, p 108.

[104] George Vass, S.J., "Divorce and Remarriage in the Light of Recent Publications," *Heythrop Journal* 11 (1970) 251–77.

practice." And there is no way to change the practice except by deepening the theology. As for pastoral practice, Vass is convinced that "remarried divorcees, under prudent conditions, should be admitted to the sacraments." We will return to this point shortly.

Wilfrid Harrington examines Jesus' teaching on divorce.[105] He argues that Jesus' teaching underwent modification in the living, everyday circumstances of the early Church. This modification of the "impossible ethic" surfaces in Matthew's tempering of the total prohibition of divorce as Mark and Luke record it. Harrington's reading of Matthew is, I take it, the rather standard "Protestant" view toward the exceptive clauses: they are redactional interpolations into the Gospel.

Harrington's presentation of the New Testament view of marriage is interesting. He contends that the Church has fixed more on the requirements against divorce than for marriage. If we had concentrated on the latter, many of our problems might be dissipated. In the New Testament, marriage is much more than consent vowed at one finalizing moment and then consummated by the first act of sexual intercourse. It is an ongoing commitment of man and woman to live a real life under changing circumstances. In this process real weaknesses and difficulties can enter and destroy a true marriage, so that it is dead. With this as background, Harrington concludes that "Jesus prohibited divorce and that prohibition is absolute. But he prohibited divorce under the assumption that the marriage involved is a true marriage."[106] Obviously, Harrington believes the Church can and should grant the right to remarry where a marriage is not a true marriage but is dead.

Peter McEniery turns to Trent's teaching on divorce.[107] His study concludes that Piet Fransen was correct in saying that Trent's statement did not involve a dogmatic definition. It was intended only to condemn the Reformers, especially the Lutheran attitude to the Church's canonical procedures.

John Noonan looks at indissolubility from the viewpoint of historical practice. His findings:

Looking at present papal practice it is evident that the scripture teaching "What God has joined together, let no man put asunder" is not taken literally or absolutely by the Roman curia. By the same token it appears that the natural indissolubility of marriage, so little regarded by the classic canon law and

---

[105] Wilfrid Harrington, "Jesus' Attitude toward Divorce," *Irish Theological Quarterly* 37 (1970) 199–209.

[106] *Art. cit.*, p. 209.

[107] P. McEniery, "Divorce at the Council of Trent," *Australasian Catholic Record* 167 (1970) 188–201.

some of its greatest commentators, and so recently asserted in polemic, is no longer the basis of papal action.[108]

Noonan's conclusion clearly raises the question: What is the basis of papal practice if it is not Scripture or natural indissolubility?

Denis O'Callaghan is concerned with a single question: Is divorce admissible?[109] He approaches the question first by studying the structure of marriage. This structure is really derived from an analysis of the overall human values which it serves. We conclude to what marriage is by examining the values it serves in the person, in the family, in the community. Moral responsibility means taking account of all the factors of moral significance in a given decision. However, decisions are sometimes unable to safeguard all values; they may have to subordinate one value to another. With this in mind, is divorce admissible? O'Callaghan believes that natural law does not outlaw *responsible* divorce, one which takes account of all the human values (personal, familial, social).

When he discusses the question in Christian perspective, his conclusions are very close to those of Harrington. For instance, the Christian community began to see the need for oaths as a guarantee of honesty and fidelity among sinful men, of self-defense for protection, etc. Why should divorce be excluded from this type of interpretation? The real danger in adapting Christ's radical teaching to men's limitations O'Callaghan finds in the possibility that men will begin to view divorce as a right, as something having merit in itself.

Canonist Jean Bernhard has written a fascinating and potentially very important article.[110] He espouses a modification of the notion of *ratum et consummatum* for two reasons. First, traditionally the indissolubility of a *ratum et consummatum* marriage has been argued by appeal to its symbolism. Such a marriage symbolizes the perfect and unbreakable union of Christ with His Church. However, Bernhard rightly wonders whether physical consummation is sufficient to realize in the most perfect manner the union of Christ with the Church. Obviously, physical consummation adds something to the merely moral

---

[108] John T. Noonan, Jr., "Indissolubility of Marriage and Natural Law," *American Journal of Jurisprudence* 14 (1969) 79–94, at 94. Cf. also Rudolph Weigand, "Unauflöslichkeit der Ehe und Eheauflösungen durch Päpste im 12. Jahrhundert," *Revue de droit canonique* 20 (1970) 44–64.

[109] Denis O'Callaghan, "Theology and Divorce," *Irish Theological Quarterly* 37 (1970) 210–222.

[110] Jean Bernhard, "A propos de l'indissolubilité du mariage chrétien," *Revue des sciences religieuses* 44 (1970) 49–62. He pursues the same point in "A propos de l'hypothèse concernant la notion de 'consummation existentielle' du mariage," *Revue de droit canonique* 20 (1970) 184–92.

(by consent) union. But just as the union of Christ with the Church transcends (while including) both the physical and the moral, so it cannot be excluded a priori that "consummation" would demand an element that transcends these categories.

His second argument is more telling. The standard understanding of *ratum et consummatum* is the result of an intervention by Alexander III to reconcile two divergent schools of thought. Gratian held that exchange of consents did not create the conjugal bond; for this, intercourse was also required. This appoach characterized the thought of the University of Bologna and through it filtered down to Roman practice. Peter Lombard (and the theologians at the University of Paris) taught, by contrast, that a nonconsummated marriage was absolutely indissoluble. Consent was seen as the efficient cause of the bond. Obviously, such a difference on a matter of great practical concern required an authoritative synthesis. Alexander III provided just this in stating that the formation of the bond occurred through a duality of modes: by both consent and sexual intercourse. But marriage concluded without intercourse was not absolutely indissoluble. This distinction led Alexander III to create the new juridical category of consummated marriage. However, the immediate practical purpose of Alexander's intervention led to oversight of the larger dimensions of the notion of consummation.

Bernhard levels several arguments against the one-sidedly physical understanding of consummation. But his strongest point is that the traditional notion of *ratum et consummatum* is not reconcilable with the doctrine of Vatican II on marriage. *Gaudium et spes* speaks of marriage as a "community of love" (n. 47), an "intimate union of their persons and their actions" (n. 48). This love, "by its generous activity, grows better and grows greater" (n. 49). And so on. Now if this is the object and finality of marriage, if this is what marriage is, it is difficult to see how the culminating point of its consummation is the first conjugal act.[111]

Pope Paul VI's *Renovationis causam*,[112] dealing with the renovation of formation for religious life, provides Bernhard with an analogy. In this document the Holy Father proposed a gradualism (whether by temporary vows or not) in preparing for the ultimate commitment of perpetual vows. Both the personalistic emphasis of Vatican II on mar-

---

[111] A similar point of view is taken by canonist Jacques Delanglade in "L'Indissolubilité du mariage," *Etudes*, Aug.–Sept., 1970, pp. 264–77. In his excellent article on marriage in *Sacramentum mundi*, W. Molinski, S.J., describes *matrimonium consummatum* as one which "reaches fulfillment in complete marital dedication" (3, 395). Cf. also Joseph Ratzinger, "Zur Theologie der Ehe," *Theologische Quartalschrift* 149 (1969) 53–74.

[112] *AAS* 61 (1969) 103–20.

riage and a gradualism with regard to the undertaking of definitive commitments lead Bernhard to believe that a revision of *ratum et consummatum* will occur. His view of the revision is as follows. Let those be admitted to sacramental marriage who are persons capable of giving true marriage consent and who are firmly decided to progress toward absolute indissolubility. The marriage will be considered consummated when the spouses have brought conjugal love to a certain human and Christian level, when they have established a fairly profound community life.

Bernhard recognizes the difficulty of translating these ideas into juridical terms. But he suggests some negative helps for determining nonconsummation: brevity of common life, infidelity from the beginning and during the whole of common life, difficulty of establishing an authentic conjugal, person-to-person relation, intolerance of common life. Perhaps even the definitive rupture of the marriage would provide a presumption of nonconsummation.

William W. Bassett has put together a thorough bibliography and excellent summary of recent trends on divorce and remarriage.[113] His study ranges farther and is better than Bernhard's very good one. Bassett distinguishes two questions: (1) Can the Church dissolve a consummated sacramental marriage? (2) Can the Catholic Church allow a second marriage while a former spouse is living? Bassett's response to the first question, after a careful overview of recent work, is that "recent studies have not proven this possibility." When he turns to the second question, his major concern is that the question be conceived as distinct and different from the first. In other words, if one says "yes, the Church can allow, in healing forgiveness, a second marriage," this need not mean the the first marriage is or can be dissolved. I believe Bassett leans to an affirmative answer himself, but at the point where one might expect his own clearly expressed opinion he turns to the notion of marriage itself and calls for "a deepening awareness of the central mystery of Christian marriage itself—a positive theology and a positive catechesis."

In discussing this positive theology, Bassett is extraordinarily good. In discovering what is a truly Christian (and "valid" in this sense) marriage, he points to four lines of study. First, there is the difference between marriage conceived as a lived relationship and as a legal contract. If marriage were freed from its narrowly legal conceptualizations and viewed as a lived relationship, the grounds of decision (about its validity) would be considerably broadened and evidential processes simplified. "We could more easily decide that there was no real Chrisitian

---

[113] Cf. n. 101 above.

marriage and so give freedom."

Secondly, Bassett turns to the notion of consummation and states a position very close to Bernhard's on broadening the concept of consummation so that it is "expressive of a human act, the psychological commitment and perfection of the marital bond." Thirdly, he discusses the very capacity to marry and brings contemporary psychological evidence to bear on the mental and emotional capacity to marry. Finally, he questions the identity of marital consent with sacramentality. Bassett concludes with a rather shocking and depressing picture of the state of tribunal procedures in the United States.

If one were to try to summarize the direction of contemporary Catholic writing on divorce, I believe it would not be inaccurate to say that two threads of thought are constantly present: (1) the absolute indissolubility of marriage as taught by Jesus; (2) the nearly universal admission in recent writings that certain unions *ratum et consummatum* in traditional terms never reach the truly Christian notion of marriage and hence fall outside the ideal of indissolubility. This literature is young and groping, depending as it often does on Vatican II's recovery of a more integral notion of marriage. Yet it is enormously important, not just in itself, but for our pastoral approach to the divorced and remarried.

The question of divorce and remarriage has also been approached from the viewpoint of pastoral practice, especially in terms of administration of the sacraments. Should those who are involved in a second marriage after a valid and sacramental first marriage be admitted to, or be encouraged to receive, the sacraments? If so, on what grounds? If not, why not? Several years ago in these Notes I stated: "It is not clear to me how anything but a negative answer to this [first] question is possible."[114] Recent literature is a chastening reminder that the matter is certainly more difficult and debatable than that sentence would indicate. Indeed, as will be clear, I would substantially modify that opinion. Since 1966, any number of theologians have reapproached the question and many have come to a different conclusion. Because the practical problem is frequent and urgent, because it unavoidably opens on the deeper doctrinal question, and because we stand to learn a great deal from continued discussion, the chance to reconsider the subject is a welcome opportunity.

Kevin T. Kelly has set up the problem very well.[115] He points out that pastoral practice could easily lead to "liturgical schizophrenia"—

---

[114] THEOLOGICAL STUDIES 27 (1966) 624.

[115] Kevin T. Kelly, "The Invalidly Married and Admission to the Sacraments," *Clergy Review* 55 (1970) 123–41, at 136–41.

a separation of sacraments from life. For the person whose first marriage was certainly valid and is now living in a stable second marriage, this second marriage is without doubt and existentially a part of this person's life. Kelly is right when he says that "simply to offer to give the sacraments without facing the problem of the Christian significance of this part of life would seem to be evading the issue." That is why moral writings have always focused on the status of this second marriage. Kelly notes that there are two general approaches:

The more traditional view would hold that this second union is "living in a state of sin" and hence must be given up. This view is slightly modernized by stressing the notion of growth in the moral life and so it would allow for the fact that the abandonment of this second marriage might take time. It would also cater for the "impossible situation" by offering the brother-sister alternative. The other view does not deny that the breakdown of the first marriage is at least objectively sinful and that, to the extent that this second union contributed to it, it too must be seen to be infected by sin and a legitimate object of repentance. But this second view would advocate a pastoral approach accommodated to man's frailty. Once the first marriage is dead and the second marriage is truly a "human marriage," this existing reality must now be recognized for the good thing it is—even though man's weakness and sinfulness might have played a part in its birth. It cannot be fully integrated into the witness of the Church's life because of the lack of fidelity it manifests. Nevertheless, it must not be seen as an evil thing to be given up but as a good thing to be cherished and developed, even though it lacks the full sacramental character of indissoluble Christian marriage.[116]

This is an extraordinarily accurate summary of two pastoral tendencies in recent literature. However, I think there is a third identifiable position. It is one which admits aspects of both of these positions, yet faces the pastoral problem of sacramental life in terms of what can broadly be called good faith. That is, reception of the sacraments (presuming absence of scandal) is argued on the grounds that the couple cannot accept evaluatively the fact that their second marriage is, in the eyes of the Church, an unholy alliance at root. Here I shall review some examples of the second and third positions in an attempt to focus the issues more sharply.

A good example of this third point of view (good faith) is the article by Innsbruck's H. B. Meyer.[117] In a rather difficult and ponderous essay, Meyer argues that the two possible reasons for excluding the

[116] Ibid., pp. 136–37.

[117] H. B. Meyer, "Können wiederverheiratete Geschiedene zu den Sarkamenten zugelassen werden?" Zeitschrift für katholische Theologie 49 (1969) 122–49. A good summary is found in Vass, art. cit., pp. 272–75.

divorced and remarried from the sacraments are not conclusive. First, there is their own subjective moral guilt about adultery. Here Meyer leans heavily on Rahner's distinction between objective "guilt" and subjective guilt, a distinction founded on the difference between theoretical and real morality. What is assented to as theoretically true does not necessarily permeate to the level of personal, evaluative realization. Concretely, the changed circumstances of collective morality concerning married life can have introduced a situation where individuals may be more or less habitually in a state of objective guilt without a corresponding subjective guilt. If this is the case with an individual couple, their state of conscience does not of itself prohibit reception of the sacraments.

The second reason for exclusion is the symbolic significance of reception of the sacraments. However, Meyer believes that just as it is morally proper to give the Eucharist to a separated brother at times, so too it is occasionally in place for the remarried to receive the sacraments. The central point of Meyer's argument seems to be the question of subjective guilt—and in this sense good faith.

Bernard Häring could be cited as another example of the third approach.[118] And yet, whether he really belongs here rather than in the second approach is not clear. His essay is vintage Häring, which is to say that it is characterized by obvious Christlike kindness and compassion, pastoral prudence, a shrewd sense of the direction of things, and a generous amount of haziness.[119] Häring allows for (secluso scandalo) the reception of the sacraments when a person is in a second marriage after a canonically valid Christian marriage. He does this on the grounds that these persons can be in genuine good faith, are truly repentant, and "make good the evil they have done as much as they can." By "good faith" Häring seems to envisage two distinct situations. First, under this title he includes the remarried couple who view their present marriage as "made in heaven," as a true marriage. Secondly, there is the couple who realize that their marriage was not and is not all right, yet are "convinced that God does not impose total continence on them while they have to live together and to educate their children."

It is not clear, however, to what extent the basis for Häring's conclusion is really the subjective good faith of the individuals; for in the course of his essay he raises a point which leaves the very status

118 B. Häring, "Internal Forum Solutions to Insoluble Marriage Cases," Jurist 30 (1970) 21–30.

119 Ladislas Orsy, S.J., says in the same issue (p. 6) of Häring's article: "If I read Fr. Häring correctly (and I am not sure of this)."

of the first and second marriages in considerable doubt, and to that extent one has to wonder whether he is basing his conclusion on this doubtful status rather than on good faith. Häring cautiously proposes as theoretically probable that marriage is "destroyed—more than by physical death—by mental death, by civil death (a lifelong condemnation to jail for a criminal) and by the total moral death of a marriage."[120] When a marriage is hopelessly dead or "thoroughly destroyed," Häring thinks that the Church might "tolerate a 'real' marriage, that is, a marriage that really can be lived." Here Häring is suggesting that a marriage which is thoroughly destroyed is not an existing marriage, is not a sacrament of God's presence among these two people.[121] He is further asserting, I would think, that a second marriage undertaken after such a "dead" marriage can be a sacrament of God's presence among these two people.

Probably a fair number of theologians would agree that Häring has accurately sniffed the direction of the winds of doctrinal development or, more accurately, pastoral practice. My only point, however, is that this opinion leads one to believe that the ultimate basis for encouraging reception of the Eucharist in Häring's thought is not the subjective good faith (though clearly this must be present) but rather an underlying judgment that when the first marriage is really dead, then the second, to that extent, is the true marriage. The notion of the "dead" marriage, especially if it means the Church's ability to tolerate a second "living" marriage, needs a great deal more study. It is, of course, at the very heart of the meaning of marriage and its indissolubility.

Now to some examples of the second approach. George Vass, S.J., provides a good example here. He is "convinced that remarried divorcees should be admitted to the sacraments."[122] Vass is a careful worker and realizes that it is not one's conclusion that is enlightening, but the reasons which led him there. How does he argue the point? Somewhat as follows. The Church, as protosacrament, is incarnate in our changing world, as the sacrament of marriage in the love of the Christian couple, as the sacrament of the Eucharist in the living unity of the faithful, etc. But this human love, this unity, inasmuch as it is human, can be frail and is capable of further development. It is the task of the sacraments to further this love and unity. Where divorcees are concerned, we must ask whether the second marriage can ever be

---

[120] Art. cit., p. 22.

[121] Häring said something similar in an interview in Der Spiegel 24 (April 6, 1970) 188–200.

[122] Art. cit., p. 277.

sacramental in the sense of symbolizing the union of Christ and the Church. Vass thinks it can.

The reason would be that the sacramental grace of marriage does not theologically speaking come from the fact that the individual partners are destined to a Communion with Christ, but rather from their mutual relationship in love. Since the human relationship in love of the first marriage has now ceased to exist and a new relationship is now taking place in the second, this new relationship in love can gradually become a human reality able to symbolize the significance of Christian marriage.[123]

Vass grants that this symbolizing cannot achieve fulness, since there was a former commitment before God and this commitment is not wiped out by admission to the Eucharist. But if it is "the historical relationship of love which is called to this act of symbolism, and not the static historical fact of a former engagement, then the new relationship can become a partial source of a sacramental grace."

Of the three participants in the very intriguing *Clergy Review* "Moral Forum," two definitely lean heavily in the direction of the second approach. James McManus, C.SS.R., puts great stress on the "marital state of mind." He says: "It is creative. In the couple themselves it creates true mutual love (something which may have been entirely lacking in their first marriage); it fosters in them true parental love for their children (they cannot see their children as the 'fruit of their sinful union'); it creates in fact a true human family in which life and love are fully shared."[124] McManus admits that serious sin may have been committed in contracting the second marriage, but he insists that "we can nevertheless accept the possibility of true interior conversion while realistically recognizing that a 'permanent situation,' i.e., a family, has been created and that this 'permanent situation' is not, nor can be changed by conversion."

In the same "Moral Forum" Henry Allard, S.C.J., argues that "human love and mutual attraction are matters which must have priority of consideration over our legal norms which then bring order into our human relationships."[125] Eventually he concludes that the sacraments should be administered to the divorced and remarried because "the relationship itself contains features which are similar to those of a marriage which is valid by law." Behind this conclusion is the distinction between what Allard calls an older and a more modern

[123] *Art. cit.*, p. 276.
[124] James McManus, C.SS.R., "The Invalidly Married and Admission to the Sacraments," *Clergy Review* 55 (1970) 123–31.
[125] Henry Allard, S.C.J., *ibid.*, pp. 450–53, at 452.

approach. "The modern approach would primarily consider the individual aspects of a relationship and test them on authenticity, honesty, and commitment. Instead of a uniform, essentialist conception of marriage, the modern approach prefers a pluriform conception."

The study of Leo Farley and Warren T. Reich, S.T., is a final example of the second approach.[126] The authors modestly offer what they term a "position paper." The position: in the present state of the question, reconciliation to full sacramental life is possible in certain cases for individuals involved in a second marriage after a first marriage certainly *ratum et consummatum*.

The heart of their presentation is in their assessment of the present marriage.[127] Here they make two points. First, they are speaking only of "deserving couples." Such couples, besides being sensitive to the inherent wrongness of divorce and desirous to participate in sacramental life, must fill this description:

Before their consciences and before God the couple truly consider themselves as married to each other, and intend to be faithful to each other. Thus, the present union appears to be both stable and enduring, and to be characterized by genuine love. The couple conduct themselves in a Christian manner; they are faithful to each other; they are generous in responding to the demands of conjugal intimacy; they are dedicated to their children and want to give them a good education; they are concerned about creating a true Christian atmosphere in their family.[128]

Secondly, the canonically invalid union of these deserving couples exists under the "sign of forgiveness." By this the authors mean that the marriage "was conceived in sin and would have remained under the power of sin but for the merciful forgiveness of God in Jesus Christ." What does the forgiveness of Christ do to the union? Of itself, the second marriage only memorializes the sin of divorce, all the more so the more successful the couple are in fashioning a true bond of love. But under the sign of forgiveness, it becomes "good and holy and salvific, for now it sounds the note of *repentance* for sin and thanksgiving for *redemption* from helplessness and hopelessness. Only in the light of Christ's merciful forgiveness can the original sin of divorce become a *felix culpa*."

[126] Leo C. Farley and Warren T. Reich, S.T., "Toward an Immediate Internal Forum Solution for Deserving Couples in Canonically Insoluble Marriage Cases," *Jurist* 30 (1970) 45–74.

[127] I say "heart" because the rest of their considerations are subordinate to this main point.

[128] *Art. cit.*, p. 52.

Farley and Reich emphasize that the repentance must be genuine and concrete. Therefore it must honor whatever demands continue from the first marriage (e.g., support of children) and it must view the first marriage as a "disclosure experience" from which the couple continues to learn.

This review will conclude with a few personal reflections. There are two instances where canonically invalid unions present problems which can be handled via the internal-forum route and where reception of the sacraments is not impossibly difficult to justify. The first is the situation where there is good reason to doubt that the first marriage was a valid Christian marriage, even though this fact cannot be established according to the criteria of present canonical jurisprudence. Anthony Kosnick has treated this situation in a thorough and balanced way.[129] The second situation is one of a previous *ratum et consummatum* marriage but where the parties are presently in good faith about their second marriage: they really believe that this, not their former marriage, is their true marriage. Though the matter could be extremely delicate in practice, Häring has handled this situation with admirable prudence.[130]

The really thorny instance is the case of the couple remarried after an apparently valid Christian marriage who sense that all was not and is not well with their present marriage. Whatever "good faith" they have is decidedly different from the second instance mentioned above. The couple believe that the first marriage was a genuine Christian marriage. They know it failed and they know about indissolubility. They know something is wrong with their present marriage. This is an extremely touchy matter, because it cannot be approached in terms of the standard understanding of good faith. Sincerity, repentance, marital mentality—all these, yes; but not total good faith about the present marriage. No one with a sense of realism, compassion, and his own limitations will feel complacent and secure in his reflections on this type of situation. It fairly bristles with problems.

The articles brought under review (Vass, Allard, McManus, Häring, Farley-Reich) have attempted to construct a pastoral approach by trying to reassess the present marriage. McManus stresses the marital mentality within it. Vass tries to establish its capacity to symbolize, even if imperfectly, Christ's union with the Church. Allard finds in it features similar to a marriage valid by law. Farley and Reich view it as a marriage under the sign of forgiveness. Helpful and enlightening as

---

[129] Anthony Kosnick, "The Pastoral Care of Those Involved in Canonically Invalid Marriages." *Jurist* 30 (1970) 31–44.

[130] *Art. cit.*

these attempts truly are, they are not without difficulties.

For instance, the weakness of Vass's position is that it is not merely the historical relation of love which is capable of symbolizing Christ's union with His Church, as he contends, but only a historical love relationship which begins with the capacity for and involves actual growth toward permanence and indissolubility. Otherwise, could not a whole succession of love relationships symbolize the *fidelity* of Christ to His Church? In the instance under discussion, either the first marriage had this capacity and was involved in this growth, or it did not. If it did not, one could argue (persuasively, I think) that it was hardly a marriage in any more than an empty legal sense. And the root problem of the second marriage disappears. If it did, however (and therefore inchoatively symbolized Christ's union with His Church), then to say that the second marriage can also be this symbol even if imperfectly fails to explain why a third and fourth union could not do the same. Is this not to begin to dissolve the very notion of Christ's fidelity to His Church? At least there is a problem here which Vass has not explored adequately.

The same difficulty could be urged in different terms against Allard's notion of a "pluriform approach" to marriage which judges the second union in terms of authenticity, honesty, committedness. What if the first marriage relationship was, at least for a time, authentic, honest, committed? And what if a third relationship becomes these things? Perhaps I have misunderstood Allard. This is easy to do in a short summary, especially where the problem is difficult and the discussion multifaceted. The same difficulty might be urged against Farley-Reich's second marriage "under the sign of forgiveness."

To say that there may be difficulties in these approaches is not to deny their value. Quite the contrary; they say something essential. It is to suggest only that they may be incomplete. I see their possible incompleteness as follows. Nearly all the authors reviewed have concentrated almost exclusive attention on the second marriage and its qualities (marital mentality, sign of forgiveness, symbolization of Christ's union with the Church).[131] This is very understandable, since the second marriage is an enormously important part of the lives of the individuals involved, and therefore the pastoral problem generally pre-

---

[131] I would add also the presence of children. Everybody writing on the subject supposes such a permanent situation with children. But what if there are no children? The man is simply in love with the woman, and the only reason preventing their breaking up is this fact. To my knowledge, no one addresses this point. The result of this neglect is that it is the presence or absence of children which seems to determine the *marital status* of the individuals, their sexual conduct, etc.

sents itself in terms of this second union. On the other hand, in doing this these authors have presumed that the first marriage is *ratum et consummatum* and hence insoluble. That is, they have accepted traditional theology and traditional legal categories in determining whether the first marriage was a true Christian marriage. Or so it seems to this reviewer.

Is is necessary to do this? I think not—not at least at the level of a general policy. The presumption which most accept in stating the problem can be challenged. It is here that the reflections of Bernhard and especially Bassett become very helpful. Given both the admitted immaturity of the theology of marriage and the inadequacy of existing law in embodying a fully Christian concept of marriage, it is at least quite possible, even probable, that the first marriage was not a truly Christian marriage in any more than a canonical sense.[132]

Concretely, if marriage is viewed as a lived relationship (rather than as a mere contract), if consummation is seen in fully human terms (rather than in exclusively physical ones), if capacity to marry is judged in the light of contemporary psychological evidence (rather than in terms of dated categories), there is substantial reason to believe that many of the first marriages under discussion may not have been true marriages at all. This may not be true of all instances, of course. But if it is true of some—and I would argue that this is very much a possibility—is this not enough for the establishment of a policy which refuses to unite canonical marital status with sacramental practice? I think so. In other words, an over-all policy-attitude allowing for the possibility of admission of divorcees to the sacraments need not imply any approval in principle of second marriages, for the simple reason that it need not be based on the supposition that two true marriages are involved. There are grounds for refusing to make or accept this supposition.

In summary, then, I am suggesting that the practical pastoral problems be approached not exclusively in terms of the qualities of the second union, important as these are, but also in terms of the possibly doubtful status of the first union. Such an approach would not unite in a sweeping and universal way canonical marital status with sacramental practice. Once such a policy-attitude were established, each individual case would demand individual attention from a confessor or

[132] This analysis is suggested, though it is far from explicit, in the theses proposed through Franz Böckle to a study group in Königstein, West Germany. The theses referred to the fact that many first marriages in contemporary circumstances really resemble "trial marriages." Cf. *Idoc*. June 13, 1970, pp. 48–52, at 50.

counselor.[133] At least this approach to the problem would seem to merit more attention than it has received, not least because it avoids the need to confront head on, at the policy level, the ancient tradition of indissolubility.

A commission appointed by Cardinal Koenig to consider the question of admitting divorcees to the Eucharist met in Vienna Feb. 4, 1970.[134] All the members agreed on the pastoral need of admitting some divorcees to the sacraments, but the theologians did not achieve a consensus on the moral and theological reasons for this conclusion. This is exactly the picture in recent literature as I read it.

Given the difficulty and delicacy of the problem, Koenig's move was a wise one. Therefore this review might well conclude with a suggestion: a similar commission should be appointed immediately in this country. Otherwise there is the danger that individuals will go their own way, solving difficult practical problems off shaky theological premises or destructive sentimentalism. If we do not rise above the insularity of our own reflections in this matter, grave harm can be done to the effectiveness of Christian witness and to countless individuals. Emphasis should be put on the theological reasons for the conclusions proposed. The very fact that prudent and informed theologians believe that some remarried divorcees should be able to receive the sacraments is good reason for leaning in this direction. However, the fact that these same theologians differ so much on their reasons means that it will be extremely difficult to educate the faithful in this area, a task of the utmost importance if scandal is to be avoided, as Häring has rightly emphasized. The commission should therefore study carefully the proper pastoral presentation of its conclusions, so that theological thought will live up to its pastoral responsibilities.

---

[133] Everyone underlines the need to individualize judgments when dealing with remarried divorcees. And rightly so; for there will certainly be instances, perhaps many, where remarried divorcees would themselves judge that they should not participate in the sacramental life of the community, or at least not frequently.

[134] Vass, art. cit., p. 275.

CURRENT THEOLOGY: 1971

NOTES ON MORAL THEOLOGY: APRIL–SEPTEMBER, 1971

The present six-month survey will focus on four principal themes; (1) norms and consequences; (2) norms, experience, and the behavioral sciences; (3) divorce and remarriage; (4) theology and liberation. In each of these areas the literature is enormous, and some of it is quite significant.

NORMS AND CONSEQUENCES

Christian man is a being of principles. For he always has experienced and always will experience the need both to manifest his faith in action and to communicate to others the implications of his faith convictions. But to manifest and communicate an experienced value means eventually to formulate it into a value judgment or norm. Clearly, overemphasis on norms can degenerate into a neolegalism at odds with the Christian idea. Nevertheless, when cultures resist norms or formulate them badly, they begin to wallow in a bed of moral marshmallows. So while morality cannot be reduced to decisions[1] and the norms which guide them, still moral norms play an important part in any life that hopes to remain human.[2] But if normative statements are to function constructively in human life, they must be properly understood and interpreted. This takes us to the heart of methodology in theological ethics as it relates to decision-making. Last year these "Notes" reviewed several important contributions to this question.[3] Here I should like to review at considerable length several articles which continue the discussion, particularly in terms of the key part played by consequences in the development of norms.

In another of his valuable and creative contributions, Bruno Schüller, S.J., discusses two understandings of moral norms and emphatically rejects the second.[4] Both appeal to what is "according to nature" but use the phrase in remarkably different ways. The first understanding

[1] On this matter see the thoughtful suggestions of Stanley Hauerwas, "Situation Ethics, Moral Notions and Moral Theology," *Irish Theological Quarterly* 38 (1971) 242-57. Also D. F. O'Callaghan, "The Meaning of Moral Principle," *Furrow* 22 (1971) 555-63.

[2] Using a Kantian model of norm (as universal), Roger Mehl somewhat overdraws the distinction between an ethic of norms and an ethic of values. Properly understood, the two (values, norms) are complementary, not competitive. See his "Universalité ou particularité du discours de la theologie morale," *Recherches de science religieuse* 59 (1971) 365-84.

[3] THEOLOGICAL STUDIES 32 (1971) 80-97.

[4] Bruno Schüller, S.J., "Typen ethischer Argumentation in der katholischen Moraltheologie," *Theologie und Philosophie* 45 (1970) 526-50.

can be summarized as follows. The good of man comprises several values, e.g., knowledge, health, wealth. Only one such value is an absolute value: man's "salvation" or his moral good; for in this good man realizes the sense of his existence. It is without exception that value which deserves preference. Therefore one who wishes to seek the good of another *never* has a justifiable reason to lead a person to act against his conscience. Other values are relative. Whether it is morally good to realize a relative value in or for another depends entirely on the relationship of this relative value to other concurring values. Therefore ethical norms which impose the realization of a certain relative value always include a built-in exception clause. They have binding force unless the value they impose competes in the situation with a value which is to be preferred. For example, the norm imposing the keeping of entrusted secrets should be understood as follows: one must keep the entrusted secret unless the only way to prevent a greater evil is to reveal the secret. Obviously, the meaning and binding force of norms concerned with relative values is being determined consequentially here.

Now when man acts in this way, he is, says Schüller, acting "according to his nature," because he is acting according to the judgment of his reason. In taking the *ordo bonorum* as the determining factor of his choosing, man makes reason the binding measure of his activity. Therefore to act "according to nature" is simply a synonym for to act "according to reason."

The second understanding of norms makes use of "according to nature" (and "contrary to nature") in an ambiguous sense and is therefore guilty of doubling the middle term of its argument. This form of argument has frequently been used in the past and had a prominent place in the debates before and after *Humanae vitae*. An example will help. "Every action contrary to nature is morally evil. But falsehood and contraception are contrary to nature. Therefore falsehood and contraception are morally evil." It is Schüller's point that "contrary to nature" has a different meaning in the major than in the minor. In the major it must mean and does mean "unreasonable." In the minor it can only mean a "relative disvalue," even though the argument intends it to mean more. If that is the case, then the argument is simply invalid; for it equivalently says that to cause a disvalue is unreasonable. The heart of Schüller's case is that falsehood and contraception (e.g.) are only relative disvalues, and whether it is unreasonable and immoral to cause them can only be determined by seeing what disvalues would occur if we did not cause them, i.e., by a consequentialist calculus.

Last year, after reviewing some of Schüller's work, the compositor of these "Notes" stated: "If Schüller's ultimate justification for causing or permitting physical harm is a preference-principle, it is not clear what role or importance the traditional notions of directness and indirectness play in his analysis."[5] Schüller has now turned his attention to this problem.[6] He points out that the direct-indirect distinction has been used in several areas: scandal, co-operation, killing, contraception. But it was used for a different reason where scandal and co-operation are involved than where killing and contraception are involved. Once we isolate this reason we will see the extent to which we can abandon the distinction, even though it will retain its descriptive function.

The sin of another, Schüller notes, is a moral evil and as such is an absolute disvalue. It would seem to follow that an action which has such a disvalue as a foreseen effect must be absolutely avoided. But this would lead to impossible consequences. No lawmaker, e.g., could attach a punishment to violation of law because he would know in advance that this would be the occasion of sinful bribery for a certain undetermined number of people. More fundamentally, it is hard to reconcile an absolute duty to avoid foreseen sin with the will of the Creator who created a being capable of sin. The way out of the dilemma has always been sought in distinguishing will, intention, and purpose from permission and toleration—or direct from indirect. The absolute disvalue of sin demands only that one not will and intend it under any circumstances. However, for a proportionate reason it may be permitted.

Schüller admits that there is something mysterious here but insists on the distinction where active scandal is concerned. But the reason the distinction is necessary is that we are dealing here with *moral* evil. The absoluteness of the disvalue forces some such distinction. However, where we are dealing with nonmoral evils (error, pain, sickness, death etc.), the reason for the distinction disappears precisely because these disvalues, fundamental as they may be, are relative disvalues. Concretely, sickness must be avoided but not at any price, not, e.g., at the price of plunging one's family into destitution. Schüller argues that when we justifiably cause a relative disvalue in our activity, we should not call it "indirect." Use of this traditional term flies in the face of the meaning of words. For instance, when one administers physical punishment to a refractory child from purely pedagogical motives, should we call the punishment and pain "indirect"? Hardly. Rather it has the character of a means and we speak of an intending will, a direct choice where means are concerned. We should not abandon this usage. Indeed, it brings out clearly the difference between the attitude to moral evil

[5] THEOLOGICAL STUDIES 32 (1971) 94.

[6] Bruno Schüller, S.J., "Direkte Tötung—indirekte Tötung," *Theologie und Philosophie* 47 (1972) forthcoming.

and nonmoral evil. For a proportionate reason we may *permit* a moral evil, but we may directly will and directly cause a nonmoral evil if there is a proportionate reason for doing so.

Schüller then turns to killing and contraception. Why did traditional theology feel it necessary to use "direct" and "indirect" when dealing with these subjects? It was because traditional theology viewed these actions as "evil *in se*." This can be sustained, however, only if the death of a person is an absolute evil in the sense of a moral evil. Once it is granted that the killing of an innocent person is the destruction of a fundamental but nonmoral value, there is no need for the distinction direct-indirect. Rather the assessment is made "teleologically," i.e., from consequences.

Schüller is correct, I believe. But the matter is of such practical importance that a rewording may not be out of place. Only if we study the origins of the terminology direct-indirect will we see to what extent it can be abandoned. It can be argued that its origins are in the value-conflicts inevitable in human choice. Whenever one chooses to do a good, he leaves another undone. Right reason tells us that we may choose to pursue this good of our neighbor only if it is at least as beneficial to him as the value we leave undone. This same analysis began to be applied also to the instance where human action caused a disvalue in a positive way, not simply by omission. Concretely, if some important value or good could be effected only by causing simultaneously some measure of harm, then that was judged morally proper if the good chosen was at least as important as the harm unavoidably caused. In other words, there was a proportionate reason for choosing the disvalue. The disvalue was not to be imputed to me precisely because it was unavoidable.[7]

Now what should not be imputed to one because it was humanly unavoidable does not enter his purposes and aims, or at least not in the same way as what is to be imputed. Therefore what should not be imputed to one should not be called voluntary, or at least not voluntary in the same way as disvalues which are to be imputed; for the moral order is properly the order of voluntary actions. This choice, as nonimputable, began to be called *indirecte voluntarium*. But it should be noted that "indirect" was (or should have been) first of all a way of saying that there was at least a proportion between the value pursued and the value left undone or the disvalue caused. It was not primarily a psychological analysis.

---

[7] If there was no truly proportionate good at stake, it was and is reasonable to conclude that the disvalues caused were avoidable, hence that they were chosen not as unavoidable means to a higher value but for themselves (*propter se*), hence that they entered and infected the agent's purposes and aims—and were direct *in that sense*.

However, in the course of time the term began to be interpreted in a psychological way.[8] It was natural, then, to associate it with certain forms of conduct that seemed to elicit this psychological intention. Thus eventually certain interventions into pregnancy came to be called direct killings and therefore illicit. That is, "direct" and "indirect" became terms which *decided* what actions are licit or illicit rather than terms used to summarize such a conclusion drawn on other grounds (presence or absence of proportionate reason).

In summary, if it is true to say that it is, above all, proportionate reason which gave rise to the terms "direct" and "indirect," it will be clear to what extent they can be abandoned. There is never any reason for choosing the sin of another in order to realize a "higher value," because there is no higher value. No good is greater for man than his moral good. Or negatively, sin is an absolute disvalue for man in light of which all other disvalues (e.g., sickness, poverty, death) are relative. Hence we may never choose and intend it as we may choose and intend other disvalues.[9] And yet we know that at times sin will occur on the occasion of our pursuit of the good of another. The terms "direct" and "indirect"—or their equivalent—when applied to scandal still seem to be morally relevant and utterly essential.

Joseph Fuchs, S.J., has written a lengthy study which appears to contain a significant shift in his methodology toward a morality of consequences.[10] As one would expect from Fuchs, the essay is a careful, subtle, ranging, and balanced piece of writing. There are times, however, when it is less than absolutely pellucid. Fuchs is primarily concerned to discover whether there are any concrete norms which are absolute, i.e., without exception. His key ideas can be distilled as follows.

First, he distinguishes premoral evil from moral evil and insists on the crucial nature of the distinction.[11] Killing, wounding, deceiving, sterilizing, etc. are premoral evils, not necessarily moral evils. "Whoever sets up negative norms, but regards exceptions as justified, by reason of overriding right, or warranted compromise, or for the sake of the lesser evil (or the greater good), shows by this that the *malum* repudiated by the norm is *not* (yet) to be understood as *moral* evil."[12]

---

[8] Cf. P. Knauer, S.J., "The Hermeneutic Function of the Principle of Double Effect," *Natural Law Forum* 12 (1967) 132–62.

[9] Thus it seems clear that direct and indirect are ultimately nonfunctional in Knauer's analysis.

[10] Joseph Fuchs, S.J., "The Absoluteness of Moral Terms," *Gregorianum* 52 (1971) 415–58.

[11] Fuchs uses "premoral" where Schüller had used "nonmoral."

[12] Fuchs, *art. cit.*, p. 443.

Secondly, Fuchs asks: when do these premoral evils become moral evils? Or—which is the same—when is human action or the man in his action morally evil? His answer: when he *"has in view and effects* a human non-good, an evil (non-value)—in the premoral sense, for example, death, wounding, wrong etc."[13] The next question clearly is this: when must one be said to "have in view and effect" premoral evil? The answer: when he causes it without proportionate reason. Thus Fuchs says:

 surgical operation is a health measure, its purpose is to cure, but it is at the same time the cause of an evil, namely wounding. This, however, appears to be justified in view of the desired cure and is capable of being incorporated in the *one human* act—a curative measure. The surgical operation is *morally* right, because the person acting desires and effects only a good—in the *pre*moral sense—namely, restoration of health. If the surgeon were to do more than was required in performing this operation, that "more" would not be justified by the treatment indicated; that is, it would be taken up *as an evil*—in the *pre*moral sense—into the surgeon's intention; it would be morally bad.[14]

Therefore for Fuchs premoral evil caused becomes moral evil when it is "taken up as an evil into one's intention." This happens when there is no proportionate reason for causing the premoral evil.

Obviously, then, intention has a great deal to say about the moral quality of an act. Indeed, Fuchs says that the moral quality of an act cannot be determined without reference to the intention. And in this sense he qualifies the traditional understanding of object, end, circumstances. Traditional moralists said that certain actions were morally evil *ex objecto* in the sense that no good intention could purify them. The basic morality of such acts was determined by the object. Fuchs says, in contrast, that "a moral judgment of an action may not be made in anticipation of the agent's intention, since it would not be the judgment of a 'human' act."[15] In other words, the object must be taken with the intention before the meaning of the action, its true moral character, can be stated. In light of this Fuchs asks:

What value do our norms have with respect to the morality of the action as such, prior, that is, to the consideration of the circumstances and intention? We answer: they cannot be moral norms unless circumstances and intention are taken into account. They can be considered as moral norms only because we

[13] *Ibid.*, p. 444.
[14] *Ibid.*
[15] To what extent this departs from the traditional understanding is not altogether clear. That depends on how many circumstances traditional moralists allowed to enter the statement of the *objectum* and how many Fuchs excludes.

tacitly assume to judge the action in the light of possible circumstances and intention.[16]

However, since this tacit advance judgment is theoretically impossible, we cannot rule out the possibility that in practice there will be an exceptional instance. Therefore, when treating of the traditional notion of intrinsic evil, Fuchs notes: "Viewed theoretically, there seems to be no possibility of norms of this kind for human action in the inner-worldly realm." For a behavioral norm universally valid would presuppose that those who arrive at it "could know or foresee adequately *all the possible combinations* of the action concerned with circumstances and intentions, with (premoral) values and non-values."

Even though there can be no theoretically exceptionless norms of behavior, Fuchs sees a genuine practical worth in norms properly formulated as universals. First, they do point out values and disvalues. Secondly, certain norms can be stated as universals "to which we cannot conceive of any kind of exception; e.g., cruel treatment of a child which is of no benefit to the child." Thirdly, in a specific culture or society universal norms can develop which "suffice for ordinary use in practical living." However, the existence and validity of such norms does not mean that we are exempt from rethinking them. Such rethinking is warranted where faulty evaluations in the past generated faulty norms or where a norm grew out of a culturally conditioned situation which no longer obtains. In this latter case moral reformulation is not only conceivable but demanded.

Fuch's debt to Knauer and Schüller is obvious and acknowledged. Because I agree with so much of what he says, it might be helpful to indicate some remaining areas of unclarity.

First, because Fuchs has followed Knauer so closely, the question of what he means by "intending" premoral evil arises, much as it did with Knauer. Knauer, it will be recalled, proposed that when there is a commensurate reason for causing premoral disvalue, the evil is *indirectly* willed. When there is no commensurate reason, the evil caused is *directly* willed. As noted above, Schüller has rightly challenged the usefulness of this terminology. Fuchs states that when there is no proportionate reason, the premoral evil caused "would be taken up *as an evil.*" He also says that premoral evil must not be "intended as such." Is "intending evil as such" equivalent to direct intent? Fuchs nowhere says this, but his heavy reliance on Knauer leads me to raise the question. Would it not be clearer and more precise to say that it is legitimate to intend premoral evil *in ordine ad finem proportionatum*? I may

[16] *Ibid.*, p. 446.

choose and intend the pain of a child or a patient if it is the only way or the most reasonable way to secure his greater good. This "greater good" (proportionate reason) does not mean that the premoral disvalue is not intended; it means that it is not intended *propter se*. Therefore would it not be better to say that it is legitimate to intend a disvalue *in se sed non propter se*? When there is no proportionate reason, the disvalue caused is chosen and intended *in se et propter se*, and it is this *propter se* which makes the act immoral. I believe this is what Fuchs means by "intending evil *as such*," but his occasional use of the simple and unqualified word "intend" leaves the matter a bit murky.

The second question raised by Fuchs's analysis is closely connected with the first. It is also a question Knauer did not face satisfactorily. In treating premoral evil (wounding, deceiving, killing), Fuchs insists in the examples he gives that the evil or disvalue is not an isolated action "but only an element of the one act." Thus he notes: "In the *one* human action (health care, transplant) the performing of the evil is not an isolated (human) action, but only an element of the one action. Therefore, a morally bad (human) action is not being used as a means to a good end."[17] The evil is justified because it "is capable of being incorporated in the *one human* act—a curative measure." The example of surgery serves Fuchs well, for obviously the harm (or "wound") is part and parcel of the one healing act or process.

Yet, if I understand Fuchs correctly, there is some unclarity here. There are two elements Fuchs appeals to in justifying the doing of premoral evil: proportionate reason and the fact that the evil is simply an element of one human action. What does it mean to say that the evil must be "incorporated in the *one* human act"? Does he mean to say that every time there is a proportionate reason, the act is really one by reason of the intent of this good, and therefore the evil caused is really only an element of one human action? Or does he mean that first we must discover whether there is in human terms one single action (as, e.g., in surgery) into which the premoral evil is "capable of being incorporated"? If Fuchs means the first alternative, it would seem that he is pushing language too far; for if an action is truly one human action, it is realistically describable as such. Thus we can say realistically that a leg amputation is a "healing action." If, however, the intended effect does not allow one to redescribe the action in terms of this effect, then are we still dealing with a single human action? If so, in what sense? Not all actions with good consequences are describable in terms of the intended results—a point Paul Ramsey has made very sharply.[18] And

[17] *Ibid.*

[18] Paul Ramsey, *Deeds and Rules in Christian Ethics* (New York: Scribner's, 1967) p. 196.

when they cannot be so redescribed, can we really speak of the premoral evil caused and chosen as only an element in *one human action*? Or if we do, what does this mean? The earlier analysis of Knauer never got off this reef.

Take the now classic case of Mrs. Bergmeier. Can her extramarital intercourse and subsequent pregnancy (whereby she was able to achieve her release from a Soviet concentration camp) be said to be simply an element of one human action describable as "bringing her family happiness"? Can it be called this simply because this is her ultimate intent? Hardly, I should think. Not only does this stretch human language beyond its limits, but it ignores all the other possible or probable consequences and describes this act in terms of just one. Rather it seems we should say that she performed one human action (extramarital intercourse) which had, among other effects, the intended good consequence of bringing her to her family. If this is a correct rendering of the example, what does it mean to say that premoral evil must be only an element of "one human action"? The example of surgery is a bit too simple; for in surgery the very same physical act which amputates also removes a threat to life. Obviously the healing intent is present, but it is not precisely this intent which makes the amputation one human action.

Therefore how far is Fuchs willing to stretch this example? I am not sure what he would say to the case of Mrs. Bergmeier; but if the ultimate justification is that the premoral disvalues must be an element of "one human action," then this one human action should be describable in terms of the intended value—much as amputation can legitimately be called a "curative procedure." Perhaps Fuchs's insistence that the premoral evil be incorporated into the one act overstates the requirements a bit. However this may be, such insistence either (1) very sharply limits the premoral evils one may cause in the pursuit of good or (2) expands the notion of "one human action" to the point where human language will no longer sustain the unity.

The third reflection constitutes a matter of emphasis. In treating the notion of intrinsic evil, Fuchs rightly claims that theoretically "there seems no possibility of norms of this kind for human action in the inner-worldly realm." He refers to *behavioral* norms—i.e., norms which take a materially described action (killing) and say of it that it is always unjust. The reason for this: an action cannot be judged apart from circumstances and intention. This seems certainly correct, but three reflections are called for.

First, it must be said that the theological problem only begins here. For instance, a prohibitive behavioral norm (e.g., against killing) is based on the perception of the value of human life and the disvalue of taking human life. Where exceptions are concerned, the real problem is to show that there are higher values involved, and what they might be. Fuchs admits this clearly when he says: "Hence the attempt on the part of moral theology to discover which values realizable in this world can justify 'killing' and which cannot."[19] Circumstances and intention justify exceptions only when they are concerned with higher, nonpostponable values. If we moralists seriously propose exceptions as possible (and they are), our most basic task is to discover those values which do and do not justify causing the disvalue. Unless we do so, are we not inviting people to except themselves without providing any hierarchy which would make such a decision rational, and therefore promotive of greater humanization? The point is emphasized here because recent literature has understandably been concerned with the fact of exceptions, while it has almost never treated the extremely difficult and unfinished task of describing the kinds of values which alone make the causing of disvalues reasonable.

A second point. While it is true that it is impossible to foresee all the possible combinations of concurring values and disvalues (circumstances and intention), still through experience and reflection it is possible to foresee at least very many of them. Therefore Fuchs is certainly correct when he says of concrete behavioral norms that "they suffice for ordinary use in practical living." They "suffice" because they include the ordinary circumstances in practical living. This is the same as saying that the significance of the action (drawn from object and ordinary circumstances) is ordinarily clear. And this in its turn is the same as saying that *ordinarily* a person will achieve the greater good by following the norm, because it incarnates the greater good. Negatively stated, this means that one who makes an exception of himself has the burden of proof that his case is truly exceptional.

Thirdly, Fuchs does admit "norms stated as universals . . . to which we cannot conceive of any kind of exception." In this sense I suppose he is admitting a kind of "relative absolute."[20] But his example is "cruel treatment of a child which is of no benefit to the child." One could and should argue that cruel treatment of a child (or anyone) is never permissible, although a treatment which visits hurt, harm, or deprivation on someone need not be cruel. Here Fuchs has introduced a formal element (cruel) into the description; this makes his example a very poor one.

[19] *Ibid.*, p. 450. Cf. also Franz Böckle, "La morale fondamentale," *Recherches de science religieuse* 59 (1971) 331-64, at 358.

[20] On this point cf. David Blanchfield, "Balancing in Moral Theology," *American Ecclesiastical Review* 164 (1971) 90-96.

A final observation. Fuchs has obviously taken a rather giant step in the direction of a consequentialist methodology. But how far this stride takes him is not altogether clear. In discussing the formation of concrete moral norms, he mentions that the significance of an action is a prime criterion. He then continues: "It is not only the 'meaning' itself of experienced realities that constitutes a criterion for the evaluating *ratio*, but also practical knowledge of the outcomes and consequences which determined modes of conduct can have. . . ."[21]

Here Fuchs seems to contrast meaning and practical knowledge of consequences. Actually these should not be contrasted in this way; for the very "meaning" of an action can only be gathered when all aspects of the action, especially its consequences, have been weighed as far as possible. The fact that Fuchs contrasts meaning and consequences implies that he is willing to speak of the meaning of an action apart from its consequences. This raises the question of just what importance he does want to attribute to consequences. The matter remains obscure.

Charles Curran rejects a morality of consequences (the so-called "teleological" model) as proposed by John G. Milhaven, i.e., one built on the same model which functions in the empirical sciences.[22] His concern is to show that a model adequate for judging the empirical sciences is not necessarily adequate for judging Christian morality. That is certainly true. But need a teleological model evoke the technological model wherein all things are means for "man the artisan"? That is not clear. To indicate that a consequentialist model is insufficient, Curran appeals to the just-war theory. This theory maintains not only the principle of proportionality, where consequences play the decisive role, but also of discrimination, "which forbids the direct killing of innocents whatever the consequences."

Here one must ask, I believe, whether the principle of discrimination, rather than being in contrast to a consequentialist analysis, is not itself possibly a conclusion of such an analysis. Its meaning then would be: we can conceive of no proportionate reason for killing innocent people even during war. Behind such statements would be the conviction that even though certain short-term military advantages (in terms of saving lives) would possibly follow from killing the innocent, still the results in the long run would be more humanly disastrous and destructive. This is a possible rendering of the principle of discrimination and it is obviously consequentialist in character.

Putting the matter another way, Knauer–Fuchs–Schüller would have

[21] Fuchs, *art. cit.*, p. 435.

[22] Charles Curran, "La théologie morale et les sciences," *Recherches de science religieuse* 59 (1971) 419–48.

to say that the principles of proportionality and discrimination are really a single principle—much as Knauer has argued that the principle of totality in medical matters is really identical with the principle of double effect.

The two arguments Curran brings elsewhere against consequentialism do not seem decisive. They are: "No one can know beforehand all the consequences of his action, and there always remains the problem of appraising the hierarchical importance of the various consequences involved."[23] These are formidable difficulties, of course, but they only point up the imperfect character of human norms, the need for careful homework and Christian sensitivity in working out a hierarchy of values within which one makes value judgments, the need for tentativeness, and the abiding readiness to admit a mistake and backtrack. Our norms are perhaps much more norms of responsibility than of morality.

Nicholas Crotty, C.P., in the course of a long study on conflict situations, exposes his methodology on rules and decision-making.[24] Since his original study appeared in this journal, a brief précis will suffice to recall the substance of his ideas. Crotty faults the manualists for a method and world view which denied the possibility of a conflict of moral values. For them, "moral value and moral disvalue consist respectively in the conformity and difformity of the moral agent's will with the perfectly ordered demands of natural law." Crotty agrees with many contemporary theologians that there are genuine conflict situations. These arise not only because of human limitations but because of the sinfulness of the world. Therefore "we need to be repentant not only of the sinfulness we bring to our conflict situations but of the very existence of these situations and the confusion, clash, and incompatibility of the moral values in any given response to them."[25] Crotty then takes issue with those who would say that in such a world an act is "quite simply morally good" even though it involves the causing of disvalues. A love-centered ethic cannot tolerate this. Rather its prime concern will be "the actual implications and consequences of our behavior for human persons and human fellowship," for its supreme norm is the "actual, concrete welfare of others."

In light of this Crotty rejects the distinction between direct and indirect as morally irrelevant. What is morally relevant is that a harmful effect occurs or does not occur, not whether it occurs *per accidens* or

[23] Charles Curran, *Contemporary Problems in Moral Theology* (Notre Dame: Fides, 1970) p. 25.

[24] Nicholas Crotty, C.P., "Conscience and Conflict," THEOLOGICAL STUDIES 32 (1971) 208–32.

[25] *Ibid.*, p. 215.

per se with relation to my activity. After all, it matters little to the enemy whether he expires as a result of my direct or indirect activity. Therefore the "justification or nonjustification must stem from an appreciation and assessment of all the values and disvalues in the total consequences of the behavior under consideration... regardless of how they relate physically to the good we are expressly intending."

In view of this consequentialism Crotty insists that on the level of concrete, specific actions there are no actions intrinsically evil, hence no moral absolutes at this level. That is, any action can *in principle* be the most loving response in a given situation. Our moral rules, therefore, are empirical generalizations, rules of thumb that arose out of the observation of a number of instances and are applicable only when the same values and disvalues are implicated in a way that is not significantly different. Therefore, in final analysis, decision-making "will be a matter of assessing all the moral good and all the moral evil implicated in each of the options available as feasible responses to one's situation and of electing and following out that alternative which appears most favorable to human welfare."[26]

Crotty's piece has packaged a good deal of the contemporary discussion about norms in a way that is interesting and challenging, though not always free of caricature. Because I agree with the substance of Crotty's approach, it is all the more important to suggest some areas where a continuous exchange might hope to bring greater clarity.

1) *Use of the term "moral."* Throughout the article Crotty refers to the exclusion of values or the causing of disvalues as "moral evil." Thus, he says: "Where these implications and consequences are detrimental to persons and community, the behavior is to that extent morally evil behavior. The evil implications and consequences may be unavoidable.... But they are there and morally they are evil."[27] The obvious consequence of this usage—and one Crotty accepts—is that such morally evil consequences "need to be recognized and deplored in true Christian repentance." However, he notes that this repentance "will mean something different from the repentance we should have for moral evil that clearly flows from our own deliberate activity."

Crotty contrasts this position with the manualist usage. In this latter view, when harmful effects occur as the result of our activity (e.g., the death of another), they are not moral disvalues but simply "physical evils." Crotty seems to understand this as the rough equivalent of "not really humanly important." In my opinion this is certainly not what traditional theologians meant. True, the term "physical evil" is not the

---

[26] *Ibid.*, p. 231.
[27] *Ibid.*, p. 219.

best term for the unavoidable disvalues our actions or omissions produce at times. For one thing, it too easily restricts the notion to tangible and material harm. Secondly, it can indeed carry the aroma of "not really important," especially to those who rightly see man's moral good as his absolute value.

But the term "moral evil" is, if anything, worse yet. First of all, it is at least confusing to speak of human disvalues such as death, suffering, poverty—regardless of how they are caused—as *moral* evil; for the word "moral," while analogous, has always referred to the sphere of voluntariety, and more narrowly to the sphere of human freedom and responsibility. When we sever this relationship, we get into the absurd position of having to talk about events as moral which have no relationship to moral beings and their activity. Fuchs and Schüller have made this clear.

Secondly, I believe the usage is dangerous; for ıı the term "moral" is used of unavoidable disvalues, we are getting perilously close to a Protestant tradition of unavoidable sin. This danger is suggested by Crotty's call for repentance where human acts have caused unavoidable human disvalues, even though he distinguishes the notion from genuine repentance. Schüller and Trigg have recently insisted on the essential difference between true repentance and regret at causing human disvalues through our activity.[28] Furthermore they believe this profound difference should manifest itself in our language. I believe they are right. If there is such an essential difference in these two reactions, then there is certainly an essential difference in the human activity which gives rise to them and this difference should also manifest itself in our language. But to refer to human disvalues as "moral evil" whether they are avoidable or not is to neglect this distinction and plant the seed of confusion, perhaps even of false consciences.

2) *Direct and indirect intent.* Crotty's use ɔɪ the term "moral" is possibly responsible for another imprecision. He rejects the notion of direct and indirect as morally irrelevant: "There is no ethical significance in the distinction, so basic to the manualist approach, between evil that is *directe voluntarium* and *indirecte voluntarium tantum....*"[29] What he is after here is clear. Crotty is rejecting an understanding of direct-indirect which says that a disvalue directly caused is one which is therefore directly intended, and thereby part of our purpose or aim. In this I believe he is correct. The terms "direct-indirect" have gotten almost identified with physical causality and therefore with certain

[28] Bruno Schüller, S.J., "Zur Rede von der radikalen sittlichen Forderung," *Theologie und Philosophie* 46 (1971) 321–41, at 338 ff.; Roger Trigg, "Moral Conflict," *Mind* 80 (1971) 41–55.

[29] Crotty, *art. cit.*, p. 231.

concrete actions. But Crotty has rejected not only this distorted understanding but also "any ethical significance in the distinction." That this goes too far seem clear from Schüller's study noted above. Some such distinction is truly essential where scandal (involving the *sin* of another) is involved. But since Crotty does not distinguish moral disvalue from nonmoral or premoral disvalue, he can establish no difference between choosing someone's sin and choosing his physical hurt.

3) *The meaning of actions*. In his discussion of moral norms, Crotty proposed that at the level of concrete specific actions there are no absolutes, simply because at this level "actions ... cannot be judged ethically without a reading of the situation in which they occur and of its demands in terms of Christian love." This is true, I believe, if it is carefully understood. In some earlier writings which commented on Joseph Fletcher, I had written the following:

> I am suggesting that human sexual intercourse has a sense and meaning prior to the individual purpose of those who engage in it, a significance which is part of their situation whether or not the partners turn their minds to it. It is an act of love, and therefore has a definitiion which relates it immediately to the love of man and woman—with all the demands of this love.[30]

This appears to cross swords with Crotty's statement about absolutes. And so he criticizes it as attributing to an action "significance independently of the human context in which it occurs." The statement, he contends, speaks of "sexual intercourse as such," which is to speak of mere physical behavior and give it a meaning. Rather, he notes, "we cannot say that sexual intercourse has, in itself as a physical act, a meaning that can be honored only in marriage," which means that "any argument against premarital sex cannot take its starting point from the nature of coitus."

We are faced here with an extremely interesting methodological point and it would be fruitful to pursue it. Those who speak of sexual intercourse (which is only an example) as having a meaning "prior to the individual purposes of those who engage in it" are not attributing a human meaning to an act described merely physically or in abstraction from its situation. What they are doing is supposing an underlying value judgment and formulating it in this way. Perhaps we could put the matter as follows. It has been and still is common to refer to sexual intercourse as "the marital act." There is here a hidden value judgment: this action ought to be restricted to the marriage relationship. The same is true of the usage "human sexual intercourse has a sense and

---

[30] "Human Significance and Christian Significance," in *Norm and Context in Christian Ethics*, ed. Paul Ramsey and G. Outka (New York: Scribner's, 1968) p. 619.

meaning etc." What this really *au fond* says—or better, supposes—is that this action *should be* restricted to those who are in the relationship we know as marriage. This is the meaning of those who speak this way. If the underlying value judgment is correct, then it is quite proper to speak of "the marital act" and it is proper to say that "intercourse has a meaning etc."

How legitimate is the underlying value judgment? That can, of course, be questioned. One who questions it immediately raises the more interesting methodological question: how was this judgment derived? It seems that it is the conclusion of long experience and reflection, especially about consequences. In other words, the experience of centuries has led us to conclude that unless this type of intimacy is restricted to the marriage relationship, the integrity of sexual language will be seriously threatened. Such a judgment is clearly a form of consequentialism. "What would happen if ...?" It is precisely here that a consequentialist methodology appears to me absolutely correct. We are concerned with what is promotive or destructive of human welfare and we judge this by observing and reflecting on the effects of conduct on this welfare. But once it becomes clear from experience that the continuing viability of sexual language calls for the permanent and exclusive relationship of marriage, I think it is legitimate to speak of "the marital act" in this value-laden sense, i.e., this act should be restricted to marriage. And in so far as one can speak this way, he can also speak of the "nature of sexual intercourse." It can even be said that "it has a meaning etc.," providing we understand the roots of this judgment. This is all that is (or should be) meant by such usage.

This analysis leads to two additional reflections. First, traditional theologians over the past centuries were more consequentialist than their language at times would indicate. For instance, the standard approach to theft ("taking another's property *against his reasonable will*") is an approach which could have been refined in this way only by considering consequences. Similarly the whole treatment of excusing causes shows a sensitivity to the conflict of values, hence of consequences involved in formulating moral obligations. Consequentialist suppositions are so pervasive by implication in traditional treatises that the real question is why these suppositions were apparently resisted in the treatises touching innocent life and sexuality. In these areas we encounter concrete pieces of conduct one may never do regardless of the consequences. Perhaps it was because these are matters of great public concern. Perhaps it was the form of argument used—e.g., *ex defectu juris* where killing is concerned, as Schüller notes.[31] At any

---

[31] Cf. n. 6 above.

rate, it is true that traditional treatises were often only apparently more deductive (or deontological) than contemporary theologians.

Secondly, when one speaks of "the marital act" or (which is the same thing) when one attributes a sense to sexual intercourse, it must be understood that such value-laden language represents a cultural judgment; i.e., this normative judgment has been concluded from experience within a culture over the centuries. That is only to say that our sexuality, like everything else about us, is given to us by our culture. In this sense the meaning of our sexuality is indeed independent of our free choice. It would be as absurd to think we could live a Neanderthal sexuality as one proper to the year 5000 A.D. We cannot simply endow sexuality with any meaning we care to. To accept this fact is not to indulge in "merely physical descriptions" of behavior, as Crotty contends. It is to accept the value judgments concluded from experience and then to designate our behavior with normative language built on such judgments. It is not to describe actions "independently of the human context." It is simply to accept the fact that the dominating aspect of this context comes to us through our culture and is, in fact, monogamous marriage.

Obviously, if such underlying value judgments are cultural in character, they can change. One's sole concern then is whether the direction of the change is humanly promotive or destructive.

4) *Rules and situations.* In speaking of decisions in the situation, Crotty writes:

If they [acts of premarital intercourse] are to be condemned, such condemnation cannot rest on the fact that they do not do justice to the meaning of conjugal intercourse but only on the fact that, given the sort of persons we are and given the relationship that exists between this man and this woman in this situation, abstaining from intercourse serves better the cause of human welfare, their own and others', than engaging in intercourse. There must be, once again, a weighing of all the values and disvalues that are foreseen to flow from such behavior in the given situation. The moral agent must discern these values and disvalues, assess them, and decide in the light of them whether sexual intercourse constitutes the most loving of the options open to him as possible responses to the situation.[32]

I have suggested that the two criteria mentioned by Crotty are really not different if one understands the intent and consequentialist underpinnings of the phrase "do justice to the meaning of conjugal intercourse." What is of concern here is rather the meaning of a general value judgment or rule of action in Crotty's view. If one has constantly to weigh all the values and disvalues of his situation, there seems to be no real utility in a rule or value judgment he brings to the situation. If moral

[32] Crotty, *art. cit.*, p. 228.

rules are of any value at all, it is that they establish presumptions, a point Crotty himself makes. Why then this insistence on a constant personal verification of the rule in my case? Certainly we do not want to exclude the exceptional instance. But if our basic value judgment is correct, we would not urge weighing all the values and disvalues to see *whether* premarital relations are morally in order. Rather would we not have to challenge a couple to show convincingly on what possible grounds they are an exception to the rule?

This point has deep pastoral and educational as well as methodological implications. Perhaps the matter might be formulated as follows. Human sexual expression provides us with an unparalleled form of self-disclosure, sharing, and growth. Therefore we have always been concerned with the conditions for protecting and enhancing this mode of self-disclosure. If long experience and reflection have built the conviction that the profound human values involved in sexual intimacy are best protected and enhanced by conditions describable as marriage, then this means precisely that the values and disvalues of other options have already been sifted over the centuries. Must it not be supposed that the values the individual unmarried couple might find for initiating sexual relations are, by and large, the very values experience has weighed and rejected as sufficient to outweigh the eventual disvalues? To ask the couple to do this all over again is to suggest that reasons similar or identical to theirs had no part in the establishment of the norm. Contrarily, quite the opposite has to be presumed if we want to prevent a balanced empiricism from plunging into an unreal individualism.

Therefore, from the fact that concrete norms *can* have exceptions (or that certain actions do not fall within the norm properly stated), it does not follow that one must weigh all the values and disvalues in his situation to see whether he should follow the norm. *That* conclusion depends on how much strength, what content, and therefore what presumptions we give to the underlying value judgment. For instance, from the fact that killing is not always morally wrong it does not follow that there must be a weighing of all the values and disvalues that are foreseen to flow from such behavior in the given situation. That would only follow if the death of another were a relatively insignificant value frequently in conflict with higher values. Rather I enter the situation with a strong presumption that I may not kill, and I am budged from this conclusion only by the most extraordinary and tragic instances. Therefore, if Crotty is going to frame his advice as he has, it would be necessary first to get involved in a careful discussion of premarital relations to determine whether and why they are (1) most always destructive and wrong, (2) generally not destructive and wrong. He should discuss the underlying value judgment and not presuppose this matter has been solved.

In summary, then, if a couple are to except themselves from an accepted norm, they bear a double onus: (1) to show that the values and disvalues they adduce are *different* from those which gave birth to the original value judgment, and (2) to show that these different values would outweigh the disvalues in this instance—in terms of both long-term individual and societal considerations.[33] They may, of course, choose a different route. They may argue that the norm was formed under certain one-sided and incomplete considerations of sexuality, or that times have changed and our culture needs a different value judgment.[34] Perhaps so. But these are different matters and they are far from established. Indeed, one need not be a latter-day Cassandra to suggest that just the opposite is the case and that the rush of contemporary attitudes and mores in this matter is toward trivialization.

NORMS, EXPERIENCE, AND THE BEHAVIORAL SCIENCES

One of the major problems with a consequentialist methodology is the value structure in light of which decisions are made. That is, if one concludes that more value than disvalue will come from a certain choice, how does one know that his evaluation of these consequences is objective? In an interesting article John G. Milhaven seizes this problem by the forelock and concludes that one's proportionate assessment of values can be tested only in experience.[35] Briefly, lived love or concern generates objective insight into the respective worth of values. But the problem still returns: "affective dispositions can generate what looks like objective insight but is in fact subjective illusion." How submit the affective experience to critique? Milhaven suggests, if I understand him correctly, that this critique will come by way of sharing experiences. Thus one whose formal education is complete might, through weekend visits to the poor, "break through his social prejudices, awake his com-

[33] That the individual couple might be precisely the ones least likely to make such an assessment with genuine objectivity seems obvious.

[34] For some recent literature, cf. Francis V. Manning, "The Human Meaning of Sexual Pleasure and the Morality of Premarital Intercourse," *American Ecclesiastical Review* 165 (1971) 18–28; Denis Read, "The Human Sexual Context," *ibid.* 164 (1971) 257–64; James R. Moore, "Sex and the Supernatural," *Christianity Today* 15 (1971) 7–10; Maurice Bellet, "Réalité sexuelle et morale chrétienne," *Etudes*, March, 1971, pp. 437–56; Richard R. Roach, S.J., "Sex in Christian Morality," *The Way* 11 (1971) 148–61, 235–42; Warren T. Reich, "Whither Sexual Ethics?" *Linacre Quarterly* 38 (1971) 184–92. This last entry occurs in an issue of *Linacre Quarterly* entirely devoted to questions of sexuality.

[35] John Giles Milhaven, "Objective Moral Evaluation of Consequences," THEOLOGICAL STUDIES 32 (1971) 407–30.

passion ... and eventually make more objective his appreciation of the evil of their condition."

Milhaven's emphasis on experience is certainly healthy. Sensitizing oneself to values and disvalues by experience and sharing is an essential step if moral reflection is to be anything more than hothouse concept-shuffling. But this sensitizing is only the first step—and in this sense Milhaven has not answered the question he put to himself, or at least not completely; for the precise problem was how to test the value judgments of those who have properly sensitized themselves through experience. At least two other steps seem essential.

First, we must reflect upon our experience and put it into as communicable a form as possible. Secondly, we must submit it to the testing of others' analysis and reflection. In these processes we may hope for the clarification of a moral policy which will best do justice to all the values involved. This is not to suggest that we are judging experience by prepackaged legal rules; we are only trusting that rational discussion will truly allow a blend and balance to emerge in our assessment of values. The supposition here is that while the concern of this or that individual may be illusory or unbalanced, and lead to erroneous judgments about what consequences are good, the possibility is reduced in the exchange of whole groups of intelligent and sensitive people.

Therefore, where there is question of determining what consequences are good, I would agree with James Gustafson's critique of Milhaven: "If there are disputes (and there are), then M. has to help us see how we should go about trying to settle them; for the answer to their settlement will not come from an appeal to 'experience' *as a single entity*."[36]

I would like to urge this problem further in the hope that Milhaven would continue his already fruitful pursuit of the matter. Perhaps he did not intend to present experience "as a single entity" and has been misunderstood. But if he did, could not the approach easily open on the type of moralism not altogether absent from, e.g., *Humanae vitae*? It would be summarized as follows: "if you are open-minded, loving, and have a sense of marriage, you will see and accept the position proposed here." It is the constant temptation of people with deep conviction to think they can validate concrete moral conclusions by use of the broader themes which nourish their convictions. We see the phenomenon at the level of student protest, in political discourse, and in all kinds of liberation movements. Awareness of this does not deny that these broader themes are somehow operative in determining what is right and wrong. It is only to say that if this is all we can adduce to support a concrete conclusion, we have not as yet begun to do genuine ethics. For instance,

---

[36] Cf. THEOLOGICAL STUDIES 32 (1971) 524, emphasis added.

it is no rational argument to say that one who rejects *Humanae vitae* "has no sense of the Cross." Such an argument serves only to raise voices, but not the level of rational discourse. Rather we should say: if *Humanae vitae* is right, then one with a sense of the Cross will attempt to live up to it even though this entails suffering.

Let us put the matter another way. Suppose two highly sensitized, loving, mature people disagree on a value judgment. By what criteria or method can they resolve this? It is the precise task of theological ethics to explain why the accenting of certain values, the shadowing of others, is not arbitrary. There is surely a correlation between true understanding and "getting involved" (experience). But this correlation can be carried just so far. We know, e.g., that several genuine saints had rather dreadful views about sexuality. We know of the invincibly erroneous conscience, i.e., a loving, mature, experienced person who is simply wrong. Profound love and concern, while very helpful, are no guarantee for the objectivity of value judgments. Indeed, it is known that a too close involvement can hinder objectivity and that a certain distance must be preserved if the larger aspects of a problem are to emerge and be weighed proportionately.

Concretely, Milhaven says that "to know whether the Church has reached the moment in history to modify its position on divorce, the moral theologian must share, in particular, the experience of present-day people who have divorced, are debating whether to divorce, or have decided not to do so."[37] Yes, but if that is all he knows, he is just as likely to make a mistaken judgment as not. He must also understand thoroughly the why of the Church's traditional position. He must know whether or not, and to what extent, the personal experience of individuals takes account of the public good. He should know the effects of contemporary divorce practices on child-raising, on personal stability, and on religious living. He must be acquainted with contemporary psychological and sociological studies on marriage and divorce. And perhaps more.

To test in a rational way the value assessments implicit in our choices, we must have some structure within which to discuss our experience. A good beginning might be certain established preference-principles. The following are examples. (1) Other things being equal, a nonpostponable value is to be preferred to a postponable one. (2) In conflict situations we must give preference to the lower but more "foundational" value, even while continuing to acknowledge the higher as higher. For instance, we must feed a starving man before trying to preach the good news of salvation to him. (3) Other things being equal, the common good

[37] *Art. cit.*, pp. 427–28.

is to be preferred to the good of the individual. Obviously, great sensitivity and discernment are needed here to avoid a crushing collectivism. (4) Other things being equal, we should undertake tasks for which we are better suited than ones for which we are not. (5) Other things being equal, we should prefer the good of those with a special relationship to our responsibility.[38]

Furthermore, this sifting and sorting of experience by use of preference-principles must be done in an atmosphere highly charged with Christian intentionalities such as the cruciform spirit of Christian life, resurrection destiny, the eschatological kingdom, the following of the poor and humble Christ. It is precisely the relation of these intentionalities to human value judgments that is an unfinished theological task. For instance, when Mr. Profumo (the British politician involved in adultery) lied and was later compelled to admit his actions, it was said that he was simply following the advice of Bishop John Robinson: he was lying to protect his family. Robinson replied that this has nothing to do with Christian love. He argued that love would not prevent the loved ones from bearing the burden and extending forgiveness. What is the bearing of basic Christian perspectives on situations of this kind?

Personal experience is but one ingredient of an adequate theological ethics. Another is the aid provided by the empirical sciences. There are very few theologians left who believe that theology can grow and mature in isolation from the social and behavioral sciences. These sciences are essential to an illumination of many morally relevant aspects of human activity. A truly contemporary theological ethics is impossible without them. But this is to say neither that scientific "findings"[39] constitute morality nor that the use of contemporary research is easy. James Gustafson, in his usual ranging and shrewd way, has in two places pointed out the problems involved in making use of empirical studies.[40] For instance, what interpretation of a field should be accepted and on what grounds? Does the theologian elect Rollo May or B. F. Skinner? If a moralist accepts one interpretation on its "scientific" adequacy, he has the burden of establishing the scientific grounds for this choice. If he chooses studies which have an affinity with his own philosophical or theological point of view, he must be ready to defend such points of view. How does he deal with the value biases of the studies he uses?

[38] For these suggestions I am indebted to Hans Reiner, *Pflicht und Neigung* (Meisenheim/Glan, 1951) pp. 166–72. The book is now out of print.

[39] "Findings" is put in quotation marks because the word would otherwise connote a measure of agreement among scientists and researchers which is not always there.

[40] James M. Gustafson, "The Relationship of Empirical Science to Moral Thought," *Proceedings of the Catholic Theological Society of America* 26 (1971); also "What is the Normatively Human?" *American Ecclesiastical Review* 165 (1971) 192–207.

Gustafson's counsel is not one of despair. But he insists, and rightly, that a theologian's use of empirical studies must be critical. When it is, "he is more likely to be a better moralist by being widely and deeply informed from the side of empirical research. But empirical research will never replace ethical arguments in the resolution of moral issues."

Charles Curran notes that although traditional theology was always open in principle to the contributions of other sciences, it often neglected this in practice.[41] Now we realize more clearly the need for a greater openness. Why? Theoretically, contemporary theology sees a greater continuity between this life and the afterlife. Furthermore, we have moved from a classical world view to a more historical one.

What is the precise relationship between moral theology and the sciences? Besides saying it is close, Curran does not fully answer this question; he is content to cite R. Springer, K. Rahner, and Max Stackhouse. But he offers several important reasons for the limits of the contribution of the empirical sciences. First, moral norms are not simply statistical norms, because the Christian faith views the present in the light of the full salvation event, which embraces also the future. The eschatological pull of the future exercises a negative critique on every existing structure of reality. The sciences of themselves do not share this vision of man and the world. Secondly, there is the reality of sin. History shows us the operations of sin in the past, and there is generous evidence that the present is not immune to the effects of sin. Thirdly, there is an element of transcendence in man which surpasses the cold rationality of science. Finally, a single science gives us but a partial perspective of reality. In light of these limitations, Curran criticizes Milhaven's tendency to reduce morality to scientific findings.[42]

These two sections may be concluded with the summary statement that contemporary theological writings have moved very markedly in the direction of a consequentialist methodology. It would be foolish to deny that there are problems in such an approach, a fact made clear by the decades-long discussion of utilitarianism. However, there is an important place for a balanced empiricism in theological ethics. If this place is to be achieved and if contemporary moral theologians are to avoid the traps of a secularist-individualist calculus, they must turn their attention to the problem that all recognize but few enlighten: the relationship of human values and disvalues to an over-all Christian concept of life, or the significance of the Christian ethos for evaluating consequences.

[41] Charles Curran, "La théologie morale et les sciences," *Recherches de science religieuse* 59 (1971) 419–48.
[42] Cf. also Charles Curran, "Homosexuality and Moral Theology: Methodological and Substantive Considerations," *Thomist* 35 (1971) 447–81.

DIVORCE AND REMARRIAGE

Last year these Notes discussed at length the problem of divorce and remarriage.[43] There has been no letup in the flow of literature during the past year. Both the profound importance of the problem and the groping character of earlier writings suggest that a continuance of the discussion is in place. The studies generally approach the question from one of three points of view: the power of the Church to dissolve sacramental and consummated marriages, revision of the notion of a sacramental and consummated marriage, the pastoral ministry to the divorced and remarried. An example of each type of article will provide an opportunity to bring the recent literature under review.

Johannes Gerhartz examines the internal theological reason for the juridical indissolubility of a sacramental-consummated marriage.[44] More precisely, must the absolute moral imperative (marriage *ought not* be dissolved) preached by Christ be translated into absolute juridical indissolubility (marriage *cannot* be dissolved)? The fact that the Church allows separation in certain cases shows that she recognizes in the juridical order that higher values can at times give spouses the right to separate. This is a dissolution of the marriage according to its positive content. The only obligation on the spouses is not to marry again. Therefore their marriage continues only in this single effect: the obligation not to marry. This indicates that the problematic of the broken marriage is the problematic of the impediment of the bond (*impedimentum ligaminis*). Can this bond be dissolved by the Church? If not, why not?

The traditional answer is, of course, no. But Gerhartz is dissatisfied with the underlying argumentation. For instance, the sacramentality of the marriage yields what Gerhartz calls *peculiaris firmitas* of the bond, but not *absoluta*. Other authors appeal to the divine positive law whereby God is said to grant dissolving powers to the Church, but not with regard to sacramental-consummated marriages. Gerhartz rejects this as a "positivistic" notion wherein God is seen as a human legislator. He finds it impossible to discover the objective foundation of the Church's practice in Scripture, natural law, the good of the children, or sacramentality. Rather the practice of juridical indissolubility must be argued from the common good. Here Gerhartz notes: "if the law of absolute juridical indissolubility of marriage is founded on the common good, it is founded on something essentially variable and hence it is essentially submitted to human judgment and power."

This means two things. First, it says that juridical indissolubility,

---

[43] Cf. THEOLOGICAL STUDIES 32 (1971) 107–22.

[44] Johannes G. Gerhartz, "L'Indissolubilité du mariage et la dissolution du mariage dans la problématique actuelle," *Revue de droit canonique* 21 (1971) 198–234.

while it traces back to the moral demands of Jesus and the sacramental signification of marriage, is ultimately a law established by the Church. Therefore no marriage is absolutely juridically indissoluble in itself. Such indissolubility exists only in virtue of regulation by the community. Secondly, it says that whether the community of faith should continue to maintain absolute juridical indissolubility is dependent on historical and empirical factors which are subject to change.

Bruno Primetshofer is in basic sympathy with Gerhartz' conclusion, though he does not argue the matter systematically.[45] He believes there is a real contradiction in an attitude which proposes a principle of indissolubility applicable to all marriages but narrows it to a single category (sacramental-consummated marriages). We are in a stage of transition during which the Church will (or should) become conscious of her power to dissolve all marriages.

An analysis different from but congenial to Gerhartz' is that of Louis de Naurois, S.J.[46] Extension of dissolving power to all marriage cases is often argued from a notion of delegation of divine powers to the pope which is embarrassingly anthropomorphic. God is envisaged in such doctrine as a temporal sovereign—indeed, one out of the Middle Ages. A heavy voluntarism underlies this analytic structure. De Naurois believes that if the Church judges that certain marriages are susceptible of dissolution, then the principle (law of God) is not simply indissolubility. The possibility of dissolution is not exterior to the law but included somehow in it. If some marriages are not susceptible to dissolution, it is necessary to say why. De Naurois does not think this has been done. But when he suggests that our conception of marriage, our juridical categories, our civilization and aspirations are not those of other eras, he is leaning toward a notion of indissolubility not far from that of Gerhartz.

J. M. Salgado will have none of this.[47] The cutting edge of G.'s presentation is the distinction between Christ's absolute moral imperative (*lex mere moralis*) and absolute juridical indissolubility (*les inhabilitans*). Gerhartz refuses to reduce Christ's teaching to an ideal; no, it is a true *Erfüllungsgebot*. But the question still unanswered is: how is this imperative to be interpreted in the juridical order? Salgado thinks that to make such a distinction would be to ask the Church to make of herself a laughingstock. She would equivalently say: "Christ demands

[45] Bruno Primetshofer, "Zerbrochene Ehe und Ehescheidung," *Theologisch-praktische Quartalschrift* 119 (1971) 117–30.

[46] Louis de Naurois, S.J., "Le problème de la dissolution du mariage par l'église," *Nouvelle revue théologique* 93 (1971) 50–77.

[47] J. M. Salgado, O.M.I., "La chiesa potrebbe, un giorno, sciogliere il matrimonio rato e consumato?" *Palestra del clero* 50 (1971) 339–49.

absolute indissolubility; but I can and will dissolve these marriages." He concludes that the Church has not touched sacramental-consummated marriages because to do so would be to remain untrue to the explicit will of Christ.

The *Palestra del clero* has never been accused, to my knowledge, of being a creative comet in the theological firmament. Salgado's essay will provide further protection against such accusations; for his rejection of Gerhartz' distinction fails to explain how the Church can accept Christ's imperative and still dissolve all marriages not *ratum et consummatum*. Surely her widening practice of dissolving true marriages demands some difference between Christ's imperative and its juridical implementation. In this sense the will of Christ is not in question. Rather the question is: what is the appropriate juridical vehicle for confronting men with Christ's imperative without inhumanly crushing them in the process?[48]

Jean Bernhard may be taken as an example of the second approach.[49] He has problems with Gerhartz' point of view, because he fails to see how the sacramental marital bond can be reduced to a purely juridical abstraction—a reduction Gerhartz seems to make. Furthermore, Bernhard believes that it is not certain at all that the Church can dissolve this "juridical abstraction." Therefore he prefers his way in on the contemporary problem. This is an updating of the notion of consummation from a narrowly physical to a more existential one.[50]

In summary, Bernhard's idea has two skeletal supports. First, the traditional notions of "consummated, nonconsummated" are profoundly modified to reconcile them with Vatican II. Even a new vocabulary is required. Bernhard suggests *mariage instauré* and *mariage consacré*. *Mariage instauré* would result from exchange of consents. Only those would be admitted to a religious marriage who consent to a fundamentally indissoluble union and promise to do all in their power to move to it. After the couple had achieved a certain level of human and Christian growth, their marriage would be *consacré* and absolutely indissoluble. Secondly, *mariage instauré* would be dissoluble by the Church in

---

[48] Cf. F. Böckle, "Morale fondamentale," *Recherches de science religieuse* 59 (1971) 353.

[49] Jean Bernhard, "Réinterprétation (existentielle et dans la foi) de la législation canonique concernant l'indissolubilité du mariage chrétien," *Revue de droit canonique* 21 (1971) 243–77.

[50] In an excellent article Walter F. Kenny shows how the basis for recent Rotal decisions in cases of homosexuality is moving away from older legalism—e.g., from *jus in corpus* as the formal object of the marriage contract to the community of life and love. Cf. "Homosexuality and Nullity—Developing Jurisprudence," *Catholic Lawyer* 17 (1971) 110–22.

case of breakdown. Such a dissolution would be both declaratory (of the irremediable failure of the marriage) and constitutive (in so far as it pertains to the Church to dissolve a bond created by the original consent).

Bernhard has written enough on this idea to get some feedback. He acknowledges two objections.[51] First, it is all but impossible to translate this notion of *consacré* into juridical terms. Bernhard grants the point but argues that canon law must use increasingly fewer juridical formulae. Furthermore, it is easier than we think to discover that a marriage has not achieved this growth. Some provisional indications: brevity of common life, continual infidelity, absence of every conjugal and familial characteristic, intolerance of common life. Such signs, especially cumulatively, provide a presumption of nonconsummation. The second objection runs as follows: why hold to two states of marriage? Why not just say, as Gerhartz does, that the Church can dissolve all marriages? Bernhard sees his approach as more consistent with a fundamental kernel of tradition: the distinction between a consummated and nonconsummated marriage.

J. P. Jossua, O.P., seems to have in mind something similar to Bernhard's idea.[52] He notes that "in life-long fidelity, clear-sightedly undertaken at the beginning and kept alive in spite of crises, the unremitting love of Christ for the Church and of God for men lives on and is borne witness to in the world. *This is the understanding of indissolubility in ancient tradition.*"[53] Therefore his distinction: "Man *should* not undo what God has built up, but that does not prevent its being undone in fact." Jossua feels keenly the need to set up in this matter a discipline that is "both new and traditional." He suggests the recognition of the ecclesial status of a second marriage by means of a "positive act re-

---

[51] Cf. J. Bernhard, "A propos de l'indissolubilité du mariage chrétien," *Revue des sciences religieuses* 44 (1971) 49–62; and "A propos de l'hypothèse concernant la notion de 'consummation existentielle' du mariage," *Revue de droit canonique* 20 (1970) 184–92; THEOLOGICAL STUDIES 32 (1971) 110–12.

[52] J. P. Jossua, O.P., "The Fidelity of Love and the Indissolubility of Christian Marriage," *Clergy Review* 56 (1971) 172–81.

[53] *Ibid.*, p. 176, emphasis added. With respect to the tradition of the first five centuries, cf. Henri Crouzel, S.J., "Remarriage after Divorce in the Primitive Church: A propos of a Recent Book," *Irish Theological Quarterly* 38 (1971) 21–41. Crouzel takes dead aim at Victor Pospishil's thesis that a distinct majority of the Fathers and ancient ecclesiastical authorities permitted the remarriage of husbands of adulterous wives, while generally they denied it to all wives, even the innocent. Crouzel's conclusion: "It is intolerable to hear so many respectable canonists affirming as an evident fact that the present eastern discipline concerning divorce and remarriage was substantially that of the Greek Fathers of the 4th and 5th centuries; in fact this is simply false" (p. 40). Pospishil returns to the fray ("Divorce and Remarriage in the Early Church," *Irish Theological Quarterly* 38 [1971] 338–47) and contends that Crouzel's conclusions are "at least extreme."

ceiving the partners back into communion." But he would not allow a full ecclesial second marriage; for something of the expression to the world of God's love is irretrievably lost in the breakdown of fidelity. "It is to signify this that marriage is indissoluble (as a demand), and the traditional refusal of sacramental re-marriage is the social expression of this demand."[54]

U. Navarrete, S.J., in his continuing studies on marriage, finds Bernhard's notion of consummation unacceptable.[55] He distinguishes three dimensions in marriage: the existential, juridical, and sacramental. From the existential point of view, conjugal love should always continue to grow, be "consummated" more and more. But juridically speaking, one must first distinguish the formational process of marriage (*in fieri*) and constituted marriage (*in facto esse*). Once this distinction is made, it becomes clear that there must be a moment when marriage, with all its juridical effects, is fully constituted. This point is consummation. Therefore consummation, from a juridical point of view, is necessarily a determined and knowable act or deed, "since from it flow juridical effects, at least indissolubility." Navarrete argues that with Bernhard's notion of consummation, it would be necessary to say that no marriage is ever consummated, since it is always open to further growth and maturation.

Labourdette is certainly right when he suggests that there are still many problems to unravel in Bernhard's approach.[56] However, there is a good deal to be said in favor of the basic direction of Bernhard's work, a point Labourdette also admits. One thing to be said for an existential concept of consummation is that it reflects the way in which very many contemporary couples factually judge their marriages. This does not say everything, of course. But does it say nothing to us? In this sense Navarrete's objection gets things backwards, I believe. Whether this particular juridical effect (absolute indissolubility) occurs must indeed depend on a juridical determination, but on a juridical determination which attempts to reflect the realities of marriage at a particular point in history. If "consummation" is to be more than just a legal category, if it is to refer to a human reality, then its juridical meaning must take shape around this reality. Canonical clarity must not have the prime priority in making this juridical determination.

In other words, it is not at all clear that the existence of this particular effect (indissolubility) demands "a determined act or fact" as Navar-

[54] Jossua, *art. cit.*, p. 181.
[55] Urbanus Navarrete, S.J., "De notione et effectibus consummationis matrimonii," *Periodica* 59 (1970) 619–60.
[56] M.-M. Labourdette, "Problèmes du mariage," *Revue thomiste* 71 (1971) 99–120.

rete understands these words. That would only be true if it is utterly necessary to be able to say at any and every moment whether or not the juridical effect actually has occurred. Traditional jurisprudence felt bound to this type of clarity and certainty. But does a balanced Christian protection of the values of marriage in the juridical sphere really demand it? That is far from clear.

Nor can it be argued against Bernhard that an existential notion of consummation means that no marriage would ever be consummated since it is always open to greater growth. There is a difference—difficult as it may be to translate juridically—between a sufficient level of stability and the fullest measure of stability. If this were not true, one could never speak, e.g., of a virtuous man or a mortal sinner, since it is always possible to penetrate our acceptance or rejection of God from greater depths of our liberty.

The third approach is exemplified by H. Heimerl, George A. Maloney, S.J., Richard de Ranitz, O.P., and John D. Catoir. Heimerl speaks only of established second marriages which have reached stability and involve children while the first marriage is hopelessly broken.[57] There is in these situations a conflict of duties: on the one hand, to maintain and nourish the love so badly needed by the partners and the children; on the other, to respect the indissolubility of marriage. Because of this conflict, Heimerl believes that the spouses should be able to continue to live together as husband and wife, and receive the sacraments if scandal can be avoided. He insists that his solution be restricted to the internal forum, but asks bishops to give their priests guidelines to cover these tragic situations. The only thing new or different in Heimerl's pastoral approach is his analysis of consent. A true marital consent is present in such unions, a fact supported by the possibility of a *sanatio in radice* if the spouse of the first marriage dies. Because of this consent, Heimerl feels that it is inconsistent to allow the couple to remain together, yet not live as husband and wife.

In an extremely interesting presentation, George A. Maloney, S.J., argues that the Church must face the problem of marriage breakdown not through dissolution but by use of the principle of economy.[58] In this context the essence of economy is "the pardon through the Church of faults committed by children of the Church or those outside the Church who wish to return to the Church in order to facilitate a restoration to full Christian life." In marriage cases, Maloney argues, the Church

[57] Hans Heimerl, "Sakramentenempfang für Wiederverheiratete," *Theologische Quartalschrift* 151 (1971) 61–65.

[58] George A. Maloney, S.J., "Oeconomia: A Corrective to Law," *Catholic Lawyer* 17 (1971) 90–109.

should not divorce couples but mercifully recognize civil divorces and remarriages and restore couples in such marriages to full communion with the Church. Even though this second union would be an imperfect sign of Christ's love for His Church, still such a pastoral adaptation is necessary, especially in view of the "new forces in society that tend to make a long-range commitment to another person or way of life most difficult."

The pastoral perspective of Richard de Ranitz, O.P., never uses the term "economy," but his analysis moves in that direction.[59] The "stuff" of the sacraments (matter, gestures, and words) are an anthropological given. Revelation raises these aspects of man's life to be paradigmatic signifiers. This means that we must theologize not on the basis of what marriage is but what marriage is *today*. "The present phenomenological given must take precedence over the acculturated system of laws which developed from a past given"; for it is the present social phenomenon that must be seen as a paradigmatic symbol of God's continual loving presence. This phenomenon, however, has altered drastically in purpose, motivation, and meaning. "Marriage today is becoming the phenomenon of a man and a woman who choose to live together as growth motivated people in an interpersonal relationship of self-giving love. This is the 'stuff' of marriage which attains the paradigmatic symbolization of God's loving presence. Since it is the 'stuff' of marriage, when it ceases, marriage ceases." De Ranitz believes that ecclesial refusal of a second marriage when this "stuff" has ceased "would have far more dreadful symbolic consequences, both theologically and psychologically, than the broken symbol of a marital breakdown could ever have."

John Catoir, presiding judge of the Marriage Tribunal of the Diocese of Paterson, N.J., treats the "internal forum solution" in a balanced and prudent way.[60] Because of the imperfection of existing marriage law and the cumbersome character of tribunal procedures, there are many couples who deserve annulments but cannot get them. In these instances, Catoir argues (correctly in my opinion), these couples are justified in marrying civilly and such a marriage (if the partners are baptized) is a sacramental marriage. After such a marriage, Catoir suggests, a blessing-ceremony or renewal of vows before a priest is quite in place. However,

it would not be right for a priest to presume to marry the couple himself, i.e., to eliminate the need for a civil or religious ceremony outside the Church, because when acting as an agent of the state in the matter of marriage, the priest is under

---

[59] Richard de Ranitz, O.P., "Should the Roman Church Recognize Divorce?" *Listening*, Winter, 1971, pp. 60–70.

[60] John D. Catoir, "When the Courts Don't Work," *America* 125 (1971) 254–57.

oath to obey the laws of the Church judicatory to which he belongs. If the priest knowingly witnesses a union which is juridically invalid in the eyes of his Church, he is exceeding his rights under state law as well as Church law, and even the civil validity of the marriage could be challenged later in certain states.[61]

According to Catoir, therefore, a twofold remedy exists for the problems surrounding divorce and remarriage: the tribunal and the internal-forum solution. Catoir admits that this latter pastoral remedy is far from ideal. "It is patronizing and imperfect since it does not totally vindicate the deserving couple." But something is better than nothing.

Catoir's essay is an excellent piece of pastoral writing. I agree totally with his attitudes, analysis, and conclusions. Perhaps a few points call for additional comment. First, it is especially important that this type of study get into the more popular literature and be explained from the pulpit; for everyone writing on the problem of divorce and remarriage insists on the need of avoiding the scandal generated by misunderstanding. Catholics, therefore, must be educated to the idea that the tribunal system is severely limited in determining precisely what unions are truly binding and hence to the occasional legitimacy of internal-forum solutions. If they are properly educated, they will understand that there is no justification for shock or judgment when they see an acquaintance (divorced and remarried) receiving the sacraments. This education is particularly important for Anglo-Saxons, whose strong legal tradition accustoms them to view law as an exhaustive measure of what is possible and right. When this legal tradition combines with a highly juridical notion of Church, the result is the remarkable view that Church law provides the answer to all problems, the only answer and a fully adequate answer.

Secondly, when Catoir refers to a twofold remedy for divorce problems (tribunal, internal forum), he does not mean to propose a simple option. The internal-forum route is legitimate precisely in so far as the public forum is inadequate. This priority of the public forum (be it tribunal or other vehicle) is grounded in the indispensable necessity of social regulation of marriage. Without some such social regulation the integrity of marriage and the imperative of indissolubility would be seriously threatened. Therefore the internal-forum solution demands a threefold condition: (1) that there are good, though not legally demonstrable, grounds for challenging the first marriage; (2) that the public ecclesial forum has not worked or would not; (3) that scandal is avoided.

Thirdly, the first condition mentioned above emphasizes a point in Catoir's study. He repeatedly refers to "annulment," "invalid mar-

[61] *Ibid.*, p. 256.

riage," etc. when speaking of the first union. At one point, however, he refers to a "broken marriage." There is a difference here. Not every broken marriage would fit the category of one whose validity could be challenged. It seems that some "dead marriages" have to be judged as true Christian marriages which collapsed after perhaps many years. It is clear that Catoir's analysis would not apply to these. It is possible to argue persuasively about many "dead marriages" that their death traces back to a radical incapacity to sustain the duties and obligations of marriage. Such incapacity, difficult as it may be to determine, argues to the invalidity of the marriage. But it can be doubted that *all* "dead marriages" automatically fit this category. For this reason I find it hard to agree with the sweeping statement of Stephen J. Kelleher: "Once a marriage is dead ... the persons can responsibly marry again and continue to receive the Eucharist."[62] This may eventually prove to be our discipline, as Maloney and de Ranitz suggest it should be; but Kelleher has given us no satisfactory reasons that it is so now. The basis for his conclusion seems to be his own personal espousal of the practice of the Orthodox Church. If that were enough for practical counsel and conclusions in the Roman Church now, the literature reviewed in this section would not exist.

Thus far the current literature; now to a personal reflection. It seems clear that a good number of tragic situations can be handled along the lines of Catoir's and Heimerl's suggestions. As for the more radical question raised by Gerhartz about the Church's power to dissolve sacramental-consummated marriages, two things strike one immediately. First, theologians have not succeeded in showing persuasively why a sacramental-consummated union is absolutely indissoluble. Gerhartz makes this quite clear. Secondly, the history of the Church's widening use of dissolving power reflects a *facit, ergo potest* pattern of justification in theological thought. These two considerations in combination suggest that we will probably learn whether power over sacramental-consummated marriage resides in the Church only if and when it is used. This is not to detract from the importance of Gerhartz' question. It is only to suggest that if his question is to be more than an exercise in abstract thinking, it immediately raises another and possibly more fruitful avenue of enquiry: *should* the Church use such power even if she has it? In raising the question of *can* in the face of contemporary pastoral problems, one is, almost willy-nilly, suggesting to some extent *should*. Otherwise why raise the problem?

The answer to this question is, of course, extremely difficult. It must be elaborated out of a rich experience and a careful reflection, not ex-

[62] Cited in *National Catholic Reporter*, Oct. 8, 1971, p. 3.

cluding that of the Orthodox churches. But the basic structure within which the enquiry should proceed seems increasingly clear. I would propose it as follows. If there is a distinction between the radical moral demand of Christ and its sociojuridical implementation, there is also a deep interpenetration of the two. That is, how clearly and integrally the Church maintains and proclaims the basic moral demand will depend very much on how this is translated into a social or juridical policy. In this perspective the question of *should* (or *should not*) concretizes itself as follows: how much juridical dissolution of marriage (and in what circumstances) is compatible with the Church's proclamation of the moral imperative of indissolubility? Or again: would use of her dissolving power in sacramental-consummated marriage cases threaten the integrity of the teaching of Christ? If it would—in our time and culture—it seems clear that it is not a possible form of the Church's pastoral ministry of forgiveness, for it would undermine the common spiritual good. But before concluding that it certainly would, there remains the extremely challenging task of showing that the doctrine of Christ is threatened by dissolution of sacramental-consummated marriages, but not by the many other dissolutions currently practiced by the Church.

If I have framed the question properly, it raises the distinct possibility that the Church should really dissolve no marriages at all, that she erred pastorally in the past in doing so and should cease and desist in the future. We cannot reject this out of hand. The *facit, ergo potest* analysis is a deeply juridical approach to a question which extends far beyond juridical considerations. Furthermore, it is a juridical analysis which built heavily on a theory of divinely delegated power, a theory under heavy theological assault these days.

This all means that what the Church *can* do (*potest*) is very likely identical with what she *should* do. And this *should* is an empirical question involving the relationship of her acts of mercy to the integrity of her proclamation of Christ's demand. It just might be that she should look elsewhere (than in the dissolution of the bond) for pastoral solutions to marriage problems, a point of view advanced by Maloney and to a lesser extent by de Ranitz. A refusal to dissolve any true marital bond is not the same as refusing to accept and forgive those who have found it impossible to live the demands of this bond.

OF THEOLOGY AND LIBERATION

"The word 'liberation' is on everyone's lips today." Thus Pope Paul VI in an address to the participants of the 50th anniversary world congress of Pax Romana, July 21, 1971.[63] That the Holy Father was not just

[63] *The Pope Speaks* 16 (1971) 170.

noting a vocabulary but also endorsing it seems clear from his own increasing use of the idea. After adverting in the same address to Christ's concern with evils of all kinds that weigh on men, Paul continued:

But it is the profound cause of evil that Jesus attacks on every occasion; it is from sin that He wishes to free man: from the influence of evil which each person discovers within himself and which chains him to his selfishness, his pride, his sensual appetite. Christ wishes to free man from collective influences which multiply individual sin, and in which we must seek the source of oppressions and enslavements that human societies generate . . . . [64]

This analysis—freedom from all enslavements, but above all from sin as the root of other oppressions—is identical with the conclusions drawn several years ago[65] and more recently[66] by Gustavo Gutierrez M.: "Christ thus appears as the Saviour who, by liberating us from sin, liberates us from the very root of social injustice." We shall return to this analysis shortly.

Liberation is indeed a much less antiseptic notion than development where the various social implications of Christianity are concerned. It better reflects the urgency of man's aspirations in the face of oppression. Furthermore, it is a notion which accommodates easily to areas other than the economic and sociopolitical.[67] For instance, an article submitted to the convention of the Catholic Theological Society attempted a critique of the contemporary notion of leadership in the Church by use of the notion of liberation.[68] There has been in the past a constant tendency to identify authority and leadership in the Church. When this identification is made in the thought patterns and day-to-day operations of a group, somewhat paradoxically a factual separation between authority and leadership begins to occur; for the more there is reliance on mere authority, the less one does those things required of true leadership. The result: as authority wanes, authority figures appeal all the more loudly to their authority and position.

This careless identification of leadership with office yields two remarkable results. First, an independent value is attributed to mere office, with, of course, a dominant concern for the prerogatives of office

[64] Ibid.

[65] Gustavo Gutierrez M., "Notes for a Theology of Liberation," THEOLOGICAL STUDIES 31 (1970) 243-61.

[66] G. Gutierrez M., "Liberation and Development," Cross Currents 21 (1971) 243-56. The entire issue is devoted to "Latin America in Search of Liberation."

[67] Cf. the interesting article of Donald Evans, "Gregory Baum's Theology of Liberation," Studies in Religion 1 (1971) 45-60; also the volume Christ the Liberator (Downers Grove: Inter-Varsity Press, 1971).

[68] Richard A. McCormick, S.J., "Leadership and Authority," Proceedings of the Catholic Theological Society of America 26 (1971).

and a corresponding insensitivity to the goals it serves. Secondly, we begin to experience the "controlled" group or society. The symptoms of the controlled group are well known: dominance of the negative in teaching; oppressive centralization at the administrative level; avoidance of risk in decision-making; derivativeness and enslavement to the traditional formula in theologizing; secretiveness in the use of power. The personality traits of the controlled group are equally well known: fear, anxiety, joyless security, rejection of risk, apathy.

If leadership cannot be identified with office or authority, what is its basic element? The study proposes:

We have said that leadership can assume any number of forms: administrative, executive, charismatic. But beneath all of them and common to all of them (in so far as they are leadership and not control) is a single element: the release, stimulation, evocation, maximization of the potential of the individual. True leadership, in whatever form it is found, calls forth the best in those led. It *liberates* them into the fullness of their potential as individuals and as a group.

This concept of leadership can be seen clearly in the notion of theological leadership. A man is a theological leader because of the depths of his insights into the faith and the power of his communication of these. Now depth of insight and power of communication constitute leadership precisely because they liberate us from the confinements of our own imaginations and formulations, from our ignorance and doubts.

In an age of specialization and diversification, authoritative position is no longer the locus of many competencies. Competence has been cut up and spread around. It is in this context that authority finds its contemporary challenge to become leadership. Authority will begin to coincide factually with leadership in our times if it makes its overriding concern the liberation of others to be leaders in all areas where we recognize a true competence and a Christian concern. For instance, the bishop who makes it possible for a theologian to be a better theologian, the layman to be a better educator, parent, or community organizer, the priest to be a better apostolic instrument, is a true leader. He has conjoined authority and leadership because he uses authority to liberate the group into its maximum potential. The theologian whose work makes it possible for youth to grow out of the traps of fadism, whose research and writing make it possible for bishops to cut adrift from secular power-models of authority, whose insights free other theologians from the tyranny of a single formulation, has joined competence and leadership because he uses competence (office, so to speak) to liberate. And so on.

We are all victims of the oppression of our own limitations and need liberation to that extent. One of these limitations is the tendency to experience another's need for liberation while not sensing our own. Nothing daunted, and with some risk of arrogance, I should like to underline a one-sidedly juridical notion of episcopal teaching authority as a contemporary form of episcopal captivity where some amount of liberation appears appropriate. As an example, I shall use an essay by the Most Rev. John F. Whealon, episcopal chairman of the NCCB's Committee on Doctrine.[69] This is chosen as an example because one may suspect that very many bishops would agree with its emphases while very many theologians would not, and because it deals with a matter of practical concern in the American church.

Speaking of ethical and religious directives for Catholic hospitals, Archbishop Whealon asks: "Who has the right to teach and to legislate concerning such moral and pastoral matters? The Roman Catholic Church places this right and obligation on the bishop of the local diocese, to the extent the he is in union with and in doctrinal harmony with the Bishop of Rome."[70] True enough, but not quite enough of the truth. The contemporary question is not precisely who has the right to teach, but rather what means must be used, what processes employed if that authority is to be used responsibly and effectively. Gregory Baum has correctly pointed out that a highly intellectualistic understanding of teaching has dominated the theology of the magisterium.[71] This makes a juridical emphasis much easier to maintain. The right to teach does not tell us much about the manner of teaching. For one thing, this right does not eliminate but rather implies the duty to learn. And if a bishop must learn, presumably there are also other teachers from whom he can and must learn. And presumably these teachers have the right to teach also. Their right is their competence. The day is past when teaching can be defined by and reduced to authoritative position. But does not a uniquely juridical emphasis do just that?

Later Archbishop Whealon remarks: "Because of the moral content and teaching effect of the code, the approval of the Committee on Doctrine, NCCB, is essential." Would it not be a better account of things in the contemporary world if the statement were fleshed out as follows: "Because of the moral content and teaching effect of the code, the approval of the Committee on Doctrine is only meaningful if it is well attuned to contemporary medical and theological thought, and very sensitive to a host of values other than institutional conformity."

Finally, in discussing an individual Catholic who does not follow "the

[69] John F. Whealon, "Questions and Answers on the Ethical and Religious Directives for Catholic Hospitals," *Hospital Progress* 52 (1971) 70–75.

[70] *Ibid.*, p. 7.

[71] Gregory Baum, "Does Morality Call for the Church?" *Proceedings of the Catholic Theological Society of America* 25 (1970) 159–73.

authorized code for Catholic morality," the Archbishop states: "It is possible to find these days a Catholic writer on speculative moral theology advancing in nearly every subject a theory contrary to traditional Catholic doctrine. You cannot 'follow' him because he is not an authorized leader of the People of God.'"[72] Once again we encounter the authority emphasis. It is not precisely because one is an *authorized* leader of the People of God that one may or should follow him, but rather because being such and being collegially such, it can be presumed that his sources of wisdom and experience generate something closer to the truth than the resources of an individual. In this sense we may and indeed must follow anyone who speaks the truth, whether authorized or not. Whether he speaks the truth and by what criteria we know this is the question, and it is a question that cannot be collapsed into a question of mere authorization. Authorization, before it can be spoken of as a right, must first be seen as a responsibility to the many components of the learning process where truth can be discovered. I have belabored this point because I am convinced that before bishops can become the truly effective teachers we so badly need, they must be liberated from a one-sidedly juridical notion of their teaching prerogatives.[73]

The status of women is another area where profound human (and thereby moral-theological) concerns are at stake. As Janet Kalven points out, women's liberation has come into existence against the background of the black movement, student movements, and the third-world emergence and has adopted very often their heady rhetoric, guerilla tactics, and shrill anticapitalist ideology.[74] But surely it would be a pity if these sometimes bizarre tactics and the violent rhetoric blinded us to the genuine moral dimension cast up by the new feminism. That we have a true moral concern here is clear from at least three facts. First, when half the population of a country is deprived of opportunity for full human development, we clearly have a moral problem. Secondly, to some extent or other the Church, in her theology and practice, has con-

[72] Whealon, *art. cit.*, p. 75.

[73] In a similar vein, cf. Andrew Greeley, "After the Synod," *America* 125 (1971) 424–26. This same unfortunate juridical emphasis appears in the preamble of the recently approved *Ethical and Religious Directives for Catholic Health Facilities*. The last paragraph states: "The moral evaluation of new scientific developments and legitimately debated questions must be finally submitted to the teaching authority of the Church in the person of the local Bishop, who has the ultimate responsibility for teaching Catholic doctrine." Because the local bishop has "ultimate responsibility for teaching Catholic doctrine" hardly means that legitimately debated questions must be submitted to him for his evaluation. This heavy juridicism of outlook suggests that teaching really means "deciding" in the new directives. The ecclesiology operative here is, well, quaint.

[74] Janet Kalven, "Women's Liberation: Some Issues for Parents and Educators," *Living Light* 8 (1971) 6–19.

tributed to this situation of oppression. Thirdly, Daniel Maguire is certainly right when he says of women's liberation that it is "clearly one of the most important developments in the field of ethics today because it is dominated by the most fundamental of ethical questions: '*What does human mean?*'"[75]

Even the most recent literature on this subject is enormous[76] and difficult to organize. It might be helpful to approach it under three titles: the oppression, the causes, proposed solutions.

1) *The oppression.* In what sense do contemporary women really need liberation? What is the oppression? In his thoughtful article Maguire underlines the fact that they are victims of a bad myth: "*die Küche und die Kinder.*" Domesticity is woman's identifying essence. Cut off from the child-filled kitchen, she is a creature exiled from her natural habitat. Not only is woman defined in terms of this limited function, but we then proceed to distort this function. Maguire finds plenty of evidence for this distortion in early theological writings, right up to Thomas' teaching that the generation of women is due to the indisposition of the reproductive materials, or perhaps to adverse weather conditions.

Sidney Callahan, who has done some of the most insightful and sensitive writing on this subject that I have encountered, agrees with Maguire that women have been reduced to pure function: to satisfying men and to producing children.[77] Regardless of their differences, all women's-liberation people have one thing in common: "anger that women are socially defined and limited by male definitions." Women who aspire to something unrelated to men and children are said to be "masculine." Once a woman is defined in terms of sex-based stereotypes, the doors of political, economic, educational, ecclesiastical opportunity close in her face one by one. This "Myth America" is not only reflected but abetted by television. Kalven points out that woman is defined by six customary roles on the contemporary TV screen: mother-housewife, sex-seller, spender, secretary, civic actor, social psychotic.

The mother-housewife bears and rears the children, soothes her husband after his hard day's work, and seems to spend a great deal of her time learning from her

[75] Daniel C. Maguire, "Different but Equal: A Moral Assessment of Women's Liberation," *Living Light* 8 (1971) 35–47, at 35.

[76] E.g., the entire issue of *Journal of Marriage and the Family* 33 (1971) is given over to a study of "Sexism in Family Studies." Scholars from the women's-liberation movement examine the field of family studies critically and in a style often acerbic and polemic. A superb introductory bibliography is that of Peggy Ann Way, "Women, the Church and Liberation: A Growth-Oriented Bibliography," *Dialog* 10 (1971) 93–103.

[77] Sidney Callahan, "Feminine Response to Function," *Humanitas* 6 (1971) 295–310; also "Toward Liberating Families," *Living Light* 8 (1971) 54–60.

neighbor the secrets of spotless laundry, shiny floors, and perfect coffee. The sex-seller is slim, sweet-smelling, eternally youthful and alluring; her decorative presence is used to promote everything from cigarettes to farm machinery, and to encourage women to vast expenditures on cosmetics to achieve the approved image. The spender plays a crucial role in the consumer economy, fortifying her ego as she increases the sales volume in the shopping plaza .... The secretary is channeled into jobs that are essentially extensions of either the housewife or the sex-object role, e.g., receptionist, airline hostess, waitress, teacher, nurse (in these latter roles generally under male supervision). Then there is the civic actor, who finds an outlet for her energies in community work, only to discover that the work itself is often ineffectual, failing to reach the levels where the real decisions are made. Finally, when a woman is unable to find fulfillment in the accepted roles, she becomes a social psychotic, seeking escape in drink, pills, drugs, or perhaps the psychiatrist's couch.... [78]

This scathing scenario is all too true and reveals a profound and dehumanizing (for both men and women) sex-based discrimination. It has led Susan Brownmiller to conclude: "Women are an oppressed class. Our oppression is total, affecting every facet of our lives. We are exploited as sex objects, breeders, domestic servants, and cheap labor. We are considered inferior beings whose only purpose is to enhance men's lives."[79]

2) *The causal factors.* How did things get this way? It is often contended, as Jaroslav Pelikan points out,[80] that theology itself provided justification for the inferiority of women in the twofold assertion that Eve was created after Adam and was the one responsible for bringing sin into the world. Joseph A. Grassi reviews the New Testament evidence and concludes that "many statements about women are time-bound to the inferior economic, social and religious position of woman in the ancient world, as well as time-bound to an old theology that held this to be the result of woman's sin."[81]

Margaret Maxey traces much of the problem to the theological models of women which have prevailed.[82] The first model was Augustinian and it placed woman somewhere between Eve and Mary. At the root of this model is the Augustinian equation of original sin, concupiscence, and sexual passion. Such an equation builds on a dualistic psychology which

[78] Kalven, *art. cit.*, pp. 12–13.

[79] Susan Brownmiller, "Sisterhood Is Powerful," *New York Times Magazine*, March 15, 1970, p. 27.

[80] Jaroslav Pelikan, Jr., "Eve or Mary: A Test Case in the Development of Doctrine," *Christian Ministry* 2 (1971) 21–22.

[81] Joseph A. Grassi, "Women's Liberation: The New Testament Perspectives," *Living Light* 8 (1971) 22–34.

[82] Margaret Maxey, "Beyond Eve and Mary: A Theological Alternative for Women's Liberation," *Dialog* 10 (1971) 112–22.

awards primacy to rational control as an index of man's superiority over women. Though St. Thomas sloughed off much of the sexual pessimism of Augustine, he continued the distortion in his own way. While woman is no longer the incarnation of lust, the carrier of evil and guilt, she is reduced in Thomas to a natural function (reproduction). In the contemporary Church, woman acquires theological significance because of her sexuality, but it is still a liability. This might be called a "utility model" in a male-dominated institution. According to this model, implicit as it may be, "women are considered an institutional liability and a personal impediment in the ministrations of an androcentric, power-oriented, hierarchically-controlled 'divine institution.'" Maxey concludes that we shall never liberate woman unless we can induce theology to liberate her.

Sidney Callahan argues that the view of Freud and the orthodox psychiatric tradition that "anatomy is destiny" supported the sexual reductionism that has imprisoned women.[83] However, this is being reversed by men like Erik Erikson who highlight other than sexual factors in human development, e.g., the need to be *somebody*. In this sense contemporary psychology is a powerful ally in women's protest at being reduced to sexual function. Their ego-based needs are being viewed as valid *human* aspirations.

It is widely argued that the Church has contributed more than her mite to the sexism of our culture by her long practice of fixed roles drawn up on the lines of sex (Grassi, Kalven, Callahan, Maxey, Bowers).[84] Perhaps the most telling statement of this is that of Mary Daly:

As long as the Church maintains a significant distinction between hierarchy and laity, the exclusion of woman from the hierarchy is a radical affirmation of their inferior position among the People of God. By this exclusion the Church is in a very real and effective way teaching that women are not fully human and conditioning people to accept this as irremediable fact. It is saying that the sexual differentiation is—for one sex—a handicap so crippling that no personal qualities of intelligence, virtue, or leadership can overcome it.[85]

Esther Woo probably comes closest to a satisfactory explanation of the origins of sexism in history.[86] She points out that muscular strength was a prime value in primitive society because of the need for survival. The

---

[83] Sidney Callahan, as in *Humanitas* (cf. n. 77 above).

[84] Marilyn Bowers, "Women's Liberation: A Catholic View," *Theology Today* 28 (1971) 24–35.

[85] Mary Daly, *The Church and the Second Sex* (New York: Harper & Row, 1965) p. 155.

[86] Esther Woo, "Theology Confronts Women's Liberation," *America* 124 (1971) 257–59.

priority of this value carried, however softly, the implication of the inferiority of women. Now once a value is established, it tends to perpetuate itself. Psychologically we grow in the image of what we feel and are made to feel. Hence the gulf between male superiority and female inferiority became wider and wider until machines began to take over for muscle. Perhaps Woo should also have adverted to the basic value of fecundity. The urgency of both muscle and fecundity suggests how functional definitions along sexual lines could settle and become stereotypes. In this light perhaps it must be said that the myth of female inferiority does not trace to religious sources and theology, but was only supported and perpetuated by them.

3) *Some proposed solutions.* How will change come about? Sidney Callahan, arguing that *la petite différence* must be preserved, rightly insists on the other hand that the bedroom is not the boardroom.[87] There must be equality and neutrality in certain areas of life. Some slight headway can be made by attempting to live this equality in one's own family, but ultimately institutions must provide massive support to these isolated family efforts. Callahan suggests (with several others) that women bishops, priests, chancery officials, etc. would help. Child-care centers, maternity leaves, greater availability of higher education, equality in job promotion—these are but a few of the practical steps that must be taken. Ultimately, however, Callahan believes that change will come about only through the growing example of women who are happily married mothers and lawyers, doctors, engineers, and so on.[88]

Janet Kalven suggests several ways in which parents and educators can purge our attitudes of misogynist prejudices and our structures of institutional sexism.[89] We must, e.g., emphasize the primacy of individual persons over the generic sex roles, avoid linking temperament

---

[87] Sidney Callahan, as in *Living Light* (cf. n. 77 above).

[88] There are those who associate abortion with women's liberation, especially abortion-on-demand. Just how "liberating" abortion-on-demand would be is, at best, highly questionable. For the fetus it would be liberating, but only in the sense that it would free him definitively from parents who would do this to him. For the mother it could easily represent a subtle form of enslavement to male sexuality. Some recent literature on abortion: Paul W. Rahmeier, "Abortion and the Reverence for Life," *Christian Century* 138 (1971) 556–60; Rachel C. Wahlberg, "The Woman and the Fetus: 'One Flesh'?" *ibid.* 138 (1971) 1045–48; Howard Moody, "Abortion: Woman's Right and Legal Problem," *Christianity and Crisis* 31 (1971) 27–32; Kenneth J. Sharp, "Abortion's Psychological Price," *Christianity Today* 15 (1971) 4–6; *ibid.*, pp. 36–37; R. Troisfontaines, S.J., "Faut-il legaliser l'avortement?" *Nouvelle revue théologique* 93 (1971) 489–512; Hans Rotter, S.J., "Die Geistbeseelung im Werden des Menschen," *Zeitschrift für katholische Theologie* 93 (1971) 168–71. The *Review for Religious* carries an ongoing bibliography which contains many entries not mentioned here—on all matters of concern to the theological ethician.

[89] *Art. cit.* (n. 74 above).

and qualities to sex roles, avoid sex-typing of occupations, promote the idea of marriage as partnership. Interestingly, several studies (Callahan, Bowers, Kalven) note that the celibacy of religious women can be a strong affirmation of the value of the person independently of sexual roles. Paul VI, referring to a "fictitious equality which denies differences established by the Creator Himself," still urges that there must be laws which "recognize [woman's] due measure of personal liberty and her equal rights to participate in cultural, economic, social and political life."[90]

Gregory Baum recently underlined the fact that the Church teaches powerfully through her institutional policies and priorities.[91] Nearly every writer on the new feminism asserts that the Church must drastically revise her institutional policies on women. For instance, Grassi notes that "there is no reason in the New Testament to keep the Church from moving as quickly as possible, locally and internationally, toward complete equality of women with men in all that concerns the ministry (especially the priesthood) and leadership in the liturgy and life of the people."[92] This is supported by Callahan, Bowers, Maxey, and a host of others. Furthermore, there must be much greater discretion in the use of biblical images (God the Father, God the Son) which reflect the male dominated culture of biblical times.

Paul Palmer, S.J., argues convincingly that Jesus made a radical contribution to the liberation of women in reversing the old double standard where divorce is concerned.[93] In the cultural setting at the time of Christ, the husband enjoyed the right to divorce his wife, but not vice versa. The wife belonged to the husband, so that adultery was not infidelity toward the wife, but was viewed exclusively as a violation by another man of the husband's right over his wife. Jesus reversed this: "Whoever divorces his wife and marries another commits adultery against her" (Mk 10:11). Palmer does not draw the implicit conclusion but he could have: the double standard should be eliminated everywhere else too. Pelikan believes that Christianity undermined the inferiority of women by the image of Mary, the highest of creatures. He believes that a more constructive view of women must involve a development of this tradition.

I hope it is not male chauvinism to say that the most fascinating article on women's liberation from a theological point of view is that of

---

[90] In "Octogesima adveniens," *The Pope Speaks* 16 (1971) 144.

[91] Cf. n. 71 above.

[92] Grassi, *art. cit.*, p. 32.

[93] Paul F. Palmer, S.J., "Christian Breakthrough in Women's Lib," *America* 124 (1971) 634–37.

Carl Braaten.[94] Braaten first insists that liberation is a misnomer. Money and careers can be the gauge of justice in society, but not of liberation. If women's liberation does nothing more than loose women into the job market, it will simply transfer their enslavement to a new locale. Real liberation will come about when we discover new ways to realize the full human potential envisioned in the high Christian ethic of sex, love, and marriage. This will sound like heresy to some within the "movement," but Braaten refuses to pull his punches. Therefore he sets out to offer the conditions under which the liberation movement ought to proceed.

Since *vive la différence* is a biblical concept, and since male and female in their sexual differences are an image of God, Braaten argues that "sexuality is not the source of sin; overcoming it is not the way of liberation." After describing the fickle, fleeting, and frustrative character of libido and eros, he centers his attention on *philia* (friendship). It is friendship that generates constancy, loyalty, fidelity. What is at stake, then, in true liberation is the chance for *philia*-love. "This is the criterion of real liberation." This *philia*-love must itself be supported by the forgiving love of *agape*, the quiet acceptance of the challenge to fulfil the other person. "The quest for liberation not carefully guided by the demands of love in its multidimensional reality will only lead to new forms of alienation and oppression .... Our contention is that women's power can bring justice, as it is doing in all fields, but only love can bring liberation."[95]

Hinging liberation on love, not just justice, links it immediately to marriage and the family. These structures can be liberating frameworks or confining straitjackets. But Braaten is convinced that marriage must be a norm in the quest for liberation of women. "If marriage is getting in the way of women's liberation, then liberation is wrongly conceived or marriage is not realizing its potential." And it is clear that Braaten does not mean serialized monogamy, but a vigorous countercultural union lived in the promise of lifelong fidelity. However, he argues that a variety of patterns in the concrete ordering of marriage is possible and desirable. A new type of family situation "is what I think women are looking for." Braaten suggests new family structures where children can grow up also with the elderly and single people, wherein domestic chores are shared, and new collective homes with a network of supportive relationships; for everyone is in need of liberation, and all will be liberated together or no one will be liberated—a note sounded by much recent literature. If we

[94] Carl Braaten, "Untimely Reflections on Women's Liberation," *Dialog* 10 (1971) 104-11.
[95] *Ibid.*, p. 108

do not find new ways to realize the potential envisioned in the Christian ethic of sex, love, and marriage, liberation will turn out to be a subhuman venture.

In summary, it can be said that theology has an important part to play in facing the moral problem of women's liberation, though I believe its contribution can be exaggerated. The task is at least threefold. First, as Margaret Maxey notes, theology must critique past models dominating women's self-interpretation and reconstruct new models out of the richness of the Christian tradition. Secondly, theology must put its own house in order by encouraging the emergence of women theologians of competence and influence in far greater numbers.[96] This will occur only if theological positions are open to women on an equal basis with men— e.g., in colleges and seminaries. Thirdly, theological disciplines are very well positioned to insist that the Church, the continuation of the human Christ, must teach what it is to be human by her own inner life. If her own structures and ministry continue to speak of humanity in terms of but one sex, must we not think that the Church is seriously compromising her mission in the contemporary world? I believe so. Granted, there are hosts of practical pastoral problems to work out; but here is a chance for genuine leadership. Too often in the past the Catholic community has almost reluctantly accommodated after everybody else has shown the way. If the "official Church" continues to turtle across the finish line in this way, is she not but a pale image of her radical and innovative Founder? In an age of faceless impersonality and bureaucratic hugeness, we long for the fresh, the bold move. However, the number of black bishops in this country gives little cause for optimism about the Church's promotion of women's liberation.[97] Nonetheless, we have here a serious moral problem and, it would seem, an idea whose time has come.[98]

[96] Cf. *Christian Century* 88 (1971) 648.

[97] The subject did surface at the recent Synod of Bishops (1971). And some very promising interventions were made, particularly by Cardinal George Flahiff (Winnipeg) and Archbishop Leo Byrne (St. Paul-Minneapolis); cf. *Catholic Chronicle*, Nov. 12, 1971. Bishop John Gran (Oslo) and Archbishop Samuel Carter (Kingston, Jamaica) were also very positive. In light of this opening, one can wonder whether Mary Daly is totally correct when she says that "the religious dimensions in the movement are going to be outlined by the women inside it and not by Church authorities outside it" ("The Church and Women," *Theology Today* 28 [1971] 349–54, at 353).

[98] On women's ministry cf. the excellent articles in *American Ecclesiastical Review:* John J. Begley, S.J., and Carl J. Armbruster, S.J., "Women and Office in the Church," 165 (1971) 145–57; Agnes Cunningham, "Women and the Diaconate," *ibid*, pp. 158–66. The Armbruster-Begley study concludes that "the question of ordination of women is not theological but pastoral ('What is best for the service of the Church and mankind?')." It is clear that Armbruster and Begley move in the direction of the ordination of women; yet they are balanced and realistic in their assessment of the situation.

From women's liberation to "Gay Liberation" may seem an enormous step. Be that as it may, the proponents of the "lavender revolution" have come out of hiding, have turned militant in anything but a limp-wristed way, and have laid their cause ("Gay is Good") at the door of the Church. As Elliott Wright points out, "the Church will have to make some response, even if it is total, negative silence."[99] What is this response to be? Both Wright and John A. Coleman[100] report the contemporary attempts at dialogue with and/or ministry to the homosexual.

The *Christian Century* gave its directions to the churches when it editorialized:

it is time to get out of the business of being judgmental about our fellow human beings . . . . It is important to take a stand in support of homosexuals' freedom from discrimination and persecution. Moreover, it is essential to move from words to deeds. On this level nothing less than full and complete acceptance will serve: not tolerance, not sympathy—these smack of judgmental self-righteousness.[101]

The responses to this were predictable: applause and indignation.[102] The basic weakness of the editorial appears if we juxtapose "their bid for acceptance as normal human beings" with the exhortation that we "take a stand in support of homosexuals' freedom from discrimination and persecution." For the militant homophile community, any judgment which does not accept their condition as normal is discriminating and an act of persecution. A correspondent caught this and noted that the inner logic of the *Century*'s position would lead to the removal of the homosexual condition from critical clinical assessment. Anything else would be "judgmental self-righteousness."

As the *Century*'s editorial showed, the word "acceptance" is slippery and extremely difficult to deal with in this context. If it means full acceptance of the person in spite of the condition, there should be no human or Christian quibble with it. If it means freedom from oppression and dehumanizing persecution, still no quibble. If, however, it means acceptance of the condition as normal and good (and this is the only

---

Cf. also *Clergy Review* 55 (1971) 866–93. This section of the issue is devoted to "God and the Feminine." Also Sarah B. Doely, ed., *Women's Liberation and the Church* (New York: Association Press, 1970).

[99] Elliott Wright, "The Church and the Gay Liberation," *Christian Century* 88 (1971) 281–85.

[100] John A. Coleman, "The Churches and the Homosexual," *America* 124 (1971) 113–17.

[101] "To Accept Homosexuals," *Christian Century* 88 (1971) 275.

[102] Cf. *ibid.*, pp. 497–500.

rendering the militant homosexual will accept, because he believes his self-integrity demands this), that is a different thing. Whether a condition (and the acts consequent upon it) is "good and normal"—and hence promotive of an individual's good and growth—is subject to a closely related double scrutiny: clinical and moral. To ask a Christian to accept a condition as "good and normal" without such scrutiny is asking him to act irresponsibly and ultimately uncharitably. For if the condition is "good and normal," impartial enquiry will establish this and help to blast the stereotypes so oppressive to homosexuals. If it is not "good and normal," then to call it such would be to imprison the homosexual in a reverse sort of sexism and make any true liberation impossible.

Francis H. Touchet has caught this point very cleanly.[103] The homophile organizations (such as Gay Liberation Front, Gay Activist Alliance, The American Church) ignore the prime focus on persons for a chosen focus on sexual preference and in doing so are guilty of an enslaving sexism. This monochromatic view jeopardizes any acceptance of the homosexual and in this sense the homophile militants are their own worst enemies.

What is the proper attitude of a Christian in this matter? Much depends on how one reads the evidence. A brief sampling of recent literature will reveal this. For instance, Paul Popenoe shows no hesitation or uncertainty in his judgment.[104] The homosexual should change "for the same reason that society tries to change other persons who are sick with a dangerous communicable disease." Relying on Irving Bieber,[105] Popenoe states flatly that "where he *wants* to be changed, he can be changed." It is because so many therapists are behind the times in techniques that the condition has been judged irreversible. His final judgment: "Homosexuality is, for every possible reason, neither necessary nor desirable. It is a definite evil, from every point of view, and should be looked on as much."[106]

Joseph A. McCaffrey has a different report to make.[107] Under the dominating influence of Freud, homosexuality has long been viewed as symptomatic of a serious flaw in the personality. Recently, however, it is seen as indicative only of an erotic impulse toward the same sex. "There is no research which categorically indicates that homosexuality is *per se*

[103] Francis H. Touchet, "A View from the Other Side of the Garden," *Listening*, Winter, 1971, pp. 42–48.

[104] Paul Popenoe, "Are Homosexuals Necessary?" *Marriage* 53 (1971) 38–43.

[105] Irving Bieber, *Homosexuality* (New York: Basic Books, 1962) p. 358.

[106] Popenoe, *art. cit.*, p. 43.

[107] Joseph A. McCaffrey, "Homosexuality in the Seventies," *Catholic World* 213 (1971) 121–25; "Homosexuality, Aquinas and the Church," *ibid.*, pp. 183–86.

symptomatic of severe emotional problems." As for the attitudes within the Church toward the homosexual, McCaffrey believes they were given shape by St. Thomas. Aquinas viewed homosexuality from the perspective of a narrowly procreational sex ethic. McCaffrey wants to reopen the question within the context of orthodox Church thinking. He asks: "What is the evidence which so strikingly and clearly condemns the practicing homosexual? No answer at present which purports to defend the Church's position is solidly based. In fact, it is precisely at the juncture of *sound reasons* that Church theorizing collapses."[108]

Two things remain dissatisfyingly unclear in McCaffrey's essays. First, what is to count as evidence or sound reasons? McCaffrey notes the inadequacy of Thomas' sexual ethics. Furthermore, he repeatedly states that "there is nothing in the literature that proves that where there is homosexuality there is mental illness." The inference seems to be that once it is established that Thomas' approach was inadequate and that homosexuality does not *per se* involve mental illness, there remain no "sound reasons" or "evidence" for hesitancy about homosexuality. That is a bit much. Secondly, it is not clear what kind of approval McCaffrey's reopening of the question would call for.

Charles Curran, in an extensive study, notes that there are three Christian positions on the morality of homosexual behavior.[109] The first states straightforwardly that homosexual acts are wrong. Generally this is based on the basic procreativity of sexuality. Moral theologian John Harvey is cited as an example of this approach. Secondly, a small but significant group sees homosexual acts as neutral. Thus *Towards a Quaker View of Sex*[110] argues that homosexuality is no worse than left-handedness. Some who argue neutrality are rather unnuanced,[111] others more informed.[112] Still Curran, rightly I believe, rejects these approaches as contrary to the radical significance of human sexuality, which "has its proper meaning in terms of the love union of male and female." There is a meaning to man and his relationships which cannot be described as totally neutral.

The third position is a "mediating" one which states that in general homosexual acts are wrong but that homosexual behavior for some might not fall under the condemnation. Curran agrees with the con-

[108] McCaffrey, *art. cit.*, p. 186.

[109] Charles E. Curran, "Homosexuality and Moral Theology: Methodological and Substantive Considerations," *Thomist* 35 (1971) 447–81.

[110] *Towards a Quaker View of Sex* (London: Society of Friends, 1963) p. 26.

[111] E.g., Robert W. Wood, *Christ and the Homosexual* (New York: Vantage Press, 1960).

[112] E.g., Neale A. Secor, in *The Same Sex* (Philadelphia: Pilgrim Press, 1969) pp. 67–79.

clusion, but not the reasoning. For example, he faults H. Kimball Jones (who judges homosexual acts legitimate at times because there is nothing else a person can do) for a notion of sin which overwhelms original structures.[113] "There is a basic meaning of human sexuality which sin neither eradicates, neutralizes nor reduces to the same ethical significance as homosexual relations." Similarly Curran rejects John McNeill's idea that some homosexual acts can be viewed as falling under the principle of choice of the lesser evil,[114] for "in this opinion the act is still objectively wrong." Rather Curran returns to his principle of compromise. Sin forms a part of objective reality. "The presence of sin means that at times one might not be able to do what would be done if there were no sin present." In one sense, then, the act is not objectively wrong, "because in the presence of sin it remains the only viable alternative for the individual."

John Harvey, O.S.F.S., objects to this compromise approach.[115] His objection does not seem to be against the principle of compromise as such, but against its application to the homosexual situation. Briefly, homosexual activity is not the only viable alternative. First, Harvey believes that "a homosexual accepting and living a fully embraced chastity out of love for God and nourishing that life in prayer and community can sublimate freely homosexual tendencies." Secondly, Harvey appeals to recent studies and argues that therapists have found that the young homosexual who is strongly motivated to change his orientation "has an excellent chance of success." Therefore to approach his situation with a principle of compromise is a pastoral disservice to him.

This face-off between Curran and Harvey is basically factual: whether there are humanly viable alternatives for the homosexual. Situating the problem at this point means that both Curran and Harvey view homosexual activity as a deviation from the ideal or normal. Little evidence that I have seen would seriously shake that view. Therefore the heart of the pastoral problem seems to be the existence of viable human alternatives. This has to be settled before individuals or the community (Church) can hope to adopt a constructive pastoral attitude; for until this matter is clear, pastoral attitudes featuring rejection or modified acceptance of the homosexual condition could be equally inhuman and therefore equally nonliberating.

[113] H. Kimball Jones, *Toward a Christian Understanding of the Homosexual* (New York: Assocation Press, 1966).

[114] John J. McNeill, S.J., "The Christian Male Homosexual," *Homiletic and Pastoral Review* 70 (1970) 667–77, 747–58, 828–36.

[115] John F. Harvey, O.S.F.S., "The Pastoral Implications of Church Teaching on Homosexuality," *Linacre Quarterly* 38 (1971) 157–64.

Two phenomena make the discovery of the truly human and Christian path more difficult than it should be and both originate from the homophile community itself. One is the unilateral emphasis on sexual preference and genital sexuality to the neglect of the broader personal aspects of the problem. The second is the militant insistence that the condition is irreversible, or, at any rate, good and normal.[116] These emphases will only tend to mobilize societal resistance, and delay liberation from oppression. More importantly, since they by-pass the key problem, they attempt to gain civil liberation at the serious risk of deepening enslavement at a far more profound and more human level.

McCaffrey is certainly right when he concludes: "If society meets the homosexual with a factual understanding, the seventies will witness a much more humane, cogent, and healthy statement of the place of the homosexual in the United States."[117] But if liberation is to prove more than a cruel slogan, the emphasis must fall heavily on the word "factual."

Another area where the concept of liberation is proving extremely rich is that of social ethics. Some very interesting literature has appeared recently. Only a few items can be reviewed here.[118]

Two recent working papers use liberation as their key organizing concept. One is "Justice in the World," submitted by the Secretariate of the Synod of Bishops to the national hierarchies.[119] The other was produced by William F. Ryan, S.J., and Joseph Komonchak for the Inter-American Bishops' Meeting in Mexico City (May 18–21).[120] At several points there is a remarkable similarity in both papers in the way they present the Church's social mission.

First, both draw upon an incarnational view of the Church as the basis for social action and social ethics. For instance, the synodal document notes that the Church was intended by its Founder to be a sign of, a

---

[116] That there is a measure of inconsistency in arguing irreversibility and normalcy seems clear.

[117] McCaffrey, art. cit., p. 125.

[118] Cf. also Edward G. Bozzo, "The Relevance of Hope for a Person-centered Moral Theology," American Benedictine Review 22 (1971) 326–52; American Ecclesiastical Review 164 (May, 1971) entire issue; Louis de Vaucelles, "Nouvelles perspectives chrétiennes en matière socio-politique," Etudes, Aug.-Sept., 1971, pp. 241–52; J. Ermel, "Y a-t-il une éthique sociale chrétienne?" La foi et le temps, May-June, 1971, pp. 257–87; William H. Lazareth, "The Church as Advocate of Social Justice," Lutheran World 18 (1971) 245–67; Charles C. West, "Salvation: Divine and Human," Princeton Seminary Bulletin 64 (1971) 14–21; Bradley C. Hanson, "The Church's Mission in a Secularized World," Religion in Life 60 (1971) 225–35; Fernand Arsenault, "L'Ethique sociale chez Teilhard de Chardin," Studies in Religion 1 (1971) 25–44; Rubem A. Alves, "Some Thoughts on a Program for Ethics," Union Seminary Quarterly Review 26 (1971) 153–70.

[119] Cf. Catholic Mind 64 (1971) 29–42. For comment quite critical of the more practical aspects of the document, cf. Idoc, June 26, 1971, pp. 51–76.

[120] Cf. ibid., pp. 13–28.

means to, God's presence among men. But "Christ died and rose again to liberate man from sin and death. This liberation ought to be realized here in this world, as an anticipation of our definitive salvation." In this same spirit the Ryan-Komonchak study states that "authentic Catholic tradition has always resisted tendencies to separate human enterprise from the divine. Creation and redemption, nature and grace are complementary, not competitive." On this basis the study asserts that whenever man fulfils his nature, God's kingdom is realized on earth. Thus, "God's will for each person is fulfillment through human efforts, rooted in the enabling gifts of grace." For this reason the "kingdom begins to be realized wherever the poor and the weak experience justice and peace."

Secondly, both studies see unjust social structures and systems as the embodiment of sinfulness and selfishness, a point that was mentioned at the outset of this section. For instance, Ryan-Komonchak note that "structures and systems, the ambiguous creations of ambiguous men, embody mankind's collective failures and sinfulness." Thirdly, both documents agree that "the Church's principal mission is to manifest, in its teaching, its life and its activity, the liberating work of Christ." Fourthly, as Ryan-Komonchak note, this liberation is twofold: "the rescue of the enslaved, both rich and poor; and the conversion and development of all. One is not less a missionary responsibility than the other. They are inseparable in an integrated, incarnational Christianity." Fifthly, both agree that the role of the Church is not to provide technical solutions, ready-made, to injustices that exist. Rather it is to be the conscience of the world, denouncing sin wherever it reigns, "whether over an individual's selfish heart or throughout an unjust social order." Finally, the two insist, in the words of the synodal study, that "the Christian who fails in his earthly obligations fails thereby in his obligations toward his neighbor, more so still toward God Himself, and he endangers his eternal salvation."

What is particularly satisfying in these papers is the integral view of man which is their basis. Christian theologians have too often in the past been unable to provide a satisfying theological foundation for social ethics.[121] They have vacillated between a natural-law perspective (which too easily neglects the eschatological perspective of Christian action as well as the existence of sin) and a narrow biblicism (which at times

---

[121] As witness to this, cf. *Christian Social Ethics in a Changing World*, ed. John C. Bennett (New York: Association Press, 1966). Of Catholic social doctrine Oswald von Nell-Breuning states: "it is ... almost entirely social philosophy and only in a limited way social theology. It needs further development on the theological side" (*Sacramentum mundi* 6 [New York: Herder and Herder, 1970] 108).

became so other-worldly that it was inhuman). The concept of liberation is an excellent vehicle for synthesizing these false polarities. For (1) if personal sin embodies itself in unjust and enslaving structures, (2) if Christ is the liberator supreme, (3) if the Church is the continuance of His liberating presence, then clearly the Church's main task is one of liberation and clearly this means freedom from *all* enslavements—both its roots in sin and its appearance in unjust human structures. The two are not separable; they are continuous. In other words, just as there is a continuity between sin and social enslavement, so there is a continuity between inner personal liberation through grace and concrete Christian social action. To conceive of the good of man in terms of only one is to misread reality as Christ illumined it.

One of the finest social statements I have seen from an American prelate is that of Most Rev. Humberto Medeiros.[122] Archbishop Medeiros notes that an ethic which hopes to appeal to the conscience of contemporary men must be both "comprehensive in scope and consistent in substance." The remarkable aspect of the Archbishop's text is its repeated emphasis on the fact that consistency in an ethic of life demands a strong stand on issues touching the quality of life. Thus, "if we support the right of every fetus to be born, consistency demands that we equally support every man's continuing rights to a truly human existence." Medeiros applies this down the line to problems of housing, education, welfare, race, warfare, etc., where the quality of life is continually threatened. An excellent example of a truly holistic perspective.

It is the annual experience of the compositor of these Notes that they never really end. They simply grind to a halt. This means that a good deal of valuable literature has been necessarily omitted in organizing the overview. Perhaps partial compensation can be made by listing some of the more significant entries.[123]

[122] Humberto Medeiros, "A Call to a Consistent Ethic of Life and the Law," *Pilot*, July 10, 1971, p. 7. Unfortunately this fine address seems otherwise unavailable.

[123] Michael Moloney, S.J., "Sin and Christian Morality," *African Ecclesiastical Review* 13 (1971) 122–26; Thomas F. McMahon, C.S.V., and Raymond Fecteau, "The Morality of Whitelisting," *American Ecclesiastical Review* 164 (1971) 171–84; Daniel Callahan, "What Obligations Do We Have to Future Generations?" *American Ecclesiastical Review* 164 (1971) 265–80; Michael Allsopp, "Authority of Conscience," *Australasian Catholic Record* 148 (1971) 116–26; Robert Hall, "Legal Toleration of Civil Disobedience," *Ethics* 81 (1971) 128–42; Bruno Ribes, "Ethique, science et vie," *Etudes*, June, 1971, pp. 823–43; Clyde L. Manschreck, "Control and Freedom: The Individual and Society,"

Encounter 32 (1971) 183–207; Denis O'Callaghan, "The Meaning of Conscience," *Furrow* 22 (1971) 78–86; "Christ and Conscience," *ibid.*, pp. 188–97; "Boston Province Bishops on Vietnam War," *Idoc*, Aug. 28, 1971, pp. 91–96; P. J. McGrath, "On Not Re-Interpreting 'Humanae vitae,'" *Irish Theological Quarterly* 38 (1971) 13–143; George A. Kanoti, C.R., "Ethical Implications in Psychotherapy," *Journal of Religion and Health* 10 (1971) 180–91; Wm. R. Albury and Richard J. Connell, "*Humanae vitae* and the Ecological Argument," *Laval théologique et philosophique* 27 (1971) 135–49; Hugh Trowell, "The Good Death' versus 'Euthanasia,'" *New Blackfriars* 52 (1971) 346–51; B. Downing, "The Case for Voluntary Euthanasia," *ibid.*, pp. 351–54; E. Hamel, S.J., "Lux evangelii in constitutione 'Gaudium et spes,'" *Periodica* 60 (1971) 103–20; George C. Kerner, "The Immorality of Utilitarianism and the Escapism of Rule-Utilitarianism," *Philosophical Quarterly* 21 (1971) 36–50; Richard G. Henson, "Utilitarianism and the Wrongness of Killing," *Philosophical Review* 80 (1971) 320–37; William J. Tobin, "Personal Character of the Moral Act," *Priest* 27 (1971) 78–80; Walfred H. Peterson, "The Courts and Freedom of Conscience," *Religion in Life* 60 (1971) 247–56; William F. Allen, "New Approaches in Moral," *Pastoral Life* 20 (1971) 28–35; G. Bourgeault, "La spécificité de la morale chrétienne selon les Pères des deux premiers siècles," *Science et esprit* 23 (1971) 137–52; Ph. Delhaye, "Dogme et morale: Un cas de fédéralisme théologique," *Seminarium* 11 (1971) 295–322, R. Hofmann, "Anthropologie de la morale," *Le supplément* 97 (1971) 141–49; C. Robert, "La situation de conflict." *ibid.* pp. 150–75; Peter Harris, "Faith and Morals," *The Way* 11 (1971) 211–18; Charles A. Joël, "Die therapeutische Insemination," *Zeitschrift für evangelische Ethik* 15 (1971) 215–26.

GENETIC MEDICINE: NOTES ON THE MORAL LITERATURE

T HE MORAL literature on genetic controls is enormous.[1] Furthermore, it touches on several different problems with ethical implications: eugenic engineering (both positive and negative), genetic counseling and screening, genetic abortion,[2] *in vitro* fertilization, cloning, etc. Much of the occasional writing is general in character.[3] The more systematic moral studies on genetics remind one of a masked ball: new disguises but behind them familiar faces. The familiar faces in this instance refer to the methodologies of well-known theologians on the (especially) American scene. Hence, even in the face of the exciting and/or frightening possibilities of contemporary biomedicine, there is a lingering sense of *déjà vu* in the moral literature. Briefly, since ultimate attitudes and judgments vis-à-vis various genetic interventions depend heavily on how the author builds his approach, the emphasis falls heavily on methodology. Three approaches are discernible: a consequentialist calculus, a more deontological attitude, a "mediating" approach.[4]

[1] Literature of the 1960's can be found in Rosalind P. Petchesky's *Issues in Biological Engineering*, ISHA Bulletin no. 7 (Institute for the Study of Science in Human Affairs; New York: Columbia Univ., 1969). Cf. also THEOLOGICAL STUDIES 30 (1969) 680-92, where I review the recent periodical literature. This literature will not be reviewed here. Another valuable bibliographical source is Sharmon Sollitto's "In the Literature," which appears regularly in the *Report* of the Hastings Center.

[2] A conference at Airlie House, Va. (Oct. 10-14, 1971) was devoted to "Ethical Issues in Genetic Counselling and the Use of Genetic Knowledge." It dealt heavily with counseling, screening, and abortion. The papers, currently in the process of publication, include thoughtful essays by Daniel Callahan, Paul Ramsey, James Gustafson, Leon Kass, and John Fletcher. For a brief report of this conference, cf. W. G. Peter, "Ethical Perspectives in the Use of Genetic Knowledge," *BioScience* 21 (Nov. 15, 1971) 1133-37.

[3] Cf., e.g., Donald Huisingh, "Should Man Control His Genetic Future?" *Zygon* 4 (1969) 188-99; S. E. Luria, "Modern Biology: A Terrifying Power," *Nation* 209 (1969) 406 ff.; Kenneth Vaux, "Cyborg, R. U. Human? Ethical Issues in Rebuilding Man," *Religion in Life* 39 (1970) 187-92. Articles of this kind abound in the medical journals and journals such as *Science* and *Science News*. Cf., e.g., *New York Times Magazine*, March 5, 1972, pp. 10 ff.

[4] The very problems theologians decide to discuss are important, for a false move here could bring theology and its important contributions to biomedical decisions into disrepute with the scientific world. Furthermore, too great a futurism would allow existing problems to get solved by default. The matter is complicated by the fact that theologians are at the mercy of the scientific world in deciding what problems are realistic and this very world gives ambiguous answers. For instance, James D. Watson reports of

CONSEQUENTIALIST CALCULUS

Joseph Fletcher, after reporting on some earlier writing on the subject,[5] sees the whole difference of opinion in terms of "apriorists" and "consequentialists."[6] This is, he says, "the rock-bottom issue... the definitive question in the ethical analysis of genetic control." The apriorists, relying on some kind of religious or nonempirical cognition, "would say, therefore, that therapeutic goals are not enough to justify *in vitro* fertilization, positive eugenics, or designed eugenic changes, no matter how desirable they might be." In contrast to this is a pragmatic or consequentialist ethics, which Fletcher claims as his own. "We reason from the data of each actual case or problem and then choose the course that offers an optimum or maximum of desirable consequences." Or again, "results are what counts and results are good when they contribute to human well being," a point to be situationally determined.

Fletcher then looks at a few cases and delivers his verdict. "I would vote for laboratory fertilization from donors to give a child to an infertile pair of spouses." As for cloning, Fletcher is a veritable cheerleader for the enthusiasts. "If the greatest good of the greatest number [i.e., the social good] were served by it," he would "vote" both for specializing the capacities of people by cloning and bioengineering

---

Joshua Lederberg's attitude toward cloning that "to him, serious talk about cloning is essentially crying wolf when a tiger is already inside the walls" ("Moving toward the Clonal Man," *Atlantic*, May, 1971, p. 52). Many authors view cloning as too far into the future to merit serious discussion now. On the other hand, statements such as that of Bernard D. Davis, M.D., are not infrequent: "Cloning is thus the aspect of genetic intervention that most requires public discussion today" (*New England Journal of Medicine* 285 [1971] 800).

[5] Inaccurately in at least several places. Speaking of "genetic engineering," Fletcher states that "Richard McCormick condemns it because, he believes, only monogamously married heterosexual reproduction is morally licit." The reference is to THEOLOGICAL STUDIES (cf. n. 1 above), where a position on "monogamously married heterosexual reproduction" is indeed endorsed; but this endorsement is far from a condemnation of all "genetic engineering," as even a quick reading will reveal. Similarly of Dr. Andre Hellegers Fletcher writes: "A Catholic obstetrician...has complained that it is 'arbitrary' to start regarding a fetus as human at the 20th week or at 'viability,' and yet the physician himself insists on the even more arbitrary religious doctrine that a fertilized ovum before implantation is human." Fletcher has misread Hellegers' point (*Washington Post*, Jan. 9, 1971, p. A21). Hellegers was simply challenging the *Post*'s concern over test-tube babies, since that paper had for years supported the proposition that fetuses before the 20th week could be destroyed. If fetuses can be destroyed before this time, Hellegers rightly wonders why it is improper for scientists to create such blobs of tissue. The point is the *Post*'s consistency, nothing more.

[6] Joseph Fletcher, "Ethical Aspects of Genetic Controls," *New England Journal of Medicine* 285 (1971) 776–83.

parahumans or modified men. There then follows one of the most remarkable sentences in the contemporary literature on genetics: "I suspect I would favor making and using man-machine hybrids rather than genetically designed people for dull, unrewarding or dangerous roles needed nonetheless for the community's welfare—perhaps the testing of suspected pollution areas or the investigation of threatening volcanoes or snow-slides."[7]

Fletcher acknowledges several possible objections to all of this. First, it could be objected that since "fertilization or cloning result directly in human beings, or in creatures with nascent or proto-human status," the entailed practice of their sacrifice in the course of investigation is immoral. He dismisses this as "a priori metarational opinion," "belief in a faith assertion."

Having thus dismembered the first objection, he confronts the second, i.e., that there might be something inhuman about the laboratory reproduction of human beings. If one has a sneaking suspicion that behind Fletcher's enthusiasm there lurks a concept of "the human," he is absolutely right. "Man is a maker and a selector and a designer, and the more rationally contrived and deliberate anything is, the more human it is." This opens on a judgment which is at least competitive for "most remarkable statement of the year": "Laboratory reproduction is radically human compared to conception by ordinary heterosexual intercourse. It is willed, chosen, purposed and controlled, and surely these are among the traits that distinguish *Homo sapiens* from others in the animal genus, from the primates down. Coital reproduction is, therefore, less human than laboratory reproduction . . . ."[8]

To those who might object or hesitate, Fletcher has the reassuring word that "fear is at the bottom of this debate." But really we should fear not, for "to be men we must be in control. That is the first and last ethical word." Therefore, where cloning, donor insemination, etc. are concerned, "all this means that we are *going to have to change or alter* our old ideas about who or what a father is, or a mother, or a family."

Thus far Fletcher. I have cited him liberally because one has to, as it were, see it to believe it.

The time has come, I think, to blow the whistle on this type of thing. It is not a question of whether this genial Christian and gentlemanly ethician is right or wrong. We have all been a little bit of both, and much more of the latter. Rather, Fletcher continues to propose to do theology by setting up dubious polarities, promulgating unexamined premises,

[7] *Ibid.*, p. 779.
[8] *Ibid.*, p. 781.

and flourishing rhetorical *non sequiturs*. The whole thing is then baptized into contemporary personalism with a now familiar ritualistic jargon: responsible, loving, pragmatic, personal. This is, of course, enormous fun; but it could be painfully expensive. If theologians are to retain any realistic hope of a dialogue with the scientific community, they must resolutely dissociate themselves from a type of discourse that too often dissolves into theology-by-anecdote.

First, the dubious polarities. An example is "apriorists vs. consequentialists." The former are accused of "religious, metaphysical, nonempirical" thought. They "would say, therefore, that therapeutic or corrective goals are not enough to justify *in vitro* fertilization, positive eugenics or designed genetic changes no matter how desirable they might be.... Good consequences could not, to the a priori moralist, justify such acts or procedures since they are wrong as means...." Here Fletcher's typologies, while retaining a certain pedagogical utility, simply ignore the possibility that it is precisely a form of consequentialism that could lead to a rejection of these things. In other words, what some theologians are saying is that the very desirability of therapeutic or corrective goals is not an isolated factor but must be weighed in light of the personal and social costs involved in moving toward such goals. They are saying that *in vitro* fertilization, cloning, etc., no matter what long-term pragmatic advantages and reliefs they would seem to provide, reveal the decisive disadvantage of containing an attack on the *humanum*, and for this reason (or consequence) are to be avoided. This is hardly metarational apriorism.

Second, the unexamined premises. At the very time Fletcher tells us that the notion of humanness "may well be the most searching and fundamental problem that faces not only ethicists but society as a whole," he announces that the search is really over: "The more rationally contrived and deliberate anything is, the more human it is." This is at best ambiguous and at worst a distortion of the human. Rational control, it is true, is a distinctive achievement of man. But he can use this rationality in inhuman ways. Deliberation and rationality tell us only that a human being is acting, not that he is acting humanly. One can, with utter control and deliberateness, do the most monstrously inhuman things. The Third Reich showed us how. Theology has always known that sin, by definition, is a deliberate, rational, controlled choice—but the most inhuman of acts. Rational control, therefore, is not the guarantor of humane choices but only the condition of their possibility. What happens to man in and as a result of his rationality and deliberate choices tells us whether these choices were more or less human, more or less desirable.

Similarly, Fletcher has argued that "if the greatest good of the greatest number ... were served by it," he would approve cloning, bioengineering of parahumans, etc. This remains an "unexamined premise" in several senses. (1) Have we not repeatedly experienced the fact that the greatest good of the greatest number, unassailable as it might be as a theoretical criterion, is practically the warrant for present practices and policies which all but guarantee that this greatest good will not be served? (2) How is the social good to be spelled out even if we accept it as a goal? Who makes the determination? On what basis? (3) How would laboratory reproduction, cloning, etc. serve it? True, Fletcher has said "if," but his failure to confront the serious, indeed decisive, problems buried in this "if" means that for him proportionate good too easily translates "anything to get the job done." He seems not to suspect that it just might be more human to exist with volcanic threats or pollution than to create parahumans to help us overcome these things. It is possible, after all, that by engineering the engineer we would become very competent barbarians. Not to raise such an issue is, in a sense, to have solved it. The editorial page of a subsequent issue of the prestigious *New England Journal of Medicine* carried a (by and large favorable) commentary on Fletcher by Bernard D. Davis, M.D.[9] At one point Davis notes: "One therefore wishes that Dr. Fletcher had discussed the conflicting interests and values that lie at the heart of ethical problems." Exactly.

Finally, the rhetorical *non sequiturs*. Fletcher informs us that in view of the new biomedical achievements "we are going to have to change or alter our old ideas about who or what a father is, or a mother, or a family." Here it must be said that we *have to* change these notions only if what *can* be done biomedically *ought* to be done humanly. Fletcher has given us no persuasive reasons why these things ought to be done, because he has not seriously examined what would happen to the doers in the process. For this reason his "have to change" is an unwitting but two-handed surrender to the scientific imperative. The contention here, then, is not precisely that Fletcher is a consequentialist, but rather that he has provided us with no grounds for thinking that he is a good one.

DEONTOLOGICAL ATTITUDE

Paul Ramsey and Leon Kass can be taken as examples of the second approach. The writings of Princeton's Ramsey are about as contrary to Fletcher as it is possible to be. If there is a practical issue in moral

[9] Cf. n. 4 above. For other reactions to Fletcher's article, cf. *New England Journal of Medicine* 286 (1972) 48–50.

theology, chances are Ramsey has been there digging, sorting, and giving forth with his version of Christian wisdom ahead of the pack. There is, it can be said, hardly anyone who has not learned a good deal from him. It must also be said that there is hardly anyone who has not snapped at Ramsey's pedagogical hand in the process, a point verified by the recent literature on biomedicine.

Ramsey's weighing of the issues raised by the new biology draws heavily on two basic principles.[10] First, there is the "nature of human parenthood." Human parenthood demands that the spheres of procreation and marital love not be separated. This means that we may not procreate apart from the union of marital love, and that sexual love may not be expressed apart from a context of responsibility for procreation. Repeatedly Ramsey asserts that the inseparability of these two spheres is human parenthood "as it came to us from the Creator,"[11] that we dare not put asunder "what God joined together in creation."[12] On this score alone he rejects AID (donor insemination), cloning, reproduction *in vitro*.[13]

His second basic principle concerns the difference between therapy and experimentation. It might be formulated as follows: we may never submit another human being to experimental procedures to which he cannot consent when these procedures have no relation to his own treatment. On this basis Ramsey believes that we could never *morally* get to know how to do certain things (e.g., cloning) because the very first attempt would have the character of an experiment on the child-to-be. Thus he says:

Because we ought not to choose for a child—whose procreation we are contemplating—the injury he may bear, there is no way by which we can *morally* get to know whether many things now planned are technically feasible or not. We need not ask whether we should clone a man or not, or what use is to be made of frozen semen or ovum banks, or what sort of life we ought to create in hatcheries etc. since we can *begin* to perfect these techniques in no other way than by

[10] Paul Ramsey, *Fabricated Man* (New Haven: Yale Univ. Press, 1970).
[11] *Ibid.*, p. 124.
[12] *Ibid.*, p. 38.
[13] Ramsey approves of AIH in a sterile marriage (p. 112). How this is consistent with his basic principle is somewhat hazy. He writes: "Their response to what God joined together ... would be expressed by their resolve to hold *acts* of procreation ... within the sphere of *acts* of conjugal love, within the covenant of marriage" (p. 36). AIH is certainly an act of procreation, and it is certainly within the covenant of marriage; but that it is "within the sphere of *acts* of conjugal love" is far from clear. Perhaps Ramsey stated his principle poorly here.

subjecting another human being to risks to which he cannot consent as our coadventurer in promoting medical or scientific "progress."[14]

Similarly it is the distinction between therapy and experimentation that governs Ramsey's whole treatment of genetic surgery. Such treatment on an existing child, however drastic, is permissible if it does "not place the child at greater risk than now surrounds him as one of a specially endangered population." Here we are dealing with therapy. Where there is question, however, of an as yet unconceived child, Ramsey is rightly much more demanding. There would have to be *no discernible risks* in prospective genetic surgery before one could procreate a child likely to be burdened with Huntington's chorea, PKU, amaurotic idiocy, etc. Until such time as corrective genetic surgery is risk-free, the proper prevention of these diseases is "continence, not getting married to a particular person, not having any children, using three contraceptives at once, or sterilization." Any other procedure would be tantamount to illicit experimentation with human beings. Ramsey's study constantly returns to these two basic principles.

Ramsey's analysis is well informed, precise, and searching, even if frequently repetitious. Furthermore, one wishes that he were more successful in resisting the titillations of his own obiter dicta and neologisms. These more purple than persuasive asides simply blunt his theological punches. This being said, I would say that I find myself very close to nearly all of Ramsey's value judgments.[15] For this reason it is all the more important to raise several issues which seem to call for further attention.

First there is the manner of argument where Ramsey's two controlling principles are concerned. The first (the nature of parenthood as involving inseparability of the two spheres of love and procreation) he views as parenthood "as it comes to us from the Creator." He draws upon the Prologue of St. John and Ephesians 5 as loci where this divine plan is made clear.

The Prologue of John's gospel (not Genesis) is the Christian story of creation

[14] *Ibid.*, p. 134.

[15] I say "nearly all" because I cannot agree with Ramsey that "we cannot rightfully *get to know* how to do this [use an artificial placenta] without conducting unethical experiments upon the unborn" (p. 113). If a pregnant woman with a nonviable fetus is dying and the only even remote hope of bringing her otherwise doomed child to term is an artificial placenta, I would think it legitimate—as therapy, not experimentation, or at least not exclusively experimentation.

which provides the source and standard for responsible procreation, even as Ephesians 5 contains the ultimate reference for the meaning and nature of conjugal love and the standard governing covenants of marriage. Since these two passages point to one and the same Lord—the lord who presides over procreation as well as the lord of all marital covenants—the two aspects of sexuality belong together.[16]

Ramsey contrasts this nature-of-parenthood perspective with a method which would weigh AID (etc.) in terms of consequences.

Perhaps Ramsey is right. But the question can be raised whether the two approaches are that different, a point suggested in the discussion of Fletcher's work. Ramsey is equivalently saying that there are some principles which hold no matter what the consequences. Others might argue that the principles have been arrived at and do indeed hold precisely because of the intolerable consequences. Specifically, Ramsey seems to say that the two spheres of sexuality are inseparable because God made them this way and told us so. Others would say that they are inseparable because to separate them would dehumanize us and *for this reason* we may say that God has joined them. It seems to me that Ramsey is not clear on how he derives this principle (and therefore, by implication, other principles). He seems to gather it from a reflective reading of Scripture and contrasts this with a consequentialist procedure. Yet over and over again he states it consequentially.

For instance, while discussing cloning Ramsey states: "The conquest of evolution by setting sexual love and procreation radically asunder entails depersonalization in the extreme. The entire rationalization of procreation—its replacement by replication—can only mean the abolition of man's embodied personhood."[17] I agree, but is it not precisely because of these effects (alienation, depersonalization) that the statement is valid? We see more deeply into these things from John's Prologue and Ephesians 5, but the conclusion is not drawn independently of a consideration of effects or consequences, unless one has a very narrow notion of consequences.[18] Rather is it not precisely conse-

---

[16] *Ibid.*, p. 37.

[17] *Ibid.*, p. 89. Ramsey reveals a similar approach in many places. For instance, on cloning, he says it would not be right "because of its massive assaults upon human freedom and its grave violation of the respect due to men and women now alive and to human parenthood as such" (p. 61). Again, speaking of the separation of procreation and marital love, he notes: "Herein men usurp dominion over the human—the dominion they hold rightfully only over the animals. This is bound to pierce the heart of the *humanum* in sex, marriage and generation" (p. 88).

[18] By "consequences" I include two things: the immediate entailments or implications of an action, the more mediate aftereffects.

quences which lead us to this conclusion? The dominating effect or consequence is the depersonalization of man, and this simply overrides any long-term eugenic goals. Therefore it is far from clear that Ramsey should speak of his principle as valid independently of consequences.

To say that a certain procedure is depersonalizing or dehumanizing demands, of course, both some notion of the *humanum* and the predictable effects on the *humanum* of prospective procedures. I shall return to this shortly.

Ramsey's second principle (the immorality of experimentation without consent) raises a somewhat similar problem. In *The Patient as Person* he has argued—dealing explicitly with infants—that the reason for this conclusion is that such experimental procedures make an "object" of an individual. In these cases, he contends, the parents cannot consent for the individual. Consent is the heart of the matter. If the parents could legitimately consent for the child, then presumably experimental procedures would not make an object of the infant and would be permissible. Therefore the basic question is: why cannot the parents provide consent for the child? Why is their consent considered null here while it is accepted when procedures are therapeutic? To say that the child would be treated as an object does not answer this question; it presupposes the answer and announces it under this formulation.

Adults may donate an organ to another (*inter vivos*) precisely because their personal good is not to be conceived individualistically, but socially—that is, there is a natural order to other human persons which is in the very notion of the human personality itself. The personal being and good of an individual does have a relationship to the being and good of others, difficult as it may be to keep this in a balanced perspective. For this reason, an individual can become (in carefully delimited circumstances) more fully a person by donation of an organ; for by communicating to another of his very being he has more fully integrated himself into the mysterious unity between person and person.

Must not something analogous be said of experimentation for the good of others? It can be an affirmation of one's solidarity and Christian concern for others (through the advancement of medicine), though it is easy to be naive about the dangers and abuses of this idea. Becoming an experimental subject *can involve* any or all of three things: some degree of risk (at least of complications), pain, associated inconvenience (e.g., prolonging the hospital stay, delaying recovery, etc.). To accept these for the good of others could be an act of charitable concern.

If these reflections are true of adults, must not the same be said of infants and children in so far as they are human persons? Therefore, precisely why is parental consent illegitimate in their case? Or perhaps more sharply, the parents' consent to therapy directed at the child's own good is both required and sufficient because it is the closest we can come to a *reasonable presumption of the child's wishes*. The fact that the therapy or surgery is for the child's good could be but a single example of a reasonable presumption of the child's wishes. Are there others? According to Ramsey, no. But I wonder.

Perhaps the following approach is not totally without merit. It was suggested that organ donation and participation in experimentation (both within limits) could contribute to the personal good of the individual involved if his personal good is defined within its proper social setting. This is a general and abstract statement. It must be concretized and qualified.

The first qualification is that whether it is personally good for an individual to donate an organ or participate in experimentation is a very circumstantial and highly individual affair. For some individuals these undertakings could be or prove to be humanly destructive. Much depends on their personalities, backgrounds, maturity, present or future position in life, etc. The second and more important qualification is that these procedures become human goods for the donor or subject precisely because and therefore only when they are voluntary; for the personal good under discussion is the good of expressed charity. For these two reasons I would conclude that no one else can make such decisions for an individual, i.e., *reasonably* presume his consent. He has a right to make them for himself.

But are there situations where such considerations are not involved and where the presumption of consent is reasonable? I think it is quite possible. For instance, if the only way a young child could be saved were by a blood transfusion from another child, I suspect that few would find such blood donation an unreasonable presumption on the child's wishes. The reason for the reasonableness of the presumption is not precisely that the blood donation is in any way a good for the donor. Rather it is that a great good is provided for another at almost no cost to the child. *Parum pro nihilo reputatur*. Could the same reasoning apply to experimentation? Concretely, when a particular experiment would involve no discernible risks, no notable pain, no notable inconvenience, and yet hold promise of considerable benefit, would not parental consent be a reasonable presumption of the child's wishes—not because it is in any way for the child's good, but because it is not in any realistic way to his harm? *Parum pro nihilo reputatur*. This is certainly to "use" the child, but in a way in which it is reasonable to presume he would want to be used, or not object to being used.

But we may not stop here. Since the individual has the right to make for himself decisions which involve risk, or pain, or notable inconvenience—a right which invalidates any presumption of his wishes—then he has a right to be protected against any possible violations of such a right, any dangers to it. It is here that one might argue the possible absoluteness of the personal-consent requirement. That is, our times are times of eager scientific research, enthusiastic eugenic ambitions, strong if subtle collectivistic tendencies, and growing impersonalization of health care. Thus it could be argued that we have a cultural situation with a built-in escalatory tendency to expose nonconsenting persons to violations of their rights. This means that there is a real danger of exceeding those limits to which the infant (e.g.) could be *reasonably* presumed to consent. He has a right to be protected against such a danger.

This danger is not sufficiently removed, it could be further argued, by the protections of parental consent, because this consent itself is in our day too often unstable and vulnerable to many noxious influences. Therefore, putting the nonconsenting person simply out of bounds where pure experimentation is concerned *might* be the only way to hold the delicate relation of individual to society in proper balance. I say "might" because if these dangers could be countered, then it would seem that some experimentation might be a reasonable presumption of the child's consent. If so, then this reasonableness would provide the basis for validating parental consent.

At this point it must be said parenthetically that in these matters it is always better to err, if err one must, on the side of conservatism. Hence if there is any doubt about the reasonableness of the presumption or, more basically, about the validity of these reflections, the personal-consent requirement should be viewed as a practical absolute. More specifically, whether there is any risk, pain, or inconvenience involved is a matter which cannot be left exclusively in the hands of medical researchers. The terrible examples in M. H. Pappworth's *Human Guinea Pigs* make this clear. Some of the researchers regard as "trivial" or "routine" procedures the ordinary patient would, with good reason, view as seriously bothersome and notably risky. Because a complication can be handled by subsequent therapy does not mean it is no longer a complication. Medical technology can dazzle us into distorted human judgments.

The approach proposed here moves away a bit from the absoluteness of Ramsey's analysis, though not necessarily from the absoluteness of his conclusions. Ramsey's analysis must conclude that *any* experimentation, even the most trifling and insignificant such as a buccal smear, on nonconsenting persons is beyond the reach of parental consent because it involves us in "treating another as an object." Perhaps. But this latter seems to be a rhetorical way of formulating a judgment concluded on other grounds.[19] I have suggested that we might approach the morality of risk-free, pain-free, inconvenience-free experimentation, rare as such experiments might be, through the notion of reasonable presumption of the child's wishes. In other words, is it not possible that the inviolability against all experimentation (if we ought to maintain such inviolability) of those incapable of consent is only a relatively necessary conclusion of human prudence rather than of intrinsic morality? At least I believe the question must be examined further.

The writings of Leon Kass reveal moral tendencies and judgments very close to those of Ramsey. For this reason he would probably fall into Fletcher's apriorist pigeonhole. In his major writings Kass realistically limits himself to the two questions which have some practicality in the future: *in vitro* fertilization (with eventual uterine implantation) and cloning.[20]

As for the first, its least controversial use will be the provision of their own child to a sterile couple. At first glance the intramarital use of artificial fertilization seems to resemble ethically AIH (artificial insemination by husband). But Kass raises two moral objections. First, the implantation of the embryo fertilized *in vitro* involves the hazards of deformity and malformation. These hazards are being imposed nontherapeutically on a child-to-be without his consent. This, Kass argues, "provides a powerful moral objection sufficient to rebut the implantation experiments." Secondly, discarding unimplanted embryos raises another problem. Kass is undecided as to whether we are dealing with a protectable humanity at this (blastocyst) stage, but we certainly will

[19] That Ramsey himself might agree with this and the underlying method is suggested by his attitude toward exceptional instances in situations of consent. He notes: "In the grave moral matters . . . a physician is more liable to make an error in moral judgment if he adopts a policy of holding himself open to the possibility that there may be significant, future permissions to ignore the principle of consent than he is if he holds this requirement of an informed consent always relevant and applicable" (*The Patient as Person* [New Haven: Yale Univ. Press, 1970] p. 9).

[20] Leon. Kass, "Making Babies—the New Biology and the 'Old' Morality," *The Public Interest*, Winter, 1972, pp. 18–56. This long study is nearly identical with Kass's "New Beginnings in Life," an occasional paper privately published by the Hastings Center (Institute of Society, Ethics and the Life Sciences). Cf. also Leon R. Kass, "The New Biology: What Price Relieving Man's Estate?" *Science* 174 (1971) 779–88, and his "What Price the Perfect Baby?" *Science* 173 (1971) 103–4.

be at a later stage and therefore "had better force the question now and draw whatever lines need to be drawn." Apart from these objections, Kass finds no *intrinsic* reason to reject *in vitro* fertilization and implantation. But the argument must not stop here. A procedure possibly unobjectionable in itself makes possible other procedures. This is not an "argument from abuse." Rather he insists on

the fact that one technical advance makes possible the next and in more than one respect. The first serves as a precedent for the second, the second for the third—not just technologically but also in moral arguments. At least one good humanitarian reason can be found to justify each step. Into the solemn and hallowed tent of human sexuality and procreation, the camel's nose has led the camel's neck and may some day soon, perhaps, even lead the camel's spermatozoa.[21]

I suspect that Pius XII had something like this in mind when he condemned AIH.

As for cloning, Kass again raises the twin issues of production and disposition of defectives and contends with Ramsey that they "provide sufficient moral grounds for rebutting any first attempt to clone a man." He further urges the serious psychological problems of identity and individuality and finds them "sufficient to reject even the first attempts at human cloning."[22]

Kass eventually goes beyond this piece-by-piece approach and brings a broader cultural analysis to bear on the two questions. Here his writing is most powerful and persuasive. He argues that "increasing control over the product is purchased by the increasing depersonalization of the process" and that this depersonalization is dehumanizing. Against Fletcher's contentions he would insist that "human procreation is not simply an activity of our rational wills ... it is more complete human activity precisely because it engages us bodily and spiritually, as well as rationally."[23]

The separation of reproduction from human sexuality Kass sees as a dehumanizing threat to the existence of marriage and the human family. "Transfer of procreation to the laboratory undermines the justification and support which biological parenthood gives to the monogamous (or even polygamous) marriage. Cloning adds an additional, more specific, and more fundamental threat: the technique

[21] "Making Babies," pp. 38–39. The last sentence of the citation occurs only in the earlier ("New Beginnings in Life") version. Either its frivolity annoyed the editor of *Public Interest* or Kass waxed formal when he went public.

[22] *Ibid.*, p. 45.

[23] *Ibid.*, pp. 48–49.

renders males obsolete. All it requires are human eggs, nuclei, and (for the time being) uteri; all three can be supplied by women."[24]

Kass's concern for the family is not blind institutionalism. Rather he is concerned that "the family is rapidly becoming the only institution in an increasingly impersonal world where each person is loved not for what he does or makes, but simply because he is. The family is also the institution where most of us, both as children and as parents, acquire a sense of continuity with the past and a sense of commitment to the future."[25] For these and other reasons Kass urges that "when we lack sufficient wisdom to do, wisdom consists in not doing." He is sharply critical of theologians-turned-technocrats (e.g., Karl Rahner[26]) whose notion of man as "freedom-event" provides no standards by which to measure whether self-modifying changes are in fact improvements.

Those unfamiliar with Kass will find his writings both enlightening and entertaining. Charles Stinson of Dartmouth College demurs.[27] He takes a rather dim view of the attitudes and analyses of Ramsey-Kass. He sees both of them as biomedical pessimists. Behind Kass's pessimism he finds a body-soul dualism which contends: if mental-spiritual life is not a "separate entity" beyond genetic manipulation, it is some-

---

[24] *Ibid.*, p. 50.

[25] *Ibid.*, p. 51.

[26] The reference to Rahner is to "Experiment: Man," *Theology Digest* 16 (1968) 57–69. (Cf. "Experiment Mensch: Theologisches über die Selbstmanipulation des Menschen," *Schriften zur Theologie* 8 [Einsiedeln: Benziger, 1967] 260–85.) Rahner's position is not accurately presented if it is drawn from "Experiment: Man" alone. His "Zum Problem der genetischen Manipulation" (*Schriften zur Theologie* 8, 286–321) must also be read. In this latter essay Rahner develops positions very close to those of Ramsey and Kass, and manifests a deep skepticism, even negativism, where eugenic genetic manipulation is concerned. He insists, e.g., that not everything that can be done ought to be done (p. 318). In applying this to donor insemination, Rahner argues that personal sexual love has an essential relationship to the child; for the child is the expression and realization of the abiding unity of the spouses. But "genetic manipulation does two things. First it separates on principle the procreation of a new person (as the abiding expression of the love-union of the spouses) from marital union. Secondly, it transfers procreation (sundered and separated from its human source) outside of the human sphere of intimacy" (p. 313). That Rahner would reject this is obvious. Furthermore, he speaks repeatedly of resisting "the temptation of the possible" and calls "immunity against the fascination of the newly possible" a virtue contemporary man must develop, and apply in the area of genetic manipulation. One of Rahner's major concerns is how his basic "No" to some of these possibilities can be made persuasive amid the existing moral pluralism. The Ramsey-Kass criticism of Rahner is, therefore, not only misleading in itself; it also *seems* to provide the support of a great theological name for utopian schemes and eugenic experiments which Rahner would resolutely disown.

[27] Charles Stinson, "Theology and the Baron Frankenstein: Cloning and Beyond," *Christian Century* 89 (1972) 60–63.

how not as true as we had thought. Behind Ramsey's outlook Stinson sees a faulty theology of creation "which assumes that God *intended* certain aspects of natural structures and forces to remain *always* beyond the control of man's intelligence." Stinson then repeats in a variety of ways what he mistakenly takes to be a counterstatement to Ramsey-Kass: increased empirical knowledge about the processes of life need not erode its divine meaningfulness. On the basis of such general assertions and the conviction that sooner or later we will be involved in "the socially regulated cloning of individuals," Stinson opts for the Rahnerian view that man's limitless power to experiment on himself is really a sign of the creaturely freedom given him by God.

Granted that the writings of both Ramsey and Kass do at times achieve liturgical fervor and leave them vulnerable to the accusation of both overstatement and pessimism, still Stinson's essay, interesting as it is, meets the serious issues they raise with little more than a gathering of evasions and begged questions.

Item. "No doubt, as Ramsey points out, accidental miscalculations and ignorance of variables will result in fetal monstrosities. Not a pretty picture to contemplate. Moreover, there will inevitably be abuses of power on the part of a small minority of insensitive or rash scientists and technicians. But are we to conclude that, because of its *risks* and possible abuses, all such work is intrinsically immoral?"[28] Since when is the certain ("no doubt") production of fetal monstrosities reducible to a mere risk? Ramsey may be wrong, but to talk of bench-made monstrosities as "risks" is hardly a persuasive way of showing it.

Item. "Ramsey's outlook is grounded . . . in a faulty theology of creation which assumes that God *intended* certain aspects of natural structures and forces to remain *always* beyond the control of man's intelligence."[29] Ramsey claims nothing of the kind. He does, indeed, argue (not "assume") that God intended certain aspects of natural structures as permanent, but he would insist that this is not to put them "beyond the control of man's intelligence;" it is only to say that certain controls may not be intelligent.

Item. "And why would a cloned human being not feel himself (or herself) to be a 'person' or 'embodied'? Possibly for a number of reasons, but Ramsey does not specify any."[30] To which two things must be said. First, when Ramsey refers to cloning as involving "the abolition of embodied personhood," he need not and does not refer primarily to the feelings of the cloned product, but to the parents and their concept of

[28] *Ibid.*, p. 60.
[29] *Ibid.*, p. 61.
[30] *Ibid.*

parenthood. Secondly, he does indeed with Kass specify reasons about the feelings of the cloned human being.[31]

Item. "Let me hazard a key theological concept for the future: it is the ongoing content of human life that is spiritually significant—not its origin whether natural or artificial."[32] Comment: it is precisely the Ramsey-Kass point that artificial origin will affect the "ongoing content of human life." One must wrestle with this contention if one is to meet Ramsey-Kass where they are.

Item. "This feat [the first cloning of a man] would certainly not invalidate Ramsey's ethical norms but it would make them irrelevant speculatively."[33] Does the first use of the atomic bomb make it speculatively irrelevant to urge the question "should we ever have done it?" If such a question is utterly urgent—as it is—then the more urgent question was: should we do it? Our mistakes of the past should teach us at least to take these earlier questions more seriously—unless one wants to hold the disastrous view that we can learn only from our mistakes.

Item. Of genetics a hundred years hence Stinson notes: "And this will *no doubt* include the socially regulated cloning of individuals who are deemed to be especially valuable to the community."[34] Here, I believe, is the real and ultimate pessimism: that because we *can* we certainly *will* do. Is there a better way to render any present ethical reflection irrelevant than to think it really makes no difference anyway, and therefore to reduce the issue to "what shall we do after we have cloned men?"

MEDIATING APPROACH

James Gustafson and Charles Curran are examples of the third approach. A methodology midway between the rather structureless utilitarian calculus of Fletcher and the Ramsey-Kass insistence on the absolute immorality of some means is that of Gustafson. Under a nine-point division Gustafson lays out the many ethical issues in biomedicine.[35] Repeatedly he sets up groups of alternative approaches, states the warrants for them, unravels their latent presuppositions, and notes the questions they raise.

For instance, in perhaps the most substantive sections of his study,

[31] Cf. Ramsey, *Fabricated Man*, pp. 71–72.
[32] *Art. cit.*, p. 63.
[33] *Ibid.*, p. 62.
[34] *Ibid.*
[35] James M. Gustafson, "Basic Ethical Issues in the Bio-Medical Fields," *Soundings* 53 (1970) 151–80.

Gustafson approaches genetic medicine from the contrasting positions of inviolable individual rights and the benefits which might accrue to others and society in general. He proposes three contrasting options. (1) The rights of individuals are sacred and primary and therefore under no circumstances are they to be violated in favor of benefits to others. (2) Anticipated consequences judged in terms of the "good" that will be achieved or the "evil" avoided ought to determine policy and action regardless of the restrictions on individual rights that this might require. (3) Both 1 and 2 are one-sided. Decisions require consideration both of individual rights and of benefits to others. One of the two will be the base line, the other will function as the principle justifying exceptions to the base line.

It is clear that Gustafson would opt for the third alternative, indeed for third alternatives in nearly every case where opposing methods or stances have been proposed. Thus, as between "restricting the kinds of experimentation that will be permitted through civil legislation . . . and clearly defined moral rules" and "ensuring the maximum possible freedom for research," Gustafson goes for a bit of both: maintaining maximum possible freedom but at the same time formulating principles and values which provide guidelines for procedures and for the uses of research. Similarly, he values summary rules but is uncomfortable with absolute rules. Or again, he argues that "the value of human physical life is primary" but this does not "entail that no other values or rights might override the right to bodily life." He wants societal benefits to count in genetic decisions, but not at all costs, just as he wants individual rights to be respected, but not at all costs. And so on.

What I believe Gustafson is doing is trying to hold in balance or bring to terms two intransigent elements of moral discourse: the complexity of reality, yet the abiding need to attempt to bring our decisions under objective rational scrutiny if our moral policies are to remain truly human. These two elements constantly surface as Gustafson's profound concerns. Equivalently he is suggesting that moral reasoning is neither as fixed and rational as Ramsey would sometimes lead us to believe, nor as shapeless and arbitrary as Fletcher's writing suggests.

Where does this leave him? With a goal and a means to it. The goal is the counsel that for man the experimenter and intervener "the chief task is to develop with both sensitivity and clarity an understanding of the qualities or values of human life and a conception of the basic human rights that will provide the moral guidelines or touchstones for human development."[36] That is why Gustafson's recent work has been concerned with the "normatively human." The means: ongoing, rigor-

[36] *Ibid.*, p. 178.

ous conversation between those who best pose ethical questions and those who are shaping developments in the biomedical field.

Gustafson's study — subtle, sensitive, sophisticated — resolutely avoids the blandishments of the shock statement and asks all the right questions. But there is one aspect of his approach which seems at least incomplete, even dissatisfying. For instance, he states that while the right to physical life is primary, "this would not entail that no other values or rights might ever override the rights to bodily life...." Thus he endorses an "ordering which gives *some* guidance in particular decisions." Precisely at this point it is necessary to say what these other values and rights might be and why they may be said to override the primary right.

Similarly, in dealing with biomedical procedures, Gustafson says that both individual rights and societal benefits must be considered. One of the two is the base line, the other functions as a principle justifying exceptions. Thus he says: "It might well be that under certain circumstances it is morally responsible to make the thrust of individual rights the base line, and under other circumstances the accounting of benefits." What are these circumstances? What is the criterion to make individual rights decisive in some instances, social benefits decisive in others? Until we know this, Gustafson's middle position is incomplete and fails to provide even "some guidance." It represents more a rejection of the opposing alternatives than a satisfying synthesis of the two.

This point should be urged because of its further implications. Let me put it this way. To say that there are overriding values *without stating what they might be*, to state that there are circumstances in which the base-line priority shifts *without stating what they might be*, is to do two things: (1) to empty the notions of "primary" and "base line" of most of their significance for decision-making; (2) to suggest that these overriding values can only be discovered in individual decision. I do not think that these are true. What Gustafson wants (and rightly) to say is that rational moral discourse is limited, that there comes a point when the complexity of reality leads us beyond the formulations of traditional wisdom. That, I think, is true. And I believe that we have always known it, even though we have not always admitted it. But where that point is located is very important. Failure to specify at least some of the values which can override a primary value or right all too easily suggests that there is no point to which rational deliberation can lead us, that we cannot specify these values, and that this can only be done in individual decisions. Does this not remove moral discourse in principle from objective and rational scrutiny? Gustafson does not want this, not at all. But how his admirable pastoral[37] sensitivities do not find their way to this theological cul-de-sac I fail to see.

I urge this point with a fear and trembling born of unqualified admiration for Gustafson's remarkable talents and work, of fear that the question may reflect my own overrationalization of the moral life, of the conviction that he as well as, and probably better than, any theological ethician on the American scene can bring light to those aspects of these remarks which hover in darkness.

Charles Curran states that moral theology, in facing biomedical problems, must proceed from a historical point of view, emphasize the societal aspects of the issues, and accept the self-creative power as a gift of equal importance with creatureliness.[38]

As for historical consciousness, we need a more "open" concept of man. For example, where Ramsey rejects Muller's eugenic proposals because they separate procreation and marital love, Curran agrees but believes that "the teaching Ramsey finds in Ephesians 5 might also be historically conditioned."

Similarly, in the past we were guilty of an individualist reading of the principle of totality. The task of contemporary moralists is to do justice to the social, cosmic aspects of man without falling into collectivism. Contemporary genetic possibilities force on us a realization of responsibilities beyond the individual.

Thirdly, where the question of man's dominion is concerned, we must hold in tension man's greatness and creatureliness. Curran does not believe that Ramsey grants man enough dominion, just as he would believe that Fletcher uncritically grants him too much. Ramsey's one-sidedness Curran traces to an eschatology developed only in terms of apocalypse (discontinuity between this world and the next). Eschatology, Curran insists, must include three elements: the apocalyptical, prophetic, and teleological. After shaking and mixing these three ingredients, he ends with an eschatology where man's final stage is not totally continuous with man's present existence (against the utopians) and not totally discontinuous with it (against the apocalyptic likes of Ramsey).

On the basis of these broad strokes Curran emerges with a position

---

[37] I use the word "pastoral" because I wonder to what extent Gustafson is lifting the anguish of personal decision (to which, of course, it is all too easy to become insensitive) into the larger sphere of moral policy and general moral reasoning.

[38] Charles Curran, "Theology and Genetics: A Multi-faceted Dialogue," *Journal of Ecumenical Studies* 7 (1970) 61–89. (This also appeared as "Moral Theology and Genetics" in *Cross Currents* 20 [1970] 64–82.)

which states on the one hand that "there are important human values which would stand in the way of the geneticist on some occasions" (e.g., adhering to the bond between procreation and marital union), on the other that "one can envision certain historical situations in which *it might be sacrificed for greater values.*"[39]

The italicized words are interesting, for they indicate two things: (1) that Curran's basic position is very close to that of Ramsey and Kass; (2) that it is held on consequentialist grounds. This latter seems clear even against Curran's explicit denial, because if a value is "sacrificed for greater values," clearly a calculus model is operative. This leads one to force a question on Curran which his essay does not satisfactorily answer: *why* hold in the first place that the spheres of procreation and marital love must in our historical time be held together? Ramsey gets this from a reflective reading of Scripture, the kind of argument Curran would reject as ahistorical and eventually deontological. Yet he also rejects the more experiential (consequentialist) model. What is left?

Curran's essay, like Gustafson's, is a helpful "both-and" balancing act, but at a different level—the level of broad cultural contrasts (e.g., between the narrowly scientific and the fully human, the utopian and the pessimistic, etc.). Ultimately, however, it finesses several of the hard questions and is less than complete in analyzing its own methodological presuppositions.

Thus far some recent moral literature; now to a concluding personal reflection. The two most commonly discussed issues seem to be fertilization *in vitro* and cloning.[40] The first is almost upon us and the second is possibly only decades away, though expert opinion differs about this. Furthermore, many of the moral issues in the more distant and exotic possibilities are essentially present in these problems. In both instances Ramsey and Kass have seen a serious issue in the production and destruction of embryos. I do too, though I am not certain of the exact way the issue should be formulated. But given the cultural attitudes now prevalent toward fetal life, I have little confidence that these points will be taken very seriously by most biotechnicians. In one sense, of course, this is all the more reason for raising them. However, because the discussion surrounding production and disposition of the

---

[39] *Ibid.,* p. 83.

[40] Though with regard to *in vitro* fertilization several variations must be weighed distinctly for their differences: (1) with husband's seed or donor's; (2) with implantation in wife's uterus or someone else's; (3) with no implantation but use of artificial placenta (etc.)—a development apparently rather far off. For differing views on *in vitro* fertilization, cf. *Medical-Moral Newsletter* 8 (March-April, 1972) entire issue, and *Hastings Center Report* 2 (1972) 1–3.

"failures" to some extent suggests that in other respects we should go ahead and that "artificial children" are desirable if these objections can be met, the more basic moral issue strikes earlier. It is that of marriage and the family.

Briefly, I am in deep sympathy with the views of Ramsey-Kass and (less explicitly) Curran that these procedures are inimical to marriage and the family (Ramsey says the "nature of parenthood") and that therefore in terms of their immediate implications and foreseeable effects we should not take such steps (nor *allow* them to be taken, since a public good of the first order is involved) unless a value the equivalent of survival demands it.

If there is, among the eugenic dreams and apocalyptic fears surrounding biomedical technology, a single certainty, it is this: *in vitro* fertilization and cloning do factually debiologize marriage and the family. Ramsey and Kass have argued that this is depersonalizing and dehumanizing. I believe they are right, and for two reasons.

First, by removing the origin of the child from the sphere of specifically marital (bodily, sexual) love, that love itself is subtly redefined in a way which deflates the sexual and bodily and its pertinence to human love, and therefore to the human itself. The artificially produced child can obviously be the result of a loving decision, even a deeply loving one; just as obviously it can be loved, cared for, and protected within the family. And precisely for these reasons is it quite valid to say that this child is the "product of marital love." But at this point that term has undergone a change, a change which has to some extent debiologized and "debodified" the word "marital." The term has moved a step away from its full bodily and therefore *human* connotations. Man is everything we say of him: freedom, reason, body, emotions. He is the sum of his parts. To reduce his humanity to any one of these or, what is the same, to suppress any one of these from his humanity is dehumanizing. And that is what is happening here.[41]

Secondly, moving procreation into the laboratory "undermines the justification and support which biological parenthood gives to the monogamous marriage," as Kass puts it. In other words, the family as we know it is basically (not exclusively or eminently) a biological unit. To weaken the biological link is to untie the family at its root and therefore to undermine it. That this is dehumanizing and depersonalizing depends entirely on what one thinks of the family (or Kass's monogamous marriage).

The family, I would argue, embodies the ordinary conditions wherein we (parents, children, and others) learn to become persons. In the

[41] Cf. Rahner, "Zum Problem der genetischen Manipulation," p. 313.

stable, permanent man-woman relationship we possess the chance to bring libido and eros to the maturity of *philia*-friendship. Through monogamous marriage we experience the basic (not the only) form of human love and caring, and learn thereby to take gradual possession of our own capacity to relate in love. That is why marriage is a sacrament: it is the human stuff eminently capable of mirroring God's own covenant-fidelity, His love. It is the ordinary societal condition of our coming to learn about responsibility, tenderness, fidelity, patience, the meaning of our own sexuality, etc. Without its nourishing presence in our midst, we gamble with our best hope for growth and dignity, our chances of learning what it means to love and be loved. For those created by and in the image of a loving God, and therefore destined to a consummation in this image, such a gamble is humanly suicidal. To undermine the family in any way would be to compromise the ordinary conditions of our own growth as persons, and that is dehumanizing.

Obviously marriages (and families) fail. And just as obviously the surrogate arrangements which pick up the pieces of our weakness, failure, and irresponsibility can and do succeed. Furthermore, it seems undeniable that the contemporary shape of family life cries out for restructuring if monogamous marriage is to survive, grow, and realize its true potential. But these facts do not negate the basic necessity of the monogamously structured family for human growth. They only say that it is worth criticizing vigorously because it is worth saving.

These reflections are not likely to be very persuasive to a culture which, it can be argued, is comfort-bent, goal-oriented, technologically sophisticated, sexually trivialized, and deeply secularized. But if they are true, they suggest that the moral theological analysis of the biomedical problems discussed in these pages must attend much more than it has to a Christian critique of the culture which not only generates such remarkable possibilities but above all shapes our reflection about them.[42]

[42] This bulletin was composed at and supported by the Kennedy Center for Bioethics, Georgetown University, Washington, D.C.

CURRENT THEOLOGY: 1973

NOTES ON MORAL THEOLOGY: APRIL–SEPTEMBER, 1972

The articles and studies on moral questions during the past semester are, if the word is not too suggestive, legion. This survey will touch four areas of contemporary concern: (1) the continuing reform of theological ethics; (2) death and dying; (3) premarital sexual relations; (4) the sociopolitical mission of the Christian.

MORALITAS SEMPER REFORMANDA

The Second Vatican Council, after speaking of the renewal of theological disciplines through livelier contact with the mystery of Christ and the history of salvation, remarked simply: "special attention needs to be given to the development of moral theology."[1] During the past six or seven years moral theology has experienced this special attention so unremittingly, some would say, that the Christianity has been crushed right out of it. When reform is in human hands, the results will inevitably bear the imprint of human handling. Be that as it may, much recent writing on Christian morality will fit no tidy category but ranges over a whole list of general concerns that represent a continuation of the "special attention" requested by the Council. Some examples follow.

Stanley Hauerwas contributes what he calls a "modest diatribe" against the new moral theology.[2] His first concern centers around the potential of the new moral theology, because of its highly general character, to be captured by conceptions of the good alien to the gospel. Too many theologians have reduced the ethical task to suggesting compelling slogans such as "conform to God's dynamic action in the world." If the concrete implications of such phrases are not spelled out, they remain homiletic flourishes capable of providing ideological justification for all kinds of things foreign to Christianity. The vacuous character of much moral reflection is reflected in the "politicization of morals," that is, the idea that the primary response to moral questions is to take a liberal or conservative stance. Thus, being "for" *Humanae vitae* is associated with legalism and authoritarianism, being "against" it makes one a participant in the love-and-freedom ethic.

---

[1] *The Documents of Vatican II*, ed. Walter M. Abbott, S.J. (New York: America, 1966) p. 452.

[2] Stanley Hauerwas, "Judgment and the New Morality," *New Blackfriars* 53 (1972) 210–21. Practically the same article appears as "Aslan and the New Morality," *Religious Education* 67 (1972) 419–29.

Hauerwas' second stricture is against the confusion of ethics and apologetics. Apologetics is, for Hauerwas, the baptism of the secular in an attempt to be relevant to the contemporary world. This represents capitulation to the assumption that conventionality defines the real. Christian ethics is that modest discipline that attempts to break this type of intellectual bewitchment by insisting that we see ourselves and our world rightly only if we view them in the light of what God has done in the person of Jesus Christ.

The final problem Hauerwas raises is the assumption that an ethical response is the same as pastoral compassion. For instance, a man whose marriage has never been happy, whose wife is frigid, etc., develops a friendship with a secretary at the office. Their genuine caring finally leads them to share a bed. The reaction to an older judgmental attitude is a type of compassion that leads the spiritual counselor to see this as a positive good, a fulfilling experience. Hauerwas finds this an ethically insufficient approach. His point is not that we should point judgmental fingers but that unless we are clear about what has gone on here, we will not be able to minister to this man at all. We will not be able to raise the painful questions that lead to the deepening of one's moral life. When the ethical is completely identified with pastoral compassion, then ironically there is no basis for pastoral concern. Behind this ethic of sentimentality there lurks the distortion that the aim of the moral life is not the good but adjustment. To Hauerwas this means the triumph of the therapeutic over the moral.

Hauerwas has made some excellent points, even if with some degree of caricature at times. His study culminates in a kind of theological haymaker: "I suspect that contemporary Christian ethics is superficial precisely because it is an all-too-faithful witness to the shallowness of our own individual lives." What Hauerwas has done is to provide some stinging correctives for a type of moral reflection that has grown sloppy and accepted uncritically the assumptions of modern humanism, especially the assumption that the moral life is primarily the securing of our own happiness.

These correctives are needed, I believe; for it can be argued that the history of theology reveals the Hegelian syndrome of action-reaction, extreme to extreme. Our escape from legalism involves us in the real danger of antinomianism. Flight from a one-sided supernaturalism too often leaves us secular pagans. Rejection of authoritarianism too easily leads us to a type of ecclesiastical anarchy. And so on. Is not heresy frequently but the reaction to a one-sided orthodoxy?

Perhaps we cannot altogether avoid this teeter-totterism in moral thought, but the best way to try is to lift out and acknowledge humbly and honestly the traps into which we are likely to fall at this moment in history. Some are: neospiritualism (that disguises or ignores the human and concrete character of sin and virtue); selective responsibility (that collapses responsibility in one sphere to emphasize it in another); narrow consequentialism (that ignores the fact that my neighbor is everyman); secularism (that depresses the deep influence of Christian realities on the moral life); individualism (that is insensitive to the communitarian dimension of moral knowledge and discernment).

Moral analysis in the past too often discussed human acts in isolation from the historical subject. One of the shifting emphases in recent moral writing is a greater concern with the moral subject. Enda McDonagh continues his illuminating exploration of morality using his own experience as the basis for reflection.[3] In an earlier study he had described the nature of the moral call as basically an interpersonal situation, a situation involving two personal centers or poles, whether individuals or community groups.[4] One of these centers was described as the subject who experiences the moral call, the other as the source of the call, though a certain reciprocity prevents us from speaking of one exclusively as subject of the call, the other as source. The present study delves into the moral response itself, especially the subject's relation to the source.

McDonagh sees this as involving three phases, though these phases are not altogether distinguishable. The first phase is other-recognition and self-identification. This recognition of the other as source of a moral call is first of all very concrete—a call to feed the hungry, care for the sick, etc. But implicit in this is the awareness of the other as other, as constituting a different world, as both gift and possible threat.[5] And simultaneously one achieves a fuller awareness of self as self.

The next phase in the dynamic process is respect for the other as other, as an independent (gift) world, and, as unavoidable concomitant, respect and acceptance of self. The third phase is the subject's response. The response is the subject's effort to meet the immediate need of the source as manifested in the moral call experienced by the subject. In responding to the other, the subject brings into being a new feature of himself; he actualizes himself. Thus, "other-response

---

[3] Enda McDonagh, "The Moral Subject," *Irish Theological Quarterly* 39 (1972) 3–22.

[4] E. McDonagh, "The Structure and Basis of the Moral Experience," *Irish Theological Quarterly* 38 (1971) 3–20.

[5] For an interesting study of the dynamics of love, cf. Esther Woo, "Subjective Love and Objective Charity in the Thought of Gabriel Marcel," *American Benedictine Review* 23 (1972) 40–55.

is self-developing or self-creative," even though this may not always or frequently be perceptible. If the response is predominantly other-centered, it is good; if it is predominantly self-centered, it is bad. The response is "critical" if it has conversion-capacity, that is, a capacity to turn the subject's basic direction or orientation from self-centered to other-centered or vice versa.

Of this basic moral orientation McDonagh says that it is the fruit of a person's historical responses. In the development of a disposition or basic direction, time plays a key role. He distinguishes this from what theologians call the fundamental moral option. This latter, he believes, "suggests some grand dramatic choice and the literature generally does not seem to one to do justice to the gradual, historical, mainly implicit formation of the basic orientation which my experience suggests."[6]

McDonagh writes with subtlety and sensitivity about moral response, and I believe the main lines of his analysis are very enriching. Two points, however, call for comment. First, there is the matter of the basic orientation. This is a *moral* orientation according to McDonagh, yet his treatment of it all but identifies it with psychological realities. I have always felt a certain discomfort with this complete identification. O'Neil and Donovan made a similar identification of "attitudes, habits, and values" with one's moral position, a term that must refer to one's posture before God.[7] The problem with this is the following: Is it not possible to experience a genuine conversion, to accept Christ's empowering grace in the depths of one's person, without shattering immediately this cluster of "habits, values, and attitudes"? One's habitual dispositions and values are, it is true, long in building, and therefore long in changing. When this cluster is dominantly self-centered, it remains, of course, as a challenge to be fought and transformed. But should we say that until it is changed it represents one's *moral* position? This is not clear. If we simply identify a moral position with a cluster of habits, values, and attitudes, we must eventually say that one is morally bad up to the point where he has managed to change these. Is there not a good deal in Christian attitudes and practice, as well as in human experience, that would find so close an identification a foreshortening of the reach of divine grace? At least the matter needs much more attention than it has yet received.

Secondly, McDonagh refers to "critical responses" as those capable of changing the subject. He is making reference to what was known in

[6] McDonagh, "The Moral Subject," p. 22.

[7] Robert P. O'Neil and Michael A. Donovan, *Sexuality and Moral Responsibility* (Washington, D.C.: Corpus, 1968).

more vintage language as "serious matter,"[8] though he has relativized (to the subject) the notion in a way most appropriate and realistic. Of these critical responses he says: "The change in basic orientation will be through a critical response but one which is prepared for in time, in history. The critical action is the culmination of a process which may not be adverted to until the critical action itself occurs."

This provides an altogether realistic understanding of a serious moral act. McDonagh's discomfort with the fundamental option as some "grand dramatic choice" is justified. But the reaction to this can too easily smother the importance of concrete actions. Or again, if in the past, serious sin was all too mechanically identified with the performance of certain actions, the contemporary reaction (no single action can be a grave choice or sin) remains precisely a reaction that tends to spiritualize the notion of moral choice. McDonagh has found the middle ground: critical action—but one that is the culmination of a process. A seriously evil choice is not a surprise phenomenon, an isolated, fragmented choice. It seems much more the culmination of a process of growing unconcern, an action wherein one embodies an accumulating unconcern and rejection.[9] It does not so much cause this unconcern as it provides the occasion to sum it up, embody it, intensify it, and seal it. The process that has been going on is ratified and manifested in this concrete, critical action.[10] When we speak of serious matter (or critical choices) as that apt to occasion a serious response, a use of core freedom, it should be understood, I believe, in this more dynamic way, a way that gives importance to the single act, but within and as part of a process of deterioration.[11]

[8] A balanced understanding of this as touching Church law is that of John O'Callaghan, S.J., "Christian Conscience and Laws of the Church," *Chicago Studies* 11 (1972) 59–71.

[9] A good statement of this is found in Thomas N. Hart, S.J., "Sin in the Concept of the Fundamental Option," *Homiletic and Pastoral Review* 71 (1970) 47–50. Eugene J. Cooper's "The Fundamental Option," *Irish Theological Quarterly* 39 (1972) 383–92, arrived too late for review.

[10] Cf. also Ralph J. Tapia, "When Is Sin Sin?" *Thought* 47 (1972) 211–24; William F. Allen, "Second Thoughts on Sin" *Priest* 28 (1972) 46–52; Martin A. Lang, "Penance Is for Penitents," *America* 126 (1972) 167–73; F. Podimattam, "What Is Mortal Sin?" *Clergy Monthly* 36 (1972) 57–67.

[11] Recent literature on the sacrament of penance includes "Les nouvelles normes pour l'absolution général." *Documentation catholique* 69 (Aug. 6–20, 1972) 713–15; M. Desdouits, "Une absolution collective est-elle invalide? illicite?" *Esprit et vie* 82 (1972) 9–11; "Pastoral Instruction on the Sacrament of Penance," *Furrow* 23 (1972) 497–501; William F. Allen, "First Confession: When?" *Pastoral Life* 31 (1972) 33–38; P. Jacquemont, "Bulletin de théologie: Le sacrement de pénitence," *Revue des sciences philosophiques et théologiques* 56 (1972) 127–46; Karl-Josef Becker, S.J., "Die Notwendigkeit des vollständigen Bekenntnisses in der Beichte nach dem Konzil von Trient," *Theologie und Philosophie* 47 (1972) 161–228.

Closely connected with an understanding of the moral act is the specifically Christian character of morality. This subject has been the center of a lively discussion during the past few years.[12] Helmut Weber (Trier) regards this as "one of the most significant questions" in moral theology.[13] Approaching the question from the perspective of social morality, he reviews the thought of preconciliar authors in Germany. Over a period of time there occurred a development from the natural-law approach (Fellermeier, von Nell-Breuning, Gundlach) to an attitude more specifically Christian (Gecks, Monzel, Ermecke, J. Höffner), even if the specifically Christian remained dissatisfyingly obscure. Finally, Weber seeks an answer in *Gaudium et spes*. The specifically Christian is the biblically inspired understanding of man and the world that the Christian brings to concrete issues and that can affect his solutions to concrete problems.

The editors of *Civiltà cattolica* argue that faith and grace characterize Christian morality and that they will necessarily "translate themselves into new moral conduct and new commands."[14] Examples offered are: love of enemies, nonresistance to the wicked, renunciation of wealth, love of the cross, the value of virginity.

Gerard J. Hughes explores the Christian justification for moral beliefs.[15] Does the Christian base his moral beliefs upon grounds not available to the non-Christian? Hughes discusses carefully and ultimately rejects three theses that derive the substantive content of our moral knowledge from specifically Christian sources. The teaching and example of Christ provide, rather, a stimulus, a context, and a motivation. For instance, we cannot read the New Testament seriously without being forced to re-examine our current moral values and beliefs. The Christian revelation continues to inject a divine discontent into our secular moral thinking and to throw light on the status of the moral life as a whole, though the implications of this discontent must be sought by the ordinary methods of ethical reflection.

D. Tettamanzi summarizes the opinions of various authors (F. Böckle, A. Jousten, J.-M. Aubert, R. Simon, J. Fuchs, Charles Curran)[16] and

---

[12] Cf. THEOLOGICAL STUDIES 32 (1971) 71–78.

[13] Helmut Weber, "Um das Proprium christlicher Ethik," *Trier theologische Zeitschrift* 81 (1972) 257–75.

[14] "Esiste una morale 'cristiana'?" *Civiltà cattolica* 123 (1972) 449–55.

[15] Gerard J. Hughes, S.J., "A Christian Basis for Ethics," *Heythrop Journal* 13 (1972) 27–43.

[16] F. Böckle, "Was ist das Proprium einer christlichen Ethik?" *Zeitschrift für evangelische Ethik* 11 (1967) 148–59; A. Jousten, "Morale humaine ou morale chrétienne," *La foi et le temps* 1 (1968) 419–41; R. Simon, "Spécificité de l'éthique chrétienne," *Supplément* 23 (1970) 74–104; Ch. Curran, "Y a-t-il une éthique sociale spécifiquement chrétienne?" *Supplément* 24 (1971) 39–58.

then presents the directions of his own thought.[17] The foregoing authors have by and large affirmed the identity of Christian and non-Christian morality at the level of material content and sought the specificity of Christian morality at the intentional level.[18] Tettamanzi fears that this overlooks the fact that faith has not merely a revealing function but a personally transforming one. Insisting on the tight connection between being and action, he suggests that the transformation of being will appear in conduct. "The newness that characterizes the Christian as a 'new creature in Christ' cannot fail to appear in 'newness' of conduct." He does not say what this newness of conduct is at the level of material content—the very issue raised by the authors he discusses. Rather he is content to say that whatever this difference is, it is the moral norm for historically existing man; for the grace of Christ, as gift and demand, assumes and perfects every human value. Rewarding as Tettamanzi's essay is, it ultimately fails to show just what a Christian morality adds, at the level of material content, to a human ethic.

In a remarkably fine article Norbert Rigali has, I believe, truly advanced the state of this discussion.[19] First he engages James Bresnahan. Bresnahan, it will be recalled, had argued to the nondistinctiveness of Christian ethics on the basis of Rahner's supernatural existential and anonymous Christianity.[20] The created consequence of God's universally salvific will in Christ is a universally experienced directedness toward God who is offering Himself in intimacy to man, even though a non-Christian may be only implicitly aware of this. Since this is the experience of everyman in his subjectivity, Bresnahan had concluded that the resources of Christian revelation (the objectification in Jesus of this subjectivity) could add to human ethical self-understanding nothing that is new or foreign to man as he exists in this world.

Rigali attacks the form of the argument, not for the moment the conclusion. The argument leans on Rahner's notion of "anonymous Christianity" and ultimately on the supernatural existential as they are developed in Rahner's early thought. Rigali rejects Rahner's earlier formulations as being individualistically biased. An atheist's orientation by grace to the God of eternal life may be a reality, but it does not deserve the name of Christianity. Christianity is essentially both

[17] Dionigi Tettamanzi, "Esiste un'etica cristiana?" *Scuola cattolica* 99 (1971) 163–93.

[18] Most recently Laurance Bright, O.P., "Humanist and Christian in Action," *Theology* 75 (1972) 525–33.

[19] Norbert J. Rigali, S.J., "On Christian Ethics," *Chicago Studies* 10 (1971) 227–47.

[20] James F. Bresnahan, S.J., "Rahner's Christian Ethics," *America* 123 (1970) 351–54.

God *and people*. Therefore one can employ the term "anonymous Christianity" legitimately only where, besides this anonymous personal relation of the non-Christian to God, there is also a relation to people which is anonymously identical with that of the authentic Christian. Rahner advanced to this position later when he came to maintain that the primary act of love of God is love of neighbor.[21] Since it is this love of the human thou that is for Christian and non-Christian alike the primary act of love of God, the basis and quintessence of morality are identical for Christian and non-Christian alike. The inference is that Christian revelation cannot add to human ethical self-understanding any material content foreign to man as he exists in the world. Rigali believes that Bresnahan had argued off an "early Rahner," one whose notion of Christian was too utterly vertical, and hence that the argument did not follow.

But Rigali does not stop there. The question of the distinctiveness of a Christian ethic has, he believes, been pursued within a single notion of ethic—an essential ethic.[22] By this term he means those norms that are applicable to all men, where one's behavior is but an instance of a general, essential moral norm. However, this notion of ethic does not exhaust the notion. There are three more understandings that must be weighed. First, there is an existential ethic, the choice of a good that the individual as individual should realize, "the experience of an absolute ethical demand addressed to the individual." At this level not all men of good will can and do arrive at the same ethical decisions in concrete matters.

Secondly, there is "essential Christian ethics." By this Rigali refers to the ethical decisions a Christian must make precisely because he belongs to a community to which the non-Christian does not belong. These are moral demands made upon the Christian *as Christian*: for instance, to receive the sacrament of penance, to participate in a liturgy, to establish a Catholic school. These are important ethical decisions that emerge only within the context of a Christian community's understanding of itself in relation to other people. Thus, "to the extent that Christianity is a Church in the above sense and has pre-ordained structures directly relevant to morality (e.g., the sacrament of penance), to this extent there can be and must be a distinctively

---

[21] Cf. also Ph. Delhaye and M. Huftier, "L'Amour de Dieu et l'amour de l'homme," *Esprit et vie* 82 (1972) 193-204, 225-36, 241-50.

[22] Thus, Timothy E. O'Connell, summarizing the literature on this matter, states: "There is no action which is demanded of Christians but is not, in fact, demanded of all men as well." This statement is true only within an essentialist concept of ethics. Cf. "The Search for Christian Moral Norms," *Chicago Studies* 11 (1972) 89-99.

Christian ethic, an 'essential ethics of Christianity' which adds to the ordinary essential ethics of man as member of the universal human community the ethics of man as member of the Church-community."

Finally, there are those ethical decisions that the Christian *as individual* must make, e.g., the choice to enter religious life. Such choices fall within "existential Christian ethics."

Rigali is insisting that the first step toward clarifying the relationship between Christian and non-Christian ethics is an adequate understanding of the term "ethics," one that allows the term to include more than essential ethics. This is an aspect of the discussion too often overlooked. But when all is said and done, Rigali's analysis represents a change in the state of the question.

Are there exceptionless moral norms? This question has been treated by many authors over the past four or five years. In one sense the question is of only peripheral importance because of the sheer irrelevance of a rule-morality for much of our moral life. However, in another sense the question is very important, because at its heart is the discussion about the deontological or teleological character of normative statements. And practical conduct can be decisively affected at key points by the resolution of this question. For example, if direct sterilization is always wrong because "contrary to nature," as Catholic tradition held for decades, then one direction of a solution for quite a few practical problems has been closed off. Three examples of this discussion follow.

Bruno Schüller, S.J., continues his already fruitful reflection on the meaning of moral norms with a synthesis of many of the things he has written before.[23] He frames the question in terms of changeable moral norms, though the substance of his study makes it clear that he is concerned with the existence of exceptional instances. In approaching the problem, he states that we must first distinguish between a factual judgment and a value judgment. When only a factual judgment changes, there is no change in the norm. We have difficulty keeping these two judgments distinct, because facts are often of great moral significance. For example, whether and when the fetus is a human being is a factual judgment, but it determines the moral character of interventions into pregnancy. The formulation of moral prohibitions and prescriptions often contains both fact and value judgments. Therefore, when the facts change, so could the norm.

But how about norms in which ethical value judgments are not composed of both value and fact, but are uttered purely as value judgments?

[23] Bruno Schüller, S.J., "Zum Problem ethischer Normierung," *Orientierung*, April 15, 1972, pp. 81–84.

Schüller answers this by distinguishing between nonmoral values and moral values. Examples of the former: life, health, appearance, success, wealth. Their nonmoral character is clear from the fact that a person is not morally good because he is healthy, etc. Examples of moral values: justice, truthfulness, fidelity. These are predicated directly of the person. Although nonmoral and moral values are distinct, a person's moral character is determined by his freely established relationship to both. However, the norms that state what this relationship ought to be are very different depending on whether moral or nonmoral value is involved. Since moral value is by definition unconditioned value, the exceptionless validity of norms stating it is analytical. Thus, one must always be just; one may never approve of the injustice of another; and so on. Norms dealing with nonmoral value, however, necessarily have exception clauses built into them. For example, one should not cause pain unless causing pain is the only way to avoid a worse (than pain) evil. This type of statement is obviously a teleological assertion, i.e., one that evaluates alternative choices from their consequences.

By contrast, a deontological norm is one that evaluates an act by a characteristic that cannot be gathered from the consequences. Catholic tradition has served up deontological norms where some nonmoral values are involved. What is the characteristic (distinct from consequences) that has led to this? Where human life and sacramental marriage are involved, it is lack of right. Where prevention of conception is concerned, this characteristic is "contrariness to nature." Schüller is clearly very uncomfortable with deontological norms. They lead to the possibility that a morally proper act could increase the number of nonmoral evils in the world, and a morally improper one could decrease them. The history of moral theology reveals a continuing attempt to contain the negative effects of deontological norms by a restrictive reading of them. Thus, indirect killings are not murders; use of the Pauline privilege is not contrary to the indissolubility of marriage.

Recently Catholic theologians have begun to judge three instances teleologically where before they judged deontologically: falsehood, organ transplants, prevention of conception. Schüller is convinced that all actions involving nonmoral values must be judged teleologically. We hesitate to do this because the areas in question (e.g., sacramental marriage) were judged deontologically before, and therefore we have no experience of what would happen. We say: "What will be the consequences if we do judge teleologically?" But this warning itself reveals the right teleological instincts.

Schüller's analyses are always well reasoned and enlightening. For this reason it would be helpful if he turned his attention to the question left unanswered in his recent writings: Are there behavioral norms that we ought practically to hold as exceptionless, even though theoretically they are not? And on what grounds?

This very question has been discussed by Donald Evans in a very careful and tightly written article.[24] He engages Paul Ramsey on the question of exceptionless rules. Ramsey had earlier argued that there are some rules that we ought to hold as exceptionless, and this for a variety of reasons. Evans first explains what "exceptionless" rule must mean. It must fulfil three conditions: (1) the prohibited action must have a definite, nonelastic meaning; (2) it must allow no quantity of benefits exception clauses; (3) it must not be open to any feature-dependent exception clauses. Thus, where we accept the prohibition "Thou shalt not steal" but give the word "theft" a plastic meaning that allows for nuancing and modification of its meaning, we have an unrevisable rule, but not an exceptionless one; for our rule is open in a way that amounts practically to the same as a less plastic definition with stated exceptions.

Evans agrees with Ramsey that the real question is whether there is adequate moral justification for *holding* that a moral rule is exceptionless. After examining the reasons that Ramsey adduces for holding certain rules "significantly closed to future exceptions" (e.g., "Never experiment medically on a human being without his informed consent"; "Never punish a person whom one knows to be innocent of that for which he would be punished"; "Never force sexual intercourse on someone who is totally unwilling"), Evans concludes that such moral rules are "virtually exceptionless." By this he means that the theoretically possible exceptions are virtually zero in their practical probability. Here the conclusions of Evans and Ramsey are very close, indeed practically indistinguishable. For Ramsey's argument assumes the possibility that in a particular instance the consequences of adhering to the rule could be so disastrous as to warrant a revision of the rule. As for Evans, he contends that there can be genuine conflicts between obligations where one is overridden by another.

A careful reading of Evans and Ramsey will, I believe, lead to the conclusion that the only significant difference between them with regard to exceptionless rules is the way their thought is trending. Ramsey fears creeping exceptionism. That is, he has a greater fear of morally disastrous consequences if we admit the need for openness in certain fidelity-rules. Therefore he gathers metaethical arguments for holding that some rules must be held as exceptionless. Evans fears creeping legalism. That is, he fears the morally disastrous consequences if we do not admit the

[24] Donald Evans, "Paul Ramsey on Exceptionless Moral Rules," *American Journal of Jurisprudence* 16 (1971) 184–214.

need for such openness in these rules. Therefore he goes about qualifying the metaethical arguments of Ramsey. In particular, Evans believes that the deontological tone that surrounds Ramsey's treatment "leaves unresolved the problems of priorities and conflicts." He is convinced that Christians have New Testament warrant for being concerned not only about covenant-bonds between men, but also about human suffering. Therefore exception-clauses on the basis of a calculation of quantity benefits have Christian, not merely utilitarian, warrant.[25] Evans' study is one of the most enlightening I have seen on the meaning of moral norms.

Denis O'Callaghan, in discussing exceptionless norms, makes two interesting points.[26] First, he argues that if there are (negative) moral absolutes, it is not that these actions are intrinsically evil; rather they have been made absolute by a teaching authority. Why? "It formulates its principles in this absolute manner because there is no other effective way of safeguarding the important values at stake. Exception would mean precedent and experience teaches how precedent tends to ladder in some areas of life."[27]

Secondly, when it comes to putting these absolutes into practice, O'Callaghan does not fault the casuistic tradition as such; some such system is necessary to face the intractability of reality without abandoning moral norms. The fault of the casuistic tradition was lack of self-criticism. "If it was honest with itself it would have admitted that it made exceptions where these depended on chance occurrence of circumstances rather than on free human choice. In other words, an exception was admitted when it would not open the door to more and more exceptions, precisely because the occurrence of the exception was determined by factors of chance outside of human control." He gives intervention into ectopic pregnancy as an example. The casuistic tradition, he believes, accepted what is in principle an abortion because it posed no threat to the general position, though this tradition felt obliged to rationalize this by use of the double effect. Tubal pregnancy, as a relatively rare occurrence and one independent of human choice, does not lay the way open to abuse.

[25] Recent literature on utilitarianism: Rolf Sartorius, "Individual Conduct and Social Norms: A Utilitarian Account," *Ethics* 82 (1972) 200–218; R. E. Ewin, "What Is Wrong with Killing People?" *Philosophical Quarterly* 22 (1972) 126–39; Peter Singer, "Is Act-Utilitarianism Self-defeating?" *Philosophical Review* 81 (1972) 94–104; R. Stephen Talmage, "Utilitarianism and the Morality of Killing," *Philosophy* 47 (1972) 55–63.

[26] Denis O'Callaghan, "Moral Principle and Exception," *Furrow* 22 (1971) 686–96.

[27] This is very similar to the analysis of Timothy O'Connell, "The Search for Christian Moral Norms" (n. 22 above).

If I understand him correctly, O'Callaghan has done two things in this study. First, he has accepted the principle of the lesser evil as determinative in conflict situations. Secondly, he has specified this principle by arguing that when crucial values are at stake (e.g., human life), the evil that is done in protecting the value at issue remains factually the greater evil if it is likely to escalate into other exceptions. I think there is something to this, though the criterion of what exception is likely to expand into others remains problematic. O'Callaghan's distinction between chance occurrence and human choice needs much more study before its adequacy is clear and certain. His over-all analysis leads to the conclusion that if there are concrete absolutes, the exceptionless character of the norm is the equivalent of *lex lata in praesumptione periculi communis*, a matter to be touched on at greater length later in these notes. If such a notion of an exceptionless norm will survive systematic analysis, the remaining problem would be to discover what actions fall into this class.

OF DEATH AND DYING

The over-all care for the dying has surfaced as a concern of much recent literature. I say "surfaced" because this subject has been for too long a contemporary form of pornography: on everybody's mind but repressed from our cultural consciousness by every myth, taboo, and ritual we can bend to this purpose.[28] There are many dimensions to this subject more important than the ethical question about prolongation of life.[29] But given the remarkable supportive and resuscitative devices now available, it is not surprising that this single point is gathering a literature all its own. A few examples will reflect the major drifts of the discussion.[30]

Merle Longwood notes that the answer we give to the ethical issues related to death will depend on the meaning we give to death.[31] He sees two different ways (ideal-types) in which Christian tradition has at-

[28] Cf., e.g., E. Mansell Pattison, "Afraid to Die," *Pastoral Psychology* 23 (1972) 41–51; Geoffrey Gorer, "The Pornography of Death," in *Death, Grief and Mourning* (Garden City: Doubleday, 1967).

[29] For a general essay on the ethical problems raised by technology, cf. Hans Jonas, "Technology and Responsibility: Reflections on the New Tasks of Ethics," in *Religion and the Humanizing of Man*, ed. James Robinson, pp. 1–19. This volume contains the plenary addresses of the International Congress of Learned Societies, Sept. 1–5, 1972.

[30] An interesting report on the life-death issue of infants suffering from meningomyelocele and on euthanasia in certain other cases of defective infants is that of E. Freeman, "The God Committee,'" *New York Times Magazine*, May 21, 1972, pp. 84 ff.

[31] Merle Longwood, "Ethical Reflections on the Meaning of Death," *Dialog* 11 (1972) 195–201. The whole issue is devoted to a study of death.

tempted to interpret death. These differing emphases correspond roughly to the writings of Paul and John. In the first ideal-type, death, as intimately related to sin, is not a natural phenomenon. It is unnatural, abnormal, opposed to God; it is the "wages of sin" and is the enemy. In the second perspective, death is viewed as an accepted part of the natural fabric of created order. It is a necessity for the continuation of creation and history. Longwood proposes that these emphases are not mutually exclusive alternatives but rather complementary perspectives that provide correctives to each other. In our culture we have over-emphasized the strand of death-as-enemy,[32] and this shows in the de-cisions made in medical practice—for instance, in the impersonal and almost brutal scene of a comatose patient surrounded by intravenous stands, suction machines, oxygen tanks, with tubes emanating from every natural and several surgical orifices. If this view of death were balanced by the second perspective, "then when the dying process has begun, a person can be helped to die with dignity, respect and a mini-mum of suffering." As it is, our "terminal wards" in hospitals are, Longwood shrewdly observes, the institutionalized expression of our inability to relate meaningfully to those who have entered this final stage of life.

When he faces the question of euthanasia for the terminally ill and intolerably suffering patient, Longwood leans heavily in the direction of Bonhoeffer, Barth, and traditional Catholic moral theology, but is ultimately content to say that our answers to the entailed questions reflect our understanding of the moral meaning of death. Longwood does not say it, but his article fairly screams a single conclusion and one I think is absolutely correct: until our culture has a healthy Christian attitude toward death, it cannot trust the answers it gives and must give to the many extremely difficult questions involved in *any* acceptance of positive euthanasia.

A different point of view is advanced by psychiatrist J. William Worden.[33] If one had only the choices between unbearable pain, an un-dignified death before one's family (brought about by surgical interven-tion to kill pain), and the chance to end life with a pill, "one would be hard pressed not to choose the latter."

In the past few years several Catholic moral theologians have probed into the possible liceity of "hastening the dying process" by acts of

[32] Emil J. Freireich writes: "In my opinion death is an insult; the stupidest, ugliest thing that can happen to a human being." Cf. "The Best Medical Care for the 'Hopeless' Patient," *Medical Opinion*, Feb., 1972, pp. 51–55.

[33] J. William Worden, "The Right to Die," *Pastoral Psychology* 23 (1972) 9–14.

commission and inched closer to Worden's point of view.[34] The prodigious Paul Ramsey is not one who allows a passing probe to expire unattended by the rather massive care he brings to such questions. Are there, he asks, any exceptions to our duty always to care for the dying?[35] He finds two. First, there is the case of those "irretrievably inaccessible to human care." The duty to care for those people is suspended, Ramsey believes, because of their inaccessibility to any form of care. When a patient is in this condition, the "crucial moral difference between omission and commission as a guide to faithful actions has utterly vanished."

The second instance is that of the dying person undergoing deep, prolonged, and intractable pain. Ramsey's reason is the same as that given for the first instance: a terminal patient beyond the reach of available palliatives "would also be beyond reach of the other ways in which company may be kept with him and he be attended in his dying. . . ."

Ramsey's analysis of our duty only to care for the dying is the finest statement of this matter I have ever seen. It is shot through with human and Christian good sense and highlights the compassion that euthanasiasts have mistakenly claimed exclusively for their view. What is to be said of Ramsey's exceptions? Since he admits that his second instance is very likely a supposable class without any members, I shall limit myself to the first class. In theory, I think Ramsey has good reason for his exception. If our duty is to care for the dying and if they are no longer within the reach of care, it would seem to follow that *nemo tenetur ad impossibile*. And when the duty to care ceases, the difference between omission and commission would seem to lose moral meaning; for the stricture against commission (positively causing death) is but a negative concretization of our duty to care.

Before this conclusion is accepted, however, several discussable difficulties should be cleared away. First, is the permanently and deeply unconscious person dying? Nothing in Ramsey's analysis seems to demand this. Would it make any difference if he were or not? Once he is

[34] Kieran Nolan, "The Problem of Care for the Dying," in Charles E. Curran, ed., *Absolutes in Moral Theology* (Washington, D.C.: Corpus, 1968) 253; Thos. A. Wassmer, "Between Life and Death: Ethical and Moral Issues Involved in Recent Medical Advances," *Villanova Law Review* 13 (1968) 765–66; Charles E. Curran as in *Sign*, March, 1968, p. 26. For "death as a process," cf. Robert S. Morrison, "Death: Process or Event?" and Leon Kass's response, *Science* 173 (1971) 694–702 and also 175 (1972) 581–82.

[35] Paul Ramsey, *The Patient as Person* (New Haven: Yale Univ. Press, 1970) pp. 157–64.

beyond care, he is beyond care, whether he is dying or not. Secondly, there is the notion of inaccessibility to human care. This inaccessibility is understood by Ramsey in terms of some kind of communication. One might argue that our duties of caring are limited not by the possibilities of communication but by the self-consciousness of the patient. Helmut Thielicke, arguing that it is self-consciousness that is the characteristic sign of human existence, suggested that consciousness of self can find expression in dimensions beyond our hermeneutical grasp. "It is conceivable that a person who is dying may stand in a passageway where human communication has long since been left behind, but which nonetheless contains a self-consciousness different from any other of which we know."[36] If this were the case, would genuine caring demand that we not put an end to this self-consciousness?

Thirdly and much more substantively, even if we accept inaccessibility as a limit on our duty to care, Ramsey is positing an exceptional instance for whose existence there is very probably no reliable evidence—and, it would seem, there can be no evidence. The only conceivable source of certainty that a person is beyond the reach of human care is, I would think, the one who experienced care and now no longer does so. But this source of certainty is excluded by the very nature of things. Ramsey says that moralists cannot say whether there are such cases as he posits, but "this would be for physicians to say." On what grounds would physicians make this judgment? They would have to guess, would they not? They are in no better position than anyone else to tell us whether the patient is experiencing anything or is beyond care. Ramsey admits that we should not lightly assume that the comatose patient is not aware of the sound of voices, the touch of a loved one's hand, etc. "But must it be assumed," he asks, "that this is always so?" No, it need not be assumed. When evidence to the contrary undermines the assumption, it is dissipated. But, once again, where does the evidence come from? What or who tells us whether our assumption is "light" or well founded? Perhaps Ramsey would have us set up commonly accepted criteria for determining when a patient can be judged to be beyond the reach of care. That is a different matter and it might possibly satisfy as an answer to the problem raised here.

This difficulty, not frivolous, raises a further point. When we have no concrete cases on which to build our exception-making clauses, or at least no evidence for them, the exception tends to gather in instances that have no place there at all. That this can erode our adherence to the

---

[36] Helmut Thielicke, "The Doctor as Judge of Who Shall Live and Who Shall Die," in Kenneth Vaux, ed., *Who Shall Live?* (Philadelphia: Fortress, 1970) pp. 147-94.

original principle seems clear. Ramsey would certainly have something to say to these remarks, and we would all profit by having it said.

P. R. Baelz, Regius Professor of Moral and Pastoral Theology at the University of Oxford, discusses the various possible structures of a Christian moral judgment on euthanasia.[37] Some Christians, for instance, will hold voluntary euthanasia to be intrinsically evil. Others, while denying that it is intrinsically evil, believe it might be forbidden either on the grounds that the general good will be better served by a proscribing rule than by permitting alternative decisions, or that the delicate structure of the doctor-patient loyalties and expectations will be damaged if exceptions are allowed. A third attitude might discriminate between individual cases. Baelz takes no position but simply unpacks some of the issues involved in any of the positions taken.

Harvard's Arthur J. Dyck reviews the underlying presuppositions of the ethic of euthanasia and rejects them utterly.[38] Some are: an individual's life belongs to that person to dispose of as he or she wishes; the dignity attaching to personhood by reason of freedom to make moral choices demands also the freedom to take one's own life; there is such a thing as a life not worth living whether by reason of distress, illness, physical or mental handicap, etc.

Dyck then outlines an ethic of "benemortasia," a term he invents to escape the ambiguities involved in the term "euthanasia."[39] This ethic does not oppose the values of compassion and human freedom. Rather it differs from euthanasia in its understanding of how these values are best realized. Certain constraints on our freedom actually enable us to increase our compassion and freedom. One such constraint, clarified in

[37] P. R. Baelz, "Voluntary Euthanasia," *Theology* 75 (1972) 238–51.

[38] Arthur J. Dyck, "An Alternative to the Ethic of Euthanasia," in Robert H. Williams, ed., *To Live or to Die: When, How and Why?* (forthcoming).

[39] For instance, in "The Right to Choose Death" (*New York Times*, Feb. 14, 1972, p. C29), O. Ruth Russell rightly criticizes keeping dying incurables alive by artificial means when they want to die. A few paragraphs later she refers to "the assistance of a physician in mercifully terminating his life." "Passive" and "active" euthanasia are qualifiers that attempt to avoid this confusion, but the fact remains that the term "euthanasia" is used to describe indiscriminately procedures that have, in the minds of very many, decisive moral differences. E.g., while Cheryl A. Forbes clearly distinguishes passive from active euthanasia (this latter is rejected), still at one point removal of artificial support systems ("pulling out the plug") is referred to as "practicing euthanasia" ("Death: No More Taboos," *Christianity Today* 16 [1972] 833). The same is true of the discussion of Lord Raglan's bill in the House of Lords (1969); cf. *Proceedings of the Royal Society of Medicine* 63 (1970) 659–70 and *Journal of the American Medical Association* 214 (1970) 905–6. Normal L. Geisler distinguishes mercy-dying and mercy-killing. He repudiates this latter in all instances and bases his rejection on a rather fundamentalist reading of biblical passages; cf. *Ethics: Alternatives and Issues* (Grand Rapids: Zondervan, 1971) pp. 231–49.

the Decalogue-covenant, is that against killing, the act of taking human life. This constraint does not mean that killing may never be justified. Where death results from our action, "we can morally justify the act of intervention only because it is an act of saving a life, not because it is an act of taking a' life. If it were simply an act of taking a life, it would be wrong."

Dyck insists on the distinction between "permitting to die" and "causing death." When should a decision be called a deliberate act to end life or "causing death"? Dyck's answer: when the act has the immediate intent of ending life and has no other purpose. Causing one's own death, he argues, does violence to oneself and harms others. It repudiates the meaningfulness and worth of one's own life. Moreover, it is the ultimate way of shutting out all other people from one's life, of irrevocably severing any actual or potential contact with others. However, when a dying patient chooses to forgo medical interventions that prolong dying or to accept drugs that alleviate pain, he is not choosing death but how to live while dying. It is our Christian task to support a person in his dying, not to encourage his suicide.

Dyck's ethic of "benemortasia" is a careful and balanced formulation of moral attitudes and judgments that have been traditional in Catholic circles for some years. His essay leans heavily on the distinction between permitting to die and causing death, and that between direct and indirect intention in our actions. These distinctions have a prima-facie descriptive validity that recommends them to common sense. But are there limits to their usefulness? That is, does the patient ever arrive at a point when the distinction becomes meaningless, as Ramsey argued? Dyck gives no hint that he thinks so.[40] If there is a single weakness to his study, it is one that plagues all moral writing on this subject: lack of a profound and precise understanding of the moral relevance of these distinctions. Dyck does not enlarge our understanding of this matter in his otherwise very fine presentation. We shall know the limits of the distinctions in question—if limits there be—only when we have grasped more satisfactorily the moral relevance of the descriptive difference between commission and omission, direct and indirect.

Daniel Maguire asks whether there are circumstances in which we may intervene creatively to achieve death by choice, whether by positive act of omission or commission.[41] Maguire puts the question to four different dying situations: the irreversibly comatose patient now sustained

---

[40] Neither does John R. W. Stott, who distinguishes the capacity to become human from "the human being who has become deprived of human powers." To this latter we may allow a natural death, but we may not directly kill him ("Reverence for Human Life," *Christianity Today* 16 [1972] 852–56).

[41] Daniel Maguire, "The Freedom to Die," *Commonweal* 46 (1972) 423–27.

by artificial means; the conscious patient whose life is supported by means of (e.g.) dialysis or iron lung; the conscious but terminally ill patient now supported by natural means; self-killing in a nonmedical context.

Where the patient is irreversibly comatose and the "personality is permanently extinguished," Maguire contends that without justifying reason it is immoral to continue artificial supportive measures. Furthermore, he endorses Ramsey's opinion that in these instances it is a matter of complete indifference whether death gains victory by direct or indirect action. As for the gravely ill but conscious patient whose life is artificially supported, Maguire asserts that "we owe them in justice and charity the direct or indirect means to leave this life" with dignity and comfort if their artificially supported life becomes unbearable to them.

What about the conscious and terminally ill patient whose life systems are functioning naturally? Maguire's answer: "direct action to bring on death in the situation described here may be moral." He rejects the contrary absolutist stand on the grounds that this practical prohibition has not been proved, and cannot be. And since it has not been proved, it must be said that "its absoluteness is at the very least doubtful. And then in accord with the hallowed moral axiom *ubi dubium ibi libertas*, we can proclaim moral freedom to terminate life directly in certain cases."

Maguire's essay represents an attempt to provoke discussion. Anyone familiar with the agonizing problems discussed here, with the sophisticated and sometimes dehumanizing life-support systems currently available, and with his own human and intellectual limitations will realize the difficulty and delicacy of the discussion and approach it with an extra measure of tentativeness. That being said, I should like to detail some difficulties I find in Maguire's study.

The notion of "the permanently extinguished personality" raises the same question occasioned by Ramsey's reference to a patient "irretrievably inaccessible to human care." Here, however, I should like to explore the question of the proof for the practical conclusion that we ought never terminate innocent life by direct action. Maguire contends that this must be proved, but that it has not been and cannot be proved.[42]

[42] In an interesting if complicated article Lonnie D. Kliever uses the model of Stephen Toulmin (*The Uses of Argument*) to approach the writings of Joseph Fletcher and Paul Lehmann. Toulmin was convinced that all rational arguments were measured by the analytic paradigm. To break the power of this model in moral argument, Toulmin replaces the mathematical model with a jurisprudential one in which logical form becomes a matter of proper procedure rather than necessary connections. Rational argument ("proof") in this model is more like a legal case than a geometric proof. Cf. "Moral Argument in the New Morality," *Harvard Theological Review* 65 (1972) 53-90.

That is probably true, but only if one understands and accepts a certain idea of proof. The only proof that I know of for any practical moral assertions is different from what Maguire might easily be implying and resembles a convergence of probabilities that leads us to rest satisfied with an assertion until it has been shown to be either humanly unwise (as absolute) or to rest on false or now-changed suppositions. Put another way, we build exception-clauses into concrete behavioral norms when we see clearly that a higher human value is being compromised, or at least can be, by failure to allow for exceptions. To do this with intellectual rigor and satisfaction, it seems that we must grasp clearly two things: the reason why the behavioral norm is generally valid in the first place, and the particular conflicting value that puts a limit on this validity. Specifically, why is it generally true that we should not directly terminate innocent human life? And what competitive value leads us to conclude that what is generally valid is not valid in some instances?

This same problem occurs with Maguire's analysis of suicide. He says: "It may not be excluded that direct self-killing may be a good moral action, in spite of the strong presumptions against it." Until we know exactly what these presumptions are and why they are strong, are we in any position to assert that direct self-killing may be a good moral action? I do not see how.

Maguire has not answered these questions with the clarity necessary. He does offer one attempted "proof" for the practical absoluteness of the prohibition against direct termination of innocent life: the cracked-dike argument (if X is allowed, then Y and Z will also be allowed). This is rejected for two reasons. First, it ignores the real differences between X, Y, and Z. Secondly, it is fallacious to say that if an exception is allowed, it will be difficult to draw the line and therefore no exception should be allowed. Good ethics is the art of knowing where to draw the line. On this basis Maguire regards the practical negative as "doubtful," and where there is doubt, there is freedom.

Maguire has, I believe, moved too fast here. Granted, good ethics is a matter of knowing where to draw the line. But good methodology is showing why and with what criteria the line is drawn here rather than there. While agreeing with Maguire's analysis of the vulnerability-to-logic of all wedge arguments, the cracked-dike approach as he presents it is not the only form of moral reasoning available to support the possible practical absoluteness of the type of normative statement involved here. We must seriously examine the possible usefulness of the traditional notion of *lex lata in praesumptione periculi communis*. Perhaps a concrete prohibition like the one in question cannot be "proved," but it might well be the conclusion of prudence in the face of dangers too momentous to allow the matter to the uncertainties and vulnerabilities of individual decision. In other words, it might be the type of conclusion we *ought* to hold as exceptionless even though it cannot be proved theoretically to be such.

The notion of a presumption of universal danger is one most frequently associated with positive law. Its sense is that even if the act in question does not threaten the individual personally, there remains the further presumption that to allow individuals to make that decision for themselves will pose a threat for the common good. For instance, in time of drought, all outside fires are sometimes forbidden. This prohibition of outside fires is founded on the presumption that the threat to the common good cannot be sufficiently averted if private citizens are allowed to decide for themselves what precautions are adequate. Hence the individuals are held liable in spite of the efficacy of individual precautions, for the primary presumption of danger still holds.

Is there place for a notion such as this as a support for the practical absoluteness of the prohibition against directly causing death in terminal situations? I am not at all sure. The matter has not received much attention, though moral reasoning very similar to this has been used now and then.[43] Its usefulness and validity will depend at least partly on how one assesses the importance of the matter and the dangers associated with it at a given point in history. Maguire's rejection of the necessary connection of X, Y, and Z is theoretically true. But practically, is it a realistic account of the many extremely important and delicate questions associated with direct termination of the terminally ill patient? Possibly not.[44]

What are some of these questions? Longwood has stated them as well as anyone:

How does one know whether a patient is only temporarily depressed and might change his mind about wanting to die in a day, a week or a month? What if the

[43] Paul Ramsey, "The Case of the Curious Exception," in G. Outka and P. Ramsey, ed., *Norm and Context in Christian Ethics* (New York: Scribner's, 1968) pp. 67–135.

[44] A classic text in this respect is Leo Alexander's statement about Nazi medical cases. "Whatever proportion these crimes finally assumed, it became evident to all who investigated them that they had started from small beginnings.... It started with the acceptance of that attitude, basic in the euthanasia movement, that there is such a thing as life not worthy to be lived. This attitude in its early stages concerned itself merely with the severely and chronically sick. Gradually the sphere of those to be included in this category was enlarged to include the socially unproductive, the racially unwanted and finally all non-Germans. But it is important to realize that the infinitely small wedged-in lever from which this entire trend of mind received its impetus was the attitude toward the non-rehabilitable sick" ("Medical Science under Dictatorship," *New England Journal of Medicine* 241 [1949] 39–47, at 44–45).

physician made a mistake in diagnosing the hopelessness of a case? If euthanasia were to be permitted, what effect would it have on the doctor-patient relationship? Who would make the decision as to when euthanasia should be administered? The patient? The patient's family? The doctor? If one decides that the patient should make this decision, are patients in fact capable during such severe crises of 'consenting' to their own death? If the family is involved in the decision, would this encourage them to 'weigh' heavily considerations of costly hospital care or children's education sacrificed against the sufferer's life? Would some unscrupulous persons be tempted to request the ending of another's life if they stood to gain large insurance benefits or an inheritance from the patient's will? Or would a society that allows euthanasia begin to measure all of life according to some qualitative standard or utilitarian calculus, cheapening life and preparing the way for the easy disposition of all those who fall below the minimal standard or because of age or illness are no longer useful or are otherwise a burden upon society?[45]

One might reason that an enormous good is at stake in the answer to these questions, and that they are unanswered questions and are destined to remain so, and *for this reason* that it is more humanly reasonable to regard the direct termination of any human life as a practical absolute. At least this approach deserves serious attention before it is concluded that the prohibition in question is "at the very least doubtful."

The question of how we treat dying patients and, by inference, patients trying to be born, reflects an underlying conviction about the make-up of humanhood. Joseph Fletcher tackles this metaethical question with his customary verve and flare.[46] He first makes precise the sense of the question. It is not whether defective fetuses, defective newborns, and moribund patients are human lives; they certainly are human. The problem, Fletcher argues, is whether we are to assign personal status to them. "What is critical is personal status, not merely human status. . . . It is not what is natural but what is personal which has the first-order value in ethics."

On this premise Fletcher sets out to establish an operational profile of personhood. He lists fifteen positive human criteria and five negative. With no importance in the ordering, the positive criteria are: minimal intelligence (I.Q. "below the 20-mark, not a person"), self-awareness, self-control, a sense of time, a sense of futurity, a sense of the past, the

[45] Longwood, *art. cit.* (n. 31 above) pp. 200–201.

[46] Joseph Fletcher, "Indicators of Humanhood: A Tentative Profile of Man," *Hastings Center Report* 2 (1972) 1–4. The full text of this paper will appear in *Proceedings of the Conference on the Teaching of Medical Ethics* (Government Printing Office, forthcoming).

capability to relate to others, concern for others, communication ("completely and finally *isolated* individuals are subpersonal"), control of existence ("to the degree that a man lacks control he is not responsible, and to be irresponsible is to be subpersonal"), curiosity ("to be without affect, sunk in anomie, is to be not a person"), change and changeability, balance of rationality and feeling, idiosyncrasy (a distinctive individual vs. a cloned carbon copy), neocortical function.

Fletcher's negative assertions are: man is not nonartificial, essentially parental, essentially sexual, a bundle of rights, a worshiper. In explanation of these negative assertions, Fletcher includes ideas well known to those familiar with his writings. Item: all rights are "imperfect" and may be set aside if human need requires it. Item: "A baby made artificially, by deliberate and careful contrivance, would be more *human* than one resulting from sexual roulette—the reproductive mode of the subhuman species." This tenet is, in my judgment, utterly ridiculous.

Fletcher admits that he has not produced a gospel of personhood and that more questions need to be asked. For instance, how are we to rank the items in this profile? Which are essential, which only optional, etc.? But he is convinced that we are apt to find good answers from medical science and the clinicians rather than from the humanities. "Divorced from the laboratory and the hospital, talk about what it means to be human could easily become inhumane."

Anyone who would attempt an even tentative personhood inventory is trying to catch, bottle, and display what most men have regarded as ultimately a mystery. But Fletcher is nothing if not courageous. I am in sympathy with the felt need to attempt what he has attempted. No additions, subtractions, or qualifications of his listing will be attempted here. That task can be left for those who accept the key metaethical assumption made by Fletcher in this essay.

I do not. Fletcher's purpose is to build an operational notion of personhood for use in medical decisions about abortion, euthanasia, etc. That is, those who do not achieve personhood according to his, or some such, criteria are candidates for these procedures. In other words, personhood in this context means protectable humanity. This reveals the assumption with which I have problems. Fletcher states (of a fetus) that the question is not whether it is a life or even whether it is a human life. "The question is whether we may assign personal status to fetal life. . . ." And later: "What is critical is personal status, not merely human status." Fletcher has nowhere shown us that this is the crucial question. His equation of protectable humanity with personhood remains a metaethical assumption. There are still very many who believe that human life prior to and regardless of its share in the *bene esse* that some call "personhood" makes profound claims on our loyalty and care—indeed, the more profound because of the weakness, dependency, and vulnerability due to a lesser share in this *bene esse*. It is the pride of Christian tradition and practice that such have been viewed and treated as our neighbor in greatest need. Fletcher has rushed right over this and assumed that it is not merely human life that we ought to respect and protect, but only a certain qualitative level of such life. Fetuses, beware!

This is not to deny that life and death decisions based on the quality of life are necessary in contemporary medicine. They are, and perhaps frequently. It is only to say that the weight of Christian tradition and wisdom has been to keep as wide as possible the category of protectable humanity and to urge that life-death decisions should be (1) restricted to dying patients; (2) about allowing to die; (3) left to the individual concerned, if possible. Fletcher is clearly going in a different direction. His distinction between protectable humanity and personhood assaults or at least undermines each of these contentions. Briefly, he has excluded from the category of protectable humanity many who really belong within this category.

In ethical reflection one of the greatest and most difficult tasks is to identify the cultural shaping of our moral judgments. Our temptation is unwittingly to inject into our notion of the human what our culture dictates. If the culture has a pronounced functional evaluation of man, those who are weakest and most defenseless will suffer and eventually get excluded from protectable human status. This has happened in Fletcher; for if the matters of euthanasia and abortion are solved in terms of his inventory, abortion has ceased to be a moral problem at all. When that happens, I think we are in serious trouble.

These are examples of but a single question touching death and dying. This and similar questions cannot be dealt with adequately in isolation from an over-all understanding of the meaning of death, as Longwood noted. This raises a final and very unsettling point. There is a virtual consensus in recent literature that in America we have successfully conspired to repress death into the realm of the unreal. As Richard Doss has pointed out, this denial of death has brought about a separation of death from life. "The dying are isolated from the living and given a new status of patient instead of person. The ageing are isolated geographically by their move to the 'leisure worlds' and 'sunset villages.' The dead are isolated in a realm of unreality created by modern funeral practices."[47] This repression constitutes the atmosphere in which our moral

[47] Richard W. Doss, "Towards a Theology of Death," *Pastoral Psychology* 23 (1972) 15–23, at 16.

reflection on the more practical ethical questions occurs and it is bound to affect our deliberations. If this is so, clearly our first moral task is to acknowledge and then challenge the cultural attitudes and values that generate and support this repression and prevent clear and Christian thinking about death. This task is far more important than any particular moral conclusion about preserving or not preserving life. Indeed, it is simply essential if our more detailed ethical assertions are to be something more than symptoms of our cultural malaise. Failure to attack this problem at its source means that our practical normative statements will remain isolated, useless, and dangerous moralisms.

Daniel Callahan, in a very thoughtful essay, has underlined this dimension of the ethics of biomedicine.[48] He argues that a satisfactory resolution of the moral problems posed by the life sciences must be cultural. Our decisions are not simply the result of "reasons"; man feels, senses, imagines, relates. At this level he acts from "reasons" that have sunk so deeply into the self that they inform the arational or unwitting side of man as much as the rational. Callahan believes that recently it has been the gospel of unlimited technological progress that has above all formed man's self-image and informed his unwitting responses. Until these values can be lifted out, examined, and altered where necessary, we will not have an ethical system capable of meeting the problems of the life sciences. Callahan concludes with a paragraph that would be an appropriate conclusion to this section:

To my mind, the least interesting piece of information about any person's ethical views is his conclusions, where he comes out on this or that problem. The most interesting part lies in the dynamics of moral decision-making, the way in which the issues are conceived in the first place, the ingredients which are used and the way they are mixed. It is at that point that a person's whole way of looking at the world is revealed; and it will be his whole way of looking at the world which will shape his conclusions. But the finding of a viable way to do this is both an individual problem and a cultural problem, and both must be solved simultaneously.[49]

PREMARITAL SEXUAL RELATIONS

That there has been a sexual revolution in the past decade seems beyond doubt.[50] Certainly there has been a significant modification in the

[48] Daniel Callahan, "Living with the New Biology," *Center Magazine* 5 (July–Aug., 1972) 4–12. Cf. also his "Normative Ethics and the Life Sciences," *Humanist* 32 (Sept.–Oct., 1972) 5–7.

[49] Callahan, "Living with the New Biology," p. 12.

[50] *Time* 100 (Aug. 21, 1972) 34 ff.; George Gallup, "Is There Really a Sexual Revolution?" *Critic* 30 (March–April, 1972) 72–75. Cf. also David R. Mace, "The Sexual Revolution: Its Impact on Pastoral Care and Counselling," *Journal of Pastoral Care* 25 (1971) 220–32.

attitudes of at least some people, and this modification appears ill at ease with traditional Christian moral convictions. Therefore it is easy to understand why sexual morality has been the subject of a good deal of theological writing over the past months, notwithstanding John L. McKenzie's invitation to "popes, cardinals, bishops, priests (including monsignori, pastors, and theologians) and laymen like Joe Breig and Dale Francis" to abstain, so to speak, from excessive concern with sexuality and talk more about "other things like justice, mercy and faith."[51]

Andrew Greeley would probably second McKenzie's invitation;[52] for in an article not totally purged of splenetic vigor, he underscores the loss of credibility of official teachings attributable to their imprisonment in "certain rigid formulations" upheld by "the overwhelming force of a rigid, static, authoritarian church."[53] The enduring symptom of this is *Humanae vitae*,[54] which Greeley sees as an "appeal to pure authority, a pure authority which the Pope mistakenly assumed that he still had." This document is, Greeley insists, a dead letter simply incapable of dealing with "the massive world population problem or the development of sexual personalism that has occurred in the wake of the dramatic new insights of depth psychology." He calls for a whole new theory of sexual morality, one less concerned with specific negative prohibitions and more concerned with the fascinating religious symbolism of human love as an image of the relationship between Christ and His Church and vice versa.

Eugene Kennedy is not nearly so optimistic about the "dramatic new insights of depth psychology."[55] Rather he sees our state of confusion and uncertainty about sex as "almost staggering in its proportions and effects." Kennedy sighs and wonders "if science has not given us more white-coated bad advice ... than all the crimson-sleeved church-

---

[51] John L. McKenzie, "Q.E.D." *Critic* 30 (March–April, 1972) 9.

[52] Andrew Greeley, "Is Catholic Sexual Teaching Coming Apart?" *Critic* 30 (March–April, 1972) 30–35.

[53] Much the same attitude is found in Eugene Fontinell's "Marriage, Morality and the Church," *Commonweal* 97 (1972) 126–30.

[54] For some recent related writings, cf. R. M. Cooper, "Vasectomy and the Good of the Whole," *Anglican Theological Review* 54 (1972) 94–106; Kevin T. Kelly, "A Positive Approach to *Humanae vitae*," *Clergy Review* 57 (1972) 108–20, 174–86, 263–75, 330–47; W. Finnin and Donald Huisingh, "Population Control Begins with You," *Duke Divinity School Review* 37 (Winter, 1972) 32–39; Leon F. Bouvier, "Catholics and Contraception," *Journal of Marriage and the Family* 34 (1972) 514–22; James R. Hertel, "'Humanae vitae' Four Years Later," *Priest* 28 (1972) 18–26; J. F. Costanzo, S.J., "Papal Magisterium, Natural Law, and *Humanae vitae*," *American Journal of Jurisprudence* 16 (1971) 259–89.

[55] Eugene Kennedy, "The Great Orgasm Hunt," *Critic* 30 (March–April, 1972) 39–56.

men in history. . . . No religion has ever exceeded psychoanalysis in dogmatization."

James Hitchcock inteprets the sexual revolution as critically related to the apparent decline in concern for transcendental religion.[56] Christianity has always stood as a balanced voice for sexual restraint. Such restraint, in whatever context, is only justifiable and supportable, Hitchcock argues, for the sake of some larger purpose. "When the purpose itself comes to be doubted, the discipline begins to seem merely repressive and cruel." At this point our obvious cultural obsession with sex takes the form of a clinical therapeutic that states: personal self-fulfilment is impossible without an active sex life.

An atmosphere of ecclesiastical noncredibility, scientific myth, and cultural obsession is hardly conducive to enlightening theological reflection on sexuality. However, that reflection has continued and much of it puts heavy emphasis on premarital sexual relationships. Roughly and in general it can be said that two approaches are discernible: deontologically founded restatements of the classical tradition, teleologically argued modifications of this tradition. I shall gather a few examples of each approach from recent writings.

First, the restatements of the classical tradition. In a paper that he accurately assesses as "un modesto contributo di approfondimento in linea teologica e pastorale," P. Bongiovani repeats the rather standard arguments against premarital intercourse.[57] For instance, the procreative character of sexual intercourse demands that the couple be in a condition to render naturally secure the education of the child. Similarly, as an expressive act, sexual intercourse between the unmarried is an "existential lie," because there is a "donation of bodies" without a corresponding stable and definitive gift of the persons "which alone on the human plane can justify and guarantee the bodily gift." I am not arguing that these reflections are without their degree of validity, but only that they are not developed by Bongiovani beyond the condition in which he found them in other authors.

This is not true of the study of Richard R. Roach, S.J. In a very thoughtful essay, he contends that the orthodox tradition in Christian morality still makes the best sense.[58] He attempts to show this by exposing the meaning of sexuality in Christian tradition. All Christian

[56] James Hitchcock, "The Church and the Sexual Revolution," *America* 127 (1972) 197–201.

[57] P. Bongiovani, "Fornicazione e rapporti tra i fidanzati," *Palestra del clero* 51 (1972) 25–41.

[58] Richard Roach, S.J., "Sex in Christian Morality," *Way* 11 (1971) 148–61, 235–42.

thinkers insist on some degree of sexual restraint. But this restraint cannot be derived from the Christian doctrine of love without further specification; for the Christian command is to love as richly, deeply, and widely as possible. The result would therefore be not to restrain the use of sex but to encourage it. We must therefore find something more within the doctrine of love which, when related to sex, will build a Christian ethic. Since Christian love governs all Christian morality, we should expect to find one expression of Christian love, among the many possible, which coincides with an important characteristic of human sexuality. What is this special characteristic?

Since all expressions of Christian love require fidelity (the sign of faith), fidelity alone cannot be this characteristic, though obviously it is essential to married love. Roach concludes: "I suggest that according to the Christian tradition sex primarily expresses *exclusive fidelity.* ... " Marriage does not, however, justify itself solely because it is a relationship of exclusive fidelity. Other interpersonal relationships could have this quality. "Marriage requires, rather, other additional justification through its social aims, which are greater than the personal aims of the faithful couple. These are the traditional aims of bearing and rearing children."[59]

Roach then adds two important points. First, the bearing and rearing of children "justifies" marriage as an institution, and not the individual marriage. Human and personal values "justify" the individual marriage. Secondly, apart from Christian faith the arguments for preferring monogamous marriage over other means for providing for children are inconclusive. That is, "it is fitting that children begin life in an institution and a society built up with such institutions designed to show forth sacramentally the exclusivity of God's love for man and the fidelity required in man's response."

In summary, Roach contends that sexual intimacy is the sign of exclusive fidelity, but that men and women may create this bond and give this sign of exclusive fidelity only because marriage has a further justification: "it is the basic unit of a society in which children are meant to be born and raised under a sign of the *one* relationship of *exclusive fidelity*, that between God and man."[60] This means, of course, that for Roach full sexual intimacy should be limited to the married state. When sex is legitimized by love alone or love in general, he argues, either we limit our loving, or we do not limit our sexual activity, or we choose not to be consistent.

Roach applies this conviction pastorally to several areas. Here his re-

[59] *Ibid.*, p., 157.   [60] *Ibid.*, p. 158.

marks are very perceptive and realistic. For instance, he points out, as Hitchcock had done, that a contemporary cultural assumption either consciously held or unconsciously assumed is that "bad sex is better than no sex." If this assumption is operative, there is a tendency to evaluate any mental or moral obstacle in the way of premarital intimacy as a hang-up. While his own evaluation of premarital relations is within the classical tradition, Roach rightly notes that there is a scale of greater and lesser evils where sex is concerned. Premarital (when marriage is to follow) relations are preferable to extramarital, homosexual fidelity to homosexual promiscuity, etc.; for "the more fidelity that one expresses in the uses or non-uses of sexuality, the more easily God may use the occasion as an instrument of his grace."

John M. Finnis, in a careful article that escaped my attention earlier, derives the radical immorality of certain sexual acts from their relationship to the basic value of procreation ("the procreative good").[61] A sexual act can involve either an inadequate response to, or a basic closure to, this good. Premarital intimacy, e.g., involves an inadequate openness to procreation because "procreation may follow but not within an assured *communio personarum*."

The interesting feature of Finnis' study is that it is not a piece-by-piece analysis of different sexual acts but the elaboration of an entire ethical theory. Finnis follows closely Germain Grisez's account of the origin of moral obligation, but adds interesting and enlightening Christian nuances to it. According to this account, there are basic values that define the scope of man's possibility, that appeal to man for their realization. The natural law is nothing more than the conclusions of practical reason about how a person ought to relate to these values.[62] As Finnis puts it:

When one of these irreducible values falls immediately under our choice directly to realize it or to spurn it, then, in the Christian understanding we must remain open to that value, that basic component of the human order, as the only reasonable way to remain open to the ground of all values, all order. To choose di-

[61] John M. Finnis, "Natural Law and Unnatural Acts," *Heythrop Journal* 11 (1970) 365-87.

[62] Recent literature on the natural law includes: Jerome G. Hanus, O.S.B., "Natural Law—Indispensable or Not?" *American Benedictine Review* 23 (1972) 85-97; David-Hillel Ruben, "Positive and Natural Law Revisited," *Modern Schoolman* 49 (1972) 295-317; Thomas Rukavina, "Natural Law and Veatch's Recent Book," *New Scholasticism* 46 (1972) 384-401; Eugene F. Miller, "Political Philosophy and Human Nature," *Personalist* 53 (1972) 209-21; F. Gerald Downing, "Ways of Deriving 'Ought' from 'Is,'" *Philosophical Quarterly* 22 (1972) 234-47; Philippa Foot, "Morality as a System of Hypothetical Imperatives," *Philosophical Review* 81 (1972) 305-16.

rectly against it in favor of some other basic value is arbitrary, for each of the basic values is equally basic, equally and irreducibly and self-evidently attractive.[63]

Thus, of life he says: "So, no suicide, no killing of the innocent: for human life is a fundamental value." The Christian grasp of this law of reason is distinctive in its concern for the *form* of one's choices, that is, "its adherence to these premoral values ... in certain circumstances *whatever the foreseeable consequences* on the horizontal plane of history." Finnis grants, however, that there is often room for dispute about whether a choice is indeed directly and positively against a basic value, whether it has such and such a form or not. But he resolutely rejects any understanding of moral norms that would make room for a calculus where the basic values are concerned.

Finnis then applies this normative theory to the area of sexuality. He rejects all the arguments which build on the unitive (expression of total giving, etc.) character of sexual intercourse.[64] What eventually makes sense of the conditions of the marital enterprise, its stability and exclusiveness, "is not the worthy and delightful sentiments of love and affection which invite one to marry, but the desire for and demands of a *procreative* community, a family." Therefore it is sensible to reserve complete and procreative self-giving to the context of a stable and exclusive union. But this does not show that all sexual intercourse must be reserved to that context. How establish this latter? Finnis grants that we have the capacity to give meaning to our acts, and therefore we might regard sexual intimacy as a sign only of regard or friendship. Ultimately, however, our choice must take account of a plain fact, "viz., that intercourse may bring about procreation." We can accept this fact, ignore it, proceed regardless of it, or try to reverse it. "But in any case, one is willy nilly engaged, in sexual intercourse, with the basic human value of procreation."[65] And in Finnis' judgment, premarital relations involve an inadequate openness to this value.

But what if procreation is contraceptively excluded? Finnis sees this as "always, and in an obvious and unambiguous way ... a choice directly and immediately against a basic value." What, then, if the intercourse is certainly and naturally sterile? Finnis argues, weakly I believe, that all sexual activity is a kind of reminder of the procreative potency

[63] *Art. cit.*, p. 275.

[64] For an interesting discussion of such formulations, cf. William F. May, *A Catalogue of Sins* (New York: Holt, Rinehart and Winston, 1967) pp. 130–37. See also Michael Taylor, S.J., ed., *Sex: Thoughts for Contemporary Christians* (Garden City: Doubleday, 1972).

[65] *Art. cit.*, p. 383.

of full sexual intercourse, and is sufficient to bring a sensitive person "within the range of the procreative value for that value to make its ordinary imperious claim ... to a sufficient openness and respect toward it."

Finnis' study is carefully wrought. His account of the origin of moral obligation and the meaning of natural law (reasonableness) is very persuasive and easily amenable to the Christian symbols to which he relates it. With no desire to challenge his normative conclusions, I believe, however, that there are some unanswered problems in his general theory.

The problem centers around the matter of choice "directly and positively against a basic value." Finnis admits that there is room for dispute about whether a choice actually is directly against a basic value or not. But he does not pursue the matter and ask why there is room for dispute, and what the methodological implications of this fact might be. The crucial question one must raise with both Grisez and Finnis is: What is to count for turning against a basic good, and why? At this point I find them both unsatisfactory. Finnis argues that whenever one positively suppresses a possible good, he directly chooses against it. And since one may never do this, he argues, there are certain actions that are immoral regardless of the foreseeable consequences. This is a sophisticated form of an older structuralism. A careful study of Christian moral tradition will suggest that an action must be regarded as "turning directly against a basic good" only after the relation of the choice to all values has been weighed carefully.

An example will illustrate this. Finnis states: "So, no suicide, no killing of the innocent: for human life is a fundamental value." Why does he insert the word "innocent"? After all, even the lives of the criminally guilty are fundamental values. The reason Finnis can insert the term "innocent" and thus delimit those killings that involve a choice directly against a fundamental value is that he has first weighed the life of the criminal (or combatant, aggressor) against other possibly competitive and more urgent values and decided that when a more urgent value (e.g., the common good) is threatened by a human life, then taking *that* life need not involve one in choosing directly against a basic value, regardless of the structure of the action involved. Is it not some such calculus that leads to the restriction "innocent"?

Finnis realizes that this approach involves a calculus, a balancing of possible goods and values, and he fears this. He says: "The human mind is capable of revising the meanings it attributes to acts in order to escape the characterization of its acts and choices as directly opposed to a basic value." It is true that the human mind is capable of both the subtlest and grossest types of rationalization to distort the meaning of its conduct. But this only means that the process of revising meaning is risky, not that it is unnecessary or disallowed, unless our view is that reality is always so neatly ordered that it never involves us in conflicts and tragic choices. In the constant effort to clarify what is to count as a choice directly against a basic value, a calculus seems certainly called for at times. Our real problem is to discover the criteria and controls to keep this unavoidable calculus or revision of meaning fully human and Christian, and to prevent our slipping into policies that are only symptoms of a desire to avoid discomfort. It is precisely here that we need the wisdom and checks that a believing community can generate by its reflection and discernment, a community led and challenged by a healthily functioning magisterium.[66]

In view of these reflections, one can challenge Finnis' assertion that "the choice to exclude the possibility of procreation while engaging in intercourse is always and in an obvious and unambiguous way ... a choice directly and immediately against a basic value." If not every killing involves one in a choice against a basic good, but only killing of the "innocent," then not every suppression of procreative potential need involve one in directly choosing against the basic value of procreation. What would seem to involve such a choice is the *unjustified* exclusion of procreation. It is precisely at this point that Finnis' argument against premarital sexual relations is somewhat vulnerable; for to the objection that procreation can be prevented in premarital relations he insists that this prevention always involves a choice against a basic good. Not clear.

Bernard Häring is the final example of the classical approach.[67] He states his agreement with the traditional norm but believes it has not always been well argued, or presented with pastoral prudence. For the Christian, Häring asserts, marriage is a sacrament. It is the expression of an irrevocable covenant of fidelity, of a total sharing of life, and it is within this covenant that sexual union achieves its full integration and a special share in sacramental significance. As a community of love and covenant fidelity, marriage is ordered to the vocation of parenthood. Hence sexual union is only true and genuine where the partner is accepted and loved (at least basically and in principle) with a view to possible parenthood. But a true yes to the parental vocation and to its responsible exercise is only possible within the covenant bond of mar-

[66] Cf. Jerome Murphy-O'Connor, O.P., "Moral Discernment," *Doctrine and Life* 21 (1971) 127–34.

[67] B. Häring, "Voreheliche geschlechtliche Vereinigung?" *Theologie der Gegenwart* 15 (1972) 63–77.

riage. From this perspective premarital intercourse always retains a negative quality in Häring's judgment.

Häring admits that many people have real difficulties in understanding and accepting this traditional norm. He attributes this to a process of radical desacralization, whereby sexuality has been ripped from the context of a truly sacred function in marriage and dissolved into a multitude of more or less human purposes and its use then asserted as a basic right even of the unmarried. The major emphasis of his very balanced article is on the need for patience and understanding when dealing with those who do not accept the traditional norm. Both pastors and theologians must disown a gavel-pounding moralism of attitude and build upon the positive, if incomplete, insights that contemporary youths bring to this problem.

Now for some modifications of the classical tradition. It is probably inaccurate to refer to the positions that follow as "modifications" of the traditional norm, for they really accept the norm but vary in their applications of it. For instance, Franz Böckle had earlier argued that a true understanding of sexual intercourse, as a total gift of love, demands marriage if sexual expression is to be true to its full meaning.[68] However, he saw in canon 1098 an opportunity to face the problems of many youths who could not as yet marry. This canon asserts the validity and liceity of marriage contracted with only two witnesses if the pastor, bishop, or delegated priest cannot be approached without grave inconvenience. A broad interpretation of this extraordinary form of marriage would include under it, according to Böckle, the situations of many modern youths not yet able to go through a full ecclesiastical wedding. This opinion of Böckle was echoed by V. Schurr.[69] K. Kriech carries the analysis a step further and claims that the demand of ecclesiastical form for marriage falls under the principle *lex non obligat cum gravi incommodo*.[70] Thus the sexual relations of those who cannot marry may appear juridically as premarital but are really marital.[71]

These early probings have been pursued in some recent literature. Several years ago Johannes Gründel outlined his approach to the ques-

[68] F. Böckle and J. Köhne, *Geschlechtliche Beziehungen vor der Ehe* (Mainz: Matthias-Grunewald, 1967) pp. 7–36.

[69] V. Schurr and H. V. Pohlmann, "Vorehelicher Sexualverkehr," *Theologie der Gegenwart* 11 (1968) 207–16.

[70] K. Kriech, "Vorehelicher Geschlechtsverkehr in moraltheologischer Sicht: Eine Zwischenbilanz," *Schweiberische Kirchenzeitung* 19 (1970) 274–78. Cf. also John F. Dedek, *Contemporary Sexual Morality* (New York: Sheed & Ward, 1971) pp. 41–42, for a similar analysis.

[71] Paul Ramsey, "A Christian Approach to the Question of Sexual Relations Outside of Marriage," *Journal of Religion* 45 (1965) 100–118.

tion, an approach very close to that of Böckle.[72] The distinctive characteristic of a true inner self-gift of one person to another—that which is proclaimed in sexual intercourse—demands a permanent bond. Therefore sexual relations are inappropriate without the marital consent (*Ehewille*). And since marriage is so important a social institution, "this consent needs public assertion before society in so far as possible." Formally, Gründel asserts, marriage begins where this consent is publicly proclaimed and legally sanctioned by the appropriate authority. However, the actual existence of this consent need not always coincide with the formal public statement of the consent. Rather it can take shape in growing stages. Gründel then says: "Without wishing to contest the legitimate place that belongs to the formal legal marriage contract, it is an unanswered question whether and how far there are responsible forms of sexual intimacy that already contain this stable marital consent but have not yet completed the legal consent."[73] Ultimately, therefore, Gründel would disapprove of strictly premarital sexual intercourse but he refuses to identify this with preceremonial intercourse, or at least he states that the matter is an "unanswered question."

C. Jamie Snoek rightly insists that sexuality must be socialized and institutionalized.[74] But what form should this take in our culture? After having noted that there is nothing precise in the biblical precepts on the point,[75] Snoek proposes a re-examination of the notion of *matrimonium in fieri*. Concretely, in the traditional concept of marriage there are three distinct elements: the yes of the partners, the yes of the Church, consummation. Snoek then states: "In view of the greater continuity felt today to exist between engagement and marriage, I should ask whether in some circumstances, it would not be permissible for the partners to place the consummation before the assent of the Church."[76] Snoek is certainly leaning in one direction. But he leaves mysteriously undeveloped what he means by the "greater continuity felt today be-

---

[72] Johannes Gründel, "Voreheliche Sexualität aus der Sicht des Moraltheologen," in *Lieben vor der Ehe?* ed. F. Oertel (Essen: Fredebeul & Koenen, 1969) pp. 66–81.

[73] *Op. cit.*, p. 76.

[74] C. Jaime Snoek, C.SS.R., "Marriage and the Institutionalization of Sexual Relations," in *The Future of Marriage as an Institution* (*Concilium* 55; New York: Herder and Herder, 1970) pp. 111–22.

[75] Bruce Malina, "Does *Porneia* mean Fornication?" *Novum Testamentum* 14 (1972) 10–17, concludes that "there is no evidence in traditional or contemporary usage of the word *porneia* that takes it to mean pre-betrothal, pre-marital, heterosexual intercourse of a non-cultic or non-commercial nature, i.e., what we call 'fornication' today."

[76] This is opposed by V. Schurr, who sees in it the figure and reality of clandestine marriage ("Wieder klandestine Ehen?" *Theologie der Gegenwart* 13 [1970] 172–74).

tween engagement and marriage" as well as the notion of "some circumstances." At least many Americans might desire a long conversation with Snoek on this "greater continuity" before proceeding
further. As for the future, Snoek believes that while monogamous marriage must remain the ideal institutional setting for sexual relations, still
the validity of new patterns of behavior will "depend on the extent to
which they contribute to the greater stability of marriage and the
family."

Francis V. Manning is fairly close to the analysis of Snoek.[77] In a long
study he acknowledges and passes in review three general viewpoints:
premarital sex is (1) always wrong, (2) almost never immoral, (3) sometimes permissible. It is this last position that Manning studies in a variety of formulations (Harvey Cox, British Council of Churches, S. Keil,
V. Punzo, R. F. Hettlinger, W. N. Pittenger). He then expresses his
own view. It is a view hard to detail because it is composed of several
statements whose compatibility is not immediately obvious. Manning
clearly views "the reservation of coital intimacy for the married state"
as the ideal, something to be striven for. Why so? His reason must be
gathered from oblique phrases such as "appropriate expression of the
love that exists" and "the sole place in which it can uniquely fulfill its
human meaning: the existential bond of marriage."

But once he has stated the normative ideal, he begins to qualify it.
First, marriage is not a moment; it is a process. As he puts it:

Like most of life's decisions, becoming married is not an instantaneous action,
but a process that takes time. At a certain point in the process coitus becomes
an appropriate expression of the love that exists and of the will to place all that
one is in the service of the other. How is this point to be determined? The couple must judge for themselves. . . . As a *general* rule of thumb, however, it might
be suggested that the couple should have manifested to others their sincere
intention to marry, and that the ceremony itself is not too far distant.[78]

The second qualification is that "this [ideal] does not mean that refraining from coitus is always best for every couple prior to marriage, for
individual differences, weaknesses, pressures etc. have to be taken
into account." At another point Manning speaks of reserving sexual intercourse "*more or less* exclusively for the sole place in which it can
uniquely fulfill its human meaning."[79]

Aside from the fine pastoral observations within which Manning situ-

[77] Francis V. Manning, "The Human Meaning of Sexual Pleasure and the Morality
of Premarital Intercourse," *American Ecclesiastical Review* 165 (1971) 18-28; 166 (1972)
3-21, 302-19.

[78] *Ibid.*, p. 317, emphasis added.   [79] *Ibid.*, p. 319, emphasis added.

ates his opinion, I find the moral reasoning inconsistent and puzzling. First, if the existential bond of marriage is "the sole place in which it [sexual intimacy] can uniquely fulfill its human meaning," then how is it in any way clear or consistent to say that the "certain point in the process [when] coitus becomes an appropriate expression" is the manifestation to others of the *intention* to marry? Manning would answer: marriage is not a moment but a process. And when the intent to marry has been manifested to others, the process is sufficiently far along to say that sexual intimacy is its appropriate expression.

Will this stand up? I think not. The intention to marry, however sincere and intense, is not constitutive of the existential bond of marriage, for the simple reason that this intention, as experience has often shown, can be, often is, and not infrequently should be revoked. This is the weakness of the notion of *matrimonium in fieri* proposed by both Manning and Snoek, and less explicitly by Gründel. The intention to marry is, indeed, part of the process leading to marriage. But the process leading to marriage cannot be converted that easily to read marriage-as-process. And unless this conversion can be made, it seems inconsistent to propose the intention to marry as the moment when sexual intimacy is appropriate.

Behind this there lurks, I suspect, an overreaction to the notion of the marriage ceremony. Every mature and reflective person knows that a ceremony does not "make the marriage" in this broader sense. Similarly, we may well have oversold the significance of the ceremony in the past to the neglect of the stability, maturity, sincerity, and authenticity in the personal relationship. But the contemporary trend is an individualistic neglect of the important social and ecclesial dimensions of marriage. Treating the ceremony as if it were *merely* a ceremony—a thing that is easy to do when the emphasis falls so heavily on marriage-as-process— is an unhealthy symptom of an eventually destructive individualism.

My second problem with Manning's position is pastoral and touches the exceptions he introduces. If marriage is "the sole place in which [sexual intercourse] can uniquely fulfill its human meaning," then why should sexual intimacy be reserved "*more or less* exclusively" to this sole place? Similarly, after stating that reservation of intercourse to marriage is the ideal, Manning states that this does not mean that "refraining from coitus is always best for every couple prior to marriage." Why not? Manning answers by making reference to "individual differences, weaknesses, pressures etc." This should be spelled out in much greater detail. And this spelling out ought to take full cognizance of two facts that experience has pretty well established: (1) that the major task of the engaged is to get to know each other's strengths, weaknesses, in-

terests, to drain off those elements in the relationship that stifle communication—a task likely to get sidetracked by the experience of full sexual intimacy; (2) that the engaged (inexperienced) are the very ones
likely to overemphasize the importance of sexual intimacy in the growth
of their relationship.

Marciano Vidal objects against both the broad interpretation of
canon 1098 suggested by Böckle-Schurr-Schillebeeckx and the notion
of *matrimonium in fieri* as proposed by Snoek-Manning-Gründel.[80] He
grants that the extraordinary form is quite acceptable in theory, and
its application to some restricted cases quite proper. But he rejects
its application to the generality of cases under discussion, because marriage is a sacramental and therefore ecclesial reality. A theological
solution that reduces the ecclesial aspects of so many marriages to a
minimum is unacceptable. As for *matrimonium in fieri*, Vidal sees this
as a recrudescence of clandestine marriage, a practice that fails to do
justice to the ecclesial dimension of marriage. Behind the recent suggestions concerning implicit marriage there lurks, he believes, an exaggerated personalism, a modern version of the old consensualist
theory of marriage involving a regression to a theology of marriage we
have long since abandoned as inadequate.

Vidal then outlines the structure of his own moral-theological reflection on the problem. It builds upon the utter necessity of institutionalizing sexual relationships. Marriage is, he insists, the institution within
which the values of sexual authenticity are best realized. But prior to
marriage two different types of unions can be distinguished: regressive
and progressive. The former do not realize and do not even tend to realize the values of marriage, whereas the latter do contain an effective
tendency toward the ideal. If premarital relations occur within the
progressive type of union, they should be viewed pastorally in terms of
their tendential value, i.e., accepted in their actuality without institutionalizing them.

Thus far some recent literature. It is an interesting literature fleshed
out with a good deal of common sense and pastoral understanding. Now
to a personal reflection. Häring is correct when he insists that this problem is not the most important of moral problems, and not even the most
important problem in sexual morality. But how it is approached and discussed can reveal a whole attitude to sexual morality, and indeed to all
moral problems. All the authors cited above are basically at home with
the classical Christian tradition that reserves full sexual intimacy to marriage (though some tinker with the definition of marriage). I am, too. In

[80] Marciano Vidal, "Moral de las relaciones sexuales prematrimoniales," *Razón y fe*,
June, 1972, pp. 517–32.

this sense the problem is above all pastoral, as Manning has rightly emphasized. Contemporary youths and young adults are not going to make their decisions in terms of the judgments of their elders. That much is clear. Not only have we disappointed them too often and too long, but education by edict has probably had its day. I agree with Manning that what we need here is a different form of communication, not prescription and preachment. One form of communication is the open, patient, nonjudgmental exploration with young adults of the meaning of marriage and human sexuality, as Häring suggests. Another form is lived example by the few so that "its value can be sensed by others, catching them up in the web of authenticity, and winning them to a challenge worth the courage required to meet it" (Manning).

Yet the constant temptation is moralism. The basic problem with moralism is that it bypasses and therefore effectively subverts the processes leading to understanding. This is as true of the new exceptionism ("Thou mayest if . . . ") as it was of an older negativism ("Thou shalt not . . . "). For this reason, the attempts to approach the phenomenon of premarital intimacy through appeal to the extraordinary form of marriage or to the notion of *matrimonium in fieri* can easily be judged as thinly disguised neolegalisms. Valid as these notions might be in theory and for some scattered instances, they approach a widespread practice that has its roots in deep attitudinal shifts through tight exception-making casuistry. This too easily plays host to the sexual obsessionism of our culture and thereby denies our youth a full if gradual exposure to the challenge of the values found in Christian tradition.

But the avoidance of moralism does not doom us to silence. The question that must be put to our generation is this: In what circumstances should the sexual experience of intimacy occur if sexual language is to retain its viability as truly human language?[81] Behind such a question is the common-sense conviction that we are quite capable of trivializing sexuality and depriving ourselves in the process of an unparalleled form of sharing and growth. A sex-obsessed culture such as ours is particularly liable to be trapped into banalization, and there are many who argue that we have already gone a long way toward emptying sexual exchange of its nourishing and humanizing capabilities.

The answer given by Christians to the question stated above is, of course, clear, even though it is elaborated in a variety of ways, as we have seen. It is simply this: sexual expression is the language of relation-

---

[81] For some interesting suggestions on the discovery of moral norms, cf. Philipp Schmitz, S.J., "Normenfindung in der Sexualmoral," *Stimmen der Zeit*, March, 1972, pp. 165–76; P. Schmitz, "Freisein in der Entfremdung," *Theologie und Philosophie* 47 (1972) 229–44.

ship. It gets its full human meaning from the relationship it expresses and fosters. And the relationship which provides us with our best opportunity to integrate and humanize our sexuality is the covenant relationship of marriage; for it is friendship that generates constancy, loyalty, fidelity. And these are the qualities that allow sex to speak a truly human language.

If sex is to have any chance at all to help us bridge the separateness of our lives and to escape the loneliness and isolation of our individuality, it cannot be lived merely in the present. It must celebrate the past and guarantee and nourish the future. It is as affirmation and promise that sexual exchange achieves quality. It has been a Christian conviction that it is a relationship lived in the promise of permanency that prevents the collapse of sexual expression into a divisive, alienating, and destructive trivialization. This is not, obviously, a terribly popular idea these days; but we must face squarely the fact that this could well be all the more reason why its strong countercultural statement is more necessary than ever now—if only that statement is constructed to invite understanding and aspiration rather than obedience.

It has been said that sex is the easiest language to speak but the most difficult to make meaningful. I would add "to keep meaningful." For Americans are notoriously the clinicians of quality where quality escapes the mere clinician. We are constantly in danger of using sexuality in essentially autonomous (independent of relationships) and depersonalizing ways: to support our insecurity, to mask or assuage our frustration, to express our anger and vindictiveness, to prop our masculinity or femininity, to promote upward mobility, to secure a husband, etc. At a recent symposium between Catholics and humanists, Lester Kirkendall adverted to the changing meaning of sexual acts on college campuses. They are now viewed, he reported, as "an experience in closeness and intimacy." Is there something to fear here? The relief of loneliness can easily be one more "use" of sexuality and perhaps the most subtle form of its autonomy and depersonalization. The dehumanization of life in our large urban conglomerates generates a desperate need for nearness and closeness. At a time when marriage is in a state of crisis and when the cultural gospel is that sexual expression is required for self-fulfilment, it seems clear how our overriding need for nearness and closeness will be met. But is it not the almost universal human experience that sex does not lead to and create closeness and intimacy, but rather that the loyalty, constancy, and fidelity of covenanted friendship allow sex to speak the language of intimacy and to be an experience of closeness? It is precisely a world with an overwhelming need for nearness and closeness that is likely to slip its grasp on the values of sexuality and to use genital sex as a self-defeating medicine for loneliness.

When all is said and done, the root crisis behind this discussion is not precisely the "shifting sexual attitudes" or "the new permissiveness" of the pollsters. The more we speak of sex, the less we address what I think is the real problem. It is plainly and simply the meaning of marriage. Marriage is the crisis. If men and women in increasing numbers are abandoning the desirability of the permanent relationship of exclusive fidelity,[82] then clearly the meaning of sexual relationships before marriage is bound to be affected. Therefore it is the man-woman relationship and the conditions for growth in intimacy that we ought to be discussing.

Eugene Kennedy has stated this very well. He writes:

What we have not grasped nearly enough are the distinctive qualities of human exchange which give meaning to sexual experience. When we fail to place marriage in the context of our more generalized efforts to become human we emphasize sex in a naive and sentimental way.... It is the foundation and atmosphere of trust and concern, the repeated cycle of dying and rising in order to grow together that we must understand in order to see sex in perspective and to speak with any deep and moral sensitivity about marriage.[83]

It is this type of thing that we must learn to explore with young adults if the values underlying the Christian tradition are to have any chance to attract them.

THE SOCIOPOLITICAL MISSION OF THE CHRISTIAN

In his letter to Cardinal Maurice Roy in early May of 1971 Pope Paul VI stated: "It is to all Christians that we address a fresh and insistent call to action.... It is not enough to recall principles, state intentions, point to crying injustices and utter prophetic denunciations; these words will lack real weight unless they are accompanied for each individual by the livelier awareness of personal responsibility and by effective action."[84] This rather widely overlooked document deserves a place among the great papal statements on social questions.[85] It forces us to ask several questions. What is the exact character of a Christian's involvement qua Christian in social and political life? What is the social

---

[82] Eugene Fontinell, "Marriage, Morality, and the Church," *Commonweal* 97 (1972) 126-30. The replies to Fontinell are more interesting and substantive than his own piece.

[83] Eugene Kennedy, "Fidelity Remains Vital," *Commonweal* as in n. 82 above.

[84] "Octogesima adveniens," *Catholic Mind* 69 (1971) 37-58. The document is followed by a perceptive commentary by George Higgins.

[85] Cf. C. Mertens, S.J., "La responsabilité politique des chrétiens dans la lettre de Paul VI au Cardinal Roy." *Nouvelle revue théologique* 94 (1972) 183-94.

mission of the institutional Church qua Church? These questions have deservedly received increasing attention in recent literature.[86]

Since the preparation of the last edition of these "Notes," the Synod released its fine document "Justice in the World."[87] The statement builds on several skeletal assertions. (1) There is the notion of social sin. The synodal statement never uses that precise term,[88] but it refers repeatedly to "personal sin and its consequences in social life," "unjust structures," "sin in its individual and social manifestations," "the social dimension of sin." (2) The Synod asserts that action on behalf of justice is "a constitutive dimension of the preaching of the gospel." (3) Why? Because in the Christian message love of God and neighbor are inseparable. And love of neighbor is inseparable from justice to the neighbor. (4) The Church's specific responsibility is not to offer concrete solutions in the social, economic, and political spheres. Rather it is to defend the dignity of the human person by denouncing injustice wherever it appears and by positively witnessing to justice through her own structures and manner of life. The one criticism that could be brought against the synodal statement is that it did not get sufficiently down to specifics.[89]

Is there anything new in this? Peter Henriot, S.J., argues that the theme of social sin is new, at least in the sense that it has never before been so clearly explicated in an authoritative Roman document.[90] Henriot then asks how the Church should be socially involved. Since social sin is the object of involvement, the actions of the Church should be seen in terms of conversion from social sin. There are three approaches to conversion: prophetic word, symbolic witness, and political action.

---

[86] E.g., the entire issue of *Christus* 19 (1972) is devoted to the notion of liberation and political action. See also Dorothee Sölle, "The Role of Political Theology in Relation to the Liberation of Men," in *Religion and the Humanizing of Man* (cf. n. 29 above) pp. 131–42; *Toward a Discipline of Social Ethics*, ed. Paul Deats, Jr. (Boston: Boston Univ. Press, 1972). The entire issue of *Lumière et vie* 105 (1971) 2–139 is devoted to "Options politiques de l'église."

[87] *Catholic Mind* 70 (March, 1972) 52–64. For the theology involved in the prepartory documents, cf. P. Cosmao, O.P., "Théologie sous-jacente au document de travail du Synode épiscopal sur la justice dans le monde." *Documentation catholique* 68 (1971) 638–40.

[88] The Canadian bishops do in their excellent statement issued at their April 17–21, 1972 meeting in Ottawa; cf. *Catholic Mind* 70 (Oct., 1972) 57–61.

[89] Thus Vincent McNamara, "The Church, Promoter and Exemplar of Justice and Community," *Furrow* 23 (1972) 578–92. In a fine and forthright article McNamara states: "It is a well-known fact that many hoped that the synod document would condemn specific injustices rather than engage in generalities. This does involve taking sides, opting for the poor, offending people. But this is the very tradition which the Church has inherited in this matter from the prophets and Christ" (p. 587).

[90] Peter J. Henriot, S.J., "Social Sin and Conversion: A Theology of the Church's Social Involvement," *Chicago Studies* 11 (1972) 115–30.

The prophetic word is denunciation of injustice wherever it appears. The major obstacle to social change is our failure to perceive the sinfulness of the situation. This failure in perception is rooted in the values and behavioral standards of our culture.[91] Hence the prophetic word shatters the images and mindsets that shade our perception of reality. To the objection that we are often prevented from speaking out by "lack of knowledge of all the facts," Henriot urges Schillebeeckx' notion of a "contrast-experience." This is the experience of a concrete social evil (racism, war, torture, hunger) to which the Christian can only respond: "This should not be so." The individual may not have all the facts, but he can know, from the values which the gospel expects to be integral to the life of a follower of Jesus, that this particular evil must not be allowed to continue. From this conviction there arises the moral imperative for a political stand. Henriot faults the American bishops for not speaking more specifically in the 1960's on the war. Their reason: they lacked sufficient information to make a concrete judgment. Though this might have been true when it was first uttered, Henriot believes the bishops should have taken the steps necessary to get the information.

Symbolic witness refers simply to acting out concretely in our own individual and community lives the values of justice. Henriot refers this above all to a sparing-sharing life-style in a consumer society. Finally, there is political action. Since social sin is a structural phenomenon, conversion is possible only through the political process. Therefore he urges "the acceptance of political action as a *religious imperative*." As for priests in political office, Henriot does not push the idea, but he argues that the synodal exclusion of it has to be read in the context of the Church's already deep involvement in political action, i.e., with a grain of salt.[92]

In another article Henriot repeats several of these emphases but turns to the specific political responsibility of the priest.[93] By "political responsibility" he means "all efforts to affect public policy, to speak to the issues of public values, to have an impact on the constitution and

---

[91] Our moral catechesis both reflects and supports these values. Archbishop J.-A. Plourde, in his address to the Synod on Oct. 19, stated: "Its [the Church] moral teaching must at all costs stop giving privileged treatment to private ethics, wherein sin is seen primarily as a private matter, rarely as association, consciously or not, with the forces of oppression, alienation and physical violence" ("Making Justice a Reality," *Catholic Mind* 70 [1972] 7).

[92] For a contrary view, cf. Donald Wuerl, "The Priest as Politician," *Priest* 28 (1972) 52-59; his arguments deserve serious attention. Cf. also "An Interview with Daniel Berrigan," *Commonweal* 96 (1972) 376-82.

[93] Peter J. Henriot, S.J., "Politics and the Priest," *Commonweal* 96 (1972) 495-98.

operation of the structures of society." Political responsibility, therefore, is social concern taken seriously precisely because we relate
effectively and efficiently in the United States to the policies and processes that deal with injustice and poverty through political responsibility. From the synodal statement that action on behalf of justice is a constitutive dimension of preaching the gospel he argues that all priests
must be socially concerned and involved.

Henriot then proposes three models of priestly action: working politically to change social structures, serving as advocate (not just arbitrator) for the poor and powerless in political disputes, living according
to a sparing life-style that has political effects both in its symbolic value
and through its sensitizing influence.

Henriot's emphasis on social sin and the need to get at the structures
that perpetuate it is right on target and badly needed. Particularly important is the notion of advocacy for the poor and powerless. A beautiful example of this is the action of Mgr. Huyghe, Bishop of Arras, and
his priests.[94] They publicly denounced the injustice done to 2,200 factory workers in an area of northern France. When accused of meddling
in politics, the bishop responded with a magnificent statement that
stands as a model of what advocacy ought to mean. Bishop Huyghe
granted that his social gesture on behalf of the workers had some political import, but added: "I could have ceased to stand with those who
are victims of the recession. This abstention would also have been a political act, less conspicuous perhaps, but heavy on the conscience. All
actions of 'engagement' are ambiguous. Speaking out is a political act,
certainly. But silence? Whether it be that of prudence or fear, it is also
a political act."

Because the basic lines of Henriot's message are so important and so
utterly valid for the American scene, a few fringe points can be disengaged for comment. First, there is the reference to the passing of the
specialized "social-action priest." The possible implication of this reference is that all priests must now be active *in that way*. Or at least it is
possible that Henriot will be read in this sense. If he actually intended
this implication, then the matter seems overstated. Because social action is a constitutive dimension of preaching the gospel, it does not logically follow that every priest must or should be involved in it in the
rather intense and full-time sense suggested by yesterday's social-action
priest. What does follow is that each priest ought to look at his own
work, talents, and concrete situation and seriously ask whether at the
three model-levels mentioned by Henriot he is doing the best he can,
whether he has not shaped and channeled his priestly attitudes and

[94] "L'Eglise fait de la politique," *Documentation catholique* 69 (1972) 329-31.

apostolate with his eyes closed to the existence of social sin. What Pope Paul said of every Christian is true of priests: "Let each one examine himself to see what he has done up to now, and what he ought to do."[95]

Secondly, there is the matter of advocacy. After distinguishing legitimately between the role of arbitrator and advocate, Henriot urges the priest to enter political controversies as an advocate for the poor and powerless. Politically, what does this advocacy mean? It means, he says, that the priest "has the obligation to become very particular, very concrete." He "speaks out in favor of a particular political program," and takes "a definite side in a controversy over a specific solution to a social program." To those who object that this would be divisive, Henriot states that Catholics must be educated "to accept the fact that a priest's choice of one political option among several does not mean that it is the *only* choice for the Christian community."

Here I think something more must be said. Certainly the priest ought to be an advocate for the poor and powerless (and not just an arbitrator) and this advocacy should be particularized in concrete policy judgments. But there comes a point when taking a side over "a specific solution to a social program" changes advocacy into arbitration—arbitration between what is the better strategy for advocacy. Henriot obscures this by contrasting advocacy with the *status quo*, as if most political decisions conformed to one or other alternative. Many, if not most, political judgments do not fit this rather desperate either-or option. They are often concerned with the most effective form of advocacy. When the question concerns not whether the poor should be helped, etc., but what is the more effective way of achieving this, we are dealing with strategy within advocacy. The options are not advocacy vs. nonadvocacy, but this form of advocacy vs. that form. I believe one could question the wisdom and ultimate effectiveness of a priest's putting the moral authority of his priesthood into politics at this point. Why? For the simple reason that by giving to a particular strategy the moral support of this priesthood, he is thereby saying to some unavoidable extent that this is indeed the only choice for a Christian. Otherwise why should he espouse it publicly qua priest?

The Chilean bishops made this point clearly.[96] Eighty priests conducted a press conference stating their intention to align themselves with the socialist government. They stated: "The profound reason of our involvement is our faith in Jesus Christ, which deepens, renews, and incarnates itself in historical circumstances. To be Christian is to

[95] "Octogesima adveniens," *Catholic Mind, loc. cit.* (n. 84 above) no. 48.
[96] "L'Eglise et le socialisme," *Documentation catholique* 68 (1971) 636-37.

be in solidarity. To be in solidarity at the moment in Chile is to participate in the historical project that its people are outlining." The Chilean
bishops, after strongly supporting the whole liberation movement and
work supportive of it, insisted that their priests not take public "partisan political positions." They added: "The political choice of the
priest, if—as in this case—it is presented as a logical and ineluctable
consequence of his Christian faith, implicitly condemns every other
option and constitutes a blow to the liberty of other Christians." They
see in this a regression to an outmoded clericalism. The French bishops
seem to have been moving in the same direction in their deliberations.[97] They wonder if the priest's first duty is not rather to arouse
Christians to their political responsibilities.

This point demands serious attention. The more one's political activity is viewed as a faith involvement—and this is strongly emphasized
in recent literature—the more does it seem to exclude other options.
And when a priest qua priest espouses the position, the more does it
appear as a faith involvement. That is why it seems important to distinguish between political positions that represent advocacy (in contrast to those that do not) and those that represent only strategic
choices within an over-all advocacy posture.[98] Strategic-advocacy options are often rooted in ideological and party differences, a fact that
means that the priest would be immersed in purely partisan politics.
At the very least, this matter needs a good deal more discussion than it
has yet received.

The point made here is that the effort to view human problems and
to respond to them from the perspectives of the weakest and most oppressed members of society should avoid identifying any concrete option or strategy of advocacy with God's kingdom, any particular economic, political, or social program with the gospel. In an age when the
transcendent has been almost totally immanentized,[99] it is all too easy
to approach a concrete form of advocacy as if we were the agents of the

[97] *Documentation catholique* 68 (1971) 645.

[98] This is the sense, I believe, of the Synod's statement contained in the document on
"The Ministerial Priesthood": "In circumstances in which there legitimately exist
different political, social and economic options, priests like all citizens have a right to
select their personal options. But since political options are by nature contingent and
never in an entirely adequate and perennial way interpret the gospel, the priest, who is
the witness of things to come, must keep a certain distance from any political office or
involvement" (*Catholic Mind* 70 [March, 1972] 44). Similarly, Vatican II argued that
"in building the Christian community, priests are never to put themselves at the
service of any ideology or human faction" (*The Documents of Vatican II*, p. 546). The
general character of these statements is, however, to be noted.

[99] For a provocative discussion of this, cf. Walter B. Mead, "Restructuring Reality:
Signs of the Times," *Review of Politics* 34 (1972) 342-66.

eschaton. C. Penrose St. Amant has made this point well in noting that self-interest and sin affect not only structures but the estimates, judgments, and political strategies of those who would modify them.[100] If an unconcerned pietism is unchristian, one-eyed concretism can itself be a disguised idolatry that forgets who man is. This point has been made by Pope Paul VI, the Synod, and the Canadian bishops.[101]

This discussion will undoubtedly continue, as it should, and it is bound to open on the larger question of the relation of Church and state. There are probably those who believe that the traditional form of American separation is in a stage of transition, or ought to be. Not so R. Coste. The involvement of the Church in politics has always been, in his judgment, a very delicate affair.[102] The Church should not become "une église politisée." Otherwise a politico-religious amalgam will occur, leading us backwards to the days of the sacral city, which "misunderstood the revolutionary and liberating disjunction willed by Christ between the political and eccles al community." Coste contends that the Church has no general political responsibility, but that she cannot remain a total stranger to politics. Her responsibility in politics is exactly the same as it is in the economic, cultural, and social sphere: prophetic and diaconal.

Finally, there is, in the call for universal priestly political involvement and in a very concrete way, some assumption made about how structural change occurs. Henriot's assumption would have to be that lasting structural change occurs through political activity. Others might put the emphasis elsewhere. And this difference provides an excellent opportunity to draw out the theological implications and limitations of human effort toward the kingdom.

For instance, Garry Wills, arguing that the best way to effect cultural change is to work outside the system, states that change comes through prophets. He further argues that prophets cannot be educated, programmed, or produced. But they can be stunted "by exerting this tremendous pressure which tells them that if they want to make a change they can do it only within the system."[103]

[100] C. Penrose St. Amant, "The Christian Ministry and Social Responsibility," *Southeastern Baptist Theological Seminary Bulletin* 21 (1972) 3-15.

[101] "Octogesima adveniens," *loc. cit.*, no. 50; "The Ministerial Priesthood," *loc. cit.*, p. 44. The Canadian bishops state that "without espousing any particular program, we invite Canadians to accept the social goal of an equitable redistribution of income" (*Catholic Mind, loc. cit.*, p. 59).

[102] R. Coste, "L'Eglise et le défi du monde," *Nouvelle revue théologique* 94 (1972) 337-64.

[103] Garry Wills, "Working within the System Won't Change Anything," *Center Magazine*, July-August, 1972, pp. 34-37, at 36.

This could easily be interpreted as a charter for the socially dormant conscience and as a direct rejoinder to Henriot. Actually, both Henriot and Wills are right. Lasting structural change does seem to occur through prophetic persons and actions.[104] But prophetic persons do not "just turn up," as Wills maintains, not at least if our view of history is informed by Christian hope. It is here that the attitudes accompanying social involvement have theological implications. Though God's ways are mysterious, do we not have to believe—to avoid presumption—that He allows us prophets only if we nonprophets have done what in us lies?[105] *Facienti quod in se est Deus non denegat gratiam.* The task of overcoming the present belongs to man; but it is also given him by God. If Christian social involvement is to avoid Pelagian arrogance, it must be deeply stamped with the conviction that the final validation and transformation of human effort is God's doing. This point is forcefully underlined by both James E. Wood, Jr.[106] and Arthur G. Gish.[107]

If individuals and the community are to be morally responsive to the cry for liberation, they must hear it. Patrick Kerans, S.J., argues convincingly that how we hear a message depends on the images that shape and control our perceptions of reality.[108] For instance, we can hear the theology of liberation as an invitation to negotiate with potential competitors. Behind this is the controlling image of man as a forceful, creative entrepreneur. According to this image, men make shrewd business deals with each other, with profit as a motive. They deal from strength, etc. Kerans feels that it is this poker-game model that is negotiating (and vitiating) relations between North and South America. It is a dominance-dependence model. The dominance is achieved not pri-

---

[104] The literature on revolution continues to grow. The most useful recent piece is the excellent study of James F. Childress, "Nonviolent Resistance and Direct Action: A Bibliographical Essay," *Journal of Religion* 52 (1972) 376–96. Cf. also Michael Wallace, "The Uses of Violence in American History," *American Scholar*, Winter, 1970–71. pp. 81–102; Maurits de Wachter, "Ethics and Revolution," *Irish Theological Quarterly* 39 (1972) 43–59; Jesús García Gonzalez, "Development and/or Liberation?" *Lumen vitae* 27 (1972) 11–34; Gerard J. Hughes, "A Christian View of Revolution," *Way* 12 (1972) 222–32.

[105] Perhaps this is a poor way of formulating the point. C. G. Arevalo, S.J., states it as follows: "What man does, bears, in God's design, an intrinsic relationship to God's kingdom as it will be given" ("Love in the Service of Hope," *Philippine Studies* 20 [1972] 417–37, at 430).

[106] J. E. Wood, Jr., "A Theology of Power," *Journal of Church and State* 14 (1972) 107–24.

[107] Arthur G. Gish, *The New Left and Christian Radicalism* (Grand Rapids: Eerdmans, 1970) p. 134.

[108] Patrick Kerans, S.J., "Theology of Liberation," *Chicago Studies* 11 (1972) 183–95.

marily by military or economic coercion, but by our ability to control the key images in such a way that the existing dominance seems a wise and good arrangement.

Over against this model he proposes that we must, as Christians, begin with the fundamental Christian mystery of forgiveness. "Then we will be led to try to understand the political dimension along with all the other dimensions of human life in the light of the controlling image of brother forgiving brother." Thus he views the call for transformation of the system as a call for new controlling images of men and reality.

Kerans makes an important point. If structural sinfulness is maintained and supported by controlling images of man and reality, a basic ethical task is to get at those images. This notion is so important and so often overlooked that a restatement may be in place. It is said that "structures are sinful, structures enslave, and therefore structures must be changed." This is certainly true, but unless the term "structure" is unpacked a bit more, we will not appreciate the enormity of the ethical task in the social sphere.

"Structures" can be understood as either operational or ideological. Operationally understood, they are things like zoning laws, welfare systems, international monetary systems, tax systems, trade agreements, health delivery systems, and so on. They are the concrete patterns of behavior that make up a person's environment. This environment is made up of interrelated sets of communities: political, social, economic, familial, religious. Our well-being is determined by the harmonious functioning of these communities. Hence they can be liberating or enslaving.

The operational structures enslave when the ideological structure implicit in them and supportive of them enslaves. The ideological structure enslaves when some value other than the individual persons who constitute these communities is the organizing and dominating value. By "organizing" I mean that it is this value that generates reciprocal expectations, patterns of actions, decisions, policies.[109] By "dominating" I mean that individuals are subordinated to this value. This process need not be and most often is not explicit or conscious. But it is this value-scale that generates and maintains the reciprocal expectations etc. that feed and support unjust operational structures. When Kerans refers to controlling images, he is referring to something very close to what have been called here ideological structures. It is these that have to be changed if unjust operational structures are to be altered permanently.

[109] It seems that Edward Schillebeeckx has in mind an analysis very close to this in "The Christian and Political Engagement," *Doctrine and Life* 22 (1972) 118–27, at 122.

For instance, it can be argued that the single dominating and organizing value in American culture is economic—the good life. Our American culture promotes and rewards this and thereby educates to it. Even our universities have capitulated to this value. Too often they simply train for the job market. Practically, then, this means that other values will be pursued and promoted only within this overriding priority. Thus, justice in education, housing, medical services, job opportunity is promoted within the dominance of the financial criterion—"if we can afford it," where "afford" refers to the retention of a high level of consumership. The dominance of the economic value is the root of enslavement, the ideological structure.

It is not suggested here that the operational structures do not merit direct and decisive action. They obviously do. But the lasting success of this action is inseparable from modification of the ideological structure. It is precisely here that the prophetic witness of a sparing-sharing use of material goods assumes its importance. This life-style is not just good example, alongside of other more practical and direct tasks. It appears to be an essential way of getting at a society's value assumptions, and hence becomes a social ethical responsibility of the first magnitude, a point made sharply by the Synod, the Canadian bishops, and Henriot.

But it is not the only way. Among several ways for the Christian community to exercise influence on the decisions made in society, James Gustafson mentions the impact on the ethos or cultural values of a society.[110] Gustafson sees this occurring as a somewhat unintended effect of a concerted effort to achieve a direct aim. For instance, the anti-war movement had a direct aim (immediate end to the war) but also indirectly brought about rather massive shifts in widely-held values. Throughout his study Gustafson is attentive to an aspect of social morality that is easily neglected: the moral affections. Unless there is the awakening and expansion of vigorous moral sensibilities, responsible social action will not occur. From this perspective Gustafson sees the problem as one of developing more imaginative forms of communication than the sort of moral reasoning ordinarily associated with theological ethics.[111] I agree, but I do not think we have found these forms.

In an excellent study, J. Bryan Hehir puts heavy emphasis on just this point.[112] Moral awareness or moral consciousness is a prerequisite

[110] James M. Gustafson, "Ethics and Faith in the Life of the Church," *Perkins School of Theology Journal* 26 (1972) 6–13.

[111] For some educational suggestions toward this end, cf. T. A. Mathias, "Education for Social Change," *Social Action* 22 (1972) 237–46; Joseph J. Blomjous, "Christians and Human Development in Africa," *African Ecclesiastical Review* 14 (1972) 189–201.

[112] J. Bryan Hehir, "International Affairs and Ethics," *Chicago Studies* 11 (1972) 197–208.

for serious moral analysis or action. One major difficulty in achieving social justice is the constriction placed upon our moral imagination, our capacity to sense and see an issue from a perspective other than our own. This privatizing of the imagination is, Hehir argues, aided and abetted by technology and language. For example, "surgical air strike" is a phrase that really shields the untrained observer from the reality of what is described, just as "terminating a pregnancy" is sanatized language that constitutes a barrier to the development of moral consciousness. As for technology, it places a mechanical shield between ourselves and the effects of our acts, and therefore tends to shrivel our consciousness.

The problem of moral consciousness can be partially[113] met through the mediation of those who have been involved in social thought and work. A fine example of this mediation is the paper entitled "The Quest for Justice" published by the Center of Concern under the principal authorship of William R. Callahan, S.J.[114] One of the intriguing features of this concrete response to the synodal challenge is the attitude taken toward Catholic identity. Since Vatican II, American Catholics have experienced a dissolution of many of the structures, attitudes, behavioral patterns that gave them identity as Catholics. The authors suggest that the most powerful and relevant quest which could build this unity and identity in our time is the quest for justice.

These are some recent writings on the sociopolitical responsibility of Christians. What they both call for and reflect is a healthy shift in the focus of our moral concern. Pope Paul left no doubt about this when he stated: "These are questions that because of their urgency, extent, and complexity must, in the years to come, take first place among the preoccupations of Christians. . . ."[115]

---

[113] "Partially" because a strong case can be made for saying that moral sensibility needs, in most cases, some direct experience of the deprivation, suffering, and injustice experienced by others. Cf. José C. Blanco, S.J., "Aggiornamento and the Works of Liberation," *Philippine Studies* 20 (1972) 439–48, at 447.

[114] William R. Callahan, S.J., *The Quest for Justice*, published by the Center for Concern, Washington, D.C., 1972.

[115] "Octogesima adveniens," *loc. cit.*, no. 7.

CURRENT THEOLOGY: 1974

NOTES ON MORAL THEOLOGY: THE ABORTION DOSSIER

On Jan. 22, 1973, the Supreme Court handed down its historic decisions on abortion (*Roe* v. *Wade*, *Doe* v. *Bolton*). The reactions to these decisions were swift and predictable. Paul Blanshard and Edd Doerr, apostles of a rather tedious and faded anti-Catholicism,[1] exulted that "we feel like a champagne dinner in honor of the United States."[2] Flushed with victory, they were in a "festive mood" and called the Court's action "the most direct defeat for the Catholic hierarchy in the history of American law." J. Claude Evans regarded the decision as "a beautifully accurate balancing of individual rights gradually giving way to community rights as pregnancy progresses. It is a decision both proabortionists and antiabortionists can live with, as it leaves the decision up to the individuals most closely involved. ..."[3] Lawrence Lader, chairman of the National Association for the Repeal of Abortion Laws, spoke of "a stunning document . . . a humanitarian revolution of staggering dimensions."[4]

On the other hand, the Administrative Committee of the National Conference of Catholic Bishops rejected the opinion as "erroneous, unjust, and immoral."[5] Similarly, the episcopal Committee for Pro-Life Affairs branded the Court's action as "bad morality, bad medicine, and bad public policy."[6] John Cardinal Krol, president of the National Conference of Catholic Bishops, referred to the decision as "an unspeakable tragedy" and added that "it is hard to think of any decision in the 200 years of our history which has had more disastrous implications for our stability as a civilized society."[7] For Most Reverend Edward D. Head, chairman of the Committee on Health Affairs (USCC), it was a "frightening decision."[8] *Christianity Today* editorialized that the decision "runs counter . . . to the moral sense of the American people . . . [and] reveals a callous utilitarianism about children in the womb that

---

[1] Cf. Paul Blanshard and Edd Doerr, "Parochaid, Abortion, School Prayer," *Humanist* 33 (1973) 34–35. The authors refer to "Pope Paul . . . their anti-sexual chieftain." They note that "the hierarchy is doubly embarrassed because celibate bishops are not recognized as the most natural guardians of a woman's womb."

[2] Paul Blanshard and Edd Doerr, "A Glorious Victory," *ibid.*, p. 5.

[3] J. Claude Evans, "The Abortion Decision: A Balancing of Rights," *Christian Century* 90 (1973) 195–97.

[4] Lawrence Lader, "The Abortion Revolution," *Humanist* 33 (1973) 4.

[5] Cf. *Hospital Progress* 54 (1973) 83 ff.

[6] Cf. *Catholic Lawyer* 19 (1973) 31–33.

[7] Cf. *ibid.*, p. 33.

[8] Cf. *Hospital Progress* 54 (1973) 96a.

harmonizes little with the extreme delicacy of its conscience regarding the imposition of capital punishment." [9] And so on.

Whatever one's opinion of the Court's action, one thing is clear: in *Wade* and *Bolton* we are dealing with "one of the most controversial decisions of this century," as the Hastings *Report* phrased it.[10] With other nations contemplating or having completed similar liberalization, it is understandable that the literature on abortion in the past months has been enormous. In the many years that I have composed these "Notes," I have never seen so much writing in so concentrated a period of time on a single subject.

Abortion is a matter that is morally problematic, pastorally delicate, legislatively thorny, constitutionally insecure, ecumenically divisive, medically normless, humanly anguishing, racially provocative, journalistically abused, personally biased, and widely performed. It demands a most extraordinary discipline of moral thought, one that is penetrating without being impenetrable, humanly compassionate without being morally compromising, legally realistic without being legally positivistic, instructed by cognate disciplines without being determined by them, informed by tradition without being enslaved by it, etc. Abortion, therefore, is a severe testing ground for moral reflection. It is transparent of the rigor, fulness, and balance (or lack thereof) that one brings to moral problems and is therefore probably a paradigm of the way we will face other human problems in the future. Many of us are bone-weary of the subject, but we cannot afford to indulge this fatigue, much as the inherent risks of the subject might be added incentive for doing so. Thus these "Notes" will be devoted entirely to this single issue.[11]

To order this review, four subdivisions may prove of use: (1) critiques of the Court's decision; (2) legality and morality; (3) moral writings on abortion; (4) personal reflections.

CRITIQUES OF THE COURT'S DECISION

I shall limit this overview to seven or eight critiques, since it is fair to say that they raise most of the substantial issues. David Goldenberg, in a good review of the legal trends leading to *Wade* and *Bolton*, takes no moral position but faults the Court on legal grounds.[12] For instance, on the basis of lack of direct reference to the unborn in the Constitution, the Court asserts that the fetus is not protected by constitutional guarantees.

[9] "Abortion and the Court," *Christianity Today* 17 (1973) 502–3.

[10] "Abortion: The New Ruling," *Report* 3 (1973) 4.

[11] Much interesting and important literature must be overlooked at this point; I hope to include it in a future survey.

[12] David Goldenberg, "The Right to Abortion: Expansion of the Right to Privacy through the Fourteenth Amendment," *Catholic Lawyer* 19 (1973) 36–57.

"If this is so, how could a state satisfy the compelling interest test in purporting to protect the fetus at the stage of viability?" A similar criticism of the Court's consistency is made by Emily C. Moore of the International Institute for the Study of Reproduction.[13] After saying that "person" does not cover the unborn, how can the Court segment pregnancy by trimesters and permit the state a controlling interest in the third trimester? This point is repeated throughout the literature.

Daniel Callahan rightly contends that the Court did for all practical purposes decide when life begins: not in the first two trimesters, possibly in the third.[14] He scores the Court for making it impossible to act in the future even if a consensus on this point were achieved. He shrewdly notes that there is a hidden presumption that when the state withdraws from resolving "speculative" questions, freedom is somehow served. If this were true, all decisions touching equality and justice would be up to the individual conscience, for these notions are highly speculative in their final meaning. Callahan argues that the entire matter should have been left to state legislatures. I agree and will return to this point.

Dr. Andre Hellegers (Kennedy Institute for the Study of Reproduction and Bioethics) resents in the entire debate the falsification of embryology for the purpose of avoiding the fundamental question: "when shall we attach value to human life?"[15] Hellegers, therefore, argues that the basic question is not, when does life begin? It is, when does dignity begin? The Court fudged this. "They have used terms like 'potential life' trying to say that life wasn't there, when the reason for saying that life wasn't there was because they didn't attach any value to it. The abortion issue is fundamentally a value issue, not a biological one."[16] If the Court is to be truly consistent, Hellegers contends, there is no reason to worry about the *health* of the fetus. This implies that experimentation on the fetus *in utero* is perfectly acceptable. It also renders uncomfortably inconsistent the FDA's strict rules about drugs during pregnancy.

Several longer critiques round out this review. In a stinging but congent rebuttal to the Court, John Noonan raises several serious questions.[17] First, if the liberty to procure termination of pregnancy is "fundamental" and "implicit in the concept of ordered liberty," how is it that this liberty has been consistently and unanimously denied by the people of the United States? Second, with many commentators, Noonan argues that the Court, in spite of its contrary allegations, allowed

[13] *Report* (n. 10 above) p. 4.

[14] *Ibid.*, p. 7.

[15] Andre Hellegers, "Amazing Historical and Biological Errors in Abortion Decision," *Hospital Progress* 54 (1973) 16–17.

[16] *Ibid.*, p. 16.

[17] John Noonan, "Raw Judicial Power," *National Review*, March 2, 1973, pp. 260–64.

abortion-on-request; for the viable fetus was denied personhood and the state was granted the right to proscribe abortion in the third trimester "except when it is necessary to preserve the life or health of the mother." Then the Court describes "health" as involving a medical judgment to be made "in light of all the factors—physical, emotional, psychological, familial, and the woman's age—relevant to the well-being of the patient. All these factors may relate to health." Briefly, in the third trimester a child may be aborted for the mother's well-being. As Noonan reasonably notes, "what physician could now be shown to have performed an abortion, at any time in the pregnancy, which was not intended to be for the well-being of the mother?"

Noonan's next objection is aimed at the Court's schizoid style of judicial interpretation. That is, the Court was evolutionary in its reading of the notion of liberty, but utterly static and constructionist in its interpretation of the term "person." Finally, Noonan, with Callahan, argues that the Court was inconsistent on its own competence. "The judiciary," *Wade* reads, "is not in a position to speculate as to the answer [as to when life begins]." [18] Yet Texas is said to be wrong in "adopting one theory of life." Clearly, if Texas is wrong, then the Court does indeed know when life begins, especially "meaningful life."

Underlying this decision Noonan sees a whole new ethic of life wherein it is appropriate for the state to protect beings with the "capability of meaningful life." We used to contend that all life is a sacred trust. Now, however, only "persons in the whole sense" are protected. Noonan warns that the mentally deficient, the retarded, the senile, etc. are now exposed; for each could be described as lacking "the capability of meaningful life."

P. T. Conley and Robert J. McKenna accuse the Court of a "foray into the legislative domain." [19] After confessing its own incompetence about life, the Court should have, on this basis, declared the matter nonjusticiable. Furthermore they argue that the Court has failed to practice what it preaches. In several recent decisions it had decided that the more fundamental the right, the more compelling must be the state or government interest in excluding certain groups from enjoyment of the right. After criticizing the Court's utilitarian valuation of life, its inconsistencies and intellectual sloth, they contend that while the unborn's right to life is not explicit in the Constitution, still, unlike the right to abort, it is recognized by law, custom, and majority opinion and could rather easily be inferred from the Declaration of Independence. There it is stated that "all men are created equal and endowed with

[18] *Roe* v. *Wade*, p. 44.

[19] P. T. Conley and Robert J. McKenna, "The Supreme Court on Abortion—A Dissenting Opinion," *Catholic Lawyer* 19 (1973) 19–28.

inalienable rights." But creation is traditionally associated with conception. They conclude that "the decision was patently unsound from either a logical, biomedical, moral or legal perspective."

Many of the points raised by Noonan and others are covered by Edward Gaffney in a devastating critique of the Court's use of history and of its defective anthropology.[20] For instance, using three of Lonergan's imperatives for the operations of human consciousness (be attentive, be intelligent, be reasonable), he finds the Court's use of history in violation of all three.

Blanshard and Doerr state that "the Court proved in long and scholarly footnotes that the Church had permitted abortion for centuries." [21] Footnotes may be lengthy, but whether they are scholarly is another question. The footnoting in *Wade* does, indeed, appear imposing and could be very deceptive. But John R. Connery, S.J., in a careful study of the animation, nonanimation debate, notes that "from the beginning of Christianity abortion has been condemned as morally wrong. The only issue was one of classification." [22] As for the Court's historical presentation, Connery says that it "is too fragmentary, misleading and erroneous to be of any real value." His conclusion: "Rather than rely on such a travesty, it would have been far more honest if the honorable justices admitted openly that they were simply departing from the past, and not just the past that began in the early nineteenth century. The decision has no precedent in either Christian moral or legal tradition." Those familiar with both the care of Connery's research and the softness of his critical touch will see this particular salvo as a deathblow to the Court's pretensions to historical scholarship.

Finally, Robert M. Byrn accuses the Court of inartistic and unpersuasive historical revisionism "before it could administer the fatal blow." [23] The controversy is about the value of human life, and the Court refused to protect unborn children "because there is a controversy over whether their lives are of value—whether they are 'meaningful.'" Social convenience and utility decided the day. If there is any doubt about the Court's shabby utilitarianism, Byrn acidly reminds the justices of William O. Douglas' dissent in *Sierra Club* v. *Morton*. In this dissent Douglas urged that "swamps and woodpeckers should be considered legal persons entitled to due process of law." Douglas continued: "The problem is to

[20] Edward M. Gaffney, "Law and Theology: A Dialogue on the Abortion Decisions," *Jurist* 33 (1973) 134–52.

[21] Blanshard and Doerr, *art. cit.* (n. 2 above) p. 5.

[22] I am indebted to Fr. Connery for use of this manuscript, which, as these "Notes" go to press, is still forthcoming in *Theology Digest*.

[23] Robert M. Byrn, "Goodbye to the Judaeo-Christian Era in Law," *America* 128 (1973) 511–14.

make certain that the inanimate objects, which are the very core of America's beauty, have spokesmen before they are destroyed." [24]

In summary, the critiques available thus far attack the Court's reasoning from almost every conceivable point of view: logic, use of history, anthropology. As William J. Curran, J.D., of the Harvard Medical School, notes, "The abortion decisions are already under a good deal of attack by constitutional lawyers, not so much for their result as for their reasoning." [25] At some point there must be a relationship of dependency between conclusion and reasoning; otherwise the conclusion is simply arbitrary. Whether another form of reasoning is available to support the Court's conclusion is, of course, what the legal discussion is all about.

From the point of view of the Christian ethician, what is most interesting (and appalling) is the utilitarian form of argument adopted by the Court and its one-dimensional value scale within the utilitarian calculus. For the Court, the overriding value is privacy. Three points here. First, if traditional attitudes toward abortion have been one-dimensional in their deafness to the resonances of other (than the sacredness of fetal life) values, the Court is no less one-dimensional. Secondly, one may legitimately ask with Albert Outler "just how private an affair is pregnancy, after all—since, from time immemorial, it has been the primal *social* event in most human communities?" [26] This is not to negate the value of privacy; it is merely an attempt to hierarchize it. Finally, the Court's reasoning on privacy raises a much broader cultural issue. Are *Wade* and *Bolton* simply symptoms of a highly individualized and ultimately antisocial notion of rights? There are many other indications in American life that such a notion of rights does indeed dominate our cultural and legal consciousness. If this is the case, there is much in the Catholic tradition, particularly in the recent social encyclicals, to redress the imbalance.

The discussion of *Wade* and *Bolton* will continue for years to come. And as with so many other profoundly divisive issues, it will inevitably be boxed and labeled with the misleading terms "liberal" and "conservative." For this reason Donald Nugent is right on target when he lobs a few mortars into the so-called liberal camp. [27] In an amusing but dead-serious essay he argues that, even if we do not know when human life begins, "in a matter of life and death the only humane position is to give life the

[24] Cited in Byrn, p. 514.

[25] William J. Curran, "The Abortion Decisions: The Supreme Court as Moralist, Scientist, Historian and Legislator," *New England Journal of Medicine* 288 (1973) 950–51.

[26] Albert C. Outler, "The Beginnings of Personhood: Theological Considerations," *Perkins Journal* 27 (1973) 28–34, at 28.

[27] Donald Nugent, "Abortion: An Aquarian Perspective," *Critic* 31 (1973) 32–36.

benefit of any doubt." Liberalism's cozying to the abortion cause is, he believes, symptomatic of a more general disenchantment with liberalism. Anglo-Saxon liberalism is a tradition of rationalized self-interest. "Abortion is in a tradition of interests, and it is inapposite that its exponents present themselves as the paladins of human values."

LEGALITY AND MORALITY

The Court's decision opens on the larger question of the relationship between morality and law, or what may be called the morality of law. More specifically: what is the responsibility of law where abortion is concerned? What is the appropriate strategy, what the criteria, when moral sensitivity attempts to translate itself into social policy in a pluralistic society? These questions have been approached in a variety of ways in recent literature.

Gabriel Fackre approaches the question as an ecumenical peacemaker and suggests that three "perceptions" must be shaken and mixed if the Protestant and Catholic communities are to cease casting glances of hostility across an abyss.[28] The first is the dignity of fetal life. "The central thrust of this perception is the weightiness of any aggression against fetal life with its incarnationally derived dignity." The second is a certain sobriety or realism that realizes the need to translate visionary commitments into norms that take account of our sinfulness and temporality. Thus, just as we have a just-war doctrine to qualify our eschatological moral expectations, so too we need a doctrine of "just abortion." Finally, there is the perception of liberation, the movement from necessity to self-determination.

On the basis of these "perceptions," Fackre proposes a doctrine of just abortion with the following motifs. (1) The dignity of the fetus is to be honored and protected with a zeal commensurate with its development toward fulness of time. (2) The limits of that protection are determined by fetal peril to others who live in the land of ripened humanity, *plene esse*. (3) The definition of that peril should be worked out in each case by those affected by it: personal (mother, father), medical (physician, psychiatrist), social (moral resource or community representative). (4) The final decision about the future of fetal life rests with the one most intimately involved, the mother. (5) The dignity of the fetus and the stake of society is so great as to necessitate fetal law. The law should require the consultative process of no. 3, guarantee self-determination of no. 4, and assure the best medical care. (6) Fetal dignity is best served through raising the consciousness of the society about that dignity and

[28] Gabriel Fackre, "The Ethics of Abortion in Theological Perspective," *Andover Newton Quarterly* 13 (1973) 222–26.

attacking the social and educational conditions that nourish the abortion problem.

Briefly, then, Fackre endorses a law that requires and supports the constraints of a consultative process. Fackre was writing before the Court's decision, and when compared to that decision his proposals look downright stringent. Ultimately, however, Fackre's doctrine of just abortion contains both moral and legal ingredients. Whether the legal constraints he proposes (consultative process) are sufficient will depend to some extent on his moral position. For instance, the retarded and the aged certainly would not be reassured if their dignity were acknowledged by policy proposals similar to Fackre's. He might respond that fetuses are not the aged and retarded. Correct. But what are they? Here I find Fackre evasive. His "to be honored and protected with a zeal commensurate with its development toward fullness of time" is just vague enough to be comfortable with almost any legal implementation. And that eventually is the weakness of the legal conclusion. It is proposed as a doctrine of "just abortion" without a rigorous exposition of the claims that allow us to decide the issue of justice-injustice. In other words, it builds on and reflects an uncertain or at least undeveloped moral position. And therefore his conclusions lack the lively sense of being accommodations to our sinfulness and temporality. When this sense of tension is lacking, legal tolerance tends to get simply identified with moral propriety.

J. Claude Evans seeks to defuse what he calls "Protestant and Catholic polarities" on abortion by "taking abortion out of the statute books altogether, a position earlier endorsed by Robert Drinan, S.J." [29] He believes that proabortionists and antiabortionists could unite on this point. Somewhat unaccountably, then, he adds that all we need is some limiting law "perhaps stating that no abortions are permitted beyond 18-week gestation" and guaranteeing personal and institutional protection against abortion-on-demand. Evans' suggestion that the disputants can unite by taking abortion off the statutes is another example of an invitation to unity by unilateral surrender. The precise contention of very many disputants is that the state has the duty to protect infant life, both before and after birth, with legal sanctions.

This is the very point made by C. Eric Lincoln as he recounts his remarkable change of mind on abortion away from a position based rather exclusively on a woman's autonomy over her own body.[30] Without

[29] J. Claude Evans, "Defusing the Abortion Debate," *Christian Century* 90 (1973) 117-18.

[30] C. Eric Lincoln, "Why I Reversed My Stand on Laissez-Faire Abortion," *Christian Century* 90 (1973) 477-79.

detailing what the law should be, Lincoln insists that the state, as party to every marriage contract or implied contract[31] (and therefore burdened with certain responsibilities), does have something to say about the interruption of pregnancy. The state is the guardian of the public welfare and in that capacity exercises control over our bodies in many areas (e.g., drug and beverage control, medical practice, seat belts, inoculations, water treatment, helmets, etc.). The desire to privatize and individualize the abortion decision totally Lincoln sees as a retreat from personal and social accountability. He makes no secret that he is appalled at the present levels of bloodletting.

This same point is underscored by A. Jousten as he discusses the situation in Belgium.[32] The law, he argues, acts as a support for morality in order to guide the exercise of liberty and responsibility to the common good. Not all men are saints who spontaneously seek the good of others. However, the more complex and pluralized a society is, the more distinction there is between law and morality, without there being separation. And with distinction comes tension. Concretely, in the definition of the rights and duties of each, it is not always possible to take account of the individual interest. If the state tries to satisfy every individual interest, it renounces certain socially useful values in the process. In explanation of this, Jousten agrees with M. T. Meulders: "in the case where two individuals are at stake, and where one risks causing a grave harm to another, there is no longer question of a 'private' matter and the law may not turn away from this situation." [33]

After reviewing the pros and cons of liberalization, Jousten tends to side with those authors who oppose liberalization and believe the situation is best handled by trusting the honesty of physicians and the jurisprudential process without trying to codify all tolerable indications.

Harvard's Arthur J. Dyck argues that one who is for civil rights, sound population policy, and compassion for unwanted children need not be committed to a policy of abortion-on-request.[34] Quite the contrary. Where civil rights are concerned, Dyck notes that women's rights encounter an evolution in property, tort, and constitutional law favoring the recognition of the fetus as a living entity. It is now clearly recognized,

---

[31] By "implied contract" Lincoln refers to the situation of an unmarried woman consenting to intercourse. In this instance the partner may be liable for support, etc. Since in reasonable societies rights and responsibilities go in tandem, the consenting woman is involved in an implied contract.

[32] A. Jousten, "La réforme de la législation sur l'avortement," *La foi et le temps* 3 (1973) 47–73.

[33] Cited in Jousten, p. 54. Cf. M. T. Meulders, "Considérations sur les problèmes juridiques de l'avortement," *Annales de droit* 31 (1971) 507–19.

[34] Arthur J. Dyck, "Perplexities for the Would-Be Liberal in Abortion," *Journal of Reproductive Medicine* 8 (1972) 351–54.

for example, that the "unborn child in the path of an automobile is as much a person in the street as the mother."[35] Dyck is convinced that it would be a considerable step backwards "if governments, which have acknowledged all of these rights, were now to deprive the fetus of any legal protection of its most fundamental right, i.e., its right to life."[36] As for population growth, permissive laws do not significantly affect this in the long run, since population growth depends upon the number of children people want. For these and other reasons, Dyck favors laws that would permit abortion only where the life or the physical and mental health of the pregnant woman is seriously threatened.

The editors of *America*, obviously convinced that whatever the law ought to be, it should not be the simple abortion-on-request policy adopted in *Wade*, discuss resistance through amendment.[37] Two amendments are possible. First, the absolutist type resembling the 13th Amendment's prohibition of slavery: "No abortion—period." The difficulty here is that such an amendment goes beyond even Catholic formulations. And if "our" exceptions are written into law, then why not the exceptions of other groups? Secondly, there is the state's-rights type of amendment that leaves regulation to the individual states. The difficulty here is that the fight to preserve the sanctity of fetal life would have to be waged in fifty states. *America* asks: "Why should an enormous national effort be made to secure a constitutional amendment, the only result of which will be to guarantee 51 more struggles?" The most immediate answer to that question would be simply: because it is worth it.

But is it really? Albert Broderick, O.P., constitutional lawyer at Catholic University, has his doubts. In a very interesting article Broderick argues that the Court was simply substituting its own moral values for those of the community. In justifying its undervaluation of life, "the Court scorned current medical and biological evidence . . ., distorted history, distorted or misconstrued contemporary social and professional morality as represented in legislation of every state and the medical associations, positioned itself again as supreme arbiter of a nation's social ethics and theology. . . ."[38] How are we to face this revival of judicial supremacy? Broderick sees the amendment route as the

[35] Here Dyck is citing *Prosser on Torts*, 3rd ed., 1964, Sect. 56.

[36] In support of this, cf. "Declaration of the Rights of the Child," proclaimed by the General Assembly of the United Nations, Nov. 20, 1959. It states: "Whereas the child, by reason of his physical and mental immaturity, needs special safeguards and care, including appropriate legal protection, before as well as after birth." Cf. T. W. Hilgers and D. J. Horan, *Abortion and Social Justice* (New York: Sheed and Ward, 1972) p. 133.

[37] "Abortion: Deterrence, Facilitation, Resistance," *America* 128 (1973) 506-7.

[38] Albert Broderick, O.P., "A Constitutional Lawyer Looks at the *Roe-Doe* Decisions," *Jurist* 33 (1973) 123-33.

"by-way of frustration," because an amendment is practically impossible of enactment. Instead he discusses two alternative strategies. First, the very internal defectiveness of the decisions provides some hope that the Court will reverse itself. Therefore, the first strategy is to provide it with every opportunity for doing so. Broderick is not optimistic here, but more so than he is about the heavily-loaded amendment process. Secondly, he argues that if a constitutional amendment is indicated, it ought to move in on judicial supremacy. An example he gives: allow Congress (through a majority of both houses) to override any decision of the Supreme Court which declares unconstitutional on 14th Amendment grounds legislation of the several states.

The Supreme Court's reasoning in *Wade* relied heavily on the right of privacy. Indeed, much prior campaigning had emphasized the abortion decision as private, and therefore not a matter for legislative regulation. Behind these and similar assertions is an entire philosophy of law. Paul J. Micallef traces two different approaches to the relation of law and morality, the positivistic and the Thomistic.[39] The former found its champions in Bentham and Mill and surfaced practically in the Wolfenden Report. It is clear that Micallef is unhappy with the distinction established, indeed almost canonized, by Wolfenden between crime and sin and then raised "to the compendious sphere of the relationship between law and morality." The relationship of human actions to criminal law, he argues, is not to be determined simply on the basis of the distinction between "the private act" and "its public manifestation."

In contrast to this analysis, Micallef carefully and thoroughly exposes Thomas' theory of law based on the common good of all persons. For Thomas, though law and morality are distinct, law has an inherently moral character due to its rootage in existential human ends. Once this has been said, the one criterion of legislation is feasibility, "that quality whereby a proposed course of action is not merely possible but practicable, adaptable, depending on the circumstances, cultural ways, attitudes, traditions of a people etc. . . . Any proposal of social legislation which is not feasible in terms of the people who are to adopt it is simply not a plan that fits man's nature as concretely experienced."[40]

Therefore, within Thomas' perspectives, all acts, whatever their nature, whether private or public, moral or immoral, if they have ascertainable public consequences on the maintenance and stability of society, are a legitimate matter of concern to society, and consequently

---

[39] Paul J. Micallef, "Abortion and the Principles of Legislation," *Laval théologique et philosophique* 28 (1972) 267–303.

[40] *Ibid.*, p. 294.

fit subjects for the criminal code. But it is feasibility that determines whether they *should be* in the penal code, and this cannot be collapsed into the private-public distinction. Therefore, while Thomas does not tell us whether abortion ought to be in the criminal code, his philosophy of law tells us what questions to ask. These questions were put very helpfully by the late John Courtney Murray. He wrote:

A moral condemnation regards only the evil itself, in itself. A legal ban on an evil must consider what St. Thomas calls its own "possibility." That is, will the ban be obeyed, at least by the generality? Is it enforceable against the disobedient? Is it prudent to undertake the enforcement of this or that ban, in view of the possibility of harmful effects in other areas of social life? Is the instrumentality of coercive law a good means for the eradication of this or that social vice? And, since a means is not a good means if it fails to work in most cases, what are the lessons of experience in the matter?[41]

Micallef and Murray present a tidy account of Thomistic perspectives on law and morality. What makes the matter so terribly complicated is that at the heart of the feasibility test is the fact that there is basic disagreement on the moral character of abortion to start with.

Charles Curran faces these complications with insight and restraint. He summarizes very well the relationship of law and morality in pluralistic societies by walking a middle path between the "idealist" tradition (wherein the natural law simply translates into civil law and merely tolerates deviations) and the purely pragmatic tradition (wherein law merely reflects the mores of a particular society).[42] Laws must root in both prophetic ideal and pragmatic reality. Thus in pluralistic societies governments will acknowledge the right of the individual to act in accord with the dictates of his conscience, but "the limiting principle justifying the intervention of government is based on the need to protect other innocent persons and the public order." In determining what this means concretely, especially with regard to innocent persons, Curran adduces other important factors: enforceability and equity. Laws which are unenforceable or have discriminatory effects compromise their contribution to the over-all good of a society.

On the basis of this understanding of the relationship of law and morality, Curran believes that those who hold strongly antiabortion moral positions could arrive at any of three possible legal positions on abortion: almost absolute condemnation, modified regulation, no law at all. His own legal position, in light of the factors adduced above, is close

[41] J. C. Murray, S.J., *We Hold These Truths* (New York: Sheed and Ward, 1960) pp. 166–67.
[42] Charles E. Curran, "Abortion: Law and Morality in Contemporary Catholic Theology," *Jurist* 33 (1973) 162–83.

to that proposed in 1961 in the Model Penal Code drafted by the American Law Institute.

Roger Shinn, in a painstakingly fair article, attempts to relate social policies to personal decisions in a pluralistic society.[43] Shinn first asks: what morality is it *right* to legislate? Behind the question is, of course, Shinn's realistic thesis that it is both possible and desirable to legislate and enforce *some* morality. The crucial question concerns only *what* morality to legislate where abortion is concerned. Both opposing positions on this question (legal freedom of abortion, legal constraints) root their case in moral convictions. Shinn discusses these with remarkable objectivity and concludes that we have a profound conflict of convictions and values and that the most we can do is learn to live with these conflicts.

He then turns to the second question: what is it *possible* to legislate? Here Shinn emphasizes the fact that law must rest on a fairly broad shared conviction or, if there is not such consensus, on a very fundamental moral or constitutional principle that people are reluctant to deny. Without these broad bases—which do not exist in our society on the immorality of abortion—prohibitive laws will be futile. For this reason Shinn argues that the Court's decision is a reasonably adequate framework for this society at this point in history. Shinn is not arguing that the decision was good history, good logic, or good judicial practice; he suggests only that "the decision offers a better way of living with a profound conflict of moral convictions than most alternatives."

Perhaps Shinn is right. Perhaps the Court's decision is a better way of living with a profound conflict of values. But before this is too readily concluded, two cautions seem in place. First, what represents a better way of living with a profound conflict will depend to some rather intangible extent on what one supports as the direction of the solution of this conflict. And this gets us right back to moral positions. For instance, if I grant that there is presently conflict in moral positions rendering strongly prohibitive laws impracticable, but if I believe (as a moral position) that nascent life is human life deserving of protection and possessed of the rights we attribute to other human beings, and if I hope that others will eventually share this conviction, then I might easily believe that the Court's decision simply deepens the difficulty of ever arriving at this conclusion. Thus the decision is, in some sense, calculated to freeze the situation of present conflict, to settle for it without providing any hope of a resolution.

If, on the other hand, my moral position were that of Shinn, I would

[43] Roger L. Shimm, "Personal Decisions and Social Policies in a Pluralist Society," *Perkins Journal* 27 (1973) 58–63.

more readily see the Court's conclusion as the best oasis during moral conflict. What is his position? Shinn believes that "the fetus has *some* rights, especially in the later stages of pregnancy, but that the woman also has rights to freedom. . . ." On this basis he states his own preference for weighting the law on the side of the woman's rights, not because fetal rights are insignificant but because the "problems of defining the health of the mother are extremely difficult." If I held that moral position, then I might conclude with Shinn that the Court's "decision offers a better way of living with a profound conflict of moral convictions than most alternatives."

My point is that Shinn's acquiescence in the Court's decision traces back, to some extent, to his moral position. Therefore, in these terms, whether one can agree with this acquiescence depends on whether one is satisfied with Shinn's moral position. Shinn has not argued this position sufficiently to invite agreement. To say that the fetus has *some* rights—without explaining what these are, how strong they are, why, etc.—and then to weight the law in favor of a woman's rights, leaves many unanswered questions. Until Shinn has argued his moral position more thoroughly and persuasively (which he professedly did not want to undertake in this essay), his conclusion about the Court's decision as a way of living with conflict remains moot if not arbitrary. What Shinn should have said is that for those who hold his moral position the Court's decision "offers the better way of living with a profound conflict of moral values."

The second caution is closely connected with the first. What is the best way of accommodating legally to moral conflict should hardly be left exclusively to those who obviously side with one side of the conflict. This is as true of the Court's decision as it is of the traditional prohibitive legal stands. The reasoning of the majority of the Court left little doubt where this majority stood on the substantive issue of fetal value. For such a group to determine what is most equitable for the country is at least as objectionable as allowing the classical prohibitionist to make this determination. The better way of discovering the appropriate legal position at the present time of moral pluralism is to leave the matter to the state legislatures, even though this procedure itself is not without problems.

Papal and episcopal statements on abortion have abounded in the recent past, and since their context has been that of threatened or actual liberalization of abortion law, there is a decided, though far from exclusive, emphasis on the relation of morality and law. Pope Paul VI, in an allocution to Italian jurists, noted that the state's protection of human life should begin at conception, "this being the beginning of a new human being." [44] This is an emphasis that reappears in nearly all the national episcopal statements.

When relating abortion to women's liberation, Pope Paul insists that true liberation is found in the vocational fulfilment of motherhood. There follows an extremely interesting analysis of the pertinence of relationships to human dignity and rights, an analysis that in its way anticipates some of the theology to be reported below (especially the *Etudes* dossier). The Pope notes:

In such a vocation there is implicit and called to concretization the first and most fundamental of the relations constitutive of the personality—the relation between this determined new human being and this determined woman, as its mother. But he who says *relation* says *right;* he who says fundamental relation says *correlation between a right and an equally fundamental duty;* he who says fundamental human relationship says a universal human value, worthy of protection as pertaining to the universal common good, since every individual is before all else and constitutively *born of a woman.* [45]

If I read him correctly, the Holy Father is insisting that the relationship constitutive of the personality and generative of rights and duties is not basically and primarily at the psychological or experienced level—a point I shall touch on later.

The Belgian bishops make this very same point. [46] Relationships—and by this they obviously mean experienced relationships—important as they are, are not the source of the dignity and rights of the nascent child. Rather, this source is the personality in the process of becoming. They cite *Abortus Provocatus*, a study issued by the Center of Demographic and Family Studies of the Ministry of Health: "There is no objective criterion for establishing, in the gradual process of development, a limit between 'non-human' life and 'human' life. In this process each stage is the necessary condition for the following and no moment is 'more important,' 'more decisive,' or 'more essential' than another." [47] Therefore they are puzzled at the fact that at the very time we are eliminating discrimination between sexes, races, social classes, we are admitting at the legal level another form of discrimination based on the moment, more or less advanced, of life.

As for the law itself, the Belgian hierarchy is convinced that liberalized abortion law does not solve the real problems. Indeed, by seeming to, it

[44] Pope Paul VI, "Pourquoi l'église ne peut accepter l'avortement," *Documentation catholique* 70 (1973) 4-5; *The Pope Speaks* 17 (1973) 333-35.

[45] *Art. cit.*, p. 5.

[46] "Déclaration des évêques belges sur l'avortement," *Documentation catholique* 70 (1973) 432-38.

[47] *Ibid.*, p. 434.

leads society to neglect efforts on other fronts to get at the causes of abortion. Therefore they are opposed to removal of abortion from the penal code, because such removal would, among other things, imply the right to practice abortion and put in question one of the essential foundations of our civilization: respect for human life in all forms.

The Swiss bishops, after noting with other national hierarchies that God alone is the judge of consciences and that no one has the right to judge other persons, put great emphasis on corporate responsibility for the abortion situation.[48] Those who neglect the social measures for family protection, for aid to single women, etc. are more culpable than those who have abortions.

The Italian hierarchy sees abortion as part of a general trend of violence against man.[49] Its legalization will not only not eliminate the personal and social evils by getting at their causes; it will augment the harm in many ways—for example, by misshaping our moral judgments. The bishops of Quebec echo many of these same points and make it clear that what is at stake is the very idea on which our civilization is built: the conviction that all men are equal, whether young or old, rich or poor, sick or well, etc.[50] They associate themselves with all men who seek truly human solutions through establishment of a more just and humane society.

The German episcopate, after noting that protection of human life is an "absolutely fundamental principle," registers its opposition to the liberalization before the Bundestag.[51] Not only is the legislation morally unacceptable, but it will not solve the alleged difficulties it is supposed to solve. In the course of this interesting statement, the bishops turn to the relation of morality and law. Clearly, not every moral imperative should be in the penal code (e.g., envy, ingratitude, egoism). But where the rights of others are at stake, the state cannot remain indifferent. "Its primordial duty is to protect the right of the individual, to assure the common good, to take measures against the transgressions of right and violations of the common good, if necessary by means of penal law." In doing this, the state becomes a *constitutional* state.

But legislation is not enough. The difficulties leading to abortion must be overcome by other measures. It is here that genuine reform ought to occur. And in undertaking these reforms, the federal republic becomes a *social* state. "It is only when the state is disposed to recognize the principle according to which no social need, whatever it be, can justify

[48] "Déclaration des évêques suisses sur l'avortement," *ibid.*, p. 381.
[49] "Déclaration des évêques italiens sur l'avortement et la violence," *ibid.*, p. 245.
[50] "Déclaration des évêques du Québec," *ibid.*, pp. 382–84.
[51] "Le problème de l'avortement," *ibid.*, pp. 626–29.

the killing of a human being before birth, that it merits the name of social state. It is only when the state is disposed to protect the right to life of a human being before birth and to punish violations of this right, that it merits the name of constitutional state." [52] Only within these parameters and on these conditions should legislators withhold penal sanctions for conflict cases—cases that ought to be precisely determined in law.

More recently the Conference of German Bishops (Catholic) and the Council of the Evangelical Church (EKD, Protestant) produced a common statement on abortion.[53] The most remarkable thing about the document is its common endorsement by the leadership of the vast majority of Christians, Catholic and non-Catholic, in Germany. Once again there is insistence on the fact that a social state will approach abortion reform positively, scil., in terms that attempt to reorder social relationships in such a way that pregnant women receive the type of support that will prevent their seeing abortion as the only way out of difficult situations. The bishops underscore the fact that no society can long exist when the right to life is not acknowledged and protected. "The right to life must not be diminished, neither by a judgment on the value or lack thereof of an individual life, nor by a decision on when life begins or ends. All decisions that touch human life can only be oriented to the service of life."

The document resolutely rejects simple legalization of abortion in the first three months ("Fristenregelung") as a form of abortion reform. Rather, the task of the lawgiver is to identify those conflict situations in which interruption of pregnancy will not be punished ("straflos lassen"). By this wording the document insists that the moral law is not abrogated by legal tolerance but it remains to guide individual decisions in exceptional situations where the state decides not to punish abortion. Throughout, the document lays emphasis on the fact that positive law regulating abortion roots not merely in considerations of utility and party politics, but in basic human values ("Grundwerte menschlichen Zusammenlebens"). An excellent pastoral statement on all counts.

The Permanent Council of the French Episcopate calls attention to the difference between legislation and morality.[54] The task of the legislator is to see how the common good is best preserved in the circumstances. But in drawing up legislation, the government will necessarily express a certain concept of man; for this reason the bishops feel impelled to speak up. Recalling that abortion, no matter how safe and clean it is, always

[52] *Ibid.*, p. 628.

[53] "'Fristenregelung' entschieden abgelehnt," *Ruhrwort*, Dec. 8, 1973, p. 6.

[54] "Déclaration du Conseil permanent de l'épiscopat français sur l'avortement," *Documentation catholique* 70 (1973) 676–79.

represents a personal and collective human defeat, the bishops remind the legislators that in widening the possibilities for abortion they risk respect for human life, open the door for further extensions, and consecrate a radical rupture between sexuality, love, and fecundity. Ultimately, the remedy for the problem of widespread clandestine abortions in France is neither legal constraints nor liberalization. Women tempted to abortion must experience, really and personally, the fact that they are not alone in their distress. Any reform of abortion law must provide for this.

The statement of the Administrative Committee of the National Conference of Catholic Bishops of the United States in response to the Supreme Court's *Wade* and *Bolton* decision is the strongest, and in this sense most radical, episcopal statement I have ever encountered.[55] After detailing the Court's assignation of prenatal life to nonpersonhood, the pastoral states: "We find that this majority opinion of the Court is wrong and is entirely contrary to the fundamental principles of morality." The document continues: "Laws that conform to the opinion of the Court are immoral laws, in opposition to God's plan of creation. . . . " After citing the fundamental character of the right to life as guaranteed in the Declaration of Independence and buttressed in the Preamble to the Constitution, the bishops conclude that "in light of these reasons, we reject the opinion of the U.S. Supreme Court as erroneous, unjust, and immoral." While the statement contains no protracted discussion on the relation of law and morality, it is clear that the American bishops utterly reject the implied doctrine of the Court on the question.

Even this brief roundup probably justifies the conclusion of Michael J. Walsh, S.J., that we have here an "impressive example of the Magisterium in action." [56] It would be useful to list the common and dominant themes of this sprawling papal and episcopal literature. I see them as follows:

1) There is total unanimity in the recent teaching of the Pope and bishops on the right to life from conception. Furthermore, as Ph. Delhaye points out,[57] there is the pronounced consciousness that this teaching is the fulfilment of the commission received by Christ to teach and witness to the constant teaching of the Church.

2) There is repeated emphasis on the fact that we are dealing with a fundamental value, one at the very heart of civilization. The documents

---

[55] *Hospital Progress* 54 (1973) 83.

[56] Michael J. Walsh, S.J., "What the Bishops Say," *Month* 234 (1973) 172-75.

[57] Ph. Delhaye, "Le magistère catholique et l'avortement," *Esprit et vie* 83 (1973) 449-57 and 434-36. The first part of this two-part article contains a rather full dossier of papal and episcopal statements on abortion.

generally place the fight against abortion in the larger context of respect for life at all stages and in all areas.

3) It is the task of civil society to protect human life from the very beginning.

4) For human life is a continuum from the beginning. As Walsh puts it, "Essential continuity of a human being from conception to death is the presupposition of every episcopal argument." [58] In light of this we encounter terms such as "person in the process of becoming." And to this individual there is repeatedly ascribed the *droit de naître*, as Pope Paul puts it, a relatively recent rendering of the more classical right to life.

5) The protection provided for this *personne en devenir* must be both legal and social. With regard to the law, there is the practically unanimous conviction that legalization of abortion on a broad scale will not solve the many problems associated with abortion, but will rather bring further devastating personal and social evils, particularly through miseducation of consciences. Beyond that, the pastorals are rather reserved in their demands about legislation, except for the American statement, which Delhaye regards as "assez dur." By "social protection" I refer to the unanimous and strongly stated conviction of the episcopates that we must do much more, personally and societally, to get at the causes of abortion. If there is a single major emphasis in all of the documents, it is this.

6) In arguing their case for respect for nascent life and for its protection through public policy, the hierarchies suit the argument to the local situation, as Walsh notes.[59] For instance, the Americans appeal to American legal traditions and the declaration of the United Nations. The Scandanavians, in opposing further liberalization, are deeply concerned to protect individuals against pressurization.

7) The statements generally note that their teaching is not specifically Catholic, though the Church has always upheld it and though it can be illumined, enriched, and strengthened by theological sources.

8) While urging the teaching clearly and unflinchingly, the bishops manifest a great compassion for individuals in tragic circumstances and a refusal to judge these individuals. On the other hand, there is a rather persistent severity with society in general, whose conditions so often render new births difficult or psychologically insupportable.

In the finest piece of writing I have seen on abortion in some time, the editors of the *Month* propose a new strategy on abortion.[60] It is simply this: make abortion as unnecessary as possible. "If one assumes that in a

[58] *Art. cit.*, p. 174.
[59] *Ibid.*, pp. 173-74.
[60] "A New Catholic Strategy on Abortion," *Month* 234 (1973) 163-71.

pluralist society the law cannot be repealed, then all recommendations will be designed to mitigate the evil rather than eliminate it." This duty to ensure the conditions for humanized life falls in a special way on those who have refused the facility of abortion. It involves two steps, one short-term, the other long-term. The immediate response envisages practical care for mothers-to-be. The editors cite the remarkable pastoral of Bishops Eric Grasar and John Brewer (diocese of Shrewsbury) as an example. It deserves quoting.

We recognize that, for one reason or another, a pregnancy can cause a problem, distress, shame, despair to some mothers. Perhaps, in our concern to uphold the sanctity of life, we have failed to show sufficient practical concern for the mother-to-be who feels herself to be in an intolerable situation. That is all over. The Diocese of Shrewsbury publicly declares its solemn guarantee. It is this: Any mother-to-be, Catholic or non-Catholic, is guaranteed immediate and practical help, if, faced with the dilemma of an unwanted pregnancy, she is prepared to allow the baby to be born and not aborted. This help includes, if she wishes, the care for her baby after birth. All the resources of the diocese are placed behind this pledge.[61]

As for long-term measures, the editors note that the motivations behind most abortion requests are social and economic. This being the case, it is absolutely essential that we so modify the social and economic conditions that these motivations will disappear. "Society should treat these requests as a *symptom of its own sickness*."

In developing their presentation, the *Month* authors have an excellent treatment of fetal personhood. They note that a widespread contemporary view sees personhood as stemming from social interaction, from relationships. On this view humanity is an achievement, not an endowment. Thus the justification of abortion has reshaped the definition of what it means to be human. The authors reject the idea that achievement is to be preferred to potentiality, and for two reasons. First, no one believes this and no one acts on it, a fact evidenced in our treatment of children. They are prized and valued for their potentiality. Secondly, the preference of achievement over potentiality affirms the rights of the big battalions over the defenseless. "To weight the debate a priori in favor of the mother who can then deal with the fetus as though it were a malignant growth is to sanction a drastic exercise of power. In all other fields, we would recognize this and stop it at once. But here, and for most of us, the victims die unseen, and so consciences are easily tranquillised."[62] The authors see this as an unevangelical failure to rise to the love of the intruder, the unwelcome guest—as a racism of the adult

---

[61] *Ibid.*, pp. 169–70.   [62] *Ibid.*, p. 167.

world. If one decides to read but a single article on abortion, this is in my judgment the one to read.

The realistic, temperate and persuasive study by the editors of the *Month* contrasts with Rachel Wahlberg's brief report of a conference on abortion held at Southern Methodist University.[63] Distinguishing between the abstract and the personal, she concludes that those not involved with a specific unwanted pregnancy tend to discuss the philosophical, medical, or moral questions. Abortion debates must move from these "ivory-tower formulations to the gut-level issues." This fairly common attitude, while it does contain an obvious truth, is, I believe, ultimately mischievous. It opposes the "person" and "immediate crisis" to moral discourse—as if morality had nothing to do with the personal dimensions of problem pregnancies and were unrelated to immediate crises. Morality is, more than inferentially, associated with ivory-towerism. Ms. Wahlberg has not really abandoned morality to deal with the "gut" issues. She has rather collapsed morality into the "gut" issues and thereby opted for her own form of morality, and one with enough only half-hidden assumptions to rock many a tower into response. But that brings us to the recent work on the morality of abortion.

THE MORALITY OF ABORTION

The study that has provoked the most interest on the Continent in many a year is the *Etudes* dossier.[64] It is a summary of the deliberations of a pluricompetent group gathered by Bruno Ribes, S.J., editor of *Etudes*. The report delves into many aspects of the abortion question. For instance, with regard to a desirable law, they recommend that the French law bear essentially on the objectivization and maturation of the decision, on "conscientization" of the responsibility involved. A permissive law will not lead to a collapse of public morality, if the experience of other countries is any indication.

But it is their moral probing that is especially interesting. Noting that the two positions on the humanity of the embryo (developmental vs. one continued vital process) have led to a dialogue of the deaf, they propose their own solution. It is based on a distinction between "human life" and "humanized life." Since we are essentially relational beings, it is in relation to others that we discover, exercise, and receive our singularity and proper being. The very existence of the fetus is a kind of injunction to the parents. Their recognition of fetal life gathers this injunction into a new call. The parents call the child to be born. It is this recognition and

[63] Rachel C. Wahlberg, "Abortion: Decisions to Live with," *Christian Century* 90 (1973) 691–93.

[64] "Pour une réforme de la législation française relative à l'avortement," *Etudes*, Jan. 1973, pp. 55–84.

call of the parents (and beyond them, of society) that *humanizes*. Prior to this event the fetus is a "human being" but is not humanized.

Refusal to humanize, .the group argues, is intolerable; for it dissociates the biological from the human, the generating function from the humanizing. However, interruption of pregnancy is "socially justifiable" if it represents the refusal to bring about a dehumanization; for there are instances where genuine humanization is impossible. The terms "dehumanization" and "inhuman situation" are not definable or codifiable except for the obvious cases: for instance, of fetal deformity which will deprive the fetus of all social relations. The authors conclude that no abortion situation is "socially justifiable" unless accompanied by an attestation of the impossibility for the parents to give birth without creating an inhuman situation.

Reactions to this study were many and swift. The Belgian bishops, as noted above, explicitly rejected such a distinction.[65] A subsequent issue of *Etudes* published the interesting reader response, especially on the distinction between *vie humaine* and *vie humanisé*.[66] Bruno Ribes repeated once again the contention that, while a person certainly cannot exist without the individuality he has prior to humanization, this individuality does not suffice to specify him. Ph. Delhaye regards the *Etudes* distinction as only the clearest formulation of an objection against which the episcopal texts are aimed.[67] He cites the Archbishop of Rouen as branding the distinction "inadmissable casuistry," as at once "subtle and coarse." Cardinal Renard, adverting to the distinction in a speech to journalists, noted that if the fetus can be humanized, it is because it is fundamentally human to start with.[68]

R. P. Corvez, O.P., believes that the thought of the *Etudes* group is clearly insufficient on the key point;[69] for human life is present in its essentials even without "recognition" of the parents. "The child is really man, even in the womb of his mother, sharing human nature before receiving a humanizing formation. It is humanity which humanizes. It is [human] nature which humanizes."

Michel Schooyans rightly claims that abortion discussions faithfully reflect the cultural climate in which they occur, and in the West they reflect the axioms and ideology of a consumer culture.[70] In this light he

---

[65] *Ibid.*, pp. 434 ff.

[66] Bruno Ribes, S.J., "Dossier sur l'avortement: L'Apport de nos lecteurs," *Etudes*, April 1973, pp. 511-34.

[67] *Art. cit.*, pp. 449-57.

[68] Alexandre C. Renard, "Allocution prononcée par le Cardinal Renard," *Documentation catholique* 70 (1973) 183-84.

[69] R. P. Corvez, O.P., "Sur l'avortement," *Esprit et vie* 83 (1973) 97-102.

[70] Michel Schooyans, "La libéralisation de l'avortement," *ibid.*, pp. 241-48.

sees liberalization of abortion as a form of "the medicine of luxury." He then turns to the human being vs. humanized being of the *Etudes* study. After granting the importance of relationships as constitutive of personality, Schooyans accuses the authors of a surreptitious slip from a distinction to a division. The distinction, valid enough in itself, results from an analysis of a unique process, an integral one. But a corresponding *division* lacks any foundation, for in concrete reality there is no stage marking the passage from one mode of being to another. This point is repeated by Outler (below).

Schooyans should have stopped there, for his final reflections represent a painful collapse of theological courtesy. He accuses these attempts of sterilizing the gospel of its intransigence. "The premises," he contends, "are forged for the needs of the cause." There are references to theologians in the service of princes and so on. In this instance, to illustrate is to deplore.

That being said, I believe Schooyans is correct in asserting that a distinction is not a division. Furthermore, it seems that the notion "humanize" is being used in two different senses by the *Etudes* group. First, it refers to a recognition and call by the parents. As a first relation, that recognition is said to humanize. Secondly, there is reference to the "impossibility to humanize." Here "humanize" implies something more than the first relation of recognition and call. It refers to a quality of life after birth.

Ribes returned to the abortion discussion later and took a somewhat different approach.[71] The thought of some Catholics is changing on abortion because the context (cultural, political, sociological) is changing. He describes the situation in terms of a thesis (the classical position) and a growing antithesis (an ensemble of affirmations that modify or move away from the classical position). At the heart of the thought of many contemporaries, Ribes argues, is the refusal of undue generalization, a rejection of moral norms that seem independent of scientific, sociological, and political data. The good is ultimately the function of many approaches and currents; therefore the moral act must integrate diverse and sometimes contradictory principles.

Concretely, where abortion is concerned, it is obviously necessary to insist on the principle of respect for nascent life. But Ribes contends that this principle must be proposed along with others that are equally valid. His chief complaint is against "the enuntiation of a principle while appearing to neglect another *equally valuable* principle." [72] It is the responsibility of the individual to balance and compose the various

---

[71] Bruno Ribes, S.J., "Les chrétiens face à l'avortement," *Etudes*, Oct. 1973, pp. 405–23.
[72] *Ibid.*, p. 420 (emphasis added).

competitive principles in the situation. And when he does so, his decision is not simply the choice of the lesser evil; it relates to what is more human, therefore to the order of duties. This latter assertion is targeted at Gustave Martelet, S.J., who in interpreting *Humanae vitae* had argued that the choice of the lesser evil, while tolerable and understandable at times, never pertains to the order of objective values and hence to the order of duties.[73]

Ribes is, I believe, correct in his criticism of Martelet. Martelet's delineation of "objective values" pertains to an unreal, almost platonic world. Nevertheless, my impression is that Ribes has confused two things: motivation and justification. Motivation refers to the perception of a person about why an abortion is necessary or desirable. In our insistence on the immorality of abortion, we may well have tended to overlook these perceptions and their underlying causes. Justification refers to an assessment of the perception of the person in light of a value scale that transcends and challenges individual perceptions.

The confusion of motivation and justification reflects an inadequate distinction between the pastoral and the moral—a point to which I shall return below. In pursuit of this point, Ribes could be confronted with two alternatives. (1) The respect for nascent life prevails over other values in most situations—as the classical tradition maintains. (2) The respect for nascent life does not prevail over other values in most situations. These are moral statements. If Ribes denies the first statement, as he seems to, then he must hold the second. But if he does want to endorse the second statement, he should get into a thorough discussion about the relationships of values, not about the complex web of motivations and perceptions that are the personal filter for the assimilation of values. These latter are basically pastoral concerns. Contrarily, if Ribes accepts the first statement, then why all the tortured concern about "other principles" of equal value which can only be composed by the individuals? Briefly, what Ribes has failed to argue convincingly is that other principles are of *equal* value. He has shown only that they are perceived as such by many of our contemporaries.

In a long study Bernard Quelquejeu proposes that a change in method is called for in facing the contemporary abortion situation.[74] If we consult the concrete perplexed conscience, we may discover there a new principle, not yet perceived and formulated. This would provide the basis for a new attitude toward abortion. Quelquejeu then argues that any judgment that prescinds from the right to exercise one's sexuality isolates the problem out of context. Concretely, if the preceding will not

[73] Cited in Ribes, *ibid.*, p. 414.
[74] Bernard Quelquejeu, O.P., "La volonté de procréer," *Lumière et vie* 21 (1972) 57–71.

to conceive was reasonable and responsible, then interruption of pregnancy is justifiable. "To affirm that an accidental conception, not desired, is in itself enough to cancel out in every case, the will not to conceive—to the point of constituting an unconditioned obligation of procreation and education—is equivalent to denying this antecedent will, in its reasonable freedom. . . . " A biological fact is allowed to prevail over a reasonable will, a felt and well-founded freedom.

V. Fagone, S.J., will have none of this.[75] He admits that a concrete solution to an abortion problem has to be found in the general context of responsible procreation. However, equating an accidental pregnancy with a biological fact rests on a false supposition and vitiates the whole argument. Quelquejeu holds that if the will to procreate is absent, the fetus is merely a biological fact. Against this Fagone urges that the will not to procreate can claim rights after conception "only if the intention to procreate is required, ontologically, for the fruit of conception to be truly human." The ontological status of a being cannot depend on a subjective decision exterior to its being. Therefore Fagone contends that two things have been confused by Quelquejeu: the legitimacy of the will to procreate or not to procreate (a *moral* question), the relationship of parental will and intent to the constitution of fetal humanity (an *ontological* question). Furthermore, how in consistency could Quelquejeu rebut the contention that even a born child is only a "biological fact" as long as the will not to procreate still persists?

Bernard Häring evaluates the main theories about the moment of hominization and concludes that each of them has some probability.[76] He grants that the data of embryology seem to buttress the position of biologists, philosophers, and moralists who view the moment of fertilization as the most decisive moment in the transmission of human life. "They are convinced that everything is directed by a typically human life principle which we may call 'soul' or the life-breath of the person."

Häring believes, however, that the theories that give prime importance to implantation and/or to the final establishment of individualization cannot be simply ignored. When does this individualization occur? Häring discusses at length the theory favored by Teilhard de Chardin, Karl Rahner, and P. Overhage,[77] and strongly advocated by Wilfried Ruff, S.J., physician and professor of bioethics.[78] They believe that

[75] V. Fagone, S.J., "Il problema dell'inizio della vita dell'uomo," *Civiltà cattolica* 124 (1973) 531–46.

[76] Bernard Häring, *Medical Ethics* (Notre Dame: Fides, 1973) pp. 81 ff.

[77] Karl Rahner and P. Overhage, *Das Problem der Hominisation* (Freiburg, 1961).

[78] Wilfried Ruff, S.J., "Individualität und Personalität im embryonalen Werden," *Theologie und Philosophie* 45 (1970) 24–59, and "Das embryonale Werden des Menschen," *Stimmen der Zeit* 181 (1968) 331–55.

hominization of nascent life should be related to the development of the cerebral cortex; for it is the cerebral cortex that constitutes the biological substratum for personal life. Since, Häring argues, a considerable percentage of embryos turn out anencephalic (characterized by lack of essential parts of the typically human brain) and therefore simply incapable of any personal activity, and since the maternal organism automatically rejects nearly all cases of such embryos, it seems to follow that before the formation of the cerebral cortex "there exists merely a biological center of life bereft yet of the substratum of a personal principle." The basic structure of the cerebral cortex is outlined between the fifteenth and twenty-fifth day, or, as Häring notes, "at least after the fortieth."

What does Häring make of all this? First, he grants that the theory "which presents hominization as dependent on the development of the cerebral cortex has its own probability." That is, "before the twenty-fifth to fortieth day, the embryo cannot yet (with certainty) be considered as a human person." Secondly, Häring proposes this as a theory or opinion only, and not something that can be acted on until it gains greater acceptance by "those in the field." Or, as he puts it, "the theory . . . does not provide sufficient ground for depriving the embryo of the basic human right to life." [79] In other words, Häring believes that at present the fetus enjoys the favor of doubt and that fetal life must be protected *ab initio*, but that the uncertainties surrounding the very early stages of embryonic development "could contribute greatly to the resolution of those difficult cases involving conflict of conscience or conflict of duties."

Kevin O'Rourke, O.P., regards this opinion as "outmoded." [80] Whether or not that judgment is too strong depends on one's assessment of the development of the cerebral cortex. If cortical development is viewed as a qualitative leap determinative of *personal* existence, then the theory does indeed have its probability. If it is not viewed in this way, then another conclusion is warranted. On the basis of the evidence I have seen (though I have not seen it all, by any means), I am inclined to see individualization as the crucial developmental stage—and individualization seems to occur prior to the development of the cerebral cortex. Be that as it may, what calls for our protection is *personne en devenir*, a contemporary rendering of Tertullian's "he is a man who will become a man." To this Häring would certainly agree.

In a good review, Charles Curran ultimately rejects delayed hominization based on either relational analyses (Pohier, Quelquejeu, Beirnaert,

[79] *Op. cit.*, p. 84.
[80] Kevin O'Rourke, O.P., "Häring on Medical Ethics," *Hospital Progress* 54 (1973) 24–28.

Ribes's earlier writing) or cortical development (Ruff).[81] Against the relational school, Curran argues that there is no reason to draw the line, for example, at birth. "After birth these relationships could so deteriorate that one could judge there was not enough of a relationship for truly human existence." Furthermore, he contends, the relational criterion proposed does not accept a full mutuality of relationships. For instance, why not press the argument and say that before a truly human relationship constituting "humanized life" is present, the child must acknowledge and recognize the parents? Finally, the exclusively relational account of the origin of life encounters problems when dealing with the other end of the cycle: death. Has death occurred when relationships deteriorate or cease?

Against Ruff and Häring, Curran argues that the *basis* for personal relations and spiritual activity (which admittedly occur only after birth, and considerably thereafter) "is not qualitatively that much more present because there is now a cortex in the brain." Therefore the emergence of these organs is not a threshold that can divide human life from nonhuman life.

I find Curran's objections very persuasive. As for his own position, Curran argues that individual human life does not begin until after the possibility of twinning and recombination has been concluded.[82] Thereafter life may be taken only if necessary "to protect life or other values proportionate to life." Curran argues, and I agree, that this phrase ("other values proportionate to life") must be interpreted in a way consistent with our assessment of the values justifying the taking of extrauterine life. In summary: a useful survey and a carefully argued statement of his own position—one I find very close to my own.

In an excellent[83] article, Albert Outler also rejects as arbitrary all "magic moment theories" as to when the defenseless deserve to be defended.[84] Such magic moments, whether they be ensoulment, cortical development, viability, birth, achievement of rationality, or acquisition of language, are merely prolongations of the body-soul dualism that has caused so much mischief. Outler grants that the distinctions are

[81] Charles E. Curran, "Abortion: Law and Morality in Contemporary Catholic Theology," *Jurist* 33 (1973) 162–83.

[82] Cf. Andre E. Hellegers, "Fetal Development,". THEOLOGICAL STUDIES 31 (1970) 3–9.

[83] I realize that terms of approval such as "excellent," especially in this context, very often betray the fact that the article in question corresponds to or reinforces the position of the commentator. Whether this is the case here, one will know only if he tests the essay, and I urge such testing.

[84] Albert C. Outler, "The Beginnings of Personhood: Theological Considerations," *Perkins Journal* 27 (1973) 28–34.

sometimes illuminating but that the radical disjunctions built on them do not make sense. In this he agrees with Schooyans.

From a theological perspective Outler sees terms such as "person," "personality," "personhood," and "self" as code words for a transempirical or self-transcending reality. This self-transcendence has been valued as a sign of life's sacredness in Christian tradition. It is not a *part* of the human organism nor is it inserted into a process of organic development at some magic moment. "It *is* the human organism oriented toward its transcendental matrix." Therefore Outler sees personhood as "a divine intention operating in a life-long process that runs from nidification to death." For this reason abortion must be seen as "a tragic option of what has been judged to be the lesser of two real evils."

Since abortion is now legal, the moral issue is more urgent and agonizing than ever. This shift from legal to moral grounds might be an advance, according to Outler, "*if* the value-shaping agencies in our society were agreed that abortion is a life-and-death choice; *if* there were legal and social supports for conscientious doctors in their newly appointed roles as killers as well as healers; *if* we had a general will in our society to extend our collective commitments to the unborn and the newly born; and *if*, above all, there were any prospects in our time for higher standards of responsible sexuality. What has actually happened, however, is that in our liberation from abortion as a 'crime,' many of us have also rejected any assessment of it as a *moral evil*—and this will further hasten the disintegration of our communal morality." [85]

Notre Dame's Stanley Hauerwas studies three questions that enlighten the abortion issue: When does life begin? When may life be taken legitimately? What does the agent understand to be happening? [86] Having answered in rather classical terms the first two, Hauerwas turns to the third question, which is at the heart of his interesting article. He contends that there is more "in an agent's deliberation and decisions that is morally important than is in the spectator's judgment." What is this more? Briefly, the agent's perspective. To illustrate how this perspective functions, he takes a situation earlier presented by James Gustafson. [87] It is a very tragic instance of pregnancy resulting from multiple rape in a situation of poverty, illness, and lack of employment. After very

[85] *Ibid.*, p. 32.

[86] Stanley Hauerwas, "Abortion: The Agent's Perspective," *American Ecclesiastical Review* 167 (1973) 102–20.

[87] James M. Gustafson, "A Protestant Ethical Approach," in John T. Noonan, ed., *The Morality of Abortion* (Cambridge: Harvard Univ. Press, 1970) pp. 101–22. For a different perspective on Gustafson's essay, cf. Frederick Carney, "The Virtue-Obligation Controversy," *Journal of Religious Ethics* 1 (1973) 5–19.

sensitively describing the values involved, Gustafson had concluded that abortion could be morally justified—or, more accurately (for Gustafson strongly resists being a spectator-judge), that if he were in the woman's position, he could see how it would be morally justified.

The special warrants for this exception Gustafson stated as follows: (1) pregnancy resulted from a sex crime; (2) the social and emotional conditions for the well-being of mother and child are not advantageous.

Hauerwas defends Gustafson's approach, not on the basis that abortion is a good thing, but rather because "abortion morally is justified under an ethical perspective that tries to pull as much good as possible from the situation." It might be a different thing if societal conditions and the woman's biography favored and supported carrying the pregnancy to term. "Yet Gustafson does not think such moral possibilities are present in this girl, at least not at this time." Behind this Hauerwas sees Gustafson's conviction that "the good and the right are found within the conditions of limitations. Present acts respond to the conditions of past actions, conditions which are usually irrevocable and unalterable." [88] Hauerwas agrees and states that our moral choices do not occur in ideal conditions where right and wrong are apparent, but rather the right must be wrenched from less than ideal alternatives.

I wish to pursue this point with Gustafson and Hauerwas, because further clarification may allow us to turn an ecumenical corner on the matter by bringing together two traditions that look rather sharply different but perhaps are really not. The point of concentration will be the phrase "moral justification." I would suggest that Gustafson has not "morally justified" abortion if we press that wording; for to do that he would, on his own terms, have to show what values are "higher in order to warrant the taking of life." I do not believe this has been shown. Gustafson–Hauerwas have rather shown that this girl in a real and understandable sense can do nothing else; that is, she has not (in her personal and societal situation) the resources to do what might in other conditions be the good thing to do. I should like to suggest that, if the emphasis falls on the woman's personal perspectives, strengths, and biography, then we are dealing with pastoral understanding or tolerance, not precisely with moral justification.

It is precisely in dealing with Gustafson's approach to abortion that Bernard Häring explains very well the distinction between moral theology and pastoral counseling.[89] Moral theology, he states, operates on a level "where questions are raised about general rules or considera-

---

[88] Gustafson, *op. cit.*, p. 115.
[89] Häring, *Medical Ethics*, pp. 112 ff.

tions that would justify a particular moral judgment." Pastoral prudence, however, looks to the art of the possible. Catholic tradition has always been familiar with the notion of "invincible ignorance" (surely a poor term because of its one-sidedly intellectual connotations and its aroma of arrogance). Häring rightly notes that this term refers to the existential wholeness of the person, the over-all inability to cope with a certain moral imperative. This inability can exist not only with regard to the highest ideals of the gospel, but also with regard to a particular prohibitive norm. On this basis Häring concludes that he would "not pursue the question once it had become evident that the woman could not bear the burden of the pregnancy."

Gustafson is thoroughly familiar with this discussion; for that reason it would be illuminating to have his further reflections on the point. In the altogether worthy cause of eliciting these reflections, I would like to continue to suggest, as a basis for discussion, that it seems more accurate to refer to Gustafson's conclusion in the case described not as "moral justification" but as "pastoral justification." For in dealing with concrete instances, are we not at the level where inprincipled values are assimilated by the individual in her situation, with her background, etc.? Behind Gustafson's use of "moral justification" is, perhaps, his strong reluctance to be a judge. But here I believe a distinction is called for. The moralist is a judge of necessity, a point made excellently by Hauerwas. But a moralist is not only a moralist in dealing with concrete situations. He is also a pastoral counselor, and *as such* is not a judge, if by "judge" we mean one who dictates what must be done regardless of a person's capacities and situation.[90] Could it be that because of his remarkable pastoral instincts Gustafson too quickly identifies the moral and pastoral role and therefore uses the term "moral justification" where something else is involved? Possibly.

Every priest who has heard confessions knows the difference between moral judgment and pastoral compassion, between the good that ought to be and the good that cannot be as yet, between aspiration and achievement. When some segments of the Protestant community say that every human choice stands in need of forgiveness, they are saying something unfamiliar to Catholic *moral* tradition (especially the manualist moral tradition) but not to Catholic *pastoral* practice. If Gustafson would speak more of the good that ought to be, and his Catholic counterpart would speak (as well he can) more of what cannot yet be and

[90] A balanced presentation of the counseling approach to abortion is that of Harry E. Hoewischer, S.J., "A Counselling Approach to the Problems of the Unwanted Pregnancy," *Inquiry* (Regis College), Oct. 1973 (no pagination given).

why, the twain could easily mate into a position identifiable as catholic, because human and compassionate, yet evangelically uncompromising and radical.

J. Robert Nelson writes that discussion of abortion among Christians would be considerably helped if "sanctity of life" were understood as including both *bios* (mere sustenance for mortal existence) and *zoe* (the qualitative dimension of life).[91] According to Nelson, *zoe* always has the higher value. If this is remembered, "Christians would never think of the fetus, at whatever stage of development, as a disposable 'thing'; nor would they have so strong a fixation on the preservation of the fetus 'at all costs' that they would be callous to either the pregnant woman's *zoe* or to the well-being of society."

Nelson's elaboration of "sanctity of life" is shot through with Christian insight and common sense. However, two points deserve comment. First, there is the meaning, or rather the implications, of the contention that *zoe* always has the higher value. Physical life is, to be sure, not the highest good for man, if one can use such language without plunging into dualism. But it is, as Schüller has recently insisted,[92] the most fundamental, and as such it is to be preferred over other conflicting goods which, even though they rank higher on a scale, are less fundamental.

Secondly, in terms of the basic moral issue, Nelson's treatment leaves the matter pretty much where it was; for the issue is precisely, how much *bios* can be sacrificed to *zoe* without undermining *zoe* itself? And on what warrants, with what controls, developed out of what form of moral reasoning? Nelson does not help here.

In a long and rather strange article Judith Jarvis Thomson tries to establish the moral justification for abortion by assimilating the procedure to a situation where one need not continue to provide his body as a source of lifesaving sustenance to someone who cannot be saved without it.[93] Thus, refusing to allow a pregnancy to continue can be the moral equivalent of refusing to be a Good Samaritan. If there are times when one may legitimately argue that the cost is too great to demand that one be a Good Samaritan, so too with continuing the pregnancy. "I have been arguing," she writes, "that no person is morally required to make larger sacrifices to sustain the life of another who has no right to demand them, and this even where the sacrifices do not include life itself."

---

[91] J. Robert Nelson, "What Does Theology Say about Abortion?" *Christian Century* 90 (1973) 124–28.

[92] Bruno Schüller, S.J., "Zur Problematik allgemein verbindlicher ethischer Grundsätze," *Theologie und Philosophie* 45 (1970) 1–23, and "Typen ethischer Argumentation in der katholischen Moraltheologie," *ibid.*, pp. 526–50.

[93] Judith Jarvis Thomson, "A Defense of Abortion," *Philosophy and Public Affairs* 1 (1971) 47–66.

To the objection that the mother has special responsibilities and obligations to the child and that the child has certain rights, Thomson argues that we do not have special responsibilities for a person unless we have assumed them, explicitly or implicitly. This means that "if a set of parents do not try to prevent pregnancy, do not obtain an abortion, and then at the time of birth of the child do not put it out for adoption, but rather take it home with them, then they have assumed responsibility for it, they have given it rights, and they cannot now withdraw support from it...."[94] Contrarily, "if they have taken all reasonable precautions against having a child, they do not simply by virtue of their biological relationship to the child ... have a special responsibility for it." They may wish to assume this responsibility, but "if assuming responsibility for it would require large sacrifices, then they may refuse."

Thomson's essay stirred two formidable combatants into activity. Baruch Brody (M.I.T.) replies that Thomson has overlooked the distinction between our duty to save a life and our duty not to take a life.[95] The former duty is much weaker than the latter. In another article Brody sets out his own understanding of when it is legitimate to abort.[96] Hypothesizing that the fetus is a human being whose life may not be taken except in the most extreme circumstances, he seeks a rule that would best state what these circumstances are. After rejecting any justification based on fetal aggression, Brody concludes with a norm which states that it is permissible to abort to save the mother's life if the fetus is going to die anyway in a relatively short time and taking its life is the only way to save the mother. The whole rationale for taking some life to save others "is that he whose life will be taken loses nothing of significance and [he] is not therefore being treated unfairly." But he insists on tightening this rule by adding the requirement that taking the mother's life will not save the child, or even if it will, it has been determined by a fair random method that the mother, not the child, ought to be saved.

While Brody's reasoning will appear quaint to a world whose attitudes toward abortion have been profoundly influenced by a variety of pressure groups (sexual freedom, population control, women's liberation, etc.[97]), it strikes me as being a very useful attempt to deal with the morality of conflict situations in a disciplined and controlled way without falling into the standard traps of utilitarian analysis. Unfortunately, however,

[94] *Ibid.*, p. 65.

[95] Baruch Brody, "Thomson on Abortion," *Philosophy and Public Affairs* 1 (1972) 335–40.

[96] B. A. Brody, "Abortion and the Sanctity of Human Life," *American Philosophical Quarterly* 10 (1973) 133–40.

[97] Cf. David R. Mace, *Abortion: The Agonizing Decision* (Nashville: Abingdon, 1972) pp. 60–62.

the whole thing looks a bit too much like an academic game, since Brody begins by admitting that there are "others who claim, *with equally good reason*, that a fetus is not a human being. . . . "[98] His study would be much more persuasive if he had explored and validated that judgment.

Philosopher John Finnis also takes on Thomson.[99] He claims that Thomson has muddied the discussion by conducting it in terms of rights. The dispute is properly about what one "must" do, is "morally required" to do. After such determinations have been made, we will be able, by a convenient locution, to assert the child's right. Furthermore, Thomson's constant appeal to rights obscures the weak point in her defense of abortion. That point is seen in her contentions that (1) rights typically or essentially depend on grants, concessions, etc.; (2) special responsibilities likewise depend on grants, concessions, etc.; (3) therefore the whole moral problem here concerns one's *special* responsibilities. Finnis rejects utterly the idea that the mother's duty not to abort is an incident of a special responsibility she undertook. It is rather a straightforward incident of an ordinary duty everyone owes to his neighbor.

Finnis then sets out his own understanding of the morality of abortion, the moral "musts" and "mays." It builds along the lines of the analysis elaborated by Germain Grisez that there are basic human goods which demand, among other things, that we never choose directly against them. Finnis spends the rest of the article lifting up the considerations that reveal whether and when our choices must be characterized as directly against a basic good. His answer is that destruction of life is inescapably antilife and against a basic good when it is intended.

Finnis has scored some telling points against Thomson, a judgment I would defend in spite of a subtle response-article in which she attempts again to equate not saving with killing.[100] However, two points merit notice here. First, Finnis refers to "traditional nonconsequentialist ethics which has gained explicit ecclesiastical approval in the Roman Church these last ninety years. . . . " This overstates the matter, I believe. The moral formulations of the Church are, above all, practical guides for the formation of conscience and direction of the faithful. Since they are teaching statements, moral reasoning and various forms of persuasion will be, indeed must be, used. And moral reasoning does imply ethical structure. But because a structure or system may be implicit in the way a teaching is formulated, this should not be taken to mean that this system is being taught or approved. It remains, as did scholastic language in the

---

[98] *Art. cit.* (n. 96 above) p. 133 (emphasis added).

[99] John Finnis, "The Rights and Wrongs of Abortion," *Philosophy and Public Affairs* 2 (1973) 117–45.

[100] Judith Jarvis Thomson, "Rights and Deaths," *ibid.*, pp. 146–59.

past, a vehicle only more or less inseparable from the substance of the teaching. In this sense it is incorrect to refer to nonconsequentialist ethics as gaining "explicit ecclesiastical approval." Furthermore, there are those who would argue that if there are practical absolutes in the moral domain, their absoluteness can be argued precisely on consequentialist grounds.

Secondly and very substantially, in discussing those actions that must be seen as choices against a basic good, Finnis notes that "the 'innocence' of the victim whose life is taken makes a difference to the characterizing of an action as open to and respectful of the good of human life, and as an intentional killing. *Just how and why it makes a difference is difficult to unravel;* I shall not attempt an unraveling here." [101] This is a crucial point. If Finnis were to attempt to unravel this—as applied, for example, to capital punishment in the past—he would encounter a consequentialist calculus at work in creating this exception, one that ultimately allows for the destruction of an individual's life if it is a threat to the common good and there is no other way of preventing this threat. On the basis of this and other forms of exception-making in the development of traditional norms, one has to conclude that a form of consequentialism cannot be excluded.

In a tortuous and ultimately very vulnerable study, Michael Tooley rejects both the "liberal" position of Judith Thomson and the more classical views of Finnis and Brody.[102] The former position is weak because of the impossibility of establishing any cutoff points that are acceptable. The classical position is rejected because it rests on the "potentiality principle" (the fetus deserves protection not for what it is physiologically but because this physiology will lead to psychological differences later that are morally relevant).

Tooley attacks this principle through a strange analogy. Suppose it might be possible at some future date to inject kittens with a chemical that would cause them to develop into cats possessing a brain similar to that of humans (with psychological capabilities, thought, language, etc.). One would not argue that they have a right to life just because of this potentiality. "But if it is not seriously wrong to destroy an injected kitten which will naturally develop the properties that bestow a right to life, neither can it be seriously wrong to destroy a member of *Homo sapiens* which lacks such properties, but will naturally come to have them."

Tooley then elaborates his own position. Briefly, it contends that "an

---

[101] *Art. cit.*, p. 141 (emphasis added).

[102] Michael Tooley, "Abortion and Infanticide," *Philosophy and Public Affairs* 2 (1972) 37–65.

organism possesses a serious right to life only if it possesses the concept of self as a continuing subject of experiences and other mental states, and believes that it is itself such a continuing entity." This concept of self is required by Tooley because right is defined in terms of a desire—and desires are limited by the concepts one possesses. Thus "an entity cannot desire that it itself *continue* existing as a subject of experience and other mental states unless it believes that it is now such a subject." On this basis Tooley accepts not only all abortions but even infanticide.

What is wrong with all this? Several things. First, a simple test of an analysis is the fit of its conclusions with the moral convictions of civilized men. To the best of my knowledge, most civilized men would recoil in sheer horror at the wholesale infanticide justified by Tooley's analysis. Secondly, in his animal analogy, Tooley has doubled his middle term ("potentiality"), well, monstrously. Finally, Tooley's key mistake is connecting inseparably rights and desires. He correctly notes that to ascribe a right is to assert something about the prima-facie obligations of other individuals to act or refrain from acting. But he then asserts that "the obligations in question are conditional ones, being dependent upon the existence of certain desires of the individual to whom this right is ascribed." Thus, he continues, if an individual asks me to destroy something to which he has a right, one does not violate his right to that thing if one proceeds to destroy it; for the owner no longer *desires* the object. On this basis desire, and therefore capacity to desire, is said to be essential to the possession of rights.

Here Tooley has forgotten that the notion of right is an analogous one, not a univocal one. Basically this analogy traces to one's understanding of moral obligation, its source and meaning. Here Finnis is absolutely correct. Before one can move securely within the vocabulary of rights and their limits, he must return to their source; for rights are a convenient locution for the existence of obligation. At the level of moral obligation, Tooley must examine why it is wrong to kill a person. To say that it is wrong because it is in violation of a person's right is patent circularity. In his deliberations I believe Tooley will soon discover two things: (1) that any viable analysis will apply to all men, neonates and uterine babies not excluded; (2) that material goods (as goods that are subordinate to persons and can become one's *property*) generate different moral assertions than human life itself. It is these different moral assertions that are the basis for the analogy of rights. For example, we speak of *jus connaturale* (a right natural to man, e.g., to his life) and *jus adventitium* (a right which arises from some positive event, e.g., from buying, selling, finding, etc.). There are other such distinctions. Tooley treats them as if they were all the same, and basically because he has not traced their origin to a systematic theory of moral obligation.

Therefore, when he says that the obligations connoted by the term "right" are "dependent upon the existence of certain desires of the individual to whom the right is ascribed," he is guilty of confusing apples and oranges, or better, of reducing all of them to prunes. One cannot, in other words, argue that what is true of one right is true of all rights. Tooley is correct in saying that I violate no right of ownership when I destroy property the owner desires destroyed. Scholastic philosophy has long been familiar with the axiom *consentienti non fit injuria* (no injustice is done to one who consents or waives his right). However, scholastic tradition has, no less than the Declaration of Independence, regarded certain rights as inalienable. If certain rights are alienable, others inalienable, then clearly one must return to the drawing boards if he treats them as all the same.

In a long and closely-argued review article, Paul Ramsey takes up the books of Daniel Callahan and Germain Grisez.[103] He criticizes as "idiosyncratic" Callahan's use of the notion of sanctity of life and his espousal of the developmental school's answer to the question about the beginning of life. Callahan's analysis, Ramsey argues, has eroded the notion of equal justice. Behind it all Ramsey sees an incorrect premise, scil., the idea that there can be inequality between life sanctities pitted against one another in conflict. Ramsey regards this as the major flaw in Callahan's defense of a legal policy of abortion-on-demand. Noting that Callahan regards the use made of his book on abortion as a "personal disaster," Ramsey contends that the book can and should be read in this abusive way and calls for a retraction of the structure of Callahan's moral argument.

I share Ramsey's discomfort with Callahan's analysis, an analysis to which he recently returned.[104] As I read his book (*Abortion: Law, Choice and Morality*), it seems that Callahan is still trying to have it both ways. His sanctity-of-life principle yields a "strong bias against abortion," instils "an overwhelming bias in favor of human life." One "bends over backward not to eliminate human life." Abortion is the last resort of a woman, "to be avoided if at all possible." And this as a *moral* position. And yet we find him saying that it is "possible to imagine a *huge* [my emphasis] number of situations where a woman could, in good and sensitive conscience, choose abortion as a moral solution to her personal and social difficulties." In other words, Callahan feels the wrong of abortion; yet he feels the desperation of its need. Armed with these, he states in his recent essay that the moral problem is *balancing* the right of the fetus with the right of the mother. However, his ultimate moral

[103] Paul Ramsey, "Abortion: A Review Article," *Thomist* 37 (1973) 174–226.

[104] Daniel Callahan, "Abortion: Thinking and Experiencing," *Christianity and Crisis*, Jan. 8, 1973, pp. 295–98.

position is hardly a balance; it comes close to eliminating one right altogether. Therefore Callahan ends up (since he cannot divest himself of his knowledge of and deep sensitivity to what is going on) cursing the rotten decisions imposed by a world most of us never made or chose.

What I miss here, then, is not sensitivity. Callahan's writings on abortion are utterly honest, appropriately corrective, and profoundly sensitive. I miss the moral reasoning that would explain his phrase "often necessary choice." Something is necessary, first of all, in terms of competitive values and available alternatives. But, unless I have misunderstood him, Callahan explains this necessity almost exclusively in terms of the woman's perception of it. Important as these perceptions are, they do not constitute the heart of an ethical or moral position on abortion. Rather, I believe that they pertain to an ethics of an individual's response to a morality of abortion—what above was called pastoral counseling. Does not a true morality of abortion have to provide the possibility for expansion of an individual's perspectives and value commitments? I think so.

Ramsey next turns to Germain Grisez. Grisez, it will be recalled, argued that the traditional understanding of the principle of the twofold effect was too restrictive. It demanded that in the order of physical causality the evil effect not precede the good. Grisez proposed that the intention of the agent remains upright (not choosing directly against a basic good) as long as the evil aspect is part of an indivisible process. The test of this indivisibility is whether no other human act need intervene to bring about the good effect.

Thus, as Ramsey interprets him, Grisez would allow abortion in a case of primary pulmonary hypertension where the woman could not oxygenate both herself and the fetus. However, in the instance of aneurysm of the aorta in which the wall of the aorta is so weakened that it balloons out behind the pregnant uterus, the physician must first kill the fetus (in a separable act) to get at the aneurysm. On Grisez's criterion, this second procedure would not be allowed. Ramsey sees this as too restrictive and not "confirmed by common sense or intuitive moral judgment."

The crucial question, Ramsey believes, is whether the target of the deadly deed is upon fetal life or upon what that life is doing to another life. "While the life is taken with observable directness, the intention of the action is directed against the lethal process or function of that life." Thus, in terms of its meaning, the action is describable as "removal," not precisely as "death-dealing." But Ramsey limits this to situations where both lives cannot be saved but only the mother's. "My view," he writes, "is that 'removal' is what *is done* and is justified in all cases where 'necessity' foredooms that only one life can be saved. . . . "[105]

[105] *Art. cit.*, p. 223.

Ramsey contends that Grisez's analysis would afford little or no guidance "where there is no necessity to do the intended action"; for every abortion could be arguably concerned with removal of the child, not its death. Therefore he equates Grisez's view to that of Judith Thomson, of all people. Here I think he has misread Grisez. Grisez insists throughout that indirectness is but a single condition of the twofold effect; proportion is another. For instance, Grisez repeatedly asserts that we do not take life for the sake of health.

Ramsey's limitation of his analysis to instances where only one life can be saved (the mother's) leads one to ask whether the really operative factor is the intention of the action as he has struggled to analyze it. Is it not more broadly the proportionate reason? That is, it seems better to sound reasoning to save one life than to lose two in a situation where the fetus cannot be saved anyway.

I am not contesting Ramsey's conclusions; that is not the point here. It is the form of moral reasoning that deserves attention. Ramsey argues that interruption of pregnancy, *direct* in its external observableness, is aimed at stopping the fetus from doing what it is doing to the mother. He is inclined to call this a justifiable direct abortion, but presumably an indirect killing. And he explicitly rejects the idea that fetal death must be indirect in Grisez's sense—an inseparable aspect of a single act. Fetal death could be, in other words, the result of a prior separable action.

Actually, it seems clear that directness and indirectness do not really function critically in Ramsey's analysis, though he continues to use the distinction;[106] for Ramsey repeatedly restricts abortion to those instances where only one (the mother) can be saved. This suggests that what is really the justification in the case under discussion is the broader principle of doing the lesser evil in a tragic conflict situation, the principle of proportionate reason. This has to be the meaning of Ramsey's phrase "what the fetus is doing to the mother." Otherwise why could we not extend this to other cases short of life-threats where pregnancy is a hardship (psychological, physical, economic), where the fetus is indeed "doing something to the mother" but something far short of a life-threat?

In this connection the Belgian bishops have an extremely interesting but somewhat ambiguous paragraph on the moral principles governing abortion situations.[107] They write:

In the case—today fortunately quite rare due to the progress of science—where the life of the mother and that of the child are in danger, the Church, concerned to meet this situation of distress, has always recognized the legitimacy of an

[106] "I agree with Grisez that any killing of man by man must be 'indirect'" (*art. cit.*, p. 220).

[107] *Art. cit.* (n. 46 above) p. 443.

intervention, even if it involves the indirect loss of one of the two lives one is attempting to save. In medical practice it is sometimes difficult to determine whether this misfortune results directly or indirectly from the intervention. This latter [intervention], from the point of view of morality, can be considered as a whole. The moral principle which ought to govern the intervention can be formulated as follows: since two lives are at stake, one will, while doing everything possible to save both, attempt to save one rather than to allow two to perish.

I say the paragraph is ambiguous because there are at least two ways of reading it. (1) Intervention in these desperate instances is legitimate *providing it is indirect in character*. Its indirectness is determined by viewing it "as a whole." (2) Intervention to save one where the alternative is to lose two is *for this very reason* (the desperate alternatives) *indirect*. The first rendering is close to that of Grisez. If the second is the proper reading, it comes very close to the analysis of Peter Knauer. One can only ask what meaning the terms "direct" and "indirect" have if the crucial moral principle is to be formulated as in the last sentence of the episcopal statement; for what seems obviously at the heart of this principle is the conflict model of human choice, a model ultimately governed by the principle of the lesser evil. I have tried elsewhere, though with considerably less than total satisfaction, to explore the very thorny problem of the moral relevance of the direct-indirect distinction.[108]

In discussing this very question, William May appeals to the writings of Joseph Fuchs, S.J.[109] After pointing out that a person becomes morally good when he intends and effects premoral good (life, health, culture, etc.), Fuchs asks: "What if he intends and effects good, but this necessarily involves effecting evil also?" The answer given by Fuchs is: "We answer, if the realization of the evil through the intended realization of good is justified as a proportionately related cause, then in this case only good was intended."

As a gloss on this citation May states: "At first it might seem (and unfortunately has so seemed to Richard McCormick . . .) that Fuchs is saying that we may rightfully intend and effect a premoral evil (e.g., death) provided there is some proportionate good that will be achieved." May denies that this is the way Fuchs is to be read, and for two reasons. First, Fuchs insists that *only* good is intended in an act that has evil effects as well as good consequences. "He refuses to say that the evil effected was properly intended in the moral sense." Secondly, May

[108] Richard A. McCormick, S.J., *Ambiguity in Moral Choice* (Milwaukee: Marquette Univ., 1973).

[109] William E. May, "Abortion as Indicative of Personal and Social Identity," *Jurist* 33 (1973) 199–217.

points out that Fuchs insists that the evil must be a part or element of *one* human act. "He is saying, in short, that the act in question must be describable as one ordered of itself to the good and that the act in question is itself the means to the end."

Here two points. First, Fuchs is saying, I believe, that premoral evil may indeed be intended—as the word "intend" has been used traditionally in applications of the twofold effect, scil., in a psychological sense. He is saying it is not intended "in the moral sense." At this point, however, one must ask what it means to intend something "in the moral sense." It seems to be nothing more than a convenient and post-factum way of saying that the good pursued was fully proportionate to the evil effected within the choice. If there is true proportion, then, as Fuchs notes, "only good was intended." This is much more a post-factum ascription than an analysis of human intending.

Secondly, there is question of what is meant by saying that the evil must be a part or element of *one* human act. When I criticized Fuchs on this very point,[110] he answered[111] that an action can be taken in three ways: physically, psychologically, humano-morally. This last is the only description of an action that suffices for its moral assessment. But taken in a humano-moral sense, the *one* choice or action includes also its intended results and foreseen circumstances. What is intended in a choice (not necessarily achieved) pertains to the *oneness* of that action. Thus, in the famous case of Mrs. Bergmeier, the action was not simply adultery, as a means to a good end. Rather, it was sexual union with a certain intended effect and in certain circumstances. Viewed in this way, the extramarital intercourse was a part of *one* action which included the intended good also. I have some problems, or at least further questions, about this; but it is what Fuchs means; and it is a bit different from the interpretation given Fuchs by May.

In an interesting article Louis Dupré grapples with this very problem.[112] He first argues that inchoate personhood is present in fetal life from the beginning but that it must be evaluated differently according to a developmental scale. He then rejects the direct-indirect analysis as a "purely verbal solution" to the abortion problem. "I prefer," he writes, "to consider abortion always a direct killing of human life and then to ask under which circumstances it could be licit." What are these circumstances? As a general rule, Dupré seems satisfied with the norm that it is permissible to kill "only to prevent a person from

---

[110] Cf. THEOLOGICAL STUDIES 33 (1972) 72 ff.

[111] Personal communication.

[112] Louis Dupré, "A New Approach to the Abortion Problem," THEOLOGICAL STUDIES 34 (1973) 481–88.

inflicting a *comparable* type of harm to others." However, the implications of that norm depend on one's reading of "comparable." What values are comparable to life? In making this assessment, he contends that "the degree of development inevitably enters into the evaluation of the life value." He then goes on to suggest that personal liberty is a value comparable to that of life to many people and that a minimum degree of mental health is a condition for personal liberty. Thus he moves away from the traditional position.

I find Dupré undecided and ambiguous about what is the really decisive norm in abortion decisions. He presents two considerations as central: the developmental evaluation of personhood and the values comparable to life itself. But what constitutes the heart of his opening of perspectives is not clear. At one point he states that "an identical risk to a woman's health decreases in moral weight as the pregnancy progresses. What would constitute a sufficient factor during the first two days after conception no longer does so after two months." This suggests that what justifies the abortion is a sliding scale of evaluation of fetal life. But then he immediately adds that "no abortive action, early or late, becomes ever permissible under our principles *unless* a value comparable to life itself is at stake." This means that *any* abortion is justified because the competitive value is comparable to life itself. Which of these two considerations is decisive?

Dupré's own example illustrates this unclarity. He notes: "In cases of rape of an adolescent, the presumption of serious mental damage appears strong enough to warrant the general use of an abortifacient at least during several hours following the coitus. But the same presumption cannot be taken for granted at a later stage of development . . . . " Now the problem here is that according to Dupré "serious mental damage" can qualify as justifying abortion only because it is a value comparable to life itself. That point can be defended, and perhaps successfully. But then, why relate it to a stage in fetal growth? An equivalence is, after all, an equivalence—unless serious mental damage is a value comparable to life when compared to some lives but not to others. This seems to be what Dupré would have to hold, but I fail to see how this avoids eroding the notion of equal rights, an erosion Dupré wants desperately to avoid.

Frederick Carney (Perkins School of Theology) believes that Dupré has confused two concepts of person, concepts that lead to unacceptable results when substituted for each other.[113] The first concept centers in the attribution of rights and responsibilities. When this notion of person is used, we are speaking of a few basic concerns common to all men, such

[113] Cf. *Beginning of Personhood*, ed. Donald G. McCarthy (a booklet of the Institute of Religion and Human Development, Houston, Texas) pp. 36–40.

as life and liberty, and the relation of individuals to each other in respect to these concerns is one of moral and legal equality.

The second concept of person describes the development of individuals and highlights special competencies or achievements. Here the relationship of individuals is one of disequality. Carney believes that Dupré's approach makes the abortion decision hinge on the second concept of person (personality development) rather than on the first.

There are other problems in which the second concept of person is very appropriate, for example, admission to a college, or the assignment of awards for some achievement. For these problems Dupré's concept of person seems to me to be the central one. But in the consideration of the basic protections of social life the second concept just cannot function in any appropriate way. In fact, I would say it will undermine our social life to try to substitute that concept as Dupré apparently wishes to do.

There are, Carney argues, instances within the first concept of personhood when it is legitimate to take life, but these are never instances of a balancing of capacities, merits, or achievements over against basic rights.

Carney then proposes his own approach. Rather than beginning with biological facts (e.g., conception, quickening, viability, birth) to which we assign decisive importance for personhood, he suggests we begin with moral theory. That is, rather than first defining personhood and then attributing rights, he wants first to attribute rights and then assign personhood to those to whom rights are attributed.

What are the reasons for wanting to put anybody within the category of individuals possessing rights? Carney finds three types of reasons for such attribution. First, there is the notion of fairness. If "x" is a rightholder and "y" is like "x" in all relevant characteristics, why should "y" not be a rightholder? This is a kind of deontological argument. Secondly, there is a teleological argument, one concerned with ends. What individuals fundamentally are or are destined to be cannot be fully acknowledged and enhanced without the attribution of basic rights. The third reason is from revelation, a theological argument. One believes that God wills that certain beings be protected in this fundamental way and therefore assigns basic rights to these beings.

Carney's suggestion is extremely interesting. Starting with biological fact is quite legitimate, as he notes. But it has not proved very helpful in achieving acceptable clarification and consensus in the body politic. If clarification and consensus in the body politic is what Carney wants from a switch in approach, then I seriously doubt that he is going to get it; for the supposition underlying such a switch is that people come out this way or that on abortion because of the rational persuasiveness of the arguments made. That can be doubted.

At any rate, a reading of recent episcopal and theological literature will lead to the conclusion that both approaches suggested by Carney are used, both by those who support the classical position on abortion and by those who would modify it. For instance, Pohier attempts to move away from the traditional position by showing two things:[114] first, that there are reasons in reproductive biology—for example, the number of spontaneous miscarriages—for saying that the fertilized ovum is not "être humain déjà"; secondly, that God's providential concern for life and man's share in this responsibility are not necessarily best described and supported by an absolute position on abortion.

If one impression is inseparable from this interesting literature, it is that abortion is a moral problem far more complex and anguishing than any one-dimensional approach (e.g., right to privacy, woman's right to dispose of her body, absolute prohibition of abortion etc.) would suggest.

PERSONAL REFLECTIONS

Exposure to such a rich and varied literature inevitably leaves one with some more or less settled reactions and opinions. The compositor of these "Notes" would order his as follows.

Moral Position

Human life, as a basic good and the foundation for the enjoyment of other goods and rights, should be taken only when doing so is the lesser of two evils, all things considered. In this Outler is, I believe, correct. "Human life" refers to individual life from conception, or at least from "the time at or after which it is settled whether there will be one or two or more distinct human individuals" (Ramsey). As this qualifier receives the continued discussion by theologians that it deserves, the benefit of the doubt should ordinarily be given to the fetus. To qualify as the lesser of two evils there is required, among other things, that there be at stake a human life or its moral equivalent. "Moral equivalent" refers to a good or value that is, in Christian assessment, comparable to life itself (cf. Dupré and Curran). This is the *substance* of the Christian tradition if our best casuistry in other areas (e.g., just warfare) is carefully weighed and sifted; for the permissible exceptions with regard to life-taking (self-defense, just war, capital punishment, indirect killing) are all formulations and concretizations of what is viewed in the situation as the lesser human evil.

This position represents an achievement which, in terms of existing evidence, it would be unscientific to deny and uncivilized to abandon. I

---

[114] Jacques-Marie Pohier, O.P., "Réflexions théologiques sur la position de l'église catholique," *Lumière et vie* 21 (1972) 73–107.

am comfortable with it as a normative statement. Recent attempts to extend exceptions through notions of delayed hominization and gradual personhood are, it seems, but contemporary analogues of the earlier theories about delayed animation. To this commentator they appear strained, though continued discussion is certainly called for. On this matter I am in agreement with Curran.

The determination of the moral equivalent of life is both difficult and dangerous.[115] It is difficult because it is very difficult to compare basic human values. Furthermore, such comparisons are a shifting thing reflecting our change in value perceptions.

It is dangerous for several reasons. First, because such evaluation is vulnerable to unrecognized cultural biases. Cultures are more or less civilized, more or less violent, more or less hedonistic, etc., and hence will be more or less human in their value judgments. We can never completely transcend the distorting influences embedded in our culture. Secondly, it is dangerous because such formulations are hard put to resist abusive interpretation. In general, it can be said that while the casuistry of the tradition shows that there are other values comparable to human life, the thrust of the tradition supports an inclination (and only that) to narrow rather than to broaden the comparable values. To make this comparison with prudence in our time calls not only for honesty and openness within a process of communal discernment, but also for further careful studies of past conclusions and present evaluations.

Pastoral Care

The position thus delineated is a *moral* position, to be equated neither with pastoral care nor with a legal position, but to be totally dissociated from neither. Pastoral care deals with an individual where that person is (cf. Häring) in terms of his perceptions and strengths. Although it attempts to expand perspectives and maximize strengths, it recognizes the limits of these attempts.

There are two aspects profoundly affecting the determination of where many people are. First, we live in a society with structures that often do not support and aid women with unwanted pregnancies, a society that heavily contributes to the factors that make pregnancies unwanted—a society with not only broad areas of structural poverty, repression, injustice, but also with subtle escalating pressures against childbearing. Secondly, perception of the existence and value of fetal life differs. Wertheimer is probably right when he notes that it is the severely limited possibilities of natural relationships with the fetus that generate the

[115] For some extremely interesting suggestions on comparable values where abortion is concerned, cf. James J. Diamond, "Pro-Life Amendments and Due Process," *America* 130 (1974) 27–29.

unlimited possibility of natural responses to it.[116] In combination, these facts mean that many people will perceive the abortion problem above all in terms of the inconvenience, hardship, or suffering a prohibitive position involves, and will tend to find that position unacceptable *for that reason.*

Since the sum total of these influences, then, is an attitude that increasingly tends to frame the moral question almost exclusively in terms of the sufferings resultant on a prohibitive moral position, it is important to distinguish two things: (*a*) whether a moral position is right and truly embodies the good; (*b*) whether standing by it and proposing it as the object of aspiration, both personal and societal, entails hardships and difficulties. In a highly pragmatic, technologically sophisticated, and thoroughly pampered culture the latter point (certainly a fact) could lead many to conclude that the moral position is erroneous. This must be taken into account in any sound pastoral procedure.

Abortion, like any humanly caused disvalue, is sought not only for a reason, but within a culture which either sanctions or not the reason, and alters or not the conditions, that give rise to the abortion. One of the most important functions of morality is to provide to a culture the ongoing possibility of criticizing and transcending itself and its limitations. Thus genuine morality, while always compassionate and understanding in its meeting with individual distress (pastoral), must remain prophetic and demanding in the norms through which it invites to a better humanity (moral); for if it ceases to do this, it simply collapses the pastoral and moral and in doing so ceases to be truly human, because it barters the good that will liberate and humanize for the compromise that will merely comfort.

Legal Regulation

Law is analogous to pastoral practice in that it must look not merely to the good, but to the good that is possible and feasible in a particular society at a particular time. However, just as sound pastoral care takes account of individual strength and limitation ("invincible ignorance") without ceasing to invite and challenge the individual beyond his present perspectives, so the law, while taking account of the possible and feasible at a particular time, must do so without simply settling for it. Simple accommodation to cultural "realities" not only forfeits altogether the educative function of law, but also could leave an enormous number of people without legal protection. For this reason I find the legal positions of both Grisez and Callahan unpersuasive. Grisez has not sufficiently attended to the feasibility dimension of legislation and therefore his

---

[116] Roger Wertheimer, "Understanding the Abortion Argument," *Philosophy and Public Affairs* 1 (1971) 67–95.

position seems to represent a confusion of morality with legislation. Callahan, on the other hand, has by implication weighed only this dimension and therefore his position seems to represent a total dissociation of the moral and the legal, and an ultimate undermining of the moral by the legal, as the statement of the German bishops (both Catholic and Evangelical) notes.

Thus there is and probably must be this side of eternity a constant tension between the good and the feasible. A healthy society attempts to reduce this tension as much as possible. But it is only more or less successful. This leads me to three observations where abortion law is concerned.

First, the feasibility test (of law) is particularly difficult in our society. Ideally, of course, where we are concerned with the rights of others and especially the most fundamental right (right to life), the more easily should morality simply translate into law. But the easier this translation, the less necessary is law. In other words, if this represents the ideal, it also presupposes the ideal. And we do not have that, above all because the moral assessment of fetal life differs. And ultimately law must find a basis in the deepest moral perceptions of the majority or in principles the majority is reluctant to modify (Shinn). This means that it is especially difficult to apply the test of feasibility to an abortion law, for the good itself whose legal possibility is under discussion is an object of doubt and controversy. Given this situation, a totally permissive law in the present circumstances would tend only to deepen further the doubt and confusion, and in the process to risk unjustifiably further erosion of respect for human life. On the other hand, a stringently prohibitive law (such as the Texas law declared unconstitutional in *Wade*) in our circumstances would have enormous social costs in terms of other important values.

Secondly, no law will appear to be or actually be adequate (whether permissive or prohibitive) if it does not simultaneously contain provisions that attack the problems that tempt to abortion. Our mistake as a nation and that of many countries has been just that: to leave relatively untouched the societal conditions and circumstances that lead to abortion, and to legislate permissively, usually on the basis of transparently fragile slogans created by a variety of pressure groups. This has been shown to be destructive in every other area of human planning. It can be no less so here.

Thirdly, and as a consequence of the above considerations, in designing present legislation we are confronted at the present time with a choice of two legal evils. No choice is going to be very satisfactory, because the underlying conditions for truly good legislation are lacking. What is to be done when one is dealing with evils? Clearly the lesser evil should be chosen while attempts are made to alter the circumstances that allow only such a destructive choice. How one compares and weighs the evils, where he sees the greater evil, will depend on many factors, not excluding fetal life. That is why a moral position on fetal life, while distinguishable from a legal position, will have a good deal to say about what one regards as a good or tolerable legal position, at least at the present time. But here again we reach an impasse, for there is profound disagreement at the moral level. For instance, given the moral position I find persuasive, I believe that the most equitable law would be one that protects fetal life but exempts abortion done in certain specified conflict situations from legal sanctions (cf. the joint Catholic-Protestant statement from Germany). In other words, I believe that the social disvalues associated with such a law (a degree of unenforceability, clandestine abortions, less than total control over fertility) are lesser evils than the enormous bloodletting both allowed and, in some real and destructive sense, inescapably encouraged (*teste experientia*), by excessively permissive laws. However, I realize that very many of my fellow citizens do not share this judgment.

What, then, is to be done? In our pluralistic atmosphere, legal provisions tracing back to almost *any* moral position (whether it be that of Vatican II or that of the Supreme Court—this latter I use deliberately because the legal conclusions so obviously reflect a moral position, though they need not do so) are going to be seen and experienced as an imposition of one view on another group. In such an impasse, the only way out seems to be procedural. Two procedures recommend themselves. First, the matter should be decided for the present through the state legislatures, where all of us have an opportunity to share in the democratic process. We have learned in our history that while this process is often halting and frustrating, sometimes even corrupt, still it provides us with our most adequate way of living with our differences—a way certainly more adequate than a decision framed by a Court that imposes its own poorly researched and shabbily reasoned moral values as the basis for the law of the land.[117]

Secondly, I used above the phrase "for the present." It is meant to suggest that our societal situation is such (both in terms of the conditions provoking abortion and in terms of the pluralism about its moral character) that any legal disposition of the question now must be accompanied by hesitation and a large dose of dissatisfaction. This means that it is the right and the duty of conscientious citizens to

---

[117] Philip B. Kurland, professor in the law school at the University of Chicago, wrote recently: "The primary defect of the Burger Court so far revealed is the same defect that was observed in the Warren Court. It has failed to account properly for its judgments. It has issued decrees but it has not afforded adequate rationales for them; it has attempted to rule by fiat rather than reason" (*University of Chicago Magazine*, July/August 1973, pp. 3–9, at 9).

continue to debate this matter in the public forum. The values at stake are fundamental to the continuance of civilized society. For this reason, to settle for the *status quo* is to settle for societal sickness. Much as we are individually and corporately tired of this subject, continued rational discussion is essential. It is one means—but only one—that will allow us, as a nation, to arrive at a position that is compatible with the fundamental moral principles undergirding our republic.

Whatever the proper answer to the legal question, one final point must be made. We sometimes think of certain problems like abortion as pertaining to individual morality, and others like poverty and racism as being social morality. The Supreme Court decision only reinforced this perspective. The contemporary emphasis is on the need to solve the so-called "bigger" and "less domestic" problems. Catholics, it is averred, have for too long been fascinated by and preoccupied with micromorality.

The matter is far more complex than this. As the literature brought under review here has shown, economic insecurity, racism, oppression, and abortion share a common root: the quality of the society in which we live. In this perspective abortion is a *social* problem of the first magnitude in so far as the factors so often involved in abortion decisions are societal in character. Similarly, poverty and racism are *individual* problems in so far as we bear as individuals responsibility for their existence and continuation. To say anything else would be unchristian; for it would deny that we are, by our Christian being, *individual members of a community* who have, as a community, responsibilities toward individuals and who have, as individuals, responsibilities toward the community. These responsibilities, while distinguishable, are continuous. Abortion exists because of a cluster of factors that make up the quality of a society. It will disappear only when that quality is changed. Hence true abortion reform must begin here. Unless and until it does, any law on abortion will be more or less inhumane.[118]

---

[118] In a review such as this a good deal of literature is necessarily overlooked, some of it because it was published as this survey was going to press. An instance of this is Sissela Bok, "Ethical Problems of Abortion," *Studies* (Hastings Center) 2 (1974) 33–52. Cf. also John T. Noonan, "Responding to Persons: Methods of Moral Argument in Debate over Abortion," *Theology Digest* 21 (1973) 291–307; Peter A. Facione, "Callahan on Abortion," *American Ecclesiastical Review* 167 (1973) 291–301; G. Caprile, "Il magistero della Chiesa sull'aborto," *Civiltà cattolica*, May 19, 1973, pp. 359–62; "Déclaration des juristes de France sur l'avortement." *Documentation catholique* 70 (1973) 749; Francis Dardot, "L'Adoption, une alternative méconnue à l'avortement," *Etudes*, May 1973, pp. 701–14; A. Théry, "L'Avortement dans la législation française," *Esprit et vie* 83 (1973) 293–95; Michael Alsopp, "Abortion—the Theological Argument," *Furrow* 24 (1973) 202–6; Stefano Tumbas, S.J., "Ci sarà anche un aborto 'cattolico'?" *Palestra del clero* 52 (1973) 662–71.

CURRENT THEOLOGY: 1975

NOTES ON MORAL THEOLOGY: APRIL–SEPTEMBER 1974

The present survey will restrict itself to the following areas of moral concern: (1) the state of moral theology; (2) the understanding of moral norms; (3) divorce and remarriage; (4) questions in bioethics.

THE STATE OF MORAL THEOLOGY

Several areas of moral theology that have been the subject of discussion over the past years continue to receive attention. Just two examples: the specificity of Christian morality;[1] and the political mission of the Church and the Christian.[2] Furthermore, a new and important journal, *The Journal of Religious Ethics*, has made its appearance.[3] The stature of the editors and the quality of the articles published thus far are most promising. *Chicago Studies* has devoted an entire issue to a catechetical (question-answer format) summary of some key areas of Christian morality.[4] In addition to this mass of material, important individual statements on a variety of special moral questions have been published in the past few months.[5] Several well-known theologians have

[1] Michael Simpson, "A Christian Basis for Ethics?" *Heythrop Journal* 15 (1974) 285–97; Norbert Rigali, "The Meaning of Freedom: Dialogue with John Giles Milhaven," *Homiletic and Pastoral Review* 74 (1974) 61–68; Jordan Bishop, "Anthropology and Ethics: The Thomist Vision," *New Blackfriars* 55 (1974) 248–53; G. de Finance, "Morale e religione," *Rassegna di teologia* 15 (1974) 161–73; Ph. Delhaye, "S. Thomas, témoin de la morale chrétienne," *Revue théologique de Louvain* 5 (1974) 137–69; Eduardo Lopez Azpitarte, "El hombre como tarea y base de la moral," *Sal terrae* 64 (1974) 355–65; R. A. Iannarone, O.P., "Si può ancora parlare di una 'dottrina sociale' cattolica?" *Sapienza* 27 (1974) 159–75; Teodoro Lopez, "La existencia de una moral cristiana específica: Su fundamentación en Santo Tomás," *Scripta theologica* 6 (1974) 239–71; G. B. Sala, "L'Etica cristiana s'interroga sulla propria identità," *Scuola cattolica* 102 (1974) 24–49; Felix Gils, "Foi et morale chez saint Paul," *Spiritus* 15 (1974) 63–74; Hans Rotter, S.J., "Kann das Naturrecht die Moraltheologie entbehren?" *Zeitschrift für katholische Theologie* 96 (1974) 76–96; J. Fuchs, S.J., "Esiste una morale non-cristiana?" *Rassegna di teologia* 14 (1973) 361–73.

[2] Dana W. Wilbanks, "The Church and Social Responsibility: Where Do We Go from Here?" *Christian Century* 91 (1974) 363–66; A. Tillet, "Chrétiens et églises dans la vie politique," *Esprit et vie* 84 (1974) 417–29; Pierre Le Fort, "La responsabilité politique de l'église d'après les épîtres pastorales," *Etudes théologiques et religieuses* 49 (1974) 1–14.

[3] *Journal of Religious Ethics*, CSR Executive Office, Waterloo Lutheran University, Waterloo, Ontario, Canada N2L 3C5. The editor is Charles Reynolds; associate editors are Arthur Dyck, Frederick Carney, and Roland Delattre.

[4] "An American Catechism. Part II: Moral," *Chicago Studies* 13 (1974) 229–350. Authors of the articles are John F. Dedek, Norbert Rigali, Cornelius J. van der Poel, Charles E. Curran, Bernard Häring, Joseph J. Farraher, J. Bryan Hehir, Thomas F. Sullivan, and Richard A. McCormick.

[5] *Principles to Guide Confessors in Questions of Homosexuality* (National Conference of

published new volumes of essays.[6]

This proliferation of moral writing could lead one to the conclusion that things were never better in moral theology. But if scientific interest is high, it is accompanied by an uneasy sense of confusion and crisis. Watergate is seen as the practical working-out of Fletcherian situationalism.[7] What Jacques Leclercq stated some twenty years ago about Christian morality strikes many as pervasively true today.[8] Gustave Ermecke, for example, feels the matter has assumed crisis proportions.[9] But his essay appears, in too many places, to confuse a moral crisis with certain disagreements with his own formulations. Thus the essay is too often an example of parenesis rather than analysis.

Nevertheless there are many who believe we are faced with a genuine moral crisis. Thomas Dubay, S.M., may serve as the vehicle for this discussion. Writing in this journal in 1973, Charles Curran attempted a survey of the status of moral theology in the Catholic community.[10] It was, by and large, an optimistic report. Dubay does not share Curran's optimism.[11] Indeed, he believes that Curran's study, for all its knowledge of the trees, misses the major outlines of the forest. And the forest Dubay sees as dark and foreboding.

Since Dubay's response appeared in these pages, it will be unnecessary to detail its contents. His major concerns, I think it fair to say, were the following: a contradictory and destructive pluralism inconsistent with the magisterium's notion of pluralism; the disappearance of the prophetic element in moral theology for an unevangelical ethics of accommodation to the expectations of the majority; the inadmissible appearance of two magisteria in the Church (theologians, hierarchy); the failure of

---

Catholic Bishops, 1973); *Declaration on Procured Abortion* (Sacred Congregation for the Doctrine of the Faith). At this time the text of this latter document is available in full only through wire-service releases etc.

[6] For instance, James M. Gustafson, *Theology and Christian Ethics* (Philadelphia: United Church Press, 1974); Charles E. Curran, *New Perspectives in Moral Theology* (Notre Dame: Fides, 1974); Bruno Schüller, *Die Bergründung sittlicher Urteile* (Düsseldorf: Patmos, 1973); Stanley Hauerwas, *Vision and Virtue* (Notre Dame: Fides, 1974). This is but a sampling, but apologies are due to those authors whose names have been omitted from this sampling.

[7] Erwin W. Lutzer, "Watergate Ethics," *Christianity Today* 18 (1974) 26–27.

[8] "Im Unterricht in der Moral und in der sittlichen Bildung liegt in unseren Tagen das vielleicht heikelste Problem der Kirche" (Jacques Leclercq, *Christliche Moral in der Zeit* [Einsiedeln, 1954] p. 10).

[9] Gustav Ermecke, "Krise der Moral—Krise der Moraltheologie," *Theologie und Glaube* 64 (1974) 338–56.

[10] Charles E. Curran, "Present State of Moral Theology," THEOLOGICAL STUDIES 34 (1973) 446–67.

[11] Thomas Dubay, S.M., "The State of Moral Theology," THEOLOGICAL STUDIES 35 (1974) 482–506.

moral theology to include in its concerns the ascetic and spiritual dimensions of Christian living. In the course of developing these objections against Curran—and to some extent against a large segment of the community of moral theologians—Dubay touches on a whole series of delicate and difficult theological themes: dissent in the Church, the existence of moral absolutes, the formation of conscience, etc.

I am glad Dubay composed his thoughtful critique and that THEOLOGI-CAL STUDIES published it. Moral theology does need criticism from outside its own ranks. Furthermore, and more importantly, Dubay has formulated his objections in a way that represents the attitudes and theological presuppositions of very many concerned and intelligent thinkers, Catholic and non-Catholic. Therefore the attempt to bring these issues into sharper focus at some length may throw light on matters that are a cause of concern and even division in the contemporary Church. Dubay has raised some very good questions. For instance, his insistence that the notion of *sensus fidelium* be made more precise is altogether salutary. However, I have very serious reservations about several of the substantial points in his study. The following remarks may be organized under three titles: pluralism, theologians and the magisterium, prophecy.

Pluralism

Dubay has some important things to say here. One certainly is the distinction between complementary and contradictory pluralism. The latter, which he attributes to Curran, he regards as inconsistent with scriptural insistence on unity, destructive of practical pastoral guidance, and deadening to the Church's commission to speak out authoritatively on important moral matters.

For instance, where unity is concerned Dubay writes: "Not by the widest stretch of imagination could we call that ecclesial community 'completely one' [Jn 17:23] if in it some members are at odds habitually and in important moral and disciplinary matters with those whose duty it is to articulate the faith and morals for and to the community. A pluralism in moral theology that fails to reckon with this New Testament insistence is failing to reckon with its sources."[12] Or again, with a contradictory pluralism "a secure knowledge of the moral implications of many acts becomes impossible."

Dubay is looking for unity in "important moral and disciplinary matters," a unity based on "a secure knowledge of the moral implications of many acts ...." Here I believe we must ask, what are these "important moral and diciplinary matters," what are these "basic matters or norms" confused by a contradictory pluralism? Are they

---

[12] *Ibid*. p. 486.

rather detailed and concrete conclusions representing the application of moral general norms? Or are they the more general norms themselves? His terminology ("basic matters or norms") suggests the latter, but I suspect he really is looking for unity and security at the level of application; for he speaks of "a secure knowledge of the moral implications *of many acts* ...." So, how basic is basic?

Here three points. First, a past tradition easily led us to believe that "basic" had to do with matters such as self-stimulation for sperm-testing, removal of ectopic fetuses, actions that are *per se graviter excitantes*, co-operation in contraception, punitive sterilization, and a host of very concrete applications. We felt we ought to possess and did possess a kind of certainty and subsequent security in these matters, and that our certainty was founded on the natural law. These, I submit, are not "basic matters or norms," if by this term is meant material on which we must agree if our Christian unity is to remain integral. There is plenty of room for doubt and hesitation and change, even contradictory pluralism, at this level of moral discourse. And yet, because the magisterium did get involved in such detailed practical applications in the past (e.g., the moral allocutions of Pius XII, responses of the Holy Office), and in a way that was authoritative, it gave credence to the notion that our moral unity is or ought to be located at this level, and that disagreement or pluralism at this level is a threat to unity. It is unclear to me whether Dubay is insisting on unity at this level. But there are certainly many who are so insisting and who will use Dubay and the biblical texts he cites to support the necessity of such unity. If it is unity at this level that Dubay has in mind as necessary when he says "'In my opinion' is hardly going to be prophetic," it must be urged that the best way to eviscerate true prophecy is to attempt to be prophetic in areas where true prophecy cannot be objectively founded and persuasively argued.

Second, in the contemporary world we are faced with a great number of truly new moral problems. The scope and many-sidedness of these problems means that we must struggle our way through to new insights and a new vocabulary capable of conceptualizing new data within the value perceptions and commitments of the Christian tradition. To approach this task with an overriding concern for unity and a corresponding intolerance of pluralism is in some sense to suppose that we already have the answers. In other words, in many areas of contemporary moral concern unity is not a present possession but a difficult, often elusive, perhaps impossible goal.

Third, Vatican II reinserted the Church into the world, into history, and into Christendom, as the eminent editor of this journal is fond of saying. This insertion calls necessarily for a rethinking of certain moral formulations and pastoral practices. A process of rethinking, because it is in human hands, is precisely a process—often halting, painful, imperfect. It requires a tolerance for the tentative and ambiguous. Many persons in the Church experience this as "confusion" because there has been very little in our past ways of doing things that educates to this tolerance.

Theologians Versus the Magisterium

This theme runs throughout Dubay's study. Only a few of the more important items can be raised here. First, he criticizes Curran for supporting a right to frequent and habitual dissent from authentic, noninfallible teaching. Dubay argues that this equivalently establishes two magisteria in the Church. I agree with this, but much more needs to be said. I have always been uncomfortable with the term "right to dissent." We are concerned, as believers, with the behavioral implications of our being-in-Christ, with moral truth. The magisterium is a vehicle for this purpose and therefore subordinated to it. To isolate this vehicle from other sources of reflection and knowledge in the Church is to forget this purpose, to subordinate the vehicle to superior-subject relationships, and thus to juridicize the search for truth. To speak of a "right to dissent" tends to accept this juridical narrowing by establishing rights against the teacher or his authoritative teaching. Therefore it would be much better, I believe, to speak of a duty and right to excercise a truly personal reflection within the teaching-learning process of the Church, a duty and right that belong to all who possess proportionate competence. Bishops, as well as theologicans, are not exempt from this arduous task. To reduce this duty to "supporting Rome," "being loyal to the Holy Father," is both to misconceive loyalty and to undermine the magisterium.

This personal reflection can end in inability to assent to the formulations of the magisterium, as any number of episcopal conferences have pointed out. How frequent and habitual this might be depends on several factors. First, if the magisterium is functioning in a healthy manner, such dissent ought to be relatively rare, a point made convincingly by Schüller.[13] Otherwise it would cease to be authoritative in any theologically acceptable sense of the word. Second, the notions of "difference" and "dissent" demand a distinction, clearly made by Pope John XXIII and Vatican II, between the substance of a teaching and its formulation. Dissent with regard to substance will be a rare phenomenon, though it might occur with regard to formulation somewhat more frequently. For instance, the substance of the Church's teaching on abortion is one thing;

[13] Bruno Schüller, "Bemerkungen zur authentischen Verkündigung des kirchlichen Lehramtes," *Theologie und Philosophie* 42 (1967) 534–51. Cf. also *Theology Digest* 16 (1968) 328–32.

its formulation by Pius XI and Pius XII or even the Sacred Congregation for the Doctrine of the Faith is not necessarily identical with that substance (e.g., where the life of the mother is at stake). Finally, how much qualification and dissent is present will likely depend on how detailed the documents of the magisterium become. There has been a real difference here in recent pontificates. Pius XII, in his many allocutions and discourses, went into some very detailed applications of medical ethics; this has not been the style of Pope John XXIII or Pope Paul VI. Indeed there are many theologians who believe that the detailed application of perennially valid moral principles should generally not be the concern of the magisterium, or that if the magisterium chooses to undertake this, it must do so with a tentativeness proportionate to the contingency of the material.

But Dubay's concern with the existence of two magisteria needs yet further comment. Speaking of the prophet as one who is sent, Dubay notes that a Catholic theologian is always sent, if not by diocesan faculties, then "at least through being in communion with the bishop and through the bishop with the Holy See." He then adds that "insofar as theologians are at odds with the sending magisterium, they are not sent." Being at odds with the magisterium, they constitute a second magisterium, a notion Dubay rejects.

I do too, but I believe he has not explored the possibility of a third alternative. If the magisterium can *per accidens* err in its authentic, noninfallible teaching (and it can), and if such error is detectable by someone other than the magisterium (and it could be), then it is clear that others in the Church do participate in the teaching-learning process of the Church without thereby becoming a second, competitive magisterium. By framing the matter as he has (either the hierarchical magisterium or the magisterium of dissenting theologians), Dubay has fragmented the teaching-learning process in the Church into camps of competitive interests and prerogatives. That is improper. We all have a part to play in a healthily functioning magisterium, and to view that part—even and especially when it takes the form of dissent—as a second and competitive magisterium, is to fail to see the teaching-learning function of the Church in appropriately processive and co-operative terms. It is to see one group in the Church in prior and independent possession of the truth. One need not hold that notion to treasure and support a genuinely authoritative teaching office in the Church and to locate that office in the person of the pope and the bishops in communion with the pope. For this reason I think it is simply false to say that theologians who disagree with the magisterium on a particular point "are not sent." They are honestly, even if very noninfallibly, making their contribution to the teaching-learning process of the Church. And that is their proper task, that for which they "are sent." In this sense there are indeed two magisteria in the Church, but two that have different if not unrelated functions. When these two functions are confused and identified and the magisterium seen in either-or terms (either bishops or theologians), the response should not be denial of one magisterium, but a clarification of both.

Prophecy

My most serious reservations on Dubay's study are in this area. First, in discussing theologians who have found themselves in a position of dissent, Dubay uses phrases such as "tailoring ethics to the expectations of majorities," "theologians who seem to begin with 'what modern man will accept,'" "the curious assumption . . . that Christian ethics should be acceptable to the majority." This Dubay sees as unworthy of the true prophet.

Since the theologian is human, there is always the danger that such tailoring will occur. But that being admitted, one could wish that such phrases with their motivational overtones would disappear from serious theological discourse. This or that theologian may be wrong—and the better the theologian he is, the more ready he is to admit this. But it is precisely rightness or wrongness that is his concern and should be the issue, not attitudes of accommodation and compromise alleged to be his point of departure by those who disagree with him.

Second, Dubay contrasts "prophetic" with "conformism." "The prophet of the Lord is never a slave to popularity or style." True enough. But there is a hidden and, I believe, false argument buried in such statements. It is this: all that is difficult is right; all that is not is conformism.

Third—and very similar to the above—Dubay, in speaking of moral prophecy, makes it appear that the more alone, isolated, and rejected a position, the more prophetic and true it is. Here great caution is required. Prophetic statements and actions, it is true, are often lonely ones. But the fact that prophetic statements are countercultural does not guarantee that every countercultural statement is truly prophetic.

Fourth, Dubay repeatedly warns that the prophet (i.e., prophetic theologian) is faithful to the gospel. "The full gospel has never been popular." He cites Stöger: "He who tampers with the teaching of Christ condemns himself." In the context of the discussion, one must wonder what Dubay has in mind. Disagreements on things like contraception, masturbation, direct-indirect killing, artificial insemination, sterilization, pastoral policies for homosexual problems are the areas of liveliest disagreement cited by Dubay. But if the gospel dictates one particular answer to these problems, I am not familiar with such an answer. Thus to face these problems with appeals to the uncompromising and prophetic demands of the gospel is either to suggest that the gospel answers these questions or is overkill. In these areas the gospel informs reasoning processes; it does not replace them. Therefore in all of the above points Dubay seems guilty of *ignorantia elenchi*; he misses the point.

Fifth, Dubay insists that the prophet (and the prophetic theologian) proclaims absolute precepts. Hence theologians who question these absolutes are departing from the gospel and abandoning their own prophetic responsibility. In developing this, he states that "Scripture takes absolute moral norms for granted" and "there are so many absolutely worded precepts in both Testaments that I shall not mention one." He cites and supports Bright's study on apodictic prohibitions that bind always and everywhere. His conclusion: "It seems to me that the alternative to an ethics with some apodictic teaching is an ethics of exhortation."[14]

It would have been well if Dubay had become specific here, for the term "absolute" is treacherous when applied to biblical or any morality.[15] For instance, when speaking of "absolute moral norms," does one mean formal (e.g., never act unjustly) or material norms (e.g., never tell a falsehood)? Put somewhat differently, in discussing norms we must be careful to distinguish between parenetic discourse and explanatory discourse or moral reasoning.[16] Explanatory discourse deals with the pros and cons of a position, with argumentation, with the normative validity of a precept. Parenetic discourse is not concerned with the normative validity of a moral command. Such validity is taken for granted and then the precept is used to pass judgment on a person's behavior. A good instance is the Johannine pericope on the woman taken in adultery. The question is not whether adultery is right or wrong; all the participants agree that it is wrong. The validity of the command is acknowledged. The only question is whether the woman has committed the act and what should be done.

Thus parenetic discourse makes use of rules to accuse, convict, condemn, urge repentance. Positively, rules are used to praise, advise, implore, encourage, strengthen. Such discourse can succeed only if genuine agreement exists on what is right or wrong.

Because parenesis supposes agreement on what is morally obligatory

---

[14] *Art. cit.*, p. 504.

[15] There is a sense, for instance, in which every moral norm is "absolute." That is, it is absolute because it imposes a categorical imperative in contrast to a mere prudential suggestion.

[16] I owe these remarks to Bruno Schüller's lectures at the Gregorian University in 1973. For some helpful remarks on parenesis cf. Norman Perrin, *The New Testament—An Introduction* (New York: Harcourt Brace Jovanovich, 1974) pp. 20–21.

and what is not, its language can be very concise and clipped. For instance, in the commands "You shall not kill. Neither shall you commit adultery. Neither shall you steal" (Dt 5:17-19), the words "kill," "adultery," "steal" contain compressed and complicated value judgments. "Killing" (or better, "murder") must be defined in terms of what killing was regarded as morally licit by Israel. Similarly, "adultery" is understood only if one first understands the institution of marriage that prevailed in Israel. For example, a husband having intercourse with an unmarried woman was not considered an adulterer.[17]

Now the Decalogue presumes that all these matters are settled and contents itself with uttering the words "kill," "adultery," "steal," etc. Thus the emphasis falls on the "You shall not," an emphasis highlighting the absolute, unconditional character of the precept. But this absoluteness is that of parenetic discourse. It does not convey information about the specific content of various moral demands. That it takes for granted.

The upshot of these remarks is that Dubay's opposition between absolutes (apodictic teaching) and exhortation is a false opposition; for the precepts of biblical morality are themselves heavily parenetic—hortatory to what is presumed to be known and agreed on. One can hardly use their absolute and unconditional character to discredit the contemporary discussion of absolute moral norms; for this discussion is concerned precisely about what ought to count as "murder," "theft," "unchastity," etc., about what is the content of parenetic discourse. It is a discussion within the area of *moral reasoning*. So when Dubay says "When an ethics knows only a contradictory pluralism and/or a whole series of 'maybes,' it ceases to be interesting. It becomes quite unlike biblical morality...,"[18] he is identifying and therefore confusing in the term "ethics" two forms of discourse, parenesis and moral reasoning.

THE UNDERSTANDING OF MORAL NORMS

In 1971 Joseph Fuchs, S.J., published his important essay on the absoluteness of moral terms.[19] In this study Fuchs concluded that theoretically speaking "there can be no universal norms of *behavior* in the strict sense of '*intrinsece malum*.'" He concluded this on a twofold basis: (1) an action "cannot be judged morally at all, considered purely in itself, but only together with all the 'circumstances' and the 'intention'"; (2) we cannot foresee adequately all the possible combina-

---

[17] Dubay's rather sweeping statement about extramarital sex is, I believe, in error. He writes: "It [an ethics without absolutes] becomes quite unlike St. Paul, who terms extramarital relations fornication or adultery..." (p. 504). Cf. Bruce Malina, "Does *porneia* Mean Fornication?" *Novum Testamentum* 14 (1972) 10-17.

[18] *Art. cit.*, p. 504.

[19] Joseph Fuchs, S.J., "The Absoluteness of Moral Terms," *Gregorianum* 52 (1971) 415-58.

tions of circumstances and intention. Practically, however, there can be norms stated as universals "to which we cannot conceive of any kind of exception."

Gustav Ermecke has made Fuchs's careful study the object of a rather free-swinging theological attack.[20] Asserting that Fuchs's essay touches on most of the crucial-points in moral reasoning, Ermecke lays out his own understanding of these points. For instance: there is a distinction between the unchangeable essence and core of man and his changeable incarnations; all norms are determined by the *humanum*; precisely because all men are men, there must be norms valid for all; never must man act contrary to his being as man; and so on. Such statements are footnoted by references to Fuchs's study, references in which Ermecke systematically associates Fuchs with a whole litany of errors and misunderstandings that either are or lead to pragmatism, positivism, functionalism, relativism, and a nominalism that is not all that far removed from heresy. Ermecke asserts that the stimulus behind Fuchs's study is the desire to legitimate certain changes in sexual morality. Therefore he refers to Fuchs's assertions as "*ad hoc* theories."

For instance, Fuchs had written that "the critical question, then, is not one of relativism but of objectivity, or the 'truth' of the action which must be in conformity with the whole concrete reality of man (of society)."[21] Of this Ermecke states: "What J.F. indicates here unavoidably approaches, in my judgment, relativism." Similarly, Fuchs had stated: "1) An action cannot be judged morally in its materiality (killing, wounding, going to the moon) without reference to the intention of the agent; without this we are not dealing with a human action, and only with respect to a human action may one say in a true sense whether it is morally good or bad; 2) the evil (in a premoral sense) affected by a human agent must not be intended as such, and must be justified in terms of the totality of the action by appropriate reasons." Ermecke brands this as "dangerous relativism."[22] Finally, Fuchs had written: "On the other hand, if there is question only of evil in the *pre*moral sense, such as death, wounding, dishonor, etc., the intention and the realization of a good can possibly justify the doing of an evil."[23] Ermecke rejects this as simply false, because when there is question of a freely caused evil, it is evil in a moral sense.

Behind many of Ermecke's criticisms of Fuchs stands a single dis-

[20] Gustav Ermecke, "Das Problem der Universalität oder Allgemeingültigkeit sittlicher Normen innerweltlicher Lebensgestaltung," *Münchener theologische Zeitschrift* 24 (1973) 1–24.

[21] *Art. cit.*, p. 439.

[22] *Art. cit.*, p. 19, n. 44.

[23] *Art. cit.*, p. 446.

agreement, a point hinted at by Ermecke himself.[24] It has to do with the *fontes moralitatis*. Ermecke feels that Fuchs has moved the emphasis away from the object to put more on the intention and circumstances. If the moral quality of the action is determined ultimately by the intention alone (Ermecke says: "eine letzlich *allein* entscheidende Bedeutung ..."), then clearly we have moral relativism in Ermecke's judgment, because intentions of individuals vary limitlessly. And this variation makes universally valid moral norms impossible. Against this Ermecke argues that the action has its own inner sense or intentionality, what traditional theology refers to as the object of the act. For this reason he asks: "How will one judge a concrete action other than according to the fonts of morality, among which there is in the first place the object, then the circumstances, finally the intention?"

Fuchs, somewhat perplexed and, I suspect, slightly aghast, responded to this vigorous and far-reaching attack with several clarifications.[25] First, Ermecke has misrepresented and falsified Fuchs's basic theses. Second, Ermecke's very general statements—which few would care to deny—simply do not come to terms with the true problematic of contemporary moral writing, nor with Fuchs's nuancing of traditional categories. Fuchs then painstakingly repeats his contention that a final moral judgment can be made only of the total concrete action, not of the individual components in isolation. Thus, when Ermecke talks about the inner sense ("metaphysicher Sinngehalt") of the action and states that this determines the morality of the action, Fuchs insists that this must be understood of the whole action, not simply of a single aspect; for it is the whole action, with circumstances and intention, that is the object of one's free choice.

Fuchs shrewdly notes that Ermecke accepts the principle that a lesser or less urgent value may be sacrificed for a higher or more urgent one. Thus, Ermecke agrees that not every killing is murder, not every taking of another's property is theft. This means that the inner sense and hence the moral judgment of killing and appropriation of another's property is drawn not simply from these factors alone—as object—but from additional elements of the whole action. Fuchs wonders why Ermecke is unwilling to apply this in other areas such as contraceptive behavior.

Fuchs flatly denies Ermecke's contention that he is putting heavier accent on the intention and circumstances, and above all that he is allowing to the intention *alone* a determining influence. He is insisting only that it is the entire action that is the basis for ethical judgment. This is not to give greater emphasis to circumstances and intention. Rather it

[24] *Art. cit.*, n. 31.

[25] Joseph Fuchs, S.J., "Sittliche Normen—Universalien und Generalisierungen," *Münchener theologische Zeitschrift* 25 (1974) 18–33.

is to assert that the object (as traditionally understood) is *never realized as such* but only as a whole. Since it is the whole action (including circumstances and intention) that is to be judged, and since concrete (Fuchs calls them "concrete-operative") norms cannot envisage and include all possible combinations of these factors, these norms have their limits. They are generalizations that hold most of the time (*valent ut in pluribus*).

In this rather remarkable exchange I agree with Fuchs. Ermecke has misinterpreted Fuchs and "responded" with a series of generalizations that simply bypass the problem raised by the eminent Roman moralist. What is at the heart of the discussion is the interpretation of the traditional *fontes moralitatis*. Ermecke contends in effect that prior to a consideration of the intention and circumstances the object has an inner sense and hence a decisive determining influence on the morality of the action—an influence, it is important to note, that resists specification by the intention and circumstances. In contrast to this, he accuses Fuchs —erroneously—of giving decisive determining influence to the intention *alone*. Fuchs does not do his. Indeed, if the intention were the only determinant of meaning, it is difficult to see how Fuchs could refer, as he does, to premoral *evil* in the object. Furthermore, Fuchs repeatedly insists that the premoral evil within the entire action must be proportionately grounded. If the intention alone had decisive influence, then any good intention would justify the causing or permitting of any disvalues. There is nothing in Fuchs that would lead to this conclusion. Rather Fuchs is insisting that the disvalues present in our conduct at times cannot receive an ultimate moral assessment until the action as a whole is weighed. In this I believe he is absolutely correct.

What, then, has Fuchs done? What nuancing has he brought to the traditional understanding of the *fontes moralitatis*? It seems to me that he has equivalently denied that the object can be an independent source of the moral quality of the action—independent, that is, of the intention and circumstances. In this sense, he has tightened the relationship between the traditional object-end-circumstances and argued that it is only the combination of the three that yields the total object of choice. The good intended in one's choice specifies the object without smothering it out of existence, and thus in a sense becomes an integral part of the total object. Manualist usage (e.g., Ermecke), though not the over-all tradition, attributed a moral quality to the object independently of the whole action, and a moral quality that at times would be uninfluenced by circumstances, including the end. Fuchs is arguing that we cannot cut up the action so finely and sharply, and that any element of the total act (whether object, end, or circumstance) remains abstract and therefore premoral when taken in separation from the other elements.

Two points. First, why did some within traditional usage treat the object as an independent source of the moral quality of the act? I suspect it was because frequently enough they smuggled the intention (or some circumstance) into the very description of the object. Take the case of one who takes food from another in order to save his own life. What is the object here? There are two possible descriptions: (1) taking another's food (property); (2) taking another's food in order to save one's life. Traditional usage equivalently used the second alternative to describe the object, for it defined theft as "taking another's property against the owner's reasonable will." But this definition obviously includes the intention and circumstances in a general way. Therefore a rather full moral quality could be attributed to the object so defined. In other words, what was included in the object or excluded from it depended on what one wanted to condemn or approve.[26]

Second, if it is only object-end-circumstances together that can yield a final moral evaluation, the implication is that it is a proportion within the entire action between the values and disvalues that justifies the causing or permitting of the disvalues. Thus, it is "saving one's life" that justifies "the taking of another's food (property)." It is precisely this emphasis on over-all proportion that Fuchs's study highlights. In this light it is not morally wrong to kill an innocent person directly regardless of the reason, but because the reasons we might have are, all things considered, disproportionate within the whole action.

It is the matter of proportion that Louis Janssens emphasizes in an important recent study on moral norms not previously reported in these pages.[27] Janssens first analyzes the Thomistic notion of the human act and points out that Thomas never abandoned the position that the inner act of the will must be considered the starting point. With this as the starting point, Thomas stresses that it is the end of the inner act of the will that determines the concrete structure of the action. *Finis dat speciem in moralibus.*

However, the human act is not simply the intent (*intentio*) of an end or goal. It also includes the choice (*electio*) of means. But the will of the end and the choice of means constitute only one act of the will, but an act that is a composite act. Since the human act is not restricted to the inner act of the will but also involves an exterior event or act, how is the inner act of the will related structurally to the external act? Janssens notes that for Thomas "the end which is the proper object of the inner act of the will is the formal element; the exterior act, as means to this end, is

[26] Cf. John R. Connery, S.J., "Notes on Moral Theology," THEOLOGICAL STUDIES 20 (1959) 591-92.

[27] Louis Janssens, "Ontic Evil and Moral Evil," *Louvain Studies* 4 (1972) 115-56.

the material element of the very same human act."[28]

He then turns to the morality of the human action. Just as the inner act of the will (end) and the exterior act (means) are one and the same concrete act, so it is with the morality of the action.[29] Janssens notes: "For this reason he [Thomas] reacts sharply against those who are of the opinion that the material event of an act can be evaluated morally without consideration of the subject, of the inner act of the will or of the end . . . . This object-event becomes a concrete *human* act only insofar as it is directed towards an end within the inner act of the will. Only this concrete totality has a moral meaning." This is the same point Fuchs correctly urged against Ermecke. Clearly, then, acts that have the same features as object-events can have a different morality "determined by the kind of end of the *will* towards which the matter-event has been directed."

After showing that the end is the formal element that specifies the morality of the action, and that the object-event (external act) is the material element, Janssens argues that Thomas insisted that "not any kind of exterior action, however, can become the material element of a morally good end." It must be material "apt" to this end. Since the exterior action is related as means to the inner act of the will (end), it must be adequately proportionate to this end. When it is, it participates in the moral goodness of the end. When is it "adequately proportionate" to the good end according to human reason? The answer given by Janssens: when there is no contradiction between the material (means) and formal (end) elements of the act. He puts it as follows: "Put into terms of the philosophy of values, this means that the means must be consistent with the value of the end. Or, according to a more abstract formulation, the principle which has been affirmed in the end must not be negated by the means."[30]

Janssens illustrates this by several examples of actions involving what he calls "ontic evil" (Fuchs's "premoral evil," Schüller's "nonmoral evil," the manuals' "physical evil"): self-defense, taking another's property. Not every taking of another's property is theft, but only that which undermines the very value of private property. Not every false statement is a lie, but only that which corrodes the meaning and purpose of human speech. Thus, when the means involving ontic evil is not proportionate, the ontic evil itself becomes the object of the will and is intended. But this may never be, since it vitiates the action.

[28] "Finis autem comparatur ad id quod ordinatur ad finem, sicut forma ad materiam" (1/2, q. 1, a. 4).

[29] "Actus interior et exterior sunt diversi secundum genus naturae. Sed tamen, ex eis sic diversis constituitur unum in genere moris" (1/2, q. 20, a. 3, ad 1m).

[30] *Art. cit.*, p. 142.

It is here that Janssens explains his notion of intending and not intending the ontic evil. He states: "Ontic evil should never be the end of the inner act of the will *if by end is meant that which definitively and in the full sense of the word puts an end to the activity of the subject.*"[31] Or again, it can be right to intend an ontic evil, to make it the end of one's inner act of the will, "if that end is not willed as a final end, but only as a *finis medius et proximus* to a higher end."[32] This is, in my judgment, identical with intending an ontic evil *in se sed non propter se.*

It is interesting to note how Janssens applies this to marital sexuality:

According to *Gaudium et spes* the marriage act must be ordered to conjugal love and to the human transmission of life, viz., to responsible parenthood. This must be the end of marital intercourse; each conjugal act must include a'*debita proportio* to this end. Consequently, if the marriage partners engage in sexual intercourse during the fertile period and thereby most likely will conceive new life, the marital act may not be morally justifiable when they foresee that they will not have the means to provide the proper education for the child. The rhythm method, too, can be immoral if it is used to prevent the measure of responsible parenthood. But the use of contraceptives can be morally justified if these means do not obstruct the partners in the expression of conjugal love and if they keep birth control within the limits of responsible parenthood.[33]

In summary, then, Janssens with Fuchs is arguing that it is impossible to pronounce a final moral judgment on an exterior action containing ontic evil (e.g., a killing, falsehood, contraception) without attending to the end of the inner act of the will. For a true moral evaluation, two things must be considered: (1) the end of the agent, the moral goodness or badness of the end; (2) the *debita proportio* of the external action to the end. Because the action in its entirety must be evaluated morally, Janssens concludes, exactly as does Fuchs, that concrete moral norms (generalizations about such actions) *valent ut in pluribus.* They forbid only that ontic evil which exceeds the boundaries of the measure of means to the realization of good ends.

Janssens' study puts him unmistakably in the camp of Knauer, Schüller, Fuchs, and others who have attempted—successfully in my judgment—to re-examine and nuance the meaning of concrete moral norms.

For some years the compositor of these "Notes" has been struggling with this problem. I have learned much from Knauer, Schüller, Fuchs, and Janssens, as well as from those who disagree with these authors, e.g., Germain Grisez. I find myself at home with the conceptual directions

[31] *Ibid.*, p. 141 (emphasis added).
[32] *Ibid.*, p. 141.
[33] *Ibid.*, pp. 143–44.

being taken by Knauer, Schüller, Fuchs, Janssens, and others. In an attempt to avoid the misunderstandings too easily associated with the terms *finis operis, finis operantis* (misunderstandings laid bare very neatly by Janssens), I have repeatedly turned to the notion of the significance or meaning of an action as that which generates concrete moral norms and contains the seed of their limitations. In an interesting and thoughtful study, David Blanchfield passes these efforts in review.[34] Accepting the methodology as "basically sound," he suggests that it must be more flexible than I have allowed. This greater flexibility would allow the intention to "enter much more into the formulating of significance and meaning," but within limits. Blanchfield states the limits as follows: "the intention may not determine the significance when it would involve violating an absolute value."

Thus Blanchfield argues, in the now classic case of Mrs. Bergmeier (Soviet prison, away from family, etc.), the attempted pregnancy could be allowed under two conditions: (1) the absolute value of the welfare of the resultant child be protected; (2) the absolute value of the warden's dignity not be violated.

I fully accept Blanchfield's suggestion that the intention must have its appropriate place in the determination of over-all significance. This is what both Fuchs and Janssens argue. However, I wonder if Blanchfield has formulated the matter well.[35] He argues that the intention should enter much more into the formulation of significance, except when it would involve violating an absolute value.

Three points. First, if the intention ought to function in determining significance, it must function in the assessment of all actions. Therefore the question is not whether the intention may be allowed to function or not where certain values are involved, but whether the significance of the whole action (the intention having its appropriate function in determining this significance) involves an inner contradiction, a lack of *debita proportio* (Janssens) or proportionate grounding (Fuchs).

Second, I believe Blanchfield's emphasis on absolute values could easily be misplaced. It would seem that it is a disproportion between the exterior action (means) and *any* value (end) that renders an action involving premoral or ontic evil morally wrong.

Third, even when the intention has been granted its proper place in determining over-all meaning, it is far from clear how this would necessarily decide the Bergmeier case in the direction of Blanchfield's solution; for *debita proportio* within the action must consider all the

[34] David W. Blanchfield, "Methodology and McCormick," *American Ecclesiastical Review* 68 (1974) 372-89.
[35] This is undoubtedly due to the constraints imposed upon him by the unlikely subject he chose as the focus of his study!

values and disvalues. It might come out on Blanchfield's side, but it might not. After these footnotes on Blanchfield's study, I should add that the essay is helpful and—which is hardly to the point—flattering.

John R. Connery, S.J., has reviewed the work of Fuchs, Schüller, Knauer, and others and related it to the whole utilitarian school of thought.[36] Since his study appeared in this review, it will suffice to recall a few of the highpoints of his critique. Basically Connery sees these authors as representing a form of consequentialism, "a moral system that makes the judgment of an act depend solely on its consequences." After exposing and criticizing in highly knowledgeable fashion the two prevailing forms of consequentialism (act-utilitarianism, rule-utilitarianism), Connery judges both as vulnerable to allowing acts that go against common convictions, especially convictions about justice. He then associates Knauer, Fuchs, and Schüller with rule-utilitarianism in the sense that "all rules are subject in one way or another to the principle of consequences." The basic problem he finds in this is that "it seems to call for, or at least allow, exceptions which go against commonly held convictions."

When faced with this problem, rule-utilitarianism appealed either to hidden effects or to long-range effects. Connery's explicit conclusion is: practically, so-called secondary rules are more reliable guidelines than "the principle of consequences." Theoretically, such rules "cannot be explained entirely in terms of consequences." His implicit conclusion is that the arguments of Fuchs, Schüller, and Knauer are vulnerable to these same challenges, i.e., those urged against utilitarianism.

Bruno Schüller presents a long and careful reaction to Connery's study.[37] He agrees with Connery that utilitarianism as a theory of moral norms is untenable, but he insists that no one should conclude from the contemporary critics of utilitarianism that traditional moral theology has found new allies in its defense of its deontological norms; for the very critics of utilitarianism reject (as "naturalistic fallacy") the way traditional theology defends as exceptionless the prohibitions against, for example, contraception and homologous artificial insemination. Rather, a philosopher such as H. J. McCloskey suggests that such norms are prima-facie duties (or conditioned norms) much as Peter Chirico and Denis Hurley had done earlier but in different language.[38] So one need

[36] John R. Connery, S.J., "Morality of Consequences: A Critical Appraisal," THEOLOGI-CAL STUDIES 34 (1973) 396–414.

[37] Bruno Schüller, S.J., "Neuere Beiträge zum Thema 'Begründung sittlicher Normen,'" *Theologische Berichte* 4 (Einsiedeln: Benziger, 1974) 109–81. Schüller's review includes much more than a response to Connery. It surveys and critiques much of the literature on this entire subject, e.g., Curran's principle of compromise and Hurley's principle of overriding right.

[38] Cf. Denis E. Hurley, O.M.I., "In Defense of the Principle of Overriding Right,"

not move to utilitarian theory to hold different conclusions than traditional theology held on these points. Indeed, one need not enter the larger theoretical discussion of moral norms at all to contest such conclusions.

However, Connery has made his argument against Schüller, Fuchs, and Knauer by appeal to the critics of utilitarianism and by use of the arguments they make. The argument in substance is this: teleological grounding of norms = reductively utilitarian theory = untenable, as the long discussion in Anglo-Saxon philosophical circles has shown.

Schüller brings several objections against this. First, he objects to forcing the discussion into the logically elegant division deontological-teleological as defined by C. D. Broad. Broad had defined teleological theories as those that determine the moral character of an action exclusively by its consequences. Deontological theories, by contrast, are those that claim there are actions that are morally wrong whatever the consequences. Schüller protests the apparent neatness of Broad's division. It simply overlooks the vast differences between those who regard themselves as deontologists. For instance, Kant and W. D. Ross are regarded as being in this category; but there is a chasm between them. Kant held that the duty not to speak falsehood is absolute; Ross holds it to be a prima-facie duty (bedingtes Erfüllungsgebot). What is it, then, that divides Kant, Fichte, and the Catholic tradition from Ross, McCloskey, and other critics of utilitarianism? Schüller's answer:

Only Kant, Fichte, and the Catholic tradition assert that there are actions that are morally wrong without any regard for their consequences. W. D. Ross and the modern critics of utilitarianism, on the contrary, assert that for the moral rightness of an action consequences always play a determining role, but not alone.... In this light, only Kant and the Catholic tradition, but not the modern critics of utilitarianism, know deontological norms as defined by C. D. Broad.[39]

So, by accepting Broad's definition of deontologist and teleologist, Connery has made it appear that all teleological tendencies conform to Broad's model, and therefore can be faced with the standard arguments brought against utilitarian theory. Schüller rejects this.

Second, with many critics of utilitarianism, Connery asserts that an action's moral rightness or wrongness cannot be determined by the amount of good it does. He uses the example of a person who promises money to a young man to cut his lawn. Should he give the young man the money? If *that* action is morally right which does more good, then he should give it only if he finds no better use for the money. This type of

---

THEOLOGICAL STUDIES 29 (1968) 301–9; Peter Chirico, S.S., "Morality in General and Birth Control in Particular," *Chicago Studies* 9 (1970) 19–33.

[39] *Art. cit.*, p. 177.

argument has led critics of utilitarianism to deny that only one principle determines the morality of any act. Thus Frankena calls for two principles: love (benevolence) and justice; David Lyons calls for three: love, justice, fairness. And so on.

Here Schüller says that the Christian theologian is perplexed by the notion of love implied in such fragmentation. "The Christian theologian who, under the influence of Romans 13:8-10, declares that love as benevolence and beneficence must be seen as the final criterion for the moral rightness of an action, does not understand under 'love' something next to justice and fairness. Rather he understands by this term the general root of all other particular principles." [40] It is a strange concept of love that has nothing to do with justice and fairness, as if these were separate and independent sources of moral rightness. Schüller accepts the identity of the principle of utility—when adequately understood —with love-as-beneficence.

Several examples are used by Connery and the critics of utilitarianism to show the impossibility of a teleological theory of norms. One concerns justice, the other fairness. Schüller speaks to both. The justice example is that of a sheriff in a Southern town faced with the alternatives in a rape case of framing a Negro suspect (whom he knows to be innocent) or carrying on a prolonged search for the real culprit. The immediate indictment and conviction of the suspect would save many lives and prevent other harmful consequences. If an action's moral rightness is determined solely by consequences, it is argued, the sheriff ought to frame the one innocent man—a conclusion that shocks our moral sensitivities, but one that a teleologist would be forced to draw.

Schüller argues that a teleologist would not be forced to draw any such conclusion. Overlooked completely is the fact that in the example not only is there question of the life of one versus the lives of many others; the entire institution of criminal law is at stake. The conclusion that the sheriff should frame the one to save others is only justified if this conclusion, raised to a universally acknowledged and practiced rule, would actually promote the common good. Since that is at least highly doubtful, such an exception must be judged contrary to the common good and unjust.

This is clearly a form of teleological argument and it is, Schüller contends, familiar to Catholic tradition. To illustrate this, he cites de Lugo's defense of the absoluteness of the confessional secret.

If it [revelation of sins] were allowed in some circumstances because of some extremely important need, this alone would be sufficient to make sacramental confession always difficult. Penitents would always fear that the confessor would

[40] *Ibid.*, p. 170.

reveal their sins because he would think this is an example of the exceptional instance. To avoid this evil, it was necessary to exclude any exception. That rare evil which would be obviated by revelation of sins is in no proportionate relationship to the perpetual evil and continuing harm which would be associated with the difficulty of confession if an exception were allowed.[41]

The example of fairness is that of a person who wants a certain candidate elected. He knows that the vast majority of his fellow citizens feel the same way and will vote for this candidate; so he himself stays home. Viewed in terms of consequences, his vote would be useless. Therefore, as useless, it is not morally right if it is viewed within a teleological framework. Yet it is unfair, for the stay-at-home enjoys the good of getting his candidate elected even though he spares himself the trouble of a trip to the polls. Therefore, it is asserted, beyond love (as usefulness, *beneficentia*) there is required a principle of fairness.

Schüller does not deny that fairness demands the person's vote. Rather he is amazed that one thinks such fairness has nothing to do with what we Christians call love of neighbor. Furthermore, he is perplexed at how narrowly the critics of utilitarianism interpret the term "useless." Of course, the vote is in one sense useless (it will not change results). But precisely because the vote is useless, it has the peculiar aptitude to be an expression of solidarity, much as the gesture of the woman who poured perfume over the head of Jesus (Mk 13:3–19) was seen as useless by some but was actually an act of love. One should not confuse the principle of utility (*beneficentia*) to one's neighbor and neighbors with mere efficiency.

In summary, then, Schüller leans heavily toward a teleological theory of moral norms if the term "teleology" is not too narrowly understood. Connery, he urges, can find justification for a deontological theory neither in traditional morality nor in the critics of utilitarianism; for the grounds on which these critics demand, in addition to love (*benevolentia* and *beneficentia*), principles of justice, fairness, etc. are mistaken. He summarizes as follows:

Traditional moral theology factually represents a deontological theory. Frankena does the same thing. But they do this from reasons that have nothing in common. Frankena believes he must hold a deontological theory because the necessary principle of justice is logically independent of the principle of love. Traditional moral theology states, on the contrary—so it seems to me—that the principle of justice is contained already in the principle of love. Therefore traditional moral theology must deny that Frankena has a legitimate ground for counting himself a deontologist. This theology itself represents a deontological theory, because it believes that there is, first, a class of actions that are morally wrong because of

41 Cited in Schüller, p. 174, from *Tractatus de fide*, disp. 4, sect. 4, n. 57.

their unnaturalness (contraception). Second, there is a class of actions that must be seen as wrong because of a lack of divine permission (e.g., killing of the innocent). As far as I can see, Frankena, on the basis of the rest of his ethics, must contest that these two classes are justified. Therefore he could not admit that Catholic tradition has a legitimate ground for holding to a deontological theory. If one admits that Frankena is correct, yet if he holds with Catholic tradition that the principle of justice (and fairness) is contained in the principle of love, *then the result is a teleological theory of moral norms.*[42]

Because Connery's work is so economical, precise, and disciplined, and because the points he raises are so important to this entire discussion, I should like to attempt my own formulation of a few problems that seem to remain.

First, after noting that the Catholic authors discussed are all "tending toward consequentialism," Connery repeatedly describes this approach as "a morality based *solely* on consequences."[43] If we understand by consequences "intended consequences," we have here the same objection raised by Ermecke against Fuchs on the place of intention ("eine letzlich *allein* entscheidende Bedeutung...". This is not what these authors are saying nor, in my judgment, what they can be forced to say. All would admit, for example, an inherent value in keeping secrets and an inherent disvalue in breaking them. The question is not that it is morally wrong to break secrets simply because of bad consequences. It is rather: when is it legitimate to bring about the admitted disvalue of breaking secrecy, and why? Schüller, Fuchs, Knauer, and Janssens insist that we are talking about an *evil* (nonmoral, premoral, ontic) where revelation of a secret is concerned. Therefore, as soon as the action involved is seen as containing such evil, it is no longer a matter of "consequences alone," but of the proportion between the evil involved and the good sought. If they regarded the action as "based on consequences alone," revelation of secrets would have to be seen as neutral in itself, not as an ontic evil.

Second, Connery notes that it is the position of Knauer—and actually of Fuchs also—that the intent (Fuchs) or commensurate reason (Knauer) is included in the moral object of the act. Apart from such a reason the act has only a physical object.[44] Thus, killing can be morally justified or not depending on the reason or intent behind the act. Of this Connery notes: "This presents no problem in regard to killing, which can be morally good or morally bad. But it does raise questions in regard to actions which have been traditionally regarded as wrong, e.g., adultery,

---

[42] *Art. cit.*, p. 176.

[43] Connery, *art. cit.*, p. 398.

[44] Schüller criticizes this language in his review of W. Van der Marck, *art. cit.*, p. 137–38. Killing, e.g., even when its moral evaluation is left totally open, is not merely a physical act; it is a kind of human action.

direct killing of an innocent person, etc., independently of whatever reasons the agent might have had.[45]

It is to be noted that Connery refers here to "direct killing of an innocent person." But it must be asked: where did such a qualified and circumscribed description come from? Why is only "direct killing of an innocent person" regarded as wrong at all times? Why is this not true of any killing? The only answer seems to be that in some instances of conflict[46] (self-defense, warfare) killing can represent the better protection of life itself, can represent the lesser evil when compared to the only other available alternative. Obviously such a conclusion roots in the weighing of the effects of two alternatives. It traces to a judgment about what would happen if some killing were not allowed. Now if such a calculus is necessarily implied in the sharpening of forbidden killing down to "direct killing of an innocent person," then it seems that this sharpened category itself must be similarly tested; otherwise we are inconsistent. So when one says that "direct killing of the innocent" is forbidden, he need not and should not imply that such killing is morally wrong "independently of whatever reasons the agent might have had." He may and ought to imply that the conceivable reasons for killing in such circumstances are, under careful analysis, not proportionate to the harm done; for if it was a weighing of alternatives that honed the rule to its present precision, it is a weighing of alternatives that must test its continuing viability.

In this regard Connery notes that "Fuchs would therefore have to attach a rider to every rule, e.g., killing is wrong except when there is a proportionate reason." Exactly so. But has traditional theology not done exactly this—and then gone about deciding which reasons are proportionate and which not? I believe so. Otherwise we would not have a theory of just warfare, a theory of self-defense, a theory of tolerable indirect killing.

Third, in supporting certain claims of justice (e.g., against direct killing of an innocent person in a situation where great good might seem to accrue as a result), Connery notes that one who develops and restricts his rules by considering the only alternatives (teleologist) and in this case prohibits the killing must appeal to hidden bad effects, "although this is often not very convincing." I agree that it is not always very convincing. But then the issue is one of clarity and certainty. How much clarity and certainty do we need? The underlying supposition seems to be that we must have rather exhaustive clarity to support a justice norm. Scholastic

---

[45] *Art. cit.*, p. 399, n. 7.

[46] For a much broader study of the notion of conflict, cf. H. Thielicke, "Anthropologische Grundtatbestände in individuellen Konfliktsituationen," *Zeitschrift für evangelische Ethik* 18 (1974) 129–45.

analysis supports this tendency of thought. However, even a strong suspicion that taking life in these circumstances may undermine rather than support (may be disproportionate to) the value of life seems sufficient to uphold the prohibition. The norms of justice and their limits, no more nor less than other norms, are the conclusions of a type of prudence that involves or can involve feared or suspected implications in alternative courses of action.

Finally, Connery concludes that Fuchs, Schüller, *et al.* "might be forced to acknowledge in the end that it would be better to rely, for instance, on considerations of justice than consequences in assessing certain classes of conduct." I do not see that the two are that distinct. It must be noted that "considerations of justice" involve an appeal to a certainty that is achieved only after another alternative has been, to the best of our ability, weighed. For example, why is not indirect killing a violation of the right (justice) of the one "only indirectly killed"—e.g., the innocents indirectly killed as I blast at the enemy's war machine? What do fish, so to speak, think of the morality of fishing?

Traditional moral formulations say that indirect killing need not be a violation of right, that it is morally legitimate when proportionately grounded. It can say this, I believe, only after having considered the alternative, scil., what would happen in conflict cases if we did not allow such killing? Because the answer to that alternative possibility is more disvalue to life itself, more ontic evil, it was concluded that such killing may be tolerated, and is not therefore a violation of the right of the one indirectly killed. Therefore behind and before the ascription of what is just and unjust is a prudential judgment—in a world of conflict and tragedy—of where the lesser evil lies.

I address these questions to Connery because we have already learned so much from his work that his continuing attention to these problems promises only gain.

After stating in different words many of the same essential ideas, Daniel Maguire speaks of the "tools and faculties" that converge on the total moral object and "aid in the delicate task of weighing the values contained in that object."[47] Alongside inprincipled moral wisdom, he lists reason and analysis, moral *Gemüt* or feeling, and creative imagination. Of affective perception, for example, he writes: "Moral enquiry will go astray if it proceeds from either headless heart or heartless head. *Gemüt* is the *votum* of the heart. *Gemüt* may need to be corrected or overruled by reason, but it should always be heard."

This is important and is easily overlooked. James Gustafson has been

---

[47] Daniel C. Maguire, "Ethical Method and the Problem of Death," *Anglican Theological Review* 56 (1974) 258–79. This is an excerpt from Maguire's book *Death by Choice* (New York: Doubleday, 1974).

calling it to our attention for years in different language. Emotions and religious commitments do function in our value judgments in a way that is sometimes beyond reduction to reasoning processes or analytic arguments. In pursuit of this point, Maguire refers to the sense of profanation. His example: the rounding up and slaughtering of civilians in wartime in reprisal for a sniper-killing. Some moralists, he notes, would condemn this in terms of "a calculus of the short and long term effects." Maguire believes this is true as far as it goes; but it does not go far enough. "At this point the sense of profanation enters." It is a reaction of moral shock, a sense of profanation of the sacred, not a reaction born of discursive reasoning. "It is an experience that is by its nature prior to ethical deliberation which might or might not follow from it."

Maguire is correct in pointing up the sense of the sacred (and its profanation) as a key source of moral knowledge. But here it could be suggested that rather than being in contrast to an assessment of proportion, moral shock is itself a way whereby the basic disproportion of certain actions is revealed to us.

This discussion of the meaning of moral norms may seem to many an abstract, academic affair. Actually it is at the heart of many polarizations between men of good will inside and outside the Catholic community. It is the core of contemporary discussions on abortion, sterilization, contraception, capital punishment, warfare, etc. This commentator's participation in the discussion in these "Notes" is particularly perilous, for he attempts objective reviewing at the very time his own leanings are rather apparent. To admit this is not to neutralize its effect; it is more in the nature of an apology.

DIVORCE AND REMARRIAGE

The problem of divorce and remarriage is one of the most difficult and urgent tasks of the contemporary Church. It has been estimated that there were 120,000 valid Catholic marriages that ended in civil divorce in the United States in 1971.[48] The divorce rate among Catholics—to say nothing of Christians more generally—is close to that of the population at large. We have been groping and struggling with this problem for some years. The literature continues to abound. Here I will review just a few of the articles that give a good idea of the tone and direction of the literature.[49]

[48] Taken from Lawrence G. Wrenn, "Marriage—Indissoluble or Fragile?" in *Divorce and Remarriage in the Catholic Church*, ed. Wrenn (New York: Newman, 1973) pp. 144–45.

[49] Some further entries on this problem: Anastasio Gutierrez, "Matrimonii essentia, finis, amor conjugalis," *Apollinaris* 66 (1973) 394–445, 97–147, and 67 (1974) 92–130; William J. LaDue, "Conjugal Love and the Juridical Structure of Christian Marriage," 34

Joseph Mac Avoy notes that in face of the many marital tragedies of our time the Church has a double mission: to propose the ideal day in and day out, and to save a world of sinners in imitation of her Master, the Good Shepherd.[50] After reviewing some recent canonical and theological attempts to render the Church's pastoral mission more adequate (especially attempts focusing on the widening of dispensing powers and admission of the divorced and remarried to the sacraments),[51] Mac Avoy raises the three questions he believes are the directions of the future: (1) What foundation and obligational value is to be attributed to indissolubility? (2) When love is irremediably dead, is there a power that can relieve the spouses of their marital commitment? (3) Very many marriages apparently fail to fulfil the conditions of a sacramental marriage. In what does a true sacramental marriage consist?

In discussing the first question Mac Avoy simply raises another. If the Church allows, for example, the remarriage of widows, is this not to admit that the marital project ceases when mutual presence is sundered by death? And if this is so, is it impossible to conceive of a sundering of mutual presence when love is irremediably dead, when there is a radical affective separation?[52]

Mac Avoy's answer to the second question is an extremely interesting affirmative. He first states that the power in question is not exactly a power to dissolve a bond; rather it is declaratory. The marital commitment emerged from the depths of free human choice. There is really no power that can reach in and nullify what the partners have done. "To destroy an irreversible act, it would be necessary that the Church, in God's name, accord to the spouses the faculty of taking back their word. But this vicarious power has no biblical foundation ...." Therefore, dispensing or dissolving power is really not that at all; it is a legal fiction that is declaratory in nature. "The couple being dead by the total disappearance of the bond of love that was generated, it pertains to an

---

(1974) 36–67; *ibid.* (no author given), "Remarriage after Psychic Incapacity" pp. 107–11; Klaus Demmer, M.S.C., "Decisio irrevocabilis? Animadversiones ad problema decisionis vitae," *Periodica* 63 (1974) 231–42; B. Primetshofer, "Zur Frage der psychischen Eheunfähigkeit," *Revue de droit canonique* 24 (1974) 203–22; Francis G. Morrisey, O.M.I., "The Incapacity of Entering into Marriage," *Studia canonica* 8 (1974) 5–21; *The Future of Christian Marriage* (*Concilium* 87 [1973]); *Perspectiva teológica* 4 (1972) 225–87; *Theologische Quartalschrift* 151 (1971) 1–86.

[50] Joseph Mac Avoy, S.J., "Mariage et Divorce," *Etudes*, Aug.–Sept. 1974, pp. 269–89.

[51] Mac Avoy admits his heavy reliance on several articles in *Recherches de science religieuse* 62 (1974), especially Joseph Moingt, "Le mariage des chrétiens," pp. 81–116, and Pierre Nautin, "Divorce et rémariage dans la tradition de l'église latine," p. 7–54.

[52] Karl Lehmann has adverted to the "extremely problematical category" of the definitively dead marriage; for such a category seems to include what is, from a Christian point of view, something of an impossibility—the inability to forgive (as cited in Schüller, *art. cit.*, p. 121).

authority officially to declare this demise, with a view to permitting the spouses a new start. Its role is not to break the bond, but to notarize the fact that its juridical effects have ceased." Behind such a legal fiction, such a gesture of authority, is the return of the spouses to their own consciences, then the legal endorsement of their separation.

Once this is realized, two things follow. First, not only does the Church have this power (for she has been "dissolving marriages" for centuries) but her use of it must mean that for centuries she has been declaring marriages dead with freedom to remarry implied. The Church's limitation on the use of this power must, therefore, be for educational reasons above all. That is, her purpose in narrowing dispensing power to a rather tight list of indications or situations was to prevent spouses from being tempted by a wide-open door before them—an opening that would destroy their efforts at mutual support during crises. The limitation did not originate with and is not tied to a well-elaborated doctrinal thought.

Second, the state also has this power; for since marriage is a fundamental unit of human society, its protection belongs to all authority charged with the protection of the common good.

Third, Mac Avoy accepts the fact that very few marriages are sacramental. A sacramental marriage is not just a human marriage solemnized with Christian trappings; it is a commitment to being a witness to the world of the covenant of God with the world through His Son. In this perspective spouses accept a true lay ministry, complementary to priestly ministry consecrated by ordination. Such a commitment can be undertaken only by a relatively few of the baptized. For the vast majority of Christians, religious marriage does not go beyond an *officium naturae*. The Church in her pastoral ministry must distinguish between these two levels.

In light of this, Mac Avoy draws several concrete conclusions. First, civil marriage must be recognized by the Church as an authentic marriage. This means suppression of the requirement of form. The Church will leave to the couple the decision as to whether they wish to celebrate the marriage religiously. Second, if the couple wish to celebrate their marriage religiously in the presence of a priest, this must be able to remain catechumenal, i.e., nonsacramental. Finally, there is the last level, that of sacramental marriage, corresponding to the real level of faith of the couple, a couple capable and desirous of making their lives a prophetic statement to the world of God's unfailing love.

Mac Avoy claims no answer to the enormous problem of marital failure. His emphasis falls on the Church's need to adapt her pastoral procedures constantly to the changing times.

Charles Robert treats of the admission of divorced and remarried persons to the sacraments.[53] Several factors constitute a new context for the discussion. For instance, there is a new sensitivity to the right of conscience decision. Second, public opinion about what is scandalous has changed (85% of French people polled believed that "under certain conditions" a remarried Catholic should be allowed to receive the sacraments). Then there is the fact of the departure of priests and religious who are dispensed and remain in full communion with the Church. These and similar events have qualified the consciousness of the faithful on the problem of sacramental practice for the remarried.

Robert then reports the answer given by Cardinal Hoeffner (Cologne): every divorced and remarried person lives in a permanent state of grave sin. To the objection that there could be a conflict of values leading the individual to conclude that he/she is obliged to remain in the second marriage, Hoeffner replies that if the Church took account of such conscience judgments, she would abdicate all control over the reception of the sacraments. Robert rightly criticizes this on two grounds: it injudiciously attributes to the Church a diagnostic power where formal sin is concerned, and it caricatures the notion of a conflict of values.

Robert then turns to his own analysis. The heart of the discussion is the state of serious sin. It is Robert's thesis that there are divorced-remarried persons who are convinced they are not in a state of serious sin. Robert believes such conscience convictions can be well founded in objective conflicts, e.g., breakdown of a marriage accompanied by the impossibility of remaining single or of abandoning a second union already contracted.

When faced with such conscience convictions grounded in objective conflict, what should the Church do? The answer is one of pastoral prudence. Robert uses the analogy of *communicatio in sacris* to enlighten the function of pastoral prudence. In its decree on Eastern churches (*Orientalium ecclesiarum*) Vatican II noted that where the Eastern brethren are concerned "various circumstances affecting individuals should and can be taken into consideration." Concretely, the Council concluded that "in view of special circumstances of time, place and personage, the Catholic Church has often adopted and now adopts a milder policy, offering to all the means of salvation and an example of charity among Christians . . . ."[54]

This represents a compromise between the two basic functions of common worship as detailed in the Decree on Ecumenism: signification

[53] Ch. Robert, "Est-il encore opportun de priver des sacrements de la réconciliation et de l'eucharistie indistinctment tous les divorcés remariés?" *Revue de droit canonique* 24 (1974) 152–76.

[54] No. 26 (*Documents of Vatican II*, ed. Walter M. Abbott, S.J., p. 384).

of the unity of the Church and sharing in the means of grace. Balancing these two finalities in our times, the Council concluded that "the fact that it should signify unity generally rules out common worship. Yet the gaining of a needed grace sometimes commends it."[55] Robert sees in these texts a dialectical oscillation between the two finalities of the sacraments. Neither finality can erase the other. Not being able in the concrete circumstances to realize fully the two finalities, the Church feels obliged within limits to admit a compromise. She softens the demands of full integration that she proposes in principle. Why not afford a similar favor to the divorced-remarried who remain within the unity of the Church?

Robert admits that the direction of pastoral prudence does not impose itself with the insistence of theoretical evidence. He admits the dangers and problems. We must, for example, grant that the divorced-remarried would share an incomplete integration in the Church. But this is the mark of the pilgrim Church, a Church that will always be characterized by the unachieved and imperfect, as the Council noted so accurately. Robert urges the hierarchy to put their confidence in the faithful. "In a community of faith this confidence rests on the relation that, in their intimate consciences, is established between the faithful and the Lord. It is a matter of constant catechesis to recall to the faithful that they walk before the face of God."[56]

In September 1970 the *Association de théologiens pour l'étude de la morale* (A.T.E.M.), which includes the vast majority of professors of moral theology in France and priests knowledgeable in matrimonial problems, met to discuss the problem of divorce and remarriage. The meeting evinced a virtually unanimous consent that the Church had to re-examine the reasons for excluding the divorced and remarried from full sacramental participation in the life of the Church. A commission was charged with drafting a document to be sent to all the French bishops on this matter, accompanied by a request for a personal reaction and suggestions. During February 1972 all the bishops of France received the document, but efforts were apparently made to dissuade the bishops from responding. Hence *Vie spirituelle: Supplément* decided to publish a slightly modified version of the document because of its inherent importance and the stature and number of the signatories.[57]

The French theologians begin by admitting that all agree on two points: the indissolubility of marriage is clearly taught by Christ and Catholic tradition; the Church has the duty to aid all the baptized to live

---

[55] No. 8 (*ibid.*, p. 352).

[56] *Art. cit.*, p. 174.

[57] "Le problème pastoral des chrétiens divorcés et remariés," *Vie spirituelle: Supplément* 109 (May 1974) 125–54.

the life of the children of God. However, the Church sees no way of honoring these two charges except by renunciation of the second marriage or withdrawal from full participation in the sacramental life of the Church. This position (which the group calls the "official position of the Church") translates into a variety of theoretical and practical attitudes constitutive of what the French theologians call an "urgent and grave question." The good of the faith is at stake.

For example, there are widespread differences and practices. Some in the Church see the death of the first spouse as the only answer. Others want to attack the first marriage—a situation that leads to use of the letter of the law against its spirit (scil., canonical dispositions considered as supports of the permanence of marriage are used to nullify it). Still others see the only solution in abandonment of the second union. Then there is the brother-sister approach. The upshot of all of this is a practice incoherent and disconcerting, which leads to a confusion deeply threatening to the faith.

How is one to explain, for instance, a policy that denies sacramental participation to the divorced and remarried but allows the sacraments to one who has killed his spouse, repented, and remarried? How explain, ask the French theologians, the policy of denying the sacraments to the divorced and remarried when there is no problem with priests and religious who have been dispensed from their vows and have married?

When faced with such problems, some want to challenge the teaching on indissolubility, a view the French theologians reject, not least because such a challenge supposes that this doctrine can lead to only one pastoral implementation. Similarly, they see an approach that concentrates on more controlled administration of the sacrament and on annulments and dissolutions as valid but inadequate.

The document analyzes the problem as involving Christians whose situation has these three characteristics: (1) the first union seemed to have all the guarantees and supports one would expect of a sacramental marriage; (2) the first marriage broke up and a second, apparently stable one followed—so stable that the Church would rather see the couple deprived of the sacraments than broken up; (3) these couples want to live their faith and the Church wants them to.

Such couples, by official policy, are advised not to receive the sacraments. The A.T.E.M. document sees this as full of contradictions. For instance, if brother-sister living is the condition for sacramental participation, the Church is equivalently advising the couple to remain together, deepen their life together, without really living a conjugal life. Or again, some pastors urge the couple to receive the sacraments privately. This clandestinity contradicts a profound aspect of the meaning of sacrament. Moreover, the very diversity of pastoral practice puts the faithful in a position of inequality before the law.

The two main problems with a change in pastoral approach are the doctrine of indissolubility and the notion of "the state of sin." As for the first, the French moral theologians note that historically the absolute demand of indissolubility has issued in a variety of pastoral implementations. There is nothing, they argue, in the New Testament to indicate that violation of the absolute demand of indissolubility is an unforgivable sin. Both Scripture and tradition yield not only indissolubility as an absolute demand of Jesus' teaching, but also the fact that the Church has the power to decide to which unions this demand should be applied. Therefore the French see the problem not as a questioning of indissolubility but rather whether "the consequences one draws from this demand apropos of divorced and remarried Christians are or are not favorable to the good of the faith."[58]

If one thinks that readmission of divorced-remarried to the sacraments denies indissolubility, it is because one concludes that whatever the state of the second marriage, the first still endures. The document regards this as strange reasoning. Before a thing can be indissoluble, it must exist; this cannot be said of a marriage that has lost all its other properties. Furthermore, such a notion of indissolubility contradicts the actual pastoral practice of the Church, a practice that urges the couple in the second union to nourish conjugal affection for each other, to be good parents, to fulfil their duties to each other (with reservations about a sex life), etc. Apropos of reservations about a sex life, the authors find it absurd to say that the principle of indissolubility is not threatened by a second marriage without a sexual life and with sacramental participation, while it would be threatened by a second marriage with a sexual life and sacramental participation.

The second problem is the "state of sin" characterization of the second union. This does not make sense to the authors, since the Church acknowledges that the couple often have the human and Christian duty to live their second union and fulfil its responsibilities. How can the couple (according to actual practice) not be in the state of sin with reference to their human and Christian duties to each other and the family, and yet be in it with regard to reception of the sacraments?

In conclusion, the A.T.E.M. statement urges a cautious policy of readmission of divorced-remarried to the sacraments. The stability of the second union and the couple's faith and over-all responsibility should be the focus of discernment. The only ones who can establish such a *policy* are the bishops—a point made also by Mac Avoy. Therefore the document pleads with them to act now. It insists repeatedly that such a

[58] *Art. cit.*, p. 141.

solution does not change the doctrine of indissolubility, because it is a pastoral solution. And where a variety of pastoral implementations are possible, it is the good of the faith that dictates what the pastoral practices ought to be. Thus the authors note:

There is no question of saying that henceforth sacramental marriage does not imply absolute indissolubility, nor that the rupture of such a marriage is not objectively what Christ called adultery. The Church cannot be involved in the least compromise on this point. Rather it is a question of knowing if the good of the faithful involved and that of the Church does not render it preferable to readmit these faithful to the sacraments . . . .[59]

Charles M. Whelan, S.J., argues for the readmission to the sacraments of the divorced-remarried under four conditions: (1) the first marriage is irretrievably lost; (2) present methods of official reconciliation are unavailable; (3) the parties to the second marriage have demonstrated by their lives that they desire to participate fully in the life of the Church; (4) there are solid grounds for hope that the second marriage will be in all other respects a Christian marriage, scil., stable.[60] Whelan sees only two reasons to support present official policy: Christ's denunciation of divorce and remarriage, and the high social interest in preserving the stability of marriage. But these do not, he argues, prevent a change in discipline.

Whelan sees the Church faced with two values: the rights of individuals and the common good (the stability of marriage). In the past four centuries pastoral policy has put too much emphasis on the common good, too little on the rights of individuals. Thus he proposes a middle ground.

The Church can avoid the dilemma of being unfaithful to Christ's teaching or of violating the rights of individual second-marriage Catholics by taking a middle ground between denunciation and blessing. In its necessary concern for fidelity to Christ's teaching and for the common good involved in the stability of marriage, the Church can refuse to give official blessing to the second marriage as such until the first marriage has been certainly dissolved or proven invalid. In its necessary concern for the rights of the individuals involved, the Church can rely on the present dispositions and good consciences of those second-marriage Catholics who meet the four conditions I have described.[61]

In a rather unusual move, the editors of *America* editorially endorsed Whelan's proposal and urged that it be adopted promptly.[62]

[59] *Ibid.*, p. 148.
[60] Charles M. Whelan, S.J., "Divorced Catholics: A Proposal," *America* 131 (1974) 363–65.
[61] *Ibid.*, p. 365.
[62] *Ibid.*, p. 362.

Karl Lehmann briefly but accurately summarizes the standard conclusions drawn from the doctrine of indissolubility (break-up of second union or live as brother-sister) and the strong objections raised against them.[63] Present practice he views as inadequate. The way out of this irreconcilable opposition of attitudes is to be found in fundamental dogmatic considerations.

In the scriptural evidence Lehmann sees both an absolute precept (not just an ideal or goal) and the awareness of Paul and the Matthean church that they are authorized to make certain concessions. This same duality of outlook is found in tradition. In finding ways of escape for distressing cases "they were always aware of the contradiction to Scripture, and saw in this action the possibility of avoiding even greater evil (in other words, they applied the principle of the lesser evil)."[64] The tension between the precept of indissolubility and human failure always remained.

Lehmann next turns to the Tridentine formula wherein it is stated that the teaching and practice of the Western Church are "in accordance with (juxta) the teaching of the gospel." The Western practice is not simply the teaching of the gospel; therefore it is left open whether there are other modes of response "in accordance with" Scripture. Anyone who fails to admit this possibility is untrue to the established facts of history.

Lehmann insists that the two lines of unbroken certainty (Jesus' absolute requirement, the practice of toleration) are not simply parallel, as if they were "equally justified." Rather the principle of indissolubility claims an inherently higher normative force, while the concessions are viewed as "not entirely without foundation." Thus the concessions have the function of drawing attention to the obligatory character of Jesus' directive. From this Lehmann concludes a key principle: "The concession of milder practice must not turn into an independent system, relatively or at least in fact indifferent to the principle of indissolubility. For it is outside the limits of what in faith indubitably ought to be the case, and consequently there is no place for it *purely and simply in itself.* There is, therefore, fundamentally no intrinsic 'right' to divorce, remarriage and eventual subsequent readmission to the sacraments."[65] To legitimize exceptional situations by general legal dispensations is to destroy marriage before it is contracted, for to put into a regulation what ought not to be is to give it a normative character. The concession becomes too easily preponderant and hides the original sense of Jesus'

---

[63] Karl Lehmann, "Indissolubility of Marriage and Pastoral Care of the Divorced Who Remarry," *Communio* 1 (1974) 219–42.

[64] *Ibid.*, p. 229. Schüller cites J. Ratzinger as narrowing indissolubility as follows: "The Church can in clear situations of distress allow controlled exceptions in order to avoid still worse evils" (*art. cit.*, p. 124).

[65] *Art. cit.*, p. 234.

requirement. Therefore Lehmann totally rejects pastoral concessions that come to constitute a self-contained system or a separate set of guidelines. This would simply legalize a rejection of indissolubility. Only on the basis of Jesus' original precept can something that ought not to be be regulated.

What, then, does he propose? "In situations of obvious distress and difficulty the Church can in principle admit clearly delimited exceptions to avoid worse evils."[66] But what Lehmann is opposed to is establishing a *general norm* which would make generally possible what is "in itself" impossible. The distress instances are a matter of pastoral counseling at the individual level. Lehmann details with care and prudence some of the conditions to be weighed in arriving at judgments of toleration.

In summary, I think it can be said that for Lehmann toleration of second marriages and admission to the sacraments linked to it is to be pastorally approached in terms of the principle of the lesser evil applied to the individual person(s). This cannot be and should not be codified, though pastoral guidelines are called for.

Charles Curran has written an excellent survey of recent literature on divorce and remarriage.[67] The article first correctly criticizes the shortcomings of the present legal approach (tribunal system) to marriage problems, even with the new simplified procedures. Curran next turns to the internal-forum solutions. He properly distinguishes two different situations of broken marriages: first marriage arguably null from the beginning, first marriage rather clearly a true Christian marriage, at least in terms of existing criteria.

Before continuing with a résumé of Curran, a personal aside is in place. The first instance is relatively easy to handle, both with regard to reception of the sacraments once a second marriage exists and more radically with regard to entrance into this second marriage. The moral right to marry is a basic right and should not be denied to an individual unless it is certainly clear that he is morally not free. This point was successfully argued by the CTSA committee report,[68] has been repeated by Charles Whelan, and represents a theological consensus in recent literature.

It is the second instance (clearly a Christian marriage from the beginning) that constitutes the truly difficult problem. It has two dimensions. The first is reception of the sacraments by a couple in a second marriage. There are reasons—and good ones, I believe—for arguing with the literature cited above that such a couple may receive

---

[66]*Ibid.*, p. 238.

[67] Charles E. Curran, "Divorce: Catholic Theory and Practice in the United States," *American Ecclesiastical Review* 168 (1974) 3-34, 75-95.

[68] Cf. *America* 127 (1972) 258-60.

the sacraments if they are in other respects properly disposed. The arguments proposed in some of the earlier literature—imperfect but genuine symbolization in the second marriage, second marriage "under the sign of forgiveness," etc.—were very incomplete and vulnerable; for the same arguments could be made for a third, fourth, and fifth union. However, we have moved beyond such arguments.

The second and really thorny issue is entrance into a second marriage. Here Curran believes one might argue (though he does not do so, as will be immediately clear) the permissibility of entering a second marriage by appeal to the forgiveness of God. "The forgiveness of God is offered for whatever failures brought about the breakdown and separation of the first marriage. This forgiveness is extended to the recognition that the forgiven but frail person needs a new marriage."[69] Curran does not develop systematically this suggestive line of thought. He simply states that it "has its weaknesses, but it appears to be the best argument that can be made for justifying such a second marriage without disagreeing with the Catholic teaching on the indissolubility of consummated, sacramental marriages."

Curran then turns to his own position on this difficult case. After reviewing in knowledgeable fashion the scriptural, historical, and theological evidence, he concludes that they will not support absolute indissolubility. It is his contention that permanency is a radical demand of the gospel that must be viewed as a goal but not as an absolute norm. Therefore he concludes that "the Roman Catholic Church should change its teaching and practice on divorce."

Why? As I read him, Curran would answer: (1) the evidence does not support an absolute precept; (2) the internal-forum solutions now used are incongruous, scil., are themselves a remove from the traditional understanding of indissolubility; (3) dissolution as now practiced is really a legal fiction, i.e., it is not dissolution properly so called, because the marriage bond is not a juridical entity existing apart from the marital relationship. Thus "dissolution" is but a recognition and acknowledgment that the marriage has broken down and that remarriage is possible.

Curran pursued his thought in more positive form at a recent meeting of the Canon Law Society of America.[70] He drew upon five major reasons which when "taken cumulatively ... call for a change in the teaching on indissolubility." This change will mean that "indissolubility of marriage in such perspective can only be the goal which is imperative for all ... but which without their own fault, might at times be unobtainable."

The first reason Curran appeals to is the "signs of the times." The

[69] Art. cit., p. 31.

[70] Charles E. Curran, "Divorce from the Perspective of Moral Theology." Curran very kindly forwarded me a copy of this study, which at this writing remains in manuscript form.

most important of these is the enormous interest in and prolific writing on the subject of divorce in recent years. Much of this writing defends the possibility of a return to the sacraments by a couple living in a second and irregular marriage. Curran believes that such a pastoral step is only a middle step. Earlier when Catholics divorced, they often did not remarry because they thought it would mean their exclusion from the sacramental life of the Church. "If they know such an exclusion is not necessary, then there would be less reason for them to abstain from entering such a second marriage in the first place." Furthermore, many of the very arguments proposed to allow readmission to the sacraments of the divorced-remarried can be used to allow the second marriage itself.

Curran then appeals to the proper understanding of Scripture, a new historical consciousness, a new personalism in the understanding of marriage, and eschatology. With regard to this last factor, he argues that the Christian understanding of the world views it as between the two comings of Jesus—short, therefore, of the fulness of the final coming. "This side of the fulness of the eschaton, the perfection of Christian love cannot always be attained.... Christian marital love in this world remains the love of pilgrim Christians who have not yet come to the fulness of love." The limitations stemming from this fact require more than just "toleration of a pastoral practice." They affect our objective understanding of what marriage is. How? They force us to see its indissolubility as a goal. This "calls for a changing in the teaching on indissolubility."

Curran's argument stands or falls with the notion of goal or ideal (*Zielgebot*) as contrasted with absolute precept (*Erfüllungsgebot*).[71] In his long monograph Bruno Schüller addresses this subject and finds the notion of goal-commandment as applied to such things as marriage simply insupportable. First, the notion of a goal-commandment (ideal) originally applies to moral dispositions and basic attitudes such as selflessness, courage, forbearance. Were Schüller in conversation with Curran, he might, I believe, argue that the fact that married Christians do not achieve but only grow toward the "fulness of love" (Curran's constant phrasing) in this world does not immediately touch the question of the indissolubility of marriage.

Second, Schüller cannot understand how a moral precept which

---

[71] For the following remarks of Schüller, cf. *art. cit.*, pp. 129–35. Bernard Häring describes the distinction as follows: "The prohibitive precepts (contained essentially in the decalogue) lay down the minimum requirements. They fix the boundaries which all must respect (prescriptive precepts). The Sermon on the Mount determines the ideals and goals toward which we must strive (purposive precepts). Unlike the prescriptive precepts of the external law, these purposive precepts emerge and clearly reveal their obligatory boundaries only as one progresses interiorly in the new life" (*The Law of Christ* 1 [Westminster, Md., 1960] 403–4).

cannot be fulfilled under certain conditions *thereby* becomes a goal-commandment or ideal. Take the case of falsehood. The fact that it is sometimes necessary and licit to speak falsehoods must be traced primarily to the priority of human life (for example) over the prohibition of falsehood, not to the growth or lesser moral maturity of the individual who uses speech in this way. For this reason Schüller argues that we should speak of presumptive precepts (*prasumptiven Erfüllungsgeboten*) rather than goals or ideals. One does not speak of the fifth commandment as an ideal, even though there are times when killing is justified.

Finally, Schüller believes that it cannot be argued that precepts such as that about indissolubility must be interpreted as ideals because we live in an imperfect world (Curran's "between two comings of Jesus"). Why? Because it is only in such a world that a deontological or deontological-sounding precept makes any sense at all. If such precepts fully applied only in a perfect world, a married couple who are living a healthy marriage would, for that very reason, have no existential sense of the indissolubility of marriage as traditionally understood. In a totally healthy world it is, for example, merely academic luxury to say "Do not oppose evil with force"; for by definition there is no force in a perfect world.

Therefore Schüller does not admit the notion of goal-commandment as a defensible way of facing the enormous problem of divorce in the contemporary world. Everything in his writing suggests that he would approach the problem through some form of value-ordering.

This literature is extremely interesting and rich. A sense of tension pervades it, that grows out of and reflects the tragic and contradictory character of reality itself. It seems to me that the literature is in some sense still groping to ask the right question. My own deepening understanding and consequent modification of opinion over the past seven or eight years suggests that the following personal reflections must be viewed as highly tentative and exploratory, very much in the category of a thought-experiment. They will be organized around four ideas, all present in the literature in one form or another: (1) indissolubility as precept; (2) dissolution of marriage *in favorem fidei*; (3) dissolution as declaratory; (4) the social nature of marriage. In developing these ideas, I am concerned with a first marriage now broken down that was, as far as we can judge, a true Christian marriage.

First the notion of indissolubility must be examined. For many centuries this was understood in a highly juridical sense, not least of all because marriage, as a basic human institution, needs legal supports and controls. When a marriage was sacramental and consummated, a *vinculum* was said to come into existence which no human power, neither the pope (extrinsic indissolubility) nor the marriage partners themselves (intrinsic indissolubility), could untie. Thus one form of pastoral accommodation was "dissolution of the bond." Once indissolubility is conceived in this way, it dictates inexorably certain practical conclusions. Modification of these conclusions is then seen as inconsistent with and a departure from the teaching on indissolubility. Furthermore, in facing contemporary marital breakdown the only alternative is seen to be the treatment of indissolubility not as an absolute demand but as an ideal, or as a demand that allows exceptions.

But should indissolubility be conceived in such juridical fashion? Perhaps not. Here I suggest that indissolubility is an absolute moral precept, a *moral ought* inherent in the marriage union. Because marriage represents the most intimate union of man and woman and is inseparably bound to procreation and education of children, it ought to be one and permanent. That is, from the very beginning there is a most serious obligation upon the couple to support and strengthen this marriage. They are obliged not to let the marriage fall apart and die. This is particularly binding on those who have made their union a sacrament to the world because they have undertaken a true ministry to the world: to mirror Christ's love for and fidelity to his Church.

Some marriages, of course, are mistakes from the beginning and should never have been attempted. The Church has always recognized this in her diriment impediments and her declarations of nullity. There still remains a place, and a necessary one, for such procedures.

Indissolubility as a moral ought implies two things: (1) the couple must strengthen and support their union and not allow it to die; (2) when the relationship has fallen apart and separation occurs, they must resuscitate it. A too quick conclusion that the marriage is dead is itself a violation of this ought, much as a premature pronouncement of death in a heart donor is a violation of his life. Furthermore, the Christian is especially slow to pronounce the death of a marriage, because he believes that behind God's ought is His generous grace. What appears "impossible" to men God's grace will often supply. The Church lives in this hope. Thus the very concept of a "dead marriage" is somewhat problematical to the Christian. A second marriage is a kind of nail in the coffin of the first, an act of despair about its resuscitation. For this reason I do not believe the Church through her juridical structures should undertake to pronounce a marriage dead. She could say that it never existed, that separation is justified—but not that the marriage is dead. That judgment is the responsibility of the couple, and when they make it they are before God. It is they who must accept the responsibility of saying that there is no hope of resuscitation.

But a marriage, like a human body, can die without any hope of resuscitation. When it is the couple's decision that this has happened, several things can be said. First, it seems clear that at least one of the partners (whether through weakness or sinfulness can be left, indeed must be left, to God's merciful understanding) has failed to live up to the precept of indissolubility. What ought not to be has come to be. Because what ought not to be has come to be, a serious disvalue has occurred. This disvalue is both personal and social, because marriage is both personal and social.

When marriage is truly dead, then it seems meaningless to speak of the moral ought of not letting the marriage die. If indissolubility is conceived in highly juridical fashion, the unbreakable *vinculum* continues and subsequent remarriage is in violation of this *vinculum*, is an objective state of sin, must not be allowed, etc. If, however, indissolubility is viewed as obligation, an ought on the couple, the obligation continues to urge resuscitation of the relationship as long as this is possible.

When the couple has made this decision before God, the Church only notarizes it; for marriage is also a social institution with social effects. I say "only" because "dissolution" must be viewed as declaratory, as public notification of what the couple has concluded.

Is one free to remarry when the marriage is dead? Here I believe the answer must be no.[71a] At least this must be the first response. Marriage is both a personal and a social reality. Its death is, therefore, both a personal and a social disvalue. It represents a failure to achieve and live the permanence Christ enjoins. Similarly, every remarriage after such a breakdown contains elements of disvalue. Why? Because as a *second* marriage it continues and memorializes the failure of the first marriage and thus tends to blunt the radical character of Christ's demand. In doing this it tends to undermine the stability of marriage itself. This is paradoxically all the more so the more successful the second marriage is.

[71a] Häring presents a point of view very similar to the one outlined here: "In past centuries the church has justified separation of spouses on various grounds. The separation, however, excluded remarriage. One reason for this was the hope of future reconciliation. In a patriarchal family system the separated or abandoned spouse was reintegrated in the original family. In today's urban society with its nuclear family, the abandoned spouse is often left alone, exposed to many frustrations and temptations. This has led many Christians to think that, for some divorced people, it would be better to remarry than to 'burn.' The issue is under theological, pastoral and canonical investigation, and sharply divides the different currents in the church. All agree that divorce must be avoided wherever humanly possible. There seems also a consensus that the abandoned spouse *should try to live a celibate life* if reconciliation is impossible. Many would, however, apply here the word of the Lord: 'Not everyone can accept this teaching, only those to whom it is given to do so.... Let him accept this teaching who can' (Mt 9:11–12)" ("Human Sexuality," *Chicago Studies* 13 [1974] 306, emphasis added).

Thus out of consideration for others and their stability in marriage one ought not to remarry. But this ought is an implication not of the indissolubility of the first marriage but of the indissolubility that others are trying to live. It is an implication of the social character of marriage— the neighbor as the self, so to speak.

How strong is this "ought not remarry"? It is here that I see the possible relevance of dissolution *in favorem fidei*. If dissolution must be viewed as declaratory, then the above practice suggests that the Church accept freedom to remarry after marital breakdown only on the grounds of a truly proportionate reason—in this instance, the spiritual good of the individual. In other words, if divorce is a disvalue and if subsequent remarriage necessarily contains elements of disvalue (undermining of the stability of marriage), then it seems clear that one must have a proportionate reason for introducing this disvalue into the world. Underemphasis of marriage as a social institution could lead one to overlook this dimension of the divorce-remarriage problem and conceive it one-sidedly in too personal terms. However, if one judges that remarriage is called for by the over-all good of his Christian life ("qui potest capere capiat"), then this would justify the threat a second union would visit on the institution of marriage.

If the Church's dissolution in cases of the Pauline Privilege is merely declaratory, then it is a structure similar to the one I have outlined that is revealed. But if her action is merely declaratory, two things follow. First, it is the couple alone who can decide that the first marriage is dead. Second, it is the individual alone who can decide before God whether a second marriage is justified by the over-all good of his/her faith, whether there is in his/her case a truly proportionate reason. This judgment, by its very nature, can be made only by the individual, since it is his/her faith that is involved, his/her strength, his/her proportionate reason. The Church in the public sphere must respect this decision of the individual, though for over-all educational purposes it is understandable that she would refuse to witness to this second marriage.

I am suggesting, therefore, that the Church's policy would be to respect the conscience decision of the individuals in question even as she attempts to enlighten this decision. This does not mean she is tolerating second marriages—at least no more so than in her past pastoral practice, if my understanding of dissolution *in favorem fidei* is accurate. It means only that the Church asserts that freedom to remarry after the death of a marriage is something essentially related to individual strengths and biographies and that therefore such freedom must be left to the individual before God.

This approach transfers a great deal of responsibility to the individual couple. But that is where I believe it belongs. To expect the Church to institutionalize and make laws for exceptions is to operate within a framework that says that the Church in her policy must cover and control all human relationships. This could easily represent an excessively juridical approach. It is to desire that laws carry the responsibility that properly belongs to individuals. The Church can all too easily think she stands in the place of the individual before God. She does not.

The reflections above are merely probes. They need far more attention and criticism than can be given here. But in light of the general outlines suggested, I should like to reapproach Curran's formulation. He has drawn the conclusion that when a marriage breaks down, is dead, the individuals are free to remarry, and on this basis he has called for a change in Church "teaching and practice on divorce."

I am ill at ease with this formulation of the matter. The root of my discomfort is Curran's possible neglect of the social dimension of marriage. If marriage is not only a personal reality but also a social one, surely this social aspect must be taken into account in developing a pastoral practice. The social aspect of a pastoral practice concerns above all the stability of marriage as an institution. Concretely, what response the Church adopts in the face of the contemporary instability of marriage will either strengthen or undermine marital stability. It must, I believe, be calculated to strengthen it. I do not see how Curran's formulation does this. In other words, by institutionalizing exceptions would not the Church take a long step toward introducing reservations as couples enter marriage, and weakening resolve as they face crises? I am afraid so.[72]

If there is in Curran's formulation a neglect of the social aspect of marriage, it is traceable possibly to a false polarity. He says that divorce and remarriage must be seen not in "juridical and ecclesiological perspective" but in "moral and personal perspective with ecclesial overtones." Thus Curran contrasts moral and personal with the juridical. This strikes me as a false contrast or opposition. The personal is not contrasted with the juridical; it is contrasted with the social. Thus marriage is both a personal and a social reality, with this or that type and number of juridical controls, supports, etc. By opposing personal to juridical, Curran makes the social dimension of marriage all but disappear from his analysis. He does not want this, but I believe it happens—and it appears in his conclusion that when a marriage is dead, the individuals are *without further qualification* free to marry. Does not the social aspect of marriage demand that we consider the over-all stability of marriage as an institution before that freedom is asserted?

---

[72] On this point cf. James Hitchcock, "Family Values and Moral Revisionism," *Communio* 1 (1974) 309–16.

In summary, then, where marriage is concerned the Church has a double mission: to be a prophetic teacher, to be a healing reconciler. She must mediate to the world both Christ's demanding challenges and his merciful forgiveness and understanding—and she must perform both tasks without undermining either. Her response to the contemporary problem of divorce does not, I believe, call for a change in her teaching. This response must remain essentially at the pastoral level. What form such a pastoral response takes depends on many factors, chief of which is, of course, the integrity of the teaching itself. In our time I suggest that the appropriate form is to turn over much more responsibility to the individual(s) involved.

QUESTIONS IN BIOETHICS

My original intent was to conclude this survey with a section on bioethics. Yet the literature is so large and intractable[73] that both wisdom and fairness suggest that only a narrow and quite arbitrary sampling be attempted, to point up the direction of some of the concerns in this field.

Several years ago Paul Ramsey published *The Patient as Person*,[74] in which he correctly argued that there comes a time when the shape of moral responsibility is *only* companying with the dying in their final passage. He then discovered that altogether too many people were agreeing with him and that he was caught up in a social trend that used as its model "death with dignity." As a self-styled "generally happy prophet of the doom facing the modern age," Ramsey returned to the

---

[73] A few examples: James J. Gill, S.J., "Euthanasia: A Reflection on the Doctor and the Hospital," *Catholic Mind* 72 (1974) 25–30; Michael Hamilton, "Medical Research: Some Ethical Issues," *Christian Century* 91 (1974) 744–46; J. Card. Villot, "La médecine et la protection de la vie," *Documentation catholique* 71 (1974) 60–61; Friedrich Tennstädt, "Euthanasie im Urteil der öffentlichen Meinung," *Herder Korrespondenz* 28 (1974) 175–77; Markus von Lutterotti, "Der Kranke denkt anders über den Tod als der Gesunde," *ibid.*, pp. 393–99; James B. Reichmann, "Planned Death and Professor Fletcher," *Homiletic and Pastoral Review* 74 (1974) 50–56; Norman D. West, "Terminal Patients and Their Families," *Journal of Religion and Health* 13 (1974) 65–69; Merle Longwood, "Ethics and the Taking of Life," *Lutheran Quarterly* 26 (1974) 64–76; Guy Bourgeault, "Expérimentation humaine et manipulation de l'homme," *Relations* 34 (1974) 240–44; Marcel Marcotte, "Le droit des mourants à la vérité," *ibid.*, pp. 142–47; W. Ross Yates, "Toward a New Morality of Death," *Religion in Life* 43 (1974) 79–91; Roger Mehl, "La signification éthique de la mort," *Revue d'histoire et de philosophie religieuses* 54 (1974) 249–60; F. Böckle, "Eutanasia: Riflessioni sugli equivoci di un termine," *Studia Patavina* 20 (1973) 455–63; J. Moltmann, "L'Influence de l'homme et de la société sur le progrès bio-médical," *Vie spirituelle: Supplément* 108 (Feb. 1974) 27–45; Joseph Fletcher, "Medicine, Morals, Religion," *Theology Today* 31 (0974) 39–46. Cf. also the useful bibliographies provided by the *Report* of the Hastings Center and the many helpful articles in *Linacre Quarterly*.

[74] Paul Ramsey, *The Patient as Person* (New Haven, 1970).

subject and stated his thesis in the provocative title "The Indignity of 'Death with Dignity.'"[75] Here Ramsey argues that we do not keep human company with the dying if we interpose between them and us most of the current notions of death with dignity. These notions are shallow and crass, often implying that death achieves dignity when tubes are withdrawn, respirators stopped, and heart-thumping omitted. These are only preludes to a dignified death, a term Ramsey rejects under any circumstances. According to Ramsey, our notion of "death with dignity," if it is to go beyond such technological preludes, must include and encompass the final indignity of death itself. Death itself is the final indignity. There is no way around this. Attitudes that attempt to beautify death, to make it a rhythm of nature or a part of life, are simply false. So while we can keep company with the dying, we can never make death itself dignified.

Ramsey's essay is responded to by two formidable thinkers, Robert Morison and Leon R. Kass.[76] Kass's study is particularly enlightening, since it advances in much more detail and with many more arguments the point also made by Morison. Noting that Ramsey's basic thesis really is "The Indignity of Human Mortality," Kass first analyzes the notion of dignity, then sets out several arguments why we may not view death as an indignity in itself. For instance, many instances of heroism and martyrdom show that "death can be for some human beings the occasion for the display of dignity, indeed of their greatest dignity." Moreover, human mortality is a spur to human excellence. It is Kass's contention that death is indeed a natural thing, a necessary part of the life cycle. Ramsey's view he sees as stemming from Ramsey's faith, rooted in this matter on the doctrine of original sin and its wages as found in St. Paul. On the Aristotelian, Jewish, and modern scientific views (especially with the theory of evolution), death is "natural" and "proper to man." On the basis of the arguments he raises in support of this contention, Kass suggests that the dread of death may be but one form of Christian humanism, and that, therefore, companying with the dying need not view death as an indignity in itself to remain truly human.

Ramsey returned to this discussion using Marya Mannes' *Last Rights* and Stewart Alsop's *Stay of Execution* as his vehicles.[77] Behind the remarkably different attitudes toward death in these books Ramsey sees a whole philosophy of life. Mannes endorses rationalized or administered

[75] Paul Ramsey, "The Indignity of 'Death with Dignity,'" *Studies* (Hastings Center) 2 (1974) 47–62.

[76] Robert S. Morison, "The Last Poem: The Dignity of the Inevitable and the Necessary," *Studies* 2 (1974) 63–66; Leon R. Kass, "Averting One's Eyes, or Facing the Music?—On Dignity in Death," *ibid.*, pp. 67–80.

[77] Paul Ramsey, "Death's Pedagogy," *Commonweal*, Sept. 20, 1974, pp. 497–502.

dying. She argues that those who "opt for life on any terms have never known life in its fullest terms." Commenting on that, Ramsey notes that her illustrations are mainly drawn from those whose passion for a full life turns suddenly into an embrace of death. To which he says: "That's a fair proof that neither true life nor real dying has been the instructor." Behind the counsels of Mannes Ramsey sees a sterile, antilife elitism that has nothing to do with *the human*. If death is truly dreadful, if it is the last indignity, then the term "euthanasia"—"good death"—"should be wholly jettisoned from all our talk about death and dying." "Death with dignity" only adds cosmetics to the dubious rhetoric of "euthanasia."

Contrarily, in Alsop's moving book Ramsey sees death as it ought to be thought of. "Death is nothing but dreadful to any human being; it is not a fact of life negotiable or manageable like other facts of life." It is Ramsey's conviction that what we have done with sexuality we are doing with death. We hoped to improve matters, he contends, by chatting about sex all day for three decades. All we have managed to accomplish is "calisthenic sexuality." Without a sound understanding of the *humanum*, we will do the same thing with death. We will have "calisthenic dying"—that is, deliberate and administered death.

Ramsey is making an extremely important point. Our actions, our care for the dying (ourselves as well as others), our ethical judgments of various alternatives are but extensions of our attitude toward death and life. And the attitude of our culture is one that turns "mysteries to be contemplated and deepened altogether into problems to be solved." This is gross submission to the requirements of "instrumental social rationalism," as he puts it. On the other hand, I believe, one need not take sides on the Ramsey-Kass disagreement about whether death is natural or is rather the last indignity; for we find both themes (death as natural, death as enemy and wages of sin) suggested in the New Testament. So I believe that both Ramsey and Kass are right if their emphases are read in a way that is not mutually exclusive. Some hint of this is found in the fact that at the level of policy with respect to the dying there is little difference between them. Moreover, it must be remembered that as above all a person with normative concerns, Ramsey is primarily concerned not with whether we call death natural, part of life, and so on, but with what people judge they are warranted to do with such a notion. There is no *necessary* connection between "death as natural" and the type of administered death Mannes promotes. Once again, the practical identity of the positions of Ramsey and Kass at the policy level indicates this. Nor is there any *necessary* connection between "death as indignity" and the type of medical vitalism Ramsey would certainly reject.

If attitudes toward life and its meaning shape attitudes toward death and its meaning, and if these attitudes largely determine the type of support and care that is extended to those who are ill or dying, it is reasonable to think that these attitudes will also influence the care a society provides for disadvantaged infants. John Fletcher reports the literature on attitudes toward defective newborns.[78] The attitude is at first one of rejection; it then evolves very often into feelings of anger, guilt, self-rejection on the part of the parents. After a lapse of time and given proper interchange between health professionals and parents, a kind of "re-presentation" of the child often occurs leading to acceptance and care.

The advent of amniocentesis and selective abortion is likely to affect this attitude in a pronounced way. As Fletcher puts it, "The basic question is, will the initial proclivity to reject the child, which we studied earlier, be reinforced by the obvious conclusion that the child might (or 'should have') been prevented?. . . Will parents of defective newborns be more inclined to abandon them because they feel more guilty than ever because of omitting an opportunity to diagnose?" Fletcher suspects that the feedback from amniocentesis will be more negative than positive where defective children are involved.

With the availability of advanced and sophisticated life-support systems, it is possible to keep many newborns alive who in earlier years would have died shortly after birth. Instances of this kind raise extremely delicate moral problems. David Smith weighs carefully the various options (neonatal euthanasia, withholding treatment).[79] He rejects euthanasia. Turning to withholding of treatment, he concludes that it is wrong "unless (1) it can be argued that the action is necessary to protect the personal life of at least one specifiable other person or (2) the infant cannot receive care in any other form." Practically this amounts to a prohibition of "letting infants die" in the case of the vast majority of newborns.

Perhaps Smith is right, but I should like to raise a problem with the form of argument he uses. At one point he states: "The error we want to avoid is the notion we should solve our limited resource problem simply by assessing the 'quality' of the output." In other words, Smith feels it necessary to stay a long arm's length from "quality of life" judgments. Yet in another place he argues: "I do not want to argue for an obligation on physicians and families to use extraordinary means on all newborns. In the course of care-cure of some babies it *may* become clear that additional therapy will cost the baby more than he can gain." It seems

[78] John Fletcher, "Attitudes toward Defective Newborns," *Studies* 2 (1974) 21-32.

[79] David H. Smith, "On Letting Some Babies Die," *Studies* 2 (1974) 37-46.

difficult to maintain consistently both of these statements. Take the phrase "cost the baby more than he can gain." What does this mean except to impose on the baby survival and a *quality of life* judged unacceptable? His life can be saved but it costs him too much. That "cost," and that "gain," it would seem, can refer only to a quality of life, much as that rendering is associated with some other objectionable practices.

I have attempted to face this problem by unpacking the terms "ordinary" and "extraordinary" as applied to lifesaving procedures.[80] It has always been acknowledged that these terms are highly relative to time, locale, and many circumstances of the patient. They are really code words to summarize several other value judgments. The two basic value judgments constituting a means extraordinary are hardship to the patient and hope of benefit. Thus, if a certain procedure (surgical, medicinal, etc.) *either* imposed too great a hardship on the patient *or* offered no reasonable hope of benefit, it was said to be extraordinary and per se nonobligatory. Thus, in the case of a comatose terminal-cancer patient, it has been concluded that artificial life-sustainers such as oxygen and intravenous feeding need not be used *because there is no reasonable hope of benefit for the patient*, not because there would be grave hardship in obtaining or using these supports.

Once one grants that in such instances artificial life-sustainers could actually prolong the physical life of the patient (for a day, two days, a week, etc.) and yet that there is no reasonable hope of benefit for the patient (he stands to gain nothing), it is clear that one is talking about the *kind of life* the patient would have in those remaining days or weeks. This is, in my judgment, a quality-of-life statement. And it has been decisive in determining whether oxygen is ordinary or extraordinary.

On the basis that quality-of-life judgments are packed into the distinction ordinary-extraordinary and are often decisive in the way these terms are applied, and on the further basis that in Christian perspective the meaning, substance, and consummation of life is found in human relationships, I have proposed that the quality-of-life criterion that ought to be applied to these decisions is "potential for human relationships." In the Christian tradition, life is not a value to be preserved in and for itself. It is a value to be preserved precisely as a condition for other values and therefore insofar as these other values remain obtainable. Since these other values cluster around human relationships, it seems to follow that life is a value to be preserved only

[80] Richard A. McCormick, S.J., "To Save or Let Die," *Journal of the American Medical Association* 229 (1974) 172–76, and *America* 130 (1974) 6–10. Cf. also the correspondence in *America* 131 (1974) 169–72.

insofar as it contains some potentiality for human relationships. On this basis I concluded, with several important caveats, that "when in human judgment this potentiality is totally absent or would be, because of the condition of the individual, totally subordinated to the mere effort for survival, that life can be said to have achieved its potential." In other words, it may be allowed to die.

Reactions to this study were—it can be said in the cozy confines of these "Notes"—interestingly disproportionate to the modest claims of the author and the essay.[81] Actually the position proposed is quite traditional, or at least in tight continuity with traditional categories, if only the implications of traditional terms are examined carefully.

Thomas J. O'Donnell, S.J., states his "substantial agreement" with my proposal, "except perhaps whereas he says that I had 'hinted at' the same solution in my book, I thought I had pretty well arrived at and explored it, in the course of some twenty pages."[82] The only difference O'Donnell sees in his formulation and mine is one of mode of expression and vocabulary. Perhaps that is so. But O'Donnell continues to talk in terms of extraordinary means in these instances, whereas the thrust of my remarks involved a move beyond the language of ordinary-extraordinary means to the quality-of-life judgments so clearly indicated in them.[83]

O'Donnell's interesting and thoughtful comment continues as follows:

There is one other dimension of the matter that perhaps Father McCormick did not explicitate sufficiently, and it is this: when we begin to identify means as ordinary and extraordinary in relation to the condition of the patient, then moral clarity demands the introduction of another category of means which I have chosen to call "minimal means" and *which must always be used, irrespective of the condition of the patient.* By such minimal means I understand basic sustaining and hygienic measures such as normal feeding, resting and other usual assistance (such as clearing the air passages of the newborn). The human composite is a dependent dynamism, and the neglect of such minimal means would be equivalent to an act of positive destruction.

This proposal is also endorsed by Frank J. Ayd, Jr., editor of the *Medico-Moral Newsletter.*[84]

[81] E.g., an editorial in the *Priest* (Oct. 1974) was titled "Nazi Morality." The editorial is unfortunately and embarrassingly uninformed about the medical and moral dimensions of this problem.

[82] Cf. *Medical-Moral Newsletter* 11 (1974) 5–8.

[83] Marc Lappé writes: "Clearly the question of non-treatment in these cases cannot hide behind an arbitrary distinction between ordinary and extraordinary care since both cases require the same intervention. It is rather a case of who deserves that care. Where 'medical indications' based on an understanding of physiology begin to be laced with 'social indications' of whom to treat, it is crucial that we consciously and judiciously deal with the question of assigning values to human lives" (*Tufts Medical Alumni Bulletin* 33 [1974] 27).

[84] Cf. n. 82 above.

Here I believe a distinction is in order. While I agree in substance with the notion of "minimal means," the matter could be formulated more precisely. When it is judged morally justifiable not to extend certain life-sustaining measures to a patient (whether adult or neonate), the obligation is then to care and comfort. What form this care and comfort takes can vary. There are instances, e.g., where what O'Donnell calls "normal feeding" could cause great discomfort or even (in some neonatal problems) kill the patient. In such cases these minimal means must *not* always be used.

Andre Hellegers, M.D., director of the Kennedy Institute (Georgetown University) is in basic agreement that some such criterion as I suggested does indeed function behind the relativity of the terms "ordinary" and "extraordinary."[85] His concerns are more at the level of application. First, he fears that mindsets about individual cases easily become social policies, with all the abuses inseparable from such generalization. Second, as for "potential for human relationships," there are great differences in what people set as the criteria for whether such relating is going on. Finally, "how do you ever *not* have a doubt in a newborn's case?" These are good questions and continued attention to them is likely to prove the usefulness or uselessness of the criterion I proposed.

In summary, these decisions are being made, sometimes perhaps abusively. And they are being made in terms of human judgments expressed by the medical profession in a variety of ways: e.g., "viable baby," "no realistic human future," "functionally incompetent," "meaningful life," and so on. It is clear that such terms contain a whole value system. It is the task of contemporary theologians, in interdisciplinary dialogue, to lift up those value systems and test them in the light of the value perceptions of the Christian tradition.

The attitudes one brings to research on fetuses and children (and the unprotected in general) are not discontinuous with those shaping moral judgments on the support of infant life. In 1970 the British Government established a special Advisory Group on the Use of Fetuses and Fetal Material for Research. This group, under the chairmanship of Sir John Peel, published its report in May 1972. In 1973 (Nov. 16) an interagency study group within the Department of Health, Education and Welfare (DHEW) published in the *Federal Register* a long document containing proposed guidelines for the protection of special subjects in biomedical research. Among these special subjects were "the fetus" and "the abortus." In an excellent study LeRoy Walters critiques these two documents and in the process raises some of the more fundamental moral

[85] Andre Hellegers, "Relating Is the Criterion for Life," *Ob. Gyn. News,* Oct. 15, 1974.

issues involved.[86] For instance, where there is question of use of a dead fetus (after an induced abortion), Walters concedes that most observers would see less serious ethical problems than those involving live fetuses. However, he raises the ethical issue of co-operation as being possibly relevant. "Ought one to make experimental use of the products of an abortion-system, when one would object on ethical grounds to many or most of the abortions performed within that system?"

Walters sees several fundamental presuppositions operative in the documents and in discussion of this matter in general. One is that the results of fetal research will be *medical* and *good*. He argues that serious *social* consequences will follow and that they will be *mixed* at best. Another presupposition is that prematurity (an admitted major cause of infant death in this country) must be stopped; otherwise those who could have prevented it (by any means?) are responsible for these deaths. A premise behind these and similar questions of Walters is the inherent value of fetal life. On the basis of the Judeo-Christian tradition, Walters contends that "it is at least not *implausible* to argue that fetal life ought to be highly valued." If that is the case, certain moral conclusions apropos of experimentation flow rather spontaneously from such an evaluation. An enlightening analysis.

In this connection I should like to call attention to a thorough, carefully reasoned study by Paul Ramsey to appear soon.[87] After a scathing denunciation of the secrecy surrounding the production of the DHEW proposed guidelines mentioned above, Ramsey turns his attention to the substance of the two documents Walters had commented upon. He likens the living previable human fetus to an unconscious patient. Furthermore, the previable fetus (in cases of spontaneous or induced abortion) resembles a dying patient. Finally, the human fetus resembles, in cases of induced abortion, the condemned. Accepting the fetus as a human being, Ramsey then approaches nontherapeutic experimentation on the fetus by asking whether it is morally appropriate to experiment on the dying, the unconscious, the condemned. Anyone familiar with Ramsey's thought can guess rather accurately where he stands on these issues. Which is not to say that his study is unenlightening; quite the contrary. It is a helpful and disciplined piece of moral reasoning.

One interesting point Ramsey makes is that the question of fetal

[86] LeRoy Walters, "Ethical Issues in Experimentation on the Human Fetus," *Journal of Religious Ethics* 2 (1974) 33–75.

[87] Paul Ramsey, *The Ethics of Fetal Research*, to be published soon in paperback by the Yale University Press. Ramsey kindly forwarded me a copy of the manuscript. See also Gary L. Reback, "Fetal Experimentation: Moral, Legal, and Medical Implications," *Stanford Law Review* 26 (1974) 1191–1227.

experimentation is different from that of abortion. He writes:

Unavoidably the morality of abortion converges with and diverges from other appropriate themes or considerations in any discussion of our question. Indeed this ought to be the case. Still I suggest that someone who believes that it would be wrong to do non-therapeutic research on children, on the unconscious or the dying patient, or on the condemned may for himself have settled negatively the question of the morality of fetal research, while someone who believes that most abortions performed today are wrong may be tending but he has not yet arrived at an ethical verdict upon that question.

In other words, even if the abortion is morally justifiable, nontherapeutic research on the living abortus is really research on the dying. And that is a question different from the morality of the abortion itself.

Here a comment. There is an almost irresistible tendency to argue here that *qui potest maius, potest et minus* (he who is empowered to do the greater thing is also empowered to do the lesser). That is very often true. Concretely, if one has the right to perform the ultimate harm (abortion), it would seem that one has the right to perform the lesser harm (harmful nontherapeutic experimentation). However, the application of this to the abortion and experimentation problems needs a distinction. If one believes that abortion is justifiable *because the fetus is not human* (or need not be treated as such), *is only maternal tissue*, etc., there is no problem with any kind of experimentation on "it" at any time, providing maternal health is safeguarded. *Qui potest maius, potest et minus.* If, however, the fetus must be seen as human, then the issues are separable, as Ramsey notes. Ramsey's insistence that they are different issues reflects his acceptance of the protectable humanity of the fetus. I agree. But that is the key issue. Interestingly, the restrictions on fetal experimentation (the *minus*) in the documents studied by Walters and Ramsey may stimulate our culture to a return to sanity where abortion (the *maius*) is concerned.

At this point a word about the "Declaration on Procured Abortion" issued Nov. 18, 1974 by the Sacred Congregation for the Doctrine of the Faith and ratified by Pope Paul VI himself.[88] This is the most detailed and authoritative utterance on abortion in some years. It seems rather obviously occasioned not only by the liberalization of abortion law throughout much of the world, but also by the heavy theological literature of the past few years. For instance, the document notes of the right to life that "it is not recognition by another that constitutes this right. This right is antecedent to its recognition; it demands recognition

[88] At this time I am reliant on the text kindly forwarded by Msgr. James McHugh, Director, Family Life Division, United States Catholic Conference.

and it is strictly unjust to refuse it." Somewhat later we read (of the fertilized ovum) that it "would never be made human if it were not human already." These statements are rather obviously aimed at the *Etudes* dossier published in January 1973.[89]

Two further theological points in this otherwise splendid Declaration call for comment. Speaking of the immorality of abortion, it states: "It may be a question of health, sometimes of life or death, for the mother.... We proclaim only that none of these reasons can ever objectively confer the right to dispose of another's life, even when that life is only beginning." If this wording states—as it clearly seems to—that abortion is morally wrong even when the only alternative is to lose both the mother and the child, then it would find itself in disagreement not only with a great number of theologians, but even with a number of bishops.[90]

Further, "From a moral point of view this is certain: even if a doubt existed concerning whether the fruit of conception is already a human person, it is objectively a grave sin to dare to risk murder." This statement is based on the traditional axiom "idem est in moralibus facere et exponere se periculo faciendi" (In moral matters it is one and the same thing to do a thing or to expose onself to the danger of doing it). The quite traditional example used to illustrate this is the case of the hunter who shoots into the brush at a moving object, uncertain as to whether it is a man or animal that moved. I believe it can be convincingly shown that the above axiom must be restricted to two instances: (1) acting with an uncertain *conscience*; (1) *rash* (scil., unjustified) exposure to the danger of doing harm.[91] Thus, in the example above, if the hunter were a dying (starving) hunter and his last chance for food was in that brush, his shot would not necessarily be rash. Something similar could be argued with regard to abortion. In the Declaration's words, "it is objectively a grave sin to dare to risk murder"; yes, if that risk is capricious and not justified by a truly proportionate reason.

Ramsey's position on fetal experimentation roots in his position on nontherapeutic experimentation on children. We may not, he argues, submit a child to procedures that involve any measure of risk of harm or to procedures that involve no harm but simply "offensive touching." "A

[89] "Pour une réforme de la législation française relative à l'avortement," *Etudes*, Jan. 1973, pp. 55–84.

[90] The Belgian bishops note: "The moral principle which ought to govern the intervention can be formulated as follows: since two lives are at stake, one will, while doing everything possible to save both, attempt to save one rather than to allow two to perish" (cf. THEOLOGICAL STUDIES 35 [1974] 350).

[91] Cf. my *The Removal of a Fetus Probably Dead to Save the Life of the Mother* (Rome, 1957).

subject can be wronged without being harmed."[92] This occurs whenever he is used as an object, or as a means only rather also as an end in himself. Parents cannot consent to this type of thing regardless of the significance of the experiment.

Why is this so? Ramsey argues as follows: "To attempt to consent for a child to be made an experimental subject is to treat a child as not a child. It is to treat him as if he were an adult person who has consented to become a joint adventurer in the common cause of medical research. If the grounds for this are alleged to be the presumptive or implied consent of the child, that must simply be characterized as a violent and a false presumption." Thus he concludes that no parent is morally competent to consent that his child be submitted to *any* nontherapeutic experimentation. In other words, proxy consent to purely experimental procedures is without moral warrants.

I have attempted to argue not a contrary position but a modified one that would allow for nontherapeutic experimentation on children where there is no discernible risk or undue discomfort.[93] The heart of the argument is this: if we analyze proxy consent where it is accepted as legitimate—scil., in the *therapeutic* situation—we will see that parental consent is morally legitimate because, life and health being goods for the child, he would choose them because he *ought* to choose the good of life. In other words, proxy consent is morally valid precisely insofar as it is a reasonable presumption of the child's wishes, a construction of what the child would wish could he do so. The child would so choose because he *ought* to do so, life and health being goods definitive of his flourishing.

Once proxy consent in the therapeutic situation is analyzed in this way, the question occurs: Are there other things that the child *ought*, as a human being, to choose precisely because and insofar as they are goods definitive of his well-being? As an answer to this question I have suggested that there are things we *ought* to do for others simply because we are members of the human community. These are not precisely works of charity or supererogation (beyond what is required of all of us) but our personal bearing of our share that all may prosper. They involve no discernible risk, discomfort, or inconvenience, yet promise genuine hope for general benefit.

[92] Cf. *The Patient as Person*, pp. 27–40. Ramsey has also continued his discussion of this matter in *Biological Revolution: Theological Impact* (proceedings of a conference [April 1973] of the Institute for Theological Encounter with Science and Technology [ITEST]).

[93] Richard A. McCormick, S.J., "Proxy Consent in the Experimentation Situation," *Perspectives in Biology and Medicine* 18 (1974) 2–20. Charles Curran has arrived at a conclusion very close to the one I defend: "Some would argue that children and those who cannot consent on their own should never be used in experimentation. I would maintain that children can be used in experimentation if there is no discernible risk to them, and their parents consent" ("Human Life," *Chicago Studies* 13 [1974] 293).

In summary, if it can be argued that it is good for all of us to share in these experiments, and hence that we *ought* to do so (social justice), then a presumption of consent where children are involved is reasonable and proxy consent becomes legitimate.

William E. May, in a carefully wrought study, reviews fully and accurately this exchange between Ramsey and the author of these "Notes."[94] The position I have summarized above he sees as "attractive at first reading" and "it seems quite reasonable." Yet he finally disagrees with it because it must regard the subject in whose behalf consent is given as a moral agent. An infant or child, however, is not a moral agent. When he analyzes the diagnostic-therapeutic situation, May insists that proxy consent is legitimate not because of any constructed moral obligations the child has, but simply because a good is at stake in the child, a need is there, and the parents and medical profession are in a position to meet this need. In the purely experimental situation, however, the child is not in any need. Therefore proxy consent is not justified.

May's point is persuasively argued. I shall leave to others the task of refereeing the exchange. Before doing so, however, two points can be made to help the referees. First, I do not believe the position I presented must necessarily regard the infant as a moral agent. Nor need it imply that he has obligations. It need only suggest that what it is reasonable and legitimate to do experimentally with youngsters might be constructed off what others who are moral agents *ought* as humans to do; for though they are not yet moral agents, infants are humans in the fullest sense.

Second, at some point this discussion must come to grips with the fact that Ramsey's position ("offensive touching")—the one preferred by May—could not allow any nontherapeutic experimentation whatsoever, even the most trivial such as a buccal smear or routine weighing. This is the logical and necessary conclusion to Ramsey's argument. However, most theologians and researchers with whom I have discussed this matter see this as unreasonable and at variance with common sense.

Completion of these "Notes" is always accompanied by a sense of incompletion and regret. So much has to be bypassed that one's only recourse is to acknowledge the fact and call the reader's attention to the material neglected.[95]

---

[94] William E. May, "Experimenting on Human Subjects," *Linacre Quarterly* 41 (1974) 238–52.

[95] Albert R. Di Ianni, "Is the Fetus a Person?" *American Ecclesiastical Review* 168

(1974) 309–26; "The Formation of Conscience," Canadian Catholic Conference, *Catholic Mind* 72 (1974) 40–51; Norman Pittenger, "Homosexuality and the Christian Tradition," *Christianity and Crisis* 34 (1974) 178–81; Norbert J. Rigali, S.J., "Morality as an Encounter with God," *Cross and Crown* 26 (1974) 262–68; *Dialog* 13 (Summer 1974), whole issue on liberation; John Macquarrie, "Ethical Standards in World Religions: X, Christianity," *Expository Times* 85 (1974) 324–27; Denis O'Callaghan, "What Is Mortal Sin?" *Furrow* 25 (1974) 71–87; Robert Egan and John Navone, "Theological Reflections on the Social Apostolate," *Homiletic and Pastoral Review* 74 (1974) 53–59; Hans-Eduard Hengstenberg, "The Phenomenology of Meaning as Approach to Ethics," *International Philosophical Quarterly* 14 (1974) 3–24; Harry S. Silverstein, "Universality and Treating Persons as Persons," *Journal of Philosophy* 71 (1974) 57–71; Christopher Cherry, "Describing, Evaluating, and Moral Conclusions," *Mind* 83 (1974) 341–54; Judith Jarvis Thomson, "Preferential Hiring," *Philosophy and Public Affairs* 2 (1973) 364–84, with a response by Robert Simon in 3 (1974) 312–20 and Gertrude Ezorsky, *ibid.*, pp. 321–30; William N. Nelson, "Special Rights, General Rights and Social Justice," *Philosophy and Public Affairs* 3 (1974) 410–30; David A. Conway, "Capital Punishment and Deterrence: Some Considerations in Dialogue Form," *ibid.*, pp. 431–43; Marvin Bergman, "Moral Decision Making in the Light of Kohlberg and Bonhoeffer: A Comparison," *Religious Education* 69 (1974) 227–42; P. R. Hughes, "Loi naturelle et contrôle des naissances: Une nouvelle recherche," *Revue des sciences philosophiques et théologiques* 58 (1974) 58–65; Eugene Hillman, "Nouvelle approche de la polygamie," *Spiritus* 15 (1974) 44–62; Gotthold Müller, "Die 'Krisis' der Ethik und die Nachfolge Christi," *Studia theologica* 28 (1974) 57–67; M. Sanchez, "Sobre la división del pecado," *Studium* 14 (1974) 119–29; Josef George Ziegler, "Das Verständnis menschlicher Geschlechtlichkeit in der sexualethischen Diskussion," *Theologisch-praktische Quartalschrift* 122 (1974) 36–45; Gotthold Müller, "Luthers Ethik und die ethische Situation der Gegenwart," *Theologische Zeitschrift* 29 (1973) 117–27; Vernon J. Bourke, "Right Reason in Contemporary Ethics," *Thomist* 38 (1974) 106–24; Ralph McInerny, "Prudence and Conscience," *ibid.*, pp. 291–305; Ludwig Berg, "Das neutestamentliche Liebesgebot—Prinzip der Sittlichkeit," *Trier theologische Zeitschrift* 83 (1974) 129–45; S. Meurer, "Das Problem der Homosexualität in theologischer Sicht," *Zeitschrift für evangelische Ethik* 18 (1974) 38–48.

CURRENT THEOLOGY: 1976

NOTES ON MORAL THEOLOGY: APRIL–SEPTEMBER 1975

Since the last edition of these "Notes," the literature dealing with moral questions has shown no inclination to slow up. There are interesting entries on sin[1] and, as was to be expected, on the new rite for the sacrament of penance.[2] Marital and sexual ethics never escape treatment.[3] The notion of natural law continues to receive attention in a variety of forms,[4] as does the relationship between faith, reason, and morality.[5] The place of authority in morality is another subject of

[1] Paul Martin, "Sin, Guilt, and Mental Health," *Christian Century* 92 (1975) 525–27; Timothy E. O'Connell, "The Point of Moral Theology," *Chicago Studies* 14 (1975) 49–66; Eric W. Gritsch, "Bold Sinning: The Lutheran Option," *Dialog* 14 (1975) 26–32; Klaus Demmer, M.S.C., "Theologia peccati anthropologice mediata," *Periodica* 64 (1975) 75–98; Donald Evans, "Moral Weakness," *Philosophy* 50 (1975) 295–310; Alfons Auer, "Ist die Sünde eine Beleidigung Gottes?" *Theologische Quartalschrift* 155 (1975) 53–68; Marciano Vidal, "Definición teológica de pecado para un mundo secularizado," *Sal terrae* 63 (1975) 563–72.

[2] Robert Coffey, "Why a Reform of the Sacrament of Penance?" *Furrow* 26 (1975) 259–69; Ludwig Bertsch, "Sakrament der Wiederversöhnung—Zur Neuordnung von Busse und Busssakrament," *Geist und Leben* 48 (1975) 63–72.

[3] James Downey, O.S.A., "Polygamy: Wrong Reasons," *African Ecclesiastical Review* 17 (1975) 147–53; Eugene O'Sullivan, O.P., "Humanizing Sexuality," *Catholic Mind* 74 (1975) 11–17; Guy Charles, "Gay Liberation Confronts the Church," *Christianity Today* 19 (1975) 1142–45; G. M. Debuisson, "Théologie mariale et mystère du couple," *Eglise et théologie* 6 (1975) 195–240; L. C. Bernal, "Génesis de la doctrina sobre el amor conyugal de la Constitución 'Gaudium et spes,'" *Ephemerides theologicae Lovanienses* 51 (1975) 49–81; Antonio Vargas-Machuca, "Los casos de 'divorcio' admitidos por San Mateo: Consecuencias para la teología actual," *Estudios eclesiásticos* 50 (1975) 5–54; David R. Cartlidge, "1 Corinthians 7 as a Foundation for a Christian Sex Ethic," *Journal of Religion* 55 (1975) 220–34; Richard Sherlock, "Creation, Procreation and the Gift of Life," *Linacre Quarterly* 42 (1975) 38–53; Hans Rotter, S.J., "Zur Grundlegung einer christlichen Sexualethik," *Stimmen der Zeit* 193 (1975) 115–25; Adolfo F. Diaz-Nava, "Paternidad responsable," *Sal terrae* 63 (1975) 601–8.

[4] Edward A. Malloy, C.S.C., "Natural Law Theory and Catholic Moral Theology," *American Ecclesiastical Review* 169 (1975) 456–69; Raymond Bradley, "The Relation between Natural Law and Human Law in Thomas Aquinas," *Catholic Lawyer* 21 (1975) 42–55; William E. May, "The Natural Law, Conscience, and Developmental Psychology," *Communio* 2 (1975) 3–31; Bernice Hamilton, "A Developing Concept of Natural Law," *Month* 236 (1975) 196–200; Robert B. Ashmore, Jr., "Aquinas and Ethical Naturalism," *New Scholasticism* 49 (1975) 76–86; John F. Harvey, "Law and Personalism," *Communio* 2 (1975) 54–72.

[5] James J. Walter, "Christian Ethics: Distinctive and Specific," *American Ecclesiastical Review* 169 (1975) 470–89; Donald J. Keefe, "Toward a Eucharistic Morality," *Communio* 2 (1975) 99–125; Pietro Palazzini, "Gli autentici valori morali del vangelo," *Divinitas* 19 (1975) 16–34; Raimondo Spiazzi, "Fede e morale nella prospettiva teologica di San Tommaso," *Doctor communis* 27 (1975) 123–36; Edouard Hamel, S.J., "La théologie morale entre l'Ecriture et la raison," *Gregorianum* 56 (1975) 273–319; Joseph de Finance,

abiding importance.[6] This survey will confine itself to three areas of concern where the literature has been especially heavy: behavioral moral norms (their meaning and limit), care for the dying and euthanasia, human rights and the mission of the Church.

MORAL NORMS: MEANING AND LIMITS

The question of moral reasoning and the norms that result from it continues to be one of burning interest. In his address to the members of the International Theological Commission (Dec. 16, 1974), Pope Paul VI called attention to the fact that the very principles of the objective moral order are a matter of controversy.[7] After noting the importance of biblical teaching for moral theology, he stated: "Theological reflection will then have to move from the Scriptures to a proper definition of moral norms in accordance with the established principles of faith and of exegesis and hermeneutics."

This concern with norms and their permanence was of particular concern to the Commission. It is sometimes said that all the directives and value judgments of the New Testament must be questioned because they are historically conditioned. M. Schürmann's careful study addresses this question and concludes that the vast majority of Pauline value judgments retain permanent validity.[8] This is so because they are transcendental in character; that is, they are concerned with the gift of self as love of God and neighbor.

S.J., "Il valore morale e la ragione," *Rassegna di teologia* 16 (1975) 305–16; John P. Boyle, "Faith and Christian Ethics in Rahner and Lonergan," *Thought* 50 (1975) 247–65; Volker Eid, "Befreiende Rede von Gott in der praktizierten Moraltheologie," *Theologische Quartalschrift* 155 (1975) 117–31; Frederick Carney, "On Frankena and Religious Ethics," *Journal of Religious Ethics* 3 (1975) 7–26; Stanley Hauerwas, "Obligation and Virtue Once More," *ibid.*, pp. 27–44; William Frankena, "Conversations with Carney and Hauerwas," *ibid.*, pp. 45–62.

[6] John E. Skinner, "The Meaning of Authority," *Anglican Theological Review* 57 (1975) 15–36; Luigi Ciappi, "Libertà di pensiero e magistero della Chiesa in San Tommaso d'Aquino," *Doctor communis* 27 (1975) 64–73; "Décret au sujet de la vigilance des pasteurs de l'église sur les livres," *Documentation catholique* 72 (1975) 361–62; Jeremy Moiser, "Law, Liberty, Church, and Gospel," *New Blackfriars* 56 (1975) 100–110; G. Martelet, S.J., "Praxis humaine et magistère apostolique," *Nouvelle revue théologique* 97 (1975) 525–28; Bernhard Fraling, "Die moralische Autorität der Kirche," *Theologie und Glaube* 65 (1975) 89–99.

[7] Pope Paul VI, "Membris Commissionis Theologicae Internationalis Romae plenarium coetum habentibus," *AAS* 67 (1975) 39–44; cf. also *The Pope Speaks* 19 (1975) 333–39.

[8] Heinz Schürmann, "Haben die paulinischen Wertungen und Weisungen Modellcharakter?" *Gregorianum* 56 (1975) 237–71. This was a presentation to the 12th Congress of Polish Bible Scholars (Breslau, Sept. 3–5, 1974) and was part of the dossier of the International Theological Commission. A shortened French version is available in *Esprit et vie* 85 (1975) 600–603 and *Documentation catholique* 57 (1975) 761–66.

Interest in norms is manifested in other quarters. An entire issue of *Dialog* (with essays by Franklin Sherman, Larry Rasmussen, and James Burtness among others) is devoted to decision-making in the contemporary world.[9] Kenneth W. Thompson believes that the "one art most needful of restoration is the ancient art of moral reasoning, of wrangling not about personalities or policies, but about the moral propositions and values underlying them."[10] New facts and possibilities force us to ask new questions, or at least to test old formulations in light of such developments.[11] This concern need not imply that ethical reflection does or ought to begin with the question "What ought I do?" as Stanley Hauerwas suggests.[12] Hauerwas believes that in approaching the fascinating problems of, e.g., modern medicine, one is involved in a kind of moral engineering that only reinforces the assumptions behind modern medicine. Of course, that can be the case. But it need not be. It is the function of good moral discourse to lay bare and challenge the assumptions involved in the very statement of the problem. Be that as it may, only a few recent contributions on norms can be reviewed here and other pertinent material footnoted in the process.

Timothy E. O'Connell argues that the recent discussions on material moral norms (e.g., the work of Knauer, Fuchs, Schüller, and others) represent an emphasis that is not justified.[13] The implicit premise of this concern for the importance of material norms, he contends, is that formal norms are unimportant. Contrarily, O'Connell's thesis is that "for the Christian moral life formal norms are, if anything, more important than material norms."

He offers several arguments for this thesis. First, the primary thrust of Catholic emphasis on natural law is that moral obligation is objective, not primarily that it is immutable. Secondly, and more positively, he believes that formal norms are very important, a point he thinks is widely missed by contemporary authors because they presuppose that the primary function of moral norms is instruction, whereas he believes that it is motivational. "I would assert that the primary function of moral

[9] *Dialog* 14 (1975) 21 ff. Cf. also T. Urdanoz, O.P., "La moral y su valor objectivo," *Angelicum* 52 (1975) 179–227; Denis O'Callaghan, "What Has Happened to the Ten Commandments?" *Furrow* 26 (1975) 36–42; Charles Curran, "How My Mind Has Changed: 1960–1975," *Horizons* 2 (1975) 187–205.

[10] Kenneth W. Thompson, "Right and Wrong: A Framework for Moral Reasoning," *Christian Century* 92 (1975) 705–8.

[11] Bernhard Stoeckle, O.S.B., "Das Problem der sittlichen Norm," *Stimmen der Zeit* 100 (1975) 723–35.

[12] Stanley Hauerwas, "The Ethicist as Theologian," *Christian Century* 92 (1975) 408–11.

[13] Timothy E. O'Connell, "The Question of Moral Norms," *American Ecclesiastical Review* 169 (1975) 377–88.

norms is not instruction at all, but rather motivation. . . . "[14] The
reasons he proposes for this are: (1) Value systems are pivotal in the
development of the person, as is clear from many disciplines; but it is
formal norms that articulate these values. (2) The kind of norms that
have a motivational focus (formal norms) seem to be more universal
within the family of man. (3) At the level of the commonplace activities
of life, the occasions requiring moral information are outnumbered by the
occasions where moral motivation is needed.

There are two aspects of O'Connell's useful essay that are somewhat
puzzling. First, it is not at all clear that the implicit premise of recent
concern for material norms is the unimportance of formal norms. The
more obvious premise is simply that material norms are more problematical. The vast literature in moral philosophy on moral norms is sufficient
testimony to this. Add to this the fact that the problematical character of
some moral norms is inseparably associated with some moral concerns of
the first magnitude (the magisterium and the use of authority in the
Church, the theological weight of tradition, dissent, the meaning of
sensus fidelium in moral matters, pluralism in theology, the weight and
meaning of reasoning in theological ethics, pastoral guidance, etc.) and it
is easy to see why recent Catholic literature has devoted the attention it
has to such matters.

The second reason is closely related to the first and concerns moral
norms as motivational. O'Connell argues that the presupposition of
contemporary concern with material norms is that "the primary function
of norms is instruction." He denies this and says that the primary
function is motivational. When one says that moral norms are primarily
motivational in function, he is saying something rather obvious, if it is
understood that formal moral norms are in question. No one, as far as I
know, has ever doubted this. However, such a statement is not true of
material moral norms. It is the precise function of material norms to be
instructional of what formal norms state in general and even trivial
terms.

For instance, "Thou shalt not murder" is a truism, for the term
"murder" is a highly compact value term that means "unjust killing."
Therefore, when one uses such propositions (truisms), it is clear that the
purpose is not to convey information about the specific content of the
proposition; the purpose is parenetic: to remind one of what he is
presumed to know and to exhort him to do (or avoid) it.

This raises once again the important distinction between parenetic
discourse and explanatory discourse. Formal norms fall into the category

[14] *Ibid.*, p. 385.

of parenetic discourse. They invite, exhort, judge. They do not primarily ⤬ inform or instruct, because they presume that the specific content is clear and known. This does not mean that they are "useless." [15] The New Testament is full of parenetic discourse. St. Paul found it not only useful but indispensable. For instance, the works of the flesh are enumerated in Gal 5:19–21: "immorality, impurity, licentiousness, idolatry, sorcery, enmity, strife, jealousy, anger, selfishness, dissension, party spirit, envy, drunkenness, carousing, and the like." These terms are compact value terms like "murder" and "adultery." They do not convey information ⤬ about the exact content of what is prohibited, but presuppose this. They are still useful, but for a different purpose: to remind, exhort, etc.

When, therefore, O'Connell argues that formal moral norms are "more important" than material norms, he is in a sense comparing the incomparable; for the two types of norms have different purposes, just as parenetic and explanatory moral discourse do. Formal moral norms ⤬ (parenetic discourse) remind of the right and exhort to it. Material moral ⤬ norms (explanatory discourse) attempt to state specifically what the ⤬ formal norms state in compact value judgments. They attempt, e.g., to ⤬ specify what is to count for "murder." Therefore they are instructional. One form of discourse is not "more important" than the other; they are simply different in terms of function and purpose. Therefore, the presupposition of concern with material moral norms is not, as O'Connell contends, that "the primary function of norms is instruction," but only that the primary function of *material* norms is instruction.

What O'Connell is probably saying is that concern with the problematic aspects of material norms should not lead us to de-emphasize the importance of parenetic discourse in the moral-spiritual life. I believe all would agree with that. Bernard Häring, in a ranging treatment of moral norms, makes exactly this point.[16] Distinguishing between prohibitive (limitative) norms that define the minimum always demanded, and goal-commandments (*Zielgebote*, e.g., the Sermon on the Mount), Häring argues that the latter deserve more stress in a truly Christian moral theology. But the term "norm" then takes on a different sense: "the liberating norm of the 'law of faith,' 'law of grace.' In this sense Christ is our life, the way, the life-giving truth. We follow his 'law' if we are on the road with him. . . . "

Yet it is interesting to note that at the very time Häring says this, he

---

[15] The reference is to John Giles Milhaven's review of *Naturrecht in der Kritik*, THEOLOGICAL STUDIES 35 (1974) 200.

[16] Bernard Häring, "Norms and Freedom in Contemporary Catholic Thought." This study, a lecture at Fordham University, is in the process of publication; it should appear shortly.

spends most of his time discussing material norms. He underlines the many considerations (experience, related sciences, historical and cultural knowledge) behind them and hence their provisional character. This provisional character, he notes, is "generally accepted within the community of moral theologians all over the world" but not by all priests and bishops trained in a more static notion of natural law. Häring then notes:

> If we understand the provisional character of norms laid down in the past, the provisional character of the data available, and the different historical contexts, then a solid hermeneutics and new efforts by theologians do not have the character of dissent from the teaching of the official magisterium; they are a solidaric part of the continuing effort of the whole Church to find the best possible norms for the ever new historical context. . . .

This is an important point and I will return to it later. Häring uses it as the context of his disagreement with Thomas Dubay. Dubay, he believes, views the sometimes disturbing phenomenon of pluralism in moral theology from a "merely institutional point of view"—one that, under analysis, gives a higher priority to institutional efficiency than to the quest for truth.[17] Häring grants that we must accent the many points on which we are united, "but this agreement should never be won by lack of sincerity or lack of courage to face the real problems of today's world, even when the hierarchy (or rather a part of it) seems not to realize the new situation."

In a long study on the relationship of conscience to moral norms, M. Huftier asks whether it is possible to draw up a list of objectively grave sins.[18] His answer is affirmative. He first notes that the moral quality of human actions is derived from both general/objective and individual/ subjective considerations. The study is primarily concerned with establishing a proper balance between conscience and objective morality. In this it succeeds very well and provides an abundance of useful scriptural and papal texts to the point.

In the course of his essay, Huftier turns to the fonts of morality (object, end, circumstances) to establish the proper balance between the general and individual considerations. Some actions, he argues, have a morality *ex objecto* that no good intention can change. "Hate, e.g., is directly opposed to God who is love; the lie is of itself opposed to God

---

[17] Cf. Thomas Dubay, S.M., "The State of Moral Theology," THEOLOGICAL STUDIES 35 (1974) 482–506. Charles Curran's response to Dubay ("Pluralism in Catholic Moral Theology"), a manuscript copy of which Curran kindly forwarded to me, will appear in *Chicago Studies.*

[18] M. Huftier, "Conscience individuelle et règle morale," *Esprit et vie* 85 (1975) 465–76, 481–89.

who is truth."[19] Therefore, although the subjective intention is a source of morality, it does not purify an action that is evil by its object. To say anything else would be to say that a good end justifies evil means.

Huftier then turns to Paul, Augustine, and Aquinas to support his contention that it is indeed possible to draw up a catalogue of objectively grave offenses. He cites Gal 5:19–21 as evidence. Augustine refers to the Pauline list and states of the sins mentioned there: "coetera mortifera peccata, quae uno ictu perimunt." Augustine further affirms: "There are certain actions that are good or bad according to the perversity of the causes that lead us to perform them.... But when our actions are sinful in themselves, as are adultery, theft, blasphemy, who will dare say that if we perform them with the intent to do good they are not sins...?"[20]

Few would want to deny that there are objectively evil actions; but two points must be made. First, in developing this thesis, Huftier has confused parenetic discourse with explanatory discourse. He uses the Pauline list from Galatians to bolster his contention that certain actions are evil *ex objecto* in the traditional sense. That is, prior to a consideration of any circumstances or intent they are morally wrong. The text of Augustine cited above is used in the same way. However, the question is not whether adultery is justified by a good intent. It is rather how the circumstances and intent must be weighed before an action is called adultery (or theft, or blasphemy). Parenetic discourse such as that found in Paul and Augustine does not tell us that. Somewhat similarly, Huftier gives as a general criterion for acts intrinsically evil their opposition to the virtues. No one can question this as a general statement. But the question is: which actions are to count as contrary to the virtues?

The second reflection concerns the axiom "a good end does not justify an evil means." Huftier repeatedly uses this to establish the fact that the intention plays only an attenuating or aggravating role if the means is already morally wrong. That is certainly true. But it is not the crucial question. The crucial question is: what makes the means *morally* wrong? One does not answer that question by referring to texts condemnatory of murder, adultery, theft, etc.; for these terms contain value judgments, scil., that the evil in question (e.g., the killing) is not justified.

Therefore the axiom under discussion must be carefully understood. If it means that a nonmoral good (end) does not justify a morally bad means, it is correct. If, however, it is understood to mean that no good end (whether the good be moral or nonmoral) can justify a *nonmoral* evil

---

[19] *Ibid.*, p. 470.

[20] *Ibid.*, p. 475. The reference is *De baptismo contra Don.* 2, 6, 9 (*PL* 43, 132).

means, it is false; for it is precisely the good end envisaged that justifies causing or permitting a nonmoral evil.[21]

This point is made clearly by Franz Scholz.[22] He notes that "the sentence 'a good end can justify a physically evil means' stands in agreement with the thought of Aquinas, who sharply distinguishes moral evil from innerworldly (scil., nonmoral) evil." Scholz's study is an interesting summary of the attitudes of Thomas and Bonaventure on exception-making. He begins by noting several problem areas where earlier formulations are undergoing modification. For instance, the formulations of many manualists (e.g., Prümmer, Noldin-Schmidt, Zalba, Ermecke) and of the magisterium (e.g., Pius XII) forbade direct abortion even to save the life of the mother. Now, however, we see statements similar to that of J. Stimpfle, the Bishop of Augsburg: "He who performs an abortion, except to save the life of the mother, sins gravely and burdens his conscience with the killing of human life."[23] Scholz sees this as a process of adjustment, a shifting of marginal instances which, logically speaking, converts an exceptionless behavioral norm into a rule of thumb. He cites other areas where such development is occurring: e.g., the suicide of an intelligence agent whose disclosures can gravely harm his country.

Is such development justified? It is at this point that Scholz refers to the thought of Thomas and Bonaventure as a basis for an affirmative answer. For Thomas, the order of reason is the criterion of the morally right and wrong. It is reason that constitutes the natural moral law. Thomas distinguished two senses of the natural moral law, the strict (and proper) and the broader. In the strict and proper sense it refers to those principles of practical reason that are intuitively clear (we must act according to reason, good is to be done and evil avoided, etc.) and to those conclusions that follow from them without discursive reflection. These are exceptionless principles because they correspond to the initial intention of the lawgiver or law. In the broader sense there are derivative applications of these formal principles (e.g., "Thou shalt not directly kill an innocent human being"). It is Scholz's thesis that for both Thomas and Bonaventure these more concrete norms can suffer exceptions.

[21] In this respect I believe Karl Hörmann has misunderstood and therefore misrepresented the position of Joseph Fuchs (cf. K. Hörmann, "Die Bedeutung der konkreten Wirklichkeit für das sittliche Tun nach Thomas von Aquin," Theologisch-praktische Quartalschrift 123 [1975] 118–29.) Hörmann writes as if Fuchs (and to some extent Knauer and Schüller) would say nothing about the moral quality of a class of acts prior to the weighing of the intention. This is not Fuchs's position.

[22] Franz Scholz, "Durch ethische Grenzsituationen aufgeworfene Normenprobleme," Theologisch-praktische Quartalschrift 123 (1975) 341–55.

[23] From the Kirchenzeitung für die Diözese Augsburg, cited in Scholz, p. 342.

Thomas treats the matter when asking about the possibility of dispensations from the Decalogue.[24] An exception is possible only when there is a difference between the original sense of the norm and its verbal formulation. Scholz argues that this possibility exists even where concrete prohibitions such as the fifth to seventh Commandments are involved. Thomas seems to deny this in the corpus of the article, but Scholz believes his final word on the point is contained in the answer to the third objection, where the distinction between original sense and formulation appears.

Scholz takes the fifth Commandment as an example. The formulation of this prohibition forbids the taking of human life. Yet there are the instances of war and capital punishment. How do these make sense if the Decalogue is "beyond dispensation" (exceptionless)? For Thomas, so Scholz argues, the divine intention is aimed only at the unjust destruction of life ("occisio hominis . . . secundum quod habet rationem indebiti"). Thus the verbal formulation is not precise enough. As imprecise, it must be viewed as conditional, scil., applicable to those cases in which the taking of life contradicts the original divine intent. For this reason the formulated norm must be regarded as a rule of thumb where exceptions cannot be excluded.

On this basis Scholz argues that Thomas clearly distinguishes the factual notion (*Tatsachenbegriff*, killing) from the value notion (*Unwertbegriff*, murder). The only thing that is exceptionless is the sense of the norm that underlies the notion of murder. Thus, eventually it is for men to determine what physical actions are to count as "murder," "adultery," and "theft." This cannot be determined a priori.

How is it, Scholz asks, that an action which appears to be murder really is not? Thomas uses the axiom "change of matter" (*mutatio materiae*) to explain this. The object or matter of the fifth Commandment is not simply killing, but unjust killing. Therefore, when a killing is justified, it no longer falls under the matter of this prohibition. The "matter" has changed. This change is possible because of the difference between the sense and the formulation of the norm.

Therefore Scholz concludes that Thomas clearly distinguished between physical and moral evil. The evil remains physical (better, nonmoral) when there is no proportionate reason for its existence. In this Thomistic analysis Scholz sees the basis for the rejection of actions that are intrinsically evil (a rejection, however, that Thomas himself did not accept). Something very similar must be said of Bonaventure, though this will not be detailed here. Ultimately, then, Scholz suggests that it is the task of reason to determine whether and which proportionate reasons

[24] *Sum. theol.* 1–2, q. 100, a. 8.

remove concrete human actions from the class of prohibited actions; for he thinks it clear that some of our formulations (e.g., "never directly kill an innocent person") do not possess the precision demanded by Thomas to make them altogether exceptionless.[25]

Walter G. Jeffko of Fitchburg State College approaches the question of norms from out of a processive view of reality (the total human situation is itself in process).[26] This would seem to deny the very foundation of any moral absolutes. Jeffko sets out to show why this is not so.

After explaining why he believes community is the ultimate standard by which we can judge the morality of any action, Jeffko argues that this absoluteness or ultimacy of community as a value does not mean that other values are provisional or relative. To explain this, Jeffko distinguishes between intrinsic and prima-facie good and evil. Intrinsic evil denotes a specific act which is universally and necessarily evil, or evil in all actual and realistically possible situations. In contrast to such a notion, prima-facie evil denotes an act that is "significantly evil and therefore evil in general, or evil in the ordinary run of situations." Where prima-facie evil is concerned, it is necessary to distinguish between the common and particular features of an act. The common features refer to those shared by all instances of a class of acts. For instance, an individual war is included within the class "war" because of certain features which apply to all wars and without which they would not be called wars. These common features are the "essential core" of the act. The particular features of an act denote the individuating circumstances of a singular, concrete act within a given class, which circumstances make it that act or occurrence and no other: e.g., the Vietnam War. The notion of prima-facie evil applies to the common features, the essential core of an act.

"It is," Jeffko argues, "the evilness of this essential core which makes a given class of acts evil in general, or evil in the ordinary run of situations. However, since prima-facie evil as such does not apply to the particular features of an act, we cannot say that the evilness of the common features makes every instance of that act evil."[27] It is possible for the particular features of an act to possess more good than the evil contained in its common features. According to Jeffko, this happens relatively rarely because the essential core tends to override or outweigh the particular features.

[25] Cf. also Bernard Häring, "Dynamism and Continuity in a Personalistic Approach to Natural Law," in Norm and Context in Christian Ethics, ed. Gene Outka and Paul Ramsey (New York, 1968) pp. 210–11.

[26] Walter G. Jeffko, "Processive Relationism and Ethical Absolutes," American Benedictine Review 26 (1975) 283–97.

[27] Ibid., p. 294.

He then turns to intrinsic evil. This notion applies to the act *as a whole* (including common and particular features). That means that an act is intrinsically evil "when its essential core is so gravely evil that no actual or possible set of circumstances, whatever goodness they may contain, could render an instance of that act good in the concrete. . . . " In the concrete the act always possesses more evil than good. Jeffko gives slavery as an example of something intrinsically evil. It so gravely violates the constituent values of community (equality, freedom, justice) that one cannot conceive of situations where it is morally right. War, by contrast, is a prima-facie evil only; the particular features can outweigh the evil of the common features.

Jeffko believes that his moral theory speaks to the situation-ethics debate. The fundamental doctrine of Fletcherian situationism is that moral quality is an extrinsic predicate. That is, no act has an essential core which is morally right or wrong prima facie. It is neutral and gets moral quality according as it is "directed by 'love.'" Jeffko therefore contends that Fletcher's basic weakness is that he denies prima-facie wrongfulness and locates all morality "within the particular features of an individual concrete act."[28]

Several things are interesting about this article. First, it is in substance a linear descendant of the work of Schüller–Knauer–Fuchs–Janssens and others. But it uses the language (prima-facie evil) most recently associated with W. D. Ross in *The Right and the Good*,[29] much as Schüller had. This brings the theological discussion closer to the philosophical—which is all to the good. A step further in this direction would be to point out that the manualist notion of evil *ex objecto* really should have been interpreted as prima-facie evil. I believe this is what Fuchs and Schüller have been driving at.

Secondly, Jeffko retains the notion of intrinsic evil but uses it in a way slightly at variance with the traditional understanding. An act is intrinsically evil if its essential core is "so gravely evil that no actual or possible set of circumstances, whatever goodness they may contain, could render an instance of that act good in the concrete. . . . " This insistence that it is the act as a whole that is to be judged is certainly correct. Fuchs is most recently associated with such an emphasis.[30] And the notion of intrinsic evil, applied to the act as a whole, is not an inaccurate rendering. However, I wonder if it is all that useful. The term has a history. One of the dominant understandings of the term in recent history is that an action is morally evil prior to a consideration of

[28] *Ibid.*, p. 297.

[29] W. D. Ross, *The Right and the Good* (Oxford, 1965) pp. 18–36.

[30] Joseph Fuchs, S.J., "The Absoluteness of Moral Terms," *Gregorianum* 52 (1971) 415–58.

circumstances and end.[31] That is not what Jeffko wants, nor, I believe, what he should want. But to continue to use the term could all too easily suggest the validity of its traditional interpretation. Terms such as "practical absolute" and "virtually exceptionless" are probably more useful.

Finally, there is Jeffko's criterion as to whether the good in the entire act outweighs the evil. This criterion is community. Thus, he says of slavery that it "so gravely violates the constituent values of community —equality, freedom and justice—that I cannot conceive a situation in which it would be morally justified." Contrarily, the ultimate justification of war lies in community, its preservation and protection. It would have been helpful if Jeffko had applied this to other problems (abortion, self-defense, business ethics, sterilization, sexual ethics) to test not its legitimacy but its usefulness. There is probably little doubt that conduct which is morally wrong affects community destructively, at least indirectly. But it is not always easy to move backwards from community to see whether an act is morally right or wrong. In this sense it is true to say that Jeffko's study does not tell us how one determines more proximately whether the good in an act outweighs its evil aspects.

These "Notes" have taken issue with Joseph Fletcher more often than not, sometimes because flamboyant rhetoric has been used as if it were moral reasoning. It is a pleasure, therefore, and a kind of verbal restitution to note that with no sacrifice of his beloved pyrotechnics Fletcher has produced what I believe is a very perceptive study.[32] In the wake of Watergate, there were those who argued that the whole mess was a working-out of Fletcherian situationism in public life. In the course of his long response to this accusation, he compares Daniel Ellsberg's violation with that of Nixon's "plumbers" to see which can be said to be justified. In both examples the accused appealed to the end as justification of the means. Ellsberg reasoned that he was justified in letting the American people know the hidden facts about the conduct and engineering of the Vietnam War. The "plumbers" who burglarized the office of Ellsberg's psychiatrist appealed to national security.

In analyzing these and other instances, Fletcher points out that the true question is not exactly stated when one asks whether the end justifies the means; the question is "does a worthy end justify *any* means?" He correctly says that the answer is a resounding "no." A proper proportion must be preserved. As a guide to whether the means is proportionate, he cites the advice of Arjay Miller, Dean of Stanford

---

[31] I say "dominant" because the term has been used in a variety of ways in the past.

[32] Joseph Fletcher, "Situation Ethics, Law, and Watergate," *Cumberland Law Review* 6 (1975) 35–60.

University's Graduate School of Business: "When, if ever, does the end justify the means? As a guide in answering such questions, I propose a very simple test: do that which you would feel comfortable explaining on television."[33] In other words, submit both your goals and means to the scrutiny of the public conscience. This is useful as far as it goes. That is, one who would be unwilling in principle to submit actions involving evil to public scrutiny as a test would be highly suspect. More positively, such scrutiny is a generally valid test of proportionality; but it is no guarantee. Furthermore, if the moral theologian settles for such indirect tests of proportionality, he spares himself the hard work of developing criteria for the hierarchizing of values and the development of a concrete *ordo caritatis* in our time. This sparing is comfortable, but moral science is the loser.

Where Fletcher is particularly perceptive is in his contention that neither Ellsberg nor the "plumbers" raised the issue of whether the end justifies the means. "Both Ellsberg and those who burglarized his doctor's office were in agreement that an end could justify a means. . . . What set them against each other lay at a deeper level—their values and ideals—the ends they were serving."[34] He is absolutely correct in pointing out that it was not the flexibility of the Nixonites that was wrong, but their motivation. Their first-order priority was to stay in power. The response of revulsion to the arguments used by the Watergate defendants was not traceable to the attitude that the end was thought to justify the means (national security does justify doing some damage if this security is truly at stake) but rather that these means were used to prosecute a thoroughly questionable end (retention of power by Nixon) and then this end was deceptively sanctified as "national security." Whatever objections one may have to Fletcher's ethical system, it would be grossly inaccurate and unfair to say it spawned that type of moral collapse.

In summary, then, here we have three more studies (Scholz, Jeffko, Häring) that are moving in the direction of the thought of Fuchs, Schüller, Janssens, Böckle, and others already reported in these "Notes." I believe this is of great practical significance, and for two reasons, one touching procedure, the other content.

First, this development in moral thought is occurring at the same time that certain concrete actions are being proscribed by ecclesiastical authorities as "intrinsically evil" or at least "never justified." This dichotomizing of thought means that certain official positions will

---

[33] Cited by Fletcher, *ibid.*, p. 54, from *Harper's*, Oct. 1974, at p. 84.
[34] *Art. cit.*, p. 55.

continue to be proposed without the support of the theological community. That is an unhealthy situation in all respects.

One could, of course, respond to this phenomenon (as indeed some have) by saying that theologians ought to get in line, that their reflections have not been sufficiently influenced by pronouncements of magisterium, and so on. I believe this is far too simple an answer and one that is profoundly juridical at its root (i.e., one that faces questions of truth in terms of a dominant concern for superior-subject relationships).[35] The task of theologians is not to repeat formulations of the magisterium. It is rather to question, probe, hypothesize, analyze, in an effort to aid the magisterium in keeping its formulations not only consistent with substantial traditional values but also accurate and persuasive in a constantly changing world.[36] No single theologian's reflections are the final word on the execution of this indispensable task. In this sense it is improper to take any individual's reflections or writings as decisive. (It should be added here that the faithful need education on this point, as do some of us theologians.) But when there is a growing and, I believe, widespread convergence of opinion in the theological community about the meaning and limits of concrete moral norms, it would be profoundly counterproductive if the hierarchical community, or at least significant numbers of this community, were to speak and act as if this convergence did not exist or need not be attended to. This is not to advocate theological arrogation of hierarchical prerogatives, for the two teaching functions in the Church are distinct. It is simply to say that neither can be exercised without the other.

An excellent example of the co-operative character of these functions is *Dignitatis humanae* of Vatican II. Without the theological perspectives of John Courtney Murray and Pietro Pavan, it is unlikely that this document on religious liberty would exist at all.[37] But without the co-operation of the American bishops and the ultimate seal of the Council fathers, it would not exist as an authentic Church document.

[35] Cf. Richard McBrien, "Catholic Theology, 1974: Problems and Prospects," *Proceedings of the Catholic Theological Society of America* 29 (1974) 397–411.

[36] This task was stated beautifully by Pope Paul VI in his allocution to the International Congress on the Theology of Vatican II, Oct. 1, 1966; cf. *Documentation catholique* 63 (1966) 1738.

[37] On Nov. 16, 1975, the Woodstock Theological Center sponsored a symposium commemorating the tenth anniversary of *Dignitatis humanae*. Msgr. Pietro Pavan ("Ecumenism and the Declaration of Vatican II on Religious Freedom") and Most Rev. James Rausch ("*Dignitatis humanae*: The Unfinished Agenda") delivered the major papers, with responses by George Lindbeck, Manfred Vogel, and Walter J. Burghardt, S.J. The proceedings will be published at a later date. An abbreviated version of Pavan's talk is found in *Origins* 27 (1975) 357–59.

There can be little doubt that the document is in some respects discontinuous with authoritative Church teaching of another era, a point made by Walter J. Burghardt, S.J., in his comments on Pavan's paper. For that reason among others, it took an uphill fight and much personal pain for it to see the light of day. But it could do so only because theologians had questioned earlier formulations of the matter and because this questioning occurred in a context of conversation between these theologians and the episcopal community. Archbishop Joseph L. Bernardin, in his report to the 1974 Synod of Bishops, drew attention to this when he recognized "the need for a new dialogue between the theological and episcopal communities in the Church for the welfare of God's people."[38]

In this respect it is worth calling attention to a remarkably fine paper by B. C. Butler.[39] After describing and carefully distinguishing authority and constraint, Bishop Butler turns his attention to the present situation in the Church. He sees it as a "crisis of authority." Authority speaks "with one voice in the Council and with another voice in its day-to-day performances after the Council." The result is that the measure of consent from the faithful, on which authority depends for its efficacy, is diminished.

What can be done? Obviously, the mature Christian must constantly remind himself of the response due to authority in the Church, an authority derived from the divine authority incarnate in Christ. But Butler then insists that authority is not located exclusively in the pope and bishops. "The authority of Christ in the Church is as extensive and as multifarious as the life of Christ in his mystical body. Thus there is a kind of authority appertaining to theology and sound scholarship despite the fact that theologians as such do not constitute an ordained ministry in the Church."[40] This diffused or "unofficial" authority, as Butler phrases it, is not confined to matters of practical discipline "but extends to the sphere of Christian doctrinal and theological teaching." Thus he sees the present understanding of the term "magisterium" as unfortunate. "Magisterial authority is not confined in the Church to official magisterial authority"; for we all belong to both the *ecclesia discens* and *docens*. "Everyone in the Church who has reached maturity has, at some time or another, to play the role of the teacher, the *magister*, the *ecclesia docens*."

He then turns to the response due to official Church authority in doctrinal matters. The claim of some teachings is, of course, identical

---

[38] Cf. *Catholic Mind* 73 (1975) 17.
[39] B. C. Butler, "Authority and the Christian Conscience," *Clergy Review* 60 (1975) 3–17.
[40] *Ibid.*, pp. 12–13.

with the claim of divine revelation itself. However, he continues, "to require the same adhesion for doctrines that are indeed taught by officials with authority but to which the Church has not irrevocably committed herself is to abuse authority." What is the proper response? Butler refers to the "respect that is due to the considered actions and utterances of those in positions of legitimate and official authority." More specifically, "the mood of the devout believer will be . . . a welcoming gratitude that goes along with the keen alertness of a critical mind, and with a good will concerned to play its part both in the purification and the development of the Church's understanding of her inheritance. . . . "[41]

It will come as no shock to readers of these pages to learn that the compositor considers this essay superb. When Bishop Butler speaks of "respect" and "welcoming gratitude" combined with a "critical mind" and "good will concerned to play its part in the purification and development," he has put the matter as well as it can be put. The theologian is in the service of the Church. He serves it well neither by uncritical obedience nor by disrespectful defiance, for neither of these contributes to the "purification and development of the Church's understanding of her inheritance." If Butler's "keen alertness with a critical mind" means anything, it implies the possibility of disagreement, and precisely as part of that "good will concerned to play its part both in the purification and development. . . . " If such disagreement is experienced as a threat and treated as such, something is wrong.

In other words, the effort to articulate our faith and its behavioral implications in our time is a dialogical and processive one. This point was specifically highlighted by Bernard Häring in the essay reported above.[42] He concluded: "There is no doubt that for her own growth, for her abiding in the truth, and for the fruitful exercise of her pastoral magisterium, the Church needs an atmosphere of freedom to examine the enduring validity of traditional norms, and the right of a sincere conscience humbly to doubt about norms which, in many or even most of the cases, are not accepted by sincere Christians." Here Häring and Bishop Butler are at one.

The second point I should like to raise concerns content and is of some urgency. It touches the difference between two types of moral reasoning and therefore teaching in a concrete area. Direct sterilization, as it is commonly understood, can serve as an example. Most, or at least many, members of the theological community believe that direct sterilization is not always morally wrong. The official position, however, is that it is never justified. What is "never justified" can be argued in two ways—

---

[41] *Ibid.*, p. 16.   [42] Cf. n. 16 above.

and these two ways represent different types of teaching, the second coming very close to what one might call moral policy.

The first type is a kind of act analysis which concludes that direct sterilization is a violation (as contraceptive in intent) of the purpose of the sexual endowment and therefore intrinsically evil. The analysis can be made in any number of ways, e.g., from a faculty-finality approach to Grisez's direct choice against a basic good (procreation). I do not believe that the conclusion ("never justified") can be taught on bases such as these. Why? As I read the literature, the answer would be as follows: such sterilization is a nonmoral evil which, like all nonmoral evils, may be caused or permitted for a truly proportionate reason. If we say anything else, we are attributing a value and an inviolability to the sexual endowment which tradition has refused to give to life itself.

However—and this brings us to the second type of teaching—even though individual acts of direct sterilization cannot be shown to be intrinsically evil, such sterilization is certainly a disvalue to be avoided in so far as such avoidance is compatible with other urgent values at stake. Indeed, there could be cultural and atmospheric reasons why its total exclusion could be taught (a policy) as the better path to follow, all things considered. The type of reasoning used by many sixteenth- and seventeenth-century moralists (e.g., danger of abuse, the consequences *ex semel licita*, etc.) leads one to believe that many prohibitions they said were "against nature" and "intrinsically evil" were really conclusions drawn on what I have called policy grounds.[43] But if this is the case, it is the reasons for the policy that ought to be weighed and argued.

For instance, would a moral stance permitting individual exceptions lead, in our atmosphere, to so much abuse, to such mushrooming of "sterilization mills," that the course of prudence is a policy of total exclusion? That is a possibility. But as a possibility, several things must be noted about it. First, it must be argued on its own grounds—and the grounds of such policy would necessarily be the following two: (1) foreseen and unavoidable harmful effects from any other policy; (2) harmful effects which would outweigh the possible goods to be achieved. Secondly, since general prohibitive policy (in contrast to teaching about

---

[43] E.g., Thomas Sanchez, S.J. (1550–1610) argued that it was never licit to "expel semen" even to save one's life, because of the intense pleasure involved. If such a possibility were ever conceded, he argued, the danger would be such that, blinded by lust, man would easily persuade himself that he had such reasons on many occasions, and thus fornication, adultery, etc. would damage the common good (*De matrimonio* 9, disp. 17). John de Lugo, S. J. (1583–1660) applied similar reasoning to abortion (cf. *De justitia et jure*, disp. 10, sect. 5). See also Dominicus Viva, S. J. (1648–1726), *Theses damnatae*, prop. 34, and Patricius Sporer (+ 1714), *Theologia sacramentalis*, 4, cap. 4, sect. 1. I am indebted to John R. Connery, S.J., for these references.

the inherent moral wrongness of individual actions) is formulated out of consideration of beneficial and harmful general effects, it is clearly dependent on historical and cultural factors that are changeable. Therefore policy is reformulable. Thirdly, such teaching would seem to be close to Church law. As such, it resists exceptions or excusing causes only if it can be successfully argued that the policy is in the category of *lex lata in praesumptione periculi communis*, effectively removing the very discretion of the individual for exception-making. The burden of proof rests on the one who would interpret his policy in such a way, and it is, in the case in question, an extremely heavy burden.

In summary, if one does not make this distinction, the absoluteness of the official position all too easily reverts to and rests on its authoritative proposal. If one makes the distinction but does not rigorously pursue its implications, the same result occurs. In either case the position is held as exceptionless largely in terms of authoritative statement. Eventually this too easily implies that the conclusion is as valid as the authority is legitimate. This represents a kind of juridicizing of the ongoing search for moral truth and is ultimately harmful to the magisterial function of the Church, and therefore to those to whom this function is both unique privilege and absolute necessity.

CARE FOR THE DYING AND EUTHANASIA

The case of Karen Ann Quinlan focused worldwide attention on the problem of care for the desperately ill and dying patient.[44] To a lesser degree this happening was foreshadowed by the predicament of Dr. Urs Peter Haemmerli, a Swiss physician.[45] He was accused of mercy killing when he refused to use artificial life-prolonging measures with dying patients, but sought to give his patients peace and comfort in their dying. Haemmerli stated: "What has happened to me could just as easily happen to any other doctor in Europe or America."[46]

A host of factors, not least of which is the technological sophistication of modern life-sustaining devices, have propelled the problem of care for the dying to center stage.[47] In some countries groups have formed to

[44] Cf. "A Right to Die?" *Newsweek*, Nov. 3, 1975, pp. 58 ff.; Peter Steinfels, "The Quinlan Decision," *Commonweal* 102 (1975) 584; Patrick F. and Carol Berger, "Death on Demand," *ibid.*, pp. 585–89; Thomas A. Shannon, "A Triumph of Technology," *ibid.*, pp. 589–90; Charles M. Whelan, "Karen Ann Quinlan: Patient or Prisoner?" *America* 133 (1975) 346–47.

[45] *Washington Post*, Feb. 3, 1975, A1. Also "Diskussion um Sterbehilfe und Euthanasie in der Schweiz," *Herder Korrespondenz* 29 (1975) 108–10.

[46] *Washington Post, loc. cit.*

[47] Some recent literature: K. S. Satyapal, "Should a Patient Be Allowed to Die?" *Journal of the Irish College of Physicians and Surgeons* 4 (1975) 164–68; Jerry J. Griffen, "Family Decision," *American Journal of Nursing* 75 (1975) 795–96; Norman St. John-Stevas,

sponsor and lobby for voluntary euthanasia. Most people are familiar with several versions of the living will and with attempts to get legal recognition for it.[48] The very definition of death has become problematic, especially as attempts are made to define death with a view to transplantation of organs.

There are many difficulties in discussing this problem in a disciplined way. First, the matter is inseparably intertwined with deep emotional responses and commitments. Several authors see this—especially in circles promoting voluntary euthanasia—as a natural and quite understandable reaction to the senseless prolonging of life to which people are sometimes exposed in their dying. Then there is the term "euthanasia" with its annoying ambiguities. Recent literature from Germany adopts the term *Sterbehilfe* (help in dying) but even that has been clouded by the attempt to include under it what is called *Sterbenachhilfe* (a form of active euthanasia). These ambiguities have not been dissolved, I believe, by Gustave Ermecke's inclusion under "active euthanasia" of the administration of pain relievers where the intention is pain relief and not directly death, though death is foreseeably hastened.[49] Nor does Albert Walkenbach's reverse usage help very much.[50] He applies "euthanasia" to those forms of care that have been regarded traditionally as morally licit (e.g., noninstigation of artificial life-supports, pain relief during dying) and argues that killing is not truly euthanasia. This is all right, of course, but it will leave Walkenbach talking to himself.

The Quinlan case proved to be the gathering place of unique importance and intensity for the rehearsal of contradictory and confusing statements and claims. Symbolic of this was the statement of Daniel Coburn, Miss Quinlan's court-appointed attorney. He is reported to have remarked that death with dignity in her case is a "complete shell game. This is euthanasia; one human being, by an act or lack of an act, is going to cause the death of another."[51]

"Euthanasia: A 'Pleasant Sounding Word,'" *America* 131 (1975) 421-22; Aneka Lant, "Euthanasia—A Patient's Point of View," *Nursing Mirror* 140 (1975) 73; "An Easy Death" (editorial), *British Medical Journal*, March 29, 1975, p. 704; Andres M. Tornos, "Para un morir 'autentico,'" *Razón y fe* 191 (1975) 62-70; Charles A. Curran, "Death and Dying," *Religion and Health* 14 (1975) 254-64; *Linacre Quarterly* 42 (1975) 86-122 (special issue devoted to care for the dying, with articles by Ned H. Cassem, S.J., Garth F. Tagge, M.D., William Shoemaker, M.D., George J. Annas, J.D., and Richard A. McCormick, S.J.).

[48] For the Catholic version of the living will, cf. "Christian Affirmation of Life," *Catholic Mind* 74 (1975) 5-6.

[49] Gustave Ermecke, "Grundüberlegungen zur 'Sterbehilfe,'" *Die neue Ordnung* 29 (1975) 128-33.

[50] Albert Walkenbach, "Lebensverlängerung um jeden Preis?" *Lebendiges Zeugnis* 30 (1975) 21-29.

[51] *Washington Post*, Oct. 21, 1975, A4.

Whatever may be said for the accuracy of Mr. Coburn's analysis, it certainly has not been the way the matter has been viewed for many years. A moral policy with its own widely-accepted vocabulary (ordinary, extraordinary means) had for years enjoyed a kind of pacific possession. By saying this, I do not wish to canonize such language; the point is rather that the value judgments behind the policy were accepted and the policy was implemented, at times not without anguish and doubt to be sure, within an atmosphere of trust and communication between doctor, patient, and family, and above all with the confidence that the best interests of the patient were being sought and served. The pacific possession has been eroded by many factors, prominent among them being the destructive malpractice situation in the United States.[52] Be that as it may, one of the staples of this policy is the moral difference between not instigating or withdrawing certain life-supports (omission) on the one hand, and active intervention to bring about death (commission) on the other. The distinction is sometimes stated by the use of the terms "active" and "passive" euthanasia, though this terminology is itself objectionable, as will become clear in this roundup. While care for the dying must issue from perspectives far broader than these and while the moral problems of this care range far beyond this distinction, I shall, in reporting recent literature, constantly return to it in one way or another—especially since several key articles attempt to challenge the distinction.

In an interesting article Kenneth Vaux contends that "widespread acceptance of euthanasia will not occur because man is constitutionally unable to acquiesce in the face of death."[53] This inability has profound biological and spiritual roots that synthesize into a medical commitment to preserve life and the social prohibition of euthanasia. What will emerge from the present crisis, Vaux believes, is a wholesome corrective to the excesses of life-prolonging technology.

However, if there would be a general acceptance of euthanasia, both active and passive, Vaux foresees three things to follow: there will be a corrosion of the unique value of the individual; the physician is likely to become in increasing measure a technician and a tool of public policy; we will erode our responsibilities as a society to deal constructively with health problems.

Vaux's study is a thoughtful bit of social history. At one point,

[52] Cf. Richard A. McCormick, S.J., "The Karen Ann Quinlan Case," *Journal of the American Medical Association* 234 (1975) 1057.

[53] Kenneth Vaux, "The Social Acceptance of Euthanasia: Prospects and Problems," in *Euthanasia Symposium* (proceedings of a symposium sponsored by the Catholic Hospital Conference of Saskatchewan, Alberta, and British Columbia, Oct. 3-4, 1974, mimeographed) pp. 11-18.

however, in dealing with a possibly new ethos in which people wish against life for death, he notes that the language will be "couched in very pious and moral language. The quality of life will be a frequently used phrase. We will probably talk about death in terms of the person's own good."[54] The term "quality of life" conjures up all kinds of abusive possibilities; therefore I wish we could find a better phrase. But to associate the notion, and the perspectives on life and death that generate it, with a destructive euthanasist ethos is a kind of overkill. There is a humanly valid and thoroughly Christian rendering of that notion, and to make it the language of a single and reprehensible ethos is to push us back to a form of vitalism that is neither human nor Christian.

A somewhat similar linguistic phenomenon occurs in the document on euthanasia first published in the *Humanist* and then in *Figaro* (July 1, 1974).[55] It is signed by three Nobel Prize winners: Jacques Monod, Linus Pauling, George Thomson. The document comes out in favor of euthanasia "for ethical reasons." It continues: "We appeal to enlightened public opinion to pass beyond traditional taboos and evolve toward a compassionate attitude with regard to the useless sufferings at the moment of death." The second part of the manifesto concerns itself with practical consequences and qualifications of such a position.

Paul Valadier, S. J., director of studies for the Jesuit philosophical and theological faculties of France, responds to this statement by highlighting its ethical method and implications.[56] He does this because he feels that many may be duped into accepting a discussible *moral* position under cover of *scientific* authority. First, the document does not discuss the traditional arguments; rather it gathers to itself adjectives like generosity, goodness, and justice. Valadier sees in this the classic strategy of putting any opposing view in a defensive posture where it must fend off accusations of being inhumane, barbarous, and unreasonable. Furthermore, the ethical reasons advanced are really a cover for the implicit postulate of the authors: "the morality of the authors is guided by that which science and technology make possible." In doing this, Valadier believes the authors have enslaved themselves to science in principle and forfeited the possibility of ever giving it moral direction. He also protests that the entire text "rests on an identification between the superiority (scientific or technological) of our societies and maturity of the moral conscience." By implication this means that tradition equals barbarity and inhumanity.

Such a peremptory attribution of virtue to the position one defends

[54] *Ibid.*, p. 9.
[55] Cf. "Le manifeste des Prix Nobel," *Cahiers*, July 1975, pp. 411-13.
[56] Paul Valadier, S.J., "Implications éthiques de ce manifeste," *ibid.*, pp. 414-19.

Valadier regards as a closed morality closely related to authoritarianism. He is concerned not to enter the debate about the problem of euthanasia—which he considers a genuine problem—but only to show that the authors have not done so. Thus the postulates of the authors "imply an ethical and philosophical position which is not self-validating, while the vigor of their position consists in its presentation as the only humane and enlightened one.'

Franz Böckle discusses humanly-dignified dying.[57] Key to Böckle's thought is the distinction between death and dying. Death is an end, a condition. Dying is a part of life, its last phase. Since this is so, "the companying we provide to the dying person is therefore always a life-help (Lebenshilfe), a help in the last difficult part of our life." Böckle fears that our debates over fringe cases can lead us to overlook the true nature of aid to the dying. The personal help we provide must correspond to the desire of the dying person for company. If it does, then the difficult decisions about concrete medical means are seen in a different perspective. This companying, he argues in another essay,[58] must aim at helping "the dying person discover the meaning of the last phase of life so he can believe it is worth living it."

In the course of his altogether balanced presentations, Böckle approaches the question of killing and allowing to die. He makes two interesting points, the first with regard to killing in general, the second its application to the euthanasia discussion. As for the prohibition against killing, Böckle notes that it is not absolute but conditional. He writes:

This conditional character of the prohibition against killing is not removed through the theological grounding of the prohibition. The life of man is for our human community the most fundamental of goods, a good that underlies all other values. But as concrete bodily existence it is not the highest of goods. In this concrete form it does not represent a value that can never concur with another more important and to-be-preferred value. Thus traditional theology balances the life of the individual who has offended community justice against the common good and so justifies capital punishment.[59]

Thus for Böckle any killing is justified by what he calls a "rigorous weighing of values." Applying this to suicide, he continues: "'To ask about the eventual licitness of suicide is to ask about the good whose realization could justify the evil of causing the loss of life' (Schüller).

[57] Franz Böckle, "Menschwürdiges Sterben als Problem," Die neue Ordnung 29 (1975) 293–99.
[58] Franz Böckle, "Recht auf menschwürdiges Sterben," Evangelische Kommentare 8 (1975) 71–74.
[59] Ibid., p. 72.

Hence, in view of modern methods of extortion, suicide to ward off a great harm to one's own countrymen is widely held to be morally permissible." Böckle rejects such a conclusion when speaking of the dying; "for the Christian knows about the promises of the gospel, that redemption grows out of difficulty and affliction. . . ."[60]

In conclusion, Böckle accepts the distinction between commission and omission, but he feels that the true ethical problem revolves around the question of when omission is morally right or wrong. And the answer to this cannot be preprogramed but must emerge from a consideration of all the circumstances.

What are some of these circumstances? Albert Ziegler identifies them within the over-all ethic of care for the dying.[61] Biological existence is not simply and in itself a value, but it is a value as the basis of human existence. In this light, care for the dying (Sterbehilfe) must be the attempt to preserve biological existence as long as possible *as the basis for human existence*. If it is truly human existence that is controlling, then all the goals or goods that comprise such existence must be a part of care for the dying. Ziegler identifies three: prolonging life, lessening suffering, preserving freedom. All must be considered and so no one can be absolutized. Thus, there is no true care for the dying if life is inconsiderately prolonged (with no consideration of increased suffering and diminished liberty). Similarly, there is no true care for the dying if freedom is inconsiderately maximized (scil., with no consideration of whether and how suffering is increased and life shortened). It is the task of care for the dying to balance all of these values in the use of means, a task that is more than clinical-technical in nature.

Ziegler puts a heavy emphasis on companying with the dying. Such companying is only help-in-dying if it helps life, not death. However, it is senseless to prolong life artificially when either pain is increased or freedom is not maintained. "Such a considerate rejection of further 'artificial' life-supports is, however, in no way 'artificial' death-causing" (Sterbenachhilfe). One who no longer administers artificial life-supports "does not perform death-causing but allows a person to die."[62] Thus Ziegler accepts the traditional distinction as morally crucial.

One matter strikes me as odd in Ziegler's very helpful study. He insists that it is not biological life for its own sake that is to be protected, but biological life in so far as it is the basis of human existence. On the other hand, when dealing with the worth of the human person, he argues that

---

[60] *Ibid.*, pp. 73–74.

[61] Albert Ziegler, "Sterbehilfe—Grundfragen und Thesen," *Orientierung* 39 (1975) 39–41, 55–58.

[62] *Ibid.*, p. 40.

this worth is not grounded in personal traits or life qualities but simply in the fact that the human being is there. Thus no definite value makes life worth living; it is life itself that is worth living. Therefore there is no such thing as a life not worth living (*lebensunwertes Leben*). Either I have misunderstood him or Ziegler is moving in two different and inconsistent directions; for how do his latter remarks square with his insistence that it is not biological life as such that is to be protected but biological life as the basis of human existence?

Two interesting statements of episcopal conferences touch the question of care for the dying. In a brief letter the English hierarchy note that it is not necessary to prolong indefinitely a life that is near its end.[63] Furthermore, they state—as did Pius XII—that the resources of medicine can be used to relieve suffering even if such treatment inevitably hastens the process of death.

However, this positive and compassionate aid brought to the dying is altogether different from the deliberate and direct suppression of one's own life or that of another. This manner of killing (sometimes called euthanasia or mercy killing) is murder. It is forbidden by the law of God as well as that of our country. The disposal of life is the prerogative of the God who gives life.

Clearly, for the English bishops "disposal of life" is the middle term of the argument. That is, killing is disposal of life, whereas withdrawal of artificial life-supports after a point is not such a disposal. We shall return to this point shortly.

A pastoral letter of the bishops of the Federal Republic of Germany was read in all the churches June 15, 1975.[64] The bishops are alarmed that euthanasia is being presented as a form of care for the dying (*Sterbehilfe*). Therefore they outline what should be regarded as true care for the dying. It includes the following: alleviation of suffering; creation of an atmosphere of solidarity and trust so that the sick person realizes that his humanity is esteemed; provision of spiritual solace and support. Finally, a death worthy of man means that

not all medical means are used if death is artificially postponed by doing so. This is the case, for example, when life can, in fact, be lengthened by means of medical measures, an operation perhaps, but when, unfortunately, despite the operation, or as a consequence of it, the sick person will suffer from severe physical or mental disturbances in the period thus wrung from death. In this situation the

[63] "Déclaration des évêques anglais sur l'euthanasie," *Documentation catholique* 72 (1975) 46.

[64] "Das Lebensrecht des Menschen und die Euthanasie," *Herder Korrespondenz* 29 (1975) 335–37. This is also available in the English edition of *L'Osservatore romano*, July 31, 1975, p. 3 ("Man's Right to Life and Euthanasia").

decision of the sick person not to undergo another operation is to be considered morally justifiable.[65]

The bishops then pose the question about the moral duty to use indefinitely artificial supports such as the respirator. Their answer is extremely interesting and deserves to be cited in full.

As long as there is any possibility of the sick man recovering in this way, we will have to use all such means. Also, it is the duty of the state to ensure that even costly apparatus and expensive medicines are available for those who need them. It is quite another matter when all hope of recovery is excluded and the use of particular medical techniques would only lengthen artificially a perhaps painful death. If the patient, relatives, and doctors decide after considering all the circumstances not to have recourse to exceptional measures and means, they cannot be accused of usurping illicitly the right to dispose of human life. The doctor must, of course, obtain first the consent of the patient or, if this is no longer possible, of his relatives.[66]

The document concludes by rebutting the contention that there is only a gradual difference between withdrawal of artificial supports and giving injections intended to cause death. "There is an essential difference between letting someone die and killing him. . . . " Thus what we owe the sick is not help to die (*Hilfe zum Sterben*) but help in dying (*Hilfe im Sterben*).

Several things are interesting about this pastoral. First, it is noteworthy that the bishops place on the government the duty to provide even expensive means for recovery. Secondly, there is explicit recognition of the prerogatives of the family to make decisions where the patient is incapable of doing so. This has been traditional in Catholic and other circles for some time, but it is assuming a new importance in an era of malpractice threat, scil., an era when doctors and the patient's family are sometimes cast into a competitive relationship of fear and mistrust. Thirdly, like the English bishops, the German episcopate sees a different type of disposal of human life going on where killing and allowing to die are involved.

Finally, and most interestingly, there is the term "recovery." The possibility of recovery determines, in the bishops' statement, whether certain life-supports and interventions need be used or not. If recovery is possible, they should be used. However, it must be noted that the notion of "recovery" is not without problems. "Recovery" can mean at least three things: (1) return to the state of health enjoyed prior to illness, a full state of health; (2) return to a lesser state, perhaps one characterized

[65] *Art. cit.*, pp. 335–36 of the German version.
[66] *Ibid.*, p. 336.

by "severe physical or mental disturbance" (how severe?); (3) return to spontaneous vital functions without consciousness. All of these represent forms of recovery in the sense that death has been stayed. Now it seems clear that if the bishops would not deem obligatory (for the patient) the medical interventions that produce the latter two categories—a point they explicitly make—then they would not include them under the term "recovery." This suggests that "recovery" implies a certain level of recovery or quality of life; for if the means need not be used by the patient and the reason is that they do not produce "recovery," then the term clearly means not just staving off death, but also a certain quality of life. What the term "recovery" really means, then, in the pastoral is "*sufficient* recovery" and that is subject to quality-of-life assessment.

Along these lines another article has attempted to show that the terms "ordinary" and "extraordinary" are really code terms for other value judgments and that increasingly the most prominent value judgment involved is about the benefit to the patient to be derived from a surgical intervention or various life-support systems.[67] This same judgment is made by Bridget Nuttgens when, speaking of infants, she suggests "that the operation should not be pursued if there is no chance of restoring the child to a life other than one of extreme disability. Clearly here we are making a decision not on the strength of the extraordinariness of the measures taken, but on their chance of success. Our criteria have changed with the development in medicine."[68]

Under analysis, benefit to the patient refers not simply to sheer physical survival but to a level of human survival defined above in terms of pain and freedom, as Ziegler has rightly noted. What mix of these values qualifies as *sufficient* recovery (German bishops) or *human* survival (Ziegler) depends very much, though I think not exclusively, on personal perspectives, personal history, personal circumstances. It is very probably this fact that is responsible for the conflict that can occur in some instances of life-prolonging. That is, the physician brings a dominantly, and at times a narrowly exclusive, life-preserving attitude to the case, whereas such an attitude must be qualified by and tailored to some very personal and individual circumstances and perspectives if it is to remain truly humane. That is, at any rate, the thrust of Catholic tradition on this matter.

In diaglogue with Marvin Kohl, Arthur Dyck continues his helpful essays on care for the dying and again contrasts the ethic of beneficent

[67] Richard A. McCormick, S.J., "A Proposal for 'Quality of Life' Criteria for Sustaining Life," *Hospital Progress* 56 (1975) 76–79.

[68] Bridget Nuttgens, "The Ethics of Living and Dying Today," *New Blackfriars* 56 (1975) 74–81.

euthanasia with the ethic of "benemortasia."[69] Against the former he urges several difficulties. First, there is the wedge principle. The wedge argument is not precisely that certain practices will actually follow from one another; it is rather concerned with the form or logic of moral justifications. Concretely, the argument for beneficent euthanasia applies *logically* to a wide range of cases, "and the reasons for keeping the range of cases narrow are not reasons on which people will easily agree." For instance, the notion of dignity is open to a very wide range of meanings. Since this is so, "moral and legal policies that justify mercy killing can in principle justify a very narrow and/or a very wide range of instances" in which it is thought justifiable to kill.

Dyck's positive attack on beneficent euthanasia is through the notion of mercy that he believes is present in the Good Samaritan ideal. This ideal understands mercy as a pledge not to kill one's neighbor and, secondly, to be the kind of person who provides care for those who need it. The care is at least fourfold: (1) relief of pain, (2) relief of suffering (e.g., loneliness), (3) respect for the patient's right to refuse treatment, (4) provision of health care regardless of ability to pay.

Behind the ethic of beneficent euthanasia and the ethic of benemortasia, according to Dyck, stand two criticially different sets of suppositions. The first concerns the notion of dignity. In the euthanasist ethic, only a certain kind of life (one with dignity) has value, whereas Dyck urges that "life as such retains some value whatever form it takes." Secondly, the notion of mercy in the ethic of benemortasia is controlled by what is considered right, "particularly the injunction not to kill on which a wide moral and social consensus exists." In the euthanasist ethic it is controlled by the concept of human dignity, a notion about whose content there are serious and widespread differences.

I agree with Dyck's conclusions where beneficent euthanasia is concerned and I think he is onto something fruitful in approaching the matter through the notion of dignity and its underlying controls. But to bring the matter into sharper focus, two possible problems in moral reasoning can be raised. The first touches dignity. Dyck asserts that in a benemortasial ethic "life as such retains *some value* whatever form it takes. The dying or handicapped person is always worth *caring for*."[70] If "caring for" means preserving and sustaining, and if this is argued precisely because the life has "some value," then the decision to allow a dying person to die must imply that his life no longer has "some value." I think this is an unfortunate way of wording the matter. If, however,

---

[69] Arthur Dyck, "The Good Samaritan Ideal and Beneficent Euthanasia: Conflicting Views of Mercy," *Linacre Quarterly* 42 (1975) 176–88.

[70] Emphasis added.

"caring for" does not mean preserving and sustaining, but only comforting while allowing to die, then how does one allow to die if the life still has some value? In other words, I do not believe that the question of whether life has value or not should be the terms in which the euthanasia vs. allowing-to-die discussion is couched.

Secondly, there is the question, what controls the notion of mercy in the contrasting ethics? Dyck says that the notion in the euthanasist ethic is controlled by the concept of dignity, about which people disagree, whereas in the traditional ethic it is controlled by what is considered right, especially by the prohibition of killing, about which there is widespread moral and social consensus. The contrast between "what is considered right" and "the notion of dignity" might strike some as odd; for presumably those who control mercy with the notion of dignity consider that this is right, that it is precisely dignity that is the chief right-making characteristic of the form mercy ought to take when dealing with the dying. To object to this, and on the grounds that people disagree widely about what constitutes human dignity, is to suggest that what really operates as a control of the term "mercy" in the benemortasial ethic is not precisely and necessarily what is considered right—for that is the whole issue—but what most people now think is right. In other words, it seems too easily to suggest that what is considered right is so precisely because there is a wide moral and social consensus on the point. (Are these quibbling points in the teeth of a very thoughtful study? Probably so.)

Two voluntary-euthanasia bills have been presented to the English Parliament, one in 1936 and one in 1969. It was probably this latter that stimulated the organization of an Anglican "Working Party" on voluntary euthanasia. Its report was recently published and it represents, in my judgment, a model of how the question of care for the dying should be faced.[71] Legal, philosophical, theological, and medical considerations are weighed in a way that is experienced, fair, and disciplined. For instance, moral arguments are given their full force but their limits and counterpositions are stated with honesty and equanimity.

Several things stand out in this perceptive booklet. First, the report rightly registers a "strong dissent from the use of the expression 'right to die.'" In its dangerous ambiguity this usage masks three distinct demands: (1) that the individual should in principle be free to determine whether he shall live or die, with the implication that should he choose to die, he is entitled to be assisted by the medical profession; (2) that a doctor should be free, with the patient's consent, to end his life in cases

[71] On Dying Well (Church Information Office, Church House, Dean's Yard, SW1P 3NZ, 1975) 1–67.

(if there are such) where it is impossible to manage the pain; (3) that a dying patient should not be subjected to troublesome treatment that cannot help the patient, and that doctors may use pain-relieving drugs even at the risk of shortening life. I believe the Anglican report is absolutely right in highlighting the misleading and ultimately irresponsible character of the phrase "right to die." The report also rejects the term "negative euthanasia." Such usage suggests that the question is whether to treat or not to treat, whereas it is rather how to treat. Decisions to cease curative attempts are not abandonment of a patient but a part of good medicine.

Secondly, the report admits that there are extreme situations outside the medical field (e.g., soldiers fatally trapped in a blazing gun-turret, wounded individuals who face certain death by torture) where it is impossible to say that those who have killed to prevent pain have acted wrongfully. However, the authors are reluctant to admit such exceptions in the medical field, and for two reasons. First, it is doubtful that there are any such cases. Secondly, even if there were, it would be impossible to specify them precisely enough to prevent continuous and abusive expansion—a point made also by Dyck. "It is for reasons of this sort that a professional ethic cannot be built on altogether exceptional circumstances, even if in some such exceptional cases a man who contravenes it might rightly be held not to be morally culpable."[72]

Thirdly, the report insists on the difference between killing and relieving the pain of the dying, whether by withholding life-supports or by administering pain relievers that may hasten death. In this they are, of course, echoing Pius XII and the tradition that preceded and followed him. There is a clear distinction "to be drawn between rendering someone unconscious at the risk of killing him and killing him to render him unconscious." Killing involves a "definite and in its implications momentous change of policy." In another place the difference is said to be "decisive." The authors agree that those who do not have to make the decisions "regard such discrimination as unnecessarily fine, but its importance tends to be intuitively evident to those upon whom the burden of decision rests." Thus it would seem that the report appeals to intuitive experience to establish the moral significance between killing and allowing to die.

Fourthly, one of the most illuminating aspects of the report is its emphasis through concrete instances on the management of pain and depression. Many of the initial requests for euthanasia are not that at all. They are requests for appropriate management, a fact the report repeatedly documents. Anyone reading this report will be struck by the

[72] Ibid., p. 12.

realization that the moral theologian must be aware of the enormous strides in the management of pain and depression; otherwise his moral reflections, originating in a nonreal world, will easily be destructive within the real one.

Finally, the report faces the euthanasist plea for compassion. The authors admit that the plea is a deeply human and a highly moral one and must not fall on deaf ears. But they then insist on two points which represent some of the finest reflections in the report and deserve to be quoted at length. The first consideration runs as follows:

The value of human life does not consist simply of a scale of pleasure and pain. Such may be the value of an animal's life. A dog's life, for example, may be valuable in so far as it is filled with doggy pleasure and devoid of doggy pains. But the value of human life consists in a variety of virtues and graces as well as in pleasure. These together constitute man's full humanity. They grow in soil in which action and passion, doing and suffering, pleasure and pain are intermixed. What a man is consists not only of what he does, but also of how he endures. A fully human life is inescapably vulnerable, as every lover knows, and even suffering may by grace be woven into the texture of a larger humanity. It is not that Christians believe that suffering is in itself a good, or that it necessarily ennobles. It may indeed destroy, and the alleviation of pain is a Christian as well as a human duty. But suffering as exposure to what is beyond one's voluntary control, suffering as undergoing, even as diminishment, is part of the pattern of becoming human. Even dying need not be simply the ebbing away of life; it may be integrated into life and so made instrumental to a fuller life in God.[73]

That says beautifully what many have been struggling to put into words when discussing care of the dying. It provides the context for the use of technology in this care. This context is one that refuses to absolutize any one consideration and thereby represents, I believe, a more fully human response to the condition of the dying person.

The second consideration is the fact that we achieve our humanity in interdependence. In the words of the report:

There is a movement of giving and receiving. At the beginning and at the end of life receiving predominates over and even excludes giving. But the value of human life does not depend only on its capacity to give. Love, agape, is the equal and unalterable regard for the value of other human beings independent of their particular characteristics. It extends especially to the helpless and hopeless, to those who have no value in their own eyes and seemingly none for society. Such neighbor-love is costly and sacrificial. It is easily destroyed. In the giver it demands unlimited caring, in the recipient absolute trust. The question must be asked whether the practice of voluntary euthanasia is consistent with the fostering of such caring and trust.[74]

---

[73] *Ibid.*, p. 21.   [74] *Ibid.*, p. 22.

The authors are totally candid and realistic in their assessment of the force of these considerations. They may not foreclose the moral debate but "they are sufficient, we believe, to show that there are strong grounds from the Christian point of view for hesitating long before admitting any exception to the principle forbidding killing human beings."

It is already clear that the compositor of these "Notes" regards this report as a splendid piece of work, not only because of the balance and insight of its medical, moral, and legal perspectives on care for the dying, but also because of its attitude toward its own reflections and arguments. It is appropriately hesitant when hesitation is called for; it refuses to absolutize when the evidence will not support an absolute. That illumines the nature of moral argument. Discussion about the moral rightness or wrongness of human action rarely leads to conclusions that are so absolute and compelling that little is left to be said or explored. Rather it adduces warrants from a variety of perspectives that issue in a convergence of probabilities around a particular value. If that is what moral discourse is, it is all that we should generally expect and what we should regard as sufficient for the discovery of norms and policies to guide human decisions. It is in expecting more or settling for less that moral argument begins to disintegrate. The Anglican study group has admirably avoided these pitfalls.

The concluding part of this section will be devoted exclusively to the distinction between killing and allowing to die. Albert Moraczewski, O.P., director of the Pope John XXIII Medical-Moral Research and Education Center, accepts the moral relevance of the distinction.[75] In active euthanasia the doctor is the cause of the death of his patient. "Without his intervention, death would not have ensued or ensued so quickly. A cause is that without which the effect would not be. . . . " Contrarily, where artificial life-supports are removed, "the individual was dying because of some existing pathology or injury. . . . " The crucial point for Moraczewski is that active euthanasia "brings about the patient's death." Why is that crucial? Because the state of mind and intention that sets out actively to terminate life is different from the state of the person who sees that continued efforts to keep someone alive are to no avail.

Three philosophers have challenged this traditional and widely-accepted approach. The first is Peter Singer. In an article dealing with the place of moral reasoning and the philosopher in ethical discourse, Singer uses the distinction between killing and letting die as an example of the type of debate that would gain needed clarity from philosophical

[75] Albert S. Moraczewski, O.P., "Euthanasia in the Light of a Contemporary Theology of Death" (cf. n. 53 above) pp. 19-38.

input.[76] After criticizing the formulation (traditional) of the American Medical Association's House of Delegates (1973), Singer reports that philosophical discussions "have shown" that when we get down to cases that embody a distinction between killing and letting die, then "without any other irrelevant considerations to influence our judgment, it becomes implausible to say that there is a great moral difference between the act and the omission."

Several reasons are offerred by Singer for this conclusion. First, in either case "we must take responsibility for what we do . . . a decision not to do something is as much a decision as one to do something." Secondly, Singer reports that "most people agree that this intuitive feeling [that it is worse to kill than to let die] is unreliable." Finally, he argues that "avoidance of pointless suffering must take precedence over a rigid adherence to a prohibition on killing."

It would be unfair to Singer to regard these remarks as his developed position; for he uses the problem only as an example and explicitly states that the "issue is not settled by what I have said so far." Nevertheless, the few remarks he does make indicate where he would come out and how he would make his argument.

Several comments seem in order. First, the fact that we must take responsibility for both decisions hardly means that they are identical decisions. Nor does the fact that both decisions entail "doing something." In this sense Singer is rebutting a position no one has ever held. Secondly, as for the opinion of most people about the unreliability of our intuitive acceptance of the distinction, the Anglican Working Party would certainly have something to say to that. Moreover, I am not sure what weight Singer would want the "opinion of most people" to carry. He himself would be the first to criticize acceptance of such opinion; for he writes that "no conclusions about what we ought to do can validly be drawn from a description of what most people in our society think we ought to do." Indeed, Singer rightly insists that if our moral theory is soundly based, we must be prepared to accept its implications even if they force us to change our moral views on issues; for unless we are, we have lost the capacity to generate radical moral criticism of prevailing standards and attitudes.

Finally, one must advert to Singer's introduction of rhetorical language which only thinly disguises (but hardly proves) certain value perspectives: e.g., "*rigid* adherence" to a prohibition on killing. If the prohibition is right, then adherence to it ought to be rigid. In such language there is the contrary suggestion that a prohibition is inappro-

[76] Peter Singer, "Philosophers Are Back on the Job," *New York Times Magazine*, July 7, 1974, pp. 6 ff.

priate because it calls for "rigid" observance. This does not enlighten, but only pre-empts the issue. Some of the same things must be adduced about the usage "*pointless* suffering."

James Rachels urges four arguments against the distinction.[77] His essay takes on added importance because it appeared in the nation's most prestigious medical journal. First, letting die may take the patient longer, and so the patient may suffer more than he would if more direct action were taken. Thus, once the initial decision not to prolong life is made, active euthanasia is preferable. "To say otherwise is to endorse the option that leads to more suffering rather than less and is contrary to the humanitarian impulse that prompts the decision not to prolong life in the first place."

Rachels' second argument is that the traditional doctrine leads to decisions concerning life and death made on irrelevant grounds. He gives as examples two babies with Down's syndrome, one with easily corrigible intestinal blockage, the other without it. The one with the blockage is allowed to die, the one without is not. However, Rachels argues, the blockage is irrelevant to whether the baby should live or not. "It is the Down's syndrome and not the intestines that is the issue." The killing–letting-die doctrine has led to these results and therefore should be jettisoned.

Thirdly, Rachels directly attacks the moral relevance of the distinction by two examples. Smith wants the inheritance he is to get from the death of a six-year-old child. He wants the child dead. So he drowns him in the bathtub. Jones wants the inheritance he is to get from the death of a six-year-old child. He wants the child dead. As he enters the bathroom, he is delighted to see the child slip in the tub, hit his head, and end up with his head submerged. He allows the child to die. "If the difference between killing and letting die were in itself a morally important matter, one would say that Jones' behavior was less reprehensible than Smith's. But does one really want to say that? I think not."[78]

Finally, Rachels attacks the idea that in active euthanasia the doctor does something, whereas in allowing someone to die he merely ceases treatment. Rachels argues that by allowing someone to die the doctor truly does something. He concludes as follows:

The reason why it is considered bad to be the cause of someone's death is that death is regarded as a great evil—and so it is. However, if it has been decided that euthanasia—even passive euthanasia—is desirable in a given case, it has also been decided that in this instance death is no greater an evil than the patient's

[77] James Rachels, "Active and Passive Euthanasia," *New England Journal of Medicine* 292 (1975) 78–80. Responses to Rachels are in the same journal, pp. 863–867.

[78] *Ibid.*, p. 79.

continued existence. And if that is true, the real reason for not wanting to be the cause of someone's death simply does not apply.[79]

Without for the moment passing judgment on Rachels' conclusions, several things must be said about the arguments he marshals. Rachels' first argument absolutizes the removal of suffering in the dying as follows: whatever course removes or lessens suffering most efficiently is morally right. With no desire or need to canonize suffering, I believe this begs the question; for it supposes that the fact of suffering, not the way it is removed, is morally decisive. That is the precise issue. The report of the Anglican Working Party is far more realistic and balanced in its approach to suffering. Furthermore, Rachels' conclusion rests on factual assumptions about the limits and inadequacy of the management of pain that many physicians and much literature would challenge, especially in our time.

Secondly, I would argue that whatever the merits of the commission-omission distinction, it does not factually lead to the conclusions Rachels draws from it. It is indeed the Down's syndrome and not the intestinal blockage that is relevant to the examples he gives; but it is an oversimplistic assessment of this condition, not the use of the commission-omission distinction, that leads to the results Rachels rightly disowns.

Thirdly, with regard to the Smith and Jones examples, to say that their actions are "equally reprehensible" is to say only that we have moral responsibility for both our acts and our omissions, and that the abuse of this responsibility can be homicidal in either an action or an omission. No one to my knowledge has ever denied this. But one must inquire further why Jones's conduct (omission) was reprehensible. Obviously, his motive was wrong (he *wanted* the child dead); but in this he does not differ from Smith. But in addition to this he *could* have and *should* have saved the child. For this reason his conduct was morally wrong. But to conclude from this that commission and omission are morally equivalent is to assume that all cases of dying patients are situations wherein the physician *could* have and *should* have saved the patient. But this is not the case; there are many instances where one cannot save the patient or, all things considered, need not do so.

Finally, when Rachels says that "the reason why it is considered bad to be the cause of someone's death is that death is regarded as a great evil," two things must be added. First, the proponents of the traditional distinction would say that death is, of course, a great nonmoral evil; but they would add that when disease or pathology takes a patient, we are

[79] *Ibid.*, p. 80.

not *causing* the death or not causing it in the same way as when positive euthanasia is performed. They would then add that what is to be considered morally wrong is not just the occurrence of the evil but its relation to our causality. And we are back to the original argument.

Secondly, and more radically, some would argue that it is not just the fact that death is a great evil that makes "causing" it morally wrong, but that this evil stands in no proportionate relationship to a good to be achieved by it. It is not, in these instances, the life of this person (patient) against the common good, or against the life of another whom he unjustly attacks. If Rachels wants to argue that there is a proportionate good at stake, he would have to get into a long discussion about the meaning of life, of death, of suffering to establish it.

Philosopher Gerard J. Hughes, S.J., does not challenge the distinction; rather he reinterprets its meaning.[80] He first points out what is obvious: the distinction is not simply tantamount to that between what is morally right and morally wrong; for there are times when doing nothing (and thereby allowing someone to die) is morally wrong, indeed morally homicidal. From this Hughes concludes that the distinction between doing something that results in death and failing to do something as a result of which someone dies is not of moral importance simply because one is an act and the other an omission. "The moral difference is logically independent of any particular metaphysical truths about causation." Actually, he argues, we tend to describe as "killing" those cases where we feel the conduct is morally reprehensible, even if the person did not actually do anything. Contrarily, we avoid the terms "suicide" and "killing" where a person acted in such a way as to bring about his certain death but did so in circumstances which made his behavior morally admirable (e.g., saving others in a burning building). Thus "the distinction between 'killing' and 'allowing to die' seems almost to depend on our moral judgment of the cases concerned rather than to provide a basis for that moral judgment."

Hughes next turns to the intention. It has been argued that killing someone involves intending his death, whereas allowing him to die involves only permitting the death. What is morally wrong is intending another's death. Against this Hughes argues, first, that it does not square with traditional attitudes on death-intending conduct (e.g., the just war).

His second argument is more interesting. He considers two hypothetical patients. Both are and will remain comatose. The first patient is stabilized with artificial life-supports. Without them he would die within minutes. The second patient is terminally ill and will die within a few

[80] Gerard J. Hughes, S.J., "Killing and Letting Die," *Month* 236 (1975) 42–45.

days. If, however, he is given an injection, he will die in just about the same length of time that the first patient would take to die were the machines shut off.

The doctor of the first patient decides, in light of all the factors to be weighed, to switch off the machines. If his estimate of all the factors differs from the moral standards we expect, he lays himself open to the charge of killing his patient. "It will not help him much to say that it was the illness which killed the patient, and that all he, the doctor, did was permit the patient to die." If, however, his estimate of all the factors coincides with ours, he could state his case by saying there was no point in doing anything more. He will come in for moral criticism only if we discover that for some disreputable reason he actually *wanted that patient dead*. "The mere fact that the doctor performed an action—switching off a machine—will not in itself sway our moral judgment one way or the other, even though that action quite certainly results in the death of the patient in a very short time."

Hughes feels that the doctor of the second patient could produce a parallel set of arguments. The patient will die in a few days, so there is no point in doing anything more. He, too, has at his disposal an action that will quite certainly result in the death of his patient in a very short space. If it is objected that by administering the lethal dosage he intends the death of the patient, he would reply that it is not true, any more than it was in the case of the other doctor, that he *wanted the patient dead*. He had no ulterior motives etc. and did not in *that* sense want the patient dead. Hughes concludes: "I can see no moral grounds for distinguishing the two cases, stated simply and out of context as I have described them. . . . " He adds: "The distinction between killing and allowing someone to die, as it is usually interpreted, will not bear the weight which has often been put upon it."

The conclusion would seem to be either that euthanasia is morally permissible in those instances in which a decision not to maintain life is permissible, or that neither euthanasia nor refusal to prolong life is permissible. However, Hughes rejects these alternatives and argues that there may be other ways of distinguishing the two cases. He suggests that allowing doctors to take more active steps would undermine the general moral climate. Thus the distinction between commission and omission is not a matter of logic or metaphysics but of psychology and social climate.

Hughes concludes as follows: "To sum up, it appears to me that the distinction between 'killing' and 'allowing to die' may serve to indicate the important difference between an agent who wants someone dead, and another agent who does not." But to apply it in all cases as if it were crucial Hughes sees as hairsplitting, when the real importance of the distinction is its inculcation of a moral and legal climate which we cannot do without.

If I understand him correctly—and I am not sure I do—Hughes is arguing that the really crucial things are the attitudes of wanting a person dead or not wanting him dead. It is the agent who wants someone dead who is the threat to human life, to our rights. The distinction between killing and allowing to die is the practical way of maintaining this deeper distinction intact. Concretely, I suppose that Hughes would argue that unless we maintained such a distinction in practice, we would lose sight of the more vital distinction and loose upon the world many more people who "want persons dead." That is what I take the italicized words to mean when Hughes writes: "The distinction between 'killing' and 'allowing to die' *may serve to indicate* the important difference between an agent who wants someone else dead, and another agent who does not." Thus the traditional distinction is important not of itself but instrumentally. It is, in a sense, only the best policy formulation we have for keeping the more crucial distinction alive and central in decisions involving life and death.

Hughes's presentation is extremely interesting and he may well be right. Certainly, the distinction between killing and allowing to die (commission-omission) is open to problems similar to those that have been brought against the direct-indirect distinction; for killing is often said to be wrong because death is intended, whereas allowing to die can be permissible at times because in the noninstigation or withdrawal of life-supports one does not intend death but only permits it.

However, before completely endorsing Hughes's conclusion, one might care to raise a problem or two. The first revolves around the rather vague terminology "may serve to indicate." Does "indicate" mean "point out" or the stronger "maintain"? Furthermore, does "may serve" mean "*necessary* to maintain" (or indicate) or "*helpful* to maintain" (or indicate)? If it is necessary to the maintenance of the more crucial distinction (between wanting and not wanting people dead), why is it necessary? If it is indeed necessary, there must be some causal relationship between the traditional distinction and the more crucial one. But if the traditional distinction had no moral meaning in itself, how would its retention be a necessary support for the more crucial one and for our whole moral climate? Hughes might say, indeed might be forced to say—unless he can establish more clearly the link between omission-commission and the more crucial distinction—that if the crucial distinction is threatened by loss of the traditional one, this is because among those who would kill terminal patients there would be more who want people dead than among those who allow people to die at times. Otherwise, why would abandonment of the distinction threaten the more crucial one and our moral climate? In other words, how can one assert that among killers of terminal patients there would be more who *want people dead*, especially if the traditional distinction has no moral relevance in itself?

Secondly, there is the crucial character of the notions of "wanting people dead" and "not wanting people dead." This is what Hughes thinks ought to be our real concern. However, I believe Hughes would admit that "wanting people dead" is not what is radically objectionable. It is wanting them dead *for the wrong reason*, for base motives, etc. If that is indeed the case, how does the omission-commission distinction relate to and affect the motivation of the one who kills or allows to die? More specifically, how does it function to inhibit or eliminate the bad motivation?

These questions are meant in no way to negate the possible validity of Hughes's conclusions. They are rather an indication of the extremely complex character of the problem we face, and of the fact that the discussion is far from over. I myself believe that there is moral significance in the traditional distinction, in the minimal sense that we ought to maintain the distinction in practice, though I am far from sure how we ought to analyze it. Although it has moral bite, perhaps we cannot demand that it do all the work we ask it to do. As this discussion continues (and as it should), one thing ought not to be overlooked. Just as there are dimensions to life that are beyond the neatness and tightness of our moral concepts and categories, and are in this sense mysterious, so there are mysterious dimensions to the last phase of life, dying. This suggests that there will also be elements of the mysterious to the acts through which we care for and comfort the dying. To think otherwise could easily be to attribute to rational analysis and argument powers they do not have. To act otherwise could easily collapse a human experience into the technological qualities (efficiency, cleanliness, painlessness, swiftness) that are to serve and support human experience, not replace it.

HUMAN RIGHTS AND THE MISSION OF THE CHURCH

Two anniversaries of special significance occurred in 1973: the tenth anniversary of *Pacem in terris* (1963) and the twenty-fifth anniversary of the United Nations Declaration of Human Rights (1948). These anniversaries were duly noted in some interesting documents and can provide the occasion for gathering some recent literature on human rights and the Church's mission in this area, especially since 1975 represents the tenth anniversary of *Gaudium et spes*.

The fourth Synod of Bishops met in the fall of 1974 (Sept. 27–Oct. 26). The *Catholic Mind* has put together a useful issue on the major documents of the Synod.[81] Included are Pope Paul's opening address, an overview of problems (Archbishop Aloisio Lorscheider of Fortaleza in Brazil), three regional reports (South America, Africa, North America–Australia–Oceania), two important speeches (John Cardinal Dearden, Dr. Philip A. Potter of the World Council of Churches), two synodal documents (human rights, evangelization), and Pope Paul's response to the work of the Synod.

Throughout these deliberations there is an undercurrent of concern about the formulation of the Church's proper mission in the sphere of the defense and promotion of human rights. Two extremes are possible in stating this mission: simple identification of the Church's mission with human liberation and development, a dualism that unduly separates the two.

In the past there may have been at least verbal leanings toward the latter extreme. Pius XI wrote to Fr. M. D. Roland-Gosselin: "It is necessary never to lose sight of the fact that the objective of the Church is to evangelize, not to civilize. If it civilizes, it is for the sake of evangelization."[82] Pius XII in an address (March 9, 1956) stated: "Its divine Founder, Jesus Christ, has not given it [the Church] any mandate or fixed any end of the cultural order. The goal which Christ assigns to it is religious. ... The Church can never lose sight of the strictly religious, supernatural goal. ... "[83] Vatican II itself noted: "Christ, to be sure, gave His Church no proper mission in the political, economic, or social order. The purpose which He set before her is a religious one."[84]

Terms such as "proper mission" and "strictly religious" cry out for clarification; for they are capable of yielding a very dualistic meaning which ends up restricting the mission of the Church to instruction in the faith, liturgy, preaching, and sacraments—in brief, a kind of "sanctuary Christianity." In this view those directly concerned in one way or another with righting unjust social structures would not be involved in the Church's "proper mission" or with something "religious."

Pope Paul once again struggled (I believe the word is not inaccurate) with the formulation of these matters in his opening address to the Synod. While speaking of the "specific finality" of evangelization, he made the following suggestion to the assembled bishops: "It will be necessary to define more accurately the relationship between evangelization properly so called and the whole human effort towards development for which the Church's help is rightly expected, even though this is not

---

[81] *Catholic Mind* 73 (1975) 2–64. Cf. also *The Pope Speaks* 19 (1975) 182–99, 216–19.

[82] *Semaines sociales de France* (Versailles, 1936) pp. 461–462, as cited in Abbott, *The Documents of Vatican II*, p. 264, n. 192.

[83] *Acta apostolicae sedis* 48 (1956) 212.

[84] *Gaudium et spes*, no. 42 (Abbott, *The Documents of Vatican II*, p. 241).

her specific task."[85] Now if it is necessary to define this relationship more accurately, clearly such a definition seems not yet to have been achieved. He warns against forgetting the priority of the message of salvation and thus reducing "their own action to mere sociological or political activity, and the message of the Church to a man-centered and temporal message." His final statement about evangelization and human progress is that "there is no opposition or separation, therefore, but a complementary relationship between evangelization and human progress. While distinct and subordinate, one to the other, each calls for the other by reason of their convergence toward the same end: the salvation of man."

Here one is tempted to ask: If human progress and liberation converge toward the salvation of man, why are they not the proper mission of the Church?

In his report to the Synod, Archbishop Joseph L. Bernardin stated that no one (from the region he represented) questions the integral relationship between evangelization and human liberation; however, there was a difference in the emphasis to be given to this relationship. In developed countries "the need for the Church to deal with the themes of justice and peace is felt as a demand of the gospel...."[86] Speaking for the bishops of South America, Bishop Eduardo Pironio referred frequently to "complete liberation in Christ," "liberation of the whole man."[87] He referred to a "dualism between faith and life," but cautioned against a "superficial identification between evangelization and human advancement" (which he saw as a real danger in South America).

After these preparatory statements, the Synod issued (Oct. 23) its statement "On Human Rights and Reconciliation."[88] This statement is extremely interesting. It refers to the fact that the "integral development of persons," the "complete liberation of man," makes clearer in man the divine image. "Hence she [the Church] believes firmly that the promotion of human rights is *required by the gospel* and is *central to her ministry*."[89] Then, speaking of the relationship between evangelization and liberation, the document first notes that the Church as evangelizer must conform to Christ, who was sent "to announce glad tidings to the poor, to give prisoners their freedom, the blind their sight, to set the oppressed free" (Lk 4:18). Faithful to this mission, the Church "can draw from the gospel... ever new incentives to... eliminate the social consequences of sin which are translated into unjust social and political structures."[90] Thus, for the Synod, correction of unjust social and political structures is *part* of evangelization, though evangelization does not stop there but leads to "full communion with God and with men."

[85] *Catholic Mind* 73 (1975) 6.
[86] *Ibid.*, p. 20.
[87] *Ibid.*, p. 35.
[88] *Ibid.*, pp. 50–52.
[89] *Ibid.*, p. 51; emphasis added.
[90] *Ibid.*, p. 56.

Pope Paul felt compelled ("We could not allow false directions to be followed") to return to this subject at the close of the Synod. After noting that human liberation had been rightly emphasized as part of that love Christians owe their brethren, he warned that the "totality of salvation is not to be confused with one or other aspect of liberation. . . . Hence human advancement, social progress, etc. are not te be excessively emphasized on a temporal level to the detriment of the essential meaning which evangelization has for the Church of Christ: the announcement of the good news."[91] Obviously, the Pontiff felt that this or that aspect of liberation was being confused with the totality of salvation and that there was excessive emphasis on the temporal aspects of social progress.

I have cited these documents extensively because they manifest a very human and understandable groping toward a balanced formulation of the Church's mission in the social sphere. One can sense in this movement from "no proper mission" to "required by the gospel and central to her mission" a kind of consciousness-in-transition. Where is that consciousness now? It is hard to say, but perhaps it could be put as follows: elimination of the social consequences of sin is essential to the Church's evangelizing mission but does not exhaust this mission—and therefore should not be "excessively emphasized." As noted, this matter is of more than speculative interest. It has everything to do with how ministry is conceived, implemented, and supported at all levels. For instance, unless I am mistaken, the phrase "genuinely priestly work"— taken exclusively to mean preaching and administration of the sacraments—must be seen as a relic.

Here attention should be called to a long and very detailed document issued by the Pontifical Commission Justice and Peace.[92] The document reviews the Church's teaching on human rights from the time of Pope Leo XIII to the present and shows how these rights, rooted in the dignity of the person, receive new light and depth through the Incarnation which so luminously affirmed this dignity (*imago Dei*). At one point the document notes that "although the Church with her religious role has no proper mission in the political, social, or economic order, she is far from looking on religion as purely private. . . . " A bit later the study states that to imitate Christ and to be his true continuation in the world "the Church as a whole, like every Christian community, is called to work for the dignity and rights of man, both individually and collectively; to protect and promote the dignity of the human person; and to denounce and oppose every sort of human oppression."

[91] *Ibid.*, p. 63.
[92] "The Church and Human Rights," *L'Osservatore romano* (English edition) 1975, Oct. 23, pp. 6–8, Oct. 30, pp. 8–9, Nov. 6, pp. 6–8, Nov. 13, pp. 9–10.

One has to wonder whether the borrowed phrase "no proper mission" is really appropriate. If it is integral to the Church's mission to protect and ɾromote human rights, and if these rights are violated precisely by unjust political, economic, and social structures, does not the Church have a proper mission, at least in some sense, in the political, economic, and social order? Otherwise, what does it mean to say that the "Church . . . is called to work for the dignity and rights of men," that this is integral to her mission? Indeed, at one point the study refers to "a continuously growing awareness of the Christian's special vocation in the social and political community. . . ." Again we read: "To take part in the process of liberating the whole man, as seen in the light of the gospel, is an indispensable element in any genuine pastoral mission of effective and authentic proclamation."[93] Now if this liberation is from every form of slavery (sin and selfishness and their effects in the social sphere), as the document insists, then it seems that the Church does indeed have a proper mission in the social, political, and economic areas. I realize that the word "proper" (as in the phrase "proper mission") can be understood to mean "exclusively the Church's," "hers and no one else's," etc. But this is not the way the term is generally understood and will be understood.

The single question raised here should not obscure the fact that the document of the Pontifical Commission is an excellent summary of the Church's commitment to human rights and could be a very useful tool for study and motivation[94] at regional levels—the very purpose for which the study was drafted.

The struggle to formulate the Christian mission where social change is concerned has not been limited to the Catholic community. This struggle has a long theological history. Hans Schwarz reviews recent criticism of Luther's doctrine of the two kingdoms.[95] Barth had criticized placing the spheres of Church and state parallel to each other as a dangerous type of isolation. H. Richard Niebuhr, while more appreciative, saw the doctrine as ultimately dualistic and culturally conservative. Carl E. Braaten asserted a similar dualism because the eschatological dynamic of the kingdom on the right had no effect on the kingdom on the left. Lawrence K. Kersten accuses the doctrine of individualism and of social impotence.

Schwarz undertakes what he calls a "partial vindication" of the

[93] *Ibid.*, Nov. 6.

[94] On motivation cf. Geiko Müller-Fahrenholz, "Overcoming Apathy," *Ecumenical Review* 27 (1975) 48–56; Richard A. McCormick, S.J., "The Social Responsibility of the Christian," *Australasian Catholic Record* 52 (1975) 253–63.

[95] Hans Schwarz, "Luther's Doctrine of the Two Kingdoms—Help or Hindrance for Social Change," *Lutheran Quarterly* 27 (1975) 59–75.

doctrine. Whether he succeeds can be left to the curious reader; for Luther was, as Schwarz notes, a dialectical thinker. This means practically that when all is said and done, the objections leveled against the two-kingdoms theory remain far clearer than the partial vindication. Nonetheless, the theory was an attempt to avoid two extremes, the Christianization of the state and the secularization of the Church.

Much of the concern over formulating the Church's proper mission in the social sphere stems from the emergence of the theology of liberation. The literature on liberation theology is already out of control.[96] Only a few recent entries can be touched here and they will be viewed uniquely from the perspective of the Church's mission. The purpose, therefore, is neither to defend nor to attack liberation theology. There are already sufficient combatants in that arena. Among the attackers, e.g., Andrew Greeley and Michael Novak are, if not *facile principes*, very upward-mobile contenders.[97]

Francis P. Fiorenza presents a useful comparison between political theology and liberation theology.[98] He uses Metz, Moltmann, and Sölle as examples of the former, Gutierrez, Segundo, Boff, and Assmann as examples of the latter. Fiorenza finds three common elements in the political theologians. "The contemporary situation is secularized, the existential response is inadequate, and a political (public) theology is not a theology of politics, but a hermeneutical task . . . . " The inadequacy of the existential response refers to the fact that a theology of transcendental subjectivity privatizes the Christian message and confirms the withdrawal of religion from societal life. The "hermeneutical task" refers to the discovery of those principles of the Christian message that reveal its meaning for the life of all men, not just the individual.

By contrast, the situation of the liberation theologians of Latin America is remarkably different. It is not one of secularization and consequent privatization of faith, as in Europe. Thus, Gutierrez criticizes Metz for predicating of the world what describes only parts of it, and not Latin America. The Church still has power in Latin America and the question is: how is it to be used in the service of society? Secondly, liberation theologians are at one in criticizing "developmentalism," scil.,

---

[96] For a bibliography cf. Francis P. Fiorenza, "Latin American Liberation Theology," *Interpretation* 28 (1974) 441–57; Egidio Vigano Cattaneo, "Fe y liberación," *Estudios teológicos* 2 (1975) 139–215; "Latin American Liberation Theology," *Theology Digest* 23 (1975) 241–50.

[97] Michael Novak, "Theology of Liberation," *National Catholic Reporter*, Nov. 21, 1975, p. 12; Andrew Greeley, "Liberation without Freedom?" *Catholic Chronicle* (Toledo), Nov. 28, 1975, p. 5 (a syndicated column, found in many diocesan papers).

[98] Francis P. Fiorenza, "Political Theology and Liberation Theology: An Inquiry into their Fundamental Meaning," in *Liberation, Revolution, and Freedom*, ed. Thomas M. McFadden (New York, 1975) pp. 3–29.

the attempt to achieve social advances within existing structures without altering these structures. Thirdly, where political theology concentrates on the proper hermeneutic, liberation theology is "concerned with the interpretations of the Christian symbols of faith."

Here Fiorenza notes that "at the center of all the deliberations by the liberation theologians stands the question of the Church and its mission."[99] The heart of this mission is to be a sign of universal salvation. The Church realizes this mission in so far as it signifies and proclaims that salvation. How does it do this? In many ways, but "its confrontation with the oppression and injustice of its concrete situation is an integral part of its mission to be the sign of salvation."

Fiorenza concludes that the critics of liberation theology (e.g., Richard Neuhaus, who warns that Gutierrez ultimately equates the mission of the Church with revolutionary struggle) have misunderstood it; for even though liberation theologians insist on a direct, immediate relationship between faith and political action, they also argue that if faith is to develop norms and criteria for political action and options, it can do so only on the basis of a concrete historical and societal analysis. A very thoughtful article.

René Coste reviews many of the key books on liberation theology, including several that are highly critical (e.g., uncritical acceptance of the terms "praxis" and "history," tendency to identify the kingdom of God and political liberation, uncritical use of Marxist categories, selective use of scriptural texts for prefixed theses, etc.).[100] Coste then gives his own evaluation: liberation theology is fecund, yet quite discussible. Among the discussible aspects Coste includes the fact that this theology is "insufficiently clear" on the mission of the Church. That is, he believes the Church ought to have a liberating political impact "on the condition that it remain faithful to its specific mission, which is a mission of salvation and not a mission directly political." Otherwise, Coste is convinced, the Church will fall into a new form of social messianism.

A pastoral session met in Paris (Sept. 13–15, 1974) to discuss the social apostolate. It included many bishops, representatives of lay movements, priests, religious, and some theologians. Following this lively discussion, the Permanent Council of the French Episcopate proposed its own reflections under title of *Les libérations des hommes et le salut en Jésus Christ*.[101] The document attempts to relate liberation movements to

---

[99] *Ibid.*, p. 21.

[100] René Coste, "Foi et société: 'Liberation et salut,'" *Esprit et vie* 85 (1975) 577–88. The article is marked "a suivre."

[101] Paris, 1975, pp. 1–107. I am using Coste's summary and also "Liberazione degli uomini e salvezza in Gesù Cristo," *Civiltà cattolica* 126 (1975) 3–12.

salvation, that is, it searches for the specificity of the Church's mission. The episcopal document first cautions against either dissociating or confusing liberation and Christian salvation. Some oppose these dualistically, some identify them uncritically. Such errors are analogous to deviations of the past wherein either the divinity or humanity was isolated in Christ's salvific activity. The relationship, the document states, "cannot be expressed either in terms of a radical rupture or in those of a continuity without breaking points."

How, then, is the relationship to be understood? The French episcopal analysis begins by describing salvation. "In so far as he is savior, Jesus introduces us to the life of the Trinity and associates us with the work of the Father in which he is incessantly at work. In Jesus Christ salvation is already given, the kingdom of God is already present in the gift that inaugurates communion with God."[102] But this salvation cannot be conceived in a "spiritualistic" way; rather, by grace it is the transfiguration of everything human. It should not be seen as a salvation to be realized in the future and elsewhere, but rather as the mysterious growth of the kingdom already present, even though not fully revealed and realized. For this reason, the document argues, "the essential link between salvation and liberation consists in this meeting between man who aspires to freedom and fights to be himself, and the God of the Alliance, who is present in the heart of history to lead it to its final term. Thus man does not reach God by leaving the world, but by inserting himself in it and collaborating with the Creator's plan."[103]

In conclusion, the French document insists, on the one hand, on the irreducibility and radicality of salvation. On the other, it asserts that "Christians would be unfaithful to their mission of evangelizing if they did not mobilize effectively to work with all their brothers, believers and nonbelievers, for the liberation of men, of each person and all persons." But the means it uses are proper to itself: "announcing the good news, service of the word of God, communication of the riches of the paschal mystery through the sacraments and prayer."

It is highly doubtful that liberationists from Latin America would rest satisfied with such a formulation. Segundo Galilea, writing in the Mexico City monthly *Servir*, has a good summary of what liberation theology is all about. He notes that the appeal of the Medellín *Conclusions* "was meant to remind the Church of its proper sociopolitical role, which it had quite forgotten in recent decades."[104] He sees this theology as an at-

[102] *Les libérations des hommes et le salut en Jésus Christ*, p. 33.

[103] *Ibid.*, p. 36.

[104] Segundo Galilea, "Liberation Theology Began with Medellín," *Ladoc*, May 1975, pp. 1-6.

tempt to move beyond dualism, yet to preserve both the autonomy of the sociopolitical and the transcendence of salvation.

Even though liberation theology is no monolith, Galilea sees three presuppositions in it: (1) the condition of underdevelopment and unjust dependence; (2) a Christian interpretation of this as a "situation of sin"; (3) the pressure on the conscience of Christians to commit themselves to remedying the situation. On the basis of these three themes, liberation theology's "fundamental objective is to clarify the intrinsic relation there is in God's plan between sociopolitical, economic, and cultural liberation and the eschatological salvation by Jesus Christ."

Galilea acknowledges the criticisms that this theology has encountered. He argues, however, that it must not be seen as a single, uniform school, but as a pluralistic current. Furthermore, one muŝt carefully distinguish in this current the truly theological literature from the abundant documentation on the sociopolitical liberation theme. Failure to make the distinction has hurt liberation theology.

In his presentation to the 1974 Synod of Bishops, Peruvian Bishop Germán Schmitz asked the Synod to "declare the word 'liberation' and its integral meaning *an* essential—if not *the* essential—element in the notion of salvation."[105] For him, this integral meaning includes positive liberation (freedom for full communion with God and neighbor) and negative liberation (the break with sin in the heart of man and in the unjust structures of society "that keep people from thinking and acting as children of God and brothers in Christ"). The Bishop does not say so, but if liberation is "an integral part of God's salvific plan," it would seem to follow that the Church has a "proper role" in all aspects of liberation.

If this is so, the Church must get involved in politics to some extent. Dom Helder Camara, Archbishop of Olinda and Recife, addressed this subject in the Synod bluntly and stirringly.[106] He acknowledged the risk to the Church in being considered political and subversive, but added: "The time has come now for the Church to stop worrying about the accusation of getting into politics. 'Politics' is simply a synonym for working for the common good, i.e., advancing the dignity of the human person and the concrete conditions that insure that dignity."

A pamphlet published by Mons. Miguel Obando, Archbishop of Managua (Nicaragua), faces the same problem, "getting into politics."[107] The Church simply has to get into politics in the sense of seeing to it "that the subject and object of the economy is man." She ought not to be in politics if this means speaking for or against a given

[105] Germán Schmitz, "Let's Officialize the Word 'Liberation,'" *ibid.*, pp. 7–8.

[106] Helder Camara, "The Gospel and Liberation," *Ladoc*, Sept.–Oct. 1975, pp. 30–34.

[107] Miguel Obando, "Should the Church Be in Politics?" *Ladoc*, June 1975, pp. 29–31.

political system that is simply trying to translate into effective and productive terms the laws of economics. Economic structures, the Archbishop points out, will either be constructive for man's dignity or they will not. "If they are not, then the Church, to safeguard the very value of man, who is willy-nilly caught up in and dependent on economic activity, must take steps to combat those structures. That is its mission. A mission that the entire Church must fulfill—hierarchy, lay people, and religious, each according to the nature and function of his particular vocation in the Church." Thus the Church must speak and act concerning the justice and injustice of given situations, but it can do so freely "precisely because it refuses to be captured by any one faction or party." This is a far cry from those approaches that speak of the relation of the Church to the economic and political spheres through means "proper to herself."

In the foregoing sampling of a huge literature, the center of concern has been the relation of salvation to human liberation in all its forms (economic, political, racial, sexual, etc). This relationship obviously determines the basic meaning of evangelization and its appropriate methods. One senses a tension throughout this literature, almost a foreknowledge of the fact that the attempt to formulate the matter is, given the mysterious depth of our salvation in Christ and its "already" but "not yet" character, doomed to failure. When the transcendence of salvation is emphasized, its immanent claims seem to be minimized. When the immanent claims (liberation) are urged, there is the ever-present danger of collapsing salvation into a particular socioeconomic policy. Thus the literature represents a series of *sic et non* statements, with the *sics* getting much stronger emphasis in the Latin American version of liberation theology than elsewhere.

When this literature is viewed from the perspective of the Church's mission, the following emphases would represent, I believe, the thrust or direction of thought: (1) a move away from statements asserting that the Church has "no proper mission in the political, economic or social order." (2) This move is made, above all, in terms of the rights of man. (3) These rights are founded on the dignity of man. (4) This dignity is stated in and sharply illumined by the gospel—a dignity rooted in what man already is in Christ. (This represents a slight de-emphasis in the vocabulary associated with the natural-law presentation of rights, though by no means its denial.) (5) Therefore, to preach the gospel, the Church must be concerned with rights. (6) Rights are at stake in many ways, but especially in unjust and oppressive social structures. (7) Therefore the Church is necessarily concerned with such structures. (8) Since these structures are affected, shaped, and often controlled by social, economic, and political factors, the Church is, in her concern for rights, necessarily concerned with these factors, though she must remain beyond any merely partisan or ideological approaches. (9) This concern is not preparatory to evangelization but is an essential part of it, even though such concern for and promotion of rights does not exhaust the notion of salvation.

If one were to attempt to bring these emphases together into a theological synthesis, the connecting link between evangelization and liberation in all forms would be, I believe, man's dignity as we know it from the Christ-event and the Church's commission to spread this good news. Man *is* redeemed in Christ. He shares the unspeakable life of God's love, His sonship—mysteriously and inchoatively, but nonetheless really. His life must be a free and deepening embrace of this reality. The Church, the extension of Christ's presence, is in the business of spreading this great good news.

However, if the person as person truly *is* what we say he is (and not merely an imprisoned spirit who will be this in a hereafter if he behaves), then to tell him this (evangelization) is to do all those things that remind him of his true dignity; for if the person *is* someone of dignity, he must be treated as such. To deny him his rights or to tolerate this deprivation is to tell him in a practical way that he is not worth these rights, that he is not dignified. We are reminded of our true worth and dignity by being treated in accordance with this dignity. (It is axiomatic that we expand and become capable of love by being loved). Hence the Church's proclamation is necessarily action. She does not civilize in order to evangelize (a kind of *removens prohibens*), if one may for the moment use the phraseology of Pius XI to depart from it. She civilizes because that is an essential aspect of evangelizing. It is the most concrete and effective, indeed the indispensable, way of communicating to human beings their real worth—scil., the good news. For if the Church proclaims to people what they truly are here and now, and yet tolerates a variety of injustices visited upon them, she literally does not mean what she says. Proclamation of the gospel is by inner necessity concern for those to whom the gospel is proclaimed; for that gospel is about the kingdom already aborning. In this sense it is true to say, as has long been admitted, that the Church's ethical action is *anticipation* of the kingdom and, as such, proclamation of it.

The power of sin and selfishness remains and it becomes concrete in the social structures that oppress and enslave. These structures are a daily reminder to man of his worthlessness. If it is not important that the person have equality of opportunity, reasonable security, religious freedom, sufficient food, medical care, etc., if it is of no moment that persons in some countries are desperately poor while others are comfortably affluent, then clearly man's real present dignity is of little moment. Enslaving structures are, purely and simply, unevangelical structures; they factually deny what the gospel affirms.

That is why the Church at all levels must be involved in liberation (one can choose his own word). It is the human way, and therefore the only way, of communicating dignity and therefore of proclaiming. That is why the Church of the past has been involved in orphanages, the redemption of captives, the care of the sick, and all kinds of social concerns. And that is why, it would seem, we must eventually say that she has a proper mission in the political, economic, and social order; for it is these orders that tell persons in our day and in a very concrete way what they are. And that is what the Church is about. If she renounces this mission, she renounces proclamation of the good news; and this she cannot do.

This is not to say that salvation is reducible to, e.g., economic liberation or that the Church has a special economic competence. Nor is it to say that one can leap from eschatology into practical economics and politics with a ready-made evangelical solution, ignoring the hard work of social ethics and spurning the achievements of a tradition of civil liberties. It is to say only that the Church's concern in evangelization is man and that if man is being countereducated by economic, social, and political structures (counter = told of his real lack of worth and dignity), then she must speak and act. In this sense liberation is absolutely essential to evangelization. I believe this is what the literature is attempting to say, and in ways far richer than this brief synthesis.

However this matter is to be formulated, one thing is clear: unless the Church, at all levels, is an outstanding promoter of the rights of human persons in word and deed, her proclamation will be literally falsified.[108]

---

[108] Some recent literature touching rights would include the following: Sebastian MacDonald, "The Meaning of Abortion," *American Ecclesiastical Review* 169 (1975) 219–36, 291–315; Dennis J. Doherty, "The Morality of Abortion," *American Ecclesiastical Review* 169 (1975) 37–47; Thomas R. W. Longstaff, "The Ordination of Women: A Biblical Perspective," *Anglican Theological Review* 57 (1975) 316–27; John F. Dedek, "Two Moral Cases: Psychosurgery and Behavioral Control; Grossly Malformed Infants," *Chicago Studies* 14 (1975) 19–35; J. Robert Nelson, "New Protection for the Unborn Child," *Christian Century* 92 (1975) 725–26; Peter Monkres, "Just-War Theology: Rejected by the Court," *Christian Century* 92 (1975) 547–49; James M. Wall, "Capital Punishment: A 'Moral Consensus'?" *Christian Century* 92 (1975) 483–84; Roy Branson, "Is Acceptance a Denial of Death? Another Look at Kübler-Ross," *Christian Century* 92 (1975) 464–68; Joseph Thomas, "Combat politique, épreuve ou lieu de la foi," *Christus* 22 (1975) 260–73; Virgilio Fagone, S.J., "Vita prenatale e soggetto umano," *Civiltà cattolica* 126 (1975)

441-60; Angelo Serra, S. J., "La realtà biologica del neo-concepito," *Civiltà cattolica, ibid.*, pp. 9-23; Dave Llewellyn, "Restoring the Death Penalty: Proceed with Caution," *Christianity Today* 19 (1975) 828-31; H. McHugh, "The Pastoral Care of Those Confronted with Abortion," *Clergy Review* 60 (1975) 218-23; Charles C. West, "Faith, Ethics, and Politics," *Dialog* 14 (1975) 169-80; Pope Paul VI, "La femme dans la société et dans l'église," *Documentation catholique* 72 (1975) 403-4; Charles West, "Justice within the Limits of a Created World," *Ecumenical Review* 27 (1975) 57-64; David Jenkins, "A Theological Inquiry concerning Human Rights: Some Questions, Hypotheses and Answers," *Ecumenical Review* 27 (1975) 97-103; Burgess Carr, "Biblical and Theological Basis for the Struggle for Human Rights," *ibid.*, pp. 117-23; Edward Rogers, "The Right to Live," *ibid.*, pp. 128-33; Julio Barreiro, "In Defense of Human Rights," *ibid.*, pp. 104-10; James V. Schall, "'Conditional' Right to Life," *Furrow* 26 (1975) 455-61; Manfred K. Bahmann, "Liberation Theology—Latin American Style," *Lutheran Quarterly* 27 (1975) 139-48; R. Coste, "Foi et société industrielle," *Nouvelle revue théologique* 97 (1975) 385-414; Raymund Schwager, "Gerechter Krieg?" *Orientierung* 39 (1975) 76-78; Margaret Farley, "The Role of Women in the Church," *Origins* 5 (July 3, 1975) 89-91; Robert N. Wennberg, "Act Utilitarianism, Deterrence and the Punishment of the Innocent," *Personalist* 56 (1975) 178-94; Ferdinand Schoeman, "When Is It Just to Discriminate?" *ibid.*, pp. 171-77; Salvatore Loi, "Originalità cristiana e liberazione umana," *Rassegna di teologia* 16 (1975) 327-41; Armando Oberti, "La salvezza cristiana come 'liberazione,'" *ibid.*, pp. 201-14; J. L. Gonzalez Faus, "Tesis sobre cristianismo y lucha por la justicia," *Razón y fe* 191 (1975) 71-79; Remi J. DeRoo, "Le rôle de l'église touchant les droits de l'homme au Canada," *Relations* 35 (1975) 35-41; "Démographie et morale politique," *Vie spirituelle: Supplément*, no. 112 (1975) 5-56 (no author given, since the document is a report of a theological meeting on population, as is the next entry); "Les problèmes démographiques et la responsabilité catholique," *ibid.*, pp. 57-89; Francis X. Winters, S.J., "Morality in the War Room," *America* 132 (1975) 106-10; Arthur Dyck, "American Global Population Policy: An Ethical Analysis," *Linacre Quarterly* 42 (1975) 54-63; Francis X. Winters, S.J., *Politics and Ethics* (New York, 1975).

CURRENT THEOLOGY: 1977
NOTES ON MORAL THEOLOGY: 1976

As has become usual, the literature touching moral theology is so vast that an adequate survey is impossible. For instance, in the past months there are interesting entries on liberation theology,[1] the Church and politics,[2] fundamental moral theology,[3] and bioethics.[4] I shall limit

[1] J. Salguero, O.P., "Concetto biblico di salvezza-liberazione," *Angelicum* 53 (1976) 11-55; Brian V. Johnstone, "Eschatology and Social Ethics: A Critical Survey of the Development of Social Ethics in the Ecumenical Discussion," *Bijdragen* 37 (1976) 47-85; Francisco F. Claver, S.J., "The Christian Gospel and Human Rights: A Praxis Perspective," *Catholic Mind* 74, no. 1305 (Sept. 1976) 14-23; Philip J. Scharper, "The Theology of Liberation: Some Reflections," *Catholic Mind* 74, no. 1302 (April 1976) 44-51; Robert Faricy, S.J., "Salvation, Liberation and Christian Responsibility," *Chicago Studies* 15 (1976) 105-18; Robert T. Osborn, "Jesus and Liberation Theology," *Christian Century* 93 (1976) 225-27; Dow Kirkpatrick, "Liberation Theologians and Third World Demands," *Christian Century* 93 (1976) 456-60; J. Deotis Roberts, "Contextual Theology: Liberation and Indigenization," *ibid.*, pp. 64-68; Dorothee Sölle, "Faith, Theology and Liberation," *Christianity and Crisis* 36 (1976) 136-41; Jürgen Moltmann, "An Open Letter to Jose Miguez Bonino," *ibid.*, pp. 57-63; Clark H. Pinnock, "Liberation Theology: The Gains, the Gaps," *Christianity Today* 20 (1975-76) 389-91; G. Caprile, "I cristiani e l'ordine temporale," *Civiltà cattolica* 127 (1976) 584-92; Ph.-I. Andre-Vincent, O.P., "Les 'théologies de la libération,' " *Nouvelle revue théologique* 98 (1976) 109-25; Fr. H. Lepargneur, O.P., "Théologies de la libération et théologie tout court," *ibid.*, pp. 126-69; R. P. André-Vincent, "Libération des hommes et salut en Jésus-Christ: Un document de l'épiscopat," *Pensée catholique*, no. 160 (Jan.-Feb. 1976) 57-65; Enrico Gilardi, "Teologie politiche e della liberazione: Osservazioni metodologiche," *Scuola cattolica* 104 (1976) 137-91.

[2] U.S. Catholic Conference, "Political Responsibility: Reflections on an Election Year," *Catholic Mind*, 74, no. 1306 (Oct. 1976) 2-9; Paul Weber, S.J., Kent A. Kirwan, "Christian Values and Public Policy: A Proposal," *Chicago Studies* 15 (1976) 199-209; James Armstrong, "The Politics of Abortion," *Christian Century* 93 (1976) 215-16; Paul Abrecht, "The U.S. Christian and the World Struggle," *Christianity and Crisis* 36 (1976) 186-91; John B. Anderson and Archie Penner, "Get Active Politically? [Two Views]," *Christianity Today* 20 (1975-76) 658-60; "Carter and the Bishops" [editorial] *Commonweal* 103 (1976) 611-12; Ferdinand Klostermann, "Kirche und Politik," *Diakonia* 7 (1976) 73-76; Gervasio Gestori, "Fede e politica nei congressi nazionali della Democrazia Christiana," *Scuola cattolica* 104 (1976) 211-42; Giuseppe Angelini, "Ideologia, prassi politica e fede," *ibid.*, pp. 243-68; Wolfgang Seibel, S.J., "Kirchliche Erklärungen im Wahljahr," *Stimmen der Zeit* 101 (1976) 433-34.

[3] W. Conn, "Bernard Lonergan's Analysis of Conversion," *Angelicum* 53 (1976) 362-404; Daniel C. Maguire, "Credal Conscience: A Question of Moral Orthodoxy," *Anglican Theological Review*, Supplementary Series 6 (1976) 37-54; Timothy E. O'Connell, "A Theology of Conscience," *Chicago Studies* 15 (1976) 149-66; Douglas John Hall, "Towards an Indigenous Theology of the Cross," *Interpretation* 30 (1976) 153-68; Joseph Sittler, "Space and Time in American Religious Experience," *ibid.*, pp. 44-51; Enda McDonagh, "Technology and Value Preferences," *Irish Theological Quarterly* 43 (1976) 75-90; James F. Bresnahan, S.J., "Rahner's Ethics: Critical Natural Law in Relation to Contemporary Ethical Methodology," *Journal of Religion* 56 (1976) 36-60; David J. Leigh, "Newman,

myself to four areas: (1) Christianity and morality; (2) norms and conscience; (3) theologians and the magisterium; (4) the "Declaration on Certain Questions concerning Sexual Ethics."

CHRISTIANITY AND MORALITY

How does Christian faith relate to moral reasoning? There are many ways of phrasing this question: What is the relationship of moral theology to moral philosophy? Is there a specifically Christian ethics? Does Christian faith add material content to what is in principle knowable by reason? Is Christian morality autonomous? Is Christ the ultimate

---

Lonergan and Social Sin," *Month* 9 (1976) 41–44; Alfred H. Wiater, "Ethik und Naturwissenschaften," *Die neue Ordnung* 30 (1976) 171–78; P. Toinet, "Conscience et loi objective," *Nouvelle revue théologique* 98 (1976) 577–91; Henry B. Veatch, "The Rational Justification of Moral Principles: Can There Be Such a Thing?" *Review of Metaphysics* 29 (1975) 217–38; Luis Vela, "Consciencia y ley," *Sal terrae* 64 (1976) 483–90; Hans Jürgen Baden, "Moralismus und Moral," *Stimmen der Zeit* 101 (1976) 445–56; E. Schweizer, "Ethischer Pluralismus im Neuen Testament," *Theologie der Gegenwart* 19 (1976) 13–17; Friedo Ricken, S.J., "Die Begründung moralischer Urteile nach R. M. Hare," *Theologie und Philosophie* 51 (1976) 344–58; Wm. E. May, "What Makes a Human Being to Be a Being of Moral Worth?" *Thomist* 40 (1976) 416–43; Walter G. Jeffko, "Action, Personhood, and Fact-Value," *ibid.*, pp. 116–34; Ralph McInerny, "Naturalism and Thomistic Ethics," *ibid.*, pp. 222–42; Walter E. Conn, "H. Richard Niebuhr on 'Responsibility,'" *Thought* 51 (1976) 82–98; F. Furger, "Katholische Moraltheologie in der Schweiz," *Zeitschrift für evangelische Ethik* 20 (1976) 219–31; Christofer Frey, "Natürliche Theologie und christliche Ethik," *ibid.*, pp. 1–24.

⁴ Cf. *Linacre Quarterly* (passim) and Hastings *Report* (passim) as well as the *Journal of Medical Ethics.* In addition: "A Vatican Statement on Sterilization," *Catholic Mind* 74, no. 1306 (Oct. 1976) 13–14; Stanley Hauerwas, "Having and Learning How to Care for Retarded Children: Some Reflections," *ibid.*, 74, no. 1302 (April 1976) 24–33; Lawrence B. Casey, "A Statement on the Case of Karen Ann Quinlan," *ibid.*, 74, no. 1301 (March 1976) 12–18; Thomas C. Oden, "A Cautious View of Treatment Termination," *Christian Century* 93 (1976) 40–43; Kenneth Vaux, "Beyond This Place: Moral-Spiritual Reflections on the Quinlan Case," *ibid.*, pp. 43–45; Cathie Lyons, "The Quinlan Decision," *Christianity and Crisis* 36 (1976) 103–4; Douglas K. Stuart, " 'Mercy Killing'—Is It Biblical?" *Christianity Today* 20 (1975–76) 545–47; "Should Karen Ann Quinlan Be Allowed to Die?" [editorial], *ibid.*, p. 33; A. Fonseca, "Sterilizzazione obbligatoria in India?" *Civiltà cattolica* 127 (1976) 153–65; S. Lener, "Sui diritti dei malati e dei moribondi: È lecita l'eutanasia?" *ibid.*, pp. 217–32; Donald P. Warwick, "Compulsory Sterilization in India," *Commonweal* 103 (1976) 582–85; Daniel C. Goldfarb, "The Definition of Death," *Conservative Judaism* 30 (1976) 10–22; Seymour Siegel, "Updating the Criteria of Death," *ibid.*, pp. 23–30; Patrick Verspieren, "La muerte y el morir en la era technológica," *Criterio* 49 (1976) 167–73; John Giles Milhaven, "Christians and the Permanently Mentally Ill," *Critic* 35, no. 1 (Fall 1976) 10–13, 95; James M. Childs, Jr., "Euthanasia: An Introduction to a Moral Dilemma," *Currents in Theology and Mission* 3 (1976) 67–78; Robert M. Cooper, "Abortion: Privacy and Fantasy," *Encounter* 37 (1976) 181–88; William May, "Ethics and Human Identity: The Challenge of the New Biology," *Horizons* 3 (1976) 17–37; Kevin O'Rourke, "Active and Passive Euthanasia: The Ethical Distinctions," *Hospital Progress* 57, no. 11 (Nov. 1976) 68–73; S. C. Papenfus, "Christianity and Psychiatry: Some Ethical Considerations," *Irish Theological Quarterly* 43 (1976) 211–16; Patrick

norm for the morally good and right, and in what sense? These questions may appear academic, at the margin of real life. Actually the proper answer to them (and as I have worded them, they may represent substantially different questions) is of great importance.

For instance, the answer affects public policy. Public policy, while not identical with sound morality, draws upon and builds upon moral conviction. If Christian faith adds new material content to morality, then public policy is even more complex than it seems. For example, if Christians precisely as Christians know something about abortion that others cannot know unless they believe it as Christians, then in a pluralistic society there will be problems with discussion in the public forum. The answer affects the Church's competence to teach morality authoritatively, and how this is to be conceived and implemented. Thus, if Christian faith adds material content to what is knowable in principle by reason, this could provide support to a highly juridical notion of the moral magisterium. Also affected is our understanding of what has been traditionally called "the natural law." Similarly, the very processes we use, or do not use, to judge the moral rightness or wrongness of many concrete projects (e.g., donor insemination, *in vitro* fertilization, warfare, poverty programs, apartheid) can be affected. Our relationship to Marxists can be deeply influenced by this discussion.

Several interesting articles directly touch this matter, e.g., those of William Van der Marck, Vernon Bourke, and Daniel Maguire.[5] Others do so indirectly. Perhaps the best way to exemplify its importance is through a study by Norbert Rigali, S.J.[6] He tries to discover the historical meaning of the *Humanae vitae* controversy, i.e., to see how future historical theology may view the matter. Future theologians will ask: How convincing was the case for change? Rigali's conclusion: *Humanae vitae* was a fitting historical response, because the challengers failed to prove their case.

Rigali faults the papal commission's report on two major points. First, the report shows a Western, technological bias in neglecting the possible

---

Logan, "The Right to Die," *Month* 9 (1976) 199–202; Leonard J. Weber, "Moral Decisions in Medical Situations," *New Catholic World* 219 (1976) 214–17; Charles E. Curran, "An Overview of Medical Ethics," *ibid.*, pp. 227–32; Ronald G. Alexander, "Can a Christian Ethic Condone Behavior Modification?" *Religion in Life* 45 (1976) 191–203; Albert Keller, S.J., "Sterbehilfe und Freiheit," *Stimmen der Zeit* 101 (1976) 253–60; Josef Georg Ziegler, "Prinzipielle und konkrete Überlegungen zum Problem der Euthanasie," *Trier theologische Zeitschrift* 85 (1976) 129–49.

[5] Daniel Maguire, "Catholic Ethics with an American Accent," in *America in Theological Perspective*, ed. T. M. McFadden (New York: Seabury, 1976) pp. 13–36; William Van der Marck, "Ethics as a Key to Aquinas' Theology," *Thomist* 40 (1976) 535–54; Vernon J. Bourke, "Moral Philosophy without Revelation," *ibid.*, pp. 555–70.

[6] Norbert Rigali, S.J., "The Historical Meaning of *Humanae vitae*," *Chicago Studies* 15 (1976) 127–38.

moral demands of harmony with nature. "Is it self-evident that the religious-ethical notion of harmony with nature should simply vanish in the presence of the notion of human control over nature?" Secondly, the commission restricted its considerations to natural law. However, there is more to Christian morality. Thus the proponent of change would in addition have to do one of two things: "(1) He must disprove the traditional view that there can be Christian secular obligations which arise from a source beyond natural law, namely, charity. (2) Or he must prove that charity cannot require in this particular matter of sexual morality any behavior other than that required by natural law."[7] In either case the proponent of change must "engage in the theological analysis of the supernatural virtue of charity," an analysis untouched by the commission.

Rigali then turns to what he thinks ought to be future developments in moral theology regarding contraception if Christ is put at the center of the moral life. In general, moral theology must become "the science of the life of Christ," the perfect revelation of what Christian life ought to be. "Christian morality must become identified with doing the will of the Father and following Christ rather than with observing the moral law."

In this perspective the new moral theology will not be just adaptation of traditional formulas; it becomes a "science of the life of striving." Different persons are at different stages and levels in this growth process toward the ideal, perfect charity. For this reason "no one is existentially obligated to do the impossible and live as if he or she were already perfect in charity." The new moral theology will realize this. Thus it will do two things. First, unlike the papal birth-control commission (which spoke of contraception as involving a "negative element of physical evil"), the new theology "will see it as including a *morally* negative element": the act is incompatible with Christian perfection, with a "degree of charity possible in this world." Secondly, however, it will know that there is a difference between being incompatible with Christian perfection and being incompatible with a particular state of striving toward that perfection.

Thus the new moral theology will take the perfect love of Christ as its measure. It will examine all matters in light of this love and the different moral obligations that are generated by its progressive stages. "It will relegate to philosophy, or consign to its own corollaries, considerations of moral matters in terms of natural law. Then the new moral theology will have become at long last *theology* instead of philosophical ethics."[8]

No Christian wants seriously to deny that Christ should be at the

[7] *Ibid.*, p. 133.
[8] *Ibid.*, p. 136.

heart of the moral life. But how this is understood and formulated is important. It is what the discussion on the specificity of Christian ethics is all about. For this reason I should like to put some questions, perhaps even objections, to Rigali.[9]

First, there are the notions of charity, natural law, and moral law as he uses them. I believe they are confused. For instance, Rigali contrasts the natural law with charity as follows: "Distinguishing the natural from the supernatural, moral theology noted ethical obligations which it considered to be founded exclusively on supernatural charity, not on natural law. It taught, for instance, that an act of almsgiving, although not demanded by justice, can be required by charity."[10]

Moral theology did indeed teach that almsgiving can be required by charity. But the charity of which it spoke was not first of all *supernatural* charity. The natural law, as it has been commonly formulated, includes not simply obligations of justice but also of charity. For example, F. Hurth and P. M. Abellán write: "All moral commands of the 'New Law' are also commands of the natural moral law. Christ did not add any single moral prescription of a positive kind to the natural moral law. . . . That holds also for the command of love. . . . The ethical demand to love God and one's neighbor for God's sake is a demand of the natural moral law."[11]

Therefore, by restricting natural law to justice claims, Rigali effectively makes all claims of charity supernatural (his term), "founded exclusively on supernatural charity." This is not the traditional understanding of natural law on this matter. Thus, when Rigali says that after showing that contraception was not contrary to natural law, the proponent of change still had another task ("disprove the traditional view that there can be Christian secular obligations which arise from a source beyond natural law, namely, charity"), he is appealing to a nonexistent tradition; for tradition denied that there are "Christian secular obligations which arise from a source beyond natural law." And in the process of making this claim, Rigali is annexing all charity claims to Christian revelation in a way that would render other religious traditions a bit uncomfortable.

Something similar happens with the term "following Christ." Rigali

[9] There are some minor arguable points in the study. E.g., Rigali refers to traditional Catholic teaching in these terms: "Artificial contraception is *per se* contrary to natural law" (p. 128). Most theologians understand *per se* to mean "as a general rule." But this was not the tradition; rather, contraception was seen as intrinsically evil.

[10] *Art. cit.*, p. 132.

[11] F. Hurth, P. M. Abellan, *De principiis, de virtutibus et praeceptis* 1 (Rome: Gregorian Univ., 1948) 43. This thesis is the traditional one. It is found in Suarez, Genicot, Vermeersch, Zalba, etc. It is also broadly shared by non-Catholic authors like Bultmann, Cullmann, E. Troeltsch. Cf. B. Schüller, S.J., "Zur Diskussion über das Proprium einer christlichen Ethik," *Theologie und Philosophie* 51 (1976) 331.

states: "Christian morality must become identified with doing the will of the Father and following Christ rather than with observing the moral law." The same contrast ("rather than") appears here that was noted between natural law and charity. But it is a valid contrast only if one restricts "observing the moral law" in a way that the tradition did not: to justice claims, or to minimal negative prohibitions. Actually, most theologians would and should equate "doing the will of the Father" with "observing the moral law." So it is only by restricting the term "moral law" that Rigali can make it *appear* that Christianity makes specific claims that "moral law" does not.

My second problem is closely connected with the first: relegating to philosophy "moral matters in terms of natural law." (By natural law I understand those moral claims that are referred to as *naturaliter nota*[12] and the more detailed, even if changeable, applications of these claims as derived through discursive reasoning.[13]) The problem with Rigali's suggested relegation is at least twofold. First, a certain separationism ensues wherein "the law revealed by Christ" has nothing to do with the *naturaliter nota*. I think this is an inadequate account of things, as the Pauline catalogues of vices and virtues suggest, and, when pushed, could imply some highly dubious things about Christology. Secondly, the major moral problems of our time (e.g., racism, poverty, deprivation of civil rights, warfare, violence) are approachable through considerations that fall within the domain of what we call natural law. This does not mean that Christian perspectives cannot illumine and reinforce these considerations; they can. But to relegate to philosophy all "moral matters in terms of natural law" is easily to isolate theology from any influence on our major moral problems. Is not our challenge rather to illumine the undoubted relationship between the *naturaliter nota* and the following of Christ, and in this sense to bring them closer together? This point has been made by any number of commentators on the "Declaration on Certain Sexual Questions" (see below).

My third question to Rigali concerns his analysis of an "act intrinsically incompatible with a degree of charity possible in this world." That is how he describes a contraceptive act and, I would think, by extrapolation any action involving nonmoral evil. Using the measure of charity (or following of Christ etc.), this action must, he says, be seen as "including a *morally* negative element" (whereas theologians commonly speak of this negative element as "physical evil," "nonmoral evil," "ontic evil," as did the papal commission). This "morally negative element" consists in the fact that such "imperfect behavior" (Rigali's phrase) is "incompatible with a degree of charity possible in this world" or "Christian perfection."

---

[12] A. Vermeersch, *Theologia moralis* 1 (Rome: Gregorian Univ., 1947) nos. 146 ff.
[13] For further discussion of this point, cf. Bourke (n. 5 above).

I have several problems with this formulation.[14] I agree that there is a "moral duty to transcend what is imperfect," to strive constantly to achieve a personal and world situation where these imperfections are unnecessary. Indeed, that is the very thrust implied in the usage "nonmoral *evil*." But to call imperfect acts "*morally* negative" and to attribute this to incompatibility with perfection (charity) is to relate the conflicts we experience to our imperfection in charity rather than to creaturely limitation and an imperfect world. Imperfect acts, if one does not smuggle in the notion of *morally* imperfect, are incompatible with a *perfect world*, i.e., one without objective conflict, not with the fulness of charity.

Let me use an example. Carcinoma may require a mastectomy or an amputation. Everyone admits that such an operation visits a disvalue or physical (nonmoral, ontic) evil on the person and in this sense is an imperfect act. Yet everyone admits that this life-saving surgery is justified. Now if Rigali's formulation is correct, we should say that it has "*morally* negative elements," and precisely because it is incompatible with "a degree of charity possible in this world." But no one would say that, because no one would relate the existence of possibly metastatic carcinoma and the physical evils (surgery) it necessitates to an individual's[15] nonachievement of a "degree of charity possible in this world." Even saints can get cancer and require surgery. Therefore, the physical evils visited by mastectomy are incompatible not with "a degree of charity possible" but with a perfect world where no conflicts occur. Much the same has been said for centuries about other nonmoral evils, such as killing in self-defense, *falsiloquia*, taking another's property, etc. Their possible justification is related to the conflictual character of some human situations.

Rigali could respond that contraception is different: it is a *moral* evil. But that is, of course, the matter in dispute. One does not solve that dispute by stipulation; otherwise we have a begged question.

My second problem: if Rigali's formulation were correct, the justification for *any* imperfect act (involving nonmoral evil) would be found by examining the state of one's charity. Not only is this an impossible measure, but it diverts attention from the very factors that ought to be considered, scil., the values in conflict. In summary, then, when Rigali sees a contraceptive act, and, in principle, any imperfect act, as incompatible with a possible degree of charity, and as thereby having a "*morally* negative element," he has gotten us very close to the notion of

---

[14] I say "formulation" because practically Rigali comes out where most theologians do today; for he admits that imperfect acts can be compatible, if not with perfection, with "the striving, at any stage, for a yet unattained Christian perfection" (p. 136).

[15] I say "individual's" because a long and honored tradition relates sickness and death to original sin.

necessary sin. We should distinguish two things: the determination of what is right and wrong (and this is related to the conflictual character of reality) and the ability to do what is right (and this is or could be related to one's growth in charity).

I address these as questions to Rigali; for it is essential that Christ be the center of the moral life, but it is not clear that the "future developments" he describes should be part of this centering.

In contrast to Rigali, Henry Allard, S.C.J., cites no. 51 of *Gaudium et spes:* "moral behavior does not depend only on a sincere intention and the evaluating of motives, but must be judged by objective standards. These are drawn from the nature of the human person and his acts."[16] On this basis Allard suggests that we must incorporate knowledge from the sciences into moral theology (psychology, biology, sociology of knowledge). As an example of psychological knowledge useful to moral theology, he cites the appreciation of the various stages of the individual's growth (infancy, puberty, adolescence, adulthood, old age). "Each stage has its own specific features which constitute objective criteria to determine the nature of the human person." On this basis he proposes the notion of "limited responsibility," which differs fundamentally, he argues, from diminished responsibility in traditional moral theology. "Various stages of growth" is a notion different from "imperfection in charity," though it is not altogether clear what "limited responsibility" means in Allard's presentation.

Vernon J. Bourke asks "whether ethics may be autonomous in relation to Christian ethics."[17] After reviewing the question as treated by any number of philosophers (Frankena, Richard Brandt), he concludes that "a philosophical ethics working in the service of moral theology must have its own independent validity." As for the relationship of such an ethics to Christian realities, Bourke states somewhat tantalizingly that it "is open to development on a higher level of human experience, in terms of the spiritual values inherent in Christianity." I say "tantalizingly" because his "open to development" does not specify the relationship.[18]

This discussion on the specificity of Christian ethics is livening up in Europe, particularly in Germany. Dietmar Mieth (Fribourg) gives a

[16] Henry Allard, S.C.J., "Recent Work in Moral Theology: In Defense of Objective Morality," *Clergy Review* 61 (1976) 191–95.

[17] Bourke, *art. cit.*, p. 558.

[18] Cf. *ibid.*, p. 570. In the course of his study Bourke misunderstands my statement that "there is no such thing as a natural law existentially separable from the law of Christ, and there never was" (*Norm and Context in Christian Ethics*, ed. Paul Ramsey and Gene Outka, p. 241). Of this and similar statements (e.g., by George Regan) Bourke argues: "These and similar writers so restrict the scope of natural law that it becomes available only to those who know the law of Christ and are supernaturally elevated by divine grace" (p. 565). Bourke reads us as saying that the natural law is *knowable* only

report.[19] Everyone admits, he notes, that faith and ethics have something to do with each other. They cannot be separated, but they must be distinguished. This European discussion is often couched in terms of autonomy (a term rooted in developments in philosophical ethics since Kant) and theonomy (attributable especially to Tillich). Thus some recent theologians discuss the question in terms of "an autonomous moral in a Christian context."

Such an autonomous morality has been presented in its most detailed form by Alfons Auer (Tübingen). Similar positions have been developed by Joseph Fuchs, R. Hofmann, Dietmar Mieth, Franz Böckle, Bruno Schüller, and others. The first attack on such positions, issued by Gustave Ermecke, has been intensified by the addition of B. Stoeckle, K. Hilpert, J. Ratzinger, and Hans Urs von Balthasar to the list of attackers.[20]

Mieth first presents some general theses representative of the direction of those arguing for an autonomous morality. Then he shows how these have been distorted by the dissidents. Finally he reviews their alternatives and concludes with some rules about theological discussion, which he feels are being violated by Stoeckle, Ratzinger, and others. For example, critics should present the position they oppose in a manner recognizable to those who hold it; there should be no nameless allegations; and so on.

The most basic thesis of the autonomous-ethics theologians is that *Christian* ethics does not consist in insights available only to believers. Rather, Mieth reports, the specific character is located in a new horizon of meaning ("im Sinne eines neuen Sinnhorizontes") and a specific intentionality. They do not deny the competence of the magisterium for the entire moral order, as Ratzinger asserts. Rather they (especially Auer) suggest that the magisterium expresses itself in an *original* way in the area of the intentionality and horizon of meaning specific to Christians, but only in a *subsidiary* way in the realm of innerworldly reality. Thus "a statement of the magisterium will be less necessary the more autonomous morality itself offers arguments, and all the more necessary the greater the deficiency of ethical awareness."[21]

However, Mieth claims, Stoeckle and Ratzinger distort these writ-

---

by Christians. That is not the point. What we are asserting is that there is a single existential order of salvation, and that the natural moral law, however understood and derived, must not be conceived as separate from it but immersed in it. This point is made repeatedly by Fuchs in his studies on natural law.

[19] Dietmar Mieth, "Autonome Moral im christlichen Kontext," *Orientierung* 40 (1976) 31–34.

[20] Cf. Joseph Ratzinger, *Prinzipien christlicher Moral* (Einsiedeln: Johannes Verlag, 1975). Ratzinger's essay is also published (without footnotes) in *Problems of the Church Today* (Washington: U.S. Catholic Conference, 1976) pp. 74–83.

[21] Mieth, *art. cit.*, p. 32.

ings. Thus, Ratzinger is simply wrong in asserting that "an autonomous moral in a Christian context" leaves no room for a magisterium. Moreover, Mieth believes, the only difference between Ratzinger and Auer on the function of the moral magisterium is the pejorative language Ratzinger uses to describe the positions of Auer, Küng, and others.

When Schürmann, Ratzinger, and Balthasar (Mieth regards Balthasar as the most extreme separatist of all) get around to formulating what they believe the specific Christian character of morality to be, they indulge in generalities which Mieth finds "not false but of little help." As an example, he cites Balthasar's statement that the absolute norm of the crucified Christ "makes himself present as the only norm in every situation."

Since Ratzinger had cited Schüller as among those holding to a "rationalistic thesis," Schüller recently returned to this discussion by directly engaging Ratzinger, Schürmann, and von Balthasar.[22] The traditional thesis has been that moral rules incumbent on a Christian are materially identical with the precepts or prohibitions of so-called natural law. Ratzinger *et al.* deny this, and for two reasons that Schüller lifts out. First, God's and Christ's love is presented as a *standard* of our love. Thus Ephesians 5:1: "Be imitators of God as His dear children. Follow the way of love, even as Christ loved you." This implies that only by referring to Christ's behavior and preaching can a Christian learn how to behave morally, a conclusion drawn explicitly by Schürmann and Balthasar. The second reason: as experience shows, faith is reliable, but reason is not. We need only recall the blunders made by philosophers throughout history to see this unreliability.

In a long and careful rejoinder, Schüller argues that these objections fail to draw two important distinctions. The first objection fails to distinguish between parenesis and normative ethics; the second fails to distinguish the truth value (or validity) of moral judgments and the genetic explanation of true and false moral judgments. A word about each.

To the first objection Schüller argues: the referring of the moral law to the gospel has nothing to do with normative ethics but is a specific sort of parenesis. To establish this, he notes that the golden rule (always treat others as you would want them to treat you) can be formulated parenetically in two ways, retrospectively and prospectively. Retrospectively: you have been treated well by others; therefore you ought to treat others well. Biblically it would be: obedience is required by recalling God's doing good to us—gospel and law. Prospectively: treat others well and you will be treated well by others. Biblically it would be: obedience is required by recalling God's judgment—law and judgment.

[22] Bruno Schüller, S.J., "Zur Diskussion über das Proprium einer christlichen Ethik," *Theologie und Philosophie* 51 (1976) 321–43.

Once we include among those "others" God and Christ, it becomes clear that the famous relation between gospel and law is an application of the golden rule in its retrospective form: God or Christ has treated you well; therefore you ought to treat others well (e.g., Eph 4:32). The main point of this first type of parenesis is not the concept of imitation (Christ's love is the moral standard) but the concept of grace (Christ's love is the ground of our love). Even as it touches imitation, it is like the golden rule, parenetic, i.e., it supposes the matter of normative ethics settled and exhorts to performance.

It is because these authors, especially Ratzinger,[23] confuse and iden- tify normative ethics and parenesis that they think the traditional thesis (no new material content unavailable to reason) robs the Chris- tian message of its specifically Christian character. Schüller grants, of course, that "Christ is the concrete categorical imperative" (Balthasar), that his "behavior is the example and measure of serving and self-giving love," that his word is "the ultimate decisive moral norm" (Schürmann). He insists only that with such statements one does not raise the issue of *how* one originally knows God's will, "whether through faith alone as a distinct manner of knowing or through human reason. Jesus' word is the 'ultimate decisive norm' even when one accepts the fact that 'Christus sua auctoritate haec praecepta (naturalia) denuo confirmavit et maiorem vim obligandi eis addidit.' "[24] Where morality is concerned, Schüller argues, Scripture is largely parenesis. That is why so many rich and excellent studies in biblical ethics never come to grips with the problem of normative ethics.

Schüller's second distinction is between the truth value or internal validity of moral judgments and the genetic explanation of true and false judgments. Thus we may distinguish between: (1) Christian ethics in the normative (truth value) sense — what Christ said and did. In this sense this ethic is absolutely true. (2) Christian ethics in the genetic- historical sense — e.g., St. Thomas' interpretation of what Christ said and did. In this second sense it remains questionable whether the ethic is truly Christian. Indeed, this level includes heresies.

Similarly one can distinguish (1) philosophical ethics in the norma- tive sense, scil., the law of reason, and (2) philosophical ethics in the genetic-historical sense, scil., Kant's understanding of this. It is an open question whether this latter is correct.

In saying that faith is more reliable than reason, Ratzinger confuses

---

[23] Schüller shows that Ratzinger mistakes parenesis for normative ethics. An indica- tion of this is that Ratzinger unaccountably relates deontological theories (of normative ethics) with parenesis by recalling the gospel. He relates teleological theory with parenesis by recalling the judgment to come. Actually these theories have nothing to do with parenesis; they are concerned with normative ethics.

[24] From Hurth–Abellan (n. 11 above) p. 43.

these two levels. Reason is more reliable than faith if philosophical ethics is taken in the normative sense and Christian ethics in the genetic-historical sense. However, faith seems more reliable if taken in the normative sense and philosophical ethics in the genetic-historical sense. With this in mind, Schüller recalls that the traditional teaching on concrete moral norms (i.e., revelation does not add anything concretely to them) concerns only the epistemological status of norms, not the sociological, historical, psychological conditions that may hinder reason from arriving at true value judgments. This is overlooked by Ratzinger, Balthasar, and Schürmann.

In a lecture (Nov. 12, 1975) before the theological faculty of the Johannes Gutenberg University (Mainz), Polish theologian Tadeusz Styczen took a different point of view.[25] He argues that the proliferation of writing on this subject is symptomatic of the fact that "we are not clear enough on where the problem itself lies." Concretely, he argues that if we have no clear and clean-cut picture of ethics as a theory of moral obligation, we will remain unclear about the specific character of *Christian* ethics.

What, then, is the essence of moral obligation? Styczen proposes three different understandings, each with "a particular shape that cannot be reduced to the others": the deontological, the eudaimonist, and the personalist. For instance, those who explain moral obligation in terms of God, the author of moral law (Christians), or in Hegelian terms of history (Marxists) are classed as deontologists. Or again, a eudaimonist theory of moral obligation would include all those who explain the moral ought by appeal to man's final end—whether this be said to be self-fulfilment, happiness, or "status omnium bonorum aggregatione perfectus" (Boethius). In this category would be almost all Thomists (with the exception of J. Maritain and Joseph de Finance) and those Marxists who are uncomfortable with the Hegelian interpretation of morality. The personalist ethic derives moral obligation ultimately from nothing other than the affirmation of the person. If other considerations play a role (e.g., authority commanding this affirmation), they are not constitutive. "The one and only constitutive for the moral 'must' is that one person reveals himself simply as a person to another, that is, as no mere thing that can be used as means to end, but as a self-value *sui generis* or as an end in himself."[26] The representatives of this ethic would include Jesus himself.

Styczen concludes: "The consequence of this [threefold differentiation] is that the question about the specifically Christian character of ethics

---

[25] Tadeusz Styczen, "Autonome und christliche Ethik als methodologisches Problem," *Theologie und Glaube* 66 (1976) 211–19.

[26] *Ibid.*, p. 217.

or about its autonomy, as well as the question about their mutual relationship to each other, is a different problem than has been thought the case up to now." It is only the third type of analysis of moral obligation that can, Styczen suggests, be completely autonomous.

Perhaps Styczen has something; but I am not sure what it is. The question is whether the revealed word engages in normative ethics, and if it does, whether this normative ethics is beyond what is accessible to human reasoning processes, *whatever be the understanding of obligation undergirding these reasoning processes.* And if this normative ethics is beyond human reasoning processes in principle, just what is it? The answer traditionally given is that there is indeed something specifically Christian in Christian ethics, but it is not at the level of normative ethics (concrete behavioral norms). The denial of this is relatively recent (Ratzinger *et al.*), and to deal with that denial one need only show, as Schüller has done convincingly, that the reasons they adduce pertain to the level of parenesis, not normative ethics. In other words, it is not clear to me that Styczen has clarified the question.

There are probably many ways of viewing and formulating this matter; no one way ought to claim a monopoly. My own tentative view, expressed elsewhere[27] and drawing on several sources, can be summarized as follows. With regard to those claims that are considered to apply to all men, Christ added nothing new. This means that at this level there is a material identity between Christian moral demands and those perceivable by reason. At this level, then, whatever is distinctive about Christian morality is found essentially in the life style, the manner of accomplishing the moral tasks common to all persons. The experience of Jesus is regarded as normative because he is believed to have experienced what it is to be *human* in the fullest way and at the deepest level. Christian ethics does not and cannot add to human ethical self-understanding as such any material content that is, in principle, strange or foreign to man as he exists and experiences himself.

Therefore, the Christian tradition is, or better, ought to be, an outlook on the human, a community of privileged access to the human. The Christian tradition is anchored in faith in the meaning and decisive significance of God's covenant with persons, especially as manifested finally in the saving incarnation of Jesus Christ and the revelation of his final coming, his eschatological kingdom, which is here aborning but will finally only be given. Faith in these events, love of and loyalty to their central figure, yields a decisive way of viewing and intending the world, of interpreting its meaning, of hierarchizing its values, of react-

[27] Richard A. McCormick, S.J., "The Insights of the Judaeo-Christian Tradition and the Development of an Ethical Code," in *Human Rights and Psychological Research*, ed. Eugene Kennedy (New York: Crowell, 1976) pp. 23–36.

ing to its apparent surds and conflicts. In this sense the Christian tradition only illumines human values, supports them, provides a context for their reading at given points of history. It aids us in staying human by underlining the truly human against all cultural attempts to distort it. In other words, it steadies our prethematic gaze on the basic human values that are the parents of more concrete rules and ethical protocols.

In summary, we do not, I believe, find concrete answers in revelation to the complex moral problems of the day. We do find a world view that informs our reasoning—especially as this reasoning touches the basic human values. This world view is a continuing check on and challenge to our tendency to make policies and choices in light of cultural enthusiasms that sink into and take possession of our prediscursive selves. Such enthusiasms can reduce the good of life to mere adjustment in a triumph of the therapeutic, collapse an individual into his functionability, exalt his uniqueness into a lonely individualism or crush it in a suffocating collectivism. In this sense it is true to say that the Christian tradition is much more a value-raiser than an answer-giver.

Ultimately, then, the Christian tradition involves two assertions. First, it admits that our reasoning processes are "primi hominis culpa obtenebrata" (*DB* 1670) and that revelation is necessary so we can know "expedite, firma certitudine et nullo errore admixto quae in rebus divinis humanae rationi per se impervia non sunt" (*DB* 1786). Secondly, it refuses to bypass or supplant human deliberation and hard work in developing normative ethics. Thus normative ethics is reasoning informed by faith, not replaced by it. If we look for more in our tradition, we will not, I think, find it. But if we settle for less, we are in trouble.

NORMS AND CONSCIENCE

Several studies deal with moral norms and their relation to conscience. Jeremy Miller, O.P., of Emory University, has a tidy summary of Rahner's approach to decision-making.[28] Rahner found both an essentialist ethic (which sees individual choices as merely instances of general moral norms) and a situational one (which sees the individual as absolutely unique and thus denies any general moral norms) inadequate. He moves between the two extremes with his formal existential ethic, precisely because an individual is more than an instance of commonly shared humanity. The person is unique and this uniqueness roots in the spirit.

This uniqueness of the person means two things. First, there are times when the application of general moral norms ("the conclusion of

---

[28] Jeremy Miller, O.P., "Rahner's Approach to Moral Decision Making," *Louvain Studies* 5 (1975) 350–59.

the syllogistic technique") still leaves open several "permitted possibilities." Still, among these possibilities "there is only one choice at this moment expressing how God calls one." Secondly, even if the application of a general norm yields what one ought to do here and now, still this one imperative "could be realized with the most diverse inner attitudes." Thus Rahner's distinction between a principle and a prescription. This latter is directed to the concrete person in a concrete situation. Because it calls one in that person's uniqueness, a prescription "is beyond the reach of general normative maxims explicative of an essence, *though not in contradiction to them,* for, of course, it cannot be really distinct from what in the individual is the individualized realization of the universal essence."[29] The morally-demanded response of a unique situation is what Rahner means by an existential ethic.

Where such prescriptions are concerned, conscience recognizes them; it does not formulate (i.e., create) them. Thus, for Rahner, conscience has two functions: (1) it brings to our awareness the relevant moral principles for a situation and applies them; (2) in the individual sphere, conscience enables the individual to hear God's call to him alone (prescription). How does conscience recognize a prescription? Here, Miller notes, Rahner relies heavily on Ignatian discernment of spirits, especially the experience of peace and consolation.[30]

Miller finds this faulty for three reasons. First, the method requires too much time for ordinary moral decisions. Secondly, how many are really receptive to the consolations against which one weighs a hypothetical choice? Thirdly, and above all, Rahner asserts an irreducibly self-evident character to God's speaking to the individual. "I am sure because I am sure." Miller sees this as unduly reducing the possibilities of self-deception. Therefore he feels that at this level Rahner underlines the problem but does not solve it. "That his proposal is existential separates it from the essentialist ethic. That it might be formalized separates it from situation ethics. But it remains a *project.*"[31]

E. Hamel, S.J., does not speak of a "formal existential ethic," since his study is much more biblical than Miller's.[32] But he arrives, through a fine study of spiritual discernment in St. Paul, at remarkably similar perspectives. His essay is concerned with discernment of God's will. He points out that in the New Testament Church there was a double teaching, internal and external. The internal refers to the teaching of

---

[29] These are Rahner's words cited in Miller, p. 355.

[30] For an interesting study on Ignatian discernment, cf. Michael Buckley, "Structure of Ignatian Rules for Discernment," *Theology Digest* 24 (1976) 280–85.

[31] Miller, *art. cit.*, p. 359.

[32] E. Hamel, S.J., "La scelta morale tra coscienza e legge," *Rassegna di teologia* 17 (1976) 121–36.

the Lord, in the Spirit, given interiorly to each individual. The external refers to the divine demands externalized especially in the words of the apostles. These are not two separate sources of knowledge of God's will, but complementary ways in which the Spirit influences the Christian to discover God's will.

As for the first and chief source of discernment, it is the Spirit within us deepening agape. "The facility of the Christian in growing to better discernment of God's will depends on the growth in him/her of this divine gift." As it deepens and abounds, so the moral and spiritual sense of discernment (knowledge by connaturality) grows. And Paul underlines the communitarian aspect of this search for God's will.

As for external laws, these are secondary. They do not substitute for conscience but aid it by illuminating it. But Paul's emphasis is heavily on the capacity of the Christian to discern. Thus St. Thomas, commenting on Paul, insists that the principal element of the new law is the presence of the Spirit. Hamel sees two operations of the Holy Spirit: aid in applying external norms, of seeing their importance, and aid in discerning within the total situation "the personal invitation *hic et nunc* offered by God." Two dangers are to be avoided: legalism (the only way to know God's will is revealed law) and inspirationism (the Christian has a kind of personal "direct line" to God's will). "The Pauline way avoids these excesses. For the apostle, the discovery of God's will is not something automatic, exclusively charismatic; it is the result of a process of spiritual discernment, realized in the heart of the community, guided by a double teaching, internal and external."[33] Hamel's study is refreshing and, like Miller's, it points the moralist's attention to the profound importance of the notion of discernment in the moral-spiritual life.

Normative ethics presupposes a method of analyzing human behavior. And where the discussion is of method, the name of Joseph Fletcher is rarely long absent from the discussion. Fletcher's *Situation Ethics* has been around almost ten years now, yet he continues to get precious little peace and quiet from his commentators. Two recent entries review his methodology and may serve as contrasts to what has been occurring in the Catholic community of moral theologians. Seton Hall's Gerard J. Dalcourt discusses the pragmatism of Dewey and the situationism of Fletcher (I shall treat only Fletcher here).[34] After describing the basic characteristics of Fletcher's position, he notes its strengths and weaknesses. Among the former is Fletcher's emphasis on the concrete situation and the increase in moral sensitivity it can foster; after that,

---

[33] *Ibid.*, p. 136.

[34] Gerard J. Dalcourt, "The Pragmatist and Situationist Approach to Ethics," *Thought* 51 (1976) 135–46.

Dalcourt finds little to recommend in Fletcher's variety of situationism.

Some of the weaknesses are the following. First, to hold as he does that love is the sole absolute is untenable, because it just does not work; for love is not an objective and effectively consistent guide to moral judgment. Even if Fletcher admits, as he does, that love must be guided by wisdom and knowledge, "this would bring him back to the sort of objective morality which he refuses to allow." Again, "love as absolute" fails the very pragmatic test this ethic insists on. Why? "Love is certainly one of our very greatest goods. But its value is a function of what is loved." Thus love itself is really only an instrumental, not an absolute, good. It does not tell us what constitutes a full and satisfying life, but is "rather a necessary precondition to the application of the pragmatic test."

Then there is the nominalism espoused by Fletcher. According to this theory, we cannot grasp the nature of things intellectually or make certain, universal, and necessary statements about them. Dalcourt objects: "But if this is so, then the situationist has no grounds for affirming, as he does, that we should always act in a loving way. For, to apply such a general rule we would have to understand the nature and consequences of love and other acts."[35]

Dalcourt details other objections, most of them quite well known; but his article is a very useful synthesis. At this point, an aside. In many contemporary discussions (especially oral) the term "situationism" or "situation ethics" is used and almost always as a condemnatory philosophical category. Thus the word functions as a kind of polemical sledgehammer. Actually, the term is almost totally useless. Before it takes on meaning, one must know the methodology and conclusions it is meant to describe, and the validity of the methodology and conclusions. *Those* are the real issues, and they are not illumined by referring to them as "situationist." Rather, the real issues are bypassed by such usage. To illustrate dramatically what I mean, I would argue that the moral theology of St. Thomas is "situationist" in a very real and profound way. But by saying that I achieve two things, neither of which is very helpful: I fail to reveal what I mean by the term, and I associate Aquinas with a term that has acquired sinister connotations. For the sake of disciplined discourse, we ought either to abandon the term or always qualify it to the point where it has meaning: e.g., the situation ethics of Fletcher, of Aquinas, of Gustafson. I am for abandoning the term, because I think it realistically beyond rehabilitation—and unnecessary; for once the qualifier has been added ("of J. Gustafson"), what does the term add or illumine?

James J. Walter studies the end-means problematic in Fletcher's

---

[35] *Ibid.*, p. 144.

writings, especially his repeated usage of the axiom that the end justifies the means.[36] Building on Eric D'Arcy's *Human Acts: An Essay on Their Moral Evaluation*, Walter contends that Fletcher is involved in a process of "description and redescription" in order to show that the end justifies the means and to discredit absolute norms. Fletcher repeatedly does two things: he describes a physical action in synthetic value terms (lying, adultery, suicide) and he redescribes the action in terms of intention or consequences.

Take the case of Mother Maria. She chose to die in a gas chamber in place of a young ex-Jewish girl in the Nazi camp of Belsen. The young girl had been arrested by the Gestapo on the charge that she was running an underground escape route for Jews. Fletcher calls Mother Maria's action "suicide," but he also calls it "sacrificing her life on the 'model' of Christ." By first classing the action within a species term ("suicide"), then redescribing the action in terms of the intention, Fletcher makes it appear that lying, adultery, etc. can be justified.

Now what is wrong with this? Walter argues: "His initial description of these physical activities never entails a consideration of the relevant circumstances which are connected with the activities." Thus, actions are *first* called murder, adultery, lying (synthetic value terms) independent of circumstances and intention. Walter continues: "It is only in his re-characterization or re-description of the act that he refers to the relevant circumstances, for example, the intention." In other words, Fletcher never really determines the meaning of such terms as "suicide" and "lying" in their *moral* sense, but constantly uses these value terms to describe only the physical or external aspects of activity. Walter sees this as dualistic, scil., the subject and his/her physical activity are separated from each other. I agree. A useful study.

Some basic aspects of normative ethics have also occupied Catholic moral theologians in the past decade. During this period, at the invitation of Vatican II, Catholic moral theologians have been re-examining certain aspects of their discipline. It is no secret that some of the results have not been to the liking or comfort of all in and out of the Church.

Paul Quay, S.J., has made this re-examination the object of a long study.[37] He focuses on six moral theologians[38] and sees their writings—what he calls a "theology of values"—as attempts to "'relativize' so-called 'absolute prohibitions'" against defrauding laborers, adultery,

---

[36] James J. Walter, "Joseph Fletcher and the End-Means Problematic," *Heythrop Journal* 17 (1976) 50–63.

[37] Paul M. Quay, S.J., "Morality by Calculation of Values," *Theology Digest* 23 (1975) 347–64.

[38] The six mentioned are Joseph Fuchs, Richard McCormick, Giles Milhaven, John Dedek, Charles Curran, Bruno Schüller.

abortion, and the like." He states explicitly that his purpose is "to show that, whatever their intentions, the shift is important, inept, and often deleterious."

Quay first summarizes "the elements in their argument." Moral norms embody and protect values. While these norms are not absolute, it is highly unlikely that "any congeries of oppositely directed values" will arise that will countervail them. In principle, however, the idea is that a moral agent looks at all the values of two alternative courses of action and "sums these values." Quay continues: "That is judged to be bad which has a negative total value; and that to be good which has a positive total value." Having decided what course of action embodies the "greatest total value," the agent directs his intention to the positive total value. Quay gives abortion as an example. "One may rightly will an abortion, for example, but only when the death of the child is seen as but one of many premoral elements whose values when summed result in an overriding positive value for the action as a whole."[39]

Quay's response to this "thread" or direction is twofold. First, it overlooks the fact that there are elements in human situations not reducible to values. He mentions several: qualitative difference between values, relations of cause and effect, persons and their uniqueness. Quay then specifies these. For instance, he notes that premoral good cannot be treated simply as a positive value. A value is not just what is good for men, but *what is good for him in terms of his needs, desires, purposes*. Thus, standing as it does in relation to one's already accepted goals, it implies the possibility of weighing and exchange. This is not true of the good. The same analysis, Quay argues, is true of the terms "premoral evil" and "disvalue." They are not the same. By treating them as such, the "value theologians" get involved in seeing "the determination of moral good as a merely quantitative process." As Quay words it: "Everything can in principle be evaluated and scaled in accord with utility, worth and price; as values are balanced, exchanged, and traded off for one another, the moral judgment becomes a commerce and merchandizing in human conduct and Christian behavior."[40]

This mercantilist spirit and calculus, Quay argues, cannot deal adequately with the relation of cause and effect and the realities of human intentionality. For instance, "The values, individual and aggregate, of someone's dying and my escaping with my life would seem to be the same, all else being equal, whether there is a causal link between them or not." Furthermore, this approach, in putting a value on persons, does not deal adequately with the uniqueness of persons. Indeed, in regarding a person as a "value for others," it is contrary to the gospel.

[39] Quay, *art. cit.*, p. 349.
[40] *Ibid.*, p. 352.

Secondly, Quay attempts to show the unfortunate consequences of confounding irreducible values. For instance, whose values are to count, the individual's or someone else's? On what grounds? Again, systems built on a "quantitative summing of values" can submerge the individual in favor of relatively minor values touching millions of others. The many objections Quay levels cannot be detailed here, but he concludes that the approach of these theologians is no different from "the crudest sort of empiricism." I think it fair to say that Quay sees the basic error of these theologians in the reduction of premoral goods and evils to values and disvalues. Once this move has been made, everything follows: the weighing of values (including persons) against other values, the quantitative summing up of net values, the neglect of causal relations, intentionality, and intrinsic consequences.

Any serious study that concludes that the recent direction taken by some theologians is "inept, even deleterious," "no different from the crudest sort of empiricism," "to undo the gospel," must be taken with utmost seriousness. I intend to do that; for there are probably many who share the fears that lie behind this study and therefore there is real danger that it will be taken seriously. First, an introductory remark. Quay has adopted a device unfamiliar to the academic community: an indictment of individual theologians, without citation or footnote references, in terms of global or over-all tendencies. Though Quay may repeatedly disown the fact, and insist that he is concerned only with a "global tendency" or a "flaw which, to different degrees and in different manners, is found in the works of each of these men," the impression is unavoidable that each is vulnerable to the alleged implications Quay adduces. The serious theologian is justifiably uncomfortable with such lumping; for if one denies the allegation, Quay can always say: "Yes, but Milhaven (or Fuchs, or Curran) words it that way." If one is going to level such utterly serious moral indictments against *individuals,* careful documentation is called for. Having noted that, I turn to a few specifics in as fair a way as possible, though it would be impossible in so short a space to attend to all the deficiencies I believe are present in Quay's study.

1) *Relativizing so-called absolute norms.* Quay asserts that several moralists "have been seeking to eliminate 'absolutely binding' moral norms." His examples: defrauding laborers, adultery, abortion, "and the like." Here several remarks. First, there is a confusion here between fact-description (*Tatsachenbegriff*) and value-description (*Wertbegriff*). "Defrauding laborers," like adultery, murder, theft, is a value-description; indeed, a morally pejorative one. To state the contemporary discussion as if it were an attempt to justify what has already been labeled as morally wrongful is to indulge in circular discourse closely resembling

homiletics. The issue is: What concrete conduct is to count for murder, for "defrauding laborers," etc.? And on what criteria, with what implications? Quay's study repeatedly confuses such questions.[41]

Secondly, what recent Catholic theologians are attempting is to approach their own tradition from within the tradition itself, not with some outside system. Acknowledging the undeniable achievements of that tradition and the over-all validity of its value judgments, they are testing its formulations at key points to see whether the formulation accurately conveyed the substantive value judgment. These theologians could be wrong in their analysis, but to neglect the task is to freeze moral theology in a way repudiated by Vatican II. This effort does not deserve to be labeled "seeking to eliminate 'absolutely binding' moral norms," even if elimination is the outcome of the rethinking; for such language seems to impute motives.

2) *Good and value (evil and disvalue)*. Quay faults recent theologians for not distinguishing these notions carefully. Failure to do so leads to assessing certain goods as values for man in terms of his needs and goals. In other words, it makes what is good for man a measurable and hence negotiable thing. This is at the heart of Quay's objection, for from it follows everything else he says.

I cannot answer for all the indicted theologians individually; but I can say that the contemporary discussion uses "premoral good" and "value" *synonymously* (as also "premoral evil" and "disvalue"). There may be a dictionary difference in the notions and words, and indeed the difference Quay describes: value implies value to man in terms of his needs and desires. But that is not the way these terms are used by Schüller, Fuchs, myself *et al.* We understand by "value" an intrinsic good to man, not something that is good simply because it is evaluated as such by human beings.[42] And it is only if premoral good and evil are understood as value

---

[41] The same confusion is notable in Quay's treatment of sexuality. He notes that "an act of sexual perversion . . . damages the properly human personality of the agent." If one knows this and still performs the act, then "he intends these [harms]." Quay then concludes: "To call these negative values and to perform the action for some extrinsic good is simply to do evil that good may come." So it is—at least it is to do premoral evil. But the entire issue is, what forms of sexual conduct are to count as "perversion"? One does not define the action as "perversion" and then set about seeing how we can justify it; for "perversion" = morally unjustifiable.

[42] In this respect cf. Ph. Delhaye, "A propos de '*Persona humana*,'" *Esprit et vie* 86 (1976) 197. He writes: "Il existe une liste universelle des valeurs capables de susciter l'attention et l'amour de tous les êtres humains et dès lors objectivement fondées. Elles sont, *en même temps*, des 'biens-en-soi' et des 'valeurs-pour-nous.' Pourquoi? Parce qu'elles prennent naissance dans les exigences, les besoins, l'inspiration à la dignité de *tous les êtres humains*" (emphasis added). Cf. also a declaration of the German bishops, "Les valeurs fondamentales de la société et le bonheur humain," *Documentation catholique* 73 (1976) 868-71.

and disvalue *in Quay's sense* that the multiple aberrations he details would follow. If one is going to enter and understand contemporary moral discourse, the terms used must be accepted as the authors use them, not as one thinks they ought to be used.

There is a long and honored tradition identifying "premoral good" and "value" in the philosophical community. It can be found in contemporary philosophers such as William Frankena. It is used repeatedly in Vatican II. Take the Decree on the Apostolate of the Laity: "All of these [elements of the temporal order] not only aid in the attainment of man's ultimate goal but also possess their own intrinsic value. This value has been implanted in them by God, whether they are considered in themselves or as parts of the whole temporal order. 'God saw all that he had made, and it was very good.' "[43] Here "value" = "own intrinsic value" = "implanted by God" = "good." In a similar vein Paul VI spoke recently of the "value of every human life."[44] The recent pastoral letter of the American bishops (*To Live in Christ Jesus*) repeatedly uses value and good synonymously. With such impeccable precedents, I will continue with peaceful grammatical and philosophical conscience to use these terms synonymously, and hence to deny that usage of value (as identical with premoral good) collapses the "what is good for man" into a negotiable thing in the way Quay adduces. Once that has been said, most of Quay's subsequent objections fade into the genre of *non sequitur*.

3) *Quantification of values.* Quay repeatedly asserts that the determination of moral goodness (the more accurate term is "rightness") for value theologians is a "merely quantitative process." Thus, over and over again we read of "greatest total value," "net positive values," "quantitative calculus," and so on. First, I know of no one who does this, who understands the resolution of conflict of values in such a quantitative sense. There are times, of course, when there is commensurability along quantitative lines. For instance—to use Philippa Foot's example—if one is steering a runaway tram and there are two directions in which it can be turned (both involving killing people), one ought to steer the tram in the direction where the smaller number will be killed, other things being equal. I believe there is a similar commensurability in some rare abortion decisions where the alternatives are to save one or lose two.

Secondly, the authors in question cannot be *made to say* that moral judgments are a "merely quantitative calculus." They do not understand the terms "value" and "disvalue" as Quay does, as goods (or evils) to persons only in terms of their needs, desires, purposes, and therefore as

[43] Cf. *The Documents of Vatican II* (tr. Abbott) p. 497.

[44] Address in St. Peter's Square, Sept. 26, 1976. Cf. *Catholic Chronicle* [Toledo] Oct. 1, 1976; cf. *L'Osservatore romano*, Oct. 7, 1976 (English edition).

goods that can be balanced, exchanged, and traded off. That there are serious and unresolved theoretical problems involved in the use of terms such as "the lesser evil," "proportionate reason," and so on, I do not doubt. But these problems are common to all philosophers and theologians who would, e.g., make *any* exception to the proscription "Thou shalt not kill." They are not restricted to the so-called "value theologians."

4) *Intentionality*. Quay believes that "they" seem overly insistent that all intentions be considered before a meaning is assigned to an action, rather than considering merely the "physical nature" of the action. To this he says: "Yet, who of moral theologians of past or present has held that the intention of the agent is less important than the physical structure of his action?" I shall not cite the many examples from manualist literature; let one suffice: self-stimulation for sperm-testing. This was explicitly condemned as *contra naturam* and illicit masturbation by many theologians, the Holy Office, and implicitly by Pius XII in my judgment. Very many contemporary theologians—I would say most of my acquaintance—believe that such a procedure for testing and treating infertility is a different human and moral act than masturbation as generally understood, and it is different precisely because of its purpose or intention. To Quay's question ("Who of moral theologians past or present . . . ?") I answer: very many, or, as we used to say, *consulas auctores probatos*.

5) *Moral evil and nonmoral evil*. Quay repeatedly overlooks this distinction. E.g., he writes: "One element of evil, not necessarily obvious or easily discernible, can vitiate a whole act. If I cannot choose to do something without willing directly, even if implicitly, what is evil, then the concrete act is evil. If, further, the evil is an intrinsic consequence of the action, then the action is intrinsically evil."[45]

These statements hold ("the concrete act is evil") only if "what is evil" is understood as *morally* wrongful. There is, e.g., a long tradition that allows us to *intend* the deception of another (*falsiloquium*) if this is a necessary means for the protection, e.g., of the confessional secret. Similarly, we may *intend* the amputation of a leg when this is necessary to prevent spread of cancer. We may *intend* the death of the criminal as a necessary means in capital punishment (or so tradition argued) and in self-defense (as very many theologians argued against what is taken to be the Thomistic understanding of things). We may *intend* the pain of the child as we spank him/her pedagogically. Now these are all evils, but nonmoral in character. By stating, as he does, that the concrete act is evil "if I cannot choose to do something without willing directly . . . what is evil," Quay must *suppose* that the evil in question is *morally*

[45] *Art. cit.*, p. 361.

evil. But that is to overlook the distinction between nonmoral (ontic, premoral) and moral wrongfulness. Doing that, one begs the entire question of intentionality.

There is, then, a long tradition that nonmoral (tradition called them "physical") evil may be intended *in se sed non propter se*.[46] Two categories of actions were excluded from this: (1) actions *against nature* (certain sexual actions, e.g., contraception, masturbation); (2) actions wrong because of a *lack of right* (direct killing of the innocent, dissolution of a sacramental and consummated marriage). As Schüller has shown,[47] these actions were regarded as intrinsically evil because of the unnaturalness or lack of right. And it was for this reason that indirectness was required in the tradition when an action involved the death of an innocent person or sterilization of the sexual power. It is these qualities (unnaturalness, lack of right) that we ought to be discussing. One does not help the discussion by first describing the act as a "perversion" and *then* saying it ought never be directly willed.

Much else in Quay's presentation calls for comment,[48] but the above must suffice. I have spent a good deal of space on this article because it is important that recent probes and revisions by Catholic theologians be not misunderstood and distorted. Theologians such as Janssens, Fuchs, Schüller, Curran, Dedek, *et al.* may be wrong—that is a risk we all run; but first they must be properly understood.

For that reason it may help to cite two examples of what two of the indicted theologians think they are about. The first is drawn from a conference of European moral theologians held at Strasbourg.[49] There Franz Böckle stated several theses on moral norms. One was drawn from Schüller's writings and was stated as follows:

All ethical norms that concern interpersonal behavior rest on a judgment of preference. They are so many reflex and formulated applications of the following preference rule: 'Put in the presence of two concurring but mutually exclusive values, a person ought to examine which of the two merits the preference.' Concretely, therefore, what is involved is hypothetical imperatives, even if this does not always get expressed verbally.[50]

[46] Cf., e.g., W. Brugger, *Theologia naturalis* (Pullach, 1959) p. 412.

[47] B. Schüller, S.J., "Direkte Tötung—Indirekte Tötung," *Theologie und Philosophie* 47 (1972) 341–57.

[48] E.g., his understanding of premoral evil. He insists that this refers to a "true privation of a *good called for*." This is not the way the notion is understood in contemporary moral discourse. Louis Janssens puts it as follows: "We call ontic evil any lack of a perfection at which we aim, any lack of fulfillment which frustrates our natural urges and makes us suffer. It is essentially the natural consequence of our limitation" ("Ontic Evil and Moral Evil," *Louvain Studies* 4 [1972] 134).

[49] Cf. *L'homme manipulé*, ed. Charles Robert (Strasbourg: Cerdic, 1974).

[50] *Ibid.*, p. 180.

Schüller wrote a brief reply indicating that he himself was not fully satisfied with this formulation, it being a first attempt.[51] He restated the problem. Where concrete norms for conduct are concerned, some norms were interpreted as moral absolutes or in a deontological manner. He gives the two examples noted above (intrinsically evil because unnatural, e.g., contraception; intrinsically evil because of lack of right: direct killing of an innocent person). The reasons given by tradition for the exceptionless character of such norms involve, he believes, fallacies. In the case of contraception, the fallacy consists in the assertion that pre-established (natural) finalities of certain organs or functions are untouchable. In the case of killing, the fallacy consists in an undue restriction of human powers.

However, he continues, tradition has known other norms as well, teleological ones. These are understood as those which judge an act *also* by its consequences. The crucial problem is to discover the criteria that allow proper assessment of consequences. The great danger is naiveté; where this exists, the preference rule (above) is rendered unintelligible. One needs other rules as mediations of the preference rule. The moral-theological problem of today, as Schüller sees it, is to discover plausible teleological justification for norms in control of actions that were interpreted deontologically in the past. This is the case precisely because the traditional reasons adduced for deontological understanding of these norms will not bear scrutiny. Schüller does not regard this as discontinuous with traditional value judgments, if one is careful not to confuse a value judgment with a historical formulation of it.

My second example is Charles Curran. In an article that appears in *Concilium* (December 1976) in several languages, but not as yet in English, Curran relates recent writings by contemporary Catholic moralists to a similar discussion in the field of moral philosophy.[52] He first points out that the objections of philosophers such as Rawls, Frankena, and Williams to "utilitarianism, teleology, or consequentialism" are threefold: (1) aspects other than consequences must be taken into account; (2) the good cannot be determined independently of the morally right; (3) not only the consequences of the action but also the way in which the actor brings about the consequences have moral significance. Thus to oppose utilitarianism, teleology, consequentialism (Curran uses the terms as synonymous), these philosophers need not maintain that certain actions are right whatever the consequences.

Secondly, Curran points out that the antiutilitarian argues that, in addition to consequences, other aspects of the action must be considered,

[51] *Ibid.*, pp. 194–96.
[52] Charles E. Curran, "Utilitarianism and Contemporary Moral Theology: Situating the Debates," forthcoming, as I write, in *Concilium*, Dec. 1976.

e.g., the obligation of fidelity in promise-keeping. Something other than consequences counts as important in assessing right and wrong, even if these other considerations do not yield an absolute behavioral norm. It is these other considerations that separate Frankena, Rawls, etc. from the utilitarian.

Thirdly, there is a third current in philosophical literature represented by G. E. M. Anscombe, who indicts all of contemporary philosophy because it is even willing to consider the possibility of exceptions based on consequences. Concretely, Anscombe condemns modern moral philosophy "for proposing a philosophy according to which the consequences of such an action could be morally taken into account to determine if one should do such an action." In other words, there are actions that are right or wrong whatever the consequences. Thus, in her terminology, W. D. Ross is a consequentialist.

In summary, then, Curran believes there are three positions. The first is properly described as utilitarian, strict teleology. The position of Anscombe *et al.* may be described as nonconsequentialism or even deontology. The second Curran calls "mixed teleology" or "mixed consequentialism." This second and middle position, Curran states, differs from strict teleology because it maintains the following points: (1) moral obligation arises from elements other than consequences; (2) the good is not separate from the right; (3) the way in which the good or evil is achieved by the agent is a moral consideration. Since such an opinion does not necessarily hold that certain actions are always wrong no matter what the consequences, it has been called consequentialism by Anscombe.

When I first encountered Curran's threefold division of positions within modern philosophy, I was pleasantly astounded. I had arrived independently at a similar division. Specifically, I had concluded to the usefulness of the following divisions: (1) absolute deontologists: Kant, Catholic tradition on certain points (e.g., contraception), Grisez, Anscombe; (2) absolute consequentialists: J. Fletcher, some utilitarians; (3) moderate teleologists: Ross, McCloskey, Frankena, Fuchs, Knauer, Schüller, Böckle, Curran, and a host of others.

Curran next asks where "reforming Catholic moral theologians" fit into this division. Exactly as I had, he concludes that "as the debate progressed it became quite evident that the reforming Catholic theologians, generally speaking, do not embrace utilitarianism or what Rawls, Frankena, Williams and others have called teleology or consequentialism." They are Curran's "mixed consequentialists" or my "moderate teleologists." Why? Because these theologians, in their explanations of *materia apta* (Janssens), commensurate reason (Knauer), proportionate reason (Schüller), insist that elements other than consequences function in moral rightness and wrongness. I include myself among those who so insist.

Somewhat similarly, Schüller lists three general approaches.[53] (1) The moral rightness of all actions is exclusively determined by their consequences. (2) The moral rightness of all actions is always also but not only determined by consequences. (3) There are some actions whose moral rightness is determined in total independence of consequences. The first position, he notes, is called "teleological" or "utilitarian" (though Schüller argues that the latter term needs rehabilitation), the second and third "deontological." He regrets that there is no terminology distinguishing the second and third positions—a fact that does not disturb Anglo-American philosophers, since practically no one (except, e.g., Anscombe) holds the third position.

William May has, I believe, accurately identified the second approach listed by Schüller as a "mixed deontological" approach (Frankena's phrase).[54] It might just as well be called "moderate teleology," as I suggested above. Whatever the term used, the type of moral reasoning involved is shared by many moral philosophers and theologians, and is the type present in Catholic tradition except in the two general areas mentioned. May contrasts this with the approach of Ramsey, Grisez, and himself.

I think he is right in this contrast, but his development calls for comment at several points. First, May uses the preservation of life to illustrate his problems with the type of "mixed deontologism" he associates with Schüller, Janssens, Curran, and others. After noting my statement that life "is a value to be preserved only insofar as it contains some potentiality for human relationships,"[55] he writes: "In other words . . . life itself, in the sense of physical or biological life, is what an older terminology would have called a *bonum utile*, not a *bonum honestum*, whereas such relational goods as justice and friendship and compassion are 'higher' goods, *bona honesta.*"[56]

May is troubled by this usage. Among other reasons he adduces is that we are images of God, "and God is absolutely innocent of evil. He *permits* evil but does not directly intend it . . . ." Furthermore, he sees a dualism in the position; for it considers life as a *conditional* good, whereas it is a *personal* good, "not something subhuman or subpersonal."

[53] Bruno Schüller, S.J., "Anmerkungen zu dem Begriffspaar 'teleologisch-deontologisch,' " *Gregorianum* 57 (1976) 315–31.

[54] William May, "Ethics and Human Identity: The Challenge of the New Biology," *Horizons* 3 (1976) 17–37.

[55] Richard A. McCormick, S.J., "To Save or Let Die," *Journal of the American Medical Association* 229 (1974) 172–76.

[56] *Art. cit.*, p. 35.

This is not the place for a prolonged discussion of the intricate matter of the direct and indirect voluntary, but several remarks are in order. First, to say that life is a good to be preserved insofar as it contains some potentiality for human experience is not to make life a *bonum utile,* a kind of negotiable thing, as Quay suggests. It is merely to talk about our duties – and especially the why of those duties – toward the preservation of a *bonum honestum,* the dying human person.[57] Secondly, I believe it is inaccurate to say what May says of God and evil ("God *permits* evil but does not directly intend it") unless one distinguishes between physical (nonmoral) and moral evil. Finally, it seems inaccurate to contrast life as a conditional good with life as a personal good. The proper pairs are conditioned-unconditioned, personal-nonpersonal. Life is a personal good, yet it need not be, even as personal, unconditioned.

In conclusion, I would suggest that Paul McKeever has the matter very well in hand when he refers to contemporary Catholic discussions as an "evolution," with an organic relation to the past, rather than a "revolution."[58]

THEOLOGIANS AND THE MAGISTERIUM

The Church is and ought to be a teacher of Christian morality; no one doubts this. But what is a matter of continuing adaptation and perennial dispute is how this is to be done most effectively. This "how" touches closely and sensitively on the very notion of magisterium, especially as the notion relates to several components in the Church, most particularly theologians. Thus the relationship of theologians and bishops will have a good deal to say about how Christian morality is conceived, implemented, and received in the Church.

This relationship has always been somewhat tense. Robert B. Eno, S.S., in a useful historical study of the early Church, passes in review some of the conflicts of the time.[59] It was in the third century that the Church saw the rise of what Eno calls "conscious theologizing." The rise of theological reflection as another form of expertise or authority was

[57] Here an interesting text of Thomas is in place. "Some change could happen that would entirely take away a man's happiness by hindering virtuous action altogether. For example, some sickness could cause madness or insanity or any other mental breakdown. Since happiness may not be attained except by living humanly or in accord with reason, when the use of reason is gone, human living is not possible. Consequently, in what concerns living humanly, the condition of madness must be equated with the condition of death" (*Commentary on the Nicomachean Ethics* 1 [Chicago: Regnery, 1964] 85).

[58] "Moral Theology: Evolution or Revolution?" *Priest* 32, nos. 7-8 (July-Aug. 1976) 12-13 (an unsigned editorial, but moral theologian Paul McKeever is editor).

[59] Robert B. Eno, S.S., "Authority and Conflict in the Early Church," *Eglise et théologie* 7 (1976) 41-60.

almost bound to lead to tension with established authority, and that tension has been with us ever since. Eno has no pat answers to the problem except to hold up the patristic ideal stamping the consciousness of both theologian and bishop. The theologian is above all a churchman; the bishop is one who is above all concerned with *prodesse*, not *praeesse* (care for others, not precedence over them).

The magisterium, the Church's teaching function, will reflect the situation of the world in which it lives. How one analyzes this situation differs markedly, apparently with the preoccupations of the analyzer. Francis X. Murphy, C.SS.R., reviews this situation, with its tensions and inconsistencies, through the attitudes and actions of Pope Paul VI, which he paints as full of tensions and inconsistencies.[60] George Kelly blames it all on dissenting theologians.[61] In the face of such differences, I recommend an essay by Bishop B. C. Butler.[62] It takes the form of a letter to a convert distressed by changes in the Church. He points out, with historical precedents and great compassion, how the shift to a more historical understanding requires patience. It is a cultural, not a faith, crisis. Incidentally, it is refreshing to see an intensely loyal Catholic bishop write that "it is possible to have grave reservations about particular papal decisions and policies" at the very time he is insisting on the indispensability of papal authority.

Paul VI has repeatedly addressed himself to this subject. For instance, in his general audience of Aug. 4, 1976, he reasserted the hierarchical structure of the Church as deriving from Christ.[63] He expressed his grave concern for those who deny "the existence within the Church of legitimate, or rather obligatory, authoritative functions," and in some of the strongest language he has ever used castigated those who sit in judgment on this hierarchical function. It is hard to believe he did not have Archbishop Lefebvre in mind.

Before turning to the longer, more systematic studies, I note several interesting entries. Cardinal François Marty (Paris) argues that the dialogue between theologians and bishops must be "institutionalized."[64] Jerome Theisen, O.S.B., proposes the notion of "reliability" as best

[60] Francis X. Murphy, C.SS.R., "The Pope and Our Common Future," *Catholic Mind* 74, no. 1300 (Feb. 1976) 29–38.

[61] George A. Kelly, "An Uncertain Church: The New Catholic Problem," *Critic* 35, no. 1 (Fall 1976) 14–26. One commentator (Andrew Greeley) referred to this article as "demented drivel." To this Kelly responded that "the article is serious." One hates to be confronted with such desperate alternatives; but if pressed, I would have to say that the article is not "serious," represents the collapse of theological courtesy.

[62] B. C. Butler, "Letter to a Distressed Catholic," *Tablet* 230 (1976) 735–36, 757–58.

[63] Cf. *L'Osservatore romano*, Aug. 12, 1976, p. 8 (English edition).

[64] Cardinal François Marty, "La charge particulière du théologien dans l'église," *Documentation catholique* 73 (1976) 572–75.

describing the Catholic attitude toward the ministry of the Holy Father.[65] In a study remarkably different in tone, Dario Composta (Pontificia Università Salesiana) insists, against what he takes to be the position of Franz Böckle, that the magisterium does not "merely inform" but teaches.[66]

The following literature touching the relation of theology and the magisterium falls into two divisions: groups (International Theological Commission, Sacred Congregation for Catholic Education) and individuals (Coffy, Whealon, Palazzini, Congar, Dulles, Lanne).

During October 1975, the International Theological Commission met in Rome. The subject of its deliberations: the relationship between the magisterium and theologians. The Commission drafted twelve theses in an attempt to state this relationship.[67] In its introductory statement it noted that this relationship has shown considerable variations through history. In the patristic age, e.g., popes and many bishops were often the great theologians. At other times a greater separation of functions could be noted, research into matters of faith pertaining to the function of specialists. Faculties of theology were at times in conflict with popes — e.g., with John XXII on eschatology. This separation of expertise probably peaked in the Councils of Constance and Basle. At the thirty-fourth session of Basle (June 25, 1439) there were 300 doctors of theology, 13 priests, and 7 bishops.

The International Commission treats three points: (1) elements common to theology and the magisterium; (2) differences between theology and the magisterium; (3) principles of a trusting collaboration between the two. Under the second heading, the Commission points out that the magisterium "draws its authority from sacramental ordination." Theologians, on the other hand, owe their "specifically theological authority to their scientific qualification." The Commission admits that tensions can arise between theologians and the magisterium but sees this realistically as a vital creative force in the Church. It concludes by urging more efficacious dialogue and lists some threats to such dialogue.

Maurizio Flick, S.J., has provided a thoughtful commentary on this document.[68] He concentrates on the relationship between the magisterium and theologians. There are two functions the theologian performs in the Church: (1) he mediates between pope-and-bishops and the peo-

[65] Jerome Theisen, O.S.B., "Models of Papal Ministry and Reliability," *American Benedictine Review* 27 (1976) 270–84.

[66] Dario Composta, "Il magistero ecclesiastico informa o insegna la morale?" *Divinitas* 20 (1976) 199–203.

[67] "Theses de magisterii ecclesiastici et theologiae ad invicem relatione," *Gregorianum* 57 (1976) 549–63; also *Documentation catholique* 73 (1976) 658–65.

[68] Maurizio Flick, S.J., "Due funzioni della teologia secondo il recente documento della Commissione Theologica Internationale," *Civiltà cattolica* 127 (1976) 472–83.

ple; (2) he contributes to the magisterium's formation of opinion. What I find refreshing about Flick's presentation is his ability to spell out these functions in a realistic, satisfying way.

As for the first function, he notes two objections against this notion of theology. First, it "reduces" the theologian to a vulgarizer of magisterial opinion. Flick responds convincingly in several ways, especially by showing the absolute necessity of an "ascending communication" ("divulgazione ascendente"), the need to relate basic ecclesial judgments to the community of the well-informed. The second objection sees this theological function as a kind of ideology — an approach which forms its positions to support the interests of an institution or movement. Not so, he says, because the theologian exercises his interpretative function in a *critical* way. Here Flick is especially good. This function requires that the theologian show not only the authority behind the teaching but also its incomplete and to-be-completed aspects. Indeed, where dogma is not involved, "the theologian can and ought (in particular circumstances) to manifest his own dissent."[69]

The second task of the theologian, to precede and prepare the opinions of the magisterium, derives from the fact that revelation "is not to be considered as a static deposit . . . but is always confronted with new questions which demand that it be continually developed." In this development, the actions, opinions, and inclinations of the People of God have a special place, but not without discernment. In this discernment both the magisterium and theology have a true *authority*.

Flick next notes that the two functions of theologians (mediation and preparation) "are not separate," i.e., normally theological research reflects and supports both functions. Thus, in dealing with the crisis of the sacrament of penance, the theologian interprets the past teaching of the Church, but in doing so also suggests to the magisterium the proper way to explain reconciliation with the Church.

In trying to relate this double function of the theologian to the magisterium, Flick cites the interesting condemnation of George Hermes (*DB* 2738–40). Some of Hermes' disciples, so goes the anecdote, came to Rome to determine why he was condemned. A Roman official asked whether "they had come to the Holy See to instruct the Holy See or be instructed by it." Flick sees this as a false statement of the question, since it presupposes that the truth is in the prior possession of one of the conversationalists. After insisting on the need for dialogue, Flick shows that classical ecclesiology had the tendency to describe the relations of magisterium and theologians in juridical terms: "the duty and therefore the right of the magisterium to direct the entire theologi-

[69] *Ibid.*, p. 476.

cal project." The Commission has qualified this, and this switch in the methodological aspect of the question "constitutes the principal novelty of the document."

On February 22, 1976, the Sacred Congregation for Catholic Education issued a fifty-page document, "The Theological Formation of Future Priests."[70] Within it the relationship of the magisterium and theologians is explicitly treated. Several statements are made about theology and its relation to the magisterium. First, the Church has the "right and duty to demand of theologians a loyalty to the magisterium," which has the function of guaranteeing that research will promote the authentic building-up of the Body of Christ. Secondly, the *munus docendi* belongs to "the bishops united in collegiality with the supreme pontiff." This episcopal magisterium cannot be replaced by individual thought. The latter has the "limited function only of investigating, illustrating, and developing objective data which comes from God." Thirdly, theologians have the task of research and critical reflection. But "they can receive from the magisterium a share in its *munus docendi (missio canonica docendi)*." However, the magisterium must maintain its "authority to judge the relation of theological speculation to the word of God."

If I interpret this document correctly, its view of the relationship between theology and the magisterium seems to be that theology is at the service of the magisterium. This is a view explicitly rejected by Archbishop Coffy (see below) and the episcopal discussions that followed his study. As will be clear, Coffy sees the relationship as one of complementarity. Whatever the term used, the substantial idea is that both the magisterium and theology are at the service of the revealed word of God; they have the same tasks (*custos* and *promotor*) but from different levels, with different tools, and sometimes with different conversation partners.

The Congregation's perspective is one of subordination, wherein the official magisterium grants a share in its charge to theologians. Thus, the Congregation says that "the episcopal magisterium cannot be replaced by individual thought." True, and every theologian knows it and ought to admit it. But "replaced by" seems a defensive and uneasy way of framing the matter. One wonders why it was not immediately added that the magisterium cannot fulfil its function without theological thought.

Another problem sharpens the issue. The document states that the magisterium has the power to judge the conformity of the results of research etc. with revelation. Few would deny this; but the problem is more complex. If, as nearly everyone concedes, it is impossible to conceive and speak of revelation without a theology (i.e., the very

[70] *Origins* 6 (1976) 173–80, 181–90.

statement of revelation, *Glaubenssprache,* implies *a* theology, as is clear from the Gospels themselves), then clearly those who judge the conformity of theological research and reflection with revelation are doing so *with a theology.* That there are problems here is obvious. For instance, what is the theology of the Congregation for the Doctrine of the Faith when it issues a decree on human sexuality, or apostolic succession, etc.? Is it self-validating as a theology because it is official? I do not raise this question out of any desire to undermine the function of the magisterium. I raise it only to sharpen the issue and thus to strengthen the function of the magisterium in the Church. The question raised suggests that the real issue is not captured with words like "replaced by individual thought" etc. This is a juridical vocabulary that ends up pitting theologians competitively against bishops. The real issue is what form their indispensable co-operation ought to take if the word of God and its implications in our time are to be preached (*promotor*) and protected (*custos*).

In the spring of 1975, the third Symposium of European Bishops met outside of Rome to discuss the relationship of bishops and theologians. Archbishop Robert Coffy (Albi) delivered a very interesting paper, which first appeared in the *Bulletin du secrétariat de la Conférence épiscopale française* but is now available in *Orientierung.*[71]

Coffy proceeds in two steps: the problem, then suggestions toward a solution. Some of the causes of the problem are: the changing cultural climate, which demands a new faith-language (*Glaubenssprache*); theological pluralism involving different language, different philosophical assumptions, different use of empirical sciences; the demand by theologians that "the ecclesial office be executed in a new way" more in keeping with our time. Furthermore, the very understanding of the faith is involved.

Every understanding of the faith necessarily implies a theology. There are no sharp lines of demarcation between the faith and the theological understanding of the faith. This clarifies the reaction of theologians to certain interventions of the magisterium. Theologians have the impression that the magisterium imposes its own theology. Therefore they demand that the magisterium admit its theological preferences and then grant that it is not the only way to express the faith.[72]

The most profound cause of the magisterium's problems Coffy sees in the very notion of revealed truth. In the recent past, perhaps under certain Platonic influences, revelation was conceived in a way that

---

[71] Robert Coffy, "Lehramt und Theologie—die Situation heute," *Orientierung* 40 (1976) 63–66, 80–83.
[72] *Ibid.,* p. 65.

allowed it to be encapsulated in objective formulated truths. Thus by the very statement of the question the magisterium was positioned to distinguish clearly between the true and the false. It conceived its task as comparing certain formulations with eternal truths thus conceived (*ewige Wahrheiten*). Our time, however, is much more sensitive to the historical character of truth—which means that magisterial interventions can no longer be beyond discussion, as they were thought to be in the past.

Against this background Coffy sees the relationship of theology to the magisterium as one of complementarity. Both the magisterium and theologians are involved as guardians (*custos*) and promoters (*promotor*) of the faith, not as rivals but in different ways. Coffy rejects the idea that theologians are in the service of the magisterium; both theologians and the magisterium are in service of the word of God. After insisting on respectful co-operation, he suggests that fewer magisterial interventions might be in order. In our time "must we not allow for a long-enduring, indispensable maturing process for many questions?" Clearly Coffy thinks so.

Coffy's presentation was followed by individual discussion groups drawn up along common-language lines. This is reported by Ludwig Kaufman.[73] For instance, the bishops noted that pluralism existed not only among theologians but also among bishops. The suggestion was also made that episcopal conferences need theological commissions chosen by theological societies and faculties. Furthermore, there was broad agreement with Coffy that magisterial interventions ought to be reduced if the magisterium is not to undermine its own authority.

Archbishop John F. Whealon (Hartford) presents an interesting study of the magisterium, not the extraordinary magisterium, but the year-to-year reformable teaching of the pope, the college of bishops, and the local diocesan bishop in union with Rome.[74] After stating that relations between bishops and theologians ought to be better, Whealon makes several points. First, the priest (and bishop and deacon) are expected to "teach and preach as the Church's doctrine only that which the magisterium has presented as the Church's doctrine . . . not our own ideas or speculations, or the ideas and speculations of theologians." Secondly, where do we find this teaching? "A rule of thumb for the Catholic laity is to accept the teaching of a deacon or priest if he is in agreement with the local bishop, and to accept the teaching of the local bishop if he is in agreement with Rome."[75] Thirdly, Whealon sees the source of confusion

[73] *Ibid.*, pp. 83–84.
[74] John F. Whealon, "Magisterium," *Homiletic and Pastoral Review* 76, no. 10 (July 1976) 10–19.
[75] *Ibid.*, p. 15.

in the contemporary Church as located in those priests who do "not reflect or express the official teaching in [their] public and private utterances." Finally, he adds a few afterthoughts on the magisterium. Statements of national episcopal conferences do not have juridical authority of themselves. They have "magisterial import only if accepted by the local bishop and taught by him to the local Church. A statement from another episcopal conference has no direct relevance for bishops, priests, and laity of another nation—and in every instance enjoys validity only if it is in harmony with Peter."[76]

Archbishop Whealon then mentions the imprimatur. The guarantee that the faith is being safeguarded "is the *imprimatur*—a review of the manuscript by a *censor deputatus* who notifies the bishop that this manuscript holds nothing contrary to Catholic teaching." For this reason he faults the recently published *An American Catholic Catechism*. "It demonstrates sadly the lack of external discipline through an *imprimatur* granted after needed revisions were made." His judgment of the book is extremely severe, especially in its "cavalier attitude toward the magisterium."[77] In summary, then, Archbishop Whealon concludes, contrary to Archbishop Coffy and others, that "theologians are at the service of the magisterium."

I have cited this interesting study at some length because I believe it represents the approach of very many nontheologians and at least some bishops. It is in rather sharp contrast to the approach taken by Archbishop Coffy, Bishop Descamps, Congar, and Dulles (see below), as are the remarks of Cardinal Pietro Palazzini on the subject.[78]

Specifically, what I miss in Whealon's reflections is a sense of magisterium rooted in the history of teaching in the Church such as one notes in Congar, Dulles, Coffy, and others. The sense of the term "magisterium" as defined by a single, recent, historically conditioned theological current and formulated only by recent popes is accepted as normative, as God's will for things. In other words, it seems to me that Archbishop Whealon has accepted a *theology* of the magisterium without attending

---

[76] *Ibid.*, p. 16.

[77] He states: "The special problem in this book is its occasional attempt to set up 'reputable theologians' as a second teaching authority in the Church, and its occasional presentation of the hierarchical magisterium as that which a Catholic should *in conscience be schooled not to obey rather than to obey* (pp..181-187)" (emphasis added). A curious reader who consulted the pages referred to would discover that they were written by the author of these Notes. I shall leave it to the reader to determine whether the italicized words bear any relationship to the content of those pages. But one thing needs saying: the material presented there on the magisterium and theologians represents by far the dominant theological position in the Church today.

[78] Pietro Palazzini, "Roma e l'insostituibile magistero universale del Papa," *Divinitas* 20 (1976) 5–8.

to the possibility that there have been and still can be other such theologies. And the theology he adopts is precisely the theology identified by Congar, Dulles, and others as one which has a history dating to only the nineteenth century. I respect this view and its proponent; indeed, with many others, I have been brought up with it and still "think it," I am sure, in many ways without adverting to it.

The over-all approach, however, is heavily juridical and this appears in Archbishop Whealon's presentation of it. Item: the emphasis on the imprimatur. This too easily overlooks the fact that a *censor deputatus* will make his assessments within the confines of his own theology. Item: the attitude toward statements of national episcopal conferences. While they may have no juridical status, it seems clear that they are used by many episcopates as genuine teaching devices.[79] Furthermore, I know of no theologian who would accept Whealon's assertion that "a statement from another episcopal conference has no direct relevance for bishops, priests and laity of another nation." It has a great deal to say about the status of a particular conviction or formulation of conviction *in the Church as a whole.*

Finally, a one-sidedly juridical approach to the teaching office of the Church, while it has elements of truth, hides more problems than it solves. Item: it opposes the doctrine of the Church and the opinions of theologians. I believe all would admit that no theologian can speak for the Church; but that is not really the issue. The issue is the truth or, in the context of doctrine, the completeness or even accuracy of a particular officially-proposed teaching. If what is officially proposed is true up to the point where it is officially changed, then "officialness" has assumed a primacy in our thought patterns that distorts the teaching function of the Church and eventually the truth.

Concretely, was the teaching of *Mirari vos* and that of the Syllabus of Errors on religious liberty right until they were corrected by *Dignitatis humanae?* Or is it not that we came to see through experience and theological reflection what is right and then it could be authenticated by the magisterium? Even more concretely, what was John Courtney Murray to say when he was convinced of the truth of the doctrine eventually enshrined in *Dignitatis humanae?* Should he have said that it is not the doctrine of the Church but it is right — or it is not the doctrine of the Church and *therefore not right?* Surely not this latter. But unilateral emphasis on past formulated doctrine too easily leads to this cul-de-sac.[80]

The more important point in all of this is that our problems in relating

[79] Cf. my "Abortion Dossier," THEOLOGICAL STUDIES 35 (1974) 312–59, where the point is made by many episcopates.

[80] Something similar could be said about Archbishop Whealon's criterion ("accept the teaching of the local bishop if he is in agreement with Rome"). The question immediately

the magisterium to theology depend on our ability to see the recent shape of the magisterium as but a single, culturally conditioned way of viewing the magisterium, and hence, too, its relationships to other segments of the People of God. If we fail here, we are victimized by ecclesiastical ideology, i.e., the use of time-conditioned formulations to support present practices and concepts in a way that sacralizes the *status quo* and thereby makes it difficult, if not impossible, to speak meaningfully of a *living* teaching office in the Church.

These brief footnotes on Archbishop Whealon's reflections are less a critique of the theology of these notions than an occasion for a respectful invitation to all of us (bishops, theologians, lay people) to be more open, not to lock ourselves into a single, historically-conditioned understanding of magisterium. In openness we may be able to discover understandings that are better calculated to serve the word of God in our time. And that is what this discussion is all about.

Yves Congar submitted a paper (really two papers) to the International Theological Commission, and his colleagues rightly urged him to publish it.[81] What distinguishes the study is the profound historical learning out of which it originates. It is both detailed and ranging, and in both aspects richly documented. There is no way the study can be adequately digested; it can only be translated. All I can do here is indicate *some* points of interest and emphasis.

Let us start at the end of Congar's paper. He concludes his historical study as follows:

The relationship between theologians (*docteurs*) and the magisterium calls for a reconsideration. This supposes first that the status of the "magisterium" in the Church is made more precise, that it is not isolated in the living reality of the Church. . . . One cannot define the dependent condition of theologians solely with reference to the "magisterium," even though there is a truth here. In this domain, as in that of obedience, one ought not frame the question in two terms only: authority, obedience. It is necessary to think in three terms: above, the truth, the apostolic faith passed on, confessed, preached, celebrated; beneath it, at its service, the "magisterium" of the apostolic ministry and the work or teaching of theologians, as well as the faith of believers.[82]

How did Congar arrive at this conclusion? Historically. He first

---

suggests itself: Rome at what time — under Pius XII perhaps? I mean to suggest, of course, that there are some formulations of the popes that are commonly qualified or rejected by nearly all theologians. And if that is the case, *when* was such qualification or rejection appropriate? Was it not when the matter became reasonably clear? But that is not simply convertible with "agreement with Rome."

[81] Y. Congar, "Pour une histoire sémantique du terme 'magisterium,' " *Revue des sciences philosophiques et théologiques* 60 (1976) 85–98, and "Bref historique des formes du 'magistère' et de ses relations avec les docteurs," *ibid.*, pp. 99–112.

[82] *Ibid.*, p. 112.

studies the use of the word "magisterium." Until the nineteenth century, the word signified the activity of one in authority in a specific area (*magister equitum, magister militum*). "Never before the nineteenth century did the word signify what we call '*the* magisterium,' even though the reality existed."

Congar next approaches the forms which teaching in the Church assumed at various times. In the early Church there were *didaskaloi*, whose activity was more catechetic than speculative. In the second and third centuries the schools began to appear and with them a certain element of theological speculation. But from the same period "that which characterized the bishop is the *cathedra*, the chair." This was the guarantor of the transmission of the apostolic message. But, Congar argues, this was not conceived primarily as juridical authority "possessing a power to obligate, but as a function by which the Church receives the faith inherited from the apostles." The tradition, in the sense of transmitted truth, was the true authority. There was no statutory separation or opposition between pastors and doctors. Thus, Athanasius participated at Nicaea as a simple deacon.

The Middle Ages witnessed the full development of the schools and the birth of scholasticism — a form of doctrine analytic and questioning. Thus there was formulated the distinction between teaching that is scientific in character and that which is pastoral. Thus, too, Thomas' distinction between *magisterium cathedrae pastoralis* and *magisterium cathedrae magistralis*. This latter was a true public office in the Church, but one based on scientific competence, whereas the "pastoral magisterium is tied to the public office of *praelatio*, i.e., of superiority or authority." Thus it is from this time that we can date a "magisterium of theologians in the Church." Theological faculties judged doctrinal theses. Gerson affirmed the right of theologians "scholastice determinare ea quae sunt fidei." This development, Congar notes, took onesidedly unhealthy turns (e.g., Council of Basle, 1439).

In the course of time, properly theological theses, the positions of theological schools, had a place in condemnations issued in the name of the faith itself (e.g., Luther). This development continued into recent times, so that Congar notes: "The encyclicals of Leo XIII and Pius XII are theological. They are not purely the expression of apostolic witness according to the needs of the time, but a *doctrine* of the 'cathedrae magistralis' incorporating data from natural law, human wisdom, and classical theology."[83]

Congar traces the historical currents from Trent to our time, currents that led to Vatican I and subsequently to *Humani generis*, with the growing unilateralism represented in these developments. *Humani ge-*

[83] *Ibid.*, p. 105.

neris brought these developments to a high point in two ways: (1) "The ordinary magisterium of the pope demands a total obedience — 'he who hears you hears me.' " (2) "The (or one) role of theologians is to justify the pronouncements of the magisterium." Pius XII did not view the theologian as teacher, Congar notes, "except by delegation of the 'magisterium' and purely, narrowly at its service and under its control. Is this in conformity with that which nineteen centuries of Church life tell us about the function of the 'didaskalos' or doctor?" Congar's answer: "No, not exactly."

Congar sees in these developments a gradual supremacy of the *quo* (formal pastoral authority) over the *quod* (the word of God).[84] This was all the more threatening, he believes, because since 1832 the modern popes have done theology — and a theology identified with that of the Roman schools, "whose personnel was recruited and watched according to a well-defined line." Vatican II, however, has restored the supremacy of the *quod* over the *quo,* and with it raised afresh the question of the true magisterium of theologians.

This article is indispensable and will, I hope, eventually be made available in English.

Many of the same themes are taken up by Bishop A. L. Descamps in a very long study.[84a] He describes what he calls the classical view of the relationship between theologians and magisterium. The task of the hierarchy is to preserve and define the essentials of revelation (the *minimum minimorum*) and its habitual mode of expression is preaching. Thus in the Middle Ages the episcopate was called the *ordo praedicatorum*. According to classical views, "the theologian — nearly always a priest — drew his authority from his share in the sacred power of the bishop, which could concretize itself in a more explicit delegation (*missio canonica*)." Both this *missio* and his own competence was subordinate to the magisterium.

These and other emphases, he states, have changed in our time. The response to authoritative pronouncements is much less obediential. Instead of the classical *missio canonica* (a product of mixing the episcopal teaching and jurisdictional functions), Descamps states that "in a sense every theologian — even the lay person — providing that that person works within the faith and in the communion of the Church, can be said to be called by God, by revelation, by the Church, even by the hierarchy."[85] Thus, without becoming an elite or challenging the princi-

---

[84] Cf. also Robert B. Eno, S.S., "Ecclesia docens: Structures of Doctrinal Authority in Tertullian and Vincent," *Thomist* 40 (1976) 96–115; John F. Quinn, "St. Bonaventure and the Magisterium of the Church," *Miscellanea Francescana* 75 (1975) 597–610.

[84a] A. L. Descamps, "Théologie et magistère," *Ephemerides theologicae Lovanienses* 52 (1976) 82–133.

[85] *Ibid.*, p. 109.

ple of doctrinal authority, the theologian no longer views himself as "sent by the hierarchy" but as the "word-bearer of the People of God."

Avery Dulles, S.J., begins his forthright but courteous study of the magisterium and theologians by noting that the relationship is still fraught with tension, misunderstanding, distrust, and occasional bitterness.[86] Dulles notes two symptoms of this malaise. First, "certain official statements seem to evade in a calculated way the findings of modern scholarship. They are drawn up without broad consultation with the theological community. Instead, a few carefully selected theologians are asked to defend a pre-established position. . . . " Secondly, many Catholics have lost all interest in official ecclesiastical statements and do not expect any light from the magisterium on their real problems. Dulles sees this situation as alarming, and so do I.

Many factors and causes are at work here. Dulles highlights one: the notion of tradition and the magisterium being followed by the pope and many bishops. It is a neo-scholastic theory which was "devised by the theologians of the Roman school in the second half of the 19th century," as Congar also notes. According to this theory, the pope and bishops have the "charism of truth." Theologians are subordinate and instrumental, their chief function being to "set forth and defend the teaching of the papal and episcopal magisterium." They are not teachers in the Church or part of the magisterium.

While Vatican II did not directly (in *Lumen gentium,* no. 25) undermine this theory, Dulles believes it did so in practice, modifying or reversing previously-taught views and rehabilitating the very theologians who made this possible.[87] Thus, the Council "implicitly taught the legitimacy and even the value of dissent. In effect," he continues, "the Council said that the ordinary magisterium of the Roman pontiff had fallen into error and had unjustly harmed the careers of loyal and able theologians." Contemporary theological developments have revealed the weaknesses of this neo-scholastic theory, especially as making insufficient allowance for error in the ordinary teaching of popes and bishops.

Dulles' second step is to recover from history some elements that may aid in the construction of the postjuridical magisterium. He notes that Thomas used the term *magisterium* primarily for those who are licensed to teach theology in the schools. Thus Thomas distinguishes *officium praelationis,* possessed by the bishop, and the *officium magisterii,* which belongs to the professional theologian. Thus, too, the distinction already noted between *magisterium cathedrae pastoralis* and *magiste-*

---

[86] Avery Dulles, S.J., "What Is Magisterium?" *Origins* 6 (1976) 81–87.

[87] Cf. Cl. Dagens, "Le ministère théologique et l'expérience spirituelle des chrétiens," *Nouvelle revue théologique* 98 (1976) 530–43. This article studies the work of Congar and M. Chenu.

rium cathedrae magistralis. The former has juridical authority behind it but is concerned with preaching and public order. The latter is concerned with teaching by argument and knowledge rather than official status. So Thomas would not say that prelates alone possess the charism of truth. Theologians have their own sphere of competence. "Within this sphere the theologian is a genuine teacher, not a mouthpiece or apologist for higher officers." Dulles finds this more in conformity with the great Catholic tradition and biblical evidence than the neoscholastic theory.

On the basis of the existence of many charisms in the Church, Dulles admits that bishops have a "legitimate doctrinal concern," but they are not the dominant voices on all doctrinal questions. Rather, "the *magistri,* teachers by training and by profession, have a scientific magisterium but they are subject to the pastors in what pertains to the good order of the Church as a community of faith and witness."[88] These two magisteria are complementary and mutually corrective.

Dulles' third step consists in a variety of reflections and suggestions on the magisterium in the postjuridical world. For instance, the theological community itself should have a greater voice in who is to represent it. Similarly, in certain areas where the preaching of the faith and technical theology are inseparably intertwined and a pronouncement is called for, it "could most suitably be drawn up by co-operation between representatives of the pastoral and of the theological magisterium." In brief, Dulles is very close to the historical perspectives of Congar. Congar is more historically detailed, Dulles more constructive in that he draws from history to create the outlines of a model of the future magisterium.

Archbishop Joseph Bernardin, in a symposium at Notre Dame University (January 1976), granted that we have much to learn about the way others besides pope and bishops fit into the "magisterial function in the Church." But he denied that this meant "multiple magisteria." Not only does this cause confusion; "it undermines valid complementarity— between the respective roles of the magisterium and the scholarly community—and at its worst could actually lead to painful and broadly destructive competition at the expense of the entire Church."[89]

Dom Emmanuel Lanne points up certain recent changes in emphasis in the notion of magisterium (e.g., collegiality, theology of the local Church).[90] Recent challenges to magisterial documents (*Humanae vitae,* 1968; *Mysterium ecclesiae,* 1973; *Persona humana,* 1976) do not

---

[88] *Art. cit.,* p. 86.

[89] Cf. *Origins* 6 (1976) 87.

[90] Dom Emmanuel Lanne, "Evolution of the Magisterium in the Roman Catholic Church," *One in Christ* 12 (1976) 249–58.

represent a questioning of the privileged role of the magisterium, but "disappointment at the result of the exercise of the teaching authority." In the course of his essay Lanne discusses the function of theologians in the magisterium. That function is "not that of 'doctor' (teacher) in the full sense of the term. The bishops alone are the 'doctors' of the faith." But then Lanne raises precisely the questions to which such assertions lead, e.g., is it possible to dissociate the content of faith, taught by the magisterium, from its theological presentation? Furthermore, what does the Church mean in declaring St. Teresa of Avila a doctor of the Church?

Thus far the literature; here a final comment or two. First, all the literature would agree that there is a "magisterial function" (Bernardin's phrase) in the Church. Similarly, all would agree that the pope and the bishops have a special place within this function, though the "magisterial function" is not simply identifiable with hierarchical status. That is, the function necessarily includes more than pope and bishops; specifically, it must also include theologians. It is the *manner* of that inclusion that is most interesting. Some, adhering to a neo-scholastic or classical view, describe the inclusion in terms of "subordination" and often in a highly juridical way. Others speak of pertinence of theologians to the "magisterial function" as one of complementarity, of convergence, or even of another distinct (scientific) magisterium. What these latter phrases—shared by bishops (e.g., Coffy, Descamps) and theologians (e.g., Congar, Dulles)—have in common is fear that the term "*the* magisterium," because of its relatively recent history, too easily identifies the teaching function of the Church with, and limits it to, a single group in the Church, and by implication excludes or seriously underestimates the indispensable place of theology and the theologian, to the ultimate detriment of the "magisterial function" of the Church.

There is probably a variety of ways of formulating the relationship between bishops and theologians. But recent literature agrees on two points: the relationship reached an enviable and ideal peak in Vatican II, and it has worsened since and needs improvement. For that improvement to occur, I believe, with Coffy and others, that "a new status is necessary for theology" in our time. That probably means also a new (different from the neo-scholastic) status for the hierarchy. What these statuses ought to be will probably have to be discovered *in the process of co-operation*. As Archbishop Basil Hume of London put it, "The Church is so riddled with tensions and problems at the moment that any man who says he can give final answers to these problems is deluding himself. I really hope to be able to call on the best minds to guide me in forming attitudes and statements that I should be expected to make. I don't see myself as a great person. I see myself far more as a member of a team."[91]

"Members of a team" may be an identifiably American, but not altogether bad, way of formulating the matter: members with different but converging functions. If it is not the best formulation, it is a good way to begin a co-operative relationship that might eventually yield a more adequate theological formulation. Whatever the case, several things can be done to move toward a more harmonious co-operation. First, there should be broad dissemination of the studies of Congar, Dulles, and Descamps. These essays reveal the historically conditioned and very late character of the neo-scholastic understanding of magisterium. Secondly, we theologians need to be more critical of one another — in a courteous and disciplined way, of course — so that the hierarchy does not bear the whole responsibility of correcting one-sidedness or irresponsibility, and therefore get forced into a dominantly negative role. Thirdly, it is important that our best theologians devote themselves to stating more clearly papal and episcopal prerogatives and duties within the "magisterial function" of the Church. In rejecting the heavily juridical notion of these prerogatives, we must not reject their substance. Appeal is made repeatedly to no. 25 of *Lumen gentium,* but it is widely, even if quietly, admitted in the theological community that this paragraph represents a dated and very discussable notion of the Church's teaching office.

Finally — and this is delicate — something must be done to liberate Roman congregations from a single theological language and perspective. The International Theological Commission was conceived in part to perform this service; yet there is little evidence that this has worked.[92] More radically, one can wonder whether congregations as such should be involved in doing theology. The temptation is almost irresistible for such groups to support the theological views of the officeholders whom they serve, as Dulles observes. Concretely, there is danger of a rather narrow notion of orthodoxy, one which compares present vocabulary with past vocabulary, thus unduly narrowing revelation to "statements" and disallowing an active, historical notion of the revelation event, "acculturation of faith," as Coffy words it.

To some, this continuing theological concern with magisterium may seem otiose, a sterile postponement of the real problems of the world. I am convinced this is terribly shortsighted. More than ever, we need a *strong* "magisterial function" in the Church; but it remains an unfinished task to determine what "strong" means in our time. Indeed, some of the concerns mentioned here took concrete form — or so it is argued by

[91] Cited in Descamps (n. 84a above) p. 103.
[92] E.g., it may be questioned whether the inclusion of *missio canonica* in the theses of the International Theological Commission (n. 67 above) is due to the full Commission.

many—in the "Declaration on Certain Questions concerning Sexual Ethics" (Persona humana), to which we now turn.

"DECLARATION ON CERTAIN QUESTIONS CONCERNING SEXUAL ETHICS"

On January 15, 1976, the Sacred Congregation for the Doctrine of the Faith released the "Declaration on Certain Questions concerning Sexual Ethics" (Persona humana). For lack of space and because the document is widely available,[93] it will not be summarized here. I will present quick references to the wide and swift response the Declaration received, then summarize in more detail the more systematic theological analyses.

The journalistic response was varied and predictable. Many of the negative responses are given in Informations catholiques internationales.[94] Thus, Jacques Duquesne (writing in Le point) sees the document as a "formidable retour en arrière." Odette Thibault (Le monde) regrets that "for the Catholic Church sin (with a capital S) is still and will always be sexual sin." Henry Fesquet (Le monde) deplored the morality of fear in the statement. P. Liégé, dean of the faculty of theology at Paris, stated (La vie catholique) that the Declaration lacks "human and gospel warmth. It is cold, it is abstract, it is sad."

A group of theologians comprising the "Organisation régionale pour le développement théologique" (ORDET) issued a statement highly critical of Persona humana.[95] "Its individualistic and legalistic character, its outdated philosophical categories, its abusive authoritarianism distance it from sincere scholarly inquiry and from the call of the gospel." In the document they found "neither truth, nor justice, nor love of God who, in Christ Jesus, has not destroyed the 'tyranny of the law' only to restore it in the Church."

Such severe criticisms were responded to by the bishop of Carcassone,[96] the Permanent Council of the French Episcopate,[97] Cardinal François Marty alone[98] and together with Roger Etchegaray, president of the French Episcopal Conference.[99] Bishop Armand Le Bourgeois of Autun noted that "Evangelization in the Modern World," released about the same time, met with a thundering silence, whereas Persona hu-

---

[93] Texts may be found in Catholic Mind 74, no. 1302 (April 1976) 52–65; Documentation catholique 73 (1976) 108–14; Esprit et vie 86 (1976) 33–39; Herder Korrespondenz 30 (1976) 82–87; The Pope Speaks 21 (1976) 60–73.

[94] "Document sur l'éthique sexuelle: Réactions réservées," Informations catholiques internationales, Feb. 15, 1976, pp. 10–12.

[95] Documentation catholique 73 (1976) 181.

[96] Ibid., p. 182.

[97] Ibid., p. 208.

[98] Ibid., pp 334–35.

[99] Ibid., p. 180.

mana " 'caused a tilt' or better a 'boom'!"[100] He regretted that truly "necessary reminders" were not more positive and global. The Belgian bishops called the document "opportune and necessary."[101] The Dutch episcopate said the document must be considered a direction pointer ("indicateur de route").[102] They hoped that the reflexion provoked by the document would produce more "positive detailed teachings pastoral in character" in the future. Coadjutor Archbishop Franz Jachym of Vienna saw the Declaration as appropriately demanding but regretted its authoritarian tone.[103] The many supportive episcopal responses may be found in *L'Osservatore romano.*[104]

In England, the *Tablet* believed the response of many Catholics would be: *cui bono?*[105] "In this country, at any rate, it cannot be described as appropriate." Theologian D. O'Callaghan thought *Persona humana* places the loyal Catholic in a dilemma: the inability to subscribe to "moral absoluteness" and "intrinsic evil" because he knows these very verdicts are being questioned in our time.[106] In Canada, Gregory Baum was critical of the document as being "legalistic morality which judges acts of faculties rather than the total functioning of the person."[107] His comments elicited an immediate response from the Archbishop of Toronto.[108] In the United States, Arthur McNally, C.P., viewed the Declaration as a "masterpiece of pastoral teaching."[109] Paul McKeever, on the contrary, argued that it fails to communicate.[110] Paul Surlis, while agreeing with the basic value judgments, regretted the lack of a positive approach.[111] *America* scored the abstract language and outdated categories.[112]

L. Kaufmann and J. David of Switzerland regretted the secrecy of the Congregation, "for which the demand for greater openness still falls on

---

[100] *Ibid.*, pp. 209-10. He noted: "Il a 'fait tilt' ou mieux 'boum'! Pensez donc, il parlait du sexe!"

[101] *Ibid.*, p. 210.

[102] *Ibid.*, pp. 178-79.

[103] Cf. *Orientierung* 40 (1976) 15.

[104] Essays and supportive documents on *Persona humana* may be found in the following issues of *L'Osservatore Romano:* Jan. 29; Feb. 5, 12, 19, 26; March 4, 11, 25; April 1, 8, 15, 29; May 6, 13; July 29; Aug. 19.

[105] "A Roman Declaration," *Tablet* 230 (1976) 73-75.

[106] D. O'Callaghan, "Comment," *Furrow* 61 (1976) 126-29.

[107] Cf. *Ecumenist* 14 (1976) 64.

[108] *Ibid.*, p. 64.

[109] Arthur McNally, C.P., "Sexual Ethics," *Sign* 55, no. 6 (March 1976) 4-5.

[110] Paul McKeever, "Sex in the News," *Priest* 32, no. 2 (March 1976) 12-13 (an unsigned editorial).

[111] Paul J. Surlis, "Theology and Sexuality," *Priest* 32, no. 10 (Oct. 1976) 42-47.

[112] "Sex Declaration: Half a Loaf," *America* 134 (1976) 63.

deaf ears."[113] Whatever consultation was involved or reference made to previous episcopal documents, "nothing indicates that these were mined or anything learned from them." Where adolescent masturbation is discussed, they wondered what good is achieved by mentioning the "useful data" provided by psychology while immediately narrowing the question to a "serious violation of the moral order." The tone of the document when it speaks of premarital relations is regrettable, a tone quite different from that employed by the Swiss diocesan synods. Something very similar is true of the undifferentiated discussion of homosexuality. The authors conclude that the document is dominated by a narrow view of human actions and "a static ordering of commands and prohibitions, instead of a dynamic view of the assimilation of truth and realization of values. . . . "

Roman Bleistein, S.J., associate editor of *Stimmen der Zeit,* thought that anyone concerned about the Church's authority must wonder whether its institutions are not undermining their own authority.[114] He cited the differences in *Persona humana* and several documents of the German episcopate. In the latter the findings of contemporary sciences are not overlooked, whereas the Roman document leans above all on Church tradition and uncritical use of St. Paul ("oft ohne Rücksicht auf den jeweiligen Zusammenhang").

Beyond such differences in the over-all approach, substantive differences were noted by Bleistein. For instance, where masturbation is concerned, the pastoral letter of the German bishops (*Hirtenbrief der deutschen Bischöfe zu Fragen der menschlichen Geschlechtlichkeit,* 1973) states that it cannot be approved "as a self-evident actuation of sexuality." As for premarital relations, the German synodal document (*Christlich gelebte Ehe und Familie*) states: "These relations cannot be seen as corresponding to the ethical norm." *Persona humana* is much more abstract and apodictic. Nor can these differences be reduced, according to Bleistein, to the difference between moral theology and pastoral application. "There is revealed a different mentality in the judgment of sexual behavior." In the face of such different *official* mentalities, what is the Catholic to think? Bleistein thinks that one institution (clearly he means the Congregation) is undermining authority.

If one reads the Declaration with a tranquil soul, declared *Civiltà cattolica,* one will discover that the massive objections against it are

---

[113] J. David and L. Kaufmann, "Zur Erklärung der Glaubenskongregation," *Orientierung* 40 (1976) 14–15.

[114] Roman Bleistein, S.J., "Kirchliche Autorität im Widerspruch," *Stimmen der Zeit* 101 (1976) 145–46.

unfounded.[115] *Civiltà* cited the "moral sexual revolution" as the cause for the difficult reception *Persona humana* received. It highlighted especially the theses of S. Pfürtner, the Swiss ex-Dominican, and argued that the Church must speak out against the "grave confusion" such misleading statements cause.

Razón y fe detected a mixture of pre-Vatican II and post-Vatican II ingredients in the Declaration.[116] There is a static notion of nature, and yet an openness to anthropological evidence and a compassionate pastoral tone. If the document itself does not achieve an adequate synthesis of pre- and post-Vatican II morality, it is the responsibility of the mature Christian to do so in his/her personal life.

Jorge Mejía believed that the Latin American reaction to *Persona humana* was calmer than the Western European and American because Latin Americans have maintained a greater discernment "as to what is good and what is bad in this delicate matter of sex."[117] He defended the document as a necessary corrective to contemporary confusion and saw its chief value as a witness value to a world that has lost its bearings.

For Jose A. Llinares, O.P., the argumentation is legalistic and the style abstract, elements that distract from the Declaration's power to persuade.[118] He sees the dominant point in the document in its constant emphasis on the need of focusing on the specific circumstances of each personal case. Firmness of principle does not release pastors and educators from the duty to learn from the human sciences.

Now to some of the more detailed studies.

John Harvey, O.S.F.S., is in agreement with the moral-theological conclusions and spends most of his time on pastoral applications.[119] Working within the objectively-wrong-but-not-always-culpable perspective, Harvey shows himself a compassionate counselor. I agree with his contention that the biblical norm ("heterosexual marriage is the proper form of sexual activity") does not depend on individual texts of Scripture. I make only two points. First, against those who are cautious about using Pauline texts (because Paul was unfamiliar with the *condition* of homosexuality, as we know it in at least some cases), he remains unconvinced because "the sacred writers did not attempt to analyze

[115] "Sessuofobia o difesa dell'uomo? La Chiesa e la sessualità," *Civiltà cattolica* 127 (1976) 209–17 (editorial).

[116] "Sexualidad y moral cristiana," *Razón y fe,* no. 938, March 1976, pp. 198–201.

[117] Jorge Mejia, "La Declaración de la Santa Sede sobre la ética sexual," *Criterio* 49 (1976) 110–12.

[118] J. A. Llinares, "Etica sexual y magisterio de la Iglesia," *Ciencia tomista* 103 (1976) 465–78.

[119] John F. Harvey, O.S.F.S., "Pastoral Insights on 'Sexual Ethics,' " *Pastoral Life* 25, no. 4 (April 1976) 2–8.

personal *motives* . . . " (emphasis added). I do not believe motivation is the point under discussion. Secondly, Harvey agrees with the document's reassertion that "every direct violation of this order is objectively serious." He paints the opposite attitude as follows: "After all, what harm to God . . . is found in deliberate masturbation, occasional fornication or acts of genital homosexuality between consenting adults?" If that is all the traditional thesis (no parvity of matter in direct violations) meant, there would be less problem with it. But it says that "*every* direct violation," and this includes even the smallest. It is *this* that most theologians and pastoral counselors deny.

Daniel Maguire first points up the values of the Declaration.[120] It stresses the reality of guilt in a time when feigned or strained innocence is fashionable. It correctly rejects the idea that science is the only legitimate way of knowing. It rejects custom as normative, takes sexual encounter seriously, etc. But all in all, Maguire believes it does not do justice "either to the subject or to the Catholic tradition." Some of Maguire's specific criticisms: (1) the Declaration was developed in secrecy and represents only one view of things; (2) methodological shortcomings (e.g., the separation of the idea of moral disorder from the notion of harm; abstractionism; aloofness from the empirical basis of ethics); (3) lack of intellectual modesty in its claims to certainty; (4) dominance of the notion of sin; (5) unrealism of expectation when dealing with homosexuality. Maguire concludes with some suggestions about "what might have been" in the document. I think his suggestions make eminent good sense.

R. P. Spitz, O.P., has a very positive reaction to the document and a very negative reaction to its critics.[121] After noting that many criticisms concerned not the principles involved but the fact that Rome recalled them, he states: "To formulate such criticisms is to admit implicitly that one finds obedience to commands repugnant, even if one holds them to be acceptable and true." Spitz agrees with the Congregation's "principal criterion" (the finality of each act), a principle "which the Church holds from revelation and an authentic interpretation of natural law." The rest of his article is deeply homiletic, e.g., that we must not lose the sense of sin, of asceticism, of sacrifice. In this sense he does not enlighten the document but deals with the attitudes and practices it was targeted against.

G. Lobo, S.J., notes that as between traditional doctrine in traditional terms and exposing it in terms appealing to the present generation, the

---

[120] Daniel C. Maguire, "The Vatican on Sex," *Commonweal* 103 (1976) 137–40.

[121] R. P. Spitz, O.P., "A propos de la déclaration de la Sacrée Congrégation pour la Doctrine de la Foi," *Pensée catholique*, no. 161 (March–April 1976) 11–19.

Congregation has chosen the first.[122] He feels there is no point in lamenting the style or tone but that our challenge is to present its content more persuasively. At one key point, however, Lobo would disagree with the content of *Persona humana*. He does not accept the statement that every act of masturbation must be considered an objectively serious violation, even though it is "undesirable . . . and sinful when practiced deliberately." His conclusion: "while permissiveness leads to disastrous results, too much rigidity also leads to equally harmful consequences."

Ph. Delhaye, secretary of the International Theological Commission, has a very long defense-commentary of *Persona humana*.[123] He first takes up some of the objections leveled against it. For instance, he insists on the right of the Holy Father to use his congregations for the ordinary, day-to-day administration of the Church. To those who claim that *Persona humana* was inopportune in its concentration on three practical problems, Delhaye responds that the whole purpose of the document was quite simple: to recall the doctrine of the Church on *certain particular points* to a world fast forgetting this doctrine. To those who are allergic to use of the natural law, Delhaye explains at length the notion as found in the scholastic tradition and insists that the nature of which the Declaration speaks "is not that of the cosmos or of philosophy alone but that of the human person."

I have the sense that Delhaye is answering a fair number of unasked questions. For instance, the question is not whether the Holy Father has a right to speak out through his congregations on moral or doctrinal questions. No well-informed Catholic theologian questions this. The issue is rather the nature of the input and consultative processes involved, so that the ultimate product is one that instructs, illumines, inspires. Similarly, the question is not whether the notion of natural law is appropriate; it is rather how it is to be interpreted, with what enrichment from behavioral sciences, with what theological perspectives. One does not respond to such questions by merely pointing to the long tradition of natural-law reasoning and comparing this to certain phrases in the Declaration. Again, Delhaye's lengthy rejection of the "neosociologism" of the sciences (which all theologians would share) hardly tells us much about just how the redactors of *Persona humana* did make use of contemporary scientific studies.

Throughout his essay Delhaye argues that the Declaration is trying to walk a middle path between extremes. Item: "*Persona humana* seems to

[122] G. Lobo, S.J., "Document—Declaration on Sexual Ethics," *Vidyajyoti* 40 (1976) 269–77.

[123] Ph. Delhaye, "A propos de 'Persona humana,'" *Esprit et vie* 86 (1976) 177–86, 193–204, 225–34.

me to keep an equal distance from two extremes: that which simply rejects the fundamental option, that which makes of it an unreal thing." Item: against pseudoscientific assertions that masturbation is not only permitted but necessary, Delhaye states that the response of *Persona humana* to this propaganda is contained in two major notions. "On the one hand, it recognizes that every material deviation is not necessarily a deliberate fault; on the other, the Declaration does not accept the idea of generalized sexual irresponsibility." At this point, and in many places throughout, I have to wonder whether we are reading the same document. In other words, are not Delhaye's repeated attempts to say what the document meant and was trying to do indicative of its failure?

Bernhard Stoeckle admits the need of the document.[124] He regrets its harsh tone and believes it suffers by comparison with the documents of the German episcopate. Several pluses he admits: its attempt to be restrained in using the natural-law notions that were criticized in *Humanae vitae;* attempts to deepen traditional teaching by advertence to the work of the sciences; a certain distance from the biological and philosophical arguments used in the past. But eventually he sees its arguments as insufficient. While accepting the conclusions, he believes that the arguments would have been legitimated and solidified if the double meaning of sexual conduct had been brought within the sphere of charity (agape) to be stamped by it. In a sense, he is concretizing in this sphere his attitude toward a specific Christian ethic. In my judgment he does not succeed.

A very critical response to the Declaration was drawn up by three theologians from Tübingen: Alfons Auer, Wilhelm Korff, Gerhard Lohfink.[125] Several other members of the Catholic theological faculty of Tübingen declared their agreement with the critique: H. Küng, W. Kasper, J. Neumann, and others. The critique takes the form of a comparison between the Declaration and a working paper drawn up for the German Synod (Würzburg): *Sinn und Gestaltung menschlicher Sexualität.* When *Persona humana* appeared, the head of the German episcopal conference declared that the Declaration confirmed the Würzburg Synod's document as well as the 1973 pastoral of the German bishops. The theologians from Tübingen contest that judgment and argue that a totally different climate is present in the Congregation's document. To show this, they lift out the sharp differences between the Würzburg working paper and *Persona humana.*

The working paper begins with the results of contemporary human

[124] Bernhard Stoeckle, "Erklärung zu einigen Fragen der Sexualethik," *Internationale katholische Zeitschrift* 5 (1976) 256–61.

[125] Alfons Auer *et al.*, "Zweierlei Sexualethik," *Theologische Quartalschrift* 156 (1976) 148–58.

and social sciences. It notes that all cultures have regulated sexual behavior and that, in spite of differences and qualifications, the norms achieved two goals: (1) institutionalization of sexual relations with the principles of permanence and exclusivity; (2) the concern of the partners for each other, for the continuation and well-being of the family. In the past the social aspects took precedence; now there is more emphasis on the meaning of sexuality for self-development and for a deep partnership.

The working paper then turns its attention to the many values of human sexuality, values which it sees as playing different roles at different periods of one's life. Then the biblical and theological evidence is used to put human experience in the broader context of faith. Against such a background the working paper faces practical issues. It evaluates promiscuous sexual relations differently from those between partners who are in love and "who are decided on a permanent bond but see themselves hindered from contracting it because of reasons felt to be grave." In treating of homosexuality, it speaks of a "narrowing of existential possibilities." Adolescent masturbation is seen as a phase-specific phenomenon to be passed through without an overload of guilt.

In contrast to this, *Persona humana* is entirely deductive, from eternal, objective, universal divine laws. The Tübingen theologians argue that the Declaration misuses Scripture (an "adventitious ornament for systematic assertions"), misuses its own tradition, and does not take scientific data seriously. By its moral positivism it "excludes itself from the scientific discussion." In the end, while achieving a certain stabilizing effect, it pays too great a price: not secession, but "a retreat to a position of partial identification with the Church will present itself as the only possibility for many." They conclude their severe criticism with the insistence that "the house of the Church ought to be, for people of our time, an intellectually and ethically livable place." Of the two documents studied and compared, it is clear to them that only the working paper of the Würzburg Synod passes this test.

Bernard Häring approaches the Declaration in three steps: (1) its good points; (2) the theological presuppositions; (3) evaluation of its pastoral attitudes.[126] At the outset and repeatedly thereafter, he expresses agreement with the underlying core-value judgments ("Kernerklärung") of the document, against those who would see no moral problem in premarital relations, homosexual activity, and masturbation. Furthermore, he insists that the Church must have the courage to say unpopular things. Finally, he welcomes the reference made to the insights of the sciences in these areas.

---

[126] B. Häring, "Reflexionen zur Erklärung der Glaubenskongregation über einige Fragen der Sexualethik," *Theologisch-praktische Quartalschrift* 124 (1976) 115–26.

Häring faults the document for the following theological presuppositions. There is, he argues, an ahistorical and unrealistic tone and attitude toward the magisterium and its formulation of moral truth. The use of Scripture is highly questionable. It totally neglects the distinction between a substantive value judgment and its formulation. The language, arguments, and conceptual underpinning lead to undifferentiated condemnations. The natural-law perspectives of the contemporary consultors to the Congregation are "represented as *the* constant tradition and the teaching of the Church." Häring argues that "there speaks in the document not *the* preconciliar theology, but a very distinct preconciliar theology," the type rejected by the Council in its rejection of several preliminary drafts for *Gaudium et spes*.

Häring is particularly strong in his rejection of the Declaration's presumption that individual acts, especially of masturbation, involve serious guilt. He grants that some theologians have gone too far in their reaction to an earlier rigorism; but a too facile judgment of mortal sin in sexual matters harms the faith of people. "It must never for an instant be forgotten that conversation about mortal sin, especially the mortal sins of children, is conversation about God." The image of God inseparable from the perspectives of *Persona humana* is, he believes, that of an avenging policeman. The document refers to the letter of Leo IX in which he authorized Peter Damian's *Liber gomorrhianus* as sexual teaching clean and free from error. Of that Häring says simply: "I certainly could not believe in the God who shines through that work."

Another problem Häring finds in the document is that its argument and language fail to allow for qualitative differences in human conduct. This is true of premarital intercourse, as well as masturbation, which is rejected "regardless of the motive." Häring's ultimate judgment is harsh: "The document of the Congregation, as a whole and in its individual formulations, goes far beyond the rigorism of past times. One can say that it represents the most logical and systematic piece of teaching, in so far as it brings tightly together all previous rigoristic teachings and presents them simply as *the* tradition."

In a careful and balanced study, Charles Curran reviews some of the literature recorded here and presents his own analysis of the Declaration.[127] First, Curran, like many others, faults the lack of consultation involved in its preparation. As for the criticism that followed its issuance, Curran sees it as a sign of greater maturity in the Church, "even though one wishes the negative criticism were unnecessary." I wish this last little point had been italicized in Curran's study; for there are many people in the Church who believe that criticism stems from a desire to

[127] Charles E. Curran, "Sexual Ethics: Reaction and Critique," *Linacre Quarterly* 43 (1976) 147–64.

criticize—as if truth and the good of the faithful were not one's motive, but rather victory within an imagined adversary relationship.

Curran's critique involves methodology and substance. As for methodology, he lists eight shortcomings: e.g., the deductive character; failure to use the nature of the person as a criterion; failure to pay sufficient attention to the experience of people. He concludes here with the judgment that the Declaration is "not in keeping with what . . . is the best in Catholic theological reflection."

In his substantive criticism, Curran singles out four points. First, the notion of fundamental option in the document is a caricature. E.g., the Congregation describes the opinions of some who see mortal sin only in a formal refusal directly opposed to God's call and not in particular acts. Curran rightly wonders what theologians hold this position. He knows of none; nor do I.

Secondly, Curran deals with premarital relations. He accepts the underlying substance of the Congregation on this matter. However, there could be times when the marriage ceremony is legitimately impeded. In these cases "there does not seem to be much of a problem from a moral viewpoint, although ordinarily such a covenant of love should be publicly witnessed and proclaimed." I believe many moral theologians would agree with that judgment. There even seems to be a foundation for this in canon law (can. 1098). But to prevent deleterious understanding of it, it might be well if we moralists emphasized the relative rarity of the occurrence and then struggled to specify more concretely what these circumstances are. Otherwise, little "covenants of marital love," like *entia,* risk being multiplied and consummated on warrants all of us would reject out of hand.

Curran next turns to homosexuality. The implication of the document's approach is that the irreversible homosexual "is asked to live in accord with the charism of celibacy." He then states his own well-known approach, based on a "theory of compromise," which proposes that for the irreversible homosexual "these actions are not wrong for this individual provided there is a context of a loving commitment to another." He regards this as a conclusion "on the level of the moral order," a phrase meant to distinguish it from an objectively-wrong-but-not-always-culpable analysis as well as one which regards homosexual actions as equivalent to heterosexual ones.

Curran's most marked disagreement with the Congregation is on masturbation. *Persona humana* sees it as an intrinsically and seriously disordered act. Curran denies this. "Individual masturbatory acts seen in the context of the person and the meaning of human sexuality do not constitute such important matter . . . providing the individual is truly growing in sexual maturity and integration." He sees the Congregation's approach as theologically inaccurate, psychologically harmful, and pedagogically counterproductive, and traces this to the methodology of the document, one whose approach is "limited to an analysis apart from the person."

This latter point is important and is certainly what distinguishes, and unfortunately divides, most contemporary theologians from those writing for the Congregation. Moral norms are generalizations about the meaning of our actions. But it is clear from many sources (contemporary sciences, Vatican II, wide pastoral experience) that sexual experiences *mean* far more than genital actuations of one sort or another. For instance, as Curran notes, masturbatory acts can be symptomatic of loneliness, of sexual tension, of prolonged absence from one's marital partner, of frustrated relationships and insufficient coping mechanisms in one's daily life, of growing selfishness, etc. It is only when the actions are seen from the viewpoint of the whole person that they reveal their *meaning*. While they are always a withdrawal from the full meaning (potential) of sexual behavior (and therefore an "intrinsic disorder"), in at least many of their meanings noted above, it is highly doubtful that this individual withdrawal is serious, scil., the type of action that is calculated to provoke the mature and sensitive person to a radical existential break with the God of salvation. And that is the meaning of "serious matter."

This point can be put in another, more systematic way. Two levels of moral rectitude are involved here. One we might call the general, the other the individual. The level of general rectitude prescinds from individual intentions, dispositions, qualities, and meanings, and states an over-all requirement. Thus we say that sexual expression finds its *full* meaning in the permanent relationship of covenanted love (marriage). However, while this tells us something, and something important, about the moral quality of our actions, it does not tell us everything; for it is quite possible to be objectively immoral once the requirement of general rectitude is satisfied. That is, it is possible to be *objectively* immoral within marriage (selfish, manipulatory, inconsiderate, uncommunicative, etc.). These qualities at the individual level of rectitude tell us much about the *meaning* of our activity. They fill out the meaning of our actions by viewing them within the context of the individual person. If, as Vatican II insisted, criteria for sexual activity are to be based on "the nature of the person and his acts" (*Gaudium et spes,* no. 51), then the meaning of our actions must be drawn from all dimensions of our personal life. By speaking as it does, on the level of general rectitude only, the Congregation prescinds from many aspects of the personal that yield the meaning of our actions, and therefore is able to condemn actions and assert seriousness in an undifferentiated way that does not correspond at key points with human experience. This is, I think, the key substantive difference between the approach of the Congregation and the commentators on its document.

At this point I refer to two episcopal pastoral letters that have come to my attention: one by Bishop Francis J. Mugavero of Brooklyn, the other by Cardinal L. J. Suenens of Malines-Brussels.[128] Both are excellent, but let me concentrate briefly on Bishop Mugavero's statement here. It is difficult to cite from the pastoral, because its achievement is one of over-all tone that emerges from the totality. The tone is positive, compassionate, and supportive; the language is simple and "American." Sexuality is seen as a great gift. "It is a relational power which includes the qualities of sensitivity, understanding, warmth, openness to persons, compassion and mutual support. Who could imagine a loving person without these qualities?" The attitude is realistic and encouraging. Mugavero states simply and straightforwardly: "If we are honest with ourselves as were the Christians who lived before us, each of us will recognize that it is not easy to integrate sexuality into our lives."

Mugavero is theologically and pastorally superb in his treatment of each of the problems treated by the Congregation. E.g., he sees in masturbation "a prime example of the complex nature of sexual behavior." He then states: "We wish to encourage people to go continually beyond themselves in order to achieve greater sexual maturity and urge them to find peace and strength in a full sacramental life with the Christ who loves them."

The treatment of premarital relations is excellent. But let me cite homosexuality as another example. Mugavero notes that anthropological, psychological, and theological reasoning all contribute to the Church's conviction that "heterosexuality is normative. All should strive for a sexual integration which respects that norm, since any other orientation respects *less adequately* [emphasis added] the full spectrum of human relationships." This is a way, I submit, of formulating a moral statement that is both continuous with the deepest value judgments of our tradition and sensitive to what we know, and do not know, about homosexuality.

Mugavero's language and tone meet people where they are. Tone, in moral matters, is not everything, but it is enormously important; for it reveals attitudes toward persons, norms, conflicts, God, the human condition. Because this is so, tone not only affects communicability; at some point it also cuts very close to the basic value judgments themselves, as the Tübingen theologians note. That is why a document that

[128] Francis J. Mugavero, "Sexuality — God's Gift: A Pastoral Letter," *Catholic Mind* 74, no. 1303 (May 1976) 53–58; L. J. Suenens, "Amour et sexualité aujourd'hui," *Documentation catholique* 73 (1976) 679–90.

is tonally inadequate risks being substantively incomplete or even wrong.

These are just a sampling of the reactions to *Persona humana*. One could summarize them as follows. Nearly everyone believes a prophetic but compassionate statement from the Church on human sexuality is in place. Secondly, the actual response given by the Congregation finds both defenders and critics. By and large, the defenders highlight the right of the Church to speak authoritatively, the authority of the document, the clarity of the reassertion of traditional teaching, the sensitivity of *Persona humana* to contemporary studies in the behavioral sciences, and (defensively) the fact that it was not trying to give a full theology of sexuality. The critics — and in the theological world they far outnumber the defenders — go after the process (secret) which produced the document, the dated theology and language central to it, the failure to deal with the behavioral sciences adequately, the authoritarian tone, the misuse of Scripture, and some of the pastoral applications.

Some of the reactions, particularly but not exclusively the journalistic, seem extreme, even unfair. I see their excessive character as transparent of a deep sense of failed expectations, and of a profound discomfort with the Roman way of doing things. On the other hand, some of the positive reactions were quite uncritical; they are symptomatic of a felt need "to defend Rome." My own reaction to the document is presented elsewhere.[129] I have found little to alter in that statement except to say that the burden of the literature reported here is that we are dealing with a missed opportunity.

If one's judgment is that, all things considered, the Declaration missed its target, what happened to bring this about? Some explanation is given in an interview involving James McManus, C.SS.R., Sean O'Riordan, C.SS.R., and Henry Stratton.[130] Briefly it is this. Over the years two different schools of theological approach were involved in the consultations leading to the Declaration: (1) the personalist school; (2) the traditional, norm-centered school, which begins with abstract principles and uses a deductive method.

It was found impossible to develop a coherent document based on these two different methods. "Eventually," says O'Riordan, "the modern school was dropped from consultations." The document as we have it was mainly the work of three people: E. Lio, O.F.M., Card. Pietro Palazzini, and Jan Visser, C.SS.R. According to O'Riordan, "the document reproduces in large part a chapter in a book recently published by

[129] Richard A. McCormick, S.J., Sexual Ethics — An Opinion," *National Catholic Reporter*, Jan. 30, 1976, and *Theologie der Gegenwart* 19 (1976) 72–76.

[130] J. McManus, Sean O'Riordan, and Henry Stratton, "The 'Declaration on Certain Questions concerning Sexual Ethics': A Discussion," *Clergy Review* 61 (1976) 231–37.

Cardinal Palazzini on Christian life and virtue. In this book the Cardinal follows the old methodology — principles are stated, and conclusions are drawn more or less independently of human persons and the complexities of human existence."[131]

There follows an extremely interesting discussion in which O'Riordan points out the deeply compassionate and flexible viewpoint of the older theology at the pastoral level. E.g., Visser would condemn homosexual acts as intrinsically evil. Yet, in an interview in *L'Europa* (Jan. 30, 1976) Visser stated that "when one is dealing with people who are so deeply homosexual that they will be in serious personal and perhaps social trouble unless they attain a steady partnership within their homosexual lives, one can recommend them to seek such a partnership, and one accepts this relationship as the best they can do in their present situation." Visser explains this on the grounds that the lesser of two evils is often the best thing for people in a particular situation, and he would see no incompatibility between this *pastoral* attitude and adherence to the abstract principle that homosexual acts are intrinsically evil.

O'Riordan, then, was asked this question: "So, in a sense, the good theologian of the traditional school is doing in pastoral theology and pastoral practice what the personalist theologian is doing in moral theology?" His answer was: "You have defined it exactly." That is, the personalist theology is simply "working out in a theoretical way what the good pastors have always instinctively known and done."

That may be the case; but let me offer this tentative probe. That formulation so identifies normative ethics with individual *potential* that the possibility of a general normative statement all but disappears. In other words, does it not simply identify the morally right with the individually *possible* — which means that no truly normative statement is possible except for the individual? Which could mean that it is not possible at all. We can and should distinguish between an abstract and deductive way of deriving moral norms, and one anchored in persons and their acts. But is distinguishing in this way the same as identifying a normative statement (personalistically derived) with a pastoral statement? I wonder. If we say the two are the same, we have, it would seem, abandoned any possibility of generalization, scil., of ethics. Therefore, to say that "the good theologian of the traditional school is doing in pastoral theology and pastoral practice *what the personalist theologian is doing in moral theology*" (my emphasis) could destroy the possibility of normative statements. Even if one does theology out of personalist perspectives, as one ought, must there not still remain the possibility that individuals cannot achieve this personalistically derived *norm*? In other words, must we not distinguish between a moral theology derived

[131] *Ibid.*, p. 232.

from "the nature of the human person and his acts" and an approach that considers only this or that *particular* person and his/her *possibilities*? If we must, then there still remains a norm and a pastoral practice. I raise this only as a question, in the hope that O'Riordan and others can cast light on it in the future.

CURRENT THEOLOGY: 1978

NOTES ON MORAL THEOLOGY 1977: THE CHURCH IN
DISPUTE

This report is entitled "The Church in Dispute" because that seems
an accurate reflection of much of the literature as I read it. Controversial
public events with theological ramifications have abounded in the past
year: ordination of women,[1] the rights of homosexuals,[2] Medicaid and
abortion,[3] the energy crisis, human rights and foreign policy, the Panama
Canal, the B-1 bomber, etc. Beneath discussion about such events we
inevitably find changing theological thought-patterns, those continuing
struggles of thoughtful persons to rephrase the *magnalia Dei* in a world
of change, conflict, doubt. As they always have, these struggles bring
persons of good will into dispute. For instance, there are indications of
an emerging face-off between the Tracy-Gilkey school and the Dulles-
Berger point of view. In moral theology the matter is no different. The
Catholic moral-theological community reveals various tendencies with
diverging attitudes toward theology, authority, certainty, evidence, human conflict, the nature of moral argument.[4] The disputes involve theologians with theologians, bishops with theologians, and hierarchies with
governments. It should not be surprising that in the tenth-anniversary
year of its publication, *Humanae vitae* is the vehicle for some of the
concerns expressed.

It would be both tendentious and ungracious to attempt to characterize

[1] Alan Geyer, in his fine inaugural address (Churches' Center for Theology and Public
Policy) referred to some of these concerns as "narcissism ... a scandalous introversion of
religious energy" (*Congressional Record*, Oct. 12, 1977, E 6236-6237).

[2] For some literature cf. *Anglican Theological Review* 59 (1977) 182-97; Theodore W.
Jennings, "Homosexuality and Christian Faith: A Theological Reflection," *Christian Cen-
tury* 94 (1977) 137-42; *Christianity and Crisis* 37 (1977) 116-44; James B. Nelson, "Homo-
sexuality and the Church," *Christianity and Crisis* 37 (1977) 63-69; "Can Homosexuals
Inherit the Kingdom?" (editorial), *Christianity Today* 21 (1977) 943-44; John Jay Hughes,
"Homosexuality: A New Study," *Clergy Review* 62 (1977) 69-72; John Mahoney, "The
Church and the Homosexual," *Month* 10 (Second New Series, 1977) 166-69; John F.
Harvey, "Chastity and the Homosexual," *Priest* 33 (July-Aug. 1977) 10-16; Clifford Longley,
"The Homosexual Challenge," *Tablet* 231 (1977) 322.

[3] For differing views cf. *Christianity and Crisis* 37 (1977) 202-7.

[4] Cf. William J. Parente, "A Conservative Response," *America* 137 (1977) 313. Parente
reports on the establishment of the Fellowship of Catholic Scholars and states that the
"CTSA work almost certainly served as a catalyst in the birth of the fellowship." For
some of the questions this has raised, cf. Thomas Dubay, "Pluralism and Authenticity in
Moral Theology," *Homiletic and Pastoral Review* 77 (March 1977) 10-22.

these tendencies. That should come from the literature. What is increasingly clear in the literature reported here is that what is probably more important than any single conclusion or argument or issue is the underlying perspective of which the surface differences are transparent.[5] This edition of the "Notes" will probe at these underlying perspectives from several, often overlapping focuses of concern: moral norms, the double effect, human rights, and the CTSA committee report on sexuality.

THE CHURCH AND MORAL NORMS

The question of moral norms and their grounding continues to be a subject of lively interest in moral literature. Here I shall review but a few recent examples of this continuing discussion. Franz Böckle, in discussing the relation of faith to conduct, points out that to act responsibly means to act from insight.[6] This does not mean that a person must see with perfect clarity the basic reason for a determined action. One can allow oneself to be led by competent authority. Rather, it means that "an ethical act must be, as such, basically able to be comprehended and must be understandable. Correspondingly, the *norms* (through which our conduct toward persons and the world is governed) must also basically stand open to human rational insight."[7]

This rational intelligibility of moral norms does not exclude the fact that the individual values that generate a norm can experience a special grounding and ratification in revelation. Quite the contrary. Thus, our faith that God loves each individual and calls each to salvation deepens our insight into the worth of the individual. But such a deepening hardly means that revealed morality is impervious to reason. "Rather, theological tradition says that the morality of revelation is the truly reasonable morality which receives its confirmation precisely in this way (by revelation)." Böckle insists throughout his study that while "there are mysteries of faith, there can be no mysterious ethical norms for action whose

---

[5] This is made clear in a splendid paper by Walter J. Burghardt, S.J., on the task and difficulties of theology (see n. 143 below). In discussing the difficulties theologians encounter, Burghardt distinguishes two different notions of theology: justification (of magisterial statements) and understanding. Far too many people see the first as the primary and perhaps unique task of theology. Burghardt provides a response which is utterly persuasive. Much pastoral good would be achieved were his address widely disseminated.

[6] Franz Böckle, "Glaube und Handeln," *Concilium* 120 (1976) 641–47.

[7] Ibid. 642. Eraldo Quarello has an interesting article on certainty in moral judgments: "Riflessioni teologiche sulla certezza morale," *Salesianum* 39 (1977) 77–92. The certainty required in the direct formation of conscience must be understood in a broad human sense. It consists of a kind of convergence of evidence involving also the will, human sensibilities, and "the many other conditionings to which the human person is subject." He agrees with Schüller that it is difficult to defend the type of pure deontology that views an act "in itself" independently of consequences. Since consequences cannot always be foreseen with absolute certainty, they should be considered as "converging lines toward what is licit or illicit."

substantive (content) demand with reference to interhuman conduct is not positively intelligible (*einsehbar*) and clearly determinable."

Böckle lists three ways in which faith exercises an influence on morality. First, faith in God's redemptive act in Jesus Christ gives to the radical act of self-determination (fundamental option) its basic ground and sense. This basic decision (*metanoia*) is the *fundamentum et radix* of the moral life and stamps all of our activity. Secondly, faith deepens and renders secure the insights important for individual acts. Here Böckle distinguishes "morally relevant insights" from "moral judgments." Faith has a direct influence only on the insights, not on the moral judgments themselves.

Finally, Böckle argues that faith forbids the absolutizing of any created good. There follows an extremely interesting paragraph:

An ever larger group of moral theologians is convinced that moral norms in the interhuman area can be grounded only in a teleological way, that is, exclusively through a consideration of the foreseen consequences of the action. Their chief argument lies in reference to the fact that the goods with which our conduct is concerned are exclusively conditioned, created, and therefore limited values. Therefore the moral judgment of an action can be given only after considering the conditions attaching to the value as well as weighing the other concurring values. Certainly man is *unconditionally* obligated by the absolute value of the ethical; but as a contingent being in a contingent world, he can realize the absolutely obliging *bonum* only in and through *bona* which, as contingent goods or values, are relative and as such can never be shown a priori to be the greatest value which cannot concur with another value.[8]

For Böckle, then, the basic values or goods are utterly essential. But he insists that they cannot be absolutized in a way that excludes as unthinkable any weighing of goods (*Güterabwägung*), a point that is made by other studies (cf. Scholz, Weber, Schüller below). The formulation of moral norms must take this into account.[9]

Böckle next turns to the role of the Church in proposing moral norms for concrete conduct. No theologian denies that the Church has a role here. "The only debated question is: with what authority, with what reasons, and with what certainty the Church can speak and decide in concrete moral matters." Both the First and Second Vatican Councils

[8] Böckle, "Glaube und Handeln" 644.

[9] Moral theologians, even when they do not advert to it explicitly, increasingly employ a teleological structure as they do applied ethics. A recent and excellent example of this is Guy Durand's "Insémination artificielle," *Laval théologique philosophique* 33 (1977) 151–63. Durand (along with Häring, Rahner, Troisfontaines, and many others) accepts insemination by husband (AIH) but rejects donor insemination (AID). The acceptance is, of course, an alteration of the teaching of Pius XII, who himself had excluded AIH ("absolute eliminanda est") precisely on teleological grounds (it would biologize marriage). It is the characteristic of teleological considerations that they are open to reassessment.

rooted the Church's competence in its mission to preach the faith (*fidem credendam et moribus applicandam praedicare*). The exact nature of this competence is to be sought in the structure of morality itself. "The natural moral law must in principle be clarified by argumentation." Neither revelation nor authoritative statement replaces human insight and reasoning. Böckle notes: "People will willingly trust themselves to competent leadership where they are convinced that for this authority objective reasons are its measure."

Böckle attributes the authority crisis since *Humanae vitae* to a failure in this area. Specifically, in moral matters the arguments are decisive. "If some theologians and the magisterium believe that they know more about a particular moral matter from other sources, then they must clearly inform Catholics and all persons of good will" as to the source of their greater certainty.[10] Böckle believes that the Church will win moral authority precisely to the degree that it is willing to engage in open, argumentative discussion. Obviously he is suggesting that this has not been the case in some recent decisions.

Böckle is correct, I believe, providing we understand human insight and moral reasoning in its broadest sense. I mean to suggest that discursive moral reasoning cannot always (perhaps even ever) capture and reflect adequately the fulness of moral insight and judgment. There are factors at work in moral conviction that are reasonable but not always reducible to the clear and distinct ideas that the term "human reason" can mistakenly suggest. When all these factors are combined, they suggest that the term "moral reasoning" is quite broad and is defined most aptly by negation: "reasonable" means not ultimately mysterious.

Dario Composta reacts sharply against some of these contentions.[11] He sees the opinions of several authors (Böckle, Jacob David, Enrico Chiavacci) as chipping away at the legitimacy of the competence of the magisterium where the natural law is concerned. For instance, some of these authors contend that the magisterium expresses itself through "a general judgment that does not substitute for the conscience of the faithful but can aid" these consciences. These and other claims have the effect of denying a true binding power to the magisterium.

He then cites Böckle's contention that all concrete ethical norms are conditioned and must be applied in a conflict world where a preference is sometimes called for. The proclamation of a norm by the magisterium, according to Böckle, does not alter this conditioned character.

Composta responds to these statements by pointing out that the power to teach (*potestas docendi*) is not a mere evangelical ministry; it is above all an "*officium ecclesiasticum*," which implies the exercise of a

---

[10] Böckle, "Glaube und Handeln" 646.

[11] Dario Composta, "Diritto naturale e magistero," *Euntes docete* 29 (1976) 365–77.

power to which corresponds the duty of obedience on the part of the faithful." The opposite opinion, he says, emphasizes the primacy of conscience. His response: that is correct "when one wants to emphasize the necessary interiorization of a norm ... but it is false when the interiorization of the norm would exempt the faithful from obedience." For the teaching authority is *sacra potestas*, which issues in an *imperium*.

It is easy to agree with Composta that some formulations unduly reduce the teaching authority of the Church to provision of information or to partnership in a philosophical discussion. That is an overreaction and at odds with the Catholic idea. But Böckle's assertions do not do this. Specifically, if concrete moral norms are indeed conditioned, then the fact that the Church (e.g., the Holy Father) has genuine teaching authority does not alter this. And to say this does not diminish his genuine teaching authority. To say that it does reveals a one-sidedly juridical notion of magisterium—which is the notion one finds in Composta. For instance, he argues that the "pontifical magisterium does not per se demand the technical consensus of theologians," and he gives Pope Paul's rejection of the majority of his birth-control commission as an example.

Here several points might be suggested. First, it is assuredly true that when advisors are divided, someone has to make a decision, take a position. But here we must distinguish carefully between a division over practical policy decisions and division over the accuracy of teaching formulations in a concrete moral area. In the latter instance clarity is not achieved by mere authoritative decree. Secondly, when advisors are heavily against a particular formulation of a moral teaching, then only a highly legal notion of magisterium would argue that the Holy Father is in the same position as he is with a heavy consensus going the other way. Otherwise consultation is a disposable luxury.

Finally, and in any case, the authority of the teacher is not such that it generates absolute certitude. It enjoys, rather, the presumption of certainty. The only way to test whether that presumption is verified in a particular moral matter is through the evidence and arguments, if these terms are not too narrowly construed. There has been a tendency to deny this (e.g., Composta says little about evidence and analyses). Our attempt should be to walk a middle course.[12]

Bruno Schüller continues his discussion of moral norms in an article that pulls together much of what he has developed at length elsewhere.[13]

[12] For some further literature on the magisterium, cf. Hans Geisser, "Das römische Lehramt in protestantischer Erfahrung," *Freiburger Zeitschrift für Philosophie und Theologie* 91 (1977) 23–52; Francis E. King, "Avery Dulles on the Magisterium," *Homiletic and Pastoral Review* 78 (Oct. 1977) 9–17; E. Glenn Hinson, "The Crisis of Teaching Authority in Roman Catholicism," *Journal of Ecumenical Studies* 14 (1977) 66–88.

[13] Bruno Schüller, S.J., "Typen der Begründung sittlicher Normen," *Concilium* 120 (1976) 648–54.

He notes that traditional theologians were familiar with the problems of deontological norms. Thus they indulged in restrictive interpretation to reduce the harmful effects of adhering to the norm. For instance, the concept of lying was so narrowly defined that broad mental reservation was not included. It was to be judged in terms of its consequences.

Similarly, the distinction between direct and indirect killing seemed to serve the same purpose. For instance, to interpret "Thou shalt not kill" literally and absolutely would at times involve more harm (deaths) than seems tolerable or necessary. Life itself would suffer in a conflict world from such an interpretation. Some recent theologians are interpreting the indissolubility of marriage as an ideal to be striven for (*Zielgebot*) rather than as a command to be conformed to (*Erfüllungsgebot*). If indissolubility is understood as an ideal, clearly it would not be included among deontological norms.

Catholic tradition, Schüller points out, used two different forms of argument to establish its deontological norms. The first form began with natural ends which were ascribed to speech and the sexual faculties. One saw divine providential wisdom at work in these natural purposes. *Deus (natura) nihil facit inane.* Thus, God gave us the faculty of speech so that through truthful speech we could live together in society. Falsehood frustrates this purpose. Schüller notes that basically this is a teleological perspective ("so that through truthful speech we could live etc."). When this natural end, by appeal to God's creative wisdom, was viewed as inviolable, the norm became deontological. In this way certain particular nonmoral values were elevated to the level of absolute preference. This happened with the integrity of the sexual (procreative) faculty.

Schüller admits that natural finalities do indeed reflect the Creator's providential wisdom. But "the extent to which these natural ends must be respected in individual cases depends on whether they must deserve the preference when in relationship with concurring values. To make that determination is, if one cares to put it that way, the natural end of the power of judgment given to man by God."[14]

The second form of argument used to justify deontological norms for certain actions was appeal to divine prerogatives. Suicide is the best example. God alone is the lord of life and death; man arrogates God's rights when he commits suicide. Schüller sees in this argument a *petitio principii.* That is, theologically the precise question is whether God does not dispose His lordship over life in such a way that He communicates the power to take life in certain situations.[15] Sensing the circularity of

[14] Ibid. 649.
[15] It is precisely here that the weakness of W. May's formulation shows most clearly. About direct willing of certain evils he says: "It is accepted *and endorsed* by the agent, ratified by him.... In accepting it and in ratifying it, the doer shows his willingness to take, as part of his moral identity, the doer of evil" (*Becoming Human* [Dayton: Pflaum,

their arguments, theologians sought other arguments which were thoroughly teleological in character: e.g., making the prohibition absolute because of the general danger associated with not doing so (*lex lata ad praecavendum periculum generale*).

In summary, Schüller sees Catholic tradition as heavily teleological in its normative ethics. Only in a relatively few cases were norms seen as deontological, and the constant attempt was to narrow these norms to reduce the harm a broader interpretation would involve. The reasons given for reading these norms deontologically he sees as unpersuasive and false. But he believes that some traditional norms, which at first sight have all the characteristics of deontological norms, could be justified teleologically. Thus, he would argue that the prohibition of suicide could be justified teleologically, scil., lack of proportionate reason.

The remainder of Schüller's study is an engagement with William Frankena. A proper understanding of love would include in beneficence that distribution which Frankena calls justice. Therefore Schüller rejects the deontology based on the assertion that a principle separate from love (scil., justice) is required.

Gustave Ermecke will have none of this. He continues his extremely critical reaction to contemporary efforts to probe the meaning and limits of normative statements as found in Böckle, Schüller, *et al.*[16] His brief essay concludes with a kind of moral-theological lament: "How far have some moral theologians already deviated from the ecclesial moral tradition, one never really refuted by anyone up to now! There is total silence about binding Church teaching! The moral confusion in theory and practice is in our time almost complete."[17]

What is behind this gloomy conclusion? Ermecke believes that theologians have abandoned as their point of departure the "nature of man" and adopted a functional perspective. The standard axiom *agere sequitur esse* is passed over in silence or denied, in favor of *agere sequitur actum*.

1975] 102). By this May means that there are certain acts which one cannot freely choose to do for any proportionate reason, simply because such acts are the kinds of acts that are inherently evil, so that one freely choosing to do them cannot not take on, as part of his moral identity, the identity of an evildoer (personal communication from May). To that I would say: if it is the *act itself* that makes me an evildoer by doing it, then how could God command it, e.g., command Abraham to kill Isaac? If God can command it, then clearly one does not take on the character of *moral* evildoer (and this is May's meaning) by doing it. May might respond by saying: Yes, but it is clear that for direct killing God does not allow it. And for that reason it is still inherently wrong. The obvious answer: that is the whole point of the discussion, scil., whether God does not communicate His lordship over life to us in certain exceptional instances. If He does, then the act is not inherently evil (as May uses the term). In summary, May's argument seems radically circular.

[16] Gustave Ermecke, "Katholische Moraltheologie am Scheideweg," *Münchener theologische Zeitschrift* 28 (1977) 47–54.

[17] Ibid. 54.

In other words, Ermecke accuses many theologians of abandoning basic human and Christian anthropology for an empty value morality that is a form of rationalism. He is particularly critical of any rules that attempt to establish an order of values (*Wertvorzugsgesetz*). This rationalism is not the *recta ratio* of tradition, which was not deaf to the resonances of being and order. It is a rationalism without a binding metaphysics.

This concentration on the analysis of individual acts, according to Ermecke, produces three thought-patterns in contemporary moral theology: (1) the exclusion of new material norms from the moral life, norms grounded in the New Testament and taught by the Church; (2) the narrowing of the notion of "reason" to a kind of "actionism"; (3) the abandonment of a deontologically understood essential order of things for a teleology of acts leads necessarily to the immoral principle that a good end justifies a means evil in itself. "This is the end of any solid and, above all, any Christian ethic and Catholic moral theology."

Unfortunately, Ermecke's recent writings strike this reviewer as almost totally exhortatory, and that within a Cassandraic mood. Even the formulations of his own Catholic tradition demand the type of analysis which he is here decrying. To newer probes he has nothing to offer but parenetic warnings about relativism, rationalism, abandonment of Church teaching. In other words, moral discourse to Ermecke is adherence to traditional formulations.

In another article Ermecke argues that beneath the conclusions of *Humanae vitae* is a concept of nature that is philosophical-theological in character.[18] Therefore one cannot argue directly against the encyclical from the perspective of natural science. The sciences, he argues, deal with the *physis* of persons; ethics deals with the *metaphysis*, the essential reality of man. "And this essential reality may not be directly harmed." He believes that many arguments adduced against Church teaching confuse scientific facts with moral judgments. For example, he cites the instance of a physician from Bonn (Dr. von Eiff) who invited the German bishops assembled in synod at Würzburg (1974) to consider recent scientific advances just as seriously as they did the work of Ogino-Knaus. Ermecke uses this as the occasion to set forth both the contributions and limits of the human sciences with respect to moral norms. In general, he argues that the sciences tell us not the what but the how of our duties. For instance, we know that we have a duty to nourish ourselves. But how this is to be fulfilled at a particular moment in history will be made concrete by the contemporary sciences.

More specifically, scientific advances take on a moral character in so far as they restrain or injure persons in their core or their development.

---

[18] Gustave Ermecke, "Wissenschaftlicher Fortschritt contra katholische Moral?" *Theologie und Glaube* 67 (1977) 55–70.

For example, certain military weapons, new abortion techniques, and "contraceptive devices that are contrary to nature" injure the basic *esse* of the human person. Ermecke then returns to Dr. von Eiff and says that he is correct when he notes that certain methods recommended by the Church offend against nature "if nature is understood in *Humanae vitae* in a purely biological way." It is not. "Nature," he says, "is not understood there, as unfortunately an *ad hoc* theological ideology repeatedly asserts, at the level of purely scientific data" or at the level of the *physis* which the sciences study. Rather, it appeals to the *metaphysis,* the essential being of man, in making its claims. Therefore one cannot argue against the encyclical on merely scientific grounds.

Ermecke concludes: "And this essential reality may not be directly harmed. The contrary assertions of a fashionable understanding of moral norms covering created values (an understanding which completely or very broadly denies deontological norms and grants validity only to 'teleological' ones) is false and moral-theologically misleading."[19]

Several aspects of this essay merit comment. First, there can be no doubt that when an action harms persons in their essential reality (what Ermecke calls *metaphysis*), then that action is morally wrong. However, Ermecke has simply asserted this of certain forms of birth regulation. What we need here is a reasoned and persuasive argument. Hence this aspect of his study begs the question in dispute, and therefore unavoidably leaves the impression that when he speaks of nature and "contrary to nature," the only thing these terms can mean is *biological* nature.

Secondly, Ermecke asserts of contrary views that they are teleological and therefore false. It is paradoxical to find him attacking teleological considerations when he himself proposes a teleological criterion to identify those scientific advances which are not advances at all, but morally wrong. He states: "Catholic moral theology must protect the whole man in his freedom and therefore ... must declare certain scientific advances morally wrong *if they hinder or harm persons in their essential being or in the historical development of this essential being.*"[20] That is a perfectly acceptable criterion; but I submit it is teleological at root.

Finally, Ermecke concludes by lifting out what he calls the "unsatisfactorily answered question" which must be put to those who disagree with him: How can the Church declare overnight as invalid and even erroneous a prohibition that she has taught as pertaining to salvation for nearly two thousand years? Much could be said to that question—e.g., about the changing circumstances in which the substance of the Church's concern must be formulated. However, what is immediately evident here is that this question is a *different* matter from the question under

[19] Ibid. 69.   [20] Ibid. 64.

discussion (whether an action is always injurious to persons in their essential being as persons). It is not a question of the natural moral law. But the fact that it leads Ermecke where it does shows how much our notions of such a law can be influenced by some hidden ecclesiological concerns. Whether that is regrettable or to be welcomed can be left to the reader.

Another author quite critical of these tendencies is B. Stoeckle.[21] He approaches the matter under the name used by Tübingen's A. Auer: "an autonomous morality." He argues that such a term and such a notion only play into the hands of reprehensible modern notions of autonomy. As an example, Stoeckle gives the teleological grounding of norms which provides for a weighing of values (*Güterabwägung*) in conflict situations. He has several objections to raise. First, such an approach assumes that all precepts of a concrete kind "are contingent and therefore of a conditional character." They are not. There are some norms that must not be allowed to fall victim of any value-preferences (e.g., the indissolubility of marriage, the prohibition of adultery and premarital intercourse).[22]

Secondly, Stoeckle argues that this point of view simply turns over to persons too much autonomy. "This position equips a person with a sovereignty that enjoins him to consider moral value as a matter for which he himself alone possesses competence."[23] Rather, he states, there are actions where we do not enjoy such sovereignty, actions which bind unconditionally. "That happens in phenomena like trust, mistrust, mercy, lack of mercy, uprightness, lying. These are withdrawn from the disposition of men...."

Stoeckle's study is primarily concerned with the specificity of Christian ethics; but he does treat the matter of moral norms as an example of the poverty of the school he opposes.

Three points. First, Stoeckle sees a teleological understanding of norms (proportionate reason) as individualistic. No one holds, to my knowledge, that because in certain conflict situations a weighing of values must occur, this is to be done individualistically, as Stoeckle holds. Nor need one hold this. There are certain kinds of action for which the community may judge that, practically speaking, there is no proportionate reason. Being naturally social and Christianly communal, we look to our tradition

---

[21] B. Stoeckle, "Flucht in das Humane?" *Internationale katholische Zeitschrift* 6 (1977) 312-25.

[22] In this regard see also the thoughtful article of philosopher Robert Spaemann, "Wovon handelt die Moraltheologie?" *Internationale katholische Zeitschrift* 6 (1977) 291-311. Spaemann uses indissolubility of marriage to confront recent tendencies. But he seems to overlook the Orthodox experience.

[23] Stoeckle, "Flucht in das Humane?" 317.

and to our community as the context in which moral learning is achieved, hence the context in which any weighing of values ought to occur. In summary, a weighing of values in conflict is not and should not be an individualistic weighing of values. Stoeckle attempts to get leverage by equating the two.

Secondly, Stoeckle commits the common mistake (about which more below) of giving actions a value definition, and indeed a very formal one (mercy, lack of mercy) when discussing actions always to be avoided. No one would disagree with him; but he is not addressing the question under discussion.

Finally, his entire discussion of the specificity of a Christian ethic calls out for distinctions. He argues (against Auer) that "Christian faith produces ethical content that is understandable and open to the reason of a believer but not to the reason of an unbeliever." Of course, there are things that are "reasonable to the Christian" that are not to the nonbeliever. For instance, the folly of the cross and the grace of the Spirit will lead individuals to conclusions that even other Christians may not share. But as I understand it, this is not the discussion. It pertains to *concrete* demands at the *essential* level, scil., a level stating demands considered valid for all persons. Stoeckle seems to overlook this. He would do well to give us a single example of a concrete act at the essential level that is in principle unavailable to human insight and demands faith.

In a long and very useful study, Louis Janssens sums up much of what is being said in recent studies on moral norms.[24] In order to understand the meaning and limits of concrete material moral norms, Janssens points out that we must take into account a double ambiguity in our actions. The first derives from the "presence and connection of premoral values and disvalues in reality, as well as in our actions." By "premoral values" he means life, bodily and psychic health, pleasure and joy, friendship, knowledge, technique, art, etc. "We call them premoral values (classically: *bona physica*). They are *pre*moral because in themselves they are neither moral nor immoral. . . . " Similarly, realities such as hunger, thirst, illness, death, neuroses, ignorance, error, and violence are premoral disvalues (classically: *mala physica*). These values and disvalues are sometimes inseparably connected in our conduct, so that there are times when "we cannot realize a premoral value without admitting the inseparable premoral disvalue."

The second ambiguity results from the fact that our choices are limited. Choosing one thing, we necessarily omit another. Faced with these

[24] Louis Janssens, "Norms and Priorities in a Love Ethic," *Louvain Studies* 6 (1977) 207–38.

limitations, our choices must respect the order of priority in reality (*ordo bonorum*), and since such preferences affect the well-being of others, they must be situated within the *ordo caritatis*. In summary, Janssens writes: "In the situations where premoral values are unavoidably connected with premoral disvalues or where it is impossible to avoid all of the premoral disvalues which are inseparably blended, we ought to choose the alternative which indicates our preference for the lesser premoral disvalue. Otherwise we do not exclude premoral disvalues as much as possible."[25]

Janssens gives several examples. One is the classical but now rare case where the physician is faced with the choice of losing both mother and fetus if he does not intervene, or of saving the one life (mother's) he can save. "If the doctor refuses to interfere, his free choice is a preference for an omission in which two lives (premoral values) are lost. If he intervenes, he chooses an action which expresses a preference for the lesser premoral disvalue, namely, the loss of only one life." Janssens correctly notes that this was the principle explicitly used by the Belgian bishops in their statement on abortion.[26]

He applies this reasoning to other situations, e.g., prisoners of the Gestapo during World War II who took their own lives rather than be tortured or drugged into revealing secrets that could endanger the lives of others. Their actions were not only good because they proceeded from good intentions. "Their action was also morally right, because they preferred a lesser premoral disvalue (their own death) in order to save higher premoral values (many lives, important military secrets)."

Janssens then turns to concrete material moral norms. He makes several points here. First, such norms must employ only descriptive language, not "morally qualifying terms" such as "murder," "lie," "theft." For instance, a "lie is a morally qualifying noun affirming that a false-hood—descriptive word referring to a premoral disvalue—is uttered in an immoral way (without proportionate reason)."[27]

Secondly, Janssens argues that both prescriptive and proscriptive norms are relative (scil., not always applicable). For instance, with regard to negative norms he states: "an action admitting or causing premoral

---

[25] Ibid. 214.

[26] Cf. *Documentation catholique* 70 (1973) 432–38. In a recent article M. Zalba, S.J., has followed a different path. He sees "therapeutic" abortions (to save the mother) as indirect. Cf. "El aborto terapeutico 'aborto indirecto,' " *Estudios eclesiásticos* 52 (1977) 9–38. Zalba concedes that many others have reasoned differently. Some use preference principles (Schüller, Dedek, Heylen, Molinski). Others appeal to compromise (Lopez Azpitarte, Curran, Martelet, etc.). Others argue that the true notion of absolutely prohibited abortion is not realized (Häring, Visser, Rotter, Troisfontaines).

[27] Janssens, "Norms and Priorities" 216.

disvalue is morally right when it serves a higher premoral value or safeguards the priority given to a lesser premoral disvalue. In other words, we can have a proportionate reason to depart from the norm."[28]

Thirdly, this does not prevent some norms from being "practically exceptionless." This is the case when the action described in the norm practically always deserves the priority (e.g., render help to one in *extreme* distress) or "when there is an inner contradiction between the elements forming part of the description of what is done." An example of this latter is rape. Rape means the use of physical or psychic violence in order to compel somebody to sexual intercourse against his or her will. Violence is a premoral disvalue that must be justified. Here it cannot be justified; for "truly human sexual intercourse is an expression of love and thus a free, mutual self-giving which is radically opposed to the use of violence."

Since proportionate reason plays such an utterly crucial role in Janssens' thought, he is at pains to show the many considerations that must be attended to in its determination. He lists four. (1) The relevant sciences (sociology, psychology, economics, etc.) must be studied to appreciate the true significance of our actions. (2) We must differentiate instrumental actions (work) from those having a meaning in themselves (play, research, contemplation) and those that are expressive actions or *Ausdruckshandlungen* (giving a present). These latter have a meaning in themselves. They are signs of love, support, solidarity. (3) We must appreciate the institutional character of some actions (promises, contracts) and the importance of institutions for the common good. (4) In establishing priorities or preferences, we must attend to the *ordo caritatis* and the *ordo bonorum*.

The remainder of Janssens' essay is an excellent treatment of the *ordo caritatis* and *ordo bonorum*. It is impossible here to do more than indicate several points of interest and importance. For instance, in treating the *ordo bonorum* Janssens notes that "the moral goodness of the person is an absolute value." For this reason one may never ("whatever the consequences may be") induce a person to act against his conscience. Similarly, we ourselves must "always follow the maxim: *non sunt facienda mala ut eveniant bona,* on the condition that *mala* refers to morally wrong actions and not to premoral disvalues."

With regard to priorities within the *ordo bonorum*, Janssens notes some of the standard preference rules. For instance: (1) All other things being equal, a higher value deserves priority over a lower. (2) The more urgent and basic the value, the more it deserves preference (e.g., life itself). (3) Degree of probability of realizing a value in one's action must be taken into account. (4) The preservation and support of a value over

[28] Ibid. 217.

the long run must be weighed. Thus, a person could jeopardize a value by the type of single-mindedness that leads to poor health. (5) Special attention needs to be given to values protected by institutions, for social life is at stake. Thus, before performing actions that depart from institutional rules (contracts, promises), several tests are called for. Would I or someone else make the same judgment about the moral choice in any situation which is similar in the morally relevant aspects (principle of universalizability)? What would happen if everyone were to perform a similar action in a similar situation (principle of generalizability)? What would happen if others are influenced by our action to do likewise (wedge principle)?

These do not solve problems, for ethical rules are not recipes. But they do prepare the problem-solver for the exercise of prudence.

Janssens insists, with Fuchs and others, that it is impossible to make a moral judgment about the material content of an action without considering the whole act. "A judgment about moral rightness or wrongness is only possible with respect to that totality, because only concerning that whole is it possible to argue whether or not it expresses the priority of the lesser premoral disvalue or of the higher premoral value."[29]

Nor is this new. Janssens argues that Thomas shares this same perspective. Thomas states that "there are some actions which, absolutely considered, involve a definite deformity or disorder, but which are made right by reason of particular circumstances, as the killing of a man ... involves a disorder in itself, but, if it be added that the man is an evildoer killed for justice' sake ... it is not sinful, rather it is virtuous."[30] Or, as Janssens words it more generally, "the whole action, considered in all its elements (circumstances) is morally right because there is a proportionate reason to justify the causing of a premoral disvalue."

Janssens concludes his long study with an examination of the Thomistic doctrine of sexual acts "against nature"—and therefore intrinsically wrong. He traces this to Thomas' notion of natural law as involving three levels of inclinations to goods. The second level is generic; that is, it refers to those inclinations we share with animals. At this level sexual intercourse is an *actus naturae* whose purpose is uniquely procreation. "As the use of food is not sinful when it is confined within a proper measure and order, in as much as it is subservient to the health of our body, so the use of the sexual faculty is not sinful if it happens in a right measure and order, in as much as it is subservient to its end, which is procreation."[31]

---

[29] Ibid. 231.

[30] *Quaestiones quodlibetales* 9, q. 7, a. 15.

[31] 2/2, q. 153, a. 2. There is an extremely interesting literature this past year on natural law. For instance, Michael B. Crowe presents a helpful critical study about the status of

This perspective was, Janssens persuasively argues, abandoned by *Gaudium et spes*. But it is lingeringly present in *Humanae vitae, Persona humana* ("Declaration on Certain Questions concerning Sexual Ethics"), and the *Documentum circa sterilizationem in nosocomiis catholicis* ("Document on Sterilization in Catholic Hospitals").

I have reported this study at considerable length for several reasons. First, it brings together a great deal of writing and reflection that has occurred over the past decade (Fuchs, Knauer, Schüller, Böckle, Molinski, Weber, Scholz, etc.) in a clear and helpful way. Secondly, it explains why earlier authors (e.g., St. Thomas) who held the same general principles did not apply them in the same way. Concretely, because of their notion of natural law and the biology available to them, they could not. Thirdly, the study provides a fine vehicle for responding to some of the objections that have been leveled at the understanding of moral norms shared by so many contemporary Catholic moral theologians. That vehicle is a proper understanding of the term "proportionate reason."

An example will help here. Archbishop Joseph L. Bernardin sent a letter to all his priests on the recent CTSA-committee publication *Human Sexuality*. It contained and recommended a critique by moral theologian Donald McCarthy.[32] McCarthy argues in his critique that "what does partially explain the direction taken here is this study's application of the controversial new theory of proportionalism in concrete moral

---

natural law ("The Pursuit of Natural Law," *Irish Theological Quarterly* 44 [1977] 3–29). Gian Darms, after rejecting an excessively loose understanding of natural law ("Entscheidungshilfen"), presents the moral law as found in Aquinas, scil., as building off natural inclinations ("Il problema delle norme oggetive dell' attività morale alla luce di S. Tommaso," *Divinitas* 21 [1977] 191–214). Dario Composta rejects the "existentialist anthropology" of some contemporary authors (J. Arntz, F. Böckle, E. Lopez Azpitarte, S.J., E. Schillebeeckx) and claims their notion of natural law is non-Thomistic; rather, it is "Rahnerian" ("Il diritto naturale tomistico nella più recente ermeneutica," *Doctor communis* 30 [1977] 82–100). Richard Bruch warns that "one must guard against drawing too much from the [Thomistic] natural inclinations" ("Intuition und Überlegung beim sittlichen Naturgesetz nach Thomas von Aquin," *Theologie und Glaube* 67 [1977] 29–54). A. Etcheverry approaches natural law phenomenologically and identifies two key constitutive elements of the human person: individuality and rationality ("Y a-t-il une nature humaine?" *Bulletin de littérature ecclésiastique* 78 [1977] 31–53). Paolo Valori, S.J., insists on the necessity of interdisciplinary dialogue in moral theology and outlines its stages ("Significato e metologia della ricerca morale oggi," *Gregorianum* 58 [1977] 55–85). Albert Chapelle discusses the continuity in Jesus Christ between creation and redemption. This illumines the relation of natural law to the economy of salvation ("Naturgesetz und Theologie," *Internationale katholische Zeitschrift* 6 [1977] 326–36). Finally, Andreas Laun points to the danger of biologism in interpreting the *inclinationes naturales* and argues that actions are morally right "not because they correspond to the nature of the agent, but because they respond properly to the ethical importance of the object" ("'Natur'—Quelle von sittlichen Normen," *Die neue Ordnung* 31 [1977] 97–111).

[32] The critique is public in character.

choices."[33] Noting the contention of writers like Janssens and Fuchs that the whole action is the object of judgment, McCarthy continues: "What this means in effect is that sexual actions otherwise immoral may be rendered moral when the 'subjectivity' freely decides that proportionately greater good than evil effects will follow." Thus he refers to the "inherent subjectivism" of this principle as one that easily leads to "ethical relativism and situationism."

As examples he cites adultery and infanticide. Adultery, McCarthy argues, is not wrong because of its "material object" (sexual intercourse). Rather, it is wrong because of specifying circumstances. That is, "adultery as intercourse *with the wrong person* and infanticide as killing *of the innocent*" (my emphasis). He then concludes: "Other extenuating circumstances or good intentions, as adultery for the good of marriage or infanticide to reduce population growth, can never make these actions good."

McCarthy then turns to the language of "premoral" and "moral evil." Of this he notes:

In such an ingenious solution the magisterial documents which speak of the evil of such practices as premarital sex or homosexual actions really only refer to "premoral evil." Then the moral or pastoral theologian can still approve of these actions as morally good when performed with sufficient justifying circumstances and ends.

He rewords the matter as follows:

The Church's tradition in moral theology has always recognized the possibility of human persons performing evil actions inculpably, but it has never conceded, *as proportionalists contend* [my emphasis] that these actions could coalesce into the species of morally good acts with the addition of further circumstances and ends.

Finally, McCarthy concludes by referring to the "key principle of ethical proportionalism" used in *Human Sexuality.* "It is," he says, "a very recent version of the classical principle of double effect (less than twelve years old). Its status remains highly controversial because it seems so easy to permit the ends to justify the means in ethical decision-making."

I am grateful that McCarthy made these points explicit, for they are likely to be entertained by a fair number of other theologians. However,

---

[33] This same statement is made by William May and John Harvey in their review in *National Catholic Reporter,* June 17, 1977; cf. also May and Harvey, "On Understanding Human Sexuality: A Critique of the CTSA Study," *Communio* 4 (1977) 195–225; Gerald D. Coleman, S.S., "'Human Sexuality: New Directions in American Catholic Thought,'" *Priest* 33, no. 11 (Nov. 1977) 12–21.

I am convinced that they are an inaccurate interpretation of the direction present in so many contemporary writers on moral theology. Here I should like to detail a few of the problems I have with this interpretation of things in an attempt to clarify the issues.

1) *The CTSA-committee study and the principle of proportionalism.* Whatever one thinks of the conclusions of *Human Sexuality,* it must be said that there is no *necessary* connection between those conclusions and the theoretical work on proportionate reason in the studies of theologians such as Schüller, Janssens, Fuchs, etc. What one concludes about concrete actions depends on how one reads one's proportions. That is key and has been traditional in Catholic theology for centuries. Thus, it is no indictment of the just-war theory to say that it was abused at times to justify Vietnam. Nor is it an indictment of the idea that promises made may conflict with more urgent supervening necessities (proportionate reason) if certain people interpret these necessities frivolously or uncritically. To think otherwise is to fall victim to a logical fallacy (*post hoc, ergo propter hoc*). Specifically, the indicted theologians might argue that, all things considered, there is no proportionate reason for engaging in strictly premarital relations. That is a quite acceptable formulation of the Church's substantial convictions on the matter.

2) *The subjectivism of proportionate reason.* This point was made above but deserves repeating. McCarthy refers to the "inherent subjectivism" of this form of moral reasoning. No theologian argues, as far as I know, that a reason is truly proportionate *because a particular individual thinks so.* Nor does any theologian argue that the determination of proportionality is the exclusive prerogative of the individual, as was noted above in dealing with Stoeckle. These would indeed be subjectivism. But there is nothing in the teleological understanding of moral norms that suggests such individualism. The preference principles which attempt to sort out the claims of the *ordo bonorum* and the *ordo caritatis* are the result of common reflection and discourse. Killing is a good example here, as Böckle points out. Over the centuries there developed the conviction that the only way at times to defend the public safety was through capital punishment. Thus it was concluded that such punishment was justifiable for certain crimes, scil., that the public safety was a proportionate reason for an exception to the general prohibition against killing. In our time we are, it seems, arriving at a different conclusion. But the point is that sorting out the claims of conflicting values is a community task subject to objective criteria. Because the individual must make such assessments at times does not mean that the assessment is correct *just because the individual has made it.* Thus, it is not proportionate to kill another just because I mistakenly believe it is.

3) *Value language and descriptive language.* This is the chief source of misunderstanding where the notion of proportionate reason is concerned. In effect, what one does is describe an action in value terms—e.g., adultery, theft, murder—and then indict theologians for accepting proportionate reasons that might justify it. Thus McCarthy writes: "Other extenuating circumstances or good intentions as adultery for the good of marriage ... can never make these actions good." Furthermore, he notes several categories of nonsexual actions described by Vatican II as "criminal" (genocide, slavery, abortion, euthanasia) and then adds: "It seems clear that the Church cannot open these actions to the kind of circumstantial justification that the ethical principle of proportionalism might allow...." This is presented as if it were what Schüller, Janssens, Böckle, etc. are saying or must be implying. That is not the case.

When something is described as "adultery" or "genocide," nothing can justify it; for the very terms are morally qualifying terms meaning unjustified killing, intercourse with the wrong person, etc. That is, they are tautological. The question contemporary theologians are facing is rather this: What (in descriptive terms) is to count as murder, adultery, genocide? We know from a long tradition that not every killing is murder. Therefore we know that some killings are justified. That is, we know that there is a proportionate reason for taking human life at times.

This confusion of value language with descriptive language is evident in many moral writings. It constitutes a bad argument, one known as *ignorantia elenchi*, missing the point. For instance, G. Martelet compares the evil of contraception with the use of violence and with a lie.[34] These latter are two remarkably different terms. The first is descriptive and presents a premoral disvalue (since violence is occasionally justifiable). The second is a morally qualifying term. Thus Janssens correctly concludes: "Should the first comparison be correct, the encyclical (*Humanae vitae*) would raise no problems. This cannot be said if the second comparison is to be maintained."[35]

This matter is extremely important; for if it is overlooked, recent studies do not get presented accurately or fairly. McCarthy notes: "The Church's tradition in moral theology has always recognized the possibility of human persons performing *evil* actions inculpably, but it has never conceded, as proportionalists contend, that these actions could coalesce into the species of morally good acts with the addition of further circumstances and ends." Here we see the error I am concerned with. An action is stamped as *evil* (and there is no doubt that this is a morally qualifying term, for it is associated with "inculpable performance") and then it is

---

[34] G. Martelet, *L' Existence humaine et l'amour: Pour mieux comprendre l'encyclique Humanae vitae* (Paris: Desclée, 1969) at 140 and 149.

[35] Janssens, "Norms and Priorities" 216.

stated that proportionalists would contend that the action could be justified by further circumstances. Straightforwardly, so-called proportionalists make no such contention and their thought is misrepresented when it is put that way. They would say that all things have to be considered before an act is said to be morally evil.

4) *Proportionate reason and double effect.* McCarthy states that the "principle of ethical proportionalism ... is a very recent version of the classical principle of double effect...." That confuses two things: the notion of proportionate reason and double effect. The notion of possible exceptions to concrete moral norms by the presence of proportionate reason has been a staple of Catholic theology for many centuries. For that reason Schüller has correctly noted that Catholic theology is through and through teleological in character. What is recent is the examination into those areas excluded from such teleology. Such actions (e.g., direct killing of an innocent person) were seen as intrinsically evil. Thus, if innocent persons were killed as a result of my intervention, those deaths had to occur indirectly. Contemporary moralists are, indeed, examining the crucial relevance of the direct-indirect distinction in these few areas. But that hardly makes the notion of proportionate reason a "very recent version of the classical principle of double effect."

In contrast to the approach taken by Janssens, William E. May has argued for the intrinsically evil character of certain premoral disvalues described independently of end or circumstances, scil., of other concurring or colliding values.[36] His example is direct sterilization. He correctly points out that human sexuality has a twofold dimension (unitive, procreative) and that these two dimensions are inseparably joined.[37] He further argues—and again correctly, in my view—that the life-giving and love-giving powers are integral to the human person and ought to elicit from us a response of acceptance and love.

He then constructs the minor of his syllogism: but "to act contraceptively or to intervene by surgical sterilization for contraceptive purposes is, in effect, to choose to reject the goodness of this human power. It is to say, in effect, that this power is here and now an evil, a curse, not a blessing...."[38] It is to "repudiate" these human goods. He concludes: "Sterilization is thus an act that of its very nature attacks the ethical or

[36] William E. May, "Sterilization: Catholic Teaching and Catholic Practice," *Homiletic and Pastoral Review* 77 (Aug.-Sept. 1977) 9-22. If the article seems to deal excessively with the author of these "Notes," it is because it represents a response to my paper (unpublished) on the subject.

[37] The word "inseparable" is perhaps not the most apt expression. For instance, J. Ford and G. Kelly once noted: "the marriage act has other natural and intrinsic ends in addition to procreation *which are separable* from actual procreation or any intention of actual procreation" (*Contemporary Moral Theology 2: Marriage Questions* [Westminster: Newman, 1963] 405, emphasis added).

[38] May, "Sterilization" 15.

moral good of the human person and that is, consequently, intrinsically evil."

May concludes with several supportive points and corollaries. First, to think that sterilization is even occasionally justifiable is to reduce the sexual power to a "merely utilitarian good" (*bonum utile*) and to a "merely biological function." Secondly, he sees his analysis as a good moral argument and believes that dissenting arguments have been "seriously challenged by competent theologians." Finally, since sterilization is intrinsically evil, it can only be tolerated (material co-operation) under stringent conditions in Catholic hospitals.[39]

Here a few points to help put the question in sharper perspective. First, there is May's argument. The key assumption—and fatal weakness—is this: prevention of conception by artificial intervention involves one in repudiating the good of procreation. This associates an over-all personal attitude of mind and will (repudiation) with a physical act. All would grant that repudiation or rejection of a basic human good like procreation is morally wrongful. But many would argue that repudiation of this good must be located in over-all selfish and unjustified refusal to bear children, or in selfishly limiting them, or in irresponsibly multiplying them—not precisely in the nonabortifacient contraceptive measures one uses to keep procreation within the limits of responsibility. May is heavily reliant here on Germain Grisez's formulation that one may never "turn against a basic good directly." However, the key issue is: what is to count for such a turning?

When should one be said to "turn against the basic good of procreation," to use May's rendering? I prefer the structure of reasoning proposed by Pius XII. That pontiff made two moves. First, he proposed a general duty to procreate, on the basis that the individual, society, and the Church depend on fertile marriage for their existence.[40] He concluded: "Consequently, to embrace the state of matrimony, to use continually the faculty proper to it, and in it alone, and on the other hand to withdraw always and deliberately, without a grave motive, from its primary[41] duty, would be to sin against the very meaning of conjugal life." But Pius XII immediately continued: "Serious motives, such as those which are frequently present in the so-called 'indications'—medical, eugenic, economic and social—can exempt from this positive, obligatory prestation (*prestazione*) for a long time, even for the entire duration of the marriage."[42]

---

[39] In this May is in disagreement with W. Smith, who believes—erroneously, in my opinion—that in Catholic hospitals not even material co-operation may occur. Cf. "Catholic Hospitals and Sterilization," *Linacre Quarterly* 44 (1977) 107–16.

[40] For a development cf. Ford and Kelly (n. 37 above).

[41] This terminology was dropped by theologians and Vatican II.

[42] *AAS* 43 (1951) 835–54, at 845–46.

Several things are notable here. First, "to sin against the very meaning of conjugal life" is a fair rendering of "turn against a basic good." This failure is attributed to failure to fulfil a duty.[43] Secondly, the Holy Father acknowledges that one does not contravene this duty when the serious indications he mentions are present. In other words, whether one "sins against the very meaning of conjugal life" is determined by the presence or absence of these indications—which he later described as "in truth very wide."[44] This is a straightforward form of teleology. As Ford and Kelly wrote: "As for the expressions 'grave motive,' 'serious reasons,' etc. we believe that a careful analysis of all these phrases in the context would justify the interpretation that they are the equivalent of the expression 'proportionate reasons.' "[45] What this means, then, is that in the context of periodic continence Pius XII associated "turning against a basic good" with a pattern of actions, and the presence or absence of a proportionate reason. This is, I believe, as it should be. But why should it be otherwise when dealing with sterilization?

Put negatively, it is simply incomprehensible to many (theologians and others) that a couple who have seven or eight children, then encounter serious medical (economic, eugenic, social) problems that make any further procreation irresponsible, and choose sterilization as the means, must be said to be "turning against a basic good." One would think that such a "turning against" must be understood here just as it was by Pius XII when dealing with periodic continence, by looking at the over-all performance of the couple. By answering that contraception and sterilization do this of themselves, May has indulged in a *petitio principii.* Hence I do not see that May has provided us with a good moral argument or that recent revisionist efforts have been "seriously challenged."[46]

There is a second point closely connected with the first. It is the assertion that sterilization involves reducing the procreative power to a *bonum utile,* a merely biological power. May sees this as dualistic. Actually, it is not at all clear that sterilization as such does this. Rather than reduce the sexual power to a *bonum utile,* those theologians who see sterilization as a sometimes justifiable premoral evil refuse to *abso-*

[43] I am not arguing that Pius XII saw this as the only failure. Clearly, he taught that contraception was a moral failure, but he based this on different grounds.

[44] *AAS* 43 (1951) 859.

[45] Ford and Kelly (n. 37 above) 425.

[46] Incidentally, if this is viewed as a good argument, it is interesting to note that one (Paul Ramsey) who shares May's general analytic approach about "never directly turning against a basic good" does not see that it applies here. Ramsey agrees that where the unitive and procreative values are concerned, proportionate reason rules. Ramsey removes the good of human life from such a teleological assessment; but it is not clear how he can do so or on what grounds, unless he absolutizes the value of life. My only point here is that, were the argument of May convincing, we would expect one like Ramsey to be espousing it. He does not. Indeed, he positively denies its application here.

lutize the *bonum honestum* that is the power to procreate. Indeed, they would retort—and correctly, I think—that the May position is the biologistic (and therefore dualistic) one. Why? Because this position gives biological functions the exclusive determination of rightfulness and wrongfulness (accepting or rejecting a basic good), and therefore of significance. And if one cared to urge this point even further, it could be pointed out that it is precisely because contemporary theologians see sexual intercourse as having a meaning in itself (*bonum honestum*) that they refuse to allow it to be viewed as a *bonum utile*. This is a reversal from earlier times. It was, after all, a centuries-old Catholic tradition that held that sexual intimacy was morally right, beyond the needs of procreation, *ad remedium concupiscentiae,* to avoid sin, etc.

In summary, then, there are indeed two inseparable dimensions to sexuality. But, as Francis X. Meehan notes in a perceptive article, "it is another question whether both values have to be embodied in each and every action, regardless of possible conflicts of values."[47]

How this "other question" should be formulated and solved is, of course, the core of the contemporary discussion on norms. Helmut Weber approaches the question through the notion of compromise.[48] After distinguishing several senses of compromise, he turns to the notion as found in theology. It is especially associated with H. Thielicke. For Thielicke, compromise is "a kind of law of life." Even the Christian cannot avoid compromise. But in his compromising he cannot appeal simply to the limited possibilities of the world. No, the world is sinful in its structures and we are responsible for it. Thus, for Thielicke, compromises we are forced to make are not only a personal failure but guilty ones. Behind this stands a notion of the corruption of the world and necessary sin. In face of this the Christian may compromise, because he/she is confident of God's forgiveness. But such compromises do not correspond to God's original will. They must be lived and experienced as a wound that cannot be healed.

When one turns to Catholic tradition, it does not seem that the notion of compromise functions in moral theological thought. Weber believes there are substantive parallels in the teaching on co-operation, doing and counseling the lesser evil, the double effect, and probabilism. All of these are, he argues, ways of explaining the doing of good while tolerating

[47] Francis X. Meehan, "Love and Sexuality in Catholic Tradition," *America* 137 (1977) 230–34. This thoughtful study goes beyond the evidence when Meehan states: "I believe that the Catholic tradition has taught that sexual activity has at one and the same time a life-giving and a love-giving meaning, and that these two meanings are intrinsically related." These insights and formulations are very recent. Cf. L. Janssens, *Mariage et fécondité* (Paris: Duculot, 1967).

[48] Helmut Weber, "Der Kompromiss in der Moral," *Trier theologische Zeitschrift* 86 (1977) 99–118.

a measure of evil—or what modern terminology calls "compromise."

Weber then compares the Reformed Protestant and Catholic traditions. The former tends to extend the notion of compromise as far as possible, while the latter tries to restrict it to exceptional instances. This difference is traceable to the different theological anthropologies at work (extent of corruption of nature). However, a position that sees compromise as more far-reaching than exceptional instances need not rest on such an anthropology. It need only amplify the notion of double effect the way Knauer has.

Weber does this and cites the work of Schüller, K. Demmer, and Joseph Fuchs as doing substantially the same. But Weber prefers to refer to his principle as that of compromise. He sees *all* of our choices as compromises in the sense that they achieve good at the cost of evil—even if that cost is the good left undone because of the limited nature of human choice. He rejects the Protestant Reformed notion of the sinful world and sinful self as underlying this. Rather, in Catholic theology "it is not the sin of man and of the world that is responsible for the situation but their limited character." Seen from this point of view, compromise is morally beyond objection, even though not every compromise fits this category.

Weber is certainly to be counted among those who understand moral norms teleologically. He situates norms within a conflict model of decision-making, then uses proportionate reason to interpret their binding force—though he calls this compromise. One interesting point about his essay is the fact that he sees the notion of compromise as *substantively* present in Catholic tradition in the teachings mentioned above. This suggests that those authors who sometimes depart from the individual conclusions of this tradition are really in deep continuity with the tradition in their moral reasoning, *pace* Ermecke. Ultimately, however, I wonder what is achieved or illumined by referring to this teleology of method as "compromise." This term too easily hides what is going on.[49]

Norbert Rigali continues his contribution to this discussion.[50] He had earlier argued that *Humanae vitae* was a fitting historical response because the challengers failed to prove their case. He made two substantive contentions. (1) Charity might require something more in this area than is clear from natural law. (2) Contraception includes a *morally* negative element, because it is intrinsically incompatible with a degree of charity possible in this world. The author of these "Notes" questioned

[49] Cf. also Klaus Demmer, "Entscheidung und Kompromiss," *Gregorianum* 53 (1972) 323–51; Mark Attard, O. Carm., *Compromise in Morality* (Rome, 1976); H. J. Wilting, *Der Kompromiss als theologisches und als ethisches Problem* (in *Moraltheologische Studien*, ed. Bruno Schüller [Düsseldorf: Patmos, 1975]).

[50] Norbert Rigali, "Dialogue with Richard McCormick," *Chicago Studies* 16 (1977) 299–308.

these notions. First, I argued that Rigali had separated natural law from charity in a way tradition would not. Tradition repeatedly urged that "Christ did not add any single moral prescription of a positive kind to the natural moral law." Secondly, I argued that the disvalues that are sometimes found in our actions are not traceable to our imperfection in charity but to the conflict character of the world we live in. Therefore, it is inappropriate (at least) to speak of these disvalues as involving "a morally negative element."

Rigali now responds to these critiques. To the first point, he agrees with what tradition literally says, but makes two objections. He faults its notion of natural law as being static and essentialistic. Specifically, this traditional conception of natural law divided the moral call "between the demands of what might be called minimal decency and invitations to perfection." These latter invitations were seen as counsels. Rigali believes that when the Christian life is seen as Vatican II saw it (as a life of striving for perfection), then "what were traditionally regarded as *counsels* of perfection must be seen as *within* the moral law, not beyond it."

His second objection is the very question itself ("How does Christian morality relate to natural morality?"). He believes that moral theologians answer this question differently. Furthermore, the question itself contains "very questionable presuppositions." We should abandon it and concentrate on the basic question about what the moral law is, "the law of humanity called to one, supernatural destiny, the law that has always been a law of charity." Rigali sees this as opposed "to the notion that the moral law is or is essentially what the classical world view called 'the natural law' and understood as a law independent of supernatural charity."[51] This section concludes with the following assertion: "Moral law (as historical consciousness must conceive it) makes specific claims that 'moral law' (= the classical worldview's conception of it) does not."

Rigali's response to my second objection is to question the meaning and legitimacy of the distinction between nonmoral (or premoral) and moral evil.[52] "The traditional understanding of the distinction between physical and moral evil, created out of the classical worldview and

---

[51] Here it would be well to recall the fact that "natural law" was used in two senses, one strict, one broad. In the strictest sense, it referred to natural rights. In the broad sense, it referred to the entire moral life. Or, as Etcheverry (n. 31 above) puts it: "Natural law extends to all our moral activity; natural right governs social relations and especially the practice of justice toward another" (31 n. 2) Cf. also J. Gründel in *Sacramentum mundi* 4 (New York: Herder and Herder. 1969) 157: "the natural law in a wide sense embraces the whole field of morality."

[52] Rigali states that he finds no "adequate discussion of it in contemporary theology." Whether he will consider them adequate or not, I cannot say; but to be recommended are B. Schüller, *Die Begründung sittlicher Urteile* (Düsseldorf: Patmos, 1973) and L. Janssens (n. 24 above).

antedating philosophical personalism, must be rethought today." Thus, killing in self-defense is not just a "physical, nonmoral, ontic evil ... it is a personal evil." On this basis he asks: "Does it really make sense today for moral theology to group together as the same kind of evil a surgical operation to remove cancer and killing in self-defense?" He then repeats his contention that contraception, as involving "a certain anti-personal element and as not completely compatible with the human fulfillment experienced through charity," contains a "morally negative element."

Rigali's kindness in attending to what I had written suggests reciprocation. As to his first concern—that the traditional view of the natural law artificially divided the moral call into minimal decency demands and counsels—I shall not contest it here.[53] Rigali, of course, uses this division to suggest that the moral law "might really be something more than what it (traditional view) conceived natural law to be." That may or may not be the case; but I think it is clearly not the issue. The issue is: Does Christian faith add concrete moral content to the moral law,[54] content that is in principle impervious to human insight and reasoning? That is an epistemological question.

If Christian revelation does produce such moral demands, then it must be said that they are mysterious precisely because unavailable to human insight and reasoning. I know of no moral theologian who has ever made that claim, though there are some who are coming perilously (and that is the right word, I believe) close to it. Specifically, if contraception is prohibited by the moral law—but at the level of what Rigali calls "supernatural charity"—this prohibition must still be available to human insight and reasoning, as Böckle noted above, even if this reasoning is informed by faith. Paul VI acknowledged this in *Humanae vitae* (no. 12): "We believe that the men of our day are particularly capable of seizing the deeply reasonable and human character of this fundamental principle." In summary, then, whether and how an adequate notion of moral law differs from the "classical notion" is not the issue. The issue is that a concrete moral demand, regardless of the notion of moral law that is its context, cannot be unavailable to human insight and reasoning.

I would disagree, then, with Rigali that moralists are asking the wrong question. Whether Christian belief adds concrete moral demands at the essential level not available to reason is enormously important. To the reasons already adduced for its importance,[55] this could be added: the reason-ability of concrete moral demands is a strong protection against abuse of authority in teaching morality.

[53] But cf. n. 51 above.
[54] Scil., at the essential level, the level applying to all human persons precisely as human persons.
[55] Cf. *TS* 38 (1977) 59.

That brings us to Rigali's second objection. Several points ought to be made. I know of no evidence that could support the assertion that the distinction between physical and moral evil is attributable to a "classical worldview." Some such distinction, even if in different words, is held throughout the contemporary philosophical and theological community. Secondly, when Rigali says killing is not just a nonmoral evil but a personal one, he is making a false comparison. Of course killing is a personal evil. It happens to persons, just as do deception, wounding, deprivation of property, harm to reputation. All theologians who use the terms "nonmoral," "ontic," and "premoral" understand these as personal evils. The question is only this: When is it morally right or wrong to cause or permit personal premoral evils? By insisting that they are personal evils, Rigali adds nothing to the determination of rightfulness or wrongfulness. If he thinks he does, then it would follow that it is *never* right to cause *any* evils in our conduct on the grounds that they are personal.

Thirdly, clearly a surgical operation to remove cancer differs from killing in self-defense. But are not both morally right? And if that is the case, then it means that the disvalues within these different actions are in the circumstances morally justified. And if that is the case, they ought not to be said to be *morally* evil. That is why contemporary theologians insist on calling a killing—until more is known about the circumstances—a premoral or nonmoral evil. In this sense both killing and amputation, while different, pertain to the same genre. For this reason I would deny that the antipersonal element Rigali finds in contraception is necessarily "not completely compatible with the fulfillment experienced through charity" and "is a *morally* negative element."

This section is already long and unwieldly. Before ending it, however, I would like to advert to two key notions in the discussion in an attempt to clarify continuing exchanges. They are "consequentialism" and "intrinsic evil."

As for so-called consequentialism, let the statement of William May introduce the matter. In speaking of what he calls "consequentialism," May writes that it is "at root a form of extrinsicism in ethics. It derives the meaning or intelligibility of human acts from their consequences or results, and these are not inherent or intrinsic to the acts but are extrinsic to them, added on to them. For the consequentialist, in other words, human acts are *of themselves* meaningless, neither good nor bad, neither right nor wrong."[56]

In my judgment, several things are seriously wrong with that account, and I believe that it no longer serves the purposes of constructive moral

---

[56] William May, "Contraception, Abstinence and Responsible Parenthood," *Faith and Reason* 3 (1977) 34–52.

discourse to argue as May does here. First, the statement trades on the generic and misleading term "consequentialist." There are many forms of teleology, just as there are many forms of deontology. I do not see the service to moral science to volunteer, for example, that all deontologists are at root physicalists or are guilty of a kind of naturalistic fallacy. Some may be. The same is true of teleology. Some teleologists may be extrinsicists. But there is nothing in the notion that demands it, otherwise Catholic tradition for centuries must be accused of extrinsicism; for this tradition was teleological in its understanding of norms in nearly all areas.

Secondly, it is simply erroneous to assert that writers like Böckle, Janssens, Schüller, Weber, Fuchs, *et al.* (all of whom are "proportionalists" in their understanding of moral norms) derive the meaning of actions from something "extrinsic to them, added to them," and that for such writers "human acts are *of themselves* meaningless." What these writers are asserting—and I include myself amongst them—is that the inherent goodness (and therefore meaning) of a promise is a *limited* goodness and may concur with a more urgent value demanding value preference. Catholic tradition has held this for centuries. In other words, if a promise need not always be kept, that conclusion does not deny, nor can it be logically forced to deny, the inherent meaning and value of promise-making. It denies only that this inherent good and meaning is an *absolute* value. That is what these authors mean when they refer to "breaking a promise," "deceiving another by falsehood," "killing a person," as premoral (or ontic) *evils*.

Finally, May asserts that for these writers "human acts are *of themselves* meaningless." Here he must inform us what he has in mind when he refers to a "human act." Breaking a promise perhaps? Directly killing a person? Using a contraceptive device? Obviously, no one of these is a human act. They become human acts, and patient of a judgment of rightness and wrongness, only when sufficient circumstances have been added to complete the picture. Thus, one breaks a promise (e.g., to attend a wedding) in order to give a dying accident victim life-saving first aid. *That* is patient of a moral assessment and we would all agree that the action is morally right. Now, why cannot something similar be said of, e.g., sterilization? As yet, that is not patient of a final judgment of rightness or wrongness. Or if it is, it is so only on the ground that integral intercourse is an *absolute* good, one that, regardless of conflicting goods and circumstances, always deserves the preference. One can, of course, maintain that. But in doing so, he is saying something about the integrity of intercourse that Catholic tradition has been unwilling to say about life itself. In my judgment, that is exactly what W. D. Ross has in mind when he speaks of breaking a promise or uttering a falsehood as prima facie (and that only) morally wrong.[57] In summary, proportionalists cannot be accused of holding, or being forced to hold, that actions have no meaning in themselves. They maintain only that no final assessment of rightness or wrongness can be made until more has been said of the action than that it is "breaking a promise." And if that is the case, they wonder, correctly, why this must not apply to all acts so described.

The second very misleading usage in this discussion is the central importance attributed to the notion of "intrinsic evil." Thus May, Stoeckle, Ermecke, *et al.* have accused Schüller, Fuchs, Janssens, *et al.* of espousing a methodology which does not allow for this concept, and hence one that allows for exceptions to norms proscribing, e.g., adultery.

Several things need to be said here. First, the notion of intrinsic evil has such a variety of understandings[58] that it is all but useless in contemporary discourse. Secondly, many contemporary theologians are primarily concerned with departing from the term *as it has been used in recent theological and magisterial literature,* a point that will become even clearer in the next section of these "Notes." In that literature, certain kinds of actions (directly killing an innocent person, direct sterilization) have been proscribed as always wrong regardless of circumstances or consequences. These theologians argue that these contentions have not been satisfactorily established. In other words, they are primarily discoursing with their own tradition, and arguing that one cannot isolate the object of an act and say of it that it is *always* wrong in *any* conceivable circumstances. One can, of course, begin to add a variety of circumstances to the description of an object so that such an action is always wrong. For instance: abortion of a fetus in order to avoid a medical (delivery) bill. That is always wrong—and, if one wishes, intrinsically wrong (scil., *praeceptum quia malum,* not *malum quia praeceptum*). There are a whole host of actions that fit this category; but when one says that, he must realize that he is no longer speaking of the object of the action *as used in recent theological and magisterial literature.*

Thirdly, and therefore, these theologians are arguing that when an action is always morally wrong, it is so not because of unnaturalness or defect of right (as recent tradition contends), but because when *taken as a whole,* the nonmoral evil outweighs the nonmoral good, and therefore the action is disproportionate. One can legitimately continue to call such an action intrinsically evil,[59] but I see no great gain in doing so. Indeed, it is confusing; for the term is associated unavoidably with its usage in recent tradition. This association suggests the validity of the analysis of

---

[57] W. D. Ross, *The Right and the Good* (Oxford, 1965).

[58] Cf. James Murtagh, *Intrinsic Evil* (Rome, 1973).

[59] Walter Jeffko does; cf. his careful study "Processive Relationism and Ethical Absolutes," *American Benedictine Review* 26 (1975) 283–97.

actions (described without circumstances) as morally wrong *because unnatural* (contraception) or *because of lack of right* (direct killing of an innocent person). Thus the term is tied to a kind of deontological understanding of moral norms that (*a*) has been persuasively argued to be invalid, and (*b*) has been shown to be inconsistent with the teleological grounding of norms in every other area of Catholic tradition.

These analytic differences between theologians should not blind us to the vast area of agreement we share and ought to be reflecting to the world. We are at one in treasuring basic human values such as life, the family, and childbearing, and it would be a pastoral disservice to allow our differences to usurp center stage; for more than ever in our time we need to support people in their desires and efforts to avoid failure "against the very meaning of conjugal life" (Pius XII).

THE PRINCIPLE OF DOUBLE EFFECT

For many decades, even centuries, some crucial moral conflicts have been approached and solved through use of the principle of the double effect. This is intimately associated with the discussion of moral norms, but it deserves separate treatment.

Franz Scholz approaches the moral relevance of the direct-indirect distinction through the study of two sets of notions: object-circumstances, essential effect and side effect.[60] In the narrow sense of the word, found in the manual tradition, "circumstance" referred to an aspect of human action which was "extra substantiam existens" (Thomas). Thus there grew a gradual association of the notion of circumstances with that of accident. But, as Scholz points out, some circumstances affect the very essence or substance of human action. This variability of circumstance is too easily overlooked when the idea is associated with "accident."

Scholz next turns to the notions of accidental and essential effects. Essential effects are those that proceed from the substance or essence of the action. Accidental effects are not produced by the substance but indicate that more than one cause is at work. Now when circumstances pertain to the very essence or object of the act, they cannot be said to produce side effects that are merely accidental. Thus the key question is: Which circumstances must in a given case be counted in the object itself, which remain accidental? This cannot be determined a priori; rather, reality itself is the test. Once we have determined this, we will know which actions are necessarily direct and which indirect.

To illustrate these rather fine speculative points (which he gives in considerable detail), Scholz cites three examples from the manual tradi-

---

[60] Franz Scholz, "Objekt und Umstande, Wesenswirkungen und Nebeneffekte," in *Christlich glauben und handeln,* ed. Klaus Demmer and Bruno Schüller (Düsseldorf: Patmos, 1977) 243–60. This is the *Festschrift* honoring Joseph Fuchs, S.J.

tion. (1) An unarmed person meets a deadly enemy intent on killing him. The only escape is by horse and on a road occupied by a group of blind and crippled persons. He rides down the road, killing and maiming many people as he escapes. Traditional manuals argued that the presence of the cripples was accidental; thus there is question of a circumstance that remains external to the object; hence the deaths were side effects. (2) Innocent persons are present in a fortress attacked by the enemy. The attacker says he does not will their deaths, but only the cause (the explosion) and not the effect. (3) A person performs an act *minus rectum* (scandal) and foresees that another will thereby be given an occasion of sin.

Scholz asks: Are we concerned with side effects in these examples, which are patient of indirectness? To the first two he says no; to the third, yes. In the first case, e.g., some authors describe the act as "fleeing down the road on a horse." By what principle do they set the boundaries between object and circumstances? Excluding the blind and the crippled from the object contradicts reality. Scholz sees this as "preprogrammed object." One degrades what is essential to the action to a side effect, but at the cost of a mistaken reading of reality. The presence of the blind and crippled on the road is of such significance that it pertains to the very *object*. And if it does, it is a part of essential effects, not side effects. The escaper cannot say he only "permitted" the deaths. The deaths and injuries are *means*. "But the means, just as the ends, can only be directly intended."[61] We would have a true side effect if, in the case described, the victims threw themselves at the last moment unavoidably into the path of the horse. In that case the rider could say: "I must permit what I cannot prevent."

As for the second case, the attacking general might say that he wishes only to kill combatants. But actually the one natural effect of the bombing is destruction—of soldiers, civilians, beasts. His regret at the death of innocents means only that their deaths are not *propter se sed propter aliud*. Their deaths are a *conditio sine qua non*. But "he who is ready—under the call of the end—to realize the condition *sine qua non*, acts exactly as the one who chooses the appropriate means, scil., directly."[62] Therefore, in these first two cases Scholz does not believe the deaths are indirect. Rather, they are a modified form of direct willing (scil., *secundum quid,* with regrets).

In the third case (scandal) we have a true side effect. He who seeks his goal by an *actio minus recta* does not cause the neighbor's sin. The operation of another cause is necessary for a true side effect. Therefore, the psychology of the will does not demand that the evil effect be willed either as a means or as a *conditio sine qua non*.

---

[61] Ibid. 256.   [62] Ibid. 257.

Since so many of the conflicts that were previously solved by the direct-indirect distinction really represent qualified forms of direct willing, Scholz moves to another model and espouses it: "direct, yes, but only for a proportionate reason." He sees this as not only more honest to reality but as advantageous. First, the direct confrontation of the will with the evil caused by it "ought to be to the benefit of a weighing of values" (*Güterabwägung*). Secondly, looking evil in the eye is healthy. It avoids development of an "exoneration mentality" associated with phrases such as "not directly willed," "only permitted." Finally, "the broken human condition with its tragic character appears more starkly. Unavoidably we become conscious of the fact that man not only cannot have, hold, and protect all goods simultaneously, but that he can be called, in the service of higher goods, to injure lesser premoral values, and that without any *animus nocendi*."[63]

Here, then, is yet another theologian who argues that every human choice is the resolution of a conflict, that the direct-indirect distinction is only descriptive, and that when actions were legitimated *as indirect* permitting of evil, actually they were morally direct in most cases, even if in qualified form (*secundum quid*, with regrets: "I would not be prepared to do this unless I had to"). Hence Scholz is arguing that there is no morally significant difference between direct and indirect actions where nonmoral evils are concerned.

Albert R. Di Ianni, S.M., accurately reviews the work of Grisez, Schüller, Fuchs, Janssens, Van der Marck, Van der Poel, and myself in this area.[64] He makes two moves. One is a kind of terminological adjustment. The other, the second half of his long essay, exposes his own understanding of the importance of the direct-indirect distinction.

He first insists on the distinction between a nonmoral evil (death) and the free causation of that evil (homicide). Then of homicide he states that "the concept of the free causation of death has at least minimal *moral* meaning in itself prior to consideration of intention and circumstances." This minimal moral meaning makes the act "'intrinsically evil' though in a weaker sense than that of the tradition." That is, it would not always be forbidden regardless of the circumstances. And when it is tolerable, it will generate what Di Ianni calls "creative regret." Why does he insist on this "minimal *moral* meaning"? In his own words: "To treat it as a mere nonmoral evil leans too far in the direction of act-utilitarianism or situationism which demands the voiding of the intrinsic moral meaning of all action concepts."[65]

---

[63] Ibid. 259.
[64] Albert R. Di Ianni, S.M., "The Direct/Indirect Distinction in Morals," *Thomist* 41 (1977) 350–80.
[65] Ibid. 362.

His second step is to explain positively why he believes the direct-indirect distinction (as in killing) is morally relevant. Some years ago I had argued that direct killing of the innocent, as in indiscriminate bombing, is wrong because of the long-term effects such killing would have, scil., life itself would be worse off by the brutalizing of sensitivities, the release of violence associated with it, and the ultimate unavoidable debasing of the moral currency.[66] Di Ianni agrees with this assessment of consequences but does not believe it is the reason the direct killing is wrong in the first place. It is wrong because it is violative of what he calls "dignity-values" (vs. "welfare-values"). What do these terms mean? "Values of welfare center about the fulfillment of whatever potentials for action and enjoyment an entity might have: life, health, pleasure, power, etc." Values of dignity have little to do with these things. "The values of dignity are such things as self-respect, autonomy, fidelity, justice, trust, integrity and the like."[67] These dignity values are of far greater importance and must be given greater weight in conflict situations.

What has this distinction to do with the direct-indirect distinction? Di Ianni sees the latter distinction as both valid and practically valuable. "It is valid because it generally generates conclusions which coincide with the conclusions generated by the more basic dignity/welfare value distinction. It is moreover practically valuable as a tool because of its greater tangibility."[68] By this he means that while value considerations are often murky, the direct-indirect distinction trades directly on the level of action. Concretely, Di Ianni asserts that to aim at an innocent person's death as an end or even as a means to a good end "is usually to treat him as an object, as a non-person (a non-freedom), as a mere means, whereas to aim at a proportionate good knowing that evil to another person will also arise as a not-aimed-at side-effect is to produce some illfare but is not a violation of dignity."[69]

How far would Di Ianni carry this? Not, he says, to the extent of a theoretical behavioral absolute, so that direct killing of an innocent could never be done whatever the consequences. Rather, it is a practical behavioral absolute. He cites a "fantastic case where someone threatens to kill 100,000 if you do not kill one." Of this he says that an "overwhelming quantity of welfare may override a small consideration of dignity."

This interesting study deserves several comments. First, I want to put a question to Di Ianni about the moral relevance of the direct-indirect distinction. He argues that direct killing of an innocent person, in addition to visiting illfare upon him, also visits indignity on the victim, "whereas

[66] *Ambiguity in Moral Choice* (Milwaukee: Marquette Univ., 1973).
[67] Di Ianni, "The Direct/Indirect Distinction" 370.
[68] Ibid. 372.   [69] Ibid. 377.

indirect killing when there is a proportionate reason causes illfare alone."
Why? Because, he says, direct killing is to treat him as an object, a
mere means. Here it must be asked why this is not true also of foreseen
indirect killing. Unless Di Ianni says more about the meaning of direct
and indirect intent, that difference seems stipulative. That is, it supposes
the very thing that is to be established, scil., that there is a *morally*
significant difference in the two types of action. As stipulative, therefore,
it seems to beg the question.

An indication of this is Di Ianni's statement that the distinction
between direct and indirect "is valid because it *generally* generates
conclusions which coincide with the conclusions generated by the more
basic dignity-welfare distinction." Furthermore, he says that to kill another as a means is *usually* to treat that person as an object. If the
distinction is valid as such, why is it not *always* applicable? The fact
that it is not indicates that it is not the morally decisive element.

Secondly, Di Ianni has engaged the author of these "Notes" and
disagreed with my explanation of the wrongfulness of, e.g., indiscriminate
bombing. In this I believe he is correct. Through the kind criticisms of
thoughtful colleagues, I have modified this teleological understanding of
the wrongfulness of many direct killings, without, however, abandoning
the teleology itself, as I shall attempt to indicate below. In other words,
there is another understanding of proportionate reason than the one I
gave.

Third, Di Ianni insists that actions such as homicide, prior to the
addition of circumstances, have "minimal moral meaning." He contrasts
this with the position on evil of Fuchs (premoral), Schüller (nonmoral),
and Janssens (ontic). These latter terms, he says, refer to "mere nonmoral
evil" and thus "lean too far in the direction of . . . situationism" because
they void actions of intrinsic moral meaning. Actually, we have here a
lis de verbo; for these authors all have obligational statements to offer
about our attitudes and actions with regard to nonmoral evils—scil.,
that they are to be avoided in so far as compatibly (with other conflicting
values) possible. And all would agree with Di Ianni that there is a place
for "creative regret." Several (e.g., Janssens) explicitly mention this.

Fourth, one might argue that Di Ianni has but an artificial distinction
when he contrasts dignity values with welfare values. I mean that actions
which assault or promote dignity pertain to one's welfare, are for or
against a person's welfare. Certainly, the authors who appeal to proportionate reason as that which in principle justifies disvalues in our actions
include in the notion of proportionate reason what Di Ianni calls dignity
values. This is clear, e.g., in the insistence we find in Janssens and
Schüller on the notion of expressive actions (*Ausdruckshandlungen*) in

measuring proportion. Therefore, dignity values do not eliminate teleology in the understanding of norms; rather, they form a part of it.

Fifth, it is necessary to ask Di Ianni how big a disaster would have to be before he is willing to call a direct killing of an innocent person "a small consideration of dignity." If he proposes, as he does, that a hundred thousand lives saved would be an "overwhelming quantity of welfare," why not one hundred, or even ten?

Sixth, it is clear that Di Ianni shares in the teleological tendencies of the theologians he cites, in so far as he rejects "intrinsic evil in the very strong sense." How far he departs and in what areas would be much clearer had he said more about falsehood, sterilization, and other (than killing) problems. This strong sense of the term is the sense in the writings of authors like Paul Ramsey, Germain Grisez, and William May. This rejection of "intrinsic evil in the strong sense" is what is common to theologians like Fuchs, Böckle, Weber, Janssens, Schüller, and Scholz, and is where the discussion really originated. Furthermore, I believe it is the heart of the matter. But such a rejection necessarily implies *some form* of teleology. Whether it is useful to retain the term "intrinsic evil" at all once this move has been made is highly questionable, as was noted above.

This brings us to the notion of proportionate reason. Above I suggested that it is the crucial notion in this discussion. Di Ianni would agree in principle to that statement. There are many ways in which that term can be explained, just as there are many considerations that go into its proper understanding. That is why reference was made to *some form* of teleology. For instance, Schüller and Janssens have emphasized the importance of expressive actions and institutional obligations in reading proportion. The former are very close to so-called "dignity values." The latter (institutional obligations) refer to duties that stem from the existence and necessity of institutions (like contracts) for stable social life. Thus, in the case of judicial murder (the judge who frames one innocent person to prevent a rioting mob from killing more in reprisal), Schüller argues that the action is morally wrong because the entire institution of criminal law is at stake.

Where proportionality is concerned, a further word about the term "consequences" is called for. Böckle noted above that an ever-increasing number of theologians trace rightness and wrongness to consequences. Many react immediately against such a notion, because it suggests to them all kinds of unacceptable things. It suggests, e.g., that torture or extortion or adultery may be morally right if they produce sufficiently good results or net good. In other words, it suggests in undifferentiated form that "a good end justifies an evil means." Thus the reaction.

Actually, that is not what is meant by the term in recent Catholic writing nor what the term can be forced to mean. By referring to consequences, recent writing means two things. First, and negatively, it means a rejection of the notion of intrinsic evil *in the strong sense* (Di Ianni's phrase). This strong sense states moral wrongness of an action (e.g., direct sterilization) independently of consequences and circumstances. Secondly, and positively, the term "consequences" means that all things must be considered before a final moral judgment of rightness or wrongness can be made. By saying "all things must be considered," these authors do not mean *total net good* as this term is often understood (scil., mere welfare values). The usage "total net good" (or evil) too easily excludes from consideration factors that go into determining proportion (expressive actions [dignity values], institutional obligations, etc.).

Another study suggests possible ways of reading proportion.[70] The oft-repeated argument of some authors (e.g., Ramsey, Grisez, May) for resisting analyses such as those of Knauer, Janssens, and Schüller is that the basic goods are incommensurable. Those who shift the major emphasis in cases of conflict to proportionate reason are (so the argument goes) measuring the incommensurable. If one attempts to do that, he is unavoidably involved in a form of consequentialism that determines the moral wrongness and rightness of an action according to "greatest net good"—not only an incoherent notion, as the long philosophical discussions of utilitarianism have revealed, but also one that is at odds with some basic Christian convictions. In other words, one does not suppress one basic good for the sake of another one *equally* basic. The only way to cut the Gordian knot when basic values are conflicted is to only indirectly allow the defeat of one as the other is pursued. As Paul Ramsey words it in a forthcoming study:

My own view is that the distinction between direct and indirect voluntariety is pertinent and alerts our attention as moral agents to those moral choices where incommensurable conflicting values are at stake, where there is no measurable resolution of value conflicts on a single scale, where there are gaps in any supposed hierarchy of values, and therefore no way to determine exactly the greater or lesser good or evil.... Where there is no single scale or common denominator, or where there is discontinuity in the hierarchy of goods or evils, one ought not turn against any human good.[71]

Those who put the major emphasis on proportionality in situations of

[70] Richard A. McCormick, S.J., "Le principe du double effet," in *Discerner les valeurs pour fonder la morale* (= *Concilium* 120) 105–20. This is not available in English but only in French, Spanish, Italian, Dutch, and German.

[71] Paul Ramsey and Richard A. McCormick, S.J., *Doing Evil to Achieve Good: Moral Choice in Conflict Situations* (forthcoming).

conflicted goods might respond in any number of ways. For instance, negatively they might urge that if proportionate reason involves measuring the unmeasurable, then what is the meaning and function of proportionate reason in the standard understandings of the double effect? They might ask why an "indirect killing" does not involve one in turning against a basic good? In other words, they would press the matter of the *moral* (not merely descriptive) relevance of directness as this was understood traditionally.

A concrete vehicle for bringing these questions into clearer focus is the classic, even if rare, obstetrical case where the physician faces two options: either he aborts the fetus and thus saves the mother, or he does not abort and both mother and child die. Both those who defend the moral relevance of the direct-indirect distinction in such instances (e.g., Ramsey, Grisez) and those who question it agree on the conclusion; that is not at issue. What is at issue is the reason for the conclusion. The defenders of the traditional distinction would argue that the conclusion is correct in so far as, and only in so far as, the death of the fetus can be said to be indirect. The revisionists, so to speak, would argue that the real reason for the conclusion is that *in such circumstances* the abortion is proportionately grounded, is the lesser evil. When one is faced with two options both of which involve unavoidable (nonmoral) evil, one ought to choose the lesser evil. To argue that the intervention is morally right because it is "indirect" is, on this view, to use a notion that is adventitious, unnecessary, and ultimately indecisive.

The common response to such an argument is that if this is true, then what is known in philosophical circles as "the Caiphas principle" is valid. That is, one is justified in sacrificing one innocent person to save five. The example often used is that of a sheriff or judge in a Southern town faced with the alternatives in a rape case of framing a black suspect (whom he knows to be innocent) or carrying on a prolonged search for the real culprit. The immediate indictment and conviction of the suspect would save many lives and prevent other harmful consequences. If an action's moral rightness is determined solely by the consequences (one innocent killed vs. many innocent killed), then it seems that the sheriff ought to frame the one innocent person—a conclusion that shocks our moral sensitivities, but one that a revisionist on the double effect would seem forced to draw.

At this point the revisionist would return to the insistence on the words "in these circumstances" in the abortion dilemma given above. In the abortion dilemma the situation is not simply a save-one vs. lose-two dilemma. It is not simply quantitative. It must be added that the deadly deed is intrinsically and inescapably connected with the saving of the mother's life, whether that deadly deed be a craniotomy or the removal of the fetus to get at a life-threatening aneurysm. That is to say, there is in the very nature of the case no way of saving the mother. There is an essential link between the means and the end. By contrast, however, I argue that such a link does not exist in the sheriff instance. There is no inherent connection between the killing of an innocent person and the change of mind of a lynch mob. For those who hold to the notion of free will in the doing of evil (and good), there is never an inherent connection between killing an innocent person and changing the murderous mind of a lynch mob. In other words, in the abortion case one chooses to save the life that can be saved because in such circumstances that is the lesser evil, is proportionately grounded. In other circumstances it would not be the lesser evil, would not be proportionate.

The article further argues that seeing proportionate reason as the crucial element in situations of conflict need not at all involve one in measuring the immeasurable. There are times, of course, when genuine measuring in the strict sense is appropriate: e.g., when merely instrumental goods and basic goods conflict. One sacrifices the instrumental for the basic, because instrumental goods are lesser in the order of goods. Thus, one prefers life to property. This is a strict weighing of values.

But such is clearly not possible where basic goods are concerned. But neither is it necessary. While the basic goods are not commensurable (one *against* the other), they are clearly associated goods. Thus, one who unjustifiably takes human life also undermines other human goods, and these human goods, once weakened or undermined, will affect the very good of life itself.

Let marriage and birth control be another example. Two distinct but closely associated goods are involved: the procreative good, the communicative (unitive) good. With this in mind, Paul Ramsey justifies contraception as follows: "In these matters ... there are no moral judgments for which proportionate reason is not the guiding preference-principle." He immediately explains this as follows: "Will not the manner of protecting the good (procreative) undermine it in the long run by serious injury to an associated good (the communicative good)?"[72] The "manner of protecting it" means here periodic continence or the so-called rhythm method. Practically, this means that the possible ineffectiveness[73] and forced and perhaps prolonged periods of abstention can easily harm the communicative good and *thereby* the procreative good itself. The Second Vatican Council said something very similar when it stated that "where the intimacy of married life is broken off, it is not rare for its faithfulness to be imperiled and its quality of fruitfulness ruined."[74] That seems to

[72] Cf. n. 71 above.

[73] I say "possible" in deference to those who urge that when properly practiced (precise and recent knowledge, high motivation) periodic continence has a very high rate of success.

[74] Cf. *Gaudium et spes*, no. 51.

me to be a reasonable account of things. It is precisely concern for the procreative good, but as related to and supported by the communicative good, that leads Ramsey to conclude to the moral rectitude of contraception and, if necessary, sterilization.

Clearly *some kind of measuring* is going on there. The incommensurability of goods (procreative, communicative) is reduced by seeing them in interrelationship. And it is this interrelationship that provides the context—a kind of single scale—in which decisions are possible and reasonable, and adoption of personal and community policies (hierarchy) is not completely arbitrary.

Could not something very similar be said of the case of the Southern sheriff above (and, by extension, of the immorality of obliteration bombing)? The manner of protecting the good (human life—by framing one innocent person) will undermine it in the long run by serious injury to an associated good (human liberty); for by killing an innocent person to prevent others from unjustly killing five innocent persons, one equivalently denies the freedom of these others. That is the very moral meaning of extortion. One supposes by his action that the cessation of others from wrongdoing is necessarily dependent on my doing harm. Such a supposition denies, and thereby undermines, human freedom. And because such freedom is an associated good upon which the very good of life itself depends, undermining it in the manner of my defense of life is undermining life itself—is disproportionate.

Here, again, one does not exactly weigh life *against* freedom; one merely associates the associable and reads proportion within such an interrelationship. That is why Schüller seems absolutely correct in insisting that in this and similar cases it is not simply a matter of the life of one versus the life of many others; the entire institution of criminal law is at stake. And that is how proportion must be read.

Let obliteration bombing be another test case. Those who would defend such counterpeople (vs. counterforce) attacks argue that they will save more lives. This was Truman's argument. The choice is seen as between taking a hundred thousand Nagasakian lives or losing double or triple that number from both sides in a prolonged conventional war.

If the article under review is correct (that proportionate reason reigns even where the taking of human life is concerned), then there must be a way of showing that Truman's understanding of proportion was wrong—if we hold it to be such, as I do. I believe there is.

Let us again use Ramsey's formulation. "Will not the manner of protecting the good (human life—by ending the war) undermine it in the long run by serious injury to an associated good (human liberty)?" Making innocent (noncombatant) persons the object of our targeting is a form of extortion in international affairs that contains an implicit denial of human freedom. Human freedom is undermined when extortionary actions are accepted and elevated and universalized. Because such freedom is an "associated good" upon which the very good of life heavily depends, undermining it in the manner of my defense of life is undermining life itself—is disproportionate. John Locke understood this association of goods very well:

For I have reason to conclude that he who gets me into his power without my consent, would use me as he pleased when he got me there, and destroy me too, when he had a fancy to it.... He that in the state of nature would take away the freedom that belongs to any one in that state must be supposed to have a design to take away everything else, that freedom being the foundation of all the rest....[75]

Perhaps it would be helpful to put this in another way and in explicitly Christian terms. It is the Christian's faith that another's ceasing from his wrongdoing is *never* dependent on my doing nonmoral evil; for the Christian believes that we are truly what we are, redeemed in Christ. We are still threatened by the *reliquiae peccati*, but are free and powerful in Christ's grace. We rejoice in our infirmities, that the grace of Christ may abound in us. And we know the powers of that grace—in Magdalen (and many Magdalens), in the martyrs, in the likes of Thomas More, Matthew Talbot, and a host of others. Others can cease their evil-doing without our connivance in it, without our doing harm to persuade and entice them. We are free. That is our Christian bet as persons who know our freedom in Christ.

That is why the *essential connection* between aborting and saving the one who can be saved is so important in the classical abortion case. No such connection exists in the instance of the rioting mob. They can cease their evil-doing without our doing harm to make them cease. To yield to their demands would be a denial to them of their own freedom. And that freedom is an associated good which must be asserted and protected if the good of life itself is to survive. We may lose some lives in sticking to this conviction, but that is where our trust in God's providence is on the line. Because people can, with God's gracious help, cease evil-doing, our doing harm to make them cease is unjustifiable, disproportionate. The judicious Christian reads his proportions not just by looking at numbers, but by looking at many other features of the situation within which the numerical must be interpreted.

Something very similar can be said, I believe, about the conduct of warfare. But before saying it, we must recall the teaching of Pius XII, the most extensive and detailed papal elaboration of the just-war theory

[75] John Locke, *An Essay concerning the True Original Extent and End of Civil Government,* in *Of Civil Government* (New York: Dutton, n.d.; no. 751 of Everyman's Library) 125.

in all of history. Pius XII, contrary to some earlier theological formulations, restricted the *jus ad bellum* (the just cause for going to war) to national self-defense. War, he taught, can be justified as a response *ad repellendas injurias* (to repel injury or aggression), not for settlement of other disputes, even the most serious (*ad vindicandas offensiones, ad recuperandas res*). Now the implication of this limitation of just cause to self-defense means that the other nation is the aggressor—in short, is engaged in wrongful conduct. It may at times be difficult to say who was the original aggressor, but that does not eliminate the need of *an* aggressor as the sole justification for going to war.

If a nation is wrongfully aggressing, once again it is the Christian's faith, and a well-founded one, that that nation can and must cease and desist from wrongful aggression without our doing harm to noncombatants to make that nation do so. There is no *necessary connection* between our doing harm to noncombatants (e.g., killing innocent civilians to stop that nation) and that nation's ceasing unjust aggression. To say that there is would be to insult the humanity of the aggressor by denying his liberty; for unjust aggressors are free to cease unjust aggression. Christ did not invent that idea, of course, but by his graceful redemption he powerfully restated it to a world that too often came to terms with its inhumanities as "necessary," "culturally imposed," etc. And by denying the aggressor's freedom, we deny our own by implication, thus removing the conditions for any rationality in war. That is why, I believe, the Christian judges attacks upon noncombatants as disproportionate.

Ultimately, then, the article concludes, revisionists admit a descriptive difference between actions involving nonmoral evil directly and indirectly. That is, the directness or indirectness of an effect tells us what is being sought and by what means and in what circumstances. These in combination reveal the significance of the action. Whether the action is, as a whole, morally right or wrong depends on this significance; for significance reveals what other values are at stake, and therefore whether the manner of the pursuit of the good here and now is destructive of it or not. In other words, it reveals whether in the action as a whole the good outweighs the evil, whether there is a truly proportionate reason or not. And it is the presence or absence of such a reason that determines whether the attitude of the agent is adequate or not, whether he is choosing rightly or wrongly, whether he remains open to the basic goods or closes one of them off in pursuit of another, whether or not one chooses against a basic good, or, in Pius XII's words, whether one "sins against the very meaning of conjugal life."

This analysis is quite tentative. But it seems not without points to recommend it. Moral theologians will undoubtedly clarify their analyses as this exchange progresses. But one thing seems increasingly clear: there are fewer and fewer theologians ready to defend "intrinsic evil in the strong sense," as Di Ianni phrases it.

THE CHURCH AND HUMAN RIGHTS

The advent of the Carter administration with its heavy priority on human rights has coincided with a continuing interest in human rights as embodied in liberation theology, and the concern of the Church more generally in this subject. Here I shall review a few more general statements and then turn to several specific areas where human rights have been involved.

During August 1977, twenty-two theologians (ten Catholic, ten Protestant, two Orthodox) from the Third World (Latin America, Asia, Africa) met in Tanzania at the University of Dar-es-Salaam. They issued an interesting manifesto on theology in the Third World.[76] After scoring the colonizing character of Christian roots on these continents and highlighting contemporary Christian strivings for genuine liberation from all enslavement (especially foreign), they make a strong theological protest. The theologies coming from Europe and North America, issuing as they do from situations proper to these countries, represent a form of cultural domination in the Third World. Questioning the pertinence of these theologies for their countries, the theologians declare themselves "prepared for a radical rupture in the epistemological area, in order to make engagement the first act of theology...." The task of theology in their countries, they insist, is to "practice a self-critique with regard to the condition of theology itself." For them, this means that theology must better represent God's invitations and purposes as seen in the needs of the oppressed and the poor. A very interesting, if sometimes simplistic manifesto.

The International Theological Commission has issued a long study on liberation theology.[77] It is an attempt to deal with basic issues touching the relationship between human development and Christian salvation. This attempt acknowledges that no one should condemn liberation theologies "if he or she is not listening at the same time to the cries of the poor and seeking more acceptable ways to respond." The report then asks whether "the types of theological reflection currently in vogue are, in their actual methodology, the only way of responding appropriately to yearnings for a more human world of brothers and sisters."

The report first presents the basic outlines of liberation theology. This theology maintains the profound unity that links the divine history of salvation to efforts for the welfare and rights of people. Thus, although

---

[76] "Pour une théologie dans le Tiers-Monde," *Relations* 37 (1977) 42–45.

[77] "Human Development and Christian Salvation," tr. Walter J. Burghardt, S.J., *Origins* 7 (1977) 305–13.

secular history and salvation are not identical, they should be conceived in the first instance as a unity. The construction of a just society is, in a sense, the inauguration of God's kingdom in anticipation. For this reason, Christian faith is to be understood principally as a historical praxis whereby sociopolitical conditions are changed and renewed.

The reports admits that there are here "many elements of great value." But it issues two caveats. First, the gospel of Jesus Christ must not be consolidated with secular history. The dynamism of God's word must not be reduced totally to its "function of stimulating social and political change." Secondly, theological theories attempting to build a more humane society must use sociological theories. There are risks here, particularly that of uncritically accepting the assumptions of Marxism.

There follows an excursus into biblical theology on the notion of liberation. Finally, the report attempts a systematic analysis of God as liberator and man's liberating action. It is impossible to summarize this careful study, but I think it fair to say that the following are some salient points. (1) Only God is properly liberator. (2) By His grace He sharpens our consciences to form a more just world. (3) Liberation must begin with *metanoia*. But full liberation is not accomplished in the course of earthly events. (4) The power of sin does penetrate social and political institutions. These unjust structures must be reformed.

The final point analyzed by the Theological Commission is the relation between human development and divine salvation. Here we see a series of *sic et non* assertions. For example, human activity and Christian hope must be neither "divorced" nor seen in terms of "evolutionary optimism." Or again, the earthly city and the heavenly city "ought to penetrate each other." Still again, there is unity between human effort and eschatological salvation, but a distinction. The report adverts to the usage of the 1971 Synod of Bishops which stated that the process of transforming the world must be seen "as a constitutive element (*ratio constitutiva*) of the preaching of the gospel." It grants that *ratio constitutiva* is controverted but concludes that, strictly speaking, the phrase means "integral part, not an essential part."

This document is well informed and carefully wrought. It deserves meditative study. My own reading of the document leads me to believe that the members of the Commission, while maintaining an unyielding unity that links human effort to eschatological salvation, felt it necessary "to spell out again with even sharper clarity the distinction between them." Should we conclude that this is a reflection on the emphases present in the works of other theologians? A good question.[78]

---

[78] One of the finest brief introductions to the theological emphases of liberation theology is that of Monika Hellwig, "Liberation Theology: An Emerging School," *Scottish Journal of Theology* 30 (1977) 137–51. Cf. also Michel Schooyans, "Chemins et impasses de la théologie de la libération," *Esprit et vie* 87 (1977) 81–94.

At any rate, there can be little doubt that the formulations of the Theological Commission ("integral part") reflect the views of Pope Paul VI. In the course of a general audience (Feb. 23, 1977), the Holy Father addressed a group of missionaries and reminded them that at the heart of evangelization is the proclamation that salvation is offered to all in the blood of Jesus.[79] He then added: "However, there is no doubt that everything that touches human promotion, that is, the work for justice, development, and peace in all parts of the world, ought also to be an *integral part* of the message.... Do not separate human liberation and salvation in Jesus Christ, without however identifying them...." Salvation, in Pope Paul's words, "is an end that both transcends and at the same time orients all human liberation."

In a background paper preparatory to the Commission's deliberations, Hans Urs von Balthasar discusses the notion of salvation, and especially that of the kingdom of God.[80] It is within that broader concept that liberation must be viewed. He sees modern history as a succession of attempts to secularize the message of salvation in various forms of "auto-liberation." While critical of the notion of "sinful structures," von Balthasar is far from denying the reality this term tries to articulate. Indeed, he urges that "now more than ever, competent Christians have to be engaged in the social, economic and political sectors...." The conclusion of this interesting essay:

The critique to which liberation theology is submitted does not question the urgency of the practical preoccupations that inspires it. But the totality of divine revelation to the world cannot in any case be confined to political and social liberation, nor even to the general notion of freedom. The theology of liberation has its specific place in the midst of a theology of the kingdom of God. It presents *an* aspect of all of theology....[81]

For a contrasting view, see that of S. Kierkegaard in the interesting study of Patrick Hanssens.[82] Kierkegaard, while insisting that faith and ethics were tightly interdependent, felt that the expression of charity in political activity was a waste of time. "In his eyes the realization of a more just social structure had no immediate Christian significance."

A consultation on the theology of human rights was held in 1976 by the Department of Studies of the Lutheran World Federation. At this

[79] Paul VI, in *Documentation catholique* 74 (1977) 307.

[80] Hans Urs von Balthasar, "Considérations sur l'histoire de salut," *Nouvelle revue théologique* 99 (1977) 518–31.

[81] Ibid. 531.

[82] Patrick Hanssens, "Ethique et foi," *Nouvelle revue théologique* 99 (1977) 360–80. For some considerations on justice and its relation to charity, cf. Cl. Mertens, "Charité, vérité, justice," ibid. 391–405.

consultation Prof. Heinz-Edward Tödt (Heidelberg) presented a study on this question.[83] He noted a "nuclear structure" of human rights that has persisted more or less clearly amidst diversities over the past two hundred years. That is, there are three essential elements in the basic rights-pattern: freedom, equality, and participation. All codified human rights turn out in any given case to be a concrete form of this basic pattern. For example, the habeas-corpus group of laws (inviolability of the person, protection against arbitrary arrest, right of fair trial, etc.) are related to freedom, even though questions of equality are inextricably interwoven. The prohibition of discrimination on the basis of race, sex, color, religion, or class relates to the right of equality, while the claim to have some control in and share of public affairs is based on a right to participate.

But after reading Tödt's study carefully several times, I am far from clear what his basic idea is. He is clear that human rights in the legal community are not founded on or based in theological considerations. These rights cluster around the notions of liberty, equality, and participation. Tödt sees parallels of this in the Christian community. For instance, as a human right equality asserts that individuals deserve equal protection before law. The grounds for this are often obscured in real life, because it is precisely the inequality of persons that so often practically obtrudes. Theologically, however, the Christian community has learned that "you are all sons of God in union with Christ Jesus. ... There is no such thing as Jew and Greek, slave and freeman, male and female ..." (Gal 3:26 ff.). Something similar is true of participation. By his inherent worth the individual claims a share in his own governance and in public life. In the Church the believer becomes a full participator (priesthood of the Christian) by baptism.

Yet, while there are similarities in the legal sphere and the Christian sphere, Tödt sees differences too. Let liberty be the example. In the civil sphere an individual's freedom has its limit in another's freedom. However, "the Christian view takes love of the neighbor into the very concept of freedom itself.... Instead of being just a limitation on one's own freedom, the neighbor is on the contrary also the opportunity for its fulfilment."[84] In other words, these notions (liberty, equality, participation) have a different quality in the Christian community than in the legal community.

What does Tödt make of this? If I understand him—relief from his density comes only with interpretative reading—he is saying that "human rights are an expression of something which is meant to be achieved *in a specific way in the community of believers*." This "specific way" is the

[83] Heinz-Edward Tödt, "Theological Reflections on the Foundations of Human Rights," *Lutheran World* 24 (1977) 45–58.
[84] Ibid. 55.

theological basis on which we approach human rights. What does this mean for a Christian's approach to the worldly problem of rights? Tödt is, in my judgment, very obscure here. It seems that what we might conclude is something like this. Those qualities expressed in civil rights (liberty, equality, participation) are or should be present *eminenter* (similarly but differently) in the Christian community. Therefore, the Christian community ought to be especially sensitive to the actual deficiencies in contemporary life. With such sensitivity, the Christian can or should be able to exercise a particularly constructive critical function vis-à-vis human rights; for he knows in belief that to which they point, their fulfilment.[85]

Human rights have received persevering attention in episcopal literature. On Feb. 24, 1977, the Episcopal Conference of Brazil published a lengthy document to commemorate two anniversaries: the twenty-fifth year of the Brazilian Episcopal Conference (CNBB) and the tenth anniversary of *Populorum progressio*.[86] It is a ringing social charter that merits careful study (it was the object of more than five hundred amendments before its publication). The Church's task, the document begins, is to proclaim salvation in Jesus Christ. While this will be achieved fully only in the Father's house, it must begin to show its fruits here on earth. In accomplishing its mission, the Church orients itself according to the criteria of faith, "which complete the demands of reason and of human nature." The political order is judged by the demands of the moral order, and the Brazilian bishops insist that, as pastors, they have a right and duty to lay out the basic demands of the moral order in the social sphere. This they do in the remainder of the document.

The bishops first point out that any number of models of the state are possible and that no model is perfect and beyond discussion. "Authentic dialogue is fettered when regimes pretend they are beyond discussion and when they repress all reforms beyond those they themselves instigate." After discussing the rights and duties of the state, the bishops turn to what they see as the chief negation of the common good: marginalization. This is found above all in the lack of power to liberate oneself from situations of poverty, hunger, and deprivation.[87]

The document then turns to the remedies for this type of marginalization. It puts great emphasis on participation in the political, social, economic, and cultural processes of the nation—and, above all, on free speech. Regimes too easily perpetuate themselves in the name of security.

---

[85] For an excellent introduction to two recent philosophies of right, cf. John Langan, S.J., "Social Justice: Rawls and Nozick," *TS* 38 (1977) 346–58.

[86] "Exigences chrétiennes pour un ordre politique," *Documentation catholique* 74 (1977) 315–19.

[87] Ibid. 317.

The bishops insist that while economic development has a price, that price cannot be the isolation of wealth in restricted geographic zones. Nor can it mean the denial of basic rights. The document concludes with a strong challenge:

A people develops itself when it progresses in liberty and participation; when it sees its rights respected, or at least when it retains recourse to defense (as in the rights of habeas corpus); when it disposes of the mechanisms capable of exercising control over executive authority; when it counts on the respect of intermediate representative government and the right of self-organization of social institutions such as political parties, unions, and universities.[88]

There can be no doubt that the bishops were stressing deeply disturbing aspects of Brazilian social and political life—and bravely so. If there is any doubt about this, one need only read the "Pastoral Message to the People of God" published Nov. 15, 1976, by the National Conference of Brazilian Bishops' executive committee.[89] It is one of the most beautiful and powerful pastoral statements I have ever read. It is an unflinching confrontation, out of gospel perspectives, with the cruelties and injustices associated with "the doctrine of national security," a doctrine that, in the name of protecting the nation from subversive activity, runs roughshod over basic human rights.

On May 7, 1977, the Argentinian bishops issued a similar critique of the ideology of national security.[90] They criticized the killings, kidnappings, and detention without trial that have grown so frequent in Argentina, and insisted that the maintenance of order, when it requires some abridgment of liberties, must be done within the limits of the law. Another courageous piece. Similar documents of protest have come from the bishops of Chile,[91] Peru,[92] Nicaragua,[93] and El Salvador.[94]

Several other documents appeared in conjunction with the anniversary of *Populorum progressio*. For instance, the Pontifical Commission for Justice and Peace issued an essay in which it underlined the changed world situation during the ten years since the issuance of *Populorum progressio*.[95] These changes (e.g., famine, environmental and energy crises, monetary crisis [inflation, unemployment], political malaise) have stimulated the poor countries to move from the notion of development to a more global vision symbolized in the term "new world order." The

---

[88] Ibid. 319.
[89] *Catholic Mind* 75, no. 1312 (April 1977) 55–64.
[90] *Origins* 7 (June 2, 1977) 20–22.
[91] Latinamerica Press, 1977, April 7, 3–5, and April 14, 3–5.
[92] Ibid., Oct. 14, 3–5.   [93] Ibid., Feb. 24, 4–5.
[94] Ibid., April 21, 3–7.
[95] "'Populorum progressio'—Note de la Commission pontificale Justice et Paix," *Documentation catholique* 74 (1977) 473–75.

Commission sees this as in profound continuity with the aspirations of *Populorum progressio*. This and similar documents indicate one thing very clearly: the Church's concern with rights is focusing with increasing sharpness on the national and international systems which are the context for the existence and exercise of rights and therefore either foster or undermine such rights.

Now to some specific disputes over rights. In the Oct. 3 issue of *Christianity and Crisis* there appeared "A Call to Concern."[96] It was signed by 209 scholars, most of them Christian ethicians. The document is the assertion of an "alternative position" to what it calls the "absolutist position" on abortion and abortion funding by Medicaid. This alternative position includes the following: support for the Supreme Court decision of 1973; rejection of the "absolutist position" on abortion because of its cost in human misery; support of concern for quality of life at all stages; support of Medicaid payments for abortions; sorrow at "the heavy institutional involvement of the bishops of the Roman Catholic Church" (an involvement the document sees as "religiously based" and violative of the deeply-held religious convictions of other individuals and groups); a call to other religious leaders to speak out against "the dangerously increasing influence of the absolutist position."

This is an important document and should not be taken lightly. It is the first time I know that so many religious ethicists have endorsed such a statement. Furthermore, the signatories include very highly respected names in the field of Christian and Jewish ethics. For these reasons, in addition to the important and unyielding character of the abortion problem, we might well expect this statement to be a showpiece paradigm of how serious ethicians go about facing a delicate and potentially divisive problem. There have been some reactions to the statement and I will draw upon them in organizing my own response.

The "Call to Concern" has, in my judgment, the following characteristics: (1) *rhetorically* inflammatory; (2) *factually* mistaken; (3) *legislatively* uninformed; (4) *politically* inconsistent; (5) *argumentatively* unpersuasive; (6) *ethically* unenlightening; (7) *ecumenically* destructive. In summary, it is a very poor statement on all counts. My surprise at the number and distinction of the signatories remains unabated. The following paragraphs will begin to say why.

1) *Rhetorically* inflammatory. One position is described with the following terms: "absolutist," "inflexible," "rigid," "compel the conscience," "blind," "dangerous," "extreme." The alternative position is fleshed out with the following: "moral," "sound," "responsible," "candor," "loving."

---

[96] "A Call to Concern," *Christianity and Crisis* 37 (1977) 222–24. This was eloquently responded to by James Burtchaell, C.S.C., with his "A Call and a Reply," *Christianity and Crisis* 37 (1977) 270–71, and Robert Hoyt in *Christianity and Crisis* 37 (1977) 265–66.

Perceptive ethicists know what is going on in this type of cheerleading.[97]

Beyond such colorful language, there is loose language. Thus, the Supreme Court is said to have decided not to "compel the conscience" of those who believe abortion is morally right. In ordinary usage, we "compel the conscience" when we force persons to do something they judge to be morally wrong. We do not and should not use this to describe constraints from doing things that many see as offensive. Otherwise let us cease and desist from outlawing polygamy, and skyjacking of planes by those who think they act justifiably in a noble revolutionary cause.

2) *Factually* wrong. The document is factually wrong on several counts. First, the moral and legal position opposed is presented as one held and pressed "on religious grounds." Several popes and many hierarchies around the world have made it clear repeatedly that the position they propose is not religiously derived, even though religious perspectives will support and deepen it. It is a matter of the moral law making claims on all persons, a matter of basic rights and duties at the heart of social life. The abortion position is no more religiously based than the position of the bishops on farm-workers' rights, the Vietnam war, capital punishment, and a host of other concerns.

Secondly, it is simply wrong—and at some point slanderous—to assert that the abortion position they oppose means "*total* preoccupation with the status of the unborn" and renders it "blind to the well-being and freedom of choice of persons in community." The past and present history of social concern of the indicted groups is sufficient to destroy such an accusation. The American bishops have consistently linked unemployment, the condition of the aged, food rights, etc. to their stand on abortion. I would invite the signatories to read a fine recent example of this by Archbishop Joseph Bernardin.[98]

Finally, the position opposed is described as "absolutist." Individuals are never identified, but the impression is unavoidable that the Roman Catholic Church is the "absolutist" group. It should be known to "writers of religious ethics" that no position associated with Catholic papal and episcopal statements, and contemporary theological ethicians, can be described accurately as absolutist—scil., one judging *all* abortions to be morally wrong. As Burtchaell notes: "Ethicists are expected to restrain themselves from misrepresenting positions with which they disagree."

3) *Legislatively* uninformed. The "Call to Concern" states that there is "no clear majority opinion on these fundamental issues." Prior to 1973, forty-six states had laws restricting abortion. Furthermore, in state-wide referendums which allowed the public to speak—as the Wade and Bolton

---

[97] Cf. Burtchaell, "A Call" 270.

[98] Joseph Bernardin, "Human Rights: Do We Practice What We Preach?" *Origins* 7 (1977) 201–4.

decisions do not—every instance showed rejection of abortion on demand as now protected by our highest court. Moreover, in a *New York Times*/CBS poll, only 38% thought a woman should be helped with government funds if she wanted an abortion; 55% said no.[99] Finally, the report, in speaking of a legal right, passes over in silence the enormously important distinction between a right not to be interfered with (a right to pursue) and a right of entitlement.

4) *Politically* inconsistent. The document regrets the involvement of the Catholic episcopate in the abortion issue, especially with regard to an amendment. It is seen as "a serious threat to religious liberty and freedom of conscience." An amendment would "violate the deeply held religious convictions of individual members and official bodies" about the beginning of personhood. Three points. First, this invitation to the bishops to absent themselves from the problem is asserted at the very time the signatories are getting in—and on religious grounds. Perhaps the bishops also have convictions that could be violated by the actions of the signatories. Secondly, the document admits "the legal right of all individuals and groups, both religious and secular, to seek laws that reflect their religious and ethical beliefs." Why, then, is the institutional involvement of the Catholic episcopate "inappropriate"? The document nowhere answers this. Such stipulation has the effect of disenfranchising certain persons from the democratic process. Thirdly, if denial of Medicaid funds is a "public censure of a medical service" which has the moral support of major religious groups, provision of such funds is a "public censure" of the position that argues that it is offensive to use our tax money for this purpose.

5) *Argumentatively* unpersuasive. The document is clearly not an ethical argument; it is a political manifesto. But even so, when charges so serious ("serious threat to religious liberty") are uttered, some moral reasoning ought to be given. Furthermore, the report does take a moral position ("abortion may in some instances be the most loving act possible"). It does this on the basis of "the well-being and freedom of choice of persons in community." Unless "well-being and freedom of choice" are carefully specified, I am afraid that in principle they may justify far more than the authors envisage (e.g., infanticide). Moreover, the authors take a stand on Medicaid funds on the grounds that denial of funds "makes it difficult for those who need it most to exercise a legal right." If this is to be persuasive, it must weigh this admitted difficulty against the loss of fetal life that *presumably* would occur through provision of funds.

6) *Ethically* unenlightening. The manifesto simply takes a position; it does not enlighten it. Indeed, in doing this, it obscures ethical issues. Item: it rejects a more demanding stand on abortion because of "its cost

[99] Cf. *Christianity and Crisis* 37 (1977) 205.

in human terms," and sees this as the "most compelling argument." Nothing is said about the cost to the fetus. That is not to enlighten a hierarchy of values; it is merely to promulgate a conclusion that is at odds with centuries of Christian tradition. Item: abortion is described as both "tragic" and "loving." Why is it ever tragic in the authors' perspectives if the basic warrant proposed is the "convictions of individual members and official bodies . . . *about when human personhood begins*"? If abortion is not about taking human life, why the tragedy?

7) *Ecumenically* disastrous. Candor is never ecumenically destructive. Nor is disagreement. Indeed, this author disagreed with the United States Catholic Conference in some of its procedures during the presidential campaign. What is destructive to ecumenism is latent anti-Catholicism. I honestly believe that this does not represent the attitudes of the signatories. But the document has been widely perceived in this way by intelligent, open, and sensitive people, both Catholic and non-Catholic. The conclusion is hard to avoid that there are elements in it which form the basis for such a perception.

My remarks have been vigorous and candid because I respect the signatories. Furthermore, documents such as this one have methodological importance beyond the issue they discuss. They are transparent of the way we go about moral discourse. And on this score the document is a disaster. As *America* editorialized: "The theologians who signed this document have done themselves no honor."[100]

Donald McCarthy discusses the use of DES (diethylstilbestrol) after rape.[101] He accepts the purely contraceptive use of DES, rejects the abortional (interference with implantation), but wonders about instances where it is not clear whether ovulation had occurred in the 12–24 hour period. Therefore, one does not know whether by administration of DES the outcome is contraceptive or abortifacient. Thus the problem: the use of DES with contraceptive intent but uncertain outcome. He suggests (and only that) that the use of this drug might be justified by the principle of double effect.

In responding to this study, William A. Lynch, M.D., points out that recent studies undermine the factual assumption in McCarthy's study, scil., that postcoital estrogens suppress ovulation.[102] Rather, they are "interceptors" that interfere with implantation. Therefore he rejects the use of DES as abortifacient.

Practically, on Lynch's factual assessment there is no problem. DES is

[100] "Another Double Standard," *America* 137 (1977) 274.

[101] Donald McCarthy, "Medication to Prevent Pregnancy after Rape," *Linacre Quarterly* 44 (1977) 210–22.

[102] William Lynch, "Comments on 'Medication to Prevent Pregnancy After Rape,'" ibid. 223–28.

abortifacient and its use must be judged as such. Interestingly, however, McCarthy raises a problem with which traditional theologians were familiar, but in a different set of circumstances. It is the problem of acting when one is factually doubtful about the effect of one's action. For instance, it was asked decades ago whether a physician could remove an abdominal mass to save a woman's life when he was uncertain as to whether this mass was a tumor or a fetus. The answer given commonly, though not universally, was negative.

To the best of my knowledge, no author attempted to justify the intervention by appeal to the double effect, simply because, as Vermeersch noted,[103] the effects are disjunctive—scil., either one or the other occurs, but not both. Those who did defend the intervention argued that *ordinarily* action taken in doubt of fact about the presence or existence of human life is unwarranted temerity and unjust. Thus, it would be morally wrong for a hunter to shoot at an object in the bush that is probably an animal but probably also a person. But several theologians pointed out that the case would be different were we dealing with a *starving* hunter whose life was at stake. It would not then be unwarranted temerity to risk harm to the only probable person because of the presence of a proportionate reason.[104] The case was approached, in other words, in terms of the justifiable or unjustifiable character of risk-taking.

That seems to me to be the proper approach to the question under discussion. It breaks into two questions: (1) How does DES (or other rape-treatment medication) work? (2) What is the status of the embryo immediately after fertilization? On all available evidence, DES administered to rape victims prevents implantation of the fertilized ovum. At this point the second question becomes crucial. What claims does human life at this stage make upon us and why?

In a long study, Gabriel Pastrana, O.P., has very competently and objectively reviewed the literature on this point.[105] He first reviews and critiques the opinions of major discussants (Noonan, Grisez, Ramsey, Curran, Hauerwas, B. Häring, Callahan, Sissela Bok, Tooley, Engelhardt). Pastrana next turns to the available biological data on the zygote and morula. Especially to be noted are the phenomena of twinning and conjunction (recombination of two fertilized ova), cell pluripotentiality of the blastocyst until the appearance of the primary organizer. "If this

---

[103] A. Vermeersch, *Theologia moralis principia-responsa-consilia* 2 (Rome, 1926–28) 589. In the ordinary case, therefore, it is true to say that doing and the risk of doing are morally equivalent: "Idem est in moralibus facere et exponere se periculo faciendi." Cf. Vermeersch, n. 103.

[104] V. Heylen, *Tractatus de jure et justitia* (ed. 5; Mechlin, 1950) 664.

[105] Gabriel Pastrana, O.P., "Personhood and the Beginning of Human Life," *Thomist* 41 (1977) 247–94.

organizer does not appear, or if it is removed, no subsequent differentiation will occur." That is, the behavioral characteristics and activities of the cells before and after the appearance of the primary organizer are specifically different.

He next applies to such data a philosophical analysis. Pastrana is concerned with two questions. First, when is the developing being an individual human being? Secondly, when is it a person? Using the traditional scholastic concepts of matter and form, Pastrana points to "from the second to the third week (14th to 22nd day) after fertilization as the time of the appearance of the biological individual human being, or, more strictly, indicating its nonappearance before that time...." In this conclusion he is very close to Paul Ramsey and Charles Curran.

He then turns to the notion of person and, after rejecting purely psychological (consciousness) and moral (relation to others) definitions of person for an ontological one, concludes: "the product of conception should be considered a human person." Pastrana's study is well informed, meticulously documented, and carefully analytic. It must be taken seriously. One minor point needs clarification. On the basis of his analysis, Pastrana should have formulated his conclusion somewhat more precisely, scil., that the product of conception should be considered a person after around 14-22 days, the time at which individuation is established. This is certainly what he meant to say.

Pastrana's conclusion is parallel to that of James Diamond, M.D., who claims that "the scientist has an almost insuperable inclination to identify hominization as being positable no earlier than the blastocyst stage."[106] Practically, that means not before 7 days and probably not before 14-21 days. This matter has very grave consequences. Let the treatment of rape be a single instance. In the literature reported above (McCarthy, Lynch), the assumption is that we are dealing with personal life from the moment of fertilization. The discussion, therefore, concerns the manner of operation of DES. Pastrana's conclusion (which he shares with Curran, Ramsey, and others) undermines the assumption.

I incline toward Pastrana's conclusion.[107] The numerous biological events converging during the earliest days (7-21)—e.g., twinning, possibility of recombination, appearance of the primary organizer, number of aborted fertilized ova—strongly suggest that the ontological status of

[106] James Diamond, M.D., "Abortion, Animation, Hominization," *TS* 36 (1975) 305-24, at 315.

[107] For a contrary view, cf. Michael A. Vaccari, "Personhood before Implantation," *Natural Family Planning* 1 (1977) 215-28. The moralist, to the extent that his conclusion relies on the phenomenon of recombination, is utterly dependent on empirical data. Vaccari is at pains to show that there is no evidence to indicate that recombination has occurred in humans. Others (e.g., Andre E. Hellegers and Kurt Benirschke) contest this.

human life at this stage may be different than after this period. What may one conclude practically from this? In my judgment, extreme caution is required here. I would suggest tentatively that there is sufficient doubt about the claims of nascent life at this stage to say that the use of interceptors (which prevent implantation) in emergency treatment of rape cases is not clearly and certainly wrong.

Two phrases are noteworthy here: "sufficient doubt," "emergency treatment of rape cases." In combination, these suggest that in *normal* instances of doubt about the extent of our obligations, life deserves the benefit of the doubt. But in cases of tragic conflict (rape), given the facts currently available, it would not be what earlier theologians called "temerarious risk" to draw the conclusion suggested.

We may learn more about this matter as the discussion continues. This implies a readiness to modify our judgments. But one thing needs saying: the abortion position firmly and constantly proposed by the Church is so sound and healthy, in my judgment, that it would be a disservice to it to extend its clarity and certainty into areas where there are reasons for genuine doubt.[108]

Another area where the Church finds itself in dispute is the matter of women's ordination. Rights are involved here, but in a nuanced sense. That is, if there is no persuasive theological or pastoral reason to exclude women from ordination, then the continued exclusion *of an entire class on the basis of sex* would be an injustice. Obviously, no individual can claim an unqualified right to ordination as a priest. But a class of persons could argue that, if there is no solid theological justification, this exclusion is a denial of a kind of *jus ad rem*—a right not to be *unfairly* interferred with in the *pursuit* of a possession or goal.[109]

The abundant literature in response to the document of the Sacred Congregation for the Doctrine of the Faith cannot be reviewed here.[110]

---

[108] At the legal level, it is clear that any law or amendment which proscribes intervention from the moment of fertilization is totally unworkable. It would represent conspiracy law. Why? Because pregnancy is not diagnosable until several weeks (at least) after fertilization. That means that the law would have to prosecute for the *intention* to abort—which is conspiracy law.

[109] A *jus in re* is understood as the right one has to his/her own property.

[110] Cf. Robert J. Egan, S.J., "On the Ordination of Women," *Commonweal* 104 (1977) 589-91, with Michael Novak's reply, 591-93; Michael Novak, "On the Ordination of Women," *Commonweal* 104 (1977) 425-27; "Inter insigniores" (declaration on the ordination of women), *Documentation catholique* 74 (1977) 158-64; Christian Howard, "Ordination of Women," *Ecumenical Review* 29 (1977) 234-53; "Women and the Priesthood" (editorial), *Month* 10 (New Series, 1977) 75-76; Karl-Heinz Weger, "Endgültig keine Ordination der Frau?" *Orientierung* 41 (1977) 64-67; Albert Ebneter, "Keine Frauen im Priesteramt," *Orientierung* 41 (1977) 25-26; "The Ordination of Women Controversy," *Overview*, April 1977; Luc J. Lefevre, "Sur l'admission des femmes au sacerdoce: Un document de Rome," *Pensée catholique* 167 (April 1977) 5-17; "The Ordination of Women" (English version of

But two statements from the American scene deserve attention. One was a dissent registered by the (virtually) entire theological faculty of the Jesuit School of Theology at Berkeley.[111] It is carefully worded and stems from a "profound love for the Church and for the Vicar of Christ." The other was composed by John R. Donahue, S.J., a distinguished Scripture scholar. Donahue critically probes the arguments and citations used in *Inter insigniores.*[112]

Theologians are not accustomed to perceive their writing in terms of rights. But a recent instance merits attention. It is the silencing of John McNeill, S.J., by the Sacred Congregation for the Doctrine of the Faith.[113] This may appear as an isolated instance. But all theologians have a stake in this happening. That is true whether one agrees or disagrees with McNeill's thesis—and I have substantial disagreements with it. Furthermore, the entire Church has a stake in such happenings.

Two questions that must be publicly answered are: (1) Why was this done? (2) How was it done? The first question does not intend to deny that drastic action is sometimes called for against what is thought to be pastoral irresponsibility. It means only to suggest that the parameters of such irresponsibility must be spelled out carefully, publicly, and in advance of their application.

But of perhaps even more urgent concern is how this was done. Before a person's ministry is publicly terminated or abridged in the Church—especially if that ministry is one of scholarship and the exchange of ideas—certain procedures of due process seem utterly essential if the Church is to retain its credibility as a "zone of truth." Among these procedures we must surely include discussion of the matter (especially the offending ideas, the pros and cons) *with the defendant.* Unless this occurs, suppressive measures will appear to be and actually be self-inflicted wounds by the Church—a community whose trust in the protective action of the Holy Spirit is second to none, and therefore a community where the free flow of ideas ought to occur in an atmosphere of unthreatened tranquility. This is especially true at a time when episcopates in many Third World countries are protesting prophetically and vigorously the denial of rights, among them the suppression of free speech.

---

the document of the Sacred Congregation for the Doctrine of the Faith), *The Pope Speaks* 22 (1977) 108–22; Karl Rahner, S.J., "Priestertum der Frau?" *Stimmen der Zeit* 195 (1977) 291–301; H. Küng and Gerhard Lohfink, "Keine Ordination der Frau?" *Theologische Quartalschrift* 157 (1977) 144–46. Leonard and Arlene Swidler have gathered many reactions to the Vatican's declaration in *Women Priests* (New York: Paulist, 1977).

[111] "An Open Letter to the Apostolic Delegate," *Commonweal* 104 (1977) 204–6.

[112] John R. Donahue, S.J., "Women, Priesthood and the Vatican," *America* 136 (1977) 285–89.

[113] For McNeill's response (a letter to Dignity), cf. *Origins* 7 (1977) 218–19.

At the bottom of this particular dispute may lurk different perceptions of the meaning and importance of public discussion in the Church, especially in areas where there are officially formulated teaching statements. And that brings us to the report of a committee of the Catholic Theological Society of America on sexuality.

THE CTSA COMMITTEE REPORT ON SEXUALITY

Few events of recent years have prompted as much reaction as the publication of *Human Sexuality: New Directions in American Catholic Thought* on June 20, 1977.[114] The reaction has come from many sources: the press, Catholic bishops, theologians. Even the *New York Times* deemed it advisable to editorialize on the study. It viewed it as "dramatic evidence of fresh currents in the Catholic community" and concluded that "such a profound note of dissent among those entrusted with teaching the young cannot fail to have significant implications for the Catholicism of tomorrow."[115]

The New York Archdiocese (document issued under the signature of Msgr. Joseph T. O'Keefe, chancellor) took a harsh view of these "fresh currents."[116] The study of the CTSA committee tips the balance between objective law and subjective conscience, between action and intention, and gives "a purely subjective definition of sexual love" by abandoning the procreative dimension. Theologian James Burtchaell sees the book as a "fatuous report by people who have no real scholarly standing."[117] Book reviewer Thomas P. McDonnell believes that *Human Sexuality* is "garbage under the guise of progressive enlightenment."[118] The *National Catholic Register* wrote that the "book is so bad it is almost good because it will undoubtedly drive the Catholic community... to seek from the bishops a thorough housecleaning."[119] The *Catholic Standard* (Washington, D.C.) referred to the study as "this infamous report" and saw it as an "insidious attack on fundamental Catholic moral values."[120]

Theologian William B. Smith, in an extremely black review, feels the book deserves an "X" rating, "not for pornography, but for violence—the extreme violence done to the sources of Sacred Theology: Sacred Scripture, Sacred Tradition, and the Magisterium of the Church."[121] Richard

[114] Anthony Kosnik et al., *Human Sexuality: New Directions in American Catholic Thought* (New York: Paulist, 1977).

[115] *New York Times,* July 7, 1977.

[116] *Catholic News,* July 14, 1977.

[117] *Newsweek,* July 11, 1977.

[118] *Church World,* June 23, 1977. A rather thorough roundup of these citations may be found in *Overview,* Sept. 1977.

[119] *National Catholic Register,* May 29, 1977.

[120] *Catholic Standard,* Nov. 24, 1977.

[121] *Catholic News,* June 9, 1977.

McBrien argues that the fundamental methodological shift—from unitive-procreative to creative-integrative—is not justified.[122] Editor-in-chief Albert Nevins of *Our Sunday Visitor* referred to the study as "this new aberration of the paramagisterium", and concluded that it "cannot do anything but great harm."[123] Six members of the CTSA view the work as "partisan in outlook, poor in scholarship, weak in argumentation and fallacious in its conclusions."[124]

On the other hand, theologian F. X. Murphy notes that *Human Sexuality* "marks the arrival at maturity of the U.S. theological community."[125] The principal achievement of the study consists "in its having set in a new perspective the traditional teaching of the Church on all modes of sexual expression." Journalist Frank Wessling argues that if the book is read completely, "it will vibrate as reasonable and true to the experience of most thoughtful persons."[126] Even though he offers several reservations, he concludes that "the book ... is so good that it is the only one I can think of that I would recommend to my children as openers for a dialogue on sexuality." Rosemary Ruether sees the book as a "major effort to shift the basis of sexual ethics from act-oriented to person-oriented principles.... Traditional moralists will be acutely discomfited by these principles."[127] Giles Milhaven praises the report as the result of listening "to that large segment of the Catholic people, growing larger each year, that live sexual lives in ways different from what the Church sanctions."[128]

Tom Driver of Union Theological Seminary applauds *Human Sexuality* as "the best book I have ever read that was written by a committee."[129] The book will make fur fly because it is predicated upon an understanding of human nature as dynamic. Joseph Cunneen, even amid several criticisms, judges the study as "a courageous and long-overdue achievement. Any fair reading of the text will make clear that its authors are moderates in their approach to theological ethics and that they are concerned to preserve a continuity in Catholic teaching even while presenting a more contemporary person-oriented rather than act-oriented approach to sexuality."[130]

These are but a few examples of the early press and theological

[122] *Church World,* July 14, 1977.
[123] *Our Sunday Visitor,* June 26, 1977.
[124] Cf. *Overview* as in n. 118 above.
[125] F. X. Murphy, *Tablet* 231 (1977) 695–96.
[126] *Catholic Messenger,* July 7, 1977.
[127] Rosemary Radford Ruether, "Time Makes Ancient Good Uncouth: The Catholic Report on Sexuality," *Christian Century* 94 (1977) 682–85.
[128] *National Catholic Reporter,* June 17, 1977.
[129] Tom F. Driver, "A Stride toward Sanity," *Christianity and Crisis* 37 (1977) 243–46.
[130] Joseph Cunneen, "Two Rousing Cheers," *Christianity and Crisis* 37 (1977) 247–49.

comments on this study. There are many more. It would be tedious to multiply them. Two things stand out rather clearly in the many responses I have read. First, they are sharply divided. Second, they seem to reveal as much about the perspectives of the responders as they do about *Human Sexuality* itself. That is, they lay bare what the responders expect and desire to find in a theological study of sexuality. These expectations and desires are transparent of certain attitudes toward human nature, Church authority, moral norms, the maturity of people, etc.

The response of bishops to *Human Sexuality* deserves special attention. Here we see the duly authorized pastoral leaders of the Church reacting to a theological study on a matter of concern to all, and one on which the Church has some rather well-known authoritative formulations. One can scarcely conceive a situation more likely to expose the thoughts of many hearts (Lk 2:35).

Of special interest is the response of the Committee on Doctrine of the National Conference of Catholic Bishops (NCCB).[131] After encouraging theological research in this area, the committee made several substantive points. First, it rejected the idea that a tentative study could be the basis for pastoral guidelines and conscience formation. Second, it scored the "rather impoverished concept" of the Word of God in the study. Third, it repeated Vatican II's analysis of the procreative and unitive dimensions of sexuality and criticized *Human Sexuality* for abandoning this. The study's "creative growth toward integration" is "too vague to apply with any kind of precision or assurance." And its second-level values (self-liberating, other-enriching, etc.) "offer little guidance." Finally, the Committee on Doctrine believes the study is deficient in relating the empirical sciences to value judgments and in its sensitivity to the "supernatural aspects of marital love." By this latter phrase the bishops underline the difference between moral claims rooted in Christian symbolism (marriage as symbolizing Christ's love of the Church) and those that are described as "a minimal sexual morality" or "simple duty or obligation."

The document of the Committee on Doctrine strikes this reviewer as courteous, moderate, and balanced—and happily purged of the nervousness, anger, and fear that is evident in some other episcopal responses. I believe the doctrinal committee is correct in noting the vagueness of the criteria central to the book (creative, integrative). No one will question the idea that healthy sexual expression ought to be creative and integrative. Therefore, it is not the case that these criteria are erroneous. But is that all we can say about sexuality? Such criteria apply to one's prayer life, dietary habits, athletics, study, etc. That is, they say little that is illuminative of sexuality as such. For this reason it seems that abandonment of the unitive-procreative analysis is unwarranted.

[131] The text is given in full in the *Catholic Standard,* Nov. 24, 1977.

Similarly, the doctrinal committee seems correct in questioning the second-level values (self-liberating etc.). Once again, it is not that these are wrong. Rather, it is the impression that these post-factum second-level values have to be applied in each case before an action can be said to be morally inappropriate. Have we not learned that certain kinds of actions are precisely denials of these qualities? And is that not the very meaning of the norms we have developed proscribing certain forms of conduct?

The one aspect of the doctrinal committee's response that is puzzling is its distinction in the sexual sphere between "simple duty or obligation" and the "supernatural aspects of marital love." It would have been helpful had the committee attempted to give concrete examples of this difference in the sexual sphere. I can think of none; for "duty" or "obligation" surely includes *all* aspects of the rightness or wrongness of our conduct, whatever the warrants adduced for the rightness or wrongness. And by adding "simple" to the term "duty" one does not alter that.

Individual episcopal pastorals vary all the way from excellent to embarrassing. In this latter category is the pastoral of John King Mussio (Steubenville).[132] While exhorting his people to "stick with Christ and His Church," Bishop Mussio stamps the authors of *Human Sexuality* as "prideful people," "free-wheeling people who in intellectual conceit strive to twist the Word of God...." They are "destroyers," "self-excommunicates." Finally, and inexcusably, the authors are said to uphold "false doctrines they contrive out of their efforts to gain worldly renown."

Archbishop John Quinn, president of the National Conference of Catholic Bishops, makes several points in his statement.[133] First, he notes that "some of the positions taken in the committee report are erroneous" and to be rejected as "in conflict with the faith and moral teaching of the Church." As an example in the sexual sphere of an absolutely binding precept he states: "sexual activity must be confined within the loving covenant of valid marriage."

Archbishop Quinn also believes the committee report erroneously concludes that traditional Catholic moral teaching paid little attention to the "personal factors which must enter into the consideration of moral right and wrong." Contrarily, he asserts, tradition always emphasized factors such as fear, neurosis, habit, passion, and force.

Finally, Archbishop Quinn concludes with a supportive statement for the work of theologians in the doctrinal development of the Church. However, "neither theologians nor bishops work well in isolation." He suggests that the report would have greater value and wider perspectives if bishops had collaborated in it.

[132] *Steubenville Register,* July 7, 1977.
[133] *Origins* 7 (1977) 94–95.

One small point—and this could be made about several of the episcopal statements. There are two types of "personal factors" in human conduct. The first concerns sin and guilt, and these are the factors mentioned by Archbishop Quinn (fear, force, etc.). The second refers to the individual qualities of conduct that do affect moral right and wrong: respect, courtesy, communication, tenderness, other-concern, etc. Such personal factors were indeed neglected in traditional treatises on sexual morality.

John Cardinal Dearden and the assistant bishops of Detroit regret that a speculative study is offered as "pastoral guidelines."[134] This leaves the impression that the findings of the work are conclusive and final. Secondly, many of the tentative conclusions are not in accord with Church teaching. The Detroit bishops suggest the pastoral of the American bishops (*To Live in Christ Jesus*) as an object of study and reflection. Finally, Cardinal Dearden's document concludes with an excellent paragraph that deserves citation.

A third point we wish to stress concerns the role of the theologians in the teaching responsibility of the Church. We recognize and are grateful for the invaluable service that theologians provide the Church in seeking ways to express Catholic moral teaching in ever more understandable terms for people of today. In this regard, human sexuality is but one of the areas of morality that demand always more carefully formulated guidelines and prudent counsel. . . . We must be patient with one another's attempt to formulate the truth.[135]

John Cardinal Carberry, with the four assistant bishops of St. Louis, issued a letter to all priests of the archdiocese.[136] It differs markedly in tone from the letter of Cardinal Dearden. First, it regrets the secrecy surrounding publication of *Human Sexuality*. "We find this a strange manner indeed for the CTSA to 'dialogue' with theologians and bishops." Secondly, it calls attention to errors in the study (denial of absolute norms, radical subjectivism). "The book represents a serious diluting of the basic demands of the Gospel of Jesus Christ." The very subtitle of the book "implies that there is a so-called 'American' Catholic thought which can arrogate to itself the authority to flaunt the clear teachings of the universal Church." This, the letter continues, is a serious error, "for it overlooks the fact that the bishops with the Holy Father are the magisterium, the official teaching authority of the Church." The letter concludes by noting that the principles and opinions in *Human Sexuality* are not to be used in guidance and the hearing of confessions, "not to be preached nor sustained either publicly or privately."

Humberto Cardinal Medeiros published a lengthy statement in the *Pilot* covering both *Human Sexuality* and the defiance of Archbishop

---

[134] Courtesy of John C. Nienstedt, secretary to Cardinal Dearden.
[135] Cf. n. 134 above.   [136] *St. Louis Review,* Sept. 23, 1977.

Marcel Lefebvre.[137] Both constitute "irresponsible attacks on the Church's teaching authority" and result in "weakening the allegiance in faith owed by Catholics to the Holy Father." Cardinal Medeiros cites *Lumen gentium* at length on papal and episcopal teaching prerogatives and notes that it is wrong "for a group of professed Catholic theologians to suggest that the teachings of Vatican II have opened the way for a completely new formulation of the Church's position on problems relating to human sexuality." The Medeiros letter ends with a paragraph of great interest to theologians. It reads as follows:

It is the responsibility of the teaching authority of the Church to listen to theologians and to judge whether their informed consensus is in harmony with the faith of the Church, and then to accept any fresh insights into the faith for the advancement of the Kingdom of God. And it is the responsibility of theologians to work within the Church—and not to speak to the Church from the independent platforms of the secular academic world, as if they were non-believers. The Church suffers greatly when Catholic theologians, claiming the right to speak independently of ecclesiastical supervision—seeming to reject the service of authority given to the Church of Christ—continue to present themselves as molders of Catholic opinion and as authentic counsellors for Catholics in the formation of their judgments of conscience. When theological science thus takes on the forms of secularized scholarship, Catholic theologians who speak its language find themselves usurping the authority of the Church's hierarchy as they become publicly identified with secularized efforts to legalize sexual aberrations and to make immorality look respectable. May the Holy Spirit enlighten those who inflict such pain and confusion on the Church, fragmenting it against the will of Christ.[138]

Entirely different was the reaction of Archbishop Francis T. Hurley. "Personally, I welcome the report. I commend the authors for grappling with the almost impossible task of trying to develop in writing and for public review what is more easily and safely done in the one-to-one privacy of the counselling situation."[139] Hurley criticizes the hucksterism of the publication of the book, the vagueness of the guidelines, and the overreliance on empirical evidence which the report itself says is skimpy. The move from traditional norms to new ones Hurley sees as a "gigantic leap" that is unwarranted. But the report has generated "dialogue, heat and controversy. That is to the good, even if it does cause us bishops to squirm a bit."

Bishop James J. Hogan sees the conclusions of *Human Sexuality* as "contrary to the law of God and in conflict with the authentic teaching of Christ's Spirit-guided Church."[140] Its principles he qualifies as "situational ethics," which are a threat to the family. He is especially concerned

---

[137] *Pilot,* July 8, 1977.
[138] Ibid.

[139] *Inside Passage,* July 29, 1977.
[140] Cf. *Overview* (n. 118 above).

that one of the authors is a seminary professor and another the president of the CTSA. When one openly and designedly rejects hierarchical teaching, "that dissenter acts immaturely and irresponsibly." Bishop Hogan then notes: "Theological pluralism has its place—and its limits. Legitimate dissent may be countenanced. But when in the name of loving service to the flock and of higher loyalty to the Church, clear Church teaching is challenged, there is neither service nor loyalty...."

I am somewhat confused by that wording. It is said that legitimate dissent may be countenanced. But when "clear Church teaching is challenged," then we are faced with something different—presumably, illegitimate dissent. This suggests the puzzling notion that dissent may be legitimate and countenanced when the teaching is not clear. That seems remarkable.

These are but a few examples of the many pastoral letters that have been issued in response to the CTSA committee report. They differ markedly in attitude and tone. Some of them leave this writer with several impressions. First, it seems that no matter what was said by the CTSA committee and with what arguments, it would be criticized *if it departed from official formulations*. I say this not because I agree with the authors' criteria or conclusions (in substantial ways I do not). Rather, the concern is for the task of theology and the notion of doctrinal development. If something is erroneous simply because it disagrees with existing official formulations, that says something very important—and deeply troubling—about theology's task and the possibility of doctrinal development.

Secondly, many of the pastorals are heavily preoccupied with authority: fears that authoritative positions would be weakened, fears that theologians are usurping pastoral authority, assertions that it is the pope and bishops who have authority to teach, etc. I am sympathetic with these concerns. But continued emphasis on them reveals one of the major difficulties in this entire discussion: to discourse about sexuality, not authority. This difficulty is not limited to the Catholic community, but it does surface there in a peculiarly intense way. There are all types of "authorities" subtly maneuvering for the final word: ecclesiastical, psychiatric, sociological, experienced, theological, etc. As long as this remains the context in which reflection on the mysterious gift of sexuality is done, I am afraid that the truly enlightening word will remain unspoken. For this reason one cannot but applaud Archbishop Joseph Bernardin's recent appeals for dialogue between bishops, scientists, and theologians.[141]

[141] Archbishop Bernardin's remarks were made Oct. 17 in a speech at the world Synod of Bishops and were widely reported in the Catholic press. In an address to the National Conference of Catholic Bishops (Nov. 14, 1977) he repeated his "special plea that we establish a closer relationship, both as a Conference and as individual bishops, with theologians and social scientists and other scholars."

"Official, authoritative, authentic" vs. "nonofficial, nonauthentic, paramagisterial." We constantly encounter these polarities and get locked into them. Eventually they assume the shape of theologians versus bishops. Is there no way out of such a conceptual and destructive impasse? Another article argues that there is.[142] It views the magisterium as the precious vehicle of our shared experience and knowledge. But three aspects of the hierarchical magisterium are often overlooked. First, it is pastoral in character. That is, it is concerned with prudential determinations where more basic principles are in confrontation with changing social structures and changing times. This can be seen in the difference in nuance in *Rerum novarum* and *Populorum progressio*. Secondly, the magisterium is philosophical-theological in character. That is, it uses a thought-system and a language that root in a philosophical and/or theological perspective. These systems are time- and culture-conditioned and therefore limited and imperfect. That means that the formulations of the magisterium at a given time are only more or less adequate. Thirdly, the documents of the magisterium are addressed to believers of different cultural backgrounds and with different value perspectives.

Together these three characteristics mean that there is a difference between the substance of a teaching and its formulation. This was explicitly acknowledged by John XXIII and *Gaudium et spes*. If there is a distinction between the substance and formulation, there is also an extremely close, indeed inseparable connection. They are related as body and soul. The connection is so intimate that it is difficult to know just what the substance is amid variation of formulation.

Let premarital intercourse function as an example. The following assertions have been made at one time or another about such behavior. (1) It is morally wrong, scil., there is always something missing. Hence it should be avoided. (2) It is intrinsically evil. (3) It is so because it is violative of the procreative finality of sexual exchange, scil., violative of responsible procreative atmosphere. (4) It is seriously wrong in each act. (5) There is a presumption of serious guilt in each act. From these five assertions, to what is the Church committed? What is its *substantial* teaching? The article suggests that it is contained in the first statement. The other statements variously involve philosophical and theological concepts and the data of empirical sciences, all subject to modification and change.

The article then suggests several conclusions. For instance, what the Church is teaching (the substance) cannot always be identified with a particular formulation. Thus formulation of conviction in the Church is much more a teaching-learning *process* than some suppose. Second, it is not a stunning theological putdown or an insuperably serious objection against an attempted formulation to say that it is not in accord with the doctrine of the Church *as found in the Doctrinal Congregation's "Declaration."* Finally, the article argues that the Holy Father and the college of bishops should not formulate their teaching *against* a broad or even very significant theological consensus; for such a consensus indicates at least that the problem has not matured sufficiently to allow an authoritative formulation.

The literature reviewed here and much that cannot be reviewed would not modify my conclusion in the above study: that we have not learned the gentle and patient art (cf. Cardinal Dearden's letter) of allowing a problem to mature. The events surrounding the appearance of *Human Sexuality* suggest that if we leave no room for doubt and questioning, we will have no room for the privilege of growth. "Doubt and questioning" is peculiarly the onerous task of the theologian, a task assigned to him by the Church. Or, as the elegant words of the editor of this journal render it:

A critical facet of that function is to subject any earthbound affirmation of Christian truth to the test of Christian truth: Does it square with, correspond to, adequately represent the Word of God? In doing so, we are not setting ourselves above Pope or bishop; we are collaborating with them in a joint effort to understand what God says to us and what God wants of us. The paradox, a humbling paradox, is that at times our very loyalty demands that we dissent.[143]

To disagree with Burghardt here is, I submit, to be faithless to the theological task and to disappoint the Church.

[143] Walter J. Burghardt, S.J., "Stone the Theologians! The Role of Theology in Today's Church," *Catholic Mind* 75, no. 1315 (Sept. 1977) 42–50, at 50.

CURRENT THEOLOGY: 1979

NOTES ON MORAL THEOLOGY: 1978

During the past year attention has been intensely focused on the deaths of two popes[1] and on the changes this might prefigure for the Catholic community. Much speculation—and it is just that—has centered on certain moral and pastoral problems (ordination of women, married priests, divorce and remarriage, birth control[2]). These and other problems are not faced simply by a changing of the guard, so to speak. They are prepared for by hard theological work. These "Notes" will touch on several areas where some of that work is being done. In order: (1) conscience and conflict; (2) *Humanae vitae* and the magisterium; (3) problems in bioethics. But before these specifics, the appearance of several important books that incorporate a good deal of contemporary work should be noted.[3]

CONSCIENCE AND CONFLICT

In a ranging article Archbishop Denis E. Hurley, O.M.I., addresses himself to some of the changing perspectives in Catholic moral theology.[4] Much of the disarray in Catholic moral teaching is due to a "coming to grips with the massive increase of knowledge about man in the multiple dimensions of his being, his activity and his social evolution." When one takes into account the many dimensions of the human situation (biological, psychological, domestic, social, and economic), the conclusions of moral reasoning are not always as clear as traditional theology would

[1] For the last speech of Paul VI, prepared for the feast of the Transfiguration (never delivered), cf. *Catholic Mind* 76, no. 1327 (Nov. 1978) 2–3. The Holy Father remembered those whose suffering he so often recalled and which he attempted so magnificently to reverse: the unemployed, the hungry, and "all those who in general find it hard to arrive at a satisfactory economic-social condition."

[2] John Paul II authored a book in 1960 entitled *Amour et responsabilité* (Paris: Société d'Editions Internationales, translation 1965). After discussing the meaning of procreation, he states: "Si l'on exclut des rapports conjugaux *radicalement et totalement* l'élément potentiel de paternité et de maternité, on transforme par là-même la relation réciproque des personnes" (215; his emphasis). He went on to add, as his syllogistic minor, that the use of contraception does this.

[3] Timothy E. O'Connell, *Principles for a Catholic Morality* (New York; Seabury 1978); Philip Keane, *Sexual Morality* (New York: Paulist, 1978); Daniel Maguire, *The Moral Choice* (Garden City: Doubleday, 1978).

[4] Denis E. Hurley, "The Quality of Life," *Tablet* 232 (1978) 483–84, 507–8, 529–30.

lead us to believe. Hurley then stands back from some contemporary debates and views them in a more general light.

What is emerging from these debates is that Catholic ethics must give due place to a consideration that traditionally does not seem to have received enough attention, namely, that in complex human situations there can be a conflict of moral values in which the choice must be left to the conscience of the individual. The important thing in this regard is that moral values that can come into conflict must be thoroughly weighed to ensure that the more important ones receive the respect that is their due, for example, regard for human life.

Hurley's remarks strike me as an accurate and insightful account of what is actually happening in some recent debates.

Readers may be interested in a brief self-review by Joseph Fletcher.[5] Fletcher looks back on his book *Situation Ethics* and tells us where he is now. His thesis has, he says, "been resisted by most of the church critics, accepted by most of the non-idealists in philosophy, and fully approved by those in the professions who have the responsibility of serious decision-making." What is that thesis? Let a few excerpts state it. "By rules we would hold that abortion or farm price supports are wrong (or right); by situation ethics we would say that whether they are wrong or right depends on the particular case." Or again: "In moral matters ... judgments should be made, and are increasingly made, on the basis of the facts in each particular situation, rather than by rules already adopted before the situation." Finally: situationists "determine right and wrong quite practically in terms of gain or loss in human well being, in actual cases rather than broad generalizations or metaphysical-transcendental presuppositions."

Voilà! Case dismissed. Those who have residual problems with what Fletcher calls his "act-utilitarianism" are those who do not decide "on the basis of the facts" but "by rules already adopted before the situation." They are proponents of "doctrinaire ethics," of "ideology," of "metaphysical-transcendental presuppositions." I believe there are still a few moral theologians out there who are convinced that moral judgments are made "on the basis of the facts in each particular situation," yet that such judgments can yield norms that enlighten similar situations. And they believe that such norms need not make of them "doctrinaire" ethicians or "absolutists." Or, in lay terms, is the world really divided into only black hats and white hats?

Andreas Laun presents a summary of the German literature on the understanding of moral norms.[6] He notes that a teleological direction is

[5] Joseph Fletcher, "Love and Utility," *Christian Century* 95 (1978) 592–94.

[6] A. Laun, "Teleologische Normenbegründung," *Theologisch-praktische Quartalschrift* 126 (1978) 162–68.

taken by "many authors" and correctly identifies them (B. Schüller, F. Scholz, F. Böckle, B. Häring, H. Küng, W. Korff, and many others).[7] At the heart of this approach, he states, is the notion of a weighing of conflicted goods (*Güterabwägung*); for in the realm of worldly values there is question only of "relative values which cannot be elevated to absolute values" (H. Küng). This suggests a certain relativizing of concrete moral norms, a certain opening to consideration of situations of conflict. F. Scholz, for one, sees this as anything but new; it is pervasively present in traditional analyses but disguised by the language of direct and indirect action. When there was question of indirect action (double effect), there was really a question of direct action which is the result of a weighing of values (*Güterabwägung*).[8] Bernard Häring has summarized this tendency as follows: "In many conflicting situations we cannot observe and realize all the desirable values at the same time, but we can and must give preference to those that are the most valuable and most urgent for both our own self-actualization and the actualization of the human community."[9] Readers of these "Notes" will recognize well-rehearsed themes in such statements.

Laun then summarizes some anticipated objections to these approaches. For instance, it is no serious objection to argue with analytically obvious examples such as "it is never permissible to violate marriage" (*Ehebruch*), for there is a moral judgment included in the very description of the conduct. Equivalently, as Schüller has shown,[10] this says: it is never permissible to act unethically. The question rather is: Is the sexual intimacy of one who is divorced and remarried a violation of marriage under all circumstances?

Similarly, to the objection that teleological theories know no exceptionless norms it must be stated that they do indeed. It is simply a question of stating specifically in the norm the value disproportion. For instance, abortion is never justifiable to avoid interruption of one's professional career.[11] Or again, teleological theories reject with St. Paul the doctrine that the end sanctifies the means if by evil means one means *morally* evil means. However, the authors of such theories insist that a weighing of values in conflict must precede the designation of a means as morally wrong.

To the charge that this teleology amounts to "situation ethics," the response is a resounding "no"; for the weighing of conflicted values

---

[7] He could have added Joseph Fuchs, S.J., who brings together many of his previous reflections in *Responsabilità personale e norma morale* (Bologna: Dehoniane, 1978).

[8] F. Scholz, *Wege, Umwege und Auswege der Moraltheologie* (Munich: Don Bosco, 1976) 103.

[9] B. Häring, *Manipulation* (Slough: St. Paul Publications, 1975) 76.

[10] Cf. Laun.   [11] Scholz, *Wege* 157.

"demands an objective, uncorrupted weighing of the relation of means to end" (a true judgment of proportion).[12] And so on.

Laun concludes his study with some critiques. First, there is lacking a coherent theory of values upon which to build. Second, Laun doubts that the terms "deontological" and "teleological" are central to the discussion; for teleologists hold that the action itself ("as it were, the 'first consequence' of the act") is important and deontologists believe consequences are not insignificant. Actually, both are concerned with values in the discovery of norms. The difference, according to Laun, is that deontologists believe there are certain values associated with our conduct that must go untouched in every case *independently of further consequences.*

Laun believes that recent teleological perspectives cannot handle the case of judicial murder (the judge who convicts one innocent person of a rape to call off a rioting mob that will foreseeably kill many). Schüller had argued that not only is the life of one innocent person at stake (vs. perhaps five innocents lost in the rioting) but the whole institution of criminal law. Laun is dissatisfied with this, because could the injustice remain secret, the criminal law would not be at stake. If not, it would seem to follow that the one innocent person should be killed to save many as the lesser evil. He says: "The way that Schüller relativizes in the example the prohibition of killing on the one hand, yet on the other limits its practical consequences by appeal to the administration of justice, recalls the theses against which Pascal argued in his fight against laxism."[13] Laun also believes that the idea that premarital or extramarital sexual relations are always objectively wrong is untenable in teleological perspectives. Thus he generalizes: "The weakness of the theory lies clearly in the fact that every act can be justified if only in its behalf advantages to important ethical goods can be thrown into the calculus in a plausible way."[14]

Laun also argues that a teleological understanding of norms would weaken rights, for a weighing of goods must be allowed in the area of rights also. He takes a case of abortion as an example. A white student has gotten an African pregnant. "Since there is no basis for marriage, a priest consulted for advice recommends a weighing of values to determine the lesser evil . . . . The problematic is clear: if abortion is not a morally evil means in every case, then the weighing of goods (and respectively evils) is the right way."[15] Contrary to this, deontologists, while admitting that ethical obligation can change in the face of higher competing values, "hold to prohibitions which cannot be removed simply by the presence of a concurring value."

He concludes by challenging Böckle: "Does it clearly follow from the

[12] Scholz, *Wege* 157.
[13] Laun, "Teleologische . . . " 168.
[14] Ibid. 168.
[15] Ibid. 168.

fact that all earthly, morally relevant values are contingent that there can be no exceptionless prohibition against attacking this value?"[16]

Many will agree with Laun that the terms "teleological" and "deontological" are not central to this discussion. But I would respectfully disagree with his contention that in these recent writings "every act can be justified if only in its behalf advantages to important ethical goods can be thrown into the calculus in a plausible way." It is precisely the argument of recent writers that attempts to do this are not always plausible. For this reason, his example of abortion is hardly one to support his assertion that teleology can weaken rights. There is an objective difference between *any* reason and a truly commensurate (plausible) one.

In a long study L. Cornerotte, C.I.C.M., discusses conflict situations.[17] He does this in two steps. First he discusses the various ways of formulating the morally right and morally wrong (whether in terms of laws, values, basic inclinations, etc.). There is, of course, no sharp exclusivity here, since laws or duties are derived from values or goods toward which we have basic tendencies or inclinations. Ultimately Cornerotte defines moral evil as "a free activity which destroys or damages the being of persons and which is contrary to or contradicts the basic tendencies of persons." The actual deprivations or damages (disorders) are, as such, nonmoral or premoral. They become moral evils by specification of an evil will.

Cornerotte then asks: Are there cases where a free agent may provoke such nonmoral disorders legitimately? Can one, for example, cause the death or deception of another without corresponding moral malice? Before approaching his analysis (his second step), he rightly notes that moral disorder can be found in either end or means.[18] It is located in the end if one chooses a nonauthentic end—e.g., if life is organized around the acquisition of riches. It is located in the means if one fails to proportion the means to the end—e.g., if one surpasses moderation in taking nourishment or if one causes more damage than necessary in resisting an aggressor. Moral disorder may also be found in means which are disproportionate for another reason, e.g., one commits adultery to preserve a family inheritance.

Cornerotte then moves to his second step, the conflict of values. Any principles for the resolution of value conflicts rest upon a hierarchy of values. St. Thomas states such a hierarchy[19] when he divides goods into

---

[16] Ibid. 169.

[17] L. Cornerotte, C.I.C.M., "Loi morale, valeurs humaines et situations de conflit," *Nouvelle revue théologique* 100 (1978) 502–32.

[18] "Bonum humanae virtutis in ordine rationis consistit. Qui quidem principaliter attenditur respectu finis. . . . Secundario autem attenditur prout secundum rationem finis ordinantur ea quae sunt ad finem" (2–2, q. 161, a. 5).

[19] 2–2, q. 152, a. 2.

exterior goods, goods of the body and the spirit, etc. Such beginnings were extensively developed by Max Scheler, Nicolai Hartmann, and Hans Reiner. Scheler, e.g., established a hierarchy on four levels: values of the agreeable, vital or biological values (health, vitality), spiritual values (beauty, right, justice), sacred values. Hartmann and, above all, Reiner developed preference principles for action when values are in conflict. These principles touch on the excellence of the value, the fundamental character of the value, its temporal urgency, its quantity, the chance of success, etc. These preference principles are present in traditional moral treatises under title of *ordo bonorum* and *ordo caritatis* (the determination of persons who deserve the preference).

On the basis of such a hierarchy, Catholic moral theology has developed what Cornerotte calls "operating principles" for the resolution of conflicts. He lists four. (1) *The principle of legitimate excusing cause.* This states that the obligation of positive law generally ceases where fulfilment is tied to a grave difficulty extrinsic to the law and proportioned to the importance of the law. Thus, one is excused from Sunday Mass when he/she must attend the sick. Clearly, an accurate appreciation of the respective values and duties is necessary.

2) *The principle of the double effect in the strict sense.* This involves situations in which an action aimed at a good effect is nevertheless accompanied by a negative dimension or result. Thus, a medicine necessary to health can produce sterility. In deciding what is a proportionate reason, preference principles (excellence, necessity, temporal urgency, quantity [common good]) must be considered as well as the principle of universalizability. Cornerotte says that the demand that the action be good or indifferent excludes actions that, taken in isolation, are moral disorders (lie) or premoral disorders (amputation of a limb). Thus he excludes from the rule of double effect actions such as shooting a person, hunger strikes, jumping from a high floor of a burning building, destruction of military installations in a just war. In all such cases the action is the direct cause of a premoral evil. For this reason "the will, although regretfully, is positively willing, and the premorally evil aspect is intended as the necessary condition of the appearance of the good effect." Cornerotte does not mean that such actions are morally wrong. He argues only that they cannot be solved by the principle of the double effect in the classical sense. And that brings him to his third principle.

3) *The principle of the double effect in the broad sense.* In this category of conflicts are situations whose resolution involves premoral evil. Cornerotte lists the following: cases involving the principle of totality (surgery, amputation); legitimate self-defense, capital punishment, just war; protection of secrets involving ambiguous statements and falsehood; taking the property of another when one is in extreme need. Moral

theologians have been unanimous in their conclusions about these instances but not in their justification. This means that traditional moral theology had not made explicit the deeper rationale for these conclusions.

Cornerotte formulates that rationale as follows:

In extreme cases, when a better solution is impossible, a superior obligatory value can, within limits, be protected by means of the active, even if regretful, sacrifice of a value of a lower order, or a value of the same order but one that is less urgent, on the condition that this sacrifice stand, in the present, in a connatural, necessary and duly proportionated relationship with the best possible protection of the values at stake, and, on the universal level, that the sacrifice not end up ultimately in a radical denial of these values.[20]

Some such principle underlies the solution of many cases presented by traditional moral treatises, even though the principle itself does not emerge explicitly.

4) *The principle of heroic sacrifice.* The love of Christ can inspire us to forgo our rights and sacrifice our lives. Thus, rather than defend ourselves, we may suffer the aggression. Or, like Father Maximilian Kolbe, we may offer to take the place of a condemned person. Here one does not exactly kill oneself, but out of heroic love one abandons oneself to external forces (malice of others, forces of nature) which will destroy one.

It is clearly the third principle that is of most interest. Cornerotte calls it the "double effect in the broad sense" because "the negative effect can be called indirectly voluntary in a broad sense since it is willed only with regret and not for itself." Cornerotte gives five positive rules or conditions for determining whether there is a *causa proportionata* for an action falling in this class. (*a*) There is an irreducible conflict of values. (*b*) There is an obligation to act, i.e., there is a preference which urges one to act in the present. (*c*) The means is ontologically proportioned to the protection of the obligatory, predominating value. By "ontologically proportioned" he means strictly and ontologically necessary. (*d*) Among the means, one must choose the least harmful, scil., the one best calculated to protect all the values. (*e*) The action does not amount to a denial of the values on the universal level.

In applying these conditions, Cornerotte lays special emphasis on condition (*c*), the ontologically necessary character of the means. A means is not ontologically proportioned if it destroys the very value it is supposed to affirm. For instance, an act of adultery demanded by a jailer as a condition of freedom for a married woman (Bergmeier case) is equivalently the denial of fidelity to her husband. Furthermore, it is not ontologically proportioned if it does not stand in a necessary relationship

[20] Cornerotte, "Loi morale" 518.

to the end. Thus, fornication and adultery are not proportionate means of self-defense, because they have no necessary relation to the preservation of life.[21]

In light of such possible exceptions, we must be careful to formulate negative moral principles properly; otherwise we will have forfeited their absolute character. Such principles (forbidding murder, lying, etc.) are absolute only in so far as they are well formulated, i.e., with exceptions included. For "the moral agent sometimes finds himself enmeshed in a conflict of laws all of which simultaneously demand his respect. Then it is a question of determining the greatest good realizable."[22]

Cornerotte feels that the "principle of double effect in the broad sense" is more frequent than we realize. It is operative in the punishment of children, the measured anger of superiors toward the irresponsibility of subordinates, the quarantine of those with contagious diseases, the incarceration of delinquents, the revelation of faults and failings of aspirants to high public office. We do not advert to this, because we are accustomed to and have accepted their moral appropriateness. "But all of them involve a certain premoral evil and cannot be explained by the classic principle of double effect." Cornerotte concludes his study by applying it to several practical and controversial areas (birth control, conduct in war, abortion).

This is an interesting, careful study. Several comments are called for. First, Cornerotte is quite correct, I believe, in saying that traditional moral theology indeed supposed some such principle as he proposes in its casuistry without ever making it explicit. This is what the contemporary discussion is all about. It is an attempt to explicitate this principle for situations of conflicted values.

Second, it is misleading, in my judgment, to call this the "principle of the double effect in the broad sense." This terminology suggests that there is a fairly close relationship between Cornerotte's obvious teleology and the classic principle of double effect, the former being a kind of extension of the latter. That is misleading, for in the classical understanding of double effect one could intend the evil neither as end nor as a means. Clearly, Cornerotte holds that evil (premoral) may regretfully be intended as a means (*in se sed non propter se*) if it is appropriately proportioned to the end in the conflict case.

Furthermore, referring to such justified actions (e.g., falsehood to protect a professional secret) as justified by the double effect "in the broad sense" tends to confirm that classic doctrine (double effect, indirect voluntary) as morally decisive. Cornerotte holds this to be the case ("the principle of the double effect in the classical sense retains all of its validity

---

[21] 2-2, q. 64, a. 7, ad 4: "non ordinatur ad conservationem propriae vitae ex necessitate."
[22] Cornerotte, "Loi morale" 525.

in its own proper sphere"). Actually, if Cornerotte is right in saying that we may at times intend premoral evil as means, even if regretfully (as I think he is), this shows that indirectness of intent in the classical principle of double effect was not truly decisive in solving cases. Directness/ indirectness as such become redundant. Bruno Schüller brings this out very clearly when he shows that permitting a nonmoral evil and intending such an evil as a means can both reveal the same basic attitude toward evil: disapproval.[23]

Third, Cornerotte takes issue with the author of these "Notes" on the analysis of the direct destruction of civilians in warfare. I had argued that the moral wrongfulness is traceable to long-term effects.[24] This he sees as "sérieusement incomplète." I agree with this criticism and have modified the analysis since Cornerotte authored his article.[25] He sees direct destruction of innocents in warfare as involving a denial of the very value (the saving of lives) one is attempting to achieve. Furthermore, he sees such destruction as in no necessary ontological relationship with the protection of the other innocent lives one is attempting to protect. In this I believe he is correct, though a further analysis of the disproportion is possible.[26]

Fourth, Cornerotte accurately applies his reasoning to the classical abortion case (abort or lose both mother and child). He says: "The intervention which saves the mother can be called 'the indirect cause in the broad sense' of the infant's death because this intervention is, in the circumstances, the only way to affirm one's respect for human life, and it is in a real, necessary, ontologically proportioned relationship with the charitable goal of saving one life rather than allowing two to perish."[27]

[23] Bruno Schüller, S.J., "The Double Effect in Catholic Thought: A Reevaluation," in Richard A. McCormick, S.J., and Paul Ramsey, eds., *Doing Evil to Achieve Good* (Chicago: Loyola University Press, 1978) 165–91.

[24] *Ambiguity in Moral Choice* (Milwaukee: Marquette, 1973).

[25] "Notes on Moral Theology," *TS* 39 (1978) 107.

[26] Ibid. 111–15.

[27] At this point Cornerotte states of Pius XI: "In no way did he demand that the mother die together with her child." I believe this to be inaccurate. Pius XI's formulation excluded any *direct* abortion for any reason whatever. Direct abortion was understood in a very definite way in the tradition. E.g., a craniotomy in difficult birth situations was seen as a direct killing. Interventions into ectopic pregnancies were disallowed until it was argued that they were indirect. This means that there were situations where both mother and child must be allowed to perish rather than perform a direct abortion. This was the way the teaching of Pius XI was understood by theologians. "Better two deaths than one murder" was the translation. If Pius XI did not mean this, it would have been unconscionable to tolerate such misunderstanding of his teaching. As Karl-Heinz Weger notes of this rare case (whose rarity does not reduce its methodological importance): "The Church's magisterium— and honesty demands that this be said—has disallowed the certain death of the mother as a sufficient reason for abortion. In recent years, however, the opinion of the Church on this question has been modified. So we read in a recent writing of the German bishops: 'In

Correct. But why call the intervention "indirect"? In other words, Cornerotte has made a very important, and in my judgment correct, move but has not fully accepted its implications.

Finally, when Cornerotte applies his analysis to contraception, in cases of irreducible conflict, he accepts antiovulatory pills[28] but rejects some other artificial methods (diaphragm, condom) on the grounds that they destroy the symbolism of the natural self-gift contained in sexual intimacy. This argument is not new. For instance, Louis Janssens, in his first exploratory analyses,[29] argued in much the same way, but he no longer does so. The matter of symbolism is an important and tricky one. The question it raises is this: Should the symbolism of mutual self-gift be attached to mere physical artificiality in this way? Or again, is there not an infringement of symbolism if periodic continence is selfishly practiced? What must be avoided is a recrudescence of a narrow physicalism. Is the symbolism of self-gift not a matter of a whole cluster of factors, involving above all the generous openness of the couple toward childbearing? As one experienced and insightful lay person remarked, "There are many ways in which sex can be exploitative." And therefore many aspects have to be considered if it is to be nonexploitative. Is it not there (in over-all conduct) that symbolism is to be sought? However one answers, it seems that what is a denial of symbolism in this area is to be determined from experience. Finally, even if (*dato non concesso*) certain artificial interventions do reduce the symbolism of the self-gift, is it so clear that such reduction is always morally wrong? To be so, would it not have to have the character of absolute value?

In a compact and carefully wrought study presented to the Congress of Italian Moral Theologians (Catania, April 12–14, 1977), Enrico Chiavacci studies the foundations of moral norms.[30] The notion of the "foundation" of moral norms has two aspects. First, there is the question of the basic sense of life which our individual actions ought to realize or express. Without such a basic sense (a metaethical question) "any conversation about moral duty or ethics in general makes no sense." The second step is the move from this ultimate and unifying sense or value to the generation of moral norms (their legitimacy and criteria). He treats this second step first and asks: "Is the rule to be followed that which . . . best

---

irresolvable conflict situations where the decision is between losing both mother and child and losing just one, the medical conscience-decision is to be respected' " ("Schwangerschaftsabbruch: Kirche und Gewissen," *Orientierung* 42 [1978] 66–69). Weger notes that this statement was meant as a help not only to doctors but also to the wife or spouses.

[28] On the proviso that they are not abortifacient in their method of operation.

[29] Louis Janssens, "Morale conjugale et progestogènes," *Ephemerides theologicae Lovanienses* 39 (1963) 787–826.

[30] Enrico Chiavacci, "La fondazione della norma morale nella riflessione teologica contemporanea," *Rivista di teologia morale* 37 (1978) 9–38.

approximates the basic sense? Or is it that which is rigorously deduced from this value? . . . We have, therefore, the possibility of a foundation for norms that roots in finality—teleological—or one that is deductive—deontological."

Chiavacci correctly notes that these terms (deontology, teleology) have their difficulties. For instance, those who understand moral norms teleologically can hold absolutes. Thus, "never lie" can be argued on teleological grounds (lying undermines the possibility of social life), but then it becomes for all practical purposes a fixed deontological principle ("never lie, come what may here and now").

Contrarily, a deontological ethic ought to admit some norms without any exceptions, come what may. But Chiavacci doubts that there really are any. Take lying, e.g., or, more exactly, speaking falsehood. The classical explanation was that the purpose of speech is to communicate true information. Thus any *locutio contra mentem* was contrary to nature and nature's Author. "But in the same Christian and Catholic tradition there are many authors who admitted grounds for 'exceptions': the evil use another could make of the knowledge communicated; the lack of another's right to make demands on me; the right of the accused not to betray himself; the grave harm that might come to others from knowledge of the truth."[31] Thus the categories deontological-teleological are not all that helpful. For the deontological understanding is clearly not one that takes no account of consequences; rather, it establishes once and for all the priority of certain consequences, or it establishes that certain forms of conduct produce more desirable consequences without excluding the possibility that in individual cases (not codifiable) that is not true.

Chiavacci notes that for Augustine and Thomas the teleological element prevails over the deontological in God Himself. Thus, the command not to kill oneself was "violated" by Samson through divine command. "But a command contrary to a deontological command can have no other justification than the prosecution of an end (good)—an end which as a rule ought to be achieved by observing the norm, but in individual cases, not generalizable, can be achieved by violating the norm."[32]

Chiavacci concludes this first section of his study by insisting that every norm is radically teleological (whether one tends to explain it deontologically or teleologically) "in the sense that it ought to represent conduct that better realizes (or compromises less) a certain development of the interior history of the individual and/or of the history of mankind and the world."

Chiavacci grants that the form the foundation of norms will take depends very much on the basic sense or value one assumes as the remote foundation for norms. Thus, the second part of his study deals with this

[31] Ibid. 18.   [32] Ibid. 19.

ultimate sense of life or value, and from a specifically Christian point of view. Here he uses Balthasar's affirmation that "Christ is the concrete categorical imperative." For the believer, the unifying sense of life which founds norms is faith in the risen Christ—not mere intellectual faith (*fides quae*) but the faith of total personal self-commitment and choice (*fides qua*). This faith is knowledge of the ultimate reality and is the only way of knowing it. "To know that Christ, the perfect image of the Father, is already law and not just the legislator, is already categorical imperative and not just the font of further detailed imperatives, to have grasped this is, in my view, the decisive qualitative move of contemporary moral theology."[33]

Why is this so? In what sense is Jesus "already law and categorical imperative"? He is the revelation of God's love. "In the New Testament the single duty of charity, of the self-gift to God seen in one's neighbor, is founded in the fact that God Himself is love." The mandate of love upon us is founded in nothing else but the love of God for us. "The fact that God . . . is love does not reach back for further justification; it is the ultimate fact." This is the background and root of the Christian moral life, the foundation of Christian ethics. In view of this, Chiavacci sees charity (the total gift of self) as the single supreme value, the ultimate "sense" of life which unifies all norms and is their Christian foundation.

For Chiavacci, it is also the Christian foundation of individual moral norms in the sense that individual norms are but concretizations of the demand of charity, the self-gift to God as encountered in others. As for "the process of the production" of these individual norms, Chiavacci argues that from the foundational value "there follows here a substantially teleological foundation for the process of the production of both precept and norm."[34] More specifically, he concludes:

The necessity of historicizing and making categorical the single precept or value (charity) is clearly opposed to a rigidly deductive process for individual norms, such as would be valid "come what may." It is precisely the peculiarity of the precept of charity which demands the weighing of the effects of our actions on others, so that what results is never morally irrelevant. It is precisely from this consideration that we have the substantially teleological form of the Christian ethic.[35]

Chiavacci takes masturbation as an example of how norms must be viewed teleologically. This prohibition has been justified deontologically (to be observed no matter what, "accada ciò che puo") and was proposed in this sense by Pius XII. Thus, in the situation of sterility-testing the

[33] Ibid. 27.

[34] Chiavacci distinguishes precept from norm throughout. The norm is the precept as assimilated and applied by the individual in his/her circumstances.

[35] Chiavacci, "La fondazione" 33.

deontologist would say:

The couple must remain sterile, with all the nonmorally evil consequences (perhaps even morally evil) involved, rather than violate the precept. A teleological ethics which accepts the supremacy of the precept of charity would, on the contrary, say: in this hypothesis charity does not render masturbation only *licit*, but renders it *obligatory* when it is a question of saving or enriching the couple.[36]

Chiavacci's study is careful and rewarding. He shows himself well read in Anglo-American philosophy as well as biblical exegesis. He has a fine sense of the conflict character of all moral decision-making and of the place and limits of the magisterium, of Scripture, and of moral reasoning. For instance, he asks: In the generation of moral norms, can other sources (Scripture, magisterium) *replace* moral reasoning? "My answer," he says, "is decisively negative." These sources are aids to, not replacements for, moral insight and reasoning and represent a kind of "exemplary pedagogy" for moral discernment.

It will come as no surprise that the compiler of these "Notes" regards this as a fine piece of analysis. Chiavacci is clearly to be counted among those (now a heavy majority of European theologians, if the literature is any indication) who interpret norms in a substantially teleological way. To my knowledge, he is the first Catholic to trace this explicitly in the way he does to the supreme value of charity in the moral life.

One small point. The example Chiavacci uses (masturbation for sterility-testing) would be explained differently by many theologians. It is not simply a matter of violating a precept for the greater good of the marriage. Rather, self-stimulation in these circumstances is a different human act and therefore does not involve the malice he correctly hypothesizes for the narcissistic performance of such an act.

The directions taken most recently by Cornerotte and Chiavacci and reported by Laun are linear descendents from Fuchs–Schüller–Janssens–Scholz–Böckle–Häring[37] *et al.* Not all are satisfied with these directions. Let two recent examples suffice: Frederick Carney and William May. Apologies are in order in advance for the inordinate use of the perpendicular pronoun—an unavoidable blemish, since these studies deal with my own reporting and writing.

Frederick S. Carney has written a detailed study of these developments as they have been elaborated and formulated by the compiler of these "Notes."[38] Carney describes himself first as a "surprised Protestant friend" when confronted with what he calls my "teleological monism."

[36] Ibid. 33.

[37] Cf. Joseph Omoregbe, "Evolution in Bernard Häring's Ethical Thinking," *Louvain Studies* 7 (1978) 45–54.

[38] Frederick S. Carney, "On McCormick and Teleological Morality," *Journal of Religious Ethics* 6 (1978) 81–107.

He says also that he is "perplexed." Ultimately he is overtaken by "sadness of heart." I am, of course, concerned that the tentative and humble gropings in these pages should so distress a friend and colleague. Such fluctuations of soul are, however, nonmoral disvalues. If they are the price of our more accurate grasp of moral truth, we must cheerfully, if regretfully, pay that price. In more familiar words, such disvalues should be visited on others only if, all things considered, there is a proportionate reason for doing so. Is there? That question depends on how we ought to conceptualize our duties when confronted with conflicts of values or goods.

Carney first very usefully describes four different types of teleology (teleology of virtue, of nature, of human institutions, of obligation) and correctly argues that the issue under discussion is the last form of teleology. One holds this fourth type of teleology if one asserts "that the moral rightness of an act ... depends upon its being the most effective act (or rule) available within the designated circumstances for serving good ends or bringing about good (or less evil) consequences."

Secondly, Carney tries to understand what kind of teleology I am proposing. In an earlier study I had written that in conflict situations where harm will result from either of two alternatives open to the agent, the rule of Christian reason is to choose the lesser evil.[39] Carney rejects this: "Surely it is possible to choose between two acts on grounds other than the consequential good or evil that each act would produce." He gives as an example the resignation of his son from a coaching position. His son would be personally worse off; the swimming team would be less well off without his skills, etc. Yet Carney's son felt there were "matters of principle" at stake. Carney argues that his son did not choose the lesser evil. Rather, he made "a decision of principle." Similarly, to my contention that where nonmoral evil is judged morally acceptable in human action a single decisive element (proportionate reason) explains this, Carney says: "For some people (both scholars and non-scholars) do as a matter of fact sometimes judge evil to be acceptable without employing proportionate reason in doing so." Further, Carney argues that there are no Christian warrants for saying that the choice of the lesser evil in conflict situations is the "rule of Christian reason."

He next identifies the teleology he finds in *Ambiguity in Moral Choice* (and, by extension, in Fuchs, Schüller, Janssens, Böckle, *et al.*) as utilitarian ("unquestionably a form of utilitarianism"). He then argues that St. Thomas cannot be enlisted to support such pure "teleological monism." Finally, he offers suggestions as to why this path should not be followed. For instance, a teleological morality cannot account for the very basic moral institution of promising and promise-keeping. Moreover, such

[39] Cf. *Ambiguity in Moral Choice*, n. 24.

a theory collapses moral agents into calculators of futurity "hellbent on producing beneficent (or less maleficent) states of affairs in the world."

Several points might be made to allow the issues to emerge more clearly. First, there is Carney's example of his son. Rather than choose the "lesser evil," Carney argues that his son's resignation decision was a "matter of principle." But that will not do. Specifically, what was this "matter of principle"? What goods were involved which were protected by this principle? For instance, if his son resigned because he insisted on green towels for all swimmers (his "matter of principle"), then his decision looks quite foolish, indeed looks like unnecessary harm brought on himself and others. If the principle were protecting some less trivial concern (e.g., honesty in reporting swimmers' ages), then the choice to resign from coaching even if it involves nonmoral harms is fully justified, and is, I would argue, the choice of the lesser evil in the circumstances. The point is that Carney cannot say that his son did not choose the lesser evil until he tells us clearly what is behind his son's "matter of principle." When he does unpack that notion, it will become clear that the notion of the lesser evil is indeed an accurate, even if general, way of characterizing the decision. The fact that he can exclude (or hide) the goods behind the notion of "matter of principle" indicates how narrowly Carney reads the term "proportionate reason."

That brings us to a second point: Carney's understanding of the teleology I have suggested. He refers to this repeatedly as "pure teleology," "teleological monism," "a pure teleology of obligation." This is then reworded and enfleshed in some of the following ways: "an act is wrong if it is less productive than some other act in bringing about good consequences or serving desirable ends"; "the consequences would be on balance negative"; "rightness ... depends on its being the most effective act available ... for ... bringing about good (or less evil) consequences"; "grounds other than the amount of evil (or good) their choice would bring about"; "morality of human action is to be made only by the assessment of the effects of the action."

Such phrases show the narrowness of Carney's reading of the term "proportionate reason" as this is found in Catholic tradition. He equivalates the term (which he erroneously calls a "moral norm"[40]) to a weighing of nonmoral goods and evils which excludes many of the considerations which belong under a proper understanding of proportion. Thus he is

[40] It is a structure of reasoning in a Catholic tradition of many centuries but has no concrete normative content as such. Here it seems advisable to invite participants in this discussion to cease using the phrase "the ethics of proportionate reason." That usage is terribly misleading. It suggests a whole system of ethics or moral theology. Actually, recent theologians are not concerned with "an ethics." Rather, they are viewing human actions in so far as these involve us in a conflict of values. That such conflicts occur more frequently than we think is clear, especially in the writings of Janssens and more recently Chiavacci.

able to say that the term amounts to "pure teleology." But Carney's equivalence here is violent and invalid, for the usage "proportionate reason" must include many considerations which Carney seems to overlook in his quite simplistic understanding of the term.[41] Once he has reduced the dimensions of the term to almost quantitative considerations, then it is an easy move to identify this teleology with "a form of utilitarianism." But even Carney seems to suggest that not all teleology is utilitarian, for at one point he refers to "all teleologies (including utilitarianism)." Presumably, then, not all teleologies are utilitarian.

To make this point, let me refer once again to a study by Charles Curran.[42] Curran identifies three general approaches: strict teleology (utilitarian), strict deontology (e.g., Anscombe), mixed teleology (or mixed deontology). This last position differs from strict teleology because it maintains the following points: (1) moral obligation arises from elements other than consequences; (2) the good is not separate from the right; (3) the way in which the good or evil is achieved by the agent is a moral consideration. Curran rightly concluded that recent Catholic revisionist efforts (I include myself here) fit this last category because they insist that elements other than consequences function in moral rightness and wrongness.

William May, who strongly resists these developments, as we shall see below, refers to such theologians as "mixed deontologists."[43] He could as well have said "mixed teleologists." But Carney has no such term. Either one is a deontologist à la Carney, or one is a utilitarian. And that makes it fairly simple for him to qualify recent studies as utilitarian. Had he a more adequate, richer notion of proportionate reason, he might have sensed the inadequacy, even violence, of such categorization. Until he enriches his notion of *causa proportionata*, his analysis will not succeed. And if he does enrich his analysis, his argument will change.

John Langan, S.J., has brought this point out in his interesting review of a forthcoming book entitled *Doing Evil to Achieve Good*.[44] Of my explanations of proportionate reason, Langan notes:

These warnings show that McC. wants to avoid methods of justifying actions with evil effects that rely simply on intending good effects or achieving beneficial long-

---

[41] Cf. *TS* 39 (1978) 88 and L. Janssens, "Norms and Priorities in a Love Ethic," *Louvain Studies* 6 (1977) 207–38. E.g., to be considered among other things: the distinction between instrumental acts, actions having a meaning in themselves, and expressive actions; the institutional character of some actions; the *ordo bonorum* and *ordo caritatis*.

[42] Charles E. Curran, "Utilitarianism and Contemporary Moral Theology: Situating the Debates," *Louvain Studies* 6 (1977) 239–55.

[43] William May, "Ethics and Human Identity: The Challenge of the New Biology," *Horizons* 3 (1976) 17–37.

[44] John Langan, S.J., "Direct and Indirect: Some Exchanges between Paul Ramsey and Richard McCormick," to appear in *Religious Studies Review*, April 1979.

range consequences. They should lead critics to beware of treating McC. as a utilitarian, as Frederick Carney does; and they should lead us to expect McC.'s revisionism in moral theology to be conservative and clarifying rather than radical and simplifying.

Langan even suspects that I may be a "crypto-deontologist." Such is the malleability of human concepts and language. But I think Langan has got it exactly right.

A third point that needs attention is Carney's reading of the axiom "A good end does not justify an evil means." Or, as Carney words it, citing St. Thomas, "the effects ... cannot ... change a bad act into a morally right one." His example from Aquinas is that of a lie, and of it Thomas states: "A person deserves to be condemned if he does evil that good may come."[45] Of this Carney says that we have Thomas denying precisely what recent revisionists affirm, "namely, that a person may intend 'nonmoral evil if a truly proportionate reason for such a choice is present.'" Of course, if an act is described as a *moral* evil (lie), no intended good can justify it. But is every falsehood necessarily a lie? If Carney thinks so, he will have to deal with the exceptions mentioned by Chiavacci—and, incidentally, with a considerable tradition which established (teleologically) such exceptions. In other words, and more generally, the axiom referred to is simply erroneous if it is read to include nonmoral evils. We cause (and intend) them all the time to achieve good purposes. So, when Carney reads Thomas as being "against *any evil* act ... that good may be served thereby," I think he is simply wrong.[46] Thomas had to be referring to *morally* evil acts, as his use of the term "lie" would suggest; or else Thomas needs correction.

My fourth point concerns considerations of justice. Carney states that if I mean that such considerations "necessarily entail the weighing of consequences, then [I] simply [do] not understand what the philosophical writers referred to by Connery mean by justice." I would certainly maintain that necessary entailment, as would centuries of Catholic and, I hope, Protestant tradition. It is implicit in our long traditions on capital punishment, just warfare, self-defense, etc. We cannot define an individual's right (justice) in the abstract and with no reference to conflicted circumstances. Specifically, with regard to the right to life, why is not capital punishment a denial of the right to life? Does my right to life include a prohibition of my being "only indirectly" killed in war? Does my right to property (e.g., food) not get qualified if my neighbor is starving? The mistake of many discussants is to conduct conversation in terms of rights and justice *before* the rights and wrongs have been

---

[45] As cited in Carney.

[46] Cf. F. Scholz, "Durch ethische Grenzsituationen aufgeworfene Normenprobleme," *Theologisch-praktische Quartalschrift* 123 (1975) 341–55.

explored. It is only *after* such conversation that we can define the reach and limits of rights. And that conversation will include consequences (conflicted values); else it ceases to be Christian, that is, to be concerned about what happens to the neighbor.

My final reflection is to return this discussion to the key point: the moral relevance of directness and indirectness of intent in our actions involving nonmoral evil. Carney's position (gathered from what he says about "many deontologists" and the way he disagrees with Knauer-Schüller-Fuchs) is: "To intend an evil effect is morally wrong in itself." I suppose he would restrict this to some kinds of acts, such as killing, though I find no reason for such restriction. (And I have noted that he tends to describe an act in value or moral terms—the lie—in stating his position, which, of course, prejudges and even distorts the problem.)

Let the classic abortion dilemma be the occasion of my question to Carney. I presume that Carney would say that abortion in this case (lose both or at least save the mother) is morally right, perhaps even obligatory. In at least some of these cases, the abortion is straightforwardly a means, not an incidental by-product. Furthermore, it is a means that was equated with direct killing in recent tradition. Take the real case given by Ramsey of an aortic aneurysm ballooning threateningly behind the uterus. To get at it, the uterus must be evacuated. Traditional theology would call this—and did call it—a direct abortion and would disallow it. It allowed only the "indirect abortion" involved in the case of ectopic pregnancies and the cancerous uterus. Recent theologians, however, believe the abortion is direct but permissible. What does Carney think? There are three possibilities: (1) It is direct and morally wrong. (2) It is direct and morally right. (3) It is indirect and therefore morally right. If he holds the second position—as I think he must[47]—we have a clear instance where one directly, even if reluctantly, may intend nonmoral evil as a means (*in se sed non propter se*). If that is the case, the redundancy of the direct-indirect distinction is exposed. That is, it is not morally decisive. Obviously, if one comes to that conclusion (that one may intend nonmoral evil as a means at times), then one is led into *some form* of teleology, though not necessarily what Carney calls "pure teleology" or "teleological monism."

Carney has not seen this because he has chosen to enter this discussion at the lofty level of typologies, typologies which are more often than not uninformative categories.[48] This is not to demean typologies; they can be

[47] The first is held by practically no one any more. The third has no relationship to any traditional understanding of the terms "direct" and "indirect."

[48] I have other serious problems with Carney's study which must remain undeveloped. E.g., he cites my use of the *ordo bonorum* and states that this is "never explained." Were Carney more familiar with the manual tradition, he would understand that this is a classical notion (as is the *ordo caritatis*). Similarly, he states, without ever specifying, that Schüller's

helpful. But their logical elegance sheds very little light on some utterly practical problems. Until these problems are faced, their theoretical implications will remain imperfectly explored.

William May (Catholic University) continues his discussion of these trends in two articles.[49] I shall draw on both in detailing his objections. He considers his points serious and even "devastating objections," indeed so devastating that he characterizes Fuchs–Schüller–Janssens–Bockle *et al.* "situationists in the pejorative sense." "It is an ethics," he writes, "that sees the *moral* meaning of our acts as given to them by something extrinsic to themselves, namely the ends or goods intended by the agent, rather than by their intrinsic intelligibility."[50] Common to these authors, as well as Scholz, Weber, Di Ianni, Cornerotte, Chiavacci, *et al.*, is the tenet that nonmoral evil (e.g., killing) may at times be intended as a means. May's objections can fairly be summarized as follows.

First, according to this view one could never say that there are inherently evil acts. May gives three examples of such acts: "It is always wrong to have coition with a brute animal; it is always wrong to intend directly the torture of another human being; it is always wrong to use public moneys to pay one's mistress."[51]

careful critique of John Connery "is marred by Schüller's misunderstanding of the nature . . .of the arguments raised by Connery and his philosophical sources." Statements such as this should be carefully exemplified to strengthen us against the temptation of wondering whether Carney has consulted Schüller's writing firsthand.

[49] William E. May, "Modern Catholic Ethics: The New Situationism," *Faith and Reason* 4 (1978) 21–38; "The Moral Meaning of Human Acts," *Homiletic and Pastoral Review* 79 (Oct. 1978) 10–21.

[50] "Modern Catholic Ethics" 33. May mistakenly believes that my earlier criticism of this argument reveals "antipathy, indeed hostility." I regret that he has interpreted the critique in that way. The remark he finds offensive (that the objection "no longer serves the purpose of constructive moral discourse") means only that I believe the objection has been sufficiently and repeatedly answered. Thus, to say that a promise to attend a friend's wedding need not always be kept—may be broken if the life of an accident victim prevents fulfilment—does not mean that promises have no inherent meaning. It simply means that this meaning cannot be absolutized as against any other value, a point that has been raised in the German literature over and over again. Those who say this are hardly guilty of "eviscerating our acts of their human and moral significance." They are simply facing the fact that real conflicts of values do frequently exist in our lives. Do we not quarantine patients in order to prevent other persons from contracting disease? Do we not spank children so that in the future their conduct may be less self-threatening? Do we not kill in war to preserve our political freedom? That is the human scene.—Similarly, May has misread Walter Burghardt's statement about what May calls "two different types of theology," the one an "understanding" theology, the other a "defensive" one. Actually, Burghardt's statement and my use of it were in no way intended to discuss "kinds of theology," and still less to brand those who disagree with certain contemporary directions as "defensive." The Burghardt distinction, as the text will show, is discussing two *functions* of theology, both legitimate and necessary. He is suggesting—and I agree—that in the past one function was emphasized to the detriment of the other.

[51] "Moral Meaning" 13.

Secondly, some writers have employed the phrase *in se sed non propter se* of the will's posture toward nonmoral evil justifiably caused. May argues that no one intends evil *propter se.*

Thirdly, the contention that no actions describable in nonmoral terms are intrinsically evil means that "the *moral* nature of a human act, then, is not to be discovered by discerning intelligently the intrinsic nature of the act; rather the *moral* nature of the human act is to be discovered by looking to the good that the act achieves, a good that is extrinsic to the act itself." Thus these authors are "extrinsicists." May sees this as the "major weakness" of the position.

Fourthly, to say that we may at times directly intend nonmoral evil means "that the agent is willing to take on, as part of his moral identity, the identity of an evildoer." May sees this as in direct contradiction to the very first principle of the moral law, "a principle that admits *no* exceptions, namely, good is to be done and pursued and evil is to be avoided." To the objection that Abraham was prepared at God's command directly to kill Isaac, May argues that "Abraham, in his readiness to obey God, was not intending an act of homicide." He says that were he himself to receive a command from God "to take a burning cigarette and burn the eyes out of an infant," he would refuse to do so, either because this command must be regarded as a hallucination or because the God giving such a command is not the *summum bonum.*

Finally, while May concedes that estimating proportion in conflict cases is not solely the prerogative of the individual and therefore is not necessarily subjectivistic, he does believe that this structure of moral reasoning is relativistic. That is, an act is not wrong "simply because the community deems that it is." To think so is "cultural relativism." Thus, capital punishment is not "objectively morally justifiable" but the human community failed to grasp this in the past.

A few points. As for May's examples of acts intrinsically evil, let one example suffice (direct torture of another human being). Is that unthinkable? Torture is a very slippery word. Does it mean *unjustified* pain inflicted on another? Or does it mean *any* pain inflicted on another? People talk as if the notion were clear. Actually, "torture" in most discourse refers to the type of pain that causes moral revulsion. In other words, in its most frequent usage it is a value term, already containing its own condemnation (disproportion) in the context or tone. Take an example. If I apprehend one of two thugs on their way to execute my brother or my sister (at the time, I am not sure which one), I would apply a very effective and increasingly painful armlock to find out which, so I could warn him/her. Is that "torture"? Or is it simply the *justified* infliction of pain against an unjust aggressor? I opt for the latter, and everyone to whom I have talked agrees. But they still reject "torture."

This is an indication that they are understanding the term in a particular way: e.g., torture as practiced in some South American countries by some tyrannical regimes, or the infliction of pain on political prisoners.

May's other example ("it is always wrong to use public moneys to pay one's mistress") is not to the point. Of course that is wrong, and intrinsically, if one wishes. But so are a thousand things, if we add enough circumstances to the description of the act. Thus, it is always wrong to abort a pregnancy in order to maintain a slimmer figure. It is always wrong to use public funds to obstruct justice and achieve a cover-up of malfeasance. When one says "to pay one's mistress," that use of funds is, of course, always wrong, because having mistresses is wrong. In other words, May is not describing an act in nonmoral terms.

Secondly, May argues that directly intending a nonmoral evil means "to take on, as part of his moral identity, the identity of an evildoer." The key word is "moral." The agent is indeed an evildoer, much as one who interrupts an ectopic pregnancy is an evildoer. That is, evil is done, and through the agent's activity. But that one is morally corrupted by this is not at all clear. Thus, to May's question about burning out the eyes of an infant with a cigarette if God commanded me to do so, I would not hesitate to say that I would do so, just as I would not hesitate to kill if God ordered it. All of us would assuredly have doubts about hallucinations and we would be very slow to conclude that this is a divine command. But *if it is clear that it is,* I would not hesitate. And I would not be taking on the character of a *moral* evildoer in the process, because it is incoherent to say that one rejects God in the very fulfilment of His commands. Thus, if God can command certain acts (such as killing—and I know of no one who doubts that He can), this shows that such acts are not intrinsically evil in May's sense, scil., that one necessarily takes on the *moral* character of an evildoer in performing them. One takes on the "identity of an evildoer" (May's phrase) when one causes *unnecessary* harm in his actions. Similarly, one violates the first principle of the moral law ("good is to be done, evil avoided") when one causes unnecessary or unjustified harm. Otherwise we could never go to war, we could not protect our secrets and our lives, etc., without violating the first principle of the moral law.[52]

Thirdly, the phrase *in se sed non propter se* is, in my opinion, not a vehicle for suggesting that people choose evil qua evil (*propter se*). Clearly they do not. Rather, the phrase intends to underline basic attitudes of disapproval and regret which ought to accompany our actions

---

[52] As for St. Thomas, we can recall Scholz's analysis (cf. n. 46 above) of the thought of Aquinas. He notes that "the sentence 'a good end can justify a physically evil means' stands in agreement with the thought of Aquinas, who sharply distinguishes moral evil from innerworldly (nonmoral) evil."

when harm is unavoidably intertwined with the promotion and protection of good in our actions.

Finally, a word about cultural relativism. May sees this as a problem for recent revisionists, scil., that they hold an act to be objectively wrong *"because* the community deems that it is." Of course that is untenable. But, to be blunt, no one says this nor is anyone who recommends communal discernment vulnerable to such accusations. We are a believing community; hence we learn within a community and form our consciences within a community. This does not imply that the community is always right. It says only that a realistic individual will understand the dangers of trying to discover moral truth alone, of deciding what is right and wrong in isolation from a pool of wisdom and reflection far greater than the individual's. If we err in such a communal discernment (facilitated by the magisterium), that is simply a sign of our imperfection as a community. Pilgrims are imperfect even when they join hands and minds. But no one of these reflections leads to the conclusion that an act is objectively wrong *because* the community thinks so.[53]

HUMANAE VITAE AND THE MAGISTERIUM

In the tenth anniversary year of the issuance of *Humanae vitae* it was to be expected that we would see a good number of statements and studies on that controversial document. The expectation has not been disappointed. Public reactions differ from Andrew Greeley's ("a dead letter"[54]) to John Cardinal Carberry's statement of gratitude to the Holy Father for these "courageous conclusions."[55] The late Pope Paul VI touched briefly on the matter in his address to the College of Cardinals (June 23, 1978). He said that this document "caused us anguish, not only

[53] Further literature in general moral theology would include the following: Allen Verhey, "The Person as Moral Agent," *Calvin Theological Journal* 13, no. 1 (April 1978) 5–15; James A. Fischer, "Ethics and Wisdom," *Catholic Biblical Quarterly* 40 (1978) 293–310; Leon Elders, "Morale chrétienne et nature," *Esprit et vie* 88 (1978) 187–92; B. Schüller, S.J., "Sittliche Forderung und Erkenntnis Gottes," *Gregorianum* 59 (1978) 5–37; Bernhard Fraling, "Grundwerte und Dekalog," *Lebendiges Zeugnis* 33 (1978) 5–27; Albert Ziegler, "Religiöse Grundwerte," *Lebendiges Zeugnis* 33 (1978) 28–41; Georges Thill, "Conflits en sciences et décision éthique," *Lumière et vie* 27 (1978) 53–60; Bernard Quelquejeu, "Les idéologies dans la décision morale," *Lumière et vie* 27 (1978) 61–78; Joachim Piegra, "Autonome Moral und Glaubensethik," *Münchener theologische Zeitschrift* 29 (1978) 20–35; S. Pinckaers, O.P., "Morale catholique et éthique protestante," *Nova et vetera* 53 (1978) 81–95; Hans Schwarz, "Toward a Foundation of Christian Ethics," *Religion in Life* 47 (1978) 162–70; Gustav Ermecke, "Grundwerte—religiöse, philosophische und ethische Begründung," *Theologie und Glaube* 68 (1978) 184–94; Walter Kerber, S.J., "Verallgemeinerung in der Ethik," *Theologie und Philosophie* 53 (1978) 65–69; H. Rotter, "Das theologische Argument in der Moral," *Zeitschrift für katholische Theologie* 100 (1978) 178–96; O. Höffe, "Bermerkungen zu einer Theorie sittlicher Urteilsfindung," *Zeitschrift fur evangelische Ethik* 22 (1978) 181–87.

[54] *Catholic Chronicle,* Oct. 20, 1978.

[55] "U.S. Bishops at the Vatican," *Origins* 8 (1978) 91.

because the issue treated was serious and delicate but also—and perhaps especially—because among Catholics and public opinion in general there was a certain climate of expectancy that concessions, relaxations or liberalization of the Church's moral doctrine and teaching on marriage would be made."[56] He referred somewhat puzzlingly to "confirmations which have come from the more scientific studies."[57] He concluded his reference to the encyclical by repeating "the principle of respect for the natural laws, which—as Dante said—'takes its course from divine intelligence and from its art,' the principle of aware and ethically responsible parenthood."

One might ask whether the late Pontiff thought he was referring to one principle or two. In other words, did he mean to identify "respect for the natural laws" with "the principle of . . . ethically responsible parenthood"? Or are they distinct principles, one (respect) in service of the other (responsible parenthood)? Whatever the case, it is clear that Paul VI provided no reasons to think he had changed his mind on the question. And it is clear that the association of "natural laws" with "divine intelligence" tends to yield intangibility.[58]

In his address at the opening of the spring meeting of the National Conference of Catholic Bishops (May 2, 1978), Archbishop John R. Quinn sensibly urged that the encyclical be read in a broader context: the integration of sexuality with the sacrificially selfless love that is the soul of the Christian life.[59] Quinn suggests that the tensions of "discussion, and sometimes painful and strident controversy" would be reduced in this way. I agree with his concern to provide a broader context for any ethic of sexuality. But at some point the question returns: can *Humanae vitae* be read as saying *only* this?

Cardinal Jean Villot wrote a letter in the name of Paul VI to participants in a natural-family-planning symposium (New York, May 23–24).[60] The letter emphasizes areas of papal concern: continued research; promotion of natural family planning ("in which the dignity of the human person is fostered"); personal commitment of husband and wife and

---

[56] "Paul VI Comments on Today's Church," *Origins* 8 (1978) 108–10.

[57] "Puzzlingly" because it is not clear what he means. Does he refer to the medical dangers associated with the pill? Or that there is now a better scientific foundation for periodic continence?

[58] In his homily of June 29, 1978, Pope Paul VI singled out *Humanae vitae* as a document that defends life, especially against the twin evils of divorce and abortion. "This document," he said, "has become of new and more urgent actuality. . ." (*Civiltà cattolica* 129 [1978] 181).

[59] *Origins* 8 (1978) 10–12.

[60] Jean Cardinal Villot, "La planification naturelle de la famille," *Documentation catholique* 75 (1978) 555–56. A similar letter was sent by Cardinal Villot to a conference in Melbourne on family planning (*Documentation catholique* 75 [1978] 257–58) and to the University of San Francisco (*L'Osservatore romano*, Aug. 3, 1977).

pastoral support for their efforts to lead a holy conjugal life.

The bishops of India issued a declaration (Jan. 17, 1978) commemorating the tenth anniversary of *Humanae vitae*. They note that the specific doctrines of the encyclical (on contraception, sterilization, abortion) are "integrated into a comprehensive vision of man, evangelical love, and responsible parenthood." After affirming their unqualified acceptance of *Humanae vitae*, they state that they have seen the fears of the Holy Father (about the powers that governments would have if contraception were approved) realized and his views vindicated "at least in some degree." They urge their priests to show great compassion but "from now on, they must avoid spreading any personal views which may be opposed to the teaching of the Church. This teaching is clear and admits of no ambiguity."[61]

Msgr. Matagrin, Archbishop of Grenoble and vice-president of the French Episcopal Conference, wrote in an article in *Le progrès* that *Humanae vitae* had stirred up controversy. Matagrin admits that the language used was, in the eyes of many, obsolete, but he underlines the validity of the profound intuition. Just as populations ought not to be manipulated, so procreation itself ought not be ruled by physical and chemical means. In a time of ecological awareness we ought to be sensitive to the concerns of Paul VI for "the quality of life, the biological rhythms not simply of the universe but of man himself."[62]

An anonymous moral theologian ("he will be risking his chair if his name is published, so it is withheld at his request and the shame of all of us"[63]) from a "prestigious ecclesiastical establishment" summarizes the situation for the London *Tablet*. One of the results to settle in over the past ten years is the loss of confidence in Roman pronouncements on moral questions. This "special correspondent" believes that the *sensus fidelium* must be taken more into account in the formulation of doctrinal and moral teaching. He regards the early liberal dissent as counterproductive because it hardened the traditionalism of some theologians and bishops.[64] It would have been better to interpret *Humanae vitae* very flexibly—something the Vatican could live with, provided the document is accepted in principle. As for the future, "The time is not yet ripe for the theoretic formulation of an ecclesial consensus on all the complex moral aspects of human procreativity in the present-day world, simply because as yet there is no ecclesial consensus about them."

[61] "*Humanae vitae* Ten Years Later," *The Pope Speaks* 23 (1978) 183–87.

[62] Msgr. Matagrin, "Le pape d'*Humanae vitae*," *Documentation catholique* 75 (1978) 752.

[63] "After *Humanae vitae*," *Tablet* 232 (1978) 852.

[64] On this cf. Brigitte Andre, "*Humanae vitae*: riguer et compassion," *Informations catholiques internationales* n. 530 (Sept., 1978) 28–29. Andre mistakenly refers to "l'Université pontificale de Georgetown."

Dr. Denis Cashman, an English physician and former medical advisor to the Catholic Marriage Advisory Council, takes issue with *Humanae vitae* on some very practical issues.[65] Contraception, he believes, does not lead to loss of respect for women. The discipline involved in periodic abstinence is often a source of harm to marriages. He argues that the "observance of natural rhythms" will never be more than "marginally satisfactory."

This is certainly not the prevailing view. Arthur McCormack reports on a tenth-anniversary congress (its theme: "Love, Fruitful and Responsible") held June 21–25 in Milan.[66] It is of particular interest because two of its major presenters were Gustave Martelet, S.J. (widely considered one of the major influences on *Humanae vitae*) and Cardinal Karol Wojtyla.[67] Three points became clear in the discussions about natural family planning: (1) natural methods have been very much improved; (2) many more Catholic doctors and counselors are involved in teaching such methods; (3) these methods are now more competitive with contraceptive methods.[68]

One of the more interesting points is McCormack's report of Martelet. It reads:

He said that paragraph 14 of the encyclical (which includes the ban on contraception) was only meant to clarify the position of the Church because of the "redoubtable volume of opinion in favor of contraception" which had developed in the sixties: it was not meant to harass individual Catholics who found themselves in the dilemma of having to limit their families but were unable to use methods allowed by the Church. He called their use of contraceptives a "disorder" which was not sinful if they acted in good conscience and had tried their best to obey the encyclical in the circumstances of their life.[69]

Similarly, Diogini Tettamanzi, professor of moral theology at the Seminary of Milan, is reported to have "confirmed the possibility of the

[65] Denis Cashman, "Letter to Editor," *Tablet* 232 (1978) 852.

[66] Arthur McCormack, "*Humanae vitae* Today," *Tablet* 232 (1978) 674–76.

[67] One of Italy's most respected newspapers, Milan's *Corriere della sera*, carried an article (Oct. 18, 1978) on "The Thought of the Pope on Love and the Pill." According to many interpreters of John Paul II (as reported in *Corriere*), in the Pope's thought "a natural law that imposes itself as an absolute is unacceptable." Furthermore, it continues: "it is the phenomenological philosophical formation of Wojtyla that led him to this conclusion: that which counts most is the intention inspiring the acts of husband and wife. Simply put: the differences between the use of the pill and other contraceptive methods is secondary if, beneath all, there is always a loving act." Finally, the author, Dario Fertilio, states that many believe it to be the papal view that contraception is "sempre un 'male,' ma un male a volte comprensibile" ("always an evil but at times an understandable one"). I tend to think this is idle speculation.

[68] Cf. Rhaban Haacke, "Zur Frage der Zeitwahlmethode," *Münchener theologische Zeitschrift* 29 (1978) 64–70.

[69] McCormack, "*Humanae vitae* Today" 676.

use of methods other than natural ones in the service of this love when a couple decided in sincere conscience that this was necessary in their concrete circumstances." Moreover, three or four Italian moralists argued that the use of contraceptives by couples who felt that they must was not a question of choosing the lesser evil but rather "of making a choice within a hierarchy of values: the preservation of married love, of life together, of the welfare of the family being a greater good than the methods used to achieve it."

This is all quite puzzling; for of this conference McCormack notes that "no dissenters were invited." As I read this report, the conference was fairly crawling with dissenters[70] for *Humanae vitae* presented the contraceptive act as a *moral* evil, not just a "disorder."[71] If it can be read to have said that it was a disorder (disvalue, nonmoral evil, ontic evil, etc.), many problems would vanish. Indeed, this is precisely the analysis that some prominent dissenters (Janssens, Fuchs, Schüller) have made. Furthermore, I am puzzled by the contrast stated between "making a choice within a hierarchy" and "choosing the lesser of two evils." These are simply various ways of wording the same thing, although one *sounds* better (scil., more positive).

Charles Curran rejects this approach. He does not think that contraception violates an ideal or involves premoral or ontic evil. "In my judgment both of these approaches still give too much importance to the physical aspect of the act and see the physical as normative."[72] He sees these approaches as attempts to preserve greater unity in the Church. By contrast, Curran argues that the matter must be faced from the more radical perspective of papal error. "The condemnation of artificial contraception found in *Humanae vitae* is wrong." The remainder of Curran's

---

[70] This conference is also reported by Lino Ciccone, "Congresso internazionale sul tema 'amore fecondo responsabile a dieci anni dall' *Humanae vitae*,'" *Divus Thomas* 81 (1978) 177–87. He is very critical of McCormack.

[71] This point is clear from many sources, most recently the Irish bishops. Of contraception they say: "L'enseignement de l'église est clair: elle est *moralement* mauvaise" (*Documentation catholique* 75 [1978] 424–25). Furthermore, reporting favorably on a new moral textbook by Dom Anselm Günthör, Luigi Ciappi, O.P., states: "He accepts the pastoral provisions of the encyclical, without mentioning 'conflict of duties' or 'hierarchy of values' in married life. He shows in this way that he does not consider worthy of acceptance those interpretations given by some Pastoral Conferences, which had not offered a correct and acceptable interpretation of the document of the Sovereign Pontiff" (*L'Osservatore romano* [Eng. ed.] no. 43 [Oct. 26, 1978] 11). One could, of course, draw a different conclusion from that of Cardinal Ciappi. For instance: "Günthör shows that he does not even consider the conflict character of reality" or "that he has absolutized the physical integrity of sexual intercourse."

[72] Charles E. Curran, "Ten Years Later: Reflections on 'Humanae vitae,'" *Commonweal* 105 (1978) 425–30; cf. also "After *Humanae vitae*: A Decade of Lively Debate," *Hospital Progress* 59, no. 7 (July 1978) 84–89.

study takes up the possibility and implications of dissent in the Church, and on a wide variety of topics. Curran grants that this means greater pluralism and that his model will somewhat reduce the prophetic role of the Church. He thinks the present situation, where official teaching is one thing and accepted practice another, is intolerable. It is clear where Curran thinks change is indicated. "If the hierarchical Church refuses to change here, there will probably be no change on other issues."

A different point of view is taken by Lawrence B. Porter, O.P. He has written a perceptive study comparing Martelet's work with *Humanae vitae*, particularly with regard to the underlying anthropology.[73] The study produces good internal evidence for saying that the "pope's response to the birth control controversy is indeed conceived in terms of Martelet's own thought." Rather than Curran's "physicalism," Martelet asserts in his study *Amour conjugal et renouveau conciliaire* (1967) that the "Church has never seen in nature or its functions a purely biological reality, but a living index of the demands of God and the spiritual being of man."[74] Martelet conceives the birth-control issue as a confrontation between technological domination on the one hand and human dominion on the other.

This is a careful study[75] and I have a great deal of sympathy for the broad anthropological perspectives Porter lifts out of Martelet. Technology can be inhuman and manipulative. The body does condition human love; and to avoid this does carry certain risks. But what that leads to is not clear. Martelet himself seems to have been aware of this; for he stated in *L'Existence humaine et l'amour* that "an encyclical is nothing other than a means by which the pope makes everyone and primarily Christians stop and think about something important . . . ."[76] Furthermore, Martelet concedes the inadequacy of expression in *Humanae vitae*:

It is a fact, however, that this vocabulary of "intrinsically evil" used by both encyclicals to denounce in contraception something truly wrong, sadly allows one to believe that this always represents in itself the most grave failure of love. This is one of the *lacunae* of both *Casti connubii* and *Humanae vitae*, that neither one nor the other sufficiently protects its readers from the awful errors of such a misunderstanding.[77]

A word here about Curran's rejection of the notion of contraception as

[73] Lawrence B. Porter, O.P., " 'Humanae vitae' a Decade Later: The Theologian behind the Encyclical," *Thomist* 42 (1978) 464–509.

[74] Cf. Martelet 43, as cited by Porter.

[75] At one point Porter is less than cautious. He writes: "As a dogmatist, and more than any moral theologian, Martelet was aware of the importance of. . .the comprehensive Christian anthropology that underlies *Gaudium et spes'* teaching" (483). That sweeping statement would be difficult to establish.

[76] Porter, " 'Humanae vitae' a Decade Later" 508.

[77] Ibid.

a nonmoral evil. That is technical terminology and it can strike people as "too strong," "misleading." What some contemporary authors are trying to do is discover a language which will recognize certain effects as deprivations or disvalues without calling them *moral* evils. For instance, when in the course of a just national self-defense certain enemy soldiers are wounded or killed, what are we to call those killings? They are certainly not the results of *morally* wrongful acts, for the defense is *ex hypothesi* just. Nor are they neutral happenings.

In this light we once again encounter the assertion that the basic message of *Humanae vitae* is (= ought to be) to caution couples who use contraception because they feel they must against the danger of confusing responsible parenthood with an unchristian hedonism or selfishness. In other words, it is a reminder that we are dealing with a disvalue, though not necessarily a terribly great one. In light of this, I have recently worded the matter as follows:

This, I believe, is very important. Some reactions to *Humanae vitae* framed the matter as follows: "contraception is wrong vs. contraception is right," this latter being the case since the argument for the former was seen as illegitimate. This is terribly misleading and, in my judgment, erroneous. It leaves the impression that contraception and sterilization are right, that nothing is wrong with them, and, eventually, that they are values in themselves. When compared abstractly to their alternatives, contraception and sterilization are nonmoral evils, what I call disvalues. To forget this is to lose the thrust away from their necessity. To say that something is a disvalue or nonmoral evil is to imply thereby the need to be moving constantly and steadily to the point where the causing of such disvalues is no longer required. To forget that something is a nonmoral evil is to settle for it, to embrace it into one's world.[78]

An analogy may help here. While speaking before the United Nations, Pope Paul VI prophetically and powerfully urged "no more war, never." This plea, however, would be misread if it were taken as an invalidation of the just-war theory, as a condemnation of a forceful national self-defense as intrinsically evil. It was rather a very useful cry by a highly respected spiritual leader about the disvalue (nonmoral evil) that is war.[79] Something similar is in place where contraception and sterilization are concerned, scil., constant reminders that they are disvalues, yet allowance for the fact that there is, in a world of conflict, still place for a "theory of just sterilization."

[78] Richard A. McCormick, S.J., "Moral Norms and Their Meaning," in *Lectureship* (St. Benedict, Oregon: Mount Angel Seminary, 1978) 45.

[79] James F. Childress has written a fine essay on just war, using the categories "prima facie" wrongfulness and "actual" wrongfulness. He notes that this language is similar to the language of proportionate cause. Cf. "Just War Theories: The Bases, Interrelations, Priorities, and Functions of Their Criteria," *TS* 39 (1978) 427–45.

In other and technical language, the issue is not "contraception is wrong vs. contraception is right"; it is rather "contraception is intrinsically evil vs. contraception is not intrinsically evil." This point is clear in the writings of Schüller, Janssens, Fuchs, and others.

I suspect that Curran will still want to reject this analysis. But that only raises the question: Has his language of "physicalism" not possibly carried him too far? Has it possibly led him to deny any significance to the bodily involvement of our beings in these instances? After all, no one gets sterilized for the fun of it, but only for the purpose of it. Sterilization and (to a lesser degree) contraception remain nondesirable interferences. People would welcome the chance to limit their families without them.[80] This suggests that sterilization is not merely a neutral technique. It is something people want to avoid if possible. Curran's admirable resistance to the idea of describing certain physical actions as morally evil prior to their contextualization and his term "physicalism" to convey this may have led him to deny any meaning to such interventions.[81] At least the question deserves continued discussion.

One of the more interesting recent studies is that of Joseph A. Selling.[82] Of the phrase *intrinsece inhonestum* (*HV* 14) Selling correctly remarks that "the text clearly shows that what the encyclical was speaking of was moral evil and not, as some commentators would have it, some category which would allow for choosing the lesser of two evils. The introduction of this reasoning runs directly counter to what *Humanae vitae* was saying . . . ." Thus, some of the following categories used to mitigate its conclusions are at variance with the language of the encyclical: conflict of duties, lesser of two evils, *Humanae vitae* as an ideal, redefinition of totality, and "probably most important, the distinction between moral and premoral evil." I agree with Selling here.

Selling then provides a brief but accurate history of moral tradition in this area. It is summarized in three expressions: *actus naturae, natura actus, actus personae.* That is, the earlier tradition involving Augustine

---

[80] This is increasingly clear in the medical literature in its description of the ideal contraceptive. It must be simple, easily reversible, cheap, medically safe, etc., all of which point to the disvalues involved when such qualities are absent.

[81] There is some indication of an overreaction in Curran's statement ("After *Humanae vitae*," n. 72) that he holds "artificial insemination with donor semen (AID) is not always wrong." Furthermore, in holding that contraception and sterilization are not disvalues, he reveals an inconsistency; for he says: "If contraception is morally acceptable, so is sterilization, although a *more* serious reason is required if the sterilization is permanent." If a "more" serious reason is required where permanent sterilization is involved, then clearly some reason is required even when it is not permanent. That is to say that it is not simply a neutral thing but has the elements of a disvalue.

[82] Joseph A. Selling, "Moral Teaching, Traditional Teaching and 'Humanae vitae,'" *Louvain Studies* 7 (1978) 24–44.

and Aquinas viewed sexual intercourse as an *actus naturae* (with procreation as its biological finality). Over a period of time nonprocreative purposes were introduced and tolerated as long as the nature of the act was respected (*natura actus*). Finally, in *Gaudium et spes* the analysis became that of *actus personae*. This brief outline cannot do justice to the persuasiveness of Selling's account.

It is his contention that while the basic values of marriage remain constant, the way in which they are protected and explained has gone through a real evolution. In essence, "the realization of the procreative end had become totally detached from the individual act of intercourse. Sexual relations were licit on the basis of their connection with expressing conjugal love alone. Consequently, a new set of norms was necessary to evaluate those relations." Yet *Humanae vitae* represents a continuation of the notion of *actus naturae* and "represents a regression in the evolution of concrete norms which had been elaborated in Vatican II." Selling, therefore, feels that the document was dated at the time it was promulgated, because it repeated a "physicalistic interpretation of natural law."

He concludes by asking why Paul VI did this. It is Selling's opinion that he did so because he feared that any sanctioning of contraception would be interpreted as license for any form of sexual behavior. To change norms in one area would inevitably have repercussions in all other areas. Thus he believes that Pope Paul never "intended to condemn every form of artificial birth control for the mature, responsible, loving married couple." Rather, he feared the floodgates and took a "safe" position.

The broad lines of Selling's analysis have been drawn by others.[83] Hence no comment is called for except to say that his study will probably be greeted with hails or harpoons. Neither is appropriate; just calm study.

Two of the most serious studies on contraception appeared in this journal; hence they need not be extensively summarized here. John C. Ford, S.J., and Germain Grisez, in a long and careful study, argue that the Church's condemnation of contraception (what they call the "received Catholic teaching") has been infallibly proposed by the ordinary magisterium.[84] "We think that the facts show as clearly as anyone could reasonably demand that the conditions articulated by Vatican II for infallibility in the exercise of the ordinary magisterium of the bishops dispersed throughout the world have been met in the case of the Catholic Church's teaching on contraception." The long Ford-Grisez study ex-

[83] Louis Janssens, *Mariage et fécondité* (Paris: Duculot, 1967).

[84] John C. Ford, S.J., and Germain Grisez, "Contraception and Infallibility," *TS* 39 (1978) 258–312. A popular summary of this is found in Russell Shaw, "Contraception, Infallibility and the Ordinary Magisterium," *Homiletic and Pastoral Review* 78, no. 10 (July 1978) 9–19.

plains that conclusion by examining the conditions articulated in Vatican II for infallible teaching, the statements of the papal and episcopal magisterium, and objections against this position.

In the same issue of THEOLOGICAL STUDIES Joseph Komonchak reached a different conclusion.[85] He argues that three conditions must be fulfilled before a teaching is infallibly taught by the ordinary universal magisterium: (1) it must be divinely revealed or be necessary to defend or explain what is revealed; (2) it must be proposed by a moral unanimity of the body of bishops in communion with one another and the pope; (3) it must be proposed by them as having to be held definitively. Komonchak discusses these conditions at length and concludes: "I do not see, then, how one can reply to the question of the infallibility of the magisterial condemnation of artificial contraception with anything but a *non constat*."

It is noteworthy that these two studies are basically essays in ecclesiology.[86] It would be immodest for a moral theologian to attempt to referee such a dispute, though it is clear that many theologians (what Komonchak calls "something like a *consensus theologorum*") would favor the Komonchak thesis. There is one point I would like to raise here for reflection. In an essay on the changeable and unchangeable in the Church, Karl Rahner highlights the distinction between a "truth in itself and in its abiding validity" and its "particular historical formulation."[87] By this he means that dogmas are always presented in context and by means of conceptual models which are subject to change. He uses transubstantiation and original sin as examples. For this latter, e.g., those who accept polygenism must rethink what is meant by saying that Adam is the originator and cause of original sin. Rahner then applies this to ethics. He states:

Apart from wholly universal moral norms of an abstract kind, and apart from a radical orientation of human life towards God as the outcome of a supernatural and grace-given self-commitment, there are hardly any particular or individual norms of Christian morality which could be proclaimed by the ordinary or extraordinary teaching authorities of the Church in such a way that they could be unequivocally and certainly declared to have the force of dogmas.[88]

This does not mean, Rahner states, that certain concrete actions cannot

---

[85] Joseph A. Komonchak, "*Humanae vitae* and Its Reception: Ecclesiological Reflections," *TS* 39 (1978) 221–57.

[86] Komonchak does, however, address the argument of *Humanae vitae*. Particularly enlightening are his reflections on pp. 253–56, where the *ordo generationis* is explained as a "total complex," not simply individual acts.

[87] Karl Rahner, "Basic Observations on the Subject of Changeable and Unchangeable Factors in the Church," *Theological Investigations* 14 (New York: Seabury, 1976) 3–23.

[88] Ibid. 14.

be prescribed or proscribed authoritatively. They can, as demanded by the times. But they pertain to man's *concrete nature* at a given point in history. And this concrete nature is subject to change. Rahner's analysis would deny the very possibility of infallible teaching where contraceptive acts are concerned. It would further invite us to discover—not a simple task—the abiding and unchangeable concern of the Church encapsulated in this vehicle (condemnation of contraception).

Several impressions are generated by this literature. First, there is praise for the "overall vision" of Paul VI, though that phrase is often left very general and unspecified; and there are invitations to read *Humanae vitae* within a broader context. Second, there is criticism of the language of the encyclical (*intrinsece inhonestum*), as if the pope did not find the proper vehicle for his message. Third, there is increasingly the suggestion that there is a middle position between *Humanae vitae* and some of its critics, one which would see a value in naturalness without canonizing it, which would see a relative disvalue in artificial interventions without condemning them as intrinsically evil. Equivalently, this view agrees that technology can be of great assistance to us but should not be allowed to dominate us. Finally—a personal reflection—there is need for a profounder analysis of sexuality in our time, a broad and deep systematic synthesis which can control and direct our reflections on family planning. When that is present, we may be able with greater assurance and fairness to retain what is of abiding importance in *Humanae vitae* and reformulate what is defective.

Nearly everyone who comments on the tenth anniversary of the 1968 encyclical calls attention to the fact that the past ten years have led to a reconsideration of authority in the Church, and particularly the nature of the magisterium. This traces, of course, to the fact that there was so much dissent associated with *Humanae vitae*. A few entries here will have to suffice.

Richard M. Gula, S.S., reviews the teaching of the manualists on dissent.[89] They do not see dissent as undermining the teaching of the ordinary magisterium, and at least one (Lercher) recognizes that suspending assent may be one way of protecting the Church from error.[90] Furthermore, Gula correctly notes that the responses to the *modi* on *Lumen gentium* (no. 25) state the very same thing. The charismatic structure of the Church further supports this notion. Gula argues that we must develop an approach to public dissent that is more realistic and adequate to our time.

[89] Richard M. Gula, S.S., "The Right to Private and Public Dissent from Specific Pronouncements of the Ordinary Magisterium," *Eglise et théologie* 9 (1978) 319–43.

[90] "It is not absolutely out of the question that error might be excluded by the Holy Spirit in this way, namely, by the subjects of the decree detecting its error and ceasing to give it their internal assent" (L. Lercher, *Institutiones theologiae dogmaticae* 1 [4th ed.; Barcelona: Herder, 1945] 297).

One of the more interesting statements on the meaning of dissent from authentic teaching of the magisterium was made by Bishop Juan Arzube at the Catholic Press Association Convention Mass.[91] He notes that, in contrast to infallible teaching, ordinary teaching has sometimes to "undergo correction and change." As example Arzube offers *Dignitatis humanae* and the teaching of previous popes on religious liberty. Such development could not have occurred "unless theologians and bishops had been free to be critical of papal teaching, to express views at variance with it . . . ." Our faculty of judgment cannot give assent to a proposition that it judges to be inaccurate or untrue. After detailing the conditions for legitimate dissent (competence, sincere effort to assent, convincing contrary reasons), Arzube argues that dissent must be viewed "as something positive and constructive" in the life of the Church.

Arzube's statement strikes this reviewer as being realistic, calm, and theologically correct. It is particularly encouraging because it comes from a bishop. Theologians also received very warmly the remarks of Archbishop John Roach at the opening of the Catholic Theological Society of America meeting. Roach touched enlighteningly on the publics he felt obliged as bishop to listen to carefully, even if at times critically.[92]

An entire issue of *Chicago Studies* is devoted to the theme "The Magisterium, the Theologian and the Educator."[93] It is one of the finest issues of that seventeen-year-old journal that we have had. Here only a few highlights can be reported.

After Archbishop Joseph Bernardin's introductory essay, there follow useful "setting the stage" articles by Carl Peter and John F. Meyers. Eugene A. LaVerdiere, S.S.S., has a fine treatment of teaching authority in the New Testament period. This is followed by John Lynch's detailed study of the magisterium and theologians from the Apostolic Fathers to the Gregorian Reform. During this period it was the councils that promulgated creeds and dogmatic definitions, but "it was the theological teachers who carried on the vital interpretative task." Indeed, with the exception of Tertullian, Origen, and Jerome, one cannot speak of a differentiation of the magisterial and theological functions. That came with the rise of the universities.

Yves Congar covers the following period up to Trent. It was in this period that a new form of teaching developed, "the 'magisterium' of the theologians, the schools and the universities." This reflects what Congar calls "two different modes of teaching." Thus, the University of Paris considered itself and was generally thought of as exercising an authentic

---

[91] Juan Arzube, "When Is Dissent Legitimate?" *Catholic Journalist*, June 1978, 5.

[92] John Roach, "On Hearing the Voices That Echo God," *Origins* 8 (1978) 81–86.

[93] *Chicago Studies* 17 (1978) 149–307. The issue includes articles by Joseph L. Bernardin, Carl J. Peter, John F. Meyers, Eugene LaVerdiere, S.S.S., John E. Lynch, C.S.P., Yves Congar, O.P., Michael D. Place, T. Howland Sanks, S.J., Avery Dulles, S.J., Timothy O'Connell, and Raymond E. Brown, S.S.

theological authority in Christianity. As a result, properly theological terms were employed by the councils to express the data of the faith (*transsubstantiatio, anima forma corporis*). Trent achieved a balance between *inquisitio* and *auctoritas*, but a balance conditioned by four centuries of scholastic theology. The result: "The teaching of the magisterium has been woven with 'theology' which has gone far beyond the pure witness of the Word of God and apostolic tradition." Congar concludes that the distinction of charisms must be preserved but within a necessary and felicitous collaboration.

Michael Place traces developments in the relationship between scholars and what he calls "the authoritative hierarchical solicitude" (for the faith) from Trent to Vatican I. The upshot of these developments was a growing isolation of the papal and episcopal competency from the rest of the Church. Place outlines the political and theological threads that led to an increasingly powerful papacy. For instance, in the late eighteenth century the key category by which papal action in matters of faith was understood was that of jurisdiction—the concern of one who was not first a teacher but was to provide for unity. As Place puts it: "The theologian is the teacher. The papacy is the ruler that provides for the right ordering necessary to preserve ecclesial unity." However, early in the nineteenth century, categories from Germany (teach, rule, sanctify) were introduced rather than the powers of orders and jurisdiction. With this came also the usage "magisterium" around 1830, and it was "situated in a cultural milieu where the papacy is understood as having absolute spiritual sovereignty...." In this new context the function of theologians is differently understood. He is now related not to the "governor of ecclesial unity" but to a supreme teacher. In such a context his role changes. It is Place's thesis that the relationship of magisterium to theologians is determined by the manner in which the Church perceives itself at a given time in history.

T. Howland Sanks, S.J., treats the relationship of theologians and the magisterium from Vatican I to 1978. He argues, rightly I think, that the conflicts that existed, and still exist, are between various forms of theology, various theological paradigms, not precisely or first of all between theologians and the magisterium. During this period (up to Vatican II) the ahistorical, Neo-Scholastic theology of the Roman school achieved an ascendency. It got enshrined in official statements. It is present in Vatican I (*Dei Filius, Pastor aeternus*) and continued to be the official theology used by the magisterium in its dealings with the historically conscious leanings of Loisy, Tyrrell, and Pierre Rousselot. Furthermore, it was responsible for the suppression of Teilhard and John Courtney Murray (as well as de Lubac, Bouillard, and their colleagues at Fourvière). In *Humani generis* (Aug. 12, 1950) this ahistorical approach peaked.

Vatican II constituted a definitive break with such an approach, but Sanks believes the problem is far from gone, because this theology has "formed the thinking and attitudes of many of the hierarchy."

Avery Dulles provides a theological reflection on the magisterium in history. His overall conclusion is that "the structures commonly regarded as Catholic today are relatively new and thus do not reflect God's unalterable design for his Church." Dulles passes in review the salient features of the models of the Church in various periods and uses these features to raise questions for our time. In the patristic period, e.g., what Dulles calls a "representational model" prevailed. The Catholic faith is identified with the unanimous belief of all the churches—and the bishops were the responsible heads of such local churches. The bishops were seen as teaching with full authority when they gather in councils representing the churches of the entire Christian world. On the basis of this model (not without imperfections) Dulles asks: can we reactivate the idea of a unity achieved "from below" through consensus? Furthermore, instead of thinking of the bishop as the representative of the Holy See, should we not see him more as the local community's representative? Or again, Dulles wonders whether we can credibly view the bishop as the "chief teacher" in our time. This notion fits more easily the fourth and fifth centuries, when prominent theologians were bishops.

When he discusses the medieval model characterized by the rise of the universities, Dulles asks: "Could theologians, individually or at least corporately, be acknowledged as possessing true doctrinal or magisterial authority?" The notion, he insists, is well founded in tradition. He criticizes the excessive privatizing of theology as if theologians "indulge in nothing other than airy speculations." He suggests that statements could occasionally be issued jointly by bishops and nonbishops, by the pope with the International Theological Commission. This would reduce the cleavage between the pastoral magisterium and theology.

The Neo-Scholastic period (nineteenth and twentieth centuries) saw the magisterium as a power distinct from orders and government. Thus it regarded the hierarchy not simply as judges but as true teachers, whereas in the eighteenth century teaching was viewed as a command or along more disciplinary lines. Under this Neo-Scholastic model the Holy See exercised a vigorous doctrinal leadership. But because papal teaching was drawn up by theologians of the Roman school, they "gave official status to their own opinions." Vatican II changed many of the perspectives associated with the Neo-Scholastic approach, especially the identification between magisterium and jurisdiction. It neither affirmed nor denied a complementary magisterium of theologians. However, it is clear that Dulles (along with Congar) believes such a notion is valid. "The concept of a distinct magisterium of theologians, as we have seen, is not simply a medieval theory; it is accepted in neo-scholastic manuals of the twentieth century."

These papers were discussed at a seminar of the Catholic Theological Society of America (June 1978) in Milwaukee. Timothy O'Connell reports the results of those discussions in the same issue of *Chicago Studies*. The key issue in relating theology to the magisterium was seen to be doctrinal development. Specifically, the seminarists asked: How do we account for the various changes in teaching that have occurred in the past? Can we develop a theology of church teaching which accommodates without embarrassment the twin phenomena of divided opinion and ignorance?

The issue concludes with the address of Raymond Brown, S.S., to the National Catholic Education Association (March 29, 1978).[94] The prestigious exegete argues that the dispute among theologians and bishops has been "greatly exaggerated." He identifies four fictions that surround the dispute: belief that the main opponents in matters of doctrine are the magisterium and theologians; that their prevailing relationship is one of disagreement; that theologians and magisterium can be spoken of as if they were monolithic groups; and that they conflict because even centrist Catholic theologians deny many matters of Church doctrine. Brown argues—persuasively, in my judgment—that third parties such as the secular media and the ultraconservative Catholic press are more damaging than any polarization of bishops and theologians. Furthermore, though there has been dissent (especially in matters of sexual morality), Brown asserts that this has been seriously exaggerated. With regard to centrist theologians denying many matters of Church doctrine, Brown insists that we must not inflate (as many do) what constitutes Catholic doctrine and we must realize that doctrines change. In his words, "seeking a new formulation to meet a new problem" is hardly a denial of a teaching.

Though his paper was delivered to religious educators, both theologians and bishops could read it with profit. Brown approaches delicate problems with a combination of precision, wisdom, and pastoral sensitivity that is admirable. Those on the extreme right or left will not be happy with his reflections. But that reflects more on the geography of their position than the accuracy of Brown's analysis. One point might deserve more emphasis than Brown's irenic analysis suggests: the differences on a single issue such as *Humanae vitae* have enormous implications with regard to moral theological method, notions of pluralism and authority, notions of the Church. Increasingly it is these issues that come to the fore in moral discussions and that perhaps accounts for the impression of polarization between some bishops and some theologians.

In another symposium (held in Philadelphia, Jan. 6–8, 1978) William

[94] Cf. also *Origins* 7 (1978) 673–82.

May discusses the moral magisterium.[95] He insists, quite rightly, that the Church expects that the faithful "will, in faith, make their own through acts of faithful understanding" the teachings of the Church. However, dissent remains possible. But this does not mean that there is a "double truth." He takes issue with Congar, Dulles, and this compositor, who "speak of two magisteria within the Church." The unity of the Church demands one magisterium, and the scholar must be willing to allow his/ her positions to be judged by this one magisterium.

Any differences between May and myself on this subject appear to be nonsubstantial and a matter of emphasis. But two comments might be in place. First, while May admits the possibility of dissent, he does not carry this far enough. That is, he does not relate it to the development of doctrine. It remains privatized. Concretely, if dissent on a particular point is widespread, does this not suggest to us that perhaps the official formulation is in need of improvement? To say otherwise is to say that scholarly (and other) reflection has no relation to the Church's ongoing search for truth and application of her message. As Bishop Arzube notes, we would never have gotten to *Dignitatis humanae* if the reflections of John Courtney Murray had been merely tolerated and not taken as a new source of evidence.

This leads to the second point: May's rejection of two magisteria in the Church. It is easy to understand how this can be a confusing verbal vehicle, and I, for one, am not wedded to it. Raymond Brown notes: "Magisterium is a fighting word. I think the attempt to reclaim it for theologians will not succeed; and I personally do not think the battle worth fighting so long as, under any other name, the legitimate role of theologians in shaping the teaching of the Church is respected."[96] I agree with that statement of things and with Brown's subsequent addition: "All that I want is that scholarly evidence be taken into account in the formulation and reformulation of Catholic doctrine."

What is important, then, is not the word; it is the idea beneath it. That is, the Church in its teaching makes use of (and probably must) theologies and philosophical concepts, as Congar repeatedly reminds us. In moral theology, an example would be *direct* killing, *direct* sterilization. These formulations are only more or less adequate and may even be wrong at times. It is one of theology's (and philosophy's) tasks to make that determination, not precisely the magisterium's.

Here an example is in place. Masturbation for infertility testing has been condemned officially (the Holy Office, Pius XII). Yet, very few

[95] William E. May, "The Magisterium and Moral Theology," in *Symposium on the Magisterium: A Positive Statement*, ed. John J. O'Rourke and Thomas Greenburg (Boston: Daughters of St. Paul, 1978) 71–94.

[96] Brown, as in *Origins* 7 (n. 94 above) 675.

theologians of my acquaintance see this procedure as having the malice of masturbation. When theologians say this, they are stating (at least they think they are) a truth, and in this sense they are teaching. Or must one wait until something is officially modified to recognize that it is true or false? Personally, I would have no hesitation in saying to an individual that that condemnation is obsolete, even if it has not been modified by the Church's more official teaching organs.

What theologians (and other scholars) have been searching for is a formula which would incorporate two things: (1) the practical admission of an independent competence for theology and other disciplines; (2) the admission of the indispensability of this competence for the formation, defense, and critique of magisterial statements. They are not interested in arrogating the kerygmatic function of the Holy Father and the bishops.[97] By "independent" I do not mean "in isolation from" the body of believers or the hierarchy. Theologians are first and foremost believers, members of the faithful. By "independent" competence is meant one with its own proper purpose, tools, and training. The word "practical" is used because most people would admit this in theory.

In practice, however, this is not always the case. This practical problem can manifest itself in three ways. First, theologians are selected according to a predetermined position to be proposed, what Sanks calls "co-optation." Second, moral positions are formulated against a significant theological opinion or consensus in the Church. Such opinion should lead us to conclude that the matter has not matured sufficiently to be stated by the authentic magisterium. Third, when theologians sometimes critique official formulations, that is viewed as out of order, arrogating the teaching role of the hierarchy, disloyalty, etc. Actually, it is performing one of theology's tasks. All three of these manifestations are practical denials of the independent competence of theology.

As for the third manifestation mentioned above, it ought to be said that when a particular critique becomes one shared by many competent and demonstrably loyal scholars, it is part of the public opinion in the

---

[97] William Cardinal Baum has a thoughtful paper on the episcopal magisterium. He suggests that the theology of this magisterium must be based on the evangelical notion of the proclamation of the kerygma and on the sacramental nature of the episcopal order. "The episcopal magisterium is thus not above, below, or alongside the role of theologians and others. It is a reality of a different order. It pertains to the sacramental transmission of the divine realities . . . ." Cf. "Magisterium and the Life of Faith," *Origins* 8 (1978) 76–80. A similar analysis was made by the then Archbishop Karol Wojtyla. He emphasizes the magisterium of bishops as proclamation, leading people to Christ. Bishops are first of all *fidei praecones* and only secondly *doctores*. The faithful defense of the *depositum* and its proclamation "entails its growing understanding, in tune with the demands of every age and responding to them according to the progress of theology and human science." He argues that the magisterium "as systematic and doctrinal teaching should be put at the service of the announcement of the gospel." Cf. "Bishops as Servants of the Faith," *Irish Theological Quarterly* 43 (1976) 260–73.

Church, a source of new knowledge and reflection. Surely this source of new knowledge and reflection cannot be excluded from those sources we draw upon to enlighten and form our consciences; for conscience is formed *within the Church.*[98]

An unsolicited suggestion might not be irrelevant here. Bishops should be conservative, in the best sense of that word. They should not endorse every fad, or even every theological theory. They should "conserve"; but to do so in a way that fosters faith, they must be vulnerably open and deeply involved in a process of creative and critical absorption. In some, perhaps increasingly many, instances, they must take risks, the risks of being tentative or even quite uncertain, and, above all, reliant on others in a complex world. Such a process of clarification and settling takes time, patience, and courage. Its greatest enemy is ideology, the comfort of being clear, and, above all, the posture of pure defense of received formulations.

In all fairness, at this point something should be added about theologians. Amid the variation of their modest function in the Church, they must never lose the courage to be led. "Courage" seems appropriate, because being led in our times means sharing the burdens of the leader— and that can be passingly painful. They should speak their mind knowing that there are other and certainly more significant minds. In other words, they must not lose the nerve to make and admit an honest mistake. They should trust their intuitions and their hearts, but always within a sharp remembrance that the announcement of the faith and its implications in our times must come from the melding of many hearts and minds. The Church needs a thinking arm, so to speak; but that arm is dead if it is detached.

PROBLEMS IN BIOETHICS

The field of bioethics has been livelier than ever. Besides the many studies that appear in such journals as *Hastings Report* and *Linacre Quarterly*, several areas such as life preservation[99] have received intense attention. This is particularly true of the now famous—perhaps "noto-

---

[98] In "The 'New Morality' vs. Objective Morality," *Homiletic and Pastoral Review* 79 (1978) 27–31, Joseph Farraher, S.J. states: "Most present-day liberals in both dogmatic and moral theology. . . treat his [the pope's] statement with no more acceptance than they would the statements of any individual theologian who disagrees with them." That statement is, I believe, simply false.

[99] Cf. Jim Castelli, "Death with Dignity," *Commonweal* 105 (1978) 525–27; Jacques Freyssinet, "Combien une collectivité doit-elle dépenser pour sauver une vie humaine?" *Lumière et vie* 27 (1978) 37–44; Steven E. Rhoads, "How Much Should We Spend to Save a Life?" *Public Interest*, no. 51 (1978) 74–92; James F. Childress, "Ethical Issues in Death and Dying," *Religious Studies Review* 4 (1978) 180–88; R. B. Zachary, "To Save or Let Die," *Tablet* 232 (1978) 174–75; Georg Ziegler, "Überlegungen zur Euthanasie," *Theologie und Glaube* 68 (1978) 168–83; H. Huber, "Sterbehilfe heute," *Theologisch-praktische Quartalschrift* 126 (1978) 38–46.

rious" is better—Joseph Saikewicz decision.[100] These studies can be referred to only in passing, since I want to stress the so-called "test-tube baby" as an instance calling for careful moral analysis and public-policy deliberation.

But first a general article of considerable importance. James Gustafson complains that in the study of the life sciences theologians have become moral philosophers.[101] By this he means that ethical questions are getting merely ethical answers without theological input because moral theologians are no longer doing theology. This allows the questions to be framed exclusively by nontheologians. Gustafson acknowledges that the problem traces partially to a lack of consensus among theologians as to what theological issues really are. Moral principles have some precision (e.g., rules on consent) but nothing of comparable precision exists in the theological realm of discourse.

Gustafson believes that the importance of teasing out the theological dimensions of problems is that differences between people are often matters of belief and loyalties. Such differences are not settled or even addressed by refining ethical principles. Rather, it is convictions about the character of ultimate reality and life that have more bearing on answers than particular moral principles. This is seen in discussions of genetic research, where, without adverting to it, people are often discussing competing eschatologies. In summary, then, theology forces questions we ought to be aware of but frequently are not.

This is a somewhat uncharacteristic addition to the Gustafson corpus. But I believe that beneath the sometimes querulous tone Gustafson has a valuable point; perhaps more accurately, he is raising a serious question. Our loyalties and beliefs, which are profoundly stamped by religious faith, do affect our perspectives and analyses of practical bioethical problems. And, Gustafson would argue, they should. It is the theological task to make this clear.

My question to Gustafson is: How is this to be done in contemporary reflection on these problems? Is the one person he cites (Paul Ramsey) really changing or altering the questions by explicit theological themes? Or is he but warranting reasonable (scil., able to be reasoned) positions by theological supports? Gustafson is really raising the question of the relation between explicit religious faith and moral reasoning. His own answer to the question is that such faith changes answers by expanding

[100] Cf. John J. Paris, S.J., "Withholding of Life-Supporting Treatment from the Mentally Incompetent," *Linacre Quarterly* 45 (1978) 237–48; André E. Hellegers and Richard A. McCormick, S.J., "The Specter of Joseph Saikewicz," *America* 138 (1978) 257–60; John R. Connery, S.J., "A Comparison of the Saikewicz and Quinlan Decisions," *Hospital Progress* 59 (1978) 22–23.

[101] James M. Gustafson, "Theology Confronts Technology and the Life Sciences," *Commonweal* 105 (1978) 386–92.

questions.

The Catholic tradition has generally been content to refer to "reason informed (not replaced) by faith." In this tradition it is not exactly moral philosophy *or* theology; it is moral philosophy *and* moral theology issuing in "reason informed by faith." That terribly important word "informed" has been in practice the object of systematic neglect or at least oversight. For that reason Catholic moral theologians have too often been content to face problems as moral philosophers. This is especially true since their tradition has been one with a heavy emphasis on natural law.

However, once that legitimate point has been granted, it could be suggested that there are any number of ways that "informed" can be approached. For instance, Stanley Hauerwas' procedural model is increasingly aesthetic. For him, theology is like writing a novel. One must be dominantly concerned with the character of the agent and the community, and the stories that have formed them. That is a fruitful way of getting at "informed by faith," but it is not the only one. Similarly, the theology of Augustine or Thomas (or anyone) can be a helpful way of enfleshing the notion of "informed by faith." But it is not the only way. To think so is to reduce theology to its genetic dimension. There are many helpful ways of moving toward an evaluative description of our religious experience. This seems fairly clear from the fact that those who use explicitly religious warrants rarely if ever come to concrete judgments that cannot be supported on other grounds. At least this question should be raised. In raising it, I want to suggest two extremes to be avoided in framing an answer. The first is a neorationalism which would consider Gustafson's point impractical and would forget that the term "reason" includes many dimensions of human experience. The second is a neosectarianism (or elitism) that would so soak bioethical problems in theological concepts and language that they would be beyond sharing.

And now to *in vitro* fertilization with embryo transfer. The birth of Louise Brown (July 25, 1978) at Oldham, England, was greeted with a sensationalism that rarely accompanies bioethical problems. In country after country articles announced that now thousands of couples have new hope. As I write, Louise Brown has been followed by another "test-tube baby" in Calcutta.[102]

This procedure has not only moral aspects but public-policy dimensions. What is to be thought of it? Initial reactions varied.[103] For instance, Bishop Augustine Harris, president of the Social Welfare Commission of the English and Welsh Catholic Bishops' Conference and auxiliary bishop of Liverpool, stated: "Some married couples have a deep desire for children but are unable to conceive. Science can support the loving and

[102] *Washington Post*, Oct. 6, 1978, A16.
[103] For journalistic reactions cf. *Overview* 13 (Nov. 1978).

natural ambitions of the couple to produce new life."[104] Similarly, Cornelius Lucy, bishop of Cork, stated: "Offhand, I don't see anything wrong with childless couples using the test-tube method if there is no other possible way for them to have babies."[105]

Meanwhile in Germany, in a spirit somewhat different from the above, Dr. Joseph Stimpfle, bishop of Augsburg, responded: "Technical manipulation with human eggs and sperm is worse than the atom bomb."[106] While avoiding the atomic imagery, Gordon Cardinal Gray, archbishop of St. Andrews and Edinburgh, stated his "grave misgivings" and noted that "the Church holds that a child should be the product of a loving union between husband and wife."[107] Milanese moral theologian Diogini Tettamanzi stated that the test-tube technique is not acceptable.[108] Archbishop Francis T. Hurley warned against "quick-order answers to moral questions." He very wisely suggested that "it would be immoral or at least irresponsible to condemn or bless the procedure out of hand without first anguishing over both the short and the long range implications of what has been wrought."[109]

Carlo Caffarra, a member of the International Theological Commission, argues that test-tube conception involves a radical separation between the sexual act and procreation and that this separation "could induce or confirm a substantially partial vision of sexuality, passing from one extreme to the other—from a vision of sexuality as function of the species to a vision of sexuality substantially and practically debiologized."[110] Archbishop Johannes Joachim Degenhardt (Paderborn) said "the limits of the right of human intervention were transgressed" in the Brown case. He based himself on the teaching of Pius XII. But moral theologian Johannes Hirschmann said he does not believe that Pius XII is the "last word on the subject."[111]

Rabbi Seymour Siegel noted that "if nature played a trick, as it has in this case, if we can outsmart nature, that is theologically permissible."[112] He later expanded on this by stating that the Jewish view is related to mitzvah. "If conception cannot be accomplished in the usual way, then let it be done artificially as long as no third party is involved."[113]

[104] *Washington Post,* July 27, 1978.
[105] *Catholic Review,* July 28, 1978.
[106] Cited in Johannes Gründel, "Zeugung in der Retorte—unsittlich?" *Stimmen der Zeit* 103 (1978) 675–82, at 675–76.
[107] *Washington Post,* July 27, 1978.
[108] *Catholic Review,* Aug. 4, 1978.
[109] *Inside Passage* 9 (Aug. 4, 1978) 2. For Bishop Mark Hurley's comments, cf. "The Test-Tube Baby," *Origins* 8 (1978) 224.
[110] *Catholic Chronicle,* Oct. 6, 1978, 14.
[111] *National Catholic Register,* Sept. 10, 1978.
[112] *Washington Post,* July 28, 1978.
[113] *United Synagogue Review,* Fall 1978 (pagination unavailable).

What is of more importance than one's conclusions is how one got there. And that brings us to the ethical and moral theological literature.

Dr. Andre Hellegers and this author attempted an overview of the issues.[114] The essay urges that the problem be seen not merely in terms of individual benefits but above all in terms of social implications. At the level of act analysis, we argue that artificial insemination (AIH), and to that extent *in vitro* fertilization with embryo transfer, "cannot be analyzed in a morally decisive way by exclusive appeal to the design of the conjugal act." The study then lifts out areas where there are nagging questions and problems: embryo wastage, possible fetal damage, readiness to abort, extension of technique beyond the married couple, medical priorities, publicity.

The editors of *Commonweal* have an interesting response.[115] They identify three ways of thinking about the procedure: (1) the anathema response (it is unnatural, therefore wrong); (2) the assimilation response (the means are but an extension of interventions we already accept; therefore proceed); (3) the apprehension response, which is made up of a great number of worries and questions. This last is *Commonweal's* position. It lists the following apprehensions: loosening of procreation from its personal determinants; the possible moral mischief involved in third-party ova and sperm; the readiness to abort defectives ("quality control"); consumption of precious medical resources together with stimulation of false hopes. These reservations are so serious that "the proper step now is to maintain HEW's moratorium on *in vitro* fertilization experiments and to broaden it with legislative and professional restrictions. *Then* let the researchers argue their case."

Moral theologian John Mahoney, S.J. (Heythrop College, London) recalls the two criticisms of Pius XII against husband insemination (masturbation to obtain semen; conception should occur as the result of the natural act of marriage).[116] He rejects both, the first because it is difficult to see how obtaining semen in this way frustrates the procreative purpose of sexuality. As to the second, he argues that while the child should be the expression of parental love, it is not through the marital act alone that the couple engages in married loving actions. As for risks (of deformity), Mahoney believes they can reach a tolerably low level. A couple can be justified in running certain risks even in the process of normal fertilization. His article is one of caution, not condemnation. In a subsequent study[117] Mahoney asserts that what is striving for expression

[114] André E. Hellegers and Richard A. McCormick, S.J., "Unanswered Questions on Test Tube Life," *America* 139 (1978) 74-78.

[115] "Test-tube Babies," *Commonweal* 105 (1978) 547-48.

[116] John Mahoney, S.J., "Test-tube Babies," *Tablet* 232 (1978) 734.

[117] John Mahoney, S.J., "Ethical Horizons of Human Biological Development," *Month* 249 (1978) 329-33.

in Pius XII's statements is the idea that the procreation of a new human being is from a union not just of bodies but of spirits also. Marital intercourse is not the only vehicle of such creative love. He then explores the pros and cons of *in vitro* fertilization in a very balanced and honest way and emerges with a cautious approval. As will be obvious below, I find myself in substantial agreement with Mahoney's perspectives and conclusions.

Thomas A. Shannon faults the Steptoe-Edwards achievement on several counts.[118] First, he sees a great deal of money and effort expended for the benefit of a few individuals, and this at a time of increasing population and diminishing resources. Second, the procedure involves risk of harm to an unconsenting third party. Furthermore, what is to be done with the mistakes? Abort? Finally, Shannon sees the combination of a couple's desperation and the scientific competitive urge to be the winning team as a powerfully explosive combination.

Johannes Gründel approaches the problem by viewing the Church's teaching on artificial insemination.[119] This teaching (Pius XII) condemns artificial insemination outside of marriage and in marriage with a third party (AID). Furthermore, Pius XII rejected even AIH. Thus, even though these statements did not envisage *in vitro* fertilization as we know it, their implications are negative toward it.

Gründel believes that more must be said here. He notes that, notwithstanding *Humanae vitae*, many theologians believe that it is the marriage, not the individual act, that must remain open to procreation. Therefore a mere citation of ecclesiastical documents is insufficient. Something similar must be said about artificial insemination by husband. As a general rule, the child should be conceived as the result of an act of personal sexual communion. However, Gründel does not see this as an absolute rule. Where there is "absolute" sterility in the marriage (e.g., absence of sperm), adoption is the answer (not donor insemination). Where, however, the sterility is merely functional, Gründel believes that we cannot "consider the individual act in isolation." Rather, the marriage as a whole must be weighed. When it is, "artificial insemination serves only as completion of such an act of love and of the marriage as a whole." From this perspective, AIH is not destructive to marriage at all, but rather a support. "This wholistic evaluation with a consideration of the consequences would correspond with the type of analysis widespread in contemporary moral theology—an analysis that considers not only the individual act but the entire happening including consequences . . . as the decisive element for moral judgment."[120]

---

[118] Thomas A. Shannon, "The Case against Test-tube Babies," *National Catholic Reporter*, Aug. 11, 1978, 20.

[119] Johannes Gründel, "Zeugung" (n. 106 above).

[120] Ibid. 680.

With that as background, Gründel turns to *in vitro* fertilization with embryo transfer. If one sees personhood as identical with conception, then, Gründel believes, the process is morally questionable experimentation. Many, however, hold that this is not necessarily the case. For instance, if we accept Boethius' definition of person (*individua substantia rationalis naturae*), we must deal with the twinning phenomenon. Ultimately, then, Gründel does not believe that the status of the zygote gives us a definitive answer. He warns, however, of other considerations: risk to the child, extension beyond such technology, genetic manipulation of the zygote, etc.

James Sellers argues that the acceptance of the Steptoe-Edwards achievement has been uncritical. It is not just "a way of helping out with a little fertility problem."[121] He raises five areas of ethical concern: (1) When human life begins—for many embryos are lost. (2) Experimentation without consent. No one can say what will happen to Louise Brown. Sellers feels that the first several hundred petri-dish babies should have been simians. (3) Interference with nature. He rejects the "Catholic" argument that mere artificiality is enough to condemn the procedure, but argues that there may be limits (in terms of justice and fitness) to what we ought to do to initiate life, just as there are for prolonging it at the end. (4) Some motives could be misguided. (5) Allocation of scarce resources.

Allen Verhey (Hope College) believes that the discussion has been too restrictedly conducted in terms of consequences.[122] Some see nothing but good; others quake at the creation finally of a real London Hatchery and Conditioning Center. Verhey is agnostic about the future and any script, whether optimistic or pessimistic, that argues inevitability. Therefore he thinks that moral analysis and public discussion should concentrate on the means, the procedure itself.

He rejects both techno-logic (one may if one can) and the extreme-unnaturalness analysis associated with the arguments of Pius XII. He ends up in the middle: "We are children of nature and children of spirit, and the course of moral wisdom is surely to forget or ignore neither side of our lineage." Thus, in agreement with Ramsey and Kass, he sees this procedure as suppressing "biological, sexual, bodily meaning of marital love." To do that is no less dangerous than its reverse, the trivialization of sex by suppressing its spiritual and personal components. But, he says, this leads only to caution, not to prohibition. "We may neither make the natural processes normative nor dismiss them cavalierly as merely physical."

---

[121] James Sellers, "Test-Tube Conception: Troubling Issues," *Christian Century* 95 (1978) 757–58.

[122] Allen Verhey, "Test-Tube Babies," *Reformed Journal* 28, no. 9 (Sept. 1978) 13–16.

Ultimately, Verhey faults the Steptoe-Edwards procedure on three grounds: lack of respect for life (zygotes created to be destroyed); the readiness to abort misfits (the very design of the procedure); experimentation without the child's consent. It is immoral on these grounds and "I hope that upon public discourse society will refuse to permit it."

In a companion piece to Verhey's, Lewis B. Smedes (Fuller Theological Seminary) discusses both feelings and reasons on both sides of the debate.[123] He concludes that *in vitro* fertilization is not immoral even if it is morally risky. Smedes rejects the argument that it is "unnatural" for babies to be born apart from sex. "Even if the setting shifts, the drama is still the same," scil., God is mysteriously at work. As for Ramsey's argument about imposing risks on the child without consent, he believes the rights of the parents to try to have their own child override this. He then turns to societal risks (excessive power to technology, destruction of zygotes). Smedes contends that the balance of good to be achieved outweighs these risks. In the face of such risks, we must "have the wisdom to guard ourselves against the evils."

Two points. First, Smedes hardly gives a realistic listing of the risks. Therefore he equivalently underestimates them. Second, in what sense is discarding zygotes only a "risk" and how do we "guard ourselves" against this if it is, as Smedes admits, inevitably part of the procedure?

The *Hastings Report* published four brief studies on the problem.[124] Paul Ramsey faults the Steptoe-Edwards work on three grounds: irremovable risk ("a small risk of grave induced injury is still a morally unacceptable risk"); harm to Louise Brown through publicity ("sociopsychological ruin seems invited"); the direction of the technology toward a "Brave New World." He finds in the articles and statements of Robert Edwards ample reasons to fear these developments. For instance, Edwards and D. J. Sharpe wrote in a 1971 article that "the procedures leading to replacement and implantation *open the way* to further work on human embryos in the laboratory." Later Edwards referred to "sexing blastocysts."[125] As for surrogate mothers, Edwards believes this should be avoided *at the present time*.

Ramsey presented a longer version of his objections to the Ethics Advisory Board (DHEW). He saw a further trauma to an already divided

---

[123] Lewis B. Smedes, "Test-Tube Babies," ibid. 16–20.

[124] "In Vitro Fertilization: Four Commentaries," *Hastings Center Report* 8, no. 5 (Oct. 1978) 7–14. The commentaries are by Paul Ramsey, Stephen Toulmin, Marc Lappé, and John A. Robertson.

[125] The first reference is from R. G. Edwards and D. J. Sharpe, "Social Values and Research in Human Embryology," *Nature* 231 (1971) 87–91 (emphasis added). The second is from R. G. Edwards, "Fertilization of Human Eggs in Vitro, Morals, Ethics and the Law," *Quarterly Review of Biology* 49 (1974) 3–26.

nation, because persons conscientiously opposed (to abortion) would have to pay for the service, one that is not of overriding national interest. He sees even the small risk of induced injury as a *conclusive* argument against doing these things. Similarly, the development he fears beyond what is now done is an *immediate* attack on marriage and the family and is a conclusive argument. His conclusion: *"in vitro* fertilization and embryo transfer should not be allowed by medical policy or public policy in the United States—not now, not ever."

John A. Robertson discusses the risk-to-the-prospective-child argument. He finds it unconvincing; for the act creating the risk of injury also brings about the very being that is said to be injured. From the child's perspective, the only alternative to the action that allegedly violates his right not to be harmed is even less desirable; for it means no existence at all.

Robertson is primarily interested in whether government should *ban* such procreation. If this argument is taken for the justification of banning, he fears that the state may also demand sterilization and abortion to prevent deformed births in other situations. The point is well made, but Robertson does not really discuss the moral issue: whether it is morally responsible to run procreative risks for prospective children.

Stephen Toulmin argues that *in vitro* fertilization is a good case in which to refrain from legislative paternalism. Ethically, he finds nothing wrong with it. It is no more dangerous than normal gestation. To the objection that it might lead to further unacceptable manipulation, he responds that this is a "flesh-creeping" argument. There is no greater reason to fear these things than there already is with artificial insemination and sperm banks. As for the unborn child, he states flatly: "Until implantation has taken place, there is no 'unborn child' to protect."

Regardless of where one comes out on the policy issue, it is surprising to find one of Toulmin's stature so thoroughly oversimplifying the ethical issues. For instance, even though the zygote may not be an "unborn child," it is living (not dead) and human (not canine) in its potential. This means that there is still the question of the respect and protection it deserves. Furthermore, I believe Toulmin misreads the "might lead to" point. It is not primarily concerned with empirical inevitability, but above all with the logic of moral justification. That is, the justification for *in vitro* fertilization can easily perform its task for other interventions. Finally, Toulmin seems to have no problem at all with AID and sperm banks. I do.

It is hard to tell exactly where Marc Lappé stands. He believes that absolute vulnerability demands absolute protection, but it is unclear how he relates this to the *in vitro* procedure.

Leon Kass, in a careful paper presented to the Ethics Advisory Board, discusses three aspects of the problem: the status and treatment of extracorporeal embryos; questions of procreation, lineage, and parenthood; limits of manipulation of human reproduction.[126] On the first point, he defends a middle position: the embryo is not nothing. It is, on the other hand, not clearly a person. But it is a human being demanding our respect, not because of rights but because of what it is now prospectively.[127] Such respect excludes "most potentially interesting and useful" research but does not necessarily exclude embryo loss in attempts at implantation.

Kass is deeply, and I think rightly, concerned with what he calls the "soft issues." Many contemporaries are likely to view donors, host wombs, etc., as only "little embryos that stray from the nest." Kass sees these "almost certain" practices as eroding the indispensable foundation of a sound family life ("itself the foundation of civilized community") by eroding clarity about who one's parents are, clarity about generational lines, etc.

Finally, after arguing that the so-called wedge argument is one of the logic of moral justification, he urges the Board, regardless of what it does, to state very precisely why it is doing so; for "this Board . . . may very well be helping to decide whether human beings will eventually be produced in laboratories."

This has been only a sampling of some recent literature touching the problem of the so-called "test-tube baby."[128] Perhaps it would be helpful here to summarize and comment on those areas that seem at the center of the discussion of the ethics and public-policy problems.

Ethics

1) *Technologizing marriage.* There are two forms this argument takes. The first is associated with Pius XII and his statements on artificial insemination by husband. The Holy Father excluded this, and especially

---

[126] Leon Kass, " 'Making Babies' Revisited," to be published in *The Public Interest*, Winter 1979.

[127] Clearly Kass, with nearly all scientists, accepts the *fact* that human life begins at conception. He cites Dr. Robert Edwards' interesting, if inadvertent, remark about Louise Brown: "The last time I saw *her, she* was just eight cells in a test-tube. *She* was beautiful *then,* and she's still beautiful *now*" (*Science Digest*, Oct. 1978, 9 [emphasis added]).

[128] One of the most important areas in weighing the moral character of *in vitro* fertilization with embryo transfer is the status of the zygote. Some interesting literature (often in disagreement) was published on this question in the past year: cf. Robert E. Joyce, "Personhood and the Conception Event," *New Scholasticism* 52 (1978) 97–109; Georges Cottier, O.P., "Problèmes éthiques de l'avortement," *Nova et vetera* 53 (1978) 13–36; Joseph T. Culliton, "Rahner on the Origin of the Soul: Some Implications regarding Abortion," *Thought* 53 (1978) 201–14; Larry L. Thomas, "Human Potentiality: Its Moral Relevance," *Personalist* 59 (1978) 266–72; Robert Barry, O.P., "Personhood: The Conditions of Identification and Description," *Linacre Quarterly* 45 (1978) 64–81.

on the grounds that it separated the "biological activity from the personal relation of the married couple" (World Congress on Fertility and Sterility, 1956). Rather, "in its natural structure, the conjugal act is a personal act...." (Italian Catholic Union of Midwives, 1951). In summary, Pius XII viewed the conjugal act as having a natural and God-given design that joins the love-giving dimension with the life-giving dimension. On this basis he excluded both contraception and artificial insemination, and a fortiori *in vitro* fertilization with embryo transfer. It is safe to say that this structured the negative responses of some theologians and bishops when they spoke of the "unnatural."

I believe that this is substantially the approach of Donald McCarthy.[129] He refers to the "integrity of the procreative process" and argues that artificial fertilization is among those "actions that violate human dignity or the dignity of human procreation." Such actions are inhuman in themselves.

The second form of this argument is a softer form. It is a general concern that too much technology introduced into a highly personal context (parenting, family) can mechanize and depersonalize the context. The argument issues in a prudential caution, not necessarily a moral judgment that each instance is morally wrong on this account alone. This argument is also justifiably concerned with objectifying the child into a consumer item ("what sex?" "what color eyes?" etc.).

What might be said of these arguments? I shall comment on only the first, since the second is a dictate of common sense and leaves the question fairly well open. It is clear that at least very many theologians have not been able to accept "the natural ... design of the conjugal act" as this was interpreted by Pius XII. That is, they have not viewed it as an inviolable value. Thus they can allow for contraception at times.

Similarly, and with consistency,[130] they have not been able to see that artificial insemination by husband is necessarily a violation of nature. Gründel states it well when he says that the child must be the expression and embodiment of love, but that sexual intercourse is not the only or necessary source for this expression and embodiment. Many would re-

---

[129] Donald McCarthy, letter to the editor, *Hospital Progress* 59, no. 9 (Sept. 1978) 6.

[130] Note the following from the *National Catholic Register*, Aug. 13, 1978: "It comes as anything but a surprise that moral theologians who reject *Humanae vitae* have difficulty explaining why laboratory conception is morally wrong, or that they are not even sure it is wrong, or they may even think it justified. Father Richard McCormick admits to a certain uncertainty, says that since Pope Pius XII there has been 'a long second look, a rethinking that it can be justified,' and counsels caution. Fr. Bernard Häring observes that Pope Pius condemned test-tube fertilization 'a long way back,' but thinks the Church 'takes a long time to come to positions on these matters.' " The *Register* has it just right, but *praeteritio* is called for in the face of statements such as that those who condemn "laboratory concoction" of babies are "faithful Catholics."

spond in a similar fashion to Donald McCarthy's assertion that artificial fertilization always attacks the integrity of the procreative process. How can one establish that plausibly? We can intuit it, but intuitions notoriously differ. And in this case such dehumanization has not been perceived by at least very many commentators (most recently Bernard Häring, George Lobo, Roger Troisfontaines, Karl Rahner, *et al.*).

That is not to say that the separation of procreation from sexual lovemaking is a neutral thing. To say that would be to minimize the physical aspects of our being in a dualistic way. Rather, the artificial route to pregnancy is a disvalue and one that needs justification. John R. Connery, S.J., has caught this well (though by saying this I do not imply that he should necessarily be associated with the analysis as one approving it).[131] Whether it can find such justification is the burden of some of the other arguments, especially that of the "slippery slope" involving possible undesirable future developments.

In summary, it seems very difficult to reject *in vitro* fertilization with embryo transfer on the sole ground of artificiality or (what is the same thing) the physical separation of the unitive and the procreative—unless one accepts this physical inseparability as an inviolable value.

2) Abortion and discarded zygotes. It is admitted that in the process of *in vitro* fertilization with embryo transfer more than one ovum is fertilized.[132] Those not used will perish.[133] There are those who view zygotes as persons with rights and therefore condemn the procedure outright as abortion. Others see them as simply "human tissue" and find no problem in their creation and loss, the more so because so many fertilized ova are lost in *in vivo* attempts at pregnancy. Still a third group would assess the zygote as somewhere in between these alternatives: not yet a person but a living human being deserving of respect and indeed protection. How much protection is the key question.

With no claim to saying the last word, I would suggest the following for consideration. First, the discussion ought not to center around the personhood of the fertilized ovum. It is difficult to establish this, and there are reputable theologians and philosophers in large numbers who deny such an evaluation at this stage. Moreover, it is unnecessary; for many of those who deny personhood insist that the zygote is not just a thing but deserves our respect and awe.

---

[131] John R. Connery, S.J., letter to the editor, *America* 139 (1978) 145.

[132] It is not absolutely essential to the procedure as such. *In vitro* fertilization could be done during successive cycles either by freezing ova in advance or by doing (most unlikely) successive laparoscopies.

[133] Furthermore, it is generally accepted that the parties ought to be willing to abort during the pregnancy if something goes wrong. I put this in a footnote because it is not necessary to the procedure as such.

Second, it is one thing to fertilize *in vitro* in order to experiment and study the product of conception; it is quite another to do so in order to achieve a pregnancy. It seems to me that the respect due nascent life, even if not yet personal life, rubs out the first alternative. Kass has stated that the "presumption of ignorance ought to err in the direction of not underestimating the basis for respect." That seems correct, and it is the same as the traditional principle that in factual doubts life deserves the preference.

Third, the term "abortion" must be carefully used when there is question of discarded zygotes. We know that a very high percentage of naturally fertilized ova never implant, are lost. This means that there is a tacit acceptance on the part of the couple that their normal sexual relations will lead to this as the price of having a child.

The response often given to this explanation is that we may not reproduce by artifice everything that happens in nature. Thus, though people inevitably die, we do not kill them. Though there are life-taking earthquakes in nature, we ought not manufacture life-taking earthquakes. Perhaps a distinction is called for here between replicating nature's disasters and replicating nature's achievements. Is there anything particularly wrong about achieving artificially, *faute de mieux*, what occurs otherwise naturally? We are not exactly replicating disasters, but rather achievements even with unavoidable disvalues. If it is by no means clear that couples engaging in normal sexual relations are "causing abortions" because foreseeably many fertilized ova do not implant, it is not clear that the discards from artificial procedures must be called "abortions," especially if the ratio of occurrence is roughly similar.[134]

Put this in the language of rights to life on the supposition that the zygote is a person. It is not a violation of the right to life of the zygote if it is spontaneously lost in normal sexual relations. Why is it any more so when this loss occurs as the result of an attempt to achieve pregnancy artificially? The matter of discards is serious, indeed crucial, for those of us who believe that human life must be protected and respected from its very beginning. These reflections are meant only as probes into a difficult area.

3) *Harm to the possible child.* The argument here is that the very procedure which gives life is inseparable from risks, physical and psychological. These may be small risks, but even so it is morally wrong to induce for a nonconsenting child even a small risk of great harm. This seems to be Ramsey's key argument.

[134] It might be well to recall here that we do not object to tubal reconstructive surgery. Yet, it is well known and foreseen that such surgery leads to a marked increase in ectopic pregnancies that will have to be reluctantly terminated—and at a later stage than the zygote stage.

On the other hand, the counterstatement (by Kass and others) is that the risk of harm need not be positively excluded. It is suffcient if it is equivalent to or less than the risks to the child from normal procreation.

The response to this assertion is that we could never get to know *that* without exposing a certain number of children to unknown risk to get the statistic. This seems to some to be an insuperable argument against ever starting the *in vitro* procedures. However, once this statistic is had, is the objection any longer telling? In other words, even though Steptoe and Edwards may have acted wrongfully (in ignorance of the risks), after it is clear that the risks are equivalent to normal conception, are those who follow necessarily acting wrongfully?[135]

4) *The extension beyond marriage.* This reasoning takes two forms. First, once *in vitro* fertilization is used successfully in marriage, it will go beyond marriage to third-party donors (semen, ovum), host wombs, etc.[136] This extension is seen as a radical attack on marriage, the family, human sexuality, personal identity and lineage of the child. The argument is one of inevitability, given the cultural acceptance by many of AID (donor insemination) already. As Kass says, "There will almost certainly be other uses involving third parties."

The second form of the argument, an extension of the first, is that the wedge argument is primarily a matter of the logic of justification. That is, the principles now used to justify husband-wife *in vitro* fertilization already justify in advance other procedures. The strict validity of this second argument, it seems to me, depends on the "principles now used to justify." If the principle is that an infertile couple, using their own gametes, may licitly use artificial means, that is one thing. If, on the other hand, it is less precise (e.g., couples may licitly overcome their sterility with *in vitro* procedures), then all the problems involved in the second form of the argument strike home.

In summary, then, at the level of the individual couple's decision, there seems to be no argument that shows with clarity and certainty that *in vitro* procedures using their own sperm and ovum are necessarily and inherently wrong, if abortion of a possibly deformed child is excluded and

---

[135] In this respect it should be noted that some of the experts testifying before the Ethics Advisory Board thought factually that (1) not enough animal work had preceded and (2) the risks for humans have not been sufficiently assessed.

[136] That this is not an idle fear is clear from the testimony given before the Ethics Advisory Board by Drs. Randolph W. Seed and Richard G. Seed. They propose to inseminate a third party, then wash out the fertilized ovum to be reimplanted in the wife. Moreover, Dr. Landrum Shettles, waiting to testify in the Del Zio case, stated: "I have cloned three human eggs from testicular tissue. They lived for three or four days." Cf. *Medical Moral Newsletter* 15, no. 7 (Sept. 1978) 28. In the words of Nobel Laureate James Watson, there is potential for "all sorts of unsettling scenarios" (*Reader's Digest* 113, no. 679 [Nov. 1978] 103).

the risks are acceptably low.[137] This is not to say that such procedures are without problems and dangers; they are not. And that brings us to public policy.

Public Policy

Public policy refers above all to laws or decisions that either ban, do not ban, or financially support *in vitro* fertilization. In my own, at this time very tentative, judgment, public policy should not support *in vitro* fertilization where research alone (not embryo transfer) is the purpose. Respect for germinating life calls for at least this. Granted, there is potentially a good deal to be learned from study of fertilized ova (genetic disease, contraception, fertility). But I do not see how this can be done without stripping nascent life of the minimal respect we owe it. Some research is necessary, of course, prior to implementation of transfer technology. I do not see this, given our doubts about zygote status, as incompatible with respect.

As for *in vitro* fertilization with embryo transfer, this should not be supported with government funds *in the present circumstances* (cf. below), though it should not be prohibited by law or policy. Why "not supported"? Because of the cumulative impact of many arguments: the dangers of going beyond marriage are almost certainly unavoidable; the distorted priorities of medicine this introduces (e.g., prenatal care for children already *in utero* is unavailable to very many); the almost unavoidable dangers of proceeding to independent zygote research and the manipulation of the implanted fetus (cf. our abortion culture) with the assault on nascent life this involves; the readiness to abort that this procedure presently entails; the trauma this would visit on an already deeply divided nation (on abortion) by asking that tax money be used for purposes against the consciences of many and not necessary to the public good; the disproportion of benefits (to a relatively few) with costs; the growing neglect of more radically therapeutic (oviduct reconstruction) and preventive (of gonorrhea) interventions; government reinforcement of the dubious, perhaps noxious, notion that women's lives are unfulfilled if they cannot have their "own children."

It should be remembered that funding implies fostering. Whether it is appropriate to foster depends on what is being fostered. And that depends to some extent on the circumstances. Thus, if we cannot fund *in vitro* fertilization between husband and wife without *in our circumstances* funding (and fostering) practices beyond that, we should not do so. I believe this to be the case. *In other circumstances* we could draw a

---

[137] In saying this, I am in substantial agreement both in method and content with the ethical committee of the Guild of Catholic Doctors (London). Cf. "In Vitro Fertilization," *Catholic Medical Quarterly* 24 (1972) 237–43. But note the words "seems" and "certainty."

different conclusion.

This section began with the deliverances of James Gustafson. Let it end with a return to this wise and insightful moral theologian. People are going to differ on this question, and probably vociferously, much as they do on abortion.[138] Those differences may well root in matters of loyalty and beliefs that are profoundly theological in character. Concretely, one view may see in the givenness of natural processes the creation and unalterable mandate of God. This involves a notion of God Himself and what He is doing in the world, and it must be explored.

Another perspective would see in man's being God's image the fact that God has shared His dominion and providence with us in such a way that we are to be the prudent overseers of nature. Such prudence means employing our creative capacities in a way that supports and furthers the outlines indicated in nature. This suggests that the criterion of use is what humanizes the person. That determination is the enormous responsibility of man.

Thus, statements like "violates the human integrity and dignity with which a loving and wise Creator has endowed humanity" are radically theological appeals. If there are differences on what does and does not violate integrity, and if these are to be made more intelligible, this theological warrant must be brought into the open and explored more deeply. In the process of doing this, we could well recall John Mahoney's reflection: "We are more prone to behave as those who nostalgically and selectively canonize the past than those who are called to consecrate the future."[139]

[138] Richard A. McCormick, S.J., "Abortion: Rules for Debate," *America* 139 (1978) 26–30.

[139] Mahoney, "Ethical Horizons" 329.

CURRENT THEOLOGY: 1980

NOTES ON MORAL THEOLOGY: 1979

The single most important happening in the field of moral theology in 1979 was, of course, the visit of John Paul II to several countries, including the United States. These visits were primarily pastoral in purpose, but in their course the Holy Father revealed very clearly not only the style of leadership he will exercise[1] but his approach and priorities in the moral sphere as well. This is especially true of his trip to the United States. And this was to be expected. In a fine editorial *America* noted:

Above all else, the Pope today is asked to be a moral teacher and leader, not just for Catholics but for all men and women of good will. Through a combination of circumstances—his own personal gifts, contemporary communications technology, the historical anguish of the time—John Paul II has been given an opportunity to appeal to the conscience of mankind in a manner unique in the history of the papacy.[2]

During the course of a few short days, John Paul II addressed nearly every difficult moral problem of our time—from human rights, power and peace, social morality, Catholic education, the magisterium, to marriage, sexuality, and women in the Church.

In no instance was the message unpredictable or unexpected. I am sure that people will react variously to individual items treated by the Holy Father. Be that as it may, it is important to highlight themes that run through nearly everything John Paul II said and did. The following three strike this commentator as worthy of note.

First, there is the Pope's constant emphasis on the uniqueness and dignity of the person. He returns to this again and again, whether he is discussing peace, poverty, energy, sexuality, abortion, or religious freedom. As the *America* editorial noted: "He insisted repeatedly that the welfare of the human person must be the final measure of all relationships among the nations of the world, of all economic and political systems and of all negotiations over regional boundaries or military superiority."[3] For example, in his address to the United Nations, the Pope stated of the quest for peace: "Every analysis must necessarily start from the premise that—although each person lives in a particular concrete social and

[1] For a reaction to this style, cf. *National Catholic Reporter*, Nov. 23, 1979, 3.
[2] *America* 141 (1979) 185.
[3] Ibid. 2.

historical context—every human being is endowed with a dignity that must never be lessened, impaired or destroyed but must instead be respected and safeguarded if peace is really to be built up."[4] Similarly, he rooted his traditional sexual ethic in the dignity of the person. Several articles in the past year have analyzed very helpfully the writings of the then Cardinal Wojtyla on the person as moral agent and centerpiece of our reflections.[5]

The second striking characteristic of the Holy Father's presentations is his willingness to challenge with a hard saying. Repeatedly he reminded us of the obligations of wealth, of the need to alter life-style for a more equitable distribution of resources, of the sacrifices required to bring life generously into the world and support it. The Pope was aware of the demanding character of his moral message. In his address to the American bishops he adverted to it explicitly: "Brothers in Christ: as we proclaim the truth in love, it is not possible for us to avoid all criticism; nor is it possible to please everyone."[6]

Third, there is in the papal statements a thoroughgoing compassion and love in the face of tension and polarization. In his speech at Grant Park, Chicago, he noted: "Let love for each other and love for truth be the answer to polarization, when factions are formed because of differing views in matters that relate to faith or to the priorities for action. No one in the ecclesiastical community should ever feel alienated or unloved, even when tensions arise in the course of common efforts to bring the fruits of the gospel to society around us."[7]

These "Notes" will organize around three areas of concern touched by the Pontiff on his visit to the United States: (1) the person and personal action;[8] (2) the pastoral problem of divorce and remarriage; (3) nuclear energy and nuclear disarmament.

THE PERSON AND PERSONAL ACTION

In moral discourse appeal is frequently made to the dignity of the person. For example, Vatican II based the notion of religious freedom on the dignity of the person. What is meant by this notion? Bruno Schüller submits it to a careful analysis.[9] The dignity of the person, as an image

[4] Origins 9 (1979) 262.

[5] A. Wilder, O.P., "Community of Persons in the Thought of Karol Wojtyla," Angelicum 56 (1979) 211–44; F. Bednarski, O.P., "Les implications axiologiques et normatives de l'analyse de l'expérience morale d'après le card. Karol Wojtyla," ibid. 245–72.

[6] Origins 9 (1979) 290.

[7] Ibid. 292.

[8] Cf. John Paul II, Redemptor hominis (Origins 8 [1979] 625–43).

[9] Bruno Schüller, S.J., "Die Personwürde des Menschen als Beweisgrund in der normativen Ethik," Theologie und Glaube 53 (1978) 538–55.

and likeness of God, means that the person must be respected and loved as an end in him/herself. It is the "dignity of the person" that makes the command of love of neighbor, as well as the golden rule, intelligible. Once this connection is made between the dignity of the person, love of neighbor, and the golden rule, Schüller argues that "dignity of the person" has the same argumentative function in normative ethics as the other two. That is, it determines moral goodness but not moral rightness. In other words, it is a necessary condition for moral rightness but not a sufficient one. Most of the hotly disputed questions in moral theology are in the area of moral rightness and wrongness. When "dignity of the person" is used to settle such controversies, it pertains much more to the genre of appeal or exhortation than to moral argument. If this is overlooked, an *ignorantia elenchi* (missing the point) occurs. That is, personal moral goodness becomes the exclusive area where one is to discuss and find moral rightness or wrongness.

Schüller next discusses two forms of argument that root in the notion of personal dignity. The first is: since persons are similar in their personal worth, they are also similar in other respects. As Galatians words it, "There does not exist among you Jew or Greek, slave or freeman, male or female. All are one in Christ Jesus" (3:28). Schüller argues that this appeal to personal dignity yields very little normative content. "For the insight into the personal dignity of another and into the claim to be treated in a morally right way leaves open the question about what the morally right response is and how this is to be determined."[10] There are morally relevant differences between persons that demand difference in treatment. Therefore "dignity of the person" is really an appeal to appraise correctly the different ethical requirements following upon, e.g., maleness and femaleness.

The second form of argument based on dignity of the person is inspired by Kant: a person is an end in him/herself and may not be treated only as a means. What does that statement yield in terms of normative ethics? It has been used widely and frequently in bioethics: e.g., in discussions about experimentation with children or incompetents. Schüller uses unchastity as an example. Does every failure in this area involve an individual in evaluating him/herself as a mere means or a thing? If we would have to say this, then "dignity of the person" would be equal in its generality to *recta ratio* or *natura humana qua rationalis*. Kant thought that even in the natural sexual act persons made themselves into "things." However, he thought it justifiable in marriage because personhood is recovered through the reciprocity of the action. Therefore, Schüller argues, there seem to be conditions under which a person does not destroy personal dignity while he makes himself a means or a "thing."

[10] Ibid. 541.

What might they be? Schüller gives several examples. For instance, a person fires his secretary for incompetence. Could the secretary not protest that in the reasons for her dismissal only her working competence, not her personal worth, was considered? In fact, a secretary's competence or incompetence has nothing to do with her personal worth. What qualifies one as a secretary is purely instrumental. Thus, in hiring or firing a secretary it is impossible not to treat an individual as a mere means. Something similar happens when the sick person asks for the doctor. Should the doctor not refuse on the grounds that he is called in terms of his medical competence only and is thus degraded to a mere means?

Schüller argues that a person is used as a thing or a mere means whenever the only basic reason for an action is utility or pleasure to be gotten from another. But he immediately notes that our lives are full of such actions, and they are actions we consider morally right. On the other hand, the attitude of using others for one's purposes defines the very structure of the egoist's life. These two reflections lead Schüller to conclude that the maxim about not using another as a means relates not to the sphere of the ethically right and wrong but to the sphere of intention and attitude. In other words, its function in moral discourse is similar to that of the golden rule and the command of neighbor love.

In all the actions mentioned by Kant (of actions wrong because one treats oneself or another as a thing), Schüller believes that Kant does not use his axiom to conclude that the actions are wrong. Rather he holds— for whatever reason—that certain actions are wrong and goes about showing why by use of the axiom. His "proofs" are mostly plausible. But he neglects to mention that the same axiom would apply with similar plausibility to actions he and others consider right. Schüller concludes, therefore, that the notions of dignity of the person or the person as self-end offer practically nothing to clarify the rightness or wrongness of a concrete act. In this he is at one with Ross, who says of the Kantian axiom: "It has in fact great homiletic value; it is a means of edification rather than enlightenment."[11]

Schüller's final section is a systematic presentation of how "dignity of the person" functions in Christian perspective in determining ethical rightness and wrongness. Since human beings are before all else persons in their free self-determination vis-à-vis ethical demands, the ethical good is the core of their worth and dignity. This is an unconditioned dignity and worth because the ethical good is unconditioned. Only the individual him/herself can radically protect or violate this worth as a person. In this sense "personal worth" is interchangeable (as a criterion of rightness or wrongness) with *natura humana* and *recta ratio*.

[11] D. Ross, *Kant's Ethical Theory* (Oxford, 1969) 55, cited in Schüller 548.

There are, however, actions which violate personal worth. For example, scandal or leading another to act against his/her conscience. Such actions by definition aim at getting another to violate his/her own personal value precisely in so far as this value consists in moral integrity. Improper diminishment of responsibility in another would also be an attack on that other's personal worth, as well as a violation of the golden rule. I would, in such conduct, refuse to acknowledge the other as one like me.

Where nonmoral goods are concerned, the matter is different. As goods of the person, they seem to share in personal worth or value. On the other hand, one's personal worth cannot depend finally on such goods. We cannot say that health and wealth enhance personal worth, while sickness and poverty diminish it. What are we to say when these goods are in conflict, scil., when we must deal with the interests of one as if they were merely a means to the interests of another? Or again, what are we to say when negative consequences to one are a means to the positive or good effects? In such conflict situations, Schüller argues, we necessarily relate to the harmful omission or commission as to a means only. But there is nothing really wrong with this unless we suppose that in conflict situations the use of preference principles (built on the hierarchy of goods themselves) necessarily involves us in violating personal dignity. Schüller rejects such a supposition and argues that the one decisive condition is that the goods and harms of all be considered in impartial fashion. It is in such impartiality that all are acknowledged as similar, as ends in themselves, as persons.

Whether, therefore, personal dignity is violated by an action that has nonmoral evil as a consequence cannot be determined by this consequence alone but only by the correspondence of the action to the golden rule. The golden rule defines moral goodness and thereby gives a *necessary* ingredient of moral rightness but not a *sufficient* one. Thus the error of those who appeal exclusively to the dignity of the person as sufficient grounding for a moral norm. "One accepts as a sufficient condition of moral rightness of conduct that which is only a necessary condition."[12]

The upshot of Schüller's careful study is that there are actions which do indeed treat others as a means only, yet remain compatible with acknowledgment of that person's dignity. In this I think he is correct. A simple example like quarantine of a person with a contagious disease is a case in point. And if he is correct, then the wrongfulness of actions we all acknowledge to be wrong should find a more illuminating explanation than in saying "this involves using another as a means only." It further invites us to a continued and deeper reflection on the notions of direct and indirect in moral discourse. The terms are settled, even hallowed, in Catholic moral tradition, so much so that questioning their morally

[12] Schüller, "Die Personwürde" 551.

decisive character seems to some to question the very values they attempt to concretize and protect, as will become clear below. Such, I am convinced, is not the case.

Marcelino Zalba, S.J., treats the dignity of the person as a criterion from a somewhat different viewpoint.[13] In the penultimate redaction of Vatican II's statement about the objectivity of criteria in reconciling conjugal love and the transmission of life, there was reference to human dignity. The statement read: "The moral character of action, when there is question of reconciling conjugal love with responsible transmission of life, does not depend on sincere intention alone and on evaluation of motives; but it depends on objective criteria based on the very dignity of the human person. . . . "[14]

To some Council fathers, locating the basis of objective criteria in the dignity of the human person appeared a novelty and pregnant with mischievous possibilities for unlimited autonomy and relativism. Consequently the text was revised to its present form: "It must be determined by objective standards. These, based on the nature of the human person and his acts, preserve the full sense of mutual self-giving and human procreation in the context of true love."[15]

Many interpreters had seen in this language (*ex personae ejusdemque actuum natura*) a criteriological shift from the facticity of nature to the broader notion of person. For instance, Ph. Delhaye had written that prior to the Council the prevailing criterion was the physiological integrity of the act. Similarly, Louis Janssens contrasted act of the person with the preconciliar *actus naturae*.[16] Zalba's article argues against these readings by insisting on the grammar of the phrase—that both *personae* and *actuum* are genitive objects of *natura*. Therefore both the nature of the person and the nature of the acts form the basis for objective moral norms. He rejects the notion that the criteria in *Humanae vitae* are merely biological and incompatible with the personal emphasis in *Gaudium et spes*.

The remainder of the article is a critique of several theologians who have, in Zalba's judgment, improperly interpreted the phrase *ex personae ejusdemque actuum natura* and thus seen it as in sharp contrast with *Humanae vitae*. He cites among others Bernard Häring, Ph. Delhaye, A. Hortelano, Louis Janssens, Charles Curran.[17]

[13] Marcelino Zalba, S.J., "Ex personae ejusdemque actuum natura," *Periodica* 68 (1979) 201–32.

[14] Cited ibid. 209.

[15] *Gaudium et spes*, no. 51 (*Documents of Vatican II*, ed. Walter Abbott, S.J. [New York: Association, 1966] 256).

[16] Cf. Zalba 223 and 225.

[17] Of Curran, Zalba notes: "The ecclesiastical magisterium cannot be accused of physicalism without grave injustice, since it is stated, without any demonstration or possibility

Zalba is certainly correct when he criticizes "dignity of the person" as a sufficient normative criterion. However, two comments are in order. First, the authors he criticizes are not saying that *Humanae vitae* uses the biological as normative in an explicit way. They are arguing that the only way the conclusions of that encyclical (every contraceptive act is intrinsically evil) are sustainable is through a criterion involving the biological as normative.

Secondly and similarly, Zalba denies any great leap or advance when Vatican II used the phrase *ex personae ejusdemque actuum natura* because the person is nothing more than *natura humana concretizata*. Thus human nature was and still is the basic norm. Here I believe he misses the point. In the authors he criticizes, person is not to be contrasted with human nature; rather it is to be contrasted with a single aspect of the person. To these authors it seems that this single aspect (physical integrity) has been absolutized in *Humanae vitae*.

Another aspect of the person that continues to receive attention is that of norms that enlighten personal decision. A lively exchange occurred recently in the *Deutsche Tagespost* between Franz Scholz and Gustave Ermecke.[18] Ermecke began the exchange on July 18, 1978 with an attack on teleological reasoning in moral theology. There followed on Oct. 3 another free-swinging attack (by an unnamed author) on Franz Böckle and "teleological moral theologians." In the words of this attack, "when love of neighbor demands a murder, then Exodus 20/13 no longer applies." Böckle is accused of having an unchristian notion of freedom, an earthly lawlessness and demonic wisdom. Of those who use teleology in building moral norms it is said: "These theologians truly are, it would seem, lords

---

thereof, that the magisterium 'identifies' the human and moral act with the physical structure of the conjugal act" (232). Whether there is injustice or not depends entirely on the correctness of the conclusion that *every act* must always remain open to the possibility of procreation if it is to avoid being intrinsically evil. It is Curran's argument that the only way this conclusion can be sustained is by giving a morally decisive character (normative) to physical integrity or givenness (and this he calls "physicalism"), a thing he does not believe careful moral analysis will sustain. Obviously Zalba disagrees. It would have been more helpful and enlightening had Zalba discussed the arguments for the traditional conclusion rather than justice-injustice. These latter categories suppose that the argument is clear and the conclusion correct. For the most recent statement of agreement with Curran, cf. Franz Böckle, "Biotechnik und Menschenwürde," *Die neue Ordnung* 33 (1979) 356–62, at 357. After adverting to the twofold sense or meaning of sexual intimacy (expression of love, fruitfulness), Böckle remarks: "It must be clearly stated that there is no successful proof that demands this connection between expression of love and fruitfulness in *every* act." Of interventions that separate these two senses, Böckle states that more recent moral theology "judges such interventions with the criterion of the goods at stake."

[18] The following exchanges are taken entirely from the *Deutsche Tagespost*, July 18, Oct. 3, Nov. 8, Jan. 9, May 25–26, and July 4. They were kindly forwarded to me by Dr. Franz Scholz.

over life and death." They arrogate to themselves the power to determine when the killing of an innocent person "is in order." They are accused of holding that a good end justifies an evil means, etc.

Franz Scholz calls attention to the unfairness of these allegations, even their injustice. The entire moral theology of a respected scholar (Böckle) as well as his person is blackened and with him "all teleological theologians." After all, he urges, if *benevolentia* is to become operative in *beneficentia*, we must of necessity consider the effects of our actions on our neighbor. In some cases this simply demands the type of weighing of goods (*Güterabwägung*) repudiated by the unnamed author in the *Deutsche Tagespost*. Furthermore, Scholz argues, such a weighing has always been present in traditional moral theology. For instance, there are many norms that impose an obligation only conditionally (e.g., Sunday worship), that bind only if one is not excused by a proportionately serious reason. Scholz asks: Does the fact that an individual must discern or weigh whether his reason is sufficient make him "lord over the Sunday obligation"?

Similarly, Scholz asks the objecting author to reflect more deeply on the axiom "a good end does not justify evil means." Unless a distinction is made between moral and nonmoral evil, a mother could not use a painful disinfectant on her child's wound; for that would be imposing pain (evil means) to achieve health and cure (good end).

Ermecke then responded to this. He claims that the assertion that all innerworldly goods and evils, as created goods, are contingent is unproven and is really a form of relativism. He asserts that in this entire discussion about teleology there is lacking a well-founded and valid measure for various values. Furthermore, there are absolute norms. They exist whenever the immediate consequences of an act are not decisive. That there are such acts Ermecke does not doubt. His example: direct killing of an innocent person. "That act which abolishes at its root the essential and existential order of a person, or makes it impossible, is absolutely morally reprehensible, even prescinding from all further consequences of this action." Yes, there are times when a true choice must be made between relative values; but the very being of persons cannot be thrown into such a calculus. Ermecke regrets that many moral theologians are now minimizing the principle of double effect, for it is of "absolutely fundamental importance."

Scholz chose the pages of *Theologie der Gegenwart* to repeat his claim that all "innerworldly" goods are relative and can come into conflict.[19] In such cases a basically teleological choice must be made. The article is a summary statement of many of the themes already discussed, especially

[19] F. Scholz, "Werdet kluge Wechsler!" *Theologie der Gegenwart* 22 (1979) 19–26.

the difference between deontological and teleological approaches.

During May 1979 Ermecke responded to this article, once again in the pages of the *Deutsche Tagespost*. He made several points. For instance, according to Scholz, no "innerworldly" good has an absolute character; only an individual's relationship to God has such absoluteness. However, Ermecke argues, lying, unchastity, injustice, even though they relate to such "innerworldly" goods, may never be done because "by doing such things man's highest good, his relationship with God, is destroyed." Therefore, Ermecke concludes, there is conduct (*innerweltliche Handlungen*) that is always morally wrong.

Furthermore, Ermecke rejects the kind of calculus (*Güterabwägung*) that a conflict situation imposes. What is the criterion for such a choice? Ermecke's example: "Truth is the most precious gift for human beings. I may directly deceive no one. I can permit one's deception, but I may never directly lead one into error." To say otherwise is to undermine the objective order and to say that the commandments "no longer bind if through their nonobservance better results are achieved." Ermecke sees all of this as utilitarianism pure and simple.

In July 1979 Scholz returned to the discussion. He proposes that ethical concepts reveal their value when they are put to the test in the conflict situations in which our lives abound. He lists three such conflicts and appeals to the common sense of the reader against Ermecke. The first is a transplant of a major organ (kidney) from a wife to her seriously-ill husband. Most people see such organ donation as heroic charity. Ermecke disallows it as a rebellion against God's rights in us, as intrinsically evil. Those who are not satisfied with such a prohibition Ermecke discredits as "superficial utilitarians whose Christian principles are for sale." Scholz is justifiably appalled at this.

Secondly, according to Ermecke, it is never permissible to utter a falsehood, even to terrorists hell-bent on murder and gross violations of rights. Scholz believes that the demands of theory would yield to common sense here—indeed, that they are foreign to any ethic that takes love of neighbor seriously.

Finally, Scholz takes the rare but classic abortion dilemma (save the mother or lose both mother and nonviable child). According to Ermecke, the only permissible intervention must be indirect. This means two things. First, the doctor must stand by and allow two to die. Second, the only permissible intervention is one which does more damage than necessary by removing fertility (uterus) along with the child. Principles that lead to such conclusions must be seriously re-examined. Scholz invites Ermecke to distance himself from his rigid conclusions in all three of these cases, but sees no way of doing so without relying on the teleology Ermecke has so severely criticized.

Scholz concludes by alluding to Paul Ramsey's and this author's exchanges, and, I am delighted to say, sees them as courteous and brotherly discussions. By implication he implores Ermecke to cease and desist from his name-calling.

The tone of some of these essays is indeed regrettable. But it is the substance that should be of primary concern. And in this regard I agree thoroughly with Scholz and Böckle. Ermecke repeatedly shoots out as objections statements that strike no discernible target. He describes and refutes positions no one holds. For instance, it is no particular objection against teleological reasoning to say that a value measure or scale must be based in Christian ontology and anthropology. Of course it must. Nor is anything attacked by saying that the use of prudence must conform to an objective value scale. Of course it must. And Scholz would agree. But he would ask: What does *that* have to do with a rejection of teleology? Nor is it any objection to say that unchastity, injustice, etc. must never be done, and to conclude from this that teleological considerations do not function in conflict situations. The whole discussion is about what concrete action is to count as injustice, unchastity, etc. Ermecke repeatedly misses this point.

In discussions such as that between Scholz and Ermecke, one frequently encounters the term "intrinsically evil," *actus intrinsece malus, actio intrinsece inhonesta.* Does usage of the term really enlighten very much? Clearly there are those who believe that abandonment of the concept is the rough equivalent of moral chaos. Regardless of one's leanings, it would be instructive to see how medieval theologians faced some of these problems. John Dedek gives an excellent summary of the teaching of St. Thomas and some of his predecessors (e.g., Philip the Chancellor, Peter of Poitiers, William of Auxerre, William of Paris, Hugh of St. Cher, St. Albert, St. Bonaventure, etc.).[20] According to many of these predecessors, those actions which were *secundum se* evil could receive no exceptions or dispensations. But by *secundum se* they meant actions which were done *ex libidine*, and therefore contained their own absolute condemnation in their very naming (*mox nominata sunt mala*). Thus, in exposing Bonaventure's teaching Dedek writes:

> Therefore, he [Bonaventure] concludes, God could command Hosea to copulate with a harlot (*cognoscere non suam*) but not to fornicate in so far as fornication designates a sinful act (*cognoscere aliquam ex libidine*). Similarly, God could command a man to take another's property (*accipere rem alienam*) but not with a sinful will (*accipere ex libidine*).

Dedek argues that Thomas' teaching fits harmoniously into this tem-

[20] John F. Dedek, "Intrinsically Evil Acts: An Historical Study of the Mind of St. Thomas," *Thomist* 43 (1979) 385–413.

poral context. He held that certain acts are *secundum se* evil. But these are actions whose very naming and description reveal the disordered element. Thomas held that killing is not murder unless it is unjust, that "extramarital intercourse is not adultery or fornication unless it is against the will of God who orders human generation."

Where dispensations from the Decalogue are concerned, Thomas took two approaches. The first was to view these precepts formally (scil., as forbidding unjust killing, inordinate sexual activity, etc.) and therefore disallowing any exceptions. His second approach was to distinguish between the precepts of the first tablet and the second tablet of the Decalogue. Precepts of the first tablet order persons to God; no dispensation is possible here. The precepts of the second tablet order persons to each other; from these God can dispense.

This is an interesting and very useful study. Dedek does not say it, but clearly his historical review implies that one can think of a Christian normative ethics, and even a very demanding one, without use of the term "intrinsic evil" as it has been understood in recent manualist theology and even in formulations of the magisterium.[21]

Reference was made above to some ongoing exchanges between Paul Ramsey and the author of these "Notes." Two interesting articles summarize and critique these exchanges in a way which sets out helpfully some of the issues at stake and involved in the discussions reported above.[22] There is no need to review these articles here, except, after expressing gratitude to both authors, to say that I believe John Langan has a much better grasp of the serious problems involved in the direct-indirect distinction than Joseph Allen.

Here I want to make two brief responses or clarifications for the record. Allen argues that I have seriously misunderstood Ramsey's position "at some points, sometimes surprisingly." He concretizes this as follows: "He assumes, for instance, that when Ramsey declares it a moral evil to kill a human being, he means any killing rather than only an unjustifiable

---

[21] A different view is taken by Theo G. Belmans in a very long study on the specification of human actions. He faults a whole host of theologians for misinterpreting Thomas' thought: Joseph Fuchs, B. Schüller, P. Knauer, Van der Marck, F. Böckle, C. J. Van der Poel, L. Janssens, F. Scholz, S. Pinckaers, J. Gründel, and many others. I shall leave it to others to make sense of the Thomistic texts on this matter. It seems to me, however, that Belmans has not reflected sufficiently on the implications of Thomas' acceptance of capital punishment and its relation to the Decalogue. To say (47) that Thomas did not consider this an exception (dispensation) to the fifth commandment is to say something only about Thomas' notion of the term "exception." It is not to face the more radical methodological implications, especially about the notion of intrinsic evil. Cf. Theo Belmans, "La spécification de l'agir humain par son objet chez saint Thomas d'Aquin," *Divinitas* 33 (1979) 7–61.

[22] Joseph L. Allen, "Paul Ramsey and His Respondents since *The Patient as Person*," *Religious Studies Review* 5 (1979) 89–95; John Langan, S.J., "Direct and Indirect—Some Recent Exchanges between Paul Ramsey and Richard McCormick," ibid. 95–101.

one."[23] Here Allen misses my point. I was arguing that Ramsey talks about human life in such a way that he puts any killing on the level of a moral evil. This is an argumentative point, a kind of *reductio ad absurdum*. In contrast to Allen, Langan has caught this: "Like sin [for Ramsey] the taking of human life is never to be 'the object of a directly intending will'. . . . [This] shows Ramsey's absolutizing of the value of the individual human life."[24]

The second point is a clarification occasioned by Langan's study. I had argued that what differentiates the classical, if rare, abortion dilemma (lose two vs. save the one who can be saved, the mother) from other cases (e.g., killing innocent civilians to persuade a nation to cease aggression) is the necessary connection between the good achieved and evil done. In the abortion case there is such a connection. In the case of "counterpeople" (noncombatants) bombing there is not. Langan—as well as Norbert Rigali in a thoughtful and gracious correspondence—argues that this proves too much. It would exclude also killing combatants as well. "For there is no *necessary* connection between killing enemy soldiers and a hostile nation's ceasing unjust aggression, and requiring such a connection if the doing of nonmoral evil is to be morally justified would rule out the killing of combatants as well."[25]

It seems to me that this misplaces the necessary connection in the self-defense (and combatant) case. It is not between killing the aggressor and the aggressor's ceasing unjust aggression. It is between killing the aggressor and my self-defense. The use of force is, indeed, the only way to achieve self-defense once aggression has begun against me. The same cannot be said about killing the aggressor's innocent wife, e.g., to get him to stop. It might factually achieve cessation of aggression, and my self-defense. But there is not a necessary connection between self-defense and the harm caused.

Langan concludes his thoughtful piece: "What the theory of proportionate reason needs at this point is not a necessary connection requirement, but a principle holding that harm done to another in order to prevent him from doing evil must be no more than is needed to dissuade, or if that fails, to disable him."[26] To which it might be responded: before one begins to propose a principle of *moderation* of harm caused, it is necessary first to have shown (and why) that it is morally acceptable to harm at all. A principle of justification of any force is one thing; a principle of moderation is another. The necessary-connection requirement—if it is valid, and I am far from sure that it is—pertains to the

---

[23] Allen, ibid. 92.
[24] Langan, ibid. 98.
[25] Langan, ibid. 100.
[26] Langan, ibid. 100.

former.

Norbert Rigali, S.J., treats the person from a slightly different perspective.[27] He emphasizes the historical character of our consciousness and being, and argues that moral theology must not be simply a touching up of classical theology but a transformation of it. He approaches this transformation from two points of view. First, the contemporary discussion about the distinctiveness of Christian ethics "to some extent sidetracked the required transformation of moral theology." Second, the transformation of moral theology requires "a new model of moral law." A word about each.

As for the first question, Rigali feels that it must be rejected as a bad question. It was generated out of a "classical consciousness." Historical consciousness knows the answer to the question. Of course there is a distinctive Christian ethic. Citing Daniel Maguire, and more remotely James Gustafson, he notes that "an ethic will be Mahayana Cambodian Buddhist or early Trobriander, medieval French Catholic or Swiss nineteenth-century Calvinist."[28] The very question supposes as at least possible that there is "a morality higher than human morality." Rigali sees this as a dualistic notion of the human person, involving a dichotomy between the natural (human) and supernatural. He concludes: "From the standpoint of historical consciousness, therefore, the question for moral theology today is decidedly not whether there is a specifically Christian ethic or whether Christian morality adds to human morality. To the extent that recent theology has been preoccupied with this question, it has been unregenerated moral theology."[29]

Rigali next turns to the moral law. The model of moral law that characterizes classicism is the ruler-subject relation—the moral law being seen as a code of precepts imposed on an individual by an authority to which the individual is subject. Such a notion unduly exalted universality and was insensitive to individuality and freedom. Thus "the moral ideal reflected in its conception of moral law is universal compliance with the patterns of behavior preordained by law." In this outlook, change in moral law is a matter of tampering with exceptions at the margins and fringes. Rigali sees the discussion about the absoluteness of moral norms not as a regeneration of moral theology but as a distraction. The negative answer given to the question by many contemporary theologians has "only succeeded in establishing an inverted, more liberal legalism in place of a more conservative legalism. It is the legalistic, authoritarian concep-

---

[27] Norbert J. Rigali, S.J., "Morality and Historical Consciousness," *Chicago Studies* 18 (1979) 161–68.

[28] For some interesting essays on Anglican ethics, cf. *Anglican Theological Review* 61 (1979) 8–156.

[29] Rigali, "Morality and Historical Consciousness" 164.

tion of moral law, whether liberal or conservative, that contemporary theology must challenge."[30] Historical consciousness, by contrast, sees change in moral law not as the exception but as the rule.

Rigali concludes by describing a concept of moral law rooting in the person "as an individual within history." Since history is the realm of contingency and singularity, "historical consciousness views each human life in terms of creating history rather than in terms of a universal code of behavior, preordained in a time-transcending human nature." In this perspective moral law is much more a *forma* than a *ratio*, more a work to be created than a pattern to follow. As Rigali words it:

As human persons are called to create history, they are called to create the moral law, in a very real sense. Today we are called to create the better world of tomorrow so that those who live tomorrow can be called to create, in turn, the still better world that the world of the day after tomorrow should be.[31]

Rigali then notes that the good confessor "has always known the moral law in this way on an unconscious level." For in contrast to the preacher who discusses morality in an abstract way, "the confessor ... must become *historically* involved with morality; the confessor is involved with an individual in his or her personal life." Briefly, "confessors have always known unconsciously ... that moral law is an evolving, historical 'form' within the individual personal histories of people's lives." Rigali argues that it is the task of moral theology to raise this notion to the conscious level of theory.

There are several troubling aspects of this essay that suggest questions and qualifications. First, there is the discussion about a specifically Christian ethic. Rigali sees this as a useless question—indeed, one revealing a dualistic understanding of the human person. I suggest that he has misconceived the state of the question. He conceives it as a genetic-historical question. Thus he asserts that ethics always requires a qualifying adjective such as "Swiss nineteenth-century Calvinist."

But this is not the issue. The issue is primarily epistemological. Briefly it is this: Are there concrete moral demands in our lives which are in principle unavailable to human insight and reasoning, and which therefore can only be known by revelation or its authentic custodians? One does not answer this question by saying that one is a Catholic moral theologian or an early Trobriander. Such adjectives only identify a historical belief-community; they do not raise the issue of how one originally knows God's will within such a community.[32]

[30] Ibid. 167.
[31] Ibid. 166.
[32] In this respect I wish respectfully to qualify William Cardinal Baum's statement in an address to a convention on moral theology held at Catholic University (1979). Baum stated:

The epistemological question, I would argue, is not otiose. And it is certainly not one "completely within classical consciousness," as Rigali contends. Indeed, I fear that dismissal of the question easily represents a form of retirement into modern gnosticism, a position that would hold that concrete moral claims valid for all persons are radically mysterious, simply and in principle impervious to human insight and reasoning, and intelligible only by faith.

One particularly virulent form of this gnosticism is the confusion of parenetic discourse with normative ethics. For example, I have attended many conversations where statements such as "We are a people set apart" or "We are baptized in the Spirit" were taken as adequate normative warrants for the rejection of direct sterilization as intrinsically evil.[33] Another form is the contention that a moral position is correct and unchangeably so *because* it has been proposed by the magisterium—regardless of the analyses and reasons that might suggest a different conclusion or formulation. Such a position not only freezes any development in moral science; it would also be opposed to Catholic tradition, which makes more modest claims, scil., that revelation is necessary so

---

"It should not be said, therefore, that revelation teaches nothing concerning human life which would not be discovered without knowledge of Christ Jesus. The purpose of revelation is the divinization of man. Revelation is not primarily the basis of a 'privileged access to the human'.... Rather revelation is the *only* access to the mystery of the interior life of the Triune God, and *therefore* to the fullness of what being human means" (*Origins* 9 [1979] 222–23). I believe no theologian would deny this. But it is not precisely what the discussion is about. Clearly we know of the life of God only by revelation. And clearly this teaches us something about the *humanum*. But the contemporary discussion is concerned with behavioral (concrete) moral norms such as those touching killing, speaking falsehoods, keeping promises, contracepting, etc. To claim to be able to find answers to these questions only in revelation is to confuse parenetic discourse with normative ethics, and to abandon in the process a very long-standing Catholic tradition. Something similar might be said about Cardinal Baum's remarks to the American bishops. After noting the impoverishment of certain contemporary Christologies, Baum says the effect of this is most obvious in moral theology. He continues: "It is from Christ, the New Man, that moral theology must take its cue, not from a merely pragmatic assessment of the results of certain human actions. For Christ has wrought in us an inward transformation so profound that it extends to every facet of the personality and to our physical existence, which is taken up as the sign, the symbol of the Christ who lives within the baptized Christian. Hence to dismiss the Church's teachings, especially on sexual morality, as 'biological' is to dismiss our concrete humanity as a sign of freedom and liberation from sin which Christ has revealed in His own humanity forever united with divinity" (*Origins* 9 [1979] 396). Such discourse ("physical existence... taken up as the sign... of the Christ who lives within the baptized Christian"), if taken as a sufficient warrant for *concrete* norms in the sexual sphere, has the effect of wafting moral analysis into a rarified sphere beyond human insight and reasoning. It makes such norms purely and simply mysterious—which is opposed to centuries of Catholic moral tradition. Cf. DS 1786: "quae in rebus divinis rationi per se impervia non sunt."

[33] For a review of Pauline ethics, cf. William D. Dennison, "Indicative and Imperative: The Basic Structure of Pauline Ethics," *Calvin Theological Journal* 14 (1979) 55–78.

that we can know firmly and expeditiously those things "quae in rebus divinis rationi per se impervia non sunt" (DB 1786).

Second, there is Rigali's gloss on the discussion of the absoluteness of concrete moral norms. He sees the negative answer to the question of absolutes as simply a "more liberal legalism," but still a legalism rooting in the classical consciousness. Here a distinction is in place. If this concern is thought to have the prime place in the moral life and moral theology, then Rigali is correct. But if it retains its proper place in our priorities and is still dismissed as the "legalistic, authoritarian conception of moral law," then I believe he is wrong. Not only is the question of methodological importance; it is of practical ("historical," if we will) importance. It is a matter of no small concern to many people how we word our concern for, e.g., the moral integrity of responsible parenthood—whether we use the term "intrinsically evil" of some acts or do not use such language.

Third, there is Rigali's description of the moral law. He elaborates it as follows: "The moral law of today is the concrete historical 'form' of the more human world of tomorrow." No one, I believe, would disagree with that description, not even theologians of the so-called "classical consciousness." Who could be opposed to a "more human world of tomorrow"? But this description relates to normative ethics just about the way "We are baptized in the Spirit" relates to, e.g., the problem of sterilization. It belongs in the genre of parenetic discourse.

Finally, Rigali contrasts abstract with historical. Thus, "while the preacher can discuss morality in an abstract way, the confessor, if he is performing his duty in an even minimally adequate way, must become *historically* involved with morality; the confessor is involved with an individual in his or her personal life."[34] Here we have abstract contrasted with historical and then historical defined in terms of individual or personal life. Two remarks. First, this identifies and confuses normative ethics with pastoral understanding and compassion, and raises this latter to the status of the former. The proper contrast is abstract and concrete; for a norm can be at once abstract and historical: e.g., Rigali's own cited above about a more human world of tomorrow. Second, this identification, if pushed, does away with the possibility of generalization in ethics, which means it does away with ethics as a science. In other words, unless I misunderstand him, Rigali has so described historical consciousness that it wipes out the pair right-wrong to concentrate on the pair good-bad, and at the level of individual discernment. This strikes me as an overreaction that is less than successful in avoiding some rather robust straw persons.

These concerns are clearly related to the Church's authentic teaching and its theological sources. John Paul II addressed himself to the relation

---

[34] Rigali, "Morality and Historical Consciousness" 167.

of theologians to the teaching office of the Church in his address to Catholic educators at Catholic University, Oct. 7, 1979.[35] Joseph Fitzmyer, S.J., the distinguished exegete, offers a commentary on that address.[36] The Holy Father stated his gratitude for theological work ("We all need your work, your dedication, and the fruits of your reflection"). He also insisted on high standards and freedom of investigation. Finally, John Paul II referred to theological "theories and hypotheses" and to "the right of the faithful not to be troubled" by them.

Fitzmyer points to a real problem in the papal address. "How can he insist on the 'eminent role of the university' and its 'undiminished dedication to intellectual honesty and academic excellence' and still caution the theological faculty of a Catholic university about theories and hypotheses? They are, after all, the stuff of 'scientific research' and 'freedom of investigation'. . . . We can only wish that he had addressed himself more explicitly to this tension that is reflected in his address."[37]

Fitzmyer's own approach to this tension is to put both magisterium and theologians in a position of reciprocal need and mutual stimulation. Theologians need the magisterium to keep them dedicated to honesty and responsible scholarship. The magisterium and the faithful need theologians to make them reflect on their need for constant updating. The real enemy of this harmonious symbiosis is, according to Fitzmyer, "the right-wing mass that would vie for authority in catechetics and teaching with both bishops and theologians."

Pope John Paul II returned to this subject in his address to the International Theological Commission.[38] He referred to the work of theologians as participating "to a certain extent" in the magisterium. But he then added: "We say 'to a certain extent' because, as our predecessor Paul VI wisely said, the authentic magisterium, whose origin is divine, 'is endowed with a certain charism of truth that cannot be communicated to others and for which none other can substitute.'" The Holy Father praised a "healthy pluralism" in theology and repeated what he had stated in *Sapientia christiana*: that theologians in institutions of higher education (*in altiorum studiorum sedibus*) "do not teach on their own authority but by virtue of a mission received from the Church."

Charles Curran examines the relationship between academic freedom, the Catholic university, and Catholic theology.[39] After accepting the standard definition of such freedom, he notes that the two instrumental-

---

[35] *Origins* 9 (1979) 306–8.

[36] Joseph A. Fitzmyer, S.J., "John Paul II, Academic Freedom and the Magisterium," *America* 141 (1979) 247–49.

[37] Ibid. 249.

[38] *L'Osservatore romano*, Oct. 27, 1979.

[39] Curran's study is to appear in the *Furrow*; I cite from the unpublished manuscript which he kindly forwarded to me.

ities designed to protect it are tenure and academic due process. Before the 1960's it was widely accepted that full academic freedom could not exist in Catholic institutions of higher learning. This began to change in the 1960's and culminated with the signing, by twenty-six leaders in Catholic education, of the Land O'Lakes statement "The Nature of the Contemporary Catholic University." In this statement full academic freedom is endorsed, "in the face of authority of whatever kind, lay or clerical, external to the academic community itself."

Curran's next move is to apply this to theology in the Catholic university, an area where it would seem most difficult to justify full freedom. He justifies full academic freedom by appeal to a contemporary understanding of theology (interpretation of the sources of revelation in light of the signs of the times vs. a deductive method highlighting clear and certain propositions) and of the magisterium (where the interpretative function of theology in relating to the magisterium involves the possibility of dissent).

Curran's final reflection is on *Sapientia christiana*.[40] The document requires that those who teach disciplines concerning faith or morals receive a canonical mission,[41] "for they do not teach on their own authority but by virtue of the mission they have received from the Church" (n. 27). Furthermore, to acquire a tenured position or the highest faculty rank, the candidate needs a *nihil obstat* from the Holy See (n. 27). Curran sees in these stipulations a view of the university as "a continuation of the teaching function of the hierarchical magisterium." He concludes: "In such a situation, there is no academic freedom because judgments about competence are not made by peers, and promotion and tenure depend on judgments made by church authority as such." He argues that canonically erected universities, Catholic theology, and the good of the whole Church will suffer as a result of the literal application of this apostolic constitution.

Joseph Farraher, S.J., takes a point of view poles apart from that of Curran.[41a] A questioner had asked why bishops allow their own Catholic university and some seminaries to retain teachers who contradict their teaching. Farraher replies that removal should not be the first step. First there should be a fraternal warning "that professors at Catholic universities and seminaries ... are considered and are representatives of the Church and as such should not promote opinions contrary to the teaching

[40] *Origins* 9 (1979) 33–45.

[41] For a discussion of *missio canonica* in various contexts, cf. Fráncisco Javier Urrutia, S.J., "De magisterio ecclesiastico: Observationes quaedam ad propositam reformationem partis IV, libri III, CIC," *Periodica* 68 (1979) 327–67.

[41a] Joseph Farraher, S.J., "Why Don't Bishops Take Action against Dissenters?" *Homiletic and Pastoral Review* 79, no. 7 (April 1979) 64–66.

of the magisterium." Farraher is clearly opposed to *promoting* one's ideas "while acting in a situation where he represents the Church." If dissenters feel that they must propose a contradictory opinion, they should resign their position "where they are considered a representative of the Church." If they persist, Farraher argues, "all efforts" should be used to remove them.

The key phrase in Farraher's analysis is "professors at Catholic universities and seminaries ... *are considered and are representatives of the Church*." The phrase is extremely general and loose. If it means that a Catholic theologian ought to take his/her tradition seriously, be aware of, respect, and study official Catholic documents, and be sensitive to the pastoral implications and repercussions of his/her work, then no one can question the phrase. If, however, "representatives of the Church" is taken to mean official spokespersons of the Church within the university community—and this is the implication of Farraher's conclusion—I believe it is simply erroneous to say that this is the proper description of the theologian's function.

Furthermore, the word "promote" is loaded. It suggests a political contest with the magisterium as the opposing candidate. Does one who states his/her own opinion honestly and presents the reasons for it as persuasively as possible "promote" it? Behind my problems with Farraher's analysis there are undoubtedly deeper disagreements about the notion of church, of magisterium, and of teaching in general.

Kenneth Baker goes even further. He reviews the contemporary theological scene and sees it as one of "open defiance now being shown by supposedly 'Catholic' theologians...."[42] "Rebellion by theologians against the supreme magisterium" is the rule, not the exception. His examples: Hans Küng, Charles Curran, Avery Dulles, Stephen Kelleher, Anthony Kosnik. Later the list is expanded to include Andrew Greeley, John Milhaven, John Dedek, and the compositor of these "Notes." And this list "is just to scratch the surface." In this Baker is correct. A deeper scratch would expand the list with names such as B. Häring, Joseph Fuchs, B. Schüller, Karl Rahner, J.-M. Aubert, Louis Janssens, D. Maguire, Walter Burghardt, David Tracy, Franz Scholz, Franz Böckle, A. Auer, and on and on.

After explaining the nature and function of the magisterium, Baker considers the role of the theologian. Theologians attracted an exaggerated respect during Vatican II, one that intimidated the bishops. The result: bishops have largely abandoned their teaching function to theological experts. Baker relies on the paper of the International Theological Commission in attempting to elaborate the role of theologians. But, unfortunately, he feels that the rules governing the theologian's role are

[42] Kenneth Baker, S.J., "Magisterium and Theologians," ibid. 14–23.

being violated "with impunity from coast to coast, in almost every diocese. . . ." Baker concludes that theologians and intellectuals who "refuse to submit to the magisterium of the Church" should, after adequate dialogue, be excommunicated.

"Remove," "excommunicate"—these are strong words aimed indiscriminately at all kinds of targets. One would think that there is a slight difference in questioning the divinity of Christ and questioning, e.g., the teaching of Pius XII on artificial insemination by husband. This latter has been done, and done carefully, by theologians of demonstrated competence and loyalty. The Farraher-Baker perspective would reverse the procedure and judge competence and loyalty by failure to question. This makes official formulation the judge of truth, rather than truth the judge of authentic formulation.[43]

At this point a very traditional and, in my judgment, still to be revered theology would have spoken of something like probabilism. The abiding and liberating value of such a concept is that it is issue-oriented, not primarily authority-oriented, even though its advocates had great respect for authority. They simply viewed it as the job of theologians to say what they honestly thought. And if enough people of genuine theological authority said the same thing, it was a presumptive sign that there was something to it. Perhaps those days are gone. Perhaps issues will be discussed with the stereotypic slogans loyal-disloyal, orthodox-deviant. But I hope not. For if that is the case, theology will have been transformed into institutional rhetoric, and truth will have become subordinate to the instruments of its search. That sort of thing is much more at home in a society that makes no pretenses about its objectivity and freedom.

In the matter of dismissal-excommunication, therefore, I am sure that theologians would prefer to follow the counsels of John Paul II. In urging Catholics to reconcile their internal theological differences, the Holy Father stated in Chicago, as noted above, that "no one in the ecclesiastical community should ever feel alienated or unloved, even when tensions arise in the course of common efforts to bring the fruits of the gospel to

---

[43] Norbert Rigali has, I believe, a much more realistic and balanced view of dissent in the Church. He points out that the theologian's role is that of explorer and discoverer, "of seeking for ways to advance the understanding or intellectual life of the Church, of proposing new theories." He refers to "better or fuller ways of understanding the meaning of faith in relation to an ever-changing world." Such work "must involve at times the proposing of theories that conflict with current official (noninfallible) teachings of the Church." Clearly these probes must be weighed against a background of experience and reflection much broader than that of any individual theologian; but to do so, these proposals must "get into the open." Rigali rightly notes that a theologian can act irresponsibly. He concludes: "However, it also would be irresponsible, and indeed cruel, to regard a theologian as irresponsible or disloyal to the Church simply because there is being proposed an opinion that conflicts with official theological teaching in the Church." I think Rigali has it exactly right. Cf. "Faith and the Theologian," *Priest* 34, no. 4 (April 1978) 10–14.

society around us."

This attitude of John Paul II should not come as a surprise. In his book *The Acting Person*,[44] the then Cardinal Wojtyla discusses authentic community. There are three characteristics that distinguish authentic community: solidarity, opposition, dialogue. Solidarity "is the attitude of a community, in which the common good properly conditions and initiates participation." It refers to a readiness "to accept and realize one's share in the community."

Opposition Wojtyla sees as "essentially an attitude of solidarity." It is the attitude of those who, because they are deeply devoted to the common good, disagree with official ideas and policies. Of such opposition the Cardinal of Krakow makes several statements: "The one who voices his opposition to the general or particular rules or regulations of the community does not thereby reject his membership."[45] Indeed, such opposition is vital to the community's growth and well-being. It is "essentially constructive." He continues:

In order for opposition to be constructive, the structure, and beyond it the system of communities of a given society must be such as to allow opposition that emerges from the soil of solidarity not only to *express* itself within the framework of the given community but also to *operate* for its benefit. The structure of a human community is correct only if it admits not just the presence of a justified opposition but also that practical effectiveness of opposition required by the common good and the right of participation.[46]

Then there is dialogue. Dialogue allows us to "select and bring to light what in controversial situations is right and true." Wojtyla admits that dialogue involves strains and difficulties and is sometimes messy. But a "constructive communal life" cannot exist without it. Opposed to solidarity and opposition are "inauthentic" attitudes of "servile conformism" and "noninvolvement." For example, "conformism brings uniformity rather than unity."

Cardinal Wojtyla did not apply this analysis to the ecclesial community. "But," as Gregory Baum notes, "the characteristics of authenticity defined for a true community, any true community, secular or religious, ought to apply *a fortiori* to the Church, which is the divine revelation of the model of community in the world."[47] Baum's point was also made tellingly by both Ronald Modras and Edward Cuddy.[48] For instance, Modras, adverting to *The Acting Person*, correctly asserts that "loyal

[44] Karol Wojtyla, *The Acting Person* (Boston: D. Reidel, 1979).
[45] Ibid. 286.
[46] Ibid. 286–87.
[47] Gregory Baum, "Le pape et la dissidence," *Relations* 39 (1979) 250–51.
[48] Ronald Modras, "Solidarity and Opposition in a Pluralistic Church," *Commonweal* 106 (1979) 493–95; Edward Cuddy, "The Rebel Function in the Church," ibid. 495–97.

opposition can serve the well-being of a church as well as of a state." But the situation in Poland did not allow Cardinal Wojtyla to highlight the critical function of theology. The militant hostility of a Marxist regime required a united resistance.

Baum's reflection is supported by John Howard Yoder in a different context.[49] In discussing a Christian approach to social ethics, he suggests that a powerful beginning to the problems of the wider social order has been made when Christians have seen their believing community as a paradigm and pilot processing plant for the models of culture and service which later could be commended to a wider society. As he noted:

Freedom of speech must first of all be realized in the puritan assembly before we can explain how it would be a good way to run a civil democracy. Care for the hungry must first develop as a commitment of the body of believers before it will occur to anyone to propose moving toward a welfare state. Christians must first be ready to forgive those who have trespassed against them for the sake of the forgiveness of Christ before there is any hope for a new effort to reform the treatment of offenders.[50]

Similarly, Gerard O'Connell states that the Church's proclamation of rights should first be verified in the Church itself.[51] He specifically refers this to, among other things, dissenting opinions.

Just so. If creative and courteous exchange and opposition is the ordinary way of progress in human knowledge and growth in any society, as the then Cardinal Wojtyla insisted, should it not first find its most splendid exemplar in the Church? I believe so.

One of the standard responses to this direction of thought is that the people have a "right not to be confused" ("troubled" is the word used by the Holy Father). The implication frequently made is that theologians should cease expressing their views publicly if those views deviate at all from official formulations. That is, I think, unrealistic and intolerable.[52] As for the "confusion" of the people, several things need to be said. First, reality is sometimes confusing and it takes time and groping before a truly satisfactory Christian and Catholic response can be formulated.

[49] This was a response to Scott Paradise in *Anglican Theological Review* 61 (1979) 118–26.

[50] Yoder, ibid. 125.

[51] Gerard O'Connell, "The Church and Human Rights," *Way* 17 (1979) 273–82.

[52] In an editorial in the *St. Louis Review*, Msgr. Joseph W. Baker writes: "Dissenting opinions are not to become a matter of public scandal, but are to be presented to appropriate ecclesiastical authorities, avoiding troubling the consciences of other members of the Church." In Baker's perspectives public dissent is equivalent to public scandal; for he contrasts as the only alternatives "presenting to appropriate ecclesiastical authorities" and "public scandal." And this is said to accord with the norms for licit dissent. If taken seriously, Baker's norms would utterly destroy public discussion in the Church and with it the very possibility of doctrinal development. Cf. *St. Louis Review*, Oct. 19, 1979.

Second, rather than silence free thought and speech in the Church, people must be educated to the idea that differing times do suggest differing perspectives and analyses, especially where very detailed moral norms are concerned, and that what seems a closed question very often is not.[53] Third, they must be educated to the idea that our unity as a community does not ride or fall with absolute uniformity on the application of moral norms to very detailed questions (e.g., *in vitro* fertilization with embryo transfer). Otherwise the Holy Father's notion of opposition would be only destructive.[54] Finally, they must be educated to take theologians seriously, but not all that seriously. If theologians are mistakenly thought to be the ultimate teachers in the Church, they risk losing, besides their freedom to probe and question, their humility.[55]

One final word about the notion of *missio canonica*. This term needs a great deal of careful questioning. It is a very general phrase capable of remarkably loose and eventually abusive understanding and use. As it is used in *Sapientia christiana*, it refers to "a canonical mission from the chancellor or his delegate" (n. 27). While the terms "chancellor" and "delegate" are somewhat obscure, at least in some instances they would apply to the local ordinary or religious superior (e.g., Catholic University of America). Of this *missio* it is said that they "must receive" it. Presumably that means that professors may not teach without it.

If all this means is that the *formal* appointment comes from the chancellor, who must be guided by the judgment of the professor's academic peers, then there is no problem. If, however, the chancellor may grant or deny this *missio* on his own, then the notion of academic freedom disappears as we know it in this country; for the chancellor could grant or deny the *missio* on warrants unacceptable to sound theology.[56]

For instance, does the *missio canonica* exclude the possibility of responsible dissent? There are those who argue this way[57] and undoubtedly some chancellors would act this way.[58] But that would be unaccept-

---

[53] Karl Rahner, "Open Questions in Dogma Considered by the Institutional Church as Definitively Answered," *Catholic Mind* 77, no. 1331 (March 1979) 8–26. Rahner has some illuminating things to say about the rules to be followed in arriving at formulations in moral and dogmatic questions.

[54] In an inventive editorial, *America* puts in the mouth of John Paul II the following lines in an imagined speech in the U.S.: "But I would urge you, above all, not to let those differences that divide you distract you from the central faith in the Gospel of Jesus Christ that unites you" (*America* 141 [1979] 145).

[55] Cf. Richard A. McCormick, S.J., "Moral Theology since Vatican II: Clarity or Chaos?" *Cross Currents* 29 (1979) 15–27.

[56] Cf. *National Catholic Reporter*, Nov. 23, 1979, for Karl Rahner's accusations (of injustice) against Cardinal Joseph Ratzinger; also Manuel Alcalá, "La tensión teología-magisterio en la vida y obre de Karl Rahner," *Estudios eclesiásticos* 54 (1979) 3–17.

[57] Thomas Dubay, S.M., "The State of Moral Theology," *TS* 35 (1974) 482–506.

[58] It must be remembered that there are still bishops in this country who exclude theologians from their dioceses because of dissent on this or that point.

able to all theologians of my acquaintance, and at variance with traditional manualist theology, as well as with the principles stated by Pope John Paul II in *The Acting Person*.

Or again, does this *missio* mean that in their scholarly tasks theologians are an extension of the magisterium into the academic world? Few would accept this self-description, although there are signs that some chancellors or potential chancellors might. Does the term suggest that theology's main task is to mediate the teachings of the magisterium? This was clearly the view of Pius XII in *Humani generis*, but it has been repeatedly criticized by theologians as a one-sided view.[59] Yet it is not rash to think that some chancellors might share Pius' theology. Finally, does it mean that only a theologian acceptable to the local bishop gets this *missio*? It should not mean this, or any of the above things, if academic freedom in any meaningful sense is to be preserved.

These are some of the possible senses of the term *missio canonica* and they are cumulatively the reasons why theologians legitimately fear the notion.

There is, on the other hand, a quite acceptable notion of *missio ab ecclesia*. At one point in his discussion of the common responsibilities of theologians and the magisterium, the Pope asserted:

In their service to the truth, theologians and the magisterium are constrained by common bonds: the Word of God; the "sense of faith" that flourished in the Church of the past and still flourishes now; the documents of tradition in which the common faith of the people was proposed; and finally, pastoral and missionary care, which both [theologians and magisterium] must attend to.[60]

I would think that those theologians whose work takes account of these bonds (*vinculis*) are, in the most profound sense of the term, "sent." Few theologians would have any difficulty with such "bonds." Indeed, they simply outline theological responsibility. But what many would object to is the extension of such constraints into a *missio* given by a per se nonacademic person, and into a *nihil obstat* from the Holy See.

Here it must be remembered that *Sapientia christiana* is dealing with pontifical faculties (and these are faculties involved with the training of future priests). Such faculties relate somewhat differently to episcopal authority than does the Catholic university in general. In other words, the bishop does indeed have responsibilities with regard to orthodoxy in such faculties. But it can still be doubted whether *missio canonica* is the appropriate way to implement such responsibilities. Concretely, it is an extremely dangerous weapon, especially in light of the sanctions some ultraright groups are calling for and pressuring the bishops to use.

[59] *TS* 38 (1977) 85 ff.
[60] Cf. n 38 above.

University structures are designed to protect faculty against precisely this type of thing.

One point is to be noted. Both *Sapientia christiana* and John Paul II regard theology in Catholic institutions of higher learning as a kind of continuation of the mission of the magisterium. *Sapientia* restricts this to canonically erected faculties. The Holy Father more generally speaks of institutions of higher learning (*in altiorum studiorum sedibus*). This is not the self-understanding of the Catholic university in the United States. In a 1971 report of the North American Region of the International Federation of Catholic Universities (IFCU), stress is put on the need for university autonomy. "The Catholic university is not simply a pastoral arm of the Church. It is an independent organization serving Christian purposes but not subject to ecclesiastical-juridical control, censorship or supervision."[61]

Therefore I agree with Curran that certain understandings of *missio canonica* and the requirement of a *nihil obstat* from the Holy See for tenure on pontifical faculties are incompatible with academic freedom as this is commonly understood in university circles in the United States.[62] Clearly, theologians must be responsible in the exercise of their freedom. But to threaten such freedom and thereby the causes for which it exists— amongst them the vitality and integrity of theology—strikes this reviewer as killing the patient to cure the disease. With concerns such as this in mind, the Catholic Theological Society of America, at its 1979 convention in Atlanta, passed a resolution on academic freedom that included two principles:

1. No theologian should be censured or deprived of that liberty acknowledged to be necessary for theological inquiry without due process which respects fundamental fairness and equity.
2. No theologian holding an academic appointment should be censured or otherwise deprived of any right except as a result of due process which is in accordance with publicly stated standards and is consonant with generally accepted academic practice in the United States and Canada.[63]

These views represent a sampling of theological perspectives from many points of view. It is probably safe to say that they also represent a division in the Catholic, and even larger, public. What might be said at this point? Much depends on one's ecclesiological presuppositions. But one thing is clear. The use of stereotypic language has no place in serious theological discussions. When those with whom one disagrees are sum-

---

[61] "Freedom, Autonomy and the University," *IDOC International*, North American edition, 39 (Jan. 15, 1972) 83.

[62] Cf. Josef Georg Ziegler, " 'Rolle' oder 'Sendung' des Moraltheologen: Versuch einer Selbstreflexion," *Theologie und Glaube* 69 (1979) 272–88.

[63] Cf. *Bulletin of the Council on the Study of Religion* 10 (1979) 114.

marily classified as "dissenters" or "deviants," we see an instance of such language and the collapse of theological courtesy. One is tempted to respond by dubbing other discussants as "conformers." That is a kind of game. The regrettable aspect of such semantics is, as I noted, that the issue gets lost. When that happens, nobody wins, and something seriously detrimental to the Church prevails.

DIVORCE AS A PASTORAL PROBLEM

In his speech to the American bishops, the Holy Father stated: "With the candor of the Gospels, the compassion of pastors, and the charity of Christ, you faced the question of the indissolubility of marriage, rightly stating: 'The covenant between a man and a woman joined in Christian marriage is as indissoluble and irrevocable as God's love for His people and Christ's love for his Church.'"[64] He repeated this teaching in his speech on the Mall (Washington, D.C.) in ringing tones: "When the institution of marriage is abandoned to human selfishness or reduced to a temporary, conditional arrangement that can easily be terminated, we will stand up and affirm the indissolubility of the marriage bond."[65]

I can think of no theologian who would deny this Gospel and Church teaching. But the problem remains about what it implies in terms of pastoral practice. This section can only sample some literature of the past several years on these pastoral implications. But before doing so, I should like to refer to a splendid pastoral letter on marriage issued by Bishop Walter Sullivan.[66] The pastoral deliberately acknowledges and avoids "the attempt to provide easy solutions to the needs of Catholic married couples." The letter first details the present-day experience of marriage, especially the obstacles to intimacy in modern life and to genuine family unity. It singles out a variety of family tensions, especially the many forms of brokenness experienced in family living.

Next the pastoral turns to marriage as a faith experience. Acknowledging that much of our traditional Church teaching "appears unrealistic to them [married persons] in the face of tensions and strains on marital and familial relationships," Bishop Sullivan attempts to speak a different language. He speaks of the "daily conflicts involved in freedom of conscience and responsible parenting." Going beyond the language of contract, Sullivan underlines the "deeper realities of the marriage covenant," of promises for an unknown future.[67] To a society which in many ways has turned against life, Bishop Sullivan notes that "all marital

---

[64] *Origins* 9 (1979) 289.

[65] Ibid. 280.

[66] Walter F. Sullivan, "Marriage and Family Life," *Catholic Virginian*, April 13, 1979.

[67] For an interesting commentary on the revision of the canon law of marriage, cf. Francis Morrisey, O.M.I., "Revising Church Legislation on Marriage," *Origins* 9 (1979) 209–18.

relationships must remain open to life."

The final section of the pastoral reviews the practical steps that can be taken in our time to strengthen and nourish family life. When dealing with broken families, Bishop Sullivan states: "It is necessary to make those who experience family difficulties, divisions, and separations feel welcome within the church community. We cannot look down on the separated, divorced or remarried as failures or as misfits." Sullivan's pastoral strikes this reviewer as a splendid and very rich mix of faith perspectives and common-sense realism.

The proper ecclesial response to the divorced and remarried has been touched upon in two pastoral letters. One is that of the bishops of the French-speaking cantons of Switzerland (Lausanne, Genève-Fribourg, Sion, Bâle).[68] The Swiss bishops take up several instances of what they call "situations particulières." One is the case of the couple who want to marry, yet do not feel at the time ready for the sacrament of marriage. Of this situation the bishops say that one will expose the importance of the sacrament without imposing it. The priest may celebrate in a prayer "the presence of God which they [the couple] already recognize in their search and in their love." But there should be no ambiguity or confusion created that this is the celebration of a sacrament.

Another instance is that of the couple contemplating marriage who cannot receive the sacrament of matrimony because they are divorced from a valid first marriage. The bishops make two statements on such a situation. First: "When it is clear that their way of life involves an undoubted fidelity and when all the time necessary for a thorough investigation has been taken, then we will be in a position to consider the propriety of a prayerful moment which corresponds to the truth of the situation with all the clarity that is then possible."[69] Second: "One will also strive, when the occasion presents itself, to open Christian communities to the reception of those who are in this painful situation and wish to remain members of the Church."[70]

This last rendering is, I would judge, studiously vague. What is implied in the notion of "opening Christian communities to the reception of" the divorced and remarried? The bishops do not say that they may receive the Eucharist.[71] On the other hand, they do not say they may not. It is always risky to attempt to interpret the *stylus episcopalis*. But perhaps

[68] "La pastorale du mariage," *Documentation catholique* 76 (1979) 343.

[69] The French reads: "Lorsqu' apparait la loyauté certaine de la démarche et après tout le temps d'approfondissement qui s'impose, on pourra envisager un moment de prière et de réflexion qui corresponde le plus clairement possible à la vérité de la situation."

[70] "On s'efforcera aussi, lorsque l'occasion s'en présentera, d'ouvrir les communautés chrétiennes à l'accueil de ceux qui sont dans cette situation douloureuse et veulent demeurer membres de l'Eglise."

[71] The entire text was not printed in *Documentation catholique*.

it is not rash to think that the bishops know of the theological discussions on this subject and of the accumulating consensus of this literature that reception of the Eucharist is a possibility in individual cases for the divorced and remarried. Is it a fair inference that they were acknowledging this development without really saying so?

The other directives are also interesting. Even the possibility of a prayerful moment for those who do not as yet want the sacrament of marriage and for those who are entering a second union (after divorce from a Christian marriage) is a remarkable step. The unavoidable implication is that although no sacramental marriage is involved, there is indeed a human reality, a human love, not incompatible with the presence of God.

An entirely different approach is taken by the C.E.I. (Conferenza Episcopale Italiana).[72] They first describe indissolubility as a property of every marriage, but a property enriched and reinforced in Christian marriage. The Italian bishops fear that there are "problems and discussions which risk disturbing and obscuring the traditional position of the Church toward the divorced and remarried." Therefore they want to set the record straight.

The first thing to be recognized is that the condition of the divorced and remarried is "contrary to the gospel." The second union cannot break the conjugal bond of the preceding union. However, by virtue of baptism and a faith not totally renounced, the divorced-remarried remain members of the People of God. "They are not excluded from communion with the Church even if, because of their condition which is contrary to the gospel, they do not share in the necessary 'fulness' of ecclesial communion." Furthermore, even though believers regard the condition of the divorced-remarried as a disorder, they should not judge the consciences and spiritual condition of those in this situation. Only God can do this.

The divorced-remarried should be aided in sharing in the life of faith. For example, they can share in "catechetical sessions and nonsacramental penitential services." They should be invited to attend Mass but not "to exercise in the ecclesial community those services that demand the fulness of Christian witness" (e.g., lector at Mass).

The pastoral next turns to the sacraments (reconciliation and the Eucharist) and insists that the problem be viewed within the perspective of fidelity to the Church and its Lord. Conversion is essential for the reception of the sacrament of reconciliation. Such conversion clearly demands genuine sorrow, which includes the firm purpose of amendment. "But this will does not exist if the divorced-remarried remain in a condition of life that is contrary to the will of God. How is it possible at

---

[72] "La pastorale des divorcés remariés et des personnes vivant dans une situation matrimoniale irrégulière," *Documentation catholique* 76 (1979) 715–22.

the same moment to choose the love of God and disobedience to His commandments?"[73]

As for the Eucharist, the Italian bishops note that it is the sacrament that signifies and realizes "the fulness of union with Jesus Christ and his Body." Reception of the Eucharist is equivalent to sharing in the fulness of love that binds Christ to his Church. "One cannot, therefore, receive worthily the sign of perfect unity with Christ and with the Church when one is in a condition of life that creates and maintains a rupture with Christ and his Church." The bishops state the traditional demand of a brother-sister relationship before the sacraments may be received.

The document also adds a practical argument. "In the face of a pastoral practice that unites in sacramental celebration legitimate spouses and the divorced-remarried, many people would not understand why divorce is an evil." If the Church, in her sacramental discipline, treats the divorced-remarried exactly as she treats others, "how can one say that she takes seriously the command of the Lord about the indissolubility of marriage?"

The Italian pastoral letter has been the subject of at least two extensive commentaries of which I am aware. One is by Francesco Bersini, S.J.[74] He takes the occasion of the pastoral letter to call attention to the fact that its conclusions are consistent with other episcopal documents, and he cites them to make his point. Bersini is aware of diverging theological tendencies on the problem. In the face of such divergences "there is only one secure path: the authoritative teaching of the ecclesiastical magisterium." He is in full agreement with the Italian bishops.

So is Dionigi Tettamanzi.[75] In his commentary on the Italian document, he insists on the fact that what is involved in excluding the divorced-remarried from the sacraments is the fidelity of the Church to Christ. "We do not find ourselves confronting a merely disciplinary or pastoral decision which is required by the circumstances of our historical moment but which in other circumstances could change." The "no" to the sacramental life of the divorced-remarried Tettamanzi sees as radically theological. There is a genuine falsification of the authentic meaning of the sacraments. These announce the gospel, a gospel which the concrete life of the divorced-remarried refutes and rejects. Moreover, Tettamanzi agrees with the C.E.I. document that reconciliation is required before the Eucharist can be received; but a firm purpose of amendment is necessary to true reconciliation. Tettamanzi regards this as impossible for the divorced-remarried who intend to remain such.

[73] Ibid. 718.

[74] Francesco Bersini, S.J., "I divorziati risposati e l'amissione ai sacramenti," *Civiltà cattolica* 130 (1979) 550–67.

[75] Dionigi Tettamanzi, "La pastorale della chiesa e le situazione matrimoniali irregolari," *Ambrosius* 55 (1979) 358–84.

Charles-Marie Guillet disagrees with this conclusion and explicitly with the document of the Italian episcopate.[76] His article, arguing for a more dynamic and communitarian notion of the Church (a community of growth, ongoing forgiveness, progressive incorporation into the forgiving Christ), had been written before the appearance of the C.E.I. statement. But Guillet adverts to this statement in a final footnote and repeats his contention that exclusion of the divorced-remarried on the basis of incompatibility with the unity signified in the Eucharist involves a static and "perfectionist" notion of the sacraments. In such perspectives the Eucharist and the Eucharistic sign are "thingafied" and seen as a reward for achievement, when actually we are all sinners on the way to ultimate achievement.

The difference in attitude manifested in the Swiss and Italian pastorals is rather remarkable. It could easily lead one to believe that the Church is still groping for a fully adequate understanding of her proper pastoral response to the divorced-remarried. It is with such an understanding in mind that I wish to make several comments on the study of the Italian bishops.

First, there is some ambiguity, perhaps even inconsistency, in the way the Italian episcopate speaks of the situation of the divorced-remarried. On the one hand, the bishops reject any attempt to judge the state of soul of such persons; on the other, they describe these people as "maintaining a rupture with Christ and his Church" and as lacking in a firm purpose of amendment. If these phrases do not describe a state of soul, what do they describe? This is particularly true of the purpose of amendment. The bishops never use the phrase, but their reasoning and language force them, it would seem, to regard the divorced-remarried as in a "state of sin."

Second, if this is indeed their attitude, it is difficult to see how they can urge the divorced-remarried to attend Mass, to deepen their prayer life, etc. These exhortations are those we would expect to be directed to those in a state of friendship with Christ and his Church. One hardly speaks of deepening charity if it is presumably absent to start with.

Third, the bishops say that the Eucharist is "the sign of *perfect* unity with Christ and the Church." If this is the case, it is difficult to see how the Church could adopt the policy she does toward the separated Eastern Churches. This policy allows for reception of penance, the Eucharist, and anointing of the sick by separated Eastern Christians in the Roman Church. The justification of this policy is explicitly stated:

Divine law forbids any common worship (*communicatio in sacris*) which would

[76] Charles-Marie Guillet, "Divorcés remariés et communion eucharistique," *Supplément* 130 (Sept. 1979) 355–64.

damage the unity of the Church, or involve formal acceptance of falsehood or the danger of deviation in the faith, of scandal, or of indifferentism. At the same time, pastoral experience clearly shows that with respect to our Eastern brethren there should and can be taken into consideration various circumstances affecting individuals, wherein the unity of the Church is not jeopardized nor are intolerable risks involved, but in which salvation itself and the spiritual profit of souls are urgently at issue.[77]

The Council fathers then state their "milder policy." Behind this policy stands an analysis of the Church and her sacramental actions. The Church has a double finality, which it expresses in its sacramental actions: the unity of the Church, the indispensable means of grace. Neither of these finalities can be suppressed or forgotten. But in concrete circumstances it is necessary to balance and compromise to do justice to both finalities. Concretely, the Church judges it appropriate at times to renounce the fulness of the conditions of integration which she imposes in principle in order to extend more widely the means of grace. In the Italian pastoral there is no mention of this second finality (the gaining of a needed grace).

Finally, there is the practical argument of the bishops ("many would not understand why divorce is an evil"). This clearly refers to what is known in technical terms as scandal. Concretely, people would draw certain conclusions about divorce and remarriage which would weaken their own and the Church's commitment to the permanence of marriage. What conclusions people will draw will depend on whether they are properly instructed or not. If they are clearly instructed that forgiving and reconciling need not and does not imply approval of what has gone before and even now come to be, then scandal is much less likely to occur. The precept of permanence is what the Church proclaims and what the couple must live. *That* is not affected by forgiving those who have failed, even sinfully, to live that command and find themselves in a position of irregularity as a result. Therefore, if the people are properly prepared for this change of approach by a careful explanation of its meaning, no scandal need occur. This will not be, I realize, an easy task.

An entire issue of *Revue de droit canonique* (representing the papers given at the 1977 Institut de droit canonique) is devoted to "Exceptions to the Norm in the Area of Marriage."[78] Several of these studies are interesting, but I want to review only one, that of Jean-Marie Aubert.[79] He notes three approaches to the situation of the divorced-remarried. First, there is the so-called "official" (until recently) approach that attempts to discover causes of nullity in the first marriage. Second, there

---

[77] Decree on Eastern Catholic Churches, no. 26 (*Documents of Vatican II*, 383–84).

[78] *Revue de droit canonique* 28 (1978).

[79] Jean-Marie Aubert, "Pratique canonique et sens de l'humain," ibid. 91–104.

is the pastoral path taken by some bishops. They allow couples in second marriages in individual cases to frequent the sacraments in a clandestine way. Aubert judges this to be ill at ease with the communitarian character of the sacraments of penance and the Eucharist. Third, there is the search for exceptions to the law of indissolubility. Aubert's essay—what he calls "a working hypothesis"—is in this class.

He first recalls two "canonical institutions" that are all but forgotten. The first is epikeia. Vatican II, in giving a place of honor to individual conscience, has created a climate for the reinterpretation of this teaching. According to St. Thomas, epikeia is a moral virtue, dictated by prudence, which regulates the application of law against its own terms. Thus it creates true exceptions.

The second, even more neglected in our times, is the notion of *receptio legis*. This refers above all to the need of acceptance of a law by the community to which it is destined in order that such law have efficacity.[80] This does not mean that acceptance is necessary for the validity of the law or that refusal means the law is false. It simply says that it does not contribute to the edification of the Church because it awakens no echo in the experience of the Church. Thus nonreception constitutes a true exception, because the law remains a dead letter.

Aubert gives two examples: John XXIII's *Veterum sapientia* and Paul VI's *Humanae vitae*. Of this latter he refers to the disputes "not only on the part of Christian couples and theologians but of numerous episcopates many of whose declarations and commentaries have been in fact refusals to accept without nuancing the condemnation of all contraception."[81] Noting that very many laws of the Code had their origin in lived custom, Aubert insists that ethical prescriptions cannot originate in a "purely descending route." The "ascending route," based on lived experience, must also be employed.

Aubert then asks whether these two sources of exception-making can apply to the indissolubility of marriage. He is not contesting indissolubility as such but only its absoluteness. He cites two cases where the Church has not recognized this absoluteness (marriage *ratum non consummatum* and the so-called Pauline privilege). "It is not clear why the Church cannot *extend the exceptions* to other cases within the body of traditional principles recalled above."

What stands in the way is a certain hardening or dogmatizing of the doctrine of indissolubility. Here Aubert makes several points. First, even though Trent refused to define the indissolubility of marriage in deference to the Eastern Churches, still an absolutizing tendency has been aided

---

[80] Thus the famous decree of Gratian: "Leges instituuntur cum promulgantur, firmantur cum moribus utentium approbantur."

[81] Aubert, "Pratique canonique" 97.

and abetted by a questionable reading of Scripture. The fidelity of God to humanity (of Christ to the Church) has been seen as a typology for marriage. However, rather than instruct us about marriage, Aubert argues that we should view marriage as a human experience for the revelation of God. In other words, we have transferred God's indissoluble love into a juridical human bond that continues to exist even without the only content that gives it sense (conjugal love). This is a kind of juridical fiction. However, in other areas the Church has avoided this. Thus, if the common good or the good of the interested parties demands, the Church dispenses from priestly celibacy or solemn religious vows.

Aubert next turns to the human reality underlying the indissolubility whose absoluteness is the effect of the sacrament. This human reality, destined to be transfigured by the sacrament, is fidelity in conjugal love. However, fidelity defines itself only by its human content. Aubert feels that the Church has not yet perceived the gravity of the social-cultural change that has occurred through the advent of industrialization, urbanization, and scientific progress.

Before industrialization the family (90% rural) was centered on a finality extrinsic to the couple: the survival of the social group. There was great infant mortality; life expectancy was half what it is now. There were certain social and economic imperatives such as continuance of the family and provision of sufficient working hands to support the family. Divorce was unthinkable, because love did not really figure in the program, at least not in the beginning. In these circumstances fidelity (and canonical indissolubility) was inscribed in the social structure.

All these things have changed in our time. There has been a spectacular reduction in infant mortality, a dramatic extension of life expectancy, the entrance of women into the labor force, a relativizing of the procreative function, etc. Thus the couple face many years together, frequently separated. The relationship between husband and wife can be cemented now only by mutual love. Fidelity is no longer inscribed in the social and economic structure as a given from the beginning. It can be only a task, a goal to pursue. And it can fail. It is in light of these developments that Aubert argues that the Church might extend her exceptions to indissolubility.

A position similar to that of Aubert is taken by Hans Stüsser (Bonn).[82] He engages in dialogue with Walter Kasper. In Kasper's recent book on marriage[83] he had argued that although no second marriage could be sanctioned by the Church, still those in a second, irregular marriage could under certain conditions receive the sacraments. He mentioned three

[82] Hans Stüsser, "Personales Eheverständnis und Kirchenrecht," *Orientierung* 42 (1978) 18–22.

[83] Walter Kasper, *Zur Theologie der Ehe* (Mainz: Grünewald, 1977).

conditions: (1) They have repented their past fault. (2) All humanly possible has been done to arrive at reconciliation with the first partner. (3) The second marriage has arrived at such a point of stability that it could not be broken up without further injustice.

Stüsser feels that Kasper has not gone far enough. Why exclude a second marriage?[84] This would become a real possibility if the reformers of the Code would take Vatican II's description of marriage seriously ("intimate partnership of married life and love"). Actually it is Stüsser's contention that the ecclesiastical understanding of marriage and that of the world are markedly different in our time. The Church's view is still grounded in the notion of marriage as a social institution for the procreation of children. Thus the importance of the first sexual act in canonical jurisprudence, once of great importance but not now. By contrast the modern world sees marriage as a personal enterprise.

With this as a background, Stüsser joins Edward Schillebeeckx in insisting that marriage is a historical phenomenon which cannot be defined once and for all in a single way. It must take account of the social, psychological, cultural, and economic factors that undergird it. "So also the conditions in which a marriage is indissoluble are variable." If marriage is seen in personalistic perspective, in terms of mutual and permanent love and caring, then "its indissolubility is not a property necessarily following from marriage as an institution but an inner task to be realized."[85] Frequently it is not so realized and we must come to grips, in our concepts and law, with marital breakdown. As yet we have not.

In order to do this, we must be clear on the sacramentality of marriage. We have tended to think of this in static and mechanical ways. According to Stüsser, it is the very depth and genuinity of human love lived out of the depths of faith. Its indissolubility is its love. As Schillebeeckx notes, "Human marriage is not indissoluble because it is a sacrament; rather it is a sacrament because and insofar as it contains the will to develop itself in unbreakable covenant fidelity."[86] This is something that can be irretrievably lost. It is our task to provide juridical categories that acknowledge this and take its full consequences (that when a marriage dies, this is no obstacle to a second union). Stüsser feels that the present reformers of the Code are engaged in merely cosmetic adjustments, when in reality the whole concept of Christian marriage has changed.

[84] For the Church of England's discussion of second marriage, cf. Trevor Beeson, "British Debate Remarriage in the Church," *Christian Century* 95 (1978) 681–82.

[85] Edward Schillebeeckx, "Die christliche Ehe und die menschliche Realität völliger Ehezerrüttung," in P. J. Huizing's *Für eine neue kirchliche Eheordnung* (Düsseldorf: Patmos, 1975) 41–73, at 51.

[86] Ibid. 55.

James Gaffney takes a slightly different approach.[87] Examining the pagan-Christian marriage in St. Paul (the so-called Pauline privilege), Gaffney states: "Paul shows no sign of imagining that a Christian's marriage literally cannot be dissolved. What he believes is that it should not be dissolved." Paul does not suppose, Gaffney argues, that the Christian whose marriage is in fact dissolved through no fault of his/her own should remain enslaved to a "fictitious marriage that no longer had any concrete existence." Gaffney sees Paul's attitude as the basis for sound Church policy in our time on divorce and remarriage.

But the implementation of such a policy has been precluded by three dubious assumptions. First, there is the assumption that Jesus taught it was impossible to divorce, rather than that it was wrong to do so. Second, it is supposed that this teaching pertains to consummated marriage contracted between the baptized. Finally, it is thought that the Pauline exemption describes a privileged exemption whose purpose was to encourage the adoption of the Christian religion.

Gaffney finds the entrenchment of these assumptions and the processes supporting this entrenchment very "intellectually unsatisfying." As a result, we find ourselves in the peculiar position of basing our belief "that marriage cannot be dissolved on a New Testament teaching that marriage should not be dissolved." Gaffney concludes by repeating what Jesus' teaching is: "For them [the married] to take it apart is not impossible. It is wrong." Thus the Church's effort should be to prevent this wrong, but to deal with it healingly and forgivingly when it occurs. There seems no question that Gaffney views a "subsequent lifetime of conjugal deprivation" after divorce as ethically deplorable and biblically unfounded.

Pierre Hayoit, the *officialis* of Tournai, studies existing tribunal procedures.[88] The only procedures now available are dissolutions for nonconsummation and declarations of nullity. He questions whether this is sufficient, even with simplified procedures and the expansion of the criteria of nullity. Clearly he thinks the answer is negative. Indeed, the criteria of nullity have become so broad (incapacity to assume the duties of marriage) that he believes, with Jean Bernhard, that we have really passed over from nullity to dissolution of marriages. But still the problem remains.

When he examines Rotal jurisprudence, Hayoit finds two paradoxical tendencies. The one, stressing the gravity of the marital enterprise, tends to broaden the grounds of nullity. The other, underlining the natural character of marriage—a state to which all ought to have access and

---

[87] James Gaffney, "Marriage and Divorce," *New Catholic World* 222 (Jan.–Feb. 1979) 20–23.

[88] P. Hayoit, "Les procédures matrimoniales et la théologie du mariage," *Revue théologique de Louvain* 9 (1978) 33–58.

therefore one for which a minimum is required—tends toward a narrowing of grounds. The Rota tutioristically follows the latter trend. In its decisions Hayoit perceives an increasing reliance on psychiatric evidence for "psychic incapacity"—and a radical, perpetual incapacity at that. This is a one-sided "psychiatrizing" of the decision.

Actually the decision must be one that establishes a prudential balance between the quality of consent at the time of marriage (psychic capacity) and the doctrine of marriage. The "psychiatric perspective" tends to overlook the fact that the capacity we are looking for in a party is one toward marriage *as this is understood in the Catholic Church.*

The last section of Hayoit's study is extremely interesting. It is devoted to "areas of desirable evolution." First, there must be an adjustment of the minimum requirements. In an effort to safeguard the right of all to marry, that minimum has been put at a ridiculously low level. Actually some people marry without the reflection that they would put into their vacation itinerary. Furthermore, this adjustment of the minimum is all the more the case when we are dealing with sacramental marriage. Marriage has a new significance in Christian theology. Sacramental marriage involves a mission in the Church. "It is difficult to admit that the Christian vision of marriage is without repercussions on the conditions of access to marriage, and in particular on that 'minimum' which one has the right to demand of candidates for *sacramental* marriage."[89] Sacramental theology would see as a minimum that Christian marriage have the value of a sign in the heart of the community.

This being the case, Hayoit moves to his next desirable development: the dissociation of marriage and sacrament. Since about the time of the Council of Trent, it has been Catholic teaching that there can be (*consistere*) no valid marriage among the baptized which is not by this fact (*eo ipso*) a sacrament. Hayoit sees this as the Gordian knot of all Catholic pastoral practice regarding marriage. For instance, it is responsible for the ease of admission to sacramental marriage and the severity in declarations of nullity. He argues for the rehabilitation of civil marriage so that those Christians who are not ready for sacramental marriage—or whose sacramental marriages have broken up—are no longer regarded as in concubinage.

The International Theological Commission authorized publication of a document that takes a totally different approach. Consisting of sixteen theses, the statement was authored by Gustave Martelet, S.J., and approved *in forma generica* by the Commission. That is, the essential ideas were approved, not every word or detail.[90]

[89] Ibid. 52.

[90] Gustave Martelet, S.J., "Christological Theses on the Sacrament of Marriage," *Origins* 8 (1978) 200–204.

The document is an attempt to place Christian marriage within a Christological framework. Christ draws into his own energy the conjugal love of the baptized. Thus the mystery proper to Christ as spouse of the Church radiates within the couples consecrated to him. Such marriage cannot be an image of Christ as spouse unless it shares his fidelity (indissolubility). The Church has no dissolving power over a union "that has passed into the power of him whose mystery she must announce and not hinder." As for the divorced-remarried, their reception of the Eucharist "is plainly incompatible with the mystery of which the Church is the servant and witness." Why? Because the Church would let such parties believe that they can, on the level of signs, communicate with him whose conjugal mystery they disavow on the level of reality."

A similar conclusion is drawn by E. Gagnon.[91] He sees the process of conversion after divorce-remarriage as a long and arduous one. The divorced-remarried are in a situation of irregularity, and utopian hopes should not structure the pastoral support extended to them. As for reception of the Eucharist, Gagnon says that "it loses its signification from the moment it is separated from the ongoing life of the Christian." The divorced-remarried must remember that the ecclesial life does not consist uniquely in the sacraments.

The International Theological Commission completed in 1978 its definitive text *Theses de doctrina matrimonii christiani.*[92] Because it was amended in accordance with the *modi* submitted, it was approved (I would think) *in forma specifica.* This would mean that it was a consensus statement of a committee. Such statements are like a convoy of ships in wartime: about as fast as its slowest member. That must be kept in mind while reading the document.

After treating marriage as an institution and its sacramentality as rooted in baptism, the document (section 3) turns to the relationship between "marriage of creation" and sacramental marriage. It sees the relationship as inseparable ("Inter duos baptizatos matrimonium creationis scindi nequit a matrimonio sacramento"). The reason: sacramentality is not an accident of conjugal union but "inheres in its essence." On this basis the document concludes that there can really or truly ("vere seu realiter") be no other marriage state for the baptized. "Therefore the Church can in no way admit that two baptized persons are in a conjugal state commensurate with their dignity and the manner of being of the new creature in Christ unless they are united sacramentally." Those who from ignorance try to separate contract marriage and the sacrament

---

[91] S. Ex. Mgr. Gagnon, "Situation dans l'église des divorcés remariés civilement," *Esprit et vie* 88 (1978) 241–45.

[92] I use the Latin text kindly provided by Walter J. Burghardt, S.J., Cf. also *Documentation catholique* 75 (1978) 704–18.

really achieve only a "psychological relation," not a true marriage bond. The Commission, therefore, rejects pastoral solutions which allow sacramental solemnizations after nonsacramental "marriages."

The Commission then asserts that the Church has no power to dissolve sacramental, consummated marriages. As for unions undertaken after sacramental marriages, they can be considered neither "regular nor legitimate" (this latter term meaning "valid but not sacramental"). May persons in a second, irregular union receive the sacraments? The Commission is clear and, as far as I can see, absolute: "From the incompatibility of the state of the divorced-remarried with the command and mystery of the risen Lord, there follows the impossibility for these Christians of receiving in the Eucharist the sign of unity with Christ." Thus the key argument of the Commission rests in the phrase *signum unitatis*. However, even though this "illegitimate state" does not permit full communion, "these Christians are not excluded from the action of divine grace, from a union (*conjunctione*) with the Church, and they should not be deprived of pastoral care."

Some of the same questions put to the pastoral of the Italian episcopate are appropriate here, especially that concerning the need for full integration before reception of the sacraments.

James Provost, the then president of the Canon Law Society of America, sees three obstacles to reconciling the divorced-remarried.[93] First, there is the attitude that such people are "living in sin." Second, there is the very difficult problem of balancing the Church's prophetic mission with her compassionate mission. Finally, canonically, such parties are viewed in law technically as "infamous" (bigamists). Provost gives a careful and realistic picture of the updated tribunal process. He does not see reconciliation of the divorced-remarried as easy or automatic. As for reception of the sacraments, Provost recalls that the "approved practice of the Church" can justify this on two conditions: (1) they are attempting to live their lives according to Christian principles; (2) scandal is avoided.[94] He concludes by raising some very useful questions to test the objectivity of the couple in an irregular second union. For instance: Are they fulfilling the responsibilities of the first and second unions? How committed is their Christian life? Are they not simply avoiding scandal but positively contributing to build up Christian married life in the community?

A similar position is presented by Pierre Côté, S.J.[95] He notes that the

[93] James Provost, "Reconciliation of Catholics in Second Marriages," *Origins* 8 (1978) 204-8.

[94] Provost denies that the "approved practice of the Church" necessarily involves a brother-sister relationship.

[95] Pierre Côté, "Pour une pastorale des divorcés-remariés," *Relations* 39 (1979) 112-17.

official position of the Church is clear: as long as the couple remain in the second union, they may not receive the sacraments. This exclusion of the divorced-remarried from the sacraments rests on a view of the Eucharist as "the sign of *perfect* communion with Jesus Christ and the Church."

At the pastoral level, however, the problem must be viewed in terms of the religious and spiritual experience of Jesus Christ by the couple, not in terms of norms and the politics of the Church. This means that the spiritual condition of the couple will be approached in the internal forum, with appropriate attention to their growth in love, the difference between ideal and reality, etc.

Côté ends by raising several "questions" (actually they look more like suggestions). First, if we stress the fact not of unity already achieved but of a movement toward such unity, then admission of these persons to the sacraments will be easier. Second, Côté acknowledges that education of the community is required here, but he believes it quite possible. Pastoral accommodation in other areas has not meant forfeiture of principle or confusion of the faithful. For example, access of the children of unwed mothers to baptism celebrations has not meant approval of the foregoing conduct. Therefore Côté cautions about a negative answer in the case of the divorced-remarried. Finally, he appeals to the experience of other Christian churches (Protestant and Orthodox) that "are inspired by the same evangelical values," yet conclude to a different praxis. Côté's reflections are very close in spirit to those of Provost.

A quite similar view is expressed by Theodore Davey, C.P.[96] The key question in his view is: Would the admission of *some* divorced-remarried persons to the Eucharist "fatally and irretrievably damage the Church's witness to the indissolubility of marriage"? If the answer is yes, then the matter is settled. Davey makes two points. First, genuine theological scandal (weakening of the ideal of indissolubility) must be distinguished from bewilderment, astonishment, jealousy. Second, the reason that people are excluded or exclude themselves from the Eucharist is lack of full integration in the Church. But, Davey argues, "full integration and full standing is not a condition before one can share the Eucharist." He appeals to the policy that allows non-Catholics on certain occasions to share in the Eucharist.

I agree with the conclusion of Côté, Provost, and Davey and the perspectives that yielded it. The Martelet paper, the International Theological Commission, and Gagnon base their negative conclusion largely on the reception of the Eucharist as a sign. One problem with this analysis is that it restricts the sacraments to a single finality (the signification of unity), as I noted above, and perfect unity at that. However, once the

[96] Theodore Davey, C.P., "The Marriage Debate: A Reply," *Month* 240, n.s. 12 (1979) 257–61.

need for dialectical balance is admitted in the two finalities of the sacraments (signification of unity, sharing in the means of grace), it seems that nothing in principle prevents sacramental reception by those imperfectly integrated into the Church. If that is true of our separated brethren at times—and Vatican II admits that it is—is it not at least as true for those who are not separated but have encountered marital tragedy? Such a reception of the sacraments has been admitted in the past even by those of quite conservative theological tendencies.

Another problem with the absolute negative conclusion is seen when we confront the spiritual status of those in these second, irregular unions. All admit that they should continue to attend Mass, fulfil all their other duties, and participate as fully as possible in the life of the Church. The International Theological Commission puts it as follows: "Although this illegitimate situation does not permit a life of full communion, these Christians are not excluded from the action of divine grace, from a union with the Church, and they ought not be deprived of pastoral care."[97] This is describing a state of irregularity but of grace. That means it is the *irregularity alone* (at least in some cases), not the personal spiritual dispositions of the couple, that constitutes the impossibility of "receiving in the Eucharist the sign of unity with Christ." Is that necessarily the case? Many theologians in recent years have not been so convinced. That points in the direction of what is the key problem in this terribly difficult discussion: the status of those who are divorced-remarried. Pius IX said that these are in a state of concubinage; for since the marriage contract and the sacrament are inseparable, those who cannot marry sacramentally cannot have a valid contract, scil., are *not married in any sense* in the eyes of the Church.

There are two questions that need further exploration here. (1) Is the Church irreformably committed to the notion of the inseparability of the sacrament and the contract ("marriage of creation")? The problem becomes much sharper when, instead of contract, the language of Vatican II is used to describe marriage. (2) Is it a necessary consequence of this doctrine that those in a second marriage are not married in any sense? The use of the general and soft term "irregular" would seem to open the

---

[97] The Commission refers to divorced-remarried as "status divortiatorum denuo 'nuptorum.' " The closure is used because the Commission rejects the notion that the baptized can contract a true marriage which is not sacramental. It refers to such a union as *unio psychologica* but not true marriage. For a useful history of the theological disputes surrounding the doctrine of inseparability of contract and sacrament, cf. C. Caffarra, "Le lien entre le mariage-réalité de la création et le mariage sacrement," *Esprit et vie* 88 (1978) 353–64, 369–84. Caffarra concludes in a fashion similar to the Commission when he says of the decision of the baptized to marry nonsacramentally: "elle ne produit rien en réalité" (381). That conclusion, I believe, depends heavily on the notion of marriage and of sacrament that prevailed when the inseparability doctrine took shape.

way to admitting that existentially there can be elements in that second union which, while not constituting sacramental marriage, are sufficient to allow the life of grace to flourish. Thus it has recently been suggested that these second unions "participate analogously in certain values of the sacrament of marriage."[98]

Put in slightly different words, there are two senses of the identity of contract and sacrament. We might describe these as *sensu aiente* and *sensu negante*. The first sense means that the sacrament is not distinct from human love that constitutes the fidelity bond. It is that bond lived in faith. But does it follow from such identity that (*sensu negante*) those whose marriages have failed *do absolutely nothing* in entering a second union? That is what traditional theology would say. And that is what is being increasingly questioned by a theology that views marriage and its sacramentality more in terms of personal love.

In still other (and legal) terms, marriage that is thought to be sacramental prevents the institutional possibility of another sacramental marriage. But does it necessarily prevent the possibility of another marriage? Whatever the answer to this difficult problem, it is at the heart of the renewal of pastoral practice with regard to the divorced-remarried in the Church today.

NUCLEAR ENERGY AND NUCLEAR ARMS

Two of the most interesting and urgent moral problems of the past year or so have been the problem of energy and in particular the use of nuclear energy, and the Strategic Arms Limitation Talks. Pope John Paul II addressed himself to both problems, vigorously and specifically to the latter, in principle and nonspecifically to the former. With regard to energy, his references were fairly general and touched on the unequal distribution of material goods. For instance, in his speech at Yankee Stadium, Oct. 2, 1979, he stated: "We must find a simple way of living. For it is not right that the standard of living of the rich countries should seek to maintain itself by drawing off a great part of the reserves of energy and raw materials that are meant to serve the whole community."[99] As for the proliferation of arms, he stated: "We applaud the decisions and agreements aimed at reducing the arms race."[100] Was this an endorsement of SALT II? It could be read that way but need not be. A word about both of these subjects as treated by theologians and theological literature.

First, the problem of energy. Bishop William E. McManus (Fort

---

[98] François Deltombe, "Pour une solution pastorale du problème des divorcés remariés," *Supplément* 130 (Sept. 1979) 329–54, at 350.

[99] *Origins* 9 (1979) 311.

[100] Ibid. 261.

Wayne–South Bend) issued a brief but effective pastoral letter in response to President Carter's energy speech of July 15, 1979.[101] "Our overriding moral obligation is to be serious about our nation's energy problems." McManus proposed reduction of nonessential driving, parochial car-pooling, thermostatic asceticism. He concluded by asking his people to give careful attention "to the difficult problems raised by some proposed solutions." Specifically, McManus asked whether it is right or wrong to build more nuclear-energy plants even though foolproof protection against nuclear disaster cannot be guaranteed. Is it right or wrong to accept higher pollution indices by use of coal for energy?

The "careful attention" McManus called for is both necessary and difficult, as a sampling of literature will reveal. Those who have not been following the relatively young ethical debate might well begin with a volume edited by John Francis and Paul Abrecht.[102] Abrecht's own essay in this volume traces the involvement of the churches in discussions of nuclear power. In the 1950's and 1960's there was little opposition to nuclear power. Indeed, its peaceful use seemed to be a way of redeeming what had previously been a weapons technology. But that has all changed in the past three or four years. Gradually there has emerged in the World Council of Churches' discussions on energy a consensus on two points. First, the underlying faith and value suppositions constantly appealed to in the debate had to be examined. Second, the paradox of a technology offering the prospect of immense potential and many incalculable risks still remains unresolved.

Abrecht notes that this position is in contrast with several other ethical views. For instance, one group (Mobilization for Survival) argues that nuclear energy is opposed to God's will. Another group founds its resistance on technical grounds: safe and workable alternative sources of energy are available (solar and wind power). Still others press the connection between nuclear power and nuclear weapons. Abrecht's own comments show clearly that he thinks no absolute yes or no to the proliferation of nuclear power is warranted.

There is absolutely no question in the mind of J. George Butler.[103] Nuclear energy fails the test of Christian stewardship of life and the earth. He severely faults the Rasmussen Reactor Safety Study's statement that the chance of a nuclear accident involving a thousand fatalities is extremely remote. (The Rasmussen Report is an extensive study directed by Norman Rasmussen, professor at M.I.T. It was commissioned

[101] William E. McManus, in the *Harmonizer*, July 29, 1979.
[102] John Francis and Paul Abrecht, *Facing up to Nuclear Power* (Edinburgh: Saint Andrew, 1976).
[103] J. George Butler, "Christian Ethics and Nuclear Power," *Christian Century* 96 (1979) 438–41.

by the Atomic Energy Commission to determine the probability and results of an accident in nuclear reactors.) The Nuclear Regulatory Commission has since totally rejected the study's summary. Butler argues that the lack of catastrophic accidents is more a matter of good luck than good management, that low-level radiation is likely to be far more harmful than we suspected twenty-five years ago, that the problem of nuclear waste has not been solved, that other forms of energy are less dangerous and more economical.

Included in the Francis-Abrecht volume is an essay by Roger Shinn on the ethical aspects of the energy problem.[104] Shinn lifts up seven issue-areas where factual and valuational problems must be faced in trying to decide what kind of society we want for ourselves and our children. For example: What is our proper relationship to nature ("fit into" or "replace" and transform)? What risks may we accept? Are our exorbitant demands for energy part of a suicidal life style? Is nuclear energy one of the many forces in modern society that will increase the gap between rich and poor nations? What is the relationship between nuclear energy and nuclear arms? Finally, Shinn asks the question about the very meaning of life: "Will nuclear energy offer the possibilities of a better human existence?"

Shinn has raised many good questions, questions, as he says, "that are often conveniently neglected." His essay is an excellent place to begin reflection on this subject.

Shinn returned to the subject in an address given in the spring of 1978 (Switzerland) during a World Council of Churches consultation on "Ecumenical Concerns in Relation to Nuclear Energy," but only recently published.[105] He notes that there are two different types of questions to be asked. Science can answer some, e.g., how much petroleum is left in the ground? What are the risks of fast breeder reactors? But there are other questions that science alone cannot answer, e.g., what are my rights to petroleum compared to the rights of others? What is the meaning of our patterns of consumption? Such questions quickly drive us to some rather basic issues of ethics and of faith. Shinn feels that the churches have confused these and thus "have a long record of making scientific judgments that they should not have made and of abdicating from moral judgments that they should make."

There is a third element that enters into deliberation about a problem like nucelar energy: ideology. By ideology Shinn means "a set of conceptions or a picture of the world and society that helps to guide action." Clearly Shinn accepts the term in its nonpejorative sense. Ideology is a

---

[104] Roger Shinn, "Ethical Reflections on the Use of Nuclear Energy," as in Francis and Abrecht, *Facing up* 137–55.

[105] Roger L. Shinn, "Faith, Science, Ideology and the Nuclear Decision," *Christianity and Crisis* 39 (1979) 3–8.

kind of framework into which we fit information. It determines what information we consider relevant. Thus, when people look out on the world, some see population problems; others see social inequalities; others see resource depletion; still others see future technologies that will solve problems.

It is Shinn's contention that the ultimate ethical and policy decisions occur at the intersection of faith and science, but that this intersection takes place within an ideological context. Shinn then applies this to the matter of nuclear risk. Sometimes the evidence is debated; sometimes it is unmeasurable. For instance, with regard to the risk of accident, neither faith nor science gives us certainty, and ideology cannot of its nature do this, "although it often gives its holders the psychic feeling of certainty." Therefore Shinn faults those who would demand of the churches a prophetic clarity at this time, because the basis for such clarity and certainty is not yet present.

Bruce W. Robbins agrees with Shinn that faith, science, and ideology affect debate on nuclear energy.[106] But he believes Shinn has not sufficiently penetrated the ideology within which the nuclear debate is occurring. It is an ideology generated out of the assumptions and goals of the nuclear industry and determines what facts we hear and what alternatives we see as available. Specifically, the prevailing ideology attempts to deflate any doubt that nuclear power is the only technologically feasible energy option of the future. Robbins believes that some of Shinn's arguments are typical of this prevailing ideology.

On the contrary, Robbins is convinced of two things. First, alternative energy sources are available. Second, the data on the harmful effects of atmospheric radiation are "staggering." Therefore nuclear power will not take us in the direction of a "just, participating and sustainable society" (the World Council of Churches' phrase).

Shinn responded by insisting that he was primarily concerned with the nature of ethical argument, not with energy as such.[107] Bruce Robbins, he says, is a crusader against nuclear energy. Shinn is ready to join Robbins' crusade only if he has better evidence. For instance, in well over 1500 reactor-years of experience, there have been no direct-on-the-spot deaths attributable to nuclear energy, whereas we have 100-150 deaths annually due to coal mining. This exchange is a good introduction to the types of arguments that are being advanced in this very important discussion.

In the wake of the Three Mile Island disaster, the entire faculty of Lancaster Theological Seminary (just an uncomfortable twenty-three miles from the damaged Pennsylvania nuclear plant) issued a statement asserting that four "structures of evil" became clear as a result of the

[106] Bruce Robbins, "Faith, Science, Ideology and the Nuclear Decision," ibid. 136–39.
[107] Roger Shinn, ibid. 139–42.

accident: our excessive consumerism, unthinking trust in technology, the economic and political structures that benefit from nuclear power, and our pervasive sense of impotence. One of seven calls to action was "a moratorium on construction of all nuclear power plants."

James M. Wall, editor of the *Christian Century*, reports this statement and responds that the Lancaster faculty is correct in describing our condition (which Wall redescribes theologically as selfishness, idolatry, greed, and apathy) but that "they veer off target" in their moratorium proposal.[108] The prophetic word, he reminds us, is never spoken in a vacuum. It is always spoken in a world of very complex relationships, in what the remarkable Joseph Sittler has referred to as the "webbed connectedness" of our ecosystem. Concretely, Wall argues that the Lancaster proposal ignores the fact that the closing would result in loss of family incomes and increase in the cost of living. He proposes a policy of "wait and see."

On this point I find Wall puzzling for two reasons. First, he himself has referred to the "massive problems which toxic nuclear wastes pose" and to "the precariousness of all nuclear plant safety systems." That is rather heavy language and if accurate (I do not say, for the moment, that it is) justifies *something*. Second, a moratorium is just that; it is not a death sentence. Or is it better to continue building plants with "massive problems" and "precarious safety systems" especially when it is persons' health and lives that are likely to be affected, not their pocketbook and the cost of living?[109]

The National Council of Churches has for many years supported a pronuclear policy statement. On May 9–11, 1979 the NCC's Governing Board met in San Antonio and officially reversed itself by a vote of 120–26.[110] The NCC statement describes an ecologically just society as one that involves sustainability, fairness, and participation. It then goes on to indicate seven general guidelines of the "ethic of ecological justice." For instance, the greater the risk in a technology, the less moral justification there is for its use. Or again: the survival needs of those below the minimum material standard take precedence over the wants of those above that standard; those who receive the benefits should as much as possible bear the costs, etc. There follow criteria for assessing technologies. Each technology pursued will violate as few as possible of the following criteria: safe, appropriate to human nature, flexible, nondestruc-

---

[108] James M. Wall, "Grace and the Nuclear Problem," *Christian Century* 96 (1979) 459–60.

[109] For reader response to Wall's editorial, cf. ibid. 643–45.

[110] "The Energy Crisis: Ethical Implications," *Origins* 9 (1979) 17–21. For a summary of the proceedings, cf. James M. Wall, "NCC Says No to Nuclear Power," *Christian Century* 96 (1979) 579–80.

tive to other necessities of life, resource-saving, resilient, fair, comprehensible, nonviolent, employment-producing, pluralistic (insuring a diversity of options), appropriate (matching the society to be served), aesthetic.

The Governing Board notes that in the application of these criteria "inevitably some ethically desirable goals must be 'traded off' against other goals which are also good." In its application of them, the Board urged an end to dependence on nuclear energy, supported energy conservation, and called for development of renewable energy sources.

Some of the persons prominent in the debate on nuclear energy and already mentioned in these "Notes" (e.g., Paul Abrecht, Roger Shinn, John Francis) were present at the World Council of Churches Conference on Faith, Science and the Future held at the Massachusetts Institute of Technology (July 12–24, 1979). Alan Geyer reports on the Conference's deliberations on nuclear energy.[111] After passionate and prolonged debate, the Conference adopted a compromise five-year moratorium on the construction of all new nuclear-power plants. The original draft proposal said nothing about five years, but said simply "until the overall risks and costs of nuclear power are fully determined and justified."

The arguments pro and con are now familiar. For example, M.I.T. physicist David Rose argued that a nuclear moratorium would make developed countries even more dependent on oil imports and therefore more likely to use military force to preserve fuel lines; would fail to meet energy needs of developing countries, which would be more likely than ever to go nuclear; would make nuclear war more likely, etc. Roger Shinn asserted that hazards and costs justified a moratorium on coal production as much as a nuclear moratorium. Others argued that nuclear energy is totally inappropriate in the Third World, because it serves only vested interests in developed countries.

This is a brief and impoverishing introduction to some recent literature on the energy debate. It is a difficult literature because the problem is difficult, inseparably intertwined as it is with complicated scientific calculations, inconsistent statistics, and considerations of international justice. The matter is further, and unnecessarily, complicated by the presence of high-powered interest groups and lobbying, and what Shinn refers to as ideology. If there is a single impression I carry away from this debate, it is this: faith alone cannot give an answer to these problems, but no answer can be safely elaborated without the perspectives on the meaning of the world and our responsibilities in it which faith originates and so powerfully supports. Therefore the greatest tragedy at this time of intense deliberation would be to allow the discussion to be determined exclusively by politics and economics. The presence in this discussion of

[111] Manuscript kindly sent me by Alan Geyer; it now appears in the *Ecumenical Review* 31 (1979) 372–79.

religious ethicists like Shinn and Geyer is consoling.

And now to SALT II. There is, of course, an enormous amount of literature on this subject of a purely technical and strategic character. Important as this is for a moral judgment, it cannot be reviewed here because of sheer size. Rather I will bring under review some of the literature that springs from a theological context or a faith community, and aims more directly at a moral judgment ibid on SALT II.

Sidney Lens notes that a minority of the antiwar movement (including Pax Christi, *Inquiry* magazine, the *Progressive*, certain individuals of Clergy and Laity Concerned) opposes the agreement as an escalation of the arms race it was supposed to limit.[112] He chastises the supporters of SALT within the antiwar movement and reviews their arguments.

One argument is that the treaty will place equal ceilings on the numbers of U.S. and Russian strategic delivery vehicles (missiles and bombers). Lens sees this as meaningless, since the Pentagon's obsession of the moment—to improve quality and accuracy—is not curtailed or limited. Thus, in SALT II, as in SALT I, the superpowers give up only what they regard as secondary but "allow themselves free rein to go ahead with what they consider most promising and urgent—the MIRV in 1972, weapons of accuracy in 1978."

Another argument is that without SALT II "things would be worse." Lens responds that just as SALT I did not restrain the superpowers from developing what they wanted, so neither will SALT II. History since 1972 seems to support him on this point. The escalatory steps proposed by the Carter administration are defended as necessary to appease the hawks who would not vote for SALT II otherwise. Lens sees this as equivalently stating that in order to win approval for arms control the government must agree to further escalation. What sense does that make when our stockpile can already kill every Russian thirty-six times over?

Lens concluded that peace people should not be negative to SALT II by rejecting it; rather they should propose a modification. This modification would take the shape of a moratorium, the original proposal of the SALT talks.

Dr. Harold E. Fey, former editor of the *Christian Century*, takes a different view.[113] After describing very usefully and in detail the enormous arms-spending around the world, he views SALT II positively: "SALT II will not stop the arms race, but if the treaty is completed, signed and ratified, there will be more restrictions and limitations than ever before. It is good to slow the arms race, even a little."

An interesting and in some sense classic face-off occurred between two

[112] Sidney Lens, "What Peace People Should Be Saying about SALT," *Christian Century* 96 (1979) 181–85.
[113] Harold E. Fey, "The Challenge of SALT II," ibid. 343–47.

distinguished Catholic intellectuals devoted to the cause of peace, Bishop Thomas J. Gumbleton, president of Pax Christi, and J. Bryan Hehir, associate secretary of the Office of International Justice and Peace, USCC.[114] I want to report this exchange at some length because it is a mirror of the attitude of people with deep moral concern, yet of different conclusions.

Gumbleton begins by noting that SALT II would legitimate the destructive power of 615,000 Hiroshima bombs (our present American arsenal). He then adverts to the statement of then Secretary of Defense James Schlesinger that "under no circumstances could we disavow the first use of nuclear weapons." Next he calls attention to the fact that use of destructive weapons against noncombatants is, in Catholic teaching, immoral. So is the threat to do so as a strategy of deterrence. Gumbleton sees ratification of SALT II as a repudiation of that moral stance.

To those who argue that SALT II puts a "cap" on the permissible numbers of such weapons, Gumbleton replies that this is equivalent to supporting a "cap" on the number of torture chambers permitted to governments. Another argument commonly made is that SALT II is a first step in the right direction. "We cannot extricate ourselves with one decisive action." Gumbleton responds, very much as Lens had, that the arms race is no longer a matter of numbers but of technology and sophistication. What would actually be a first step would be a change in our thinking; but that is not found in the agreement.

As an alternative to ratification of SALT II, Gumbleton proposes "simply to end formal negotiations and rely on unilateral demonstrations of arms restraint." He concludes his essay by noting areas where the churches can make a positive contribution.

Bryan Hehir moves in two steps. First, he discusses the political-moral case for SALT II, then the ecclesial case. By "political-moral" he means that the key moral value is control; the political method is negotiated limitation.

As for the political-moral case in favor of SALT II, Hehir, after conceding the agreement's limitations, presents four arguments. First, the quantitative controls are limited but not inconsequential. Proper evaluation of these controls means seeing SALT as a process with a history, a future. This process represents the first reduction of offensive weapons in the history of the nuclear arms race and as such "breaks the mind-set that the technological dynamic is beyond political control."

Second, there are qualitative controls, and limited as they may be, the key fact is the *principle* of qualitative control, which can lead to further reductions in the future.

[114] Thomas J. Gumbleton, "Is SALT Worth Supporting? No," *Commonweal* 106 (1979) 105–7; J. Bryan Hehir, "Is SALT Worth Supporting? Yes," ibid. 108–10.

Third, there is the ominous threat of what can be anticipated if SALT II controls are not imposed. The crucial significance of the SALT process is the chance to impose political control on an arms race generated by a quasi-independent technological dynamic. If SALT II fails, what framework will remain for superpower arms limitation? We may be sure that if SALT II fails, we will see B-1, Trident II, along with MX on the legislative docket.

Finally, Hehir argues that defeat of SALT II will contribute nothing to the wider process of disarmament.

As for the ecclesial aspects of the discussion, Hehir cautions against identifying any one position as Catholic. Furthermore, it would be delusory to think that the public debate will be cast in terms of the Christian exchange. It will be argued in terms of whether it "gives away too much," not whether "it achieves too little." Hehir concludes that it is well within a balanced middle Christian position to hold that SALT II is not enough, but it is imperative as a step in the process." It is a position that meshes the possible and the necessary, that blends commitment with unavoidable compromise.[115]

One of the finer and more instructive pieces of reflection on SALT II is that of Alan Geyer.[116] He describes his study as "a framework for coping with SALT II issues." Geyer begins by noting that there is no greater burden upon Christian history "than the failure of this generation of Christians to define the *nuclear arms race as a theological issue.*"

The assumption of the Geyer study is that the probabilities of nuclear war within a generation are now rising rapidly. Geyer lists seven reasons for this statement: (1) massive resort to nuclear technology by many countries since the energy crisis of 1973-74; (2) breakdown of prospects for nonproliferation; (3) mounting prospects of nuclear terrorism; (4) rising curves of hostility in nuclear-prone regions such as Korea, the Persian Gulf, South America; (5) conventional arms race; (6) deterioration of détente; (7) lack of a coherent security-disarmament policy at the highest levels of U.S. government.

Geyer believes that SALT II must be assessed in terms of its effects on these seven somber trends. Furthermore, he believes that SALT has been absolutized into an idol, a monopoly of the superpowers to the exclusion of other countries ("an imperious and arrogant nuclear condominium"). Thus he emphasizes a world view that would approach the nuclear arms race within an international framework. He is extremely critical of the whole SALT process. "Nothing in the history of SALT can efface the fact that the superpowers now have many thousands more nuclear

---

[115] For letters of reaction, cf. ibid. 226, 250–51.

[116] Alan Geyer, "Arms Limits and SALT Limits: The Superpowers' Role in Nuclear Disarmament," *Shalom Paper* 6 (1979).

warheads than they had a decade ago." SALT I gave them this license and SALT II guarantees no reversal. Behind this buildup there are "desperately shifting rationales," reminiscent of Santayana's definition of a fanatic: "one who doubles his speed when he has lost his way."

Ultimately, however, Geyer finds the most morally compelling reason for supporting SALT II the vision of the world without ratification of it. It would almost surely witness a terribly costly and dangerous acceleration. Therefore, while he sympathizes with Bishop Gumbleton (SALT II is a "cruel hoax"), Geyer ends up supporting the agreements in a spirit of "painful ambivalence."

Geyer's presentation is forceful, insightful, and shot through with the moral urgency of nuclear arms limitation and reduction. It is, however, pretheological; that is, it is much more clearly concerned with what Christians ought to do and think than with the Christian warrants for doing so.

Joseph J. Fahey, director of the Peace Studies Institute at Manhattan College, attempts to fill this theological vacuum.[117] He first cites the many documents (Pius XII through John Paul II, Vatican II, World Synod of Bishops, United States bishops) condemnatory of the arms race as itself an act of aggression. He then provides six theological assertions that "are relevant to a Catholic understanding of the need for disarmament." Briefly they are: (1) God as a loving God who wishes our common survival; (2) a theology of human nature that sees it as not totally depraved and therefore capable of peace; (3) a theology of sin that locates sin also in our corporate structures; (4) a theology of redemption that issues in a vibrant vision and hope; (5) a theology of politics that sees the political world as the sphere of God's redemptive activity; (6) a theology of nonviolence that roots in Jesus' command to love our neighbor.

Fahey makes some excellent points. I particularly appreciate his stress on the Christian basis for optimism and hope. If there is one common enemy of the cause of disarmament and peace, it is the sense of inevitability that settles into our attitudes—and practices. That leads to apathy, and apathy means abandonment of the political process to its own dynamic. Fahey has made it quite clear that there are no Christian warrants for such a response.

The first step against such apathy is public education. A New York Times–CBS news poll taken June 3–6 indicated the necessity of such education. When asked whether the Senate should vote for SALT II, 27% responded affirmatively, 9% negatively, and 64% stated that they did not know enough to have an opinion. That is startling and profoundly disturbing. For this reason the *National Jesuit News* put together a

---

[117] Joseph J. Fahey, "The Catholic Church and the Arms Race," *Worldview* 22 (1979) 38–41. Cf. also *America* 140 (1979) 127–30.

special supplement on SALT II as a service to Jesuits. It is simply excellent. The supplement includes a summary of the SALT II agreements, a glossary of terms, bibliography, the position of the State Department, and four possible positions on SALT II.[118] The four positions are those of Network (support), Admiral Zumwalt (opposition), Senator Mark Hatfield (amendment), Pax Christi (passive nonsupport).

George S. Weigel, Jr., backs off from the tactical discussion of SALT II to present the background against which any discussion of national security, arms control, and disarmament must take place among Catholics.[119] There are four arenas in which contemporary debate ought to occur: contemporary history, strategic arena, theological arena, pastoral arena. It is Weigel's contention throughout his interesting study that there has been a tendency within recent Roman Catholicism to oversimplify the historical, strategic, and theological arenas. Sophistication is utterly essential. The Church's contribution to this can be to provide the arena where sound political discourse can occur. It will be sound if it is gathered around three questions: (1) What should be the goals of American national security, arms control, and disarmament policy? (2) What are the obstacles blocking our way to these goals? (3) What steps should the country next take to break through the obstacles? Weigel's study is good. It combines moral idealism with political realism and then wraps the package in Christian hope.

In an extremely interesting issue of *America*, four authors (Daniel Berrigan, Paul F. Walker, Seymour Melman, James R. Kelly) approach the arms race from several different perspectives: moral, strategic, economic.[120] Berrigan's essay is vintage Berrigan, a desperate cry in biblical and prophetic terms at the lunacy of the arms race. Paul Walker argues that SALT II fails in limiting the qualitative nuclear arms race. Yet he believes it should be supported, "for it is a positive, albeit small, second step toward regulating an increasingly dangerous and costly nuclear weapons competition."

The editors of *America* agree. In an excellent editorial they first note that "there is no issue of more fundamental importance to the nation and the world than the control of nuclear arms."[121] There is an insane logic in the arms race, the premise being that the way to protect the possibilities of peace is to increase the dangers of war. The most successful weapons are those that are never used. *America* terms all of this an "exercise of lunacy" that is draining the human, material, and technical resources of

---

[118] *National Jesuit News*, Oct. 1979.

[119] George S. Weigel, Jr., "The Catholics and the Arms Race: A Primer for the Perplexed," *Chicago Studies* 18 (1979) 169–95.

[120] "The Arms Race: Marathon to Madness," *America* 140 (1979) 525–37.

[121] Ibid. 524.

all involved. Nonetheless SALT II should be supported because it represents "a moment in a process" and "a small, significant, even indispensable step toward sanity."

Moral theologian Francis X. Meehan and parish priest William Mattia were deeply moved by this issue of *America*. They regarded the stance as prophetic and the issue as "a great moment in religious journalism."[122] Both authors feel they must begin to do something about nuclear arms in their respective roles; for moral truth is attained by those who are, in their own lives, walking toward the truth. The remainder of this challenging article is a detailing of practical ways in which the problem of nuclear disarmament can be made urgent and practical for people.

A delegation of ten U.S. church leaders met with ten Soviet church leaders March 27–30, 1979, at Geneva's Ecumenical Center. The agenda: disarmament. In a 1200-word statement the group asserted that "we are convinced that the arms race cannot be won; it can only be lost." Alan Geyer reports the meeting and notes that the core of the statement is an appeal for early approval of SALT II.[123] The treaty, the statement continues, provides "a new and essential framework [of parity] for negotiating substantial and equal reductions in SALT III." Geyer underlines the fact that President Leonid Brezhnev and Soviet church leaders view the treaty as an absolutely vital symbol of détente and the reversal of the arms race. He concludes that "Christians in the U.S. would do well to evaluate the significance of SALT in such symbolic and political terms, not simply in terms of military hardware."

This is a sampling of religious and theological response to the SALT II debate. As I write, the Senate is about to undertake discussion of the matter. No one knows what the outcome will be. But one thing is clear: we are dealing here with what is certainly one of the most urgent moral concerns of our or any age. The possession, and a fortiori the use, of enormously destructive nuclear weapons makes no human or Christian sense. It is purely and simply a dead end for everyone concerned, an obscenity on the face of God's good earth. To those who say we cannot turn the clock back, the only answer is: we must. The question then becomes how this is most quickly and efficaciously to be done. By supporting SALT II, by passive nonsupport, by amendment, by opposition?

This reviewer sees real dangers in the latter three strategies, not the least being that, regardless of intent, they will have the practical effect of an alliance with those who want to increase and maintain our superiority

---

[122] Francis X. Meehan and William Mattia, "The Arms Race and the American Parish," *America* 141 (1979) 126–28.

[123] Alan Geyer, " 'Arms Race Can Only Be Lost' Say Ecumenists," *Christian Century* 96 (1979) 485–86.

in nuclear destructive power and who thereby inevitably intensify the arms race.

It is one of the paradoxes of this discussion that one can agree with many of the points made by Gumbleton-Fahey (Pax Christi) and yet agree with the conclusion of Hehir-Geyer and others. The modest stipulations of SALT II do indeed represent a form of institutionalized escalation. By these provisions alone the limitations on arms development will be relatively insignificant and support the fears of those who see in SALT II a missed opportunity. I agree with most of this. Yet I suspect that people with the same moral concerns and armed with the same moral teachings about the immorality of nuclear war and the nuclear arms race can disagree in their conclusions because they weight the political and symbolic importance of SALT II differently.

My own opinion, one that shares in Geyer's "painful ambiguity," is that SALT II ought to be supported. Not because it makes any significant quantitative or qualitative advances in arms control or reduction; rather it ought to be supported as the lesser evil among several not so attractive, even drastic options. Concretely it seems to be the only option that attempts to bring and keep arms development within the established process of negotiation, and as such SALT II can be seen as an extension of the very moral concerns that might lead one to oppose it. If we cannot achieve the reasonable in one fell treaty—and we certainly have not in SALT II—at least we do not forfeit the context in which the struggle toward this goal may continue with renewed vigor and with a deepened sense of moral urgency.

INDEX

857

Committee on Health Affairs (USCC), 473
Common good, 4, 695
Commonweal, editors of, on test-tube
    babies, 789
Common worship, 20-27, 547, 830-831
Communes, hippie, 330
Communicatio in sacris, 20-27, 547, 830-
    831
Communication, 438, 445, 741
Communications, mass, 74
Communicative good, 719
Communion, 25-26, 54, 61, 84, 376, *See also*
    Eucharist; Lord's Supper
Community, 82, 187, 431
Community aspect of penance, 66
Community with Christ in the Church, 83
Compassion, 79, 424, 439, 651
Composta, Dario, 654, 686-687, 697
Compromise, 694, 704-705
Compromise, principle of, 127-128, 305, 537,
    677
Conception, 8, 486, 514-515, 733, 735
Conclusions (Medellin), 619-620
Concrete human nature and natural law, 136
Concrete law, 134
Concrete nature, 133
Concrete norms, 532, 535
Concretism, 468
Concubinage, 840
Concubinarii, 84-86
Concupiscence, 122, 387
Condigna prolis educatio, 79
Conduct, 73, 136
Conference on Business Morality (1966), 92
Conference on Intra-Uterine Contraceptive
    Devices (1962), 108
Conference of Teheran, 185
Conferenza Episcopale Italiana (C.E.I.),
    828-831
Confession, 138
    common, 139, 141-144
    devotional, 87-88
    generic, 63-64, 142
    group, 138
    integral, 141
    interpersonal, 139
    lay, 138
    private, 63-65, 71
    quality of, 88
    specific, 71
    public, 139-140, 143-144
    vernacular, 66-67
Confessional practice, 230-231
Confessional secrets, 539-540
Confession of youngsters, proper age for,
    59-63
Confessions (Augustine), 139-140
Confirmation, 61
Conflict, 291, 305-322, 542, 638, 747-768
Conflict of duties, 772
Conflict model of human choice, 511
Conflict of values, irreducible, 753

Conformism, 527, 821
Congar, Yves, 654, 659-667, 779-783
Congregation for the Doctrine of the Faith,
    244, 657
Congress (U.S.) and conscientious objec-
    tion, 154
Congress of Italian Moral Theologians
    (1977), 756
Conjugal acts, 49, 216, 312, 320
Conjugal intimacy, 43, 83, 91, 343
Conjugal love, 49, 165, 209, 217, 288, 337,
    376, 406, 408, 535, 544
Conley, P. T., 476
Connell, Francis J., 67, 142
Connery, John R.
    on abortion, 477
    on evil, 591
    on moral terms, 533, 537-539, 541-543
    on norms, 763-765
    on political protest, 271-272
    on test-tube babies, 796
Connolly, Peter R., 36-37
Conscience
    authoritarian, 60
    claims of, 96-97
    conflict and, 747-768
    direction of, 87
    ethics of, 293
    freedom of, 157
    formation of, 137, 523
    maturation of, 16
    mirror, 3
    moral, 2-3
    moral education and, 2
    norms and, 626, 638-652
    personal, 60
    psychic results of violation of, 27
    public, 587
    religious, 8
    social, 60
    violation of obligation and, 1
Conscientious objection to war, 96, 153-158
Conscientious objectors, Catholic, 102
    historical, 555, 813-814, 816
    operations of human, 477
    person and, 734
    return to, 191
Consensualist theory of marriage, 459
Consensus fidelium and contraception, 109
Consent, 409-412, 433, 571, 791
Consents, exchange of, 336-338
Consequences, 295, 538, 541, 650-651, 684,
    716-717, 757
    norms and, 349-367
    principle of, 537
Consequentialist calculus, 350, 401-405, 420,
    506, 808-809
Consequentialist methodology, 359, 364, 371
Consequentialism, 237, 295, 359, 361, 364,
    402, 404, 425, 506, 537, 541, 649-650,
    708-709
Constance, Council of, 651

862

Etienne, Jacques, 132-133, 234
Études dossier on abortion, 493-495, 570
Eucharist
  after commission of mortal sin, 65-66
  divorce with remarriage and, 83, 340-342,
    347, 380, 827-830, 837-840
  statement on, 25-26
  See also Communion; Lord's Supper
Eucharistic fasts, 52-53
Eugenic engineering, 401-402, 409, 411, 419
Eugenics, 280-281, 289
Europe, Western, *Persona humanae* in, 671
European Bishops, third Symposium of
  (1975), 657
European moral theologians, conference of,
  648
Euthanasia, 5, 194-195, 224, 439, 443-446,
  563-564, 576, 592-612, 700
Euthenic changes, 283
Evangelical Church of Germany, 58, 489,
  518-519
Evangelism, prescientific, 69
Evangelization, 614, 621-623
Evans, Donald, 382, 433-434
Evans, J. Claude, 473, 480
Evidence, 262-263, 265-266, 683
Evil
  absolute, 79
  direct intent of, 318
  direct willing of, 688
  extrinsic, 43
  gravely, 585
  historical virus of, 169
  inherent, 162-163
  intrinsic, *See* Intrinsic evil
  lesser, *See* Lesser evil
  moral, *See* Moral evil
  nonmoral, 351-353, 534, 541, 581, 583,
    591, 608, 630-631, 647-648, 652, 715
  objective, 308-309
  ontic, *See* Ontic evil
  physical, *See* Physical evil
  premoral, 353-356, 511, 530, 532, 534, 541,
    643, 645, 648, 715, 754
  prima-facie, 584-585
  structures of, 844-845
  women as carriers of, 388
Evil effects, 10
Evil *ex objecto*, 10-11, 585
Evolution, 112-113, 281, 562, 747
Evolutionary character of the human person
  as sexed, 174
Ex-cathedra pronouncements, 38-39
Exception clauses, 433-434, 438, 442
Exceptionism, 460
Exceptionless rules, 433-435
Exception-making, 592
Exceptions, 811, 832
"Exceptions to the Norms in the Area of
  Marriage" (Institut de droit
  canonique), 831-832
Exclusivity, principle of, 675

Excommunication, 820
Existence, 2-3, 445
L'Existence humaine et l'amour (Martelet),
  773
Existential ethics, 430-431, 638-639
Existential human ends, 483
Existentialism, supernatural, 429
Existential order of salvation, 633
Existential theology, 178
Exodus 20:13, 807-808
Experience, norms, and behavioral science,
  349, 367-371
Experimentation, 192, 194, 433
  consent to, 409-412, 433, 571, 791
  therapy and, 406
  with incompetents, 803
Explanatory discourse, 579
Exploitation, 43, 56, 275, 325, 756
Extramarital intercourse, 135, 304, 357,
  451, 512, 529, 811
Extraordinary means, 600
Extrinsicism in ethics, 708-709, 766
Fackre, Gabriel, 281-282, 479-480
Fact-description, 644
Fagone, V., 497
Fahey, Joseph J., 850, 853
Fairness, 539-540
Faith, 22-25, 81, 178-179, 182, 186, 575-576,
  579, 657
Fallopian tubes, 108, 318
Falsehood, 535, 538, 556, 694, 752, 809
Family, 421-422, 675, 711, 742
  lying to protect, 370
  nuclear, 558
  patient's, 444
  sex and, 43, 452
Family planning, 769-770, 778
Family size, determination of, 328
Family system, patriarchal, 558
Farley, Leo C., 343-345
Farm price supports, 748
Farm-workers rights, 730
Farraher, Joseph J., 96-98, 100, 785, 818-
  820
Fast breeder reactors, 843
Fasts, 52-53
Favre, Raphael, 141
Fay, Charles, 136
FDA, 475
Fecundity, 44, 388-389, 490
Feeling, 445, 543
Fellermeier, J., 428
Fellowship of Catholic Scholars, 683
Female sexuality, biphase or cyclic charac-
  ter of, 47-48
Fertilio, Dario, 771
Fertility, 43, 165
Fertilization, laboratory, 402-403
Fertilized ova, 402, 733-734, 796
Fesquet, Henry, 668
Festorazzi, Franco, 70
Fetal aggression, 504

Fetal damage, 789
Fetal life, dignity of, 475, 479
Fetal monstrosities, 415
Fetish phrases, 75-76
Fetus at quickening, 8
Fetuses
  death of, 108-109, 446
  defective, 444
  living, nonviable, 10, 313, 407
  research on, 567-570
  right to be born of, 399
  viability of, 402
Fey, Harold E., 847
Fichte, Johann Gottlieb, 538
Fidelity, 422, 450, 454, 461-462, 714, 753, 833
  homosexual, 451
  life-long, 375, 391
  morality of, 147
Fides informis, 72
Films, nudity in, 37-38
Final-option theory, 170-171
Finis operantis, 536
Finis operis, 8-9, 28, 312-313, 536
Finn, James, 100-101, 103
Finnis, John M., 451-454, 505-507
Fiorenza, Francis P., 617-618
Fitch, Robert E., 75
Fitzmyer, Joseph A., 817
Flahiff, George Cardinal, 392
Fleck, James C., 103
Fleming, Donald, 289
Fletcher, John, 283, 401, 564
Fletcher, Joseph
  on genetic medicine, 402-405, 408, 412-413, 416-417, 419
  on humanhood, 444-446
  on the new morality, 293-295
  on norms and consequences, 363
  on organ transplants, 194-195
  situation ethics of, 74-79, 117-119, 126, 441, 585-587, 640-642, 650, 748
Fletcherian situationalism, 522, 585-586, 640-641
Flick, Maurizio, 63, 204, 654-655
Folly of the cross, 146, 150
Fontes moralitatis, 532
Fontinell, Eugene, 448, 462
Food, 622, 696, 763
Food rights, 730
Foot, Philippa, 646
Forbes, Cheryl A., 439
Force, 98-99, 156, 160, 163, 179, 182-183, 740-741
Ford, John C., 38, 66, 110, 113, 208-211, 214, 701-703, 776-777
Forgiveness, 87, 170-171, 343, 345, 470, 554
Forgiveness of six, 87
Formalism in confessional practice, 87
Fornication, 27, 456, 529, 591, 672, 754, 811
Fortas, Abe, 267-268, 271
Fourvière (France), 780

Fox, A. S., 193
Fox, Theodore, 188
Fragoso, Mons., 182
France, factory workers in, 465
Francis, Dale, 448
Francis, John, 842-843, 846
Frankena, William, 73, 539-541, 632, 646, 649-651, 689
Frankenstein, Baron, 414
Franklin, Ruth K., 189
Fransen, Piet, 141, 247, 334
Freedom, 597
  academic, 201, 245, 817-825
  contemporary psychological data on, 305
  core, 172
  human, 148-149, 281-283, 439, 720-721
  religious, 622, 801
  sexual, 504
  unchristian, 807
Freedom for research, 417, 817
Freedom involved in venial sin, 71-72
Freedom of conscience and conscientious objection, 157
Freedom of speech, 736, 822
Freedom of theological inquiry, 242-244
Freedom to kill, 273
Freeman, Harrop A., 96-97
Free moral choice and celibacy, 146, 153
Free will and lies, 71-72
Freireich, Emil J., 436
French bishops
  on abortion, 489-490
  on conflict, 310
  on marriage, 548
  pastoral of, 235
  on penance, 144
  on social questions, 467
French Catholics, medieval, 813
French episcopal commission on the family, 213-214
French Episcopal Conference, 668
French Episcopate, Permanent Council of the, 489, 618-619
French law on abortion, 493, 570
French people on divorce, 547
French rule in Indochina, 158-159
French theologians on marriage, 548-549
Freud, Sigmund, 388, 394
Friendship, 79, 391, 422, 461, 651, 693
Fristenregelung, 489
Froehlich, Karlfried, 325, 327
Frustration, 295
Fuchs, Joseph
  on Christian morality, 297-300, 302, 428-429, 633
  on contraception, 217
  on double effect, 713, 715-716
  on *Humanae vitae*, 772, 775
  on intended good, 511-512
  on the magisterium, 819
  on moral terms, 529-538, 541-543, 696-699
  on natural law, 14, 134, 136, 632

on norms and conscience, 642-645, 648, 650, 705, 709-710, 749, 759-760, 764-765
on norms and consequences, 353-359, 362, 577, 582, 585, 587
on penance, 91
on persons, 811
on renewal in moral theology, 69
on sex, 30
on sin, 304
Functionalism, 530
Fundamentalists, biblical, 290, 439
Fundamental moral option, 70-71, 426-427, 685
Gaffney, Edward M., 477
Gaffney, James, 835
Gagnon, E., 837, 839
Galatians (Paul), 579, 581, 726, 803
Galen, 234
Galilea, Segundo, 619-620
Garrett, Thomas, 92-93
Garrigou, E., 110
Gaudium et spes (On the Church in the Modern World) (Vatican II)
on Christian morality, 301, 428, 632
on contraception and marriage, 113-114, 210, 234, 535, 773, 776
on divorce, 336, 338
on double effect, 719
on human rights, 612-613, 744
on justice, 91-92, 95
on natural law, 239
no. 51, 678-679, 719, 806
on persons, 806
preconcilar theology rejected in, 676, 697
on war, 101, 103
Gay Activist Alliance, 394
Gay liberation, 393-397
Gay Liberation Front, 394
Geck, A., 428
Geisler, Normal L., 439
Geisser, Hans, 687
Gemüt, 543
Generalizability, principle of, 696
Generalization in ethics, 816
General-rule agapism, 76
General rules, 81
Genesis, 324-325, 407
Genetic engineering, 233, 278-290, 401-402, 414
Genetic medicine, 401-422
Genicot, Edward, 629
Genital sexuality, 397, 461
Genocide, 127, 700
Gerhartz, Johannes G., 372-375, 380
German bishops
on abortion, 488-489, 518-519
on authority, 250
declarations of, 645
documents of, 670, 674
Hirtenbrief der deutschen Bischöfe zu Fragen der menschlichen Geschlechtlichkeit, 670

pastor letter (1973) of, 674
pastoral letter (June 15, 1975) of, 598-600
German physicians on contraception, 49
Germans and Spanish Civil War, 160
German-speaking moral theologians on natural law, 131
German Synod (Würzburg), *Sinn und Gestaltung menschlicher Sexualität*, 674-675, 690
German synodal documents, *Christlich gelebte Ehe und Familie*, 670
Germany
discussion of Christian morality in, 632, 780
Evangelical Church of, 58, 489, 518-519
preconcilar authors in, 428
recent literature from 593, 748-749, 755-756, 765
Gerson, J., 662
Gesinnungsethik, 293
Gestapo, 642, 694
Geyer, Alan, 96, 683, 846-847, 849-850, 852-853
Ghandian Satyagraha, 99
Ghoos, J., 3-4
Gift, celibacy as, 148-152
Gilby, Thomas, 236-237
Gilkey, Langdon, 683
Gish, Arthur G., 469
Glaser, John W., 172-175
Glaubenssprache, 657
Glorieux, Paul, 170
GNP, 323, 329
Goals, direction to, 73
God
Bible as the book of the acts of, 74
creative acts of, 8
disobedience to, 72
doctrines revealed by, 5
kingdom of, *See* Kingdom of God
living, 139
love for, 43, 430
love of, 668
orthodox belief in, 154
people of, *See* People of God
sanctity of, 140
voice of, 2-3
will of, *See* Will of God
word of, *See* Word of God
work of, 15
Goldenberg, David, 474-475
Golden rule, 803
Good, 4, 46, 581-582, 645-646, 685, 695, 703
Good, James, 237-238
Good of *prolis*, 47, 307, 372
Good Samaritan, 503, 601
Gospel, 19-20, 181, 184-185, 423, 657
Götz, Ignacio L., 293-294
Government, 74, 92, 94
Gowen, Donald E., 325, 327
Grace
divine, 16-17
increase of, 87

868

Hellegers, André E., 402, 475, 499, 567, 735, 786, 789
Hellenistic philosophy, 257
Hellwig, Monika, 724
Help in dying, 599
Help to die, 599
Henriot, Peter J., 463-466, 468-470
Heresy, 22, 24-25, 424, 530
Hermeneutics, moral-theological, 256-257
Hermes, George, 655-656
Heroic acts, 33
Heroic sacrifice, principle of, 753
Heterosexual intercourse, 402-403
Heterosexuality, 679
Heterosexual marriage, 671
Hettlinger, R. F., 457
HEW's moratorium on *in vitro* fertilization, 789
Heylen, Victor L., 210, 234-235, 694, 733
Hierarchizing of values, 587, 772
Higgins, George, 462
Higuera, G., 171, 286
Hilfe im Sterben, 599
Hilfe zum Sterben, 599
Hilgers, T. W., 482
Hilpert, K., 633
Hippie communes, 330
Hindery, Roderick, 305
Hiroshima, 162, 848
Hirscher, J. B., 139-140
Hirschhorn, Kurt, 280-281
Hirschmann, Johannes B., 209, 213, 788
Hirtenamt, 252, 256
Hirtenbrief der deutschen Bischöfe zu Fragen der Menschlichen Geschlechtlichkeit (German bishops), 670
Historical consciousness, 813-814, 816
Historical theology, 627
History, 180, 388, 723-724
History of salvation, 69
Hitchcock, James, 449, 451, 560
Hitler, Adolf, 277
Hodgson, P. E., 236-237
Hoewischer, Harry E., 502
Höfer, Albert, 139, 142-143
Höffner, J., 428, 547
Hofmann, R., 633
Hogan, James J., 742-743
Holland, penance in, 64-65
Holy Office, responses of, 524, 647, 783
Holy Orders, 152
Holy Spirit, guidance of, 42, 251, 260-264, 640
Homicide, 191, 713
Homiletic and Pastoral Review, 31
Hominization, 498
Homophile community, militant, 393-394, 397
Homosexual acts, 5, 395-396, 681, 698
Homosexual fidelity, 451
Homosexuality, 374, 393-396, 527, 670-672, 675, 677, 679, 681
Homosexual literature, 5

Homosexual promiscuity, 451
Homosexuals, 5, 393-397, 683
Homo viator, 198
Hope, theology of, 180-181
Horan, D. J., 482
Hörmann, Karl, 110, 582
Hortelano, A., 806
Hospitals, Catholic, 384-385, 702
Hough, John E. T., 332
Housewives, 386-387
Housing, 399
Houtart, François, 279
Hoyt, Robert, 729
Huftier, M., 32, 83-84, 430, 580-582
Hughes, Gerard J., 428, 609-612
Hughes, P. E., 280
Hugh of St. Cher, 810
Huguera, G., 90-91
Huizing, Peter, 252, 256, 260, 333
Human acts, 354, 356-357, 541
  metaphysical structure of, 133, 135, 533-534
Human Acts: An Essay on Their Moral Evaluation (D'Arcy), 642
Humanae vitae (Paul VI)
  on abortion, 496
  challenges to, 665-666
  on conflict, 306-307, 310-312, 317
  on contraception, 208-210, 214-231, 255, 790, 795, 832
  magisterium and, 197, 199, 206, 251-266, 747, 768-785
  no. 14, 775
  on norms and consequences, 350
  on norms, experience, and behavioral sciences, 368-369
  on persons, 806-807
  reactions to, 233-242, 697, 700, 705, 707
  reform in moral theology and, 423, 627, 674, 683, 686, 690-691
  on sex, 448
  on theology and authority, 242-251
Human choice, conflict model of, 511
Human dignity, 27-38, 327, 332
  exploitative conduct offensive to, 43, 46
  Incarnation and, 15, 19-20, 479
  test-tube babies and, 795
Human freedom, 148-149, 281-283, 439, 720-721
Human Guinea Pigs (Pappworth), 411
Humani generis (Pius XII), 16, 662-663, 780-781, 824
Human institutions, teleology of, 760
Humanism, 424, 461
Humanization, 179, 196-197, 494-495
Humanized life, 493, 495, 499
Human law and celibacy, 148
Human life, 46, 80-81, 440, 515, 583, 601
Human love, 78, 342
Human nature, 133, 136, 295, 850
Human persons, inviolability of, 81, *See also* Human dignity
Human procreativity, 770

717, 723, 810-811
ex objecto, 10-11, 585
Invalid marriages, 379-380
Inviolability of life, espionage and, 31-33
In vitro fertilization, 286, 290, 401-402, 404, 406, 412-413, 420-421, 627
In vitro fertilization with embryo transfer, 787-800, 823
third party, 788-790, 798-799
In vitro reproduction 406
Irish bishops on contraception, 772
Iron lungs, 441
Irresponsibility, premarital, 224
Irreversibility of homosexuality, 397
Isaac, 689, 766
Israel, 293
Israel, Richard J., 292-293
Italian bishops
collective pastoral of, 199
on marriage, 828-831
on penance, 91
Italian hierarchy on abortion, 488
Italian jurists, allocation of Paul VI to, 486
Italian Society of Obstetricians and Gynecologists, 166
IUDs, 108-109
Jachym, Franz, 669
Janssens, Louis
on authority, 247, 254
on conflict, 759
on contraception, 48, 165, 756
on double effect, 713, 715-717
on *Humanae vitae*, 234, 706, 772, 775-776
on the magisterium, 819
on moral norms, 533-536, 541, 585, 587, 648, 650-651, 693-701, 704, 709-710
on persons, 806, 811
on relational value theory, 120
on teleology, 760-762, 765
Jealousy, 579
Jeffko, Walter, 584-587, 710
Jerome (St.), 779
Jesus, 76, 141, 179, 299
Jewish philosophy, 257, 290, 729
Jewish tradition, sexual relations and, 28
Johann, Robert O., 42-43, 46-47, 120-121
Johannine pericope on the woman taken in adultery, 528
John (St.), Gospel according to, 285, 407-408, 436, 523
John XXII, 654
John XXIII, 46, 216, 225, 525-526, 612, 744, 832
John XXIII Medical-Moral Research and Education Center, 605
John Paul II
address (October 7, 1979) to Catholic educations, 816-817
Amour et responsabilité, 747
on divorce, 826
on the magisterium, 820-825
on natural law, 771

on nuclear energy, 841
on nuclear weapons, 850
Redemptor hominis, 802
Sapientia christiana, 817-818, 823-825
speech on the Mall of, 826
visits of, 801-802
See also Wojtyla, Karol Cardinal
Jonas, Hans, 435
Jones, H. Kimball, 396
Jorge, Dom, 182
Jossua, J. P., 375-376
The Journal of Religious Ethics, 520
Jousten, A., 428-429, 481
Judeo-Christian tradition, 326-327, 477, 568, 637-638
Judgments, Factual, 431
Judicial murder, 750
Juridical notion of the moral magisterium, 627
Juridicism, 2, 117, 384-385
Jurisprudence, Rotal, 835-836
Jus adventitium, 507
Jus connaturale, 507
Jus divinum
meaning of in the Council of Trent, 138, 141-142
See also Divine law
Justice, 539-540, 543, 621, 651, 668, 689, 714, 763
abortion and, 480
equal, 580
law and, 268
natural sense of, 81
practical problems of, 91-92
racial, 117
revolution and, 186
sin and, 171
social, 123, 572
Justice and Pricing (McMahon, ed.), 92-93
"Justice in the World" (Secretariate of the Synod of Bishops), 397, 463
Just laws and ordinances, violation of, 99-100
Just-revolution theologians, 178, 183
Just war, 96, 515, 542, 752, 763
Just-war doctrine, 102, 158, 163-164, 359, 479, 699, 774
Kahn, Herman, 103
Kalven, Janet, 385-389
Kant, Immanuel, 538, 633, 635, 650, 803-804
Kantian model of norm, 349
Kasper, Walter, 138-139, 674, 833-834
Kass, Leon R.
on death and dying, 562-563
on genetic medicine, 401, 405, 412-416, 420-421
on organ transplants, 189, 195
on test-tube babies, 791-792, 797-798
Kaufmann, L., 658, 669-670
Kautzky, R., 286
Keane, Philip, 747
Keck, Leander E., 292

just, 99-100
marriage, 54-55
moral, 309, 629-630, 636
negative, 313
tax, 155
Laws concerning abortion, liberalization of, 106-109
Leadership, 382-383
Lear, John, 187
Le Bourgeois, Armand, 668
Leclercq, Jacques, 32, 522
Lederberg, Joshua, 401-402
Leenhardt, F. J., 129
Legalism, 76
Lefebvre, Marcel, 653, 741-742
Lefever, Ernest W., 161
Legal form, marital consent and, 135
Legalists, natural-law, 290
Legalism, 117, 374, 423-424, 668, 813-814, 816
Legality and morality, 4-5, 293, 473, 479-493
Legal regulation of abortion, 517-520
Legal right to civil disobedience, 97
Legal toleration of homosexuals, 5, 393
Leger, Paul-Emile Cardinal, 147, 153
Legislation, 53-55, 517
Lehmann, Karl, 545, 552-553
Lehmann, Paul L., 73-74, 118, 441
Lehramt, 252, 256, 657, 687
Leigh, David, 198-199
Leliaert, Richard, 326
Le Maire, H. Paul, 251
Lennerz, Heinrich, 141
Lens, Sidney, 847
Lenten fasts, 53, 91
Leo IX, 676
Leo XIII, 255, 615, 662, 744
Lercher, L., 778
Lesser evil, 127, 235, 353, 552, 647, 719, 750, 760-761, 772
Letting die, 564-565
Lewis, Eve, 62
Lewit, Sarah, 108-109
Lex Christi, 14-15, 129, 257, *See also* Law of Christ
Lex naturae, 13-14, *See also* Natural law
Liberalism, 106, 180, 479
Liberalization of abortion laws, 106-109
Liberation
civil, 397
confession and, 87
economic, 621, 623
gay, 393-397
metanoia and, 724
perception of, 479
political, 621
political action and, 463, 467-468, 472
racial, 621
revolution and, 179-180, 185
sexual, 621
theology and, 349, 381-400, 614, 617-620, 621

wars of, 102-103, 159
women's, 385-393, 487, 504
Les libérations des homme et le salut en Jésus Christ (Permanent Council of the French Episcopate), 618-619
Liberation theology, 617-622, 625, 723-724
Liber gomorrhianus (Damian), 676
Liberties, abridgement of, 728
Liberty, 1-3, 56, 58-59, 71, 268, 660, 731
Liégé, P., 668
Liège case, 7
Lies, *See* Lying
Life, 100-109, 268, 432, 511, 597, 711, 714
Christian moral, 117, 137
classification of permanent forms of, 74
death and, 446-447
development of, 74
disposal of, 598
ethic of, 399
good, 172, 471
human, 46, 80-81, 148, 440, 515, 583
innocent, 441-442
inviolability of, 31-33
preservation of, 651
quality of, *See* Quality of life
right to, 6-7, 489, 518, 763
sanctity of, 6-7, 31-32, 492, 503, 508
social, 178
transition to death from, 172
transmission of, 216
utilitarian valuation of, 476
Life-death decisions, 446
Life expectancy, 833
Life of the mother, 582
Life preservation, 785-786
Life projects, 3-4
Life-support systems, 599-600, 603, 605
Life-taking, 515
Lifetime commitment, sexual relations without, 28
Lincoln, C. Eric, 480-481
Lindbeck, George, 588
Linde, Shirley Motter, 107
Lin Piao, 159
Lio, Ermenegildo, 233, 680
Lippes, J., 108
Liturgy, 22, 24, 52, 140-141
Llinares, Jose A., 671
Lobo, George, 672-673, 796
Lobo, Ildefons, 136
Lochman, J. M., 179, 182-183
Locke, John, 721
Logical pluralism, 657
Lohfink, Gerhard, 674
Loisy, Alfred, 780
Lombard, Peter, 336
London Hatchery and Conditioning Center, 791
Loneliness, 461, 601
Lonergan, Bernard, 477
Longmore, Donald, 189-190
Longwood, Merle, 435-436, 443-444

Pastoral policies for homosexual problems, 527
Pastoral practices, 165, 173, 524-525
Pastoral problems, 82-91, 228-231, 392, 802, 826-841
Pastoral teaching on sex, 669-671, 680-681
Pastoral use of the distinction between mortal and serious sin, 171
Pastrana, Gabriel, 733-734
Paternalism, 183-184, 793
Patience, 422
Patient as Person (Ramsey), 409, 561
Patients, 436-437, 440-441, 444, 609
Patristic age, 654
Patristic heritage, 297
Paul (St.)
    1 Corinthians 11:21, 53
    on death and dying, 436, 562
    Ephesians, 285, 407-408, 419, 434-435
    Galatians, 579, 581, 726, 803
    on homosexuality, 671-672
    on indissolubility, 317, 552, 835
    law and, 117, 128
    on morality in reason and nature, 14, 19, 293
    on norms, 749
    parenetic discourse in, 579
    on sex, 529
    spiritual discernment in, 639-640
    uncritical use of, 670
Paul VI, 473
    on abortion, 491, 525-526, 569
    address (July 21, 1971) of, 381-382
    address (August 6, 1976) of, 653
    address of in St. Peter's Square, September 26, 1976, 646
    address of to International Theological Commission, 576
    address (June 23, 1978) to the College of Cardinals, 768-769
    addresses of to the Synod of Bishops (1974), 613-615
    allocution of on contraception of October 29, 1966, 164, 166, 168, 208-212
    allocution to Italian jurists of, 486
    allocution to the International Congress on the Theology of Vatican II, 588
    on contraception, 38, 50-51, 109, 114-115, 687, 768-770, 772
    creation on June 23, 1964 of a commission on marriage and birth control by, 210, 213
    general audience (February 23, 1977) of, 725
    Humanae vita, See Humanae vitae
    June 23, 1964 statement (on contraception) of, 109, 114-115, 209
    last speech of, 747
    on the magisterium, 817, 820
    message to College of Cardinals in 1967 of, 185
    "Octogesima adveniens," 390, 462, 466, 468, 472

Paenitemini, 88-89, 91
Populorum progressio, 164, 176-177, 185, 727-729, 744
"Pourquoi l'église ne pent accepter l'avortment," 487
Renovationis causam, 336
Sacerdotalis caelibatus, 144, 149, 151-153
    statement of February 12, 1966 of, 212-213
    visit (August 1968) to Latin America of, 185
    on war, 774
Pauline catalogues of vices and virtues, 576, 630
Pauline corpus, natural morality and, 14
Pauline ethics, 815
Pauline privilege, 316-317, 432, 559, 832, 835
Pauline theology of law, 117
Pauling, Linus, 595
Pavan, Pietro, 588-589
Pawnbroker, 37-38
Pax Christi, 847-848, 851, 853
Pax quaedam, 101
Pax Romana, 50th anniversary world congress of, 381
Peace, 4, 106, 639, 801, 847
Peace, the Churches and the Bomb (Finn ed.), 103-104
Peccatum leve plene deliberatum, 72
Peel, John, 567
Pelagianism, 297, 299
Pelikan, Jaroslav, 387, 390
Penance, 59-67, 83, 87, 89, 91, 137-144, 427, 575, 655
Pendergast, R. S., 111-113
Penitential celebrations, communal or public, 71, 137, 140-144
Penitential discipline, 88, 137, 141
Penitential rites, private, 142-144
Penitential services, nonsacramental, 828-830
People of God, 254, 385, 388, 664, 828
Pérez-Ramirez, Gustavo, 177-178
Permanence, principle of, 675
Permanence in second marriages, 82, 84
Permanent Council of the French Episcopate, 489, 618-619, 668
Perrin, Norman, 528
Persecution of homosexuals, 393
Persian Gulf, 849
Person, 500, 791, 802-826
Persona humana (Declaration on Certain Questions concerning Sexual Ethics) (Sacred Congregation for the Doctrine of the Faith), 626, 630, 645, 665-666, 668-682, 697, 745
Personal evil, 707-708
Personalism, 3, 119, 404, 448, 459
Personalist theology, privacy and individualism in, 178
Personality, 441, 500
    permanently extinguished, 441

Premarital intercourse, 27-31, 134-135, 363, 365-367, 423, 447-462, 692, 698, 744-745
Prescriptive principles, 73
Pricing, 92-93
Priestly or religious life, masturbatory activity in candidates to, 174
Priests
  celibacy of, 144-153
  confession of youngsters and, 60
  contraception and, 229-230
  human sexuality and, 31
  married, 146-148, 150, 152-153, 747
  social-action, 465-466
  women as, 389
Prima-facie evil, 584-585
Primary organizer, 733-734
Primary pulmonary hypertension, 509
Primetshofer, Bruno, 373
Principia naturaliter nota, 131, 133
Principle of compromise, 127-128, 305, 537, 677
Principle of consequences, 537
Principle of discrimination, 359
Principle of double effect, *See* Double effect, principle of
Principle of economy, 377
Principle of exclusivity, 675
Principle of generalizability, 696
Principle of heroic sacrifice, 753
Principle of justification, 812
Principle of legitimate excusing cause, 752
Principle of moderation of harm caused, 812
Principle of overriding right, 125-127, 305, 537
Principle of permanence, 675
Principle of tension, 123-125
Principle of totality, 10, 187, 226, 360, 752
Principle of twofold effect, 509
Principle of universalizability, 696, 752
Principle of utility, 539-540
Principles, 72-82, 117-128, 349
Principles, distrust of absolute, infanticide and, 106
Privacy, right to, abortion and, 474, 478, 515
Privacy and individualism in transcendental, existential, and personalist theology, 178
Private-public distinction, 484
Probabilism, 10, 213
Procreation
  act of, 28-29, 31, 406
  contraception and, 209, 234, 591
  human character of, 110-112, 165, 288
  needs of, 704
  laboratory, 403, 413
  marital love and, 419
  meaning of, 747
  nature and, 44-45
  premarital intercourse and, 451-452
Procreative meaning of coitus, 216-218, 220-221, 236, 701, 703, 719

Professional secrets, 125
Profumo, John, 370
Progestins, contraceptive use of, 51
Progressive magazine on SALT, 847
Prolis, good of, 47, 307, 372
Promiscuity, 451, 675
Promises, 650, 695-696, 709
Property, 182, 534
Property rights, 219-220, 309, 364, 481, 631, 708, 763
Prophecy, 249-250, 419, 462-463, 523, 527-529
Proportionalists, 709-710
Proportionality, tests of, 587
Proportionate reason, 315, 583, 647, 650, 689, 692, 694-695, 697-699, 701, 703, 761-762
  DES and, 733
  double effect and, 713, 722
  evil without, 9
Proportionate-reason principle, 9-13
Proportionalism, 697-701
Prosch, Harry, 98-99
Prosser on Torts, 482
Protestant churches on marriage, 839
Protestant ministers, marriages before, 55
Protestant tradition of unavoidable sin, 362
Protestant views on abortion, 479-480, 489, 502
Provost, James, 838-839
Proxy consent, 571-572
Prümmer, Dominicus M., 582
Psychic development, mortal sin and, 71
Psychological data, conscience and, 2
Psychological studies, 369-370
Psychology, 387-388, 448, 632, 670, 679, 695
Public, deception of, 35
Public consensus on morality, 4-6
Public policy, 5-6, 107, 627, 799-800
Punishment, 433, *See also* Capital punishment
Punzo, V., 457
Quade, Quentin L., 159
Quadragessimo anno (Pius XI), 255
Quaestiones quodlibetale (Thomas), 9, q. 7, a. 15, 696
Quality of life, 196, 328-329, 399, 565-566, 595, 729-730, 770
Quantitative calculus, 646-647
Quarello, Eraldo, 684
Quay, Paul M., 642-648, 652
Quebec, bishops of, on abortion, 488
Quelquejeu, Bernard, 496-499
"The Quest for Justice" (Callahan), 472
Quickening, 8, 514
Quinlan, Karen Ann, 592-594, 786
Quinn, John F., 663
Quinn, John R., 239-241, 740-741, 769
Rachels, James, 607-609
Racial problems, 43, 117, 399, 621, 630
Rahner, Karl
  on artificial insemination, 685
  on authority, 777-778

on celibacy, 146-147, 151
on Christian morality, 299-300, 302, 414-415, 421, 429-430
on contraception, 38
on dissent, 251-252, 264
on guilt, 340
on hominization, 497-498
on the magisterium, 819, 823
on moral acts, 173
on norms and conscience, 638-639, 697
on norms, experience, and behavioral sciences, 371
on penance, 64, 87
on revolutionary violence, 183-184
on test-tube babies, 796
Ramsey, Paul
on abortion, 508-509, 515, 568-569
on Christian morality, 296, 300, 786
on civil disobedience, 98
on contextualism, 73, 76, 78, 81, 118
on death and dying, 437-441, 443, 561-563
on DES, 733-734
on double effect, 716-720
on experimentation, 568-572
on evil, 810-812
on genetic medicine, 278, 283-287, 290, 401, 405-417, 419-421
on the new morality, 294
on norms and consequences, 356-357, 433-434, 651, 762-764
on relationships between the Church and the magistrate, 5-6
on sex, 28-31, 455, 703
on test-tube babies, 791-793, 797
on war, 100-106, 154, 161-163
Ranwez, E., 235
Ranwez, Pierre, 61-63
Rape, 43, 500, 513, 539, 695, 718, 732-735
Rasmussen, Larry, 577
Rasmussen, Norman, 842-843
Rasmussen Reactor Safety Study, 842-843
Ratner, Herbert, 107
Ratum et consummatum marriage, 316-317, 335-336, 343, 346
Ratzinger, Joseph Cardinal, 128-129, 336, 552, 633-637, 823
Rausch, James, 588
Rawls, John, 649-650
Realism, erotic, 36-37
Reason
  acting according to, 350
  age of, 1
  attainment of the use of, 60, 62
  commensurate, 355, 541, 650
  faith, morality, and, 575-576, 638
  law of, 16, 635
  proportionate, *See* Proportionate reason
Reback, Gary L., 568
Rebellion, 100, 180-181, 198, 809, 821
Reconciliation, 83, 140-142, 144, 343, 828, 834
Recta ratio, 804
Redemption, 16, 295, 299, 343, 685, 850

Redemptor hominis (John Paul II), 802
Reductionism, sexual, 388
Reed, John J., 17-19, 228
Reformed Protestant tradition, 705
Reformers on divorce, 334
Regan, Augustine, 187
Regan, George M., 136, 632
Regatillo, E., 90-91
Reich, Warren T., 343-345
Reiner, Hans, 370, 752
Relativism, 117, 530, 698, 766, 768, 806, 808
Religious beliefs, 82, 107
Religious freedom, 622, 801
Religious liberty, 56, 58-59, 226, 660, 731
Religious symbolism, 448
Remarriage, divorce with, *See* Divorce and remarriage
Renard, Alexandre C. Cardinal, 494
Renovationis causam (Paul VI), 336
Repentance for sin, 173, 343, 361
Representational model, 781
Reproduction, 402-403, 413, 785-800
Reputation, 33, 708
Repute, loss of, 317
Rerum novarum (Leo XIII), 255, 744
Research, 417, 695, 817
Research on children, 410-411, 567, 570-572, 803
Research on fetuses, 567-570
Resistance, active and passive, 95-96
"Responsible Parenthood: A Philosophical View" (Johann), 42-43
Responsibility, 3, 42, 75-76, 137, 296, 422, 435
Resurrection, 180, 295, 299, 326, 370
Reuss, Josef Maria, 48, 50, 109-110
Revealed morality, natural law and, 130, 638
Revelation, 14, 16, 73, 589-590, 656-657
Revolt, 1, 99, 180
Revolution, 175-187, 393-397, 447, 449, 468-469, 618, 671
Rhetoric, 75, 98-99
Rhymes, Douglas A., 74-76, 79
Rhythm method, 535
Ribes, Bruno, 493-496, 498-499
Ricoeur, Paul, 224
Riga, Peter J., 194, 196, 267, 279, 323
Rigali, Norbert J., 305, 429-430, 627-632, 705-708, 812-816, 820
Right, 125-127, 305, 537, 727
The Right and the Good (Ross), 585
Right conduct, determination of, 73
Rights, 621, 735-736
  bundles of, 445
  human, 576, 612-624, 683, 723-737, 801
  individual, 418, 514
  vocabulary of, 507
  vocation and, 92
Rights of children, 82
Right to die, 603
The Right to Life (St. John-Stevas), 6-7
Right to life, 489, 518, 763

Right to refuse treatment, 601
Right to reputation, right to silence and, 33
Right to secrecy, right to silence and, 33-35
Right to silence, 33-35
Rigorism, 676
Rinaldi, G., 52-53
Riquet, Père, 190, 196
Risk to the possible child, 791-793, 797
Rites, non-Catholic, 22-23
Roach, John, 779
Roach, Richard R., 449-451
Robbins, Bruce W., 844
Robert, Charles, 310-311, 317, 546-548
Robinson, John A. T., 66, 73-75, 370, 792-794
Robinson, Norman H. G., 117
Robots, 286
Rock, John, 104-106
Roe v. *Wade*, 473-479, 482-483, 490, 518, 730-731
Roguet, A.-M., 140, 143
Roland-Gosselin, M. D., 613
Roman curia on divorce, 334
Romans, 14, 19, 326
Roman school, neo-scholastic theology of, 780-781
Roman schools, theology of, 663-664
Rose, David, 846
Ross, D., 804
Ross, W. D., 538, 585, 650, 709-710
Rossino, G., 84, 89-90, 143
Ross-Macdonald, M., 189
Rotal decisions, 374
Rotal jurisprudence, 835-836
ROTC, 293
Rotter, Hans, 129-131, 694
Rouen, Archbishop of, on abortion, 494
Rousselot, Pierre, 780
Roy, Michel Cardinal, 49, 462
Rucker, Darnell, 97-99
Ruether, Rosemary Radford, 738
Ruff, Wilfried, 187, 192-193, 497-499
Rules, 20, 81, 94, 166-167, 294, 315, 433-435
Rule-utilitarianism, 537
Rusk, Dean, 270
Russell, John L., 237
Russell, O. Ruth, 439
Russia and Vietnam, 159
Rustin, Bayard, 97
Rutenber, Gulbert G., 102
Ryan, Columba, 136
Ryan, Leo, 92
Ryan, William F., 397-398
Sacerdotalis caelibatus (Paul VI), 144, 149, 151-153
Sacramental marriages, 82, 85, 372
Sacramental penitential celebrations, 71
Sacramental rites and formulas, revision of, 137
Sacramental signs, 139
Sacrament of Penance, *See* Penance
Sacraments, 52-59, 82-84, 338-339, 342-343, 338-339, 342-343, 346-347, 549-552

Sacraments to dying non-Catholics, 25
Sacred Congregation for Catholic Education
  on theologians and the magisterium, 654, 656
Sacred Congregation for the Doctrine of the Faith
  on abortion, 521-522, 525-526, 569
  "Declaration on Certain Questions concerning Sexual Ethics," *See Persona humana*
  on ordination of women, 735-736
  Persona humana, See Persona humana
Sacrifice, 79, 753
Saikewicz, Joseph, 786
St. Amant, C. Penros, 468
Sainte-Marcelle-d'Auvergne, Soeur, 131
St. John-Stevas, Norman, 4-8
St. Louis bishops on sex, 741
Salgado, J. M., 373-374
SALT, *See* Strategic Arms Limitation Talks
SALT I, 847, 850
SALT II, 841, 847-853
SALT III, 852
Salvation, 69-70, 170, 323, 633, 724
Samson, 757
Sanchez, Thomas (1550-1610), 591
Sanctity of God, 140
Sanctity of life, 6-7, 31-32, 492, 503, 508
Sanders, Jack T., 302
Sanks, T. Howland, 779-781, 784
Santayana's definition of a fanatic, 850
Santmire, H. Paul, 329-331
Sapientia Christiana (John Paul II), 817-818, 823-825
Satyagraha, Ghandian, 99
Scandal, 22-25, 339, 351, 712, 805, 831
Scandinavians on abortion, 491
Scheler, Max, 752
Schiffers, N., 246
Schillebeeckx, Edward, 40, 459, 464, 470, 697, 834
Schism, external approbation of, 22, 24-25
Schlesinger, James, 848
Schmaus, Michael, 114, 170
Schmidt, H. W., 129
Schmitz, Germán, 620
Schmitz, Philipp, 460
Schnackenburg, Rudolph, 14
Scholasticism, 95-96, 131, 542-543, 673
Scholz, Franz
  on evil, 807-811
  on the magisterium, 819
  on norms, 582-583, 587, 685, 697, 711-713, 716, 749-750, 759, 763, 765, 767
Schools, Catholic, 430
Schoonenberg, Piet, 170, 247
Schooyans, Michel, 494-495, 500, 724
Schueler, Robert L., 322, 328
Schüller, Bruno
  on abortion, 503
  on authority, 257
  on conflict, 314-319, 596, 755, 759-760, 764-765

on dissent, 525, 528
on double effect, 713, 715-717, 720, 755
on fundamental option, 71-72
on *Humanae vitae*, 772, 775
on the magisterium, 200-201, 819
on moral acts, 173, 534-541, 543, 545, 552, 555-556
on natural law, 15, 18, 128-130, 629, 633-636, 706, 709-710
on norms and conscience, 642, 645, 648-651, 684-689, 694, 697, 699-701, 705, 749-750
on norms and consequences, 349-353, 355, 359, 362-364, 431-433, 577, 582, 585, 587
on persons, 802-806, 811
on sin, 170-171, 174
Schürmann, H., 634, 636
Schürmann, Heinz, 576
Schurr, V., 455-456, 459
Schwartz, Herman, 33-34
Schwarz, Hans, 616-617
Sciences, 119, 671, 673-675, 680, 690
Scientific empiricism, 82
Scientific studies, 769, 817
Scientific theology, 242-243, 320
Screening, genetic, 401
Scripture, 70, 128, 372, 635, 676, 680, 759, 832-833

Second Vatican Council, *See* Vatican II
Secor, Neale A., 395
Secrecy, right to, 33-35
Secretariate for Promotion of Christian Unity, 26
Secretariate of the Synod of Bishops, 397
Secrets, 125, 541, 752
Secularism, 106, 223-224, 425
Seed, Randolph W., 798
Seed, Richard G., 798
Segundo, Juan Luis, 184, 617
Selective Service statutes, 153, 155-157
Self, 33, 438, 500
Self-defense, 10, 184, 310, 316, 515, 534, 542, 631, 707-708, 722, 763
Self-defense against unjust aggression, 12, 752, 812
Self-giving, mutual, sex as embodiment of, 43
Selfhood, discovery of, 179-180
Selfishness, 224, 579, 622, 774
Self-killing, 441
Self-sacrifice, suicide and, 32-33
Self-sacrifice for the neighbors, 191
Self-stimulation for sperm-testing, 524, 647, 758-759, 783-784, 789
Sellers, James E., 292, 791
Selling, Joseph A., 775-776
Senate (U.S.), 852
Sentimentalism, 347
Separation (of married persons), 82-83, 87, 558
Serious sin, 143, 169-173, 231, 342, 427, 547

Sermon on the Mount, 555, 579
Sex, 14, 43, 147, 236, 575, 645, 756
Sex crimes, 501
Sexual aberrations, 742
Sexual activity, inordinate, 811
Sexual acts against nature, 696
Sex ethic, procreational, 395
Sexism, 386-390, 394
Sex-object roles, 386-387
Sexual detail, obsenity and, 36
Sexual differences, 391
Sexual endowment, 591
Sexual ethics, 626, 628, 668-682, 697, 737-745
Sexual expression, 46-47, 124-125, 165, 173, 175, 225, 305, 307-308, 366, 739
Sexual faculties, 688
Sexual freedom, 504
Sexual intercourse
  as *actus naturae*, 775-777
  forced, 433
  human dignity and, 27-38
  illicit, 28
  marital love and, 217, 220, 224, 227, 334-336
  natural law and, 134, 363-365
  preceremonial, 29-30
  promiscuous, 28
  situation ethics and, 78, 81
  truly human, 695
Sexual intimacy, 366, 450, 456, 704, 756
Sexuality
  calisthenic, 563
  CTSA committee report on, 737-745
  female, 47-48
  genetic engineering and, 285, 287
  genital, 397, 461
  human, 117, 165, 174, 413, 657
  intervention into the physical or biological processes of, 51
  John Paul II on, 801
  language of, 44-45
  marital, 49, 110-116, 135, 227, 236, 238, 240, 248, 336-365, 535
  meaning of, 675, 679
  Neanderthal, 365
  physical, 36
  structure of, 44-49, 241, 490
  sin and, 172
  spiritualization of, 44
  theology of, 680
  views of saints on, 369
Sexualization, public, 49
Sexual language, 225, 364, 460
Sexual liberation, 621
Sexual love, situation ethics and, 78, 81
Sexual mastery, 85
Sexual morality, 628
Sexual passion, 387, 740
Sexual preference, 394, 397
Sexual reductionism, 388
Sexual revolution, 447, 449, 671
Sexual roulette, 445

World Conference on Church and Society (Geneva, 1966), 179, 182

World Council of Churches, 613, 842-844, 846

World Synod of Bishops on nuclear weapons, 850

World War II, 694

Worship, common, *See Communicatio in sacris*

Wounding, 353-354, 356, 530, 708

Wrenn, Lawrence G., 544

Wright, Elliott, 393

Wrightsman, Bruce, 322, 325

Wuerl, Donald, 258-259, 464

Yoder, John Howard, 822

Youngsters, confession of, 59-63

Zahn, Gordon, 102

Zalba, Marcelino, 53, 89-90, 113, 582, 629, 694, 806-807

Zamoyta, Vincent, 248, 265

Zananiri, Gaston, 176-177

Ziegler, Albert, 597-598, 600

Ziegler, G., 187, 195

Zielgebote, 579

Zinn, Howard, 267-269, 271

Zoe, 503

Zoghbi, Elias, 332-333

Zumwalt, Elmo, 851

Zygotes, 733, 791-794, 796-797, 799